Mastering™ Windows Vista™ Business

Mastering™ Windows Vista™ Business

Ultimate, Business, and Enterprise

Mark Minasi

John Paul Mueller

Wiley Publishing, Inc.

Acquisitions and Development Editor: Tom Cirtin
Technical Editor: Russ Mullen
Production Editor: Martine Dardignac
Copy Editor: Cheryl Hauser
Production Manager: Tim Tate
Vice President and Executive Group Publisher: Richard Swadley
Vice President and Executive Publisher: Joseph B. Wikert
Vice President and Publisher: Neil Edde
Book Designers: Maureen Forys and Judy Fung
Compositor: Laurie Stewart, Happenstance Type-O-Rama
Illustrator: Andrei Pasternak, Happenstance Type-O-Rama
Proofreader: Nancy Hanger
Indexer: Nancy Guenther
Anniversary Logo Design: Richard Pacifico
Cover Designer: Ryan Sneed
Cover Image: © Pete Gardner / Digital Vision / gettyimage

ISBN: 978-0-470-04615-9

For general information on our other products and services or to obtain technical support, please contact our Customer Care Department within the U.S. at (800) 762-2974, outside the U.S. at (317) 572-3993 or fax (317) 572-4002.

Wiley also publishes its books in a variety of electronic formats. Some content that appears in print may not be available in electronic books.

Library of Congress Cataloging-in-Publication Data

Minasi, Mark.
Mastering Windows Vista business : ultimate, business, and enterprise / Mark Minasi, John P Mueller.
p. cm.
Includes index.
ISBN 978-0-470-04615-9 (paper/website)
1. Microsoft Windows (Computer file) 2. Operating systems (Computers) 3. Computer networks. I. Mueller, John, 1958- II. Title.
QA76.76.O63M57465 2007
005.4'46--dc22

2007009246.

10 9 8 7 6 5 4 3 2 1

To everyone who has ever taken one of my seminars. It's probably true that I've learned more over the years from my students than from anyone else.
—Mark Minasi

To my sister Christine in celebration of her becoming an RN—as I finished this book, she graduated.
—John Paul Mueller

Acknowledgments

As you can tell by lifting this tome, a lot of work went into creating all these pages about the workings of Windows Vista.

First, I'd like to thank John Mueller, who revised, with a significant amount of new material, the lion's share of this book, and Barrie Sosinsky, who wrote the final part.

I would be remiss if I didn't also thank those at Wiley who helped get this book out on time. Thanks go to Neil Edde, publisher, and Tom Cirtin, acquisitions and development editor, for helping get the book on the road and providing guidance throughout the process. Thanks to our copyeditor, Cheryl Hauser, for making sure the manuscript was beautiful. Thanks also to the technical editor, Russ Mullen, for keeping a technical eye on the book at all times. Thanks to Martine Dardignac, production editor, for keeping the book on schedule and making sure everything was in order, and to Laurie Stewart, compositor, for making the pages look so good! Last, thanks go to the graphic artist, Tony Jonick, who contributed to the wonderful illustrations enhancing this book; the proofreader, Nancy Hanger; and the indexer, Nancy Guenther.

—Mark Minasi

Thanks to my wife, Rebecca, for working with me to get this book completed. I really don't know what I would have done without her help in researching and compiling some of the information that appears in this book. She also did a fine job of proofreading my rough draft and page proofing the result. Rebecca also keeps the house running while I'm buried in work.

Russ Mullen deserves thanks for his technical edit of this book. He greatly added to the accuracy and depth of the material you see here. Russ and I had to work through a number of technical issues for this book. Vista represented a significant challenge, and I'm happy to say that Russ was always there to help.

Matt Wagner, my agent, deserves credit for helping me get the contract in the first place and taking care of all the details that most authors don't really consider. I always appreciate his assistance. It's good to know that someone wants to help.

Finally, I thank Tom Cirtin, Martine Dardignac, Cheryl Hauser, and the rest of the editorial and production staff at Wiley for their assistance in bringing this book to print. It's always nice to work with such a great group of professionals, and I very much appreciate the friendship we've built over the last six books.

—John Paul Mueller

About the Authors

Mark Minasi, MCSE, is one of the world's leading Windows authorities. He teaches classes in 15 countries and is a much-sought-after speaker at conferences and industry-gathering keynotes. His firm, MR&D, has taught tens of thousands of people to design and run Windows networks. Mark has written more than 15 books for Sybex, including the market-leading *Mastering Windows Server 2003* and *The Complete PC Upgrade and Mainentance Guide*, and most recently *Mastering Windows Server 2003: Upgrade Edition for SP1 and R2* and *Administering Windows Vista Security: The Big Surprises*. He has won four years in a row the CertCities reader's choice award for Favorite Technical Author.

John Paul Mueller is a freelance author and technical editor. He has writing in his blood, having produced 73 books and more than 300 articles to date on topics ranging from networking to artificial intelligence and from database management to heads down programming. Some of his current books include a Windows power optimization book, a book on .NET security, and books on Amazon Web Services, Google Web Services, and eBay Web Services. His technical editing skills have helped more than 52 authors refine the content of their manuscripts. John has provided technical editing services to both *Data Based Advisor* and *Coast Compute* magazines. He's also contributed articles to magazines like *DevSource, InformIT, SQL Server Professional, Visual C++ Developer, Hard Core Visual Basic, asp.netPRO, Software Test* and *Performance,* and *Visual Basic Developer*. Be sure to read John's blog at `http://www.amazon.com/gp/blog/id/AQOA2QP4X1YWP`.

When John isn't working at the computer, you can find him in his workshop. He's an avid woodworker and candle maker. On any given afternoon, you can find him working at a lathe or putting the finishing touches on a bookcase. He also likes making glycerin soap and candles, which comes in handy for gift baskets. You can reach John on the Internet at `JMueller@mwt.net`. John is also setting up a website at `http://www.mwt.net/~jmueller/`. Feel free to look and make suggestions on how he can improve it. One of his current projects is creating book FAQ sheets that should help you find the book information you need much faster.

Contents at a Glance

Contents

Introduction

What you have in your hands is a soup-to-nuts, beginner-to-expert, end-user-to-administrator handbook—the all-in-one guide to using and supporting Vista, Microsoft's latest release in the NT family of operating systems.

This book is for you if you're upgrading from a previous version of Windows or if you're coming to the Windows world from another operating system. This book is also for you if you're new to networking or if you're thinking about setting up a network at home or in your business. In addition, this book is for you if you use a corporate client-server Windows 2000 or Windows Server 2003 network at the office. In other words, if you use Vista in any environment, including a stand-alone system at home, you'll find here information you can use—all the way from installing Vista to network-troubleshooting techniques.

What Is Covered in This Book

This book is divided into eight parts, building in a logical order from setting up your system to configuring advanced features.

Part I: Installation and Setup

Chapter 1 is an overview of Vista—what's new since the last incarnation, what makes it different from other operating systems and other versions of Windows, and what its main features are. Don't be misled if it seems there's a lot of jargon in this first chapter. I figured that power users who are already familiar with other operating systems will be looking to this chapter just to get an idea of what's different in Vista; if you're not a power user on another system, you won't miss anything if you simply skim these comparisons.

In Chapter 2, I take up the topic of *installing* Vista, on your own as well as for other users. This chapter discusses how to install Vista in these three ways:

- As an upgrade to a previous version of Windows
- As a new installation on a computer that already has installed an operating system that you want to keep
- As a clean installation on a computer that doesn't have an operating system installed

I'll also show you how you can reduce the amount of work needed to install the system—by means of an automatic, "unattended" installation. Most importantly, this chapter describes how to use the new Windows Easy Transfer feature to preserve the settings from your previous version of Windows.

Chapter 3 shows you how to get started using the newly redesigned Desktop and Start menu. It also includes information about the radically different Help system, the Help and Support Center, and how to get remote assistance help from a colleague or coworker.

Chapter 4 provides some additional information about the radically new Aero Glass interface. This new interface looks so different from what Microsoft provided in the past, that I felt it important to discuss it to a greater depth. This chapter also describes how to get a basic interface back if you're not particularly happy with Microsoft's new eye candy.

Chapter 5 shows you how to customize Vista so that it's specifically suited to your needs. You'll learn how to use the Vista Control Panel to adjust your video settings and display, customize and snazz up your Desktop, set systems sounds, and adjust your keyboard and mouse. Chapter 5 also shows you how to customize the Taskbar and Start menu so that you can work more efficiently. Readers with disabilities will want to read the section on using Vista's accessibility features.

Chapter 6 covers how to install, run, and remove programs, including how to set up an application for multiple users. You'll learn how to use Compatibility Mode to run non-native Vista applications, and you'll read about which types of programs you shouldn't install on Vista. Terminating an unresponsive application using Task Manager is also covered, as well as exchanging data between programs.

If you need to run Vista on a portable computer, you'll definitely want to read Chapter 7. Topics cover using external monitors and PC cards, setting hardware profiles, managing battery usage, saving dial-up profiles for multiple locations, and troubleshooting. And no discussion of portables would be complete without coverage of file synchronization. You'll also find new Vista features such as determining what the power button does.

Part II: Managing Applications, Files, and Folders

Chapter 8 shows you how to work with and manage your files and folders. The chapter information includes searching, compressing, encrypting, and burning CDs and DVDs. You'll also discover some of the new file features such as working with Virtual Folders and adding tags to files. Most importantly, this chapter provides you with details about the new Windows Sidebar feature.

Chapter 9 is all about printers, printing, and fonts. Step-by-step instruction is provided on installing and configuring local and remote printers, sharing a local printer, and managing a print queue. Fonts are tied closely to printers, so this chapter also shows you how to install and manage fonts. You'll also learn here how to use Microsoft Fax, a cousin to the printing features.

Chapter 10 covers installing and configuring specific types of hardware, how to assign and manage hardware resources, how to disable a device, and how to update hardware drivers. You'll also learn how to set up multiple monitors to your desktop system.

Part III: Digital Media

Chapter 11 concerns the latest version (version 11) of Windows Media Player, which you can use to play audio and video files, listen to Internet radio stations, and so on. Windows Media Player will be new to you if you were previously a user of Windows NT Workstation or Windows 2000 Professional. There have been several versions of Windows Media Player, but you can download all versions for free from Microsoft, so there's no reason not to upgrade. This chapter also discusses the new Network Projector feature that makes using a projector on your network almost automatic.

Chapter 12 describes Windows Photo Gallery. Before you quickly move to the next paragraph, consider how often businesses use photographs for presentations, inventory, and many other documentation tasks. This chapter shows how you can use this valuable new feature to work with pictures faster and easier than before.

Chapter 13 covers digital image management and Windows Movie Maker. You'll learn how Windows integrates with scanners and digital cameras and how it provides wizards for activities such as photo printing. Windows Movie Maker is a basic, few-frills digital video editor that you can use to put together simple movies.

Part IV: The Internet and E-mail

The chapters in Part 4 cover how to use the communications tools included with Vista.

Chapter 14 includes instructions for installing and configuring an Internet connection (including broadband connections) and for setting up Internet Connection Sharing. This chapter also provides a good description of Windows Firewall and shows how to configure it. Unlike previous versions of Windows, Windows Firewall in Vista is a two-way firewall, so it's a serious tool for protecting your system.

Chapter 15 covers all you need to know to use the Internet Explorer web browser.

Chapter 16 explains how to use Remote Desktop Sharing.

Chapter 17 is an overview of Windows Mail, the news and mail client that's included with Vista. You'll also find out about the new Windows Calendar program, which helps you maintain your schedule. This new feature even lets you share calendars with other people so you can schedule meetings or determine the best time to accomplish a task collaboratively.

Part V: Home Networking

This section of the book covers networking from a small-scale perspective. If you are new to networking, read this section before tackling the next one. Chapter 18 preps you for planning and setting up your Vista network. This chapter also discusses the Vista features that help you map your network and list network resources.

In Chapter 19, I show you how to set up and configure a Vista peer-to-peer network. You'll learn how to create shares, attach to network resources, and utilize user and hardware profiles. Chapter 19 wraps up with a section on network troubleshooting.

Chapter 20 addresses wireless networking, a very hot topic today in both private and public arenas. You'll learn how to configure and secure wireless networks within Vista.

One of the ways that Vista is radically different from every other operating system is that it's *secure*. Security is a great thing to have, for obvious reasons, but it can also cause problems—the first time you can't access a file on your own computer, you'll want to know why! Microsoft's main focus for Vista appears to be security—you'll find that you have to give yourself permission to perform many tasks that you didn't need permission to do before. Chapter 21 takes you through the details of security so that you can address problems quickly and directly.

Part VI: Advanced Networking

Now we get into some of the networking topics that are applicable to larger-scale situations. Chapter 22 shows you how to connect Vista machines to a domain, how to connect domain-based documents and printers, how to create user and hardware profiles, and how to troubleshoot your domain.

Chapter 23 addresses Windows Server 2003. While there's a whole 'nother book of things to be said on this topic (and, in fact, I've written one!), this chapter will give you a basic overview of its capabilities.

Chapter 24 deals with the scenario of using your Vista workstations over a non-Microsoft-based network. Microsoft has worked with Novell to provide Vista users with Client Service for

Novell NetWare tools to make it easy to operate over such systems. In Chapter 24, you'll learn the idiosyncrasies of those tools. In addition, Chapter 24 also covers working with two other major players in the networking space: Unix and Apple's Macintosh.

Part VII: Network Administration

The chapters in Part 7 provide you with the tools and skills you need to work more efficiently and to keep your Vista system and network in tip-top shape.

Chapter 25 shows you how to monitor and optimize your system using Vista's administrative and diagnostic tools, including Disk Management, Event Viewer, and Task Manager. You'll find that the Event Viewer has changed significantly in Vista, so this is a must-read chapter for administrators. In addition, you'll learn about the new BCDEdit utility used to change the boot options for your system.

In Chapter 26, I introduce you to Active Directory and show how it provides better, more flexible administration options and significant control to network administrators.

Chapter 27 explains how and when to use the Registry to change Windows applications and hardware settings. Also covered in Chapter 27 is the important topic of backing up and restoring the Registry.

Creating scripts that automate everyday tasks is explained in Chapter 28, as well as how to schedule your scripts to run at specific times.

Chapter 29 shows you how to prevent system crashes and other system disasters, how to restore a configuration, and how to recover lost data, among other topics. This chapter discusses the new Recovery Environment that Microsoft provides with Vista. You'll be amazed at how many new troubleshooting features you have at your disposal, the most important of which is the new Windows Memory Diagnostic Tool.

Chapter 30 shows you how to use Vista's security and monitoring tools to audit your security system. Apply what you learn in this chapter, and you'll be able to see if someone has logged on or off, changed security settings, created or modified users, or accessed system resources.

Part VIII: Advanced Topics

Chapter 31 is about virtual private networks (VPNs). A VPN is a tunnel through the Internet that connects your computer to a network. When you're on the road, you can dial up almost any ISP and set up a VPN session to your network over the Internet. If you're a road warrior, you shouldn't skip this chapter.

Chapter 32 discusses the Microsoft Management Console (MMC), an all-in-one administrative tool that can be set up to include everything you need to administer Vista. Vista comes with the new MMC 3.0, which provides a significantly improved interface. You can perform all of the tasks you did in the past, but it requires less effort on your part when you know how to use the new features.

You'll learn how to configure and manage services—programs that run in the background to support basic activities—in Chapter 33.

Chapter 34 addresses the two basic services you can set up and configure with Internet Information Server (IIS): web service and FTP service.

Chapter 35 looks at advanced troubleshooting principles and procedures. It also provides specific techniques for troubleshooting your Vista setup, printing, and error messages.

Part IX: Enterprise Installation Setups with Business Desktop Deployment (BDD)

The chapters in Part 9 discuss the Business Desktop Deployment (BDD) product that Microsoft now uses to make deployments easier for administrators. Rather than create the static deployment setup, you can now create a dynamic deployment that makes it easier to configure Vista for multiple systems, each of which has specific needs. You'll discover the specifics of how BDD can make your deployment easier in Chapter 36, An Overview of Business Desktop Deployment (BDD).

Now that you have an understanding of how BDD works, it's time to get your system set up to use it. Chapter 37, Getting Started with BDD, helps you get BDD installed and configured on your system. In addition, this chapter helps you understand some of the aids that Microsoft provides for using BDD, such as the Best Practices Guides and Sample and Job Aids Guides.

Once you have a working installation, you'll want to begin using BDD to create deployments for your company. Chapter 38, Defining Deployment Scenarios, describes what you need to consider in setting up a deployment.

Chapter 39, Performing Pre-imaging Tasks, gets into the details of actually performing a deployment. This chapter is the first step in creating media because you really do need to perform some pre-imaging tasks. For example, this chapter considers how to use the solution accelerators and discusses pre-imaging aids such as the Windows Automated Installation Kit (WAIK) User's Guide for Windows Vista.

Chapter 40, Using Image Engineering, gets into the actual creation of an image. For example, this chapter considers how to inject a device driver into the deployment image. Most important of all, this chapter shows how to use the Windows System Image Manager to ensure the deployment configuration you create will actually work with all of the systems in your company.

Once you have an image created, you can begin deployment. Chapter 41, Performing Remote Setups, helps you understand the requirements for deploying Vista across your organization. This chapter describes both the Remote Installation Service (RIS) and Systems Management Server (SMS) portions of the remote deployment.

Typesetting Conventions Followed in This Book

As much as I could, I attempted to be consistent throughout the book with the capitalization of menu commands and dialog-box options. All program-level filenames and command names appear in a `special font` to help distinguish them from the natural grammar of the sentence.

I've *italicized* terms for emphasis or as needed to avoid confusion. For example, terms being defined for the first time are in italic. Furthermore, when I'm presenting the syntax of a command (yes, system administrators will still occasionally be dealing with command-line entry), placeholders and variables will be represented in *`italic`*.

Finally, anything I instruct you to type into an entry field or command line will be shown in **`boldface type`**.

Stay in Touch!

I hope you find the answers to all your Vista questions here. In addition, please check out my web page for the latest information regarding Vista: `www.minasi.com`.

If you have questions I didn't cover, or if you have a comment on the book, or if I made a mistake, I'd love to hear from you. Just e-mail `help@minasi.com` with questions, comments, or suggestions for future editions. I try to answer all of the e-mail I get, but you can help me with that by doing a couple of things. First, please don't send me receipted mail. For various reasons that I won't go into here, I've set up my mail handler to automatically delete receipted mail. Sorry. Second, if you're asking for advice, please try to keep the problem statement to a few paragraphs. If it gets any more involved than that, then, well, we're sort of moving into the field of network consulting, which is partially how I make my living, so I'm afraid your request will be slotted to be dealt with *after* those of my contracted clients. As you've probably guessed by now, I *do* receive a lot of mail. Much of it is highly complimentary, and I am very thankful to all of you who have corresponded! I *will* try to reply to all mail I get—and thanks again for reading!

Part I

Installation and Setup

In this section you'll learn how to:

- **Install Windows Vista**
- **Use the Desktop and Get Help**
- **Customize the Interface**
- **Install, Remove, and Run Programs**
- **Organize Programs and Documents**
- **Use Features Specific to Notebook PCs**

Chapter 1

Introducing Windows Vista

Since the advent of the personal computer, users have wanted three things in an operating system: power, stability, and usability. Windows Vista has all these and more in abundance. It features an indefatigable 32-bit architecture, complete with built-in networking and the capability to run almost every piece of Windows software on the market, as well as a new interface. (You can also obtain the 64-bit version for your 64-bit machine that contains all of the same functionality, but offers better performance, assuming you can get the correct device drivers for your system.)

What does all this mean to the consumer, the person sitting at a desk 52 weeks a year who just wants to be a productive computer user? It means a lot. It means a fast, up-to-date operating system with a slew of advanced features that ensure the computer will almost never crash. It means an operating system that can host the emerging multitude of 32-bit software applications, some of which offer amazing facilities for professional audio and video recording, editing, and broadcasting. It means a new interface, which gives users tremendous control over how the system performs its tasks and how it maintains its connections to peripherals and to other computers.

In this chapter, I'll give you an overview of Windows Vista: what's new, what's different, and what's under the hood. I'll compare Windows Vista with previous versions of Windows. In later chapters, I'll expand on most of the topics I'll introduce in this chapter, but you'll find a lot here to whet your appetite.

- What is Windows Vista?
- What's new in Windows Vista?
- Should you upgrade to Windows Vista?
- How is Windows Vista different from other operating systems?
- What are the features of Windows Vista architecture?

NOTE I used Vista Ultimate edition when working on this book so I could explore everything that Vista has to offer. However, most business users will rely on Vista Business edition, so I'll try to point out differences whenever possible.

What Is Windows Vista?

In a nutshell, Windows Vista is the latest version of the Windows NT family of operating systems, or OSes, which includes Windows 2000 and Windows XP. Windows Vista Business comprises a feature set designed for business users. Microsoft has actually come out with five editions of Vista:

Ultimate This edition contains everything and is the most expensive (and hardware intensive) edition. I can see that many gamers and higher end users will love this edition, but it's probably overkill for most businesses.

Enterprise Microsoft has targeted this edition at large businesses with a global presence. This edition contains many features that the business with a global presence won't need, such as additional layers of security designed to prevent access from external sources. For example, this is the minimum edition that supports Microsoft's new BitLocker technology, which encrypts your entire hard drive in a way that makes it impossible for anyone stealing your machine to access the drive, even if they install the drive in another machine.

Business This is the edition that contains the features that most business users will want. Yes, it includes many of the eye-grabbing graphics such as Aero Glass, but you won't see most of the media center additions originally found in Windows XP Media Edition. Aero Glass is the new Vista interface that lets you see through title bars and other screen elements. The "Aero Glass UI" section of the chapter describes this feature in greater detail.

Home Premium This is the replacement for Windows XP Media Center Edition and will appeal to home users who need Windows to do a bit more than just let the kids do homework.

Home Basic This edition provides the basics for home users. It's the edition that you want if you really don't need Aero Glass or any of the other fancy Vista features, but do need the extra security that Vista provides.

Windows Vista does offer a lot of eye candy and other features that will certainly attract both home and business users. However, the main attraction for administrators is security. Microsoft has ripped out a considerable amount of the code that appeared in previous versions of Windows and rewrote it with security in mind. You'll find that from a security perspective Vista lets you do considerably less than Windows XP did. None of the accounts run with administrator privileges anymore, even though someone in the Administrator group can temporarily raise their privileges as needed. Users will now see additional warnings about actions they're taking and won't be able to perform some tasks at all. For example, you'll find that gaining access to the root directory of a local hard drive is much tougher with Vista. I'll show you how all of these new security features work as the book progresses, but for administrators, this is the main event.

Vista also has the distinction of being Microsoft's last 32-bit operating system. Future Windows desktop operating systems will use 64 bits (or higher). Using 64 bits provides a lot of perks for the administrator. The "Differences between 32-bit and 64-bit Architectures" section of the chapter discusses these perks in detail.

As you probably know, in the past, Microsoft offered two main categories of Windows versions for 32-bit personal computers: the Windows 95 family and the Windows NT family. In the Windows 95 family were Windows 95 itself, naturally enough; Windows 98; Windows 98 Second Edition, which despite its unassuming name was a major upgrade to Windows 98; and Windows Millennium Edition, also known as Windows Me. In the Windows NT family were Windows NT versions 3.1, 3.5, 3.51, and 4, each of which came in a Workstation version and a Server version, and then Windows 2000, which came in a Professional version and several Server versions.

The Windows 95 family, widely referred to as Windows 9*x* in a brave attempt to simplify Microsoft's inconsistent nomenclature, offered impressive compatibility with older hardware ("legacy hardware," as it's sometimes politely termed) and software ("legacy software"), including full (or full-ish) DOS capabilities for running games and character-based applications. These versions of Windows kept their hardware demands to a reasonable minimum. They were aimed at the consumer market. When things went wrong (which happened regrettably often), they became unstable. And they crashed. Frequently.

Many of those people—both professionals and home users—who couldn't stand or afford to lose their work because of Windows 9*x*'s frequent crashes migrated to Windows NT versions instead. (Others tried OS/2 while it lasted, then returned disconsolately to Windows. Others went to Linux and mostly stayed there.) NT, which stood for New Technology for a while until Microsoft decided that it didn't stand for anything anymore when NT 4.0 arrived, had a completely different underpinning of code than Windows 9*x*. NT was designed for stability, and as a result, it crashed much less frequently than Windows 9*x*. Unfortunately, though, NT wasn't nearly as compatible as Windows 9*x* with legacy hardware and software. Most games and much audio and video software wouldn't run on NT, and it was picky about the hardware on which it would run. (Actually, this wasn't "unfortunate" at all—it was deliberate on Microsoft's part and probably wise. But the result was far from great for many users.)

So, for the last half-dozen years, users have essentially had to decide between stability and compatibility. This led to a lot of unhappy users, some of whom couldn't run the software they wanted, and others who kept losing work or at least having to reboot their computers more than they should have had to.

The Windows 9*x* line culminated in Windows Me, which tacked some stability and restoration features onto the Windows 9*x* code base. NT culminated in Windows 2000 Professional, which featured increased compatibility with applications over NT (which wasn't saying all that much—many games still didn't run on Windows 2000 Professional), a smooth user interface, and usability enhancements.

Windows 2000 Professional was arguably the most stable operating system that Microsoft had produced until Windows XP came along. (Some old-timers reckoned Windows NT 3.51 was more stable.) But Windows 2000 Professional's stability came at a price: It had no interest in running any games or other demanding software that wouldn't conform to its stringent requirements. And while it was compatible with quite an impressive range of legacy hardware, many items still wouldn't work. Even up-to-date hardware could be problematic, especially if it connected via Universal Serial Bus (USB).

Since the late 1990s, Microsoft had been promising to deliver a consumer version of Windows that melded the stability of NT and the compatibility of Windows 9*x*. In Windows XP Home Edition, that version of Windows finally arrived. According to Microsoft, Windows XP Professional was a strict superset of Home Edition, as well as of all the desktop clients that preceded Professional.

NOTE Windows 2003 Server is a separate version of Windows, designed for use on servers. It does everything that Windows XP Professional does and adds a comprehensive set of tools for managing and administering a network. It's designed to run on a network file server or application server. Chapter 20, "Connecting to Domains," and 21, "Introduction to Server 2003," cover it. Vista isn't a server operating system; Microsoft designed it for desktop use. The server version, probably called Windows Server 2007, won't arrive for a while yet.

What's New in Windows Vista?

This section outlines the most striking and appealing new features in Windows Vista. Of course, the biggest feature for users is the new Aero Glass user interface, but really, that's just eye candy. Administrators will spend considerable time looking at the new security features, which are definitely a step in the right direction. Microsoft has improved security significantly in this release of Windows.

Aero Glass UI

The new Aero Glass user interface (UI) will bedazzle you with spectacular graphic effects, pure and simple. You can't point to many things that the Aero Glass user gets that the non–Aero Glass user doesn't except a little bit of added help. It can be argued that an attractive user interface does improve user productivity in much the same way that other environmental considerations do. Productivity is one of the reasons why companies have plants in the office area (even areas that a client won't visit) or paint offices in bright colors, rather than maintain a factory atmosphere. Sure, the factory atmosphere is significantly easier to maintain and dirt cheap to install, but users don't work well in such an environment. For a business user, the added user productivity is about the only thing to recommend the Aero Glass UI, except that it looks great, as shown in Figure 1.1.

The see-through title bar, brilliant colors, and graphical effects that the Aero Glass UI provides really do dazzle the eyes. In some cases, such as working with Photo Gallery, the additional graphics are also helpful, but not required. Most business users can do just fine using the non-glass UI discussed in the next section.

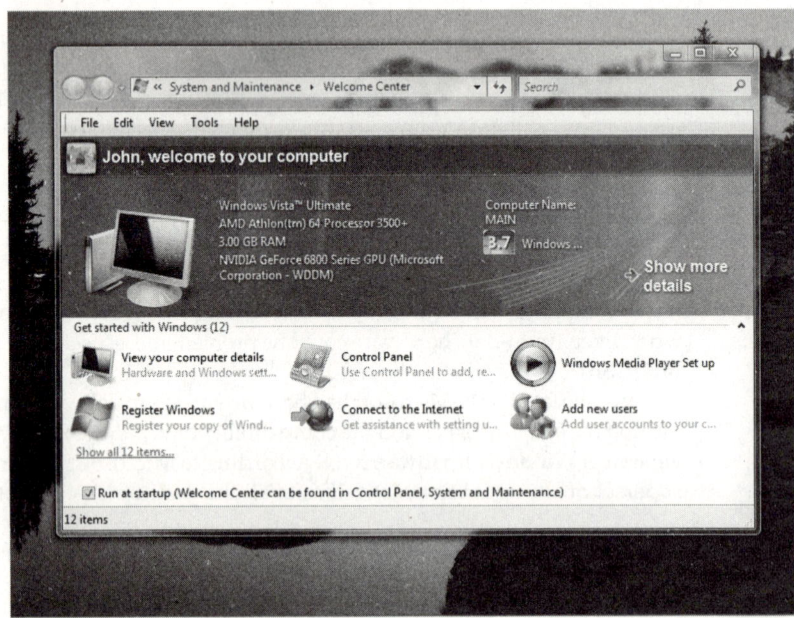

FIGURE 1.1
The Aero Glass UI looks nice, but requires a lot of hardware to run.

Non-Glass UI

Most business users will find early on that the Aero Glass UI is pretty, but not necessary. If you want to get work done quickly and with fewer resources, you really need a no-frills interface. Vista also includes a Windows Classic theme. This theme still provides most of the gizmos of the Aero Glass UI, but without the expense of the transparent effects. Figure 1.2 shows a comparison of the Windows Classic theme to the Aero Glass UI shown in Figure 1.1.

As you can see, the Windows Classic theme looks a lot like Windows 2000 with some Windows XP mixed in for good measure. However, it still includes something called the compositor, a special Vista feature that makes creating graphics faster and easier. The amount of memory that Vista uses is reduced considerably when you use the Windows Classic theme and you'll notice the CPU usage is also considerably less. The thing that surprised me is that the cabinet temperature of my system actually went down because the graphics processor wasn't working so hard. However, you can still do better by turning off the compositor and other unnecessary graphic effects, something you'll find discussed in the "Configuring the Windows Classic Interface" section of Chapter 4.

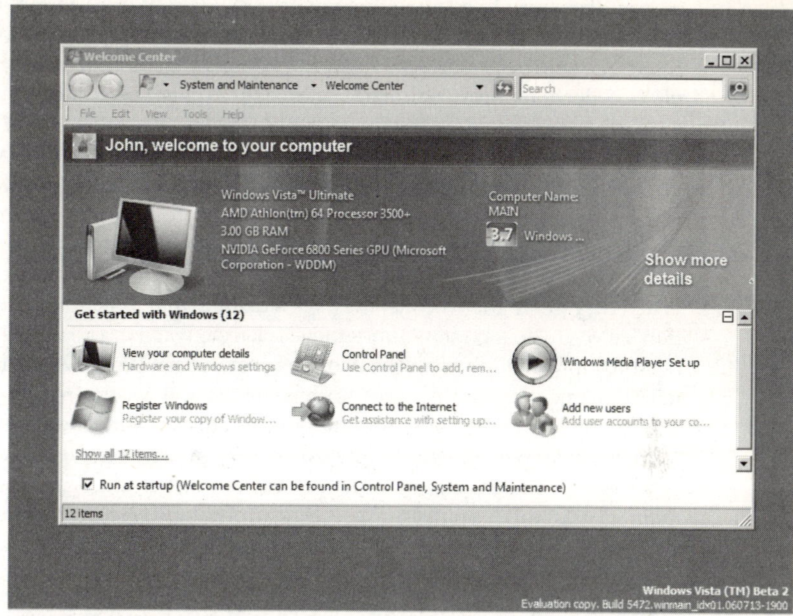

FIGURE 1.2
The non-glass UI looks a lot like Windows XP, but does include a few Vista features.

Many Administrative Tasks Have Moved

You'll still find the familiar `Administrative Tools` folder in the Control Panel and the applets it contains still do all of the tasks it did before. The interface for the applets differs. In some cases, it differs a lot. Most administrators won't recognize the interface for managing Internet Information Server (IIS). The new Microsoft Management Console 3 (MMC) interface has added some changes as well.

However, the visual changes are just the tip of the iceberg. You'll find that other tasks have moved around. For example, you'll use a different setup when you want to change the display settings, or anything that might normally be associated with the user, rather than a strictly administrative task. The command line has also changed a little. Vista no longer uses the `BOOT.INI` file to control the boot options. Consequently, you don't use the utilities you might have used in the past to modify the boot settings, you'll use the BCDEdit utility discussed in Chapter 25 to perform the change instead. You'll also notice that any scripts you have require some additional setup and even batch files have changed. The `CHOICE` and other commands (see Chapter 28) have new options under Vista that actually break existing batch files. You'll find a wealth of these changes throughout the book so you won't be surprised when you need to perform a task and find that it doesn't work the same way as before.

IE7

Internet Explorer 7 (IE7) has received considerable press because of the significant changes it provides. Vista comes with IE7 installed; you'll use Microsoft's latest browser from day one unless you choose a third-party alternative. IE7 includes a number of important additions including RDF Site Summary (RSS), antiphishing support, protected mode, and tabbed browsing. Chapter 15 discusses IE7 in detail, but the following paragraphs provide a good overview.

The Resource Description Framework (RDF) is a World Wide Web Consortium (W3C) standard (see `http://www.w3.org/RDF/`) for describing information on the Internet using Extensible Markup Language (XML). Developers use it for a wide range of tasks, everything from news syndication to photo collections. RSS (see `http://www.oasis-open.org/cover/rss.html`) is an extension of RDF technology presented by the Organization for the Advancement of Structured Information Standards (OASIS) that helps you keep abreast of the latest news without much effort. The publisher pushes (sends) the summary to you and you decide whether you want to read the whole story.

Phishing attacks are on the rise, so having protection from them is a great addition to IE7. A phishing attack is one where someone sends an e-mail claiming to be a reputable organization such as a bank. The e-mail can look quite legitimate, so many people are fooled into clicking the link. When they get to the website, they see a display that looks very much like the reputable organization's website. In fact, sometimes they look exactly alike. The whole purpose of this ruse is to obtain personal information from the user including social security number, date of birth, and mother's maiden name. The person who was phishing can now open a credit card in the user's name. As you can see, having good protection from this kind of attack is a must because a phishing attack can take any form. For example, someone might do the very same thing to gain access to your corporate network.

Protected mode is a Vista-only feature that further improves the security that IE7 provides. The main focus of this feature is to keep code from running silently in the background and prevents outsiders from damaging essential system data. This protection helps against many forms of attack, but the most important is the elevation of privilege attack that gives the hacker access to your entire system (not that User Access Control, or UAC, makes that very easy anyway). This particular feature relies on a broker to process incoming and outgoing calls. The broker prevents reading or writing data outside the temporary Internet file folder without the user's explicit permission.

A tabbed interface is the final major productivity aid for IE7. Using Tabs lets you keep multiple windows open at the same time. Earlier versions of Internet Explorer required that you open one browser for every website you wanted to visit. Not only did this make it hard to move between websites, but it also tended to waste system resources. The tabbed interface is user friendlier and makes your Web surfing experience better.

IPv6

Internet Protocol version 6 (IPv6) is a necessary and useful upgrade to the Internet as a whole. The most prominent new feature that this protocol provides is more address space, which means more websites and other uses for IP addresses. Even though IPv4 appeared to provide unlimited address space when first developed, it's all too evident that the Internet is beginning to run out of addresses today. IPv6 provides a number of other features such as automatic network configuration. You can see more information, including the IPv6 specification, at `http://www.ipv6.org/`.

Windows Collaboration/People Near Me

Windows Collaboration is the Vista feature that makes it significantly easier to work with other people. Anyone can make use of Windows Collaboration because it isn't limited to company websites or other forms of organization that people normally associate with collaboration. You can collaborate with the guy across the street on a security plan for your neighborhood should you wish to do so (this is admittedly an extreme example). You can use Windows Collaboration to invite both local and remote participants, view the participants who actually attend, distribute agendas and other documents required for the collaboration, perform activities such as giving presentations, and perform person-to-person activities such as passing notes. You can even use Windows Collaboration in unsecured environments should the need arise.

People Near Me provides an extremely easy method of creating a collaboration environment with other people on your local network. All you do is perform a simple setup and then either invite other people to join you or join other collaborations as you receive invitations. One of the principal collaboration tools associated with People Near Me is Windows Meeting Space. Chapter 20 discusses People Near Me and other kinds of collaboration using Windows Collaboration.

Identity Protection with CardSpace

Your identity is an important part of who you are. However, your identity changes by context. For example, when you go into work, your identity is based on your employee number, and when you go into the bank, it's based on your account number. Even though you don't change your identity, the way people view you does based on the circumstances. Up until now, managing all of those different identities was difficult on the Internet. Many people ended up maintaining extensive text files with critical identification information just so they could remember who they are in a particular context. CardSpace provides a standards-based method of managing identity based on connection and application context. It's part of the .NET Framework 3.0, which comes as part of Vista (Microsoft also plans to release the .NET Framework 3.0 for Windows XP and Windows Server 2003). You can discover more about this technology in Chapter 21.

File Protection with Code Integrity and BitLocker

Microsoft is making a significant effort to improve the protection of essential files on your system. The Code Integrity feature is automatic. It looks for unsigned files that act as part of the Vista kernel, the part of Vista that provides operating system services. By checking these files for problems every time you start your machine, Vista reduces the risk that you'll encounter nasty viruses and rootkits. Many hacker exploits depend on attacking the kernel in some way, so this protection is important. This feature is absolute on 64-bit systems, even for drivers. Vista will prompt administrators for 32-bit systems for permission to install unsigned drivers.

BitLocker takes protection a step further by encrypting the entire hard drive. No one can read the hard drive unless they have the required key. It doesn't even help to move the drive to another machine because the data remains unreadable. Consequently, this particular feature significantly reduces the risk of someone reading sensitive information from a stolen laptop or obtaining access to your desktop machine when you're not present. Vista supports this feature through a special chip called the Trusted Platform Module (TPM). As an alternative, you can also add BitLocker support to your system using a USB flash drive. You can read more about this feature in Chapter 21.

Better Performance with SuperFetch, ReadyBoost, and ReadyDrive

Vista provides a number of new ways to enhance performance, which means speed in this case. Even though Vista uses significantly more memory and requires more hardware than previous versions of Windows, it also has the potential to perform tasks significantly faster due to three new services.

- SuperFetch improves performance over time by analyzing your use of memory and optimizing the memory configuration. In short, you get more out of the memory your system is using.
- ReadyBoost makes your system more responsive by looking for flash memory devices and using any available memory to support system needs. Because the flash memory

device is faster than the hard drive on your system, you receive a performance boost when your system has flash memory devices attached. (This service doesn't affect your ability to use the device in any way.)

- ReadyDrive improves disk performance by using the flash memory available on hybrid hard drives. These drives store commonly used information in flash memory, making access significantly faster. This same feature can also improve laptop battery times because the system spins the hard drive up less often.

Enhanced Windows Firewall

Versions of Windows prior to Windows XP didn't include a firewall at all. Windows XP introduced a simple firewall, but it only protected you from incoming threats, not threats to outgoing messages. Windows Vista provides a significantly improved firewall that protects you from both incoming and outgoing threats. Not only do you get protection both ways, the level of protection has also increased, as have your configuration options. Chapter 14 provides you with full details on this enhanced feature.

New Ways of Organizing Your Data

Vista includes a number of new ways to organize your data and you'll learn about them in detail in Chapter 8. However, one of the most important new ways is the use of virtual folders. You create a virtual folder using Vista's search capabilities, which are significantly better than previous versions of Windows. In fact, I'd go so far as to say you won't believe your eyes. Many searches appear nearly instantaneous and provide results from your e-mail, data folders, and other parts of the system. Anything you index appears in the search. A virtual folder saves these search results so you can grab information from anywhere without knowing or caring where that information physically appears on the system.

Windows Explorer isn't as limited in categorizing your data as it has been in the past. You can create data stacks, essentially virtual folders that classify your data, to sort through your data faster. When creating a stack, you can choose a default file characteristic such as author or size, or you can create stacks based on metadata you define. The best part about stacks is that you can access them from the Windows Explorer content menu with the same ease as sorting.

Explorers help you limit your view of data. For example, Vista includes a document explorer that shows just the documents in a location without considering all of the other files that might appear there. In many respects, Explorers are simply another form of search and filtering combined. However, the view differs. What you see is an actual folder view where you know the location of the data. The Explorers don't just deal with data. The Software Explorer (Chapter 14) helps you track applications on your system, while the Game Explorer tracks your game usage and provides easy access to the games on your system.

Sometimes what you see isn't what's actually there. Windows always supported junctions since Windows 2000 (even though many people are just now beginning to use them with any regularity). A junction is a connection to another folder. For example, you can create a junction with a folder on a network drive on your local drive. Even though that folder doesn't actually exist on your drive, you can use it as if it does. Vista adds a new feature called the symbolic link that overcomes some problems with the junction. Now you can create links to files that work the same as junctions do. Even though the file doesn't exist in the location that it appears in Windows Explorer, you can use it as if it does.

Print Management Console

Microsoft has made it significantly easier to manage printers. The Print Management console lets you view the currently installed drivers, monitor printer status, add or delete printers, and perform administrative tasks such as assigning a printer to a port. Chapter 9 discusses this topic in detail.

User Account Control (UAC)

The biggest user-oriented change in Vista is the UAC. In fact, this is the most hotly debated change as well; some people feel that it's too invasive and a few feel that it's not really needed at all. UAC is a new method that Microsoft is using to protect the user from outside influences and to help the user think through tasks that might have invited attack in the past. Depending on the user's rights, UAC can also prevent the user from performing actions that could cause problems. For example, the user might not even be able to view the `Windows System32` folder, much less do anything with it. A network drive might become inaccessible unless the administrator provides specific access to it. You'll find a discussion of how to manage UAC in Chapter 3.

Tablet and Media Center Support

You won't find separate editions of Vista for Tablet PC users or for Media Center any longer. If you want the best of both technologies, you'll need to obtain Vista Ultimate edition. Tablet PC users can also upgrade to Vista Business edition, while Media Center users can update to Vista Home Premium edition.

Vista contains everything that you used in the past with some enhancements. Tablet PC users will still find the Sticky Notes, Tablet PC Input Panel, and Windows Journal. These three utilities look about the same as they have in the past, but their operation is smoother and they work fine for desktop users as well.

The Windows Media Center application has received a minor boost in functionality for Vista. You'll find that it provides support for all of the latest devices and makes it easier to perform tasks such as burning a DVD.

Built-in RAM and Disk Diagnostics

Many network administrators carried floppies or CDs around in the past so they could boot their modern systems with ancient DOS in an effort to find the errant RAM or partially functional hard drive on a system. It turns out that Windows often got in the way of performing a complete check of the system with the result that the error remained hidden from view. Vista fixes both problems by providing diagnostics that you can use to locate both RAM and hard drive problems without Windows interference. You'll find out more about these new diagnostics in Chapter 29.

Vista also introduces a new technology to help safeguard data before a failure occurs. Current hard drive technology relies on Self-Monitoring, Analysis, and Reporting Technology (SMART) to provide an early warning on machines where the user has actually activated the required support in their computer's setup. (The required support is often turned off by default and most users don't know they need to activate it to obtain the required support.) However, this system has limitations and doesn't always provide the user with enough advance notice of the hard drive failure to save the data completely. A newer technology named Proactive Reporting and Correcting Safeguard (PRCS) attempts to resolve these reporting problems and give the user more time to save data before the hard drive fails. Microsoft has submitted this technology to the T13 standards committee, and you can read more about it at `http://www.t13.org/docs2005/e05142r0-PRCS_Proposal.pdf`.

New Deployment Tools

Creating and managing setups for a large organization is time consuming to say the least. When working with previous versions of Windows, organizations often need to buy third-party imaging tools to create an image of the operating system for slipstream installations. Vista overcomes many of these old problems by providing new deployment tools and a new technology called Windows Imaging (WIM) format. This new technology helps you create a modular image of Vista that gives you better control over the installation scenario on multiple machine types with full language support. Using WIM, you can add drivers, perform updates, and change Windows components without ever booting the operating system image. The following list describes five new or updated utilities that Vista provides for making your deployment easier (you can learn the details in Chapter 2).

Application Compatibility Toolkit (ACT) This utility checks your system for potential problems before you upgrade to Vista. It also helps you understand how your system will perform with Vista installed. For example, your system might not run a game very well, but it may run Word just fine.

Microsoft Windows User State Migration Tool (USMT) Trying to migrate settings in the past was extremely difficult. Some people performed the task by hand, others tried the somewhat usable Microsoft utilities, a few tried third-party products, and a few just consigned themselves to performing all of the required configuration from scratch. Although USMT isn't perfect, it does do a lot better job of helping you migrate user state information that previous tools.

ImageX You use this tool to create and manage WIM images.

Windows System Image Manager This utility helps you configure Vista without having to perform the task manually. You create a `Unattend.xml` file that contains the required instructions instead.

Windows Preinstallation Environment (PE) You use this utility to modify the system information and perform tasks such as formatting drives without booting the operating system.

Command-Line Changes

Vista includes some changes at the command line, where many administrators still spend a lot of their time. Some of the changes are simple. For example, the `Choice` command used in batch files requires use of different switches in Vista. The changes actually break batch files, so you'll need to perform updates with this and other commands that you might not have thought much about in the past. Chapter 28 describes many of these changes.

You'll also find some new utilities. For example, Vista doesn't rely on the `Boot.ini` file any longer to make boot selections. Consequently, editing this file doesn't buy you anything, even when you do find it on the hard drive. The new Boot Configuration Data Store Editor (BCDEdit) utility provides the functionality to change boot settings and you'll find it discussed in Chapter 25.

A few of the new utilities aren't actually new; they used to appear in the Windows Resource Kit. For example, AuditPol and RoboCopy used to appear in the Windows Resource Kit, but now you have them at your disposal when using a default Vista installation. You'll find that Microsoft has enhanced these utilities as well. Make sure you check out Chapter 21 for changes in the security utilities.

Photo Gallery

With so many people getting digital cameras, it's no wonder that Microsoft added this feature. Photo Gallery helps you manage your digital pictures. You can view them, sort them, add information about them, print them locally, or send them to someone else. Chapter 12 provides complete information on this new tool.

Startup Repair Tool (StR)

The StR is Microsoft's attempt to combat some of the most common issues that cause system boot failure including incompatible drivers, missing or corrupted startup configuration settings, and corrupted disk metadata. The premise for this tool is good. It reduces the chance that you'll end up with an unbootable system. If you can at least boot your system, you can often fix any problems it might have. It remains to be seen how well this tool works in reality. Most tools of this type depend on the developer's preconceived notions of what can go wrong. However, after seeing several blue screens of death during the beta cycle, I've come to appreciate that this tool does at least some of what it claims. After the blue screen of death, the system displays a message stating that you just experienced a blue screen of death and offers to look for a solution. Clicking Look for Solution didn't find much of value for many of the errors, but I was surprised to find that even during the beta, the system returned a message stating that Microsoft had already fixed the problem in an upcoming build. You can explore this tool in detail in the "Startup Repair Tool" section of Chapter 29.

Group Policy Management Console (GPMC)

The old method of configuring group policies required that you create your own custom Microsoft Management Console (MMC) snap-in setup based on the configuration you wanted to modify. The GPMC provides a means of managing group policies with significantly fewer setup requirements. You use a tree view setup to move around the domain instead of configuring specific domain elements. GPMC makes it possible to see the Organizational Unit (OU) connections and the individual Group Policy Objects (GPOs) so you don't have to configure each GPO separately. In addition, GPMC offers these valuable features.

- Backup and restore GPOs
- Backup and restore of filters
- Create HTML-based reports of all of the settings in a GPO
- Script some group policy management actions

GPMC comes installed with Vista. However, you can also get it for your Windows XP and Windows 2003 systems at `http://www.microsoft.com/downloads/details.aspx?familyid=0a6d4c24-8cbd-4b35-9272-dd3cbfc81887&displaylang=en`. Simply download and install the product following the prompts. You can discover more about this administrative tool in the "The Group Policy Management Console (GPMC)" section of Chapter 23.

Group Policy Templates Are Now XML

If you're responsible for managing security on a large network, then you've probably run into the administrative (ADM) template file. The ADM template file first appeared in Windows NT 4.0 as a means to define and implement changes to the Registry. When Microsoft introduced group policies, the ADM template file remained with some minor modifications. The problems with ADM template files include:

- ADM bloat that occurs when the template appears in each GPO as a separate item
- ADM template version mismatches
- ADM template corruption or changes that occur when the administrator installs updates and patches
- Confusing policy and preference settings that depend on the area of the Registry that a template affects
- Lack of control over multistring and binary Registry values

Vista handles the problems in ADM template files by introducing two new features. The first is defining group policies using XML-based files (ADMX files) that are easy to modify and reference. The ADMX files chop up the ADM template files into smaller files that are easier to manage. In addition, each ADMX file can contain multiple languages so internationalization is easier. The second is using a template repository to store the templates, rather than placing a copy in each GPO. Using a central repository means that you avoid version mismatches and problems during to patches or updates.

Windows Sidebar

Windows Sidebar is one of the few Vista features that really do require the Aero Glass to work properly. This application appears on the right or left side of your display and holds any number of gadgets. The supplied gadgets include Calculator, Calendar, Clock, Contacts, CPU Meter, Currency Conversion, Notes, Picture Puzzle, Recycle Bin, RSS Feeds, Slideshow, and Stocks. The power of Windows Sidebar is that you can add more gadgets to it. Not only does Microsoft plan to introduce additional gadgets, you'll probably find gadgets from third parties as well. By keeping Windows Sidebar displayed, you can track current events without any disruption of your work. Since you can see through Windows Sidebar to your application, nothing is covered. Of course, you need Aero Glass to see through Windows Sidebar. You can learn more about this product feature in the "Working with Windows Sidebar" section of Chapter 8.

AutoPlay Enhancements

Vista makes it considerably easier to control AutoPlay functionality on your system. You'll find a new AutoPlay applet in the Control Panel. When you open this applet, you'll find a list of all of the media today; everything from audio CDs to HD DVD and Blu-ray Disc movies appears in the list. You can configure each entry with a default action or simply tell Vista to ask you what action to take with each media. You can even choose to turn off AutoPlay should you want to control disc access manually. The options you can choose depends on the Vista edition you run. However, you'll find automatic options to perform tasks such as playing a video in Windows Media Center now.

NOTE Don't confuse AutoPlay with AutoRun. AutoPlay is a feature that defines which application to use to open media when you insert it into the drive regardless of the content of that drive. AutoRun is a feature that depends on special files that appear on the media. In some cases, the effects of AutoPlay and AutoRun are the same, but you can control AutoPlay, while AutoRun is more or less automatic. For example, an application installation CD could contain an AutoRun file that starts the setup program automatically.

Sync Center

At one time, people associated the Sync Center with mobile devices. However, in Vista it provides a centralized location to sync anything with anything else. For example, you could edit a copy of a file locally on your hard drive and then sync the finished version with a file on a network drive. You can learn more about this technology in the "Using Sync Center" section of Chapter 8.

Mobility Center

Anyone who's used a laptop for a while knows what it's like to have to set up the laptop for different environments. You use one setup at work where you have a docking station, another on the ride home, and another at home where you have a network you need to protect from the kids. When you go to a business meeting, none of these settings work, so you end up creating more. The laptop that used to work efficiently is now a mass of conflicting settings. Mobility Center provides a centralized location to manage all of your laptop settings so that you don't have to remember to change settings in each area. Using this application, you can adjust these settings and more.

- Display brightness
- External display settings
- Display orientation
- Speaker volume
- Power plan
- Wireless networking on or off
- Synchronization status

The bottom line is that Vista makes it considerably easier to move from one place to another. You can read more about Mobility Center in the "Configuring Your System with Mobility Center" section of Chapter 7.

Windows Defender (Antispyware)

Windows Defender is Microsoft's upgraded (perhaps completely changed) version of Giant Software Company's antispyware product. Spyware is becoming an increasing difficult problem to control. The Vista version doesn't actually bear much resemblance to the original product. Of course, Microsoft has had to provide a means to keep definitions updated and Windows Defender will check online for updates automatically. It also tells you when definitions are outdated.

However, the upgrade mechanism and automatic start feature that Vista provides isn't the big news. Most antispyware products must run in administrator mode to perform a complete check of the hard drive. Unfortunately, the user isn't running in administrator mode in Vista. Consequently, Microsoft made Windows Defender a service that runs in the background using its own credentials. So, while the user is protected from spyware, there isn't any need to elevate user privileges to get the job done. You can learn more about Windows Defender in the "Protecting Your System with Windows Defender" section of Chapter 14.

Windows Experience Index

Microsoft's controversial Windows Experience Index (the relaunched Windows System Performance Tool) supposedly provides the user with a simple guide on what will and won't run on a particular system. The index is simply a number that tells you how your system will perform. You can see this number at the top of the Welcome Center display shown in Figure 1.1. The reason that this tool is so controversial is that not everyone agrees that it provides a valid view of system functionality.

You can see more details about the information used to create the index by clicking Show More Details in the Welcome Center and then Windows Experience Index in the System window. Microsoft uses the processor calculations per second, memory operations per second, desktop performance, 3D business and gaming performance, and hard drive data transfer rate as primary indicators. You can learn more about this tool in the "Using the Windows Experience Index to Your Advantage" section of Chapter 10.

Games Explorer

Vista includes a new kind of explorer called Games Explorer. This product performs many tasks that really aren't business related, such as tracking how many times you've played a particular game and showing you the Entertainment Software Rating Board (ESRB) rating of the game. However, it does provide one feature that is important in a home business setting: Parental Controls. You can use the Parental Controls feature to block access to any games on your system.

Windows Calendar

For years, one of the big reasons to use Outlook instead of Outlook Express has been the availability of a calendar. Vista overcomes this oversight by providing Windows Calendar, an application you can use to schedule tasks and record your appointments. Like Outlook Express, Windows Calendar isn't as fully functional as the calendar offered as part of Outlook, but it does work well for an individual or small business that doesn't need to worry about resource sharing. You can publish your calendar in order to share it with other people, but Windows Calendar doesn't quite provide all of the functionality that Outlook users might expect. It's a welcome addition, however, and will serve many people well. You can learn more about this application in the "Using Windows Calendar" section of Chapter 17.

Small Business Resources

Microsoft is trying to provide a better Windows environment for small business users. You'll find a Small Business Resources link in the Programs menu that takes you to a special website. This new small business website contains security, support, articles, research, products, and demonstrations all designed to help small business. You'll also see an advertisement for Small Business Plus, a new Microsoft business relationship product that will help small businesses with summits, online training, a newsletter, and additional online support. The direct link to this information is `http://www.microsoft.com/smallbusiness/hub.mspx`.

Windows Easy Transfer

Windows Easy Transfer is the new tool supplied with Windows Vista for migrating your settings. Microsoft designed this tool for smaller organizations and individuals, where you transfer settings from one machine to another. If you want to perform large-scale setups, when you need the Business Desktop Deployment (BDD) package, which is a separate download. This comprehensive package contains the Windows System Image Manager Tool (creates complete system images), Windows User Setting Migration Tool (USMT), and Remote Installation Service (RIS). You can learn more about Windows Easy transfer in the "Use Windows Easy Transfer to Transfer Settings " section of Chapter 2.

Connect to a Network Projector

Anyone who's given a presentation knows that it can be difficult to make the correct connections to a project. Vista makes this process easier with the Connect to a Network Project utility. The utility actually searches the network for projectors and then makes suggestions on a connection. Mind you, this connection need not be wired; you can use a wireless connection. You can discover more about this feature in Chapter 11.

iSCSI Initiator

The Internet Small Computer Systems Interface (iSCSI) Initiator helps you use storage devices on another machine. These devices (such as tapes, hard drives, CDs, or DVDs) can include anything that already supports iSCSI as a target. The iSCSI Initiator service makes a request of the remote drive using standardized methods. You can make the request from a LAN, WAN, or the Internet with equal ease. The Vista software also works with Storage Area Networks (SANs). You can learn more about working with iSCSI in Chapter 10.

.NET Framework 2.0/3.0

Developers are creating more and more .NET applications. In the past, developers created native applications where the compiler changed code from human readable form to machine code. .NET applications are managed; a special interpreter reads a tokenized form of the application at runtime and changes it to machine code form. Not only are managed applications easier to code, they also provide a significant number of advantages. For example, you can make a .NET application a lot more secure because an intermediary application is interpreting them. In addition, you can theoretically run managed applications on a number of non-Windows platforms without creating special versions for that platform. The MONO project (`http://www.mono-project.com/Main_Page`) seeks to move .NET applications from Windows to other platforms including Linux, Mac OS X, Solaris, and UNIX.

Previous versions of Windows required that you make a separate download of the .NET Framework. Many people felt this was too much work considering the size of the download. Vista comes with this support installed. You can learn more about working with the .NET Framework in Chapter 33.

Complete PC Backup

When Microsoft says that backup is now complete, you can actually believe them. The old NTBackup application was in dire need of update. Let's face it: not many people use tapes any longer for small to moderate backups. DVDs, removable hard drives, and network drives make better choices. Vista provides all of these choices.

Of course, NTBackup was always best at creating a backup of individual files and it wasn't all that easy to restore them. Vista also changes the backup and restore options. You can backup single files, groups of files, or the entire system. An entire system backup is an actual copy of everything on the drive that you can use to restore everything on your machine in the event of a hard drive failure. The restore process is just as flexible. It's actually easy to backup and restore files in Vista.

My favorite feature, however, isn't the flexibility or the media choices. Vista can perform backups automatically to whatever media you choose. Using automatic backups means that you don't have to remember to get the job done; Vista does it for you. Chapter 29 discusses this topic in detail.

Previous Versions for Files

Windows has had restore points for quite some time. However, Vista handles this functionality differently. Yes, you can still create a full restore point and you can restore from a restore point. If your system experiences a major problem installing an application or performing a configuration, you can still roll back the change. Vista adds the capability to restore just a single file. You can choose from any of the previous versions of the file to restore just that file to a known state.

Multiple Clocks

It may seem like a small feature, but I already like this one. In previous versions of Windows, you could see one and only one clock in the notification area of the Taskbar. Vista lets you have up to three clocks so you can track multiple time zones. Chapter 5 discusses this feature in detail.

Should You Upgrade to Windows Vista?

Whether you should upgrade to Vista depends on your needs, how well your current version of Windows is fulfilling them, and whether your hardware is up to the test. The decision is wholly yours (of course), but the following sections offer some suggestions, depending on where you're coming from.

NOTE As of this writing, Microsoft doesn't have an upgrade plan in place for Windows XP Professional x64. Given that Microsoft knows the world is moving toward 64-bit architectures, you can be sure that Microsoft will come up with an upgrade plan for your 64-bit version of Windows XP at some point.

Windows 3.*x*, Windows 9*x*, Windows NT, Windows 2000

Vista requires a ton of new hardware, so if you're using an old system that has one of these operating systems installed on it, you'll need to start from scratch. Microsoft doesn't offer any upgrade path for you and it's unlikely that your hardware will handle all of the requirements of Vista.

You have good reasons to upgrade to Vista. Microsoft has ended or is ending support for all of these products, including fixes for problems that viruses and spyware can use to gain entry to your system. Most new applications also require something a bit more robust than these older operating systems can provide. The hardware you're using will eventually give up the ghost, but you'll probably give up on it first because you'll want to perform the tasks that your neighbor can. These older operating systems just don't offer quite the functionality that Vista can provide (see the "What's New in Windows Vista?" section of the chapter for an overview).

Windows XP Home Edition

Interestingly enough, this version of Windows XP provides the largest number of upgrade possibilities. You can upgrade to any Vista edition. There are a lot of reasons to upgrade Windows XP Home Edition and many of you already know what they are because people have been creating workarounds for Windows XP Home Edition shortcomings for quite some time. For most people, the biggest reason to upgrade to Vista is the extra security it provides. It's a lot harder to become infested with viruses and spyware when the system is working so hard to keep itself clean. Of course, nothing is impossible.

Home business users will gain access to a number of new features, not the least of which is the small business support that Microsoft provides with Vista. You'll also like features such as Game

Explorer if you have to share access to the system with your children. All of the new applications are helpful as well. A home user doesn't need all of the capabilities of Outlook. With the addition of features such as Windows Calendar, you no longer have to decide between the cost of a full version of Windows and the functionality you require to get the job done.

Windows XP Professional, Windows XP Media Center, and Windows XP Tablet PC

Microsoft has provided less flexible upgrade paths for these other Windows XP editions. The reason is that these Windows XP editions provided specific functionality that some Vista editions don't provide. Here's the list of update choices for each of the Windows XP editions.

- Windows XP Professional: Vista Business or Vista Ultimate
- Windows XP Media Center: Vista Home Premium or Vista Ultimate
- Windows XP Tablet PC: Vista Business or Vista Ultimate

Security is a very good reason to upgrade from these other Windows XP editions. Microsoft does provide significant changes in security that makes securing your system significantly easier. The new security management tools are also a plus. For example, you can now create group policies with greater ease. In addition, the policies don't consume as much space or lend themselves to certain kinds of corruption that plagued earlier versions of Windows.

If you get Vista Ultimate, you obtain everything that Windows has to offer, including full media support. However, most business users will find that Vista Business does everything they need, including providing support for the Tablet PC. You can actually access all of the Tablet PC utilities from your desktop now.

When you're using any of these three Windows XP editions, it pays to scan through the "What's New in Windows Vista?" section of the chapter. The overview will help you decide whether there's a compelling reason to upgrade to Vista. I'm sure you'll agree that there are many good reasons, but often you'll need to add extra memory or a new display adapter to your existing system to make it work with Vista. It's important to consider the tradeoff of investment in new hardware against the new features that Vista provides. In some cases, you'll find that sticking with Windows XP for now is the best choice.

How Is Windows Vista Different from Other Operating Systems?

Many people would agree that Vista is probably the best and worst operating system Microsoft has ever put together. It's the best operating system from a security and possibly a reliability perspective. Even though it requires substantial hardware to run, Vista tends to use the hardware more efficiently so you actually get better performance. However, there are the downsides of too much security and very high hardware requirements to consider too. Just how much security or hardware do you need to perform word processing tasks? This all leads to the topic of the following sections: How does Vista stack up against other popular operating systems?

Windows Vista Compared with UNIX

Of all the operating systems under discussion here, UNIX is probably the most similar to Vista in terms of architecture. There are many different flavors of UNIX, however. Each flavor has a different user interface, and not all of them are graphical. As a group, UNIX operating systems are 32/64-bit, secure, and capable of running on a number of processor types.

UNIX is mostly a server OS these days; it's not very popular as a client OS anymore. In the past, artists and designers have used high-end UNIX-based workstations to create special effects for films. Vista, however, supports high-end 3D protocols. Running Vista on a high-powered 64-bit processor will give you equal processing power to those UNIX workstations, with the added punch of Vista, for a fraction of the price.

Vista also adds managed code to the mix. No, Vista doesn't run everything using managed code, but you'll find that the .NET Framework does appear with regularity as a requirement for Vista applications. Using managed code can improve system reliability and security. Using MONO (`http://www.mono-project.com/Main_Page`) lets you run the managed code on Linux, Solaris, Mac OS X, Windows, and UNIX systems, so in reality, these other operating systems are losing their edge in platform independence. You may eventually see Windows applications in the same places you see everything else. In short, Vista is closing any gaps it had with UNIX and is making significant improvements in the areas where it already excelled.

Windows Vista Compared with Linux

Linux is a freely distributed 32/64-bit OS, a variant of UNIX. Many shells are available that add a friendly graphical face to Linux, making it more accessible to the average end-user than standard UNIX, but with all of UNIX's stability.

A large segment of the Linux fan base is the "anti-Microsoft" crowd that sees Microsoft's industry dominance as a very bad thing and wants to counteract it in any way they can. They love Linux because of the philosophy behind it—free and constantly being collaboratively improved. There's something to be said for that. But me, I'm not political. I just want to run some applications.

In the end, the main reason for owning a computer is to run applications, right? So, it's important to choose an OS that runs the applications you need. Some business software companies have released versions of their applications that run on Linux, but the majority of applications still run only on Windows (including Vista). I'm not going to disparage Linux here, partly because I think it's a great OS and partly because I'm somewhat afraid of all those rabid Linux enthusiasts out there. However, I will say this: not all of the applications I need to run will work on a Linux system.

Windows Vista Compared with the Macintosh OS

Like Vista, the Macintosh OS is a 32/64-bit environment with built-in networking capabilities. Despite its well-known and intuitive interface, the Macintosh OS lacks many of the powerful features found in Vista. Object linking and embedding (OLE), Messaging Application Programming Interface (MAPI), and Telephony Application Programming Interface (TAPI) are all unfamiliar to Apple users. There's also a relatively limited amount of software available to the Macintosh market as compared with the Windows market.

The latest version of the Macintosh OS and Vista do have some significant changes to consider from previous editions. The Macintosh has received a well-deserved reputation for supporting magnificent graphics. That's one of the reasons that this operating system is so popular with anyone who works with graphics. In this respect, the Macintosh operating system is still superior, but Vista is definitely making inroads. At some point, you can expect Windows and Macintosh to duke it out over the graphics issue.

The Macintosh OS is also no longer limited to special Macintosh hardware. Apple made the interesting choice to give up that unique hardware and now you can find the Macintosh OS running on an Intel system near you. Consequently, Windows has lost a bit of its edge for running on open hardware. There are even reports that some people have gotten Windows and the Macintosh OS to dual boot on a single machine. Imagine that!

What Are the Features of Windows Vista Architecture?

I've already discussed some of the Vista architecture. In this section, I'll analyze it a little more closely to see what makes Vista tick and why it's different from other operating systems.

From a programmer's perspective, Vista is divided into two layers. These are actually two separate operating modes. The *kernel mode* is where Vista performs its internal tasks and controls interaction between programs and the operating system, and between programs themselves. It's generally protected from end users fiddling with it. The *user mode*, which is usually described as sitting above the kernel mode because it's closer to the end user, is where your applications run. The area is considered nonprotected because you have access to it through your applications.

Kernel Mode

Nothing happens in the Vista universe without the operating system knowing about it and giving its blessing. The kernel is the core of Vista. It acts as a "gofer" between the operating system and the computer's processor. As such, it's responsible for scheduling all the operating system's interactions with your computer. The kernel also manages all the interrelationships between the different kernel mode operations. It does this by means of *threads*. A thread is a series of instructions that are attached to a command that is executed by a program. Threads include memory addresses, scheduling for the amount of time the process will take, and anything else that describes the process.

The kernel mode is divided into three subsections: the Hardware Abstraction Layer (HAL), the kernel, and Executive Services. Executive Services is subdivided further into its own component parts; more on those parts shortly.

THE HAL AND THE KERNEL

The HAL controls the interaction between the kernel and the system hardware. One of the design goals of Vista was the capability to be easily ported from one type of computer to another. To this end, the HAL *abstracts* the hardware from the kernel so that the kernel doesn't need to know what type of hardware is installed in the computer. This abstraction extends to running multiple processors in your computer. Vista is one of the only PC-based operating systems that can take advantage of symmetric multiprocessing. The abstraction provided by the HAL gives Vista greater stability.

Because of the abstraction provided by the HAL, software that attempts to directly access the hardware isn't permitted to run. The HAL, working with the kernel, stops those programs dead in their tracks. For performance reasons, many DOS programs—particularly games—use direct hardware access. Programs written for Vista don't need to worry about how to access the hardware; they just ask the operating system for support, and Vista takes care of the rest.

Vista does have some communication that bypasses the HAL and goes directly to the hardware. In each of these cases, the communication is between the Executive Services and the individual drivers for hardware devices such as the video card and network card. But the concept of hardware abstraction is still maintained.

EXECUTIVE SERVICES

Executive Services is a set of separate components that complete the underpinnings of the Vista kernel mode. Each Executive Service controls a specific function. The following is a brief overview of each of those functions.

I/O Manager

I/O Manager handles all communication between your applications and your hard disk. Additionally, it manages drivers for different file formats (FAT, NTFS) and keeps the Vista kernel informed of the hard drive's status. I/O Manager also manages network cards and modems. In short, this manager controls any device that delivers data to or from the computer. Its components are illustrated in Figure 1.3.

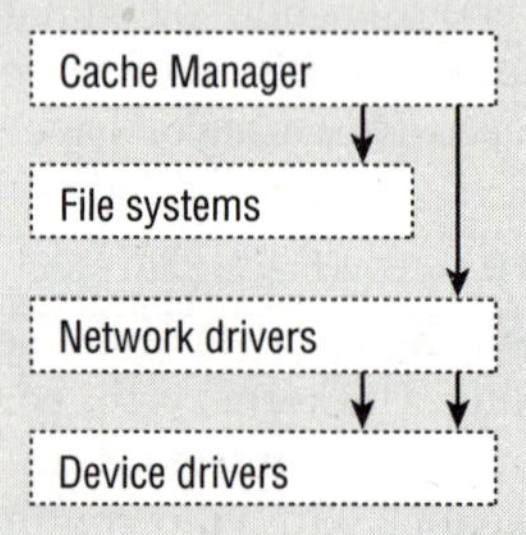

FIGURE 1.3
I/O Manager is built to simultaneously control multiple devices and drivers.

I/O Manager is divided into the following sections:

Cache Manager Monitors your use of disk cache and disk pages.

File systems Manages the file systems you have installed on your computer.

Network drivers Controls your network cards and network protocols.

Device drivers Manages the hardware you have in your computer. This includes everything from your hard drives and modem to your keyboard and mouse.

Object Manager

Object Manager manages all the system objects that Vista uses. An object is a piece of data the operating system uses to create system events. Objects are acted on by processes. Every object has a handle (yes, that's the technical term) that a process connects to in order to complete its job. The Object Manager is extensible, meaning that it can be expanded and added to as new object types are developed.

Security Reference Monitor

Security Reference Monitor is the "watchdog" for Vista. Security Reference Monitor assigns security tokens and authenticates users each time they execute a task.

Process Manager

Process Manager is the complement to Object Manager. Process Manager manages the creation and deletion of processes. A *process* is a set of threads combined with a memory address and the necessary objects needed to complete a system task. The Process Manager works in conjunction with the Security Reference Monitor to ensure that every process is assigned a security token.

Local Procedure Call Facility

Local Procedure Call facility acts as a negotiator between user mode and kernel mode. From an internal standpoint, Vista uses a client-server model to administer itself. Just as Vista connects to a server and requests services from it, the Vista user mode requests services from the Vista kernel mode. Those requests are handled by local procedure calls. Local procedure calls are also used in standard client-server networks.

Virtual Memory Manager

Virtual Memory Manager oversees how Vista uses virtual memory. To increase the amount of usable memory space, Vista uses hard-disk space as memory when it runs out of memory (which can happen fairly quickly with some high-powered programs). The disk memory is known as *virtual* memory.

Win32K and GDI

The Win32K and Graphics Device Interface (GDI) are the graphics subsystem of Vista. The graphics functions in earlier versions of Windows NT were provided by the Win32 subsystem in user mode. Microsoft moved the graphics subsystem into Executive Services for version 4 to give the graphics functions a performance boost. In fact, this resulted in the single greatest increase in the apparent speed of Windows NT 4.

User Mode

In the Vista user mode, each of your programs runs in a separate memory space, an arrangement that protects each program from the others in case one should crash. This is true for 64-bit, 32-bit, and 16-bit programs, both Windows and DOS.

NOTE The 64-bit version of Vista is far more restrictive about what it will run than the 32-bit version. While the 32-bit version will run 16-bit libraries, the 64-bit version won't. Consequently, you'll find that many of your older applications won't work with the 64-bit version of Vista. This limitation isn't due to Vista, but in the way that the 64-bit environment must work to provide the benefits that it does.

The user mode is divided into subsystems. Each subsystem handles a different type of application and can report directly to the kernel mode. The subsystems are described briefly in Table 1.1.

In addition to the subsystems noted in Table 1.1, user mode may also contain VDMs (video display metafiles). A VDM simulates a computer running MS-DOS 5, with 16 MB of RAM and conventional, expanded, and extended memory. As stated earlier in this chapter, this simulation makes it possible to run MS-DOS programs on Vista. It also enables you to run 16-bit Windows applications by simulating Windows 3.1 running on that MS-DOS computer with 16 MB of memory. By default, Vista starts all 16-bit Windows applications in the same Win16 on Win32 or *WOW* environment. This simulates exactly the environment the programs were written to operate in under Windows 3.1. However, Vista gives you the ability to start the application in a separate memory space, which creates another WOW for each 16-bit Windows application.

Remember that the WOW environment imitates Windows 3.1 so well that it even hangs just like the old Windows did! That means that if one of your 16-bit Windows applications crashes, it will take all the other 16-bit applications with it—unless you have chosen to start them in their own memory spaces, in which case the other 16-bit programs will keep running without a problem.

TABLE 1.1: User Mode Subsystems

SUBSYSTEM	DESCRIPTION
Win32	Administers 32-bit and 16-bit Windows programs.
OS/2	Administers character-based OS/2 programs.
POSIX	Administers POSIX programs, which are UNIX hybrids that can be run on any POSIX-compliant system, including Vista. They're written to a series of application programming interfaces (APIs) that are platform independent. They control interaction with system components such as hard drives and memory.
Security	Administers system security and manages security tokens, monitors, and passwords. The user mode portion of the Security subsystem runs only during a user logon.

TIP If a 16-bit application crashes, it will also crash any other program running in the same memory space. If this happens, you can stop the WOW by using Task Manager and restarting the 16-bit program. All 32-bit applications will be unaffected by the crash and continue to run normally.

Differences between 32-bit and 64-bit Architectures

From an administrator's perspective, there are a number of important differences between the 32-bit and 64-bit versions of Vista. One of the most noticeable differences is that the 64-bit version tends to run faster because Vista can make use of the full 64 bits of a machine to reduce the number of operations required to perform some tasks. A 64-bit register also provides better and easier access to memory. The system also has wider buses to transfer information. In short, a 64-bit system has all kinds of additional resources that a 32-bit system lacks and Vista makes use of them all.

A 64-bit system is also supposedly more secure because it can't run any of those 16-bit applications that caused so many problems in the past. The 16-bit applications relied on libraries that have all kinds of nonsecure code—a perfect target for hackers who want to gain entry to the system. Of course, the fact that you can't run 16-bit applications in Vista means that some applications that did run in the past won't run now. You'll find that game playing (at least older games) is a lot harder in the 64-bit version of Vista.

You'll find that having a 64-bit version of Vista can also present some support problems because now you need 64-bit drivers as well. Many vendors aren't providing 64-bit drivers yet because there isn't enough market appeal for them. The same problem occurred when the 32-bit version of Windows first appeared. Vendors tried to stay in the world of 16-bits until enough people asked for the 32-bit drivers. Eventually, every vendor started producing 32-bit drivers and it became hard to locate 16-bit drivers. The same process is likely to occur with the 64-bit version of Vista. Eventually, you'll find that you can obtain all of the 64-bit drivers you need. In the meantime, it pays to shop carefully.

Summary

This chapter has discussed what you need to know about Windows Vista in order to decide whether to upgrade to it or stay with your current version of Windows. You've discovered the new Vista editions and what they provide. The overview of new Vista features in this chapter should act as your guide to whether an upgrade makes sense.

It's time to do a little work on the upgrade of your system. First, you need to decide whether there's a good reason to upgrade. Which new Vista feature grabs your attention? Second, you need to consider your current hardware. The "Will Your Computer Be Able to Run Vista?" section in Chapter 2 can help you with this part. Once you know what you want out of Vista and whether you can update to it without changing your hardware, you're on your way to making the upgrade decision. Of course, many systems out there won't run Vista. Now you have to make the choice by weighing the cost of new hardware against the new functionality you'll receive.

Chapter 2 is all about installing Vista on your system. You'll need to consider everything about the upgrade before you even begin the installation. Many systems will require some type of upgrade to run Vista at all. Fortunately, Chapter 2 tells you about a few shortcuts you can take to make the pain of update a little easier to take. Once you know you have a system that can support Vista, you'll use the remainder of Chapter 2 to perform the actual installation.

Chapter 2

Installing Vista

This chapter discusses how to install Vista in each of the four ways in which you may want to install it: as an upgrade, as a new installation on a computer that already has installed an operating system that you want to keep, as a clean installation, or as a BitLocker installation. *BitLocker* is a new drive encryption technology that Microsoft has introduced. This technology encrypts the entire drive and makes it impossible for anyone to hijack your files, even if they move the drive to another system. Using this technology means making a few changes to the normal setup process. Chapter 21 describes BitLocker in much greater detail.

NOTE This chapter concentrates on the needs of the individual installer or someone working with fewer than 250 machines. Microsoft has provided a number of automation tools in a package called Business Desktop Deployment (BDD) for organizations with a lot of machines to maintain. You'll find a complete description of BDD in Part IX of the book. This part of the book includes a number of testing tools as well that are only referenced in this chapter.

At the end of the chapter, you'll find a discussion of how to perform an unattended installation, which can be useful if you need to install the same operating system multiple times. Unattended installations typically serve the needs of someone who has a number of machines with the same specifications to support. For example, your organization might have 20 Dell computers of the same make and model with the same configuration. An unattended install works well, in this case, because you can easily configure the setup to meet the needs of a single machine. Use BDD when you have a considerable number of machines of different types or require special support such as multiple languages.

- Preparing for installation
- Upgrading to Vista
- Performing an installation of Vista
- Using the Windows Easy Transfer to transfer files and settings
- Keeping Windows updated
- Automating the installation of Vista

Vista: What's New?

Installations in Vista are significantly different from previous versions of Windows. In previous versions, you had to answer a lot of questions and go through a number of configuration steps in a character mode setup before the system rebooted and let you continue with a graphical installation. Microsoft streamlines the whole process in Vista and makes the process friendlier. No longer do you work in the character mode setup unless you have special needs to address. Many of the special setup requirements appear as options that you can use when you need to, but don't have to pass through on your way through the installation process. It's easier to bring up a command prompt when you need it to use command-line utilities, and you generally don't have to restart the machine afterward. In short, Vista provides a new kind of installation that will require a little time to learn, but one you'll like once you get to know it.

The Order of Business

Here's the order of business for installing Vista successfully:

1. First, make sure that your computer will be able to run Vista. Start by comparing your system specifications with the minimum requirements, and see whether you need to upgrade any components.
2. Then, assuming your computer has an operating system loaded already, insert the Vista DVD in your computer and run the Windows Upgrade Advisor. As of this writing, you can only upgrade from Windows XP SP2 versions. The upgrade can require a significant amount of time to complete—even Microsoft warns you of the potential problems.
3. If you want to perform a clean installation of Vista rather than an upgrade, but you want your new installation to pick up your current settings and some of your files, run the Windows Easy Transfer to save the settings from your current version of Windows and then boot from the Vista DVD to start the installation.
4. Then perform the upgrade, new installation, or clean installation.
5. If you ran the Windows Easy Transfer, run it again to apply your files and settings.

Will Your Computer Be Able to Run Vista?

First, make sure that your computer will be able to run Vista. The following sections discuss the main requirements.

Processor

Vista requires a minimum of a 1 GHz 32-bit or 64-bit processor. You can choose a processor from

- AMD (`http://www.amd.com/us-en/Processors/ProductInformation/0,,30_118_9331_12862%5e13301,00.html`)
- Intel (`http://www.intel.com/business/bss/products/client/vistasolutions/index.htm`)
- Via (`http://www.via.com.tw/en/products/vista/cpu.jsp`)

Realistically, you'll want the fastest 64-bit processor you can get because many Vista features require a lot of processing power, especially when you use the Aero Glass user interface. The reason you want a 64-bit processor is that this is Microsoft's last 32-bit operating system. In addition, because Microsoft designed Vista from the ground up to use a 64-bit processor, you gain significant performance benefits by having a 64-bit processor in your machine.

If you don't know what processor your computer has, watch the information that comes up as it boots. This will give you at least the processor type and speed. If you have Windows installed on the system, you can also right-click Computer and choose Properties. The General (opening) tab of the System Properties dialog box tells you about the processor installed on your machine.

RAM

Vista requires a minimum of 512 MB of RAM to install and run. This, too, is an absolute minimum and delivers poor performance unless your processor is extremely fast (in which case the lack of RAM cannibalizes processor performance). For a single user running one or two tasks at a time, 1 GB is enough. For running several large applications at once, get 2 GB or more RAM.

NOTE Vista can access a maximum of 4 GB of RAM when working with a 32-bit processor. The 64-bit version of Vista can access a maximum of 128 GB of memory. The theoretical maximum memory access for current 64-bit hardware is 1 TB physical or 4 TB virtual, so Microsoft may eventually move the Vista memory limit upward.

If you don't know how much RAM your computer has, watch the count of RAM when you boot. If the number is in kilobytes (KB), divide by 1,024 to get the number in megabytes (MB). Alternatively, click Start, right-click Computer, and choose Properties from the shortcut menu. Windows displays the System Properties dialog box open at the General tab. The amount of RAM is reported at the bottom.

GET PLENTY OF RAM

Everyone knows that you need plenty of RAM to run Windows. That's true—up to a point. But most people still have too little RAM on their computers.

Vista will run—well, more like stagger along—on 512 MB RAM. If the computer has a fast processor, and if you don't use any large applications or large files, performance may be tolerable. But the hard disk will be kept busy as Windows continually uses virtual memory to store the information that won't fit in the RAM.

If you're buying a new computer, you'll be much better off saving a little money on the processor and putting it into RAM. Unless you're running the latest 3D games or performing terrain mapping or other advanced imaging, you'll notice little benefit from having a few hundred extra megahertz of CPU on your computer. But another 512 MB (better, another 1 GB or more) of RAM will make a huge difference on a system with just about any processor. For an existing PC, the slower and older your CPU, the more dramatic a difference more RAM will make in performance.

The ReadyBoost feature of Vista also makes it possible to increase higher speed memory using a flash device such as a Universal Serial Bus (USB) flash drive. Simply place the flash drive into the USB port and Vista will use it as memory that is faster than a hard drive, but not quite as fast as RAM. You can't use a flash drive as an absolute RAM replacement, but if you already have 512 MB of RAM and want to give your system a bit of a boost, a 2 GB or larger flash drive can make a difference. Of course, your system must have ReadyBoost running (it's on by default) to make use of this feature. Chapter 33 describes how to work with services such as ReadyBoost.

Free Disk Space

Vista requires approximately 15 GB of free disk space to install on a 20 GB hard drive. You'll need a minimum of a 22 GB hard drive to use BitLocker. If you're installing over a network, you'll need more free space. In addition, there has to be room for your paging file (by default, 1.5 times the amount of RAM in your computer) and for your hibernation file (the same size as the amount of RAM) if your computer supports hibernation. On top of that, you'll need space for any applications you want to install and any files you want to create.

In practice, it's a good idea to have at least 20 GB of free space on the drive on which you install Vista (for a total of 40 GB), plus space for your applications and files. To see how much space is free on a drive, right-click the drive in an Explorer window and choose Properties from the shortcut menu. The General tab of the resulting Properties dialog box for the drive shows how much free space it has. You may also see the size of the hard drive when you start your system (vendors commonly hide the hard drive size in the model number). Hard disks are so inexpensive these days, and so easy to install, that there's little reason to try to hobble along with a full hard disk.

Sometimes you can't get to Windows (it might not be installed) and must know the particulars of a hard drive. You can open a command prompt and use the `Dir` command to display the remaining space on a hard drive. If you need to know more information that `Dir` provides, use the DiskPart utility. Select a drive by typing **`Select Disk`** ***`0`*** (the number of the drive you want to check), then use the `Detail Disk` command to show the partition and space information for that drive.

DirectX 9–Capable Video Adapter and Monitor

You actually have two options for video adapter with Vista. If you want to use the Aero Glass feature, you must have a DirectX 9–compatible display adapter with at least 128 MB of memory. Vista currently supports display adapters from the following vendors.

- Intel (`http://www.intel.com/business/bss/products/client/vistasolutions/index.htm`)
- ATI (`http://www.ati.com/technology/windowsvista/index.html`)
- NVidia (`http://www.nvidia.com/page/technology_vista_home.html`)
- S3 (`http://www.s3graphics.com/en/products/vista/index.jsp`)
- Via (`http://www.via.com.tw/en/products/vista/platform.jsp`)

More graphics memory is better when it comes to Aero Glass. In fact, if you intend to perform graphics heavy tasks, you might want to use a system that allows dual display adapters in a Scalable Link Interface (SLI) configuration. The display adapter must also include these features.

- Windows Display Driver Model (WDDM)–compatible driver
- Pixel shader 2.0 support in hardware
- 32 bits per pixel graphics resolution

If you choose not to use Aero Glass, your video adapter and monitor need to be capable of SVGA resolution (800 × 600 pixels) with 256 or more colors. This is the minimum display resolution permitted, unlike in earlier Windows versions. (Safe Mode still runs in standard VGA, and you can configure individual apps to switch to that mode with Compatibility Mode, but it's not for regular use.) Beyond that, just about any Peripheral Component Interconnect (PCI) or Accelerated Graphics Port (AGP) video adapter should work (drivers permitting, of course), as should any cathode ray tube (CRT) or liquid crystal display (LCD) monitor.

DVD Drive

You need a DVD drive or access to one to install Vista. If the drive is on another computer, you can install across a network or copy the files to your local drive and run them from there. You can also do diskless network installs in a corporate environment.

Checking System Compatibility

There isn't any doubt that the upgrade requirements for Vista are considerably higher than previous Windows versions. You'll also find that you need new drivers to meet Microsoft's stricter requirements. In fact, you'll find that Vista simply won't upgrade some past Windows versions. The following sections provide the information you need to ensure Vista will run on your system.

Suggested Upgrade Paths for Previous Versions of Windows

Vista requires a significant investment in hardware, so let's face it, many machines out there today can't run it solely from a hardware perspective. In addition, Microsoft has limited the updates it supports. You can't support any past version to just any version of Vista. Table 2.1 shows the update paths that Microsoft has envisioned for Vista.

NOTE As of this writing, the Vista upgrade only supports Windows XP SP2. The upgrade process might not work if you have an earlier version of Windows XP (including SP1).

TABLE 2.1: Vista Upgrade Paths from Previous Windows Versions

PREVIOUS VERSION	UPDATE VERSIONS
Windows XP Professional	Vista Business and Vista Ultimate
Windows XP Home	Vista Home Basic, Vista Home Premium, Vista Business, and Vista Ultimate
Windows XP Media Center	Vista Home Premium and Vista Ultimate
Windows XP Tablet PC	Vista Business and Vista Ultimate

Table 2.1 contains a very short upgrade list. However, any other previous version of Windows requires that you perform a clean install. Essentially, this means starting from scratch, although, you can save your settings for future use.

Using the Microsoft Windows Vista Upgrade Advisor

To check whether Vista thinks your computer will be able to run it, run the Microsoft Windows Vista Upgrade Advisor program. Don't use the commonly available alternatives, such as the update advisor for Windows XP. The following steps describe how to check your system.

1. Insert the Vista DVD. If your computer doesn't automatically start running the DVD, open an Explorer window, navigate to the DVD, and double-click the `setup.exe` program.
2. On the opening screen, click the Check Compatibility Online link.

3. Download and install the Microsoft Windows Vista Upgrade Advisor by following the prompts provided by the installation program.
4. Check Launch Microsoft Windows Vista Upgrade Advisor on the final installation page and click Close. Vista automatically starts the program for you.
5. Click Start System Scan. The program asks you to choose the Vista features you want to use. Many of the entries are self-explanatory, such as using the Aero Glass interface. Other entries are more nebulous, such as simplifying your business.
6. Check the features that you expect to use. When you get to the bottom of the list, you'll see Microsoft's recommendation for the version of Vista that you should use.
7. Click Next (it's hidden at the bottom of the list). The upgrade advisor performs a check of your system's hardware. If the program finds discrepancies, it will display a list of the required fixes for Vista. Figure 2.1 shows a typical report.
8. Click Next. The upgrade advisor performs a check of all of the drivers and other low-level software on your system. You'll see another report similar to the one shown in Figure 2.1, but for software this time.
9. Click Next. You'll see a final report window where you can choose to save the report to disk as an HTML file or print it.
10. Click Close. Windows closes the program.

Follow the Microsoft Windows Vista Upgrade Advisor advice to get your computer ready for upgrading to Vista. In particular, you need to take care of any blocking issues that the Advisor has identified. An example of a blocking issue is not having enough disk space to install Vista. You might need to remove some existing files or reconfigure your partitions using the DiskPart utility in order to resolve such an issue.

FIGURE 2.1 Use the Microsoft Windows Upgrade Advisor to check whether your computer will be able to run Vista.

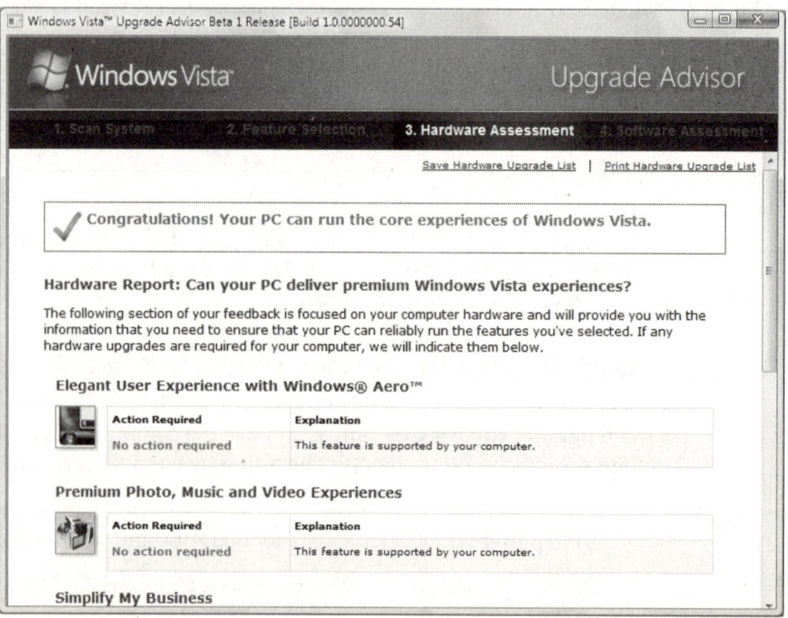

Choosing an Installation Method

Once you've decided to install Vista, your next decision is how to install Vista on your computer. You can install Vista in three ways:

Upgrade You can upgrade any of the operating system choices in Table 2.1 with Windows Vista. This means you essentially overwrite the previous version of Windows with Vista. Upgrading like this transfers all your files, settings, and applications to Vista, so (in theory) you can pick up your work or play straight away in Vista where you left off.

New installation A new installation installs Vista on a new disk or a separate partition. You can use the Windows Easy Transfer to copy your files and settings from your previous version of Windows to Vista.

Clean installation You can install Vista from scratch on your computer, deleting the previous copy that was there rather than upgrading it. Again, you can use the Windows Easy Transfer to copy your files and settings from your previous version of Windows to Vista. You'll need to install all the applications you want to use after you install Vista.

Which type of installation to perform can be a tricky decision. The longer you've been running Windows on this computer since installing it, the stronger the arguments are for both an upgrade and a clean installation:

- By now, you've probably installed all the applications you need and got them working together. By upgrading, you can transition your whole work environment to Vista, so that your Desktop, Start menu, and folder structure retain their current settings and your applications all work as before.
- Then again, you probably have applications that you no longer use, or applications that no longer work. (Techies call this a "dirty system.") By performing a clean install, you can strip your system down to only the software you need. It'll take longer, but the result may be better. Similarly, your data folders could probably do with some cleaning out and archiving.

If you need to install a new hard drive as your main hard drive, you'll need to perform a clean install. Because Vista uses a substantially different file system, you'll find that some of the old tricks such as using ghost copies don't work as well as they could and may not work at all. Of course, the vendors will eventually provide updated versions of their products that do work with Vista as long as you're not using BitLocker (which encrypts everything in a way that would make it difficult to create a ghost copy).

Preparing for Installation

Once you've established that your computer should be able to run Vista, prepare for installation by taking those of the following steps that are applicable to the type of installation you're planning (upgrade, new installation, or clean installation).

Back Up All Your Data Files

For safety, back up all your data files shortly before installation, using your usual backup medium.

Write Down Internet Connection Information

If you're planning a new installation or a clean installation, rather than an upgrade, and you use a dial-up Internet connection, write down the information you need to create the connection: your

ISP account username, your password, your ISP's phone number, and your ISP's primary and secondary DNS servers. You might also want to write down the information for connecting to your mail servers.

Plug In and Switch On All Hardware

Make sure that all the hardware you intend to use with the computer is attached to it and powered on. For example, if you'll use a printer and scanner with the computer, make sure these devices are attached to the computer and powered on, so that Setup can detect them if it's smart enough.

WARNING Make sure your hardware configuration is exactly the way you want it before activating Vista. Activation creates a code based on the installed hardware that locks that copy of Vista to that hardware, so if you make a lot of hardware changes to the system later, you might need to reactivate (by calling Microsoft). I'll explain activation in more detail later in this chapter.

Use Windows Easy Transfer to Transfer Settings

Vista includes a wizard for transferring files and settings from one computer or operating system to another. Windows Easy Transfer can save you a great deal of time when you want to transfer files and settings either to a new computer that's running Vista or to a new installation of Vista on the same computer on which you've kept your previous installation of Windows as a dual boot. For example, if you choose to test Vista on a new partition before committing yourself to it, you can use Windows Easy Transfer to transfer your work environment to the new partition so that you can use your regular settings and files.

Before you use Windows Easy Transfer, make sure you're connected to any network drive you want to use, or that you have a removable disk or recordable DVD ready. To transfer files and settings, you'll need plenty of storage. You can save settings files to a floppy drive, but most data files will be too big. The following steps describe how to use Windows Easy Transfer.

NOTE As an alternative to working with the Vista DVD, you can choose the Start ➢ Accessories ➢ System Tools ➢ Windows Easy Transfer to start the wizard. At this point, you can begin with step 3 of the following procedure.

1. Insert the Vista DVD. If your computer doesn't automatically start running the DVD, open an Explorer window, navigate to the DVD, and double-click the `setup.exe` program. Windows displays the Welcome to Microsoft Vista screen.
2. Click the Transfer Files and Settings from Another Computer link. Windows starts the Windows Easy Transfer Wizard.
3. Click Next. If your computer is running any applications, Windows Easy Transfer displays a list of them and asks to close them.
4. Click Close to close all of the open applications. Windows Easy Transfer asks whether you want to start a new transfer or continue an existing transfer.
5. Click Start a New Transfer. Windows Easy Transfer asks which computer you're using.
6. Choose My Old Computer. At this point, you have three transfer options.
   - **Use a Windows Easy Transfer USB Cable.** This option lets you transfer data directly between machines, even when you don't have a network setup.

- **Use a Network.** Use this option when you want to store the settings in some other location. A network share is the best option in most cases. When using the Connect Directly to Your New Computer Through a Local Network options, both computers must be active at the same time and you use a key to encrypt the data exchange. However, you can also choose to use an intermediate location, such as online storage, by selecting the Use a Shared Network Location option that both computers can access. Both computers must be able to access the shared location directly, even if they have no direct access to each other. In this case, one computer can save the data to the common location and the other can pick it up later. You use a password to encrypt the data file containing the settings. You can use this option when installing Vista on another partition of the current machine.
- **Use a Type of Removable Storage.** This option lets you save your settings to removable media including CD, DVD, USB flash drive, and external hard drive. This option works very well for moving common settings between machines for multiple installations. You can also use it as a method of making regular backups of your settings. This is also the option you should use when you plan to make a clean install of Vista on your machine. As with the Shared Network Location option, you must supply a password for encryption purposes when using this option.

NOTE You must use a CD-RW or DVD-RW disk when using the CD or DVD option. You can't use write-once media such as DVD+R.

7. Choose one of the types of data transfer or storage. Since the direct connections are straightforward (you begin transferring immediately), the procedure continues with the stored options described in the previous step.
8. Choose a location to store the information. You can choose a local drive, networked drive, Universal Naming Convention (UNC) location, or even an online location. Click Next. Windows Easy Transfer asks which settings to save.
   - **All User Accounts, Files, and Settings.** Saves every setting on your system that Windows Easy Transfer recognizes. Depending on your application, you may need to perform a separate save. For example, Windows Easy Transfer won't save your Firefox bookmarks. Use the Firefox features to save your bookmarks separately. In general, if an application provides a separate setting saving utility, it makes sense to use it.
   - **My User Account, Files, and Settings Only.** Saves only those settings that are related to your account on the system. This setting does preserve your user settings, but it won't save those associated with the Administrator account.
   - **Advanced Options.** Lets you decide what to save. This option can become quite complex, but it offers the greatest flexibility in saving your settings. If you want to be safe, use the first option in this list. However, if you've been using your system for a long time and want to clean up settings you no longer use, this is the option to try. You should also view this option as a means to verify what Windows Easy Transfer actually saves for you. If you don't see some very special setting in the list, you'll want to save it separately.
9. Choose one of the settings options. When working with Advanced Options, you'll normally need to wait several minutes while Windows Easy Transfer collects all of the settings and displays them to you. Choose the individual settings and click Next. You can use the Add

Files and Add Folders links to add more files and settings to the list. No matter which of the settings saving options you choose, Windows Easy Tranfer will begin collecting and saving the settings it's designed to save. Be patient, even on a fast machine this process is long and slow (think about going to lunch).

10. Click Close when you see the final dialog box.

For details of how to apply your saved files and settings to your new installation of Windows, see "Applying Your Files and Settings" later in this chapter.

Stop Any Antivirus Software or Disk Utilities

Stop any antivirus software or disk utilities before running the Windows installation, because the installation process needs direct access to your hardware and the antivirus software might see that access as an attack and prevent it. The exception to the rule is the built-in Windows software. For example, you don't need to stop Windows Defender. In addition, even if you haven't configured Windows Firewall to allow for any installation requirements, Setup will ask to configure it for you.

Export Settings for Applications that Support It

Many applications today provide a means to export your settings. For example, when working with Firefox, choose Bookmarks ➤ Manage Bookmarks and then choose File ➤ Export to save your bookmarks. Of course, this process only saves your bookmarks. You'll need a separate program, such as MozBackup (`http://mozbackup.jasnapaka.com/`) to back up all of your settings. The point is that many modern applications provide some means to back up your settings. If you don't see a built-in feature to perform this task, then look online or ask the vendor about backup functionality. Generally, you're going to find that Windows Easy Transfer does a very good job with Windows, a mediocre job with Windows applications, and a poor (or nonexistent) job with third-party applications, so this separate step is very necessary.

Upgrading to Vista

Upgrading to Vista means a lot more than simply checking your hardware for compatibility and ensuring that you can actually update your copy of Windows. Vista has stricter application requirements, so you need to perform tasks such as checking application compatibility. The following sections discuss utilities you can use to ensure a good installation and the actual installation process. All of these tools also appear as part of the BDD discussed in Part IX of the book. The text references you to the appropriate information in that part of the book where appropriate.

NOTE **Upgrade installations commonly require a large amount of space on the boot partition for your system. The boot partition is the partition that contains all of the boot files for the machine, which isn't necessarily the same as the partition where you have installed Windows. Some systems have a small boot partition to allow for a multiple boot scenario or may have a small drive from a previous setup used for booting. A typical Vista install requires about 4 GB on the boot partition for an upgrade. If you have less than 4 GB on the boot partition, you won't be able to perform an upgrade even though everything else is acceptable.**

Checking Compatibility with the Application Compatibility Toolkit (ACT)

The Windows ACT has been around for a long time now. It helps you ensure your application runs as intended on the Windows platform of choice. In fact, ACT takes you through an entire testing and deployment process prior to making the target application available to users. You get this tool as part of BDD or you can download it separately at `http://www.microsoft.com/downloads/details.aspx?FamilyID=4005DA79-933A-4CC8-BF86-FE2E28B792FD`.

Application compatibility checking is essential for Vista because many applications that ran in the past won't run at all. For example, Vista doesn't support the old HLP (help) file format. Consequently, applications that still use help files in the old format aren't as useful as applications that rely on the Compiled Help Module (CHM) file format. Likewise, some applications don't have the publisher identified, which means that you'll have to go through a security check every time you run the application (even if you run it in administrator mode). Although these changes may seem minor, they all add up to applications that simply won't run under Vista.

NOTE Make sure you download ACT 5.0 for Vista. The ACT 4.1 version is for Windows XP and older versions of Windows. In addition, through some very strange decision process, Microsoft decided to use the .NET Framework 1.1 for ACT 5.0. The program won't even install unless you have the .NET Framework 1.1 installed on your machine (despite the fact that Vista has the .NET Framework 2.0 already installed). You can download the .NET Framework 1.1 from `http://www.microsoft.com/downloads/details.aspx?FamilyId=262D25E3-F589-4842-8157-034D1E7CF3A3` or you can get it from Windows Update. Make sure you also install .NET Framework 1.1 SP 1 (`http://www.microsoft.com/downloads/thankyou.aspx?familyId=A8F5654F-088E-40B2-BBDB-A83353618B38`) or you'll experience problems getting Vista to work with the ACT 5.0 setup program correctly.

After you download ACT, you'll need to install it. ACT requires access to a copy of SQL Server. Fortunately, you can download and install SQL Server Express Edition (`http://msdn.microsoft.com/vstudio/express/sql/`) and Service Pack 1 (`http://www.microsoft.com/downloads/details.aspx?familyid=CB6C71EA-D649-47FF-9176-E7CAC58FD4BC`) or higher for this purpose. You won't want to use SQL Server Express for a real-world enterprise installation, but it works fine for a local or small business installation.

The following sections provide details on using ACT for a single machine or in a small business environment. You can find additional information about ACT in the "Testing Applications with Microsoft Application Compatibility Toolkit 5.0" section of Chapter 39.

Configuring ACT

The ACT setup process occurs when you choose Start ➤ Programs ➤ Microsoft Application Compatibility Toolkit 5.0 ➤ Application Compatibility Manager the first time. The following steps help you configure ACT for use.

1. Click Next to get past the Welcome dialog box. ACT asks what type of installation you want to perform. Generally, you need to use the Enterprise Configuration unless your organization already has a central data store configured and you have access to it.

2. Select Enterprise Configuration and click Next. ACT requires a database to store the information it collects. You must select a SQL Server instance first, and then create a database within it. Don't select one of the existing databases; the ACT database should appear as a separate entity.

3. Choose a SQL Server entry from the list. If you don't see your server, click Browse and choose one of the entries in the Select Server dialog box.

4. Type the name of the database you want to use. The example uses ActData as the name of the database.

5. Click Next. ACT also requires a log file location for your data entries. The example uses `C:\ACT_Log`.
6. Type a location for the ACT log file. Click Next. ACT asks which credentials it should use to interact with the system. This step is important because the credentials you choose can affect system security. Always choose Local System when you don't need to access a network drive. Otherwise, choose credentials that have the least privilege necessary to perform the task.
7. Choose Local System or provide other credentials for ACT to use. Click Next.
8. Click Finish. ACT is ready to use. You see the Microsoft Application Compatibility Manager window with the Configure tab selected.

Notice that the Log Processing Service settings are blank. ACT doesn't configure itself as a Log Processing Service. In order to collect data and process the resulting logs, you need to set up the Log Processing Service. The following steps get you started.

1. Click Change Settings. The Settings dialog box appears.
2. Check This Computer is Configured as a Log Processing Service.
3. Select the Local System Account unless you need to access a share on a network drive.
4. Type the path to the local or network share in the Path field. ACT automatically fills in the Share As field when necessary. You can also choose a share by clicking Browse and searching for the share.
5. Click OK. ACT locates the share and starts the service for you.

Creating a Data Collection Package

ACT must collect data to provide you with reports on application usability. You must define one or more data collection packages that tell ACT how to collect information. ACT 5.0 provides options specifically designed to help you work with Vista. The following steps tell how to create a Vista data collection package.

1. Choose the Collect tab of the Microsoft Application Compatibility Manager and then click the Data Collection Packages link. If this is your first experience with ACT, the lists in the tab are blank.
2. Click New. You'll see a New Data Collection Page dialog box. You must define the major category of data to obtain, the time to start collecting the data, the amount of time to collect data, the interval at which to save data, and the location of the data store.
3. Choose Deploying a New Operating System or Service Pack. This option chooses Vista specific evaluators. Click Advanced to see the list of available evaluators and those chosen by default. Check any additional evaluators you want to use and click OK.
4. Choose a starting time for the collection. The default setting collects data as soon as you finish installing Vista.
5. Select a collection duration. The default value of 3 Days is enough to test common applications. You'll need to select longer collection intervals for less used applications. For example, you might perform system maintenance only on Fridays. If you want to test these applications at least twice, you'll need to select an interval of at least 14 Days.

6. Select an upload interval. Longer intervals tax system resources less, but shorter intervals provide more data points that you can analyze faster. The default setting of 2 hours works in most cases.
7. Define an output location. Choose the Local (`%AllUsersAppData%\Microsoft\Application Compatibility Toolkit 5\DataCollector\Output`) setting for individual collection scenarios. As an alternative, choose a nonlocal share for group collection scenarios so the data appears on one centralized location.
8. Click Save. ACT asks you to choose a location for the self-extracting package.
9. Accept the default location or choose a network share when you want to use the same package on multiple machines.

At this point, you have a self-extracting package set up for testing purposes. You still need to start it. The executable file you created as part of the package creation process is actually an agent that you must start in order to collect data. After you collect enough data, you can organize it and then perform analysis on it.

Organizing the ACT Data

Now that you have some data to work with, it's time to organize it. The organizational tools appear on the Organize tab of the Microsoft Application Compatibility Manager. You organize the data in two ways. First, you prioritize the data. Second, you categorize the data using categories that you create. The following steps describe how to prioritize the data.

1. Select the Prioritize folder of the Organize Tab.
2. Choose an object type, Machine or Application, in the Type of Object field.
3. Select a priority from the list in the Priority field: Business Critical, Important, Nice to Have, or Do No Include in Reporting.
4. Highlight a machine or application you want to prioritize and then click Change Priority. Microsoft Application Compatibility Manager changes the priority of the item.
5. Repeat steps 1 through 4 for every data item collected for the target systems.

The next step is to categorize the data so that you can sort through it with greater ease in the reports. The Microsoft Application Compatibility Manager provides two sample categories for you: Software Vendor and Test Complexity. The Software Vendor has subcategories of 3rd-Party, Custom, and Microsoft Corporation. However, you shouldn't rely on these examples exclusively (you can delete them if you want). To manage the categories you use for reports, select the Create Categories folder of the Organize tab. Here are the basic tasks you can perform.

- **Adding a Category or Subcategory.** Type the new category or subcategory you want to create in the appropriate Name field and click Add.
- **Removing a Category or Subcategory.** Highlight the category or subcategory that you want to remove and click Remove.
- **Renaming a Subcategory.** Highlight the subcategory you want to rename and click Rename. Type the new name in the Rename Sub-Category dialog box and click OK.

Categories exist completely apart from priorities. Consequently, each data item you collect should have both a category and a priority. ACT assigns the All category to all data items at the outset, which means you always see them. The following steps help you categorize the data you collect.

1. Select the Assign Categories folder of the Organize tab.
2. Choose an object type, Machine or Application, in the Type of Object field.
3. Select a category in the Category field. You can only select categories that you have already created. When you select the All category, you can't select a subcategory.
4. Select a subcategory in the Subcategory field when required.
5. Highlight a machine or application you want to categorize and then click Assign Category. Microsoft Application Compatibility Manager changes the category and optionally the subcategory of the item.
6. Repeat steps 1 through 5 for every data item collected for the target systems.

Performing Analysis of the ACT Data

Creating a report in the Microsoft Application Compatibility Manager is the final step of the process. Performing this part of the task is painless. Begin by selecting the Analyze tab. The left side of this tab contains fields that help you create the report. The following steps help you configure a report.

1. Select a report type such as Select Deployment Type, Operating System, or Update Impact Analysis.
2. Select a subreport type, such as Windows Vista or Windows XP for the Operating System report.
3. Choose the source of the report data such as Applications, Computers, or Web Sites.
4. Choose an output format for the report such as Risk Rating, Priority, Deployment Status, Software Vendor, or Test Complexity. At this point, you see the report and report statistics. The report appears in the area in the right pane, while the report statistics appear below the selection fields in the left pane.

At this point, you can save the report for future use by clicking Save Report. You can also open existing reports by clicking Open Report. The Export Data option serves a different purpose by letting you export your data to another application. For example, you could use Excel to perform further analysis of the data.

Sometimes you'll still have too much data to view even with the categories and priorities you've applied. In this case, you can click Apply Filter to add filtering to the output. When you want to see all of the records again, click Show All.

Migrating Settings Using the Microsoft Windows User State Migration Tool (USMT)

USMT provides significantly more flexibility when transferring user information than using Windows Easy Transfer. Of course, you pay for that extra flexibility with significantly greater complexity. Consequently, if Windows Easy Transfer does the job for you, then you'll want to skip this section. You can download USMT at `http://www.microsoft.com/downloads/details.aspx?familyid=0CAA294C-29D9-4449-81D5-4B69B97DF7AE`.

Unlike Windows Easy Transfer, USMT is actually a command-line tool that you can add to everything from batch files to the task scheduler. Given the right command-line switches, you can use it to back up all of your system settings and data on a given interval. Of course, the main use for this utility is to move user settings and data from one machine to another, even if you must use an intermediate share on a network server to do it. Here are the command-line options for the USMT utility that stores the settings, ScanState.

/compress[+ | -] Enable or disable compression of the settings files. The default setting enables settings file compression.

/localonly Use only local drives for the scan. This setting overrides any settings you provide as part of an INF file.

/l:<log file> Place the log file in a particular location. The default location is the `\USMT` folder.

/v:<verbosity> Define the amount of information that appears in the log file. Adding more information provides additional details about the scanning process, but also increases the time and resources required to perform the scan. The verbosity levels are as follow:

Level 1 Enables verbose output.

Level 4 Enables error and status output.

Level 5 Enables verbose and status output.

Level 8 Enables error output to a debugger.

Level 9 Enables verbose output to a debugger.

Level 12 Enables error and status output to a debugger.

Level 15 Enables verbose, status, and debugger output.

/progress:<log> Defines the location of the progress log. The progress log informs you about the status of the scan.

/all Scan all of the users on a particular machine instead of just the current user. This setting lets you perform one scan per machine no matter how many users the machine supports. You must have administrator privileges to use this command-line switch.

/user:<user> Scan a particular user on the target machine. ScanState normally scans the currently logged on user. This command-line switch lets you scan other users. You must have administrator privileges to use this command-line switch. ScanState lets you use multiple `/user` switches on the same command line.

/ui:<timeout> Exclude any users whose accounts are inactive within the timeout value. This feature lets you get rid of any old accounts that aren't used on the current machine. The timeout value can include a number of days or appear as an actual date in Year/Month/Day format.

/i:<input inf> Use the specified INF file to configure ScanState. The INF file can define every element of the scan process. The following command-line switches augment and modify INF file use. Normally, ScanState enables all of these switches. However, if you use any of them on the command line, ScanState automatically disables the features you don't specify.

/x Remove the default migration groups from the scan. This command-line switch focuses the search on the target machine and the specified user. It applies to the [Administrator

Scripts] and [Administrator User Scripts] sections of the INF file, along with the Copy This State and Copy This User State settings.

/u Perform a full scan of the `HKEY_CURRENT_USER` hive. Use this setting to ensure that you have all settings for every application you have loaded on your system.

/s Scan all of the system settings and applications. This command-line switch refers to the [System Settings], [Applications], and [User Settings] sections of the INF file.

/f Use file rules during the scan. This command-line switch refers to the [Files and Folders], [Administrator Scripts], and [Administrator User Scripts] sections of the INF file.

/c Continue the scan process even after encountering a nonfatal error. ScanState always fails after a fatal error.

/p Generate a space estimate file (`USMTsize.txt`). You must specify `/compress-` option to use this feature. The resulting space estimate is for an uncompressed scan.

/o Overwrite any existing store data. If you don't specify this command-line switch and the selected data store (directory or other share) contains data, ScanState will fail. Use this option only when you know you want to overwrite the existing data.

/r:<count> Specify the failure retry count. The default setting of 3 works in most cases. However, you might want to increase this value in environments where you can't count on a good connection to the target machine. On the other hand, you can save scanning time by reducing the value in environments where you know the connection is completely reliable.

/w:<timeout> Specify the delay, in seconds, when retrying after a failure. The default setting is 1 second. However, you might want to increase this value when the connection between systems isn't only unreliable, but the interruption is long lasting.

/efs:<option> Specify choice of USMT behavior for Encrypted File System (EFS) files. The following list defines the standard behaviors.

abort ScanState automatically fails when it encounters an EFS. This is the default behavior.

skip ScanState skips the EFS partition and continues with any other data stores that appear in the processing list.

decryptcopy Decrypts the EFS data and stores it in an unencrypted state. This option can fail even when the files are accessible because Windows encrypts files using the user's credentials. If you're trying to save the data for another user, the scan can fail because you don't have the credentials required to decrypt the data.

copyraw Copies the EFS data in the encrypted state. This option can backfire, in some cases, because the credentials that Windows generates for a particular user can differ between installations. When this problem occurs, the data becomes permanently inaccessible. The only way to avoid problems when using this technique is to migrate the EFS certificates. The "Saving Settings with the User Setting Migration Toolkit (USMT)" section of Chapter 39 contains additional details on working with EFS.

<store path> Specify the path to the data store. You can use a local drive or save the data to a network drive using the UNC format.

/test Places USMT in a test mode so that you can perform tasks such as verifying that an INF works as expected. You can also use this command-line switch to verify that a scan won't fail due to a lack of permissions.

Using the ScanState utility to save local settings usually means relying on the command line rather than an INF file (an option discussed in detail in Chapter 39). For example, if you want to save the settings for the local drive to a local data store, you might use the following command line.

```
ScanState D:\MySettings /All /LocalOnly /V:5 /L:D:\MySettings\Scan.log
```

These settings create a store in the `D:\MySettings` folder for all users by scanning only the local drives. The scan information appears in `D:\MySettings\Scan.log` and has a verbosity level of 5.

After you install a new operating system and its associated applications, you use the LoadState utility to restore the settings that you saved using the ScanState utility. The following command-line switches work the same as the ScanState utility.

- `/compress[+ | -]`
- `/l:<log file>`
- `/v:<verbosity>`
- `/progress:<log>`
- `/all`
- `/user:<user>`
- `/i:<input inf>`
- `/x`
- `/u`
- `/s`
- `/f`
- `/r:<count>`
- `/w:<timeout>`
- `<store path>`
- `/c`
- `/test`

The LoadState utility also has a number of specialized command-line switches. The following list describes them.

/ix Don't use Scanstate INFs. This command-line switch lets you customize the restoration process. For example, you might only want to restore some users. You can't use this feature on a compressed data store.

/md:<mapping> Maps the user to a new domain. When the data store contains multiple domains, you specify the old domain first, followed by a colon, followed by the new domain such as `/md:OldDomain:NewDomain`. When you want to migrate all users to the same domain, specify only the new domain value. The old domain value can contain wildcard characters so that you can match multiple old domains, even when you don't want to match all of the domains.

/mu:<mapping> Maps the user to a new username. When the data store contains multiple users, you can match a particular user by specifying the older username first, followed by a colon, followed by the new username such as `/mu:OldUser:NewUser`.

/q Bypass the administrator account checks. This option lets any user load their own state information without administrator credentials. However, LoadState normally fails for other accounts since the user won't have access to them. In addition, LoadState can fail when the user has insufficient credentials to perform all tasks for their own account.

/lac[:<password>] Create local accounts in a disabled state. This command-line option lets you load state information even if the local account doesn't exist. USMT will create the account for you automatically and give the account the password you provide. You should use this option with caution since the password appears in plain text.

/lae Create local accounts in an enabled state. Use this command-line switch with `/lac` to enable any accounts that USMT creates automatically.

/efs:recover Recover any EFS files left in backup form. Use this option when a load fails and files remain in the backup.

/rollback Enable rollback support. This option will cost you a little extra time, but it lets you rollback a bad load. Considering migrations are seldom error proof, using this command-line switch is always a good idea when time allows.

You use the LoadState utility at the command line. In most cases, you'll use it with similar command-line switches as you used for the ScanState utility, so it pays to review the scan log. The command-line switches used for the scan always appear as the first item in the log, making it easier to retrace your steps later. Here's an example of the LoadState utility.

```
LoadState D:\MySettings /All /LocalOnly /V:5 /L:D:\MySettings\Scan.log \rollback
```

Generally, the instructions in this section are all you need to use USMT effectively on a single machine. You can find more information in the "Saving Settings with the User Setting Migration Toolkit (USMT)" section of Chapter 39. These additional instructions help you understand the complexities of an enterprise environment and work with the version of USMT that comes with the BDD.

Performing the Update Installation

When you upgrade, the installation procedure copies the settings from your current version of Windows and applies them to the installation of Vista. Remember that you can only upgrade the Windows XP Home SP2, Windows XP Professional SP2, Windows XP Media Center SP2, and Windows XP Tablet SP2 editions. Other Windows products, such as Windows 2000, Windows NT, and Windows 9*x* require that you perform a clean install (if you can install on the target computer at all). It's important to remember that the upgrade process can require a lot of time to complete.

NOTE Microsoft places all of the outdated files from your Windows XP installation in a `Windows.old` folder when you perform an upgrade. The subfolders contain the Window XP files as well as the unchanged Registry settings. Even though these files exist, you can't boot Windows XP from them. Microsoft only provides these files so that you can retrieve settings you require to customize Vista completely. When you're sure that you no longer need the `Windows.old` folder, you can delete it to save space on your hard drive.

1. Insert the DVD in a DVD drive. If AutoPlay is enabled on your computer, Windows displays the introductory screen. If not, open an Explorer window and double-click the DVD. This should trigger the AutoPlay action. If it doesn't, double-click the `setup.exe` file on the DVD to run it.
2. Click the Install Now link. Setup asks whether you want to obtain important updates before you begin the installation process. Generally, it's always a good idea to update your system. You want to be sure that everything on your system is ready for the installation process, including essential system files. Notice that this window also contains a check box that asks whether you want Microsoft to know about your installation experience.
3. Check or clear the I Want to Help Make Windows Installation Better option.
4. Click Go Online to Get the Latest Updates for Installation. You must remain connected to the Internet while Setup updates your system. After Setup completes the update process, you'll need to enter your product key. This setup screen also contains an automatic activation option that you should keep checked unless you're installing Vista on a machine that lacks an Internet connection.
5. Type your product key and click Next. Setup displays the licensing agreement next.
6. Read the licensing agreement, check I Accept the License Terms, and click Next. Setup asks whether you want to perform an upgrade installation or a custom installation. Normally, you'll perform the upgrade installation to use existing settings for your machine. The only time you need to perform a custom installation is when you want to modify your setup with Vista in mind. For example, you might choose to add Vista features immediately, rather than simply install the feature set that Microsoft thinks you need.
7. Click Upgrade. At this point, the Vista installation becomes more or less automatic. Follow any remaining prompts to perform setups for your unique machine configuration.
8. Complete the setup using the steps in the "The Installation Paths Converge" section of the chapter.

Performing a New Installation of Vista

You need to perform a new installation of Vista when you don't have one of the supported update versions or your hard drive doesn't have the required space on the boot drive. A new installation begins like an update, but requires that you perform a number of additional configuration tasks as described in the following steps.

1. Insert the DVD in a DVD drive. If AutoPlay is enabled on your computer, Windows displays the introductory screen. If not, open an Explorer window and double-click the DVD. This should trigger the AutoPlay action. If it doesn't, double-click the `setup.exe` file on the DVD to run it.
2. Click the Install Now link. Setup asks whether you want to obtain important updates before you begin the installation process. Generally, it's a good idea to update your system. You want to be sure that everything on your system is ready for the installation process, including essential system files. Notice that this window also contains a check box that asks whether you want Microsoft to know about your installation experience.

3. Check or clear the I Want to Help Make Windows Installation Better option.
4. Click Go Online to Get the Latest Updates for Installation. You must remain connected to the Internet while Setup updates your system. After Setup completes the update process, you'll need to enter your product key. This setup screen also contains an automatic activation option that you should keep checked unless you're installing Vista on a machine that lacks an Internet connection.
5. Type your product key and click Next. Setup displays the licensing agreement next.
6. Read the licensing agreement, check I Accept the License Terms, and click Next. Setup asks whether you want to perform an upgrade installation or a custom installation. Normally, you'll perform the upgrade installation to use existing settings for your machine. The only time you need to perform a custom installation is when you want to modify your setup with Vista in mind. For example, you might choose to add Vista features immediately, rather than simply install the feature set that Microsoft thinks you need. Most savvy computer users perform a custom installation, but a custom installation isn't absolutely required.
7. Click Custom. Setup asks where you want to install Vista. It shows you a listing of available partitions. Normally, you won't have any problem seeing the partitions, but you can load any required drivers as part of this step by clicking Load Driver. For example, you may need to load a driver to support a Redundant Array of Inexpensive Disks (RAID) drive setup.
8. Choose a partition and click Next. If the partition you choose contains a previous version of Windows (likely in this case), Setup displays a warning message. Click OK to close this message box. Follow any remaining prompts to perform setups for your unique machine configuration.
9. Complete the setup using the steps in the "The Installation Paths Converge" section of the chapter.

Performing a Clean Install of Vista

Unlike previous versions of Windows, Vista provides a completely new graphically based setup that automates many tasks and provides menu items to perform other tasks such as system recovery. Because Vista uses a graphical setup, the actual setup procedure follows the upgrade and other paths more closely. Consequently, if you're already familiar with one way of installing Vista, you're probably familiar with all methods because they vary only by a few steps. The following steps help you with the clean Windows setup.

1. Boot the computer using the Vista installation disk. You'll see Vista start up and Setup asks you for some basic information.
2. Provide the Installation Language, Time and Currency Format, and Keyboard or Input Method. Click Next. Setup presents the main installation option. However, below this option is a link for the System Recovery Options.
3. Click the Install Now link. At this point, you'll need to enter your product key. This setup screen also contains an automatic activation option that you should keep checked unless you're installing Vista on a machine that lacks an Internet connection.
4. Type your product key and click Next. Setup displays the licensing agreement next.

5. Read the licensing agreement, check I Accept the License Terms, and click Next. Setup asks where you want to install Vista. It shows you a listing of available partitions. Normally, you won't have any problem seeing the partitions, but you can load any required drivers as part of this step by clicking Load Driver. For example, you may need to load a driver to support a RAID drive setup.
6. Choose a partition and click Next. If the partition you choose contains a previous version of Windows (likely in this case), Setup displays a warning message. Click OK to close this message box. Follow any remaining prompts to perform setups for your unique machine configuration.
7. Complete the setup using the steps in the "The Installation Paths Converge" section of the chapter.

Performing a BitLocker Installation of Vista

BitLocker is a new disk encryption technology that comes with Vista. This technique encrypts the entire drive. However, some part of the drive must remain bootable. Consequently, what you really set up with BitLocker is a 2 GB boot partition that isn't encrypted and the remainder of the drive that is encrypted. The technology works despite the 2 GB partition because absolutely everything about your system, including Vista itself, is on the second partition. Only common boot information appears on the first partition. You may have noticed that the setups so far in this chapter are significantly easier and more flexible than previous versions of Windows. Vista really does make a big leap in ease of installation. However, the BitLocker setup requires a little more work on your part. The following sections describe how to set up your system for BitLocker.

Editing System Information and Formatting Drives Using Windows Preinstallation Environment (PE)

Previous versions of the Windows CD Setup program came with a clunky character mode interface that didn't exactly inspire confidence. Vista comes with a miniature copy of Windows that provides the graphical interface that you use normally. This mini-version of Windows is called the Windows Preinstallation Environment (PE). You use it to access all of the features of setup. In this case, you must make a detour to create a special partition setup for BitLocker. The following steps describe how to perform this task.

1. Boot the computer using the Vista installation disk. You'll see Vista start up and Setup asks you for some basic information.
2. Provide the Installation Language, Time and Currency Format, and Keyboard or Input Method. Click Next. Setup presents the main installation option. However, below this option is a link for the System Recovery Options.
3. Click System Recovery Options. You'll see a number of system recovery options, including the option to open a command prompt.
4. Click Command Prompt. Setup starts the familiar command processor. This process depends on the DiskPart utility, which lets you perform low-level manipulation of the hard drive. You can perform an amazing number of tasks, but the essential task, in this case, is creating the correct partition layout.

5. Type **`DiskPart`** and press Enter. You'll see the DiskPart prompt. It's easy to obtain help at any time by typing **`Help`** and pressing Enter. DiskPart will display a list of commands you can execute.
6. Type **`Select Disk 0`** and press Enter. DiskPart tells you that it has selected the first disk on your hard drive. You always have to select a file system object before you can work with it when using DiskPart. Selecting a drive is always the first step in the process.

WARNING This next step is permanent. It removes the partition tables from the selected drive. Make sure you have saved any data you want to save on the drive before you execute this step. Make sure you have selected the correct drive.

7. Type **`Clean`** and press Enter. DiskPart erases all of the partition information on the selected drive. This act cleans the hard drive completely; nothing remains behind.
8. Type **`Create Partition Primary`** and press Enter. DiskPart creates a new primary partition on the hard drive. This act also selects the new partition automatically so that you can work with it.
9. Type **`Assign Letter=C`** and press Enter. DiskPart assigns the letter C to the new partition.
10. Type **`Shrink Minimum=2000`** and press Enter. DiskPart shrinks the new partition by 2,000KB. This new area will hold the actual boot partition. You can increase this value to ensure the disk partition is large enough for updates later. In most cases, you'll want to set the value to at least 4,000 to ensure you can perform updates. Remember that Vista looks at the boot drive, not the data drive, as the basis for later updates.
11. Type **`Create Partition Primary`** and press Enter. DiskPart creates a second new primary partition. This smaller partition will hold the boot files and won't be encrypted when you use BitLocker. DiskPart automatically selects this new partition so you can work with it. If you want to work with the first partition you created again, you must use the `Select Partition 0` command.
12. Type **`Active`** and press Enter. DiskPart makes the second partition the active partition—the one that the system uses for boot purposes.
13. Type **`Assign Letter=D`** and press Enter. DiskPart assigns the letter D to the new partition.

NOTE The drive letter assignments are only suggestions. If you want to use C for the boot partition and D for the Vista partition, you can certainly do so. Likewise, you might choose to assign Z to the boot partition to keep it at the bottom of drive lists while working in Vista. The point is that you should assign the drive letters based on personal preference and your working habits.

14. Type **`Exit`** and press Enter to exit DiskPart.
15. Type **`Format /y /q /fs:NTFS C:`** to format the Vista partition. The Format utility formats the partition using NTFS.
16. Type **`Format /y /q /fs:NTFS D:`** to format the boot partition.

17. Type `Exit` and press Enter to close the command prompt.

18. Click the Close button or press Alt+F4 to close the System Recovery Options window. You don't have to click Shut Down or Restart to restart the setup process; Setup already recognizes the new partitions you created.

Performing the BitLocker Installation

Now that you have a shiny new partition you can use for BitLocker, it's time to install Vista. Follow the same procedure that you do for a clean install using the steps in the "Performing a Clean Install of Vista" section of the chapter. However, make sure you choose the correct disk partition for Vista. Since there are two partitions, it's easy to make a mistake. Always install Vista on the first partition you created (drive C: in the example). Setup automatically uses the second partition (drive D: in the example) for the boot files.

The Installation Paths Converge

The installation paths converge when your system reboots and prepares to work with Vista for the first time. No matter how you begin the Vista installation, eventually you'll see a "Please wait a moment while Windows prepares to start for the first time" message. This message appears after the first reboot. Next you'll see an Install Windows dialog box appear that contains a list of tasks that Setup is performing on your behalf. The first few items go fast and then you'll wait for a while at the Completing Installation task. Your system will reboot at least once during this process.

Performing the Initial Setup

Vista performs a lot of work that you used to perform manually in the background, so it may seem like it's taking a long time to complete its work. At some point, you'll see a Set Up Windows dialog box asking you to enter a name and password. The following steps take you through the installation process starting from this point.

1. Type a name and password for your account. Make sure you include a password hint to use to recover your password later should you need to do so. You can optionally choose a different icon from the ones shown. Click Next. The next dialog box asks you to choose a computer name and a background.

2. Type a computer name and optionally choose a background. Click Next. Setup asks you about automatic updates. There's a lot of controversy over setting Windows to use automatic updates after Microsoft made certain optional updates, such as Windows Genuine Advantage (WGA), part of the automatic update. My recommendation is to have Windows ask you about the setting later and then ensure you set Automatic Updates to inform you about required downloads so that you can make the choice.

3. Choose an automatic update option. Setup automatically advances to the next dialog box where you choose the time and date settings for your computer.

4. Select a time zone. Choose the current date (this feature should be set automatically) and change the time as needed. Click Next. You see a final dialog box.

5. Click Start. Windows checks your system performance at this point. Eventually, you'll see a logon screen.

6. Type your password and press Enter.

At this point, you've completed a major part of the setup. Windows will start up for the first time, display the Welcome Center, show Windows Sidebar (with the default gadgets), and perform background tasks such as performing preliminary network configuration.

Configuring the Network

One of the first tasks you'll probably want to perform after you complete the installation is getting your network setup. Fortunately, Vista makes this task very easy. The following steps tell you how to perform this task.

1. Choose Start ➤ Network. You'll see the Network window. Below the menu is a note saying that network sharing and discovery aren't enabled.

2. Choose to enable network sharing and discovery. In most cases, you'll want to choose the private sharing and discovery option. Vista normally discovers the domain or network automatically at this point. However, you might not see the new entries immediately.

3. Right click anywhere in the Network windows and choose Refresh to display the network resources you can access.

Applying Your Files and Settings

To apply the files and settings you saved by using the Windows Easy Transfer to your new installation of Windows, take the following steps:

1. Choose Start ➤ All Programs ➤ Accessories ➤ System Tools ➤ Windows Easy Transfer.

2. Click the Next button. Windows Easy Transfer asks you to select a transfer option.

3. Click Continue a Transfer in Progress. Windows Easy Transfer will ask about the technique used to connect the two computers. The choices are a local area network or a CD, DVD, or removable storage. Remember that when you use direct connection methods, such as a USB cable, you select Start a New Transfer instead and use the procedure found in the "Use Windows Easy Transfer to Transfer Settings" section of the chapter. These options are for remote or delayed transfers.

4. Choose either the local network or the removable storage options for the data retrieval. If the firewall on your new machine isn't configured to allow Windows Easy Transfer to work, you'll see a dialog box asking you to make the appropriate choice.

    1. If you're using the network method, provide the Windows Easy Transfer key you obtained when setting up your old machine. Click Next.

    2. If you're using the removable storage approach, you can choose between CD or DVD, USB Flash Drive, or External Hard Disk or Network Location. Choose which of the three options you want to use. Choose the location of the data, supply the password you used when you created the backup, and click Next.

5. No matter which method you choose to create a connection to the data, Windows Easy Transfer will display a list of user accounts on the old computer. Choose an account from the User Account on the Old Computer field.

6. Select one of the accounts listed in the User Account on the New Computer field. Click Next. Windows Easy Transfer dislays a listing of items that will get transfered from the old computer to the new computer.

7. Click Transfer. Windows Easy Transfer will begin transferring the data. The time required by the transfer process depends on the location of the data and the amount of settings that Windows Easy Transfer has to apply. Windows Easy Transfer displays a time estimate at the top of the dialog box.

8. Click Close when the transfer is complete.

Keeping Windows Updated

Vista includes a feature called Windows Update that keeps Windows up to date by automatically downloading updates, such as patches and fixes for security holes, and offering to install them. If you need to run old applications that have compatibility problems, Windows Update may be of particular interest because it also includes new fixes for applications to run on Vista.

You should know several things about Windows Update before you find it springing into action: how it works, how to configure it, and what to do when an update presents itself.

When Windows Update Runs

By default Windows Update runs automatically, but only when an Administrator user is logged on. (Microsoft assumes that you don't want Limited users—let alone guests—to install or refuse updates.) If multiple Administrator users are logged onto the computer at the same time, Windows Update runs for only one of them.

You can activate Windows Update during the installation process, in which case, it may work in the background and you'll never hear from it again unless there's a problem you must address. However, given the recent problems with Windows Update, such as the installation of unnecessary software like Windows Genuine Advantage (WGA), some people are less willing to let Windows Update run without monitoring, which means you must configure it separately from the installation process.

Shortly after Windows has first been installed, an icon appears in the system tray with a balloon telling you that your system might be at risk. If you click that balloon, the Windows Security Center appears where you can open the Windows Update setting by clicking the Windows Update link. The Windows Update window contains a Change Settings link. Click this link and you see a window where you can choose to allow Windows Update to download the updates automatically or not. The safest setting that balances the need to update your system and also keeps track of Microsoft's activity is Check for Updates but Let Me Choose Whether to Install Them, as shown in Figure 2.2.

The Install Updates Automatically (Recommended) option is the one that Setup chooses. The default setting checks for updates every day at 3:00 ≈AM, assuming that your computer is running at that time. Microsoft chose this setting to reduce the possible conflicts with activities you have to perform. You should set this interval to match your work habits if you decide to allow automatic updates.

You can use the Download Updates but Let Me Choose Whether to Install Them as a means of reducing the load on your computer. The updates download automatically when you aren't using the computer for critical tasks. You still have the option of not installing the update. The downside of this option is that the updates consume hard drive space whether you use them or not.

No matter what you might think about Microsoft's update policies, you should never choose the Never Check for Updates (Not Recommended) option unless your system is almost never connected to the Internet. Even the most dedicated user is bound to miss an update now and then. If you happen to miss the update that fixes a day-zero exploit (one where a cracker creates a virus on the same day that a security flaw becomes public knowledge), your system will be vulnerable to whatever someone decides to do to it.

Sometimes you'll hear about a new fix and won't want to wait for Windows Update to find it. You can also run Windows Update manually by choosing Start ➤ All Programs ➤ Windows Update. (If you prefer to run Windows Update manually, you may also want to turn off automatic updating. Read on.)

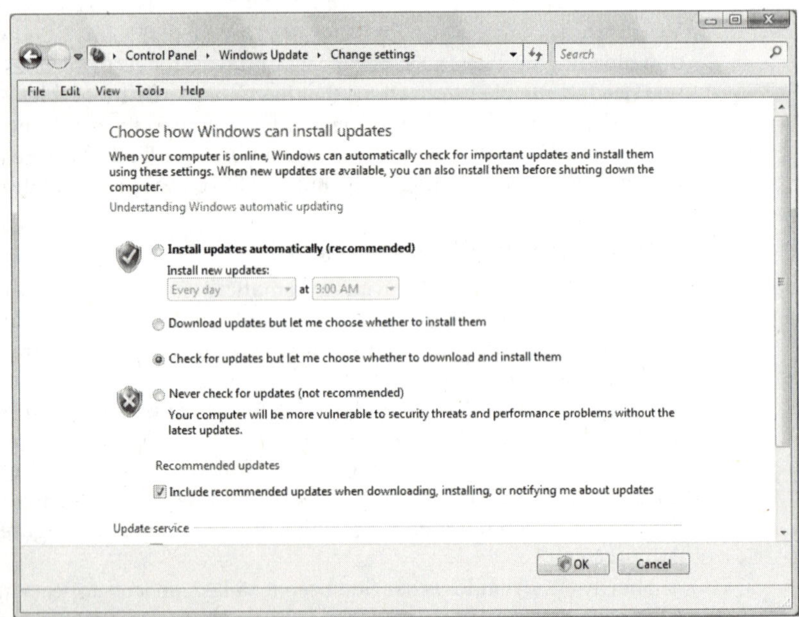

FIGURE 2.2
You can configure Windows Update using this special configuration window.

Running Windows Update Manually

If you don't want to wait for Windows Update to run automatically on schedule, or if you don't like to have your computer calling Microsoft secretly in the wee hours of dark and stormy nights, you can run Windows Update manually. You can do so either from the Start menu (Start ➤ All Programs ➤ Windows Update) or from the Help and Support Center window.

Understanding the Windows Update–Related Services

You may have tweaked your system to run more efficiently by shutting down some services and setting them to start manually. This is a common practice and it does result in a system that performs better. However, Windows Update requires two services and you must set them up in a certain way or Windows Update will behave oddly. This particular problem is so odd that many people discover it by accident and then can't find any help for it online. Before you use Windows Update (even before you open the browser to access it) make sure you verify that both the Background Intelligent Transfer Service and the Windows Update services are started. In addition, you must set the Windows Update (the renamed Automatic Updates found in previous versions of Windows) service to Automatic, even if you don't plan to leave it in that state.

Summary

The beginning of this chapter is all about planning. It's essential to plan an installation before you move ahead with the actual task. This chapter has also discussed how to install Windows as a clean install, an upgrade to your current version of Windows, an entirely new installation, or the special BitLocker installation. You've also learned how to use the Windows Update feature to keep your copy of Windows updated, compatible, and secure.

Of course, now it's time to plan your installation. Make sure you start by planning your upgrade or new installation. For example, even a new installation requires that you save settings from an older machine. Accomplish all of these planning tasks before you proceed with the installation of your choice. Of course, part of the planning process is to decide which kind of installation you want to perform. After you complete the installation, make sure you install any applications you want to use and then restore your setting using Windows Easy Transfer.

Chapter 3 helps you explore and configure the Vista desktop. The learning curve is a little steep in this update since Microsoft has decided to move just about everything to a new location. Not only will you rediscover old friends like the Windows Help Center, you'll also learn about new features such as User Account Control.

Chapter 3

Using the Desktop and Getting Help

In the first part of this chapter, I'll discuss how to get started with Vista. I'll cover how to log on and log off, how to switch from one user session to another, and how to exit Windows. I'll also discuss how you can find out who else is logged on to the computer when you're working at it, how you can get an idea of which programs the other users are running, and how you can log off another user (or all other users) in order to reclaim the resources they're using.

In the second part of this chapter, I'll discuss how to find the help you need to use Vista most effectively. Vista includes a greater amount of help than previous versions of Windows and presents that help in a new interface, the Windows Help and Support program. I'll describe how to use Windows Help and Support and the various areas it offers. I'll also mention other resources that you may need to turn to when you run into less tractable problems.

- Logging on and off
- Using the Desktop and the Start menu
- Switching users
- Seeing what other users are doing
- Overcoming new interface challenges
- Using the Winkey
- Working through User Access Control (UAC)
- Shutting down Windows
- Using the Windows Help and Support
- Using Remote Assistance
- Using the troubleshooters
- Finding help on the Internet

NOTE Before we start, here's something you need to know. Vista supports three types of users: Computer Administrator users, Limited users, and the Guest user. By default, all named users are set up as Computer Administrator users, which gives them full authority to configure and customize the computer. Limited users, which you create manually, can perform only minimal configuration and customization. The Guest user, an account that's created automatically by Windows, can perform no configuration or customization. In the first part of this chapter, I'll assume you're logging on as a Computer Administrator user, because that's most likely to be the case. Chapter 21 discusses how to create and manage user accounts.

Vista: What's New?

Vista presents a number of new user interface features. Of course, the biggest change is the interface itself. If you have the Aero Glass interface installed, you'll find that the interface does indeed look completely different. However, all of the new gizmos and fancy displays aren't the part of Vista that will help you the most. In fact, I foresee that many business users will simply turn off the extra graphics to ensure better system performance for real work.

Even with the special graphics turned off, Vista offers a lot in the way of changes. Some of the changes are simple. Microsoft has decided to change the Start menu text into an icon. Yes, it's still the Start menu, but now it has a Windows icon. I'm not entirely sure why Microsoft has made these changes, but some of them are odd enough that you'll want to know about them before you proceed too far into the book. The "Overcoming the Ten Most Confusing Vista Interface Changes" section of the chapter discusses the most important changes.

The big news for Vista is the UAC. This new security feature imposes itself into many Vista areas, including the user interface. UAC is here to stay. You can turn it off, of course, but that could be counterproductive because UAC really does serve some useful purposes, which you'll find in the "Dealing with User Access Control (UAC)" section of the chapter. In some cases, you'll want to adjust UAC to meet your particular needs, but getting warnings about potential security issues is always good.

Some of the Vista changes are very good news. For example, if you've ever tried to find something in the old Help and Support Center, you know that locating what you need can be confusing. The new Windows Help and Support is streamlined and significantly easier to use. While some power users will very likely grouse that some of their favorite features are missing, most people will appreciate the significant ease with which they can locate topics and the improved viewability of the information.

Logging On and Logging Off

Logging on and off in Vista works differently from previous versions of Windows. Logging on and off could hardly be easier, but it's important to understand what happens when you do so, and how logging on and off differs from switching users.

The first thing you'll notice is that the old Windows NT/2000 log on dialog box that was optionally available in Windows XP is now completely gone in Vista. Your only option is to choose from one of the available names and type in your password when prompted. The change means that you can no longer enter an arbitrary username or a hidden name such as Administrator. In fact, you'll find that the Administrator account is more or less inaccessible in Vista without performing some special configuration. Generally, this change means that Vista is significantly more secure than previous versions of Windows because access is more tightly controlled.

In pre–Windows XP versions of Windows, only one user at a time could be logged on to a computer running Windows. For a second user to log on, the first user needed to log off. Logging off involved closing all the open programs and files: either the user could close the programs and files manually before logging off, or Windows would close them automatically when the user issued the Log Off command (and confirmed that they wanted to log off).

Once all the programs and files were closed and all network and Internet connections were closed as well, Windows displayed the Log On to Windows dialog box or the Enter Network Password dialog box, depending on whether the computer was attached to a network. Another user could then log on to Windows, run programs, open files, establish network and Internet connections, and so on.

FAST USER SWITCHING, PERFORMANCE, AND FILE INTEGRITY

Having multiple users logged on to Windows at the same time affects performance because each user who's logged on takes up some of the computer's memory. Having a user logged on takes up relatively little memory, but each program that the user has running, and each file that they have open, adds to the amount being used.

Vista needs a minimum of 1 GB of RAM to run at an acceptable speed. For each light user, reckon another 256 MB of RAM; for each moderate user, 512 MB; and for each heavy user, 1 GB. If you have 2 GB of RAM, you should be able to have two or three users logged on and running several programs each without running short of memory.

Having multiple users logged on at once can also affect file integrity. For example, what happens when two users try to change the same file at the same time? The short answer is: It depends.

Some programs are smart enough to realize that someone else has a copy of the file open. For example, if you try to open in Word the same document that another user has open, Word displays the File in Use dialog box to warn you that the document is locked for editing and to offer you ways to work with the document (open a read-only copy; create a local copy and merge your changes later; or receive notification when the original copy is available).

Other programs aren't smart enough to spot the problem. For example, WordPad (Vista's built-in word processing program) lets you open a document that another user has open, change it, and save the changes. The other user can then save *their* changes to the same file, so the last user to save their file wins because only their changes are saved. And this is assuming that only two users are editing the document at the same time. For all WordPad knows, half the people in Delaware could be editing the document at the same time and wiping out each other's changes.

If your computer has a modest amount of RAM—say, 512 MB, 768 MB, or 1 GB—or if you're having problems with users opening files at the same time, turn off the Fast User Switching feature. Windows XP made this feature easy to find—all you needed was to clear the Use Fast User Switching check box in the User Account dialog box. In Vista, you must start a copy of the Group Policy editor. To perform this task, choose Start ➤ Run, type **`gpedit.msc`** in the Open field, and click OK. When you see the Group Policy Object Editor window, select the `Local Computer Policy\Computer Configuration\Administrative Templates\System\Login` folder. Double-click the Hide Entry Points for Fast User Switching policy entry. Choose Enabled and then click OK. Users won't be able to use Fast User Switching at this point.

In Vista, multiple users can be logged on at the same time, although of course only one user can actually be using the computer. Each of the users who are logged on can have programs running and files open. Vista lets you switch quickly between users without closing the programs and files.

Only one user can be *active*—actually using the computer—at any time. (Given that most computers have only one keyboard, mouse, and monitor, this may seem too obvious to mention—but things are very different in UNIX and Linux, in which multiple users can be actively using the same computer at the same time, some locally and some remotely.) A user who's logged on but not active is said to be *disconnected*.

This means that, for example, Jane and Jack can keep their programs open while Ross is using the computer. When Jane logs back on (in the process disconnecting Ross, who perhaps stepped away for a cup of coffee), Windows resumes her session from where she left off, displaying the programs she had running and the files she had open. Windows reestablishes any of Jane's persistent network connections, including any Internet connection that's set to connect automatically.

Being able to leave multiple users up and running is great—up to a point. But it has serious implications for performance and file integrity. The following sections discuss these considerations briefly.

Logging On

Let's assume for the moment that you're working with a stand-alone or workgroup PC. To start using Windows, log on from the Welcome screen. The Welcome screen displays a list of the users who have accounts set up on the computer. Any programs a user has running appear listed under the username, together with the number of e-mail messages waiting for them. If a user is logged on but has no programs running, the Welcome screen displays *Logged on* beneath their name.

By default, user accounts are set up without passwords, so you log on by clicking the username under which you want to log on. (If an administrator has set up Windows to require passwords, you'll need to enter the password for the account as well.)

When it accepts your logon, Windows displays your Desktop with its current settings. (The section "Using the Desktop and Start Menu" a little later in this chapter discusses the basics of the Desktop and Start menu.)

The first time you log on, Windows creates your folders and sets up program shortcuts for you—so the logon process takes a minute or two. Subsequent logons are much quicker.

If your Vista computer is connected to a domain, when you power on the computer, it will still boot to a Windows Log On screen. However, unlike Windows XP, you won't see a domain drop-down list box for your logon. Instead, you must include the domain name as part of your logon. For example, if your domain is mycompany.com, then you would log on using YourName@mycompany.com as your logon name. You must supply a valid username and password that has domain access privileges. If you don't have this information, contact your domain administrator. Passwords are required for network access; you can't have an account that has a blank password. You can only access information in the domain to which you have privileges.

Logging Off

The counterpart to logging on is (unsurprisingly) logging off. Vista provides a number of ways to log off the system. Select Start and you'll see three buttons at the bottom right of the Start menu. The first looks like an on/off switch, but it doesn't turn your computer off. Instead, it places your computer in a low power state so that you can restart the computer faster. The second looks like a lock and it does indeed lock your system so you can go to lunch. Neither of these options actually logs you off or closes your applications. Microsoft is actually trying to make it faster and easier for you to restart your system after an absence.

NOTE If you leave your computer unattended for a while, the screen saver usually kicks in—unless you have something open that prevents the screen saver from starting (or you've disabled the screen saver). For example, a dialog box open on screen usually prevents the screen saver from starting. The default setting is for the screen saver to start after 10 minutes and to display the Welcome screen. The screen saver gives you some protection against prying eyes (particularly if you're using passwords for logging on), but it also makes it harder to see who's doing what on the computer.

The third button is the one that gives you the most control. It's narrow and has an arrow on it. Click this button and you'll see options to switch users, log off, lock, restart, sleep, and shut down. If you truly want to log off the system, you must choose the Log Off, Restart, or Shut Down options. The Log Off option returns you to the Welcome screen, where you can log on as someone else. Use

Restart when you need to restart your system for some reason, such as after installing a patch. The Shut Down option is the only option that completely removes power from your system. You use this option when you're going away for the weekend or need to perform system maintenance.

Using the Desktop and Start Menu

Once you've logged on successfully, Windows displays the Desktop. Figure 3.1 shows what the Desktop looks like the first time you start Windows and start a couple of programs. Because you can customize the Desktop extensively, your Desktop might not look anything like the Desktop shown in the figure: the wallpaper might be different; the Taskbar could be located at a different side of the screen; or various toolbars might be displayed. One of the few unchanging things about the Desktop is the Start menu button—but even this might not be displayed if someone has chosen to hide the Taskbar (of which the Start button is a part).

FIGURE 3.1
The components of the Windows Desktop

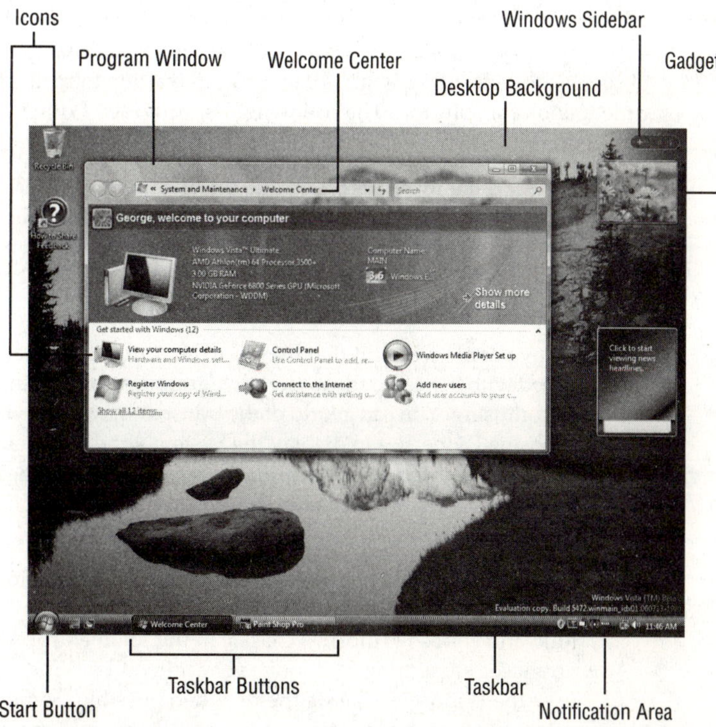

Vista also starts Windows with the Welcome Center, which contains a list of common tasks you can perform, and Windows Sidebar, which contains several gadgets that are designed to make your computing experience more enjoyable. You can get rid of both the Welcome Center and Windows Sidebar to reduce distractions and enhance your own productivity. We'll examine the Desktop in more detail in the forthcoming chapters, but these are the basic actions for navigating it:

- The Desktop contains one or more shortcuts to items. Usually, there's an icon for the Recycle Bin, if nothing else. Double-click an icon to run the program associated with it.

- The Start menu provides access to the full range of programs and features currently installed on Windows. Click the Start button to display the Start menu. Choose one of the items that appear on it, or click the All Programs button to display a cascading menu containing further items.
- The Taskbar gives you quick access to each program that's currently running. The Taskbar displays a button for each active program window. To display that window in front of all other windows, click its button. To minimize the program, click its Taskbar button again.
- The notification area contains items that are useful to have displayed all the time (such as the clock, which is displayed by default), together with information and alerts (which are displayed at appropriate times).
- The Desktop background is a graphic that you can change at will.

Overcoming the Ten Most Confusing Vista Interface Changes

Vista provides a significant number of user interface changes. Some of these changes are quite obvious—others will lurk in the background waiting to spring their surprise when you least have time to look for solution. The following list provides a quick overview and some fixes for the most common interface change complaints.

- The Start menu doesn't look like the one used by older versions of Windows, such as Windows 2000. A lot of people don't like having their application options hidden from view or categorized by Microsoft. You can get the classic menu by right-clicking the Taskbar, choosing Properties to display the Taskbar and Start Menu Properties, selecting the Start Menu tab, and choosing the Classic Start Menu option.
- Many people will find that they like the Aero Glass interface, but not the transparency associated with it. Seeing the underlying graphics poke up through various display elements can be confusing. You can get rid of the transparency by choosing Start, right-clicking Computer, choosing Properties to display the System window, clicking Advanced System Settings to display the System Properties dialog box, clicking Settings in the Performance area, and clearing the Enable Transparent Glass option on the Visual Effects tab of the Performance Options dialog box.
- You may want a bare bones Vista experience to get rid of the needless graphics. In this case, right-click the Desktop, choose Personalize from the context menu, click the Theme link, and choose Windows Classic in the Theme drop-down list box. When you click OK, you'll see something that looks very much like Windows 2000. In fact, much of this book uses the Windows Classic theme when possible. Some Vista features require all of the extra graphics to work though, so you'll see the Aero Glass interface sans transparency when needed.
- UAC pops up every time you want to perform any reasonably complex task. Even though UAC seems like the worst thing Microsoft has ever done for administrators, it does provide useful safety features for less experienced users. That said, you can tune UAC to meet specific needs. Discover how to perform this task in the "Dealing with User Access Control (UAC)" section of the chapter.

- You can't find anything in its old location. Microsoft has changed the Vista directory structure, so, yes, things have moved around. Fortunately, Microsoft provides junctions (a kind of shortcut) that lets older applications access the settings correctly. The new directory names are actually a plus for anyone working at the command line because you don't have to worry about spaces in the names. For example, `Documents and Settings` has now become simply `Users`.
- Windows Sidebar simply refuses to go away—it's there like an unloved season every time you start Vista. Closing the Windows Sidebar won't get rid of it. If you truly want to rid yourself of Windows Sidebar, right-click it, choose Properties, and clear the Start Sidebar When Windows Starts option. You must still close Windows Sidebar by right-clicking it and choosing Close Sidebar from the context menu. If you decide later that you want Windows Sidebar back, you can start it up using its applet in the Control Panel.
- All of the icons can suddenly disappear from your Desktop if you're not careful. Vista has a new feature that makes it possible to hide everything so you can gaze fondly at whatever wallpaper you have on your desktop. To get your icons back again, right-click the Desktop and choose View ➤ Show Desktop Icons.
- Running many of your applications now fails due to security issues. It's important to remember that you now run as a standard user, even if you're part of the Administrators group. The fast way around this problem is to right-click the application icon and choose Run as Administrator from the context menu. If the problem continues, you'll need to reconfigure the application to run using administrator credentials all of the time. To perform this configuration, right-click the application icon, choose Properties from the context menu, select the Compatibility tab in the application's Properties dialog box, and check the Run This Program as an Administrator option.
- You can't seem to figure out a way to adjust your display settings. Microsoft has changed the display settings around a lot. To access the new settings, you need to right-click the Desktop and choose Personalize. The Personalize Appearance and Sounds window provides everything needed to get your display tuned to your personal liking. The "Customizing the Vista Display" section of Chapter 5 describes the Personalize Appearance and Sounds window in detail.
- Network applications that used to work fine no longer work as anticipated. The issue is that Microsoft has added a number of security features that may be blocking your network applications. For example, you might run into a problem with Windows Firewall because it now blocks outgoing as well as incoming data. Vista also treats a network drive as an Internet connection, which means you might find that you no longer have permission to perform some tasks. Chapter 21 discusses Vista security issues.

Using the Winkey

As I mentioned in Chapter 1, Vista provides a number of keyboard combinations for the Winkey, the key (or keys) with the Windows logo on the keyboard. If you're comfortable leaving your hands on the keyboard, these combinations are doubly convenient, because not only can you avoid reaching for the mouse but you can also display with a single keystroke a number of windows and dialog boxes that lie several commands deep in the Windows interface.

Table 3.1 lists the Winkey combinations.

TABLE 3.1: Winkey Combinations

WINKEY COMBINATION	WHAT IT DOES
Winkey	Toggles the display of the Start menu
Winkey+Break	Displays the System Properties dialog box
Winkey+Tab	Moves the focus to the next button in the Taskbar
Winkey+Shift+Tab	Moves the focus to the previous button in the Taskbar
Winkey+B	Moves the focus to the notification area
Winkey+D	Displays the Desktop
Winkey+E	Opens an Explorer window showing Computer
Winkey+F	Opens a Search Results window and activates Search Companion
Winkey+Ctrl+F	Opens a Search Results window, activates Search Companion, and starts a Search for Computer
Winkey+F1	Opens a Windows Help and Support window
Winkey+M	Issues a Minimize All Windows command
Winkey+Shift+M	Issues an Undo Minimize All command
Winkey+R	Displays the Run dialog box
Winkey+U	Displays Utility Manager
Winkey+L	Locks the computer

Dealing with User Access Control (UAC)

UAC is possibly the most talked about feature of Vista because it most directly affects the user in an in-your-face manner. You can't escape UAC when you perform any advanced task. Actually, UAC started out far more aggressive than its current incarnation, but Microsoft has toned UAC down so it seldom intrudes when you perform common tasks on the local machine.

Considering the Costs and Benefits of UAC

Microsoft had to plead with people to leave UAC turned on during the Vista beta. The problem was so significant that there was a real concern that UAC might not get tuned properly. Finally, however, UAC became usable enough that many people did leave it on and Microsoft received the input it required. The resulting functionality is far less intrusive than the original. Many people run applications all day long without seeing it at all. This is how things should be.

When you tune UAC properly and run only standard applications, you should see it very seldom. UAC isn't meant as an annoyance or a time-robbing Vista feature; it's supposed to warn you when someone is doing something they shouldn't with your machine. In general, if you're an average user and don't need to perform administrative tasks every day, you'll gain significantly more than you'll lose by running UAC on your machine.

The biggest cost of UAC is that it's intrusive. If you're an administrator, UAC can actually prevent you from getting work done. You might find that a job that was supposed to take about 5 minutes to complete suddenly takes an hour because UAC is getting in the way. This is where tuning comes into play. However, it's also important to realize that you need to observe the proper precautions because Vista is far less forgiving than earlier versions of Windows when it comes to sloppy security. Make sure you run applications using the Run as Administrator feature when needed. In most cases, you don't need to turn off UAC completely, but you may need to turn off a particular feature to accomplish a particular task and then turn it back on so you keep getting the benefits of this security feature.

Turning Off UAC

You have a number of options for turning off UAC. It's possible to get rid of the most obnoxious features by making a single change. Choose Start ➤ Control Panel, select the User Accounts and Family Safety link, and then select the User Account Control Panel link. Near the bottom of the Make Changes to Your User Account window, click the Turn User Account Control On or Off link, clear the Use User Account Control to Help Protect Your Computer option, and click OK. At this point, Vista will inform you that you have to restart your machine for the security change to take effect.

TIP Vista may not always tell you to reboot your system after a security change, but you must reboot your system for the change to take effect. Even though Vista has accepted any change you make, your user token won't reflect the change until after you reboot the system.

Another way to turn off UAC, this time with far greater ramifications, is to disable the User Account Control entries in the Local Security Policy console. These settings affect far more than the UAC setting that Vista tracks through your user account and the changes are more dangerous from a security perspective. The next section, "Overcoming UAC as Needed," describes these settings in detail.

Overcoming UAC as Needed

Some administrators will want to tune UAC to meet their specific needs. It's still not a good idea to turn off UAC completely—even administrators make mistakes and a little safety net can prove to be a good idea for everyone. That said, you still might need to change the UAC configuration when working with certain applications, especially those that change the system setup in some way or older applications that don't always follow the rules.

All of the settings you need are found in the Local Security Policy console, which you access by choosing Start ➤ Control Panel, selecting Classic View, double-clicking the Administrative Tools folder, and then double-clicking Local Security Policy. You'll find the settings in the `Security Settings\Local Policies\Security Options` folder. The User Account Control options appear near the end of the list. The following list describes each of these options.

User Account Control: Admin Approval Mode for Built-in Administrator account This feature isn't defined by default because it only affects the administrator account. When enabled, it sets the admin approval mode for the administrator account, which means that the administrator doesn't need to manually provide permission for activities that UAC would normally request permission to perform.

User Account Control: Behavior of the elevation prompt for administrators in Admin Approval Mode The setting determines the kind of prompt that someone in the administrators group receives to perform administrator level activities. The default setting merely asks the user to approve of the action. However, you can also tell UAC not to prompt the user at all or to request a name and password. Disabling the prompt means that the activity will normally fail.

User Account Control: Behavior of the elevation prompt for standard users This setting determines the kind of prompt that a standard user receives when performing an administrator level task. The default setting asks the user to provide the name and password for an administrator account. You can also change this setting so UAC doesn't prompt the user at all, which means that the task will always fail.

User Account Control: Detect application installations and prompt for elevation This feature detects any type of application installation and requests permission to perform it. Since application installation is a somewhat rare task after a system is set up, you should probably keep this setting enabled because it helps you detect unwanted or unauthorized application installations.

User Account Control: Only elevate executables that are signed and validated Enabling this feature means that you won't be able to install most applications that aren't signed and validated. A signed application is one that has a valid digital certificate that identifies the application vendor. If you can ensure that all of your applications are signed, then enabling this feature is probably a good idea. However, since few applications are signed today, you'll probably want to retain the default disabled setting.

User Account Control: Only elevate UIAccess applications that are installed in secure locations This feature detects any application that attempts to interact with the user interface of another application. For example, an application might provide accessibility support for all of the applications run on a certain machine. The accessibility feature may require interaction with these other applications to determine what information their user interface provides. Since this feature could be used to make virus actions appear as part of another application, it's a security hazard. This setting tells UAC to ensure that any cross-application user interface access takes place only from secure locations. Using this setting won't affect the performance of bona fide accessibility applications such as JAWS.

User Account Control: Run all administrators in Admin Approval Mode Enabling this feature ensures that anyone in the administrator group is prompted before performing an administrator level task. The prompt acts as a safeguard because it ensures that someone can't perform an administrator level task without the user's knowledge and permission. However, this setting can also be a productivity drain. You could disable it before you perform a series of administrative tasks, and then reenable it later to maintain the safety it provides.

User Account Control: Switch to the secure desktop when prompting for elevation Use this feature to make all elevation prompts appear in the secure desktop environment. When you use this feature, you'll notice that the Desktop darkens and you can't perform any other activity. The purpose of the secure desktop environment is to make it a lot harder for someone to trick the user into providing permission to run an errant program. Since only the prompt appears, someone can't place text in front of the prompt that makes it appear the user is granting permission for another application.

User Account Control: Virtualize file and registry write failures to per-user locations Some older applications attempt to write file and Registry information to the wrong location. These older applications assume that they have full access to the system and can write anywhere at any time. Vista emphasizes keeping application interaction with the file system and Registry controlled. Virtualizing access means that Vista controls where the actual file and Registry writes go, making it harder for older applications (and viruses) to write to locations that they shouldn't access.

Managing Multiple Users

When multiple users share a single PC, a special set of challenges arises. How will their data be kept separate? How can more than one user log on at a time? How can you tell who's logged on and what they're doing? The following sections address some of these concerns.

USING THE CONNECT COMMAND TO SWITCH USERS QUICKLY

Switching users as described above is easy but takes a few clicks. There's a quicker way of switching—by using Task Manager as follows:

1. Right-click open space in the Taskbar and choose Task Manager from the context menu. Windows opens Task Manager.
2. Click the Users tab (shown in Figure 3.2, later in this chapter).
3. Right-click the user that you want to connect as and choose Connect from the context menu. If the user's account has a password, Windows displays the Connect Password Required dialog box. When you enter the password correctly (or if the account has no password), Windows disconnects your session and connects you as the user you selected.

Note that this works only if Fast User Switching is enabled; otherwise there won't be a Users tab.

Switching to Another User

As mentioned in the "Logging Off" section of the chapter, when you click the right arrow button on the right side of the Start menu, you see the Switch User option. When you choose the Switch User option, Windows keeps your programs running (instead of closing them, as it does when you log out) and displays the Welcome screen so that you can log on as another user or (more likely) other users can log on as themselves.

Locking the Computer

To leave your current session running but display the Welcome screen quickly, press Winkey+L. Microsoft calls this action *locking* the computer, although the term is neither accurate nor helpful with Vista's default settings. The computer isn't locked in any useful sense unless all user accounts are protected with effective passwords.

NOTE If you're connected to a domain, pressing Winkey+L locks the computer.

Checking Which User Is Currently Active

If you're in any doubt as to which user is currently active, display the Start menu (by clicking the Start button or pressing the Winkey) and check the username displayed at the top, right (immediately under the person's icon).

Seeing Who Else Is Logged on to the Computer

The Welcome screen displays details of each user logged on to the computer and the number of programs they're running. But if you don't want to display the Welcome screen (and disconnect your session by doing so), you can find out which other users are logged on by using Task Manager as follows:

1. Right-click the Taskbar and choose Task Manager from the context menu. Windows displays Task Manager.
2. Click the Users tab (shown in Figure 3.2), which lists the users and their status.

NOTE Limited users and the Guest user can't see which other users are logged on or which processes they're running. As a result, Limited users and the Guest user can't switch directly to another user's session by using Task Manager, although they can disconnect their own session or log themselves off by using Task Manager.

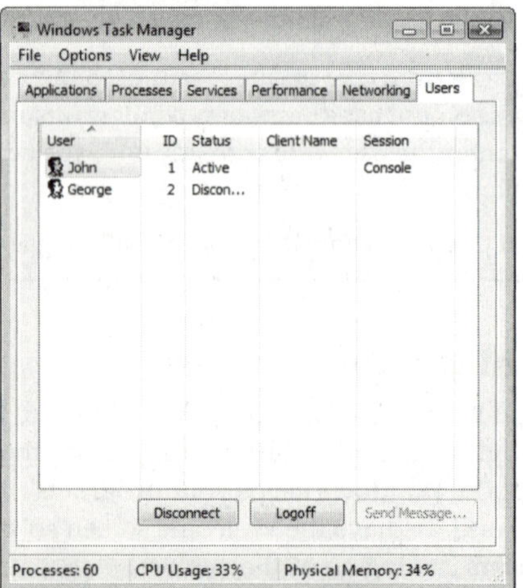

FIGURE 3.2 The Users tab of Task Manager shows you which other users are logged on to the computer. You can send them messages, switch to their sessions, or log them off forcibly.

Seeing Which Programs the Other Users Are Running

It's not easy to see exactly which programs the other users of the computer are running unless you know the names of the executable files for the programs, but you can get an idea by using the Processes tab of Task Manager. This tab also shows you how much memory each program is using, which helps you establish whether—or why—your computer is running short of memory.

Follow these steps to start Task Manager and display its Processes tab:

1. Right-click the Taskbar and choose Task Manager from the context menu to open Task Manager.
2. Click the Processes tab, which lists the processes you're running.
3. Select the Show Processes from All Users check box. (This check box is cleared by default.) Task Manager adds to the list all the processes that the other users are running as well. Figure 3.3 shows an example of the Processes tab. You can sort the list of processes by any column by clicking the column heading. In the figure, the processes are sorted by the User Name column so that it's easy to see which process belongs to which user.

As you can see in the figure, George is running a number of applications, including Windows Sidebar (`sidebar.exe`) and Windows Explorer (`explorer.exe`). These are the two largest programs, but George is running a number of other applications as well. You don't need to memorize the mapping of each executable filename to its program, but if you look at Task Manager now and then, you'll learn to scan the list of processes and see which is running. This will help you decide whether you should go ahead and log another user off Windows (as described in the next section) or whether doing so will trash their work and ruin their life.

While you're looking at Task Manager, there are a couple of other things you might as well know. Windows also has a number of processes open on its own account. The LOCAL SERVICE account is running `svchost.exe` (service host), as is the NETWORK SERVICE account. The SYSTEM account is running a dozen or more processes, of which you can see only the top few in the figure. Of these, the first, the System Idle Process, is consuming 91 percent of the processor cycles. (This is actually good news. When the System Idle Process is taking up most of the processor cycles like this, the computer is idling along—goofing off until the user does something that presses it into action.)

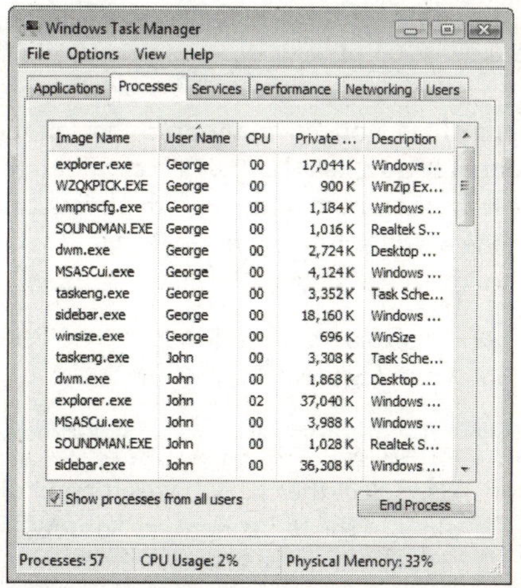

FIGURE 3.3
Use the Processes tab of Task Manager to see which programs the other users are running.

WHICH NAME CORRESPONDS TO WHICH PROGRAM?

To find out which program corresponds to each executable file, display the Applications tab of Task Manager. Right-click a program and choose Go to Process from the context menu. Task Manager displays the Processes tab and selects the process for that program.

Of course, knowing the executable name doesn't tell you anything about that application. Right-click the highlighted process and choose Open File Location from the context menu. You'll see a copy of Windows Explorer open with the executable highlighted. Knowing where the application is located on your hard drive can tell you a lot about the application. However, if you need to know more, right-click the executable file and choose Properties from the context menu. Select the Details tab and you'll discover who created the application and when. You might also see a digital signature for the application. When you don't see this information and you can't identify the application directory, it's often time to determine whether the application is a virus or an application you don't want running on your system.

Learning about applications is easy enough—but there are many more processes running than programs. Vista has a new Services tab that helps you discover those services running on your system. Right-click the process you don't know about and choose Go to Service(s) from the context menu. If the process is a service, you'll see the services associated with it on the Services tab.

When all else fails, try closing all the programs listed on the Applications tab of Task Manager, and you'll see that there's still a goodly list of processes left. Try stopping any obvious services that you can temporarily dispense with, and see if an associated process disappears. For instance, try closing your Internet connection or stopping your PC Cards. Did either of those actions lose you a process? Then you have an idea of what that process does.

If you're desperate to find out which function or service an executable runs, try searching for the executable. The folder that contains the executable may give you a clue as to the program, or there may be a comment on the executable that reveals its purpose. Then again, the executable may prove to be one of the mysterious system files stored in the Windows folder or the `Windows\System32` folder. If the latter is the case, figure it's something unknowable and leave it alone.

You may have noticed that the numbers in the Mem Usage column don't add up to anything like the amount of RAM listed as being committed (even though you can't see the whole column). That's because that committed figure is both physical memory (RAM) used and virtual memory (hard disk space being used to simulate more RAM). If you want to see how much memory each process is taking up, follow these steps:

1. In Task Manager, choose View ➤ Select Columns to open the Select Columns dialog box (shown in Figure 3.4).
2. Select the memory-oriented check boxes.
   - Also select the check boxes for any other information you want to see in Task Manager. Many of the items here are somewhat arcane, but you might want to look at CPU Time or Peak Memory Usage.
3. Click the OK button. Task Manager closes the Select Process Page Columns dialog box and adds the columns you chose to the Processes tab.

Figure 3.5 shows the Processes tab of Task Manager with all four of the memory-related columns added. Notice that the two copies of Windows Sidebar have very heavy memory usage indeed, but that the disconnected session uses far less than the connected session even though both copies of Windows Sidebar are running the same gadgets.

FIGURE 3.4 Use the Select Process Page Columns dialog box to add further columns of information to Task Manager's Processes tab.

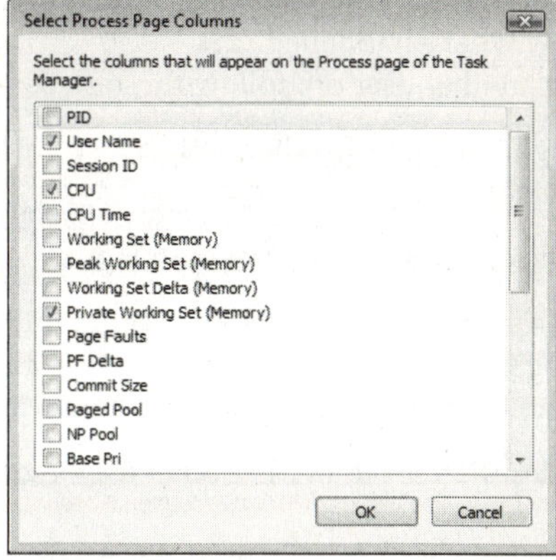

FIGURE 3.5 If you want to see virtual memory usage, add the Virtual Memory Size (VM Size) column to the Processes tab in Task Manager.

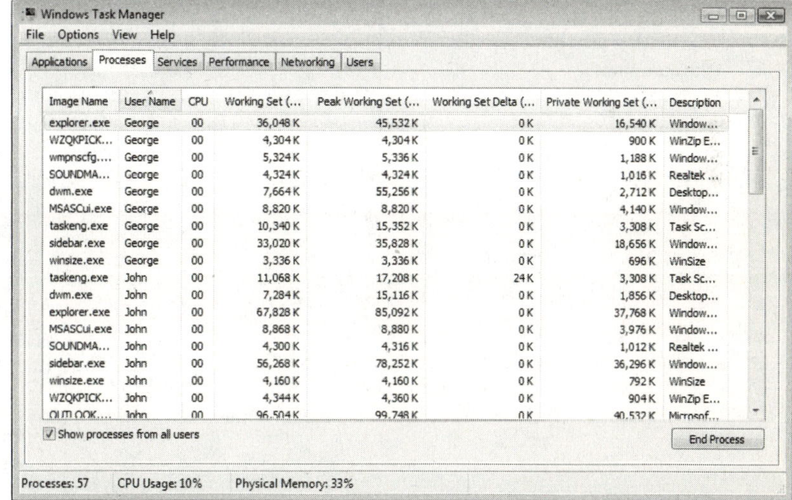

Logging Another User Off

If necessary, any Computer Administrator user can log another user off the computer.

Logging someone else off isn't usually a great idea, because although you can use Task Manager to see which processes they're running (as described in the previous section), you can't see whether they have any unsaved work in them. If you don't use passwords to log on to Windows, it's much better to log on as the other user and close the programs and documents manually. Then log off (as the other user) and log back on as yourself. If you do use passwords, you'll need to know the other user's password to log on as them, which kind of defeats the point of having passwords in the first place.

That said, you may need to log another user off if they're running enough programs to affect the computer's performance or if they have open a single-user program or a document that you need to use. If you do so, you may want to send them a message as described in the next section so that they know what's happened.

To log another user off, follow these steps:

1. Right-click the Taskbar and choose Task Manager from the context menu to display Task Manager.
2. Click the Users tab (shown in Figure 3.6).
3. Select the user and click the Logoff button. (Alternatively, right-click the user and choose Log Off from the context menu.) Windows displays the Windows Task Manager dialog box (shown in Figure 3.7), asking if you want to log the selected user off.
4. Click the Yes button. The other user's session is toast—as is any unsaved work they had open.

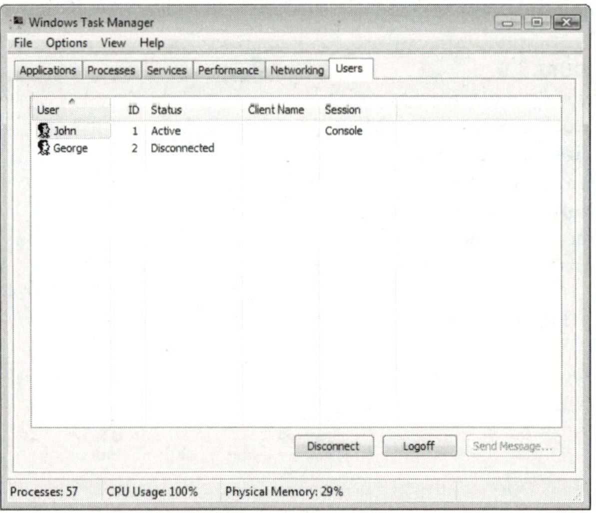

FIGURE 3.6 From the Users tab of Windows Task Manager, you can log another user off the computer.

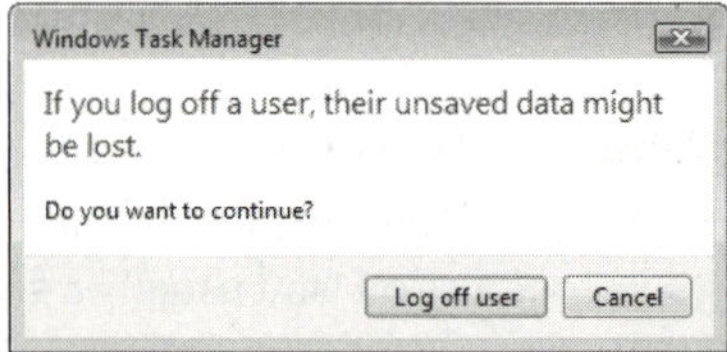

FIGURE 3.7 You can log another user off the computer—but be aware that doing so will cost them any unsaved work.

Sending a Message to Another User

You can send a message to another user logged on to this computer. Because the other user can't be using the computer at the same time as you, this feature isn't useful for real-time communication—it's not exactly instant messaging—but it can be useful for making sure a family member or a colleague gets a message the next time they use the computer. (For example, you might ask them not to shut down the computer because you're still using it.) It's also useful for notifying another user that you've had to terminate a program that they were using.

To send a message to another user, follow these steps:

1. Right-click the Taskbar and choose Task Manager from the context menu to display Windows Task Manager.
2. Click the Users tab.
3. Select the user you want to message and click Send Message. Windows displays the Send Message dialog box (shown in Figure 3.8).
4. Enter the message title in the Message Title text box and the message in the Message text box.
   - To start a new line, press Ctrl+Enter. (Pressing the Enter key on its own registers a click on the OK button, sending the message.)
   - To type a tab, press Ctrl+Tab. (Pressing the Tab key on its own moves the focus to the next control.)
5. Click the OK button to send the message.

The next time the user logs on to Windows, they receive the message as a screen pop-up.

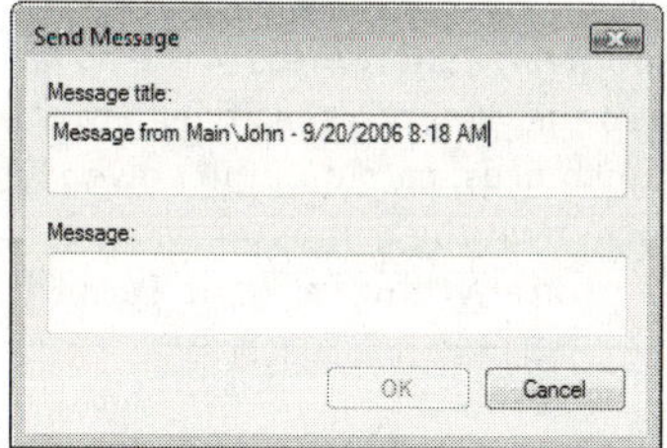

FIGURE 3.8
Use the Send Message dialog box to send a message to another user logged on to this computer.

Shutting Down Windows

Vista emphasizes hibernation over actually shutting the computer down. The controls you used in previous versions of Windows have changed. Clicking what used to be the Turn Off Computer icon now places you computer in a low power state—it doesn't actually turn your computer off. However, many people can use the low power state without problems as long as their computer is backed up by an uninterruptable power supply (UPS) or other alternative power in case of a power failure.

However, it's nice to know how to shut down Windows completely when you need to perform maintenance or you plan to be gone for the weekend. You can shut down Windows in several ways:

- By clicking the Right Arrow button at the bottom of the default Start menu or by choosing Start ➤ Shut Down from the classic Start menu. No matter which Start menu you use, you'll see a list of options, one of which is Shut Down. Choose this option to shut your computer down.
- By clicking the Shut Down Options button (has an up arrow icon) on the Welcome screen and then choosing the Shut Down option.
- By choosing Shut Down Options button (has an up arrow icon) and then choosing the Shut Down option from Windows Task Manager.
- By pressing Alt+F4 with the Desktop active, choosing Shut Down in the What Do You Want the Computer to Do field on the Shut Down Computer screen, and then clicking OK.

POWERING DOWN YOUR COMPUTER WHEN WINDOWS HAS CRASHED

If Windows won't shut down because it has crashed, you'll need to shut it down the hard way. To do so, press the power button on the computer. On Advanced Configuration and Power Interface (ACPI)-compliant computers, you may need to hold the power button down for 4 seconds or more to shut the system down—short presses of the power button may have no effect.

In some cases, you'll need to press the Reset button on the front of the case. This button reboots the computer without shutting it off and is actually easier on the computer's electronics than performing a power off restart.

On some computers, a short press of the power button may make Windows display the Turn Off Computer screen so that you can specify whether to hibernate, turn off the computer, or restart it. Under normal circumstances, catching the power signal like this is pretty smart, helping to dissuade users from powering down the computer without exiting Windows first. But if Windows has crashed, you won't be able to do anything from the Turn Off Computer screen.

Windows Help and Support

Windows Help and Support is the latest in Microsoft's efforts to provide help resources powerful enough to silence the ringing of the phones on its costly support lines. Vista's Windows Help and Support builds on the improvements introduced in previous versions of Windows. Like many other parts of Vista, some of the changes to the Windows Help and Support are graphical. The Windows Help and Support now sports an easier-to-use interface that gets you to the information you need more quickly.

Starting Windows Help and Support

Choose Start ➤ Help and Support to open Windows Help and Support at the home page. You should see something like Figure 3.9, except that it will contain some updated information. (Your hardware manufacturer may also have customized Windows Help and Support by adding content to it or by adapting its interface.)

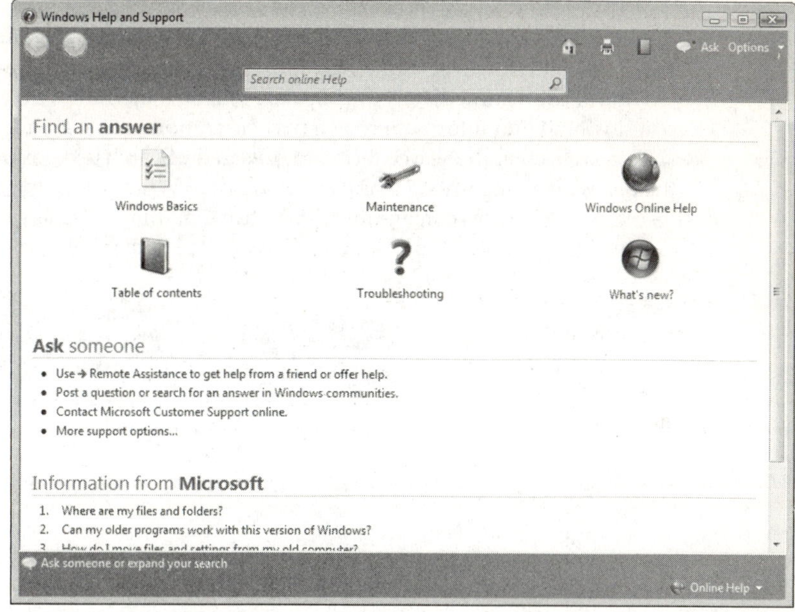

FIGURE 3.9
The home page in Windows Help and Support provides links to the many different areas of Windows Help and Support.

As you can see in Figure 3.9, the Windows Help and Support window has a toolbar (at the top, starting with the Back button) for primary navigation rather than a menu bar. This toolbar is called the *navigation bar*. Below the navigation bar appears the Search bar. The Information from Microsoft section changes frequently by drawing the latest information from Microsoft's website. They also vary depending on any customization provided by the PC manufacturer. (For example, Dell and HP both customize the Help system.)

TIP You can open multiple Windows Help and Support windows at once, which can help when you're searching for different pieces of help information or navigating different routes searching for the same piece of information.

Finding Your Way around Windows Help and Support

Windows Help and Support has access to a large amount of information in Help files that Windows installs on your hard drive, together with troubleshooters for stepping you through the process of finding solutions to common problems and links for running Windows programs (such as Remote Assistance and the System Configuration Utility) that may help you solve or eliminate problems. But Windows Help and Support's strongest feature is that it also provides a gateway to information resources on the Web and Internet.

Because of the amount of information and resources that Windows Help and Support offers, you may find that it takes you a while to get the hang of navigating around it. This section highlights the main ways of finding the information you need: searching, browsing, using the History feature, and using the Index.

Searching for Help

All of the icons and help links on the Windows Help and Support main page help you narrow your search quickly. However, these aids address common topics and might not address your needs. If you don't see an immediately appropriate link on the Windows Help and Support home page, the easiest way to find information on a particular topic is to search for it.

To search, enter the search term or terms in the Search text box and click the Search Help button (the one with a magnifying glass) or press Enter. Windows Help and Support displays the Search Results window shown in Figure 3.10. Notice that Microsoft has greatly simplified the display. All you need to do is click the link of interest to display that help topic.

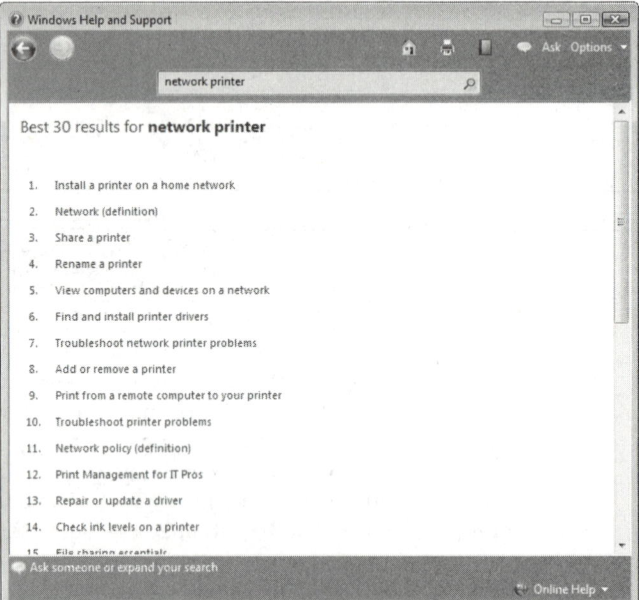

FIGURE 3.10
Click a search result in the Search Results window to display a particular help page.

Setting Search Options

Windows Help and Support lets you specify how you want it to search. To set search options, take the following steps:

1. Click the Options button on the navigation bar. Windows Help and Support displays the Options screen.
2. In the Options list, click the Settings option. Windows Help and Support displays the Set Search Options screen (shown in Figure 3.11).
3. Choose the search options you want to use.
   - The Include Windows Online Help and Support When You Search for Help options ensures that you obtain the most current information Microsoft provides about a

particular topic. However, you must have an active Internet connection to use this feature, so you'll want to clear this option when you're in a location where an Internet connection doesn't exist. Windows Help and Support still works, even when you have this option selected, but the lack of an Internet connection will produce a noticeable delay in response.

- The Join the Help Experience Improvement Program option lets you participate in the documentation process by recording the information you view most often and sending it to Microsoft. The information isn't associated with you or your machine in any way, so Microsoft won't know that you personally looked for a particular piece of information. However, this option does use network bandwidth (very little) and some companies may have a policy against using it. Check with your network administrator if you have any questions about using it.

4. Click OK. Windows Help and Support will begin using the new options immediately.

FIGURE 3.11
Choose search options on the Set Search Options screen in Windows Help and Support.

BROWSING FOR HELP

Windows Help and Support provides another feature called Browse Help. You see the button for accessing this feature at the top of the display. When you click Browse Help, you see a Contents page as shown in Figure 3.12.

You browse for help when you don't really know how to ask help a particular question. In fact, you might have tried a few search terms without much success. When you use this option, you drill down to the particular question you have. For example, you might start with the simple topic of networking, work your way into network setup, and eventually end up at a topic that discusses how to set up an ad hoc network (one between two computers that aren't normally connected). The idea behind this kind of search is not to assume anything about what information you want—you simply move one level at a time and get more specific with each level.

This is also a good way to discover more about Windows. If you have a little time to kill, you can choose a topic and drill down into the specifics to learn more about that topic. Often, you'll pick up little tidbits of information that will significantly improve your Windows experience.

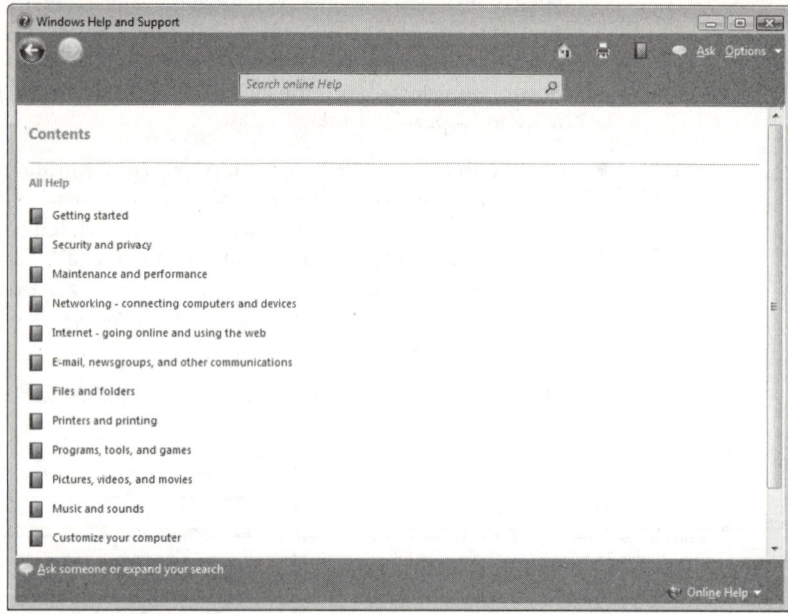

FIGURE 3.12 Browsing for helps means looking through the Contents page for a particular item.

MAKING THE MOST OF THE MICROSOFT KNOWLEDGE BASE

The Microsoft Knowledge Base is an online repository of knowledge and wisdom accumulated by Microsoft about its products. Given that the Knowledge Base is one of the main tools that Microsoft's support engineers use for troubleshooting customer problems with Windows, it's a great resource for searching for solutions to problems that Windows' local help resources don't know about. You can go directly to the standard Knowledge Base search at `http://support.microsoft.com/search/`. However, you'll find the advanced Knowledge Base search (`http://support.microsoft.com/search/?adv=1`) more useful because it provides additional search options, such as product selection and search location. For example, you can choose to search just for how-to articles, rather than for all of the content that Microsoft provides.

The disadvantage to the Knowledge Base, and perhaps the reason it's not more heavily emphasized in Microsoft's battery of help solutions, is the way it's arranged and the necessarily scattershot nature of its coverage. The Knowledge Base consists of a large number of answers that Microsoft's support engineers and other experts have written to questions that frustrated users and developers have submitted. The answers vary greatly in length, depending on the complexity of the problem and user level, ranging from beginner topics to super-advanced (developer-level) topics. Coverage is patchy, because the questions tend to be answered only when they're not covered in the Help files and other more accessible resources. This is probably the reason why the Knowledge Base no longer appears in any of the Windows Help and Support topics: the Knowledge Base's offerings may be helpful, but they may equally well be completely irrelevant to your needs.

To search for a Knowledge Base topic, go to either the standard or the advanced search website. Choose the product you're using from the Search Product field and type search terms, such as network printer, in the For field. The advanced search lets you input the search type, search method, time interval of the articles (such as last 6 months), number of results to show, and the search location (such as TechNet articles). Each article is identified by an Article ID number, which consists of a six-digit number (for example, 201950). Previously Microsoft had a Q in front of each article number but has dropped that convention.

Each article has a title that describes the problem it covers, information on which products and versions it covers, a summary that you can scan to get an idea of the contents, and the full text of the article. Beyond this, each article is tagged with keywords describing the main areas of its content. By searching for keywords, you can avoid passing references to words you might have included in the search, thus producing a more focused set of results.

Often, when you ask for help online, people will tell you to look at a particular Knowledge Base article for the answer. You can enter this article number as the search criteria and the Knowledge Base will take you directly to the article in question. You can also use this technique when you see a Knowledge Base article referenced in any documentation.

You can also use the Article ID to retrieve the article by e-mail by sending a message to `mshelp@microsoft.com` with the Article ID number in the Subject line.

If you don't know the Article ID but think you can locate it by searching article titles, you can get an index of Knowledge Base articles by e-mail by sending a message to `mshelp@microsoft.com` with the word "Index" in the Subject line.

Asking for Help

As you saw in Figure 3.10, Windows Help and Support provides a list of a dozen or so *help topics* on the home page. You can browse any of these help topics by clicking its link. Figure 3.13 shows an example of a help topic. Click one of the links in the topic area to display the links or information available.

Unfortunately, you might not always find what you need in Windows Help and Support. The Ask button displays a page that provides links to Remote Assistance, Support from Microsoft (both telephone and website), and Windows Communities. This page also provides links to advanced options that include the Knowledge Base, the Microsoft Website for IT Professionals, and Windows Online Help.

Some of these help options appear in other parts of the chapter. For example, the "Using Remote Assistance" section of the chapter describes how to use the Remote Assistance link found on this page. You'll find a complete description of the Knowledge Base in the sidebar entitled, "Making the Most of the Microsoft Knowledge Base."

WORKING WITH THE WINDOWS COMMUNITIES

The Windows Communities option takes you to Vista-specific newsgroups (the direct link is `http://windowshelp.microsoft.com/communities/newsgroups/en-us/default.mspx`). You need to sign in with your Windows Live ID (formerly called Passport) to obtain access to the website. The website, shown in Figure 3.14, provides multiple options for getting help. The best first option is to search the newsgroups for the information you need. After all, if someone else has already asked the question, you may as well benefit from it also. In addition, asking the same question multiple times tends to annoy the very people who can answer your question.

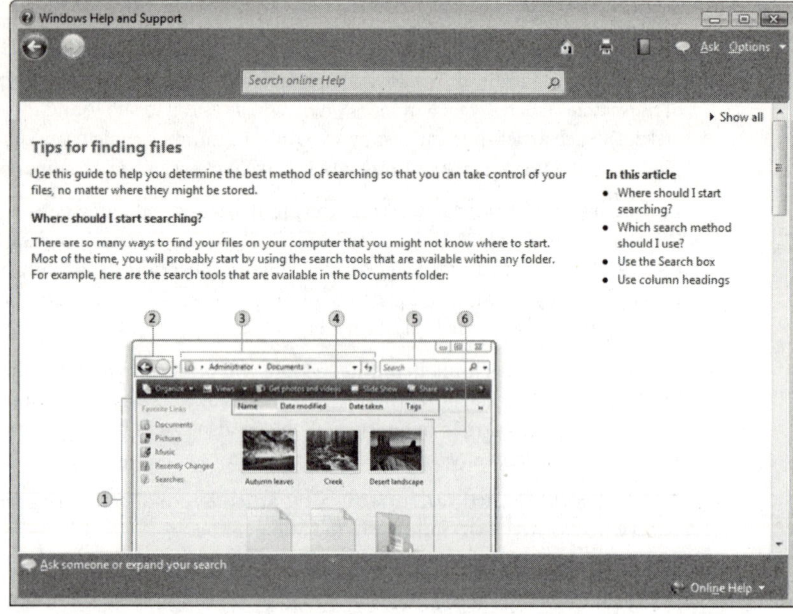

FIGURE 3.13 Follow the links in the Pick a Help Topic list to reach help topic areas.

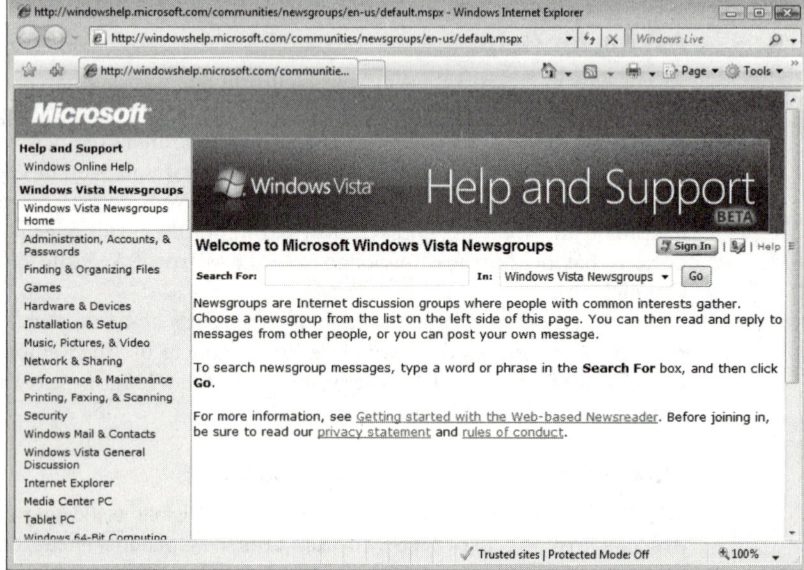

FIGURE 3.14 Locate the help you need by using the Vista newsgroups online.

When you can't find the answer to your question using the search engine, you can also choose a specific newsgroup. Sometimes, you'll spot the answer where the search engine didn't. In addition, you might find the answer you need by reviewing similar questions. Obviously, if you don't find what you need, you can upload your own question and wait for a response. Even though asking a question directly might seem like the best first choice, it usually isn't. First, you need to understand that not every newsgroup question receives an answer, so you might never receive a response. Second, there's a question of waiting for someone to respond even if your question does receive some attention. Most people need an answer now and the best way to get it is to find an existing answer to your question.

Using Windows Online Help

Many readers will remember the Help and Support Center of days past and look at the new Windows Help and Support with disdain. Actually, a version of the Help and Support Center still exists, but you need to go online to use it. This version appears at `http://windowshelp.microsoft.com/Windows/en-US/default.mspx`. As you can see from Figure 3.15, the content isn't precisely the same as before, but you do get the convenient two-pane display of days past.

You also get all of the search capability of the past. Because you're using a browser, rather than a local application to access help, you also get all of the features of a browser. This functionality includes the ability to store online help locations in your Favorites folder using the same technique that you use for any website. The newer Windows Help and Support application doesn't provide this functionality and many power users will miss it.

TIP You'll probably want to keep your Windows Online Help links in a special folder. Using a special folder (and associated subfolders for each topic) means that you can find the help topic you want far faster. It's also possible to separate the links you save from the browser by dragging and dropping them from the Favorites folder into a folder of your choice. The link will appear in the new folder you create and disappear from the Favorites folder in the browser. Clicking the link works just as you would expect, so placing the links into a separate folder won't result in any loss of functionality.

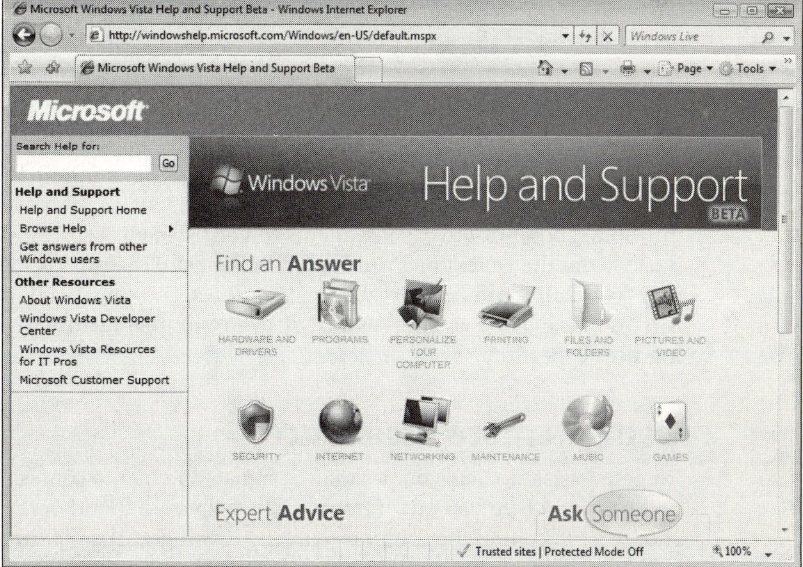

FIGURE 3.15
Windows Online Help provides a significant boost in functionality for power users.

GETTING ADVANCED HELP ON THE MICROSOFT WEBSITE FOR IT PROFESSIONALS

The Microsoft Website for IT Professionals (`http://www.microsoft.com/technet/windowsvista/default.mspx`) is less of a help center and more of an information center as shown in Figure 3.16. This website offers more than user level assistance. The website includes advanced articles on security, large site deployments, and other issues that concern IT professionals, rather than the average user. In addition, you'll find links for downloads and information on other information sources such as webcasts. Finally, you'll find a link for Windows Scripting, which is an important topic for any IT professional who wants to automate tasks.

FIGURE 3.16
Use the Microsoft Website for IT Professionals when you need something more than user level assistance.

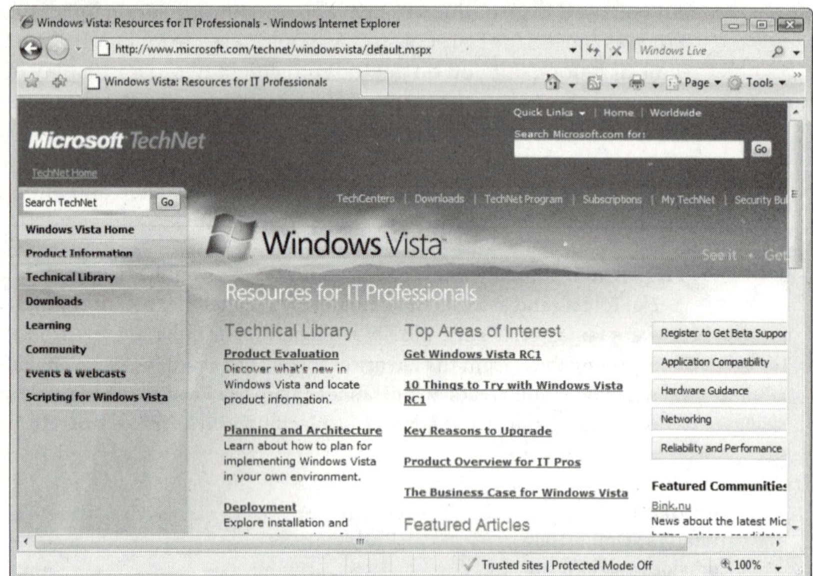

Printing Help Information

Sometimes it's handy to have a paper copy of a particular help topic, just in case Windows Help and Support becomes unavailable. For example, you might have to perform a task that requires multiple reboots or other adjustments to your system. To print the current topic, click the Print button, and then click the Print button in the Print dialog box that Windows Help and Support displays. Unlike previous versions of Windows, you can't print multiple pages at once—perhaps Microsoft is making an effort as part of an environmental initiative to reduce the amount of printing people perform.

Using Remote Assistance

Remote Assistance lets you permit a designated helper to connect to your computer, see what's going on, and help you out of trouble. The helper—a friend or an administrator, whomever you choose—can control the computer directly if you give them permission, or you can simply chat with them and apply as much of their advice as you deem fit.

To use Remote Assistance, both your computer and your helper's must be running Vista or, with the correct settings, Windows XP. You can mix these two platforms with some loss of functionality and security (you can't expect Windows XP to provide all of the support that Vista provides). You send an invitation via e-mail or save it as a file (for example, to a network location designated for Remote Assistance request files, or on a floppy or CD that you then pop in the snail mail). When your helper responds, you decide whether to accept their help.

Each of the methods of requesting Remote Assistance has its advantages and disadvantages. An e-mail invitation lets you include details of the Windows problem with which you need help—but you don't know when the recipient will check their e-mail. A file invitation, like an e-mail invitation, lets you include details of the problem, but you have no idea of when you'll receive a response to it (if ever).

On the other end of the wire, you can offer Help via Remote Assistance. All you need is for someone to send you an invitation.

NOTE Previous versions of Windows let you request help using Windows Messenger. Vista no longer supports this option due to security concerns.

Security Considerations

Like all remote-control technologies, Remote Assistance has serious security implications that you need to consider before using it.

If you give another person control of your computer, they can take actions almost as freely as if they were seated in front of the computer. You can watch these actions, and you can take back control of the computer at any time, but you may already be too late: it takes less than a second to delete a key file, and little longer to plant a virus or other form of malware.

Even if you *don't* give your helper control and instead simply chat, keep your wits about you when deciding which of their suggestions to implement. Malicious or ill-informed suggestions can do plenty of damage if you apply them without thinking. Never take any actions that could compromise your security or destroy your data. Above all, treat any incoming files with the greatest of suspicion and virus-check them with up-to-date antivirus program before using them.

One particular problem is that you can't tell that the person at the other computer is who they claim to be. For this reason alone, you should always protect your Remote Assistance connections with a strong password known only to the person from whom you're requesting help. That way, if someone else is at their computer or has identity-jacked them, they won't be able to respond to the Remote Assistance invitation you send.

Enabling Remote Assistance

Remote Assistance is enabled by default. To find out if Remote Assistance is enabled on your computer, follow these steps:

1. Display the System window (for example, by pressing Winkey+Break or clicking the System link on the System and Maintenance screen of Control Panel).
2. Click the Remote Settings link. Click Continue when asked by UAC. You'll see the Remote tab of the System Properties dialog box shown in Figure 3.17.
3. Check the status of the Allow Remote Assistance Connections to This Computer check box. If this check box isn't selected, select it.
4. Click the OK button. Windows closes the System Properties dialog box.

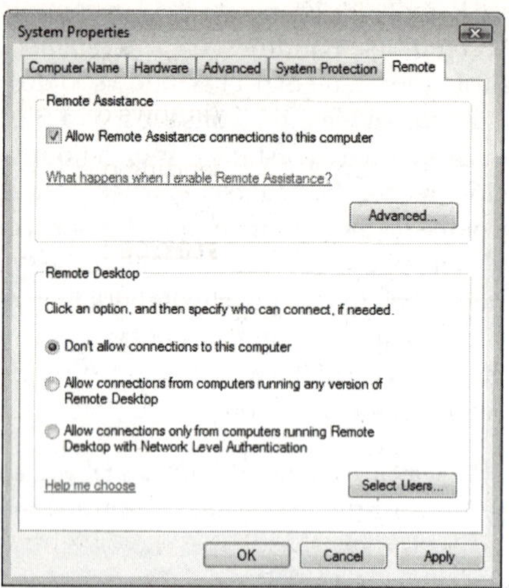

FIGURE 3.17
The Remote tab of the System Properties dialog box lets you adjust the Remote Assistance options.

Setting Limits for Remote Assistance

To set limits for Remote Assistance:

1. In the Remote Assistance section of the Remote tab, click the Advanced button to open the Remote Assistance Settings dialog box shown in Figure 3.18.
2. In the Remote Control section, clear the Allow This Computer to Be Controlled Remotely check box if you don't want your helpers to be able to control the computer. (This check box is selected by default.) Even when this check box is selected, you need to approve each request for control of the PC manually.
3. In the Invitations section, use the two drop-down lists to specify an expiration limit for Remote Assistance invitations that your computer sends out. The default setting is 6 hours; you might want to shorten this period for security.
4. Check the Allow Connections Only from Computers Running Windows Vista or Later option if you want the extra security and functionality that Vista provides. When you check this option, you can't obtain Remote Assistance from a Windows XP system.

FIGURE 3.18
Adjust the functionality that Remote Assistance provides to match your specific needs.

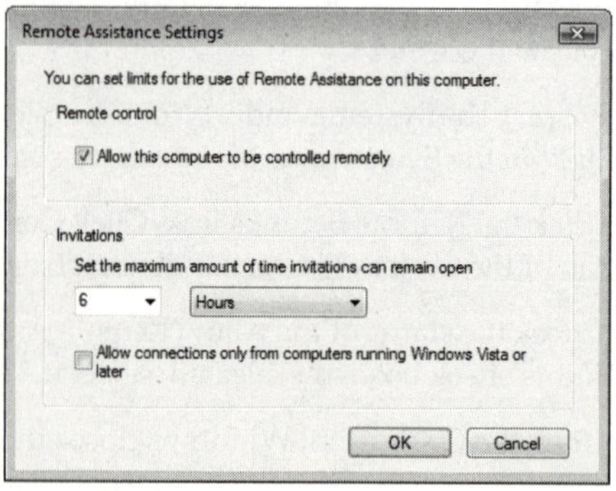

5. Click the OK button. Windows closes the Remote Assistance Settings dialog box, returning you to the System Properties dialog box.
6. Click the OK button. Windows closes the System Properties dialog box.

You're now ready to start sending out invitations for Remote Assistance.

Sending a Remote Assistance Invitation via E-mail

To send a Remote Assistance invitation as an e-mail message via your existing e-mail account, follow these steps:

1. Choose Start ➢ All Programs ➢ Maintenance ➢ Windows Remote Assistance or click Ask in Windows Help and Support and then choose the Remote Assistance link. Windows opens a Windows Help and Support window to the Remote Assistance topic.
2. Click the Invite Someone You Trust to Help You link. Windows Help and Support displays the Pick How You Want to Contact Your Assistant screen of Remote Assistance (shown in Figure 3.19).

NOTE The first time you go through these steps, Windows Help and Support displays a screen bearing Important Notes. If you want to skip this page in the future, leave the Don't Show This Page Again check box selected (as it is by default) and click the Continue button.

3. Click Use E-mail to Send an Invitation. Vista asks you to provide a password for your computer.
4. Type a password, confirm it, and then click Next. If the password you provide is too short, Vista will ask you to enter a new one. Make sure you provide a password that's at least six characters long. It's preferable to use a strong password that includes numbers, letters (both uppercase and lowercase), and special characters. See the "Using Passphrases in Place of Passwords" sidebar for a good method of creating a strong password you won't forget.

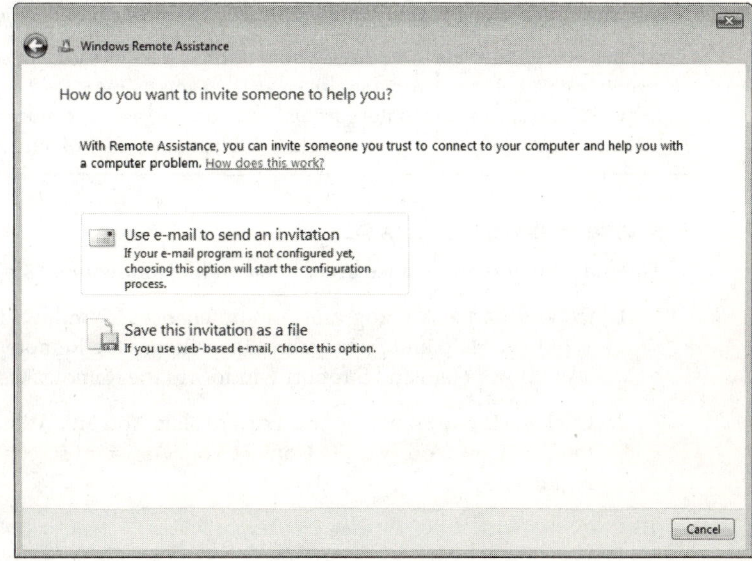

FIGURE 3.19 On the Pick How You Want to Contact Your Assistant screen of Remote Assistance, specify which type of Remote Assistance invitation to send.

5. Once Vista accepts your password, it will start your e-mail program, create a message, and add some content to it.

6. Type the e-mail address of the person you want to invite in the To field of the e-mail message. Make sure you choose this person with care.

7. Type a personal message in the "Enter a personal message here:" section of the e-mail message.

8. Click Send to send the e-mail to the person you want to invite and wait for them to respond. You'll see the Remote Assistance window shown in Figure 3.20 as you wait.

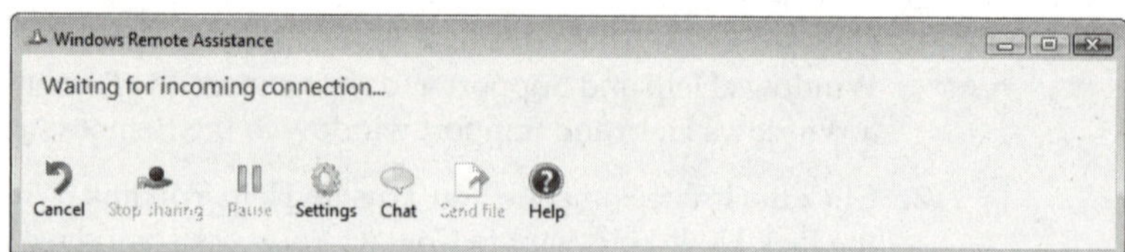

FIGURE 3.20
You'll see a Remote Assistance window like this one as you wait for a connection.

USING PASSPHRASES IN PLACE OF PASSWORDS

As more people try to gain access to your computer using any means necessary, you have to get smarter about the passwords you choose. The only problem is that choosing a password that's truly difficult to guess also makes it tough to memorize. For example, a password such as Goodby3 is decent because it combines numbers, uppercase, and lowercase letters, but it's not the easiest password to remember when you come back from vacation. If you change your password frequently, you might find yourself locked out of your own system.

An alternative, you can use a new kind of password called the passphrase. A passphrase is a sentence that you know you can remember. For example, "Mars is the 4th planet from the sun" is easy to remember, yet it combines all of the best features of a good password. Windows doesn't care that you use a passphrase and a long phrase is truly difficult for someone besides yourself to guess.

Of course, you still have to stay away from obvious passphrases. For example, "My name is Fred" isn't a very good passphrase. Everyone else knows that your name is Fred, too. However, not too many people know, "There are 6 rocks in my garden." It's not a phrase that most people would guess, even if they know you well. Yet, such a phrase is almost ridiculously easy to remember.

SAVING AN INVITATION AS A FILE

To send a Remote Assistance invitation as a file, follow these steps:

1. Choose Start ➤ All Programs ➤ Maintenance ➤ Windows Remote Assistance or click Ask in Windows Help and Support and then choose the Remote Assistance link. Windows opens a Windows Help and Support window to the Remote Assistance topic.

2. Click the Invite Someone You Trust to Help You link. Windows Help and Support displays the Pick How You Want to Contact Your Assistant screen of Remote Assistance (shown in Figure 3.19).

NOTE The first time you go through these steps, Windows Help and Support displays a screen bearing Important Notes. If you want to skip this page in the future, leave the Don't Show This Page Again check box selected (as it is by default) and click the Continue button.

3. Click Save This Invitation as a File. Vista asks you to provide a location for the file and a password for your computer. The default location for the file is the Desktop. However, placing the file in your Desktop means that someone must watch your Desktop for help requests. The more common solution is to place the file on a common network drive where support personnel know to look.
4. Provide a location for the Remote Assistance request file. Make sure the file has a msrc incident file extension. This file extension is associated with Remote Assistance and automatically starts the application when opened.
5. Type a password and confirm it. Make sure you provide a password that's at least six characters long. It's preferable to use a strong password that includes numbers, letters (both uppercase and lowercase), and special characters. See the "Using Passphrases in Place of Passwords" sidebar for a good method of creating a strong password you won't forget.
6. Click Finish. Vista creates the invitation file in the location you request. You'll see the Remote Assistance window shown in Figure 3.20 as you wait.

Accepting a Remote Assistance Invitation

You always receive a file with a Remote Assistance invitation. When using the e-mail method, the file is attached to the e-mail. Otherwise, you'll find the file in a support folder on a network. No matter where you find the file, you'll accept the invitation by opening the file. You'll see a Remote Assistance dialog box like the one shown in Figure 3.21. Simply type the prearranged password and click OK.

After you enter the password, you'll see a Remote Assistance window like the one shown in Figure 3.22. The only difference is that you'll see a full screen beneath the set of tools at the top. Vista will continue to attempt to make a connection until the requesting computer responds or you click Cancel.

In some cases, the requesting computer won't respond before a timeout occurs. At this point, Vista will tell you that the computer isn't responding. After you click OK to clear the error message, you'll see the Windows Remote Assistance dialog box shown in Figure 3.23.

FIGURE 3.21
Provide the prearranged password and click OK to accept the Remote Assistance invitation.

Windows Remote Assistance
Type the password to connect to the remote computer
You can get this password from the person requesting assistance. A Remote Assistance session will start after you type the password and click OK.
Enter password:
OK
Cancel

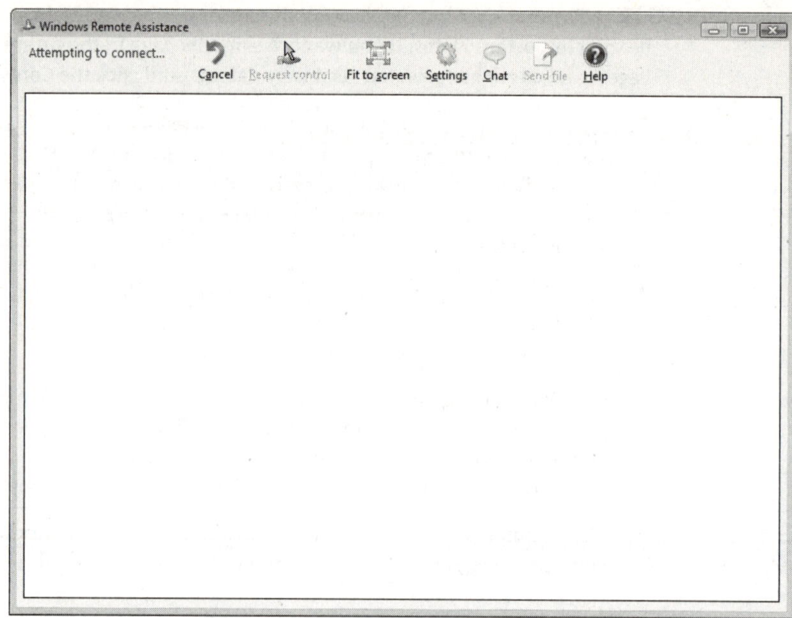

FIGURE 3.22
The helper's version of the Windows Remote Assistance window varies slightly from the requestor's window.

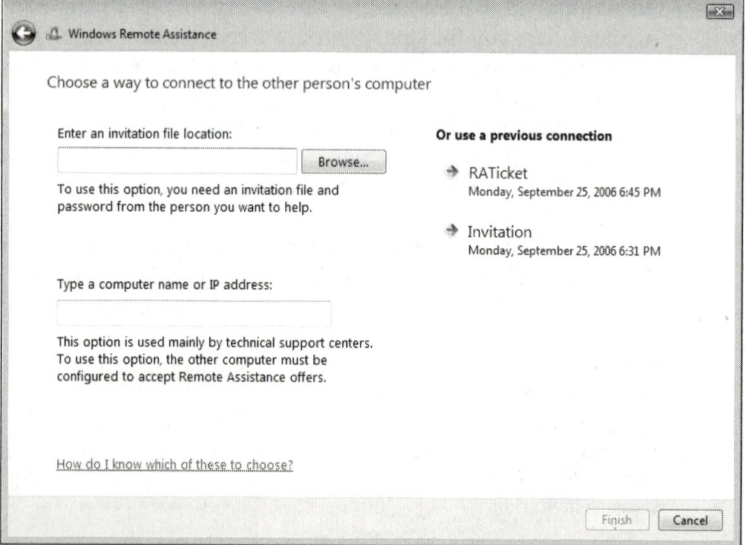

FIGURE 3.23
Choose another computer to work with or try a failed connection a second time.

This dialog box actually provides three options for support personnel. First, you can open the next Remote Assistance request file. Click Browse to locate the file, and then click Finish to try to establish contact. Second, you can type the IP address or name of a computer on the network. This option often helps with less skilled users when you must establish the connection manually. Third, you can choose one of the invitations that failed in the past.

You can also get to the dialog box shown in Figure 3.23 in a more direct manner. Simply click the Offer to Help Someone option in the initial Remote Assistance dialog box, rather than click Invite Someone You Trust to Help You.

Working with Remote Assistance

At some point, the request you send will either time out, you'll cancel it, or the person will respond. No matter how you establish a connection, both you and the helper will have access to a set of controls for a session. Figure 3.20 shows the sender controls that become active and you can begin working with the other party. The following sections provide information on using Remote Assistance after you establish contact with the other party.

Performing the Remote Assistance Setup

The level of help you receive depends on your Remote Assistance settings. You can also control how well Remote Assistance works by clicking Settings. Remote Assistance displays the Windows Remote Assistance Settings dialog box shown in Figure 3.24.

The Use ESC Key to Stop Sharing Control option determines whether you can press Esc at any time to stop the other party from doing anything with your system. This is a safety feature that you shouldn't ever have to use, but that you should always keep in place. If you can't trust the other party enough to work with your computer, then you probably don't want to ask them for Remote Assistance.

The Save a Log of This Session option lets you save a text version of everything that takes place during the Remote Assistance session. You should always keep this feature enabled because it means you don't have to take notes. Everything that occurs is recorded for later use, so you can focus all of your attention on what is happening on the display. The log will help you remember specific steps to perform a task later and can help you when you don't understand why something went wrong during a session. In other words, this feature also acts as a diagnostic when you need it.

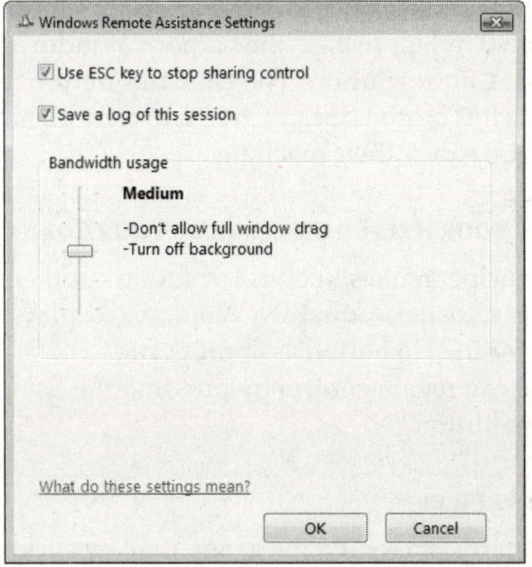

FIGURE 3.24
Make sure you get the help you need by setting up Remote Assistance properly.

NOTE Only you can control the use of the Esc key and the network bandwidth for the session. Your helper can save a log of the session using the Windows Remote Assistance Settings dialog box. This log appears on the helper's system, not your system. Consequently, if you both want session logs, then you both need to check the Save a Log of This Session option.

The hardest feature to set up is the bandwidth. You don't want to use up so much bandwidth that the entire network is brought to its knees. The best practice is to use the Medium setting as shown in Figure 3.24 unless you really need to improve performance because the other party is controlling your system. In many cases, you can actually get by with lower settings when you simply need advice on how to perform a task. Try the lowest setting you can to obtain the desired results.

Chatting with Your Helper

To chat with your helper, click Chat. You'll see a Chat window open. The helper must click Chat as well. Type a message in the Message Entry text box and press the Enter key or click the Send button to send it.

To start voice transmission, click the Start Talking button. Your helper then sees a dialog box asking if they want to use a voice connection. If they click the Yes button, Remote Assistance establishes the voice connection. Talk as usual, and then click the Stop Talking button when you want to stop using the voice connection.

NOTE The first time you use the talk feature, Remote Assistance runs the Audio and Video Tuning Wizard if you haven't run it before.

To choose voice settings, click the Settings button. Windows displays a Remote Assistance Settings dialog box. Choose the Standard Quality option button or the High Quality option button as appropriate. Alternatively, click the Audio Tuning Wizard button (if it's available) to run the Audio and Video Tuning Wizard to optimize your speaker and microphone settings. Close the Remote Assistance Settings dialog box when you've finished.

Requesting Control of the Requestor's Computer

As shown in Figure 3.22, the helper's Windows Remote Assistance window contains a special Request Control button. You click this button to request control of the remote machine. Simply clicking this button doesn't give you control, however. The requestor must specifically authorize you to take over their machine.

Giving Your Helper Control of Your Computer

If your helper requests control of your computer by clicking Request Control in his or her Windows Remote Assistance window, Windows displays the Remote Assistance dialog box. Click the Yes button or the No button as appropriate.

You can regain control by pressing the Esc key, by pressing Alt+C, or by clicking the Stop Sharing button.

Sending Files

Either party can send a file at any time by clicking Send File. When you click this button, Remote Assistance asks you to select a file from your system to send to the other party. The other party receives notification that you want to send a file. If they accept, then Remote Assistance asks where they want to store the file on their system. You can send any type file that the firewalls on both systems permit. For example, it's quite easy to send document files in most cases. However, you might find it significantly more difficult to send executables, scripts, batch files, or even source code files. Many firewalls block these files with good reason. Always contact the network administrator if you experience problems sending a file.

Temporarily Disconnecting Your Helper

You might need to perform a task quickly, and sending all of that information over the network definitely slows things down. Click Pause when you need to temporarily disconnect your helper. Your helper won't see your computer screen because Remote Assistance isn't sending any information to the helper. Click Pause again to restore the connection.

Disconnecting Your Helper

To disconnect your helper, click the Cancel button. Remote Assistance closes the connection and restores your Desktop to its full complement of colors (if you chose to optimize performance for your helper).

When your helper disconnects themselves, Windows displays a Remote Assistance dialog box telling you so. Click the OK button to close this dialog box, then close the Windows Help and Support window.

Microsoft Online Support (Get Help from Microsoft)

Microsoft Online Support lets you automatically collect information on a problem you're having and submit it to Microsoft electronically. A Microsoft technician then sends a solution, which appears as a pop-up in your notification area. You can read the response in the Windows Help and Support window and apply the wisdom it contains to fix the problem.

Microsoft Online Support lets you avoid both long waits on hold and the difficulty of explaining complex problems and system configuration over the phone.

To use Microsoft Online Support, you need a Microsoft Windows Live ID or a Hotmail account. If you don't have one, Windows Help and Support walks you through the process of getting one.

To connect to Microsoft Online Support, click Ask in Windows Help and Support, click the Contact Microsoft Customer Support Online link, and follow the steps the Windows Help and Support presents. For obvious reasons, your computer needs a working Internet connection to use this feature.

Windows Newsgroups (Go to a Windows Website Forum)

The Windows Newsgroups are an assortment of Windows-related online newsgroups that you can access through a web-based front end. Although these newsgroups are run under the auspices of Microsoft, they suffer to some extent from the problems of noise and irrelevance that characterize public newsgroups. (See Chapter 17 for a discussion of newsgroups and how to use Windows Mail to access them.)

Using the Troubleshooters

Vista includes a number of *troubleshooters* for troubleshooting common problems with hardware and software configuration. Vista will often detect a problem with your system and display the troubleshooter automatically. However, you can also start the troubleshooting process manually. Windows Help and Support provides a central starting point for running these tools, although Windows also offers you the chance to run the appropriate troubleshooter when it detects that you've run into a configuration problem.

To run one of the troubleshooters, follow these steps:

1. From the Windows Help and Support Home page, click the Troubleshooting link. Windows Help and Support displays the Troubleshooting in Windows screen.
2. In the Fixing a Problem list, click a link to display a list of troubleshooters for that problem.
3. Click a Troubleshooter, and then follow the onscreen instructions. Figure 3.25 shows the Troubleshoot Driver Problems screen.

TIP Always look at the bottom of help and troubleshooter screens for the Was This Information Helpful? section. Click the button that best expresses how helpful you found the help screen or troubleshooter and then tell Microsoft why. Providing this information might seem like a needless waste of your time, but it really does help Microsoft refine the help files. Since the help files in Vista are dynamic, a suggestion you make today could appear in a help file tomorrow. Consequently, feedback is always a good idea if you want Microsoft to make any progress at all in improving the help system.

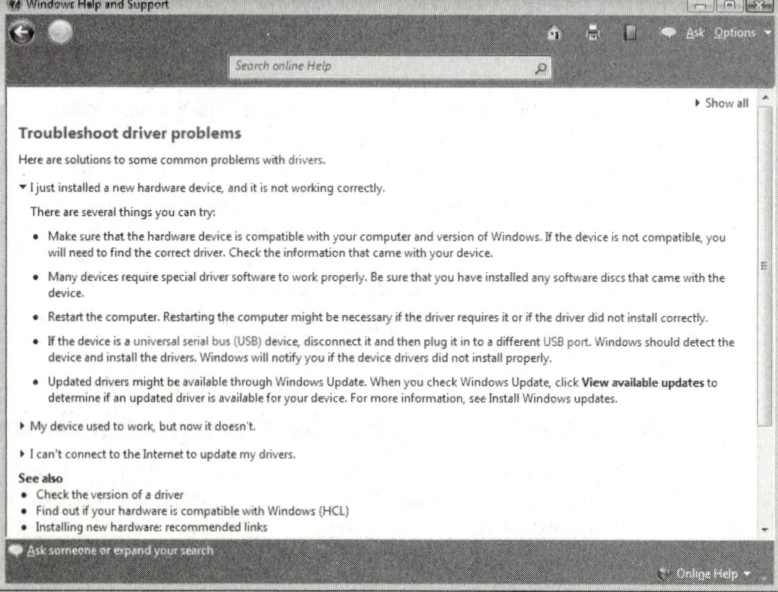

FIGURE 3.25
The troubleshooters provide a convenient way to diagnose problems using a step-by-step procedure.

Finding Help on the Internet and Web

If you can't find the information you need through Windows Help and Support, try the Internet and the Web.

TIP One of the best ways to get good information on the Internet is to perform a site search on Google. Simply go to the Google Advanced Search page at `http://www.google.com/advanced_search?hl=en`. Type the search term that you want in the Find Results fields (use one or more of the fields depending on what kind of search you want to perform). In the Domain field, type the domain for a particular website. For example, if you want to use Google to search Microsoft support, then type **`support.microsoft.com`** in this field. You'll very likely find that the Google results are not only more refined, but also more thorough as well.

Help on the Web

With earlier versions of Windows, the first port of call when looking for help on the Web was the Microsoft website, which offered all sorts of resources from the latest patches and drivers to the Knowledge Base. But now that Windows Help and Support seamlessly searches the Microsoft website and provides links to some hardware and software manufacturers' offerings, and Windows Update can automatically download and prompt you to install updates and patches to Windows, there's less reason to access the Microsoft website manually unless you need, say, the extra search capabilities that the Knowledge Base website offers.

To find information from hardware and software manufacturers not partnered closely enough with Microsoft to rate inclusion in Windows Help and Support's repertoire, to download the latest drivers, or to find other sources of information, the Web can be either more or less valuable, depending on your luck and your persistence in searching.

Chapter 15 discusses how to surf the Web with Internet Explorer.

Help in Newsgroups

Another good source of information and help are the many computer-related public newsgroups (such as the `comp.sys` hierarchy) and the Microsoft public newsgroups (in the `microsoft.public` hierarchy).

Chapter 17 discusses how to use Windows Mail to read news.

Summary

This chapter has covered a lot of ground, but now you have the information you need to navigate the Desktop and to get help when you run into a problem. Windows Help and Support gives you access to much more information than previous versions of Windows did, and it's easy to make using it your first step when trying to solve a problem.

Of course, practice makes perfect. Most people never try to use help until they actually need it. Unfortunately, that's the worst time to learn how to use help because you're probably in a time crunch and the boss is breathing down your neck. The best time to learn how to use help to resolve a problem is when there isn't a problem to solve. Take time now to become familiar with Windows Help and Support. Try the various support links, perform some searches, or set up a Remote Assistance session with a friend. All of these activities may seem to waste time until you have a real world problem to solve. Any time you spend learning the help system today will save you significant time when you really need it tomorrow.

So far we've dabbled with the new features of the Vista interface—it's time to stop dabbling. Chapter 4 tells you about the four interfaces that Microsoft supports in Vista and how to best use them in your work environment. Chapter 4 will help you explore all of those fancy new features that Microsoft has added to Vista and determine which features you want to use and when. I'm convinced that many business users can get by just fine without all of the eye candy. However, there are times when you need to use those extra graphics to achieve a particular goal. Chapter 4 is your gateway to understanding why the Vista interface is so different.

Chapter 4

Navigating the Vista Interface

Every other version of Windows has had what amounts to a single interface. Sure, you could change it around as needed, but in the end, you got what amounted to just one interface to think about. Vista changes all that. Now you have multiple interfaces to consider, each of which appears to have its own set of hardware requirements.

Most people know about the Aero Glass interface and the fact that you can turn everything off to get the Windows Classic interface. These two interfaces represent the extremes of the Microsoft offerings. Sandwiched between these two extremes are two other offerings, the Vista Standard interface and the Vista Basic interfaces. Actually, all of these terms are Microsoft-speak and this chapter clears up the confusion.

Everyone will also notice that some Windows features are suddenly missing. They aren't really missing, Microsoft simply decided to rename them and move them around. This chapter helps you find all of your old friends and make sense of the Vista organization no matter which interface you decide to use.

This chapter covers the following topics:

- Understanding the Vista Interfaces
- Configuring the Vista Interfaces
- Locating and Using the Control Panel
- Personalizing Your Computer Setup
- Accessing the System Dialog Box

Vista: What's New?

Someone at Microsoft is constantly unhappy with the current look and feel of Windows. That's the only reason I can figure for the drastic changes that Microsoft makes in every version of Windows. They're never happy to leave the interface alone—it changes at the whims of whomever is in the graphics department at any given time. Consequently, you're continually facing a new learning curve for using a product that's been a staple on desktop everywhere for a number of years. Vista's use of what at first seems like four different interfaces is just another example of this constant change from Microsoft.

As with Windows 95, the massive change of the past, Microsoft has decided to rename and change the location of many standard features. These changes are going to cause a lot of consternation for anyone who needs to get work done with Windows. Sure, starting something like Word hasn't changed much, but you're going to find significant changes in just about everything else. For example, you can't get directly to the System dialog box any longer—you have to go somewhere else first. You no longer modify the display settings on your machine; you personalize your system.

Even the Control Panel has changed. Theoretically, these changes are supposed to make Windows easier to use, but long-time users will simply find that their jobs are much harder now.

Defining the Interfaces

Depending on how you look at Vista, it has up to four interfaces. However, nailing those interfaces down has been difficult. You get two of these interfaces by default when you install Vista: Aero Glass and Vista Standard. To obtain the other two interfaces, you must reconfigure your system. Here's a breakdown of the four interfaces that are discussed in the sections that follow.

- **Aero Glass:** This is the default interface for any machine that uses one of the premium Vista editions and has the required hardware. It provides you with that see-through look on various parts, such as the title bar, of each window. This interface relies on a special Vista feature called the *Compositor* to display the snazzy effects and provide functionality such as the thumbnails of each window you select in the Taskbar. The Compositor is essentially a fancy graphics engine. You can't get the Aero Glass interface with Vista Home Basic.

- **Vista Standard:** The Vista Standard interface appears as part of the Vista Home Basic edition. This is the default interface you see when you have all of the hardware to run the Compositor. This interface provides all of the functionality and features of the Aero Glass interface, but without some of the glitz, such as see-through title bars.

- **Vista Basic:** This is the closest you get to Windows XP in Vista. You still see visual effects such as rounded buttons, but you don't see any of the effects produced by the Compositor. It's possible to use this interface with any Vista edition and it's the default interface for older systems. In some cases, this means that you won't see some of the nice graphic functionality that Vista normally provides. Moving a window might appear jerky on the display, rather than smooth as when you use the Compositor. However, this interface also makes fewer demands on your system, which means that you get better performance overall. There are always tradeoffs to consider.

- **Windows Standard/Classic:** This is what I like to term as the business interface for Vista. The display you see is very much like the display you used in Windows 2000. There aren't any fancy graphics. As a result, you obtain maximum system performance. Unfortunately, you also lose access to some of the Vista features, which includes some informational displays that rely on Vista's graphics functionality. Even so, this is the option that many business users will rely on to ensure they get the most from Vista. Interestingly enough, this option comes in two forms: Windows Standard and Windows Classic. The Windows Standard setup has a tiny bit more flash than the completely dull Windows Classic, but they're both based on Windows 2000.

Now that you have some idea of what the various interfaces will do for you, you might want to see what they look like. I'll definitely provide screenshots throughout the book, but a black-and-white image hardly does the interface justice. You can see a side-by-side comparison of the four interfaces online at `http://www.istartedsomething.com/20060919/vista-choose-own-adventure-ui/`. Simply choose the part of the interface that interests you most and select the link for the interface you want to review. You'll see a full screen view of the interface component in color.

Understanding the Aero Glass Interface

As mentioned in Chapter 2, you must have a display adapter that supports DirectX 9 and a minimum of 128 MB of RAM to use the Aero Glass interface. You might be surprised to find that many graphics adapters support these minimum requirements. However, a minimal display adapter combined with a system that isn't really up to par usually results in a poor Aero Glass experience. Consequently, even if Microsoft decides that your system can run Aero Glass, you might decide to differ in that opinion, or at least not use Aero Glass all of the time.

Fortunately, you don't have to use the Aero Glass interface all of the time, just when you need it to perform a graphics tasks or when your system isn't overloaded. You have several options for configuring the Aero Glass interface, most of which are explored in the "Using the Personalize Feature" section of the chapter. However, the following steps provide a quick way to access the Aero Glass and other interfaces supplied with Vista.

1. Right-click on any blank location on the Desktop and choose Personalize from the context menu. You'll see the Personalize Appearance and Sounds window shown in Figure 4.1.

2. Click the Window Color and Appearance link. You'll see the Window Color and Appearance window shown in Figure 4.2. Now, here's the first place you can make a performance choice. If you want to obtain an interface very much like that presented by the Vista Standard interface, simply clear the Enable Transparency check box and click OK. However, you have other options should you need them.

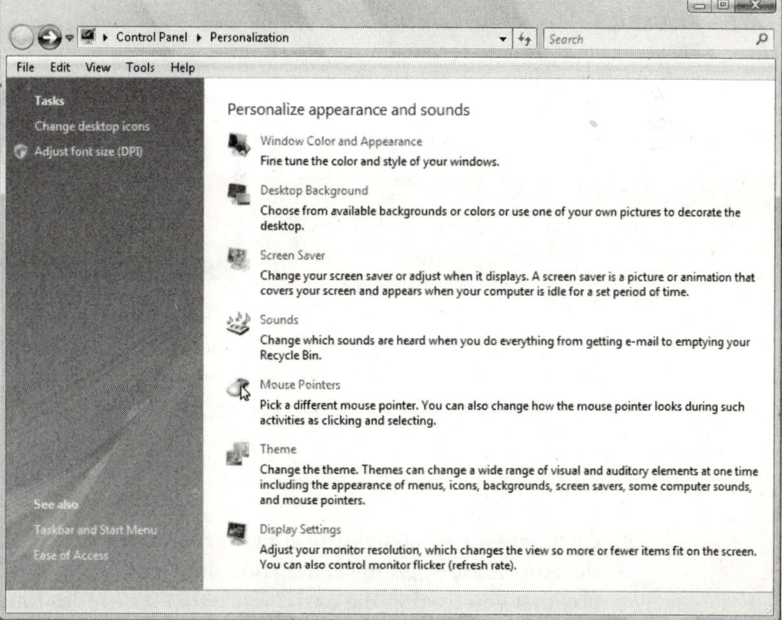

FIGURE 4.1
The Personalize Appearance and Sounds window shows common interface options.

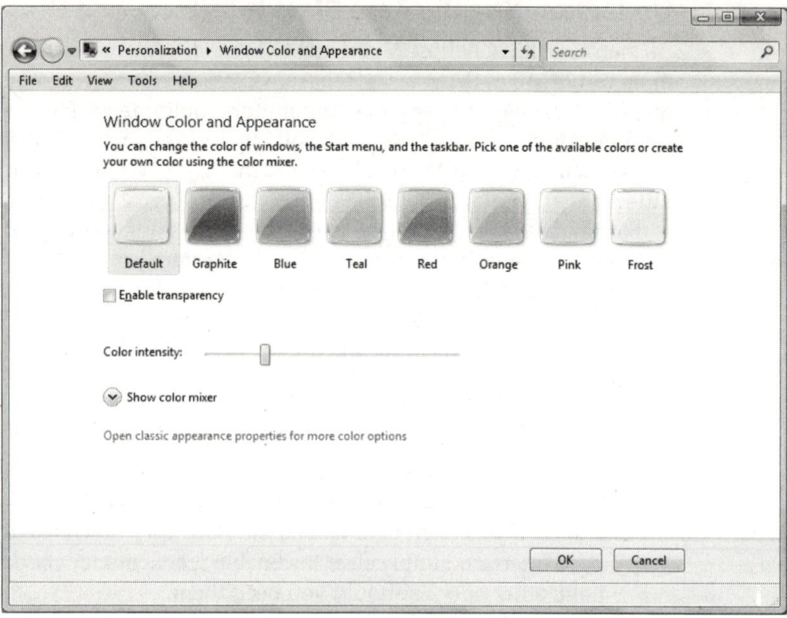

FIGURE 4.2
Use the Window Color and Appearance window to make changes in transparency.

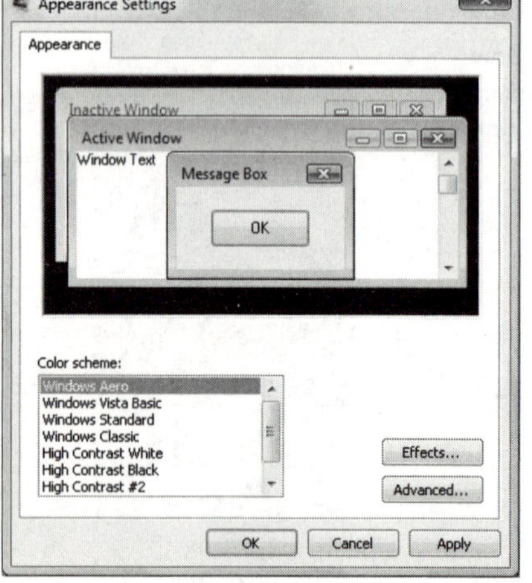

FIGURE 4.3
Choose a color scheme to change the way that Vista presents information on screen.

3. Click the Open Classic Appearance Properties for More Color Options link and you'll see the Appearance Settings dialog box shown in Figure 4.3. This is the color selection dialog box that you used in the past. Notice that it includes four new color schemes, including Aero Glass, Windows Vista Basic, Windows Standard, and Windows Classic. It's interesting to note that changing the color scheme does far more than simply change the colors that Vista uses—you'll notice changes in system settings as well. For example, when you

choose Windows Classic, the system automatically clears the Enable Transparency option in the Window Color and Appearance window.

4. Choose any of the color schemes and click OK. Your display will change as needed to support the scheme you selected. These changes include system settings changes such as enabling or disabling transparency.

Understanding the Vista Standard Interface

As previously mentioned, the Vista Standard interface only comes with Vista Home Basic edition. Consequently, you can't choose this interface when working with other editions—at least not directly. The best way to obtain the desired effect is to turn off transparency as described in the "Understanding the Aero Glass Interface" section of the chapter.

If you're using Vista Home Basic edition and find that you have turned off the Vista Standard interface (either on purpose or accidentally), you can restore it using the same procedure as found in the "Understanding the Aero Glass Interface" section of the chapter. Choosing the Vista Standard Interface option from the list of color schemes will restore the interface for you.

Configuring the Vista Basic Interface

The Vista Basic interface is essentially the Windows XP view of the world. Yes, you see rounded buttons and nice displays, but these displays don't include any of the fancy graphics that the Aero Glass interface or Vista Standard interface include. For example, if you look carefully at the Vista Standard interface title bar, you'll notice that it's subtly shaded—it has a pattern. The Vista Basic interface doesn't include these little extras because it doesn't include the Compositor. The easiest way to select this interface is to follow the procedure in the "Understanding the Aero Glass Interface" section of the chapter. However, you can also perform this task by removing support for the Compositor as described in the "Removing Other Gizmos from the Interface" section of the chapter.

You're going to notice some interesting behavioral changes when you choose this interface. For example, when you click Window Color and Appearance link in the Personalize Appearance and Sound window (see Figure 4.1) you don't see the Window Color and Appearance window (shown in Figure 4.2). What you see instead is the Appearance Settings dialog box. Vista cuts out the intermediate step because the issue of transparency is no longer relevant—the lack of compositor support makes transparency impossible. These changes in behavior appear in many different areas of Vista, which means that the steps you use to accomplish a given task change slightly based on the interface you use.

Configuring the Windows Classic Interface

There are a number of ways to get to the Windows Classic interface. Of course, you can use the procedure in the "Understanding the Aero Glass Interface" section of the chapter. However, an easier method exists if you want to use the Windows Classic look. The following steps describe this technique.

1. Right-click on any blank location on the Desktop and choose Personalize from the context menu. You'll see the Personalize Appearance and Sounds window shown in Figure 4.1.

2. Click the Theme link. You'll see the Theme Settings dialog box shown in Figure 4.4.

3. Select the Windows Classic option in the Theme field and click OK. Vista changes to the Windows Classic interface.

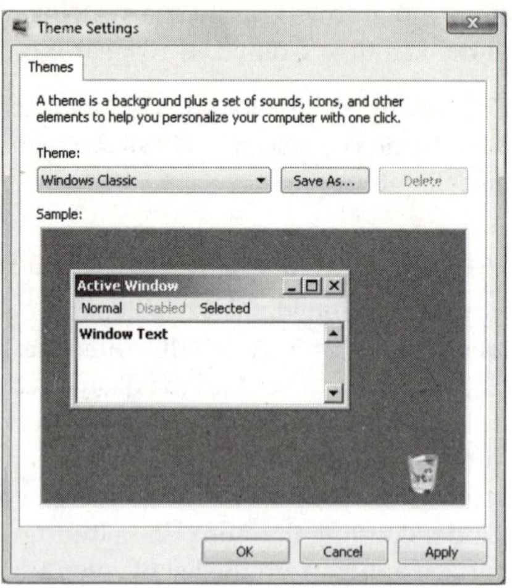

FIGURE 4.4
Make a quick change to the Windows Classic theme using the Theme Settings dialog box.

Don't get the idea that changing to the Windows Classic interface will make Vista work like Windows 2000. The same Vista menu options, dialog boxes, and windows are in place as before. Of course, a few minor changes do take place. You won't see the Window Color and Appearance window (see Figure 4.2) because there isn't any reason for it when using this interface.

NOTE The remainder of the book uses the Windows Classic interface for screenshots, unless you actually need to use one of the other interfaces for a particular application. The Windows Classic interface tends to make many interface options clearer.

Removing Other Gizmos from the Interface

Vista provides a wealth of other interface gizmos that don't add anything to the user experience, kill off valuable resources, and tend to make the display confusing. You can access these interface options from a number of places, but the best place is in the Performance Options dialog box. The following steps explain how to display this dialog box.

1. Right-click the Computer icon on the desktop or in the Start menu, and choose Properties from the context menu. You'll see the System window shown in Figure 4.5.
2. Click the Advanced System Settings link. You'll see the Advanced tab of the System Properties dialog box as shown in Figure 4.6. This dialog box should look familiar because it's changed very little in the last several versions of Windows. Microsoft has retained many interface features from previous versions of Windows—they're simply buried beneath the Vista interface.
3. Click Settings in the Performance section of the Advanced tab. You'll see the Performance Options dialog box shown in Figure 4.7. This is the dialog box that exposes many of the Vista features. Many of these features are the same as previous versions of Windows. For example, you'll still find the Smooth Edges of Screen Fonts option. However, I'll discuss later in

this section some new Vista options that you need to know about in order to get maximum performance.

4. Choose one of the overall performance options, such as Adjust for Best Appearance, or individually check or clear options as needed in the Custom list. Click OK twice to close the Performance Options and System Properties dialog boxes.

FIGURE 4.5
The System window provides access to system configuration options.

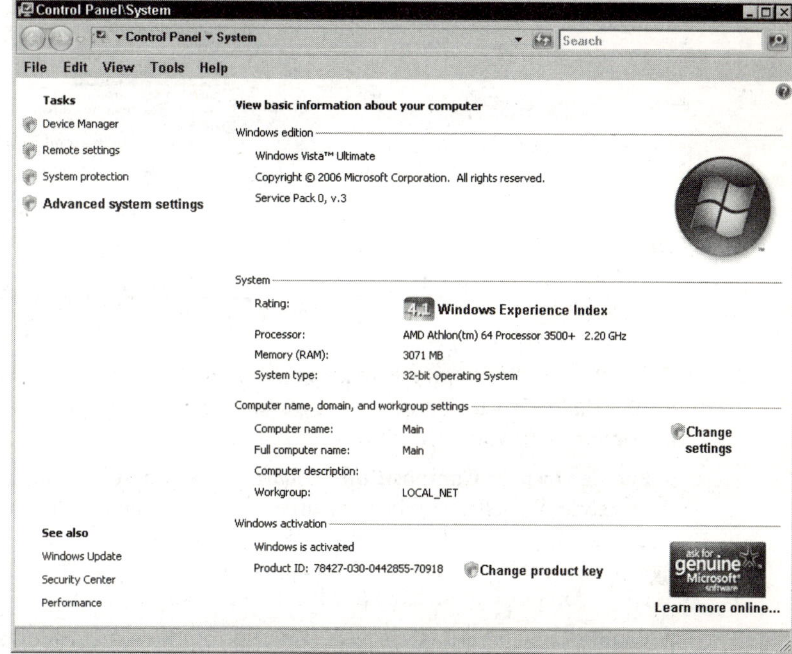

FIGURE 4.6
Use the System Properties dialog box the same way you used this feature in other versions of Windows.

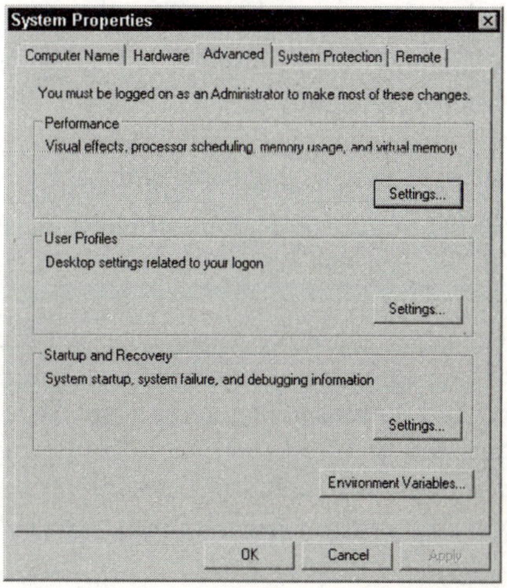

System Properties
Computer Name | Hardware | Advanced | System Protection | Remote
You must be logged on as an Administrator to make most of these changes.
Performance
Visual effects, processor scheduling, memory usage, and virtual memory
Settings...
User Profiles
Desktop settings related to your logon
Settings...
Startup and Recovery
System startup, system failure, and debugging information
Settings...
Environment Variables...
OK | Cancel | Apply

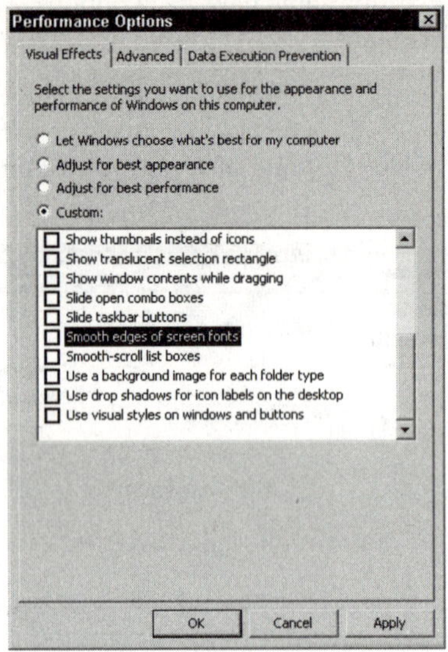

FIGURE 4.7
Enhance system performance by removing any Vista interface gizmos you really don't need.

The Performance Options dialog box does include a number of new features for Vista. You can use this dialog box to control how the interface works. The following list describes the Vista interface options that you need to consider.

Enable Desktop Composition Clearing this option will turn off the Compositor, which means that some Vista features become unavailable. Remember that many Vista graphics features rely on the Compositor. If you turn off this feature, you'll notice lower resource usage, a small increase in performance, and some degradation in display quality. For example, objects may appear jittery when you move them from one location to another.

Enable Transparent Glass Clearing this option removes transparency from the interface elements, but doesn't turn off the Compositor. You won't be able to see through title bars and other display elements, but you'll still see some of the glitz normally associated with Vista. As an example, all of the title bars will still show the pattern that Vista uses.

Use Visual Styles on Windows and Buttons Even though this setting does appear in Windows XP, the effect is slightly different in Vista. When you clear this setting, you see a Windows Classic interface. However, checking it displays a Vista interface, not a Windows XP interface. The buttons are flat, in both cases, but some of the screen functionality is different.

You'll find a number of other settings in the Performance Options dialog box such as Slide Open Combo Boxes. The vast majority of these settings provide glitz—nothing of substance at all and you can turn them off quite easily. The best way to approach this dialog box with performance in mind is to select Adjust for Best Performance. Selecting this option turns off every nonessential graphics feature and gives you a Windows Classic interface. You can then check the Use Visual Styles on Windows and Buttons to obtain the Vista Basic interface, Enable Desktop Composition to obtain a Vista Standard interface, and Enable Transparent Glass to obtain the Aero Glass interface.

It's also possible to create policies for various elements of the Vista interface. Begin by starting the Group Policy Editor (GPEdit.msc). Select Start ➤ Run, type **`GPEdit.msc`** in the Open field, and click OK. You'll see the Group Policy Object Editor window shown in Figure 4.8. Navigate to the `Local Computer Policy\User Configuration\Administrative Templates\Windows Components\Desktop Window Manager` folder. The policies in this folder control everything found in the Performance Options dialog box, albeit at a far cruder level. For example, the animations, such as Slide Taskbar Buttons, are an all-or-nothing option. You do have separate control over the Compositor.

As you work with the Group Policy Editor, make sure you check other possible problem areas for users. For example, the `Local Computer Policy\User Configuration\Administrative Templates\Windows Components\Windows Explorer` provides a number of policies that can reduce the Vista learning curve. For example, setting a policy for Turn On Classic Shell ensures that the user sees the shell that they're used to using in a previous version of Windows. For example, the user can't single click on a folder to open it—they must double-click the folder instead.

FIGURE 4.8
Set a policy regarding the Vista interface to ensure users don't add more glitz than their systems can handle.

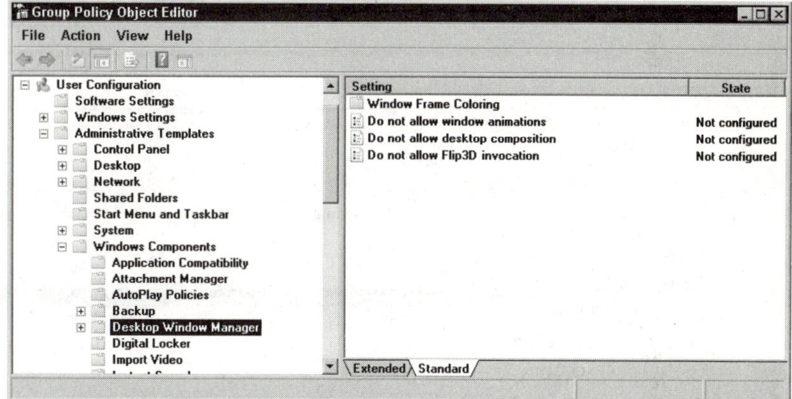

Finding the Control Panel Features

Microsoft has changed the Control Panel in an effort to make it easier to use. The new default Control Panel looks like the one shown in Figure 4.9. The emphasis of the new Control Panel is to make things easier to find for newer users. All of the applets that you're used to using are now categorized.

Each of the entries you see in a category is a link, as is the category title itself. Selecting a category displays a number of applets associated with that category. Choosing one of the sublinks displays one or two applets. Figure 4.10 shows what you'll see when you choose the Hardware and Sound category link. Notice that each entry contains a full description. Each of the entries also contains a number of sublinks. These sublinks help you perform specific tasks with that applet, such as changing system sounds. What you'll see when you click the link is a dialog box that looks surprisingly similar to those provided with Windows XP.

Of course, this arrangement isn't for everyone. For one thing, you might end up clicking yourself to death before you finally reach a destination of any sort. Notice that both Figures 4.9 and 4.10 include a Classic View link. When you click this link, you see something closer to the view that Windows XP and earlier versions of Windows provided, as shown in Figure 4.11. You can restore the new Control Panel view at any time by clicking the Control Panel Home link.

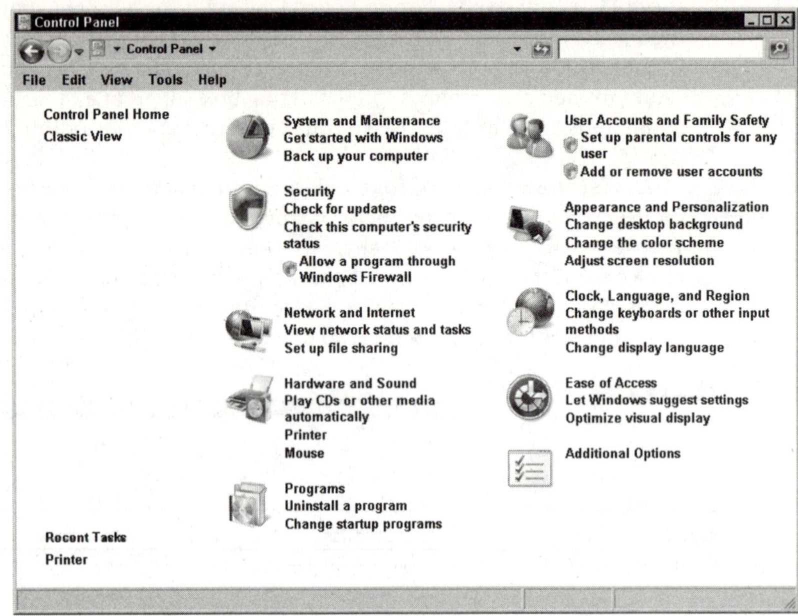

FIGURE 4.9
The new Control Panel is theoretically easier to use, but it does move things around.

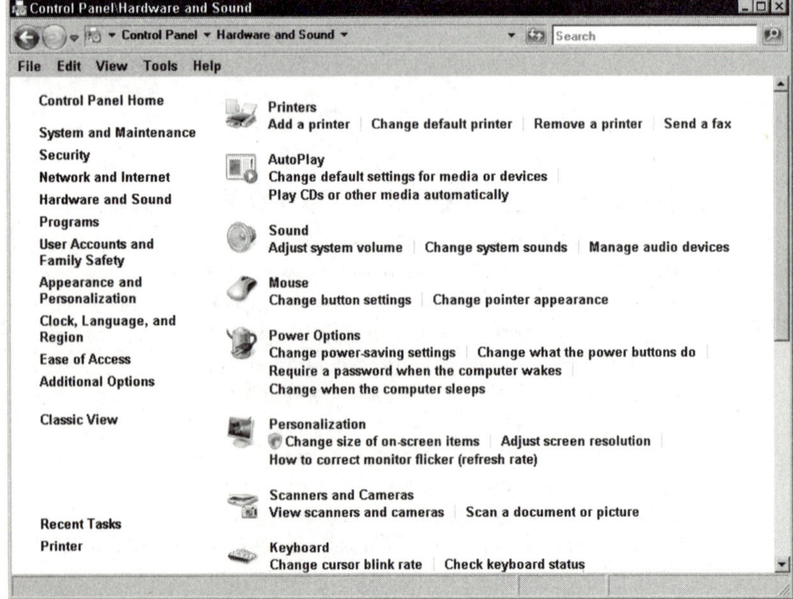

FIGURE 4.10
Choosing a link lets you drill down into the Control Panel content.

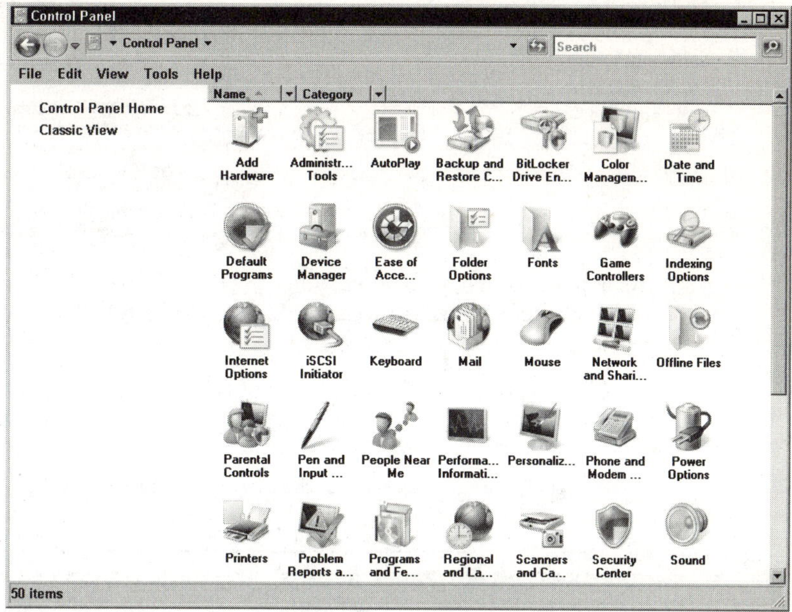

FIGURE 4.11
Many experienced Windows users will prefer the classic view of the Control Panel.

Even here, Microsoft decided to make some changes. Actually, some of the changes are nice and you should try them out. Click the down arrow next to the Name button and you'll see the drop down shown in Figure 4.12.

You can perform three kinds of applet identification using this drop down. First, click Sort and Vista will sort the Control Panel applets by name in ascending or descending order. This option is actually a toggle. If you click Group, Vista will place the applets into three groups: A – H, I – P, and Q – Z. As with Sort, this button is a toggle so you can place the groups in ascending or descending order. Click Sort to remove the groups from the display. The three check boxes let you remove some of the applets from the display so you don't have to peruse so many of them. Simply check one or more of the check boxes to display that group. Clear all of the check boxes when you want to display all of the applets again.

Vista also makes it easy to work with Control Panel applets based on category. Clicking the down arrow next to the Category button displays the drop down shown in Figure 4.13. Category might not be the best name for this feature. Think about this drop down as letting you sort the Control Panel applets based on functionality or purpose.

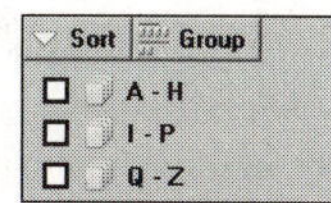

FIGURE 4.12
The Name button helps you locate applets based on their name.

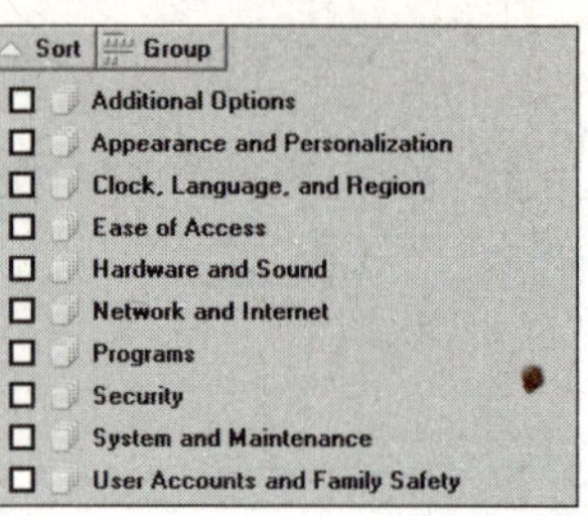

FIGURE 4.13 The Category button helps you locate applets based on their purpose.

As with the Name drop down, you can perform three kinds of sorting using this drop down. You can sort alphabetically by category, group the applets by category, or choose specific groups to display.

TIP Notice that the group names match the group names in the new Control Panel view shown in Figure 4.9. You can use this commonality to your advantage. Sort the applets by category to see which categories contain the applets you commonly use. This means it's easier to explain how to access a particular applet to users who might be using the new view.

MODIFYING CONTROL PANEL ACCESS

It isn't always a good idea to let users access all of the Control Panel applets. In addition, you might want to modify what the user can do with the applet when you do allow them to access it. Fortunately, you can use the Group Policy Editor to modify the way the Control Panel works. Begin by starting the Group Policy Editor. Select Start ➤ Run, type **`GPEdit.msc`** in the Open field, and click OK. You'll see the Group Policy Object Editor window shown in Figure 4.8. Navigate to the `Local Computer Policy\User Configuration\Administrative Templates\Control Panel` folder.

Most of the policies are straightforward. For example, you can prevent access to the Control Panel at all by enabling the Prohibit Access to the Control Panel policy. In most cases, you'll want to hide specific applets by setting the Hide Specified Control Panel Items policy. In this case, you must provide a list of applets to hide. Use precisely the name of the applet as it appears in the classic view.

Using the Personalize Feature

One of the most interesting changes to the Vista interface is the lack of a Display Properties dialog box. In past versions of Windows, you could right-click any clear area of the Desktop and choose Properties from the context menu. At this point, you'd see a Display properties dialog box that would let you change all of the functionality of the display such as the background image, the colors used for various features, special effects, the display dots per inch (DPI), the screen size, and the number of colors that the display could present, among other things. It was a very handy and consolidated way to work with the display that's no longer available as a single dialog box in Vista.

The Personalization window, shown in Figure 4.14, provides all of the functionality of the Display Properties dialog box, albeit not in an easy to access package. To access this window, right-click any clear area of the Desktop and choose Personalize from the context menu.

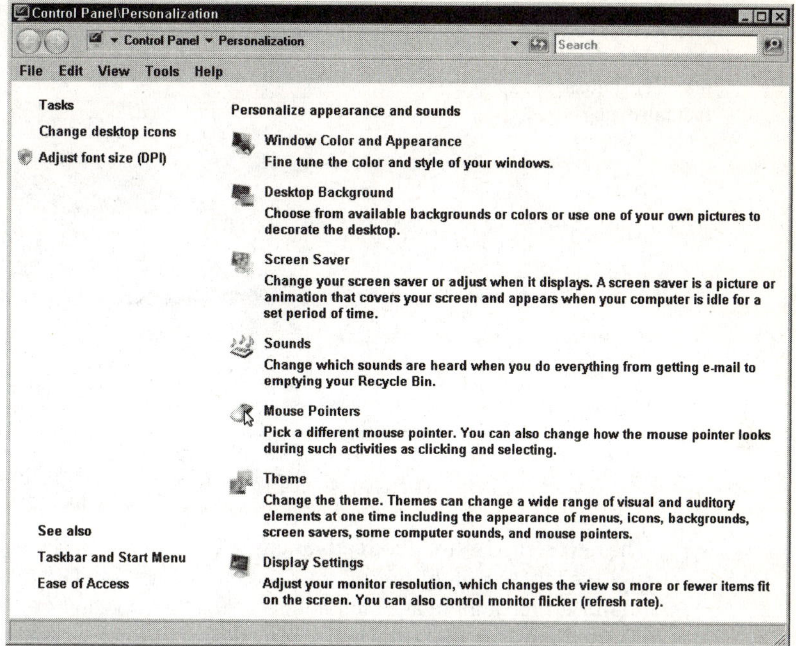

FIGURE 4.14 The new Personalization window provides all the functionality but none of the convenience of the Display Properties dialog box.

Don't get me wrong, Vista does add significant new functionality to the personalization of your system, but you have to make many extra clicks to do it now. Given that much of the functionality is the same, it might be easier to reference this Personalization window to the similar features in the Display Properties dialog box. Changing the appearance of the display (a feature that used to appear on the Appearance tab of the Display Properties dialog box) now requires more clicks. You can see the procedure for performing this task in the "Understanding the Aero Glass Interface" section of the chapter. What you actually get is a single tab view of many of the Display Properties dialog box tabs of the past. For example, when you click Screen Saver (shown in Figure 4.15), you see the same Screen Saver tab as before, only now it's a separate dialog box, which means you can't simply click Appearance as the next step in your configuration.

If you look carefully at the Screen Saver Settings dialog box, you'll see that the controls haven't changed much since Windows 2000, when all of these controls appeared on the Screen Saver tab. The only major change is that instead of a Power button, you now have a Change Power Settings link to use. The Wait and Password protected controls have also changed places and Microsoft has renamed them. That's it, that's all of the changes that Microsoft has made since Windows 2000, except now the controls are harder to access.

NOTE As with most things in Vista, Microsoft has made content changes to just about every area of the display (personalization) settings. Just as you have new pictures to use for the Windows background, you also have some new screen savers to use. One interesting change is that none of the old Open Graphics Library (OpenGL) such as 3D Pipes are available under Vista. The change is very likely due to the change in display technology—you probably won't be able to use the older screen savers.

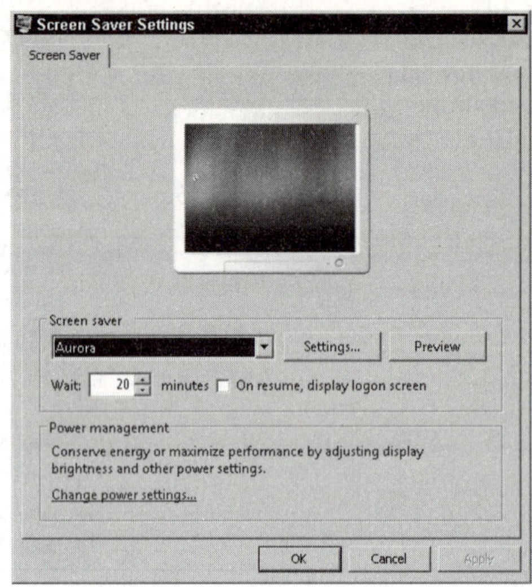

FIGURE 4.15
Microsoft has divided the Display Properties dialog box into separate tab dialog boxes.

The new setup isn't without advantages. Users with special needs often find it necessary to change the font size of the text on their screen. Using more DPI makes it easier to read the text. The standard setting, known as Small Fonts, is 96 DPI. You can also choose the Large Fonts setting of 120 DPI, which does make the text significantly larger, or a custom DPI setting based on your particular requirements. To access this feature in the old setup, you had to first display the Display Properties dialog box, select the Settings tab, click Advanced to display the display adapter's Properties dialog box, and then choose the font size you wanted on the General tab of that dialog box. With Vista, you click the Adjust Font Size (DPI) link. So, yes, it's easier, but how often are you really going to make this change?

Finding the System Dialog Box

Microsoft has replaced the System Properties dialog box with the System window as the first item you see when you select the System applet in the Control panel. You can also access this window as you always have in the past by right-clicking the Computer icon and choosing Properties from the context menu. No matter which option you choose, you'll see a display similar to the one shown in Figure 4.5.

The System window actually provides access to a number of dialog boxes. For example, click the Windows Experience Index link and you'll see the Performance Information and Tools window shown in Figure 4.16. Chapter 25 provides a detailed description of this window, but it's important to know that the Performance Information and Tools window provides you with a significant amount of information about your system. You can actually use this information to make software buying decisions without guessing as to whether the software will actually run on your system. You can also access locations such as Windows Update and the Security Center. In other words, the System window has become a one-stop location to perform many of the tasks you must perform to maintain your system.

However, there's still the problem of gaining access to the original System dialog box because you need the detailed controls it provides to perform certain tasks such as getting rid of the extra glitz that Microsoft thinks you need. Fortunately, you can click any of these links to gain access to the System Properties dialog box, which contains all of the tabs found in older versions of Windows:

- Change Settings in the Computer Name, Domain, and Workgroup Settings area (Computer Name tab)
- Advanced System Settings (Advanced tab)
- System Protection (System Protection tab)
- Remote Settings (Remote tab)

You won't find a direct link to the Hardware tab of the System Properties dialog box within the System window. When you click the Device Manager link in the System window, it takes you directly to the Device Manager window shown in Figure 4.17. This action is the same as clicking Device Manager on the Hardware tab of the System Properties dialog box. Consequently, if you want update your windows driver (a feature that also appears on the Hardware tab), you must choose one of the other options in the System window and then select the Hardware tab manually.

FIGURE 4.16
The Performance Information and Tools window is just one of many new destinations from the System window.

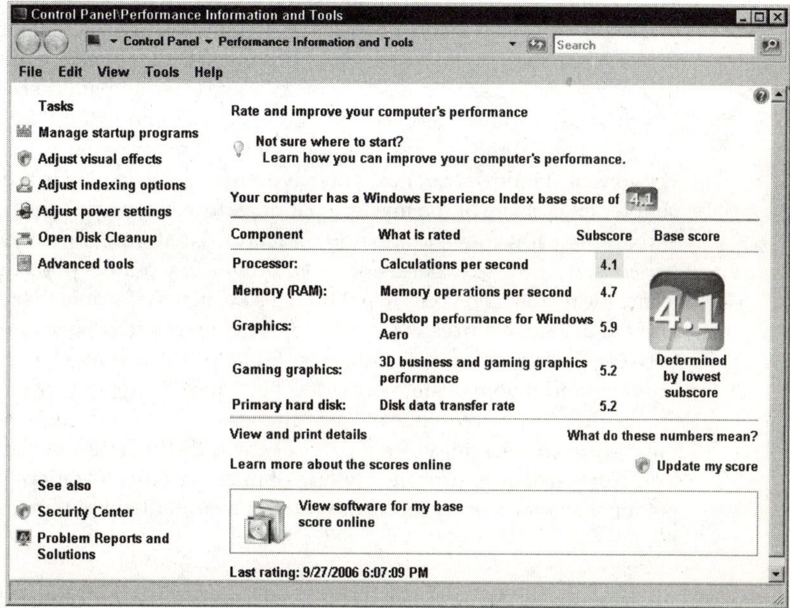

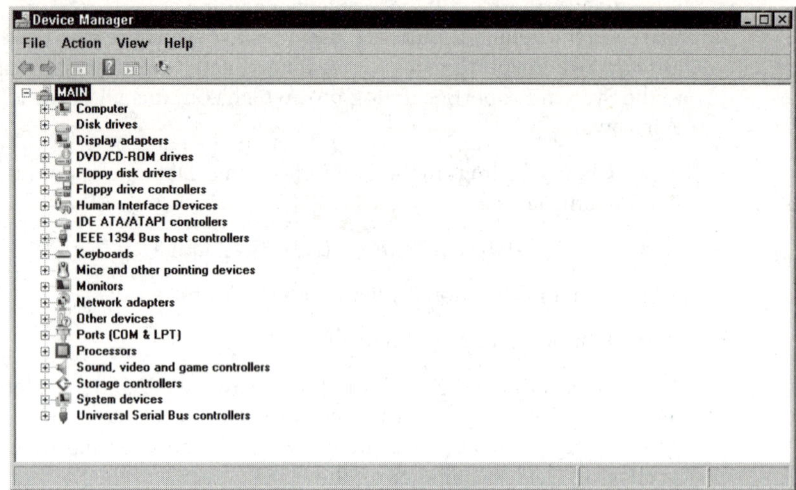

FIGURE 4.17 Clicking Device Manager takes you directly to the Device Manager window where you can manage system devices.

Summary

This chapter has helped you understand some of the changes to the Vista interface from previous Windows versions. Of course, the biggest change is figuring out which interface you actually want to use. Vista doesn't make it easy to choose a particular interface in some cases. You'll probably find that you want to use one interface for everyday use and another for special occasions. Whatever interface you choose, this chapter has helped you understand the choices. You've also discovered the location of some of those missing Windows features. Sure, they were easy to find in previous versions of Windows, but now you have a new game to play in locating the feature you need. This chapter takes some of the mystery out of feature locations.

Now that you know how to find the features that were missing in Vista from previous Windows versions, it's time to experiment on your own. Try out the procedures and tips in this chapter to locate the features on your own. You'll also want to take time to try out the various Vista interfaces and the display features. All of these issues are important because you need to strike a balance between performance and ease of use. Some people may well find that they like the Aero Glass interface and if your system provides the required support, there isn't any reason not to use it.

Chapter 4 is an overview of Vista changes to the interface. When you move on to Chapter 5, you'll gain an in-depth view of precisely how the interface works and how best to customize it. You'll discover an entirely new world of interface customizations that could greatly improve your personal productivity, keep your system safer, and help you maintain better control over system resources.

Chapter 5

Customizing the Interface

Vista can be customized in an amazing number of ways. You can move, resize, tweak, or change the color of just about everything. In this chapter, you'll learn about some of the most important interface adjustments you can make for usability, convenience, and just plain old personal preference.

This chapter covers the following topics:

- Working with the Control Panel
- Changing the date and time
- Adjusting video settings
- Customizing Vista display
- Customizing the Desktop
- Customizing the Taskbar
- Setting Start menu options
- Adjusting the keyboard and mouse
- Choosing system sounds
- Using Accessibility options

Vista: What's New?

In many respects, Vista presents the same options that you've used in the past, but they have different names. Microsoft likes renaming features for whatever reason, which creates a new and unnecessary learning curve for every product version. This chapter will provide you with the old term to new term conversions that you need to get going with Vista quickly. Of course, you'll also find that some of the old methods for accessing features have changed and this chapter tells you the new methods of accessing these features. For example, configuring your display is considerably different from times past (as witnessed in the discussion in Chapter 4).

One of the more interesting changes for those of us on the go is that you can now have multiple clocks running. That means you no longer have to figure out what time it is in Milwaukee when you're in London. You'll also find it considerably easier to synchronize your system clock with a reliable time source.

Microsoft has focused a lot of attention on accessibility aids in past years. Vista changes the old Accessibility applet into the Ease of Access applet. However, the change is more than superficial in this case. You'll find some real changes in Ease of Access that make it considerably easier to work with Vista. The most important change is that the Ease of Access applet is available at all times, not just when you're logged onto the system.

Working with the Control Panel

To open Control Panel, simply click Start ➤ Control Panel.

TIP In previous versions of Windows, there was a Control Panel icon in the Computer window (formerly known as the My Computer window). When working with Windows XP, you had to check the Show Control Panel in My Computer check box in the View tab of the Folder Options dialog box. Vista doesn't require that you use this option (and doesn't include it any longer). Instead, click Open Control Panel on the toolbar at the top of the Computer window or choose the `Computer\Control Panel` entry in the Folders list in the left pane of the display to open the Control Panel from Computer.

In previous versions of Windows, the number of applets and folders (seen as icons) in Control Panel had gotten rather large, so Vista organizes them into categories rather than simply showing all the icons at once. This new view, called Category view, is the default view in Control Panel. See Figure 5.1.

NOTE An *applet* is an application that you access using the Control Panel. In most cases, the applet performs a configuration task for the associated software, hardware, or operating system feature. The default Vista setup includes one folder, the `Administrative Tools` folder, which contains all applets for administrator-related activities, such as setting local security policies. Opening `Administrative Tools` doesn't execute an application, it simply opens a folder that contains other applets and it acts just like any other folder you have opened in the past.

If you'd prefer the traditional Control Panel layout, you can click the Classic View hyperlink to switch to it, as in Figure 5.2. The icons on your Control Panel might be different from the ones shown in Figure 5.2, as some third-party applications add icons here.

FIGURE 5.1
Control Panel in Category view.

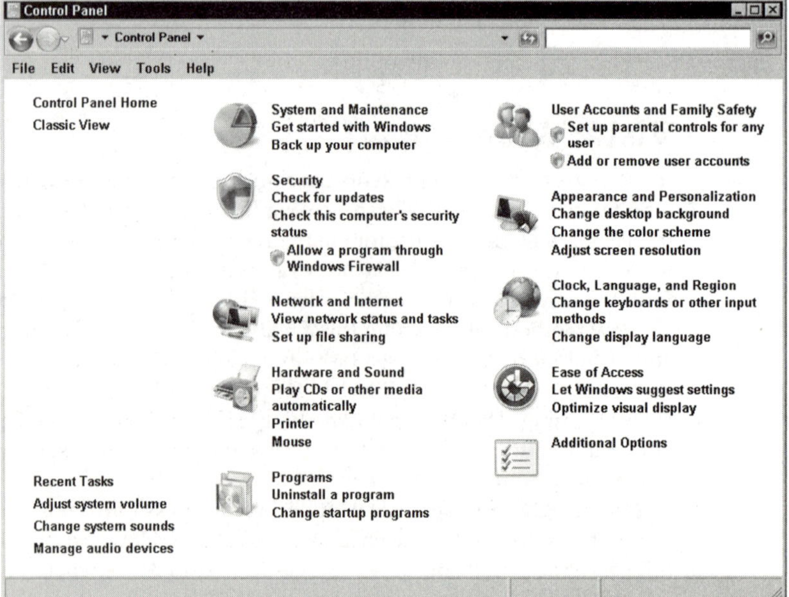

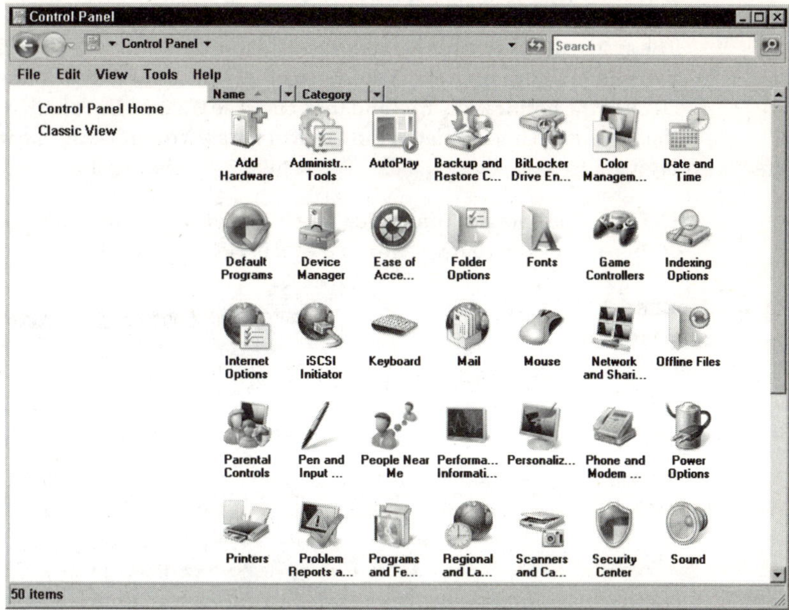

FIGURE 5.2 Control Panel in Classic view.

This book uses Category view in its figures and steps, but experienced users will probably prefer Classic view because it involves fewer mouse clicks and because the category in which an item resides is not always obvious.

If any items don't have a category assigned (such as applets added by some third-party program), you can access them from Category view by clicking the Additional Options link, or by switching to Classic view.

Changing the Date and Time

Microsoft has made a number of changes to the way in which you work with date and time on your system. Most of these changes were due to user requests. Some of them enhance security of your system by making it impossible to fool the system by performing certain tricks (such as setting the date and time to the ancient past). The following sections describe how to set the date and time, use multiple clocks, and choosing a time source for synchronizing your computer.

TIP Virus writers and other nefarious individuals have made use of the ability to change the system time to thwart some Windows security features (most notably Kerberos) in the past. Microsoft seems determined to overcome this problem with Vista by disallowing any access to the date and time by anyone other than administrators. When you attempt to change the date or time in Vista, you might see a permissions error telling you that you can't perform this task (without any explanation of why). Unfortunately, you have to modify the Registry to make it possible for non-administrators to modify the system date and time (which makes those multiple clocks even more important). You can see the Registry changes you need to make in the Knowledge Base article at `http://support.microsoft.com/?id=300022`.

Setting the Date and Time

The system clock in your PC keeps track of the date and time; you can set the date and time through your BIOS setup program. You can also set it from within Windows for the same effect. Click the clock in the notification area and then click the Change Date and Time Settings link, or double-click the Date and Time applet in the Control Panel. You'll see the Date and Time dialog box shown in Figure 5.3.

NOTE The Date and Time dialog box options only affect the main clock on your system. Any additional clocks on your system use the main clock as a starting point.

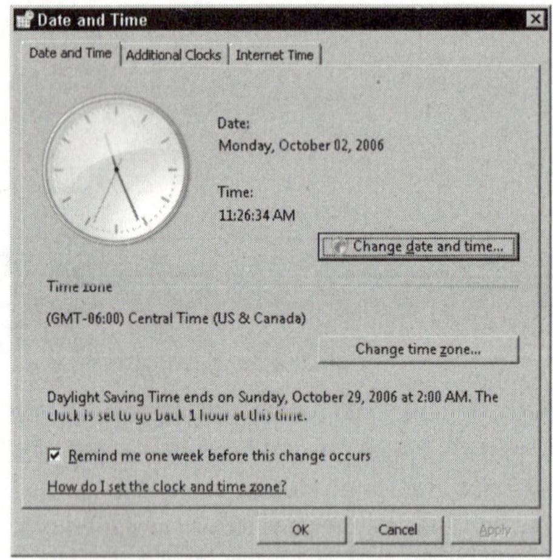

FIGURE 5.3 Vista provides a number of features not previously found in the Date and Time dialog box such as multiple clocks.

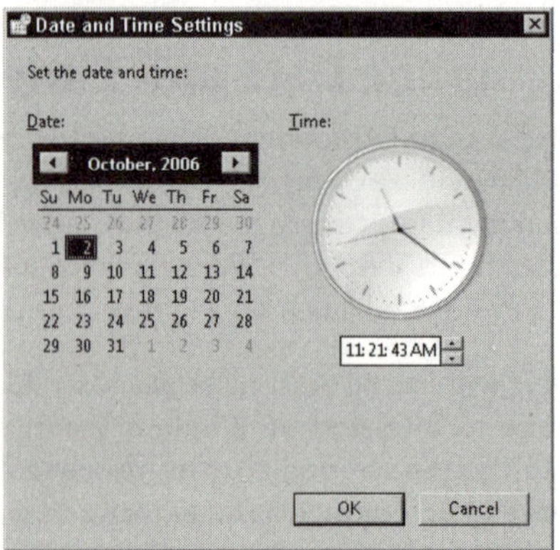

FIGURE 5.4 You can adjust the date and time from within Vista.

The Date and Time dialog box has separate controls for date/time and time zone. Anyone who needs to can click Change Time Zone to change the time zone as needed when traveling. To change the date or time, click Change Date and Time, click Continue at the User Access Control dialog box, and you'll see the Date and Time Settings dialog box shown in Figure 5.4.

Change the date and time as needed, then click OK twice to close both the Date and Time Settings and the Date and Time dialog box. Vista displays the time changes you make in the notification area.

TIP Point at the clock in the notification area to see today's date. As an alternative, you can always increase the height of the Taskbar. You automatically see the date when you increase the size of the Taskbar to three lines or greater.

Changing the Time Zone

Unlike the date and time, you can change time zones whenever necessary without having an administrator account. This feature makes it easy to reset your clock as needed when traveling. As with the date and time, you access the time zone from the Data and Time dialog box shown in Figure 5.3. Click Change Time Zone and you'll see the Time Zone Settings dialog box. Choose your time zone from the Time Zone field, choose whether you want your system to automatically compensate for daylight saving time, and click OK twice to make the change.

TIP As an alternative to changing the time zone, consider creating multiple clocks as described in the "Creating Multiple Clocks" section of the chapter when traveling. Using this technique makes it easy for you to track the time at home and in your current location.

Creating Multiple Clocks

Vista has a new feature that lets you have multiple clocks on your machine. This might not seem like a big deal at first, but it can save you considerable time and embarrassment in tracking times in other locations. Consider the problem of daylight saving time. Some areas of the world have this feature, others don't. Even those areas that use daylight saving time don't change time on precisely the same date. Consequently, tracking time in other areas of the world isn't always a matter of adding or subtracting the required number of hours. Obviously, unless you're careful, you can end up being an hour late for a meeting based on differences in daylight saving time observance alone.

To add a second or third clock to your setup, click the clock in the notification area and then click the Change Date and Time Settings link, or double-click the Date and Time applet in the Control Panel. You'll see the Date and Time dialog box shown in Figure 5.3. Select the Additional Clocks tab and you'll see places for up to two additional clocks as shown in Figure 5.5.

Check Show This Clock, choose a time zone in the Select Time Zone field, and type a name for the clock in the Enter Display Name field. Click OK to make the change permanent. You won't see the additional clocks in the notification area. To display the additional clocks, hover the mouse over the time in the notification area and you'll see a pop-up that contains the current date as well as the additional clocks.

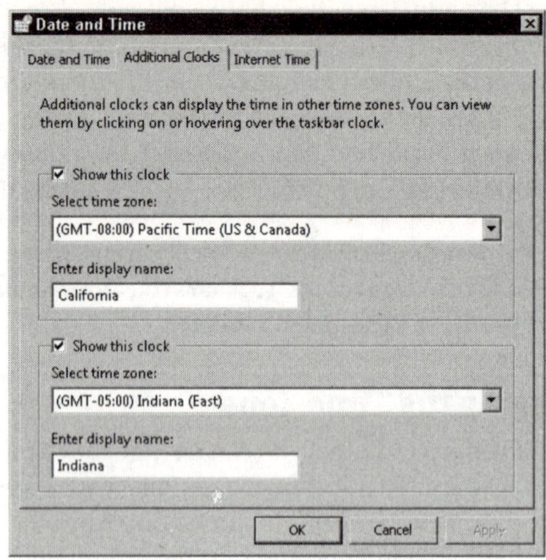

FIGURE 5.5
Adding additional clocks makes it easy to track time anywhere in the world.

Synchronizing with an Internet Clock

One problem many people have had with PC clocks over the years is their tendency to lose time. To combat this problem, Vista provides a feature that automatically synchronizes the system clock with a time server on the Internet. Vista turns on this feature by default, and updates your system clock periodically. You can turn it off, or update it immediately. Like the date and time settings, you must be part of the administrators group to change the Internet time synchronization settings for your system. In addition, to use this feature you must have the Windows Time service running (the default settings automatically start it, but some people stop this service to optimize system performance).

To configure the Internet time synchronization for your system, click the clock in the notification area and then click the Change Date and Time Settings link, or double-click the Date and Time applet in the Control Panel. You'll see the Date and Time dialog box shown in Figure 5.3. Select the Internet Time tab. Notice that this tab tells you the time of the next automatic synchronization when you have Internet time synchronization enabled. Click Change Settings, click Continue in the User Account Control dialog box that appears, and you'll see the Internet Time Settings dialog box shown in Figure 5.6. Check Synchronize with an Internet Time Server when you want to perform automatic time updates. Choose one of the time servers listed in the Server field, and click OK twice to make the change permanent. You can also click Update Now to update the time on your system immediately.

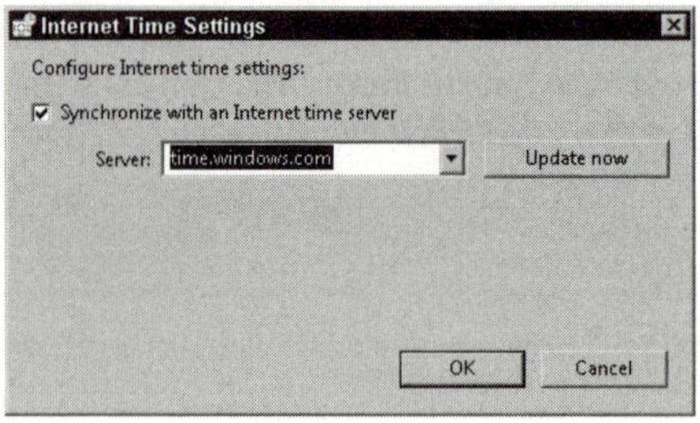

FIGURE 5.6
Choose whether to update time automatically and which time server to use.

NOTE When you update the time online, it relies on the Time Zone setting you have selected to know how to adjust the server's time to fit the correct time in your zone. The server isn't necessarily in the same time zone as you, after all! That's why the Time Zone setting in the Time Zone tab is important.

Here are a couple of useful Registry tweaks for working with the Internet Time feature.

By default, Windows checks the time against the time server once a week (that's every 604,800 seconds). If you want to use some other interval, go to `HKEY_LOCAL_MACHINE\SYSTEM\ControlSet001\Services \W32Time\TimeProviders\NtpClient` and set the decimal value of the *SpecialPolInterval* key to some other value in seconds. There are 86,400 seconds in a day, just FYI.

Five servers are available by default: `time.windows.com`, `time.nist.gov`, `time-nw.nist.gov`, `time-a.nist.gov`, and `time-b.nist.gov`. Normally, you won't need any more servers because even if one server is down you have four others from which to choose. However, you might run into scenarios, such as travel to other areas of the world, where another time server is helpful. To add more, just add them in the Registry key `HKEY_LOCAL_MACHINE\SOFTWARE\Microsoft\Windows\CurrentVersion\DateTime\Servers`. Make sure that each value you add has a unique numeric name. For example, when you add the next server to the list, use a name value of 6 because the last value in the list is 5. Not sure what other time servers are available? Check out `http://ntp.isc.org/bin/view/Servers/WebHome`.

Adding Multiple Time Servers at Once

One easy way to add a lot of time servers to the Registry at once is to create a REG file containing them in Notepad. For example, you could create the following text file in Notepad and save it as `timesrvr.reg` (or whatever name you want, as long as it has a `.reg` extension):

```
Windows Registry Editor Version 5.00[HKEY_LOCAL_MACHINE\SOFTWARE\Microsoft\Windows\
CurrentVersion\DateTime\Servers]@="1""1"="time.windows.com""2"="time.nist.gov""3"=
"clock.isc.org""4"="timekeeper.isi.edu"
```

You can keep going ad infinitum with the list, giving each time server you want to add a consecutive number. Then save your work and close Notepad. Locate the file in Windows Explorer, right-click it, and choose Merge.

Adjusting Video Settings

Video settings are the settings and options for both your video card and monitor and their drivers that affect overall display appearance in Windows. These are separate from the color schemes, fonts, and other appearance features you might choose (covered partially in Chapter 4 and later in this chapter). The following sections review some important information about video.

Installing Video and Monitor Drivers

Vista is fairly good at detecting the video card during Setup, so the correct video drivers should already be installed. (It's somewhat less adept at detecting monitors.) You can check by doing the following:

1. Right-click the Desktop and choose Personalize.

2. Click the Display Settings link to display the Display Settings dialog box shown in Figure 5.7. Notice the video card and monitor names that appear in this dialog box. The list contains one entry for each display adapter and monitor combination on your machine, so you'll have to examine the drop-down list when you have multiple display adapters and monitors on your machine. If these settings match your actual hardware, Windows has accurately detected them.

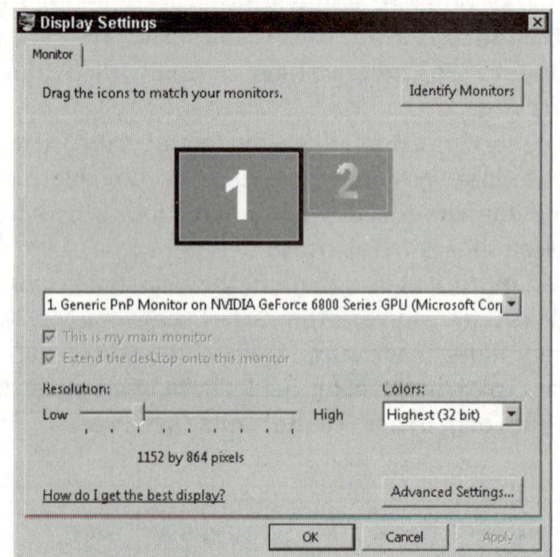

FIGURE 5.7
The Settings tab reports what video card and monitor Windows thinks you have.

If any of the settings are incorrect, see the following sections to change them.

TIP You might not know which monitors are attached to each display adapter based on the information provided in the Display Settings dialog box. Click Identify Monitors to display the number associated with each monitor on the display so you can see it. The number appears for about 3 seconds and then goes away.

UPDATING THE VIDEO CARD DRIVER

Having the right video card driver is important because the driver tells Windows what display resolutions, color depths, refresh rates, and other performance settings should be available. If Windows can't detect your video card type, it will install a driver for a standard VGA card, which will limit the display options to 640 × 480 and 16 colors. In addition, the standard VGA video driver doesn't support power management, so you won't be able to use features like Suspend or Hibernate.

An outdated or corrupted video driver can also be a problem, although there's not a simple test to look for this. If you suspect a video driver problem, your best bet is to go to the card manufacturer's website and download a driver designed specifically for Vista and for your exact model of card.

To install a video driver, do the following:

1. Right-click the Desktop and choose Personalize. Click the Display Settings Link to display the Display Settings dialog box shown in Figure 5.7.

2. From the list, select the display adapter you want to work with. Alternatively, you can click on one of the monitors displayed on the Display Settings dialog box.
3. Click the Advanced Settings button. This opens a Properties box for the selected video card and monitor.
4. Click the Adapter tab, and then click the Properties button. Click Continue when you see the User Account Control dialog box. This action opens a separate Properties box just for the video card.
5. Click the Driver tab, and then click the Update Driver button. The Hardware Update Wizard runs. You'll see options that let you choose between automatically searching for the correct driver (the best option when you don't know where to locate a driver) or installing from a local driver source (the best option when you have a disk or have downloaded the required software), as shown in Figure 5.8.

   If you choose the Browse Computer for Driver Software option, choose the starting location for the search, and then click Next. You can include subfolders in the search by checking Include Subfolders. Go to step 8.
6. Click Search Automatically for Updated Driver Software. The Hardware Update Wizards asks where to search for the device driver as shown in Figure 5.9.
7. Click Yes, Always Search Online, Yes, Search Online This Time Only, or Don't Search Online to choose one of the search options.
8. The Hardware Update Wizard automatically searches for the best driver for your system. If you already have the best driver installed, the Hardware Update Wizard shows a completion dialog box. Click Close to end the procedure.
9. When the Hardware Update Wizard does find a new driver, continue working through the wizard to install your chosen driver. (It's fairly self-explanatory from this point on.)

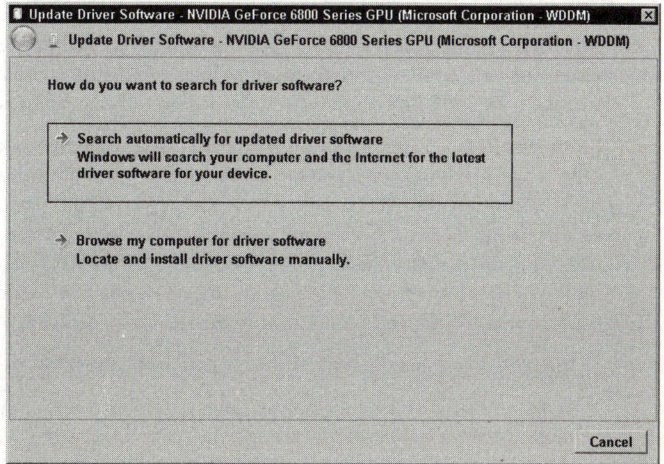

FIGURE 5.8
Choose the method you want to use to obtain a new driver for your system.

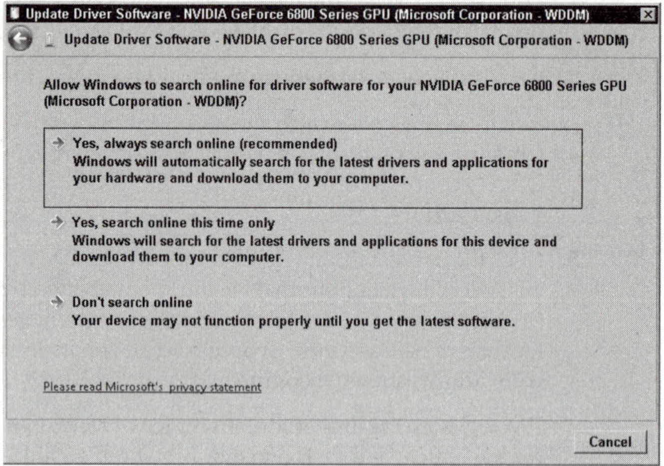

FIGURE 5.9
Select one of the automatic search options for the device driver.

UPDATING THE MONITOR DRIVER

The procedure for updating the monitor driver is very similar to that for a video card. Monitor drivers are very simple; they're basically just INF files that tell Windows what the monitor's capabilities are (resolution, refresh rate, and so on). They don't actually do anything much within Windows. So, if Windows reports that your monitor is standard VGA when in fact it's something better, the worst thing that happens is that you're limited to a lower display settings and refresh rate than you'd normally be.

USING OLDER MONITORS WITH VISTA

Most high-end monitors come with their own setup disk containing the INF files needed to set them up in Windows. However, since most people keep a monitor much longer than they do a PC, you will likely run into some fairly old monitors out there with unsigned drivers.

Under older versions of Windows, you could simply bypass any dire warnings about using the unsigned driver. The x64 version of Vista doesn't allow you to install unsigned device drivers, so you can't use these older INF files and must rely on the best matching generic driver.

The x86 version of Vista doesn't provide any such warnings by default. However, you can change the policy to warn or block unsigned device drivers in this environment as well. Begin by starting the Group Policy Editor (GPEdit.msc). Select Start ➤ Run, type **`GPEdit.msc`** in the Open field, and click OK. You'll see the Group Policy Object Editor window. Navigate to the `Local Computer Policy\User Configuration\Administrative Templates\System\Driver Installation` folder. The Code Signing for Device Drivers policy determines how the x86 version of Vista reacts to unsigned drivers. You can set any of the following three policies:

Ignore Vista installs the monitor driver without asking any questions.

Warn Vista display a message similar to the one found in Windows XP warning that the device driver could cause harm to the system.

Block Vista doesn't allow the user to install the unsigned device driver, making the system as safe as the x64 version, but also making it impossible to use the monitor's full capabilities.

To let Windows know you have a different monitor than the one currently chosen:

1. Right-click the Desktop and choose Personalize. Click the Display Settings Link to display the Display Settings dialog box shown in Figure 5.7.
2. Select the display adapter you want to work with from the list. Alternatively, you can click on one of the monitors displayed on the Display Settings dialog box.
3. Click the Advanced button, and then choose the Monitor tab.
4. Click the Properties button. Click Continue when you see the User Account Control dialog box. Choose the Driver tab.
5. Click the Update Driver button. The Hardware Update Wizard runs. It's unlikely that Vista will detect your monitor. Consequently, you usually need to select the required driver manually. The following steps assume a manual installation.
6. Click Browse Computer for Driver software. You see the manual configuration options shown in Figure 5.10. The first option is to look for the driver in a specific location on your system. You can enter the floppy or CD drive containing a vendor-supplied driver when you have one. After you type the correct location, click Next and proceed to step 8.

   The second option lets you look at the Microsoft supplied drivers first, and then use a vendor-supplied driver when Microsoft doesn't provide a driver. Use the second option when you have an older monitor that Microsoft has supported in the past.
7. Click Let Me Pick from a List of Device Drivers on My Computer. Vista generally doesn't show you many options, at this point, if it detected the monitor incorrectly at the outset. That's because it is displaying compatible hardware, a feature that seldom helps much.
8. Clear the Show Compatible Hardware option. You see an amazing list of monitor drivers, as shown in Figure 5.11.

FIGURE 5.10
Choose one of the manual configuration options that Vista provides to locate your display driver.

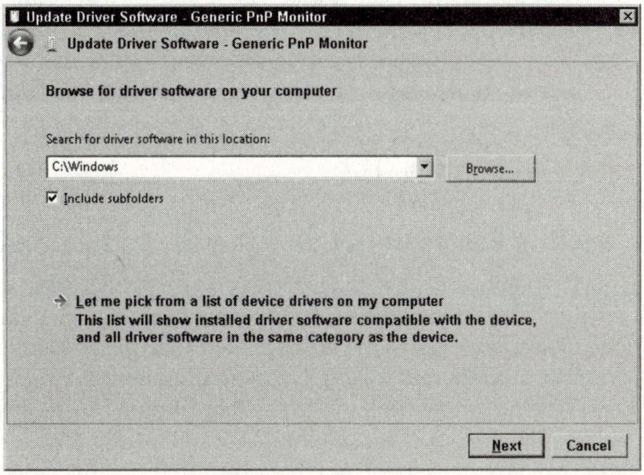

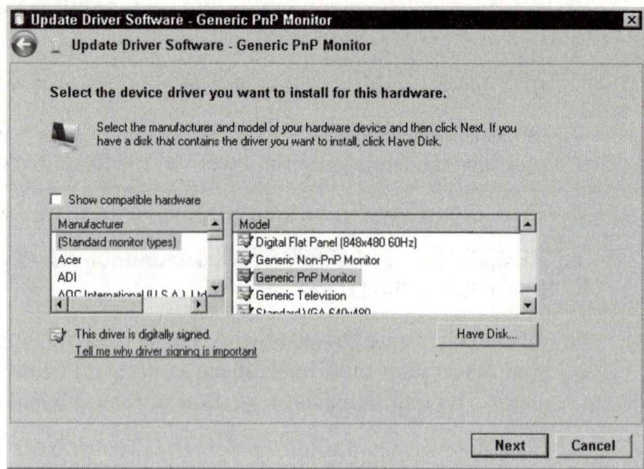

FIGURE 5.11
Select the manufacturer first, and then the model, to locate a driver for your monitor.

9. Choose the hardware vendor for your monitor in the Manufacturer field. Choose the model number in the Model field.

   If your monitor doesn't appear in the list, click Have Disk. You'll see the Install from Disk dialog box where you type the location of the device driver using an interface similar to the one shown in Figure 5.10.

TIP Sometimes, you can't find a monitor driver online because the vendor doesn't support it any longer, and you might not have the required disk. In most cases, you can use a monitor INF file from an older version of Windows as a replacement. These settings normally appear in the `Monitor.inf` files located in the `\WINNT\INF` or `\Windows\INF` folder. For example, I have an older Sony Multiscan 17sf II monitor and the information for it appears in the Monitor2.INF file. Copy the files you need to a local drive and use that location to search for the monitor. These INF files are unsigned, so you may see a warning about using them. This is about the only time where this technique works, so don't get the idea that this is a cure-all for every situation. This technique only works because all you really need are settings and not an actual device driver.

10. Continue working through the wizard to install your chosen driver. (It's fairly self-explanatory from this point on.)

Setting Resolution, Color Depth, and Refresh Rate

If you're not familiar with the terms *resolution*, *color depth*, and *refresh rate*, review the following information before you get started changing those settings in Windows.

Resolution refers to the number of unique pixels that make up the display. It's expressed in two numbers: width and height. For example, standard VGA is 640 × 480.

Vista no longer runs in 640 × 480 resolution except in Safe Mode; the minimum it supports is 800 × 600 unless a video driver is loaded that supports only standard VGA. From there the resolution can go up to whatever the maximum is that the video card and monitor can both support. On a high-end monitor, this could be as high as 2,048 × 1,536 or more. The higher the resolution, the smaller icons, windows, and text will appear on the screen. The video card has a maximum resolution it can support, and so does the monitor. The overall maximum resolution for the system is the one that both can agree on.

NOTE Why does everything on screen get smaller as the resolution goes up? It's because each item—an icon, for example—is a fixed number of pixels in size. When you switch to a higher resolution, that number of pixels takes up less space on screen in proportion to the total screen area.

Color depth refers to the number of digital bits needed to accurately describe the color of each pixel. For example, in 4-bit color, there are 4 binary digits to work with, from 0000 to 1111. There are a total of 16 combinations of 0s and 1s in four digits, so 4-bit color supports 16 colors. Standard VGA is 4-bit color. Vista supports only the much higher color depths (again, except for in Safe Mode), such as 16 bit and 32 bit. Color depth is an issue only for the video card; most monitors can support any color depth.

Refresh rate is the speed at which the monitor is able to refresh each pixel of the display. As soon as the monitor's electron gun hits a pixel, it immediately begins to decay, so each pixel must be refreshed many times a second. Refresh rates are expressed in Hertz (Hz). At low refresh rates, such as 65Hz, the monitor appears to flicker because the pixel light is decaying faster than the monitor is refreshing it. At high refresh rates (85Hz or above), flicker isn't noticeable. Refresh rate is primarily an issue for the monitor; most video cards can support any refresh rate that the monitor is capable of. The maximum refresh rate for a monitor goes down as the screen resolution goes up; a monitor that supports 120Hz at 800 × 600 might support only 85Hz at 2,048 × 1,536.

The amount of memory on the video card determines the resolutions and color depths you can use. Windows automatically detects the RAM installed on your video card and adjusts its available settings accordingly. To calculate how much video RAM a particular resolution and color depth combination will require, use this formula:

Width × Height × Number of bits ÷ 8

Dividing by 8 converts bits into bytes. So, for example, 1,024 × 768 resolution with 32-bit color depth would be 1,024 × 768 × 32 ÷ 8, or 3,145,728 bytes (approximately 3.1MB).

However, the amount of memory required to display an image isn't the end of the RAM requirement. Video adapters use RAM for many different purposes, such as creating 3D effects and storing animated effects. Consequently, the more RAM you have, the better.

Changing the Resolution and Color Depth

After all that theoretical build-up, changing the resolution and color depth is really simple:

1. Right-click the Desktop and choose Personalize. Click the Display Settings Link to display the Display Settings dialog box shown in Figure 5.7.
2. Select the display adapter you want to work with from the list. Alternatively, you can click on one of the monitors displayed on the Display Settings dialog box.
3. Drag the Screen Resolution slider to the right or left to adjust the resolution.
4. Choose a color depth in the Colors drop-down list.
5. Click OK.

TIP As I mentioned earlier, the lowest resolutions and color depths aren't available in Vista by ordinary means. However, there's a way to get to them. From the Settings tab, click Advanced; then go to the Adapter tab and click the List All Modes button. Select the video mode you want (each is a unique combination of refresh rate, color depth, and resolution).

CHANGING THE REFRESH RATE

As noted earlier, the refresh rate is more of a function of the monitor since it depends on the physical ability of the monitor's electron guns to keep up with the pixel refreshing. Therefore, as you would expect, you adjust it in the monitor properties:

1. Right-click the Desktop and choose Personalize. Click the Display Settings Link to display the Display Settings dialog box shown in Figure 5.7.
2. Select the display adapter you want to work with from the list. Alternatively, you can click on one of the monitors displayed on the Display Settings dialog box.
3. Click the Advanced button to display the video adapter and monitor Properties dialog box.
4. Click the Monitor tab and you'll see the monitor settings shown in Figure 5.12.
5. Open the Screen Refresh Rate drop-down list and select a refresh rate. Or, if there is an Optimal setting available, choose that to select the highest refresh rate that the monitor and video card can collectively support in the current screen resolution.
6. Click OK. If you see a message asking if you want to keep the current settings, click Yes. You will see this only the first time that you choose a particular setting.
7. Click OK again to close the Properties box.

TIP With refresh rate, higher is better; but don't exceed the maximum for your monitor, or damage to the monitor could result. This is where having the correct driver loaded for your exact model of monitor is handy; the driver knows your monitor's capabilities. If you don't have the right driver for your monitor and are using a driver for some other model instead, look up your monitor's capabilities on the manufacturer's website to be sure. A refresh rate of 85Hz is supported by most monitors and results in a decent display. Refresh rate is an issue primarily with CRTs.

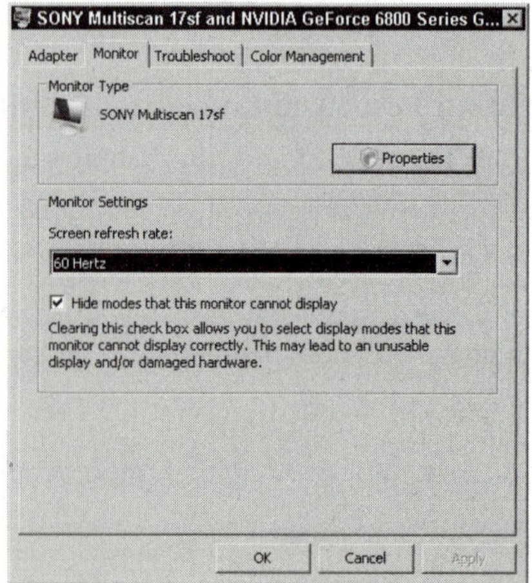

FIGURE 5.12
Choose a refresh rate that will work with your monitor and video adapter combination.

Setting Monitor Controls

Most monitors today have external controls for adjusting the size and positioning of the image. These adjustments can help you remove a black ring from around the outside of the picture and help you center the picture precisely. The positioning is sometimes called *phase*. Each monitor is different, so check the manual that came with yours.

You might have controls on your monitor for adjusting other factors, such as the straightness of the sides. Some monitor images bow out at the middle; some constrict at the middle. This adjustment is called *pincushioning*. Another adjustment you might be able to make is to tilt the entire image to the left or right slightly.

Many good-quality monitors also have controls for convergence. *Convergence* refers to the alignment of each red, green, and blue pixel. Display a pure white page in Windows (such as a blank word-processing document); if you notice a red, green, or blue tint, making a convergence adjustment may correct it.

Troubleshooting Video Problems

If you still have display problems after ensuring that the right drivers are loaded and compatible resolution, color depth, and refresh rate settings have been chosen, try the Display Troubleshooter feature:

1. Right-click the Desktop and choose Personalize. Click the Display Settings Link to display the Display Settings dialog box shown in Figure 5.7.
2. Select the display adapter you want to work with from the list. Alternatively, you can click on one of the monitors displayed on the Display Settings dialog box.
3. Click the How Do I Get the Best Display? link. Follow the instructions for your monitor type as presented in the help file.
4. If the help file doesn't provide what you need, click Advanced Settings. You see the display adapter and monitor Properties dialog box.
5. Choose the Troubleshoot tab.
6. Click Change Settings. Try various options to locate problems with your system, such as shutting off hardware acceleration.

If you're having problems only with a specific program, Windows Help and Support may be able to offer some suggestions. You might also try the DirectX Diagnostic Tool, for troubleshooting problems related to DirectX technology (which is used in many of the most popular games today). To run it, choose Start ➤ Run and type **`dxdiag`**; then click OK. You will see a box asking whether you want Windows to check to see if your drivers are digitally signed. This is a good idea, so click Yes to do that.

Figure 5.13 shows the DirectX Diagnostic tool's Display tab, which may be helpful for display-related problems. Yours may look different (for different monitors).

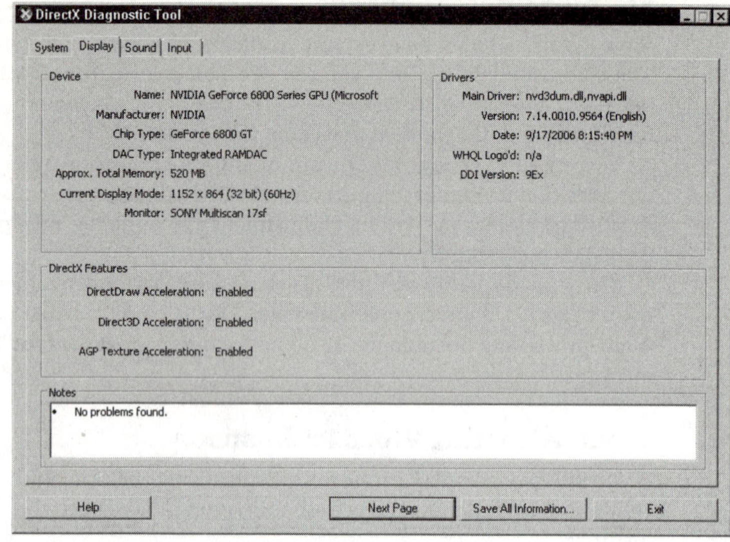

FIGURE 5.13 For problems with a game, the DirectX Diagnostic Tool may be helpful.

Customizing the Vista Display

Now we get into the "fun" display settings, the ones that affect the color choices, backgrounds, shapes, icons, and so on. Most of these settings will be old hat to experienced Windows users, but others are welcome surprises new to Vista. Chapter 4 provides you with a better view of Vista specific changes that you need to know about when you're updating from Windows XP.

Working with Themes

A *theme* is a collection of settings with complementary colors, icons, sounds, background, and so on. Rather than changing each individual aspect of the appearance separately, you can apply a theme to make a group of selections that work well together.

Themes were part of the Plus Pack for Windows 95 released back in the mid-1990s. They came standard with Windows 98, Windows Me, and Windows XP. Now in Vista, the Themes feature is alive and well, but there are only two to choose from: Vista and Windows Classic. You can get more themes by buying the Plus Pack for Vista, getting free themes from `http://www.themexp.org`, or by creating your own themes. (You will want to make sure you have a pop-up blocker running before visiting this site.)

NOTE All of your Windows XP themes work fine in Vista. If you have a Windows XP theme you want to use, simply move it to your Vista setup.

The Windows Vista theme is the default. The Windows Classic theme sets Windows' appearance to resemble Windows 2000. If you (or users you support) are more comfortable in Windows 2000, you might want to set up that theme as a transition helper.

To select a theme, follow these steps:

1. Right-click the Desktop and choose Personalize; then click the Theme link. You'll see the Theme Settings dialog box shown in Figure 5.14.

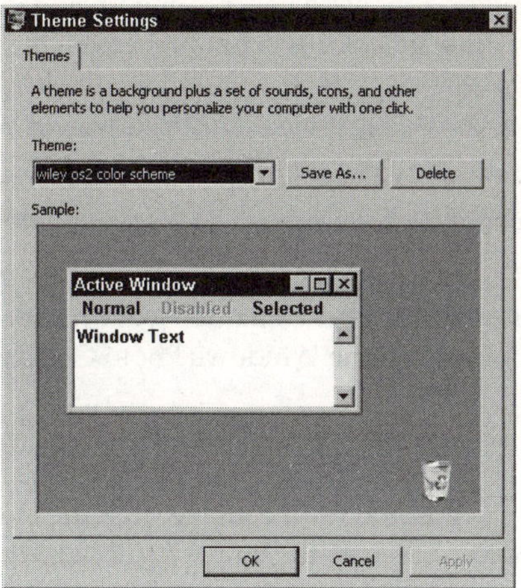

FIGURE 5.14
Choose a theme to use for your system.

2. Open the Theme drop-down list and choose the theme you want.
3. Click OK.

Applying a theme changes many different settings at once. In the next several sections, you will learn how to change many of these settings manually. After you've made your selections of these settings, you might want to return to the Themes tab and save your set of settings under a new theme name. To do so, from the Themes tab, click the Save As button.

NOTE Changing to the Windows Classic theme doesn't affect the Start menu; it remains in the Vista two-column layout. If you want to change the Start menu so it looks more like the Windows 2000 Start menu, do so from the Start menu's Properties. See "Setting Start Menu Options" later in the chapter for details.

Customizing the Desktop

The next few sections show you how to set individual appearance attributes for the Desktop. Most of these are set automatically when you apply a theme, but you can also adjust them individually.

Background

The *background* is the image (or solid color) that appears as the Desktop surface. In some previous versions of Windows it was called wallpaper. You can use a variety of formats of graphics, including bitmap (`.bmp` or `.dib`), GIF (`.gif`), JPEG (`.jpg` or `.jpeg`), and PNG (`.png`).

NOTE You might remember that past versions of Windows let you use an HTML page as a background. There are many security problems with using a Web page as a background and given Vista's mission of cleaning up security issues, you won't find this feature in Vista. Vista limits you to using graphics or solid colors for the background. If you do want to add some Web content to your display, you can do so using the Windows Sidebar. See the "Working with Windows Sidebar" section of Chapter 8 for details.

If you don't choose a background image, the Desktop will appear in whatever solid color you specify. The solid color is actually there all the time, even when a background picture obscures it; if you use a small picture, you will see the background color around the edges.

To select a background, complete the following steps:

1. Right-click the Desktop and choose Personalize; then click the Desktop Background link. You'll see the Desktop Background window shown in Figure 5.15.
2. Select a background category from the Picture Location field. You can choose between Windows Wallpapers, Pictures (your personal pictures), Sample Pictures, Public Pictures, Solid Colors, and the Windows Photo Gallery.
3. Select a background image or solid color from the Background list. If the image you want doesn't appear on the list, use Browse to locate it.
4. Set a position for the image from the How Should the Picture Be Positioned? options. Fit to Screen enlarges the image to fill the whole Desktop. Center places one normal-size copy in the middle. Tile repeats the image as needed to fill the Desktop.
5. Click OK.

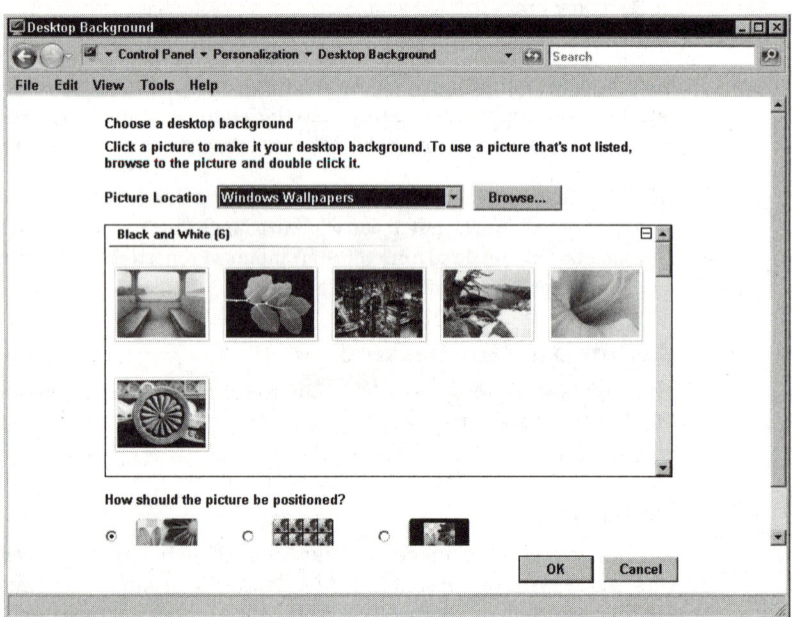

FIGURE 5.15
Vista makes it very easy to choose a background for the Desktop.

CHANGING DESKTOP ICONS AND PROPERTIES

If you used previous versions of Windows, you probably remember that there were several system icons on the Desktop, for things such as Computer, Network, and so on. Vista has only one default system icon on the Desktop: Recycle Bin. If you miss those old-style icons, you can reinstate them. You can also change their appearance.

1. Right-click the Desktop and choose Personalize; then click the Change Desktop Icons link. You'll see the Desktop Icon Settings dialog box shown in Figure 5.16.
2. Check any icons you want to appear on the Desktop.
3. Optionally, to change the look for an icon, select its picture in the middle section of the dialog box and then click Change Icon. The Change Icon dialog box opens.
4. Select a different icon for that item and click OK.

TIP You can click Browse to pick up an icon from a different source; you aren't limited to the ones shown initially in the Change Icon dialog box.

5. Click OK.

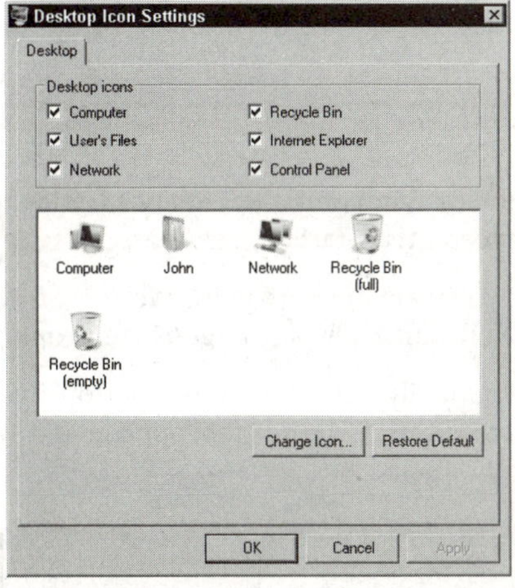

FIGURE 5.16 Select only the icons you want to see on the Desktop and their appearance.

Working with Screen Savers

Screen savers are another once-hot feature that has fallen by the wayside. Put simply, people have gotten bored with seeing images dance across their screens. The practical need for screen savers has also diminished. Originally, they were designed to keep images from burning into a monitor when a PC sat idle for a long time, but with today's monitors, burn-in isn't an issue, so screen savers are just for decoration and amusement.

Using a screen saver can provide a small amount of local security, because you can set it to return to the Welcome screen when resuming out of the screen saver display. If you have set up a password for yourself for logging in on the Welcome screen, that password must be retyped to regain entry. This can prevent casual passers-by from tampering with the system.

To set up a screen saver:

1. Right-click the Desktop and choose Personalize; then click the Screen Saver link. You'll see the Screen Saver Settings dialog box shown in Figure 5.17.
2. Select a screen saver from the Screen Saver drop-down list. If you want to preview it, click the Preview button.

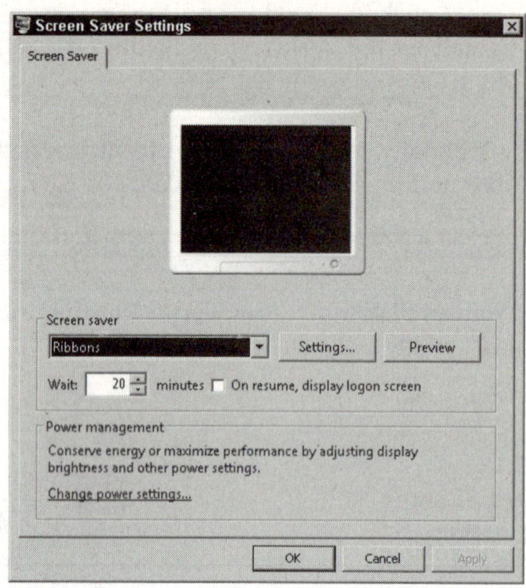

FIGURE 5.17
Set up a screen saver that provides a bit of decoration and amusement.

3. Enter a number in the Wait box for the number of minutes that should elapse before the screen saver starts.
4. If you want to return to the Welcome screen when resuming after the screen saver, check the On Resume, Display Logon Screen option.
5. Optionally, click the Settings button if you want to change any of the settings for the chosen screen saver. The box that appears is different for each screen saver because each has different options.
6. When finished, click OK.

Changing Color and Appearance Options

As mentioned in Chapter 4, Vista significantly changes the way you set the color and appearance of the display. This chapter looks in detail at some of the changes you can make. To open the color and appearance settings, right-click the Desktop, choose Personalize, and then click the Window Color and Appearance link. If you're using the Aero Glass interface, click the Open Classic Appearance Properties for More Color Options link. You'll see the Appearance Settings dialog box shown in Figure 5.18.

From here you can choose a color scheme, which directly affects the interface you use to work with Vista. See Chapter 4 for more details about these options.

But wait—there's more. Click the Effects button for an Effects dialog box where you can turn on/off various visual effects, as in Figure 5.19. Generally speaking, the more of these you can turn off, the better the video performance you'll get.

We're not done yet. Back on the Appearance tab, click the Advanced button to open the Advanced Appearance dialog box. Here's where you can customize the chosen color scheme, item by item, as in earlier Windows versions. (This works only for Windows Classic–style windows and buttons.) For example, you could choose Active Title Bar from the Item list, and then select a color, size, and font for it, as shown in Figure 5.20.

NOTE You can't save your custom color schemes in Vista, although you could in earlier Windows versions. However, you can save custom color schemes as part of a theme. Consequently, if you need to save a custom color scheme, make sure you make all of the interface changes you want first, and then save the resulting settings as a new theme.

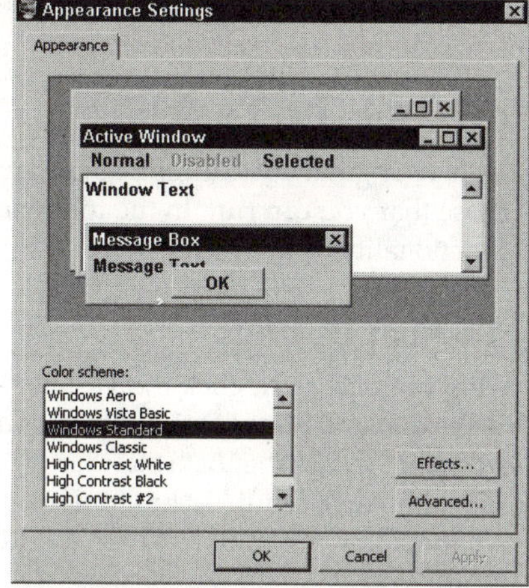

FIGURE 5.18
Choose appearance options such as color here.

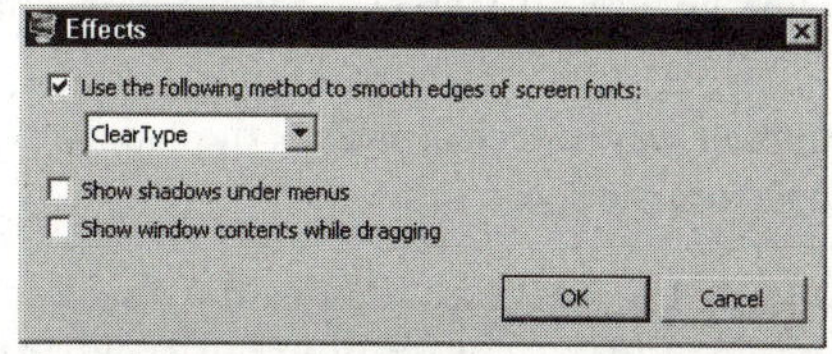

FIGURE 5.19
Choose which visual effects you want in Windows.

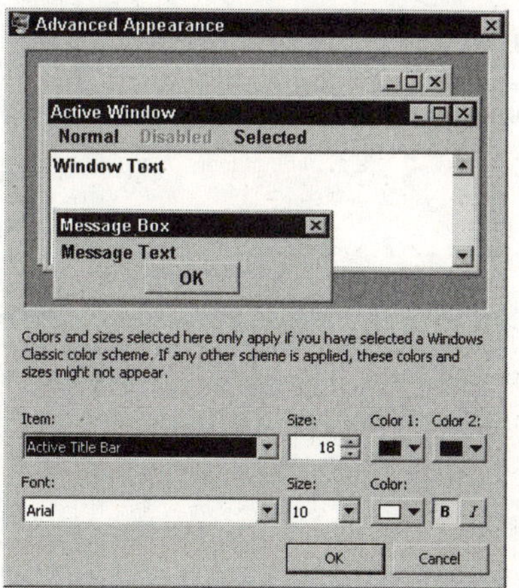

FIGURE 5.20
You can customize each aspect of a color scheme.

Removing the Desktop Icons

You may not want to clutter your Desktop with icons. After all, you have that family picture or a scene from your last vacation. One of the new Vista features lets you remove the icons from the Desktop, so you can see your pictures in all their beauty. To remove the icons, right-click the Desktop and choose View ➤ Show Desktop Icons. All of the icons will disappear from the Desktop. If you want to get the icons back, simply use the same command.

Customizing the Taskbar

The Taskbar is your gateway to all sorts of programs and windows, both those that are already running and those that you can run. In the following sections, you'll learn how to control its appearance and functionality.

Setting Taskbar Options

To set Taskbar options, right-click the Taskbar and choose Properties; then click the Taskbar tab. You'll see a Taskbar and Start Menu Properties dialog box like the one shown in Figure 5.21. Notice that this screenshot shows the Vista Standard / Aero Glass interface. The last option, Show Window Previews (Thumbnails), requires the Compositor to work.

You have the following options when working on the Taskbar tab:

Lock the Taskbar The Taskbar is locked at its current position by default so that a user cannot move it to another location. Another way to access this same setting is to right-click the Taskbar and click Lock the Taskbar to toggle it on/off.

TIP Another way to lock or unlock the Taskbar is to right-click the Taskbar and choose Lock the Taskbar from the shortcut menu.

Auto-Hide the Taskbar Hides the Taskbar until you move your mouse pointer to where the Taskbar is hidden. Auto-hiding the Taskbar is useful if you have limited screen space or if you just don't like the look of the Taskbar.

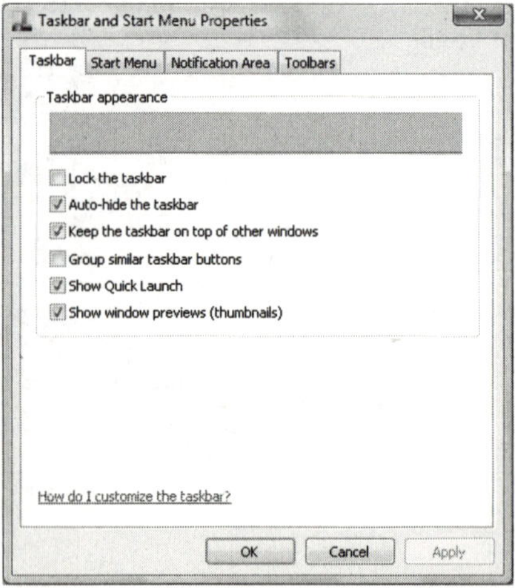

FIGURE 5.21
The Taskbar and Start Menu Properties dialog box.

Keep the Taskbar on Top of Other Windows Keeps the Taskbar visible at all times. This is the default setting. (Screen saver programs ignore this setting, however, as they cover the entire screen.)

Group Similar Taskbar Buttons Groups together buttons for files opened by the same program. This is a new feature in Vista and is on by default.

Show Quick Launch The Quick Launch area of the Taskbar contains application icons. Click on an icon and it opens the application. Some applications, such as Internet Explorer, Office, and Firefox, place icons here by default. You can also add your own application icons by right-clicking the Quick Launch area and choosing Open Folder from the context menu. When you see the Windows Explorer view, you can drag and drop application shortcuts into the Quick Launch folder. You can now access the application without using the Start menu.

Show Window Previews (Thumbnails) This option requires the Compositor to work. It displays a pop-up view of each application on the Taskbar when you place the mouse cursor over that application. For example, when you place the mouse cursor over Word, you'll see a picture of the document that you have open in Word. This feature comes in handy when you have multiple copies of the same application open and want to see which one to select without actually choosing it from the Taskbar.

If you unlock the Taskbar, you can then drag it to one of the other sides of the screen; it need not be on the bottom.

You can also make the Taskbar appear in multiple rows. (Unlock it first.) This is useful if you keep a lot of windows open at once and you would like to be able to see them more easily from the Taskbar. To do so, position the mouse pointer over the top edge of the Taskbar and drag upward.

Working with Taskbar Toolbars

Vista includes a number of toolbars, all of which provide some functionality. For example, I often keep shortcuts to my projects on the Desktop. By placing the Desktop toolbar on the Taskbar, I can open any project without displaying the Desktop first. Using this simple setup saves considerable time during the workday. Whether a Vista toolbar is actually useful, though depends on your work habits. For example, some people spend a lot of time typing Internet addresses, so the Address toolbar is quite useful.

Before you can use a toolbar, however, you must add it to the Taskbar. To set Taskbar options, right-click the Taskbar and choose Properties; then click the Toolbars tab. You'll see a Taskbar and Start Menu Properties dialog box like the one shown in Figure 5.22.

As an alternative to using the check boxes in the Taskbar and Start Menu Properties dialog box, you can right-click the Taskbar and choose one of the options from the Toolbars menu. You'll see the same options as shown in Figure 5.22, plus an option to create a new toolbar. Simply use the Toolbars ➢ New Toolbar option to create a new toolbar. Vista will ask you to choose a folder on your hard drive to act as a source of icons for the new toolbar. Your new toolbar can contain any kind of shortcut, application, or data file you want.

You can customize the Deskop toolbar (or any other Taskbar toolbar) by dragging shortcuts directly onto it and dropping them there. To remove an icon from a toolbar, right-click it and choose Delete.

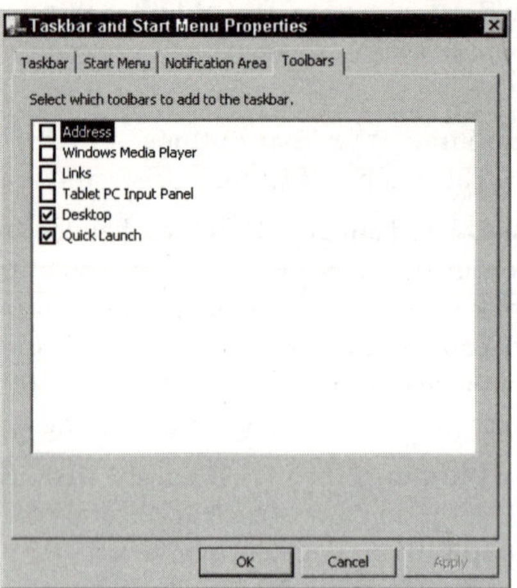

FIGURE 5.22
Add special toolbars to the Taskbar to make it easier to get work done.

Here are some things you can do to a toolbar:

- Add icons to it by dragging shortcuts onto it from the Desktop or Start menu.
- Delete icons by right-clicking them and choosing Delete.
- Resize it by dragging the dotted "handle." If you don't see any dots at the left end of a toolbar, the Lock the Taskbar setting is probably turned on.
- Drag it into the center of the screen to make it a floating toolbar, in its own window.
- Drag it to a different side of the screen to dock it there as its own separate bar.

You can also make your own toolbars, although not out of thin air. First, you create a folder; then you right-click the Taskbar and choose Toolbars ➤ New Toolbar to make that folder into a toolbar. Then any files you put into that folder will appear as shortcuts on the toolbar.

Customizing the Notification Area

The notification area, also called the system tray, is at the far right of the Taskbar and displays icons for programs and tasks that are running in the background. These might include drivers or managers for devices such as a PDA interface or satellite Internet service.

To control which programs load at startup, see Chapter 6. If you just want to control which icons appear in the notification area, however, you can right-click the Taskbar and choose Customize Notification Icons. Then set notification options in the Customize Notification Icons dialog box. See Figure 5.23.

When some icons are hidden in the notification area, a left-pointing arrow appears to the left of the area; you can click that arrow to see the hidden icons. Click it again to hide them.

In some cases, you'll want to customize the notification area to a greater degree than simply showing or hiding icons. To manage the notification area, right-click the Taskbar and choose Properties. Select the Notification Area tab and you'll see the selections shown in Figure 5.24. The check boxes in this dialog box let you choose whether the system always shows icons or hides them based on your custom settings. In addition, you can choose the system icons that appear in the notification area. Finally, click Customize to display the dialog box shown in Figure 5.23.

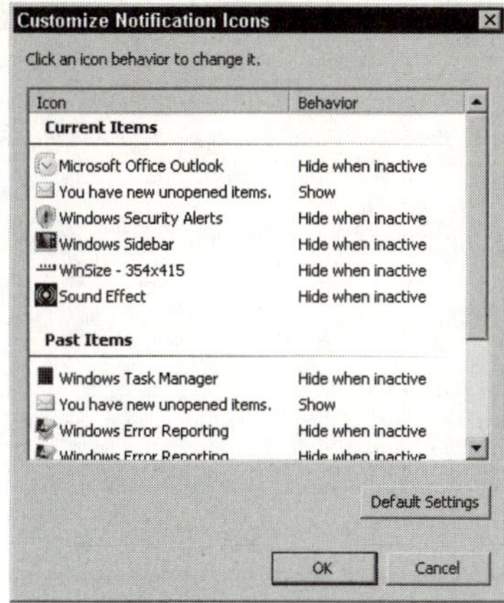

FIGURE 5.23
You can specify which icons appear in the notification area and which are hidden.

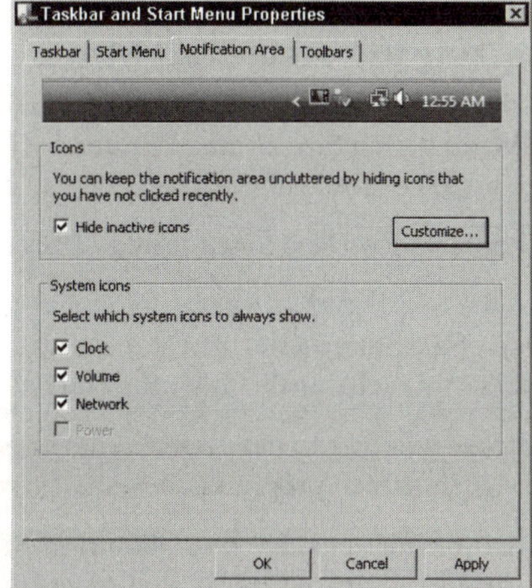

FIGURE 5.24
Determine whether to hide or show icons, as well as which system icons appear in the notification area.

Setting Start Menu Options

The Start menu's options are found in the same Taskbar and Start Menu Properties dialog box as the previous section covered, but on the Start Menu tab.

Vista has a new look for the Start menu, but you can revert to the old-style ("Classic") Start menu if you prefer it. Each has its own separate set of customization options. To switch between them:

1. Right-click the Start button and choose Properties.
2. Click Start Menu or Classic Start Menu, whichever you prefer. See Figure 5.25.

Then, to customize the appearance of the Start menu you chose, click the Customize button beside it.

NOTE This chapter's coverage of the Start menu focuses on its overall appearance and settings. In Chapter 6, you'll learn how to add, remove, and arrange shortcuts on the Start menu for the programs you want to run.

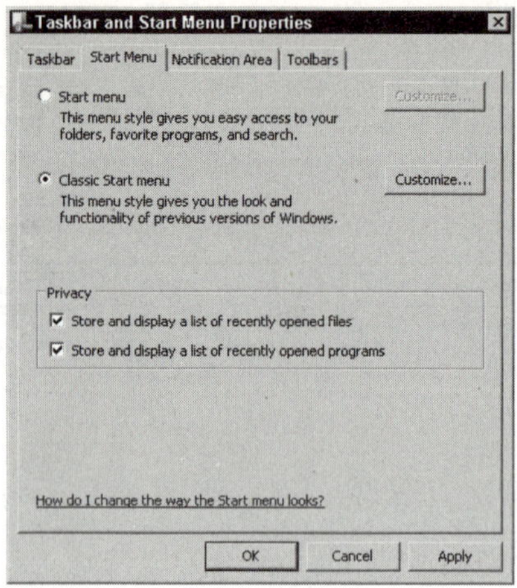

FIGURE 5.25
The Start Menu tab.

Customizing the Vista Start Menu

Clicking the Customize button for the regular (that is, the Vista) Start menu brings up the Customize Start Menu dialog box. Unlike Windows XP, Vista shows everything you can do in one dialog box. Here's a list of some of the tasks you can perform.

- Choose an icon size for programs. This controls the icons on the Start menu only.
- Set the number of programs to appear on the Start menu. This controls the area on the left side of the Start menu, where recently or frequently used program shortcuts appear. The higher this setting, the taller the Start menu will be.
- Choose whether to have an Internet or e-mail link in the top left section of the Start menu, and if so, which programs they should represent.
- Choose whether submenus should open automatically when you pause on them with the mouse. If you turn this off, you must click each submenu level to open it.
- Choose whether to highlight newly installed programs. This is on by default and makes newly installed programs and their submenus a different color.
- Choose and customize Start menu items. This is a list of various items that can appear on the Start menu if you like, such as the Favorites menu. Some of them have additional options, such as displaying them as a link versus a menu.

TIP When you install a new program, it doesn't find its place in the alphabetical Start menu hierarchy right away; it hangs out at the bottom for a while. If you're using the Classic Start menu, you can re-alphabetize it manually by right-clicking the Taskbar and choosing Properties, clicking the Customizing button next to Classic Start Menu, and clicking the Sort button. There's no equivalent button if you use the Vista style of Start menu, however. To have Windows always alphabetize the list, remove the permissions from the Registry key that controls the sort order for the Start menu. To do so, in the Registry Editor, go to `HKEY_CURRENT_USER\Software\Microsoft\Windows\CurrentVersion\Explorer\MenuOrder`. Then choose Edit, Permissions, and click the Advanced button. Deselect

Inherit from Parent, and then click Copy in the Security dialog box. Then click OK and clear the Full Control entry from your account and all security groups you're a member of. Leave only Read permission.

Customizing the Classic Start Menu

The Classic Start menu has customization options similar to those for earlier versions of Windows. The Add, Remove, and Advanced buttons enable you to add, remove, and arrange content on the Start menu. You'll learn more about changing the Start menu content in Chapter 6.

The Sort button alphabetizes the Start menu content. When you install a new program, it appears at the bottom of the menu at first; this Sort feature places it in its rightful alphabetical location.

The Clear button erases the historical usage records for the Start menu; it clears the My Documents menu and also the Personalized Menus feature if you're using it.

The Personalized Menus feature is available only when you use the Classic Start menu. It keeps track of which programs you use the most and displays them first on the Start menu. After a few seconds' pause, or when you click the down-pointing arrow at the bottom of the Start menu (present when the feature is on), the complete list appears. To turn Personalized Menus on/off, mark or clear its check box in the Advanced Start Menu Options section.

Speaking of that section, there are many other fine-tune settings you can adjust for the Start menu there. Some of these options are "Display" this or that; mark such a check box to add a certain special-purpose folder or utility to the Start menu. Others are "Expand" something; turn these on to make certain features display as a submenu rather than opening a window when you select them.

Adjusting the Keyboard and Mouse

Your mouse should work automatically in Vista, with no special drivers or adjustments. However, the default settings are n't optimal for everyone; some people prefer a faster or slower mouse pointer, greater or lesser sensitivity, or for the buttons to be switched for left-hand operation.

The adjustments for both keyboard and mouse are made through Control Panel. (If you're using Category view, you'll find them in the Hardware and Sound category.)

Keyboard Properties

The keyboard properties are rather simple. They let you adjust these features:

Repeat delay The amount of time between holding down a key and the key starting to repeat (that is, repeatedly type the character quickly on screen).

Repeat rate The speed at which repeating occurs once it begins.

Cursor blink rate The speed at which the insertion point (vertical line) flashes in a text-editing program.

Mouse Properties

There are a surprising number of adjustments possible for the average mouse. You can control what the buttons do, how fast the pointer moves across the screen, what that pointer looks like, and whether any special features are applied to its movement. Table 4.1 lists the mouse adjustments you can make.

TABLE 5.1: Mouse Properties

TAB	SETTING	PURPOSE
Buttons	Switch primary and secondary buttons	Useful for left-handed people to enable the index finger to control the primary button.
	Double-click speed	Adjusts the sensitivity for double-clicks. Useful for users who have a difficult time double-clicking fast enough.
	ClickLock	Makes the mouse button into an on/off toggle. Useful for people who have mobility problems that hinder normal dragging.
Pointers	Scheme	Enables you to select a predefined set of mouse pointers.
	Customize	Enables you to select a specific image for an individual pointer in a scheme.
Pointer Options	Select a pointer speed	Controls the distance the pointer moves on screen when you move the mouse.
	Enhanced pointer precision	Enables more precise control of the pointer through little enhancements such as assisted deceleration.
	Snap to	Automatically moves the mouse pointer to the default option in a dialog box.
	Display pointer trails	Turns on a trail for the mouse pointer to make it easier to see, especially for people with vision impairment.
	Hide pointer while typing	Makes the mouse pointer vanish while you are working in a text-editing application, so you don't get it confused with the insertion point.
	Show location of pointer when Ctrl key is pressed	Just what the name says. Useful for people who "lose" the pointer on screen due to visual impairment.
Wheel	Scrolling	Controls how much the display scrolls for every notch movement of the wheel (if present).
Hardware	Troubleshoot	Helps troubleshoot mouse problems.
	Properties	Displays properties for the mouse device installed.

Choosing System Sounds

If you have a sound card and speakers, you hear sounds when certain system events occur, such as Windows startup and shutdown, an error message, and so on. You can change these sounds individually, or you can apply an entirely different sound scheme.

To do so, right-click the Desktop and choose Personalize from the context menu; select the Sounds link. Pick a scheme from the Sound Scheme drop-down list on the Sounds tab or click an individual sound on the Program Events list and assign a sound to it from the Sounds list or with the Browse button. To play a sound, click the button that looks like a right-pointing arrow.

Using Ease of Access Options

Accessibility features in Vista help people with hearing, vision, or mobility impairments to use their PCs more easily. Microsoft has renamed the accessibility features as the Ease of Access features. You'll see the new icon associated with Ease of Access in many places in Vista that didn't previously have this feature. For example, you can change the Ease of Access features before you even log on to the system by clicking the Ease of Access icon in the lower right corner of the display.

Other display settings aren't specifically classifiable as Accessibility features, but are nevertheless useful for people with vision impairments. For example, in the Display Properties, you can choose Large or Extra Large font size on the Appearance tab, and you can click the Advanced button (still on the Appearance tab) to specify a color and size for an individual screen element.

Using the Ease of Access Center

Previous versions of Windows used a feature called the Accessibility Wizard that was supposed to make it easier to set the accessibility options. Unfortunately, this feature actually made life difficult for anyone who actually needed it because the Accessibility Wizard was a time-consuming and somewhat difficult tool to use. Vista uses the new Ease of Access Center, which is considerably easier to use and friendlier as well. You can access this feature from the Control Panel in the Appearance and Personalization category. You can also use the Start ➤ All Programs ➤ Accessories ➤ Ease of Access ➤ Ease of Access Center command to open this window. Figure 5.26 shows how this window appears.

The Ease of Access Center assumes that you have immediate accessibility needs, so it enables both the Always Read This Section Aloud and Always Scan This Section options. The Always Read This Section Aloud option starts the Narrator and reads the four application options in the upper section to you. The Always Scan This Section moves the selection from one application to the next. This combination makes it very easy to select the applications you require at the outset. The "Using Magnifier," "Running Narrator," and "Using the On-Screen Keyboard" sections describe these applications in detail. The Set Up High Contrast option simply sets your display to use the high contrast theme described earlier.

Below these four application entries, you find links to perform specific accessibility configuration tasks. The following sections describe each of these tasks.

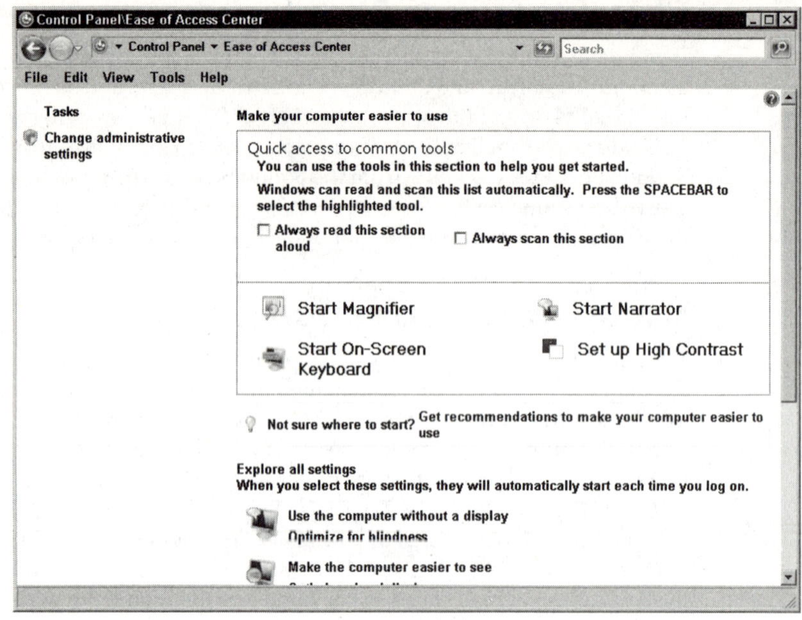

FIGURE 5.26
The Ease of Access Center makes it quite easy to configure your system to meet accessibility needs.

USE THE COMPUTER WITHOUT A DISPLAY

Here are some settings for people who won't use a display with Vista. The following settings include a couple of new features to address this need.

Turn On Narrator This application reads all of the content on the display based on information that developers provide for accessibility purposes. You must have speakers to use this feature, but don't need to perform any setup other than ensuring the speakers work.

Turn On Audio Description This feature tells you what is happening in a video. As with Narrator, all you need is speakers to make this feature work. However, in this case, the video must have closed captioning, which isn't always available in computer videos.

Turn Off All Unnecessary Animations Animations tend to confuse screen readers and make it nearly impossible for someone who can't see the screen get useful work done. Since the user can't see the animations, there isn't any reason to keep them running. This feature also closes Windows notification dialog boxes automatically after the specified time interval.

MAKE THE COMPUTER EASIER TO SEE

These settings help people who have low vision or merely tired eyes. The following settings include some favorites from past versions of Windows and a couple of new features.

Choose a High Contrast Color Scheme Turn on a high-contrast display theme by marking the Use High Contrast check box. You can then click the Settings button to select a high-contrast color scheme that includes large fonts. Note that these are Windows Classic color schemes, and if you choose one, the button and window style will change to Windows Classic. Once you enable High Contrast, you can toggle it on/off by pressing Alt+Left Shift+Print Screen.

NOTE Turning on High Contrast in the Accessibility Options is different from simply selecting a high-contrast or large-font color scheme in the regular Display Properties. When you turn it on via Accessibility Options, the on/off toggle with Alt+Left Shift+Print Screen is available, whereas normally it wouldn't be.

Turn On Narrator This application reads all of the content on the display based on information that developers provide for accessibility purposes. You must have speakers to use this feature, but don't need to perform any setup other than ensuring the speakers work.

Turn On Audio Description This feature tells you what's happening in a video. As with Narrator, all you need is speakers to make this feature work. However, in this case, the video must have closed captioning, which isn't always available in computer videos.

Use the Computer without a Mouse or Keyboard

Vista supports a number of alternative input options that previous versions of Windows didn't provide. In addition, it supports some old favorites such as the On-Screen Keyboard as described in the following list.

Use On-Screen Keyboard Starts the On-Screen Keyboard application, which lets the user provide input using any alternative keyboard setup, such as an eye gaze system or a stylus.

Use Speech Recognition This is the new addition for Vista. The speech recognition features are significantly improved. However, they aren't perfect. While you can input commands without too much trouble and could type a letter to Mom, you'll need to exercise care when using speech recognition for complex tasks.

Make the Mouse Easier to Use

Vista contains many adjustments for people who have difficulty performing common mouse activities. Actually, this feature works quite well for everyone. Some people use these features to position the mouse more accurately in drawing programs, for example. The following list describes the mouse-related accessibility features.

Mouse Pointers This feature lets you choose the mouse pointer size and presentation. For example, you may find it easier to see an inverted mouse presentation such as white on a black background.

Turn On MouseKeys The MouseKeys feature lets you use the numeric keypad to position the mouse. This particular feature provides very fine mouse control, so you can inch the mouse along or fast-forward it across the display as needed without actually touching the mouse. As far as your application is concerned, you're moving the mouse, even though you're using the numeric keypad to do it.

Activate a Window by Hovering over It with the Mouse This feature makes it possible to use the mouse to activate windows without actually clicking a button to do it. Hovering the mouse is sufficient to select the window.

Make the Keyboard Easier to Use

In real-world usage, the biggest help is Windows' ability to accept alternative input devices called SerialKey devices. These attach to the PC's serial port (most models; newer ones may be USB) and are specifically designed to help mobility-impaired people. You can turn on access to a SerialKey device. There are also numerous features that assume you're using the standard keyboard or mouse but make them work in a nonstandard way.

If you have trouble using a standard keyboard, try some of these options:

Turn On MouseKeys The MouseKeys feature lets you use the numeric keypad to position the mouse. This particular feature provides very fine mouse control, so you can inch the mouse along or fast-forward it across the display as needed without actually touching the mouse. As far as your application is concerned, you're moving the mouse, even though you're using the numeric keypad to do it.

Turn On StickyKeys Lets you use the Shift, Ctrl, Alt, and Windows logo keys as on/off toggles by pressing them twice in succession. You can also turn this feature on/off at any time without going through Accessibility Options by pressing the Shift key five times in a row. Click Settings to adjust the properties for the StickyKeys feature.

Turn On ToggleKeys Plays a sound when the Caps Lock, Num Lock, or Scroll Lock key is pressed. This is useful for someone who might accidentally press one of those keys and turn on the Lock toggle without realizing it.

Turn On FilterKeys Tells Windows to ignore brief or repeated keystrokes. This is useful for someone who might have a hard time zeroing in on a single key and releasing it quickly. Another way to turn on this feature is to hold down the Shift key for 8 seconds. Click Settings to adjust the feature's properties.

Underline Keyboard Shortcuts and Access Keys The Vista default doesn't underline keyboard shortcuts for whatever reason. Instead, you see the shortcuts when you press Alt; at least in some applications. This feature presents the underlines at all times, which is welcome news to anyone who liked this feature and wonders why it's missing in Vista.

Use Text or Visual Alternatives for Sound

In most programs, deaf or hearing-impaired users should have no problem with the default Windows settings. That's because Windows is primarily a visual operating system, and the sound cues are of minimal importance. However, such users might miss out on the warning beep that accompanies an error message or the system sound that alerts the user to incoming mail or some other event. Here are some features that might be of interest to users with a hearing need (these features work equally well for anyone who must work in a low sound environment, such as a crowded office):

Turn On Visual Notifications for Sounds (SoundSentry) Generates a visual cue on screen when a system sound plays. You can then choose what you want this visual cue to be, such as flashing the Desktop or the active window.

Turn On Text Captions for Spoken Dialog (When Available) Displays captioning for any programs that support it. When used in a supported program, this works somewhat like closed captioning on a television.

Make It Easier to Focus on Tasks

This link provides access to a number of features that I've already presented as part of other options. You gain access to the Turn On Narrator, Turn On StickyKeys, Turn On ToggleKeys, Turn On FilterKeys, and Turn Off All Unnecessary Animations options. In addition, you'll find a new feature called Remove Background Images. This feature removes all background images, no matter what their source is, to avoid confusing background and foreground information.

Using Magnifier

The Magnifier application can be very useful for people who aren't totally blind but have some degree of visual impairment. It magnifies in a special panel at the top of the screen whatever portion of the screen the mouse pointer passes over. To turn it on, choose Start ➤ All Programs ➤ Accessories ➤ Ease of Access ➤ Magnifier.

As long as Magnifier is running, a Magnifier Settings dialog box appears. You can minimize it and keep Magnifier open; however, if you click Exit in that box, the entire Magnifier program will terminate.

Running Narrator

Narrator is useful for people who have a hard time reading text in dialog boxes. When enabled, it reads the text in the active dialog box or window. To turn it on, choose Start ➤ All Programs ➤ Accessories ➤ Ease of Access ➤ Narrator.

When you turn on Narrator, a dialog box describing it appears. Read the info, and then click OK to clear it; a Narrator window appears containing options for narration. You must leave this window open for Narrator to continue to work, but you can minimize it.

You can then switch to any other program, and it will attempt to read whatever text appears in it. It works in Microsoft Word, for example, and can read the letters that you type as you type them.

Using the On-Screen Keyboard

The On-Screen Keyboard is an application that displays a facsimile of a keyboard in a window on screen. You can click the letters you want to type. This might be useful for someone who can use a mouse but cannot type on a keyboard. To turn it on, choose Start ➤ All Programs ➤ Ease of Access ➤ Accessibility ➤ On-Screen Keyboard. When you're finished with it, close its window.

Summary

In this jam-packed chapter, you learned how to customize the Windows interface—how it looks, how it sounds, and how it behaves. This chapter also helped you understand changes to the way Vista performs tasks when compared to older versions of Windows. You also learned about some of the Ease of Access features in Vista. Remember that you can access these features wherever you see the Ease of Access icon.

Of course, just knowing how to perform the task isn't the same as seeing it in action. Your task now is to try out the various settings—kick the Vista interface tires. Once you find a good setup for a particular need, save it as a theme so you can access it quickly later. You can save your themes to a network drive and use them on other machines. All you have to do is double-click the theme file to apply it to any workstation.

In the next chapter, we'll take a look at installing and running applications. You'll not only find out how to add and remove programs but also how to make old programs work well under Vista and how to control what programs run automatically.

Chapter 6

Installing, Running, and Managing Applications

However wonderful the features built into Vista—and some of them *are* pretty wonderful; some less so; see the rest of the book for details—they're not the be-all and end-all of computing. The programs bundled with Vista let you perform a few basic tasks from creating simple documents to playing music and video or to creating simple video movies of your own. But sooner or later, you're going to want to install a third-party program and run it so that you can carry on with your business and your life.

On the assumption that this is probably going to happen sooner rather than later, this chapter discusses how to install, configure, remove, and run programs—and how to shut them down when they fail to respond to conventional stimuli.

This chapter uses various programs as examples, ranging from the latest (and supposedly greatest) programs specially designed for Vista, to Windows 9*x* programs, to DOS programs that are still only just starting to suspect that graphical environments exist. The odds are overwhelmingly against these programs being those you want to use with your copy of Vista, but these programs provide examples of many of the issues you'll encounter with installing, running, and removing programs.

This chapter covers:

- Multiuser considerations
- Installing and removing programs
- Adding and removing Windows components
- Running programs
- Dealing with unresponsive programs
- Program compatibility issues
- Sharing data between applications
- Organizing the Start menu

NOTE If you performed an in-place upgrade of your previous version of Windows to Vista, the installation processes should have configured all your programs for use already, so you shouldn't need to reinstall them. Of course, the time savings in not installing the applications can be offset by the longer than normal installation time required for an upgrade, so you need to weigh an upgrade carefully. If you have old programs that you find don't run properly on Vista, you may need to run them in Compatibility Mode. If so, turn to the section "Running Programs in Compatibility Mode" later in this chapter.

Vista: What's New?

When people moved from Windows 9*x* to Windows XP, they noticed a few differences, some of which they could overcome using special settings. You'll definitely notice changes in the way Vista does things. Running programs under Vista has taken quite a twist from days gone by for three reasons.

- The User Access Control (UAC) functionality prevents some applications from running at all unless you have administrator privileges.
- Microsoft didn't work nearly as hard to maintain backward compatibility this time around and purposely broke some applications for the sake of security.
- Some Windows elements from previous versions are simply missing, such as support for HLP (help) files (your application must use a newer help file format such as the Compile HTML Help Format, or CHM, file).

These challenges aren't necessarily bad for anyone. The older software that Vista blocks from running has security holes and was designed at a time when personal computers were significantly more personal and considerably less connected. The Internet has changed things in a significant way and the new Vista method of handling these changes makes sense. Of course, the fact that some of your older applications won't run, seemingly for no reason at all, will certainly make life interesting for many IT personnel because explaining security to the boss has never been easy.

Vista also goes further in protecting the multiuser environment. Under Windows XP, it's relatively easy to bypass protections to obtain access to other user data. You won't find that Vista is very flexible in this area. Obviously, an administrator can bypass the protections, but generally, it's a bad idea to do so. The barriers between users are there for a purpose, data protection.

One of the features that you'll find has improved in Vista is the Programs and Features applet, which replaces the Add and Remove Programs applet of previous Windows versions. This new applet is easier to use and it provides a separate window that lists updates you've made to your applications. Consequently, you'll find it significantly easier to determine whether your system has a particular required update.

Multiuser Considerations

As you saw earlier in the book, Vista offers strong multiuser capabilities. From the start, Vista encourages you to set up your computer for multiple users, allowing each their own custom settings. And multiple users can be logged on to the computer at the same time (although only one user can be active). Some users can be running programs in the background (as it were) while the current user is working away unaware of them.

Vista's multiuser capabilities raise some issues for programs and files, as discussed in the next section.

Who Can Install Programs?

Vista supports four types of user accounts: computer administrator, standard user, limited, and guest. Only computer administrator users can install and remove programs for the most part (vendors are currently working to make applications work better for standard users). It's important to remember that even if you're part of the Administrators group, Vista views you as a standard user. To avoid problems with UAC, you'll want to right-click that setup program and choose Run as Administrator from the context menu. Double-clicking the setup program will always result in running the program as a standard user, which may not work. Limited users and the guest user can't install or remove programs. (You'll learn how to set up user accounts and control their type in Chapter 21.)

If a limited user or the guest user tries to install a program, Windows displays a dialog box telling them that they'll need administrator rights to do so. The user must specify a valid Computer Administrator username in the User Name text box and the appropriate password in the Password text box in order to proceed with administrative privileges. If the user tries to continue with the installation without supplying Computer Administrator credentials, Vista immediately ends the installation program.

To Whom Is the Program Available?

In some operating systems, you can install a program for some users but not for others. In contrast, by default, Vista Professional makes any program you install available to all users of the computer—provided that the program's setup routine does things in the right way. For example, if you install Office, the setup routine automatically creates shortcuts for all users to use the programs, so the next time any user logs on, they'll have a swath of new programs that they can use from the Start menu.

NOTE Many modern setup routines let you choose between installing an application for all users or just the current users. However, none of them let you install an application for one set of users and not another. The setup is an all or single-user scenario.

Of course, Microsoft Office 2007 knows all about Vista, because they're both Microsoft products and they're roughly the same vintage. Eudora Pro 4.2, on the other hand, is several years old and hasn't heard of Vista. However, it installs fine and is available to all users after installation because its setup routine was (presumably) constructed along Microsoft's guidelines.

If the program's setup routine is deficient, you may need to install the program to an explicitly shared location or create shortcuts for it manually. For example, if you install Lotus SmartSuite Millennium Edition on Vista by using its setup routine, the user who installs SmartSuite gets the full set of shortcuts for it (plus a slew of shortcuts clogging the notification area, a.k.a. system tray, plus the indescribably wretched SmartCenter program launcher and general menace). Other users get none of these—except for shortcuts to Net-It Now! Starter Edition, the little-known web-publishing companion software that was included with SmartSuite. This isn't useful, helpful, or even amusing.

TIP Windows expects all programs to be installed into the `Program Files` folder. Putting them there seems to help make them available for all users, although it's not a guarantee of success. Putting them in another folder is usually not a good idea. If you have an application that installs to another folder, you must give yourself permission to access that folder. Programs that don't require installation, such as a utility, should run fine with the appropriate permissions.

What Happens When Multiple Users Open the Same File at the Same Time?

Problems arise with some programs when different users have the same file open. For example, multiple users can open the same WordPad file at the same time, and each can save their changes into (or through) the other's changes. The result is pretty horrible.

Of course, some files are *designed* to be accessed by multiple users at the same time. For example, most database files are designed so that they can routinely be accessed by dozens, hundreds, or even thousands of users at the same time. However, the program prevents any *record* from being accessed by more than one user at a time. Some database programs prevent users from accessing records adjacent to any record being accessed by another user to avoid the problems that can occur when records are added to or deleted from the database—either of these actions changes the numbering of records. But as long as each user is (virtually) cordoned off from all other users in the recordset, all is well. Similarly, Excel lets you explicitly share workbooks with other users.

At the risk of generalizing absurdly, more complex (or perhaps more sentient) programs use some form of locking mechanism so that they can tell when another user has a file open. This locking mechanism can consist of flags on the file in question, but often it's implemented as a separate file that's created when the file is opened and is deleted when the file is safely closed. You can see this easily enough with Word, which creates a locking file in the same folder as the document you've opened (or just saved, in the case of a new document) *and* sets a flag on the document. The locking file replaces the first two characters of the file's name with the characters `~$`, so that a document named `Penguins.doc` would generate a locking file named `~$enguins.doc`. (Before you ask what happens with two-character filenames—if the file's name is six characters or fewer, Word *adds* the `~$` to the beginning of the filename. Seven characters, it replaces the first character. Eight characters, it replaces the first two.) If you open the locking file in a text editor (such as Notepad), you'll see that it contains the name of the current user (several times over, with variations in the spacing), some extended characters, and a variety of spaces.

NOTE Word's locking files are hidden, so you won't see them in Explorer or in common dialog boxes unless you've selected the Show Hidden Files and Folders option button in the Advanced Settings list box in the View tab of the Folder Options dialog box (choose Tools ➤ Folder Options) in Explorer.

When you go to open a file, Word takes a quick look through the folder that contains the file to see if there's a locking file for it. If there is, it displays the File in Use dialog box to let you know about the problem and offer you options for proceeding. When you close the file that was open, Word deletes the locking file. But if you delete the locking file while the file is open, Word still knows that the file is open because the flag is still set on the file, locking file or no. It's also important to note that Word lets another user open a read-only copy of the file you're working on, so the only lockout is to changes to the file and not the file itself.

As you might imagine, any program that doesn't use a locking mechanism so that it can tell when its files are open is going to have problems with multiple users accessing the same file. Very generally speaking, the less complex the program, the less likely it is to check that a file is open, and the more likely you are to have a problem with multiple users opening a file at the same time.

This problem also arises with files that can be opened with two or more different programs that are available on the computer. For example, if you use WordPad to open a Word document, it opens the document without any locking. You can then open the same document in Word while it's still open in WordPad. Word then locks the document, and you won't be able to save changes to the original file from WordPad.

What Happens When Multiple Users Run the Same Program at the Same Time?

By and large, having two or more users open the same document file at the same time (in the same program or in different programs) is more of a problem than having two or more users run the same program at the same time.

The brief answer to this question is as follows:

- Some programs are designed to be used by multiple users simultaneously, so they don't cause problems.

- Some programs are too dumb to notice that they're being used by multiple users at once, so each session is happy enough. Some of these programs are designed to run multiple instances for any given user anyway, so they're in good shape to run multiple instances for multiple users.
- Some programs notice there's a problem with multiple sessions and deal with it gracefully.
- Some programs notice there's a problem and sulk conspicuously.

With most programs, the problem comes not with the executable files and libraries (DLLs) but with the settings files. Vista handles the executables and libraries, running each in a separate memory space and segregating each user's programs from all other users' programs. But if a program is designed to use a central settings file rather than to implement a separate settings file for each user, the settings file can cause problems. If the program locks the settings file when the first user runs it (the program), the settings file won't be available when the second user runs the program. The same goes if the settings information is stored in a central location in the Registry.

Perhaps the easiest way around this is to use a separate settings file for each user or to keep separate Registry entries. As you'd imagine, that's what the Microsoft Office programs do. For example, if you're familiar with Word, you probably know that it stores a lot of information in the global template, which is saved in the file `Normal.dot`. The global template is always loaded when you're running Word, so Word maintains a separate global template for each user. This way, it avoids problems when users in separate sessions of the same installation of Word change their settings at the same time.

Problems also arise when separate instances of a program try to use the same hardware resources on the computer at the same time—for example, the COM ports, the audio output, or the microphone input—or the same set of data files.

How a program handles a problem gracefully depends on what the program does and what the problem is. In a program that can manage only one instance running on the computer at the same time, when you start a new instance in another user session, you'll typically see a warning dialog box that lets you choose to either cancel running the new instance of the program or forcibly terminate the other user's session of the program.

As you'd expect, some programs are smarter than others. In particular, it shouldn't come as a shattering surprise to learn that current Microsoft programs are much more aware of Vista's multiuser functionality than earlier Microsoft programs or programs from other software companies.

For example, Windows Media Player lets you switch users while you're still playing music or video or copying a CD. The music (or video) continues to run even while the Welcome screen is displayed. If you then log back on as the same user, Windows Media Player simply keeps going without interruption. Only when you log on as another user does Windows Media Player stop playing the music or video (or copying the CD). And—perhaps more important—it exits the instance that was playing or copying for the other user, freeing up the sound and video circuitry together with whatever system resources it was using. (Before you ask—Windows Media Player quits when you switch to another user even if it wasn't playing.)

Installing a Program

You have probably already installed programs, so you don't need a full-blown explanation of it. Most programs these days come on CD or DVD, and if you have AutoPlay enabled for your CD/DVD drive, the Setup program usually starts automatically when you insert the disc. If it doesn't, you can browse the disc's content, locate the `setup.exe` file, and double-click it to start the ball rolling.

TIP If you get an error when installing a program from a CD/DVD that started Setup using AutoPlay, try opening Computer, right-clicking the CD/DVD drive, and choosing Explore. This lets you browse the drive's content. (Double-clicking won't work in this case; it'll just relaunch the AutoPlay.) Perhaps you can find a file on the CD/DVD that will run the Setup program correctly; sometimes the bug is with the `Autorun.inf` file rather than with the Setup program itself. You can always right-click the `Autorun.inf` file and choose Open. The file will open in Notepad. The `Open=` entry in this file tells you which program executes the setup routine.

What happens when you run the Setup program depends on the whims of the setup routine's programmers or (more commonly) on which of the two commonly used Windows installers they used—InstallShield or WISE. Suffice it to say that the usual steps for installing a program include agreeing to its license agreement, choosing which of the program's components to install, selecting a Start Menu folder (often still called a Program Group, in an embarrassing hangover from Windows 3.*x* days), and twiddling your thumbs (or fetching a fresh cup of wheat grass). For some programs, you'll have to reboot as well.

Installing and Running Multiple Versions of the Same Application

In previous versions of Windows, any program that you wanted to run needed to be installed on that operating system, even if you dual-booted two different operating systems. For example, if you dual-booted Windows 2000 Professional and Windows 98 and had Office 2000 installed on the Windows 98 partition, you still had to install Office on the Windows 2000 Professional partition in order to run it.

No longer. Now if you dual-boot, for example, Vista and Windows XP, and have Office 2000 installed on the Windows XP partition, you can access that program while running Vista. In some cases, the program will appear on the All Programs menu in Vista. If it doesn't, you can locate its executable file in an Explorer-type window and double-click its shortcut to start the program.

Making Programs Run at Startup

If you want a program to start every time you log on to Windows, place a shortcut to it in your Startup folder. Starting programs automatically like this can save you a few seconds each time you start Windows if you always need to use the same programs. When everyone on a machine needs to start a particular application every time Windows starts, you can place a program shortcut in the all users Startup folder, rather than your own folder.

The physical location of your Startup folder varies by Windows version. Rather than having to look for it, you can use a very fast method to access this folder. Open the Start ➤ All Programs menu. Right-click the Startup folder entry and from the context menu choose either Open, for your own Startup folder, or Open All Users, for the Startup folder common to all users. You'll see a copy of Windows Explorer open with the Startup folder selected. Simply create the shortcuts you that require in the Startup folder and the application will start every time you start Vista.

TIP Don't get the idea that the Startup folder is limited to application shortcuts. If you visit the same website every day, you can include a link to it in the Startup folder. Internet Explorer will automatically start and load the website for you. You can also get a head start on your projects for the day by placing shortcuts to the data files in the Startup folder.

To prevent a program from running at startup, obviously enough, you remove its shortcut from the Startup folder.

Some programs run automatically at startup even though they don't appear in the Startup folder. Some of them run for a good reason, such as applications that start certain Windows services. Others are optional. Optional applications often provide a setting within the application configuration settings to start automatically. You can stop the automatic startup by clearing this option.

Some applications just assume you want to start them automatically, even when you don't, and don't provide a convenient configuration option. You can still disable these applications by using the System Configuration Editor (type **`msconfig`** from the Run command). See Figure 6.1. Simply deselect the check box in the Startup tab for whatever you want to disable the next time Windows starts. When you do so, Selective Startup in the General tab automatically becomes selected. If undesirable results occur, return to the System Configuration Editor (in Safe mode if need be) and reselect that item, or to reselect all items, go to the General tab and choose Normal Startup.

If you decide you want to permanently prevent that item from loading at startup, you can edit the Registry to make that so. The Location column of the System Configuration dialog box shows the location of the entry for that application in the Registry. Go to that location and remove the entry for the application to stop the application from running automatically. Note that this window also shows all of the entries in your Startup folder, so the Location column will reflect the Startup folder location should you want to view it.

TIP Surfing the Internet, you can accumulate adware and spyware that loads automatically at startup. Before you go manually stripping this stuff out of your Registry, first try some more graceful and thorough uninstall methods, such as removing them from the Add or Remove Programs applet in Control Panel and running a spyware removal tool such as Spybot Search & Destroy (`http://www.safer-networking.org`). See the next section for more information about program removal.

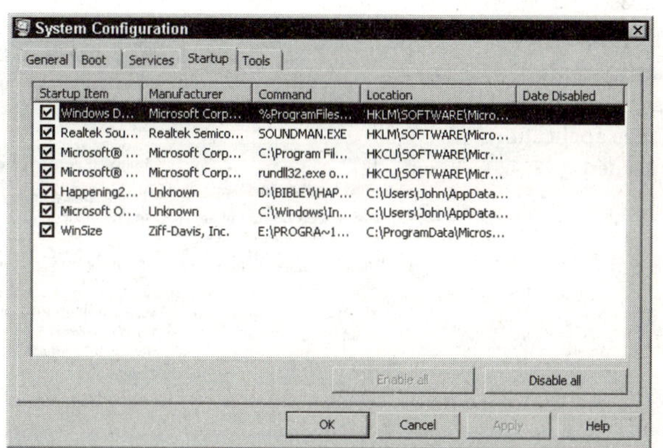

FIGURE 6.1 You can use the System Configuration utility (msconfig) to selectively disable certain items that load at startup.

Removing a Program

You should always remove a program through its Uninstall routine or through Windows' Programs and Features applet in Control Panel. This approach normally keeps your Registry tidy by deleting references in it to that program (some applications don't cooperate and leave their settings in place); it also deletes any files in the `%SystemRoot%` folder and any other non-program-specific folders that were used only for that program. If you try to delete a program by removing its folder from the hard disk and deleting its shortcuts from the Start menu and Desktop, you might not have removed all the pieces.

TIP Many applications remove their critical files and clean up their entries in the `Program Files` folder, but leave a terrifying mess in the Registry. You can see this problem occurring because reinstalling the application also restores your settings because your settings were never removed. This problem has occurred with all versions of Windows, so it's nothing new in Vista. At some point, you'll actually notice that Vista is slowing down because of all of the extra entries that reference nonexistent software. Whenever possible, look on the vendor Web site for an application to remove the registry entries. For example, Symantec provides such a solution for their products. Another solution to the problem is to use a Registry cleaning aid such as RegClean (`http://www.majorgeeks.com/download458.html`), Registry Mechanic (`http://www.pctools.com/registry-mechanic/`), and TweakNow RegCleaner (`http://www.tweaknow.com/RegCleaner.html`). However, even these solutions don't provide complete removal of all of the entries. Eventually, most people have to reformat the drive and reinstall Windows to obtain a clean environment. Vista doesn't appear to fix this problem, unfortunately. Even so, using proper application removal does slow the problem down and lets you use your copy of Vista far longer without a reinstall.

To remove a program, follow these steps:

1. From Control Panel, double-click Programs and Features. You'll see the Programs and Features window shown in Figure 6.2. This figure shows the Details view. As with any Windows Explorer display, you can choose other views, such as Medium Icons, by selecting the option from the Views menu.
2. In the Currently Installed Programs list box, select the entry for the program you want to remove.

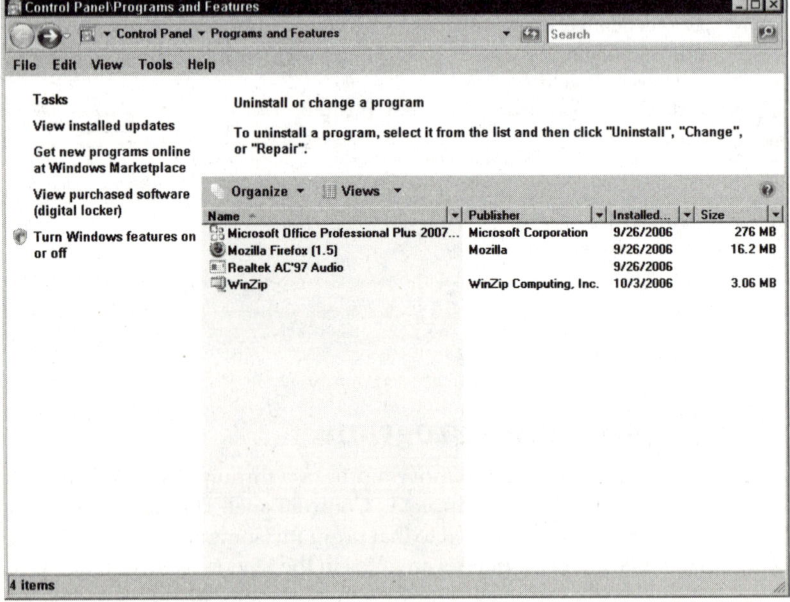

FIGURE 6.2 Vista makes it easy to remove or change applications as needed.

3. Click the Uninstall/Change button (or the Uninstall button, if they're separate). Windows checks to see if other users are using the computer (because they might be using the program that you're about to remove).
4. If any other user is logged on, Windows displays a Warning dialog box. At this point, you can click the Switch User button to display the Welcome screen, then log on as each user from there and log them off. But usually you'll find it easier to use the Users tab of Task Manager to either switch to the other users or simply log them off. When you're ready, click the Continue button if the Warning dialog box is still displayed. (If it's not, click the Change/Remove button in the Add or Remove Programs dialog box instead.)

TIP If you have a lot of programs installed, click any of the headings to sort by that value. You can sort or group by Name, Publisher, Installed On, and Size. Obviously enough, the Name category is useful for finding programs by name. The Size category is good for determining which programs are hogging disk space when you need to free some up in a hurry. The Installed On column is a very good choice when you need to find older programs that haven't received updates in a while or that you want to verify you still use.

Once you've cleared the Warning hurdle, Windows invokes the uninstall routine for the program. The next steps vary depending on the program (or on its programmers or the tool they chose), but in most cases, you either specify which parts of the program to uninstall (if the program contains discrete components) or simply confirm that you want to get rid of the program.

If the uninstall routine tells you that it was unable to remove some parts of the program that you've asked to uninstall completely, it usually lets you know which parts are left. This is often caused by someone having previously tried to remove the application manually. For example, unInstallShield provides a Details button that you can click to display a dialog box containing the names and locations of features the application couldn't remove. In this case, it's easy enough to delete these folders manually by using Explorer.

TIP If a program still shows up on the Installed Programs list after you've removed it, you can remove it from the list by going to `HKEY_LOCAL_MACHINE\SOFTWARE\Microsoft\Windows\CurrentVersion\Uninstall` in the Registry and deleting the key for that program.

Removing 16-Bit Windows Programs and DOS Programs

Windows' Programs and Features applet tracks all 32-bit programs installed on the computer, and it's able to track many 16-bit programs as well. But some 16-bit Windows programs and most DOS programs don't show up in the Programs and Features window, so you can't remove them that way.

The preferred way of removing a program that doesn't show up in the Programs and Features window is to run its uninstall routine manually. Some Windows programs add a shortcut to their uninstall routine to the program folder (or, in Vista, to the Start menu) that contains their other shortcuts. If there's no shortcut, you'll need to dig through the folder that contains the program to see if it has one. The file might be an EXE file, but it might also be a BAT (batch) file.

If the program doesn't have an uninstall routine, you'll need to remove it manually. (If you've only just installed the program, you *could* use the System Restore feature to return your system to its state before you installed the program—but usually you'll have made other changes to your computer since installing the program. Chapter 29 discusses how to use System Restore.) This usually means deleting the folder (or folders) that contains the program and removing any references to it that you can find.

There are two problems with removing a program manually like this. First, you don't necessarily know where the program has put all its files. This is usually more of a problem with Windows programs, which (following Microsoft's own recommendations) often put shared files into the Windows folder or one of its subfolders, than with DOS programs (which probably don't know that the Windows folder exists, and certainly don't care about it even if they do know). So, if you simply delete the folder or folders the program created, it may leave detritus in other folders. (This is why uninstall routines exist, of course.)

The second problem is that the program may also have added commands to configuration files of their era (such as `autoexec.bat` or `win.ini`) that will cause errors when you've deleted its files. You'll need to discover these additions manually (usually when you get an error message) and delete them or comment them out manually. Because Vista uses these configuration files only for compatibility, these errors are likely to cause you annoyance rather than grief—unlike in the old days, when a command for a missing program could make Windows 3.1 refuse to load.

Checking Program Updates

Windows XP included a feature for checking updates on your system, but it wasn't very easy to find. Vista remedies that situation. You can now find updates for applications that record them with relative ease by clicking the View Installed Updates link shown in Figure 6.2. Vista displays the Installed Updates window shown in Figure 6.3.

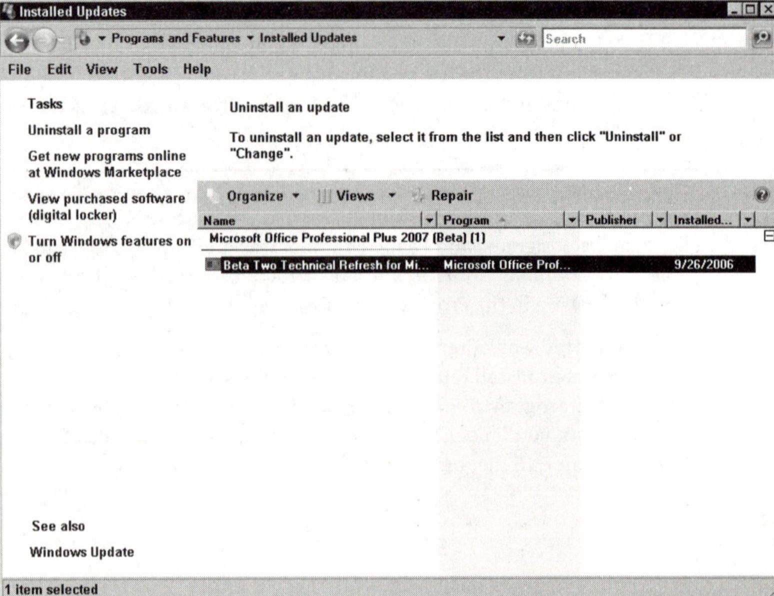

FIGURE 6.3
Review and manage updates to your applications using the new Installed Updates window.

Notice that the first line in the list has an application name. Each application appears in a separate section. Below the application name is an update. In this case, the update isn't removable, so the only button shown on the menu is Repair. You can always repair an update that has gone wrong. When an update is removable, you'll also see a Remove button on the menu.

Figure 6.3 shows a Details view of the data. As with all other Windows Explorer displays, you can choose other presentations. You can also sort or group the entries by any of the headings shown. The default settings group the entries by program. If you sort or group by another column, you might not see the name of the application associated with a particular update. In some cases, sorting by another column works to your advantage. For example, sorting by the Installed On column lets you see which updates you installed on a particular day.

Adding and Removing Windows Components

Many of the accessory programs that come with Vista are optional. You can activate them when you need them or deactivate them when you don't. Microsoft apparently considers disk space so cheap that you can't actually remove the software any longer. However, you can remove data files and folders that the software creates when you no longer want to use it, so you can save some disk space by turning a feature off.

Here are the steps to add or remove Windows accessories and other optional components:

1. In Control Panel, choose Programs and Features.
2. Click the Turn Windows Features On or Off link. A window appears showing various individual components and component categories. See Figure 6.4.

FIGURE 6.4
Select an item or category to add or remove.

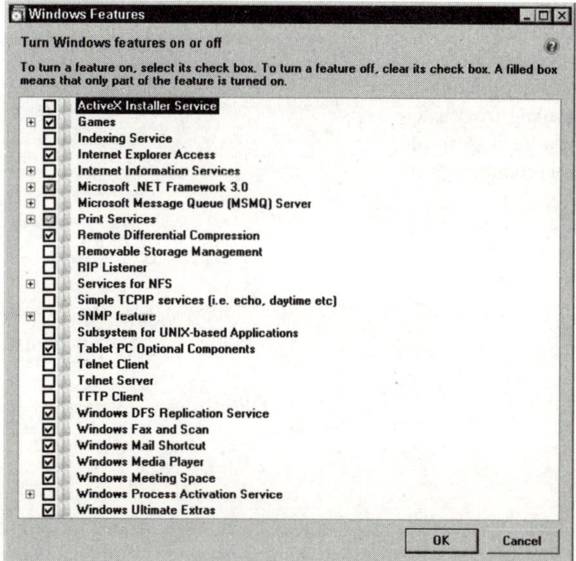

3. Place or remove the check mark next to an item to enable or disable it. Some of the items on the list are for single features, such as Telnet Client; others are for entire categories. If you choose a category, such as Games, you can click the plus (+) sign next to the category name to see a list of accessories in that category, and then select each one individually. For some categories, there are multiple levels; for example, opening the Internet Information Services (IIS) category produces three subcategories: FTP Publishing Service, Web Management Tools, and World Wide Web Services.

4. After you have made all your selections, click OK. If prompted for the Vista DVD, insert it and click OK to continue.

Depending on what you're installing, you might be asked to restart the PC at the end of the procedure; do so if needed. When Windows reboots, any items you added will be available, and any items you removed will not.

Setting Program Access and Defaults

In Windows XP, the whole concept of program access and defaults revolved around hiding certain Windows features. Microsoft claims that it can't remove the features because Windows uses them, but it can hide the features from view so the user can't access them. Vista changes this whole concept and expands it to include third-party applications. In fact, you don't even find this feature in the same place any longer (it used to be part of the Add and Remove Programs applet). You display the new program by choosing Start ➤ All Programs ➤ Default Programs. Figure 6.5 shows the Default Programs window. The sections that follow describe each of the Default Programs features.

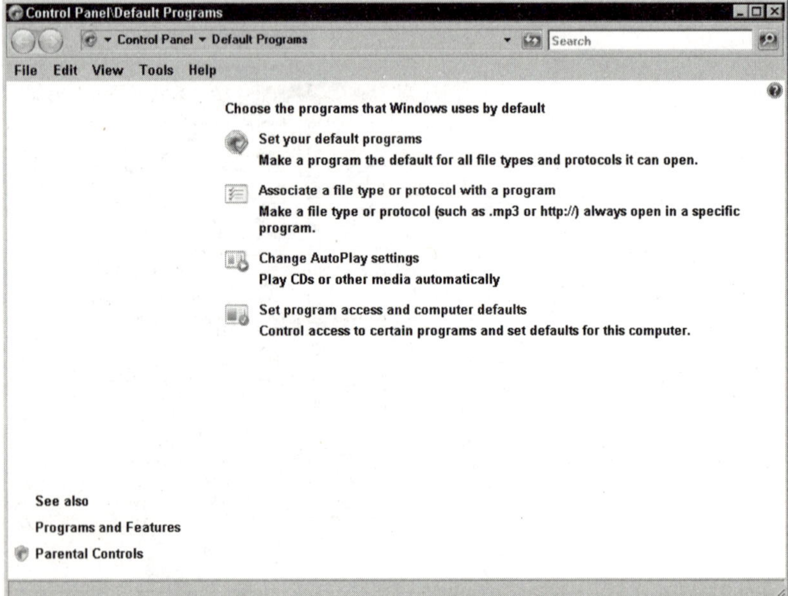

FIGURE 6.5
The concept of a default program has changed in Vista—it now includes third-party products.

Setting Default Programs

You might have run into a problem in the past where you have two applications installed that support essentially the same file extensions. The only problem is that the application you want to use most of the time isn't the default application. Your secondary application, the one with the special feature you need occasionally, is the default. Vista fixes this problem by letting you choose the default program, even if that program isn't from Microsoft. To use this feature, click the Set Your Default Programs link in the Default Programs window. You'll see the Set Default Programs window shown in Figure 6.6.

To set a default program, select it from the list. You'll see information about the program on the right side of the window. If you want the selected program to handle every data file that it can handle, then click Set This Program as Default. However, you might want one of the other programs on your system to handle a few of those data files. In this case, click Choose Defaults for This Program and you'll see the Set Program Associations window shown in Figure 6.7.

As you can see, each of the file extensions in the list has a description and tells you which application currently handles the file type. Check the file associations that you want the application to handle. After you make your selections, click Save and Vista will use the application for the file extensions that you designate.

Associating File Types or Protocols with a Program

You'll notice quite quickly that the default program settings don't include all of the applications on your system. In fact, it includes only those applications where a known conflict exists. Obviously, you need a way to create associations between other protocols and file types. In this case, you click the Associate a File Type or Protocol with a Program link in the Default Programs window. You'll see a complete list of all the file and protocol associations on the current system. The information includes a description of the file type or protocol, along with the program currently assigned to handle it as shown in Figure 6.8.

FIGURE 6.6
Choose the default program to handle specific data files on your system.

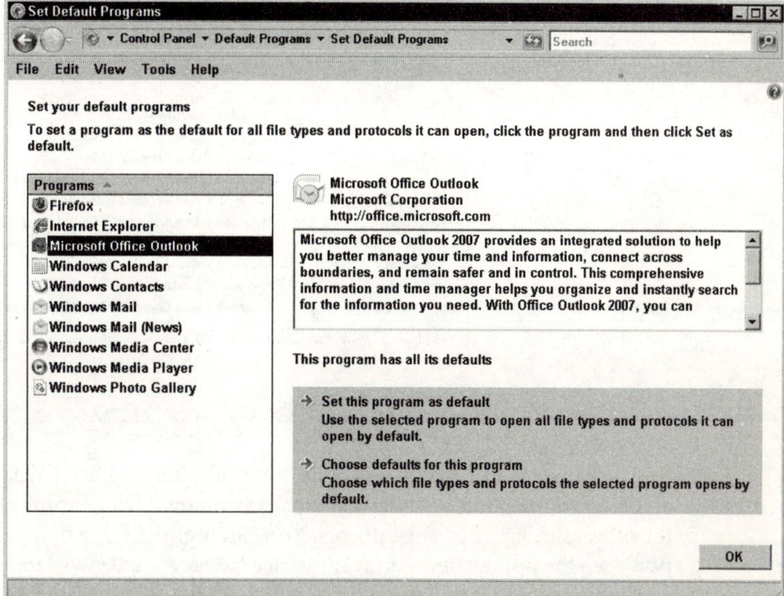

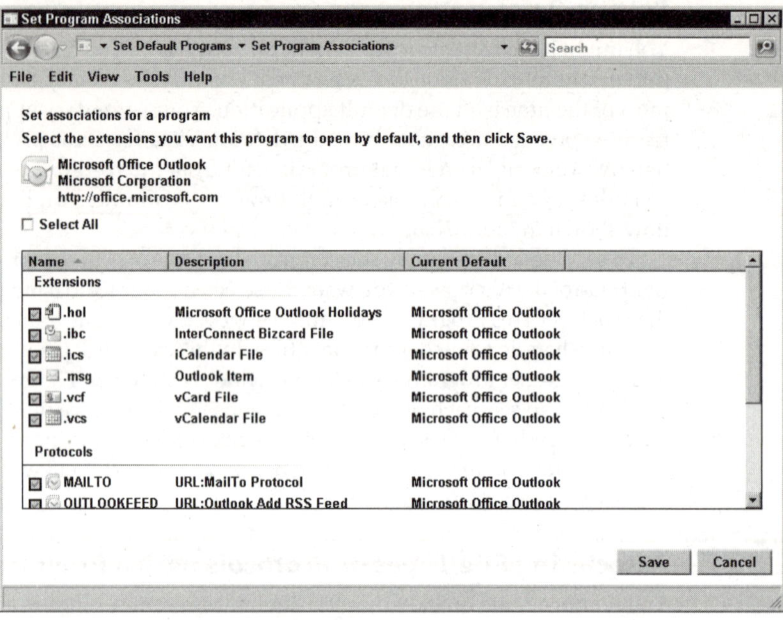

FIGURE 6.7 Vista makes it easy to associate a program with just a few file types.

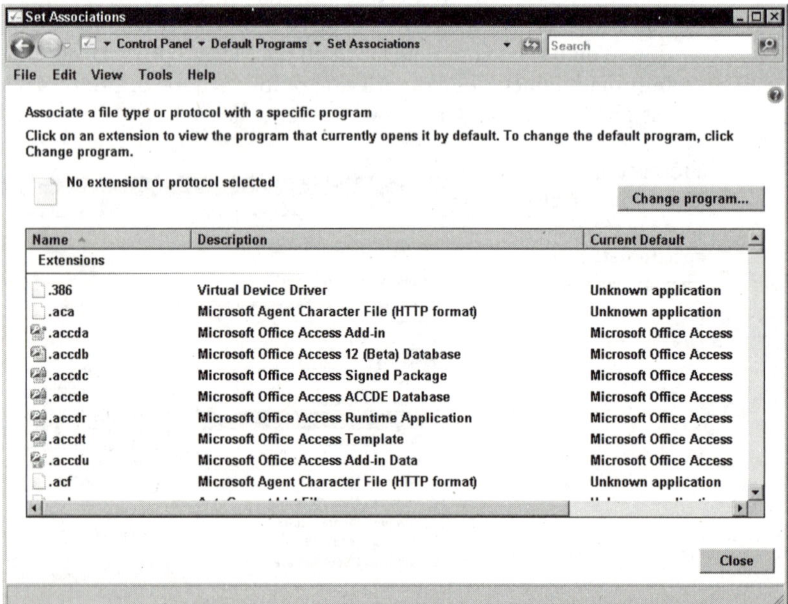

FIGURE 6.8 Associate a file type or protocol with the application you want to use to handle it.

To change one of the associations, highlight it in the list. Click Change Program and you'll see an Open With dialog box. The dialog box contains a list of applications that you're currently using for other, similar, files or protocols. You can highlight one of these programs and click OK. If you don't see the application you want to use listed, click Browse to locate it on your system and then click Open to add it to the application list. Click OK to create the association.

Modifying AutoPlay Settings

The system's AutoPlay settings control what happens when you place a disc into a CD or DVD drive. In previous versions of Windows, Microsoft followed a somewhat loose policy on the AutoPlay settings; the drive would normally automatically start an application setup or perform other tasks based on the media you provided. However, in Vista, Microsoft hasn't assumed anything. For the most part, the drive won't do anything except ask you want to do with an annoying frequency. You can change this behavior by changing the AutoPlay settings. Simply click the Change AutoPlay Settings link to display the AutoPlay window shown in Figure 6.9.

The first time you see this window, you'll notice that most of the entries have no default setting. The settings you can choose depend on the media type. For example, when working with an audio CD, you can play the CD using either the Windows Media Player or the Windows Media Center, rip music from the CD, open the folder so you can see what it contains, take no action at all, or have Vista ask you want to do. You might see other options depending on what software you have installed on your machine. The version of Vista you use also affects the choices you have. After you choose the actions you want Vista to take, click Save at the bottom of the window (you may have to scroll down to see the button).

One of the additions to note about Vista is that it has entries for both the HD DVD and the Blu-ray DVD. These new media types provide you with high definition (HD) video. Interestingly enough, at the time of this writing, there aren't any actual players for the media, but it's good to see that Microsoft is planning ahead.

FIGURE 6.9
The AutoPlay settings control how Vista reacts to various kinds of media.

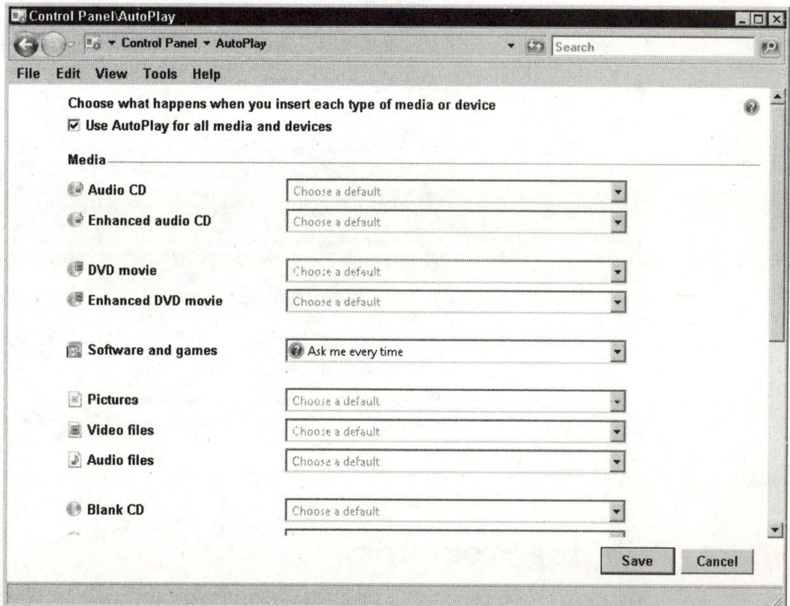

Configuring Program Access and Computer Defaults

We finally come to the feature that the Default Programs window is supposed to replace. As previously mentioned, Microsoft now considers third-party applications as part of the program access picture. Consequently, you can set the behavior of all of the applications on your system. Click Set

Program Access and Computer Defaults to display the Set Program Access and Computer Default window shown in Figure 6.10.

This window looks very much like the Windows XP equivalent and it works very much the same. The top two entries offer you the choice of using only your applications or only Microsoft's applications. Generally, you probably won't use these settings unless you have a complete suite of applications that you want to use or don't want to purchase any software at all (relying on Vista to supply everything). Consequently, Figure 6.10 focuses on the Custom setting, which lets you mix and match applications as needed.

This window asks you two questions. The first is whether you want to use the Microsoft application or your own application for a particular need. For example, you can choose to make Internet Explorer the default application even if you have another browser installed on the system. The second question is whether you want the user to see this application displayed in the Start menu. This feature only works with third-party applications; Microsoft always wants users to see their application on the Start menu. Clearing the Enable Access to This Program check box means that the user won't see the application listed, even if the application starts automatically when the user performs the required actions, such as double-clicking a file.

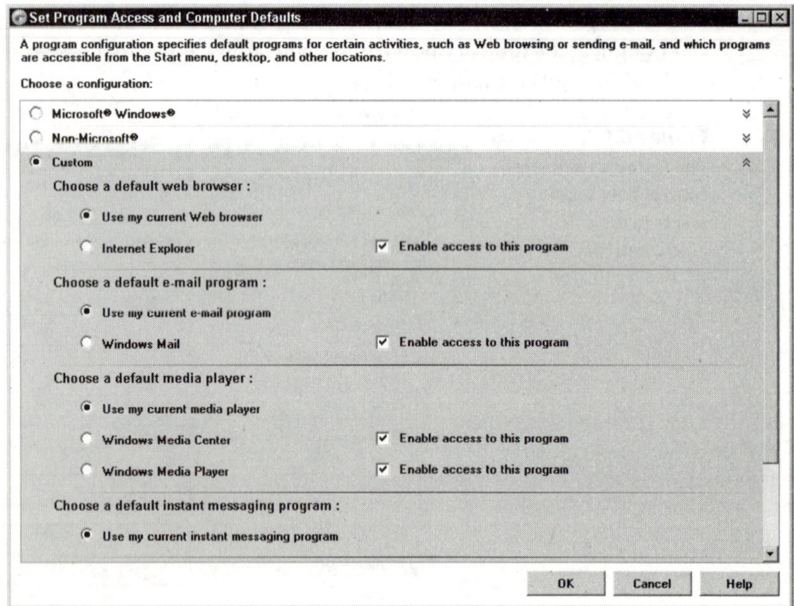

FIGURE 6.10
Modify the program access and computer defaults as needed for your system.

Running Programs

In Windows, you can start a program in any of several ways. If you've used a previous version of Windows, you'll probably be familiar with these ways. They break down into two categories: starting a program directly by opening it, and starting a program indirectly by opening a file whose file type is associated with the program.

You can start a program directly in any of the following ways:

- Click its shortcut on the Start menu.

- Double-click a shortcut on the Desktop or in an Explorer window. (Chapter 8 discusses how to create shortcuts wherever you want.)
- Click a shortcut on the Quick Launch toolbar or another Desktop toolbar. (Chapter 5 discusses the Desktop toolbars and how to customize them.)
- Choose Start ➤ Run. Windows displays the Run dialog box. Enter the name of the program in the Open text box (either by typing or by clicking the Browse button), using the resulting Browse dialog box to identify the file, and clicking the Open button. Then click the OK button.

NOTE Using the Run dialog box seems a clumsy way of running a program, but it's useful for running Windows utilities. Windows doesn't provide a Start menu entry (for example, the Registry Editor, discussed in Chapter 27, and the System Configuration utility, msconfig) and for running programs for which you don't want to create a shortcut but whose path and filename you can type (or otherwise enter) without undue effort.

- Double-click the icon or listing for the program in an Explorer window (or on the Desktop). You can also use the Search Companion (Start ➤ Search) to locate the program you want to run.

Almost all setup routines create shortcuts to their programs automatically. Usually, the setup routine puts a shortcut on the Start menu or in a subfolder of the Start menu. Some setup routines place a shortcut directly on the Desktop; some consult you first, others don't. Some setup routines offer to also put a shortcut in the Quick Launch toolbar or notification area; other setup routines do so without consulting you.

An icon in the Quick Launch toolbar is simply an alternative shortcut to one on the desktop; an icon in the notification area indicates that some portion of the program is already running. You can right-click an icon in the notification area to see a menu of choices for dealing with that running program. If there's a Properties, Setup, Options, or some similar command, it might open a dialog box in which you can prevent the program from loading automatically at startup. You can also use msconfig to prevent it from loading at startup.

Dealing with Unresponsive Programs

Programs run pretty well on Vista—but not all programs run well all the time. Sooner or later, a program will hang or crash on you. Vista generally makes it apparent that an application isn't working as expected by displaying (Not Responding) in the title bar, but this isn't always the case.

When you suspect that your application has crashed, first make sure the program hasn't got an open dialog box that you can't see. When you're working with multiple programs, you can easily get an open dialog box stuck behind another open window. If the dialog box is application modal, it prevents you from doing anything else in the program until you dismiss it. (Dialog boxes can also be *system modal*, in which case they prevent you from doing anything else on your computer until you deal with them.)

Minimize all other open windows and see if the dialog box appears. If not, you'll probably have the program that's not responding still displayed on your screen, probably with only some parts of the window correctly drawn. For example, the areas of the program that were covered by other programs or windows typically won't be redrawn (or not redrawn correctly).

"NOT RESPONDING" STATUS ISN'T ALWAYS TERMINAL

When you see a program listed as having Not Responding status in the Programs tab of Task Manager, you may be tempted to kill it off right away. But you'd do better to stay your hand for a minute or two. Why? Because Not Responding status doesn't necessarily mean that a program has hung or crashed:

- First, Not Responding may mean nothing more than that program is responding more slowly than Windows expects; if you give it a few seconds, or perhaps a few minutes, it may start responding normally again. If your computer seems unresponsive overall, back off, and give it a few minutes to sort itself out.
- Second (and often related to the first point), Not Responding may mean that Windows is struggling to allocate enough memory to the program; this often causes the program to run slowly. Task Manager is a little harsh in this respect—it's Windows' fault that the program isn't responding, but Task Manager points the finger at the program.
- Third, VBA-enabled programs (for example, Microsoft Word and Microsoft PowerPoint) are often listed as Not Responding when they're running a VBA routine or macro. In this case, Not Responding means only that VBA temporarily has control over the program. When VBA releases control of the program—in other words, when the routine ends—Task Manager lists the program as Responding again. (If the program shouldn't be running a macro, try pressing Ctrl+Break to stop it.)

TIP To quickly minimize all open windows, click the Show Desktop button on the Quick Launch toolbar (if present) or right-click an empty area of the Taskbar and choose Minimize All Windows from the shortcut menu.

Next, try using Alt+Tab to switch to the program and bring it out from behind any dialog box that's hiding it. Chances are that this won't work either, but it's worth a try. If the dialog box appears, deal with it as usual, and the program should come back to life.

If that didn't work, try using Task Manager to switch to the program:

1. Right-click an empty area of the Taskbar and choose Task Manager from the shortcut menu. Windows displays Task Manager. Or, if you can't get to the Taskbar, press Ctrl+Alt+Delete and then click the Task Manager button.
2. If the Applications tab isn't displayed, click it. The Applications tab (shown in Figure 6.11) lists each running program and its status. The status can be either Running (all is well with the program, as far as Windows is concerned) or Not Responding (Windows believes that the program isn't responding to conventional stimuli).
3. Select the program that's not responding.
4. Click the Switch To button. Task Manager attempts to switch to it, and minimizes itself in the process.

If that didn't work either, it's probably time to kill the program. Take the following steps:

1. Restore Task Manager by clicking its button on the Taskbar.
2. Decide whether the program has hung or crashed. (See the nearby sidebar "'Not Responding' Status Isn't Always Terminal" for advice on determining whether the program is still viable.)

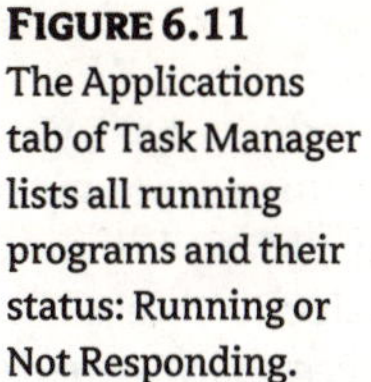

FIGURE 6.11
The Applications tab of Task Manager lists all running programs and their status: Running or Not Responding.

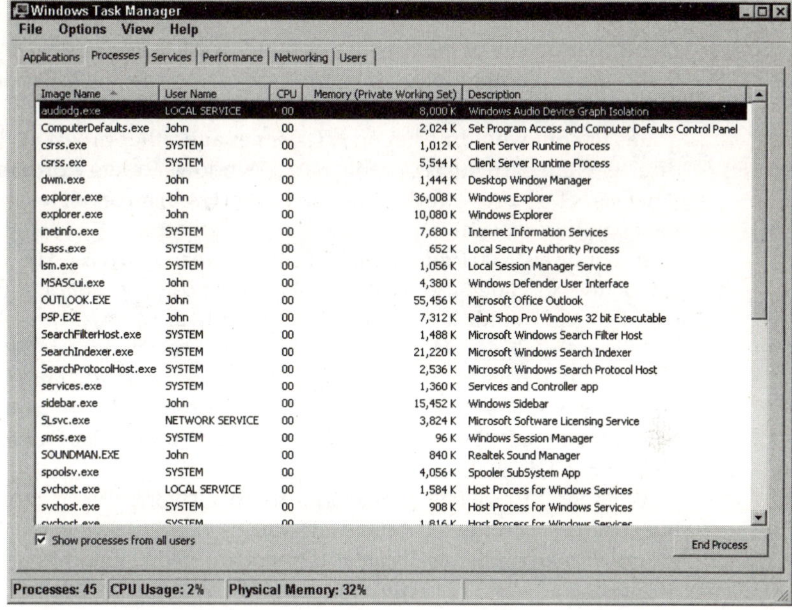

3. Select the task in the Task list.
4. Click the End Task button. Windows displays the End Program dialog box.
5. Click the End Now button. Windows terminates the program and frees up the memory it contained, at least in most cases. Sometimes, Windows won't be able to recover all of the resources that an application uses due to errors in the way that the application handles memory.

NOTE Vista may require several seconds to end the task. During this time, Vista is going to be less responsive than normal. Don't get frustrated. Vista will eventually return control to you. In some cases, you might find that the system is unstable after you end an application. Rebooting the system is always the best approach to take when you think there is any instability to overcome.

If killing the program like this doesn't work, you have several options. Here they are, in descending order of preference:

- Close all other programs that are responding. Then log off Windows. Doing this should shut down any programs you're running.
- If you can't close the program and can't log off Windows, but Task Manager is still working (apart from not being able to kill the program), use Task Manager to switch to another user, then log off the user session with the crashed program.
- At this point, you're pretty much out of options. Reach for the Reset button on your computer. When Windows restarts, check the disk for errors. (See Chapter 29.)

Program Compatibility Issues

If you've used any of the versions of Windows NT, or if you've used Windows 2000, you'll know that program compatibility has been a major issue for the NT code base. In order to make NT stable and crash proof, the designers made heavy sacrifices in compatibility. Many Windows 9*x* programs flat out wouldn't run on NT. Games and other programs that tried to access hardware directly were particularly problematic: Windows 9*x* lets a program access hardware directly, whereas NT's Hardware Abstraction Layer (HAL) forces all hardware requests to be brokered by the operating system.

In Windows 2000 Professional, Microsoft greatly increased the number of programs that would run on the NT code base—but some Windows 9*x* programs still wouldn't run, and many DOS-based games wouldn't run either. Direct hardware access was still a problem, because HAL was still there. Briefly, if the program could run in protected mode, letting HAL handle the communications with the hardware, it would usually run, although it might run a bit more slowly than on other versions of Windows (or on DOS). If the program insisted on trying to communicate with the hardware directly, HAL gave it grief. (Fill in your own *2001* joke here: "I'm sorry, Doom, I'm afraid I can't do that," and so on.)

Windows XP probably provides the best of all worlds when it comes to application compatibility, but at the cost of some reliability and security. Windows XP is able to run most 32-bit Windows programs without problems. It can also run many 16-bit Windows programs (unless you're using the 64-bit version). And it can run a number of DOS programs. Most of this happens transparently: You install the program by running its setup routine or installation routine as usual; you run the program as usual; and that's that. Behind the scenes, Windows XP provides more flexibility in providing the program with the type of environment it needs. On the surface, all is serene.

Vista adds some new wrinkles. Microsoft was far less concerned about compatibility and far more concerned about both security and reliability in Vista. Consequently, application compatibility has taken a giant leap backward in Vista. You're going to find that some of those old applications simply aren't going to run in Vista, ever, and there's nothing you can do about it.

Fortunately, you aren't powerless to get that old application running. Vista's Compatibility Mode can fool the program into thinking that it's running on the version of Windows that it expects. Vista then mimics the environment of that version of Windows for that program, sustaining the illusion that things are to the program's liking. For example, if a program expects Windows 95 and won't run without it, Compatibility Mode tells the program that it's running on Windows 95 and tries to prevent it from finding out the truth. Usually the program then runs fine, although you may notice some loss of performance as Vista soft-soaps the program to keep it happy.

NOTE If you're familiar with the Mac, you might be wondering how Vista's Compatibility Mode compares with Mac OS X and its Classic technology for running programs that won't run on OS X. Basically, there are similarities between Compatibility Mode and Classic, but Compatibility Mode is both less gruesome conceptually and far lighter on the memory. Classic essentially loads a hefty chunk of System 9.1 (on top of OS X, which isn't exactly svelte itself) and uses it to run the program, whereas Vista essentially dupes the program into a false sense of security by giving it the cues it expects. This duping requires a bit more memory and system resources, but nothing like the overhead that the Mac needs to run a program in Classic mode. But then Vista is less of a drastic change from its predecessors than OS X, which is essentially mutated Unix with a GUI interface.

Once you've set up Compatibility Mode for a program, that program runs in Compatibility Mode each time, so you shouldn't need to tweak it any further unless some of its features misbehave. (However, you might need to enable Compatibility Mode for the application's Setup program and then again for its executable after it's installed.)

Compatibility Mode is very impressive, and it's great when it works. But some ancient programs (particularly DOS programs) may never work, even with Compatibility Mode. In these cases, your choices of course of action are approximately (a) give up on the program, (b) dual-boot your system with the version of Windows with which the program was last known to work, or (c) use emulation software such as VMware to run on top of Vista. Create a session of the version of Windows with which the program works.

Programs You Shouldn't Even *Try* to Run on Vista

No matter how impressive Vista's compatibility with programs designed for earlier versions of Windows (or for DOS), there are some types of programs you should never try to run on Vista. These include the following:

Operating systems Obviously, you can't install DOS, an earlier version of Windows, or another operating system or operating environment on top of Vista—at least, not without using some kind of PC-emulation software (such as VMware). If you need to run something from a DOS-like command prompt, open a command prompt window from within Windows (choose Run from the Start menu and type **`cmd`**.)

Old antivirus programs Antivirus programs designed for previous versions of Windows, including Windows 2000 Professional, don't know how to deal with Vista. You may be able to update the program. More likely, you'll need to get a whole new version.

WARNING Attempting to install some of these antivirus programs may crash your Vista computer.

Old troubleshooting and cleanup utilities Most troubleshooting and cleanup utilities designed for earlier versions of Windows will give Vista nothing but grief. So will disk utilities (for example, Norton Utilities) designed for earlier versions. As with the antivirus programs, these utilities don't know how Vista works—in fact, most of them assume that Windows works in a completely different way. So, despite Vista's ability to restore your system after bad software goes on the rampage, it's a mistake to let old troubleshooting and cleanup utilities loose on your system in the first place. Where you still need the added functionality to supplement Vista's capabilities, invest in a new utility specifically designed for Vista.

Some potential offenders are smart enough to figure out the problem and quit on their own. When an application determines that it won't be able to install on Vista, it displays an error message. Figure 6.12 shows a typical example for the Adobe Acrobat Reader.

FIGURE 6.12 This old version of Adobe Acrobat Reader is smart enough to refuse to be installed on Vista.

16-Bit Programs and 32-Bit Programs

Okay, time-out. What *is* a 16-bit program, and what's a 32-bit program? Where does the number of bits come from, and what does it mean?

A layperson's answer to the first question might be that 16-bit programs are programs designed to run on 16-bit versions of Windows (for example, Windows 3.1) and 32-bit programs are programs designed to run on 32-bit versions of Windows (Windows 9*x*, Windows NT, Windows 2000, Windows XP, and Vista).

Actually, it's not quite that simple. To get a fraction more technical, 16-bit programs are written to the Win16 application programming interface (API) and 32-bit programs are written to the Win32 API. The APIs are sets of rules that tell programmers how they can access the functionality that an operating system exposes to them and how a program should behave so that it gets along with the operating system and other programs running on it.

Normally, 32-bit programs *are* written for 32-bit operating systems, and 16-bit programs *are* (or, you might hope, *were*) written for 16-bit operating systems (which have largely gone the way of the dodo). But by using the Win32's extensions—a 32-bit operating system extension that sat on top of the 16-bit Windows 3.1 operating environment (which in turn sat on top of the 16-bit DOS operating system)—you could run a 32-bit program on Windows 3.1. So some 32-bit programs were written for a 16-bit operating system. (Well, sort of.) And because 32-bit operating systems can normally run 16-bit programs, many 16-bit programs are used to this day, running more or less happily in virtual machines on 32-bit operating systems.

The 32-bit operating system may have to perform a process called *thunking*, essentially gearing down to run a 16-bit program. Thunking typically involves some overhead and a slight loss of performance. But if the 16-bit program ran at an acceptable speed on Windows 3.1 with, say, a 486 processor, it should run at a decent speed on even a modest Celeron or Duron processor, even with any thunking needed.

Just as 32 valves are better than 16 (for making a satisfactory engine growl if not for reaching the speed limit ahead of that pickup in the next lane at the traffic signal), 32 bits are better than 16. The advantage of 32 bits is that you can move more information at once—*much* more information. Thirty-two bits can represent a range of more than 4 billion integer values (4,294,967,296, to be precise), whereas 16 bits can represent only 65,536 integer values. Sixty-four bits can represent correspondingly more than 32 bits, and 64-bit PC operating systems are on their way. In fact, Vista Professional and Windows 2003 Server both have 64-bit versions for the 64-bit Itanium processor from Intel.

That still hasn't answered the second question: Where does the number of bits come from, and what does it mean? The *bit-ness* of a program essentially comes from the word size of the computer it's running on. The *word size* is the biggest number that the computer can handle in one operation. Those fire-breathing speed demons of the mid 1980s, 286 systems, used a 16-bit word size, enabling them to handle much more data at once than the (exhaust-breathing) 8-bit systems that preceded them. Then, 386 systems upped the ante to a 32-bit word size, at which it stayed for several generations of chips: even Pentium IV and Athlon systems use 32-bit words. The Itanium processor has a 64-bit word size, enabling it to handle impressively large chunks of data in a single operation.

When you're installing programs on Vista, you seldom need to worry about how many bits they're going to use, because Vista handles any necessary transitions between 32-bit and 16-bit code seamlessly. You *do* sometimes have to worry about *where* you install older programs so that all users of the computer can use them—but more on this a little later in this chapter.

Running Programs in Compatibility Mode

Compatibility Mode lets you tell Vista to emulate Windows 95, Windows 98, Windows NT 4, Windows 2000, or Window XP so that a program thinks it's running on the operating system it knows and likes. It's important to note that the emulation specifies a certain operating system configuration. For example, the Windows NT emulation is for Service Pack (SP) 5 and the Windows XP emulation is for SP2. In some cases, the addition of an SP makes the emulation less than ideal.

TIP Often you'll need to run the program's setup utility in Compatibility Mode. Then run the program itself in Compatibility Mode after installation.

Vista comes with the Microsoft AppCompat database of compatibility problems known about programs. AppCompat is automatically updated by Windows Update, which gives you another incentive to accept Windows Update's offers to download every update available—at least until your computer's hardware and all your software are working as perfectly as you could wish.

NOTE You can set Compatibility Mode only on files on local drives. You can't set Compatibility Mode on a program located on a network drive, on a CD drive or other removable drive, or on a floppy drive. But you can create a shortcut on a local drive to a program located elsewhere, and then specify Compatibility Mode for the shortcut.

Windows provides two ways of setting up a program to run in Compatibility Mode. The first way is formal and cumbersome, but it lets you test whether the Compatibility Mode you chose works for the program. The second way is much quicker, but you run the risk of getting a program comprehensively hung if Compatibility Mode doesn't work.

The Formal Way of Setting Compatibility Mode

Here's the formal way to run a program in Compatibility Mode:

1. Choose Start ➤ Help and Support. You see Windows Help and Support.
2. Click the Get Your Programs to Work on This Version of Windows link. Windows Help and Support opens the Make Older Programs Run in This Version of Windows help topic.
3. Click the Click to Open the Program Compatibility Wizard link. Windows displays a Help and Support Center window and starts the Program Compatibility Wizard in it.
4. Read the information and cautions on the Welcome to the Program Compatibility Wizard screen and click the Next button. Windows displays the How Do You Want to Locate the Program That You Would Like to Run with Compatibility Settings? screen (shown in Figure 6.13).
5. Use one of the following three ways to locate the program:
   - To set Compatibility Mode for a program that's already installed, select the I Want to Choose from a List of Programs option button and click the Next button. The wizard scans your hard drive and displays a list of programs (Figure 6.14 shows an example). Select the program and click the Next button.

- To set Compatibility Mode for a program you're installing from CD, insert the CD, select the I Want to Use the Program in the CD-ROM Drive option button, and click the Next button.
- To set Compatibility Mode for a program that isn't installed and whose installation medium isn't on CD, or if you're just feeling ornery, select the I Want to Locate the Program Manually option button and click the Next button. The wizard displays the Which Program Do You Want to Run with Compatibility Settings? screen. Enter the path in the text box, either by typing or by clicking the Browse button and using the resulting Please Select Application dialog box (a common Open dialog box) to select the program. Click the Next button.

  The wizard displays the Select a Compatibility Mode for the Program screen (shown in Figure 6.15).

6. Select the option button for the operating system you think the program needs: Windows 95, Windows NT 4 (Service Pack 5), Windows 98/Windows Me, Windows 2000, or Windows XP (Service Pack 2). Often, the application will tell you what it needs to run, as shown in Figure 6.12.
7. Click the Next button. The wizard displays the Select Display Settings for the Program screen (shown in Figure 6.16).

   If you know the program needs display limitations, select the appropriate options.For most programs, you don't need to select any of these display limitations. However, many older educational programs do require special screen setups.

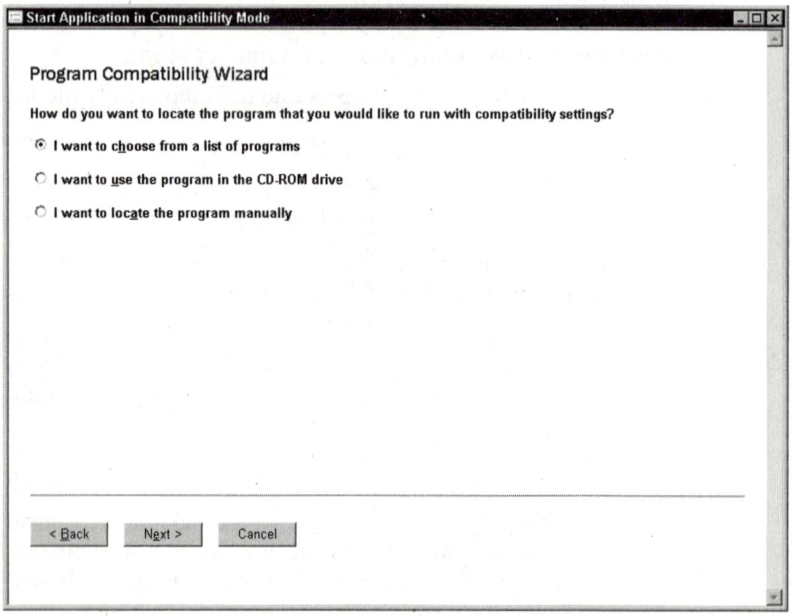

FIGURE 6.13 Choose how to select the program you want to run in Compatibility Mode.

Start Application in Compatibility Mode
Program Compatibility Wizard
Which program do you want to run with compatibility settings?
Select a program:
Program Name
Folder
Settings
Adobe Reader 7.0
Programs
Microsoft Office Access 2007 (Beta)
Microsoft Office
Microsoft Office Excel 2007 (Beta)
Microsoft Office
Microsoft Office Outlook 2007 (Beta)
Microsoft Office
Microsoft Office PowerPoint 2007 (Beta)
Microsoft Office
Microsoft Clip Organizer
Microsoft Office Tools
Microsoft Office Diagnostics
Microsoft Office Tools
Microsoft Office Picture Manager
Microsoft Office Tools
Microsoft Office Word 2007 (Beta)
Microsoft Office
Adobe Reader Speed Launch
Startup
winsize
Startup
Uninstall WinZip
WinZip
WinZip 9.0
WinZip
Refresh
< Back
Next >
Cancel

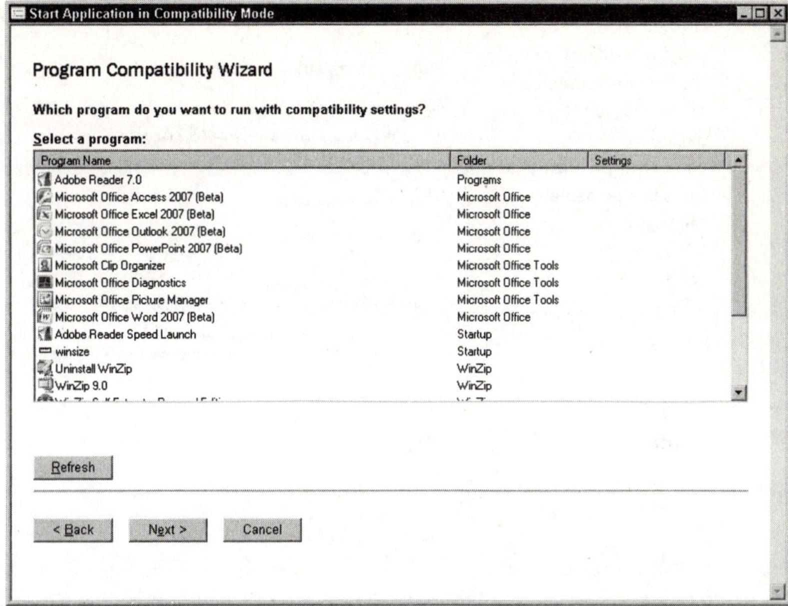

FIGURE 6.14
Select a program from the list that the Program Compatibility Wizard assembles.

Start Application in Compatibility Mode
Program Compatibility Wizard
Select a compatibility mode for the program
Choose the operating system that is recommended for this program, or that previously supported the program correctly:
Microsoft Windows 95
Microsoft Windows NT 4.0 (Service Pack 5)
Microsoft Windows 98 / Windows Me
Microsoft Windows 2000
Microsoft Windows XP (Service Pack 2)
Do not apply a compatibility mode
< Back
Next >
Cancel

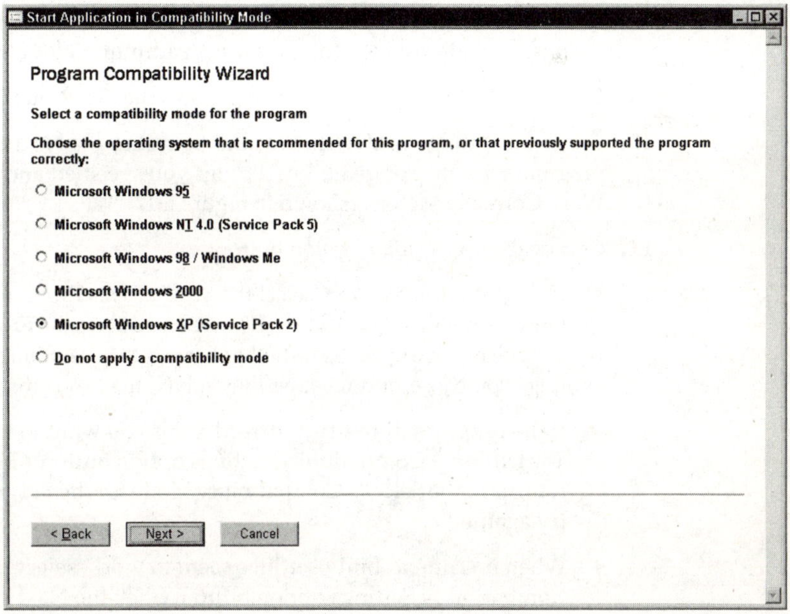

FIGURE 6.15
On the Select a Compatibility Mode for the Program screen of the Program Compatibility Wizard, select the Compatibility Mode you want to use.

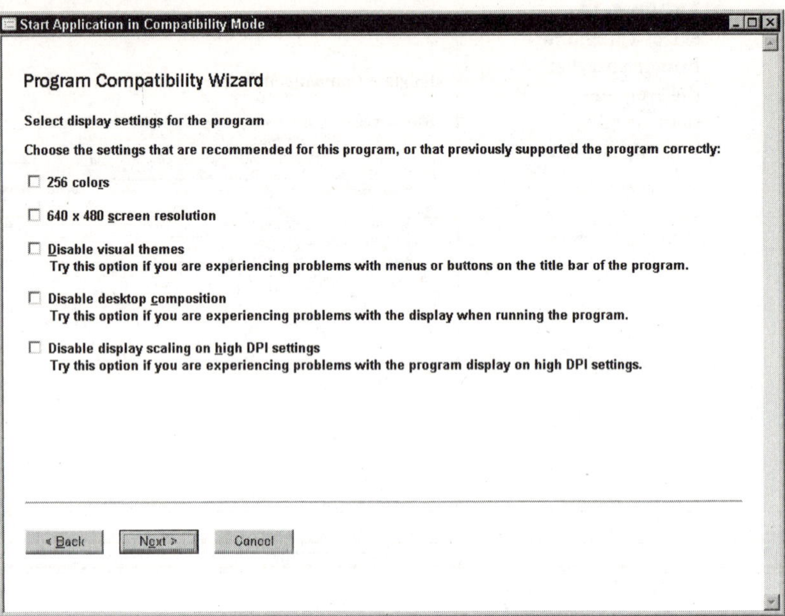

FIGURE 6.16 On the Select Display Settings for the Program screen of the Program Compatibility Wizard, you can apply limitations to the display settings used for the program.

8. Click the Next Button. The wizard asks whether you need to run the application as an administrator. Older applications that store data in nondefault locations or make Registry changes will almost certainly require an administrator account.
9. Click the Next button. The wizard displays the Test Your Compatibility Settings screen.
10. Check the settings you've chosen, and then click the Next button. The wizard launches the program with the compatibility settings you specified and displays the Did the Program Work Correctly? screen (shown in Figure 6.17).
11. Choose the appropriate option button:
    - If the program ran okay, select the Yes, Set This Program to Always Use These Compatibility Settings option button. The wizard displays the Program Compatibility Data screen, on which you can choose whether to send Microsoft information on the program, the settings you chose, and whether they solved the problem.
    - If the program didn't run correctly, but you want to try other settings, select the No, Try Different Compatibility Settings option button. Click the Next button. The wizard returns to the Select a Compatibility Mode for the Program screen. Return to step 7 and try again.
    - When no compatibility settings seem to work, select the No, I Am Finished Trying Compatibility Settings option button. Click the Next button. The wizard displays the Program Compatibility Data screen (discussed previously). In this case, you have more incentive for sending Microsoft information, as it may help them fix the problem with this program in the future.

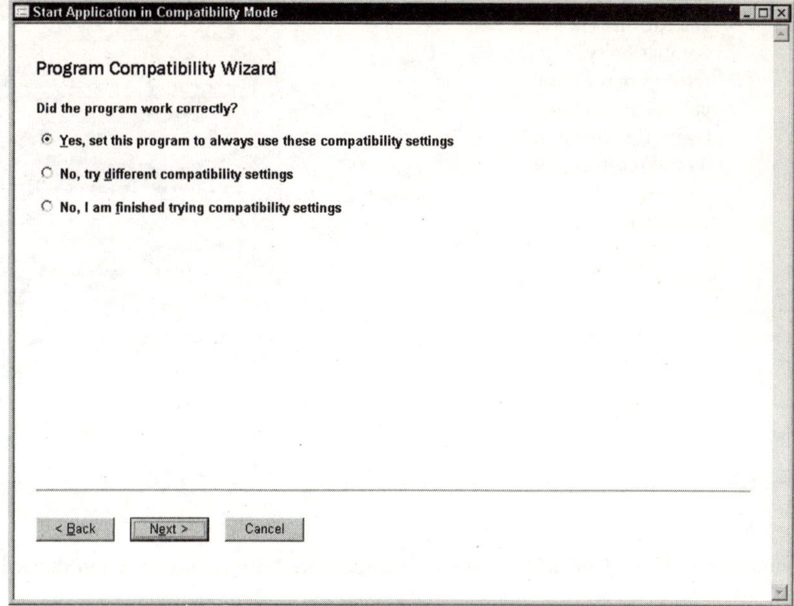

FIGURE 6.17
On the Did the Program Work Correctly? screen, tell the Program Compatibility Wizard whether the program launched correctly with the computer settings.

12. Choose the Yes button or the No button as appropriate.
13. Click the Next button. If you chose the Yes button, the wizard sends the compatibility data. Either way, it displays the Completing the Program Compatibility Wizard screen.
14. Click the Finish button. The wizard closes itself.

THE QUICK WAY OF SETTING COMPATIBILITY MODE

The quick way of setting Compatibility Mode is as follows:

1. Right-click the shortcut for the program and select Properties from the shortcut menu. Windows displays the Properties dialog box for the shortcut.
2. Click the Compatibility tab, which is shown in Figure 6.18.
3. Determine whether you want to create settings just for yourself or for all users of the machine. If you want to set up the application for use by everyone, click Show Settings for All Users and you'll see a second, Compatibility for All Users, dialog box that looks precisely like the one in Figure 6.18.
4. Select the Run This Program in Compatibility Mode For check box if it's not already selected.
5. In the drop-down list, select the mode you want to use.
6. In the Display Settings section, select the Run in 256 Colors check box, the Run in 640 × 480 Screen Resolution check box, or the Disable Visual Themes check box as necessary. (Again, for most programs, you won't need to set these options.)

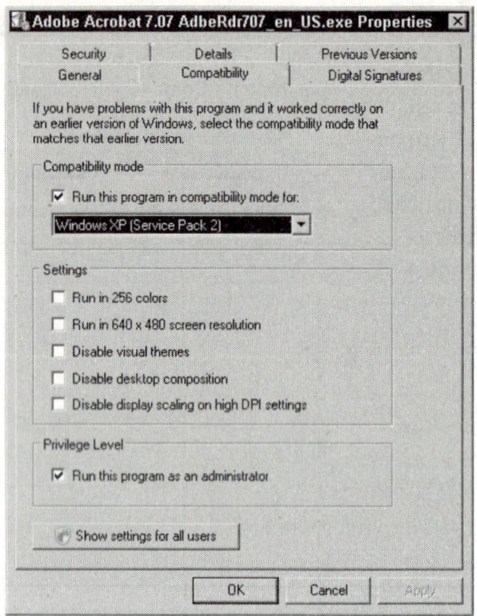

FIGURE 6.18 You can also choose Compatibility Mode settings in the Compatibility tab of the Properties dialog box for the shortcut.

7. Check Run This Program as an Administrator when the application requires administrator credentials.

8. Click the OK button. Windows applies your choice and closes the Properties dialog box.

This method of specifying Compatibility Mode settings has the advantage that you can specify different Compatibility Mode settings for different shortcuts for the same program or even for the shortcuts to different documents of the same file type.

TIP If you want to use Compatibility Mode for a shortcut that points directly to a file on CD or DVD drive, you won't be able to access the Compatibility tab for the shortcut while there's a disc in the drive. Remove it, and then open the properties for the shortcut. Then you can replace the disc in the drive before you run the program to test the settings.

Exchanging Data between Programs

Ever since the early versions of Windows, one of its great advantages has been its ability to transfer data between programs via its Clipboard.

The Clipboard can transfer data of different types that wouldn't normally be compatible with one another. For example, suppose you are writing a letter in a simple word processor such as WordPad that doesn't support the import of very many types of graphics. You have a graphic in some odd format that you want to include; it will open in a Windows-based drawing program, but not in WordPad. You can copy the graphic to the Clipboard in the drawing program, and then paste it into WordPad, bypassing the whole import/export hassle entirely.

But wait—there's more. In addition to the simple copy (or cut) and paste of the Clipboard, you can also maintain links between the original material and the copy. That's object linking and embedding (OLE).

NOTE The Clipbook Viewer application that came with previous versions of Windows appears to be missing in Vista. However, Vista does come with the new Snipping Tool, which is an incredibly easy way to grab anything from anywhere you need it.

Clipboard Basics

You're probably already familiar with basic Clipboard operation. Almost all Windows programs have an Edit menu containing commands for Cut, Copy, and Paste. These commands place and retrieve things on the Clipboard. There may be several shortcuts for these commands, depending on the program. Here are the most common ones:

- Cut: Ctrl+X or the Cut button on the toolbar
- Copy: Ctrl+C or the Copy button
- Paste: Ctrl+V or the Paste button

These common Ctrl key combinations can be used anywhere you can highlight an object, which makes it possible to copy and paste information from dialog boxes and other sources of information that don't normally have the Cut, Copy, and Paste commands.

The Clipboard isn't designed to be permanent storage. It holds only one clip at a time, so when you cut or copy something else, whatever was there before is erased. (In Microsoft Office 2000 or Office XP you have an expanded Clipboard available, which is discussed in the next section.) If you want to store something from the Clipboard for later use, check out the Clipboard Viewer, discussed later in this chapter.

TIP You can capture all or part of a screen image to the Clipboard, and then paste it into a graphics program such as Paint to save it. To do so, press Shift+Print Screen for the entire screen or Alt+Print Screen for the active window.

Using the Snipping Tool

Many of the existing ways of capturing information on screen are inconvenient. For example, you have to remember the arcane Ctrl key combinations to capture text from many dialog boxes, assuming the dialog box lets you grab the text at all. Even when you can grab the information, the clipboard limits you to a single object, such as text or a graphic. Vista comes with a new feature called the Snipping Tool, which is very adept at capturing whatever you want. You can start this application by choosing Start ➤ All Programs ➤ Accessories ➤ Snipping Tool. The first time you start the Snipping Tool, it asks whether you want to place an icon for it in the Quick Launch area of the Taskbar.

The Snipping Tool is very easy to use. All you do is draw a rectangle or other shape around the area you want to capture. It doesn't matter what that area contains, the Snipping Tool will capture it. All snips appear as graphics, so you wouldn't use this tool to grab text that you want to edit later. When you start the Snipping Tool, you see a small toolbar like the one shown in Figure 6.19.

The default setting creates a rectangular snip. Click the down arrow next to New and you'll see the other snipping choices. Here's a list of the snipping options that the Snipping Tool supports:

Free-form Lets you draw an irregular snip around any shape on screen.

Rectangular Creates a rectangular snip where the sides are all straight and even.

Window Captures the window that you point to with the mouse.

Full Screen Captures the entire display area.

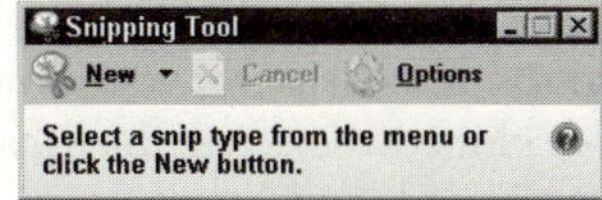

FIGURE 6.19
The Snipping Tool provides a simple interface for capturing a part of the display.

After you capture a snip, the Snipping Tool displays it in an editor as shown in Figure 6.20. You can use the pens and highlighter to augment the information presented by the clip. If you make a mistake, you can remove it using the Eraser tool. Use the Send Snip command to send the snip to someone else. You can also use the Save command to save the snip for later use.

The Snipping Tool also offers a number of configuration options that you access using the Tool ➤ Options command. Figure 6.21 shows the Snipping Tool Options dialog box. You can tell the Snipping Tool to perform tasks such as automatically saving any snips you create to the clipboard. You can also control the selection ink (the rectangle or other shape around the snip) or decide not to include it at all. If you decide later that you really don't want the Snipping Tool in the Quick Launch toolbar, you can clear the Display Icon in the Quick Launch Toolbar option.

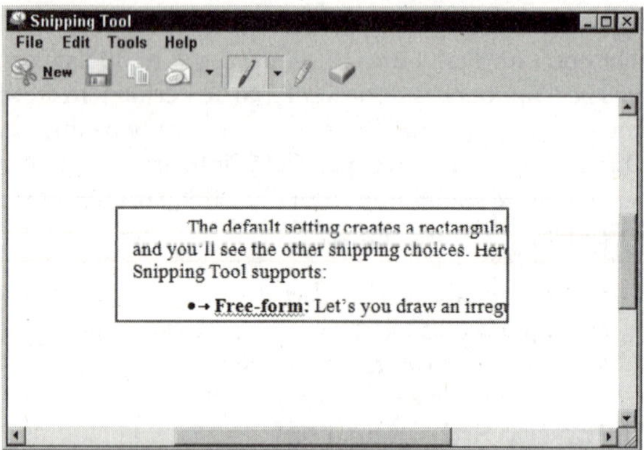

FIGURE 6.20 After you capture a snip, embellish it to meet your needs.

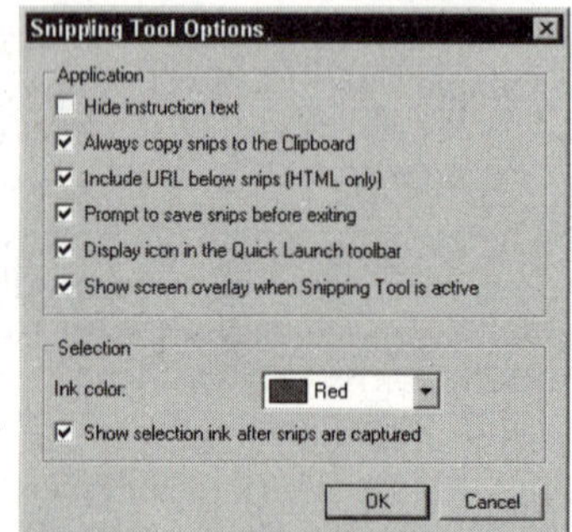

FIGURE 6.21 Change how the Snipping Tool works using the Snipping Tool Options dialog box.

Organizing the Start Menu

In Chapter 4, you learned about customizing the way the Start menu works in general; you can also customize it by selecting which shortcuts appear on it and in what positions. The Vista Start menu has several sections containing program shortcuts, pointed out in Figure 6.22:

- The pinned shortcuts area, at top left, shows Internet and E-mail shortcuts by default. You can add shortcuts here for whatever programs you like as well. Only the Vista Start menu provides pinned shortcuts; the Classic Start menu doesn't provide this feature.

- The frequently used programs list, at bottom left, contains shortcuts for the programs you use most often or have used most recently. This list is managed automatically by Windows; you can't edit it manually.
- The All Programs menu, accessible when you click All Programs, lists folders and shortcuts for all installed programs. You can add and remove shortcuts from here freely, as well as create and remove folders and rearrange items. (The All Programs menu replaces the pinned shortcuts area and the frequently used programs list on the left side of the display.)

FIGURE 6.22
Shortcuts appear on the Start menu in several places.

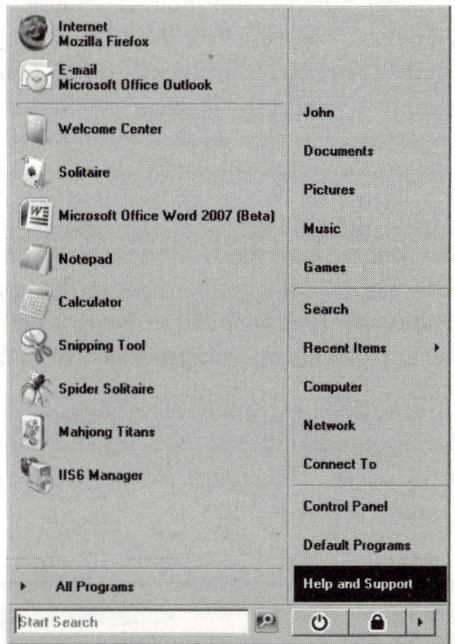

Editing Pinned Shortcuts

Vista makes it considerably easier to add pinned shortcuts to the Start menu. Simply right-click the application and choose Pin to Start Menu from the context menu. Vista will place the shortcut in the pinned area. Likewise, when you decide that you no longer want the shortcut in the pinned area, right-click it and choose Unpin from the Start Menu from the context menu. Moving applications back and forth is quite easy and you should pin and unpin applications as needed until you create an optimal Start menu setup.

Adding Programs to the Quick Launch Toolbar

You can also add applications to the Quick Launch toolbar as long as you're using the Vista Start menu (the Classic Start menu doesn't include this feature for whatever odd reason). Right-click the application you want to add to the Quick Launch toolbar and choose Add to Quick Launch from the context menu. If you decide later that you really don't want the application in the Quick Launch toolbar, right-click its icon and choose Delete from the context menu. Don't worry; removing the icon from the Quick Launch toolbar won't remove it from other locations.

Editing the All Programs List

The All Programs list is really just a set of folders nested within one another, so you can edit the structure of the All Programs menu by adding, moving, or deleting shortcuts and folders within it. For easy access to it, right-click the Start button and choose Open for a Computer-like Window, or Explore for a Windows Explorer-like Window. Then work with it as you would any other file-management window. Likewise, if you want to change settings for all of the users on the machine, right-click the Start button and choose Open All Users from the context menu.

One quirk with Vista is that the Start menu structure for all users of the PC is stored separately from that for the current user. When the Start menu actually displays, the two are combined into one Start menu, but you edit them separately. This enables any user to customize the Start menu, even if they don't have the needed permissions to change the settings for the PC as a whole. When you right-click the Start button and choose Open or Explore, you get the version for the current user. If you want to edit the version for all users, right-click and choose Open All Users or Explore All Users instead. Figure 6.23 shows the Programs menu for All Users being explored.

NOTE If you are new to file management, you may want to refer to Chapter 8 for some help.

Another way to edit the All Programs menu is to use drag-and-drop. This method has several advantages. For one, it's quicker. For another, it works with the Start menu structure as an integrated whole, so you don't need to worry whether the shortcut you want to work with is part of the current user or All Users configuration. With drag-and-drop, you can:

- Drag a shortcut from the Desktop or a file-management window into the menu system. To do so, drag it to the Start menu and pause, holding the mouse button down, until the Start menu opens. Then pause on All Programs; then continue your way through until the desired location is displayed.

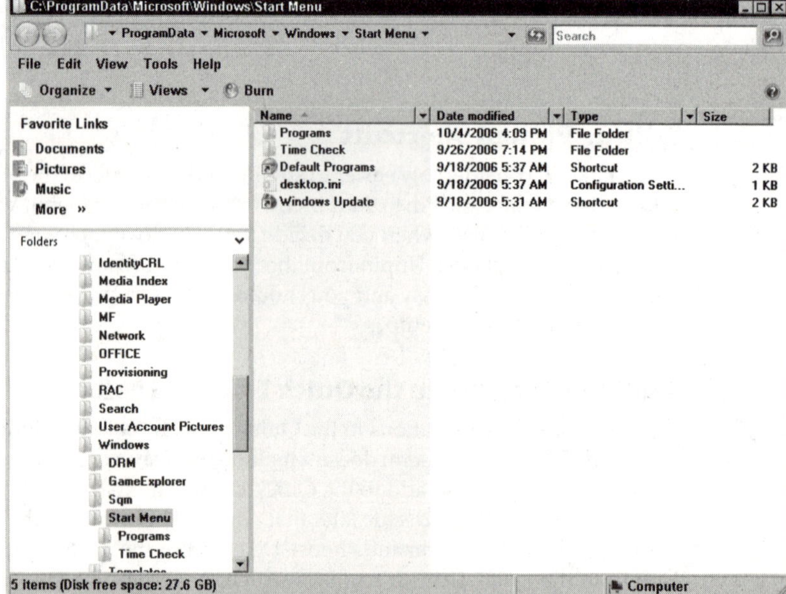

FIGURE 6.23
The contents of the All Programs menu for All Users in Windows Explorer.

- Drag an item from one folder to another on the menu. To make a folder open, drag the item to it and pause, still holding the mouse button down; the folder will open after a few seconds.
- Delete an item from the menu by right-clicking it and choosing Delete.

Summary

This chapter has discussed how to install programs, how to run them—using Compatibility Mode if necessary—and how to remove them when you tire of them. It's also touched on the types of programs you shouldn't even try to install on Vista, and it's shown you how to use Task Manager to kill a program that's crashed. Finally, you learned how to exchange data between programs and how to edit the Start menu's content.

Of course, all of these management tasks are essential for using Vista efficiently. The sad thing is that many people will never change their Start menu or learn to work with applications that are cranky under Vista. Changing your environment so that it suits your specific needs pays large dividends in enhanced productivity. When you know where to find something on your computer and feel comfortable with the layout, you can accomplish tasks significantly faster. So, the best thing you can do after reviewing this chapter is play with your Start menu and then work on those applications you can't get to run.

Chapter 7 examines how to use Vista on a notebook or other portable computer. It seems anymore that these smaller than desktop devices have so many names, it's hard to track what's what. If you have something other than a desktop machine, you'll definitely want to check out the usage tips in Chapter 7. Even if you have a desktop machine, you might find a good tip or two on performing tasks faster. For example, some people use the Briefcase effectively even with a desktop machine—think portable files.

Chapter 7

Using Vista on Notebook PCs

Vista includes many features designed to make life easier for notebook PC users. Some of these features work on all PCs but are especially applicable to portables; other features don't even appear when you install Vista on a desktop PC. In this chapter, we'll look at some Windows features that people who own notebook computers can use to make their computing experience more trouble-free.

- How notebook PCs are physically different
- Using built-in and external monitors
- Working with PC cards
- Using the Windows Mobility Center
- Working with Tablet PCs
- Working with hardware profiles
- Monitoring and optimizing battery usage
- Establishing dial-up connections from multiple locations
- Synchronizing files with other PCs

Vista: What's New?

The biggest issue for notebook users isn't getting that odd little pointing device to work right or the struggle with the keyboard. Even though these issues are a concern, the biggest problem is one of power. A notebook computer that lasts six hours on battery when you have eight hours' worth of work to do isn't quite making it as an effective tool. The good news for Vista users is that the power options that Vista provides are significantly better than previous versions of Windows and more in tune with what notebook users need. Of course, if you use that fancy interface, then all bets are off. These new power features are only useful when you combine them with other Vista features to truly save power.

Vista provides yet more support for mobile device functionality. It supports more devices and helps you configure those devices with greater ease. For example, the Windows Mobility Center provides a single location where you can find all of the tools you require to manage your mobile device. You'll also find more support for the Tablet PC and you don't even have to purchase a separate version of Vista to get it. The Tablet PC support comes with standard versions of Vista now so everyone can make use of them.

NOTE Many of the Vista notebook features aren't available as part of Vista Home Basic edition. You must have Vista Home Premium or better to obtain many of these features.

You'll also notice that hardware profiles are missing in Vista. Many users relied on hardware profiles in previous versions of Windows to reduce power consumption from devices they didn't really need when disconnected. Vista does an admirable job of reconfiguring the system on the fly, so the need for hardware profiles is reduced. However, the new setup still leaves many people out in the cold because you can no longer control devices individually. For example, many people had a no network setup so they could perform risky tasks on their systems without fear of infection from the Internet. Gamers often turned off nonessential devices to obtain the last bit of processing power from their systems.

Vista also includes the new Restart Manager. Anyone will tell you that stopping and restarting a computer consumes a huge amount of battery power. Restart Manager reduces these battery-killing restarts by only restarting the requisite services and applications after you apply a patch or update. You may still have to restart your computer sometimes, but you'll find that it happens less often, which means that your battery should last a lot longer, even if you apply updates while on the move.

How Notebook PCs Are Physically Different

Besides the obvious of "everything's smaller," notebook PCs have a few important differences from desktop PCs. Here's a quick rundown:

Fn key In addition to the normal keys on a keyboard, most laptops have a key labeled Fn. This is an additional system key, much like Control and Alt. You use it in conjunction with the function keys (F1 through F12) and sometimes with other keys as well to issue special laptop-specific commands. Figure 7.1 shows several function keys on a notebook PC; notice that they have additional writing on them that shows what they do when combined with the Fn key.

FIGURE 7.1 Some function keys have extra functionality when combined with the Fn key. For example, the F7 key here turns down screen brightness.

LCD screens Notebooks have built-in LCD monitors; most can also accept an external monitor through a built-in VGA output jack. An Fn key combination switches between the two monitors when an external one is plugged in.

TIP Near the end of Chapter 9, you'll learn about a Vista feature called ClearType that can make text on an LCD monitor appear sharper. You'll probably want to turn it on for your notebook PC's monitor.

Docking station connector Most notebooks have a connector on the back for plugging into a docking station.

Mouse alternative You can connect an external mouse via USB, PS/2, or serial port, but most notebook PCs have a built-in mouse alternative. One older style of mouse alternative is called a pointing stick. (Toshiba calls theirs an Accupoint.) A newer mouse alternative, found on most laptops sold today, is a touchpad (sometimes called a glidepad).

PC card slots Since laptops don't have expansion slots in the motherboard the way that desktop PCs do, they need a way of accepting expansion cards. The modern standard for this is *CardBus*, which is the 32-bit version of the PC Card specification, also known by its standards organization's name, PCMCIA (Personal Computer Memory Card International Association). Like USB, PC Cards are hot pluggable.

NOTE You might hear the terms *PC Card* and *CardBus* used interchangeably (I even do this myself, out of habit). In this chapter, I use the term PC Card to mean any PC Card, and CardBus to specifically refer to the 32-bit ones.

Battery In addition to using an AC adapter to feed power to your portable computer, you can choose to run your system with an internal battery. The most common substances used in computer battery packs are Nickel Cadmium (NiCad), Nickel Metal Hydride (NiMH), and Lithium Ion (LIon).

These physical features are discussed in more detail later in the chapter, in sections that pertain to them.

Using Built-In and External Monitors

Most notebook PCs have an external VGA graphics port, and you can switch between using it and using the built-in LCD display by pressing the Fn key in combination with one of the function keys. On my Compaq Presario laptop, it's Fn+F3, for example. Pressing that combo toggles between LCD only, external only, and both on at once.

If your notebook supports it, you can also use the DualView feature in Vista to extend the desktop across both monitors. Normally when you enable both monitors at once, both show the same thing, but with DualView, each can show separate content. Most modern display adapters with multiple outputs will support DualView. The biggest problem is ensuring that you have enough video memory to support two monitors from the same display adapter. In addition, you'll need a device driver that works with DualView. Some display adapters only support DualView when you download the latest driver from the vendor.

TIP Given the current state of display adapter technology, most desktop machines that support Vista can also support DualView. This means your desktop machine could have two monitors attached to it, even though you don't have two display adapters.

DualView is almost like the multiple monitors feature you'll learn about in Chapter 9, and except that on a laptop, the primary monitor is always the built-in one; an attached external monitor is always the secondary one.

Not all laptops support the DualView feature. To determine whether yours does, and to try it out if possible, hook up an external monitor to the laptop and enable both displays (with an Fn key combination). They should both show the exact same thing. That part should work even if the video chipset does not support DualView.

Then do the following:

1. Right-click the desktop and choose Personalize, then click the Display Settings link. If your PC supports DualView, there will be two separate monitor icons there. If not, there will be only one.
2. If there are two, click the one for the external monitor, and then click Extend My Windows Desktop onto This Monitor.
3. Click OK. The desktop is now stretched out over both monitors rather than them both showing the same thing.

Working with PC Cards

As mentioned at the beginning of this chapter, notebook PCs use PC Card slots as their primary means of accepting expansion devices. PC Card technology predates USB; today many USB devices are available that take the place of PC Card devices.

PC cards use software known as *socket services* and *card services*. Socket services are similar to device drivers; they handle the interaction between the PC and the card. Card services handle high-level functions and control the transfer of information from the card's memory to the CPU.

Vista handles the interface between all types of PC card devices behind the scenes, resulting in hot-pluggable functionality. You can insert a PC Card device at any time, and Windows will automatically detect it, as you'll see in Chapter 10 when we discuss adding hardware.

When you remove a PC Card from the system, you're supposed to use the Safely Remove Hardware utility to shut it down first. (You'll also learn about this utility in Chapter 10.) However, if you forget and simply remove the card, it'll probably be okay. Using the Safely Remove Hardware feature simply ensures that all the device's activities complete normally rather than being aborted in midstream.

When one or more hot-pluggable devices are attached to the PC, an icon appears in the notification area for them. You can click this icon to see the attached devices, and then click the one you want to choose to shut down for safe removal.

You can also double-click the Safely Remove Hardware icon in the notification area to open a dialog box showing the installed hot-pluggable devices and stop one from there. Simply click Stop to stop the device.

Configuring Your System with Windows Mobility Center

The Windows Mobility Center is more of a central storage area for all of the tools you use with a mobile device, than an actual application. You access features by clicking the Windows Mobility Center link in the Mobile PC applet of the Control Panel. Think of the Windows Mobility Center in the same way that you do the Personalization window—as a means of accessing settings fast. This centralized management utility helps you perform the following mobile device–specific tasks:

Brightness Helps you adjust the brightness of your display quickly, which means that you can compensate for differences between indoor and outdoor ambient light without a lot of extra effort.

Volume Lets you silence your mobile device in meetings, yet have sound when you're working alone.

Battery Status Shows the amount of power left in the battery. You can also choose a power plan for your system.

Wireless Network Shows the status of any wireless network connections to your system. In addition, you can turn your wireless connection off or on.

Screen Rotation Lets you change the orientation of your Tablet PC screen to landscape or portrait. This feature doesn't affect other portable devices.

External Display Helps you connect to an external monitor. You can also adjust the output settings for that monitor.

Sync Center Shows the status of any synchronization between the mobile computer and a desktop system. You can also use this feature to start or stop the synchronization process and to adjust the synchronization settings for your system.

Presentation Settings Helps you configure your system for a presentation. You can adjust the background image, volume, and other display features.

TIP You can also access the Windows Mobility Center by clicking the Battery icon in the notification area and choosing the Windows Mobility Center link. Another alternative is to press WinKey+X.

As you can see from this list, the Windows Mobility Center isn't providing you with any new settings, which begs the question of why you should use it at all. Most people don't have a lot of time to locate settings when they're in the middle of a presentation. By concentrating all of the settings you need in one place, the Windows Mobility Center reduces the usual fumbling about as you try to find something.

The interesting part about Windows Mobility Center is that it consists of individual blocks, as shown in Figure 7.2. Microsoft has designed the Windows Mobility Center to allow for expandability by third-party vendors. Consequently, you might have more blocks than shown in Figure 7.2 in your version of the Windows Mobility Center (consider this the minimum you'll get).

FIGURE 7.2
The Windows Mobility Center provides centralized access to essential notebook functionality.

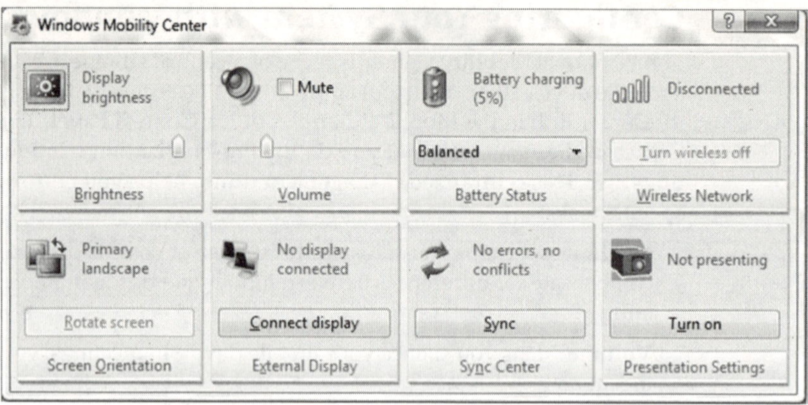

Working with Tablet PCs

At one time, you had to buy a completely separate version of Windows for the Tablet PC. With Vista, the Tablet PC functionality appears as part of the operating system. You can break the Tablet PC functionality down into two areas: configuration and special applications, both of which appear in the following sections.

TIP All of the Tablet PC applications described in this section work fine on your desktop or notebook computer. In fact, you'll probably want to try them out to determine whether they have a place in your daily activities. For example, most people use sticky notes. Vista provides the electronic equivalent in the form of the Sticky Notes application.

Adjusting the Tablet PC Settings

Vista provides specialized settings that make it easier to work with a Tablet PC. For example, you can choose where menus appear and how Vista interprets hand movements. You'll find these settings in the Tablet PC Settings applet of the Control Panel, as shown in Figure 7.3. The General tab includes settings for the handedness of the display as well as an option to calibrate the tablet display so that it recognizes pen movements with greater accuracy.

Depending on how well you write and Vista interprets your writing, you might need to adjust the settings on the Handwriting Recognition tab. The Use the Personalized Recognizer setting creates a personal profile of your handwriting habits, which should improve handwriting recognition. Generally, you want to keep this option enabled unless you notice a significant drag on system performance. You can also determine whether the recognizer should use automatic learning or not. Again, unless you notice a drag in system performance, you should keep this feature enabled. If you disable this feature, Vista deletes any past data, so you'd need to start the learning process over again if you enabled the feature again later.

The Display tab contains settings to adjust the orientation of your display. The Orientation field contains the current display orientation. Most Tablet PCs include buttons you can use to adjust the orientation of the display. The Sequence setting changes the order of orientation changes so that you can reach a desired orientation with greater ease and fewer button presses.

The Other tab includes settings that don't fit anywhere else. The default display contains a link that you can click to adjust your pen and input device settings. Figure 7.4 shows the Pen and Input Devices dialog box that you use to adjust how your input device interacts with Vista.

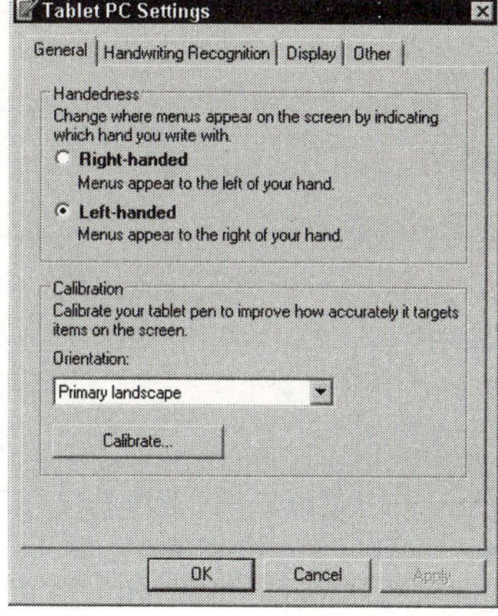

FIGURE 7.3
Set the Tablet PC configuration using the options in this applet.

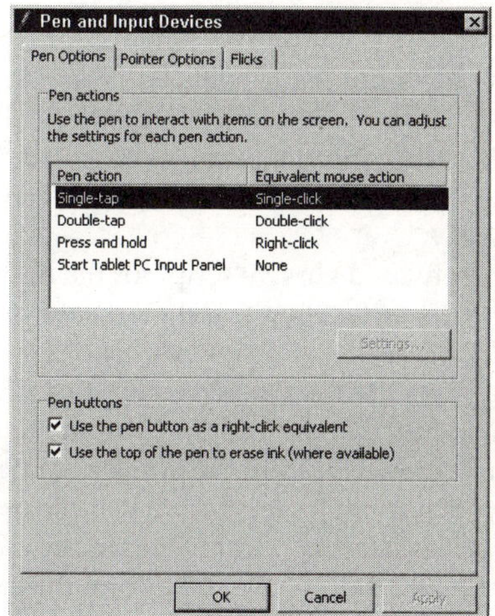

FIGURE 7.4
Use this dialog box to change how Vista interacts with the input devices on your Tablet PC.

Using Sticky Notes

The Sticky Notes application provides the equivalent of the physical sticky notes that are probably tacked on your monitor as I write this. The Sticky Notes application is actually handy for anyone who needs to write a note, so it's something that desktop users should probably consider looking at too. You start the Sticky Notes application using the Start ➢ All Programs ➢ Accessories ➢ Tablet PC ➢ Sticky Notes command. You'll see a dialog box like the one shown in Figure 7.5.

As shown in Figure 7.5, you can write out a note. However, you can also record voice notes by clicking the Record button at the bottom of the display. You can place multiple notes in the same file by clicking New Note. The Previous Note and Next Note buttons on the toolbar let you move between notes as needed.

By default, you have to start Sticky Notes after you start your computer. However, you can tell Sticky Notes to start automatically by choosing the Tools ➢ Options ➢ Open at Startup command. It's also possible to have Sticky Notes always available by choosing the Tools ➢ Options ➢ Always on Top command.

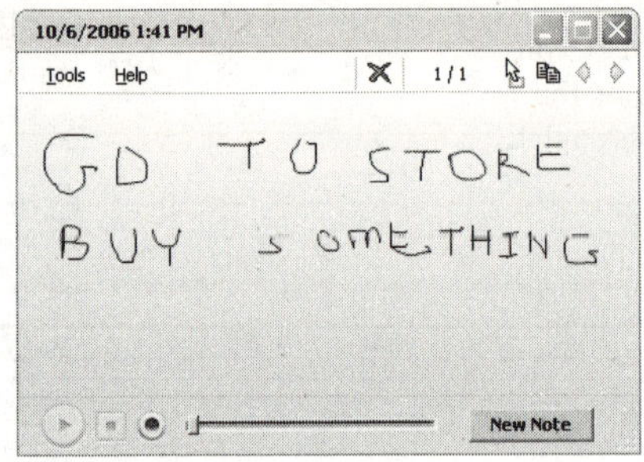

FIGURE 7.5
Use this dialog box to change how Vista interacts with the input devices on your Tablet PC.

You don't have to use Sticky Notes to read the notes you create. In fact, you don't have to display the application at all. Click on the Drag and Drop tool on the toolbar and drag the note to any location you want that can support the notes. For example, when you drop a note into Word, it appears in its original form. Some locations might display the notes as shortcuts. Double-clicking the shortcut opens the note.

Using Tablet PC Input Panel

The Tablet PC Input Panel helps you provide text input to the Tablet PC. You access it using the Start ➤ All Programs ➤ Accessories ➤ Tablet PC ➤ Tablet PC Input Panel command. The program actually has three input modes: Writing Pad, Character Pad, and On-Screen Keyboard. Figure 7.6 shows the Writing Pad mode. You select each of the other modes using the buttons on the top left of the display.

I purposely used cursive script for the figure to show that the Tablet PC Input Panel is good at reading text, even text that you should have had a hard time getting Windows to accept in previous versions. Vista seems to do an excellent job of accepting both printed and cursive text. Of course, you can always use the On-Screen Keyboard mode when all else fails.

If you do find that the Tablet PC Input Panel has significant problems recognizing what you enter, you can always report the problem using the Tools ➤ Report Handwriting Recognition Errors command. What you'll see is a form you can use to describe the problem and send it off to Microsoft. Given how much this application has improved, I'd say there's a good chance your input really will help. Although I didn't have to perform this task, you might also consider using the Tools ➤ Personalize Handwriting Recognition command to display the Handwriting Personalization Wizard where you can teach the application how to recognize your handwriting or clean up specific errors.

At some point, you'll probably see changes you want to make to how the Tablet PC Input Panel works. Use the Tools ➤ Options command to display the Options dialog box shown in Figure 7.7. Most of these options define how the application appears on screen. For example, you can change the position of the Insert button so that it works better with your writing style. You can also choose the kind of ink used for the pen and whether the Tablet PC Input Panel tries to guess the word you're entering automatically after a pause.

NOTE You'll find a few oddities when working with the Tablet PC Input Panel. For example, clicking the Close button doesn't close the application—it hides the application. To close the application, you use the Tools ➤ Exit command. The application also hides when you display any of the supporting dialog boxes. Click the application icon to display the application again. The default icon position is the center left side of your display, but you can change it to meet any requirement you might have.

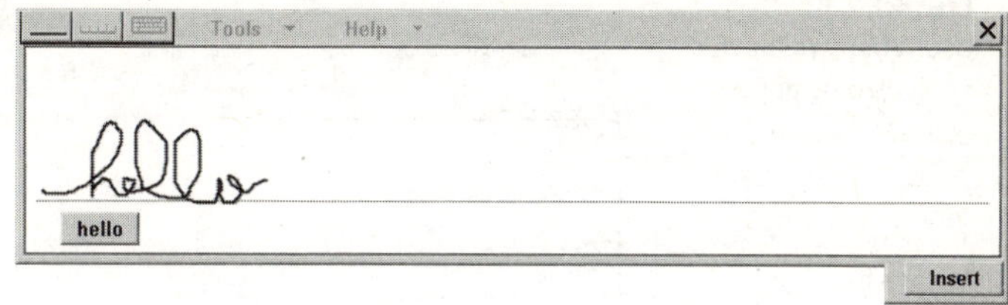

FIGURE 7.6
Type input into the Tablet PC using your stylus and this alternative input application.

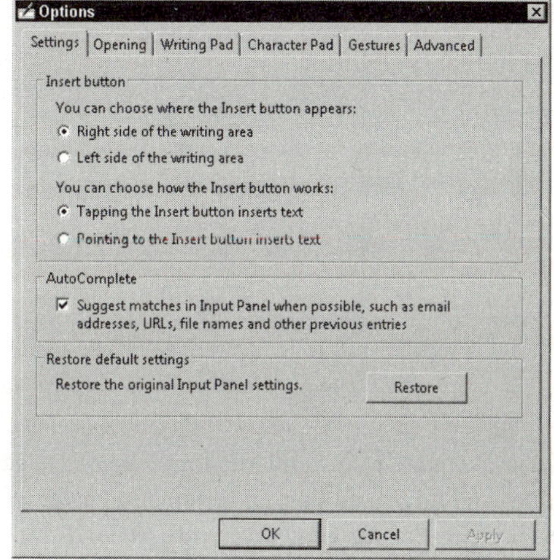

FIGURE 7.7
The Tablet PC Input Panel provides a number of options to change its appearance on screen.

Using Windows Journal

Just as Vista provides an alternative for sticky notes, you also have an alternative to real paper in the Windows Journal application. As shown in Figure 7.8, this application looks very much like a sheet of paper. Windows Journal provides a selection of pens and highlighters you can use to write or draw. You can select anything you draw to resize or copy it. Windows Journal even provides a way to flag important entries so you can locate them quickly when needed. You start Windows Journal using the Start ➤ All Programs ➤ Accessories ➤ Tablet PC ➤ Windows Journal command.

In many respects, Windows Journal is simply the paper version of Sticky Notes. You can import and export your notes, search notes for content, print notes, and even send them to others using email. The whole idea is to make it easy to communicate with others and to store your personal information in a form you'll easily recognize.

Monitoring and Optimizing Battery Usage

Vista has several features for helping you make the most of your notebook battery's charge. You don't want the screen going blank every minute that you pause to gather your thoughts, but neither do you want it to remain on using power for a long time if you get called away unexpectedly. Vista lets you adjust the settings to come up with your own best compromise between usability and battery life. Power management is available on both notebooks and desktops.

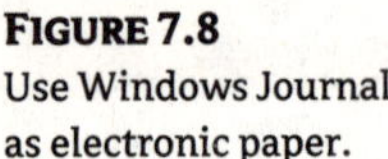

FIGURE 7.8
Use Windows Journal as electronic paper.

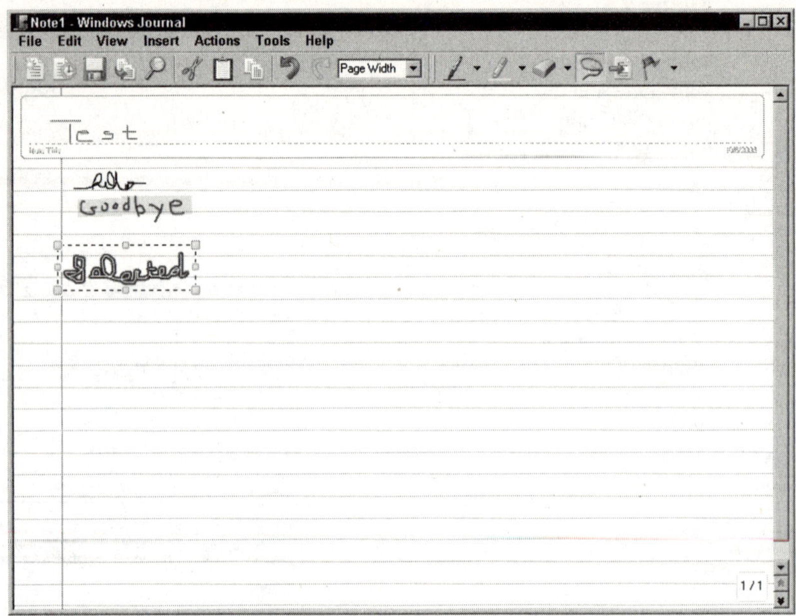

NOTE There are two standards for power management in PCs: Advanced Power Management (APM) and Advanced Configuration and Power Interface (ACPI). ACPI is the more modern one, and it works the most smoothly with Vista. If you have an older notebook PC, you might investigate whether a BIOS update is available that would switch it over from APM to ACPI. (Of course, if your computer is old enough that it still has an APM-supported BIOS, it's probably not going to run Vista very well in the first place.)

To configure power management, open the Power Options applet of the Control Panel. As an alternative, you can also click the Change Power Settings link in the Screen Saver Settings dialog box. You can also choose the Battery Status option in the Windows Mobility Center (see the "Configuring Your System with Windows Mobility Center" section of the chapter for details). Figure 7.9 shows the Power Options window you'll use to configure power options.

Choosing and Updating a Power Plan

Power plans are a combination of your need for processing speed and a requirement to manage power. Generally speaking, the more power you supply to a system, the better it performs. For example, if you keep the hard drive spinning all of the time, the system responds faster to hard drive requests. Microsoft provides three power management plans, as shown in Figure 7.9. You can easily choose any of these power plans for your processing needs.

The default settings probably aren't going to match your needs very well. I suggest clicking the Change Plan Settings link and at least reviewing the power settings. (You could also click the Choose When to Turn Off the Display or Change When the Computer Sleeps links since they lead to the same window.) Otherwise, you might get a nasty surprise when Vista powers down your system right in the middle of your thinking process. Figure 7.10 shows the Edit Plan Settings window you'll see.

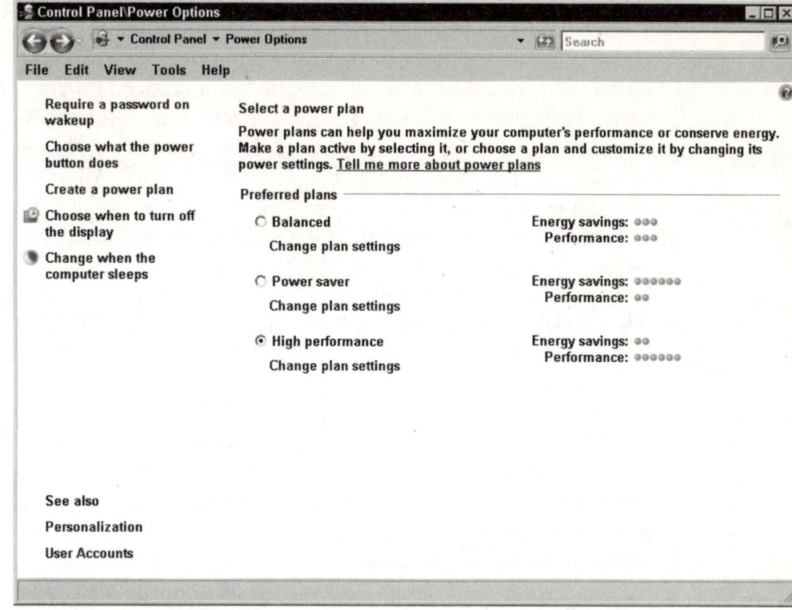

FIGURE 7.9
Choose a power plan that best matches your power needs at any given time.

FIGURE 7.10
The Edit Plan Settings window provides a simple overview of the power plan settings.

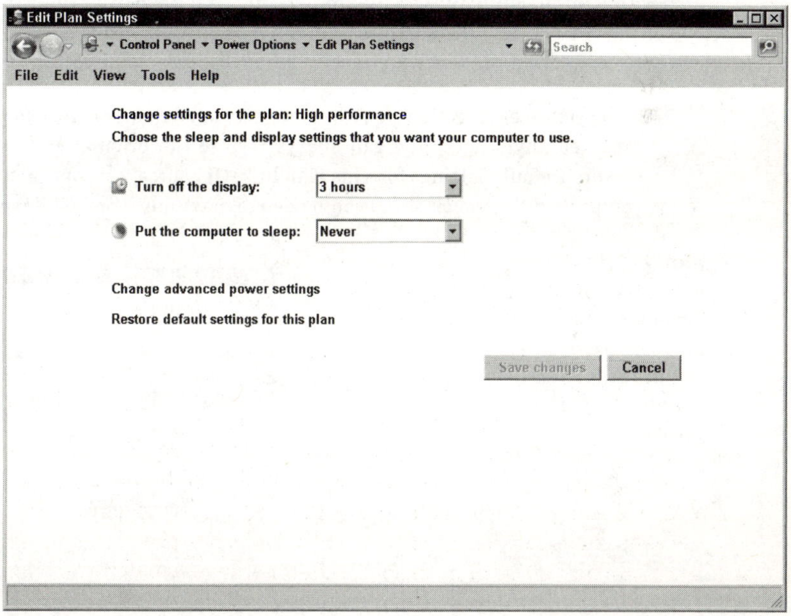

The Edit Plan Settings window lets you change the most common settings, which means the display and computer sleep time. However, you can change a considerable number of other settings. Just how many depends on your current computer setup and the devices attached to it.

To get to the real settings, click the Change Advanced Power Settings link. You'll see the Power Options dialog box shown in Figure 7.11. Each of the settings affects a different major power user in the computer system, such as the hard drive or the wireless adapter. You can also control the lid settings for mobile computers that support this feature. All of the settings provide either a drop-down list box or a text box with a spin control so you can quickly make numeric changes. In all cases, setting a value to 0 turns it off. The actual setting will say Never when you make it permanent and it isn't selected.

NOTE Make sure you check the Power Options dialog box for old favorites that used to appear as separate sections. For example, you'll find a Hibernate After entry in the Sleep folder. Setting this value to 0 effectively turns hibernation off. You'll also find some power hungry applications in the list. For example, setting Search and Indexing to the Power Saver setting greatly reduces the power that this particular application uses. Of course, less power means slower updates. Mobile users will also want to set the actions that they want Vista to take when the battery reaches specific thresholds. For example, you can set alarms to warn you about a low battery or that will even shut the system down gracefully (so you don't lose data). All of the battery-related settings appear under the Battery folder.

Sometimes you'll find that a setting is grayed out. In some cases, the setting is unavailable because of other settings on your system, such as the screen saver configuration. Other settings become unavailable when you aren't using that particular device. You can choose to change these settings by clicking the Change Settings that are Currently Unavailable link at the top of the Power Options dialog box.

TIP If you ever find that you've made so many changes that your system doesn't behave as expected any longer, you can always restore the original Microsoft settings by clicking the Restore Default Settings for This Plan link. Of course, this option is all or nothing. Any changes you've made are reversed, so you'll need to make any worthwhile settings changes from scratch.

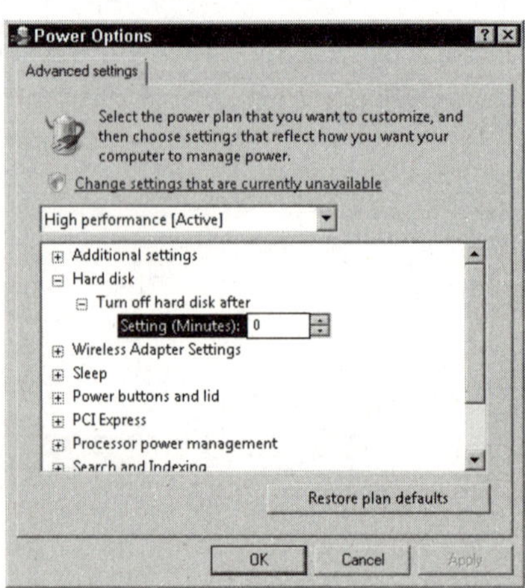

FIGURE 7.11 Vista provides extreme flexibility in choosing the power settings no matter what kind of machine you use.

Creating a Power Plan

Microsoft provides you with three plans that effectively cover the two extremes and the middle ground of performance and power management. You might decide that you need a little more control than that and don't want to adjust the power settings in the Power Options dialog box (see Figure 7.11) constantly. In this case, you'll want to create a power plan of your own. The following steps show how to create a new power plan.

1. Open the Power Options applet of the Control Panel. You'll see the Power Options window shown in Figure 7.9.
2. Click the Create a Power Plan link. You'll see a Create a Power Plan window like the one shown in Figure 7.12. This window shows all of the current plans, as well as providing a place for you to name the new plan.
3. Select the plan that most closely matches the plan you want to create.
4. Type a name for the new power plan. Whatever you do, try to come up with something a little more descriptive than High Performance. For example, I created a power plan for when I perform maintenance on my computer, so I called it Weekly Maintenance. Make sure that the name reflects how you plan to use the new power plan.
5. Click Next. You'll see a display similar to the one shown in Figure 7.10 where you can choose the default display internal and sleep time.
6. Change the Turn Off the Display and Put the Computer to Sleep settings as needed, and then click Create. Vista creates the new plan, as shown in Figure 7.13.

FIGURE 7.12
Create a new power plan when the default selections don't meet your needs.

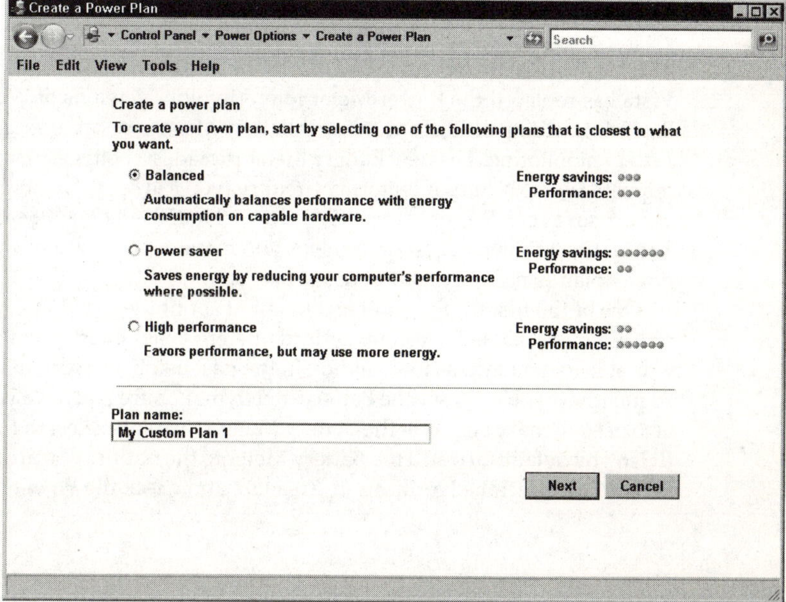

FIGURE 7.13
The new power plan replaces the power plan you chose as a starting basis.

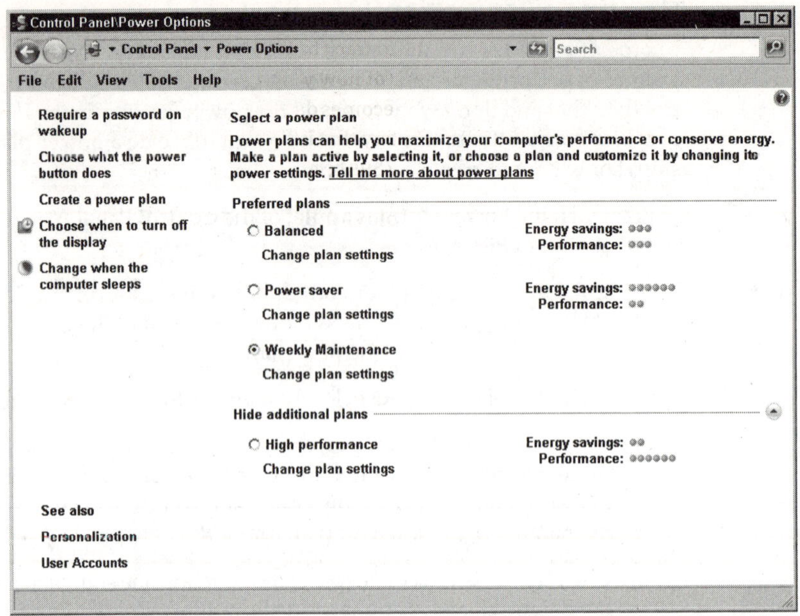

Notice that the new power plan replaces the power plan that you chose in step 3 as one of the preferred plans. You can hide the additional plans (which could be replacements for all three of the original plans) from view. At this point, you need to use the instructions in the "Choosing and Updating a Power Plan" section of the chapter to configure your new power plan.

Working with the Battery Meter

Vista has replaced the Power Meter found in older versions of Windows with the Battery Meter. Besides renaming the feature, the new Battery Meter is easier to see and provides some intelligence in battery monitoring. The new Battery Meter provides a better estimate of battery life within the limits imposed by the battery monitoring circuitry (you can see more on this topic at `http://windowshelp.microsoft.com/Windows/en-US/Help/5c39ae20-a443-4608-a0a3-fdddb9bb51631033.mspx`). The better visibility and accuracy helps you monitor your system with greater ease and modify your power plan as needed to reflect usage needs.

One of the first things you need to know about the new Battery Meter is that you can't see it unless you're using the Vista Standard or Aero Glass interfaces, which seems odd since Microsoft was able to display this information in the past using a lesser interface without any problem. Consequently, if you can't see the Battery Meter, make sure you have your display set up correctly. You also need to make sure that the Battery Meter is actually selected for display in the notification area (it isn't by default). To add the Battery Meter to the notification area, right-click the Taskbar, choose Properties, select the Notification Area tab, and check the Power option.

TIP Power is such an important consideration with laptops that someone's already come out with a Windows Sidebar gadget to track battery status. Power Meter Plus installs in Windows Sidebar and gives you a better view of how your battery is faring. One of the interesting features of this particular gadget is that it becomes darker and more noticeable as your battery discharges, so you aren't as likely to miss a battery that is nearing its limit. You can find Power Meter Plus at `http://www.softpedia.com/get/System/System-Miscellaneous/Power-Meter-Plus.shtml`.

The notification area displays a Battery Meter icon similar to the one found in other versions of Windows (just a bit spiffier). When you hover the mouse over the Battery Meter, you'll see the current power status in text. The most important change in Vista is that the Battery Meter provides you with an estimate of the time you have left to use your computer with the current battery power based on your usage patterns—I found that this estimate is fairly accurate (within about 10 minutes). Opening the Battery Meter displays a dialog box that contains the current battery level as both an icon and as text.

NOTE If you have multiple batteries in your mobile computer, Vista shows one icon for each battery. This feature lets you assess the amount of power left in each battery.

Below this display are the power options for your system. The default setting tells Vista to manage your power automatically, which means that you might find things shut down more often as the battery drains. You can also choose a specific power plan (see the "Choosing and Updating a Power Plan" and "Creating a Power Plan" sections of the chapter for details).

Finally, you'll see two links. Click the Learn How to Conserve Power link to open a Windows Help and Support topic on tasks you can perform to reduce the mobile computer's power consumption. Click Move Power Options to display the Power Options window shown in Figure 7.9.

Right-clicking the Battery Meter lets you choose from three options: Power Options (which displays the Power Options window), Windows Mobility Center (see the "Configuring Your System with Windows Mobility Center" section of the chapter for details), and Show System Icons. This last option opens the Notification Area tab of the Taskbar and Start Menu Properties dialog box where you can clear the Power option and remove the Battery Meter from the notification area.

Choosing What the Power Button Does

Most computers today come with a power button other than the one that simply removes power from the entire system. The button could be located anywhere from the keyboard to the lid of the mobile device. Of course, you don't necessarily want to remove power from the system when you press the power button. Vista lets you choose one of four actions: Do Nothing, Sleep, Hibernate, and Shut Down. To define the power button action, click the Choose What the Power Button Does link in the Power Options window (see Figure 7.9) to display the System Settings window shown in Figure 7.14. Choose the option you want from the When I Press the Power Button list.

NOTE Some applications used to veto the sleep or hibernate requests made by users. Consequently, you could possibly find yourself with a dead battery after the computer turned itself back on when you placed it in your computer bag. Vista makes it considerably harder for an application to veto a sleep or hibernate request, so you can power down your computer and store it with greater confidence.

FIGURE 7.14 Select the power down option you want to use.

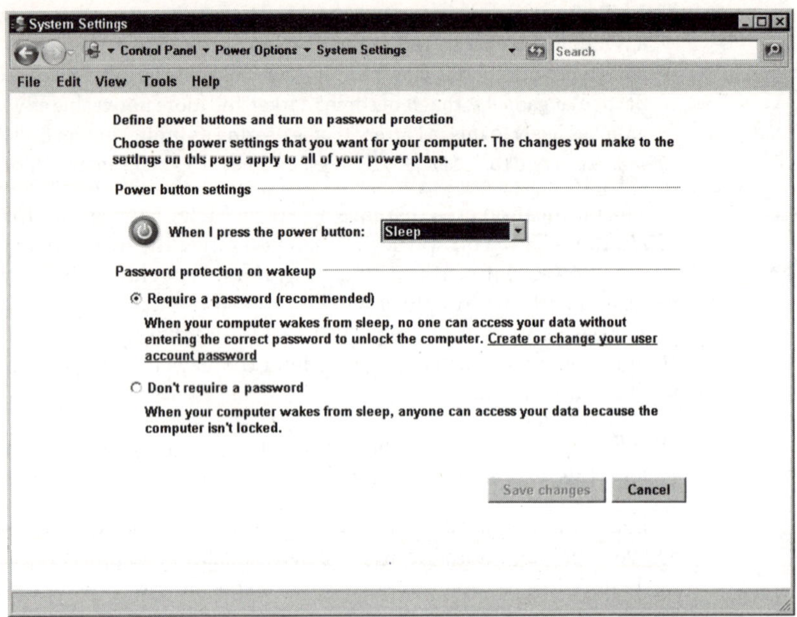

This window also lets you choose the password requirements for waking the system up from sleep or hibernation. These options are only active when you select Sleep or Hibernate. The default setting of Require a Password is the only one you should consider if you plan to keep your system safe. Notice that you can click the Create or Change You User Account Password link to create or change a password. Make sure you provide a safe password for your system.

TIP When choosing applications for your mobile device, make sure you consider how they use power. That's right, getting the wrong application can dry up your power faster than anything else will. For example, an application that constantly polls the hard drive for information is going to drain your battery quickly (and many do just that). Just in case you're a developer and want to know what all of the hubbub is about, Microsoft has set up a hands-on lab that demonstrates how to create power-friendly applications. You can find it at `http://msdn.microsoft.com/windowsvista/reference/mobilepc/hols/default.aspx`.

SLEEPING COMPARED TO HIBERNATION

Many Vista users are probably wondering about the difference between sleeping and hibernating because Vista supports them both. Both options let you reduce power consumption, yet maintain the state of your system so that you can press a single button and get back to work almost immediately without any setup.

Sleeping conserves less power, but it lets the system wake up faster. Sleeping is good for a short-term shutdown, such as when you go to lunch. A system wakes up so fast from the sleep state you might actually think that it was only using the screen saver, but it really was in a power-saving mode.

Hibernation removes power from more of the system. In addition, instead of keeping data in memory, it places the data in memory in a special file on the hard drive. Because hibernation removes power from more of the system, it conserves more power. However, it also requires a longer startup time than sleeping, but still less than starting up from a full shutdown. You'll probably use hibernation for shutting down your system overnight. The short, but noticeable delay, in starting up gives you time to get a cup of coffee in the morning.

So, where does this leave shutting the system down? Removing power from your system reduces power usage to zero, which means that it's the most environmentally friendly power usage option, but it also requires a longer startup period and you have to set your desktop up from scratch. Shutting your system down is the only acceptable option when you need to perform maintenance inside the computer cabinet. You'll also want to shut down before you go on vacation. Shutting the system down does affect the life span of the components inside the computer (you lose a little component life with every jolt of electricity from a full startup), but most people will get rid of their computer before the accumulation of startups has any effect at all on the system.

Using Multiple Dialing Locations

People who travel between cities with a notebook PC often need to connect to the Internet using different dialing settings depending on where they are. For example, in one location you might need to dial a 1 before the number, in another location a 1 plus the area code, in still another it's a local call, and so on.

To make it easier to remember the appropriate settings for each location, Vista offers Dialing Rules. Set them up through Control Panel:

1. From Control Panel, open the Phone and Modem Options applet. (The first time you do this, you're prompted for Location Information such as your area code; enter it and click OK.)
2. In the Dialing Rules tab, click New to open a New Location dialog box.
3. Enter all the details about the location you're setting up, as shown in Figure 7.15. Make sure you hit all three tabs: General, Area Code Rules, and Calling Card. The Calling Card tab is useful if you need to punch in the numbers for your calling card or credit card before each call from a certain location.
4. Click OK. Now you have a new location.

To use your new location, select it from the Dialing Rules tab.

Synchronizing Files with Other PCs

Many people use the "low tech" way of exchanging files between PCs—they copy them onto a floppy for transfer. And there's nothing wrong with that. Others hook the notebook PC into the LAN and copy files over the network.

NOTE For those of you who used the Direct Cable Connection feature in previous versions of Windows, you won't find it in Vista. Microsoft seems to have removed it and not told anyone why.

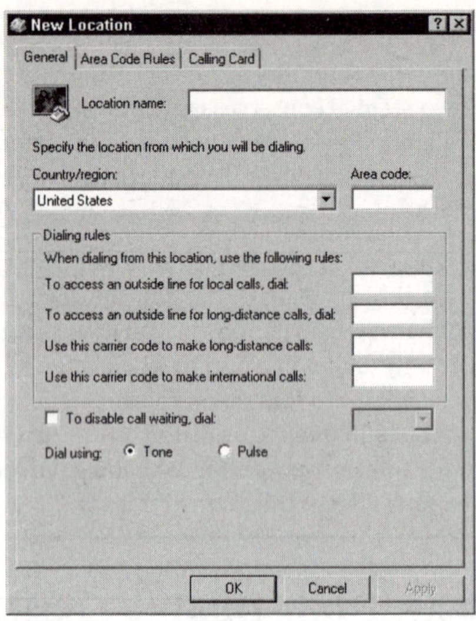

FIGURE 7.15
Set up a new dialing location for every city from which you make dial-up connections and need different settings.

However, each of those methods has a fundamental problem: What if the copy on the desktop PC or network location has changed too? How do you manage synchronization when it's possible that neither copy is in its original state? To solve this problem, Vista offers two different features: Offline Files and Briefcase.

Working with Offline Files

The Offline Files feature is useful if you need access to files and folders that aren't always available 24/7, such as files on a network that periodically goes down for maintenance or files on a desktop PC that you want to access while you're traveling with your laptop. It's designed to be an improvement over the Briefcase feature from previous Windows versions.

TIP The Briefcase feature is still available in Vista, and is discussed later in this chapter, because Briefcase offers one feature that Offline Files does not: it enables synchronization and transfer via floppy or other removable disk. The Offline Files feature works only with a network.

NOTE Don't confuse the Offline Files feature with the ability in Windows Explorer to cache websites for offline reading by subscribing to them. That capability is covered in Chapter 15.

Selecting Files and Folders to Be Available Offline

Working with Offline Files is different in Vista from previous versions of Windows. For one thing, you can always create an Offline File without having to perform a lot of setup. The process is still essentially the same; Vista caches the files you select to your local hard drive and you synchronize them later with the system that has the original file. The following steps help you create an offline file or folder.

1. Locate a file or folder in My Network Places that you want to cache.
2. Right-click it and choose Always Available Offline.

NOTE Don't try to create an offline file or folder when the file or folder is open by anyone. Vista will display an error message saying that the file or folder is in use.

SYNCHRONIZING FILES OR FOLDERS MANUALLY

Simply selecting the file or folder as described in the "Selecting Files and Folders to Be Available Offline" section works fine when you want to accept the default settings. However, in some cases, you might want better control over the synchronization process. For example, you might want to synchronize the files or folders immediately after reconnecting to the network to ensure that any changes you make appear to other users immediately. You might also want to synchronize manually immediately before you disconnect your computer from the network. When you want this level of control, you need to use the following steps.

1. Right-click the file or folder you want to make available offline and choose Properties from the context menu. Select the Offline Files tab. You'll see the options shown in Figure 7.16.
2. Click Sync Now. Vista performs the synchronization process. You might not see anything happen if Vista has already synchronized the file or folder.

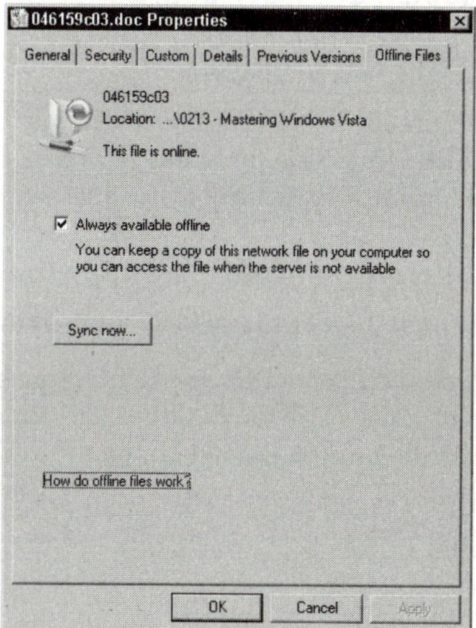

FIGURE 7.16 Synchronize files and folders manually as needed to ensure they remain current.

WORKING OFFLINE

When Offline Files is enabled, the files and folders you have set up appear as if they were online even when they are not actually available. You access them in the same way you normally do—for example, through My Network Places or via shortcuts to them. If they're available via a network, you get the "live" copy; if they aren't available, you get the cached, offline copy. An icon appears in the notification area to let you know you're working offline.

Using Briefcase

Offline Files works only if you have a network connection between the two PCs at the outset. You can disconnect a notebook computer from the network after you have created the offline file or folder and it will automatically synchronize when you reconnect to the network, but you must have the initial network connection to make Offline Files work. If you must rely on transferring files via removable disk (such as a floppy or CD-RW), you might be interested in the Briefcase feature instead.

With Briefcase, you create Briefcase folders on both PCs—the PC containing the originals (probably the desktop PC; in this chapter I'll call it the *main PC*) and the PC on which you'll temporarily work with the original files (probably the notebook PC; in this chapter I'll call it the *secondary PC*). Then you synchronize the Briefcase files with one another initially, and then again later when you're ready to return any changes you've made to the original PC.

Creating a New Briefcase File

To use Briefcase, you need to have a Briefcase icon on each of the PCs (both the desktop and the notebook). If there isn't already a Briefcase icon on your desktop, you can put one there by right-clicking the desktop and choosing New ➤ Briefcase. You can create a Briefcase anywhere, not just on the desktop, but most people prefer to store it there for convenience.

NOTE The Briefcase will have the name New Briefcase; you can change its name the same as any other icon (press F2 and type a new name).

Copying Files to a Briefcase

The procedure for copying files to a Briefcase depends on whether you plan on using a floppy disk or a network connection. In reality, if you're going to use a network connection, you're better off using the Offline Files feature instead. However, I'll explain both methods in this chapter.

Copying Files to My Briefcase for Floppy Transfer

Let's start with the steps necessary for copying files from My Briefcase to a disk.

1. Start on the main PC. Open a file management window and drag the files you want onto the Briefcase icon on the desktop. This copies those files to the Briefcase folder. You can double-click the Briefcase icon to open the folder and confirm that they are there if desired.
2. Insert a blank floppy disk (or other removable disk). Then drag the Briefcase icon from the desktop onto that drive's icon in My Computer. The entire Briefcase is moved there.
3. Take that disk to the secondary PC, and open that drive in My Computer there. Drag the Briefcase folder onto the desktop there.

Now the Briefcase is on the secondary PC's desktop, and you can open the Briefcase folder and work with the files from there.

Copying Files to My Briefcase for Network Transfer

Now that we've copied files from My Briefcase to a disk, let's try copying files from My Briefcase onto a network.

1. Make sure both PCs are logged onto the network and that file sharing is enabled on the main PC.

2. Start on the secondary PC. Open My Network Places and navigate to the files you want to copy.

3. Drag the files from My Network Places and drop them on the Briefcase icon on the desktop. If desired, you can double-click the Briefcase icon to open the folder window and confirm that the files are there.

Now you can work with the files directly from the Briefcase folder on the secondary PC's desktop.

SYNCHRONIZING BRIEFCASE FILES

When you synchronize files, you overwrite the originals with updated versions from the Briefcase. You can update all the files or only selected ones—your choice.

To see which files in the Briefcase need updating, view the Briefcase window in Details view. The Status column tells which files have changed. See Figure 7.17. Unchanged files have an Up-to-date status, while changed files have a Needs Updating status. The third file has an Orphan status. Since I have Word configured to create an automatic backup every time I change a file, this file is a new file that doesn't appear in the original folder. Therefore, it's an orphan file—one that doesn't have a home outside of Briefcase. You can always delete orphan files.

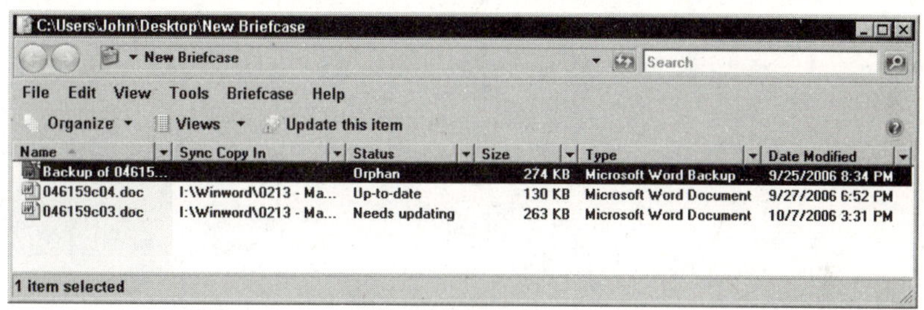

FIGURE 7.17 Use Details view to see which files have changed in the Briefcase.

NOTE If you're wondering how I obtained the single pane view shown in Figure 7.17, select Organize ➤ Layout ➤ Navigation Pane in the Briefcase folder. Vista will remove the Navigation pane on the left side of the display.

Even if none have changed on the secondary PC, you might still want to synchronize if there's any chance that the originals have changed on the main PC, and if you want to continue to have the most recent versions on the secondary PC.

Once again, the procedures for synchronizing are different depending on whether you're using the floppy disk or network transfer method.

Synchronizing with Floppy Disk Transfer

Now that you've learned to synchronize Briefcase files, let's try synching them up during a disk transfer.

1. Copy the Briefcase folder from the secondary PC's desktop to a floppy disk, and take that floppy disk to the main PC.

2. Display the floppy disk's content on the main PC, and drag the Briefcase icon onto the desktop there.

3. Double-click the Briefcase icon on the main PC desktop, opening the Briefcase window.
4. To update all files, choose Briefcase ➤ Update All. Or, to update only certain files, select them and choose Briefcase ➤ Update Selection.
5. A report appears. Make sure it lists the actions you want to perform. If you need to change the action for an item, right-click it and choose a different action. See Figure 7.18.
6. Click Update.

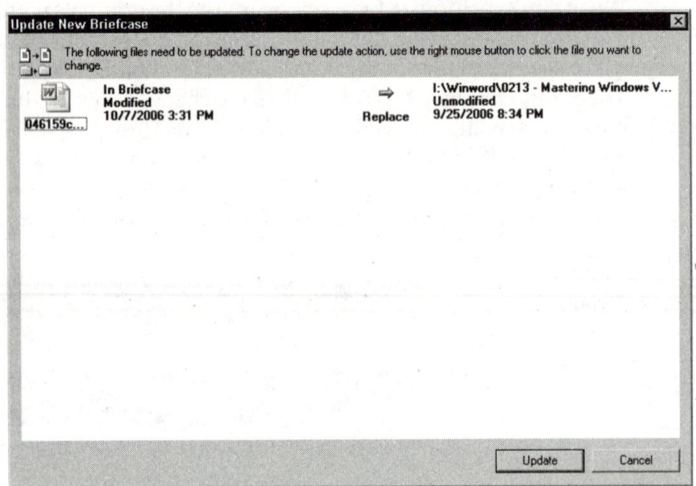

FIGURE 7.18
Confirm the update for each changed file.

Synchronizing with Network Transfer

Now let's try synching up with a network:

1. Make sure both PCs are connected to the network.
2. On the secondary PC, double-click the Briefcase icon, opening its window.
3. To update all files, choose Briefcase ➤ Update All. Or, to update only certain files, select them and choose Briefcase ➤ Update Selection.
4. A report appears (Figure 7.18). Make sure it lists the actions you want to perform. If you need to change the action for an item, right-click it and choose a different action.
5. Click Update.

Using the PowerCFG Utility

The PowerCFG utility is a command line utility that lets you perform all of the tasks that you can perform with the graphical utilities described in this section when it comes to power. To use this feature, you must open a command line prompt that has administrator privileges. Simply right-click the Command Prompt icon in the Accessories folder and choose Run as Administrator from the context menu. At the command line, you can always type `PowerCFG /?` to display a list of commands you can execute with this utility. For example, if you want to list all of the current power plans, type:

```
PowerCFG /List
```

You'll see the power configuration name, its Globally Unique Identifier (GUID), and an asterisk showing which power scheme is active. The GUID is important because you use it to identify a particular power scheme. For example, you might want to query the settings for a particular power setup, so you'd type:

```
PowerCFG /Query 637a4cca-6a7f-456f-822a-eccbf57a9aa5 > Settings.txt
```

Notice that I redirected the output to `Settings.txt`. The output for even one power configuration is likely more than you can display in the command window. In fact, you might be surprised to learn that the output contains all kinds of settings you can't access from the graphical utilities under certain circumstances. For example, the output includes all of the possible settings and all of the possible values for those settings, even if your system doesn't support them.

This chapter doesn't lists all of the command line switches because there are simply too many to list. However, you'll want to know about command line switches such as `/Change`, which lets you modify the power configuration from the command line. You can adjust features such as the monitor or disk time-out values.

However, the most important command line settings are those that let you preserve state information. You can use the `/Export` command line switch to export all of the settings for a particular machine. Likewise, you can use the `/Import` command line switch to import settings that you saved earlier.

Summary

In this chapter, you learned about the hardware, features, and issues involved in working with Vista on a notebook computer. Vista presents many changes to the administrator when it comes to mobile devices. Some older features, such as Direct Cable Connection, are missing completely in this new operating system. You'll also find that Microsoft has put a lot of effort into making some features easier to configure. For example, using the Offline Files feature is considerably simpler and faster in Vista than it was in Windows XP.

The important consideration in this chapter is discovering the features you can change on your mobile computer to make it work better with Vista. Try working with various power plans to create the optimal setup for your system. A balance between power savings and system responsiveness is a must. Don't forget to perform other kinds of research as you look for an optimal power plan, however. For example, applications that aren't mobile computer friendly will waste a lot of power, no matter how you have the system configured.

In the next chapter, we'll look at file management—not only the obvious stuff like moving and copying files, but also the techie goodies like NTFS encryption and compression. Vista includes a lot of new media options. For example, you'll find it a lot easier to burn your own CDs. Chapter 8 also discusses one of the most interesting new Vista features, Windows Sidebar. The Microsoft gadgets are admittedly not much to write home about, but look for this to change in the near future. You've already heard about one new gadget for Windows Sidebar in this chapter, Power Meter Plus.

Part II

Managing Applications, Files, and Folders

In this section, you'll learn how to:

- Organize Your Files and Folders
- Burn CDs and DVDs
- Install and Manage Local Printers
- Work with Fonts
- Set Up Fax Services
- Use Hot-Pluggable Devices

Chapter 8

Managing Files and Folders

At some point, almost all users are called on to work with files, even if it's just to copy an important document to a floppy disk or unzip a compressed archive. For those who understand how files and folders are organized on a disk, file management isn't that difficult, but the learning curve can be fairly steep for beginners.

This chapter offers something for both beginning and advanced users. Beginners will want to start with the basics of Windows Explorer; advanced users will likely skip ahead to the sections that cover more advanced operations, such as burning CDs and working with NTFS features.

This chapter covers:

- Using Explorer
- Organizing your files and folders
- Working with search folders, folder groups, folder stacks, tags, junctions, and symbolic links
- Understanding the multiuser environment
- Customizing the Explorer interface
- Setting file and folder properties
- Searching for files and folders
- Working with compressed files and folders
- Using Encrypted File System (EFS)
- Synchronizing with data found in other locations
- Creating CDs and DVDs
- Using Windows Sidebar

Vista: What's New?

Vista has a lot of old in it from previous versions of Windows. You'll still find Windows Explorer, albeit with some differences. For example, the left (Navigation) is now split into the familiar drive hierarchy and a favorites listing. Microsoft always has to change something, whether it's broken or not. One new addition that's really nice is the check box feature. Using check boxes to select files and folders makes it less likely that you'll select something by mistake.

Fortunately, you have a lot of new features to look forward to as well. Vista has a number of new ways to work with files and folders. For example, you'll find that using search folders can significantly reduce errors, while making data access significantly easier. Using search folders, you don't need to worry about data location, you simply consider the data itself. Vista also supports folder groups, folder stacks, tags (a method for identifying your data in new ways), and both junctions and symbolic links. Don't worry too much about know what these features are now—you'll find the details later in the chapter.

The Sync Center has undergone major changes and you'll find it included with Vista now, rather than as a separate download. You can use this feature to synchronize data in one location with data in any other location. It's a very cool feature for anyone who's on the road, has to deal with intermittent network connections, or simply needs to work with a local copy of data on occasion.

Windows XP lets you create CDs, and now you can create DVDs too. Vista doesn't support all of the high-definition formats for writing yet, but it does support standard DVDs. Having DVD support will make it easier to create backups using native Vista functionality, rather than relying on third-party support.

Perhaps the least attractive feature of Vista right now is Windows Sidebar, an application that relies on gadgets to perform a myriad of simple tasks. The gadgets that Microsoft supplies are cheesy, to say the least. Some people will probably like them, but they don't really show off the functionality that this feature could provide. Look for third parties to create some truly interesting gadgets in the future. In fact, we'll look at some third-party possibilities in this chapter. Don't underestimate the potential of Windows Sidebar, especially not based on the gadgets you find in Vista. That said, you still might find something useful and interesting in the gadget collection.

Using Explorer

Windows Explorer, often just called Explorer, is the formal name for the file-management window from which you can perform operations on files, like moving, copying, deleting, renaming, and so on. You access Explorer using the Start ➢ All Programs ➢ Accessories ➢ Windows Explorer command. Figure 8.1 shows a typical view of Explorer using the default options in the Vista Standard interface. The defaults include the Menu Bar, Navigation pane (left), Preview pane (right), and Details pane (bottom). You can add or remove all of these features using the options on the Organize ➢ Layout menu.

The view in Figure 8.1 relies on the Show Preview and Filters option found on the General tab of the Folder Options dialog box (see Figure 8.2) that you open with the Tools ➢ Folder Options command. Explorer provides a simpler view that you select using the Use Windows Classic Folders option. In this case, you'll see the Menu Bar and Navigation pane, but not the Preview or Details panes.

Now that the basics are out of the way, let's look at Explorer in detail. If you're a relative newcomer to Windows or simply want to see all of the new features that Microsoft has added, the following sections explain some basics of working with files in Windows Explorer for your benefit.

Opening vs. Exploring

You'll see two terms as verbs for working with Explorer, opening and exploring. These terms have come to mean different things as Microsoft has changed the feature set of Windows.

In Vista, *opening* a folder or other object means that you use the same window when one is available. For example, if you right-click a drive in Computer and choose Open, the drive contents will appear in the same copy of Explorer that holds Computer. The advantage of opening the drive is that you can easily move back to Computer later by clicking the Back button.

Exploring a folder or other objects opens a new copy of Explorer to view the contents of that object. If you right-click a drive in Computer and choose Explorer, you'll see a new copy of Explorer open with the content of that drive displayed. The advantage of this technique is that you can compare two objects when necessary by placing them side by side. Consequently, opening and exploring both have a place in Vista because they help you perform different tasks.

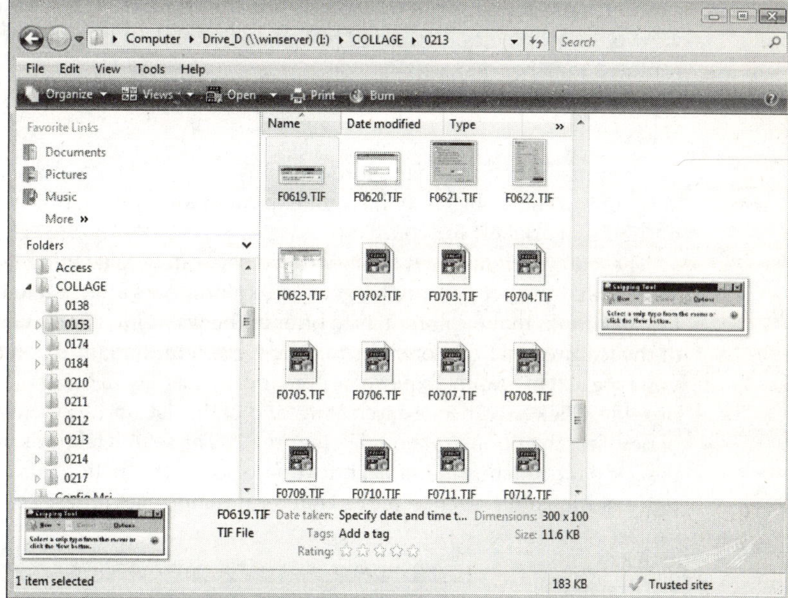

FIGURE 8.1
The Vista view of Windows Explorer with all of the gizmos intact.

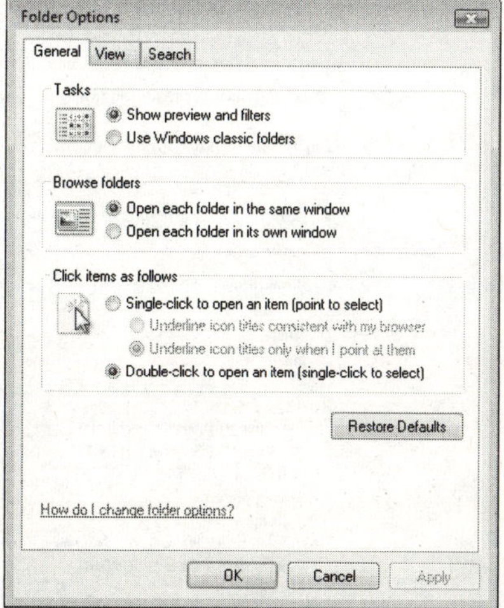

FIGURE 8.2
Choose the Use Windows Classic Folders option to get just the basics in Explorer.

Branches

It's easy to think of Windows Explorer as the filing system of Vista. It may be more accurate, though, to describe it as a *window* to the filing system of Vista. The views in Windows Explorer depict an upside down tree with its root being Desktop (this is a change from previous versions of Windows where the root was My Computer). It branches down from there showing the various connected drives and other resources.

Each item that appears in Explorer is considered an object. Every object has its own properties, many of which you can modify to suit your needs, regardless of whether you're working with a file, a folder, a program, or a network computer. Although Explorer is often thought of as a method to view or locate objects, you could just as easily think of it as the glue that holds this diverse environment together.

Views

You can arrange objects in Explorer in many ways, all of which are called *views*. The View menu not only controls how objects in the right Explorer pane appear, but also how Explorer itself can be configured to work best for you.

The left and right panes are controlled separately. One thing that you'll notice is missing from Vista is that the left pane no longer has Explorer bars attached to it. What you see in Figure 8.1 is the maximum that Explorer has to offer in the way of instantly viewable content. However, many of the features that Explorer has to offer remain hidden until you need them. For example, when you type text in Search, Explorer automatically displays a list of files matching the specification you provide. Click Advanced Search at the end of the list, and suddenly you see a considerable number of new search options as shown in Figure 8.3. The search features don't appear as an Explorer bar—the left pane remains the same, but you do see new functionality. The "Understanding the Importance of Metadata" section of the chapter describes how these search features work in detail.

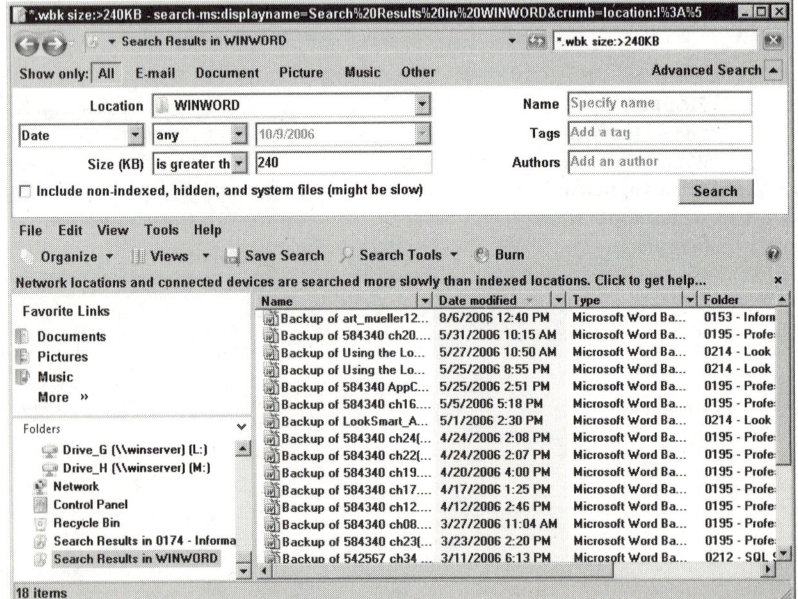

FIGURE 8.3
Special Explorer features no longer appear as Explorer bars in Vista.

The right pane shows the content of the currently selected location. Several views are available for the right pane, including Extra Large Icons, Large Icons, Medium Icons, Small Icons, Tiles, List, and Details. You may wonder what happened to the Thumbnail view from Windows XP. Vista always shows thumbnails unless you tell it not to do so. Of course, displaying thumbnails all of the time can be time consuming because Vista has to read each of the files and create a smaller version to display as an icon. You can get rid of the thumbnails by choosing Tools ➤ Folder Options, selecting the View tab, and checking the Always Show Icons, Never Thumbnails option, as shown in Figure 8.4.

The default view for Computer is Tiles, while the rest of Vista tends to use the Details view. However, you can change the view to whatever works best for you by selecting the view from the View drop-down list. Figure 8.1 shows the Medium Icons view. Figures 8.5 through 8.10 show the same folder as shown in Figure 8.1, but using the other views that the Vista version of Explorer provides (since only the right pane is important, each graphic shows only the right pane):

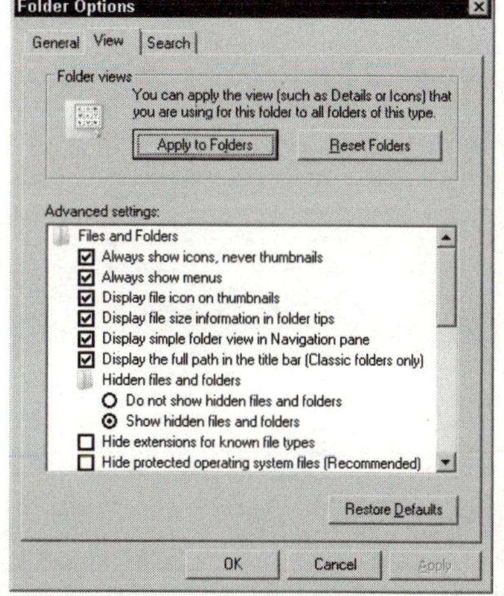

FIGURE 8.4
Explorer now controls the display of thumbnails using a folder option.

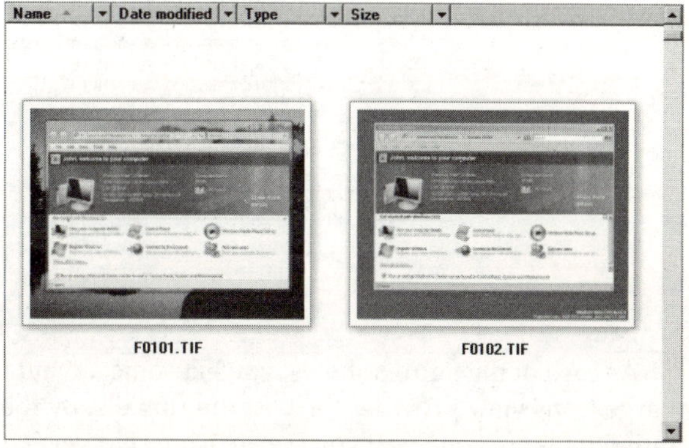

FIGURE 8.5
Using the Extra Large Icons view.

FIGURE 8.6
Using the Large Icons view.

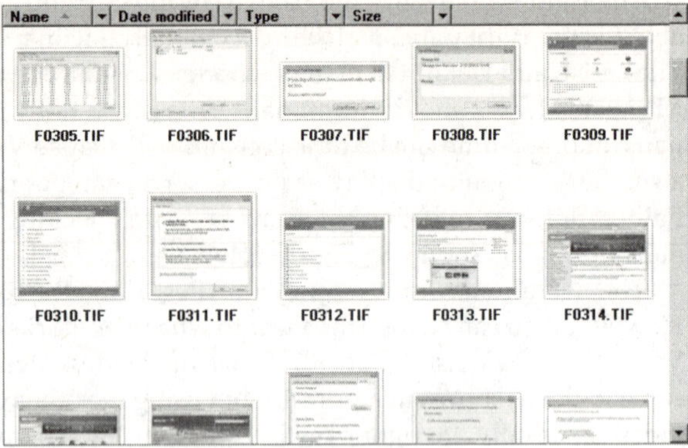

FIGURE 8.7
Using the Small Icons view.

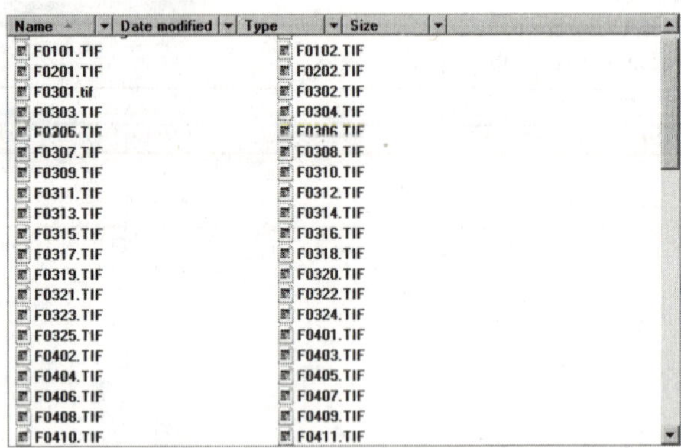

FIGURE 8.8
Using the List view.

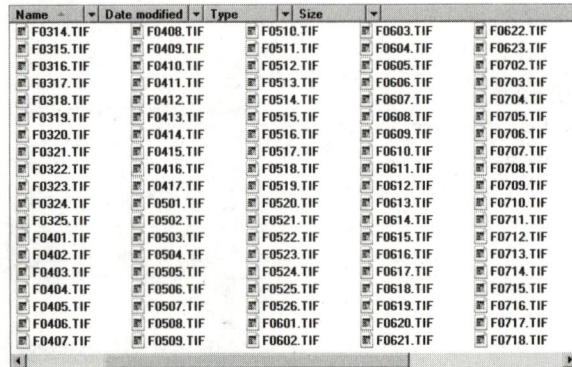

Name	Date modified	Type	Size	
F0314.TIF	F0408.TIF	F0510.TIF	F0603.TIF	F0622.TIF
F0315.TIF	F0409.TIF	F0511.TIF	F0604.TIF	F0623.TIF
F0316.TIF	F0410.TIF	F0512.TIF	F0605.TIF	F0702.TIF
F0317.TIF	F0411.TIF	F0513.TIF	F0606.TIF	F0703.TIF
F0318.TIF	F0412.TIF	F0514.TIF	F0607.TIF	F0704.TIF
F0319.TIF	F0413.TIF	F0515.TIF	F0608.TIF	F0705.TIF
F0320.TIF	F0414.TIF	F0516.TIF	F0609.TIF	F0706.TIF
F0321.TIF	F0415.TIF	F0517.TIF	F0610.TIF	F0707.TIF
F0322.TIF	F0416.TIF	F0518.TIF	F0611.TIF	F0708.TIF
F0323.TIF	F0417.TIF	F0519.TIF	F0612.TIF	F0709.TIF
F0324.TIF	F0501.TIF	F0520.TIF	F0613.TIF	F0710.TIF
F0325.TIF	F0502.TIF	F0521.TIF	F0614.TIF	F0711.TIF
F0401.TIF	F0503.TIF	F0522.TIF	F0615.TIF	F0712.TIF
F0402.TIF	F0504.TIF	F0523.TIF	F0616.TIF	F0713.TIF
F0403.TIF	F0505.TIF	F0524.TIF	F0617.TIF	F0714.TIF
F0404.TIF	F0506.TIF	F0525.TIF	F0618.TIF	F0715.TIF
F0405.TIF	F0507.TIF	F0526.TIF	F0619.TIF	F0716.TIF
F0406.TIF	F0508.TIF	F0601.TIF	F0620.TIF	F0717.TIF
F0407.TIF	F0509.TIF	F0602.TIF	F0621.TIF	F0718.TIF

As each of the figures shows, you get some advantage from each view. For example, the Extra Large Icons view provides the best thumbnails. By the time you get to the Small Icons view, the thumbnails are gone—all you see are icons. However, the Small Icons view presents you with the maximum number of files with readable filenames. The List view sacrifices on file count to ensure you see the full filename for each file. The Details view presents complete information about each file. In fact, you can easily expand the information to include details that you could never get in earlier versions of Windows (see the "Understanding the Importance of Metadata" section of the chapter for details). Finally, the Tiles view combines medium-sized icons (so you can see those thumbnails when you want) with a moderate amount of information (full filename, file size, and file type).

FIGURE 8.9
Using the Details view.

Name	Date modified	Type	Size
F0101.TIF	8/4/2006 1:11 PM	TIF File	793 KB
F0102.TIF	8/4/2006 1:12 PM	TIF File	329 KB
F0201.TIF	8/25/2006 5:16 PM	TIF File	173 KB
F0202.TIF	8/30/2006 10:46 AM	TIF File	128 KB
F0301.tif	9/19/2006 12:09 PM	TIF File	1,738 KB
F0302.TIF	9/19/2006 5:36 PM	TIF File	45 KB
F0303.TIF	9/19/2006 5:38 PM	TIF File	62 KB
F0304.TIF	9/19/2006 5:59 PM	TIF File	42 KB
F0305.TIF	9/19/2006 6:06 PM	TIF File	89 KB
F0306.TIF	9/20/2006 8:30 AM	TIF File	52 KB
F0307.TIF	9/20/2006 8:31 AM	TIF File	15 KB
F0308.TIF	9/20/2006 8:39 AM	TIF File	16 KB
F0309.TIF	9/20/2006 8:59 AM	TIF File	164 KB
F0310.TIF	9/20/2006 9:39 AM	TIF File	129 KB
F0311.TIF	9/25/2006 2:22 PM	TIF File	36 KB
F0312.TIF	9/25/2006 4:19 PM	TIF File	151 KB
F0313.TIF	9/25/2006 4:14 PM	TIF File	240 KB
F0314.TIF	9/25/2006 5:01 PM	TIF File	269 KB
F0315.TIF	9/25/2006 5:08 PM	TIF File	335 KB
F0316.TIF	9/25/2006 5:22 PM	TIF File	441 KB

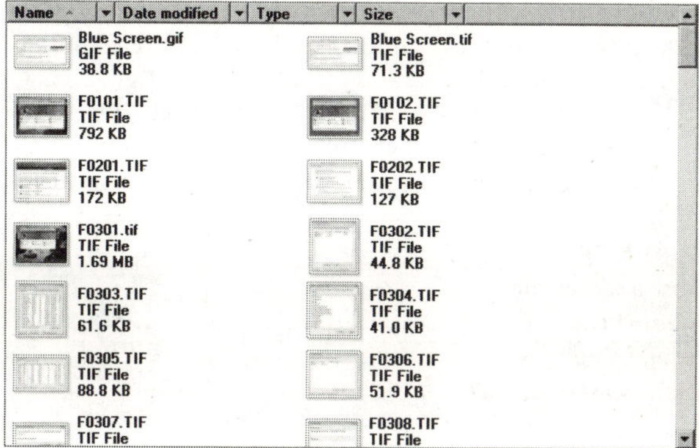

FIGURE 8.10
Using the Tiles view.

Reordering Files

What if you can't remember the name of a file you need, but you do remember the date it was created? Or, what if you know which application created the file and what the file extension is? With Explorer, you can arrange the items in the right pane so that they are sorted or organized by name, size, date, or file type. You can then see at a glance what is and isn't inside the folder. To change the actual order of the files, choose an option from the View ➤ Sort By menu.

However, you can also order the files by grouping them. You can use the same grouping options as you would for sorting, which includes attributes such as name, date, and so on. When you group the icons, you can close the groups that you don't want to see, leaving just those that fit within the list that you do want to see. Grouping doesn't work when using the List view. To change the file grouping, choose an option from the View ➤ Group By menu.

Vista also provides a virtual file feature in Explorer called stacking. Stacking creates search folders that hold the files in groups similar to that provided by the grouping feature. However, you can create subfolders within the folders, so that the stacks become progressively more particular about their content. You can learn more about using search folders in the "Working with Search Folders" section of the chapter. To change the folder stacking, choose an option from the View ➤ Stack By menu.

All of these organizational tools have one thing in common. You can organize the data using a number of standard file attributes that include Name, Date Modified, Type, and Size. You can also choose whether Explorer organizes the files in ascending or descending order. These sorting options also appear in previous versions of Windows. In addition to these sorting options, Vista adds sorting by tags and ratings for some, but not all, files. The Vista version of Explorer adds a new option simply called More. Click this option and you'll see the Choose Details dialog box shown in Figure 8.11. Using this option, you can choose any tag that the file supports as a means of sorting, grouping, or stacking the files. The "Understanding the Importance of Metadata" section of the chapter describes how to use tags in detail.

TIP When you're working in Details view, you can click a column heading to sort by that column. For example, you could sort by the Size column or the Date Modified. Click a column heading again to shift between an ascending and descending sort.

You can also set the View using the Views button on the toolbar, and you can arrange the icons by right-clicking anywhere in the right pane, clicking Sort By, and selecting an order from the submenu. Explorer also provides grouping choices in the Group By menu and stacking choices in the Stack By menu of the context menu that you see when you right-click in the right pane.

TIP Select Auto Arrange if you want the listing to always arrange automatically. Otherwise, sometimes when you create a new file or folder, it will initially appear at the bottom of the list (until you refresh the display by pressing F5 or until you close and reopen the window).

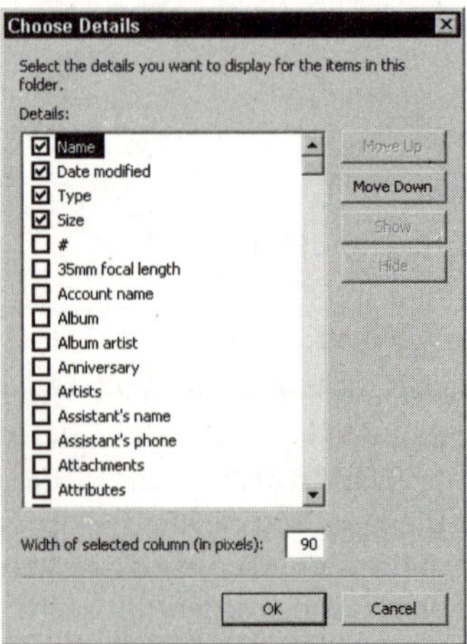

FIGURE 8.11
Choose a special file attribute to use for sorting, grouping, or stacking your files.

Working with Shortcut Menus

Right-clicking objects throughout the Vista interface displays a shortcut menu that contains options pertaining to the objects at hand. The same options are typically available from the main menus but are more conveniently reached with the right-click.

Which commands appear on a shortcut menu depends on such factors as the current folder's location, the current file or folder type, user privileges, and which programs are installed on your computer. Figure 8.12 shows a typical shortcut menu for a document file.

Some of the commands shown in Figure 8.12 were added by third-party applications, so you won't necessarily see them on your PC. For example, Add to ZIP File and the other ZIP-related entries were added by WinZip. You'll find that many third-party applications add entries to make it easier for you to work with the application.

Of these commands, most are equivalent to what you'd find on the application's File or Edit menu. Choosing Properties, which usually appears at the bottom of a shortcut menu, generally takes you to the object's Properties dialog box.

Here are a couple of the most notable ones from Figure 8.12:

- **Open and Open With.** The Open command opens a data file in whatever application is set to be the default for its file extension. The Open With command opens a submenu of all the programs that could potentially open that file, so you can choose. This is useful when you want to open a file using a different application but not change the association for all files of that type.

- **Send To.** This command opens a submenu of various locations where you might want to send a copy of the file. All your removable disks are included here, plus My Documents, Mail Recipient, Desktop, and Compressed (zipped) Folder. The latter points to Vista's built-in support for the ZIP file format. To create a ZIP file, select a group of files, right-click the group, and choose Send To ➢ Compressed (zipped) Folder.

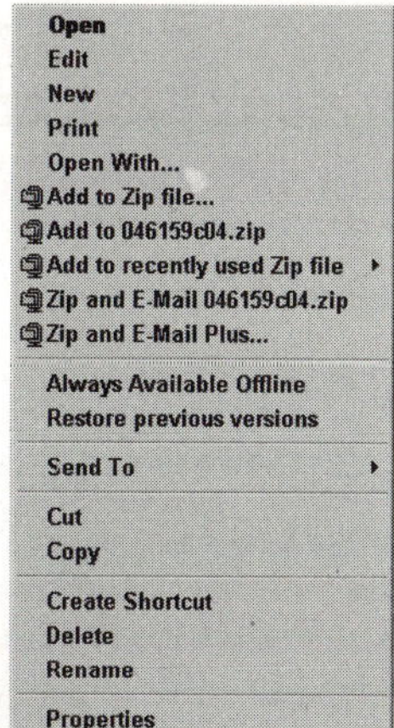

FIGURE 8.12
A shortcut menu for a document file.

TIP You can create your own Send To submenu entries by placing a shortcut to the desired application in the C:\Users\<User Name>\AppData\Roaming\Microsoft\Windows\SendTo folder. Many applications work well this way, letting you open files using a right-click rather than resorting to odd Registry manipulations. You use this technique for generic applications, such as Notepad or a hex editor (a program for gaining a low-level look at files). If you decide that everyone should be able to send files to an application, place the shortcut in the All Users account instead of your personal account folder.

The shortcut menu for a folder is very different. When you right-click the white background in a folder's file listing, you get a shortcut menu like the one in Figure 8.13. I won't go into what each of these commands does right now, because most of them are addressed throughout the remainder of this chapter.

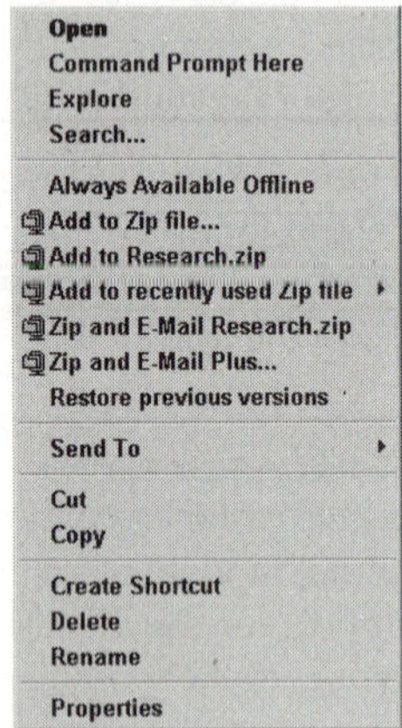

FIGURE 8.13
A shortcut menu for a folder.

Organizing Your Files and Folders

Working with files and folders might be familiar territory for you, and if so, feel free to skip this section. But if you don't have the firmest of grasps on skills like creating, deleting, renaming, and so on, stick with me here.

Creating New Folders

To create a new folder in Explorer, follow these steps:

1. Choose where you want to create a new folder. You can easily create a folder on the Desktop or inside another folder. It's also possible to create a folder at the root of a hard drive or a floppy drive, within the system folders (such as \Windows), and other areas that don't actually belong to you as a user when you have the required permissions. User Access Control (UAC) prevents you from creating a file in the root folder of a drive to reduce the risk of virus, adware, or other attack (you can create a folder in the root of the hard drive).
2. In Explorer, choose File ➤ New ➤ Folder, or right-click the drive or folder in which you want to create the folder (or the background in the currently displayed folder) and choose New ➤ Folder from the shortcut menu. To create a folder on the Desktop, right-click an empty area, and choose New ➤ Folder from the shortcut menu.

3. The folder is created with the default name New Folder. By default, the name is highlighted. To give a new name to the folder, type it now. You can always rename a folder by selecting it and choosing File ➤ Rename or by pressing F2 or right-clicking the folder and choosing Rename from the shortcut menu. (I'll discuss renaming in detail later in this chapter.)

Moving Items

You can move files and folders anywhere on your computer or over the network as long as you have permission to do so. To move a file or folder, follow these steps:

1. Select the file or folder you want to move. To select more than one object, hold down Ctrl while you click each one. If the objects constitute an uninterrupted group, hold down Shift while you click the first object and the last.
2. Choose Edit ➤ Cut (or press Ctrl+X).
3. Select the destination, and choose Edit ➤ Paste (or press Ctrl+V).

You can also drag items from one place to another:

- Drag from the right Explorer pane to the left.
- Drag from either Explorer pane to another Explorer or Explorer-type window.
- Drag from either Explorer pane to the Desktop. (Optionally, if you hold down the right mouse button while you drag, you can create a shortcut or shortcuts on the Desktop for the object or objects you're dragging.)
- Drag from the Desktop to an Explorer folder.

TIP If you drag a folder from the right Explorer pane to the left on a *different* drive, Vista defaults to copying the file instead of moving it. (As long as you're dragging the object to the same drive, Vista moves the file or folder by default.) If you don't want Vista to copy the file, hold down the Shift key while you drag the object to another drive. That way it will be moved rather than copied.

Copying Items

You can also copy files and folders anywhere on your computer or the network as long as you have permission to do so. To copy a file or folder, follow these steps:

1. Select the file or folder you're going to copy. To select more than one object, hold down Ctrl while you click each object. To select objects that constitute an uninterrupted group, hold down Shift, click the first object, and then click the last object.
2. Choose Edit ➤ Copy (or press Ctrl+C).
3. Select the destination, and choose Edit ➤ Paste (or press Ctrl+V).

You can also drag the items from one place to another, as described in the previous section, with one difference: to ensure that the objects you're dragging are copied and not moved, hold down the Ctrl key while you're dragging.

TIP If you drag a folder from the right Explorer pane to the left on the same drive, Vista defaults to moving the file instead of copying it. (As long as you're dragging the object to a different drive, Vista copies the file or folder by default.) If you don't want Vista to move the file, hold down the Ctrl key while you drag the object to another drive. It will be copied, not moved.

Using the Check Box Feature

Sometimes, choosing just the right files can be frustrating. You might find that the mouse is more enemy than friend when working in Explorer. However, the new Check Box feature can change the problem of selecting files from hard to easy. You enable this feature by choosing Tools ➤ Folder Options in Explorer to display the Folder Options dialog box, select the View tab, and check the Use Check Boxes to Select Items option. Click OK to close the Folder Options dialog box and you'll instantly notice a difference in the display.

Every time you hover the house over a folder or file, you'll see a check box in the upper left corner of the icon as shown in Figure 8.14. Check this check box to select the file. The files you check remain selected until you clear the check, so you don't have to use fancy selection methods anymore to select a group of files.

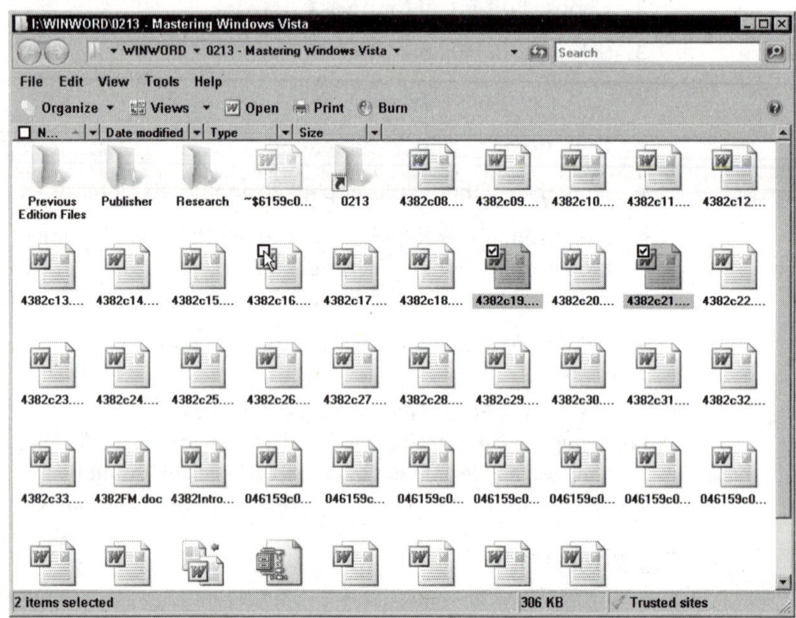

FIGURE 8.14
Use the Check Box feature to make selecting files and folders a snap.

NOTE The interesting part about the Check Box feature is that it shows up in all kinds of places. For example, you'll find it in the typical file open dialog box, even when the application you're using is old and shouldn't support the feature. Consequently, the Check Box feature is very useful for any kind of file selection process.

Saving Files and Folders to the Desktop

You can keep files on your Desktop for quick and easy access. To store files and folders on the Desktop, do one of the following:

- Drag a file from Explorer to the Desktop.
- If you're saving the file from within an application, select Desktop (it's at the very top of your local drive hierarchy) in the application's Save As dialog box.

When you right-click a file, drag it, and then release the button, you'll see a shortcut menu with the following options:

Copy Here Copies the file to the new location.

Move Here Moves the file to the new location.

Create Shortcut(s) Here Creates a shortcut to the file at the new location. As I've discussed, a shortcut is a pointer to the real file or folder and can be stored anywhere on your computer.

Cancel Cancels the operation.

TIP If you're new to Vista or are confused about when to use Ctrl or Shift when moving or copying files, the safest thing to do is to drag the file with the right mouse button. This way, you're always presented with a choice of whether to move or copy the file.

Renaming Files and Folders

You can quickly and easily rename files and folders. Because Vista keeps track of file associations, you don't have to worry about including the three-character file extensions.

WARNING The sentence above is true only if you haven't turned off the Hide Extensions for Known File Types setting in Folder Options. When a file's extension is hidden, it's not involved in the renaming process. However, for a file that does show the extension on screen, you must retype the extension when renaming the file if you select the entire filename. (A new Vista feature selects only the filename even if you display the file extensions unless you specifically highlight the entire filename.) Don't type an extension if the extensions are hidden, or you'll end up with a double extension on the file—one hidden, one showing. For example, `Mytext.doc` will become `Mytext.doc.doc`.

To rename a file or folder, follow these steps:

1. In Explorer, select the file or folder you want to rename.
2. Choose File ➤ Rename, or right-click the file and choose Rename from the shortcut menu.
3. When only the name of the file (the text associated with the icon) becomes highlighted, do one of the following:
   - If you want to simply replace the entire name, start typing the new name; the old name disappears the moment you start typing.
   - If you want to make only a correction or two to the existing name, use the arrow keys to move to specific characters within the existing name. The highlight disappears the moment you start moving within the name, enabling you to insert or delete specific characters without deleting the entire name.
4. To accept the name, press Enter or click outside the name area. If you make a mistake, press Escape.

TIP You can also rename files and folders with two single clicks (but don't click so fast that Vista interprets it as a double-click) on the name of the object so that it's highlighted. Then follow steps 3 and 4.

Deleting Files and Folders

If you decide that you don't want a file or a folder, you can easily delete it. By default, the file isn't actually deleted when you tell Vista to delete it: instead, it's compressed and sent to the Recycle Bin folder. A file in the Recycle Bin hasn't been removed from your hard drive, only placed on inactive duty, so to speak. (You can periodically delete items within the Recycle Bin to *actually* remove them entirely, or you can empty the Recycle Bin to delete everything in it.)

The Recycle Bin is a good intermediate place to keep files you're pretty sure you want to delete, because if you change your mind after "deleting" them to the Recycle Bin, you can always open the Recycle Bin and resurrect the object. Mutter your apologies for treating the item so shabbily, and it's ready for use once more.

TIP If you're the kind of person who hates being pestered by second thoughts, and you'd prefer to avoid the nice little safeguard of the Recycle Bin, you can *really* delete an item by selecting it and pressing Shift+Delete.

TIP You can turn off the Recycle Bin so that no deleted files go there at all. Just right-click the Recycle Bin icon and choose Properties; then mark the Do Not Move Files to the Recycle Bin check box in the General tab.

Sending Items to the Recycle Bin

You can send a file or a folder to the Recycle Bin in several ways:

- Select the item, and then press the Delete key.
- Select the item, and then choose File ➤ Delete.
- Right-click the file or folder, and then choose Delete from the shortcut menu.
- Select the item, and then drag and drop it on the Recycle Bin icon.

Emptying the Recycle Bin

By default, the size of the Recycle Bin folder is set at 10 percent of your hard drive. If you have more than one hard drive, or if you have a dual-partitioned drive, you'll have a Recycle Bin folder for each drive, and the size of the folder is set at 10 percent for each drive. For example, if drive C is 3.44GB, the Recycle Bin folder is 353MB; and if drive D is 6.09MB, its Recycle Bin folder is 624MB.

When the Recycle Bin folder is full, Vista automatically deletes enough items, starting with the oldest, to accommodate whatever you're currently sending to it. When an item is removed from the Recycle Bin, it's gone forever.

To better control the Recycle Bin and maintain its intended functionality (which is to provide second chances), you can periodically empty it manually. You can delete all the items it contains or only selected items.

- To delete selected items, double-click the Recycle Bin to open the Recycle Bin folder. Now delete items as you would in Explorer.
- To totally empty the Recycle Bin, right-click its icon, and choose Empty Recycle Bin from the shortcut menu.

WARNING When a file is deleted in Vista, it's *really* deleted. Other operating systems such as MS-DOS or Windows 9x delete only the first byte from a file and mark the space as available. Vista is much more thorough because of its secure nature. When you delete a file in Vista, all the bytes in the file are set to a zero value. This is like reformatting the space where the file was so that it can be reclaimed.

RESTORING ITEMS FROM THE RECYCLE BIN

To restore items from the Recycle Bin you can do one of the following:

- Open the Recycle Bin folder, select an item, and drag it to the folder of your choice.
- Open the Recycle Bin, select the item you want to restore, and click Restore This Item in the Recycle Bin Tasks bar. The item is restored to its original location.

Working with Search Folders

Depending on whom you talk to, search folders appear with several different names. The most common alternative is the virtual folder. Whenever you perform a search in Vista, Explorer creates a search folder that contains the search results. In addition, you automatically create a search (virtual) folder when you perform tasks such as creating folder stacks. If you understand the mechanics of search folders, you can create folder and file collections for any need in Vista. The idea is to collect the data you need into one search folder without regard to its physical location on the system. In fact, you can collect data across your network or even across the Internet, should you wish to do so.

Search folders use a special color so that you can identify them easily. They appear as blue folders, as shown (in black and white) in Figure 8.15. The easiest place to find search folders is in your own data folder. Simply click the folder with your name on the Desktop and then choose the Searches folder. You'll see a number of standard search folders.

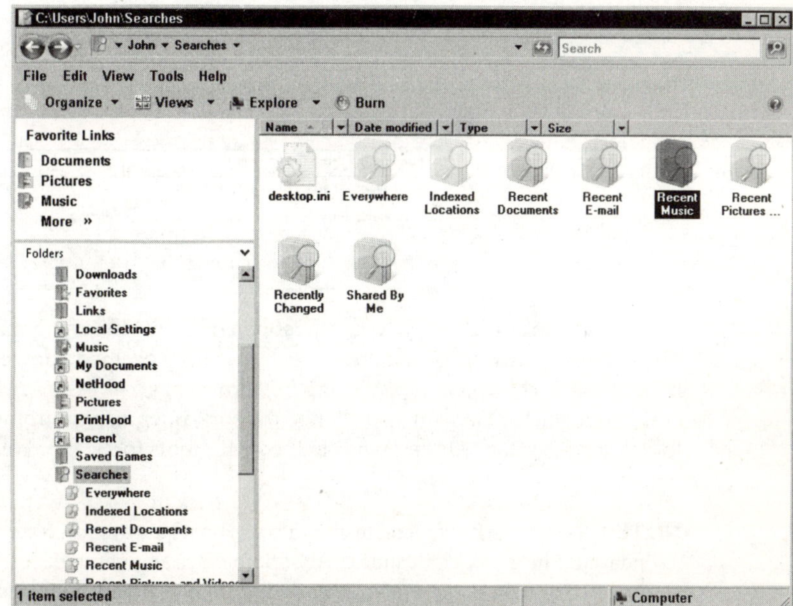

FIGURE 8.15
Vista displays all search folders as blue folders (shown in black and white) with a magnifying glass so you can identify them easily.

You already know that using certain Vista features creates search folders. A stacked folder always appears as search folder. In fact, when using stacks, you can create search folders within other search folders. The following sections describe how to create and manipulate search folders of your own.

CREATING A SEARCH FOLDER

Creating a search folder is as easy as defining a search. To begin the process, open a copy of Explorer and type a search definition in the Search field. Click the Search button (the one that looks like a magnifying glass) and you're well on your way to starting a search. You'll see a search display like the one shown in Figure 8.3.

However, a search alone doesn't create a search folder. Click Save Search and you'll see a Save As dialog box like the one shown in Figure 8.16. Notice that the dialog box prompts you to provide tags necessary to define the search content (see the "Understanding the Importance of Metadata" section of the chapter for details). The default location for saving searches that you create yourself is your personal Searches folder. You can save searches anywhere you can save any other file.

FIGURE 8.16
Saving a search creates a search folder.

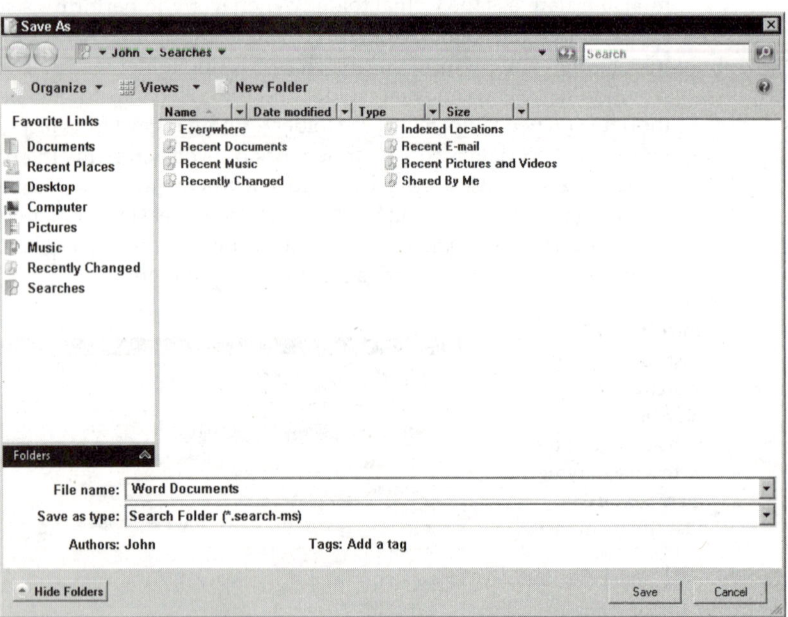

After you save the search, you can reopen it at any time using the search folder that you created. The folder will always contain the search that you specified. However, you can go further in modifying the search, which is why using the term *search folder* is more accurate. For example, you can add folder stacks. You can also change the sort order, use grouping, and even modify the search folder itself (see the "Understanding the XML Roots for Search Folders" section of the chapter for details).

NOTE Searches that you create on indexed folders always run faster than locations you haven't indexed. Since you can't index network folders, any network searches will run considerably slower. Not only do you have to consider the performance hit of searching in a location you haven't indexed, you must also consider the network overhead.

SETTING THE SEARCH OPTIONS

The search options you choose determine the efficiency and effectiveness of the search and affects the content of the search folder. For example, Explorer assumes that you only want to search the contents of indexed files, which means any data files on the network won't appear in the search folder when the content you want appears within them. Whether the default settings cause a problem or not depends on the way you work with the network. A laptop user might never have to change the default settings if they commonly work with files on the local drive.

You can access the search options in several ways. The easiest method is to choose Search Tools ➤ Search Options to display the Folder Options dialog box shown in Figure 8.17. You can also open the Folder Options applet in the control panel or choose Tools ➤ Folder Options in Explorer. In all cases, the settings you want to change appear on the Search tab. Figure 8.17 shows the default settings.

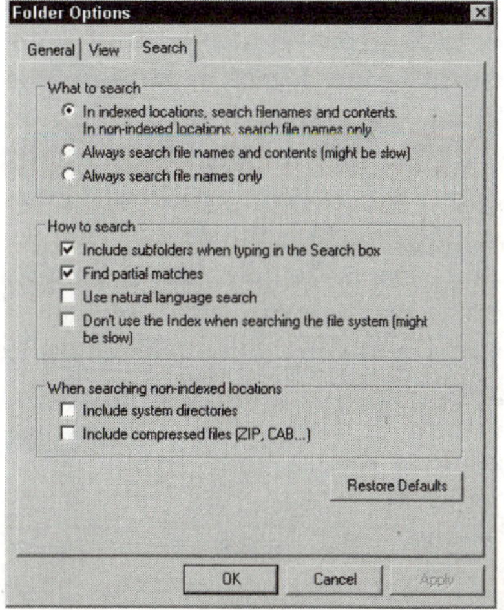

FIGURE 8.17
Set the search options to meet your needs when working with network or other unindexed data.

The What to Search section contains three options. The default setting takes the middle ground with performance by looking for content only in indexed files. You can also choose to search content for all files, which can incur a significant performance hit, or search just the filenames. In some cases, searching just the filenames can work to your benefit by delivering fast results when your only goal is locating a particular file based on extension or filename.

The How to Search section contains individually accessible options that determine what the search folder contains after the search. A subfolder search requires more time than searching just the current folder, but also produces results that are more complete when you organize your data into subfolders. The partial match and natural language searches allow for less than perfect search criteria. However, performance suffers when you use these features and the results may contain false positives. The index usually provides the fastest searching method. However, the index could also be outdated. A change to a file might not appear right away. Consequently, turning off indexed searching costs you time, but can also ensure more accurate results.

One of the complaints about previous versions of Windows was that any search automatically involved searching CAB, ZIP, and other archive files. In fact, a number of people actually wrote workarounds for this problem. Vista makes it possible to bypass both system files and archive files. The benefit is that you gain performance. However, because the default setting changes past Windows behavior, you might find that the search results don't contain all of the files and folders that you expected.

Changing Indexing Locations

Indexing can be a tricky topic because it involves tradeoffs. Some people think that indexing all of the local hard drives is the best course of action because searches are considerably faster. However, your system uses both CPU cycles and resources, such as memory, to create the index. Anything used to create the index is unavailable for other purposes. Even though indexing doesn't occur when you're physically doing something with the computer, the fact remains that you still have resources tied up in the index, so indexing everything in sight probably isn't efficient unless you spend all of your time searching for things. Likewise, most people perform searches at some point in the day. Consequently, you want to have the index available to find the items you need quickly. In short, you have to index based on the places that will most likely contain the data you need.

The default settings assume that you're going to look in your own personal folder, Office products such as Outlook, any offline files you've created, and the Start menu as shown in Figure 8.18. However, you might never search in your personal folders for anything because you already know what those folders contain and you normally share data files with other people, so creating an index of the personal folders doesn't make sense. On the other hand, Vista won't know to index the shared data folder you use to share data with other people. Customizing the index is very important. You can access the indexing locations by choosing Search Tools ➤ Modify Index Locations.

You should notice two things about Figure 8.18. First, you can't depend on the index unless you see Indexing Complete as the status. Consequently, if you find that you're getting less that perfect search results, this is the first place to look. Second, the number of search items tells you a little about the load that indexing places on your system. As the number of items increase, so does the system burden and you'll definitely see the loss of performance.

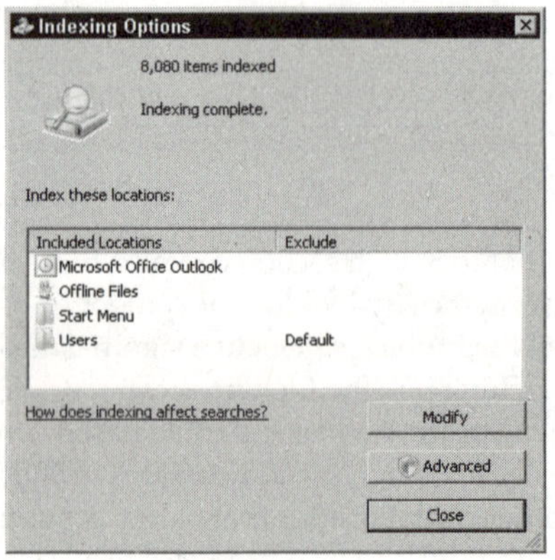

Figure 8.18
Modify the index locations so that the index your system creates matches your search requirements.

When you click Modify, you see the Indexed Locations dialog box where you can check which directories you want Vista to index. However, the initial display shows only your personal indexes. To see all of the indexes, you must click Show All Locations. After you click Continue at the UAC prompt, you'll see all of the local drives, your offline files, and any applications, such as Outlook, that offer indexing. Check or clear the directories that you want to index. It's essential to tune all of the directories on a system to ensure optimal performance.

Click Advanced to define how indexing occurs. After you click Continue at the UAC prompt, you'll see the Advanced Options dialog box. The Index Settings tab lets you choose a new location for the index. You should always place the index on your fastest drive when you have multiple drives installed on a system. Click Rebuild when you want to rebuild the index to take advantage of any changes you've made to the settings. You can also choose to index encrypted files and treat similar words with diacritics as different words.

Vista doesn't index every file on your system—it only indexes the file types that you want indexed. Adding more files to the list makes searching for every file type faster. However, very few people actually search every file type on their system. You might only search DOC files. Selecting the file types carefully can reduce indexing time without affecting search efficiency at all. The File Types tab contains a list of all of the file extensions that your system recognizes. Check the file extension to add that file to the indexed files list. You can also choose whether the index contains just the filename or the filename and content.

Understanding the Importance of Metadata

Metadata is a description of the data in a container. For example, most web pages include metadata that describe the page content. You'll also find metadata in database files and as part of many applications. However, from a search folder perspective, metadata is a description of the content of a data file. When you include the author name as part of the Properties dialog box for Word, you're adding metadata to the Word file that Vista can use to create a better index.

Not every application includes the ability to provide metadata, but a good many of the complex applications on your machine do. For example, I commonly add metadata to my Corel Draw files to make them easier to locate later. Whenever possible, you should provide complete metadata for each of the files you create. The metadata provides just one more way to identify the file and its content, which makes searches considerably faster and more accurate.

Vista also provides a method for working with metadata directly in files. Right-click any file and choose Properties. Click Details and you'll see the metadata associated with a file as shown in Figure 8.19. The metadata varies by file type. Figure 8.19 shows some of the metadata for a graphic file. Actually, this list contains a wealth of information about the picture, including the camera used to take it. Given that the computer has no way of understanding graphics, all of this metadata provides about the only way that you can search for an image on your hard drive.

FIGURE 8.19
Use metadata to define data in a way that makes it considerably easier to find.

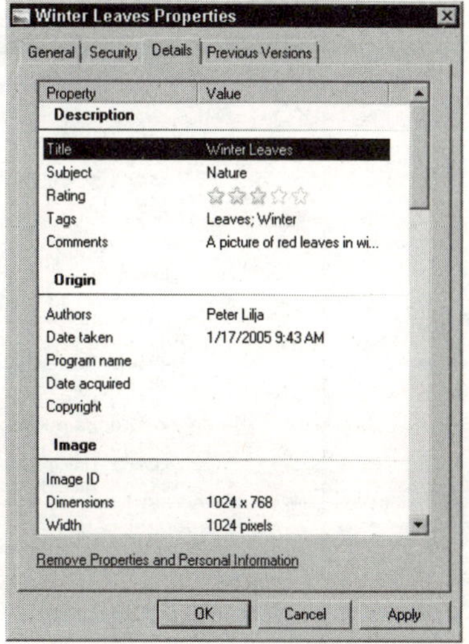

Notice that Figure 8.19 shows a special entry called Tags. A *tag* is a short descriptor that you use across multiple files. Normally, you use more than one tag to describe a particular picture and separate each tag with a semicolon. A tag need not consist of one word, but it's best to keep tags short. The Tags field in this example contains two entries, Leaves and Winter. You can enter these values in the Tags field shown in Figure 8.3 when searching to locate files faster. A tag represents another way to categorize files consistently.

Understanding the XML Roots for Search Folders

Microsoft has purposely made search folders flexible by relying on the Extensible Markup Language (XML) to define them. Search folders aren't anything too mysterious; you don't have to be an operating system guru to modify them to meet your own needs. Since all search folders rely on an XML specification, you can modify them quite easily as long as you know something about XML. If you want to see the XML in the file, use any program capable of viewing XML or text to open the search folder. Figure 8.20 shows the XML description of the Recently Changed search folder. I simply used Notepad to open it.

Search folders normally contain three main sections, each of which uses a special tag: `<viewInfo>`, `<query>`, and `<properties>`. The `<viewInfo>` tag contains children that describe how you want to display the entries in the search folder. For example, this is where you would define the sort order. The `<query>` tag contains children that describe the content of the search folder. You would include the document specification and the search location as children of this element. Finally, the `<properties>` element contains special data you want to locate, such as documents created by a particular author or tags defined as content in the file. Unfortunately, Microsoft hasn't yet published a complete specification for the search folders, so you won't be able to determine the use of every element in the file.

WARNING Always save a copy of the search folder and make changes to the copy. Otherwise, changes that have unexpected results might be difficult to undo later. It's important to work with search folders carefully.

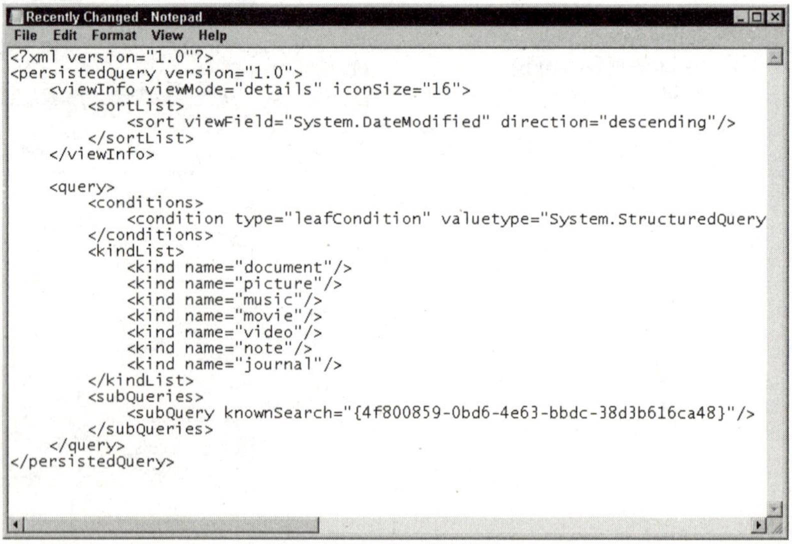

FIGURE 8.20 Search folders use XML to describe their content.

Recently Changed - Notepad

File Edit Format View Help

```
<?xml version="1.0"?>
<persistedQuery version="1.0">
    <viewInfo viewMode="details" iconSize="16">
        <sortList>
            <sort viewField="System.DateModified" direction="descending"/>
        </sortList>
    </viewInfo>

    <query>
        <conditions>
            <condition type="leafCondition" valuetype="System.StructuredQuery
        </conditions>
        <kindList>
            <kind name="document"/>
            <kind name="picture"/>
            <kind name="music"/>
            <kind name="movie"/>
            <kind name="video"/>
            <kind name="note"/>
            <kind name="journal"/>
        </kindList>
        <subQueries>
            <subQuery knownSearch="{4f800859-0bd6-4e63-bbdc-38d3b616ca48}"/>
        </subQueries>
    </query>
</persistedQuery>
```

One of the entries I modify most often is the <scope> tag. The <scope> tag contains entries for where you want Explorer to look for the files and folders you specified. Unfortunately, the <scope> tag only contains one entry usually as shown here because Vista won't let you add anything else.

```
<scope>
   <include path="I:\WINWORD"/>
</scope>
```

However, you can add as many <include> tags as you want between the scope tags. For example, if you change the code as shown here, you'll add both the C and D drives to the search.

```
<scope>
   <include path="C:\"/>
   <include path="D:\"/>
   <include path="I:\WINWORD"/>
</scope>
```

This is an example of a modification you can make to a search folder specification that you can't add in any other way. Because search folders rely on XML, you'll find that you can add to the flexibility that they provide quite easily. The important consideration is that you work with search folders within the limits that Microsoft has set for them within Vista. Unfortunately, those limits don't appear in writing today, which means that a little experimentation is usually in order.

NOTE The best way to perform a search on a network drive, such as a server, is to map the network drive. To create a mapped drive, open the connection to the network drive in the Network window (Start ➤ Network). Once you create the mapped drive, use the drive letter you assigned to the network drive for the search instead of the Universal Naming Convention (UNC) path. If Vista doesn't allow you to add the drive to your search scope, you can open the search folder and manually add the drive as an <include> child of the <scope> element.

Creating Junctions and Symbolic Links with MkLink

Vista contains a couple of features—junctions and symbolic links—that will make it easier for an administrator to create easy data access for the user without exposing the actual location of that data. A *junction* is a high efficiency shortcut to a local directory. You use junctions to provide a quick access method for local resources. Even though MkLink will let you create junctions to network drives, attempting to use them will display an error message. Here's the command line syntax for a quick shortcut I created to a personal data folder.

```
MkLink /J MyStuff \Users\Mark
```

A *symbolic link* is simply another kind of shortcut, but it requires more resources to use. You use symbolic links to point to a file or folder in any other location. However, unlike a shortcut, the symbolic link makes the pointer look like a local file or folder. As far as the user is concerned, the file or folder exists on the local drive. Most importantly for administrators of mixed systems, Microsoft created symbolic links to look just like the links on UNIX systems. The most important feature of symbolic links is that you can use them to create links to network drives. For example, the following command line creates a folder named `Test1` that is actually a link to the `\Winword` folder on drive D on a server named WinServer.

```
MkLink /d Test1 \\WinServer\Drive_D\Winword
```

A symbolic link has another different from junctions. When you right-click a symbolic link and choose Properties from the context menu, the resulting Properties dialog box contains an additional tab named Shortcut. The Shortcut tab contains settings that let you work with the original source of information. Consequently, unlike junctions, you do have some control over the link when working with symbolic links.

The important difference between shortcuts and both junctions and symbolic links is that shortcuts are a Component Object Model (COM) object that the shell understands, but that the operating system doesn't really know about. Shortcuts are useless to anyone writing scripts or development applications. Consequently, even though a shortcut gives you access to remote resources on the network it has significant limitations. That's why both symbolic links and junctions are so important.

NOTE The MkLink utility also supports Windows NT style hard links (reparse points). A *hard link* provides a direct pointer to a file on the same volume as the hard link. In other words, you can create a convenient way to access a file that might be buried several layers deep using a hard link. Any change you make to the hard-linked file also appears in the original file, so changing one is akin to changing the other. Given the power and flexibility of both junctions and symbolic links, you should avoid using hard links.

Use the MkLink utility to create junctions, symbolic links, and hard links. Here's the command line for the MkLink utility:

```
MKLINK [[/D] | [/H] | [/J]] Link Target
```

The following list describes each of the command line switches.

/D Creates a directory symbolic link. The default setting creates a file symbolic link.

/H Creates a hard link (reparse point) using the Windows NT methodology instead of a symbolic link. This option is only provided for backward compatibility.

/J Creates a directory junction instead of a symbolic link.

Link Defines the name of the symbolic link, junction, or hard link. This is the name of the local file or folder that the user sees.

Target Defines the location of the target file or folder. This is the real location of the data.

NOTE The `Dir` command can be very helpful in showing you symbolic links and junctions on your hard drive. When using the `Dir` command normally, directories have a <DIR> annotation, while symbolic links have a <SYMLINKD> annotation and junctions have a <JUNCTION> annotation. The actual location of the symbolic link or junction appears in brackets behind the directory name such as, `MyStuff [C:\Users\Mark]`. Finally, you can use `Dir /AL /S` in the root directory to list just the symbolic links and junctions on your hard drive.

Understanding the Multiuser Environment

From the ground up, Vista is designed as a multiuser-networking environment. Because security is so integral to the way that Vista operates, it's possible for two or more users to use the same workstation without stepping on each other's toes. That is, one user can log on and do the work they want to do without necessarily knowing who else has access to the computer or without having access to another user's files.

When a user logs on to a Vista workstation, the operating system assigns that user a security token. The Vista Security Manager portion of the Executive Services manages security tokens. Each time that user attempts to do something in Vista, be it open a file, send e-mail or change the way the Desktop looks, the Security Manager checks that person's token to see if they have the rights and permissions to perform the task they've requested. See Chapter 21 for a more thorough discussion of security.

As a result of the token-based security system, Vista administers multiuser environments logically. User profile information is stored in the user's folder in the `Users` folder on the drive where Vista is installed. Inside the `Users` folder is a folder for each user that logs in to a workstation, and inside each user's folder is a set of folders that customize the Vista environment for that user.

Customizing the Explorer Interface

There are many ways to change the way the Explorer window looks and acts. In the following sections, I'll outline some of the most important ones.

Setting Folder Options

The Folder Options dialog box is a rich source for customizing the Explorer interface. Changes made there affect all Explorer windows, regardless of what drive or folder's content appears there. To access it, choose Tools ➤ Folder Options.

In the General tab (shown in Figure 8.2), you can:

- Turn off the Common Tasks pane to the left of the file listing by choosing Use Windows Classic folders.
- Choose to open each folder in a separate window, instead of the default of having the next-chosen location replace the preceding one.
- Choose to have Windows (the Explorer window and the Desktop) work more like a web page, wherein you single-click to activate something and point at it to select it.

NOTE **When Windows 98 was in beta testing, the default was this single-click-to-activate behavior, but it drove most people crazy because it was so different from what they were used to. Therefore, in the final version, and in all versions since, the double-click-to-select method has been the default and this single-click one has been just an alternative.**

In the View tab, you can:

- Set a particular View option to apply to all folder listings. By default, when you change the View setting, it applies to that folder only.
- Select or deselect a wide variety of Advanced Settings for how files should be displayed. Table 8.1 lists the complete set.

NOTE **Vista doesn't provide support for the File Types tab. Instead of the File Types tab, you use the Default Programs applet in the Control Panel (discussed later in this chapter) to change file associations for an extension. The Offline Files tab, covered in Chapter 7, lets you cache copies of files available through a connection that may only be available sporadically.**

TABLE 8.1: Advanced Settings in the View Tab of the Folder Options Dialog Box

SETTING	PURPOSE/NOTES
Always Show Icons, Never Thumbnails	Displays icons when using the icon sizes normally large enough to show thumbnails. See the "Views" section of the chapter for details.
Always Show Menus	By default, Vista doesn't show menu bars for various applications including Explorer, Media Player, Photo Gallery, and Internet Explorer. Checking this option displays the menu bars as all times.
Display File Icon on Thumbnails	Displays a small version of the application icon on a thumbnail. Using this option makes it easier to determine which application opens the file by default.
Display File Size Information in Folder Tips	On by default. Includes file size in the ScreenTip that appears when you hover the mouse pointer over a file.
Display Simple Folder View in Navigation Pane	On by default. Collapses any branches open in the folder list when you move to a different branch of the folder tree.
Display the Full Path in the Title Bar	Off by default. Same as above but for title bar.
Hidden Files and Folders	By default set to Do Not Show Hidden Files and Folders. Power users generally change this to Show Hidden Files and Folders so that hidden items appear in file listings (but ghosted, to distinguish them from normal files).
Hide Extensions for Known File Types	On by default. Power users generally turn this off so that all file extensions appear.
Hide Protected Operating System Files	On by default. Excludes files with the System attribute from file listings.
Launch Folder Windows in a Separate Process	Off by default. Launches each folder window in a separate memory space, increasing stability but decreasing performance.
Managing Pairs of Web Pages and Folders	Specifies how Windows should treat web page files that have associated folders in a file management window.
Remember Each Folder's View Settings	On by default. Opens each folder to the same View setting as was previously selected for it.
Restore Previous Folder Windows at Logon	On by default. When Windows shuts down with open folder windows, they are redisplayed when Windows restarts.
Show Drive Letters	On by default. Displays both the drive letter and the friendly name for a drive. When you clear this setting, Vista displays only the friendly name.

TABLE 8.1: Advanced Settings in the View Tab of the Folder Options Dialog Box *(CONTINUED)*

SETTING	PURPOSE/NOTES
Show Control Panel in My Computer	Off by default. In previous Windows versions, this was on by default. Adds a Control Panel icon to My Computer.
Show Encrypted or Compressed NTFS Files in Color	On by default. Changes the text color for any files that use NTFS compression or NTFS encryption (covered later in this chapter).
Show Pop-Up Description for Folder and Desktop Items	On by default. Displays a pop-up ScreenTip when you hover over an item.
Show Preview Handlers in Preview Pane	On by default. Displays the contents of a file using a preview handler when the Preview pane is displayed. Clearing this option will improve the performance of your computer.
Use Check Boxes to Select Items	Off by default. Displays a selection check box whenever you hover the mouse over an object. See the "Using the Check Box Feature" section of the chapter for details.
Use Sharing Wizard	On by default. Limits the capability to assign complex permissions to files and folders in the interest of simplicity.
When Typing into List View	Lets you choose between typing the value into the Search field automatically or displaying the results in the view.

Customizing an Individual Folder

In addition to the global settings, you can also specify settings for each folder. As you've already seen, by default, Windows remembers your choice of View setting for each folder individually. You can also do the following to further customize the folder:

1. Choose View ➤ Customize This Folder. A Properties box for the folder appears.
2. Click the Customize tab and then choose a different folder type from the Use This Folder Type As a Template list if desired. See Figure 8.21. For example, if the folder will be holding pictures, you might choose that. The folder type template sets several default options appropriate for that content type, including a view.
3. If you want a picture thumbnail to appear for the folder in Thumbnails view, click the Choose Picture button and add one.
4. If you want a different icon to appear for the folder whenever icons are shown, click the Change Icon button and select an icon.
5. Click OK when finished.

NOTE Vista doesn't allow you to modify the Explorer toolbars. Previous versions of Windows provided customization options that you can't use in Vista. This policy seems to coincide with Microsoft's elimination of toolbar customization in other products such as Office.

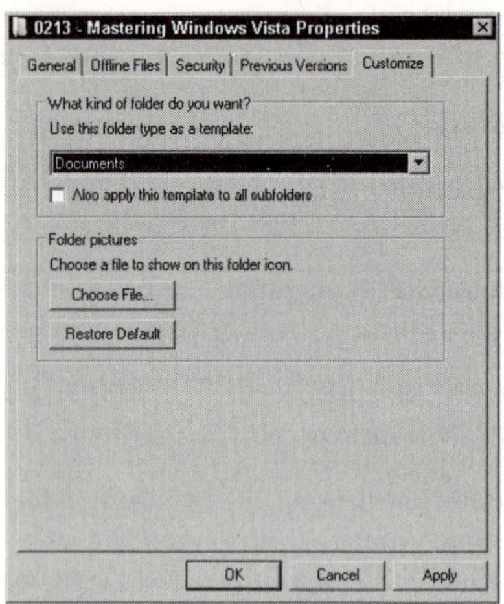

FIGURE 8.21
Properties for the current folder affect how it appears in Explorer.

Setting File and Folder Properties

Right-click any file or folder and choose Properties to display its Properties box. Files typically have five or six tabs and some have even more. You've already read about a number of these tabs in other sections of the book including the Details, Previous Versions, and Offline Files tabs. Some applications, such as Word, also provide Custom tab where you can type custom properties for the file. However, one important tab that you haven't seen yet is the General tab.

The General tab lists information about the file and lets you turn on/off three attributes for the file:

- Read-only prevents the file from being modified or deleted.
- Hidden excludes the file from file listings (unless the Show Hidden Files and Folders option is chosen in Folder Options).
- Archive marks the file as having been changed since the last time a backup operation turned off the archive attribute. (This check box is present only on FAT and FAT32 volumes; for what happens on an NTFS volume, see the following description.)

On NTFS volumes, the General tab has an Advanced button, which you can use to set NTFS options such as encryption and compression. When you click the Advanced button, you can then mark the Folder Is Ready for Archiving check box to turn the Archive attribute on/off.

For folders, the Properties box contains a General tab, the same as with files, but also a Customize tab (which you saw in "Customizing an Individual Folder" earlier in the chapter) and a Sharing tab for setting up network sharing permission for the folder. You'll learn about networking features in Part V of this book.

Working with Compressed Files and Folders

Two kinds of compressed files and folders are available in Vista. You can use Zip compression to create compressed archives of multiple files in a single ZIP file that Vista can work with as if it were a folder; you can also compress files with NTFS compression if you're using the NTFS file system on the drive. The following sections look at these compression features.

Using Zip Compression

If you have limited disk space on your computer or on your network, or if you often need to transfer files over the Internet and have a slow connection, you've probably used a compression utility. Vista includes its own version of a compression utility called WinZip, a popular program that has been widely distributed in stand-alone versions for many years.

When you compress, or "zip," a file or a folder in Vista, that file or folder can be uncompressed, or "unzipped," by almost any other compression utility. In addition, Windows treats ZIP files like folders, so you can open and browse them just like you would a normal folder. A compressed folder has a zipper on it.

Compressing a file or a folder is fast and easy. You simply right-click the file or folder in an Explorer-type window, choose Send To on the shortcut menu, and click Compressed Folder on the submenu. A compressed copy of the file or folder is placed in the folder that contains the original file. The filename is the same as that of the original file or folder, but with a `.zip` extension. If you selected more than one file or folder for zipping into a single ZIP file, the ZIP file will bear the name of the last file or folder in the selected group.

Once a ZIP file exists, you can open it in Explorer and compress other files or folders by simply dragging them to the compressed folder. When you then move the file or folder out of the compressed folder, it's uncompressed.

You can also compress files in Windows applications, and in Chapter 17, we'll look at how to do so in Windows Mail.

WARNING Even though a ZIP file appears to be a normal folder when opened in Explorer, it has limitations. For example, if a Setup program and its helper files are contained in a ZIP file, the Setup program probably won't run correctly from its ZIP file location; you'll likely need to extract the contents of the ZIP file to a real folder on your hard disk before you can run it. And if you open a document from a ZIP file, it will be read-only and you'll need to save it under a different name.

Using NTFS Compression

As you learned way back in Chapter 1, the NTFS file system has many advantages over FAT32 under Vista. One of these is the capability of compressing a folder to save disk space. Retrieving files from a compressed folder takes slightly longer than a normal folder; other than that the compression is totally invisible. You might want to compress folders that you don't use frequently if disk space is an issue. NTFS compression doesn't compress as dramatically as Zip-type compression, but is less obtrusive.

On an NTFS drive, files and folders have an Advanced button in the General tab of their properties box. It's your gateway to the NTFS properties for the item:

1. From the file or folder Properties box, click the General tab.
2. Click the Advanced button. The Advanced Attributes dialog box opens (Figure 8.22).
3. Mark the Compress Contents to Save Disk Space check box to compress the item, and then click OK.

4. Choose Apply Changes to This Folder Only, or choose Apply Changes to This Folder, Subfolders, and Files. Then click OK.

NTFS compressed folders and files appear with their names in blue rather than black to differentiate them from normal ones when you choose the Show Encrypted or Compressed NTFS Files in Color option in the Folder options dialog box. To decompress them, follow the same steps but clear the check box.

When you move or copy a compressed file or folder onto a non-NTFS drive, it's automatically uncompressed. Here are some additional rules:

- Any new files/folders created in a compressed folder become compressed.
- Any files/folders copied into a compressed folder become compressed.
- Any files/folders moved from another NTFS drive into a compressed folder become compressed.
- Any files/folders moved from another location on the same NTFS drive into a compressed folder retain the compression settings from the original location.
- Any compressed files/folders moved into an uncompressed location on the same NTFS drive remain compressed.
- Any compressed files/folders moved into an uncompressed location on a different NTFS drive become uncompressed.

TIP NTFS compression and NTFS encryption (covered in the following section) are mutually exclusive; you can use one or the other but not both. If you need NTFS compression, consider using some other method of protection such as network security; if you need NTFS encryption, consider some other method of compression such as Zip compression.

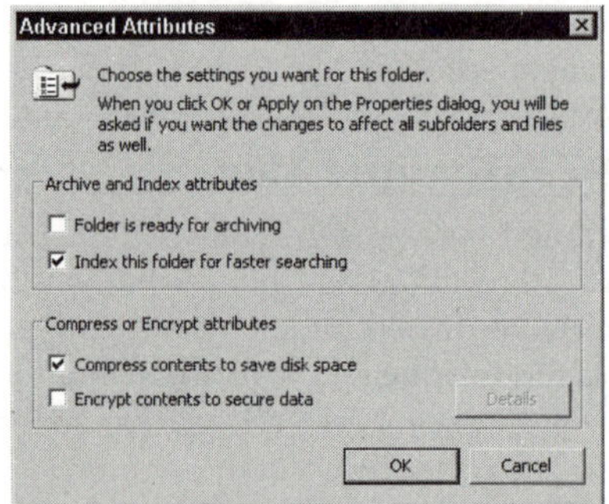

FIGURE 8.22 Set NTFS compression here.

Using Encrypted File System (EFS)

You might have noticed in Figure 8.22 that NTFS encryption is also available, in addition to compression. This encryption is sometimes referred to as Encrypted File System, or EFS. Encrypted folders and files appear with their names in green rather than black to differentiate them from normal ones when you choose the Show Encrypted or Compressed NTFS Files in Color option in the Folder options dialog box.

EFS encryption is different from network permissions because it deals with security on a local level. It's based on the logged-on user on the machine. When the user who encrypted the folder or file is logged on, it's transparent, but when anyone else is logged on, the file or folder is inaccessible. This is handy when multiple users share a PC and must work with sensitive data.

NOTE Encryption isn't limited to local machines only; there's also encryption between a web browser and a server using Secure Socket Layers and encryption between computers on virtual private networks (VPNs) and e-mail. However, this chapter will limit the discussion to local EFS.

It works like this: EFS encryption uses the logged-on user's public key to generate a file-encryption key that the encrypted file or folder must pass through in order to be accessed. When you're logged in as the same user who did the encrypting, Windows automatically accesses the needed keys, but when anyone else is logged on, there's a different public key in use, so the decryption doesn't happen.

Backing Up Your Certificates

Before you start using NTFS encryption, you should make a backup copy of the certificates needed to access encrypted files and store them on a removable disk. There's virtually no way to hack into an encrypted file if you lose the needed certificates or keys.

The first time you use NTFS encryption, Windows generates your personal encryption certificate. This certificate includes a public key and a private key. Windows can also create another certificate, for a designated recovery agent, which will also permit access to the user's encrypted files. Unlike previous versions of Windows, Vista automatically displays an Encrypted File System dialog box. Click Back Up Now and follow the instructions to back up your certificates.

At some point, you'll probably want to make additional copies of your certificates. You'll want to back up these two certificates separately. The personal encryption certificate should be stored in a safe location that you can personally access; the recovery agent certificate should be given to your system administrator.

To back up your personal encryption certificate:

1. Make sure you're logged on using the user account for which you want to back up the certificate.
2. Display the Internet Options dialog box, either from Control Panel or from Internet Explorer (Tools ➤ Internet Options).
3. In the Content tab, click the Certificates button to open the Certificates dialog box.
4. In the Personal tab, select the certificate that shows Encrypted File System in the Certificate Intended Purposes area. See Figure 8.23.

WARNING If you don't have a certificate listed on the Personal tab, you have no encrypted files or folders. Go ahead and encrypt one file just for the purpose of creating the certificate, and then come back here to continue.

5. Click Export. The Certificate Export Wizard starts.
6. Click Next, and then click Yes, Export the Private Key, and click Next again.
7. Click Next to accept the defaults on the next screen.

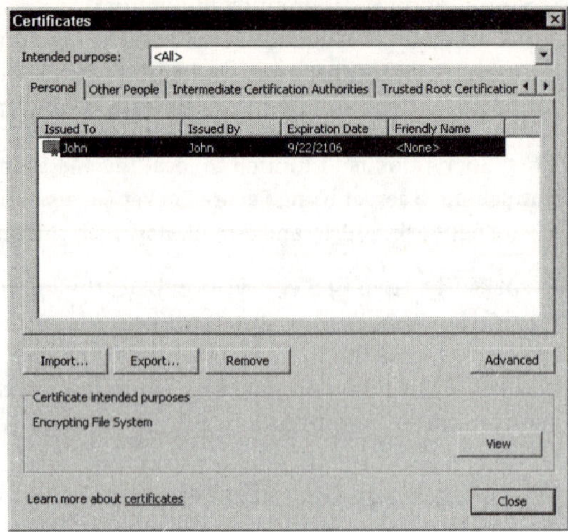

FIGURE 8.23
Manage certificates, including backing them up, from here.

8. When prompted for a password, make one up and enter and confirm it. Then click Next.
9. Enter a path and name for the exported file. You might want to export to a floppy, for example. You don't need to type a file extension, because a `.pfx` extension will be automatically appended. Then click Next.
10. Click Finish. A box appears telling you it was a success; click OK.

Encrypting and Decrypting

Windows allows you to encrypt both folders and files, but most experts recommend that you encrypt only folders. Any files you place in an encrypted folder become encrypted while they are there, but if you move them out of the folder they become decrypted. However, if you encrypt an individual file, it remains encrypted no matter where you move it.

TIP **Some programs generate temporary files as they operate that store parts of your data file. Even though you may be storing the data file in an encrypted folder, these temp files aren't encrypted because they are stored someplace else—for example, in `C:\Windows\Temp` or some other location. If you can determine where the program stores its temporary working files, you might want to encrypt that folder for added security.**

To encrypt a folder:

1. From the folder's Properties, click Advanced in the General tab.
2. Mark the Encrypt contents to secure data check box. Refer back to Figure 8.22.
3. Click OK, and then OK again. The folder's name turns green to indicate it's encrypted.

When you encrypt a file, rather than a folder, you're asked whether you also want to encrypt the parent folder of the file; you don't get a prompt like that when encrypting a folder.

To decrypt, repeat the process but clear the Encrypt Contents to Secure Data check box. Obviously, you must do this while logged on with the same user account as you used to encrypt. (You can also use an account where you've imported the encryption certificate.) A dialog box asks whether you want to decrypt only the folder or the folder and its contents. If you choose to decrypt the contents too, it will only decrypt the files for which the current user account has valid certificates.

When moving or copying, the following rules apply:

- If you move or copy an unencrypted file into an encrypted folder, it becomes encrypted.
- If you move or copy a file from an encrypted folder into an unencrypted folder, encryption is removed.
- If you have encrypted a file itself (not just the folder in which it resides), it retains its encryption no matter where it's moved or copied.
- If you try to move an encrypted file or folder to a non-NTFS drive, encryption is removed.
- If you delete an encrypted file or folder to the Recycle Bin, it remains encrypted in the Recycle Bin.

WARNING Beginners can get themselves into a fair amount of trouble by using EFS encryption without really understanding it, so don't experiment with EFS on important files, and don't use EFS unless you're confident that you understand its risks and limitations.

Sharing Encrypted Files with Other Local Users

You can set up sharing for individual encrypted files only; you can't do it for folders or multiple files at once. ("Encrypted files" here includes both files that have been individually encrypted and files that are encrypted because they reside in an encrypted folder.)

NOTE This sharing doesn't have anything to do with sharing files and folders via network. EFS is for local access only. If you want to share an encrypted file or folder via network, place it in your Shared Documents folder or set up its network sharing permissions as explained in Chapter 19.

To share an encrypted file:

1. Right-click the file and choose Properties.
2. In the General tab, click Advanced. Then, in the Advanced Attributes dialog box, click Details.
3. In the Encryption Details box, click Add. The Select User dialog box appears.
4. Select the user that you want to have access, and click OK.

NOTE Only other local users of this PC who have an EFS certificate appear here. If the person you want to designate doesn't appear, have them log in to the local PC and encrypt a file or folder.

Transferring Encrypted Files to Another PC

To work with an encrypted file on another PC, you must export your personal encryption certificate on the original PC and then import it on the other one.

1. Back up your personal encryption certificate using the steps in "Backing Up Your Certificates" earlier in this section.

2. On the computer that is to receive the certificate, open the Internet Options dialog box (Tools ➤ Internet Options from within IE) and display the Content tab.
3. Click the Certificates button, and then click Import. The Certificate Import Wizard runs. Click Next to Continue.
4. Browse to locate the exported certificate, which has a `.pfx` extension. Then click Next.
5. Enter the password you assigned when you exported it, and then click Next.
6. Click Place All Certificates in the Following Store. Then click Browse to open the Select Certificate Store dialog box, choose Personal, and click OK.
7. Click Next, and then click Finish.

Using Sync Center

Previously versions of Windows made it hard to keep files and folders synchronized. Vista remedies the problem by making synchronization almost too easy. In fact, synchronization is automatic in most cases. Synchronization occurs when Vista updates files in one location with files from another location. The key word is update. The Sync Center works with files that actually appear in multiple locations. For example, when you set up a folder for offline use, Vista sets up synchronization with that folder. If the folder becomes unavailable for any reason, you can still make changes to the content of the file. When the folder becomes available again, Vista updates the content of the original folder with the changes you've made.

You can always verify synchronization by opening the Sync Center. It appears as a green icon in the notification area or you can open it using the Sync Center applet in the Control Panel. Figure 8.24 shows the initial Sync Center display.

FIGURE 8.24
Use Sync Center to manage the synchronization between devices or network drives.

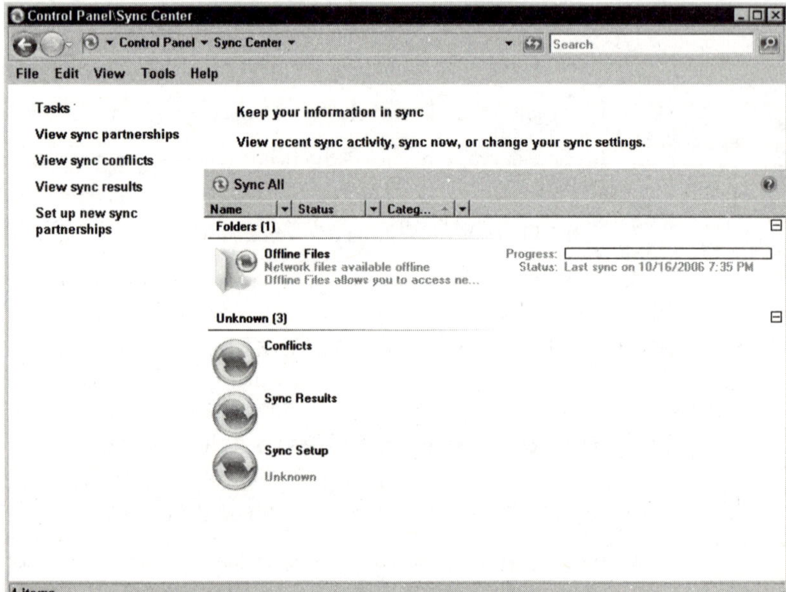

Synchronization is either one or two way. An offline folder is always a one-way synchronization. Any content you change in the folder while the folder is unavailable automatically moves to that folder when your system reestablishes contact. On the other hand, synchronization with a device is either one or two way. You may decide to provide two-way synchronization with your laptop, but only want one-way synchronization with a camera or MP3 player. In general, Vista sets up the type of synchronization automatically depending on the location or device type.

Whenever your system synchronizes with an attached device, you can choose the type of synchronization partnership. Of course, your device has to support Sync Center and since this is a new application, most older devices won't. To verify whether a device will work with Sync Center, install any software that came with it, open Sync Center, and select the Set Up New Sync Partnerships link. If the device appears in the list, then you can create one- or two-way partnerships with it.

Using synchronization isn't without risk. Since the Sync Center doesn't place a lock on any file you modify, someone else could modify it too. When this situation occurs, the file in the primary folder might contain newer data than when you last synchronized with it. Now the problem is one of which file to keep; there's a conflict between the two files. Vista lets you choose which of the files to keep or you can save your modified file using a different name (preserving both sets of changes).

Whenever you want to verify the results of synchronization, you can choose the View Sync Result link of the Sync Center. You'll see a list of started, completed, and failed synchronization. Although Vista doesn't tell you about started and completed synchronization, it will always tell you about failed synchronizations or those that result in a conflict.

Creating CDs

The recordable CD is without doubt the most cost-effective backup and transfer medium available. If you bought your computer recently, it may have come with a recordable CD drive, and you'll be interested to know that Vista includes CD-writing (also known as "burning") capability.

Burning CDs from Explorer is an easy, three-step process:

1. Copy the files to the storage area.
2. Check the files in the storage area to make sure that they're the right files and that there aren't too many of them.
3. Write the files to CD.

Copying the Files to the Storage Area

The first step in burning files (or folders) to CD is to copy them to the storage area. You can do so in several ways, of which these three are usually the easiest:

- Select the files in an Explorer window or in a common dialog box. Then right-click in the selection and choose Send To ➢ CD Drive from the shortcut menu. (Alternatively, choose File ➢ Send To ➢ CD Drive.) This technique is the most convenient when you're working in Explorer or in a common dialog box.
- Drag the files and drop them on the CD drive in an Explorer window or on a shortcut to the CD. For example, you could keep a shortcut to the CD on your Desktop so that you could quickly drag files and folders to it. This technique is good for copying to CD files or folders that you keep on your Desktop.

- Open an Explorer window to the storage area, and then drag files to it and drop them there. This technique is mostly useful for adding files when you're checking the contents of the storage area. When you insert a blank CD in your CD drive, Windows displays a CD Drive dialog box offering to open a folder to the writable CD folder.
- Place a blank CD in the drive. Vista will automatically detect that the CD is blank and ask how you want to work with it. You can choose between audio or file storage. After you choose file storage, you have an option of creating a multi-session CD using the Live File System option that might not be compatible with all systems or a CD that is only usable for one recording using the Mastered option that is compatible with most systems.

When you take one of these actions, Windows copies the files to the storage area and displays a notification area pop-up telling you that you have files waiting to be written to the CD.

Either click the pop-up or (if it has disappeared) open a My Computer window and double-click the icon for the CD drive. Windows opens an Explorer window showing the storage area, which appears as a list called Files Ready to Be Written to the CD. (For a CD-RW that already contains files, the storage area also contains a list of Files Currently on the CD.) Figure 8.25 shows an example of the storage area. As you can see in the figure, Windows displays a downward-pointing arrow on the icon for each file or folder to indicate that it's a temporary file destined to be burned to CD and then disposed of.

While Windows copies the files, the CD drive will appear to be busy, but it won't actually be writing any information to CD yet.

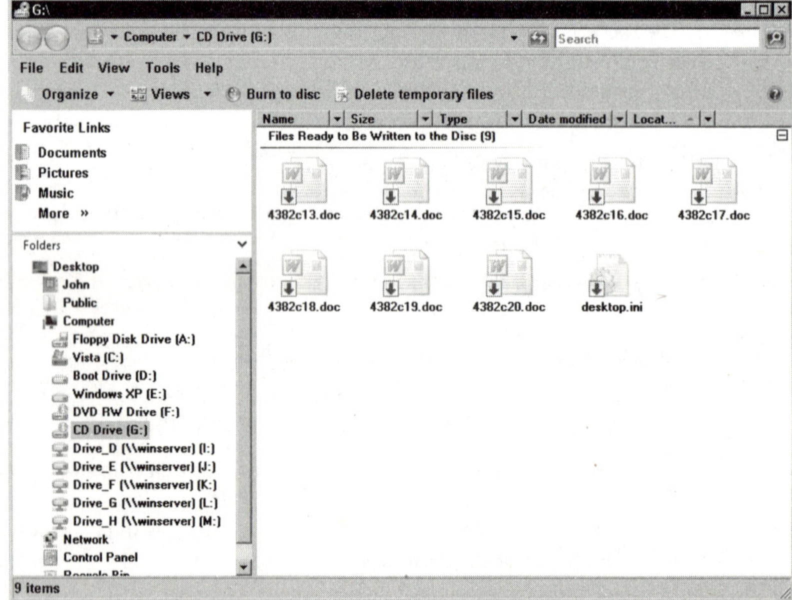

FIGURE 8.25
The storage area holds the copies of files to be copied to the CD. The downward-pointing arrow on each file icon and folder icon indicates that the item is temporary and will be deleted after being burned to CD.

CHECKING THE FILES IN THE STORAGE AREA

Once you've copied to the storage area all the files that you want to burn to the CD, activate the window that Explorer opened to the storage area and check that the files are all there, that you don't want to remove any of them, and that there aren't too many to fit on the CD. (If you closed the window showing the storage area, you can display the storage area again by opening an Explorer window to My Computer and double-clicking the icon for the CD drive.)

NOTE By default, the storage area is located in the `Local Settings\Application Data\Microsoft\CD Burning\` folder under the folder for your account in the `Documents and Settings\` folder.

To check the size of files in the storage area, select them all (for example, by choosing Edit ➤ Select All), and then right-click and choose Properties from the shortcut menu. Windows displays the Properties dialog box for the files. Check the Size readout in the General tab.

Writing the Files to CD

Once you've looked at the files in the storage area and are satisfied all is well, start the process of writing the files to CD. Take the following steps:

1. Click Burn to Disk. Windows starts the Burn to Disk Wizard.
2. Enter the name for the CD in the Disk Title field. CD names can be a maximum of 16 characters.
3. If you want the wizard to close itself when the CD is finished, select the Close the Wizard After the Files Have Been Written check box. If you select this check box, you won't have the option of creating another CD containing the same files because the wizard automatically clears the storage area.
4. Choose the writing speed for the CD. Faster writing speeds let you create CDs faster, but also incurs the risks of write failures.
5. Click the Next button. Vista begins writing the files to the CD.
6. Click the Finish button. The wizard closes itself and deletes the files from the storage area unless you selected the Yes, Write These Files to Another CD check box.

When Things Go Wrong Writing the CD

If you try to write more files to a CD than will fit on it, the CD Writing Wizard displays the Cannot Complete the CD Writing Wizard screen. You can remove some files from the storage area, then select the Retry Writing the Files to CD Now option button, and click the Finish button if you want to try to fix the problem while the CD is open. In most cases, though, you'll do best to leave the Close the Wizard without Writing the Files option button selected and click the Finish button. Then you can return to the storage area, fix the problem, and restart the writing process.

The CD Writing Wizard may also warn you that there was an error in the recording process, and that the disc may no longer be usable. This is the other reason that people like the term *burning* for recording CDs—when things go wrong, you get burned and the disc is toast. In this case, you'll probably want to try writing the files to another CD.

When you've finished creating the CD, test it immediately (preferably on a different computer) by opening an Explorer window to its contents and opening some of the files. Make sure all is well with the CD before archiving it or sending it on its way.

TIP If the CD you create won't read or play properly, it may have suffered recording errors. Try reducing the burning speed by using the Select a Recording Speed drop-down list in the Recording tab of the Properties dialog box for the drive.

Clearing the Storage Area

If you end up deciding not to create the CD after all, clear the storage area by deleting the files in it. To do so, click Delete Temporary Files. Windows displays the Confirm Delete dialog box to make sure you know the files haven't yet been written to CD. Click the Yes button. Windows deletes the files and removes the Files to Add to the CD heading from the Explorer window.

DVDs Too, Now!

Vista also offers the chance to work with DVDs. Basically everything works the same as when you work with CDs. Of course, you get a lot of extra recording space on a DVD and there are additional burning options. The most interesting new option is to burn a DVD video disk using the Windows DVD Maker. (See Chapter 11 for details on working with Windows DVD Maker.) For example, you can use DVDs to store video. However, the basics of working with DVDs are the same as CDs.

Working with Windows Sidebar

Windows Sidebar is an interesting new addition to Vista that provides nearly instant updates of various kinds of information. It appears on the right or left side of the display as shown in Figure 8.26. You can choose to have it appear on top of all of the other windows for constant display or underneath so it doesn't distract you unless you really do want to see it. (You can always display Windows Sidebar by clicking its icon in the notification area.) The information varies according to the gadgets you install. A *gadget* is a mini-application normally used as an information output, such as a clock, calendar, Really Simple Syndication (RSS) feed, or stock ticker. The gadgets supplied with Vista aren't of the sort that you could call critical. At best, most of them are fun, while some are just plain distracting. The following sections describe Windows Sidebar in detail.

NOTE Windows Sidebar works fine using any interface. However, when you decide to place it on top of all other windows, you really need to use the Aero Glass interface to see anything underneath. Some of the gadgets may also require use of the Vista Standard or Aero Glass interfaces.

Setting Windows Sidebar Properties

Windows Sidebar has a few properties that affect the application as a whole. You access these properties by right-clicking Windows Sidebar and choosing Properties from the context menu. You can also set the properties opening the Windows Sidebar Properties applet of the Control Panel or by right-clicking the Windows Sidebar icon in the notification area and choosing Properties. Figure 8.27 shows the settings in the Windows Sidebar Properties dialog box.

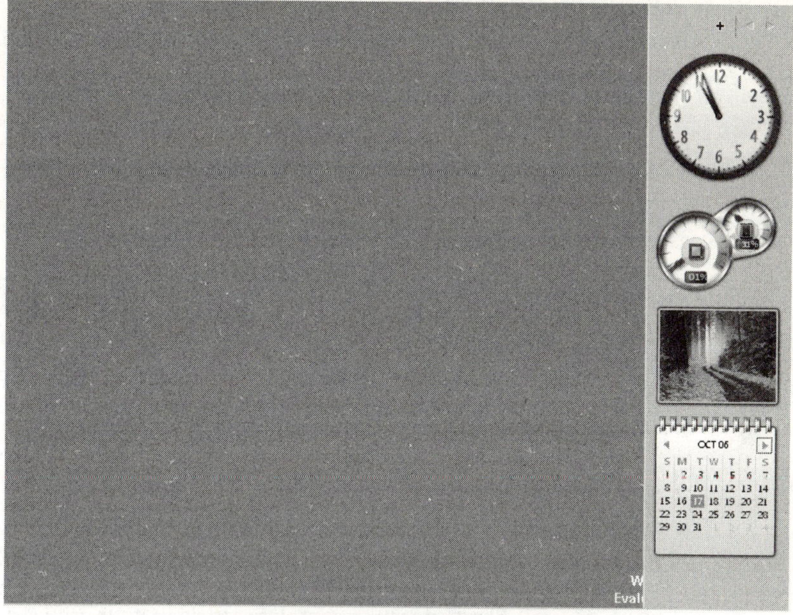

FIGURE 8.26
Windows Sidebar has the potential to provide interesting functionality, but the current gadgets aren't thrilling.

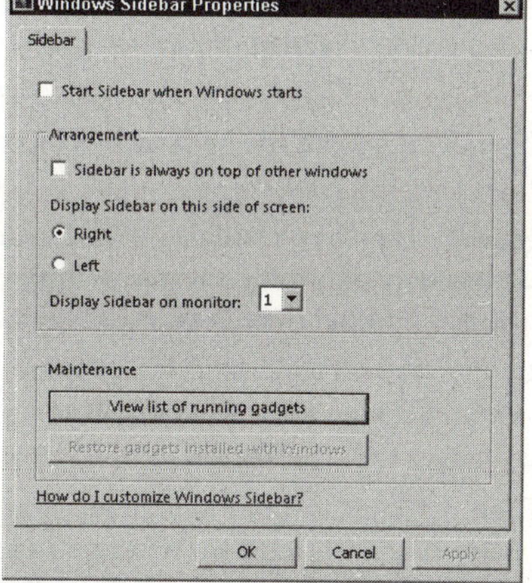

FIGURE 8.27
Change the way that Windows Sidebar works by modifying its properties.

The Windows Sidebar Properties dialog box provides settings to control when it starts (if ever), whether Windows Sidebar appears on the top of other windows, which side it appears on, and which monitor it uses for display (you could place it on a secondary monitor to make it less distracting). The Maintenance section contains two pushbuttons. Click View List of Running Gadgets to see which gadgets are running. The list includes the gadget version number and vendor. You can highlight a gadget and click Remove to remove it from Windows Sidebar. If your gadget setup becomes messy, you can click Restore Gadgets Installed with Windows to reset Windows Sidebar to its original state.

An Overview of the Standard Gadgets

Vista does come with a number of gadgets installed. They all provide some sort of simple data output or interesting diversion. The following list describes what you get with Windows Sidebar (of course, you can always add more gadgets later).

Calendar Displays the current date in large type or a view of the month. Double-clicking switches between the two date formats. You can't store appointments using this gadget; it only provides the date.

Clock Displays the current time.

Contacts Provides a list of contacts. However, you must add the contacts manually. I had expected this feature to interact with Outlook, but if you want a contact added to it, you'll need to do it manually.

CPU Meter Shows CPU and RAM usage on the current computer.

Currency Conversion Converts one monetary unit to another. For example, you can convert from U.S. dollars to Argentine pesos. Simply select the two currencies and type the amount that you want to convert.

Feed Headlines Displays a list of RSS headlines. You connect to RSS feeds using your browser. The gadget displays the headlines for the feed that you want most, or all of the feeds. Clicking a headline displays a fuller description of it in a pop-up dialog box. Clicking the headline in the pop-up dialog box opens the complete article in your browser.

Notes Provides a sticky note. You can type as many as you want and scroll through them. You can change the font face and size, along with the color of the sticky notes. Vista automatically saves any notes you create, so they appear each time you restart the system.

Picture Puzzle Creates a mini-puzzle that you solve. This is just like that game you had as a kid where you moved the various blocks around to get them in order. Once the blocks are in order, you see the picture.

Slideshow Displays a slideshow of pictures. You can select a location for the picture. The default location shows the sample pictures that come with Vista. The slideshow includes transition effects and the time Windows Sidebar displays each picture.

Stocks Provides a running display (stock ticker) of current stock prices. You can search for specific stocks. Clicking the gadget displays a pop-up dialog box where you can choose the specific stocks and see the information in a little more detail.

Weather Obtains weather information for the locality you specify. You don't get very much information—just the current temperature and whether the sky is cloudy or sunny.

Adding, Removing, and Configuring Gadgets

Windows Sidebar comes with a number of gadgets installed, but not nearly all of the gadgets that come with Vista. You can see the list of available gadgets by right-clicking Windows Sidebar and choosing Add Gadgets from the context menu. You'll see the Gadget Gallery dialog box shown in Figure 8.28. To add a gadget to Windows Sidebar, right-click it and choose Add from the context menu. This method always adds the gadget to the top of Windows Sidebar. You can also drag and drop the gadget onto Windows Sidebar. This second method lets you place the gadget wherever you want.

FIGURE 8.28
The Gadget Gallery shows you a selection of the available gadgets.

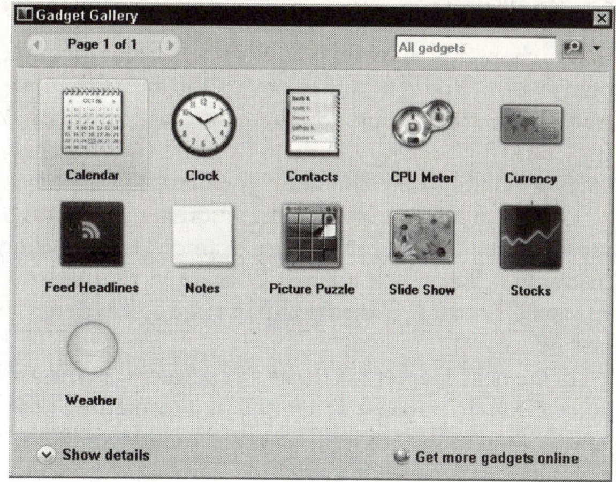

TIP You can always move gadgets around on Windows Sidebar or even move them off the sidebar if you desire. Hover the mouse over the gadget and you'll see a little toolbar appear on the right side of the gadget with two or three buttons. Click the grabber button (always the bottommost button) and drag the gadget wherever you want to see it. Moving the gadget off of Windows Sidebar often displays more gadget features. For example, the calendar gadget displays both the current date and the month view instead of one or the other.

Of course, at some point Windows Sidebar will become positively stuffed with gadgets unless you remove the ones you no longer need. To remove a gadget, hover your mouse over the gadget and click the button at the top of the little toolbar that appears. You can also right-click the gadget and choose Close Gadget from the context menu. Closing a gadget removes it from Windows Sidebar, but you can always add it back later using the Gadget Gallery.

Many of the gadgets also offer configuration options. For example, you can set the font size, font face, and background color for the notes gadget. You know that there are configuration options when you hover the mouse over the gadget and see a button with an icon that looks like a wrench. Click this button and you'll see a pop-up dialog box containing the gadget properties. In some cases, you can also right-click the gadget and choose Options or Properties from the context menu.

Obtaining New Gadgets Online

Microsoft is expecting third-party developers to produce a wealth of new gadgets. Some of these gadgets are going to be available on the third-party websites as stand-alone downloads. You'll need to find them yourself using a search engine such as Google. However, you'll also find many gadgets by clicking the Get More Gadgets Online link in the Gadget Gallery dialog box shown in Figure 8.28. In fact, even at this early date there are 67 gadgets you can download from the Microsoft website. Consequently, if the gadgets that Vista provides are a bit of a yawn, check out the gadgets online. To use one of the online gadgets, click its link to see the download page. Click the download link on the download page and Internet Explorer will ask whether you want to install the new gadget. Follow any third-party instructions to complete the installation.

Summary

In this chapter, you learned how Vista handles files and folders and how to manage them on your own system. You not only reviewed the basics of moving, copying, deleting, and so on, but also learned about searching, compression, and encryption. You also learned how to use Vista's built-in capability for burning CD-ROMs and DVDs. This chapter also discusses some new Vista features such as Windows Sidebar and Sync Center.

Of course, this is a lot of information to digest. You'll want to try out all of the new features and see how they'll work for you. For example, try out Windows Sidebar and see if it's more helpful or distracting. Whether it actually does prove useful depends a great deal on the gadgets you choose to install. Try a few of the third-party gadgets to determine whether they actually can save you time and effort.

In the next chapter, we'll discuss printers and fonts. The two topics are integrally tied together, since the main purpose of a font is as a formatting device for printouts. Even if you've been using printers and fonts for a long time, you might want to review this chapter to pick up some additional pointers and time-saving tips.

Chapter 9

Installing and Working with Printers and Fonts

Vista makes printing seem so easy that it's easy to overlook the printing subsystem. You simply issue a Print command in an application, select a printer, and out comes your hard copy. But if you need to step beyond the daily end-user routine and install or configure printers, you might need a little help. It's not always obvious what settings are best for network versus local printers, for PostScript versus Printer Control Language (PCL) operating modes, and any number of other operating details.

In this chapter, you'll learn how to install and configure printers and how to manage Windows fonts. This chapter covers the following topics:

- How Vista handles printing
- Installing local printers
- Sharing a local printer
- Installing remote printers
- Working with printer properties
- Working with the Print Management console
- Managing a print queue
- Creating and using separator pages
- Installing and managing fonts
- Changing the display font
- Sending and receiving faxes

Vista: What's New?

Actually, not a lot is new with printing in Vista. Considering how well Windows XP handled printing, that's good news for administrators already burdened with a significant number of changes in other areas. As usual, Vista does add a few new wrinkles to printing. In this case, you'll notice new printer models, as expected, and the ability to use web service devices. A web service device is one that you access through a web service. The physical device could be anywhere. The connection method that Vista uses makes the web service device look like a local printer.

Microsoft also updated the faxing capabilities of Windows in Vista. You'll find that you can use both a modem and a fax server to send and receive faxes. Working with cover sheets is no longer an arcane process because Microsoft has provided a nice editor to create cover sheets. It's also quite easy to combine a scanner with the fax capabilities in Vista. You'll find that sending a fax from your computer is no longer a hair pulling experience—it goes quite smoothly.

Vista does offer one new feature that really is a perk for anyone who needs to manage a number of printers. The Print Management console makes it very easy to find out every detail about every printer on your network. You can attach to other servers and see everything you need in one place. This one tool promises to save administrators everywhere a significant amount of time and effort.

How Vista Handles Printing

If you're interested in the theory behind Vista printing, check out the following explanation; if you just want to learn the practical stuff, feel free to skip it.

Let's start with a bit of pre-Windows history (yes, back in the dark ages—that is, the 1980s). The MS-DOS applications each interacted directly with the printer through its own proprietary driver. The PC needed a separate driver for each printer and each application. Applications typically came with at least one disk full of printer drivers, covering the bases for dozens of the most popular models, but someone with a less popular printer could be out of luck unless that printer happened to emulate one of the more popular ones. Some of the less popular printers came with driver disks for the most popular applications, so you could sometimes acquire the needed driver from that end of the equation instead of from the application side. Still, acquiring the correct driver for each application and each printer was often a dicey proposition.

Then there was the waiting. Most applications didn't include a print spooler, so when you issued the Print command, you had to wait until the print job was finished printing before you could resume using the application. And remember, printers printed much more slowly back then, so a big print job could tie up your whole system long enough for you to take a very leisurely coffee break.

Not only did the application need a printer driver, but it also needed font files. Most printers had only one or two typefaces built in; if you wanted anything else, the application had to send font files to the printer before a print job. There was a separate font file for each combination of size, typeface, and attribute. So, for example, 16-point bold Helvetica was a separate file from 16-point italic Helvetica or 14-point bold Helvetica. These font files took up space on the hard disk, and if you were going to print a document containing many fonts, the printing was delayed while the fonts were transferred to the printer's memory. To compound matters further, if you had two printers, you had to have a separate set of font files for each of them in some applications. Programs like Ventura Publisher would generate the needed font files during setup, and if you got a new printer, you needed to rerun the setup to generate a new set of fonts for it.

NOTE **Back in this era, add-on cartridges for some laser printers were popular; you could plug in a cartridge to add several typefaces to the printer that some applications could then use in addition to the software fonts (aka soft fonts).**

Then thankfully, along came Windows. Starting around version 3.*x*, Windows began solving the problem of needing a different driver for each application by taking over the printing process itself. All Windows-based applications that needed to print sent their requests to the Windows printing subsystem. Since the applications didn't interact with the printer, you didn't need a separate printer driver for each one. All you needed was a Windows driver for each of your printers.

Windows used (and still uses) the term *printer* to mean a printer driver, because to Windows, the terms are synonymous. Windows interacts with the printer driver, and the printer driver then interacts with the printer. So, when you set the properties for a printer, you're actually setting up the behavior of the driver and not the printer itself. You can have multiple drivers installed for a single physical printer, each set up for a different behavior. For example, you might have one driver set up to use separator pages between print jobs and another one set up not to do so. Windows would consider each of these separate printers, and it would look from an application's Print dialog box as though you had two printers installed on the same port.

The printer driver tells Windows a variety of things about the printer, including what its paper handling capabilities are, how much RAM is has installed, and what *Page Description Language (PDL)* it speaks. Several PDLs are popular today; two of the most popular are PCL (by Hewlett-Packard) and PostScript (by Adobe).

TIP Almost all laser printers support either PCL or PostScript, so if you don't have the exact driver you need for a laser printer, you can usually hobble through using a driver for some other laser printer that uses the same version of PCL or PostScript.

Having Windows handle the printing rather than the individual application also frees up the application for continued work more quickly after you issue the Print command. The application quickly prints the entire job to the Windows *print spooler*, basically a holding tank for print jobs. Then Windows spoon-feeds the print job to the printer as the printer can accommodate it.

Remember that the other big hassle with MS-DOS printing was the need for separate font files for each typeface, size, and attribute combination. Starting with Windows 3.1, Windows began offering generic, scaleable typefaces called *TrueType*. These font files have several advantages:

- A TrueType font file contains an outline of each letter, rather than a fixed size, so a single font file can produce any size of text.
- TrueType fonts work with the Windows printing subsystem, so they work with any Windows application.
- TrueType fonts work with almost any printer, so you need only one set of TrueType fonts no matter what printers you have.

Vista continues to support TrueType and an improved variant of it called OpenType. The improvements are behind the scenes and not significant for an end user, but you need to be aware of the two different names because when you start working with fonts (later in this chapter), you'll see two different icons for them.

Installing Local Printers

A *local printer* is one that is directly attached to your PC. It could be attached through a parallel, serial, USB, infrared, or some other port type. With a local printer, you have complete control; you can install and remove drivers for it, share it, control the permissions for the sharing, and so on. (In contrast, you might not always be able to have your way completely with a network printer, discussed later in this chapter.) The following sections explain how to install and share a local printer.

Installing a Local Printer Driver

Most printers these days come with a setup disk of their own. Running the Setup program on the disk installs the needed Windows drivers. If you have such a disk available, you should use it because some Setup programs install a proprietary print spooler for the printer. For example, many of the Epson ink jet printers have their own spooler. If you install the printer manually using the Add Printer Wizard described next, you'll miss out on any special utilities such as that. However, using the Vista drivers may be the only option in many cases, at least until vendors begin signing their drivers and catching up with other Vista requirements.

WARNING Since the 64-bit version of Vista limits you to using only signed drivers and the 32-bit version uses signed drivers by default, you'll want to check with the vendor to ensure signed drivers are available. Even though you can get unsigned drivers to work with the 32-bit version of Vista, it's not the best option.

If you don't have a setup disk for the printer, or if the Setup program won't run under Vista, the next most preferable path is to download a setup utility from the printer manufacturer's website. (Actually, this isn't a bad idea even if you do have a setup disk already, because the setup disk might have been created prior to Vista's introduction and might not have Vista-specific drivers on it, or a newer version of the Vista driver might be available.)

If no setup files are available from the printer manufacturer, you can try the Add Printer Wizard in Windows. Vista provides drivers for hundreds of different printers, so it's possible that it includes a driver for your printer.

NOTE When working with the x86 version of Vista, if no Vista driver is available for your model, try the Windows 2000 driver. If no 2000 driver is available, try the one for NT 4.0. Still no luck? Check the printer's manual to find out whether it emulates any other printers; perhaps Vista includes a driver for one of them. You might also be able to kludge through with a driver for a similar model by the same manufacturer. For example, all the Lexmark Optra S models are basically the same except for their speeds and feature sets, so you could print with a different driver using the default settings even if you couldn't reliably set printing properties. Older drivers are always risky under Vista. If your printer driver attempts to make changes to the kernel to perform tasks such as checking the ink supply, it probably won't install.

To add a local printer with the Add Printer Wizard:

1. Open the Control Panel and choose Printers. You see the Printers window.

TIP If you'd like Printers and Faxes to appear on the Start menu, right-click an empty area of the Start menu and choose Properties. On the Start Menu tab, make sure Start Menu is selected, and then click Customize. In the Customize Start Menu dialog box, click the Advanced tab, and then scroll down through the list of options there and place a check mark next to Printers. Click OK twice to close the open dialog boxes.

2. Double-click the Add Printer icon or click Add a Printer in the toolbar.
3. The Add Printer Wizard runs; click Next to continue.
4. Click the Add a Local Printer link. The Add Printer wizard asks you to choose a port, the connection between your computer and the printer. You have a choice between all of the

standard existing ports or creating a new port. A new port can include a local port that relies on the standard connection methodology or a TCP/IP connection. When creating a standard port, all you need to provide is the port name as Windows will recognize it, such as LPT1:. A TCP/IP port requires that you supply a port type, such as a TCP/IP device or a web services device. You can automatically detect the hostname or IP address, or type the information manually.

5. Choose a port and if necessary, provide the additional connection information required. Click Next.
6. Vista displays a list of printers as shown in Figure 9.1. It's important to notice two special features in this dialog box. First, if you have a disk and you haven't used it (or the vendor specifies that you need to install the printer normally using this technique), you can click Have Disk. Vista will ask you to provide the location of the disk that has the INF (information) file on it for your printer. Remember that the x64 version of Vista won't allow you to use older, non-signed drivers. Second, Microsoft is always updating its printer support. If you don't see your printer listed and you don't have a disk, click Windows Update. Vista may find your printer on the Windows Update site. In all cases, any changes you make will simply update the list of printers shown in Figure 9.1.
7. Choose the printer vendor and model number. Click Next. The Add Printer wizard asks for a printer name.
8. Type the printer name in the Printer Name field. If you've created multiple setups for a single printer, make sure you differentiate them. For example, if you've set the printer up to print to a file, you might add (File) in parenthesis after the printer name.
9. Click Next. Vista will install the printer for you. At this point, you can print a test page to test the printer setup.
10. Click Print a Test Page.
11. A box pops up asking whether the test page printed okay; click Close if it did, or click Troubleshoot Printer Problems if it did not; then work through the Printing Troubleshooter.
12. Click Finish. You'll see the new printer added to the Printers window.

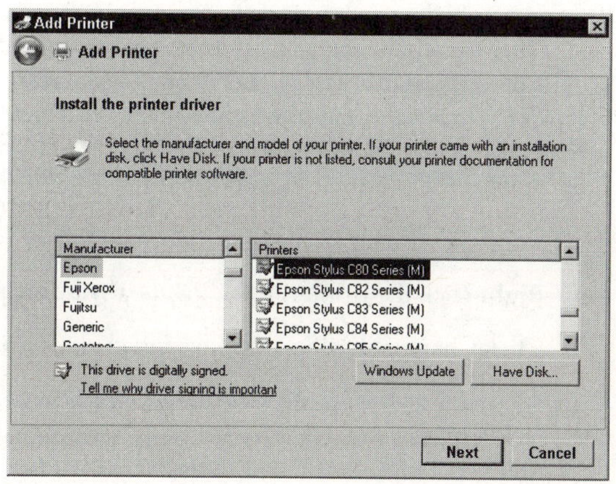

FIGURE 9.1
Choose your printer from the supplied list.

Installing Multiple Drivers for the Same Printer

As I mentioned earlier, one of the advantages in Windows printing is that Windows can accept multiple drivers for a single physical printer. You can use this capability for any number of purposes, such as:

- Installing both a PCL and a PostScript driver for a printer that is capable of using either PDL. Sometimes having two separate PDLs can be a boon when troubleshooting a problem; for example, the printer might run out of memory when printing a large graphic using one PDL but manage to print the page using another.
- Using different printer properties for certain jobs. For example, you might have one driver set up by default to pull from a paper tray containing letterhead stationery and another driver set up by default to pull plain paper from a different tray.
- Turning off the print spooler for one driver while leaving the other one to use the Windows print spooler.
- Setting one printer driver to Landscape by default and another one to Portrait so that you don't have to switch between the two orientations in the application in which you're printing.

Setting up a second driver for an already-installed printer is just like setting it up initially. The biggest difference is that you must give the printer a different name. For example, you might have MyPrinter (PCL) as the name of the first printer installation and MyPrinter (Postscript) as the second printer installation name.

Sharing a Local Printer

Unlike previous versions of Windows, you'll notice that Vista doesn't provide any means of sharing a local printer during installation. I suspect that this is one of many small changes that Microsoft has made to improve security. In the meantime, it also means that you must set up sharing manually when you want to share a printer with others.

NOTE Some printers have built-in network cards so that you can attach them directly to a network hub; no particular PC has local control over these printers. You can print to one of these using its IP address. Other printers are not network-capable by themselves, but you can hook them up to a print server that manages their network connection. (Wireless print server boxes are very reasonably priced these days, and enable you to place a printer anywhere—not just near a PC.) Then there's the shared local printer. When you share a local printer, you give other network users permission to access it, and when they do use it, the request goes through your own local copy of Windows. If the printer is heavily used, you might notice the drain on your system resources while the print jobs are spooled off to the printer. That's why on busy networks, it's preferable to have printers networked through a print server or their own network address.

To share one of your local printers, do the following:

1. Right-click the printer in the Printers window and choose Sharing.
2. Click Change Sharing Options, and click Continue when prompted by UAC. Vista will enable printer sharing for this printer, but won't activate it.

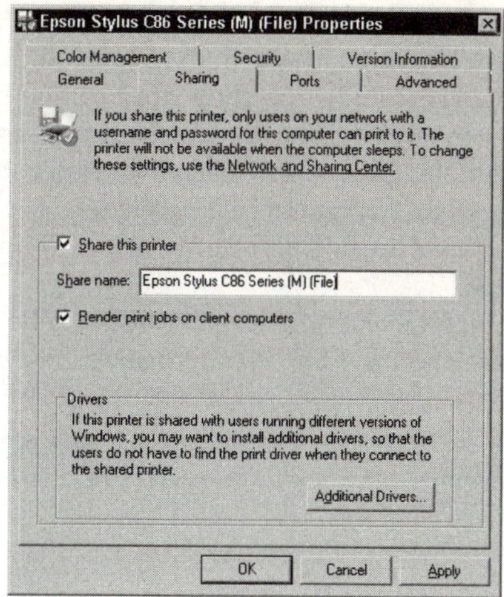

FIGURE 9.2
Use client rendering to reduce the printing load on the local machine.

3. Check the Share This Printer option and enter a share name for it (or accept the default name). Notice that by default, Vista reduces the local print burden by enabling the Render Print Jobs on the Client Computers option as shown in Figure 9.2. When you use this option, the client performs much of the work of getting the print job put together.
4. Click Additional Drivers. You'll see an Additional Drivers dialog box where you can choose additional drivers to support for other versions of Windows. See the "Installing Multiple OS Support for a Shared Local Printer" sidebar for reasons that you want to install additional drivers immediately.
5. Check all of the required additional drivers and then click OK.
6. Click OK.

Pretty simple, eh? But see the following section to gain some control over the specifics of the sharing.

INSTALLING MULTIPLE OS SUPPORT FOR A SHARED LOCAL PRINTER

When others share your local printer, as long as they have Vista installed on their PCs, everything works fine. But if they're running some other version of Windows, it's a no-go.

To circumvent this problem, users wanting to access your printer must install a printer driver for that printer on their own PCs, in a version appropriate for their operating systems. For example, Windows 98 users would need a Windows 98 driver for your printer. If they happen to have the needed driver on a disk at their local workstation, they can use it when they set up the printer. However, most people don't keep printer driver disks lying around for printers they don't own, so the likelihood of this is slim.

As a courtesy to users who might want to print to your local printer over the network, you can preinstall the needed drivers for various operating systems. Then when the person sets up your printer, the needed drivers will be copied from your PC to theirs as part of the setup process.

Setting Permissions for a Shared Printer

The simple Sharing tab shown in the preceding section might lead you to believe that no options are available for controlling how your printer is shared. However, that's not the case.

First, you can control when the shared printer is available to others in the Advanced tab. You can specify certain times of day when the printer should be available, and you can assign a priority to the print jobs coming in from other people. For example, if you set the priority to 2, and your own print jobs have the default priority of 1, your own jobs will print first, and then anyone else's. See Figure 9.3.

You can set the permissions for the printer—that is, which users can use it and what they can do to it—in the Security tab. See Figure 9.4.

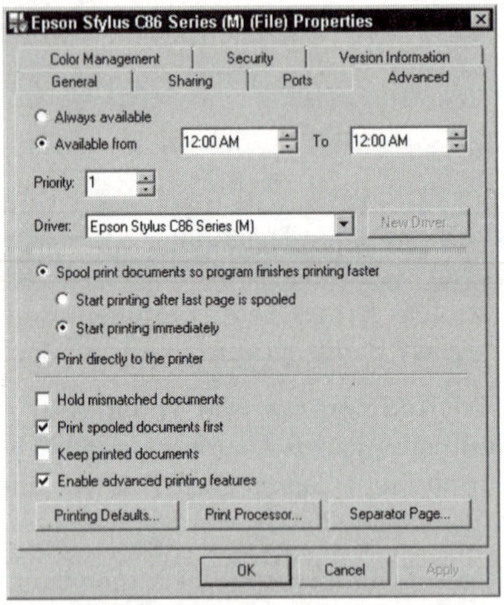

FIGURE 9.3
Control when others can use your printer and what priority should be assigned to their print jobs.

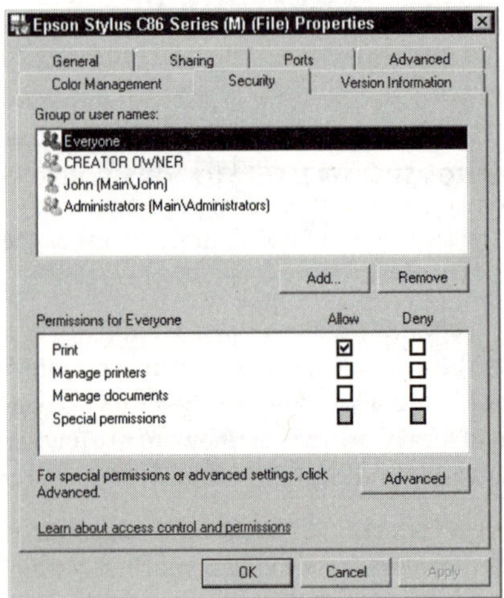

FIGURE 9.4
You can assign different permissions for the printer to different users and groups.

TIP If you don't have the Security tab in your printer's Properties box, it's probably because Simple File Sharing is turned on. (It's on by default in Vista installations.) To turn it off, from any Explorer window choose Tools ➤ Folder Options. In the View tab, scroll down to the bottom of the Advanced Settings list and deselect Use Sharing Wizard.

For each listed user or group, you can assign permissions to Print, Manage Printers, and Manage Documents. You'll learn more about users and groups in Chapter 21, but let's look at the printing-specific permissions here:

Print Can send documents to the printer's queue.

Manage Printers Can view the print queue and can pause and resume it.

Manage Documents Can view the print queue and can pause, resume, or delete print jobs in it.

You'll learn about working with print queues later in this chapter, but when you get there, keep in mind that the actions explained there can be performed only with the needed permissions to do so.

As with other network resources, you can also click the Advanced button to fine-tune the permission settings, but this is probably beyond the scope of what you want to get into right now. When you learn about advanced permissions in Chapter 21, you might want to come back here and explore the printer's permissions further.

Installing Remote Printers

A *remote* printer is one that isn't connected to your PC directly. It could be connected to another individual's PC on the network, connected directly to the network itself, or accessible through the Internet via TCP/IP.

NOTE Vista lets you install remote printers as local printers in some cases. For example, you can create a local connection to a TCP/IP printer or a web services printer in many cases. See the "Installing a Local Printer Driver" section of the chapter for details.

Setting Up a Remote Printer

Before you can print to a remote printer, you must install a driver for it on your local PC. That's actually a good thing, because then you can set your own properties for the printer and not have to rely on someone else's settings for it. For example, perhaps you always print your documents in Landscape orientation, but the printer owner always prints in Portrait. Since you maintain your own copy of the driver, you can have your own default Landscape setting without manually making the change every time.

To install a remote printer, do the following:

1. From the Printers window, click Add a Printer. The Add Printer Wizard starts; click Next.
2. Click Add a Network, Wireless, or Bluetooth Printer. Vista will automatically search the network for available printers as shown in Figure 9.5. It will continue searching for printers until you click Stop or a predefined interval elapses.
3. Click Stop. If you see the printer you want to use, highlight it and click Next. Vista will create the connection for you. Proceed to step 6.
4. Click The Printer I Want Isn't Listed. Vista shows a manual printer entry screen, as shown in Figure 9.6.

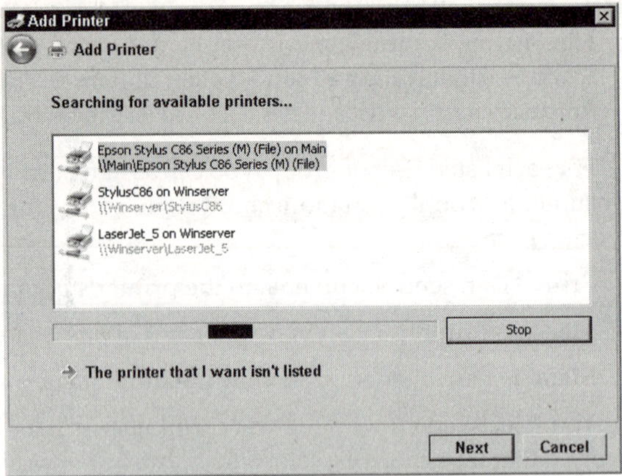

FIGURE 9.5
Vista automatically searches for network printers.

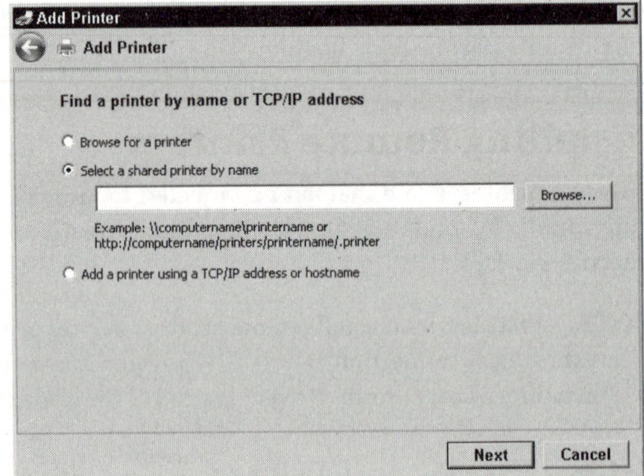

FIGURE 9.6
Provide the information required to connect to the remote printer.

5. If you have an address for the printer already, enter it. It could be a network path (such as `\\server\printer`) or a URL. If you don't know the address, choose Browse for a Printer, and then click Next and locate it.
6. Check the Set as Default Printer option if you want to make this the default printer. Type a name for the printer in the Printer Name field. Click Next. Vista displays a dialog box asking whether you want to print a test page.
7. Click Print a Test Page if you want to test the remote connection. Depending on where the printer is, you might not be able to check the results of the test. In this case, you'll need to test the connection later.
8. Click Finish. The needed drivers are copied to your PC, and the printer is set up.

Installing a Printer through a UNIX Host

If your network includes UNIX-based computers, you can print through the network to a printer attached to them, or to network-capable printers on a UNIX network, but you have to do a couple of setup things first:

1. Open the Programs and Features applet found in the Control Panel. Click the Turn Windows Features On or Off link.
2. Check the LPD Print Service and the LPR Port Monitor options found under Print Services as needed.

NOTE The Line Printer Daemon (LPD) service lets you share your printer with UNIX machines. You only need this service if you want to let UNIX systems use your printer. The Line Printer Remote (LPR) service lets you use a printer on a UNIX system. You only need this service when you want to send documents to a UNIX system for printing.

3. Run the Add Printer Wizard and start setting up a new local printer.
4. Then when asked about the port to use, create a new LPR port.
5. Enter the IP address for that printer's host in the Name or Address of Server Providing LPD box.
6. In the Name of Printer or Print Queue on That Server box, enter the name of the printer as it's known by the host device.
7. Click OK.
8. Complete the wizard normally.

Managing Installed Printers

From the Printers window you can view the installed printer drivers. The printer icons are different depending on the printer's status:

A local printer's icon is a regular printer.

A remote printer's icon has a cable beneath it, indicating that it's on the network.

The default printer's icon has a check mark on it.

A shared local printer has a group symbol underneath it.

A fax driver (such as for Windows Fax and Scan) has a fax machine icon.

A printer that sends its output to a file has a disk icon on it.

Removing a Printer Driver

To remove a printer driver, select it and press Delete, just like any other file or folder in Explorer.

Depending on the printer, you might see a message stating that some files were used only by that driver and asking whether you want to delete them. If you never plan on reinstalling this printer, answer Yes. If you think you might reinstall it, choose No; that way you might not need to reinsert the Vista or printer CD-ROM/DVD when you reinstall.

Working with Printer Properties

Through a printer's properties, you can adjust almost every aspect of the way it works, from the print quality to the paper feed. To set properties for a printer, right-click it and choose Properties.

The properties for a printer vary widely depending on the printer model. Because the printer manufacturer supplies the printer drivers, there's no real standardization in the options they include or in the layout of the various tabs. However, at least a few settings are available for all printers, regardless of model. The following sections outline some of the broad categories of settings that you might find in the properties for various types of printers.

General Properties

All printers have a General tab. In it, you can change the printer driver's name, enter comments about the printer, and print a test page. See Figure 9.7.

From the General tab you can also click the Printing Preferences button to open the Printing Preferences dialog box for the printer. The content of this dialog box will vary depending on the printer model; Figure 9.8 shows it for my ink-jet printer.

Ports Properties

In the Ports tab you can select which port a printer uses. On the surface, this seems simple enough: one printer, one port. But if you mark the Enable Printer Pooling check box at the bottom of this tab (see Figure 9.9), you can then choose multiple ports for a single printer driver. This enables you to put multiple identical printers on different ports and have print jobs sent to whichever one happens to be free through a single print driver and print queue.

FIGURE 9.7
The General tab helps you identify the printer.

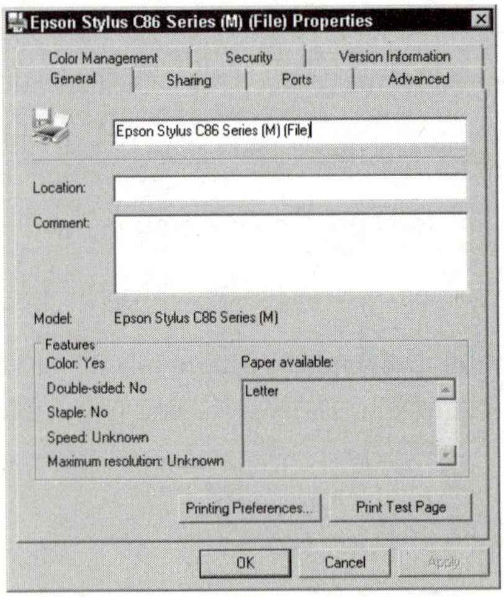

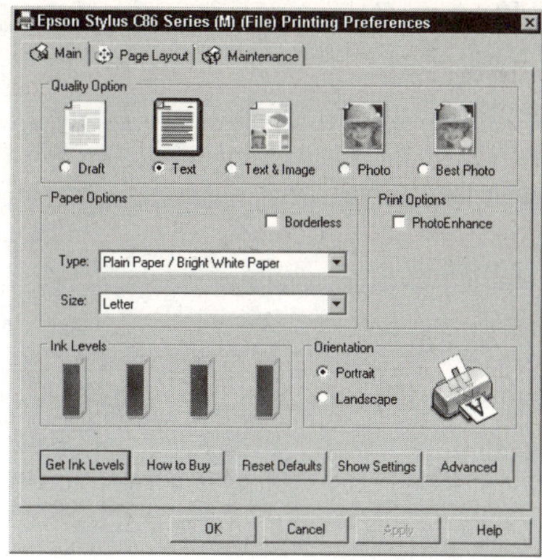

FIGURE 9.8
Printing Preferences set basic operational parameters such as page orientation.

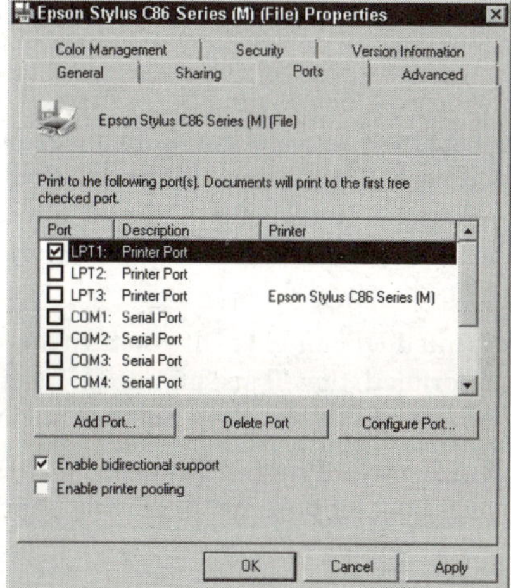

FIGURE 9.9
In the Ports tab, you can select ports to be associated with the selected printer driver.

Clicking a port and then clicking the Configure Port button brings up a dialog box with options for that type of port. With a parallel port, there's only one option: Transmission Retry. However, with a serial (COM) port you can set the communication settings (such as bits per second, parity, stop bits, and so on).

ADVANCED PROPERTIES

In the Advanced tab (Figure 9.10) are a variety of special-purpose settings. You saw earlier about the availability hours, when sharing was discussed. Some of the other options here are:

Spooling By default, a printer uses the Windows print spooler, but you can choose to print directly to the printer instead. If you do that, the application might slow down or lock up entirely while the job prints.

FIGURE 9.10
Advanced properties for the printer control special situations.

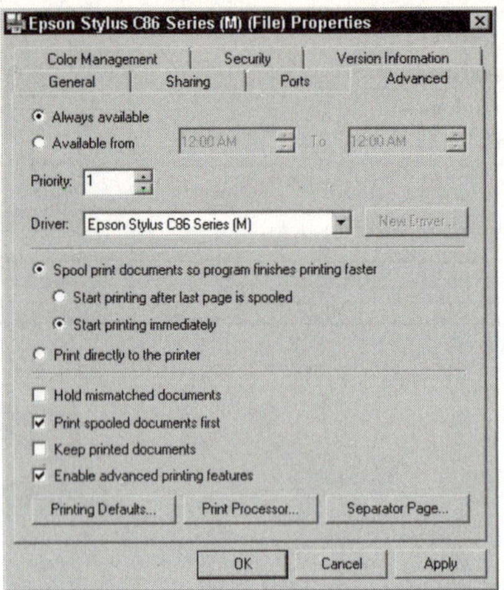

Hold Mismatched Documents When this is on, the driver checks the document to be printed to make sure it can be successfully printed on the printer (correct page size, etc.). If not, it holds it in the queue.

Print Spooled Documents First There's a delay between when a document begins being transferred from the application to the print spool. If you have the Spooling setting set so that the document will not start printing until the last page is spooled, the printer will sit idle waiting, even if other documents of a lower priority are completely spooled and waiting. If you mark this check box, however, those lower priority documents will be able to "cut in line" to allow more efficient usage.

Keep Printed Documents If you turn this on, items in the print spool will not be deleted after they are printed; they'll just go into an inactive status there. This enables you to resubmit the same print job from the spool without having to reprint it in the application.

Enable Advanced Printing Features When this is on, any special options the printer is capable of, such as booklet printing, page order, and pages per sheet, will be available.

DEVICE SETTINGS

Most printer drivers have a Device Settings tab, but the content of it varies dramatically from printer to printer. These are generally the same settings that you can control from the LED panel on the printer itself, but they're accessible through the printer driver for convenience. Figure 9.11 shows one for a laser printer.

COLOR MANAGEMENT

For color printers only, a Color Management tab may appear, enabling you to select a color profile. A color profile is a configuration file that specifies color fine-tuning for a particular source. This is handy if you're trying to match the colors on screen more closely with the actual output from the printer, so it's more of a "what you see is what you get" affair. If the printer is shared, the Color Management properties aren't usually alterable from the remote PCs using the shared printer, although the settings can be viewed from there.

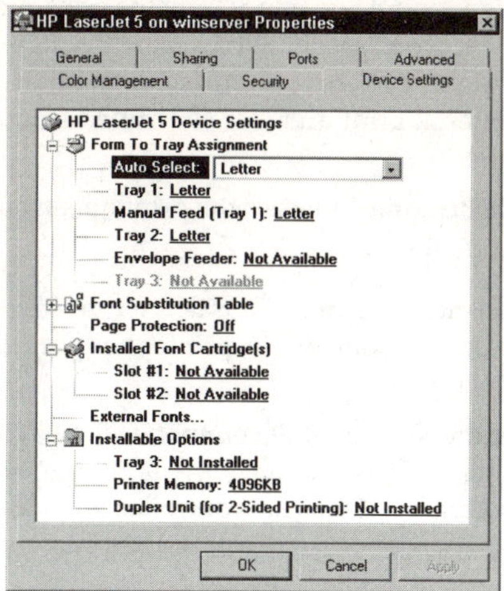

FIGURE 9.11
Device Settings are specific to the printer model.

UTILITIES

Found primarily in ink-jet printer drivers, the Utilities tab offers shortcuts to self-tests, head-cleaning routines, and other utility programs built into the printer. You can also find these utilities in other places. For example, you might find the utilities as part of the Printing Preferences dialog box shown in Figure 9.8. Most of these can also be run by pressing buttons on the printer itself or by running a separate utility application for the printer; they're provided in the driver for convenience.

Managing the Printing Process

Once a print job leaves the application, it's at the mercy of the print spooler (aka the *print queue*), a holding area where print jobs wait to be printed. The bottleneck here is the printer's speed and available memory. The more memory a printer has, the more print jobs can be stacked up in it waiting for the printer's hardware to catch up. The less memory a printer has, the more it relies on the print queue in Windows to hold the excess incoming data.

Managing a Print Queue

To open a print queue, double-click the printer in the Printers and Faxes window. Another way is to double-click the printer icon appears in the notification area when a print queue is active (that is, when it contains something to be printed). Figure 9.12 shows a print queue with several print jobs.

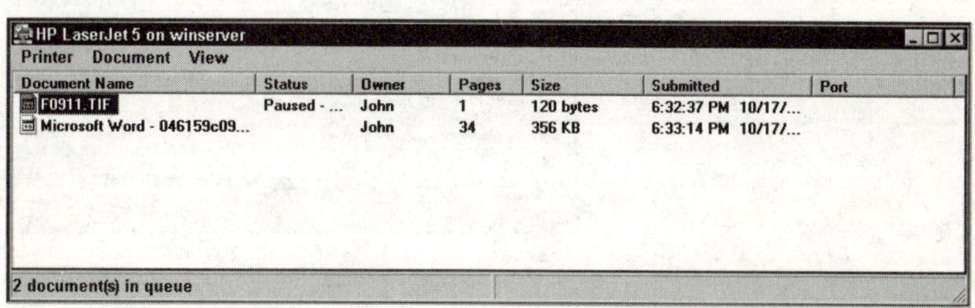

FIGURE 9.12
A printer's queue shows what print jobs have been submitted and are waiting to be printed.

You can control two things from the print queue: the queue itself and individual print jobs within it. As you learned earlier in the chapter, you can grant permissions for these activities separately when assigning sharing permissions to other users.

The overall print queue is controlled from the Printer menu. Some of the important commands are:

Pause Printing Freezes the print queue but leaves all print jobs intact.

Cancel All Documents Clears the entire queue.

Use Printer Offline Pauses the connection between the printer and the queue. The queue stops sending data to the printer temporarily, but the queue itself continues accepting incoming documents.

There are several other commands on the Printer menu, but they're all commands you've already seen in this chapter, such as Sharing and Properties.

Individual print jobs are controlled from the Document menu. The important commands are:

Pause Pauses the print job. If the job is currently printing, it also pauses the printer. If the job is waiting to be printed, it makes other non-paused jobs able to pass the paused job in the queue. So if you submit a big print job and then a small one and decide you want the small one to print first, you can pause the big one.

Resume Resumes a paused print job.

Cancel Cancels the print job.

Occasionally a document might get "stuck" in the print queue. It can't print, and you can't delete it. To fix this, you must stop and restart the Print Spooler service from the Computer Management console (in Administrative Tools in Control Panel). You'll find the print spooler under Services there. Right-click the service and choose Stop, and then right-click it and choose Start (see Figure 9.13).

Taking a Printer Out of Service with Pending Print Jobs

Suppose you have a printer with lots of jobs waiting in its queue and the printer has a blowout that requires you to take it out of service. What happens to all those print jobs? You don't want them to be lost, so you must transfer them to another printer.

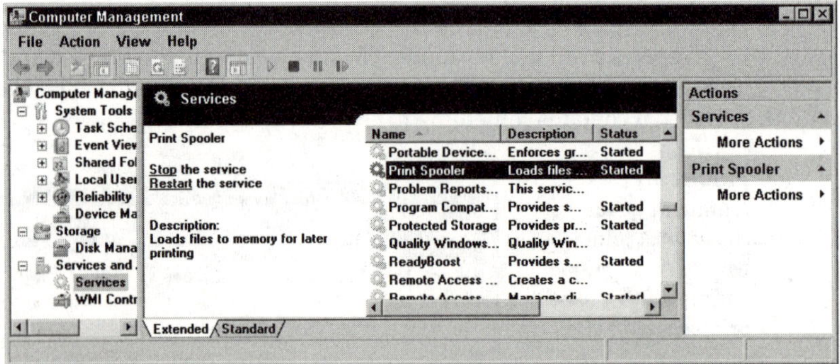

FIGURE 9.13
Stop and restart the Print Spooler from the Services window.

To do so, open the print queue for the broken printer, and choose Printer ➤ Properties. In the Ports tab, click the port to which the other printer is assigned and then click OK. You can do this to redirect to any printer on the same print server.

If you need to redirect to a printer on a different print server, you must add a port for it. Click Add Port, click Local Port, and then click New Port. Then enter the name of the other print server and shared printer in this format: **`\\`*`print_server`*`\`*`share_name`***.

Using Separator Pages

A separator page is an extra page that prints before each document. It identifies who printed it, the date and time, and so on. On a shared printer, this can be a valuable tool for determining to whom a print job belongs, even though it wastes a certain amount of paper.

A separator page also can have another purpose—it can send a printer-specific hexadecimal code to the printer. This is useful for activities such as switching the printer between PCL and PostScript modes.

Separator pages are text files with a `.sep` extension. Vista includes four separator page designs:

`Sysprint.sep` Switches to PostScript and prints a separator page with the account name, job number, date, and time.

`PCL.sep` Switches to PCL and prints a separator page with the account name, job number, date, and time.

`Pscript.sep` Switches to PostScript but does not print a separator page.

`Sysprtj.sep` Same as `Sysprint.sep` but uses Japanese fonts if available.

Selecting a Separator Page

To select a separator page to use with a certain printer, do the following:

1. Open the Properties for the printer and go to the Advanced tab.
2. Click the Separator Page button. The Separator Page dialog box opens.
3. Type the path to the separator page, or click Browse to locate it.
4. Click OK.

Designing Your Own Separator Page

You can design your own separator pages by creating text files in Notepad and saving them with a `.sep` extension. You can modify one of the existing `.sep` files or start fresh.

At the top of the file, type one single character on a line by itself. The SEP files that come with Vista use the backslash (\) for this but you can use the at sign (@) or some other character if you prefer. This defines the character that will precede all subsequent commands—the escape character. From there, just start typing your codes. Table 9.1 lists the codes you can use for separator pages and shows a \ as the escape character.

TABLE 9.1: Separator Page Codes

PAGE CODE	DESCRIPTION
`\N`	Name of the user who is printing.
`\I`	Job number.
`\D`	Date.
`\T`	Time.
`\L` *message*	Prints a message. Type your message in place of *message*. For example, `\L Acme Corporation` would print the name "Acme Corporation" on the page. It prints everything that follows the `\L` code until the next `\` is found or until it runs out of page width. (Messages won't wrap to multiple lines automatically.)
`\F` *pathname*	Prints the content of the specified file. Type your file path and name in place of *pathname*.
`\H`*nn*	Sends a hexadecimal instruction to the printer. Type the hex code in place of *nn*.
`\W`*nnn*	Specifies the maximum width of the separator page, in characters. The default is 80; the maximum is 256. Type the width in place of *nnn*.
`\B\S`	Prints in single-width block letters.
`\B\M`	Prints in double-width block letters.
`\U`	Turns off block-letter printing.
`\`*n*	Skips a number of lines (0 through 9). Type the number of lines in place of *n*.
`\E`	Ejects the page from the printer.

Make sure that `\E` is the final code of the file. Then save it with a `.sep` extension in the `%systemroot%/system32` folder.

Setting Print Server Properties

So far, you've learned about setting properties for individual printers, but you can also make global printing settings that affect all the installed printers. To do so, right-click an empty area of the Printers and Faxes window and choose Server Properties. This opens the Print Server Properties dialog box.

This dialog box has four tabs:

Forms This is a master list of the available forms that can be assigned to the various paper trays in the Device Settings tab for an individual printer. You can add new forms here.

Ports This is the same as the Ports tab in an individual printer's properties.

Drivers This tab tells what drivers have been installed for which operating systems. For example, if you've added drivers for additional operating systems for some of your shared printers, you'll see them listed here. You can add and remove drivers from here.

Advanced Here you'll find an assortment of check boxes and other controls for fine-tuning the printing subsystem on your PC. Table 9.2 lists the options here.

TIP The Spool folder you set in the Advanced tab applies to all printers. If you want to specify a different spool folder location for a specific printer, you must do so by editing the Registry. Go to `HKEY_LOCAL_MACHINE\Software\Microsoft\WindowsNT\CurrentVersion\Print\Printers\printer` key, and change the SpoolDirectory to the desired location.

WARNING If you want users to be able to receive notifications when their print jobs are complete, you must start the Alerter service using the Services snap-in in Computer Management. Alerter doesn't start automatically by default.

TABLE 9.2: Advanced Print Server Properties

SETTING	PURPOSE
Spool Folder	Specifies where the print queue's file will be stored.
Log Spooler Error Events	Creates a log file containing any error messages generated. Error messages would include things like Out of Paper.
Log Spooler Warning Events	Creates a log file containing any warning messages generated. Warnings might include things like Toner Low.
Log Spooler Information Events	Creates a log file containing information messages generated. You would not normally want to log these; they're things like Print Job Completed.
Beep on Errors of Remote Documents	Signals the print server to beep when errors occur.
Show Informational Notifications for Local Printers	Makes pop-up bubble messages appear in the notification area for routine events associated with local printers.
Show Informational Notifications for Network Printers	Makes pop-up bubble messages appear for routine events associated with network printers.

Using the Print Management Console

The Print Management console shown in Figure 9.14 is a new feature in Vista. This feature doesn't exactly add anything new to printing. However, it centralizes printing functionality and makes it possible to manage printing tasks from a remote location. The Print Management console also presents information in a different way from the standard printer utilities. You'll find that you don't do as much digging as you did in the past. The following sections describe this console in detail.

Working with Print Filters

A *print filter* shows you information about a group of printers. Printers can provide a considerable amount of information, so you don't want to try to view it all at once. Using a filter displays specific information about a printer, such as the number of print jobs that it has pending. Vista comes with four print filters installed, but you can create others as needed. To use a print filter, simply select its entry in the Print Management console. Here are descriptions of the four print filters.

All Printers Shows the printers connected to the local machine. The filter information includes the printer name, queue status, number of jobs, and the server name.

All Drivers Lists all of the drivers currently installed on the local machine. The filter information includes driver name, environment (such as Windows x86), driver version, provider (vendor), and server name.

Printers Not Ready Shows the printers that aren't ready for a particular reason (not printing). The reasons could range from being out of ink to an inoperative printer (not turned on or not functioning at all) or a printer jam. The filter information includes the printer name, queue status, jobs in queue, and server name.

Printers with Jobs Tells you which printers have jobs pending. However, this list doesn't tell you that the jobs are actually printing. The filter information includes the printer name, queue status, jobs in queue, and server name.

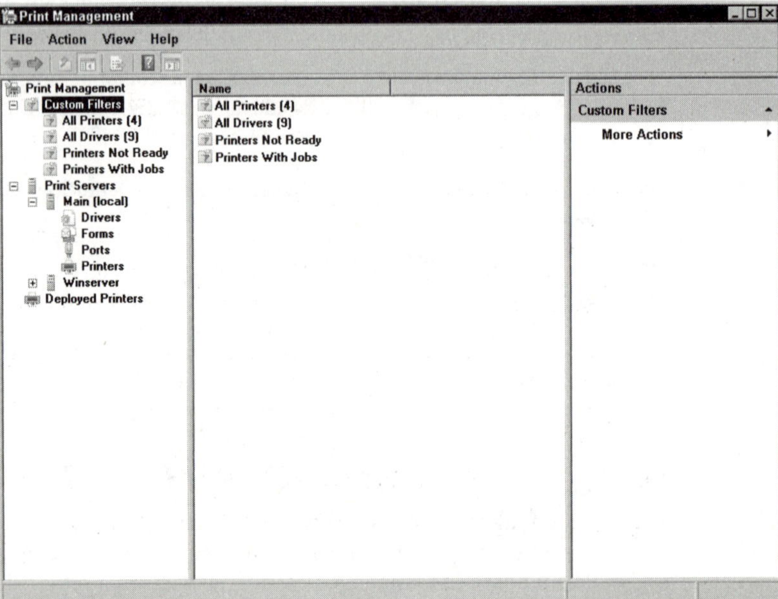

FIGURE 9.14
The Print Management console makes it considerably easier to manage large printer setups.

Creating New Print Filters

The four printer filters that Microsoft provides are useful, but probably not everything you need. You can create new print filters to display additional information about your particular setup. Every filter you create includes the printer name, queue status, jobs in queue, and server name by default, but you can change these entries. The following steps tell you how to create a filter.

1. Right-click Custom Filters in the Print Management console and choose Add New Printer Filter from the context menu. You'll see the New Printer Filter Wizard dialog box.
2. Type a name for the printer filter in the Name field and a description in the Description field. Documenting your print filter is important because you might not remember why you created it later otherwise. Check the Display the Total Number of Printers Next to the Name of the Printer Filter option if you want to display the number of filter entries in a manner similar to the All Printers filter shown in Figure 9.14.
3. Click Next. You'll see the Define a Printer Filter dialog box shown in Figure 9.15. This is where you define the filter criteria. The criteria limit the filter results. This filter will show any printer queues that have more than five jobs in them (a potential indicator of overloading or an error).
4. Choose the filter criteria and click Next. You'll see the Set Notifications dialog box shown in Figure 9.16. This is an optional filter addition that provides notifications when the filter detects the conditions you set. For example, you might want the filter to send you an e-mail message when the number of jobs exceeds five for a particular printer queue. In addition to providing notification, you can tell the filter to automatically run a script. Notice that this dialog box provides separate Test buttons so that you can check each of the entries before a crisis arises.
5. Click Finish. The New Printer Filter Wizard creates the new filter for you.

FIGURE 9.15
Choose the criteria that determine the filter output.

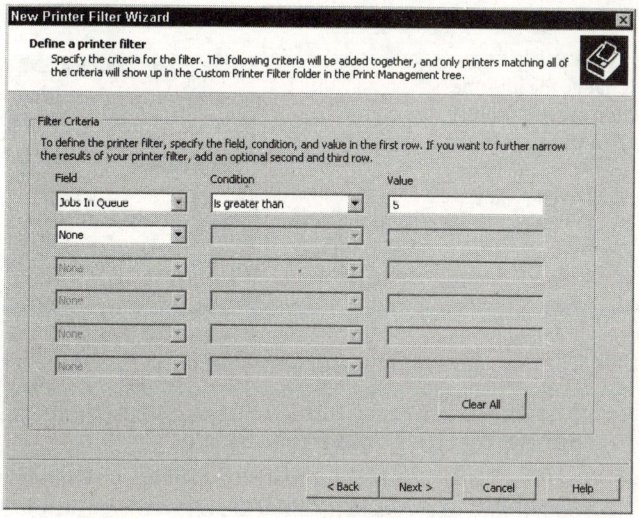

NOTE You can easily delete any errant filters by highlighting the entry in the list and pressing Delete. The Print Management console warns you that the deletion process is permanent. Click Yes to make the deletion permanent.

You might decide that you really don't like the columns that Microsoft chose for you. In this case, right-click the filter you've created and choose View ➤ Add/Remove Columns from the context menu. You'll see the Add/Remove Columns dialog box shown in Figure 9.17. To add a new column to the list, highlight its entry in the Available Columns list and click Add. Likewise, to remove a column, highlight its entry in the Displayed Columns list and click Remove. You can also change the order of the columns using the Move Up and Move Down buttons.

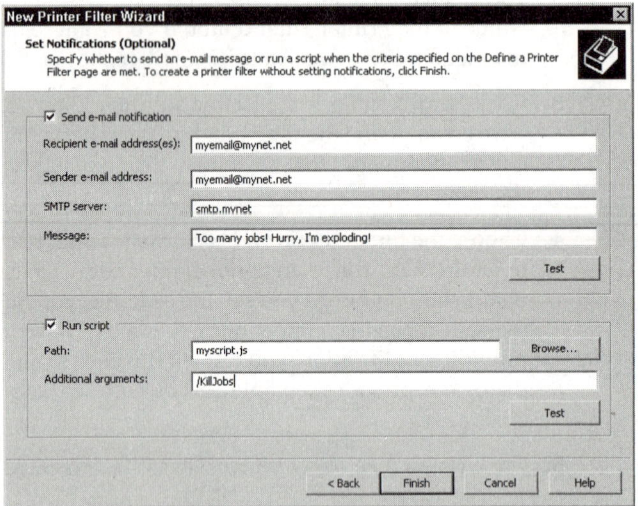

FIGURE 9.16
Provide notification and run scripts as necessary to react to filter conditions.

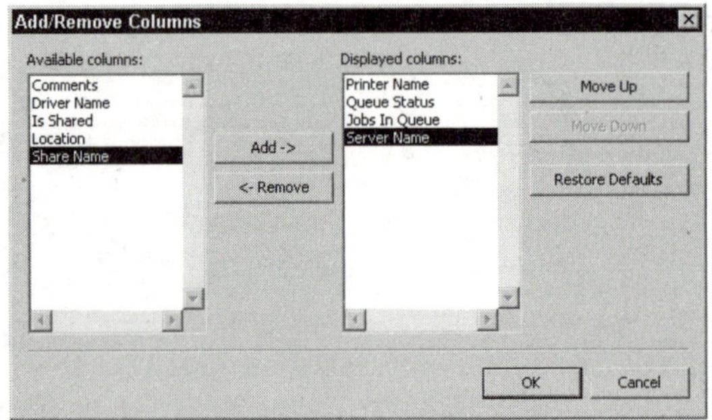

FIGURE 9.17
Change the information presentation of your filter as needed to display the information you want.

Managing the Local Print Server

The Print Management console always contains an entry for your local server as shown in Figure 9.14. You'll find the servers in the Print Servers folder. The four folders for each print server are Drivers, Forms, Ports, and Printers. This list should sound familiar because it's exactly the same list that I discussed in the "Setting Print Server Properties" section of the chapter. The only real difference is that the information appears as tabular entries, which means that it's considerably easier to work with a number of items, such as forms, without clicking yourself to death.

The displays also show you a wealth of information that you don't see when working with the Print Server Properties dialog box. For example, when you choose the Printers folder, you see the expected printer name, queue status, jobs in queue, and server name columns. However, at the bottom of the screen you see information about the jobs for a particular printer when you select one from the list. Using this additional information, you can pause, cancel, and reorder jobs with ease.

Managing Remote Print Servers

The best part about working with the Print Management console is that you can view remote locations. All you need to do is create a connection to the remote server and you get all of the same management features you get with a local server. The remote server can even be an older version of Windows (I tried it with a Windows 2000 machine and it worked great).

To add another server to the Print Servers folder, right-click the Print Servers folder and choose Add/Remove Servers from the context menu. You'll see the Add/Remove Servers dialog box. Type the name of the server you want to add to the Add Servers list and click Add. If you don't know the precise name of the server, you can click Browse to locate it.

When you decide not to monitor a server any longer, you open the same dialog box and highlight an entry in the Print Servers list. Click Remove to remove the server from the list. If you accidentally remove the local server, you can click Add the Local Server to add it back into the list.

Working with Deployed Printers

The Deploy Printers folder doesn't display anything until you configure a printer for deployment. A *deployed printer* is one that's associated with a Group Policy Object (GPO) in Active Directory; Vista automatically deploys the printer to any user machine that is part of that GPO. You can use this feature in any environment where you need to set up printers quickly and can be assured that everyone in a particular group will require the same printer setup. Unfortunately, the Print Management console only displays the deployed printers and lets you work with them; it doesn't actually let you deploy a printer. Use the following steps to deploy a printer.

1. Open the Group Policy Object Editor (select Start ➤ Run, type **`gpedit.msc`** in the Open field of the Run dialog box, and click OK.
2. Locate the `Windows Settings\Deployed Printers` folder for either the Computer Configuration or User Configuration objects.
3. Right-click the `Deployed Printers` folder and choose Deploy Printer from the context menu. You'll see the Deploy Printer(s) dialog box.
4. Type the UNC location of the printer you want to deploy in the Enter Printer Name field. Click Browse if you need to search for the printer.
5. Click Add. Click OK. You see the printer added to the Deployed Printers list.

If you want to remove a printer from the list, you open the Deploy Printer(s) dialog box, highlight the printer, and click Remove. When you click OK, Vista will remove the printer from the list.

Managing Fonts

Whenever you produce anything containing text, you select a font to specify the style of lettering. As you learned earlier in the chapter, Windows versions 3.1 and higher have included a type of font file called TrueType. TrueType revolutionized the desktop publishing industry by providing the average end user with a huge assortment of cheap, scaleable fonts. Vista includes support for TrueType fonts, but Vista comes with OpenType fonts installed.

NOTE The term *font* has a somewhat ambiguous meaning. Some people claim it refers to the style of lettering only and is synonymous with typeface. Other people claim a font is a particular typeface at a particular size with a particular set of attributes applied (bold, italic). Usage has been inconsistent over the years in the computer industry, and Windows itself is inconsistent in terminology. In this chapter, I'll use the term *font* to be synonymous with typeface.

The Fonts window in Vista, accessible through Control Panel, shows all the installed TrueType and OpenType fonts (as well as a few other types of special-purpose fonts that are neither).

Installing Fonts

Most of the fonts you'll acquire will come as part of an application. For example, when you install Microsoft Office, the Setup program automatically installs dozens of fonts in Windows. Even when you buy a disk full of fonts in a computer store, it usually comes with a Setup program for browsing the fonts and choosing the ones you want.

If the font source does not include any installation utility, you can install the fonts from within Windows' Fonts window by doing the following:

1. From Control Panel, click Appearance and Personalization, and then click Fonts. That's the only way to get to the Fonts applet in Category view; if you're using Classic view, you can simply double-click the Fonts icon.
2. In the Fonts window, choose File ➤ Install New Font. You'll see the Add Fonts dialog box shown in Figure 9.18.
3. Navigate to the drive and folder where the new font is located. If there are a lot of fonts in that location, it may take a minute for the list to populate. Click the Network button if you need to map a network drive to locate the fonts.

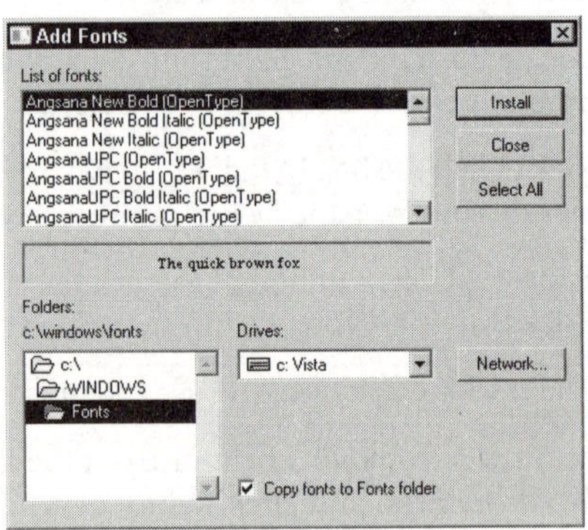

FIGURE 9.18 Use the Add Fonts dialog box to locate fonts on any drive you can access.

4. Select the font you want. To select multiple fonts, hold down the Ctrl key as you click each one, or hold down Shift to select a block.

NOTE If you clear the Copy Fonts to Fonts Folder check box, it will save the space on your hard disk by using the fonts from their source location. However, if that source location is ever unavailable, the fonts that are there will be unavailable as well.

5. Click OK to install the fonts.

TIP You can also drag and drop font files into the Fonts folder instead of going through the process just described.

Managing Your Font Collection

From the Fonts window, shown in Figure 9.19, you can browse the installed fonts, remove any that you don't want, and see previews of the fonts.

Here are some activities you can perform on fonts:

- To see a preview of a font, double-click its icon; when done looking at it, click Close. See Figure 9.20.
- To remove a font, delete its icon from the Fonts folder.
- To hide variations of the same font, choose View ➤ Hide Variations. This hides any fonts that are exactly like some other font except for being bold or italic.

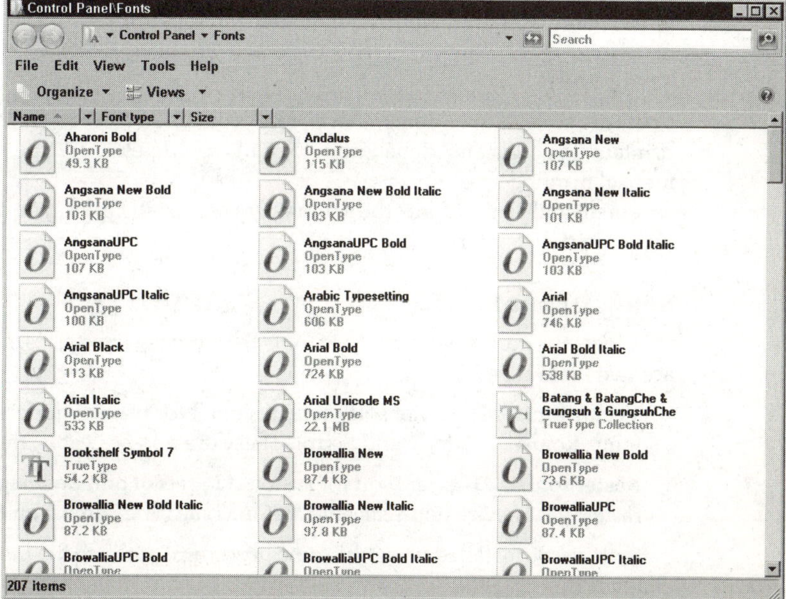

FIGURE 9.19
Browse the installed Windows fonts here.

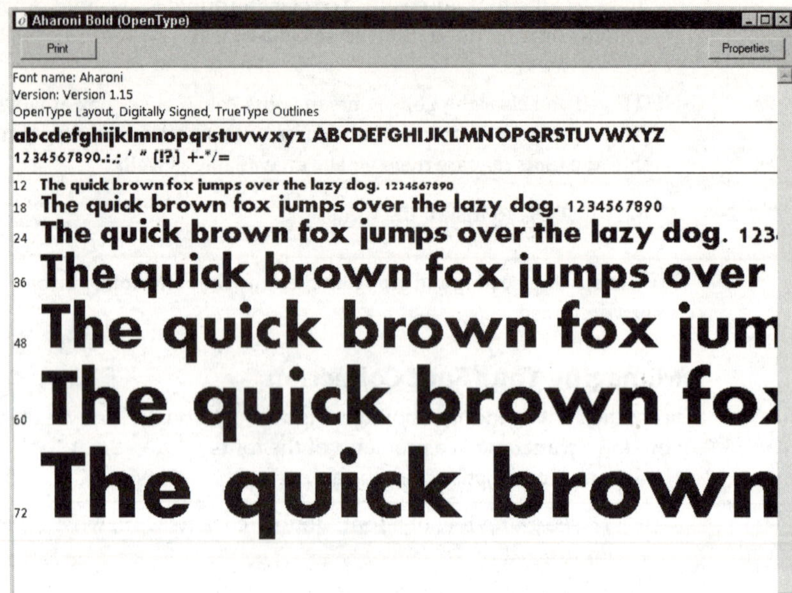

FIGURE 9.20
A preview of the selected font.

Using Other Types of Fonts

Most people think of TrueType or OpenType fonts only when they hear the term *font*, but there are, in fact, many different kinds of fonts that Windows applications can use.

TYPE 1 FONTS

These are scaleable soft fonts (that is, fonts contained in software) designed for use with PostScript printers. Type 1 is an Adobe technology that predates TrueType and is still in use today in commercial printing operations.

You install Type 1 fonts the same way you install OpenType or TrueType fonts, as explained earlier in the chapter.

NON-SCALEABLE FONTS

Windows supports several types of fonts that come in fixed sizes, rather than being scaleable. There are two main types:

Vector fonts These are soft fonts designed for use on plotters. Vista comes with three vector fonts: Roman, Modern, and Script. These are non-scaleable; they come in a fixed few sizes.

Raster fonts These are soft fonts stored in sets of bitmap images, with one size of lettering per raster file. They're non-scaleable. Before TrueType, almost all PC fonts were of this type.

Both can be installed using the same procedure outlined in "Installing New Fonts" earlier in the chapter.

If you have raster (PCL) printer fonts on a disk and you want to install them into the printer's memory, you would install them from the printer's properties. To do so, go to the Device Settings tab in the printer's Properties box and double-click External Fonts. Then specify the location from which you want to import the fonts. See Figure 9.21. These fonts would be available only for this printer, of course.

PRINTER-RESIDENT FONTS

Some printers have a number of built-in fonts. Some are scaleable (notably PostScript fonts in a PostScript printer); others are in a few fixed sizes. They're automatically available in applications but do not show up in the Fonts window.

The fonts may be stored in the printer itself, or in an add-on cartridge that plugs into a printer. Back in the early days of Hewlett-Packard LaserJet printers, cartridge fonts were very popular. Today, however, you'll seldom see them.

The printer driver knows about any printer-resident fonts automatically, but you may need to tell the printer driver about any cartridges you've installed. If your printer supports cartridges, there will be an Installed Font Cartridges option in the printer's Device Settings tab in its properties. Click it and then select which slot the cartridge is plugged into to make Vista recognize the cartridge.

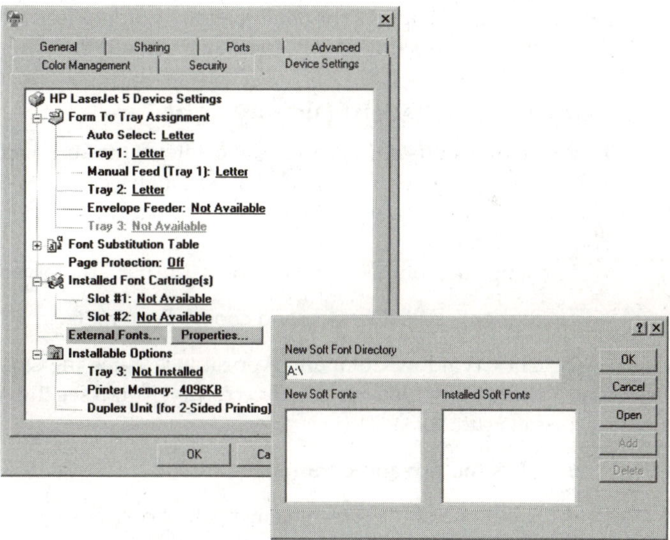

FIGURE 9.21
Install raster fonts for a printer.

Working with the Font Substitution Table

When a printer has its own resident fonts, you can choose to have them override certain soft fonts that an application might call for in a printout. This makes printing quicker because the soft font does not need to be sent to the printer prior to the print job. The table establishing the rules for which fonts should be substituted, and for what, is the *font substitution table*. Mostly you'll find it available on laser printers; ink-jet printers typically don't have resident fonts.

To work with the font substitution table, open the printer's Properties box and go to the Device Settings tab. Then locate the Font Substitutions listing, and click the plus (+) sign next to it, expanding the font list. See Figure 9.22.

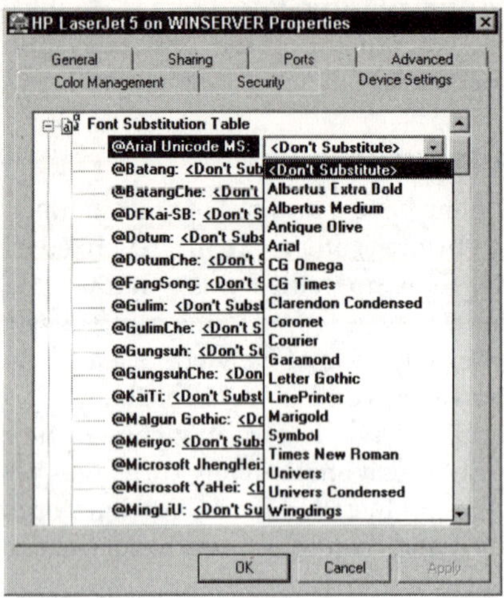

FIGURE 9.22
You can substitute printer-resident fonts for soft fonts selectively.

This font list consists of all the soft fonts in the Fonts folder in Windows. Click one of them and a drop-down list appears containing all the resident fonts in the printer. Choose one of them, and then whenever a document calls for the chosen soft font, the printer's own font will be used instead.

Selecting a Different Display Font

There are two kinds of fonts in Vista: printer fonts and display fonts. So far we have been talking only about the printer fonts. Each printer font has a corresponding display font that is used for displaying the font on screen when you use it in an application (and also when you preview it in the Fonts window).

To change the font used in Windows title bars, dialog boxes, and so on, do the following:

1. Right-click the Desktop and choose Personalize.
2. Click Window Color and Appearance. Click the Open Classic Appearance Properties for More Color Options link if necessary. You'll see the Appearance Settings dialog box shown in Figure 9.23.
3. Click the Advanced button.
4. Select one of the screen elements that contains text, such as Active Title Bar.
5. Open the Font drop-down list and select a different font to use for that element. Change the size, too, if desired, from the Size list.
6. Repeat steps 3 and 4 to change other screen elements if desired, then click OK.

Enabling ClearType for the Display Font

Vista comes with a feature called ClearType that can help with poor on-screen text appearance on LCD monitors. Normally, Vista can detect whether you have an LCD monitor and will turn ClearType on for you. However, it doesn't hurt to check. You should not turn ClearType on unless you have an LCD monitor because it can actually make the fonts appear worse on a CRT monitor. To turn it on, do the following:

1. Right-click the Desktop and choose Personalize.

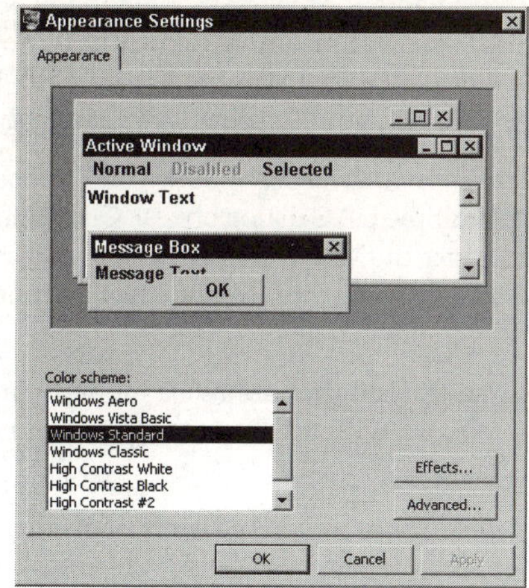

FIGURE 9.23
Use the Appearance Settings dialog box to change the font for your display.

2. Click Window Color and Appearance. Click the Open Classic Appearance Properties for More Color Options link if necessary. You'll see the Appearance Settings dialog box shown in Figure 9.23.
3. Click the Effects button.
4. Mark the Use the Following Method to Smooth Edges of Screen Fonts check box.
5. Choose ClearType from the list, and click OK twice.

Faxing in Vista

Vista comes with a Microsoft fax module that will serve adequately as a simple PC-based fax utility, so you don't have to buy a separate program like WinFax PRO just to send and receive the occasional page or two. I'm bringing it up here in this chapter because Windows tends to lump printing and faxing into the same category. Unlike previous versions of Windows, fax support is automatic in Vista, which means that you don't have to install anything.

WARNING You can install Windows Fax and Scan without having a modem installed in the PC or access to a fax server, but you can't use it to send and receive faxes.

Working with Windows Fax and Scan

Windows Fax and Scan is the core application for Microsoft Fax. You start it using the Start ➢ All Programs ➢ Windows Fax and Scan command. Because this application works equally well for faxing and scanning, Microsoft doesn't make any assumptions about your setup. You need to configure Windows Fax and Scan before you can use it for faxing. If you haven't performed the configuration, you'll see an error message, No Fax Accounts Are Configured, in the status bar. The following steps describe how to configure Windows Fax and Scan for use with a modem.

1. Choose Tools ➢ Fax Accounts to display the Fax Accounts dialog box.
2. Click Add. You'll see the Fax Setup dialog box.
3. Click Connect to a Fax Modem.

4. Type a name for the fax modem in the Name field, and then click Next. Vista will ask you how to answer incoming faxes. The options include Answer Automatically, Notify Me, and I'll Choose Later; I Want to Create a Fax Now. Unless you have a dedicated telephone line for your fax, you'll probably want to choose Notify Me.
5. Choose an answering option. You'll probably see a UAC dialog box (in fact, you'll probably see multiple UAC dialog boxes). Click Continue. You may also see a Windows Firewall dialog box since the Windows Firewall blocks requests of this type automatically. Click Unblock. Vista will install the Fax modem at this point. If it can't detect your modem, it will ask whether you want to install a modem.

Of course, you might not have a modem. In this case, you'll need to configure Windows Fax and Scan to work with the fax server on your network. The following steps describe how to perform this task.

1. Choose Tools ➤ Fax Accounts to display the Fax Accounts dialog box.
2. Click Add. You'll see the Fax Setup dialog box.
3. Click Connect to a Fax Server on My Network.
4. Type the UNC name for the fax server. Click next. Vista will attempt to connect to the remote fax server. You'll probably see a UAC dialog box (in fact, you'll probably see multiple UAC dialog boxes). Click Continue. You may also see a Windows Firewall dialog box since the Windows Firewall blocks requests of this type automatically. Click Unblock. Vista will install the fax server connection at this point.

Before you can send any faxes, you need to provide some basic information about yourself. Choose the Tools ➤ Sender Information command to display the Sender Information dialog box shown in Figure 9.24. You can use every one of these fields when creating a cover page for your fax. In fact, the default cover pages do use them. (See the "Creating a Cover Page" section of the chapter for more details on working with cover pages.)

Sending a Fax

To send a fax, you must have a fax-capable modem or a fax server account, of course, and it must be set up in the Printers and Faxes folder as a print device. Vista adds the Fax print device as part of the basic installation, so you'll never need to worry about the Fax device unless you accidentally delete it.

FIGURE 9.24
Set the sender information that you want to transmit with a fax.

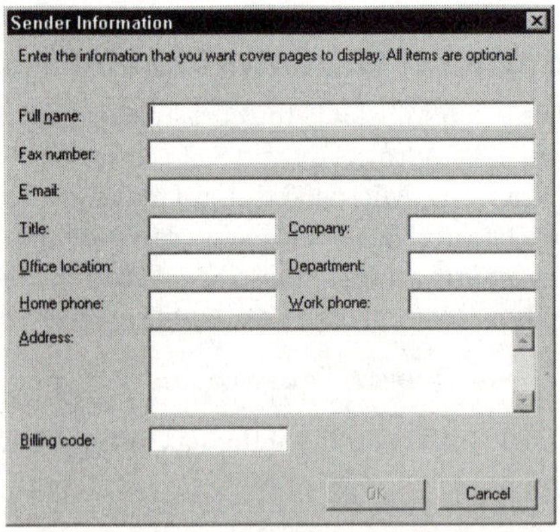

Sender Information
Enter the information that you want cover pages to display. All items are optional.
Full name:
Fax number:
E-mail:
Title:
Company:
Office location:
Department:
Home phone:
Work phone:
Address:
Billing code:
OK
Cancel

There are two ways to send a fax. You can use the Send Fax Wizard that's part of the faxing module, or you can print to the fax driver as you would a printer from within any application to fax a document from that application.

Sending a Stand-alone Fax

A stand-alone fax is appropriate when you just want to send a quick cover page with a message on it or when you need to scan existing material instead of creating the content electronically. To create a stand-alone fax, open Windows Fax and Scan. Now you have a choice to make. Choose File ➤ New ➤ Fax to send a simple message, File ➤ New ➤ Scan to scan material into Windows Fax and Scan, manipulate it, and then send it as an attachment, or File ➤ New ➤ Fax from Scanner to scan material directly from the scanner and send it immediately as a fax. In all three cases, you'll see the New Fax dialog box shown in Figure 9.25.

You might have noticed that the New Fax dialog box looks a lot like a new e-mail dialog box. In fact, when you click To, you'll see the same contact list that you use with Outlook. Just like an e-mail, you'll add a subject and you can insert files or graphics. The formatting, text editing, and other features work very much like e-mail as well. In short, if you can send an e-mail, you can send a fax.

Of course, sending a fax isn't precisely like sending an e-mail. The New Fax dialog box contains a couple of special features. First, you'll notice the Cover Page field where you can choose a cover page for your fax. Microsoft provides four default cover pages that provide all you need for general communication. You may want to create a custom cover page for a business, but these cover pages even work as a starting point when you want to create something on your own.

Second, the New Fax dialog box includes the ability to scan material directly into the fax you're creating. Simply choose Insert ➤ Pages from Scanner, when you want to include scanned material.

Third, if you're using a modem to send the fax, you can provide an entry for the Dialing Rule field. This field ensures that your fax actually gets to its destination. The modem may have to dial a special number to get out of the building, for example. When you complete your fax, click Preview to make sure that it appears as you want the recipient to see it. If you need to make changes, you can get back to the editor by choosing View ➤ Preview.

FIGURE 9.25
Define your fax and send it using a process similar to e-mail.

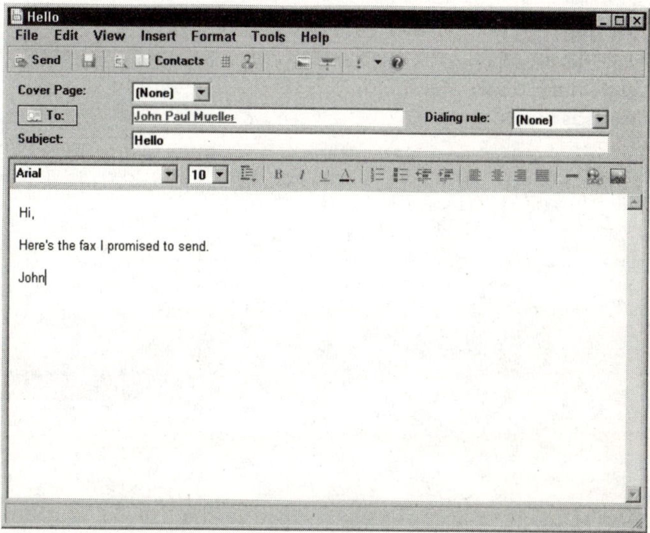

FAXING FROM AN APPLICATION

Faxing from an application is appropriate when you need to fax more pages than just a cover page. For example, you can fax from Word to send an entire Word document or any portion of it.

To fax from an application, begin printing normally in that application, but choose Windows Fax and Scan as the printer in the application's Print dialog box. The Send Fax Wizard runs, and from that point, the process is the same described as in the preceding section.

Receiving a Fax

When the Windows Fax and Scan service is installed, it adds a service that runs all the time, listening for the phone to ring. When it does, an icon pops up in the notification area letting you know. You can click that icon to answer the call with the fax driver, or ignore it to decline. From Windows Fax and Scan, you can choose Tools ➤ Fax Status Monitor to open a window that shows the monitoring system. Once the fax is received, it appears in Windows Fax and Scan and you can double-click it to view it.

Creating a Cover Page

Arc you finding the cover pages provided by Vista a little dull? They just don't seem to reflect your sense of taste and style? Maybe you want something a little flashier? In this section, you'll learn how to create a new custom cover page.

Microsoft has made it significantly easier to work with fax cover pages in Vista. To begin, choose Tools ➤ Cover Pages. You'll see the Fax Cover Pages dialog box shown in Figure 9.26 where you can manage the cover pages for Windows Fax and Scan.

One suggestion to make the editing process easier is to copy an existing cover page and change it as you see fit. Using this approach makes it significantly easier to discover all of the ins and outs of cover pages and reduces the time to create a finished product. Simply click Copy and you'll see the list of existing cover pages. Choose the cover page you want to use as a template and click Open. Of course, you don't want to change the original, so highlight it in the list, click Rename, and type a new name for the cover sheet. Make sure the cover sheet has a .cov file extension.

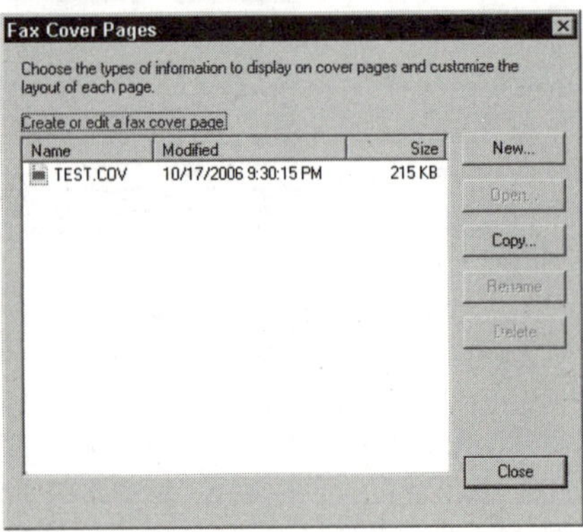

FIGURE 9.26
Add, delete, copy, and edit fax cover pages as needed.

Now it's time to edit the cover sheet. Highlight the entry you created and click Open. You'll see an editor that looks very much like a combination of a simple drawing program and a word processor as shown in Figure 9.27. All of the features work just as you might expect. You can edit text, add formatting, change the font, and do anything else you can do with a basic word processor. In addition, you can use the basic drawing tools to create circles, squares, lines, and polygons. One editing feature that seems to be missing is inserting graphics. You can accomplish this task by opening the graphic in another application, copying it to the clipboard, and pasting the image into your fax cover sheet.

You may have noticed the fields in Figure 9.27. For example, the top of the cover sheet contains a To field. Next to this field is an odd-looking {Recipient Name} entry. You don't have to worry about creating these entries yourself. Simply choose the options on the Insert menu. For example, to insert the recipient name, choose Insert ➢ Recipient ➢ Name. You can modify the appearance of the text, move the field around, modify the field name, and perform any required formatting.

After you create a cover sheet, click Save and close the editor. The new cover sheet is available for immediate use in your next fax.

FIGURE 9.27
Modify the content of the fax cover sheet so it contains the information you want to send.

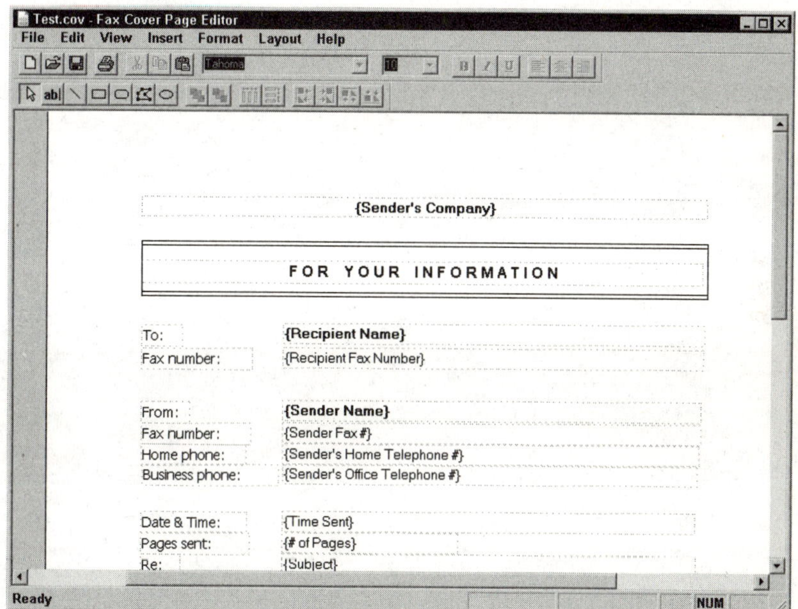

Summary

This chapter has covered printing and font management. You learned how to set up local and network printers and how to fine-tune their operation using their Properties. You also learned to manage a print queue, to install and remove fonts, and to change the display font in Windows. Most importantly, you also discovered the new Print Management console, a Vista feature that is certain to reduce your administration time.

Of course, you'll want to spend some time working with these new features. Try configuring printers for various uses. Make sure you try the new Print Management console to work with both local and remote printers. If you have a modem installed on your machine or access to a fax server, try configuring Windows Fax and Scan. Create some custom cover sheets and have a little fun with this updated feature.

Everyone thinks that Windows is all about the software. However, before you can do anything with Vista, you need to consider the hardware. In the next chapter, you'll learn how to install and configure hardware devices. This sometimes difficult task is made significantly easier in Vista, but you'll also find some interesting twists and turns due to the need for driver signing and Microsoft's focus on security.

Chapter 10

Installing and Configuring Hardware

Vista makes it easier than ever to install and configure new hardware. Its full support of Plug and Play, USB, FireWire, and other technologies makes for effortless installation of most new hardware. And for those situations where Plug and Play doesn't work quite right, Vista includes several utilities for helping identify and correct the problem.

- Considering the new Windows Experience Index
- How hardware interacts with Vista
- Using hot-pluggable devices
- Using the hardware wizards
- Disabling a device
- Uninstalling a device
- Adding some specific hardware items
- Working with iSCSI devices

Vista: What's New?

Microsoft adds new hardware support with every version of Windows. Of course, Vista is no exception because the new Aero Glass interface requires a significant improvement in hardware to run. However, there are many other changes as well. For example, Vista supports Internet Small Computer System Interface (iSCSI), a standard that lets the computer send data requests using the same Internet Protocol (IP) that you use to communicate over the Internet with a browser. The Internet Engineering Task Force (IETF) (`http://www.ietf.org/`) originally designed the specification for this technology, so iSCSI is an open standard. You'll normally find iSCSI used with storage area networks (SANs) today, but it does have a number of other uses because the technology makes it possible to see a remote drive as locally connected. You can learn more about this technology in the "Working with iSCSI Devices" section of the chapter.

Another big change in Vista is that Microsoft is attempting to help people make sense of the performance of their system. Sure, you can use the Reliability and Performance Monitor console to check system statistics, but most people can't easily interpret those statistics. The Windows Experience Index is one of several attempts by Microsoft to make performance easier to understand. Although many experts disagree with the rating and Microsoft will likely spend a lot of time trying to hone the results, the Windows Experience Index does answer the question of what your system performance means. Theoretically, you should be able to use the Windows Experience Index to determine where you need to spend on hardware updates and let you make better software purchasing decisions. Of course, that will only happen reliably when Microsoft finally gets the numbers completely tuned.

Using the Windows Experience Index to Your Advantage

The Windows Experience Index is Microsoft's attempt at helping you understand all of the performance statistics on your system with greater ease. The goal is to help you understand what it all means in a useful way. There is a lot of contention about the Windows Experience Index because many vendors feel that Microsoft hasn't tuned the numbers properly. It's very likely going to take Microsoft a while to come up with completely valid numbers, but the initial attempt does provide good information and does solve a significant problem for many people.

The idea behind the Windows Experience Index is a good one for two reasons. First, you can use the numbers to determine where your system is weak so that you can spend update dollars wisely. Second, you can use the numbers to determine whether a particular piece of software will run on your system. Yes, you can perform a line-by-line comparison of the required hardware on the software box against the specifications of your machine, but this indexing system should make things considerably easier and more accurate because the index is based on actual hardware performance.

Now that you know what the Windows Experience Index can do for you, it's time to check it out on your system. Click Show More Details in the Welcome Center window that appears automatically when you start your system. (You can also display the Welcome Center by choosing Start ➤ All Programs ➤ Accessories ➤ Welcome Center.) You'll see the System window that shows the overall Windows Experience Index for your machine in the Rating field of the System section. Click the Windows Experience Index link and you'll see the details for your system as shown in Figure 10.1.

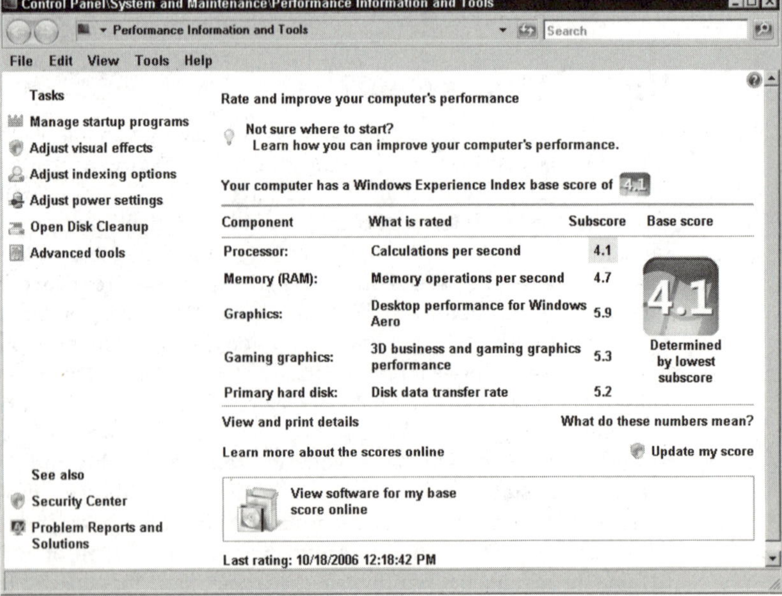

FIGURE 10.1
The Windows Experience Index is made up of a number of system performance analyses.

Using this display, you can determine which part of your system is weakest. In this case, the processor is the weakest link. Since the motherboard will accept a faster processor, I could swap out the processor for this machine and speed it up considerably. This information would have been difficult to obtain in previous versions of Windows, but the Windows Experience Index makes it easy to figure out. Microsoft also makes it easy to print out the information so you can take it to the store with you. Click the View and Print Details link and you'll see a Performance Information and Tools window that contains more details about the performance of your system and includes a complete list of the pertinent hardware. Click Print This Page and you'll get hard copy output of the contents of this window that you can take with you when buying hardware.

From a software perspective, you can obtain general information about what your computer will run by clicking the What Do These Numbers Mean? link. Generally, you need a computer with a rating of 3 or higher to use the Aero Glass interface. However, even a rating of 3 won't let you use all of the Vista features. To get the most out of Vista, you must have a computer that rates at least 4 and higher.

The big payoff from a software perspective will eventually occur when you can click the View Software for My Base Score Online link and see the list of software your system can run under Vista. Even if you decide not to buy your software from Windows Marketplace, you can at least get a quick idea of what Microsoft thinks will run acceptably (whether you agree with this list is entirely up to you). One thing to note about this link is that it contains your statistics. For example, the link for the system shown in Figure 10.1 is `http://www.windowsmarketplace.com/?CPU=4.1&MEM=4.7&HDD=5.2&DWM=5.9&D3D=5.3`. Let's say you decide that you're going to update your system and hope to achieve a CPU rating of 4.9. Simply change this number in the link to determine whether the upgrade will be enough to run the software you want to use.

How Hardware Interacts with Vista

Let's start this chapter with a little background information about Vista's support for hardware devices.

Device Drivers

Each device—whether it's a modem, a sound card, a printer, or whatever—speaks its own language. In order for Windows to communicate with a device, a *device driver* for it needs to be installed. A device driver is a program that translates between Windows and the actual piece of hardware. Most device drivers also include user-adjustable settings that you can use to fine-tune the device's behavior, as you saw in Chapter 9 with printer drivers.

The driver files themselves usually have a `.sys` extension, but there may be helper files associated with them that use other extensions. For example, there might be a file with a `.dll` extension (Dynamic Link Library), a `.chm` extension (a Help file for the device), a `.cpl` extension (for Control Panel access to the device's properties), an `.htm` extension (a web document) containing help information, and others.

For almost a decade now, nearly all hardware manufactured has included support for a standard called *Plug and Play* in Windows. It enables Windows to detect the hardware automatically and install the correct driver for it from its own internal database of drivers. Vista includes thousands of drivers for popular hardware items. If the correct driver isn't available through Vista itself, it prompts you to insert the disk provided by the device manufacturer and copies the needed driver from that location to your hard drive. From then on, each time Windows starts up, the driver for that device loads automatically.

Driver Signing

One reason that earlier versions of Windows could become unstable was because of an outdated or corrupted device driver. This was a problem because not all device manufacturers produced error-free drivers and because sometimes different devices used driver files of the same name that would overwrite one another when you installed a new device. To combat this problem, Microsoft came up with a way of attaching a digital signature to a device driver to certify that it's capable of working with Vista and hasn't been modified since its creation. Drivers that live up to this standard are known as *signed drivers*. When you install a new device, Windows will prefer a signed driver to an unsigned one. If only an unsigned driver is available, you'll see a warning before Windows installs it on an x86 system. You must use signed Vista drivers when working with the x64 version of the operating system.

Should you install an unsigned driver? It's a gamble. An unsigned driver could cause system instability, including lockups and blue-screen error messages. On the other hand, the unsigned driver might work just fine. You never know. Try searching the device manufacturer's website for a signed driver first; if you can't find one, back up your Windows configuration with System Restore before installing the unsigned driver. However, it's important to realize that Microsoft has made changes in the way it works with drivers in Vista. If a driver tries to make changes to the kernel or perform other tasks in an insecure manner, the driver installation will fail. Consequently, the piece of hardware might be inaccessible at the outset and remain that way because the driver won't install at all.

TIP The default security setting for driver signing is to let you install the driver without any kind of warning on the x86 version of Vista. If you want some other setting, such as to always warn about unsigned drivers or never allow them, open the Group Policy Object Editor. Choose Start ➤ Run, type **`gpedit.msc`** in the Open field, and click OK. Select the `Local Computer Policy\User Configuration\Administrative Templates\System\Driver Installation` folder. Open the Code Signing for Device Drivers policy and choose the Enabled option. Choose one of the options in the When Windows Detects a Driver File without a Digital Signature drop-down list box. Click OK to make the change permanent and close the Group Policy Object Editor.

In a few cases, a certain driver may be known to cause problems in Vista. If you try to install such a driver, a feature called Windows Driver Protection will kick in and refuse to allow you to install it. Vista comes with a database listing the prohibited drivers, and when you use Windows Update, this database gets updated from Microsoft.

INF Files

When Windows searches for a driver for a device, it isn't looking directly for the driver files; instead it's looking for an information file (`.inf` extension). This is a text file that tells what driver files should be used for the device and what settings for it should be entered into the Registry. Figure 10.2 shows an INF file for a 1394 (FireWire) host controller card, for example.

For some devices, the INF file is actually all there is to the driver. For example, if you have a driver disk for a monitor, chances are that there aren't any real "drivers" for that monitor; there's just an INF file that describes the monitor to the Registry for the purposes of defining the maximum resolution and refresh rate that should be allowed.

Driver Versions

Vista works best when all device drivers are written specifically for Vista. In fact, Vista drivers are your only choice when working with the x64 version of Vista. However, if such a driver isn't available for a critical piece of hardware, you may be forced to try a driver written for an earlier version of Windows.

Generally speaking, you should try to get the newest driver you can, which means starting with Windows XP drivers. If you can't find a Windows XP driver that will work, try a Windows 2000 or even a Windows NT driver. Drivers written for Windows 9*x* or Windows Me probably won't work in Vista because the operating systems are too different. As the driver gets older, you incur additional security, reliability, and performance problems. If you truly can't find a good driver for your piece of hardware, it may very well be time to replace the hardware, rather than destabilize your system.

FIGURE 10.2 This INF file tells Windows how to install the drivers for an IDE controller card.

```
1394.inf - Notepad
File  Edit  Format  View  Help
; 1394.INF  -- This file contains descriptions of
;              all supported 1394 host controllers
;
; Copyright (c) Microsoft Corporation.  All rights reserved.


;;++ Added by AddSDisk.cmd
[SourceDisksNames]
3426=windows cd

[SourceDisksFiles]
1394bus.sys            = 3426
ohci1394.sys           = 3426
;;--

[Version]
Signature="$CHICAGO$"
Class=1394
ClassGuid={6BDD1FC1-810F-11D0-BEC7-08002BE2092F}
Provider=%MSFT%
DriverVer=06/21/2006,6.0.5728.16387
;; Commented by AddSDisk.cmd
;; LayoutFile=layout.inf

[ControlFlags]
; All PnP devices should be excluded from manual AddDevice Applet list
ExcludeFromSelect=*

; ================== Table of content ========================
[DestinationDirs]
DefaultDestDir=12
1394_CopyFiles=12
OHCI_CopyFiles=12
```

System Resources

Each device requires system resources. These resources can include a range of I/O addresses, an interrupt request (IRQ) line, or a direct memory access (DMA) channel. Or, to be more precise, the controller through which the device is attached requires the resources. For example, even though you might have two hard disks on an IDE bus, that IDE bus takes up only one set of system resources. Another example: you might have six SCSI or USB devices chained together on a single interface, but that interface would use only one resource.

IRQs

When a device needs to talk with the CPU, the device must initiate the conversation. The device must signal to the CPU, "Hey, I need to talk to you!" and that's the purpose of an interrupt request (IRQ). The device is literally requesting permission to interrupt the CPU's work to perform some other task. A device has an assigned IRQ, and whenever it needs attention, it places a message on that bus. The CPU receives it and initiates a conversation. Most systems have 16 IRQs, numbered 0 through 15, but over half of them are preassigned to system devices such as the keyboard, system clock, and built-in IDE controllers.

NOTE On chipsets that use an Advanced Programmable Interrupt Controller (APIC), more than 16 IRQs might be listed in use in Device Manager. You can find a somewhat dated (2001) but still valuable article about the APIC at `http://www.microsoft.com/whdc/system/sysperf/IO-APIC.mspx`. This article is part of a larger site at Microsoft called Hardware and Driver Central, directly accessible at `http://www.microsoft.com/whdc/default.mspx`, which contains many useful articles about hardware resource allocation in Windows.

When you install a new piece of hardware, an IRQ must normally be assigned to its controller. There are some exceptions to this rule. For example, a game port doesn't require an IRQ because the system automatically monitors it at specific intervals when an application (such as a game) requests that action. In other words, an IRQ is only required when the device must independently interrupt the CPU's activity.

Some devices have a built-in controller that requires the IRQ. An internal modem would fit that description, for example. Other devices share a controller with others—for example, a SCSI device shares a SCSI interface card with up to six other devices, and a USB device can share a USB root hub. Therefore, it's advantageous to choose USB or SCSI devices when they are available.

So, what happens if all the IRQs are taken? It depends on the device. If it's an Industry Standard Architecture (ISA) device, there's not much you can do, because all ISA devices require their own separate IRQ. However, ISA is virtually obsolete, so you probably won't find yourself working on systems with a lot of ISA devices. If it's a Peripheral Component Interconnect (PCI) device, there shouldn't be a problem because PCI devices can automatically share IRQs. Windows will assign multiple PCI devices to the same IRQ, and no conflict will occur.

I/O Addresses

In addition to the IRQ, the device must have a meeting area for its conversations with the CPU. This assigned area for the device is its I/O address. This is a section of the PC's memory set aside for that device's use. Some devices have a range of memory addresses. Memory addresses are expressed in hexadecimal, so you might have a range like DF68–DF6F. Some devices might have multiple ranges. Since there's more memory to go around than there are IRQs, I/O address conflicts are rare.

DMA Channels

Some devices have a way of working directly with memory, circumventing the CPU, for faster performance. This is called direct memory access (DMA), and in order to do it, the device must have a DMA channel assigned to it. This is most common for keyboards and sound cards. Some IDE devices can also use DMA. Each device that uses DMA must have a unique DMA address (0 through 5).

How Resources Are Assigned

Plug and Play also manages the system resource assignments for the devices, ensuring that there are no conflicts. When Windows starts up, it makes a list of the available system resources and then doles them out to devices, trying for a "best fit" so that all devices have what they need.

Devices that aren't Plug and Play compatible typically have jumpers on them for manually setting resource assignments. These devices are extremely rare, and you always get documentation with them showing how to set the jumpers. If your system includes one or more such devices, you should make a note of their manually set assignments and then make sure that Windows uses those same assignments in Device Manager (covered later in this chapter).

What Happens When You Install a Device in Windows?

When Windows automatically detects a new device, or when you run the Setup program for a device or install it with Add New hardware, a number of things happen:

- Registry entries are made for the new device.
- If the device requires any drivers, they are copied to your hard drive.
- If the device requires any system resources, Windows claims them on behalf of the device so they won't be assigned to anything else.

Depending on the device, you may see some or all of these tangible signs of the device being installed:

- The device appears in the Device Manager listing.
- A New Hardware bubble appears briefly in the notification area.
- An icon for controlling the new device appears in Control Panel. Some Windows-only modems do this.
- An icon for controlling the new device appears in Computer. Some digital cameras do this, but only when the camera is physically connected to the PC.

NOTE If a device's Setup program does add a Control Panel applet, you may find it only in Classic view, not Category view. Some devices do provide a Category view icon. For example, you may find your sound card applet in the Hardware and Sound category.

Using Hot-Pluggable Devices

Hardware devices that use USB, FireWire, and PC Card connections are *hot pluggable*—you can plug in and unplug the device while Windows is running without any adverse effects. Windows automatically loads and unloads drivers for hot-pluggable devices as needed. Serial Advanced Technology Attachment (SATA) hard disks are also hot pluggable, although you wouldn't commonly connect or disconnect one while the system was running.

NOTE Limited users and Guest users can install hot-pluggable devices. This is good because it enables someone to sit down at a computer and connect a flash memory device, for example. However, only Computer Administrator users or users with administrative privileges can install devices that aren't hot pluggable.

When you plug in a hot-pluggable device for the first time, Windows displays a pop-up message in the notification area to let you know that it has noticed the device. Windows then automatically looks for a driver to let Windows and the device communicate with each other. It first checks in its capacious driver cache, which contains a wide variety of preinstalled drivers. If it draws a blank there, and if your computer is connected to the Internet, it checks the Windows Update site for a driver for the device; if it finds a driver, it downloads it and installs it. If Windows is able to find a suitable driver in either the driver cache or Windows Update, it unpacks and installs the driver, displaying a pop-up message identifying the device as it does so.

When the driver is installed and working, Windows displays a pop-up message telling you that the hardware is ready to use.

If Windows can't find a driver for the device, it starts the Found New Hardware Wizard, so that you can supply the driver for the device manually. I'll discuss how to use the Found New Hardware Wizard in just a minute.

Removing a USB device or FireWire device is as simple as unplugging it. Windows notices that you've removed the device and unloads its driver. Any data transfers that were in progress are aborted.

If the device is one through which you are transferring important data, such as an external drive, you might want to use the Safely Remove Hardware feature to ensure that all transfers have completed before you unplug the device. To do so, double-click the Safely Remove Hardware icon in the notification area. The Safely Remove Hardware dialog box opens. Select the device you are going to unplug and click Stop. Then, when a message appears that the device has been stopped, you can click Close and then unplug the device.

When you plug a hot-pluggable device in again, Windows notices it and loads the driver without displaying any pop-up message.

Using the Hardware Wizards

Vista tries to hide the details of hardware installation whenever possible. In many cases, when you restart your system after installing a new piece of hardware, you'll see a bubble saying that Vista is installing some new software for it. You can click the icon in the notification area if you want to monitor the installation, but normally you won't need to do this. Vista automatically searches its cache of local drivers and then goes to the Internet to locate a driver there. After the installation is complete, you'll normally see another balloon telling you that the device is ready to use. From a device installation perspective, Vista is about as trouble free as you can get.

For devices that aren't hot pluggable, or for hot-pluggable devices for which Windows can't find a suitable driver, you use Windows' two hardware wizards, the Found New Hardware Wizard and the Add Hardware Wizard. In addition, you might find that the driver you have today has problems, which means using the Update Driver Software Wizard to locate a newer, and hopefully better, driver.

Interacting with the Found New Hardware Wizard

When Windows discovers some hardware for which it can't find a suitable driver, it starts the Found New Hardware Wizard. The wizard lists the type of hardware it's found. If the wizard can't identify the type of hardware, it displays *Unknown Device*.

The Found New Hardware dialog box gives you three options:

Locate and Install Driver Software (Recommended) When you select this option, Vista automatically searches Windows Update for an appropriate driver for your device. Vista may also search other locations, but Windows Update is the starting point. When Vista finds the driver it needs online, you're finished. In most cases, new hardware that came out after Vista installs using this option. However, you'll also find older hardware on the list when Microsoft or the vendor provides the required support after the Vista release, so it's always a good idea to check this option.

Ask Me Again Later You're preparing an important document for someone or need to get something done now. Installing a new device driver is the last item on your list of things to do. When you're in a hurry, but want to install the device driver later, choose this option.

Don't Show This Message Again for This Device Older versions of Windows insisted that you always install a device driver for every device (or at least make an effort to do so). The message box for new hardware would appear with annoying regularity, even when you knew the hardware wouldn't install. Vista gives you an option not to install the device at all. This option comes in handy in situations where you don't want to uninstall the device, but you know Vista won't support it either. For example, you might have a dual-boot setup with Windows XP and use the device only when you have Windows XP booted.

Let's say that you do want to install a device, but Vista doesn't find any support for it online. In this case, you'll see a dialog box containing two options. The first option tells you to insert the disk with the driver software. Of course, this option assumes that you have a disk with a Vista driver (or at least a driver that will work with Vista when using the 32-bit edition). If you do have the disk, insert the disk and choose the first option. The "Installing a Driver from a Specific Location" section of the chapter describes this task in detail.

The second option assumes you still want to install the device but lack an appropriate driver. Simply select the I Don't Have the Disk. Show Me Other Options link to begin using this final alternative. In this case, you'll see another dialog box that contains a Check Online for a Solution Now link. Click this link to look for the device driver in other locations. However, you might decide that you really don't want to spend time looking for the device. In this case, you'll choose the Don't Check Online; I'll Set Up This Device Later link.

Installing a Driver from a Specific Location

There are a number of ways to install a driver from a specific location. For example, you might click the option to install the new driver manually or using a disk in the Found New Hardware Wizard. You could also click the Have Disk button or link in any of the hardware installation dialog boxes that Vista provides. The common thread for this installation type is that you're installing specific software, not a generic device driver for a device that lacks support. To install a driver from a specific location, take the following steps:

NOTE Microsoft recommends that if you have a vendor device driver on a CD or portable media, and the vendor supplies an installation program that you use the vendor-supplied installation program. Using the vendor-supplied installation program ensures that any device-specific tasks are processed properly. In addition, the vendor-supplied installation may provide extra features, such as automated error checking, should the installation fail.

1. Click the button or link that starts the process for installing a new device driver from a disk, CD, or specific location on your local or network drive.

2. If you have the driver on a floppy or a CD, insert it in the appropriate drive and select the drive when asked. If you have the driver on a local drive or network drive, click the Browse button, use the resulting Locate File dialog box (a common Open dialog box) to locate the driver file, and click the Open button to enter its name and path in the Copy Manufacturer's Files From text box.

3. Click the OK button. The wizard displays a device driver selection screen with one or two panes (shown in Figure 10.3) that contains the name of the hardware model or models identified by the driver. You'll see the two-pane version of the screen when a single disk contains entries for multiple vendors.

FIGURE 10.3
When you specify the driver to use, the wizard displays the Select the Device Driver You Want to Install for This Hardware screen.

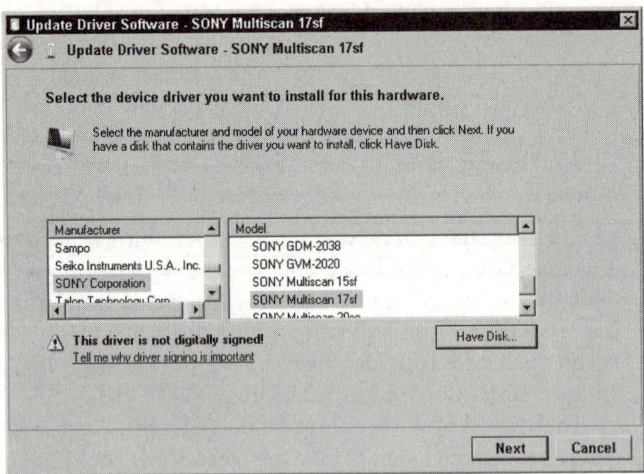

4. Select the driver and click the Next button. If Windows doesn't think the driver is correct for the device, it displays the Update Driver Warning dialog box, warning you that the hardware may not work and that your computer might become unstable or stop working. Click the Yes button if you're sure you want to install this driver. Otherwise, click the No button and select another driver.

NOTE If the wizard can't find hardware information in the location you specified, it displays the Select Device message box telling you that the location you specified doesn't contain information about your hardware. The wizard then displays the Install from Disk dialog box again so that you can specify a different location for the file. If you get to this stage, you're probably stuck. You can click the Cancel button to close the Install from Disk dialog box and return to the Select the Device Driver You Want to Install for This Hardware screen so that you can select a built-in driver, but that's about it. Click the Cancel button to cancel the wizard.

5. The wizard checks to make sure that the driver you're installing has passed the Windows Logo testing to verify its compatibility with Vista. This is basically the same thing as driver signing, explained earlier in the chapter. If the driver has passed Windows Logo testing, all is well; if it hasn't passed, the wizard displays a warning box warning you of the problem and strongly discouraging you from installing the driver. If you're sure the driver is okay, click the Continue Anyway button. If you have any doubts about the driver, click the STOP Installation button.

6. If Windows finds no problem with the driver, it installs it and displays a Completing Driver Installation screen.

7. Click the Finish button. Once the wizard closes, the hardware is ready for use.

If the Found New Hardware Wizard is unable to install the device, it displays the Cannot Install This Hardware screen telling you what the problem was.

Running the Add Hardware Wizard

If Windows doesn't find the new hardware you want to install, run the Add Hardware Wizard so that you can add the hardware manually. Microsoft uses the term *legacy* a lot with this particular wizard because Vista uses it to install older devices that don't have the best hardware support. In addition, you can use this wizard to install generic device drivers that come with Vista when your device doesn't provide its own support. The generic drivers work better with monitors and worse with complex devices, such as printers.

To run the Add Hardware Wizard, follow these steps:

1. Choose Start ➤ Control Panel. Vista displays Control Panel.
2. Click the Classic View link. Vista displays the Classic View screen.
3. Double-click Add Hardware. Vista starts the Add Hardware Wizard, which displays the Welcome to the Add Hardware Wizard screen.
4. Click the Next button. The wizard searches for new hardware.
   - If the wizard locates the new hardware, it begins looking for a driver to install. The installation procedure follows the Found New Hardware Wizard process described in the "Interacting with the Found New Hardware Wizard" section of the chapter. Complete the installation using the Found New Hardware steps.
   - When the wizard fails to locate the hardware (which is likely since Vista didn't find the device earlier), you'll see an error message stating that Vista didn't find any new hardware.
   - Click Next. Vista displays the Add Hardware dialog box shown in Figure 10.4.
5. In the Common Hardware Types list box, select the type of hardware you're installing. If the device doesn't fit any of the descriptions, select the Show All Devices item.
6. Click the Next button. If you choose the Show All Devices item, the wizard displays the Select the Device Driver You Want to Install for This Hardware screen (shown in Figure 10.5).

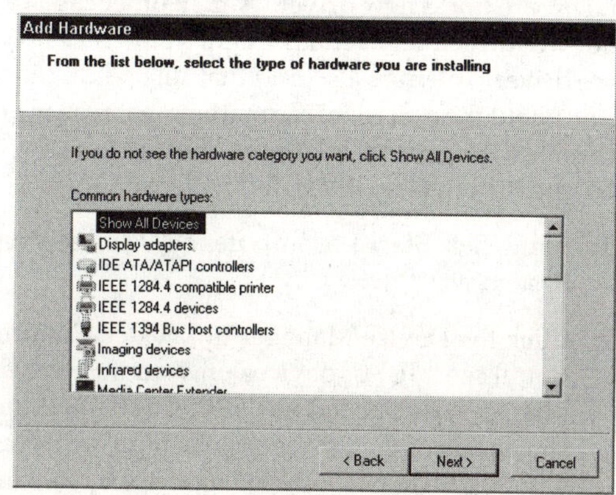

FIGURE 10.4
The Add Hardware dialog box helps you search for appropriate device drivers for your system.

FIGURE 10.5
On the Select the Device Driver You Want to Install for This Hardware screen of the Add Hardware Wizard, select the device driver.

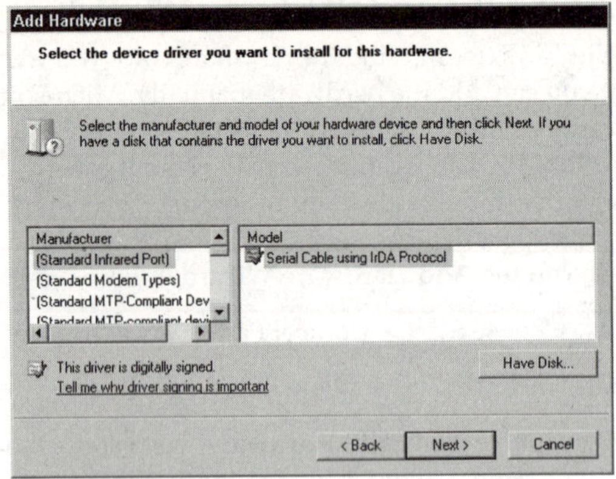

7. If Windows has a driver for the device, select it by selecting the manufacturer in the Manufacturers list box and the device in the Models list box. In many cases, you'll have to rely on a generic driver for older (legacy) devices. If you have a vendor-supplied driver, follow the procedure in the "Installing a Driver from a Specific Location" section of the chapter to install it.
8. Click the Next button. The wizard displays the The Wizard Is Ready to Install Your Hardware screen, listing the hardware that's lined up for installation.
9. Click the Next button. The wizard installs the hardware and displays the Completing the Add Hardware Wizard screen.
10. Click the Finish button. The Add Hardware Wizard closes itself. The hardware should be ready for use.

Updating a Device Driver

You may have a device on your machine that works okay, but it sometimes causes problems and you'd love to find a new driver for it. In other cases, you might read about a problem with your current device driver, or a vendor might send you a newsletter that contains information about a new device driver. You may also find that Vista didn't install support for a particular device and didn't tell you about the omission. No matter what reason you have for wanting to update a device driver, Vista makes the process relatively easy.

To update a device driver, follow these steps:

1. Right-click Start ➤ Computer and choose Properties from the context menu. You'll see the System window.
2. Click the Device Manager link. Click Continue when prompted by the UAC dialog box. You'll see a list of devices on your system as shown in Figure 10.6. Notice that Device Manager has opened one of the hardware categories, Universal Serial Bus Controllers, and shows one of the devices as disabled, USB Mass Storage Device. You can always determine whether Vista has disabled a device by looking for the yellow triangle with an exclamation mark in it.

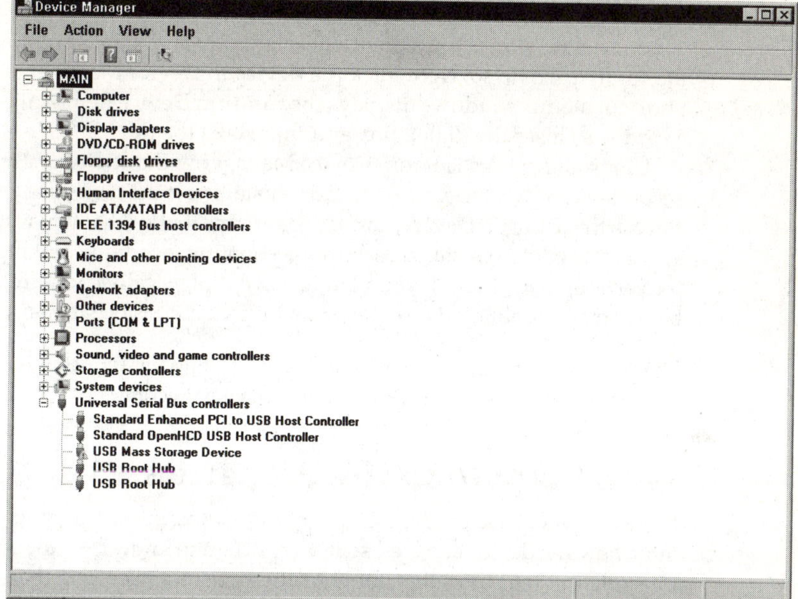

FIGURE 10.6 Device Manager shows you which devices Vista disables due to hardware or device driver problems.

3. Right-click the device you want to update and choose Update Driver Software from the context menu. You'll see an Update Driver Software dialog box where you can choose to have Vista look for the update for you or you can install the driver update manually.

   - Click the Search Automatically for Updated Driver Software link when you want to update an existing driver but aren't sure where to locate the driver or know whether an update even exists. The Update Driver Software Wizard may ask you how you want to search for the software (Yes, Always Search Online; Yes, Search Online This Time Only; or Don't Search Online). The installation process follows the process found in the "Interacting with the Found New Hardware Wizard" section of the chapter once you choose a search method.
   - Click Browse Computer for Driver Software when you've already downloaded an updated driver or have received a disk from the vendor. Follow the steps in the "Installing a Driver from a Specific Location" to complete the installation.

Disabling a Device

If you want to stop using a device temporarily, you can disable it. For example, you might want to disable a device that you think is making Windows unstable as a troubleshooting strategy.

To disable a device, open Device Manager by clicking Start, right-clicking Computer to open the System Properties dialog box, and clicking the Device Manager link. Right-click the device, and then choose Disable from the shortcut menu. Windows displays a confirmation message box. Click the Yes button. Windows closes the message box and disables the device.

Uninstalling a Device

If you want to stop using a device permanently and want to remove it from your computer, uninstall it first. To do so, right-click the device in Device Manager and choose Uninstall from the shortcut menu. Windows displays the Confirm Device Removal dialog box. Click the OK button. Windows closes the dialog box and uninstalls the device.

Uninstalling a device from Device Manager without physically removing it from the PC may result in Windows redetecting it and reinstalling it the next time you start up (or the next time you refresh the listing in Device Manager). Perhaps that's what you want, if you were removing it only so that you could reinstall it as a troubleshooting technique. But more likely, you really don't want it to appear, even though you plan to leave it physically connected. In a case like that, you would be better off disabling it (see the preceding section), since then it won't come back automatically.

NOTE You can also uninstall a device by clicking the Uninstall button on the Driver tab of its Properties dialog box; this is covered in the next section.

Working with Device Properties

Device drivers have properties, just like any other files. The properties for the device driver determine how the device behaves, so it's important to know how to set them. In the following sections, I'll explain some basics that apply to any type of device, and then we'll look at configuring some specific device types.

Viewing Device Properties

Some device types have their own applet in Control Panel, through which you can see all of the installed devices of that type and work with their properties. Modems are like that, for example.

However, you can also work with Device Manager, which lists all devices of all types. Most people find this the most expedient way to check on multiple device types. To display Device Manager (shown in Figure 10.6), do the following:

1. Right-click Computer and choose Properties.
2. Click the Device Manager link.

Click a plus (+) sign to open a category. In Figure 10.6, the Universal Serial Bus Controllers category is open. Then, double-click a device to see its properties (or click it once and then click the Properties button in the toolbar).

Viewing and Changing Drivers

You can work with a device's drivers in the Drivers tab of its Properties box. Figure 10.7 shows the Drivers tab for a satellite USB device, for example.

From the Drivers tab, you can choose:

- Driver Details to see exactly what files are being used for the device.
- Update Driver to start the Hardware Update Wizard. It's like the Add New Hardware Wizard except it searches for better drivers for an existing device.

- Roll Back Driver to revert to a previously used driver after using Update Driver.
- Disable to temporarily remove the device from service.
- Uninstall to completely remove the device's drivers.

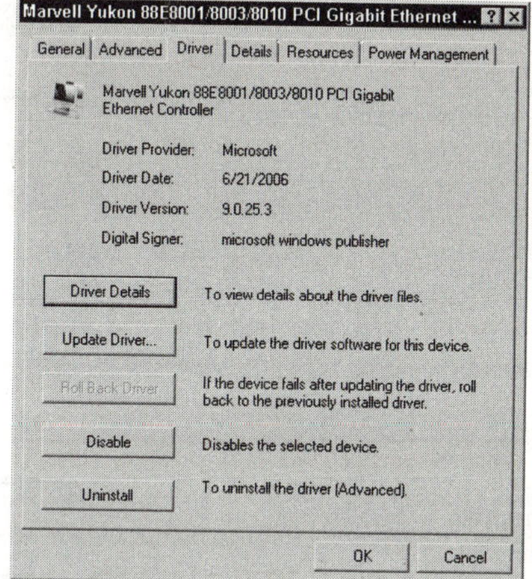

FIGURE 10.7 View, change, or remove drivers here.

Viewing and Changing Resource Assignments

Plug and Play automatically assigns resources to a device. In earlier versions of Windows, Plug and Play technology wasn't fully reliable, so it was a rather common occurrence to need to adjust the resource allocations manually. However, in Vista, Plug and Play works well nearly every time; in fact, with an ACPI-compliant system, it can be rather difficult to find a resource it will let you modify. That's because ACPI takes control of most of your Plug and Play devices and runs its own show.

If No Conflicts appears in the Conflicting device list as shown in Figure 10.8, the current resource assignments are okay. If, on the other hand, you see one or more conflicting devices listed there, you might want to try to resolve the conflict by assigning different resources either to this device or to one of the conflicting ones.

NOTE If the Use Automatic Settings check box is available, you'll be able to try manual resource assignments for the device. In Vista, however, for the vast majority of devices, this check box won't be available, and you won't be able to manually change resources.

If a device is working okay, you shouldn't change its resource assignments. Vista works best when you allow Plug and Play to handle all resource allocations automatically.

If you do need to change resources, do the following:

1. Deselect the Use Automatic Settings check box in the device's Resources tab. The other controls in the dialog box become available.
2. Open the Setting Based On drop-down list and choose a different configuration as shown in Figure 10.9. Keep trying configurations until you find one that reports No Conflicts in the Conflicting Devices list.

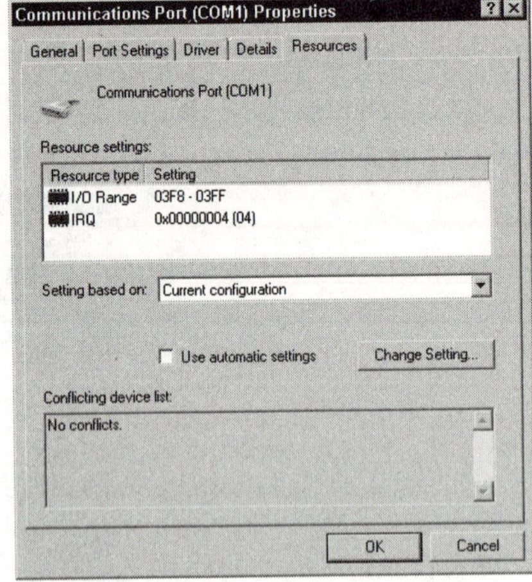

FIGURE 10.8 View resource assignments here, and change them if there are conflicts.

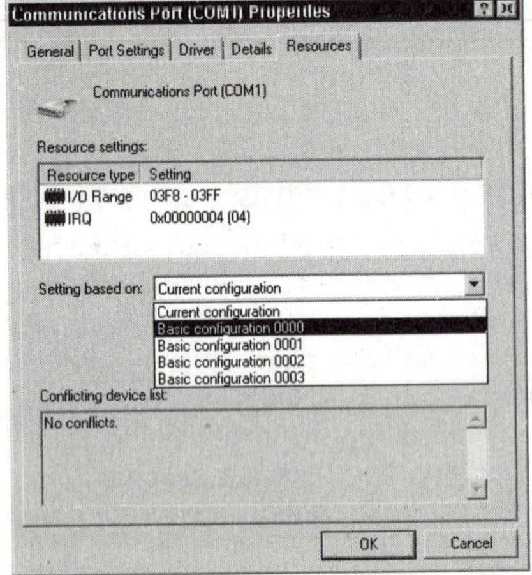

FIGURE 10.9 Choose alternative configurations as needed to avoid conflicts.

TIP If you can't find one that reports No Conflicts, you can try setting an individual resource manually. To do so, select it from the Resource Settings area and then click Change Setting. For most devices, you won't be allowed to do this; you'll see an error message. However, some devices do allow this, and if it's possible, it's one possible way around an otherwise irresolvable resource conflict.

3. Click OK to close the device's properties.

TIP Here's a little-known tweak for all you hard-core techies out there. For more control over manual resource assignments in Vista, set the ACPI driver to Standard PC instead of its default of ACPI PC. To do so, view the properties for ACPI in Device Manager (in the Computer category). Go to the Driver tab and choose Update Driver. Then choose Install from a List or Specific Location, and then choose Don't Search. In the list that appears, select Standard PC and then complete the wizard. Warning: Power management features like Standby and Hibernate will no longer work, and you'll probably need to reinstall the drivers for some of your devices.

Configuring a Modem

If your modem is Plug and Play (and it probably is if you acquired your computer within the last decade), Vista will recognize and install it automatically. If not, you can use the Add Hardware Wizard as described earlier in the chapter.

NOTE Vista uses a universal modem driver called Unimodem. Unimodem is the software interface between all your computer's 32-bit Windows-compatible communications applications (including the ones that use TAPI) and your modem or other communications hardware. It includes integrated control for port selection, modem initialization, speed, file transfer protocols, and terminal emulation. Because Unimodem handles the modem configuration, you only have to specify setup parameters once.

After you install your modem, all your TAPI-aware communications programs will use the same configuration settings. When you change them in one application, those changes carry across to all the others.

To change the modem's properties, open up Phone and Modem Options in Control Panel. (It's in the Printers and Other Hardware category if you're using Category view.) Then in the Modems tab, select the modem you want to work with and click Properties.

Here are some highlights of the modem properties you can set.

In the Modem tab:

Speaker Volume This controls the internal speaker in the modem. It does not affect the sound coming through your speakers.

Maximum Port Speed Leave this at the default in most cases. You might reduce it if your modem is having connection problems at higher speeds and you want to limit its speed for greater reliability.

Dial Control Normally you want the modem to detect a dial tone before dialing; deselect this check box if you don't.

On the Diagnostics tab:

Query Modem Click this button if you aren't sure whether the modem is installed correctly. This utility sends some test codes to the modem and shows the modem's response. This is handy because the modem doesn't have to be connected to a phone line for the test to work. See Figure 10.10.

In the Advanced tab (Figure 10.11):

Extra initialization settings You can enter AT commands here if the modem requires any special codes to be sent to it before it dials. For example, some programs like AOL send special initialization strings to the modem, and they can sometimes cause the modem to drop the carrier or have other problems. You could type **&FI** in this box to tell the modem to use its built-in factory settings instead of the initialization string that a particular program sends.

NOTE AT commands, also known as Hayes commands, are codes that tell the modem how to operate. AT is short for "Attention" because the first two letters of a command are always AT to get the device's attention. They used to be a lot more common in the days before PPP and TCP/IP Internet connections. To find out more about AT commands, see `http://www.modems.com/general/extendat.html`.

WARNING You should exercise some caution here, though, and consult the documentation for your modem to verify the actions of the command before using it. If the command isn't right for your modem, using it could cause some real damage.

Advanced Port Settings This opens a dialog box where you can turn off and on FIFO (First In, First Out) buffers, adjust the size of the Receive and Transmit buffers, and specify which COM port the modem uses. By default, the buffers are on and set to the highest settings. Turn them down or off to troubleshoot connection problems.

NOTE The Advanced Port Settings button doesn't appear with all modems. You may not see this button at all (as shown in Figure 10.11). The device driver supplied by the vendor determines whether some advanced features appear in Vista.

Change Default Preferences This opens a dialog box (Figure 10.12) in which you can set disconnect-when-idle settings and adjust some other low-level modem properties such as compression and flow control.

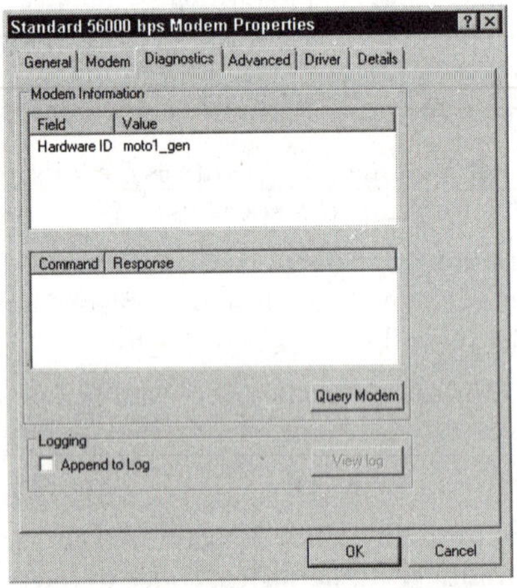

FIGURE 10.10
The Diagnostics tab of the Modem Properties dialog box lets you test your modem configuration and set logging options.

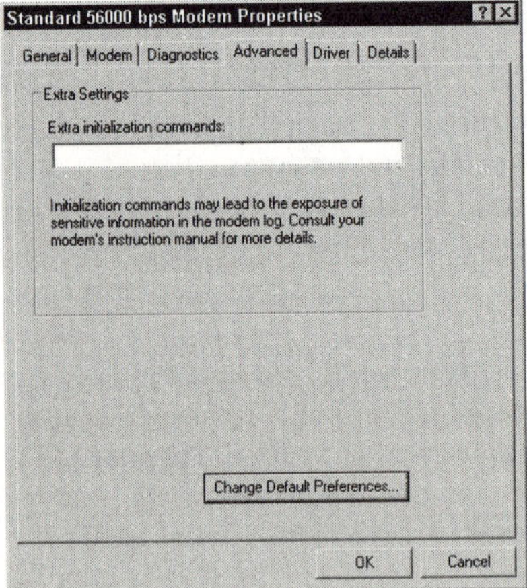

FIGURE 10.11
The Advanced tab of the Modem Properties dialog box.

FIGURE 10.12
The Default Preferences dialog box.

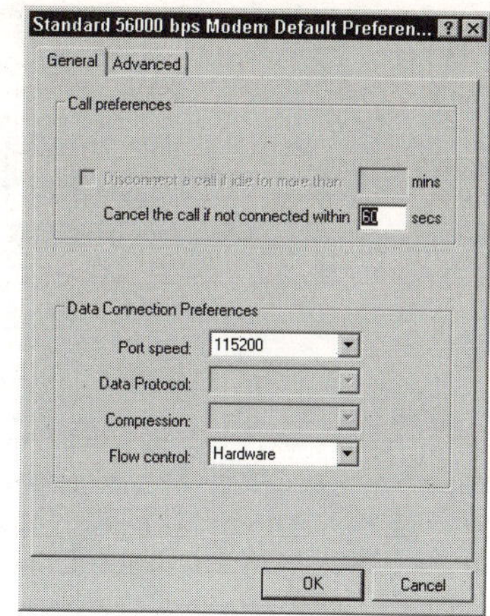

Configuring a CD or DVD Drive

Vista should detect new CD and DVD drives automatically without having to install any drivers for them. In fact, you'll find the support for both CD and DVD drives much improved from previous versions of Windows.

Depending on the model of CD or DVD drive, Vista will very likely be able to work with it directly with no special software. In addition, you can burn both CDs and DVDs without additional software in almost every case. The important criterion is to ensure your device appears on the approved hardware list for Vista. You may have to install the vendor software to access some special hardware features or gain functionality that Vista doesn't provide. For example, you might install software to perform backups as a job, rather than using the Vista-supplied software.

There are two different Properties dialog boxes for a CD or DVD drive. One is accessible from Device Manager, and the other from Computer.

CONFIGURING A CD DRIVE FROM DEVICE MANAGER

From Device Manager, double-click the drive to display a Properties dialog box that controls its driver and some of the base-level settings. Figure 10.13 shows a minimal DVD drive configuration.

A CD drive may have a Properties tab where you can change these settings:

CD Player Volume slider Drag the slider to set the volume you want the CD player to deliver when playing audio CDs. This setting controls the output of the CD drive. You can control the output volume from your sound card by using Volume Control.

Enable Digital CD Audio for This CD-ROM Device check box Select this check box if you want to use digital output rather than analog output from the CD drive for audio CDs. Digital output typically gives you higher audio quality, especially when you're copying audio CDs to your hard drive. Most newer CD-ROM drives and just about all DVD drives support digital output, but some older CD-ROM drives don't. If digital output doesn't work for you, clear this check box to return to analog output. Enabling digital output makes it possible to play an audio CD on a drive that doesn't have an audio patch cable running from the drive to the sound card inside the case.

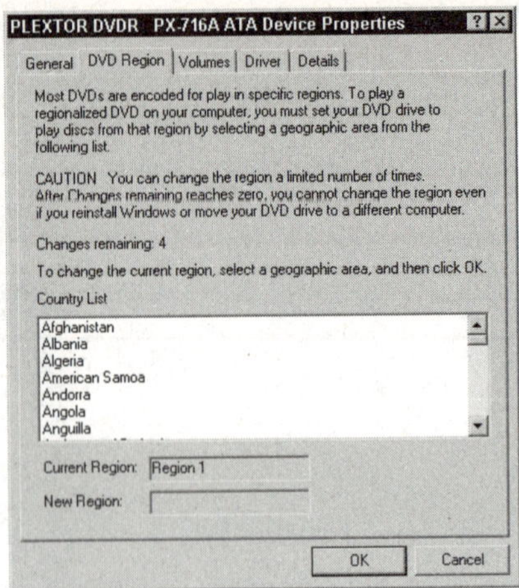

FIGURE 10.13
Selecting a country automatically configures the DVD player for the correct region.

DVD Encoding Regions

In case you've managed to avoid the question of DVD encoding regions, as far as DVDs are concerned, the world is divided into eight regions, or locales:

- Region 1 is the United States, Canada, and U.S. Territories.
- Region 2 is Europe, Japan, South Africa, and the Middle East.
- Region 3 is Southeast Asia, East Asia, and Hong Kong.
- Region 4 is Australia, New Zealand, the Pacific Islands, South America, Central America, Mexico, and the Caribbean.
- Region 5 is Eastern Europe, Mongolia, North Korea, the Indian subcontinent, and Africa.
- Region 6 is China.
- Region 7 is "reserved" (for off-world use, perhaps).
- Region 8 is for international vessels such as airplanes and cruise ships.

DVD players are encoded to play only DVDs for their region. Almost all DVDs are encoded for the region in which they're intended to be sold. (There are also all-region DVDs that will play in any region.) So to play a DVD, you need a player with a matching region code.

Most consumer-electronics DVD players are coded for one region only. Some players—typically more expensive ones—can play discs for two, more, or all regions. Other players can be *chipped*—modified—to play DVDs with different regional encoding or even to play any regional encoding.

PC DVD drives are a little more flexible. With most drives, you can switch regions a certain number of times before the drive goes into a locked state in which you can no longer change the region. The DVD Region tab of the Properties dialog box for the DVD drive (see Figure 10.13) displays the number of times you can change the region again. Use them sparingly.

Why do DVDs have regional encoding anyway? In theory, it's to let the movie studios control the release of the movie in different countries. For example, U.S.-made movies are usually released in the United States several months before they're released in Europe, and DVDs and videos of the movie are often released in the United States while the movie is still running in Europe. Regional encoding prevents most of the Europeans from viewing the movie on DVD until it's released with Region 2 encoding.

In practice, regional encoding also enables the distributors to charge different prices for DVDs in different countries without being undercut by imported DVDs from the least expensive regions. For example, at this writing, DVDs in Region 2 are substantially more expensive than those in Region 1.

The Properties dialog box for a DVD drive through Device Manager also contains a DVD Region tab, which displays the DVD encoding region currently set for the DVD player. To change the region, select the country you want in the list box and click the OK button.

Configuring a CD Drive from Computer

In Computer, you can right-click a CD drive and choose Properties to see a very different Properties dialog box, as shown in Figure 10.14.

Some of its settings and information apply to the individual disc that happens to be inserted at the moment; others are for the drive itself. Here's a quick rundown:

General Shows the space usage on the individual disc, if one is inserted.

Hardware Shows a list of all local drives (not just this one). You can click on one and click Properties for more information about it.

Sharing Enables you to share the drive on the network.

Customize Lets you customize the appearance of the CD or DVD drive.

Recording Determines the default recording drive for your system when more than one drive capable of recording exists. You can also choose the temporary drive used to hold the information you want to burn onto the CD or DVD. This tab also determines whether Vista ejects the burned CD or DVD after recording and lets you modify the global settings for the media.

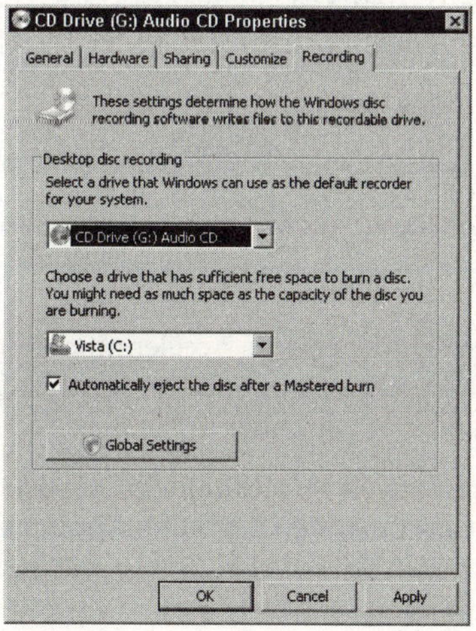

FIGURE 10.14
The Properties dialog box that is accessible from Computer tends to focus on software device properties.

There might be other tabs here, too, depending on the drive and on what software is installed. For example, you might see a DirectCD 5.0 Options tab when working with Roxio Easy CD Creator.

Configuring a Removable Drive

The first time you plug in a removable drive or a local drive and Windows finds pictures or audio files on it, Windows displays the Removable Disk dialog box or Local Drive dialog box to let you specify whether you want to set a default action to take with files of this type. The CompactFlash card contains picture files, so the Removable Disk dialog box contains actions that Windows can take with picture files: Print the Pictures, View a Slideshow of the Images, Copy Pictures to a Folder on Computer, Open Folder to View Files, or Take No Action.

Select the action you want to take. If you want Windows to take this action for every disk you add that contains this type of file, select the Always Do the Selected Action check box. Then click the OK button. Windows closes the Local Disk dialog box or Removable Disk dialog box and takes the action you specified.

Configuring a Video Card

When you install a new video card, Windows may detect it on startup and display the Found New Hardware Wizard so that you can install the correct driver for it. Other times, you may have to change the video driver manually by using the Hardware Update Wizard.

After installing the driver for the new video card, you usually need to restart Windows. When you log back on, Windows displays the Display Properties dialog box so that you can test and apply the screen resolution and color quality you want. See Chapter 5 for a discussion of how to choose a suitable screen resolution and color depth.

If you're seeing corrupt images on your monitor, or if the mouse pointer doesn't respond properly to conventional stimuli, or if DirectX isn't working, you may need to change the graphics hardware acceleration on your computer or disable write combining.

NOTE **Write combining is a method of shunting more information from the video card to the monitor at once. It can cause screen corruption by providing the monitor with more information than it can handle.**

To do so, take the following steps:

1. Right-click open space on the Desktop and choose Personalize from the shortcut menu to open the Personalization window.
2. Click the Display Settings link to display the Display Settings dialog box.
3. Click the Advanced button to open the Monitor and Graphics Card Properties dialog box.
4. Click the Troubleshoot tab.
5. Move the Hardware Acceleration slider one notch at a time from Full (or wherever you find it) toward None until the problems disappear. At each setting, click the Apply button, and check your computer to see the effect of the change.
6. Alternatively, or additionally, try clearing the Enable Write Combining check box to prevent screen corruption. Click the Apply button and see the effect of the change.

7. When the screen seems to be behaving as it should, click the OK button. Windows closes the Monitor and Graphics Card Properties dialog box, returning you to the Display Properties dialog box.
8. Click the OK button. Windows closes the Display Properties dialog box.

Viewing USB Hub Usage

USB hubs can support multiple devices. Each of these devices appear in Device Manager separately, but with no Resources tab since the device uses no system resources directly. The hub itself also appears there.

In Device Manager you may see several devices listed in the USB category. The ones associated with the motherboard (or add-on USB controller card) will have a Resources tab; it's the only one that directly draws resources. The two host controller entries in Figure 10.6 have resources in this case.

If you view the host controller Properties, you find an Advanced tab that lists System Reserved as the main user of the device. However, you'll also find the other devices attached to the host controller as shown in Figure 10.15.

You'll also see a USB Root Hub entry, which is the system interface for the above-mentioned controller. It draws no resources directly. On some systems, any USB devices that are directly plugged into the USB ports on the PC appear in this device's Power tab. On others, the General Purpose USB Hub appears on its list and then the devices plugged directly into the PC's USB ports are in turn on the Power tab for the General Purpose USB Hub.

If you have any expansion hubs connected to the root hub, they also appear in Device Manager. In Figure 10.6, that would be the USB Root Hub entry, representing a USB hub that's built into the base of my monitor. In its properties is a Power tab that lists the USB devices connected to it. See Figure 10.16.

If you have problems with USB devices, the first thing to check is the Power tab for the hub into which it's plugged. If many USB devices are chained together coming through this hub, there may not be enough power to support them all; the Power tab can tell you how much power is available and how much is used. In Figure 10.16, there's only one device, but a single USB port can support up to 127 devices, provided they have enough power.

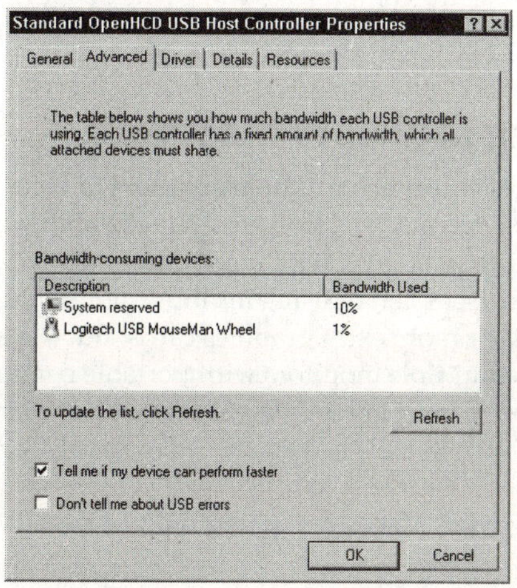

FIGURE 10.15
Use the Advanced tab content to determine resource usage by a particular device.

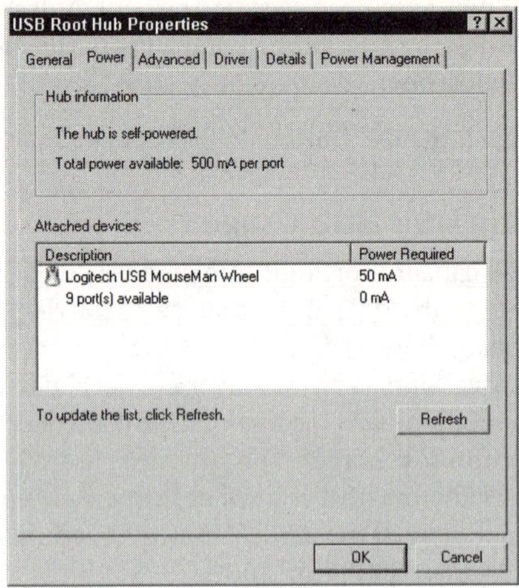

FIGURE 10.16 View a USB hub's Power tab to see what devices use it.

You would typically run into problems with power in situations where you are plugging in a device to an unpowered hub—such as the USB expansion port on a keyboard—and where the device being connected does not have its own power source and needs to draw a substantial amount of power. One example might be a USB webcam. In such a case, Windows will throw up a warning that the device is underpowered, and you would need to connect it to one of the USB ports directly on the system unit instead.

Vista also provides a new feature for getting your USB hub operating again. The Reset Hub button on the Advanced tab will restart your USB hub for you. In some cases, this action will clear up problems where the USB hub hasn't disconnected devices (because the device isn't configured properly) or enumerate the devices that are actually connected (to eliminate phantom devices).

Another new Vista feature is the ability to manage USB power. Select the Power Management tab and you'll see options for letting the computer shut down the USB hub (saving additional power). Shutting down the hub works fine when you're talking about a mouse, but may not work so well when you have devices that require power after you've left the room (such as a security system). You can also set the computer to wake when the USB hub receives the required signals from an external source.

Using Multiple Monitors

Vista lets you attach multiple monitors to your computer to increase the amount of Desktop space available to you. This feature can make both work and play much easier—but it can also lead you to loading your desk with more monitors than it can comfortably provide a footing for.

This discussion of using multiple monitors concerns only desktop computers to which you can add one or more extra graphics cards. But Vista also includes a feature called DualView that lets you use multiple monitors with portable computers and graphics cards with multiple outputs. Mentioned in Chapter 7, DualView works exactly the same way except with notebook PCs with both a built-in LCD screen and an external VGA port.

WARNING Setting up multiple monitors can be a tricky and frustrating business. With some combinations of motherboards and graphics cards, you need to install the graphics cards in the right sequence in order to get them to work. Others work fine immediately. Others never work. Before you try to implement multiple monitors, check the Hardware Compatibility List (HCL) at the Microsoft website, `http://www.microsoft.com`, for details of the graphics cards that are known to work in multiple-monitor configurations with Vista.

To use multiple monitors, you need to make sure that your graphics cards work together (some graphics cards don't) and that your computer's motherboard supports multiple monitors (some motherboards don't). In most cases, you'll want to use an AGP graphics card (or one of the new PCI Express cards in a system that supports that) and one or more regular PCI graphics cards; two or more regular PCI graphics cards without an AGP or PCI Express card can provide a satisfactory solution as well. Many of the newer video cards have two inputs: one analog (VGA) and one digital (DVI) so you can connect one CRT and one LCD (provided it has a digital input port) to a single video card. Some newer systems provide support for dual PCI Express cards in a Scalable Link Interface (SLI) configuration. These graphics cards provide very high performance and actually require specialized power supplies. An SLI setup can have up to four DVI ports to power up to four LCD displays (or CRT displays when you have the required converters).

The monitors, by contrast, don't need to know about each other—each gets its own input, so each can believe it's the only monitor in town if it wants to. So any monitors should do. You can mix CRTs and LCDs freely on a system, as long as you have the right ports to which to connect them.

NOTE In the 1990s, large monitors were so expensive that it was much cheaper to buy two, three, or even four small monitors than one large one. Now that's changed for just about every monitor configuration. LCDs have come down considerably in price and CRTs have been going down in price for quite some time. There's no reason why you shouldn't have a monster monitor and a couple of satellite monitors if you want—or even two or more monsters.

To set up multiple monitors, power down your computer and insert the new graphics card. (You *can* install multiple graphics cards and monitors at a time, but unless you're very lucky and everything works, you'll be looking at some doubly confusing troubleshooting.) Connect the second monitor, and then power everything on. Don't be surprised if the bootup display appears on the second monitor rather than your primary one. After you log on to Windows, it should discover the new hardware, which will trigger a Found New Hardware notification-area pop-up followed by the Found New Hardware Wizard. If Windows seems not to have noticed the new hardware, run the Add Hardware Wizard manually to add the graphics card and monitor.

Next, display the Monitor tab of the Display Settings dialog box. For each monitor you want to use (hint: all of them), select the monitor and then select the Extend My Windows Desktop onto This Monitor. Once you've done that, let Windows know where the monitors are positioned in relation to each other by dragging the monitor icons into their relative positions. If you get confused as to which monitor is which, click the Identify button to have Windows flash up the number of each monitor on the monitor. Then set the screen resolution, color depth, and refresh rate for each monitor as usual.

Once you close the Display Properties dialog box, you should have a substantially enlarged Desktop. By default, the Taskbar appears on your primary monitor (the one that shows the boot sequence), but you can drag it to any of the other monitors as you see fit.

Maximizing a window maximizes it for the monitor it's currently (or mostly) on. You can extend a "normal" window across two or more monitors by dragging its window border to the appropriate size.

Configuring Windows to Use an Uninterruptible Power Supply

One of the great benefits of a laptop computer is that its battery protects it from data loss when a power outage occurs. To get similar protection in a desktop computer, you need to attach a separate device—an uninterruptible power supply (UPS).

What Is a UPS?

A UPS is essentially a large battery of above-average intelligence that sits between your computer and the electricity supply and ensures a steady power stream to your computer to protect it from blackouts, brownouts, and surges. Different UPSs do this in two different ways.

The simpler way is for the device to monitor power fluctuations and kick in when the power supply falls outside acceptable thresholds. Technically, this type of device is called a *standby power supply* (SPS) rather than a UPS, but you'll often hear SPSs described as UPSs.

The more complicated—and better—way is for the device to feed power to the computer continuously, charging itself when the power supply is running within acceptable parameters. This device is technically a UPS. This way of supplying power is better because the UPS delivers conditioned power to the computer all the time, protecting it better from fluctuations and avoiding the critical moment of changeover from main power to battery power that can be a drawback with an SPS.

Choosing a UPS

If you're looking for a UPS, keep these features in mind:

Operating system support Make sure the UPS is designed for use with Vista. With operating system support, the UPS can warn Vista when the electricity supply has failed. Vista can then shut itself down automatically if the computer is unattended.

System management port Make sure the UPS has an appropriate system management port for your computer. Many UPSes use a serial port connection. Others use a USB connection.

NOTE If you don't plan on connecting the PC and the UPS, you don't need to worry about a system management port or operating system support. Some people simply ignore their UPS's capability of communicating with the PC and treat it like a dumb battery backup. However, ignoring the capability means that your system won't shut down based on battery power left, instead of some nebulous timeout value. In addition, the UPS can't tell the computer about internal errors and you won't be able to test the UPS correctly. In short, to gain full use from the UPS, you really need to have it communicate with the computer.

Indicators for line voltage and battery power The UPS should have one indicator to indicate when the incoming power to the UPS is okay and another indicator to indicate when the devices attached to the UPS are running on battery power. (Many UPSs also sound an alarm when battery power is being used.) Many UPSs include other indicators that show when the outlet you're using is incorrectly wired or has experienced a fault. These additional indicators can prove quite helpful when you're trying to understand a power problem.

Multiple power outlets Make sure the UPS has enough outlets for all the devices you want to plug into it directly. In general, a well-designed UPS includes between four and eight outlets, with six outlets being the most common.

Enough power and battery life Before buying the UPS, work out how much power and battery life you need it to have. Make a list of the computers and devices you'll need to have plugged into the UPS, and then use a power-supply template such as that on the American Power Conversion Corp. website (`http://www.apc.com`) to calculate the number of volt-amps (VA) you'll need to keep the equipment running. (You can simply add up the voltages listed on the equipment, but be aware that the power-supply rating on your computer equipment shows the maximum power rather than typical power usage.) Then decide the amount of time you'll need to shut down the computers once the power alarm goes off. Generally speaking, the more power and battery life you need, the more the UPS will cost. If you just want a few minutes to allow you to shut down Windows under control (or to have Windows shut itself down), a modest and inexpensive UPS may fit the bill. Always plan on 10 minutes' worth of backup power as a minimum.

TIP **Unless you're convinced that you'll need to print during a power outage, don't plan to plug your printer into your UPS. Printers are power hogs. Laser printers are such power hogs that they can kill a UPS.**

Installing a UPS

You might remember that previous versions of Windows included special software to manage your UPS. Vista is apparently missing this functionality. What this means is that you need to buy a third-party monitoring utility or ensure that the UPS comes with the required software. Install the UPS software according to the vendor instructions.

Working with iSCSI Devices

An iSCSI device is a combination of the Internet and Small Computer Systems Interface (SCSI) technology. SCSI is a popular technology for hard drives. You usually find SCSI used for high-end systems that require a lot of bandwidth and high reliability. Other technologies, such as SATA drives, appear with increasing regularity in desktop machines because they offer a lot in a very small package and at a better price than SCSI. To use iSCSI technology, you must have access to an iSCSI device, such as a SAN, over any network connection. (You'll find that iSCSI isn't limited to the Internet and that the Internet isn't even the most popular connection option.)

You control the client portion of iSCSI using the iSCSI Initiator applet found in the Control Panel. This applet includes six tabs that help you configure, discover, target, and use iSCSI resources. It's even possible to set up Remote Authentication Dial-In User Server/Service (RADIUS) support for the connection. This chapter doesn't describe all of the intricacies of setting up the server to provide iSCSI support and focuses on the iSCSI Initiator applet. The following sections describe iSCSI in detail.

Configuring Vista to Access iSCSI

You configure iSCSI using the iSCSI Initiator applet of the Control Panel. Whenever you open this applet, it checks to ensure that the iSCSI service is started and that the Windows Firewall will let Vista send SCSI commands to a remote device. You can start the service and configure the firewall manually, or you can let the applet ask you about these features and set them up for you automatically.

To start the iSCSI service, open the Services console found in the `Administrative Tools` folder of the Control Panel. Right-click the Microsoft iSCSI Initiator Service and choose Properties from the context menu. Set the Startup Type field on the General tab to Automatic. Click Start. Wait for the service to start and click OK.

To configure the Windows Firewall to allow iSCSI use, open the Windows Firewall applet of the Control Panel. Click the Change Settings link. You'll see a Windows Firewall Settings dialog box. Click the Exceptions tab and you'll see a list of potential exceptions, as shown in Figure 10.17. Check the iSCSI Service option and click OK.

You must restart your system for the Windows Firewall settings to take effect. After you have all of these changes made, you can open the iSCSI Initiator applet in the Control Panel to work with iSCSI devices. As usual, you'll see the UAC dialog box a number of times. Simply click Continue each time you see it.

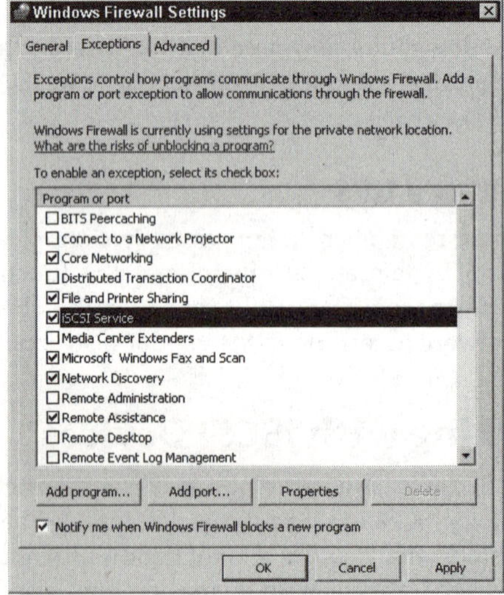

FIGURE 10.17
Configure Vista to allow use of iSCSI connections.

Discovering Servers

An iSCSI server provides an IP connection through port 3260 that a client uses to discover resources on that server. Of course, this means having software on the server that provides the required information. For a Windows server, this means installing the Internet Storage Name Service (iSNS) software found at `http://www.microsoft.com/downloads/details.aspx?familyid=0DBC4AF5-9410-4080-A545-F90B45650E20`. Once you have your server configured, you can create a connection to it on the Discovery tab of the iSCSI Initiator applet. You must provide both a portal and a iSNS server entry as shown in Figure 10.18.

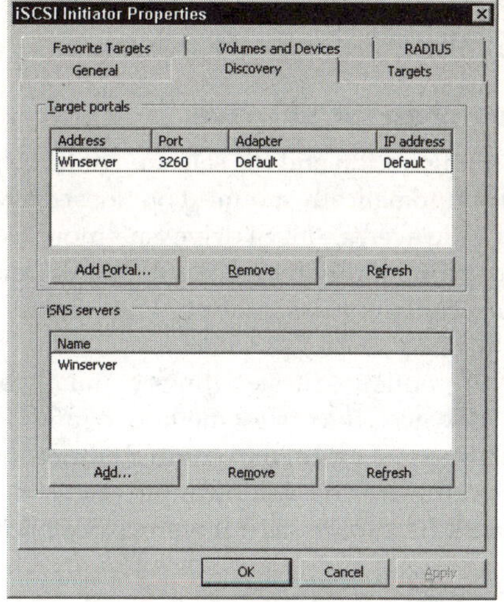

FIGURE 10.18
Begin working with iSCSI by setting up a portal and iSNS server.

The easiest way to proceed is to click Add Portal to display the Add Target Portal dialog box and type the Domain Name Service (DNS) name of the server providing iSCSI support in the IP Address or DNS Name field. Unless you've changed the default settings, retain the default port number. If you're using a standard intranet setup, you shouldn't have to do anything more than provide the server name. However, when you're using an Internet connection with additional security, you'll probably have to provide additional details to make the connection or Vista will tell you that the connection has failed (without providing any details as to why).

When you need to provide additional information, click Advanced. You'll see fields for providing both Challenge-Handshake Authentication Protocol (CHAP) and RADIUS details on the General tab. The Secure Internet Protocol (IPSec) tab contains the settings for IP handshaking, including both Internet Key Exchange (IKE) and Encapsulating Security Payload (ESP) protocol settings. The settings you use in the Advanced Settings dialog box depend on the way you have your server configured.

To add an iSNS server, click Add to display the Add iSNS Server dialog box. Provide the DNS name or IP address of the server that provides iSNS services. This entry may not be the same machine that is providing iSCSI resources. As with the portal entry, Vista checks for the presence and accessibility of the server before it accepts the entry.

Creating a Connection to a Target

After you create the required entries on the Discovery tab, you'll find that Vista populates a list of targets on the Target tab. This listing tells you about all of the resources you can access with the portals you've configured. To use a particular target, highlight its entry in the Targets list and click Log On. You'll need to provide your credentials for accessing that resource. If you don't see all of the resources you expected, click Refresh to update the list. When you want to discover additional information about a resource, highlight the entry and click Details.

You might decide that you want to connect to a particular iSCSI resource every time you start your computer. Vista calls an automatic connection a Favorite Target. A list of these favorites appears on the Favorite Targets tab of the iSCSI Initiator Properties dialog box. To create a favorite, check the Automatically Restore This Connection When the Computer Starts option when you log on to the resource. To remove a favorite, highlight its entry in the Favorite Targets list on the Favorite Targets tab and click Remove.

Mounting an iSCSI Drive

All the configuration and the selection of targets isn't much use if you can't access the drive. Your computer automatically mounts your local drives when it starts up unless you specifically tell it not to do so. However, an iSCSI drive isn't mounted (made accessible) simply because you've created the proper configuration to access it. The Volumes and Devices tab of the iSCSI Initiator Properties dialog box contains a list of the volumes, mount points, and devices that you've mounted using the iSCSI Initiator.

You can configure these settings manually by clicking Add and providing the required information. However, the easiest method to mount the resources you can access is to click Autoconfigure. Vista will make all of the required entries for you based on the targets in the favorite targets list. If you see an entry you don't want to access, highlight it and click Remove. At this point, you can use your iSCSI resource as if it were a locally connected device.

Summary

This chapter has discussed how to add and support new hardware items in Vista. You can use this information when you're having trouble with a device and need to reconfigure it as well as when you get ready to install a new monitor, a DVD drive, or some other hardware device. In addition, you've discovered how to use and work with iSCSI devices. The iSCSI device may become the next big thing in disconnected computing because you can access the device from a centralized location where an administrator can properly back up and maintain the device. Finally, this chapter has shed some light on that mysterious Windows Experience Index.

This is one of the chapters that you'll probably reference in an emergency. For example, you might have installed a new piece of software and suddenly found that a device you need is no longer accessible because the device driver doesn't like the new software (or vice versa). However, you don't want to wait until an emergency. Begin looking at the various hardware support features in Vista now so that when an emergency does arrive, you can handle it quickly and efficiently.

In the next chapter, you'll learn about Windows Media Player, the latest and greatest version of Microsoft's music and video player. Unlike previous versions of Windows, you'll find that Windows Media Player doesn't install automatically in Vista (and this is probably a new trend for Microsoft). You'll also find that Windows Media Player has added some interesting new features.

Part III

Vista Digital Media

In this section, you'll learn how to:

- Play digital music and video clips with Windows Media Player
- Play audio CDs and DVDs
- Listen to Internet radio
- Record sounds with Sound Recorder
- Manage digital photographic images
- Create movies with Windows Movie Maker
- Organize your graphics with Windows Photo Gallery

Chapter 11

Windows Media Player

This chapter discusses how to use Windows Media Player, the powerful multimedia player incorporated in Vista. A vast improvement on its predecessor of the same name, Windows Media Player not only provides features for enjoying audio and video, it also supports ripping (that is, copying CD or DVD tracks to your hard disk) and burning (making audio CDs or DVD movies from digital files). It also covers sound volume control and the Sound Recorder. In this chapter, you'll learn about:

- Configuring Windows Media Player
- Playing music in Windows Media Player
- Understanding digital rights management
- Copying a CD or DVD to your hard disk
- Creating your own CDs and DVDs
- Tuning in to Internet radio
- Backing up and restoring digital licenses
- Using Volume Control to control output and input
- Recording and converting sounds with Sound Recorder
- Connecting to network projectors

Vista: What's New?

Of course, one of the biggest new features of Vista is that you get Windows Media Player 11 automatically. However, unlike previous versions of Windows, Vista requires that you perform a setup before you can use Windows Media Player. This may be a nod to leveling the playing field for other products, but it's more likely a requirement to ensure the new digital rights management (DRM) features work as anticipated.

You can also burn DVDs in Vista. Not only can you use DVDs for data storage, you can create video DVDs as well. Of course, your hardware has to provide the required support and you have to have the required permissions. Generally, the video functionality will see more use for home videos than making copies of your movie collection.

For anyone who's had to work through the problems of getting a projector to work properly, the new Network Projector feature should be a real plus. It helps Vista detect and use any projector found on your network. Even if Vista fails to find the device, you can always create a connection by entering the projector's address.

Introducing Windows Media Player

Windows Media Player is a multipurpose player that plays music, video clips, DVD movies, and Internet radio. It rips, burns, and copies files to portable digital players. In short, it does virtually everything that most people would want a media player to do.

Vista comes with the latest Windows Media Player 11, so you don't have to do anything special to start using it. In this chapter, I'll cover only the latest version as of this writing—version 11. Version 11 is a dramatic improvement over earlier versions, incorporating features that users have been clamoring for. It also arranges features differently in the hierarchy. For example, Internet radio no longer warrants its own tab; now it's blended in with the online Guide. I'll point out some of the other differences throughout this chapter as we go along.

Start Windows Media Player by choosing Start ➢ All Programs ➢ Windows Media Player. Or, if you have the Quick Launch toolbar displayed, click the Windows Media Player icon there. Of course, you can always double-click an audio or video file, insert a multimedia CD or DVD, or perform any other multimedia-related activity to start the Windows Media Player as well.

NOTE You'll only see the Windows Media Player icon after you perform the required initial setup discussed in the "Performing the Setup" section of the chapter. Any activity that requires Windows Media Player starts the setup for you, so you don't have to do anything special to get started.

Versions 8 and 9 of Windows Media Player always started on the Media Guide page, which is essentially a browser window that displays the latest news from the WindowsMedia.com website. The trouble with that, though, was that if you had a slow Internet connection or none at all, it took awhile for that fact to become apparent to the application. In the meantime, you were stuck drumming your fingers until it decided to release you. In Version 11, as in version 10, it starts up on whatever tab it was on the last time you closed it.

Figure 11.1 shows Windows Media Player in its Full mode, with a track playing. Notice the player controls at the bottom of the window (Play, Pause, and all the usual stuff) and the tabs across the top for accessing different sections in the application (Burn, Rip, and so on). Also, notice the right pane, which is a Now Playing list of tracks I've queued up for my listening pleasure.

As you can see in Figure 11.1, Full mode takes up a serious chunk of a small screen, even when Windows Media Player isn't maximized and the menu bar and window frame are hidden. For sustained use, you might prefer Compact mode, shown in Figure 11.2. (You can also use menu commands or right-click menus.)

NOTE You might be wondering what happened to Skin mode in Windows Media Player 11. Skin mode still exists, but you won't find it in the default menus or as part of the buttons that appear in various places on the Windows. Instead, you must right-click the toolbar at the bottom of the display and choose View ➢ Skin Mode from the context menu. You can also press Ctrl+1 to enter Skin mode or Ctrl+2 to enter Full mode.

Performing the Setup

Before you can do anything with the Windows Media Player, you must perform the required setup. The Windows Media Player 11 Setup Wizard starts any time you perform a multimedia task such as double-clicking a file or inserting a CD. You can also start it by starting the application. The following steps help you perform the required setup. I'm assuming that you already see the first setup wizard screen because you've performed a multimedia activity.

1. Choose between the Express Settings (Recommended) or Custom Settings options as shown in Figure 11.3. Use the Express Settings (Recommended) option if you won't be using the Windows Media Player extensively or doing anything unusual with it. The settings that Windows Media Player uses by default work well for most people, which is why Microsoft recommends this option. If you use the Express Settings (Recommended) option, the button title is Finish. All you need to do is click it and the setup is complete. However, if you plan to make extensive use of the Windows Media Player to perform complex tasks, choose the Custom Settings option instead. You'll need to follow the remaining steps in this section.

2. Click Next. You'll see the Select Privacy Options dialog box shown in Figure 11.4. Notice that you can significantly limit Windows Media Player's interaction with the Internet to maintain your privacy. For example, if you decide that you really don't want to use the online guide, you can clear the Display media information from the Internet option. The Privacy Statement tab contains information about how Microsoft protects your privacy. You should read this information before you make any privacy decisions.

FIGURE 11.1
Windows Media Player 11, shown here in Full mode, rivals many of the best stand-alone media player applications available today.

FIGURE 11.2
In Compact mode, Windows Media Player occupies a more reasonable amount of your screen.

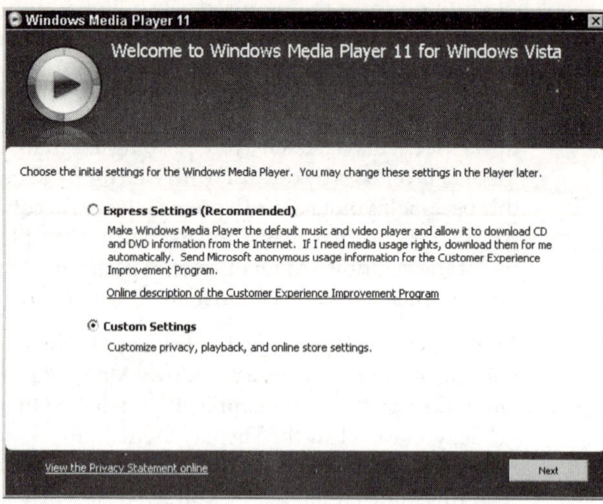

FIGURE 11.3 Select the setup mode for Windows Media Player.

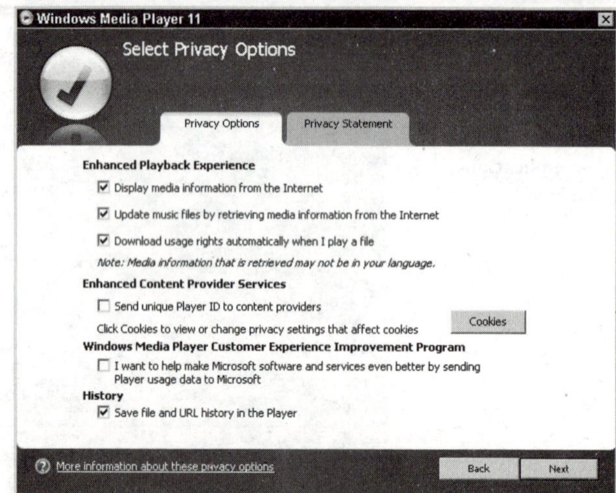

FIGURE 11.4 Choose how you want Windows Media Player to interact with the Internet and protect your privacy.

NOTE The remaining sections of this chapter assume that you've chosen the default settings. Consequently, if you decide to change any of the Windows Media Player settings, you may find that some of the features described in the chapter no longer work as anticipated or might not work at all.

3. Make any privacy selections and click Next. You'll see the Customize the Installation Options dialog box. This dialog box contains two check boxes. The first, Add a Shortcut to the Desktop, determines whether Windows Media Player places an icon on your desktop. Unlike previous versions, the setup wizard disables this option by default. The second, Add a Shortcut

to the Quick Launch Bar, places the icon mentioned in the introduction to this section in the Quick Launch area. The setup wizard enables this option by default.

4. Choose the installation options that you prefer and click Next. You'll see the Select the Default Music and Video Player dialog box. This is one of the customizations that avid music and video users will require, especially when your specialized hardware ships with high-end applications. Choose the second option, Choose the file types that Windows Media Player 11 will play when you plan to use multiple applications for your media setup. Choose the first option, Make Windows Media Player 11 the default music and video player, when you plan to use Windows Media Player as your only multimedia application. When you choose the first option, the setup wizard changes the button to Finish. Click Finish to complete the setup. Otherwise, continue with the steps that follow.

5. Click Finish. You'll see the Set Program Associations window shown in Figure 11.5 where you can choose which files the Windows Media Player will automatically open for you.

6. Check the files you want to use and click Save. Windows Media Player will only open the selected files when you double-click them.

Using the Online Stores

Windows Media Player 11 provides links to several online stores. The default store, as shown in Figure 11.1, is URGE. However, you can also use the Media Guide or browse for your favorite store. The following sections provide a brief description of these options for obtaining digital music.

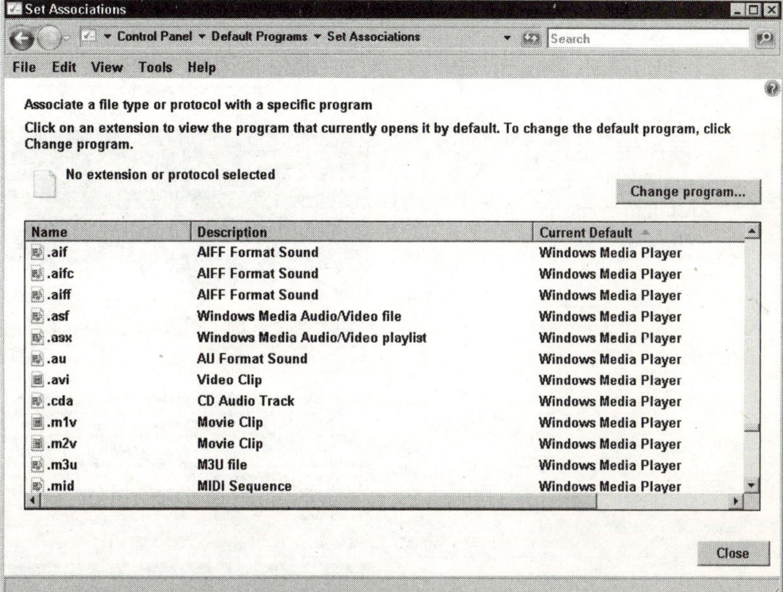

FIGURE 11.5 Select the files that Windows Media Player will open when you double-click them.

TIP You might need to install Windows Media Player for employees but not want them to have the full functionality of the application. Fortunately, you can control access to many Windows Media Player features using a group policy. To open the Group Policy Object Editor, choose Start ➢ Run, type **`gpedit.msc`** in the Open field of the Run dialog box, and click OK. The Group Policy Object Editor contains the Windows Media Player settings in two locations. If you want to control machine resources, such as the Prevent Media Sharing policy, look in the `Local Security Policy/Computer Configuration/Administrative Templates/Windows Components/Windows Media Player` folder. On the other hand, if you want to control what the user can do, such as the Prevent Radio Station Present Retrieval policy, look in the `Local Security Policy/User Configuration/Administrative Templates/Windows Components/Windows Media Player` folder. Make sure you also look at the other media-related folders in the Windows Component folder. For example, you'll find separate folders for both Windows Media Center and Windows Media Digital Rights Management.

USING URGE

The default online store for Windows Media Player 11 is URGE. To use it, simply click URGE on the menu bar. Like many online stores, URGE requires that you install special software to make it work with Windows Media Player. Consequently, you'll see a dialog box like the one shown in Figure 11.6 show up when you select this option unless you've already installed the URGE software as part of using Internet Explorer. Click I Accept after reading the agreement, and Windows Media Player installs the required software for you. The installation can require more than a few minutes as the online store downloads software (usually a lot of it) to your system. You may also see one or more Microsoft Windows Media Configuration Utility dialog boxes that ask questions about the installation process. Most of these dialog boxes will contain security information and ask your permission to perform an installation or configuration. In general, you click Run to perform the required task. You'll also likely see a number of UAC dialog boxes.

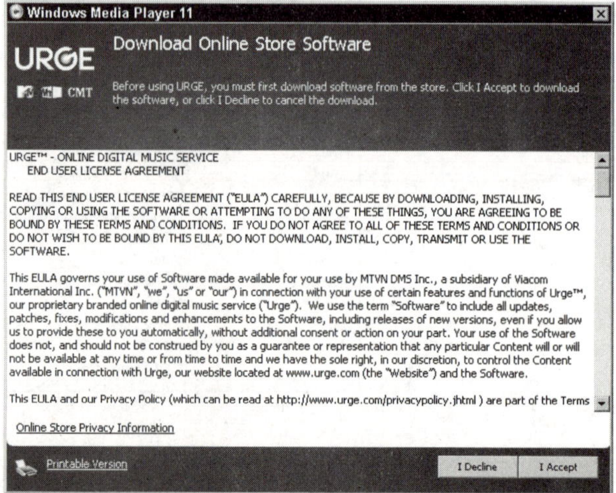

FIGURE 11.6
Most online stores require that you install their special software.

URGE and other online stores are essentially websites, so you can easily visit them using your favorite browser. Using Windows Media Player to access the online store simply provides a convenience factor. Figure 11.7 shows a typical example of the URGE website. Notice the folder structure in the left pane. You can use these folders to move from area to area in the online store. For example, when you click Charts for the URGE online store, you see a list of the current hits.

Using the Media Guide

Windows Media Player still lets you access the Media Guide. Simply click the down arrow under the URGE entry and choose Media Guide from the list. The display and the tab name will change to reflect your choice. As with URGE, the Media Guide is essentially a web page (`http://www.windowsmedia.com/mediaguide`) with hyperlinks to audio and video clips available online. If you have a fast Internet connection, it can be a fun browse, sort of like reading the entertainment section of your local newspaper but with sound and video (see Figure 11.8).

In Version 11, the Internet Radio feature is also accessed from the Media Guide tab. I'll tell you more about Internet Radio later in the chapter.

Browsing for Other Online Stores

If you find that you don't want to access either URGE or the Media Guide, you can choose other online store options. Click the down arrow under the URGE or Media Guide tab and choose Browse All Online Stores from the menu. You'll see icons for a number of popular online stores. Click any of these icons to access that store. After you make the selection, Windows Media Player will add that store to the menu so you can access it easily later. Follow any store-specific installation instructions (similar to those in the "Using URGE" section of the chapter to install the required software).

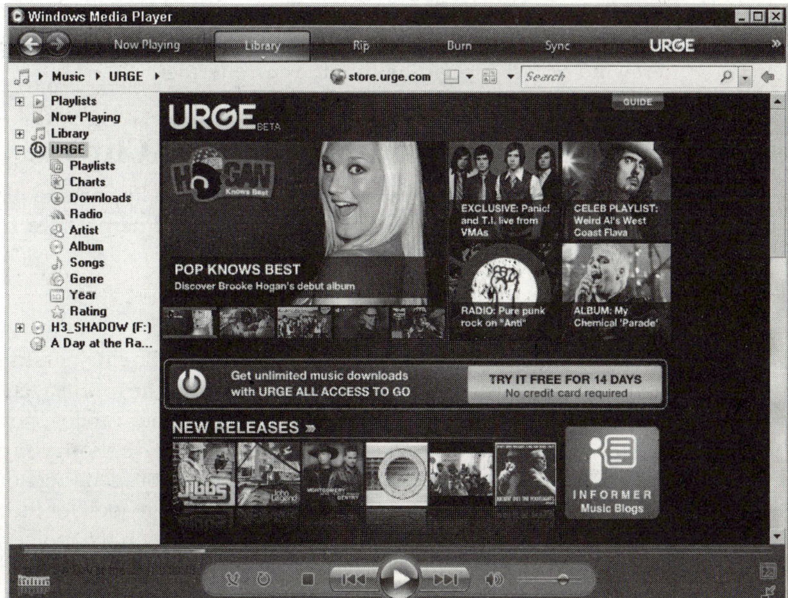

Figure 11.7
The online store software will include folders you can choose to learn more about a particular product.

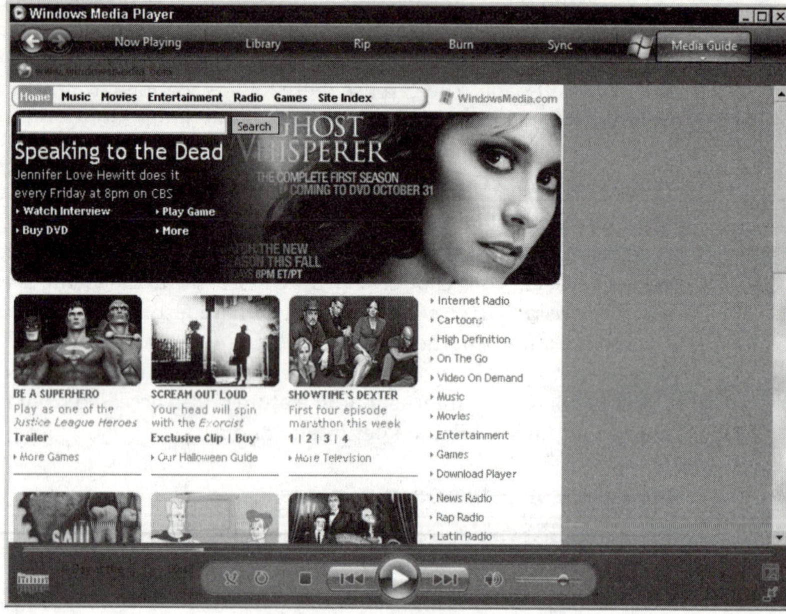

FIGURE 11.8
The Guide tab presents a constantly changing assortment of hyperlinks to downloadable media content.

Working with Player Controls

The player controls at the bottom of the Windows Media Player window are the same as on a cassette deck or audio CD player—you've got your standard Play, Pause, and Stop buttons, plus buttons for skipping forward and back among tracks. The slider bar above them can be dragged to rewind or fast-forward within the current track.

Working with Audio and Video Clips

One of the most common uses for Windows Media Player is to play audio or video clips you've stored on your hard drive. These could come from Internet sites, from audio CDs you've "ripped" (more on that later), or from other sources.

Working with Libraries

Previous versions of Windows Media Player relied on catalogs. In addition, you searched your system looking for the media you wanted to catalog. The results were often less than helpful because you ended up with the Windows sample files in your catalog, not to mention samples provided with other programs or media provided with games. In short, you ended up with a mess. Windows Media Player 11 uses a different approach. Instead of spending hours searching today's enormous hard drives, you tell Windows Media Player where to look for the media you want in your library. When you first open the library by clicking Library on the toolbar, you see a listing of potential views as shown in Figure 11.9.

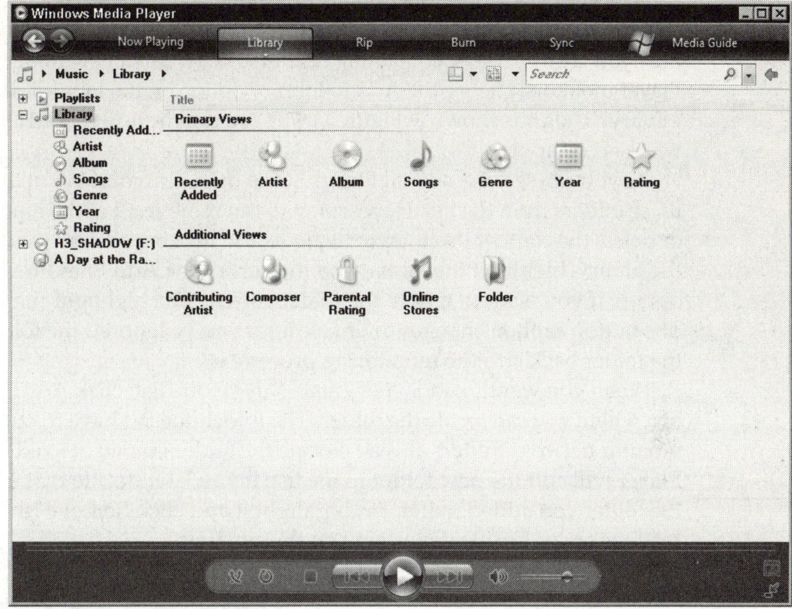

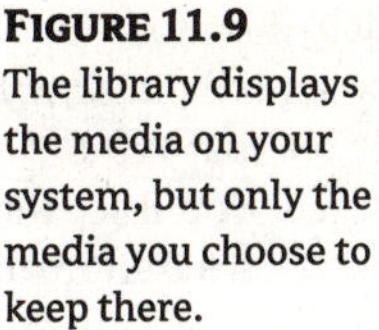
FIGURE 11.9
The library displays the media on your system, but only the media you choose to keep there.

Figure 11.9 shows the views for music. You can also display views of pictures, video, recorded television, and other media by choosing the appropriate option on the Library menu. (Simply click the down arrow to access the menu.) The list of views varies for each media type. For example, when working with pictures, you can choose Recently Added, All Pictures, Keywords, Date Taken, Rating, and Folder as views.

The library begins with a display of all of the sample files that Vista includes, as well as any media you've placed in your personal or in the `\Users\Public` folder. In fact, the sample media isn't located in your personal folder, even though it appears that it is. The sample media appears in the `\Users\Public` folder and you access it as if it were in your personal folder.

WARNING It's easy to get confused between personal and public data in the Windows Media Player. Any data you place in the `\Users\Public` folder is accessible to everyone, so you need to ensure that you want others to see anything you place there. However, other users can't access the media in your personal folder. Vista tends to enforce this limitation better than any preceding version of Windows, so any media you place in your personal folder should be relatively safe from prying eyes. Of course, a determined user will always figure out a way to overcome the security in the operating system.

You may find that you don't want all of those sample files in your library or that you only want a few pieces of it. For example, you might decide that you want some songs on an album, but not others. To delete a particular entity from the library, right-click that entity (such as an album, song, picture, or video) and choose Delete from the context menu. You'll see the Windows Media Player dialog box shown in Figure 11.10. The default option, Delete from Library and My Computer, actually removes the file from your hard drive. If you want to keep the file, choose the second option, Delete from Library Only. Click OK and Windows Media Player will perform the desired action.

Windows Media Player automatically monitors the folder that you tell it to monitor. Consequently, once you configure the library settings, you shouldn't have to do anything with them until the next time you create a folder containing new media. To add a new folder to the list that Windows Media Player monitors, choose the Add to Library option on the Library drop-down. You'll see the Add to Library dialog box shown in Figure 11.11. (You can click Advanced Options to see the entire dialog box when necessary.)

As you can see, the default library setup includes a number of default folders. You can't remove these folders from the list. However, you can remove all of the media they contain from the library or delete the content itself. If you want to add missing content that appears in the folder, but not in the library, highlight the folder, and then check the Add Files Previously Deleted from the Library option. If you want to ignore the folder completely, highlight the default folder and click Ignore. The button caption changes to Enable after you've ignored the folder and clicking Enable will add the folder back into the monitoring process.

When you want to add a personal folder to the list, click Add. You'll see an Add Folder dialog box where you can locate the folder. The folder doesn't have to appear on your computer; you can monitor network folders as well. Locate the folder you want to add and click OK. Windows Media Player will add the new folder to the list. If you later decide that you really don't want to monitor the folder you added manually, highlight it and click Remove (the same button has captions that read Ignore or Enable depending on the situation).

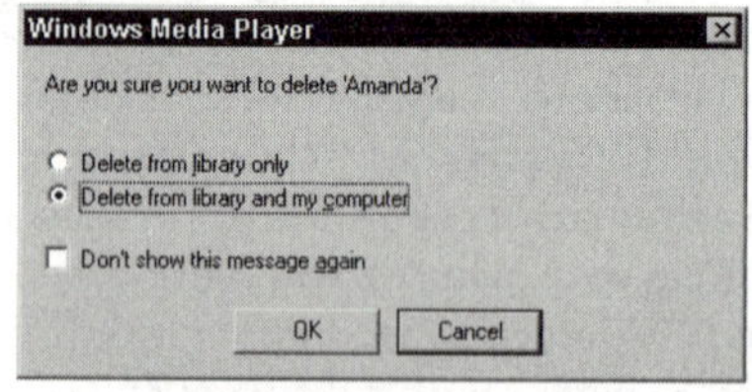

FIGURE 11.10
Remove any of the sample files you really don't want in your library before you begin adding any new files.

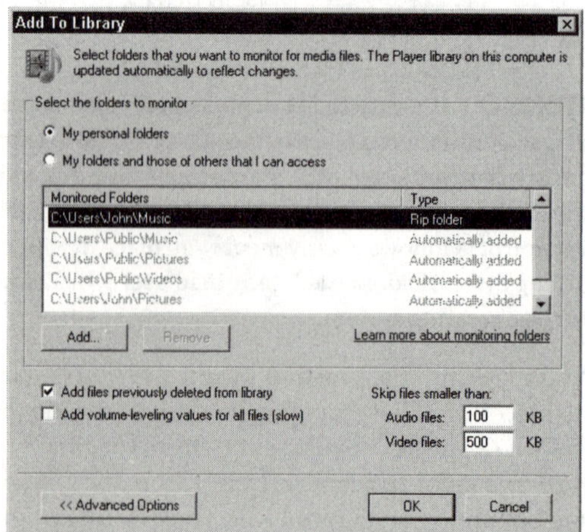

FIGURE 11.11
Choose the folders you want Windows Media Player to monitor for new content.

The sound quality of music recorded in a studio is consistent. However, music that you record yourself might not have a consistent loudness, which means that the volume will vary from selection to selection. You can ask Windows Media Player to correct for this problem by checking the Add Volume Leveling for All Files (Slow) option. Of course, having Windows Media Player check all of the volume levels will slow the system down a little.

The Add to Library dialog box contains two other options—both of which control the size of the files that appear in the library. The Skip Files Smaller Than section contains two text boxes, one for audio and another for video files. Set the smallest sized file you want to appear in the library. Using this feature makes it less likely that you'll find sound bytes such as sound effects or animations in the library. Obviously, you have to achieve a balance between the files you want and those that you don't. At some point, you'll have to remove some of the files from the library manually to obtain a complete list of all of the files you want.

After you make all of the changes you want to the Add to Library dialog box, click OK. Windows Media Player scans for any changes and updates the library display to reflect them. Click Close to close the Add to Library by Searching Computer dialog box.

Sharing Media

Media sharing is a two-way process. Vista begins by assuming that you want to find media that others are sharing, but that you don't want to share media yourself. To locate media shared by others, select the Media Sharing option in the Library drop-down list. You'll see the Media Sharing dialog box shown in Figure 11.12. Make sure you check the first option, Find Media That Others Are Sharing, and click OK. To actually locate shared media, choose the Apply Media Information Changes option in the Library drop-down list.

You may decide to share some of the media on your system with others. In this case, check the second option, Share My Media, and click OK. You'll use the familiar UAC dialog box. Click Continue and the Media Sharing dialog box changes as shown in Figure 11.13. Highlight one of the entries in the list shown in the window and click Allow. Notice that Windows Media player disables the Allow button and enables the Customize button. The default (and only) entry for Windows Media Player is Other Users of This PC. To enable sharing with the network, you must provide a network share for one or more of the media folders.

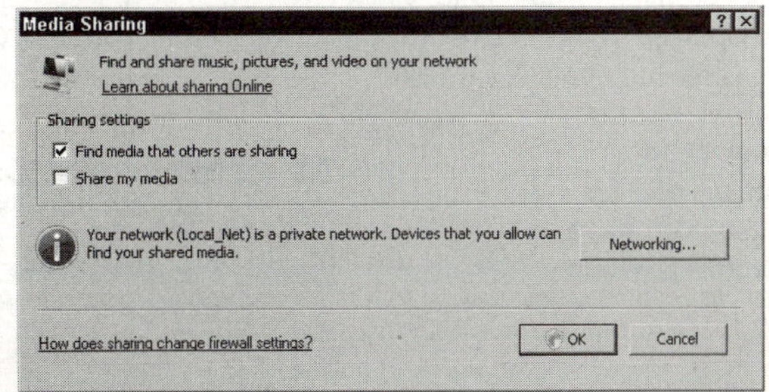

FIGURE 11.12
Choose the folders you want Windows Media Player to monitor for new content.

FIGURE 11.13
Make the media accessible to other people on your machine or even on the network.

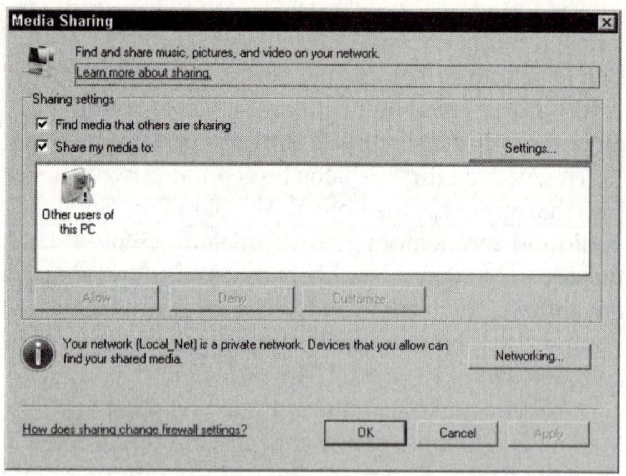

At this point, you can configure the sharing by highlighting the entry you want to configure and clicking Customize. If you want to use the same settings for all of the sharing options, you can click Settings instead. In both cases, you'll see a dialog box similar to the one shown in Figure 11.14. The title bar is slightly different, but the options are essentially the same in both cases. When working with the Media Sharing – Customize dialog box, you'll need to clear the Use Default Settings option check box. When working with Media Sharing – Default Settings dialog box, you'll need to provide a name in the Share Media As field.

Notice that you can configure the media sharing according to media type, the rating you assign to the media, and the parental settings. Consequently, you don't have to share everything, just the media you want.

You might have noticed that the examples in this section rely on a private network. Vista severely limits what you can do on other network types. If your network is wrongly configured as a public network, when in reality it's a private network, you'll find that you can't share anything at all. When this problem occurs, click Networking in the Media Sharing dialog box and you'll see the Network and Sharing Center window shown in Figure 11.15. Click the Customize link and you'll see the Set Network Location dialog box. Select the Private option and type the name of the private network in the Network Name field. Click OK. After a few seconds, you should see the new network settings displayed in the Network and Sharing Center window. Close and reopen the Media Sharing dialog box to share your local files.

FIGURE 11.14
Configure how you want to share media with other people.

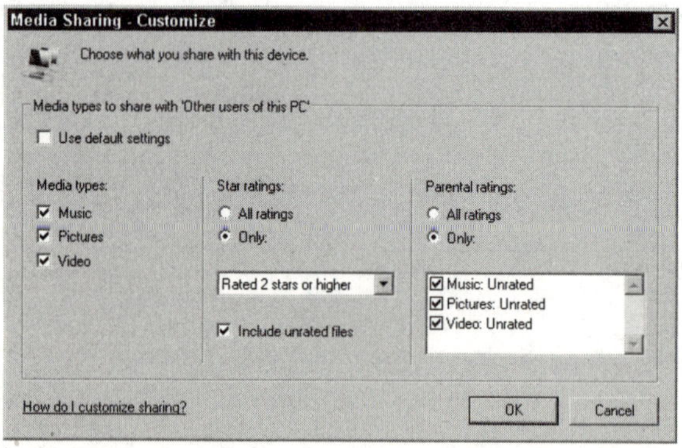

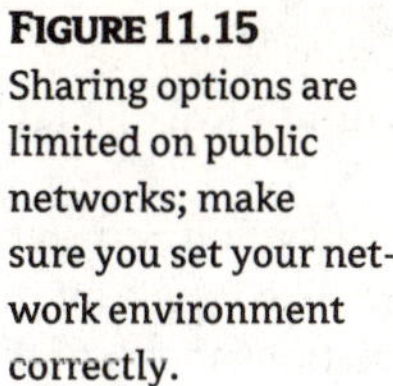

FIGURE 11.15
Sharing options are limited on public networks; make sure you set your network environment correctly.

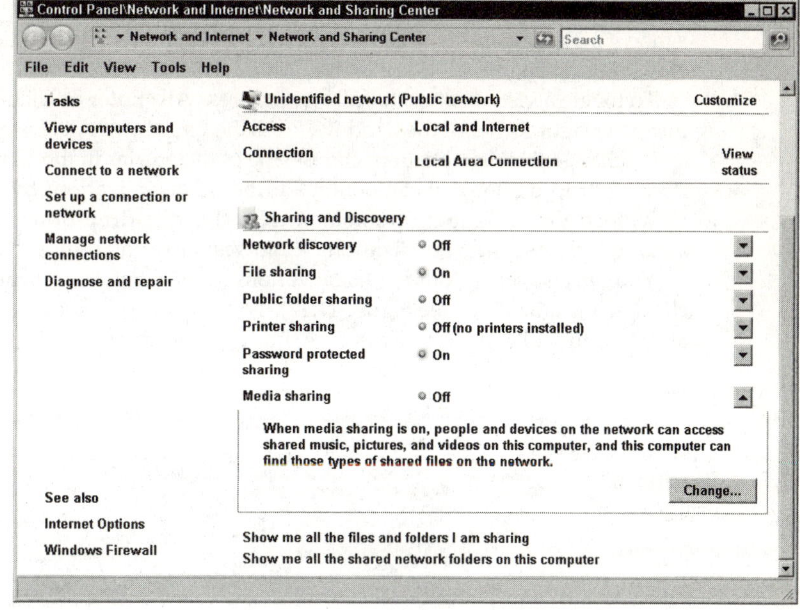

Playing Audio and Video Clips

Once you've let Windows Media Player discover the tracks that you have on your computer and list them in the Media Library, you can play any track by navigating to it and double-clicking it (or by selecting it and clicking the Play button). You can select multiple clips, right-click the selections, and choose Add to Now Playing or Add to 'Untitled Playlist' from the context menu as well. (Whether the context menu contains Now Playing or Untitled Playlist depends on whether you have the List pane displayed.)

On the Library tab, the rightmost pane lists the files queued up for playing. You may have to click the Show List Pane (the left-facing arrow) button to display this pane. This is the Untitled Playlist (or at least it is by default).

Click the down arrow below the Library tab to open a menu from which you can start a new playlist to save and more. See Figure 11.16. To clear a playlist, choose an entry in the right pane and click Clear List pane (the button that looks like an ×).

FIGURE 11.16
The Now Playing List button has a menu associated with it.

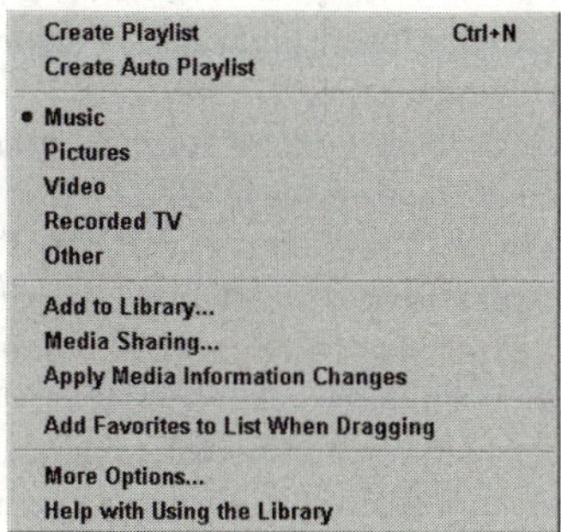

Choosing Visualizations

When it's playing audio, Windows Media Player shows visualizations (graphical displays) on the Now Playing page.

To toggle a visualization to full screen, press Alt+Enter or click the View Full Screen button in the lower right corner of the window. Press the Esc key (or Alt+Enter again) to toggle off full screen.

To change the visualization, choose one of the entries in the Visualizations menu of the Now Playing drop-down. You can obtain additional visualizations by choosing the Visualizations ➢ Download Visualizations option in the Now Playing drop-down. If you don't want to see a visualization, choose the Visualizations ➢ No Visualization option.

You can also set options for visualizations by choosing Visualizations ➢ Options entry, and then clicking Visualization (see Figure 11.17). You can add and remove visualization collections here, and for some collections, you can click the Properties button to display settings you can adjust for it.

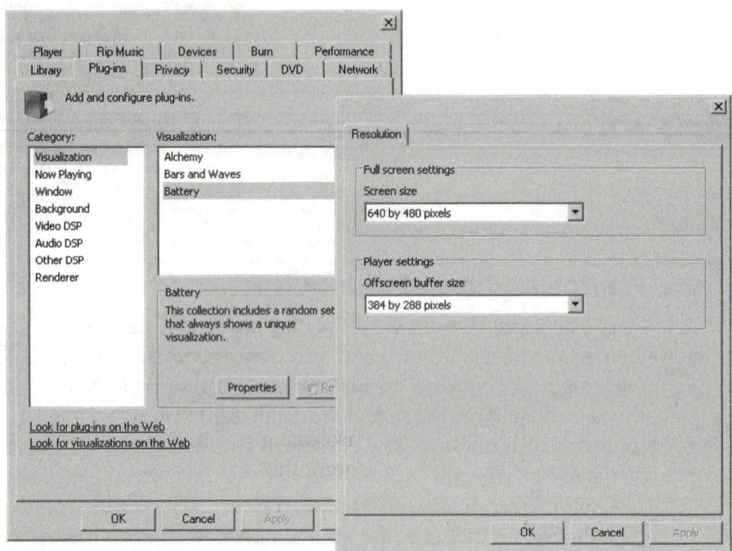

FIGURE 11.17 Choose a visualization collection on the Plug-Ins tab of the Options dialog box.

Adjusting the Quality Settings

If your digital video playback in Windows Media Player is unsatisfactory, you can try making adjustments to the Windows Media Player performance settings.Choose More Options from the Now Playing drop-down, and on the Performance tab, change the settings as needed to obtain the required performance. See Figure 11.18.

In addition to these general settings, you'll find individual device settings on the Devices tab. Highlight one of the devices in the Devices list and click Properties to display a Properties dialog box for that device. For example, a CD or DVD drive contains options to use digital or analog feedback. The Display Properties dialog box contains options for changing the screen's aspect ratio.

The Devices tab also contains an Advanced button. Click this button and you'll see the File Conversion Options dialog box. This dialog box contains options to perform file conversion tasks in the background (which means the task takes longer, but that you can also do something else while you wait). You can choose quality over speed when converting the files and you can also set the amount of disk space set aside for conversion purposes.

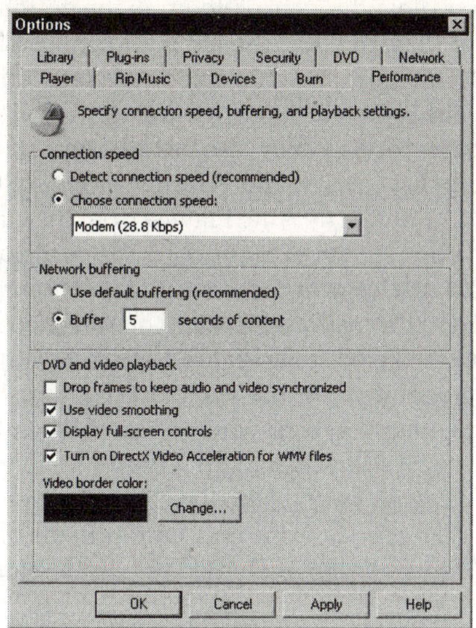

FIGURE 11.18
Adjust video playback settings.

All of these settings control the fine balance between quality, speed, and resources that affect your media experience. When you choose quality, the system always takes a performance hit and requires more resources. Likewise, when you limit the availability of resources (such as hard drive space), quality and speed both suffer.

Displaying Other Lists

The Now Playing list is not the only thing that can potentially appear in the right pane of the Library tab. You can change it to a Burn List (that is, files you've chosen to burn to CD), a Sync List (files you've chosen for synchronizing with a portable player), or a Play List (described in the preceding section). To choose among those options, click the appropriate button along the menu bar.

Creating Playlists

Playing audio files from disk is easy enough, but you can make it even easier by creating playlists of the audio files you like to play together. It's like a Now Playing list (as in the preceding section) except that you save it for later replaying.

To create a new playlist, follow these steps:

1. Choose Create Playlist from the Library drop-down list. Windows Media Player automatically chooses the Library tab for you and turns the Untitled Playlist entry in the right pane to a text box.
2. Type a name for your playlist and press Enter.
3. Drag and drop files into the playlist from the file listing (middle pane).
4. Click the down arrow next to the playlist name and choose Save Playlist As from the menu. Windows Media Player displays a Save As dialog box that has the name of the playlist as the filename.
5. Click Save. Windows Media Player saves the playlist in the default location.

To play a playlist, scroll down to the bottom of the folder tree (left pane) and locate the playlist under Playlists. Right-click it and choose Play from the context menu. To delete a playlist, right-click it and choose Delete. To make modifications to the playlist, highlight it and click Edit in List pane.

Windows Media Player also includes an automatically generated playlist. You specify the criteria for the playlist content and Windows Media Player will locate it for you. To create an automatic playlist, choose Create Auto Playlist from the Library drop-down list. You'll see the New Auto Playlist dialog box shown in Figure 11.19. (I've already filled out some entries for this playlist.)

The playlist lets you choose from a wide range of criteria, everything from the artist who created the media to the media's bit rate. You can choose other media elements to go along with the target media based on the same search criteria. Finally, you can apply limitations to the playlist, such as the number of items or the size of the content.

Unlike other playlists, you can't save the automatically generated playlist directly. However, you can add it to an existing playlist by clicking the entry in the `Playlists` folder and choosing Add to <*Playlist Name*> from the context menu. If you create a new playlist, the automatic playlist elements can appear as the only entries in the playlist to which you add the elements. You can also add the automatically generated playlist to Now Playing or play it as a separate entity.

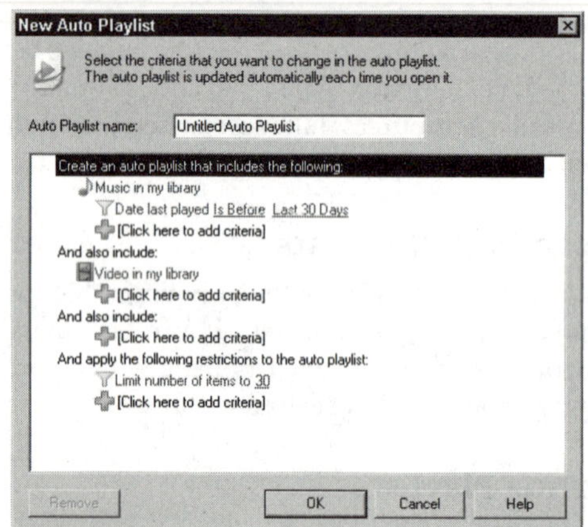

FIGURE 11.19
Create a playlist automatically based on criteria that you provide to Windows Media Player.

Customizing the Now Playing Pane

As you're playing a clip, the Now Playing tab can display a variety of things, depending on the settings you choose. You already know about the Show List pane and the visualizations from earlier in the chapter. Windows Media Player comes with a number of enhancements, such as a graphic equalizer, that you can display one at a time. To display the enhancements, choose Enhancements ➢ Show Enhancements from the Now Playing drop-down list. Figure 11.20 shows a list of the standard enhancements that come with Windows Media Player.

The enhancements normally appear in the bottom third of the area reserved for visualizations. The following list describes each of the enhancements.

Color Chooser Lets you control the colors used in the Windows Media Player window.

Cross-Fading and Auto Volume Leveling Enables you to turn volume leveling and crossfading on and off. Cross-fading has a slider for overlap between tracks, so you can eliminate the "dead air" between the tracks.

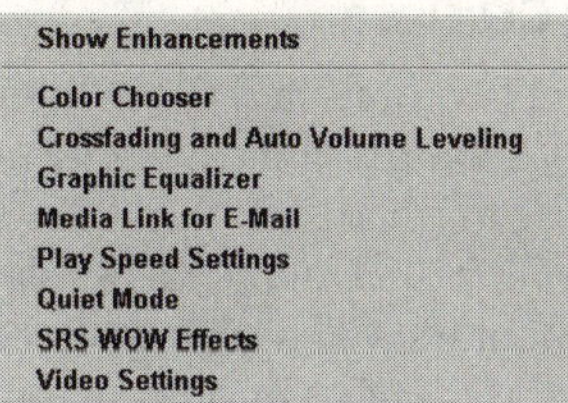

FIGURE 11.20
You can display each of these enhancements to make changes to Windows Media Player behavior.

Graphic Equalizer Defines the frequency output of the Windows Media Player so that you can accommodate various room conditions and the capabilities of your speakers.

Media Link for E-mail This is pretty cool. You can mark a section of a track (beginning and end points) to be sent to someone via e-mail.

Play Speed Settings Drag the slider to move the track speed up or slow down—without changing the pitch.

Quiet Mode Lets you set up volume adjustment that minimizes the difference between the loud and the quiet parts of a track so that you don't have to crank up the volume to hear the quiet parts, only to have your ears blasted when the loud parts come on.

SRS WOW Effects Contains sliders where you can adjust the TruBass and WOW special effects. You can also optimize for standard speakers, large speakers, or headphones.

Video Settings Drag sliders here for Hue, Saturation, Brightness, and Contrast when playing video clips.

Rating Your Library Entries

Each track in your library starts out with a default rating of three stars. You can change this to reflect your enjoyment of a particular track. This information can then be used with some of the automatic playlists generated by the program, such as playlists that consist only of tracks with a certain number of stars or higher.

To change a track's number of stars, simply click the highest star to assign to it from the Library's center window. For example, to give it two stars, click the second star. The maximum rating is five stars. Tracks you've rated have gold stars; auto-rated tracks have pale blue ones.

Working with Audio CDs and DVD Movies

In addition to playing stored audio and video clips, Windows Media Player can also read media content directly from audio CDs and DVDs. You can also transfer the content of a CD (but not DVDs) to your hard disk, in full or in part, for later playback when you don't have the CD handy.

Playing a CD

Unless you turn off AutoPlay, Vista asks you which media player you want to use to play CDs the first time you insert one into a CD drive. After the initial selection of Windows Media Player, it automatically starts playing an audio CD you insert in your CD drive. Use the player controls at the bottom of the window, or double-click a certain track in the Now Playing list to jump to that track. Right-click a track and choose Disable Selected Tracks if there's one you want to skip.

Retrieving CD Data

If your computer is connected to the Internet, Windows Media Player attempts to retrieve the CD information by submitting the CD's ID number to the WindowsMedia.com database of information. (According to Microsoft, Windows Media Player doesn't submit any information about you other than the Globally Unique Identifier [GUID] and your IP address, which is required to get the information about the CD back to your computer.)

If Windows Media Player doesn't automatically display the track names, or if it shows them as Unknown Artist – Unknown Album, you'll need to retrieve them manually. Click the Find Album Info hyperlink below the playlist on the Now Playing tab's window, and Windows Media Player leads you through a search for the artist and album or enables you to enter information for a custom-created CD.

TIP In the past, the WindowsMedia.com database wasn't very complete, but it's getting better all the time. If it can't find a certain CD, you might try Gracenote, the online database of CD information (`http://www.gracenote.com/`). Gracenote is widely used by MP3 rippers and contains impressively accurate information for a very wide range of CDs. Gracenote works in the same way as WindowsMedia.com: it uses the unique identifying code that each commercially released audio CD contains. By submitting this code, a program can download the CD information: artist name, CD name, and track titles. Most rippers handle this process automatically when you insert a CD. Part of Gracenote's wide coverage of CDs is because it receives many entries from its users. If a CD you try to look up in Gracenote doesn't have an entry, you can submit one. Many MP3 rippers have a built-in mechanism for submitting entries to Gracenote.

Copying (Ripping) a CD

Windows Media Player enables you to extract the audio data from the CD (a process normally called *ripping*) and encode it to a compressed digital format that can be played on the PC or on a portable digital player.

Configuring Rip Settings

As you probably know, CD-quality audio files are huge, taking up about 9MB per minute. (This is why about 74 minutes of audio fits on a 650MB CD.) Ripped files are much smaller than that. How small? It depends on the format and bit rate you choose.

Windows Media Player 11 can rip in either WMA, MP3, or WAV format. If you choose WMA format, you can further choose between Standard, WMA Pro, Variable Bit Rate, or Lossless WMA. (Audiophiles might have a preference.) This is a change from earlier versions of Windows Media Player, which required a third-party codec to be installed in order to rip to MP3 format. Table 11.1 details the differences between the available choices of rip format. MP3 is a very compact and popular format, but its bit rate is limited. WMA offers several choices, from very compact (Variable Bit Rate at the lowest quality setting) to very high fidelity (Lossless). Let your inner audiophile decide.

Once you've made up your mind in what format you want to rip, choose Tools ➤ Options, click the Rip Music tab, and make your selection in the Rip Settings area (see Figure 11.21). First choose a format and then drag the Audio Quality slider to the left or right to specify a bit rate.

TABLE 11.1: Media Formats Supported in Windows Media Player 11

FORMAT	BIT RATE	SPACE REQUIRED FOR AN AVERAGE CD
MPEG Layer 3 (MP3)	128 to 320Kbps	57 to 144MB
Windows Media Audio (WMA)	48 to 192Kbps (you choose)	22 to 86MB
Windows Media Audio Pro (WMA Pro)	32 to 192Kbps (you choose)	14 to 86MB
Windows Media Audio (Variable Bit Rate)	40 to 355Kbps (you choose a range)	18 to 155MB
Windows Media Audio (Lossless)	470 to 840Kbps (whatever the CD is recorded at; no choice)	206 to 411MB

While you're here in the Options dialog box (Figure 11.21), go ahead and make your other selections for rip settings:

- **Click the Change button** to browse for a different location in which to store the ripped tracks. The default is `My Documents\My Music`.
- **Click the File Name button** to specify how the files should be named. Some people like more or less information in the filename; it's up to you. Use the Move Up and Move Down buttons to reorder the information (see Figure 11.22).

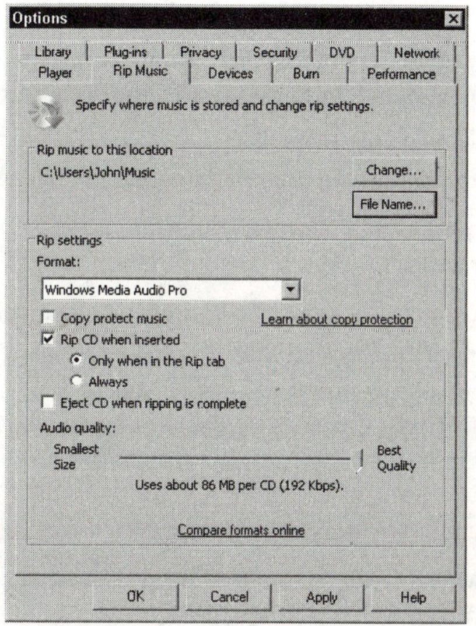

FIGURE 11.21
Specify the format and bit rate for the rip.

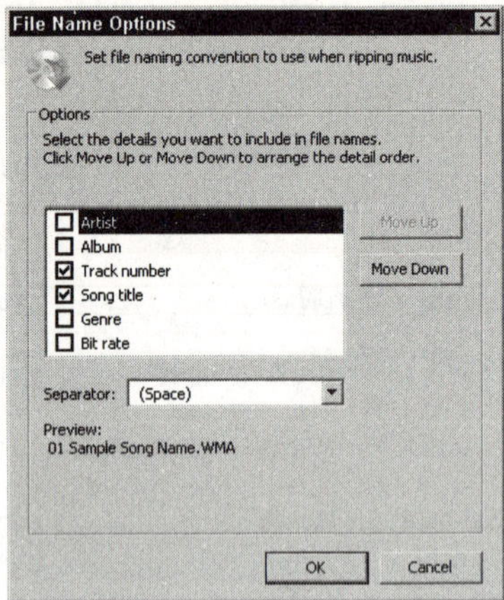

FIGURE 11.22 Choose the details about the track to be included in the filename.

WHAT CAN YOU LEGALLY DO WITH DIGITAL AUDIO?

If you're going to enjoy digital audio, you need to know what you can and cannot do with it. Here's what you can legally do:

- Listen to streaming audio from a website or an Internet radio station, even if the site or person streaming the audio is doing so illegally.
- Record audio from a medium you own (for example, a CD) to a different medium (for example, a cassette) so that you can listen to it at a different time or in a different place.
- Download a digital file that contains copyrighted material from a website or FTP site provided that the copyright holder has granted the distributor permission to distribute it.
- Download a digital file from a computer via P2P technology (for example, Napster, audioGnome, or Gnutella) provided that the copyright holder has granted the distributor permission to distribute it.
- Create digital-audio files (for example, WMA files or MP3 files) of tracks on CDs you own for your personal use.
- Distribute a digital-audio file to which you hold the copyright or for whose distribution the copyright holder has granted you permission.
- Download (or copy) MP3 files or other supported digital-audio files to portable audio devices (such as the Diamond Rio or the Creative Labs Nomad).
- Broadcast licensed audio across the Internet.

Here are some of the key things that you *cannot* legally do with audio:

- Download a digital-audio file that contains copyrighted material if the copyright holder hasn't granted the distributor permission to distribute it.
- Distribute a digital-audio file that contains copyrighted material if the copyright holder hasn't granted you permission to distribute it.

- Lend a friend a CD so they can create digital-audio files from it.
- Borrow a CD from a friend and create digital-audio files from it.
- Upload digital-audio files from a portable audio player that supports music uploading, such as the I-Jam or the eGo, to another computer. (In this scenario, you're essentially using the portable player to copy the files from one computer to another.)

Ripping Audio CD Tracks

To copy a CD, follow these steps:

1. Insert the CD in your PC. If it starts playing, stop it.
2. Click the Rip tab in Windows Media Player.
3. If you want to exclude any tracks, clear their check boxes (see Figure 11.23).
4. Click the Rip Music button. Then just wait for it to finish.

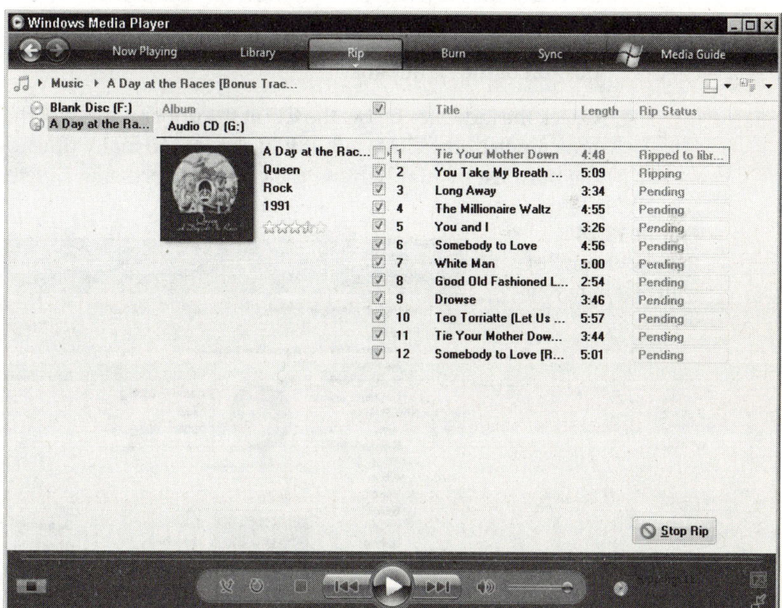

FIGURE 11.23 Select the desired tracks (or rather, deselect the undesired ones) and then click Rip Music.

Burning CDs

Ripping and burning—what violent metaphors we seem to have come up with for working with audio content on a PC. Some of this probably stems from how difficult it used to be "back in the day" to copy audio content between formats. After struggling with the software of yesteryear, a lot of users were probably ready to rip and burn anything they could get their hands on. But no more. In Windows Media Player 11, it's easy to make audio CDs.

TIP Before you decide for sure that you want an audio CD, consider this. An audio CD holds only about 70 minutes of music. On the other hand, a data disc containing MP3 or WMA files hold hours and hours of music. More and more CD players these days support digital-audio formats, including many car stereos, so check to see if the player for which you're creating the CD will support that. If so, you can do yourself a favor and make your disc a data disc, and receive many times the capacity out of the same little blank disc.

Windows Media Player creates audio CDs by running the tracks through a two-phase process. First, it converts each track to CDA format (CD-Audio); then, it burns them to the CD blank. It takes about twice as long to create an audio CD as a data CD because of the extra step of file conversion.

CREATING A BURN LIST

To make a compilation CD out of the tracks in your Library, follow these steps:

1. Click the Burn tab.
2. Drag and drop files to the burn list (showing in the right pane in Figure 11.24), or select them and click the Add Selection to Burn List button.
3. Insert a blank CD-R in your writeable CD drive and wait for it to be recognized in the upper portion of the right pane.
4. Check the indicator below the CD in the upper portion of the right pane. This indicator shows how much of the CD is left. If you choose too many titles, you'll need to remove some from the burn list by highlighting the entry and pressing Delete.

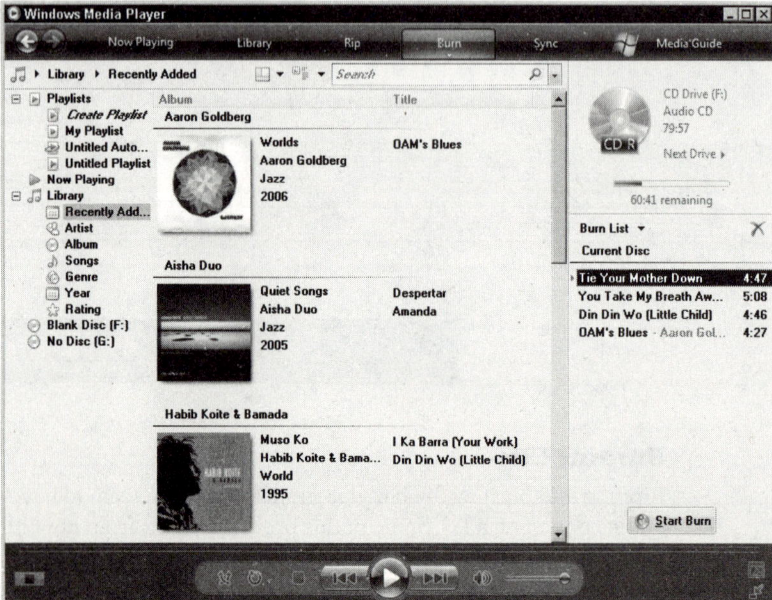

FIGURE 11.24
Build your burn list with files from your library.

5. When you're satisfied with your burn list, click the Start Burn button. Then just wait for the CD to be created. Try not to use your PC for anything else while it's burning the CD (to avoid buffer underrun errors as much as possible).

WARNING A buffer underrun error occurs when the CD is ready for more data but the PC isn't sending it fast enough. This used to be a huge problem, but now most CD drives have buffers built in that help with this problem, and some software solutions are available as well. Still, just to be on the safe side, it doesn't hurt to be cautious about overtaxing the CPU while the PC is trying to burn a CD. It's better than wasting a blank.

Burning DVDs with Windows DVD Maker

You can also burn DVDs using Vista, but you use a different application to do it. The Windows DVD Maker helps you create DVDs containing pictures. You start this application by choosing Start ➤ All Programs ➤ Windows DVD Maker. The following steps tell how to burn a DVD.

NOTE Even though you don't need to use Aero Glass with this application, you do need a better than average display adapter. It's very likely that you'll see a message saying your display adapter isn't good enough to use the Windows DVD Maker if your system can't run Aero Glass.

1. Place a blank DVD in the DVD drive.
2. Click Choose Photos and Videos. You'll see a Windows DVD Maker window that contains a blank area to hold video, audio, and picture files.

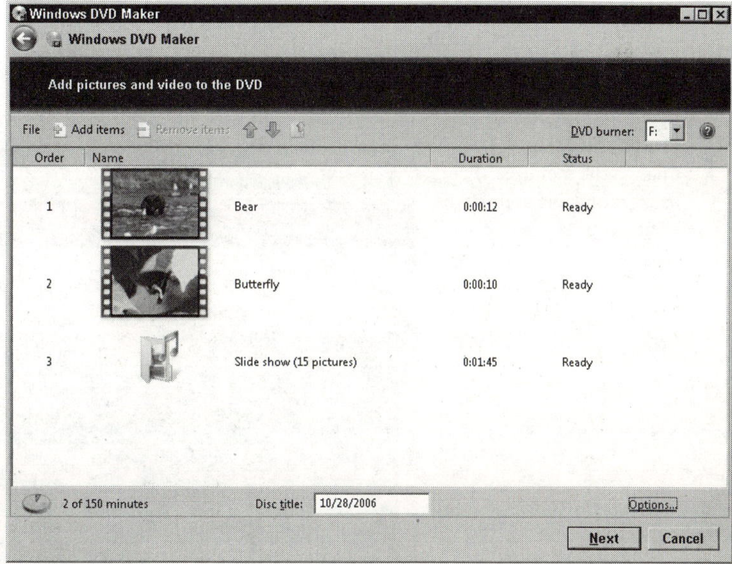

FIGURE 11.25 Choose the media that you want to appear on the DVD.

3. Click Add Items. Add any items that the Windows DVD Maker supports (approximately the same set of files that the Windows Media Player supports). Any music that you choose will get added to a slide show if you create one. Figure 11.25 shows a collection of various media files for one DVD. Notice the indicator at the bottom of the screen. Make sure that you don't place too many files on the DVD. The indicator tells you how many minutes of play time you have left.

4. Click the Options link. You'll see the DVD Options dialog box shown in Figure 11.26. Notice especially the Video format area. Make sure you choose the right output format for the video. You can also choose elements such as whether to start with a menu.

FIGURE 11.26
Make sure you set the options for the DVD you're creating.

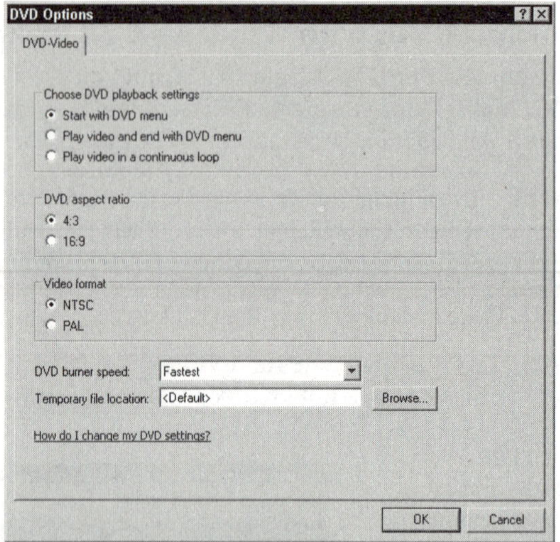

FIGURE 11.27
Change the menu background and style to suit your tastes.

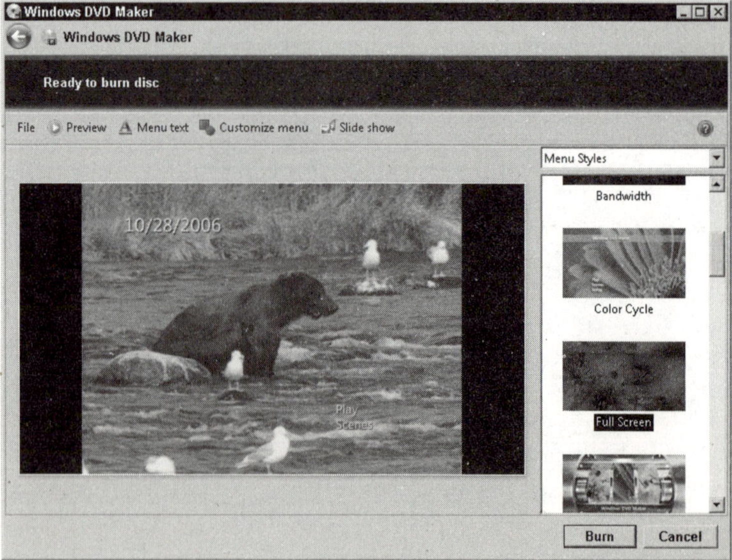

5. Select the options for your DVD and click OK. Click Next. You'll see a Ready to Burn Disk window similar to the one shown in Figure 11.27. This window lets you change the menu options, choose a menu background, and modify the menu text. At the very least, you'll want to click Menu Text, type a new title in the Disk title field, and click Change Text.
6. Customize the menu as needed, and then click Burn. Windows DVD Maker creates a DVD for you based on your selections.

After what seems like days, you'll receive a DVD you can place in any DVD player. Depending on the options you choose, the DVD will start at a menu, provide a full play option, and let you select particular scenes. Overall, the ability to create both full motion video and slideshows is impressive in Vista. However, you can't rip DVDs, which means that you can't perform manipulations of existing DVDs like you can when using other products such as Roxio's Nero.

Playing a DVD

Once you've installed a DVD drive and a DVD player, you can play a DVD by putting it in the drive. As with a CD, Vista will ask your preference for playing the DVD the first time. If you choose Windows Media Player, Vista automatically plays the DVD using it the next time you insert a DVD. Windows Media Player uses the standard Play controls for DVDs and displays a list of the DVD chapters in the playlist area. The Enhancements menu I mentioned earlier in the chapter is also available. Right-click in the viewing area and you can access all of the usual special DVD controls as part of a context menu. Windows Media Player starts all DVDs in the full-screen mode, but you can easily view them any of the other screen sizes as well. The video automatically resizes itself to the size of the viewing area you provide.

In order for a DVD drive to play DVD movies, you must have the appropriate codec installed for DVD video encoding. In earlier days, this was usually a piece of hardware because of the processor-intensive nature of the decoding process, but on modern systems, it's usually software since systems have gotten powerful enough that the burden is not so burdensome. If you get an error message when you try to play a DVD movie but you can read data DVDs, your system probably lacks the needed codec. Lots of companies would like to sell you a codec; see `http://www.microsoft.com/windows/windowsmedia` for vendors that Microsoft recommends.

TIP If you've done a clean Windows install and have deleted everything that came on your PC originally and you now find that you don't seem to have the right codec, it was probably lost in the reinstall. Check the discs that came with the PC; perhaps there's a DVD player application that will serve. Once a DVD player application installs the needed codec, you might be able to play DVDs through Windows Media Player (so you won't necessarily have to use the player you just installed if you preferred Windows Media Player to it).

Choose More Options from the Now Playing drop-down list, and select the DVD tab to set properties for the DVD player feature. The DVD tab offers these options:

DVD Playback Restrictions To implement parental control on DVDs played on the computer, click Change, choose a rating from the drop-down list, and click OK.

Language Settings Click Defaults to set the default language for audio, captions, and DVD titles.

Advanced Settings Click the Advanced button to set audio modes, such as choosing between regular stereo and Dolby Surround Sound. The options here depend on your sound cards and speakers.

Tuning into Internet Radio

Windows Media Player provides good features for tuning in to Internet radio—radio broadcast across the Web via streaming audio servers such as SHOUTcast, Icecast, or RealAudio.

As of version 11, Windows Media Player has relegated Internet radio to the Media Guide tab; it no longer has its own tab. No matter. It does somewhat make sense, given that you need to be connected to the Internet to work with it, just as you need to be connected to the Internet to see the Guide.

To listen to Internet radio, take these steps:

1. Click the Media Guide tab.
2. Click the Radio hyperlink. A list of featured stations appears.
3. If you see a station that interests you on the Featured Stations list, click it to display its details.
4. Depending on the station, there will either be a Play link or a Visit Web Site to Play link. If you have a Play link, click it and the station will begin playing in Windows Media Player; if you have a Visit Web Site to Play link, a website will appear with instructions for playing that station.

Searching for a Radio Station

From the main radio web page, you can click one of the categories to browse for stations in that category. For example, you might choose Classic Rock in the Find Radio Stations area of the web page. After you click a link, you can use the screen shown in Figure 11.28 to search by keyword or zip code. When you find a radio station you think you might like, click the Play link to listen to it.

FIGURE 11.28
You can browse for a radio station by genre or search by keyword or zip code.

You can also perform an advanced search. To do so, click the Use Advanced Search link to display the Advanced Search controls (shown in Figure 11.29). Specify whichever criteria you want—Genre, Language, Country, State (in the U.S. only), Speed, Band (AM, FM, or the Net), Keyword, Call Sign, or Frequency—and click the Search button to locate stations that match.

FIGURE 11.29 Use the Advanced Search panel to use multiple criteria in your search for a radio station.

Creating and Editing Presets

You can edit your presets by changing the My Stations list as you need. You can't change the Featured Stations list.

To add a station to your My Stations list, expand its heading and click its Add to My Stations link.

To remove a station from your My Stations list, expand its heading in the My Stations list and choose Remove from My Stations.

NOTE You can also retain a local copy of the radio stations you like. Simply right-click the entry in the Now Playing list and choose Add to ➤ *<Playlist Name>*.

Applying Skins

You can apply *skins* (custom graphical looks) to Windows Media Player to change its appearance in Skin mode. Windows Media Player comes with a selection of skins built in. In addition, you can download skins from the Internet. Unlike previous versions of Windows Media Player, Microsoft hides this configuration from plain view. Begin by placing Windows Media Player in Skin mode by right-clicking the control area at the bottom of the window and choosing View ➤ Skin Mode from the context menu. (You can also press Ctrl+2 to display Skin mode.) The display changes to show whatever skin you've configured. Figure 11.30 shows the Revert skin that comes with Windows Media Player.

FIGURE 11.30 Skin mode lets you change the appearance of Windows Media Player to suit your tastes.

To apply a skin, right-click the control area at the bottom of the window and select View ➤ Skin Chooser. You'll see a window similar to the one shown in Figure 11.31. Select a skin in the list box to see how it looks (as shown in the right pane). When you find one you like, click the Apply Skin button to apply it. You can also apply a skin quickly by double-clicking its file in an Explorer window or on your Desktop.

Unfortunately, the installed skins are woefully inadequate. To download extra skins, click the More Skins button on the Skin Chooser page. Windows Media Player opens a browser window of the appropriate page of the WindowsMedia.com website, which maintains a gallery of skins, some created by Microsoft and others by users. (You'll also find skins in online software archives such as CNET's Download.com, but WindowsMedia.com is a good place to start.)

When you download a skin package, Windows displays the Windows Media Download dialog box. From this, you can click the View Now button to display the skin or the Close button to dismiss the dialog box.

NOTE Windows Media Player skins can have the file type Windows Media Player Skin File and the `.wms` extension, but you'll usually find them compressed into files of the Windows Media Player Skin Package file type. These have the `.wmz` extension.

To delete a skin from Windows Media Player, select it in the list box and click the Delete button, then click the Yes button in the Confirm Skin Delete dialog box that Windows Media Player displays.

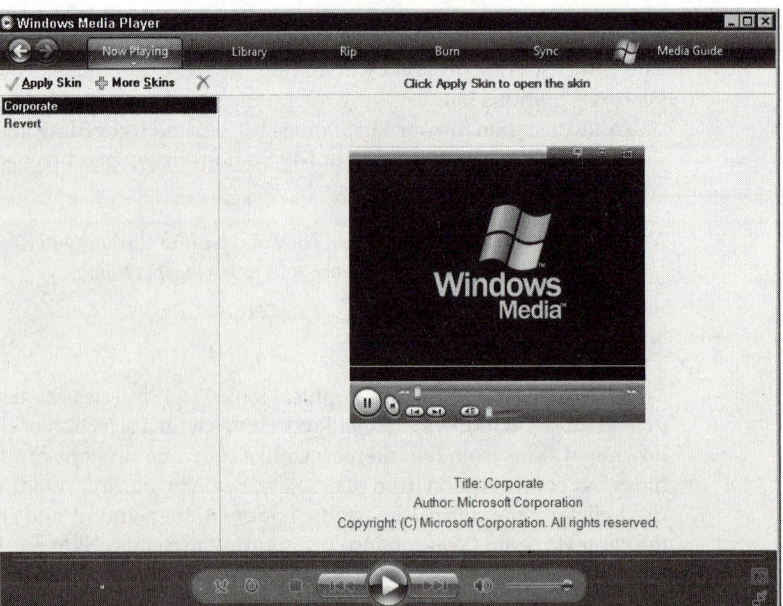

FIGURE 11.31 Select a new skin for Windows Media Player using the Skin Chooser window.

You can create your own custom skins for Windows Media Player. To do so, download the Windows Media Player Software Development Kit from the Microsoft website and follow the tutorials on the Microsoft Developer Network (MSDN; `msdn.microsoft.com/workshop/imedia/windowsmedia/wmpskins.asp`). When you've created a skin, store it in the `Program Files\Windows Media Player\Skins` folder, and Windows Media Player will automatically list it on the Skin Chooser page.

Working with Content Licenses

Being able to store audio and video in digital format on a PC, play them back easily, and even transfer them via the Internet or removable media is great for consumers of audio and video content. But it can be much less than great for creators of audio and video content: These computer capabilities pose a severe threat to their livelihoods by compromising their copyrighted works and robbing them of sales.

In the past, audio and video works have largely been distributed on physical media, such as CDs, cassettes, LPs, videocassettes, and DVDs. The tangible nature and physical presence of such media generally makes it clear when a theft has occurred: physical media can't walk out of stores by themselves. Making unauthorized copies of a work distributed on a physical medium such as a videotape involves cost (for the media, for the copies, and for any duplicating equipment needed), time (typically real-time copying), and effort. Distributing those copies involves further cost, time, and effort. And the illegality of such pirated works is widely known (and recognized, if not exactly appreciated): most consumers are aware that it's illegal to distribute (let alone sell) copies of copyrighted works. Besides, copies of works on analog media (such as videotape or audiotape) are lower fidelity than the originals, so the unauthenticity of late-generation copies is clear.

By contrast, any work stored in a digital medium accessible by a PC can be copied in seconds at almost zero cost, and the copies are perfect every time. These perfect copies can be distributed via the Internet, again at negligible cost. And they can be distributed in quantities and over distances unthinkable for physical media. For example, if someone buys a CD in Sioux Falls, makes MP3 files of its tracks, and makes them available on a file-sharing service, anyone with Internet connectivity anywhere in the world—from Vladivostok to Tierra del Fuego, from Juneau to Java—can download them and then distribute them further.

At this writing, there are several technologies intended to protect the rights of content creators (and their authorized distributors) while allowing consumers to use the content. For example, most DVDs use an encryption system called Content Scrambling System (CSS), which requires an encryption key in order to be decoded. CSS keys were licensed and tightly controlled by the DVD-Copy Control Association (DVD-CCA)—tightly controlled, that is, until Norwegian hackers in the LiVid (Linux Video group) created a utility called DeCSS by reverse engineering some unencrypted code they discovered in a sloppily constructed software DVD player. Now that DeCSS is widely available, CSS-encrypted content can be deciphered by anyone who has the code.

Perhaps the most promising of the technologies designed to protect content is the digital license. A digital license is encrypted information that links a particular copy of a downloaded work to a particular computer or individual. For example, in the current model of digital licenses for audio, if you download a track that uses a digital license, you buy or are otherwise granted a license to play the track on the computer on which you downloaded it. If you transfer the track to another computer, it won't play, because the computer lacks the necessary license information.

So far, so good. But in order to be viable enough to become widely accepted, digital licenses need not only to be easy and intuitive to use but also compatible with both generally used technology and with the prevailing laws. For example, the First Sale Doctrine laid out in the Copyright Act allows consumers to sell or give a copy they've legitimately acquired of a copyrighted work to another person. Any copyright-protection technology that prevents consumers from doing this effectively (for example, because any subsequent recipient wouldn't be able to view or listen to the work because it was locked by encryption and a nontransferable license to the first purchaser's computer) would be open to heavy-duty legal challenges.

Leaving aside such details for the moment, digital licenses are now being used to secure some copyrighted content. Windows Media Player adopts a two-pronged approach to digital licenses for audio content: it supports digital licenses for both tracks you buy and download and tracks you copy from CD. Windows Media Player automatically issues a license for each track you copy from a CD (unless you set it to copy tracks without licensing them).

Windows Media Player lets you choose whether to use digital licenses or whether to be free, easy, and possibly illegal. As long as you use those tracks on the PC with which you created them, there's no problem with using licenses. But, if you want to be able to play the tracks from another computer, you've got a problem, because the license ties the associated digital media file to the PC for which the license is issued: you'll need to acquire a new license or transfer a license from the original computer. Similarly, you may not be able to download a copy of a licensed track to a portable player without licensing gymnastics.

Simply *playing* a track from another computer should be fine, legally, because it's the same file that you created from the CD. So should moving the track to another computer that belongs to you and using it on that computer. Only if you create an illegal copy of the track—and particularly if you distribute it—should there be a problem. More on this later in the chapter, but you can see that the implementation of digital licenses tends to be problematic, partly because of the nature of the beast and partly because of the assumption of those who implemented the technology that anything unlicensed will tend to be licentious. There's no good reason for using digital licenses for the tracks you copy from CD unless you can't trust yourself (or other users of your computer) not to take illegal actions with them.

Unlike previous versions of Windows Media Player, Windows Media Player 11 apparently doesn't require that you perform a lot of extra work to obtain the licenses you need to work with content. Everything happens automatically when you check the Download Usage Rights Automatically When I Play or Sync a File option on the Privacy tab of the Options dialog box. Select More Options from the Now Playing drop-down list box to display the Options dialog box.

Working with Portable Devices

Windows Media Player can help you copy audio files to a portable digital audio device. Earlier versions of Windows Media Player treated a portable device the same as a writeable CD, but in Windows Media Player 11, a special tab, Sync, is designed for use specifically with portable devices.

TIP Most portable devices come with effective software for loading tracks and playlists onto them. Because this software is specifically designed for the portable device, it may offer enhancements that Windows Media Player does not. However, some portable device software packages can't rip, encode, and load to the portable device in one move, as Windows Media Player can with some of the players it supports.

Creating the Sync List

Creating a Sync list is the same as the process for creating a playlist or a Burn list. In fact, Windows Media Player saves the Sync list using a special name, `Sync List.wpl`. To create a Sync list, follow these steps:

1. Click the Sync tab.
2. Drag and drop files into the right pane, or select files in the center pane and click the Add to Sync List button.
3. Choose Save Playlist As from the Sync List drop-down list box in the right pane and save the Sync list using the default filename.

You can create the Sync list at any time, either before or after you connect your portable device.

Making Media Player Recognize Your Device

Media Player automatically recognizes a wide variety of portable devices, so this may not be an issue for you. When you plug in your portable device (usually to a USB port), go to the Sync tab and press F5 to refresh the device list. Then open the drop-down list over the right pane to see whether your device is listed. If it is, select it and you're ready to go. If it doesn't appear on that list, choose Refresh Devices from the Sync drop-down list.

Copying Audio Files to a Portable Player

To copy files to a portable player, follow these steps:

1. Make a Sync list as described earlier.
2. (Optional) Click the Display Properties and Settings icon above the right pane, opening the Properties box for your portable player. Then change any of its settings as desired and click OK.
3. Click the Start Sync button. The clips are copied to the portable device.

When you're tired of those clips and want to delete them from the portable device, you can use the controls on the device itself to remove the files.

Setting Output Volume and Recording Volume

As you saw earlier in the chapter, you can adjust the output volume by moving the Volume slider in Windows Media Player. If you prefer, you can put a Volume control in the notification area so that it's always handy even when Windows Media Player or your other favorite noisemaker is minimized or hidden behind other windows. Unlike previous versions of Windows, Vista makes the Volume control available by default.

Setting Playback Volume Levels

To set the volume, single-click the Volume control. Windows displays a pop-up panel bearing a Volume slider, Mixer link, and a Mute check box as shown in Figure 11.32. Drag the slider up and down to set the volume. Windows emits a ding chord when you release the slider so that you can hear the approximate loudness of that volume. Click anywhere other than the pop-up panel to make the panel disappear.

When you mute the sound by selecting the Mute check box on the pop-up panel, Windows displays a red circle and bar beside the Volume control as a visual reminder.

You can double-click the Volume control, or right-click it and choose Open Volume Mixer from the shortcut menu, to display the Volume Mixer dialog box shown in Figure 11.33. Then drag the sliders for various types of playback devices to control them individually.

You can change the devices that each have their own sliders here. To do so, clear or set the check marks next to the entries in the Devices menu.

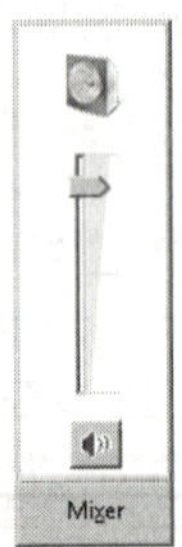

FIGURE 11.32
Single-click the Volume icon to control the volume on your system.

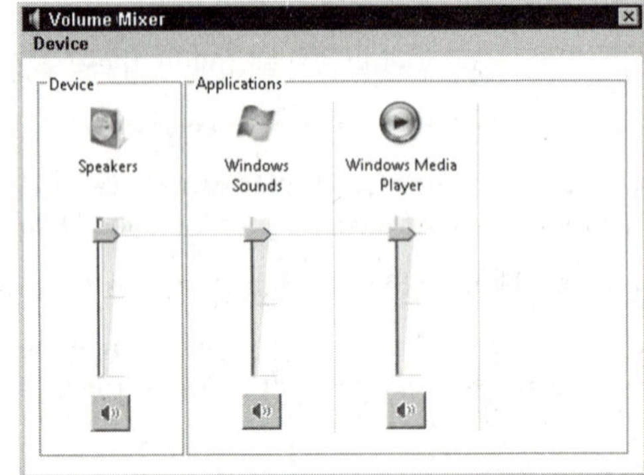

FIGURE 11.33
Mix the sounds on your system to achieve a particular balance.

Setting Recording Volume Levels

Notice that the sliders shown in the preceding section are for playback devices. If you want to set volumes for recording devices, you have to configure them using the individual properties for the device. The following steps describe how to set a recording device recording level.

1. Right-click the Volume icon in the notification area and choose Recording Devices from the context menu. You'll see the Sound dialog box and Vista automatically selects the Recording tab for you.

2. Highlight the device you want to modify and click the Properties button. You'll see the device's Properties dialog box.

3. Select the Levels tab and you'll see levels for the device as shown in Figure 11.34.

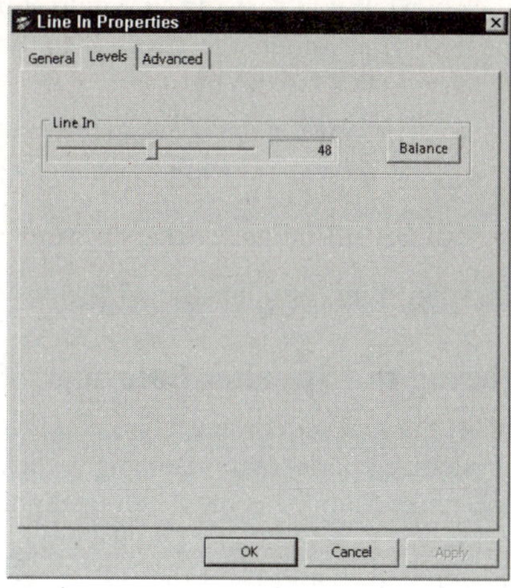

FIGURE 11.34 Set the volume for a recording device using its Properties dialog box.

4. Click Balance to display the Balance dialog box when needed to adjust the balance between the right and left inputs.
5. Click OK twice to make the change permanent.

Setting the Speaker Configuration and Layout

To set speaker balance on the signal output by your sound card (as opposed to setting it via your amplifier), use the following steps.

1. Right-click the Volume icon in the notification area and choose Playback Devices from the context menu.
2. Highlight the speakers you want to adjust and click Configure. You'll see the Speaker Setup Wizard dialog box shown in Figure 11.35.
3. Choose a speaker configuration from the list. Click Test to check the configuration. You can also click the individual speakers in the diagram to the right to test individual speakers.

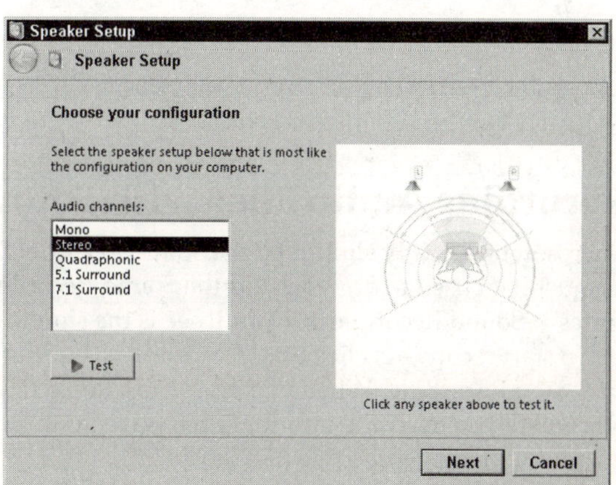

FIGURE 11.35 Adjust the configuration and balance of the speakers attached to your system using this wizard.

4. Click Next. If you're using surround sound, the wizard will ask you to choose the optional speaker types (otherwise, proceed to the next step). Check the optional speakers in your setup and click Next.
5. The wizard will ask you to choose full-range speakers—those that don't require a separate subwoofer to provide a full range of sounds.
6. Choose the full-range speakers in your setup and click Next.
7. Click Finish to complete the wizard.

Configuring the Speaker Balance

After you set the speaker configuration and layout, you'll probably want to set the speaker balance for your system. To perform this task, right-click the Volume icon in the notification area and choose Playback Devices from the context menu. Highlight the speakers you want to adjust and click Properties. Choose the Levels tab and you'll see the volume and balance settings shown in Figure 11.36. Make any required changes and click OK twice to make the settings permanent.

TIP All of the devices described in this section also include an Advanced tab on their Properties dialog box. The Advanced tab has controls that let you choose the quality of output from the device and whether applications can gain exclusive control over the device.

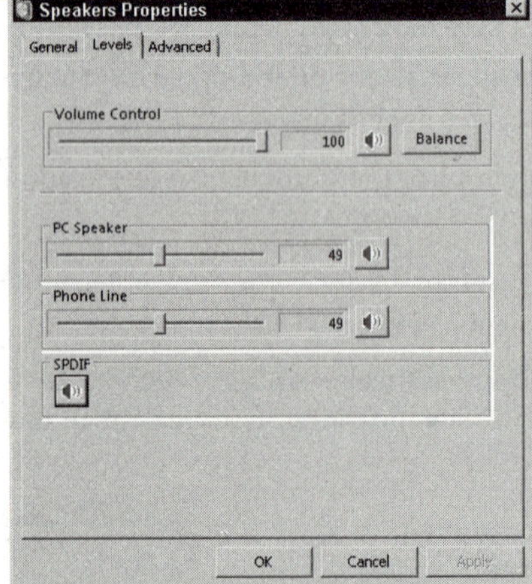

FIGURE 11.36
Modify the speaker volume and balance after you configure the speaker layout.

Recording Audio Files with Sound Recorder

Microsoft has greatly simplified the Sound Recorder for Vista and you'll find that it can't do nearly as much as it used to do. You start the Sound Recorder by choosing Start ➤ All Programs ➤ Accessories ➤ Sound Recorder. All you'll see is the simple bar shown in Figure 11.37.

To start recording, click Start Recording. The Sound Recorder continues recording until you click Stop Recording. When you press Stop Recording, Sound Recorder displays a Save As dialog box where you enter the information to save your recording. You only have one choice of format, Windows Media Audio File (`*.wma`).

FIGURE 11.37 Microsoft has made Sound Recorder considerably simpler, but it lacks functionality.

If you want to resume your recording later, click Cancel when you see the Save As dialog box. The button caption changes to Resume Recording. When you click it again, the recording will resume. As normal, click Stop Recording to stop the recording and display the Save As dialog box.

Connecting to a Network Projector

Vista provides the capability to connect with network projectors almost instantly. To use this feature, choose Start ➤ All Programs ➤ Accessories ➤ Connect to a Network Projector. The first time you start this application, Vista will display a Permission to Connect to a Network Projector dialog box because you have to set up your firewall to allow the connection. Click Yes. After you click Continue at the UAC dialog box, Vista displays the Connect to a Network Projector dialog box shown in Figure 11.38.

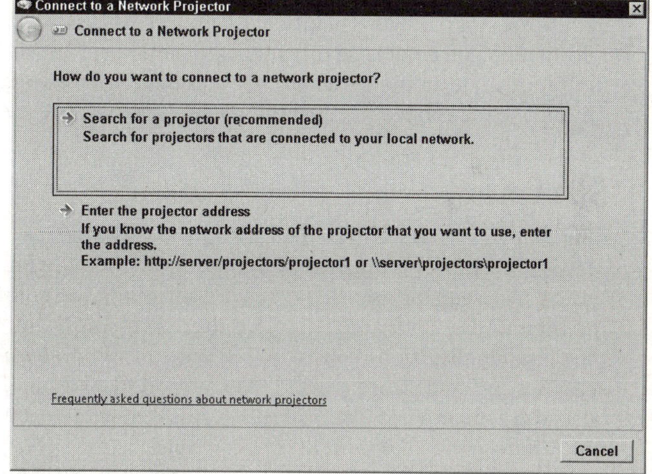

FIGURE 11.38 You have two ways to connect to a network projector on your network.

Locating a Projector Automatically

The easiest way to connect to a network projector is ask Vista to find it for you. Click the Search for a projector (recommended) option shown in Figure 11.38. Vista will search for network projectors on your network. It displays a list of these projectors in the Available projectors list. Highlight the projector you want to use and click Connect. That's all you need to do. The network projector is now available for your meeting.

Using a Network Projector Address

Sometimes Vista won't find the network projector you want to use. This problem normally occurs with older network projectors or those that require a password. In this case, enter the projector address in the dialog box shown in Figure 11.38. You'll see the dialog box shown in Figure 11.39.

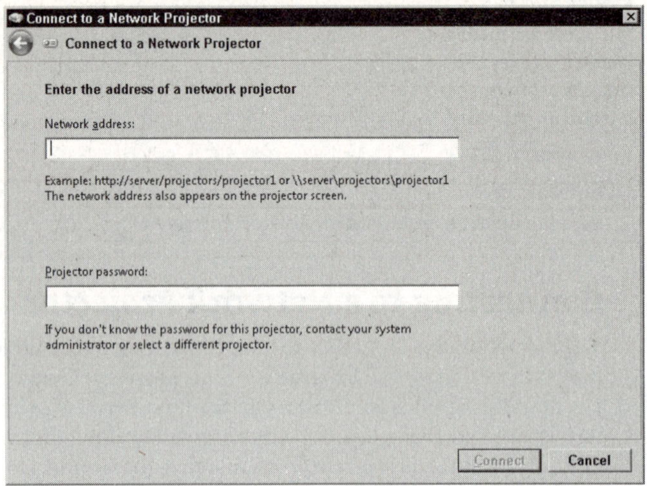

FIGURE 11.39 Some projectors require that you enter their address and password manually.

Type the address for the network projector in the Network address field. You can provide either an URL or a UNC location on a LAN. Type a password, if any, for accessing the network projector in the Projector password field. Click Connect and Vista creates the connection for you. If any of the information you enter is incorrect, the projector isn't attached to the network, there's a firewall configuration issue, or there's a hardware problem with the projector, Vista will simply tell you that it can't make the connection (leaving you to figure out the cause).

Summary

This chapter has concentrated on audio and video, discussing how to make the most of Windows Media Player for listening to CDs, copying CDs to your hard disk, and tuning into Internet radio. You've also seen the assorted ways of controlling the volume that Windows outputs and how to record sounds with Sound Recorder, the distressingly limited tool that Windows provides for the purpose. Finally, for anyone who's spent considerable time configuring their system for a presentation, Microsoft has created the Connect to a Network Projector Wizard. This is one of the best additions to Vista, from a multimedia perspective, because it has the potential for saving so much time.

What can I say? It's time to play. Multimedia is one of the fun parts of using a computer and it's a good idea if you become familiar with it sooner rather than later if you use multimedia with any regularity. Make sure you understand how the multimedia features work so you can do everything from play games to give phenomenal presentations. It's also important to realize that multimedia can represent one of the greatest threats to your computer system. After you understand what multimedia can do for your computer, make sure you set group policies that help improve the security of your system. For example, you might not want to allow downloads from online stores if you worry about downloads contaminating your network with viruses and spyware.

The next chapter delves into a new Vista feature, Windows Photo Gallery. You might initially think that this is a toy application designed to meet the needs of someone with a family and a wealth of pictures. However, Windows Photo Gallery is a great organizational tool for any kind of graphics. For example, I experimented with it as an organizational aid for the graphics in this book. Windows Photo Gallery is a good organizational tool for anyone who has pictures on their system, which is most of us.

Chapter 12

Windows Photo Gallery

Windows Photo Gallery is a tool for organizing graphics. The term *photo* in the title is unfortunate, because Windows Photo Gallery works with any kind of graphic image, not just photographs. Organization is important because no one wants to spend a day looking through one nondescript file at a time for a particular image. Unlike text, you can't search for graphics using keywords because there isn't any text within a graphic to search. Consequently, you must provide some other means of organizing and searching for graphics. Windows Photo Gallery provides the means to label and then view graphic images. Using Windows Photo Gallery, you can locate the image you need for a particular task quickly and easily. In this chapter, you'll learn about

- Looking for pictures and videos
- Categorizing the pictures and videos
- Filtering the information contained in Windows Photo Gallery
- Uploading pictures and videos to others
- Archiving pictures and videos for later use
- Printing your pictures

Viewing Pictures and Videos

You start Windows Photo Gallery by choosing Start ➤ All Programs ➤ Windows Photo Gallery. The initial view shows all of the videos and pictures in the standard locations on your system grouped by Year Taken and sorted by Date Taken as shown in Figure 12.1. Although this view works at the outset, you'll probably find it less than useful once you've added all of your pictures and videos.

Fortunately, you have a wealth of methods for reducing the eye overload that the initial windows Photo Gallery display can present. The sections that follow examine techniques you can use to make the viewing process easier on the eyes and faster as well. After all, the whole purpose of this application is to help you organize your images, not make them more frustrating to find.

TIP Each of the groups in a window has an arrow associated with it on the right side of the display. Click this arrow and Windows Photo Gallery hides the group; click it again and you see the group. This feature makes it easy to ignore groups that have nothing to do with your current search.

FIGURE 12.1
Windows Photo Gallery starts with a generic view of your media that requires configuration.

Seeing All Pictures and Videos

There are times when you really do want to view all of your pictures and videos, but you don't want to see them all at once. What you really want to do is see a subset of the videos and pictures, one group at a time. Consequently, the grouping and sorting features of Windows Photo Gallery are exceptionally important. You've already seen the effects of using proper grouping and sorting in other areas of Vista, such as the Control Panel and within Windows Explorer. Grouping and sorting work the same in Windows Photo Gallery, but there's an emphasis on making these two features work together.

Some of the groups that Windows Photo Gallery has might not apply to you. For example, if you have only one camera, then grouping the photographs by camera isn't going to accomplish much—you might as well choose None from the list of groups. In addition, the Camera grouping requires that you specify the camera-related tags (see the "Setting Picture and Video Properties" section of the chapter for details). It's also important to choose groupings that make sense for your photographic needs. For example, grouping the photographs by year if you take several thousand photographs each year simply isn't going to accomplish anything. In this case, you might choose the Month Taken or Date Taken groups instead.

After you choose a group that seems to work, your photographs will still appear in a random order within the group. The images you see in Figure 12.1 are the smallest that Windows Photo Gallery provides. Figure 12.2 shows the Tiles view that you can choose from the Choose a Thumbnail View drop-down list box (which also has groups and sorting options). As you can see, these images are considerably larger. Consequently, good sorting isn't just nice, it's a necessity if you really do want to find the image you need.

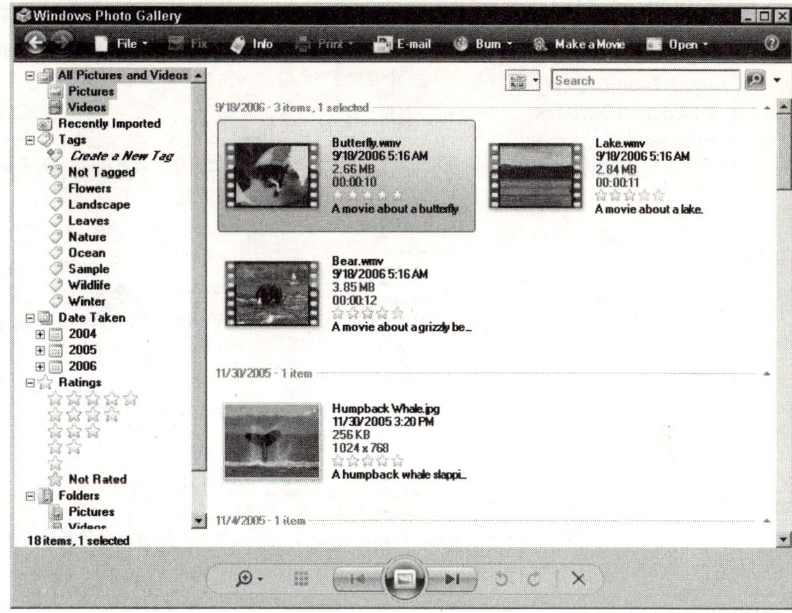

FIGURE 12.2
The Tiles view provides information about each entry, but consumes a lot of screen real estate.

TIP If the Tiles view isn't large enough to see everything you want, hover the mouse over the picture. Windows Photo Gallery produces an even larger image that includes the same basic information included with the tile. However, the print is a bit larger, making the information easier to see.

The one feature that can dramatically improve your ability to view a huge number of images quickly is the Table of Contents as shown in Figure 12.3. The Table of Contents appears to the left of the images and corresponds to the grouping you choose. If you don't see the information you want in the Table of Contents, simply change the grouping you use to obtain other information. You add this feature to the display by choosing the Table of Contents entry on the Choose a Thumbnail View drop-down list box. Clicking an entry takes you directly to that part of the listing. Use the up and down arrows to scroll through the entry list.

Filtering by Recently Imported

Windows Photo Gallery provides a number of filters to view subsets of the photographs in your collection quickly. In many cases, you'll want to review the photographs you've just taken, which is why the Recently Imported filter is so important. Unfortunately, no amount of testing would tell me precisely what "recently" means in the Microsoft mind. Anything you import today will most certainly appear in the list, but something imported last week may not appear. Unfortunately, Windows Photo Gallery doesn't provide any options for changing the meaning of recently imported either.

To view the recently imported items, select Recently Imported in the pane on the left side of the window. You'll see a list of recently imported items similar to the one shown in Figure 12.1 or 12.2 (depending on the view you choose).

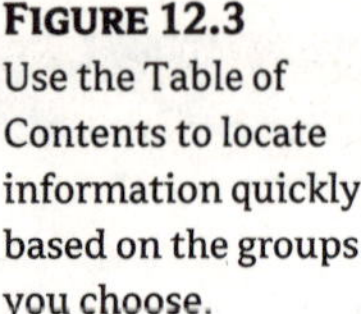

FIGURE 12.3
Use the Table of Contents to locate information quickly based on the groups you choose.

TIP When working with a filter, you always have the same grouping and sorting options that you do when using the All Pictures and Videos view. In fact, Windows Photo Gallery retains your grouping and sorting options as you move between filters so that only the number of items changes, not the way in which they're arranged.

Filtering by Tags

Filtering by tags is the most important filtering method that Windows Photo Gallery provides because tags reflect the way that you view the photographs. There are two ways to filter by tags and this section shows the simplest approach. The "Setting Picture and Video Properties" section of the chapter demonstrates a more complex approach that you'll want to use when you have many photographs to work with.

All of the tags you've defined appear in the left pane of the window as shown in Figure 12.1. When you click one of the tags, the display changes to show only the images that have tags attached to them. You'll even see a special Not Tagged entry you can choose when you want to find the photographs you haven't tagged yet. It's important that every image (even videos) have tags associated with them. Even more important, you must apply the tags consistently. After all, Vista has no idea of what the picture contains or what it means to you. Only you can make that determination.

If you're happy with one of the standard views, you can add tags directly within the main Windows Photo Gallery window. Simply highlight the image and click Info. You'll see information about the selected image appear in the right pane of the window as shown in Figure 12.4. Click Add Tags to add a new tag to the list. If you decide that a tag doesn't really apply to an image, select it and click Delete.

NOTE You can change most of the information shown in the Info pane. To change an item, select it and type a new value. Press Enter to make the change permanent or Escape to reverse the change.

FIGURE 12.4
The main window lets you add tags to your images quite quickly.

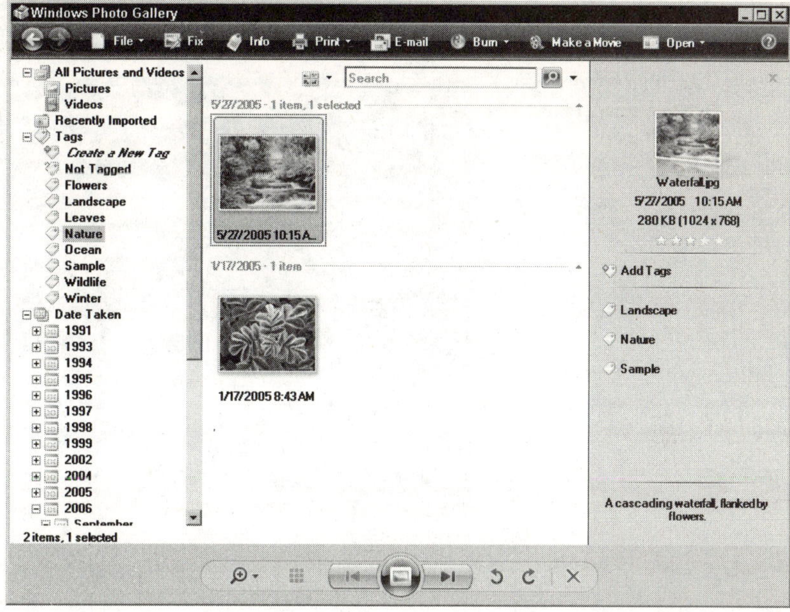

You might not always see the amount of detail that you need to add tags to your images using the main window. When this problem occurs, double-click the image to display a single image view similar to the one shown in Figure 12.5. In this case, Windows Photo Gallery automatically displays the Info pane. You enter the information just as you do in the main window. Click Back to Gallery (upper left corner) when you finish making changes to the image data. If the image still isn't large enough, you can use the Changes the Display Size control in the toolbar to zoom into the image (you can accomplish the same thing using the wheel of your mouse). Once the image is zoomed, you can access a particular part of the image by grabbing it with the mouse and dragging the image to one of the sides of the image area.

TIP It's important to keep tags short and simple to keep them effective. A short, simple tag can apply to a broader range of image types. If you only have one or two images associated with a particular tag, then the tag becomes ineffective. In addition, the left pane offers limited space to display the tags. You want to keep the tags short so that you can see the entire tag and not make selection errors.

Filtering by Date Taken

The Date Taken entry in the left pane helps you find images based on the date that you say they were taken. Windows Photo Gallery initially assumes that the date and time stamp on the file reflect the date the image was taken, but you can change this value using the techniques described in the "Filtering by Tags" section of the chapter. Why would you want to change the date and time for the images? Many people remember images based on context. A vacation taken last fall is memorable because Aunt Fannie fell into the river and you got it on film (or in digital form, as the case might be). Consequently, the date and time of an image is an important method of finding just the image you need.

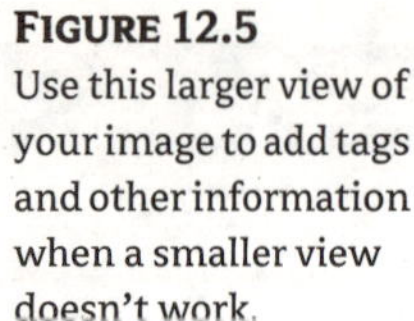

FIGURE 12.5
Use this larger view of your image to add tags and other information when a smaller view doesn't work.

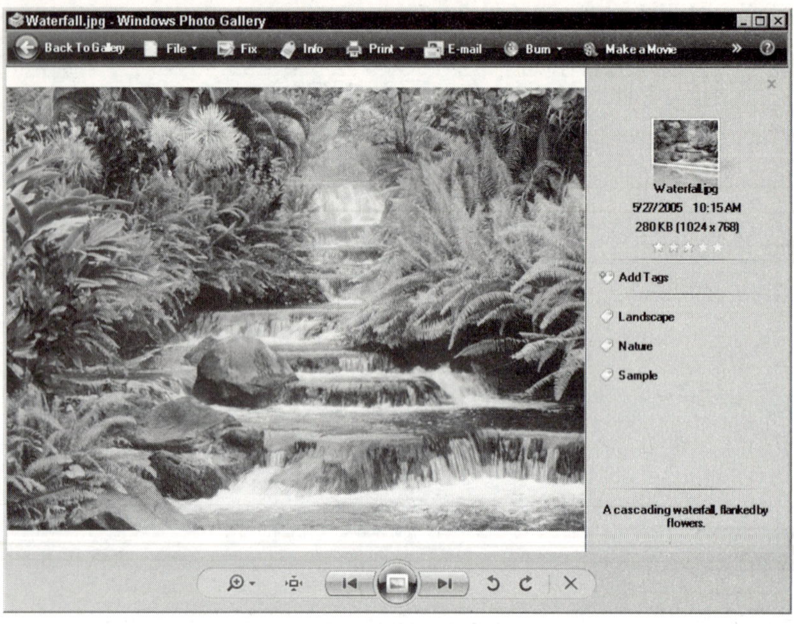

TIP You can press Ctrl+Click to select multiple items in the Date Taken (or any other) folder. However, you can't simply drag the mouse with the button down to select multiple items as you would in Windows Explorer.

Windows Photo Gallery organizes images by date at three levels. You can choose a particular year, month within a year, or a date within a month. Each level helps narrow the search for a particular image based on date alone.

NOTE An odd problem occurs when you change the date of an image. The image doesn't immediately move to the new folder. You have to close the folder and reopen it to see the image in the proper location. In addition, if the folder is now empty, Windows Photo Gallery still displays it until you close the application and restart it. The empty folder doesn't cause any problems, but the image area is empty when you select it.

Filtering by Rating

Image ratings are subjective. Ratings ask the question, "How much do you like the image?" There isn't any right or wrong answer, just your opinion of the image to consider. In fact, ratings you assign to images will change over time. The image you like today may fall out of favor tomorrow. Because ratings are so subjective, they provide a kind of soft search for images.

Ratings are probably most useful for personal or artistic images—those with aesthetic appeal. Many business users will never use this feature because the image is strictly information related. However, ratings can have a place in businesses as well. Instead of rating an image based on personal taste, you can always use the rating for other purposes. For example, you might rate an image based on the amount of customer attention that it attracted. Some websites actually provide a means for users to provide input on how they feel about a particular image. The point is that the ratings associated with images are always subjective.

Windows Photo Gallery lets you rate images from one to five stars. To see images with a particular rating, click the number of stars in the Ratings filter on the left side of the window. The Ratings filter also includes a Not Rated entry so you can quickly find the images that you haven't rated yet.

Filtering by Folder

Sometimes you know where something is located on your system and only want to work with files in that location. For example, I keep my business images completely separate from my personal images. The business images are further grouped by project in separate folders. Finally, some images appear in special folders because they contain special information. The point is that the physical location of the data is another means of organizing and filtering it.

Knowing how to work with folders is important for another reason. Unless you want those Vista sample pictures hanging around forever, you need to eliminate them from the gallery. The easiest way to get rid of these images is to right-click the `Public Pictures` and `Public Videos` folders in the Folders filter on the left side of the window and choose Delete from the context menu. Unfortunately, this action does delete the images, but at least you don't have to keep them around.

WARNING Deleting a folder or an image by right-clicking it and choosing Delete from the context menu always removes the images from the hard drive. Windows Photo Gallery actually places the images in the Recycle Bin, so you can recover them until you empty the Recycle Bin. If you want to remove a folder from the gallery, right-click its entry and choose Remove from Gallery from the context menu. For whatever reason, Microsoft chose not to include this option for the four standard folders: `Pictures`, `Videos`, `Public Pictures`, and `Public Videos` so your only choice is to delete them.

When you want to add your own images to the gallery, right-click Folders and choose Add Folder to Gallery from the context menu. You'll see the Add Folder to Gallery dialog box shown in Figure 12.6, where you can add any folder on your system or any network you can access.

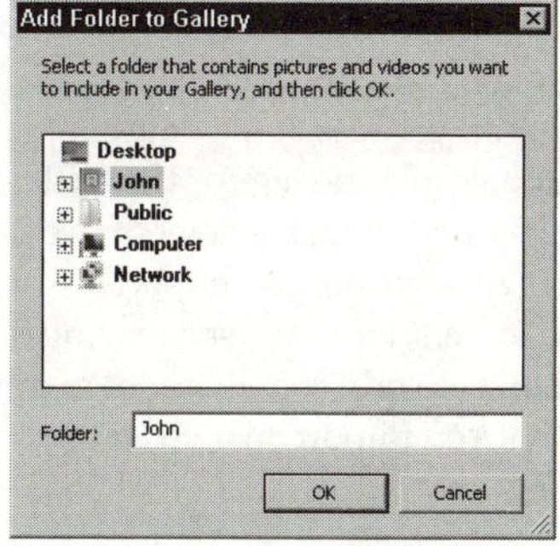

FIGURE 12.6 Add folders containing your personal images to the gallery as part of personalizing it.

Uploading New Pictures and Videos

Windows Photo Gallery doesn't just work with images that you already have on your system. You can also import images from other sources. The three sources of imports are removable media (CDs and DVDs), cameras, and scanners. In all three cases, you begin by configuring your system for the import. Choose File ➢ Options and you'll see the Windows Photo Gallery Options dialog box. Select the Import tab to see the options shown in Figure 12.7.

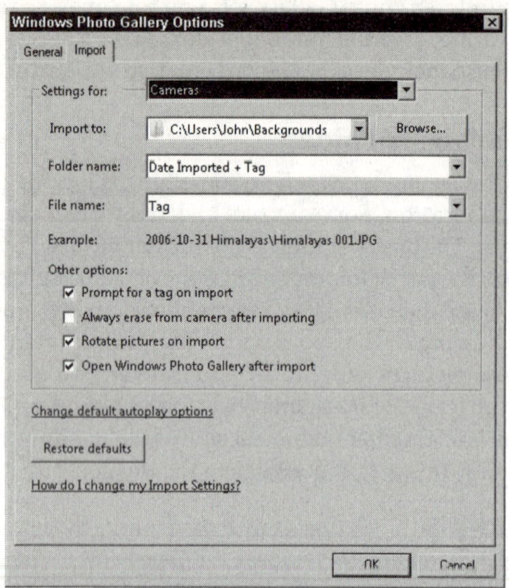

FIGURE 12.7
Configure the import options for use before you use them the first time.

Begin by choosing the kind of device you want to work with in the Settings For field. After you choose this setting, you can begin configuring the device. I find it's better not to use the standard folders that Microsoft supplies in the Import To field, because then you're stuck using other items that appear in those folders, such as sample Microsoft art. Using a separate folder is a better idea because then you can use the folder as part of your organizational strategy. To add a new folder, click Browse to display the Browse for Folder dialog box. Select a starting location (your personal folder works just fine for personal imports) and click Make New Folder. Type a name for the import area and click OK.

Every import appears in a subfolder of the folder that you just created. The Folder Name field describes how Windows Photo Gallery automatically names this folder. For example, you can choose to use the Date Imported and a special tag. Windows Photo Gallery asks you for this tag as part of the import process. If the date isn't important to you (after all, each file will include one), you can choose to use just the tag for the folder name.

The other options in this dialog box are self-explanatory. For example, you can choose to erase the camera automatically after you import the pictures. Unless you really don't want to provide a name for the imported folders, I recommend leaving the Prompt for a Tag on Import option checked. Otherwise, you can end up with odd combinations of imports when Windows Photo Gallery mixes together all of the images that you import on a given day.

Managing Pictures and Videos

By now, you have a whole host of images added to the Windows Photo Gallery as folders and imports. However, just having the images added and (hopefully) categorized isn't enough. This utility can do a lot more, which is where this section of the chapter fits in. The following sections describe some of the additional management you can perform with your gallery once you have it put together.

Setting Picture and Video Properties

The tags that you created in the "Filtering by Tags" section of the chapter are nice and may be all you need. However, as your gallery becomes more complex and your techniques for acquiring images more advanced, you'll very likely find a need to add additional properties to the images that you work with. However, you can't access these properties directly from the main window. What you need to do instead is right-click the image and choose Properties from the context menu. You'll see a wealth of properties like the ones shown in Figure 12.8.

Vista automatically provides some of these properties. For example, most of the entries in the File section of the properties are provided automatically. You can change the size of the image file simply by changing the Size field. Likewise, you can't change the Dimensions field in the Image section. However, these properties are informational and can help you discover more about the image.

You can change a wealth of other properties that aren't normally accessible. For example, you can change most of the entries in the Origin section (except the Program Name field). It's also possible to change the entries in the Camera and Advanced Photo sections.

After you make these changes, click OK. The information becomes available immediately for use in selecting the images. For example, the camera information appears as one of the groups you can use to organize the information. The point is to give you as many organizational aids as possible so you can locate images quickly.

Sharing Your Library

As with many of the media features of Vista, you'll find that you can share anything you create with Windows Photo Gallery. Choose File ➤ Share with Devices and you'll see the Media Sharing dialog box. You can learn more about this dialog box in the "Sharing Media" section of Chapter 11.

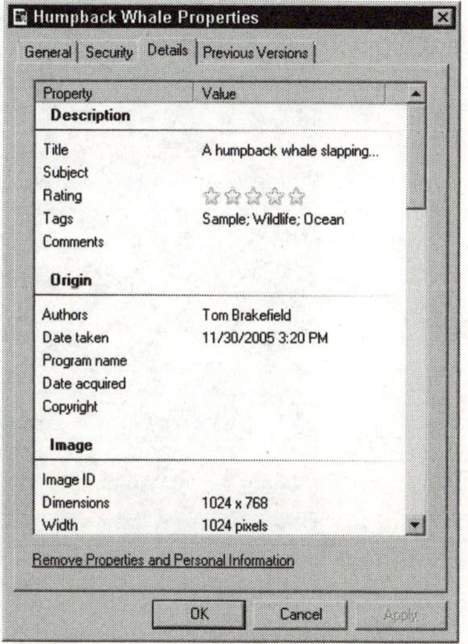

FIGURE 12.8
Add as many properties and tags as needed to images to fully identify them.

Fixing Pictures

It's important to remember that Windows Photo Gallery isn't a professional tool that helps you perform any graphic manipulation that you deem necessary. However, the number of tools you get will serve many basic needs. For example, you can fix common photographic problems such as the exposure setting for underexposed or overexposed images. To fix an image, highlight it and click Fix. You'll see a display similar to the one shown in Figure 12.9.

In many cases, you can tell Windows Photo Gallery to fix common problems by clicking Auto Adjust. The application will scan the photograph for problems, make the adjustments, and place a check mark next to the problem it solved. For example, if Windows Photo Gallery makes a change to the color, you'll see a check mark next to Adjust Color.

The other options on the right side of the display are manual. For example, when you click Adjust Exposure, you'll see sliders for adjusting brightness and contrast. These sliders affect the image as a whole, so you often need to adjust the settings to obtain a good balance, rather than a perfect image. If you don't like a particular change, click Undo at the bottom of the window.

Some changes, such as Crop, require that you interact directly with the image as shown in Figure 12.10. You can change the position of the cropping area, adjust the size of the crop, and even rotate the frame. If you want to make sure that the resulting image is a specific size, such as 4 × 6, you can choose an option from the Proportion drop-down list box.

Windows Photo Gallery doesn't leave you without recourse if you decide that you really don't like the changes you made. To return your image to its previous glory, right-click the image and choose Properties. Select the Previous Versions tab. Highlight the previous version that you want to use and click Restore. The image will appear as it did before.

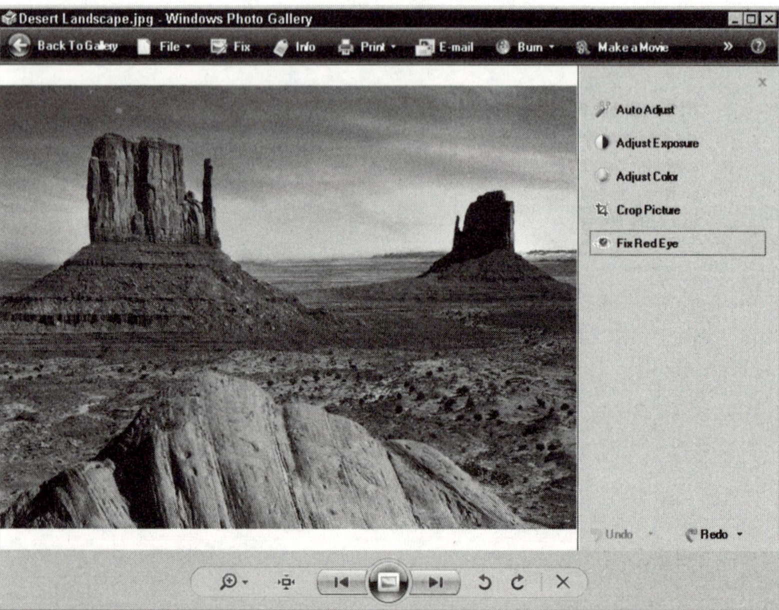

FIGURE 12.9
Make common changes to images using the simple tools that Windows Photo Gallery provides.

Of course, all of these shadow copies can quickly become a problem on your system because they keep collecting when you use the default settings. You can change this behavior by choosing File ➤ Options to display the Windows Photo Gallery Options dialog box. Select the General tab. Choose a value other than Never in the Move Original to Recycle Bin After field. Even when Windows Photo Gallery moves the file, you can still restore it from the Recycle Bin. Simply right-click the file and choose Restore from the context menu to restore it.

Creating Data Discs and Movies

You can create data discs that contain elements from your gallery. The Burn menu contains options for create a data disc or a video DVD. The process for creating either form of media is very much the same as described in Chapter 11 (see the "Burning CDs" and "Burning DVDs with Windows DVD Maker" sections of Chapter 11).

When you select either option from the Burn menu, Windows Photo Gallery checks your CD or DVD drive for the appropriate media. It then starts the standard application for working with the kind of output you want to create. Consequently, you won't find any surprises when you want to create removable media for your gallery.

Likewise, when you click Make a Movie, Windows Photo Gallery opens the Windows Movie Maker application. You can learn more about this application in the "Using Windows Movie Maker" section of Chapter 13.

In all three cases, Windows Photo Gallery automatically sends a copy of whatever you've highlighted to the target application. Consequently, when the application opens, the media you want to output is already in the application. All you need to do is create the desired media.

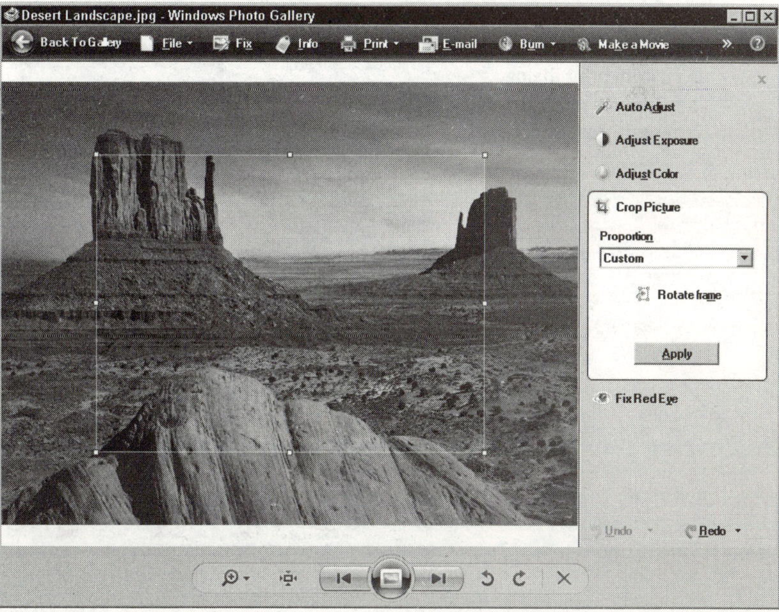

FIGURE 12.10
You can crop images so that they print out at specific photographic sizes.

Ordering Prints

At one time, you had to run down to the corner drugstore, drop off your prints, come back a week later, and pick them up. With Windows Photo Gallery, you can cut out at least part of that cycle by sending your prints to the lab directly. To send your pictures to a lab for printing, follow these steps:

1. Select the pictures you want printed.
2. Choose Print ➤ Order prints. Windows Photo Gallery looks for a lab in your area. It displays one or more of these locations in the Order Prints window.
3. Choose one of the places that you know or at least looks reputable and click Send Pictures. You'll see a warning dialog box telling you that you'll be sending the prints and that anyone receiving them may see personal information.
4. Click Send. Follow the instructions for the particular lab you choose. The instructions vary by lab. You'll need to choose picture format and so on, along with providing a credit card for the transaction.

Printing Your Pictures

Printing pictures in Windows Photo Gallery is different from printing other material. Because pictures require special handling, Windows Photo Gallery provides a customized print dialog box. Make sure you have your printer turned on because some printing choices require that Vista communicate with the printer. Choose Print ➤ Print To display the Print Pictures dialog box shown in Figure 12.11.

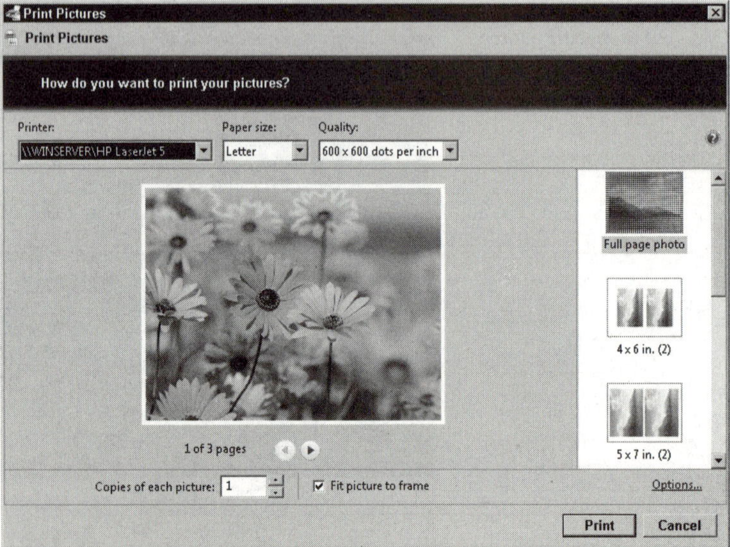

FIGURE 12.11
A custom print dialog box lets you print pictures with less effort.

Begin by choosing the printer you want to use, the paper size, and the quality of the output since these settings all affect other options you can choose. Along the right side of the dialog box, you'll see a list of common output sizes. You can create everything from wallet-sized prints to full-page output. The number of copies of each picture setting affects how many pages you need to print the size images you request.

WARNING Clear the Fit Picture to Frame option when printing standard image sizes such as wallet or 4 × 6. If you don't clear this option, the pictures end up slightly oversized and won't fit within a frame as expected.

After you make all of your selections, click Print. Windows Photo Gallery will send the output to the printer.

You do need to be aware of two options that the Print Pictures dialog box offers. Click the Options link and you'll see the Print Settings dialog box shown in Figure 12.12. Windows Photo Gallery doesn't make these options available through the Windows Photo Gallery Options dialog box (open using File ➤ Options), so you need to set them here.

The first option, Sharpen for printing, ensures that the output is as clear as possible. If you clear this option, the output will appear faster, but won't have the photographic quality you expect. The second option, Only, shows options that are compatible with my printer and reduces the selections in the drop-down list boxes to those that your printer supports. You may want to clear this option if you're using a printer driver that is almost the right one for your printer, but not quite. In this case, your printer may provide functionality that the printer driver doesn't tell Vista about. However, you'll want to use this option with care because you don't want to send incorrect output when working with more expensive papers (always create a test output with low-cost paper first).

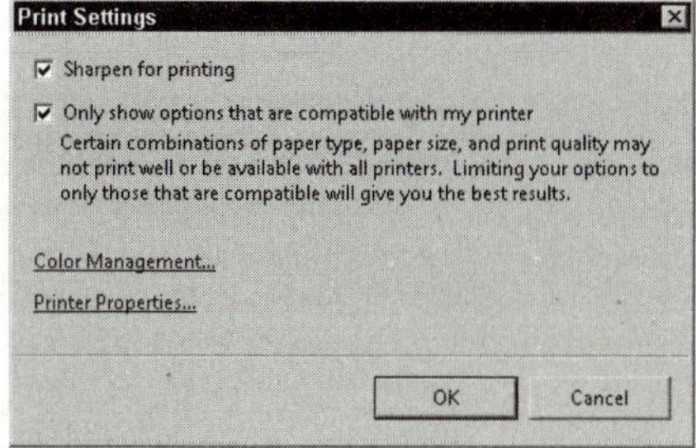

FIGURE 12.12
Set the printing options as necessary for your printer.

Emailing a Picture or Video

One of the most common ways to sent pictures or video today is through email. Using email is fast and low cost. It's not quite the same as getting a printed copy, but certainly good enough for many situations. To send a picture or video by email, use the following steps.

1. Select the pictures you want to send using email.
2. Click Email. You'll see an Attach Files dialog box like the one shown in Figure 12.13. Notice the email size estimate directly below the Picture Size drop-down list box. This value changes

as you change the picture size. It's important to monitor this value because email boxes limit the amount of data you can send. Many email setups today limit you to between 2 MB and 4 MB, although it's easy to find ISPs that allow nearly unlimited email capacity.

3. Choose one of the options from the Picture Size drop-down list. Click Attach. You'll see a standard message open with the files attached. Depending on the email client you use, you might see some special features. For example, Outlook asks how you want to share the pictures and whether you want to resize them. The message itself is in plain text, rather than using the standard HTML format.

4. Add a list of recipients, change the subject, add any special message text, and then click Send. Your email client will send the pictures.

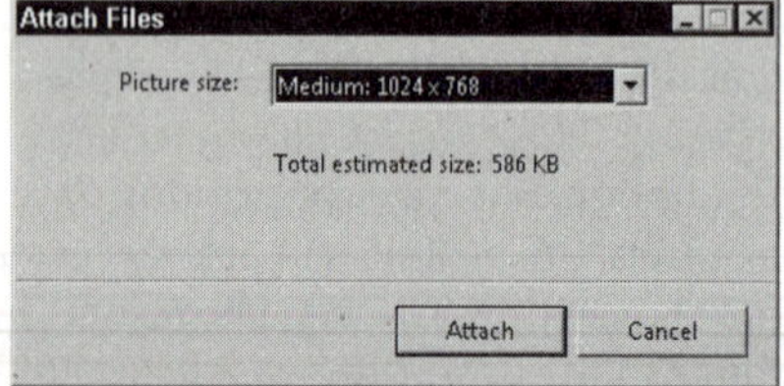

FIGURE 12.13
Choose an image size for your pictures and Windows Photo Gallery will estimate the size.

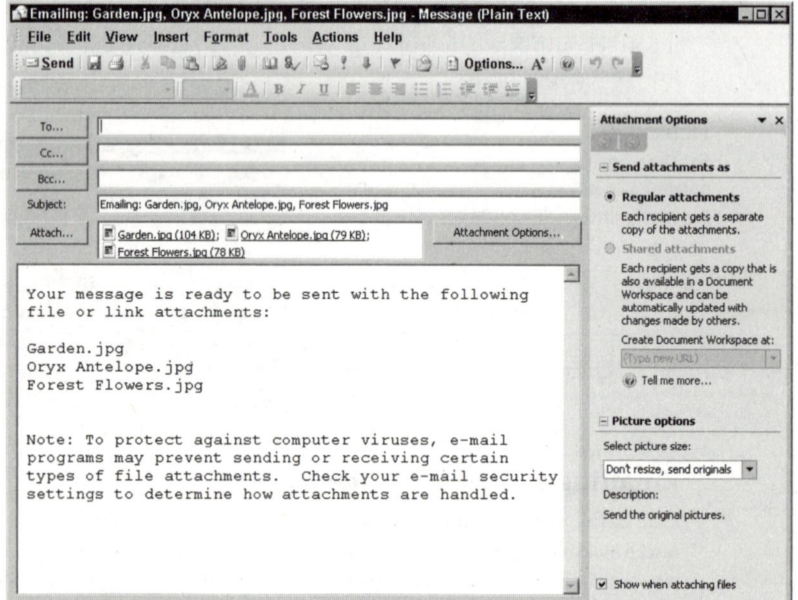

FIGURE 12.14
Your email application may provide special support for sending pictures.

Summary

This chapter has described how to use Windows Photo Gallery for various tasks. The simplicity of this application belies its ability to work in a number of situations, both professional and personal. You may find that this is one of those features that you stumble across and are glad that you did when you discover what it does. The long and short of using Windows Photo Gallery is that it helps you organize, categorize, and search for graphics in a way that no other Windows tool has done in the past.

One of the problems with using Windows Photo Gallery is that you must do some work to make it worthwhile. While it's possible to search for text files on your system using the content alone, graphics don't provide content that the computer can easily recognize. You must describe the content to the computer so that it can provide an effective means of search. Consequently, the first task you must perform after you locate your graphics files is to describe them. If you have the number of graphics files that I do, the description process can take a long time and might prove frustrating, but it's worth it in the end to avoid spend even more time looking for that one elusive graphic on your hard drive.

The next chapter describes how to acquire and view images using various techniques. For example, you'll discover how to get Vista to work with your scanner and video camera. This chapter also discusses how to use the Windows Movie Maker to create your own movies. Creating a movie can be fun and it's just another way for businesses to present information to potential clients.

Chapter 13

Digital Media and Movie Maker

In Chapter 11, I showed you how Windows Media Player helps manage sound and video files, but what about still graphics, like the ones you acquire from scanners and cameras? Sure, you can use Windows Photo Gallery (described in Chapter 12), but this new Vista application may not provide everything you need. In this chapter, we'll look at how Windows interacts with graphic files. We will also explore the Windows Movie Maker application, which enables you to build your own graphic and video presentations.

- Understanding image formats
- Acquiring images from a scanner or digital camera
- Viewing images in Windows Explorer
- Making prints of digital pictures
- Using Windows Movie Maker

Acquiring Images

Image files come from various sources, including Internet downloads, e-mail attachments, digital cameras, and scanners. If you're getting an image file that someone else has already digitized—like your Aunt Velda's photos of downtown Ketchikan that she e-mailed to you from the cruise ship—then the format and resolution have already been predetermined. When you digitize pictures on your own, however, you get to make some choices.

Understanding Image Formats

Why are there so many image formats, anyway? Here are my theories:

- Because different formats are suitable for different uses
- Because people who work with graphics a lot are always looking for ways to improve on the weaknesses of whatever format they are stuck using
- Because there are lots of companies that want to make big bucks by inventing the perfect image format

Don't laugh—these are real. There are tons of image formats, and each one was created for one of these reasons.

You don't need to know the intricate details of every image format out there, but you should know the basics of a half-dozen of the most popular ones so that you can make good choices about what format is appropriate for what job.

When evaluating an image format, here are some questions you should ask:

Size How large is the size of the file compared to the same image saved in some other format? If you're planning to use the file for the Web, you should know that using small files provides a great advantage. You can decrease file size by applying compression to the file.

Compression type Is the file type compressible? If so, does it use lossless compression (compression with no loss of quality) or lossy compression (compression that sacrifices image quality somewhat)? For Web and on-screen use, a lossy compression format is fine, but for print, you'll want something that is either lossless or uncompressed.

Compatibility Is it a well-known format that many applications support? A graphic file seldom stands alone; you need an image viewer to look at it, and it usually gets put into an application to accompany some text. The best graphic format in the world is no good if the application you use doesn't support it.

Color Depth Does the format have any limitations on the number of colors you can use? For example, GIF has a 256-color limitation, making it unsuitable for photography.

Special Features Does the format support any special features that most other formats don't? For example, does it support 48-bit color definition? Does it support animation? (For example, GIF and PNG can store several versions of a graphic in the same file and then alternate between them for a crude animation effect.) Does it support alpha channels for transparency?

Table 13.1 evaluates some of the most popular image formats based on these criteria.

Besides the image's format, the other consideration is its resolution—the number of pixels vertically and horizontally that make up the image.

TABLE 13.1: Image File Formats

	TIF	JPG	GIF	PNG	BMP
Size	Large	Small	Small	Small	Large
Compression	Lossless	Lossy	Lossless	Lossless	None
Compatibility	Excellent	Excellent	Good	Good	Good
Max. Color Depth	48-bit	24-bit	8-bit	48-bit	24-bit
Special	Alpha channel support		Can be animated	Alpha channel support	
Notes	Widely considered the best format for high-resolution print publications	Widely considered the best format for web page use	Proprietary compression algorithm	Improved version of GIF	Native format for Windows graphics

The "correct" resolution for a picture is almost entirely usage dependent. To avoid loss of image quality, you want to make sure that there will be enough pixels to display or print the image at the size you want.

For example, suppose you take a picture with your digital camera in a 1,024 × 768 image mode. (Most cameras do better than that today, but let's go with a conservative example.) Now you want to display it on a web page. Computer monitors display at 96 dots per inch (dpi), so you could display this image at a huge size on a web page without losing one iota of quality. In fact, 1024 × 768 is probably too big for optimal Web use, because it will take longer than necessary to download.

Now, let's say you want to print that picture on a 1,200 dpi color printer, and you want a regular-sized photo print (4 × 6). At 1,200 dpi, the native size for that picture would be less than 1″ wide (1,024 pixels), so to print it at 6″ wide, you would need to enlarge it sixfold. Since those extra five pixels between the actual ones don't exist, your software must create them by averaging the values of the surrounding pixels, resulting in a blurry mess.

The moral of the story: Consider the context in which you'll be using an image and resize it if you need to. Use an image-editing program such as Adobe Photoshop or Jasc's Paint Shop Pro to cut the resolution to fit the needs of the project. Unfortunately, you can't do much to increase the resolution of a picture, so try to capture or scan images in a higher resolution than you think you'll need, and then preserve that high-res original for later repurposing.

Transferring Images from a Digital Camera

When you connect a digital camera to the PC, a box pops up, as in Figure 13.1. Your choices may vary depending on what applications are installed. You might also see a proprietary screen instead of this one if you have some special application installed for photo handling (such as the one that came with your camera, for example).

You have several options to choose here, including viewing the pictures with the Windows Media Center. Vista offers the new option of using the Windows Photo Gallery (see Chapter 12 for details), but doesn't provide some of the options found in older versions of Windows. You can also choose Open Folder to View Files.

All those wizards are great, but I most often stick with the basics and choose Open Folder to View Files. This opens the camera's storage as a removable disk, much like a flash RAM drive. You can then just drag and drop the pictures onto your hard disk or desktop. Unlike previous versions of Windows, Vista uses a standard easy-to-use folder as shown in Figure 13.2.

FIGURE 13.1
Choices offered when connecting a digital camera.

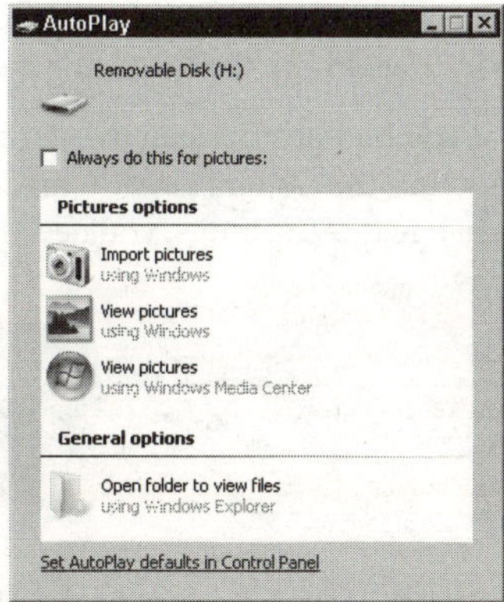

FIGURE 13.2
Open the camera like any other folder.

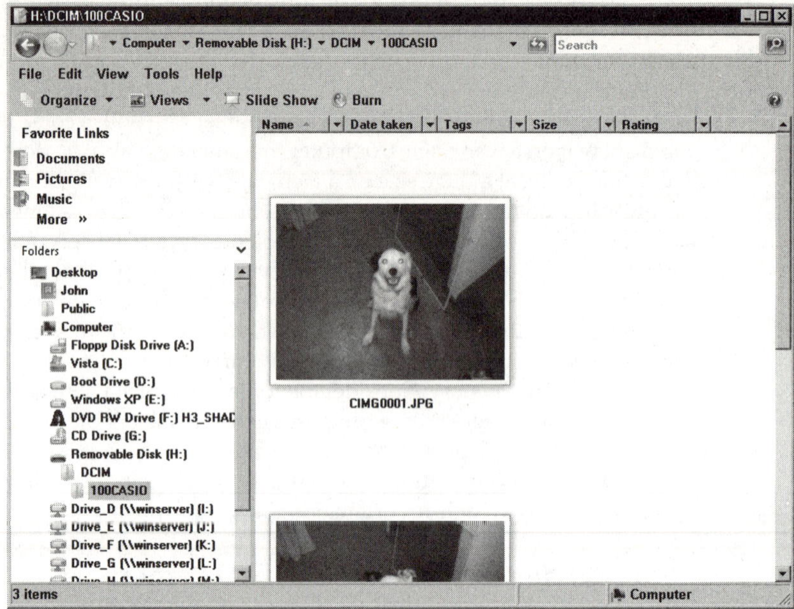

In the interests of completeness, let's look at the Import Pictures method too:

1. After connecting the camera, choose Import Pictures. Vista automatically scans the camera's hard drive and displays the first picture it finds. You'll see the Importing Pictures and Videos dialog box shown in Figure 13.3.
2. Type a tag for the picture.
3. Click options. You'll see the Import Settings dialog box shown in Figure 13.4.
4. Choose the import options that you want to use to import the pictures (the "Uploading New Pictures and Videos" section of Chapter 12 describes these options in more detail).
5. Click OK to close the Import Settings dialog box. Click Import to start the importing process.
6. Repeat steps 2 through 5 for each picture. After you complete the final picture, Vista opens the Windows Photo Gallery with the Recently Imported filter selected.

Notice that you had no choice in the steps of the preceding exercise for either resolution or file format. That's because the camera already made those decisions for you when you took the pictures. If you want to change those settings, you need to do so in the camera itself. (Time to drag out its manual.)

FIGURE 13.3
Provide a tag for the picture that you're importing from the camera.

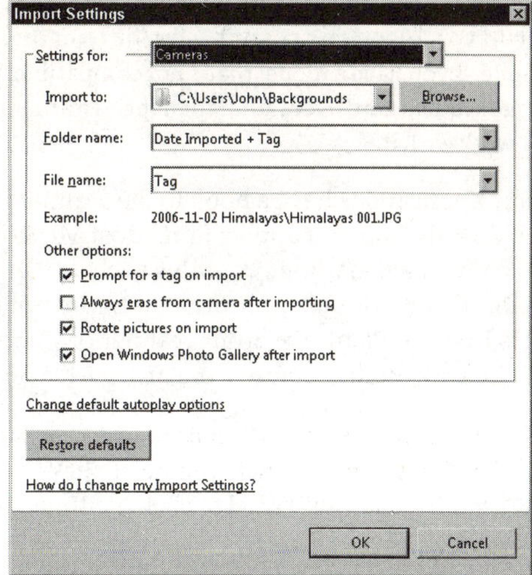

FIGURE 13.4
Set the import options for your camera.

Something interesting does happen when working with Vista. Right-click any of the pictures you imported and choose Properties. Scroll down to the Camera section. Vista automatically records all of the pertinent camera information for you, as shown in Figure 13.5.

Acquiring Images from a Scanner

When you snap a photo with a digital camera, you're digitizing the image right then and there. Any later relationship you have with the PC is strictly on a transfer basis, as you just saw.

On the other hand, with a scanner, you are digitizing the image *during* the interaction between the PC and the scanner, so you have much more control over the process. You can choose both the resolution and the image file format.

FIGURE 13.5
Vista automatically records all of the particulars of the camera for you when working with a digital camera.

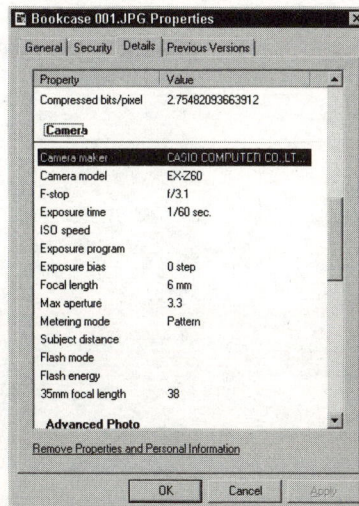

Bookcase 001.JPG Properties

General | Security | Details | Previous Versions

Property	Value
Compressed bits/pixel	2.75482093663912
Camera	
Camera maker	CASIO COMPUTER CO.,LT...
Camera model	EX-Z60
F-stop	f/3.1
Exposure time	1/60 sec.
ISO speed	
Exposure program	
Exposure bias	0 step
Focal length	6 mm
Max aperture	3.3
Metering mode	Pattern
Subject distance	
Flash mode	
Flash energy	
35mm focal length	38
Advanced Photo	

Remove Properties and Personal Information

OK | Cancel | Apply

WARNING Not all scanners work equally well with Vista. Check the Hardware Compatibility List (`http://www.microsoft.com/hcl`) for the specific models that are guaranteed to be compatible. If you have a model that's not compatible, it will still work, but you'll need to use its own image acquisition driver rather than the Vista one. The Scanner and Camera Wizard will probably not work with it.

Many applications have a hook to the scanner built into them, so you can acquire the image and place it directly into that application. Most Microsoft Office XP and 2003 applications are like that, as are many image-editing programs such as Paint Shop Pro and Photoshop. Check the documentation for the individual application to figure out how to access it. In Office applications, the command is Insert ➢ Picture ➢ From Scanner or Camera. In this chapter, however, I'll show you the stand-alone method, separate from any particular application.

NOTE The first time you attempt to use a scanner with Vista, you'll see a Windows Firewall warning. To use the scanner, you must click Unblock. Of course, Vista will display the usual UAC warning and you'll need to click Continue to clear it.

To scan an image on a Vista-compatible scanner, follow these steps:

1. Choose Start ➢ All Programs ➢ Windows Fax and Scan. You'll see the Windows Fax and Scan window.
2. Click New Scan. You'll see the New Scan dialog box shown in Figure 13.6.
3. Choose the scanning options you want to use. Begin with the Profile field first since this field controls many of the presets for your scanner. In fact, after your first scan, you'll find a Last Used Settings profile. Make sure you set the Color Format and Resolution fields appropriately.
4. Click Scan. Windows Fax and Scan will scan the image and place it in the Scan folder. After the scan completes, you can right-click the file and place it in a new folder. You can also send it to someone else using e-mail or forward it as a fax. Finally, you can right-click the entry, choose Save As from the context menu, and place the scanned image on your hard drive.

FIGURE 13.6
Choose the settings for the scan.

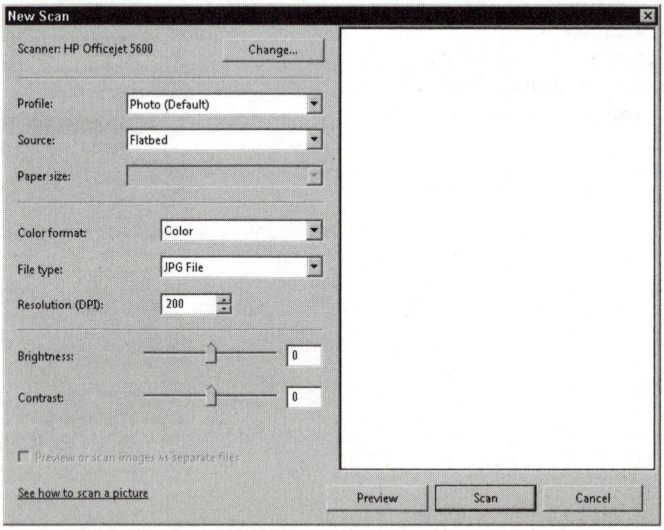

Viewing Images

Vista tries to be very user friendly when it comes to pictures, to the point where, to a hardcore techie, it can be downright insulting. There's a special utility for doing everything from looking at a picture to printing a copy of it. Still, you can't really fault Microsoft for catering to the largest segment of the Vista audience.

Viewing a Picture Slide Show

Many of my non-techie friends (yes, I have non-techie friends) seem to be really enamored with showing pictures on their monitors and televisions in full-screen mode, like the PC was a slide projector of yore. Personally, I don't understand the appeal of this.

NOTE **This feature uses the Aero Glass functionality, even if you don't have Aero Glass enabled. Consequently, you might find that you can't use this feature if your display adapter doesn't provide the capability Aero Glass requires.**

Right-click a folder containing pictures and choose Properties from the context menu. On the Customize tab, choose Pictures and Videos in the Use This Folder Type as a Template field. Optionally, you can check the Also Apply This Template to All Subfolders option. Click OK and Vista changes the folder type. To make maximum use of the change, choose Organize ➤ Layout ➤ Details Pane and Organize ➤ Layout ➤ Preview Pane. At this point, you should see the graphics options in the menu bar, as shown in Figure 13.7.

Notice that you can burn pictures now with a simple click. However, the option of interest is Slide Show. Click this button and your display will turn into a full-screen slide show. You'll see controls to pause and start the slide show. In addition, you can move between images manually. Click Exit when you don't want to see the slide show any longer.

FIGURE 13.7
Use the Pictures and Videos template for folders containing pictures.

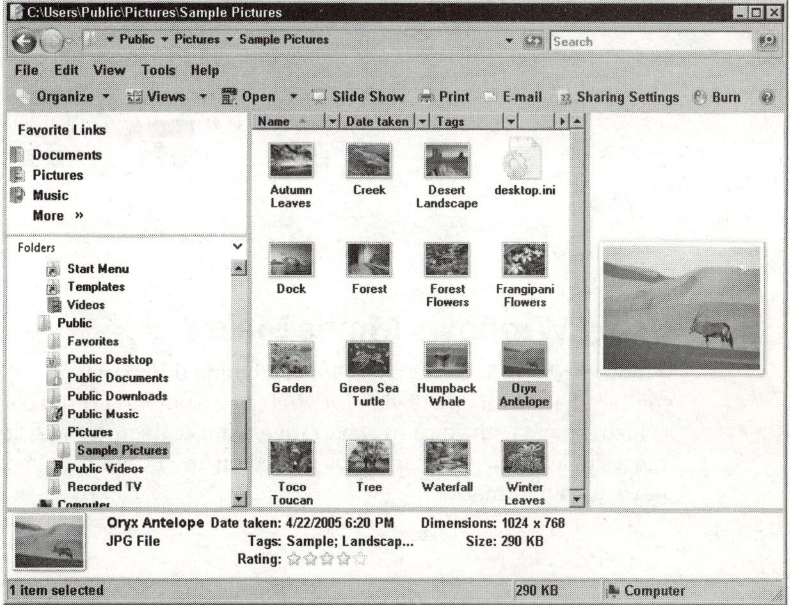

In addition to these basic controls, you can change the way the slide show moves between images and how it presents them by choosing one of the options on the Themes menu. The Properties menu (the one that has an icon that looks like a gear) lets you change the speed of presentation. You can also control whether the slide show continues in a loop and whether the slide show shuffles the images to present them in a random order.

Setting a Picture as a Windows Background

The easy way to set a picture as a Windows wallpaper background is to right-click it and choose Set as Desktop Background. You can also open up the Personalization window (right-click the Desktop and choose Personalize), click the Desktop Background link, click Browse, locate the folder you want to use for images, and then choose the image you want to use, as shown in Figure 13.8. This method has the advantage of enabling you to choose a solid background to turn off the wallpaper feature entirely. You can also choose a Position (Stretch, Center, or Tile).

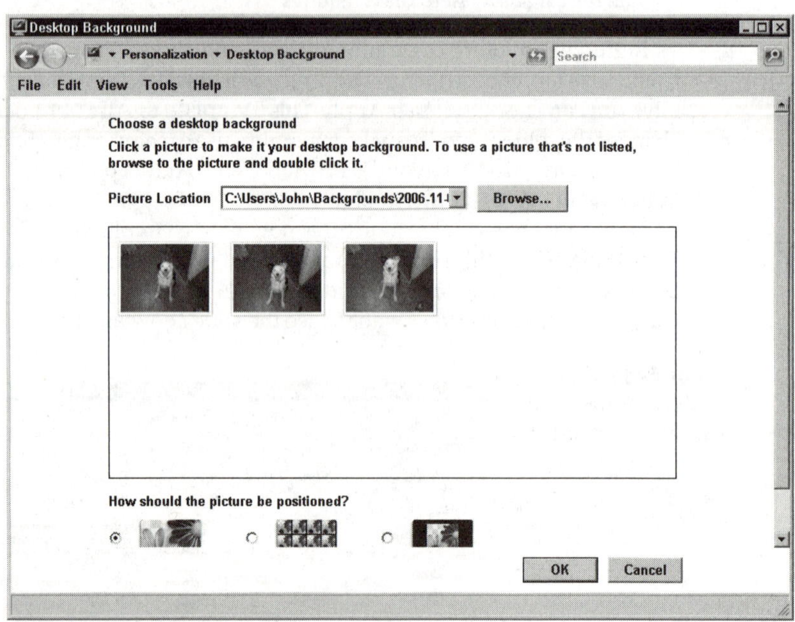

FIGURE 13.8
Choose an image that you want to use for a background on your computer.

Using Windows Movie Maker

Windows Movie Maker is a tool for combining different kinds of media clips into "movies" that you can share with others via disk, Web, or e-mail. You could combine home video footage from a video camera with voice-over narrative, a musical soundtrack, still photos, and other media types into a single movie file that can be played on any PC with a player that supports the Microsoft movie (`.mov`) format.

NOTE If you want to use footage from a video camera, you need a way of getting it into the PC. If it's a digital video camera, that's simple—just hook it up to the PC via whatever interface type it uses. (Most digital video cameras use a FireWire port, which you might need to add on a PCI expansion card.) If it's an analog camera, or you want to transfer from videotape with a VCR, you need a video interface device to convert from analog to digital format.

Here's the big picture for creating a movie:

1. Create one or more collections. *Collections* are organizational folders for content, and they are not specific to a particular movie project. Once you import a clip, it can be used again and again in different movies.
2. Import or record the content for the movie into the collections.
3. Start a new movie project, and place the media clips into it.
4. Add a soundtrack or voice narration if desired.
5. Save your project.
6. Export your project to a movie file. You can't edit a movie file; that's why you save the project first, in case you need to make changes to the movie. You can make the changes to the project and then re-export.

The following sections look at these steps in more detail. Start up Windows Movie Maker (Start ➤ All Programs ➤ Windows Movie Maker) and then proceed through these sections.

NOTE There have been several versions of Windows Movie Maker. This chapter covers the most recent version at this writing—Version 5.1, the one that came with Vista. You can download the newest version through Windows Update for free.

Creating Collections

Collections are organized beneath a master folder called My Collections. It's a lot like the folder tree in Windows Explorer. Here's what to do to create a collection:

NOTE Windows Movie Maker has a Task view and a Collections view. Click Show or Hide Collections to display the Collections view. You'll see this option in the middle pane when you have either the Task view or Collections view shown or in the right pane when you don't.

1. Click the collection you want the new one to appear under. Click Imported Media to create a top-level collection.
2. Choose File ➤ New Collection Folder.
3. Type a name for the collection and press Enter.

You might want a collection for video clips, another for still photos, one for sound files, and so on. Figure 13.9 shows several collections ready for use. You can have multiple levels in the folder hierarchy; that's the point of clicking the parent collection in step 1.

FIGURE 13.9
Set up your collections for storing incoming clips.

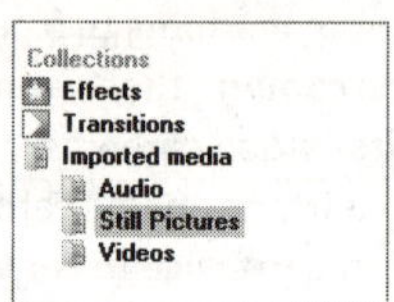

Importing Content

The easiest way to get content into a collection is to import existing content from your hard disk. To do so, follow these steps:

1. Select the collection into which you want to import.
2. Choose File ➤ Import from Digital Video Camera (to obtain pictures from your camera) or File ➤ Import Media Items (to obtain any form of media on a local or network drive). When working with a camera, you'll see a wizard for accessing it (see the "Recording Video Content" section for details). Otherwise, the Import Media Items dialog box opens.
3. Locate and select the media you want to import, then click Import to import it. You can import sounds, videos, and still images.

You can drag clips between collections if you find that you imported it into the wrong folder; it's just like working with files in Windows Explorer.

TIP You can't import CD audio directly from a CD, but you can use Windows Media Player to convert it to WMA or MP3 format and then import that file from disk.

Recording Content

If you have a digital video camera that can be used while attached to the PC, a microphone, or some other input device, you can record new content directly into Movie Maker.

Recording Video Content

You can directly record video content only if you have a supported video device—for example, a digital video camera that can record while it's hooked up to the PC, or another brand of analog-to-digital converter such as Dazzle.

Assuming you do have a supported device, here's how to record with it:

1. Make sure the device is connected to the PC and that your PC recognizes it. You may need to go through the Add Hardware Wizard, as described in Chapter 10.
2. Choose File ➤ Import from Digital Video Camera.
3. The Import from Digital Video Camera dialog box opens. Select the desired camera (if there is more than one).
4. Choose the audio input device from the Audio Device list. Adjust the audio input level by dragging its slider up or down.
5. Choose an audio input source from the Audio Input Source list. This is usually a microphone.

6. Make any other adjustments you desire. Click the Configure button to see the available settings for your video equipment.
7. Click Next. Then enter a filename for the captured video and specify a location in which it should be saved.
8. Click Next. A screen appears where you can adjust the recording quality.
9. Leave the Best Quality for Playback on My Computer option selected, and click Next.
10. The Capture Video screen appears. Adjust any settings here as desired, and then click Start Capture.

NOTE If you use Create Clips, it breaks the video into separate clips whenever it detects a different frame (such as when you turn the camera on or off or turn off the Pause feature). Otherwise, it records a single, long video clip.

11. When you're done recording, click Stop Capture.
12. Repeat steps 10 and 11 to capture more clips if desired. When you are done, click Finish.

If you marked Create Clips, it creates a separate folder containing the multiple clips. If you didn't, it creates a single file with the name you specified.

Creating a Movie Project

Now you're ready to create the movie project. Remember that the clips in collections are available to all movie projects; your collections are entirely separate from any particular project.

When Windows Movie Maker starts, it starts a blank movie project. You can go with this one or create a new one with the File ➤ New Project command.

Adding Visual Content to a Project

Simply start dragging visual content (video or still photos) from collections into the project area at the bottom of the window in the order that you want it to appear in the movie.

There are two project views. Storyboard view is the default; it's the one that looks like a filmstrip. Each clip takes up an equal amount of space in Storyboard view, regardless of its actual length. You can work only with visual clips in Storyboard view; there's no audio track displayed. See Figure 13.10.

Timeline view shows each visual clip's size according to the amount of time it will remain on screen. In Timeline view, you see a soundtrack line below the visual clips, indicating what sounds will play as each visual image appears. See Figure 13.11.

To switch between them, click the Timeline or Storyboard button.

FIGURE 13.10 Storyboard view shows visual clips only.

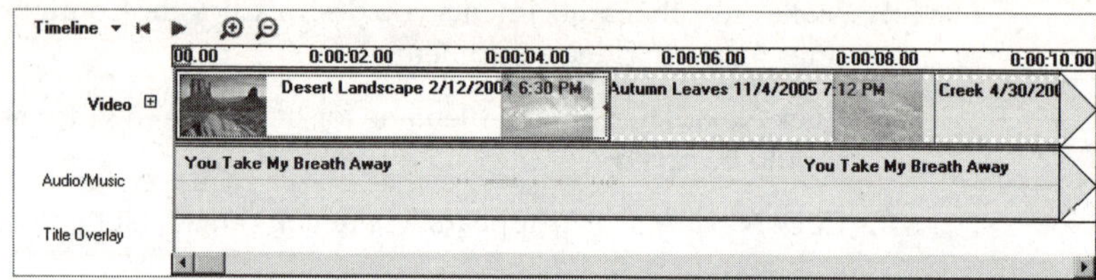

FIGURE 13.11 Timeline view shows both sound and picture and spaces them out in their actual proportions.

ADDING A SOUNDTRACK OR NARRATION

To add a soundtrack, you need to be in Timeline view. Then drag any sound clip onto the timeline. At this point, you can drag it to the left or right to adjust its position in the movie.

You'll probably want to wait to record narration at the last minute, after you've finalized the order and duration of each clip. To record narration, follow these steps:

1. Make sure your microphone is plugged in to the Mic port on your sound card.
2. Switch to Timeline view and choose Tools ➤ Narrate Timeline.
3. The Narrate Timeline controls appear in the upper pane. Drag the microphone volume slider up or down as needed.
4. Click Start Narration. Your movie displays in the Preview pane. Speak into the microphone to narrate as the movie progresses.
5. Click Stop Narration. A Save Windows Media File box appears.
6. Enter a filename and click Save. The track is saved in WMA format, just like files you create in Sound Recorder.

TIP If you've added other audio to the movie, you might find that the narration has taken its place, forcing it to move farther to the right on the timeline. Drag them so they overlap to make both play at once.

ADDING VIDEO EFFECTS AND TRANSITIONS

Windows Movie Maker has the ability to add special effects, somewhat like in Microsoft PowerPoint.

You can add video effects and video transitions. Video effects apply to the entire clip; video transitions occur as the clip is first appearing.

To apply an effect or transition, follow these steps:

1. On the Collections list, click Effects or Transitions. A list of available effects appears in the center pane, as shown in Figure 13.12.

TIP To see more of the effects listed in that center pane at once, choose View ➤ Details.

2. Drag and drop one of the effects onto a clip in the timeline or filmstrip.

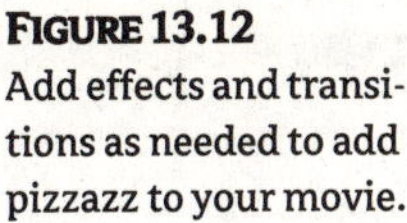

FIGURE 13.12
Add effects and transitions as needed to add pizzazz to your movie.

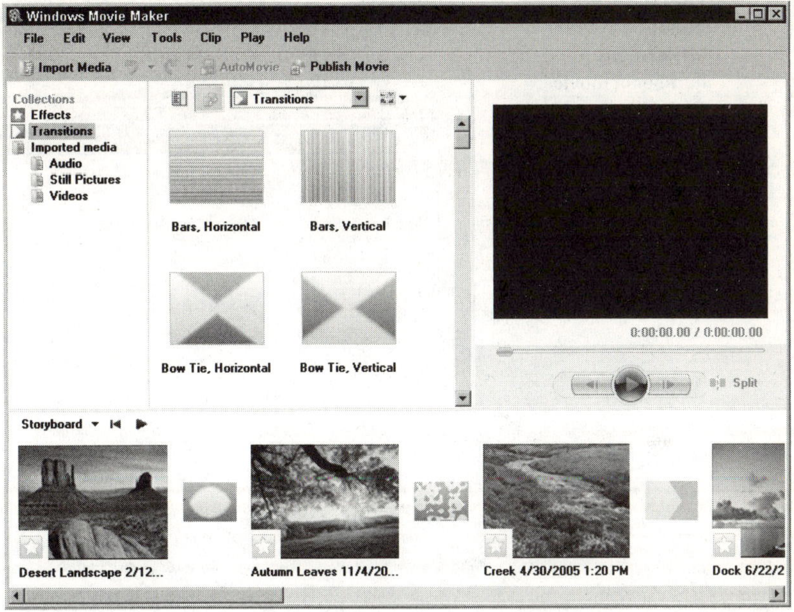

PREVIEWING THE MOVIE

To preview the movie, click the Play button under the preview pane. If you want to view it full screen, click the Full Screen button under the preview pane.

Exporting a Project to a Movie File

When the movie is exactly the way you want it, save your work on the project (File ➤ Save Project). Then export the movie by doing the following:

1. Choose File ➤ Publish Movie. You'll see a list of options for saving the movie as shown in Figure 13.13.
2. Choose the location for the movie to be saved. You can save to your hard disk, to the Web, to a recordable CD, to e-mail, or to an attached digital video camera. Then click Next.
3. Enter a name for the movie file and choose a location. Your choices here will depend on your choice from step 2. Then click Next.
4. Accept the default quality setting and click Next.
5. Wait for the movie file to be saved.
6. You're asked whether you want to watch the movie now. Click Yes to play it in Windows Media Player or click No to return to Windows Movie Maker.

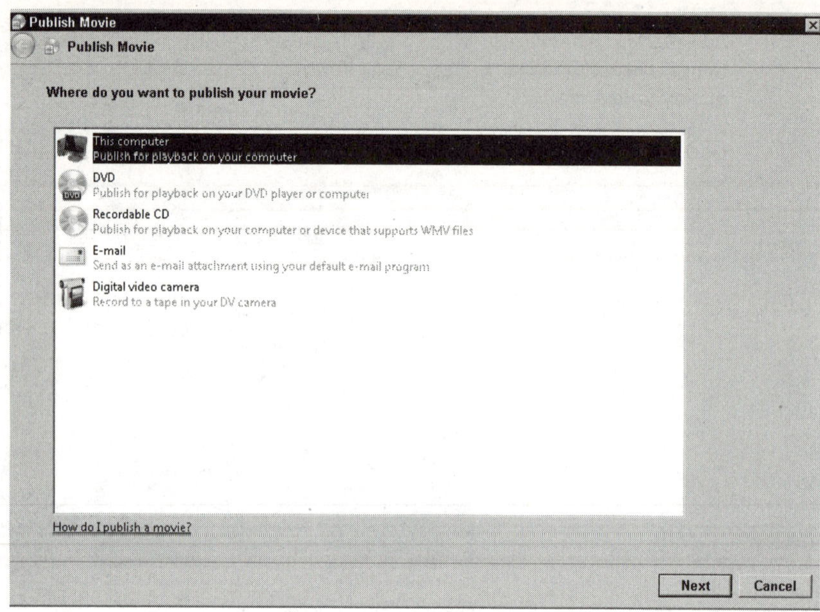

FIGURE 13.13
Windows Movie Maker offers a number of movie-saving options.

Summary

In this chapter, we looked at image file management and Windows Movie Maker. You learned how to acquire images from scanners and cameras and how to work with them in Windows and incorporate them into Windows Movie Maker files.

At this point, you have a full view of the graphics capability that Vista provides. It's admittedly significant, but professionals will probably continue to rely on third-party products. Even so, you'll want to spend some time playing with the graphics features that Vista provides to determine whether they'll work for you.

In the next chapter, we'll switch gears a bit and start looking at online functionality, starting with the Internet itself. Fortunately, Vista makes the job significantly easier than previous versions of Windows. For example, you'll find that creating an Internet connection is nearly automatic, even if you have to work through a communications server.

Part IV

The Internet and E-mail

In this section you will learn how to:

- **Connect to the Internet**
- **Use Internet Explorer**
- **Use Communications Programs such as NetMeeting and Remote Desktop Connection**
- **Use Windows Mail**

Chapter 14

Connecting to the Internet

Will Rogers once explained that the telephone is like a very big dog: when you pulled on its tail in New York, the dog would bark in Los Angeles. Radio, he said, works exactly the same way, but without the dog. In Vista, communications functions are integrated into the operating system. Maybe Will Rogers would have said that the dog is now using a keyboard and an Internet connection.

Communications capability has been part of DOS and Windows since the earliest IBM PCs. Vista includes an extensive set of communications tools that enable you to exchange electronic mail with other computers, browse the Internet, and use your computer to control telephone calls. In this chapter, I'll discuss the following:

- Using the Internet Connection Wizard
- Connecting to the Internet with a dial-up modem
- Connecting to the Internet with a cable modem
- Connecting to the Internet with DSL
- Connecting to the Internet with satellite
- Sharing an Internet connection
- Troubleshooting Internet connections

You can find more specific information about communications applications in the remaining chapters of this part of the book:

- Chapter 15 covers the Internet Explorer web browser.
- Chapter 16 covers Remote Desktop Connection.
- Chapter 17 covers Windows Mail, the Vista control center for messaging components and news.

Vista: What's New?

The big new feature in Vista is Windows Defender. This new feature makes it considerably easier to maintain system security, and it provides enough automation so you don't have to remember to perform every task. Although Windows Defender isn't a full protection system, it does help keep your system safe from outside contaminants such as spyware. You can also use it to monitor your system's activity to an extent.

Along with Windows Defender, Vista boasts a beefed-up firewall. Windows Firewall is a lot more robust and aggressive in monitoring activity with the Internet. You'll find that it provides two-way protection, now, in place of the one-way protection that Windows XP provided. In addition, fewer items are on by default, which means that you'll have to give permission to perform tasks more often. Fortunately, Vista makes the process of giving permission when necessary easier (assuming you have the proper rights).

Vista has also become significantly better at creating Internet connections automatically. Generally, if Vista can access the Internet connection at all, you'll find that you have the access you require. Vista does tend to grab the first Internet connection it can find, instead of the fastest one available. Consequently, if you have multiple connections at your disposal, you may find yourself configuring Vista to use the one you want, but this seems to be the major flaw in an otherwise good connection strategy. Of course, it still helps you to know how the connectivity works, just in case you run into a problem that Vista can't solve.

Types of Internet Connections

The most common way to connect to the Internet used to be through a cable modem or Digital Subscriber Line (DSL). Even in rural areas, dial-up connections are quickly becoming a thing of the past. People are increasingly finding better, faster ways to gain Internet access. We'll look at some of them in this chapter, along with the traditional dial-up modem.

High-speed Internet connectivity is also known as *broadband*. In theory, connecting through a broadband device can be as much as 1,000 times faster than connecting through a 56Kbps modem. Though only a gleam in our collective browsing and e-mailing eyes in the very recent past, broadband connections are now proliferating. As you'll see in the following sections, they're affordable and, with Vista, extremely easy to install and get up and running.

Connecting to the Internet

During installation of Vista, you were given an opportunity to configure an Internet connection (actually, it's very likely that Vista will simply find the connection and make it work for you). If you didn't do so then, you can do so at any later time using the New Connection Wizard, which walks you through the steps. You can use this wizard to set up a broadband connection as well as an analog modem connection, to connect to your office computer system from a location outside the office, or to set up a local area network (LAN).

NOTE Chapter 10 covers the installation and configuration of a modem driver.

If you have a connection that requires you to log on, you'll need your username and password. If you're connecting through an analog modem, you need an account with an Internet Service Provider (ISP), your username and password, and the phone number to dial in to your ISP.

To create a connection, follow these steps:

1. Open the Internet Options applet in the Control Panel. Select the Connections tab. Click Setup. If you already have an Internet connection (which is quite likely with Vista), you'll see a Connect to the Internet dialog box like the one shown in Figure 14.1. If you see this dialog box, click Cancel or Browse the Internet now to cancel the setup wizard. Generally, you only need to proceed with the wizard if you want to create an alternate connection.

2. Click Set Up a New Connection Anyway. The next dialog box (see Figure 14.2) will ask how you want to connect to the Internet. Generally, you have two options, as shown in the figure, depending on how you configure your system.
3. Choose a connection type. Depending on the connection you choose, you'll need to enter information about the connection. When working with broadband, all you need to provide is a username, password, and connection name. Figure 14.3 shows the connection information for a dial-up connection.
4. Enter the phone number (and area code if necessary) and specify whether the modem needs to dial 1 before dialing the phone number.
5. Enter your username and password. Check Show Characters if you want to see the password as you type it, rather than the usual dots. Check Remember This Password if you want to avoid entering the password each time you connect to the Internet.

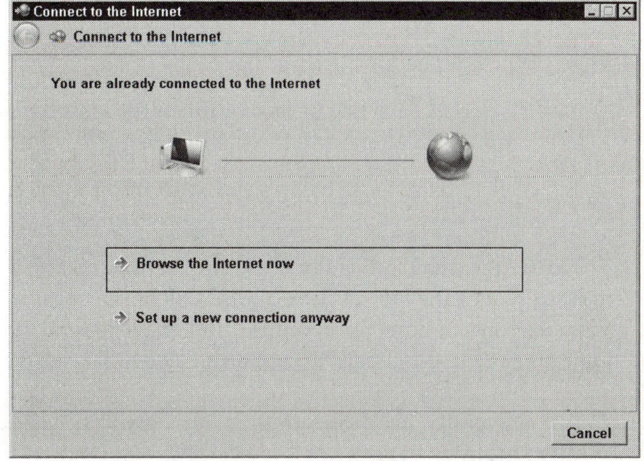

FIGURE 14.1
Vista usually makes the Internet connections you need in the background; you may have a connection already.

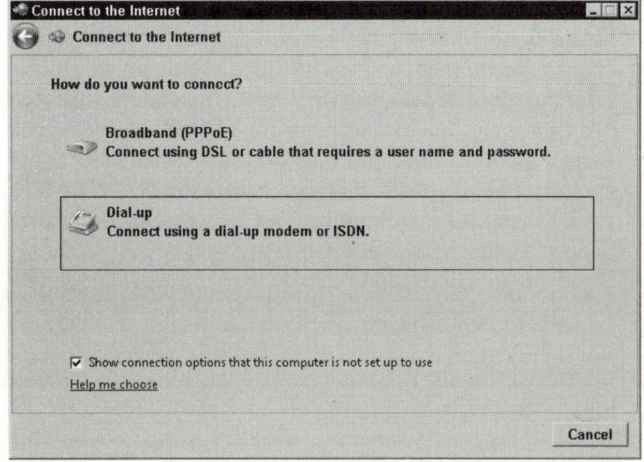

FIGURE 14.2
Choose the kind of connection you want to create to the Internet.

FIGURE 14.3
Provide the information Vista needs to create the connection.

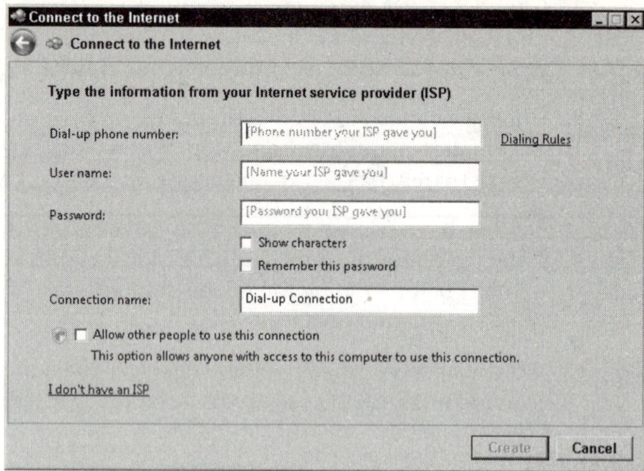

6. Type a name for the connection.
7. Check the check box at the bottom of the screen if you want to allow anyone who uses your computer to connect to the Internet using this account and password.
8. Click Create. Vista creates the connection for you. Click Close to close the final status dialog box.

No matter what connection type you want to create, you don't necessarily have to have an ISP to do it. Notice the I don't have an ISP link at the bottom of Figure 14.3. When you click this link, Vista displays options for obtaining an ISP. In general, you can either search online for an ISP in your area or choose the ISP based on a CD you've received.

THE TELEPHONY INTERFACE

Whenever you work with an Internet connection that involves dial-up, you work with TAPI (Telephony Application Programming Interface). TAPI is a set of software hooks to applications that control the way your computer interacts with the telephone network. TAPI is an internal part of Vista rather than a specific application program—it provides a standard way for software developers to access communications ports and devices, such as modems and telephone sets, to control data, fax, and voice calls. Using TAPI, an application can place an outgoing call, answer an incoming call, and hang up when the call is complete. TAPI also supports features such as hold, call transfer, voice mail, and conference calls. TAPI-compliant applications work with conventional telephone lines, Private Branch Exchange (PBX), and Centrex systems; these applications also work with specialized services such as cellular and Integrated Services Digital Network (ISDN).

End users don't usually work directly with TAPI. The closest you'll get is when you set up dialing locations, as you learned in Chapter 7. When you create a set of rules for dialing from a particular location, such as dialing a number for an outside line, you're communicating your preferences to TAPI.

Connecting to the Internet with a Cable Modem

It's amazing how much times have changed. Less than five years ago, everyone wanted the latest and greatest in computer hardware—the fastest processors, the best video, the biggest hard drives. Nowadays, if you offer someone a choice between a computer with all the best hardware on the market or an average computer with a really fast Internet connection, 9 out of 10 people would choose the computer with the Internet connection.

Internet bandwidth is king, and there's no sign that things will change in the near future. So, what can you do when you decide it's time to upgrade from your 56K modem to something a bit faster? One option is to sign up for Internet access over the same cable that brings TV into your home—provided it's offered in your area.

Cable Internet Access—How Does It Work?

A cable modem has at least two (and maybe more) interfaces on it. The first is a standard F port connector, a coaxial cable connector that's similar to the one on the back of a television or a VCR. Your cable service is connected to that port. The second interface is a 10Base-T (Ethernet) connector or USB connector, which connects your cable modem to your computer. If it's an Ethernet connector it uses an RJ-45 plug, which looks like a wider-than-normal telephone plug. If it's a USB connector, it connects to any USB port on your PC.

Once your cable modem is up and running, data comes down to your system on a special channel on your cable signal and, unlike an analog modem, it's always on.

How Fast Is It?

Being the techie that I am, I like absolutes. I like to know exactly how things work and exactly how fast something will run. So, I did a bit of research to find out how fast cable modem service actually is. What I learned is that you can't find out.

When determining how fast a cable modem will actually run, you must consider a number of factors. Some factors (but not all) are out of the control of the cable ISPs, so their common answer—if you really press them on it—will be "it depends." Of course, this doesn't prevent them from bragging that their service is up to 1,000 times faster than a 33.6 modem. In theory, it is.

Let's take a look at that theory. On a typical cable modem installation, a 6MHz analog carrier channel is dedicated to carrying downstream data from the Internet to your computer. Now, the way all the bits and bytes are put together over a cable modem yields a throughput of 36MB on a 6MHz carrier channel. So, in theory, 36,000,000bps is 1,000 times greater than 33,600bps.

Ah, but a few factors get in the way. First, let's start with your computer. A cable modem either connects to the PC via a 10Base-T or a USB connector. The former is called a "10"Base-T connection because the maximum throughput it will support is 10,000,000bps (10Mbps). That's a bit less than 36Mbps—about 73 percent less. So much for the claim of being 1,000 times faster. If it's a USB 1.1 connection, it's limited to 12Mbps. USB 2.0 is better—with an upper limit of 480Mbps—but both the cable modem and the PC's USB port have to support it.

NOTE Technology constantly changes, so the only absolutes you have for the numbers in this chapter is that they aren't absolute. Consider them as guidelines that you can use to make comparisons. It may very well be that your ISP uses a newer modem type that really can deliver the full 36Mbps to your computer. If you're using Vista, you probably have a USB 2.0 setup on your machine, which means that the USB connection isn't a limitation either. The point is that you'll need to do some research to discover what your ISP can deliver to your machine.

That's not the only possible bottleneck. The signal that is coming down the 6MHz carrier channel and into your computer is mixed in with other signals headed to other nearby computers. Your cable Internet traffic is traveling across the same cable that connects all the other homes and apartments in your neighborhood. Now, in theory, that cable can carry the entire 36Mbps of signal into your area. But how many users does it take to completely saturate that connection to your neighborhood? Four computers using 9Mbps each? What about 40 users running 900,000Kbps each? What about 400 users running 90Kbps (less than two 56K modems) each? Each combination would saturate the cable signal for your neighborhood and—believe it or not—it's not uncommon for between 500 and 2,000 cable TV subscribers to all be running on the same cable (that is, running into the same cable "head-end" or "node"). Hopefully, not all of them are subscribing to cable Internet access as well. If they are, and if everyone's using their cable modems, your connectivity might not be much better than that of two 56K modems, but I admit I'm stretching things a bit to make a point. (Actually, the stretched point is a lot less than it used to be because many people are now getting set up with cable Internet access and I know of many people who have moved on to DSL, satellite, or other solutions.) Simply put, the best neighbor to have is one who doesn't even have a computer.

There's also the potential for a bottleneck from your cable company out to the Internet itself. Now, in all fairness, this is a bottleneck point for any ISP—whether you have dial-up, DSL, a cable modem, or whatever. Just as airlines make their money by selling more seats on a plane than they actually have, ISPs make money by selling more bandwidth than they actually have. They wouldn't be able to survive if they didn't.

A close companion who has a cable modem was able to confirm my speed rating of "it depends." In his particular scenario, he was able to see average throughputs of 256Kbps to 512Kbps, with his best connection being about 1.3Mbps—roughly the speed of a T1 connection. So, cable modems are definitely faster, but don't buy into the hype about their being 1,000 times faster than a regular modem.

Cable Internet Access—Advantages and Disadvantages

A number of advantages and disadvantages are associated with cable modem service in comparison with typical analog modems. I've outlined a few of the positives and negatives for you.

Advantages of Cable Modem Internet Access

Here are the advantages:

Always on Full-time dedicated Internet access—you'll definitely appreciate this once you have it.

High speed Despite the possible bottlenecks I discussed earlier, 99 times out of 100, cable modems will give you far better speed and reliability than analog modems. Once you get connected, you'll never be willing to move somewhere that *doesn't* have high-speed access.

One less phone line required If you had a dedicated second phone line installed in your house for computer access, you can drop that phone line. This should save you $10–$30 per month, which can offset the cost of the cable modem service.

Affordable In comparison with other high-speed Internet access options, cable modems are one of the most affordable.

Disadvantages of Cable Modem Internet Access

Here are the disadvantages:

Privacy Since all systems in a "neighborhood" of cable Internet subscribers use the same connection to send and receive data, someone may be able to intercept your traffic and analyze it—a security risk. I've even seen cases where shared network folders showed up as available on their neighbors' PCs under 9*x* versions of Windows.

Few choices Unlike phone companies and Internet service providers, cable companies are more or less a monopoly here in the United States. You usually won't be able to choose from multiple cable Internet providers; you'll have to take whatever is available in your neighborhood.

Getting Hooked Up

Okay, so let's assume you've decided to take the plunge and get hooked up to the Internet with a cable modem. Here's what you might go through, from start to finish.

Questions to Ask Your Provider

You should definitely ask your cable provider a number of questions before getting hooked up. You might not get answers to all of them, but I'd want any provider to be able to answer at least some of the following questions to my satisfaction:

- How can you ensure that my neighbors won't be able to intercept my data and read it?
- Will I receive a public IP address? If so, will it be fixed or dynamic? (Fixed IP addresses are better if you need to access your computer remotely or if you plan on setting up a web server of your own; dynamic IP addresses are better from a security point of view.)

NOTE Some ISPs offer dynamic IP addresses by default and fixed IP addresses at an extra cost. Make sure you have a good business reason for the extra cost of the fixed IP address because the prices tend to be high.

- How fast can I expect it to be? Can you guarantee a certain level of service? (By all means, e-mail me if you get any provider to actually guarantee a certain level of bandwidth—I'd like to hear about them!)
- Are there any speed restrictions on my uplink speed? (*Uplink* refers to data sent from your computer to the Internet. Uploading a large e-mail message, videoconferencing, or transferring a large file to someone are all affected by slow uplink speeds.)
- Are there any restrictions on the type of services I can run on my computer? For example, can I run my own web server? If so, is there a traffic limit, above which I have to pay extra?

Service Delivery

Once you've talked with your provider and agreed to purchase the service, they will set up a time to send an installer out to your location. Now, I don't have cable modem Internet access, but I'd expect the service to be just about as prompt as my regular cable service (meaning not very prompt). Once they're at your location, they'll work with the cables a bit and hook up their cable to a box—the cable modem.

Once the box is hooked up, it's time to hook the computer up. If your computer already has an Ethernet adapter in it, they will most likely connect the cable modem to the Ethernet adapter. If your system doesn't have an Ethernet adapter, they should add one to your computer for you (make sure that you have your original Vista software handy, just in case they need it). Or, they might install a USB model of cable modem instead.

You may or may not need to run the New Connection Wizard to set up your connection. Your ISP will most likely give you setup instructions. If you do need to run the New Connection Wizard, follow the steps I gave you earlier in the "Connecting to the Internet" section.

NOTE As with anything, make sure you actually test the Internet access before you let the installers leave. It sounds like something they should do automatically, but I've actually heard about it happening where the installer provided the required connections and hardware, and then simply left without testing the setup fully. If the installer leaves before you've fully tested the connection (by actually visiting some websites and not just one), you might have to wait several more weeks for them to fix the setup at an additional cost (of course).

Connecting to the Internet with DSL

Another popular high-speed Internet option is Digital Subscriber Line (DSL) service. DSL typically comes in two varieties: Asymmetric DSL (ADSL) and Symmetric DSL (SDSL). Since the two technologies move data in a similar manner, you may also see these commonly referred to as xDSL.

Asymmetric DSL is called asymmetric because the uplink and downlink speeds are different, with more of the speed usually being allocated to the downlink (what you use to download content from the Internet). With Symmetric DSL, the same amount of bandwidth is available in both directions—up and down.

DSL—How Does It Work?

DSL uses the existing copper phone lines already in your house to send a high-speed data signal. Your plain old telephone service (POTS) typically uses a low-frequency range for all the types of signals you're accustomed to: voice, fax, and data. DSL operates on the same line—at the same time—by using a higher (inaudible) set of frequencies to transmit data. Since the DSL signal is operating in a different frequency range, you can still use your phone, fax machine, or even a dial-up modem at the same time you're using your DSL service to access the Internet.

When you have a DSL modem installed in your home, the device will have at least two or three interfaces on it. The first will be a standard RJ-11 phone connector that you're probably very familiar with. Your phone line will be connected to that port.

The second interface on your DSL modem will either be a 10Base-T connector (also known as an RJ-45) or a USB connector. Either can connect your DSL modem to your computer. If you have a 10Base-T model, your computer will need a 10Base-T port on the back of it in order to connect the two. If your computer doesn't have a 10Base-T port, your DSL provider will probably install one for you. If you have a USB model, all you need is a spare USB port.

NOTE Some ISPs now commonly use 100Base-T connections for DSL and you may see even faster speeds. In general, it's more cost effective and less troublesome to rent a modem from the ISP than to buy one of your own. DSL tends to be quite picky in the equipment that it will use when working with a particular ISP, so using the ISP-selected modem tends to reduce problems down the road.

The third port that you might have on the back of your DSL modem is another RJ-11 jack—this is for connecting your phone to the DSL modem. Your setup will rely on filtering to keep all of the functions separate. The DSL provider installs these filters for you, so you don't need to worry about installing them separately.

How Fast Is It?

Unlike cable modems, DSL service usually has very defined levels of service associated with it, from 256Kbps all the way up to 9Mbps. A speed of 1.5Mbps is the same as a T1 Internet access line, the same type of line that many businesses use for their Internet access needs, and it's probably more than enough for the average individual user.

NOTE A T1 line is a long-distance circuit that provides 24 channels of 64Kbps each, giving you a total bandwidth of 1.544Mbps.

You'll usually have at least a few providers to choose from. Compare the speed offerings from all the providers able to service your neighborhood and choose what's best for you.

Depending on how your provider's network is configured, the potential for a bottleneck exists from your DSL provider out to the Internet itself. Remember, this is a bottleneck point for any ISP, whether you have dial-up, DSL, a cable modem, or whatever. As I mentioned earlier, ISPs make their money by selling more bandwidth than they actually have, in the expectation that not everyone will use it at once.

Having DSL myself, I can tell you that—in my case—it's lived up to its service speed. I've been able to verify a full 1.1Mbps worth of connectivity on my service, which is exactly what I paid for. Being able to download Windows service packs in five minutes instead of four hours is a definite advantage in my line of business.

Depending on your ISP, DSL also has the advantage of allowing updates with a telephone call. You might decide that 1.5Mbps is a good starting point, but later decide you need more bandwidth. In most cases, all you need to make is a simple telephone call to add bandwidth to your setup (with an associated increase in cost).

Some DSL vendors can provide you with a static IP address, so that the address for your system remains the same. A static IP address lets you use your system as a web server when the ISP doesn't block port 80. Contrast this with cable modem setups where you normally can't obtain a static IP address.

DSL—Advantages and Disadvantages

A number of advantages and disadvantages are associated with DSL service in comparison with typical analog modems. I've outlined a few of the positives and negatives for you.

Advantages of DSL Service

Here are the advantages:

Always on Full-time dedicated Internet access—once you've had it, you'll never want to go back.

High speed Once you get connected, you'll never be willing to move somewhere that doesn't have high-speed access.

One less phone line needed If you had a dedicated second phone line installed in your house for computer access, you can drop that phone line because you can still use your DSL line as a voice line—even when you're on the Internet. This should save you $10–$30 per month, which can offset the cost of the DSL service.

DISADVANTAGES OF DSL SERVICE

Here's the major disadvantage:

Limited service area Due to technical limitations, your location must be within three miles (some providers say anywhere from 12,000 to 20,000 feet) of the phone company's DSL-capable switching location without a repeater. And that distance is based on the length of cabling between you and the phone company's office, not the "as the crow flies" distance. So, even if you live two miles from a DSL-capable switching location, you won't be able to get DSL if there are more than three miles of cable between you and the switch.

NOTE Many telephone companies are upgrading their systems with repeaters to make DSL a reality well outside the normal range. One of the big reasons to do this is so that you can also receive cable television using the same connection. In fact, many telephone companies now offer a package where you pay one bill for telephone, television, and Internet connectivity. Consequently, you'll want to contact your ISP to determine whether you can get DSL in your area.

Getting Hooked Up

Okay, so let's assume you've decided to take the plunge and get hooked up to the Internet through DSL. Let's take a look at what you might go through, from start to finish.

QUESTIONS TO ASK YOUR PROVIDER

Before ordering service, you should probably ask any prospective provider a few questions. Although this isn't a complete list of items you may need to consider, it's a good start.

- Will I receive a public IP address? If so, will it be fixed or dynamic? (Fixed IP addresses are better if you need to access your computer remotely or set up a web server; dynamic IP addresses are better from a security point of view.)
- Do you guarantee the level of service that I'm purchasing?
- Are there any speed restrictions on my uplink speed? (*Uplink* refers to data sent from your computer to the Internet—uploading a large e-mail, videoconferencing, or transferring a large file to someone are all affected by slow uplink speeds.)
- Are there any restrictions on the type of services I can run on my computer?

SERVICE DELIVERY

Once you've decided on a provider and agreed to a level of service, your provider will set up a time to send an installer out to your location (or, in some areas, they can send you a kit to install the DSL modem yourself—although you should have more technical knowledge than the average casual Internet user does if you're going to do this). Once they're at your location, they may have to work with your phone lines a bit before hooking up your DSL modem. DSL connections require new hardware within the outside telephone connection itself (the physical box located on the outside of your home), along with the installation of filters.

Once the DSL modem is hooked up, it's time to hook up the computer. If your computer already has an Ethernet adapter, the installer will most likely connect the DSL modem to the Ethernet adapter. If your system doesn't have an Ethernet adapter, they should add one to your computer for you (make sure that you have your original Vista software handy, just in case they need it).

The DSL connection requires a dedicated Ethernet card. Don't attempt to hook it up to your network because it won't work. If you want to connect it to a particular computer and share the connection with the rest of the network, then the host computer requires two Ethernet cards and you must set it up as a router. A better choice is to buy a hardware firewall with the required two Ethernet connections.

You may or may not need to run the New Connection Wizard to set up your connection. Your ISP will most likely give you setup instructions. If you do need to run the New Connection Wizard, follow the steps I gave you earlier in the "Connecting to the Internet" section.

Connecting to the Internet with Satellite

Cable and DSL are the preferred methods of broadband connection, but if you live in an area where neither is available, then what? Satellite Internet access may be the answer for you.

NOTE Most rural areas with a telephone cooperative (rather than a big name telephone company connection) have DSL availability. Make sure you ask your telephone company about this solution before you use a satellite connection. Unlike DSL, satellite relies on a radio link transmission that's affected by weather conditions and even innocuous problems such as trees that are in the way. Satellite usually isn't a reliable connection and you should treat it as such.

Satellite—How Does It Work?

Originally, satellite Internet was a one-way service. Over the last several years, the one-way systems have become obsolete, replaced by two-way systems. You might still occasionally see a one-way system.

One-way satellite Internet uses a satellite dish for downloads, but uploads are handled with a regular 56Kbps dial-up modem. Therefore, you need to have two Internet connections—one for the satellite and one dial-up. They must both be active at once for you to surf the Web. The satellite is available all the time, but the dial-up you must connect and disconnect with a dial-up connection. You can use your own dial-up ISP or contract ISP service for the modem through the satellite provider.

Two-way satellite is a much newer technology; it uses a different type of satellite dish, and handles both uploading and downloading through it. Two separate cables run from the satellite dish—one to a Transmit box and one to a Receive box. (Some newer models combine both functionalities into a single physical box.) These boxes hook to one another and then connect to your PC via a USB port. The end result—a connection nearly as good in speed and reliability to that of cable or DSL that doesn't require the use of a phone line. As with ADSL, upload speeds are slower than download speeds; you can expect about 128Kbps uploading and between 300Kbps and 600Kbps downloading, on the average.

Satellite—Advantages and Disadvantages

The main advantage of satellite Internet over dial-up is speed. Downloads happen at up to 1Mbps, and since you spend much more of your time downloading than uploading, this results in greater Internet productivity.

Two-way satellite is obviously better than one way because of the higher speed in uploading, and also because you don't need to tie up a phone line or contract with a dial-up ISP. Two-way satellite is also always on, with no per-hour charges.

There are no advantages for satellite over DSL and cable other than broader availability (and even that advantage is diminishing). Satellite is slower, less reliable, and more expensive than either of those.

All satellite Internet systems have the disadvantage of needing to buy and install a satellite dish. The two-way satellite dish must be professionally installed (by FCC mandate) because of its transmitting capability, and installation will cost $200 or more. The hardware for a two-way satellite connection will run $500 or more.

Satellite Internet also can't be shared via router with other PCs in your home or office, unlike cable and DSL. You can share a satellite connection through Internet Connection Sharing, but you can't hook the satellite cable directly into a router.

Setup for satellite Internet on the PC is also a bit more involved. With cable and DSL, you simply plug in the cable and it works; with satellite you must run through a configuration and registration process using an analog modem. You must redo this setup if you ever need to reinstall Windows or if you get a new PC.

In addition, weather conditions can cause problems with satellite service. Heavy rain or snow can cause the service to stop responding, and I've also observed problems on bright and sunny days due to sunspots. There's not much you can do other than wait for it to start working again.

WARNING Some people have also run into problems using satellite Internet on a dual-boot system. For example, if you dual-boot with Windows XP and Vista, and you configure the satellite in Vista, when you boot to Windows XP it won't work. So, you rerun the Setup program in Windows XP, and it starts working, but then when you go back to Vista, it doesn't work anymore and you have to run Setup there again. This is because when you connect to do the configuration, it dynamically assigns you an IP address. You keep that IP address as long as that copy of Windows is installed, but if you run the Setup on a different Windows version, it asks for another IP address and locks your user ID onto it instead.

Getting Hooked Up

Most satellite cable companies, such as DirectTV, now offer satellite Internet service. You can place an order for service online (or contact your local dealer), and they will ship your hardware to a professional installer in your area who will come to your home and do the installation. (The dish will need a clear view of the southern sky.) Other ISPs subcontract from satellite Internet service providers to offer service, such as Earthlink. If you go with a subcontractor provider, they handle all your tech support requests but pass along the hardware-related ones to the satellite company for resolution.

Depending on the installer you get, they may do the PC setup for you, or you may need to do it yourself. You'll receive a CD-ROM containing the Setup program; it's fairly self-explanatory. You'll need an analog modem to complete it; you might need to borrow one if you don't have one, just for this one usage.

Protecting Your System with Windows Defender

Vista now provides a rudimentary spyware and virus detection setup in the form of Windows Defender. In my opinion, it's a good second choice, but you'll definitely want a full-fledged virus protection product in addition to Windows Defender. Microsoft agrees and makes it quite easy to install the third-party product. Windows Defender is designed more for those who won't install a third-party virus protection product and as a second line of defense. The following sections describe Windows Defender in detail.

Obtaining Definition Updates

Besides actually using the product, the most important task you can perform with any virus or spyware detection product is to update the signatures it relies on to ferret out problems with your system. A signature is a means of detecting nefarious files based on the file content. The program checks files for this signature and tells you when it find the signature anywhere on your system. Of course, crackers are extremely prolific and change their files frequently to avoid detection, which means that you must keep the signatures updated on your system to obtain any benefit from the security program. Signatures go by various names. Microsoft uses the term *definition* for their signature files, which as good a name as any.

Windows Defender relies on Windows Update for new definitions. Every day, Windows Update checks for new definitions (along with other system updates). If you have Windows Update set the default settings, it will provide Windows Defender the updates you need automatically. However, it's important to verify that these updates actually do occur. Open the Windows Update applet in the Control Panel and click the View Update History link. If Windows Update is doing its job, you'll see entries like the one shown in Figure 14.4 for Windows Defender.

Notice that the update includes a version number. Theoretically, you'll be able to check the Microsoft Knowledge Base article that also appears as part of the update to verify that you have the latest version. I say theoretically because Microsoft is supposed to provide this information, but it hasn't actually appeared on the website yet. You can find the required Knowledge Base article at `http://support.microsoft.com/kb/915597/en-us`. If you find that your definition file is outdated, click the Check for Updates link in the Windows Update window and Windows Update will download the updated Windows Defender file for you.

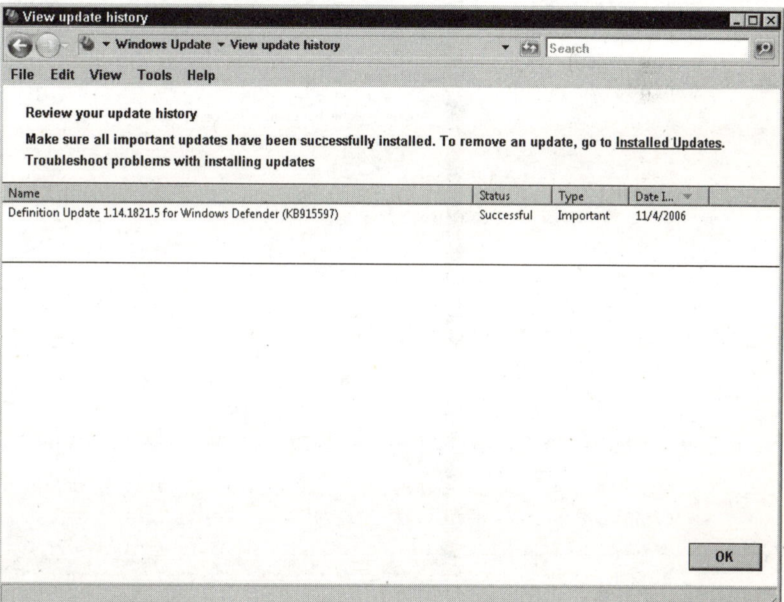

FIGURE 14.4
Make sure that Windows Defender is updated so that it can address the latest threats.

Performing System Scans

Windows Defender performs scans automatically at 2:00 AM every day, which is fine if your system is turned on at that time. Many people turn off their machines after they complete their work for the day unless a company policy dictates otherwise. Consequently, you may find that Windows Defender never actually performs a scan on your system and gives you a false sense of security.

You can avoid the scanning problem by opening the Windows Defender applet in the Control Panel. At the bottom of the main window is the last scan information as shown in Figure 14.5. If this date isn't current, you can run a scan immediately by clicking Scan. The Last Scan field also tells you what kind of scan Windows Defender performed. A quick scan probably doesn't provide optimal system protection, so you might want to change the settings to perform a full scan. Notice the other information displayed with the last scan date. You can determine when Windows Defender will scan your system next and whether you have real-time protection enabled.

To change the default scan time and type, click Tools on the toolbar and then the Options link in the Tools and Settings window. You'll see the Options window shown in Figure 14.6. This figure shows the default Windows Defender settings, which make using it as innocuous as possible, but also could make it ineffective. Make sure you set the scan time for a time when you'll actually have your machine on. I set Windows Defender to run during lunch. A scan isn't very effective if you're not using the latest definition file. That's why you'll want to check the first option, Check for Updated Definitions before Scanning, to ensure you have the latest definition files available for the scan. I also suggest performing a full scan, rather than a quick scan. When you finish making changes, click Save.

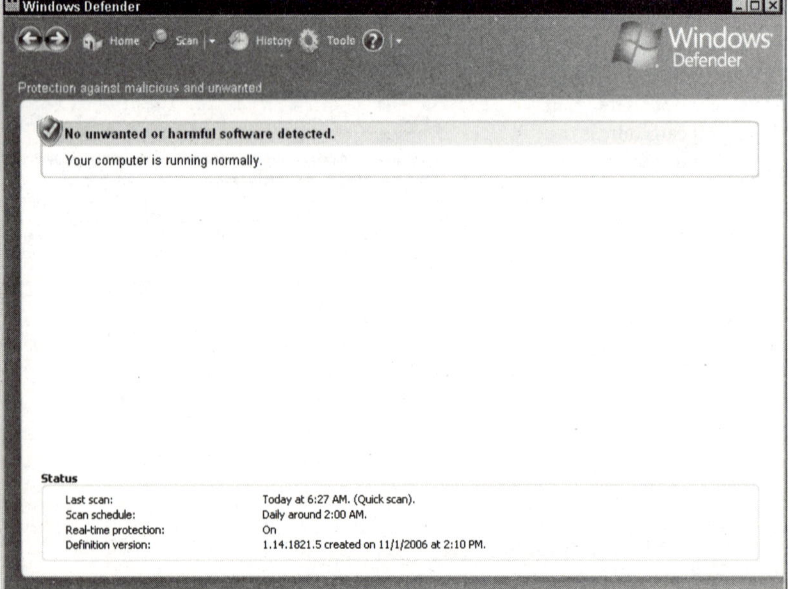

FIGURE 14.5
Windows Defender is only effective when it actually performs scans on your system.

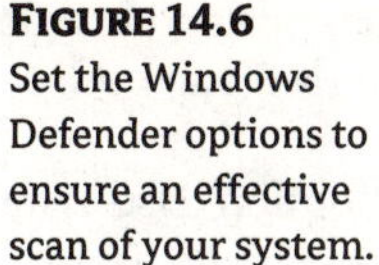

FIGURE 14.6
Set the Windows Defender options to ensure an effective scan of your system.

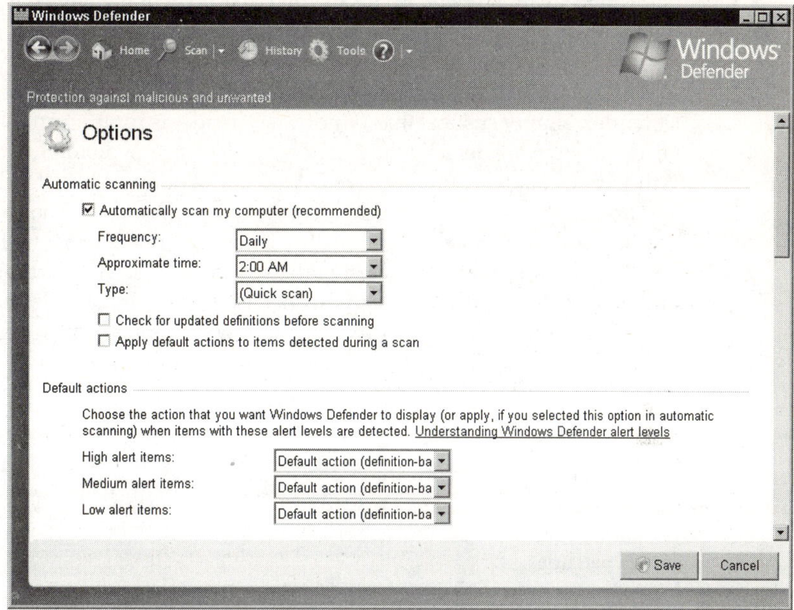

Configuring Windows Defender

You can configure Windows Defender to perform various checks and behave in certain ways when it encounters a problem. To start, click Tools on the toolbar and then the Options link in the Tools and Settings window. You'll see an Options window like the one shown in Figure 14.6.

Windows Defender comes configured to perform a number of real-time checks. For example, when you go to a website, Windows Defender checks anything that Internet Explorer downloads. It also verifies that applications have permission to run and checks application registration (essentially, interaction with the Registry). Figure 14.7 shows the default settings for the real-time checks. Even though this is the default, I normally check all of the options to provide maximum protection. Too little protection will mean hours of work eradicating a virus or spyware—assuming you see them at all.

Of course, you have to decide what to do with a threat when Windows Defender finds one. The Default Actions section of the Options window contains three levels of default actions based on the threat level of a particular item. You can choose to perform the default action as defined in the definition file, remove the item, or ignore the item. It's probably not a good idea to ignore any threat to your system. I normally set the High alert items field to Remove and leave the other two levels set at Default action (definition based).

The Advanced Options section determines how Windows Defender works. The default settings scan the contents of archived files and folders for possible threats, provide detection of odd behaviors in software that hasn't been analyzed for risks, and create a restore point before it does something with detected threats. This last option is especially important because you want to have a way to restore the system if Windows Defender works a bit too hard on your behalf. False positives, detecting a virus or spyware in a file that doesn't actually have one, do happen and you need some means of reversing the actions for false positives. Otherwise, you might find that your system doesn't boot or that applications don't behave as expected.

The Administrator Options section provides two options. The first option, Use Windows Defender, simply ensures that Windows Defender is running on the system. If you have third-party virus and spyware detection installed on your system, you might decide that you really don't want Windows Defender running as well. After all, Windows Defender does consume processing cycles and use resources, both of which affect system performance. The second option, Allow Everyone to Use Windows Defender, should really say let everyone interact with Windows Defender. Checking this option means that anyone using the system will receive alerts about possible virus or spyware problems, can choose actions to perform based on the threat, and may review Windows Defender activities. This option doesn't prevent Windows Defender from running and it certainly doesn't deter Windows Defender from taking action. If you decide that the users of the machine don't have the skills required to make good decisions about viruses and spyware, you might want to clear this check box.

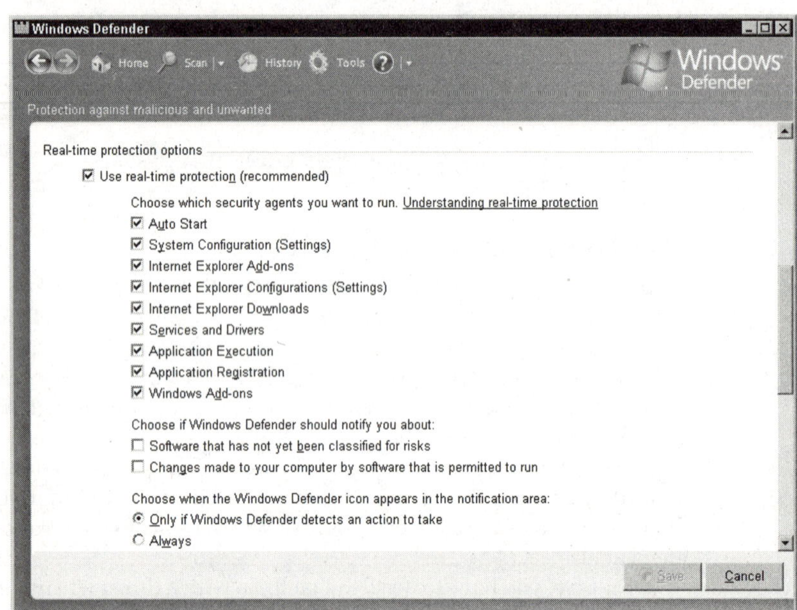

FIGURE 14.7
Real-time checks perform constant surveillance of your system for potential problems.

Checking the Application Execution History

You should regularly check on Windows Defender to determine whether it's working as anticipated. To perform this task, click History. You'll see the history of the actions that Windows Defender has taken as shown in Figure 14.8.

Some events, such as the one shown in the figure, display as unknown. Windows Defender monitors the Registry and other vulnerable parts of the system and creates entries even when the application doesn't appear in the definition file. This is the reason you need to review the history—you need to determine whether an entry is worthy of additional review. In this case, I changed the start page for Internet Explorer and Windows Defender logged the change. However, if you saw this same change and knew you didn't make it, then you'd want to investigate further.

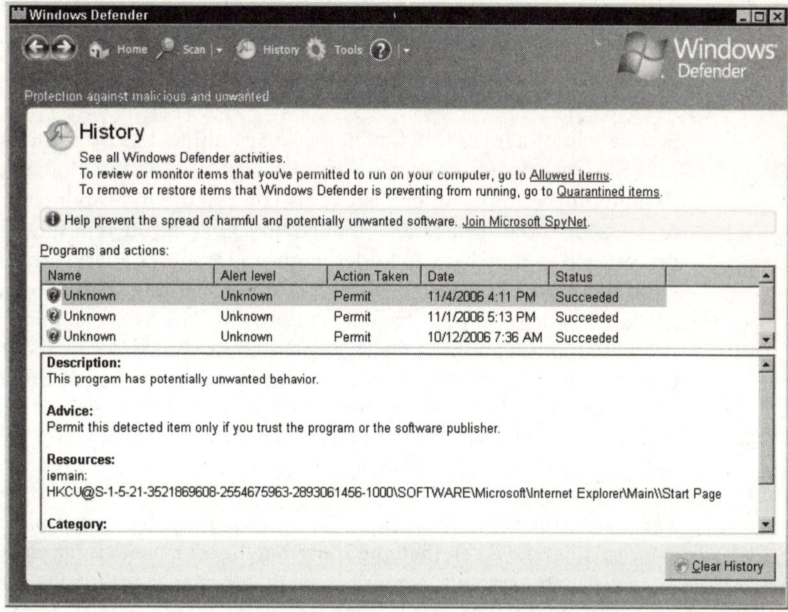

FIGURE 14.8 Verify that Windows Defender is working as planned by reviewing its history.

You should notice a few additional pieces of information about this entry. First, the change appears in the Registry and that it affects the HKCU or HKEY_CURRENT_USER hive. (The HKEY portion of this name tells you that this is a hive key—a main key in a portion of the Registry.) The at sign (@) signifies that this is the hive for a particular user, the user with a Security Identifier (SID) of S-1-5-21-3521869608-2554675963-2893061456-1000. The SID is important because each user has their own hive for their personal settings. You would actually look up the information for this entry in the `HKEY_USERS\S-1-5-21-3521869608-2554675963-2893061456-1000\Software\Microsoft\Internet Explorer\Main` key. The affected value appears after a double slash (\\). Therefore, in this example, you'd look for the Start Page value in the Main key and examine it.

WARNING If you see an entry that affects Internet Explorer, don't open Internet Explorer to view it. When the change triggers spyware or a virus attack, opening Internet Explorer will only cause the change to happen. Likewise, you really don't want to open the Internet Options applet in the Control Panel. Always open the Registry Editor to review the change by selecting Start ➢ Run, typing **`RegEdit`** in the Open field of the Run dialog box, and clicking Open.

As you work with Windows Defender, you may choose to allow certain actions to occur because they aren't spyware or virus related. You can review the list of allowed actions by clicking the Allowed Items link in the History window (see Figure 14.8). If you decide later that an action really isn't safe, highlight the entry in the list and click Remove from List.

Windows Defender won't automatically delete items that you download that might contain harmful content. Instead, it quarantines the items so that you can review them. To review the list of quarantined items, click the Quarantined Items link in the History window. You can perform one of three actions in the Quarantined Items window. The first is to remove everything by clicking Remove All, which means deleting all of the entries from your machine. Unless there's only one entry, you'll probably want to review the entries one at a time. When you decide that a particular entry is bad, highlight it and click Remove. Likewise, if the entry doesn't contain spyware or a virus, highlight it and click Restore.

TIP You can also find the Allowed Items and Quarantined Items links in the Tools and Settings window. Simply click Tools on the toolbar to display this window.

Using Software Explorer

Software Explorer is a tool that helps you examine the applications on your system from a security perspective. You access this tool by clicking Tools on the toolbar and then clicking the Software Explorer link. Unlike other Vista tools you can use to examine applications, Software Explorer reviews all of the applications that could run at the current time, including those that appear in places such as the `Startup` folder. Figure 14.9 shows a typical view of Software Explorer.

In this case, I've selected Microsoft Office Outlook. This program appears in the Startup Programs category because I have it set up within my `Startup` folder. Notice that the application is permitted to run and that the right pane shows information about it. If you decide that the application could cause problems, click Disable and it won't run during the next startup. Likewise, if you later decide that the application is fine, then you can highlight it and click Enable so it does run during the next startup. When an application proves detrimental, remove it from the system by highlighting it and clicking Remove.

TIP All of the entries in Software Explorer include a Ships with Operating System field. In general, when this field is Yes, then you know that the component is normally reliable. However, don't be fooled. Some crackers overwrite operating system files with their own versions, so you want to exercise care to also check the other statistics that come with the file such as the Digitally Signed By field. If this field is intact and the file ships with the operating system, it's unlikely that someone has tampered with the file.

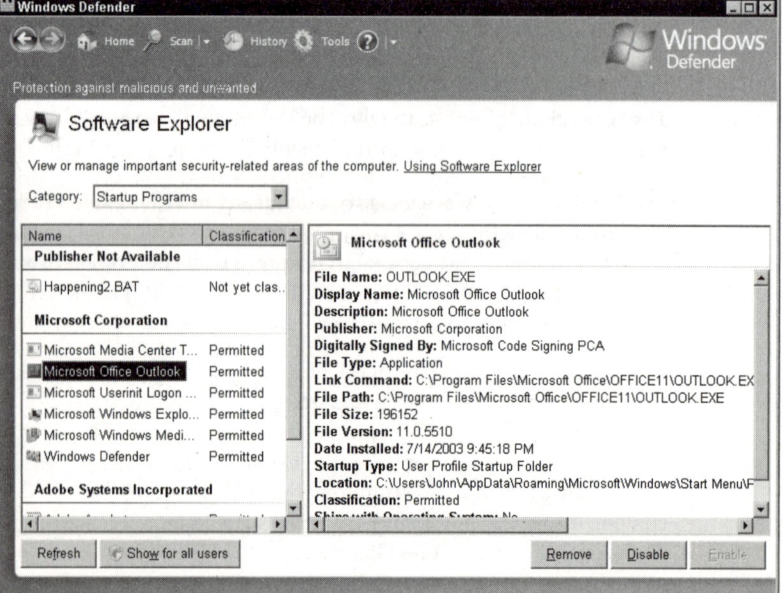

FIGURE 14.9
Software Explorer helps you examine applications on your system from a security perspective.

Each of the categories provided in Software Explorer contains different options for controlling applications. When working with the Currently Running Programs category, you can examine each application and choose whether it should continue running. When an application is detrimental, you can end it by highlighting it and clicking End Process. If you need additional information about the application, click Task Manager to obtain the Task Manager view of the application.

WARNING Ending applications by clicking End Task could result in data loss. Any application you end using the End Task button stops immediately—Vista won't give it time to save data. After all, if an application really is a virus, you don't want it to run any longer than necessary to stop it.

When working with Network Connected programs, you can choose to end the task or simply block outside communication with it. Besides the usual information, Software Explorer also tells you how the application is communicating with the outside world. In some cases, you might want the application to run, but you might want to block incoming communications with it. For example, you might want the Windows Media Player to run, but you might not want to receive the Internet information it can access. In this case, you should highlight the entry and click Block Incoming Connections.

Protecting Your System with a Firewall

A *firewall* is a security system that deters would-be mischief makers from accessing your computer system through the Internet. No matter what type of Internet connection you use, you'll want to be sure that the Windows Firewall is enabled. Windows Firewall is included with Vista and Microsoft enables it by default.

To make sure Windows Firewall is enabled, open the Windows Firewall applet in the Control Panel. If the product is running, the display is green and you'll see Windows Firewall is on as part of the status information as shown in Figure 14.10. To enable the firewall, click the Turn Windows Firewall on or off link to display the Windows Firewall Settings dialog box and choose the On (recommended) setting. When your system has no need to communicate with the Internet, check the Block All Incoming Connections option as well. Click OK and Vista will start Windows Firewall.

If you have a larger network or a corporate network, you'll need a more sophisticated firewall. You might start by asking the advice of your ISP. You can also find a wealth of information, vendors, consultants, and so forth on the Internet by searching on "firewall." A good jumping-off place is `http://www.firewall.com`.

NOTE The Windows Firewall features in Vista actually rely on two different utilities. Most users can perform tasks such as adding programs or ports when prompted. These features rely on the Windows Firewall applet in the Control Panel. However, advanced tasks such as monitoring Windows Firewall, configuring logging options, working with Internet Control Message Protocol (ICMP), and adding or removing network connections requires an administrator account. You use the Windows Firewall with Advanced Security console found in the `Administrative Tools` folder of the Control Panel to perform these tasks. Consequently, you might only be able to perform some tasks in the sections that follow when you don't have the required credentials.

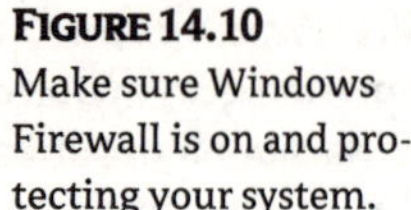

FIGURE 14.10
Make sure Windows Firewall is on and protecting your system.

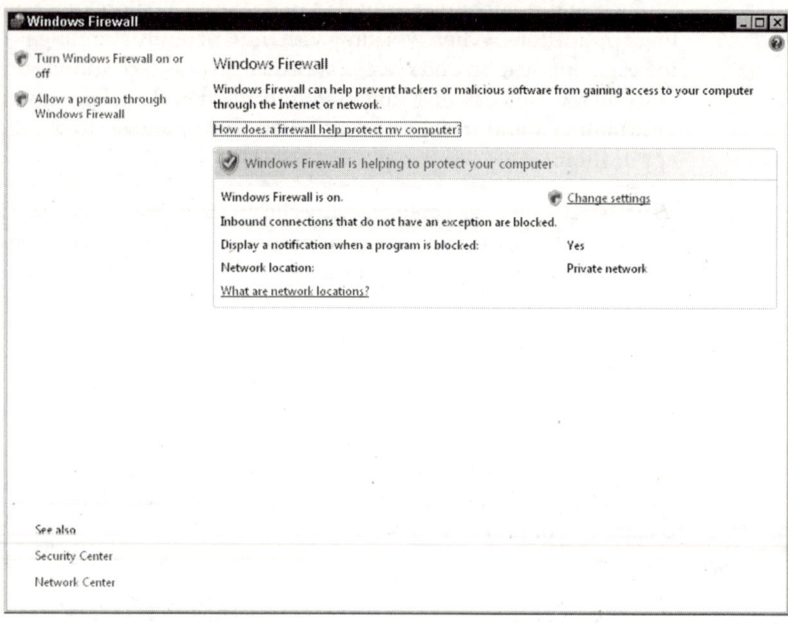

An Overview of Windows Firewall

Windows Firewall started off as a wimpy version of the commercial products called Internet Connection Firewall (ICF). It didn't provide much functionality and the protection was only one way—incoming. Any application on your system could send data out, which meant that once a cracker gained access to your system, you were pretty much out of luck detecting the cracker's activities. Still, ICF was better than nothing at all.

With Windows XP Service Pack 2, Microsoft introduced Windows Firewall, which is a two-way firewall. Now you could depend on protection for both incoming and outgoing traffic on your system. In addition, you could turn off all nonstandard communication. Consequently, Windows XP Service Pack 2 is generally better protected at the outset than previous versions of Windows.

Vista continues to improve on Windows Firewall. Microsoft tightened up things considerably in Vista. All access with the outside world is turned off by default and you have better control over how Windows Firewall works. For example, you can tell Windows Firewall to let a particular application communicate with some websites, but not with others. The level of control and the use of default pessimistic security settings make Vista considerably safer by default.

Unfortunately, Vista also requires that you play an active role in working with Windows Firewall. Now when you want to gain outside contact for Windows Media Player, you must specifically grant permission. The extra level of interaction will almost certainly confuse some users, but really, it's all for the best because it forces you to remain aware of the security setup for your system.

Adding, Configuring, and Removing Programs

As previously mentioned, Windows Firewall is pessimistic in Vista. It doesn't let any communication through unless you specifically tell it that such communication is acceptable. Consequently, you might suddenly find that some of your applications don't work and you'll definitely find that some parts of Vista don't work. For example, if you want to use all of the features of Windows Media

Player, you need to give it permission in Windows Firewall. Fortunately, Windows Firewall will generally display a message telling you that an application is requesting permission to communicate with the Internet. You can grant permission to use the Internet without additional trouble.

In a few cases, you're going to see some rather odd error messages. For example, the Event Log will tell you that it can't find an endpoint mapper and the Task Scheduler will simply claim that it can't find the other computer. Some applications will simply refuse to function because their developers assumed that you wouldn't have a firewall installed. Consequently, the application won't tell you about the lack of communication at all. In all of these cases, you need to do more than simply grant permission, you must specifically add the application to Windows Firewall. To perform this task, open the Windows Firewall applet of the Control Panel and click the Allow a Program through Windows Firewall link. You'll see the usual UAC message (click Continue) and then the Exceptions tab of the Windows Firewall Settings dialog box shown in Figure 14.11.

All of the default Windows applications that require outside communication already appear in the list. To enable outside access for the applications, locate the application you want to enable and check its entry in the list. Click OK and you're ready to go.

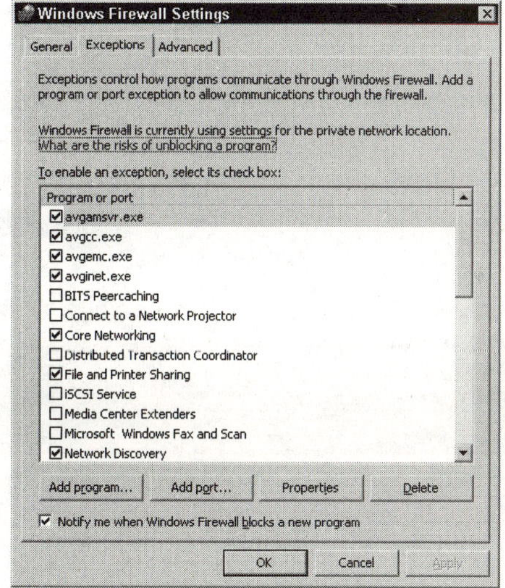

FIGURE 14.11
Windows Firewall provides exceptions for applications that must communicate with the Internet.

Other applications require that you click Add Program. You'll see the Add a Program dialog box (see Figure 14.12) where you can choose from the list of default applications or click Browse to locate the executable on the hard drive. Make sure you select the executable since Windows Firewall grants or denies Internet access based on the executable name. In some cases, it's hard to tell which application is the executable, especially when it comes to games that have a starter program and then a main program. Use Task Manager as needed to determine which application is actually making the request.

After you choose an application, you can simply click OK to give it full Internet access. However, this isn't always the wisest course of action to follow. You should give each application only the level of Internet access that it requires. To change the level of access that an application possesses, click Change Scope. The default setting is Any Computer, which means that the program can access anything anywhere. You can also limit the application to the local intranet, which is a very good idea for applications that require network access, but not Internet access. Finally, you can select Custom List. In this case, you provide the IP addresses that the application can access. This option provides the best flexibility because you decide precisely what the application can do. Windows Firewall supports both IP version 4 and IP version 6 addresses, so you won't have any problem adding just the website you want the application to work with.

You can change the scope of an application after you add it as well. Highlight the application entry on the Exceptions tab of the Windows Firewall Settings dialog box and click Properties to display the Edit a Program dialog box. In the Edit a Program dialog box, click Change Scope. Vista displays the Change Scope dialog box shown in Figure 14.13.

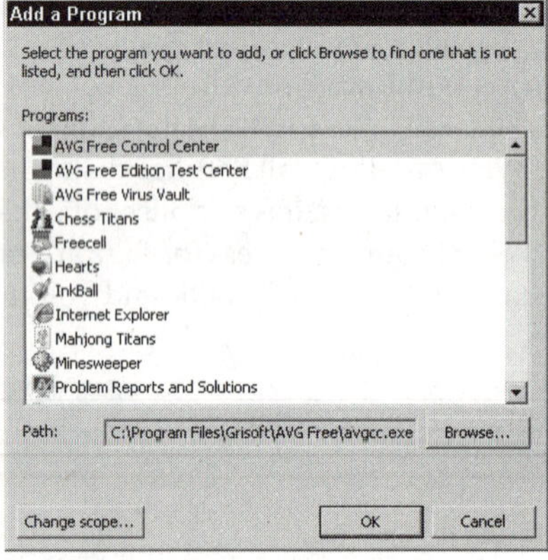

FIGURE 14.12 Choose the program you want to allow Internet access.

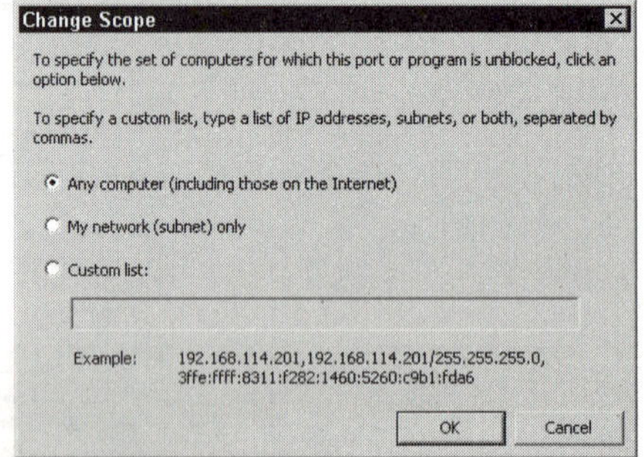

FIGURE 14.13 Define precisely how you want the application to access the Internet by providing a scope for it.

Adding, Configuring, and Removing Ports

Sometimes you need to provide communication options for multiple applications. In this case, you create a port for the applications, rather than configuring the applications individually. The application documentation normally tells you which port the application requires. The port number appears after a colon in the URL. For example, `http://www.microsoft.com:8080` tells you that the application accesses `www.microsoft.com` using the http protocol on port 8080.

Ports can also rely on either a User Datagram Protocol (UDP) or Transaction Control Protocol (TCP). Most of your communication with the Internet relies on TCP, so this is the best choice when you're unsure of which protocol to use.

Working with ports is much like working with applications. The only differences are that you click Add Port and use the Add a Port dialog box shown in Figure 14.14 to do it. Notice that this dialog box contains the same Change Scope button that an application has and it also provides the same scoping options.

FIGURE 14.14
Ports let you provide a special port for multiple applications to use.

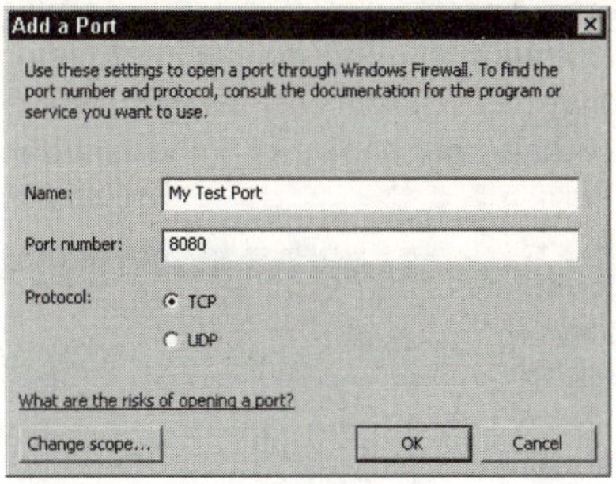

Monitoring Firewall Performance

Performance is a somewhat nebulous term that many people associate with speed. However, performance in Windows also encompasses reliability, security, usability, and other factors. An application's performance is a measure of how well the application accomplishes its stated goals. You can measure the Windows Firewall performance using the Windows Firewall with Advanced Security console in the `Administrative Tools` folder of the Control Panel. You'll need administrative privileges to open this console, which appears in Figure 14.15.

The `Monitoring` folder (shown in Figure 14.15) contains three subfolders that tell you the specifics about working with Windows Firewall. This folder also provides you with an overview of Windows Firewall. The first thing you'll notice is that Windows Firewall actually operates using one of three profiles: domain, private, and public. The domain profile takes effect when Vista works with a domain controller and uses Active Directory to manage settings. Microsoft calls this a corporate network setting. The public profile takes effect when you connect directly to a public network, such as the Internet or to the network at your local Starbucks. The private profile takes effect in all other cases, even when you connect the computer to a network. You select a profile based on your network setting in the Network and Sharing Center.

No matter which profile you use, you can obtain Windows Firewall settings from this view. For example, you can determine whether Windows Firewall is using logging and what kinds of information it's logging for you. In fact, you'll find a link for the log that you can click and view the log entries directly. See the "Configuring the Logging Options" section of the chapter for details in setting the logging options.

The first two subfolders provide status information about rules you've created. The `Firewall` folder contains a list of active inbound and outbound rules and their status, as shown in Figure 14.16 (see the "Creating Incoming and Outgoing Rules" section of the chapter for details). Likewise, the `Connection Security Rules` folder contains a list of active connection security rules that you've created and their status (see the "Creating Connection Security Rules" section of the chapter for details). The third subfolder, `Security Associations`, tells you about the Internet Protocol Security (IPSec) associations you created with previous versions of Windows. You can learn more about IPSec at `http://www.microsoft.com/technet/prodtechnol/windows2000serv/howto/ispstep.mspx` and `http://www.microsoft.com/technet/community/columns/secmgmt/sm121504.mspx`.

The view in Figure 14.16 doesn't show all of the possible columns. You can choose which columns to view by right-clicking Firewall and choosing View ➤ Add/Remove Columns. The Add/Remove Columns dialog box contains a list of available columns on the left and displayed columns on the right. Use the buttons to move columns between the two lists to hide or display them. However, the number of columns and amount of information makes the list in Figure 14.16 useful as an overview alone. To see all of the details for a particular entry, right-click the entry and choose Properties. The Properties dialog box shows all of the details for a particular entry in an easy-to-view form.

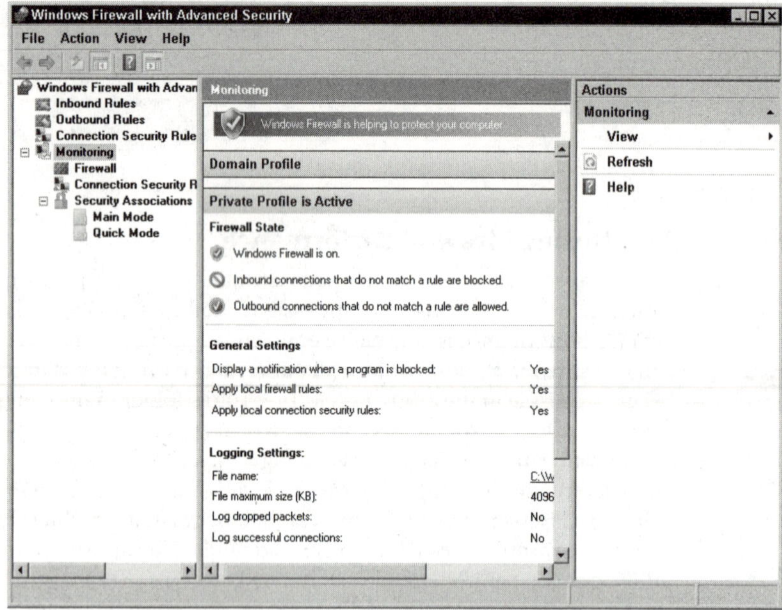

FIGURE 14.15 Use the Windows Firewall with Advanced Security console to measure Windows Firewall performance.

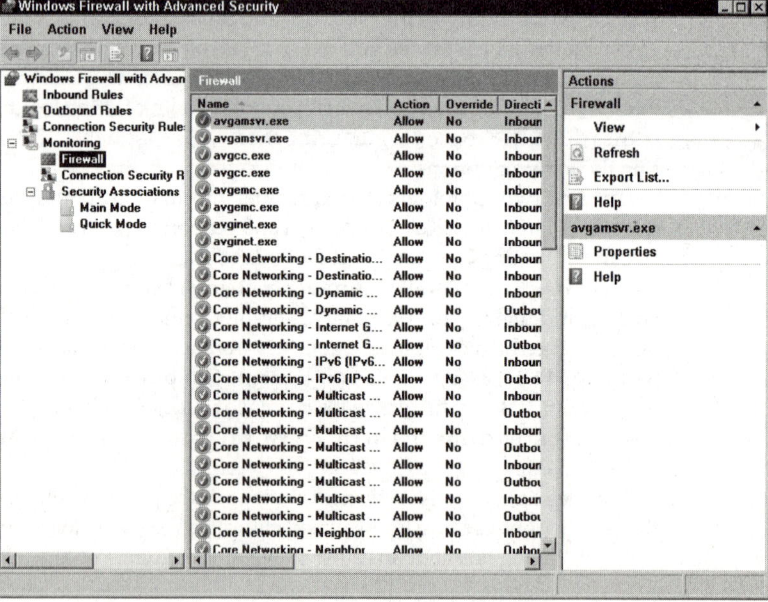

FIGURE 14.16 Check the status of individual rules and associations using the monitoring subfolders.

Configuring the Logging Options

Windows Firewall provides options for logging firewall activities. Generally, you won't need to maintain logs for the system unless you think there's a problem or you need to troubleshoot Windows Firewall. In fact, Microsoft sets the logging options off by default. To enable the firewall logging, open the Windows Firewall with Advanced Security console in the `Administrative Tools` folder of the Control Panel. Right-click the top-level folder and choose Properties. You'll see the dialog box shown in Figure 14.17.

Notice that there are settings for each profile. Consequently, you must first choose the tab that matches the profile that you're currently using. Click Customize in the Logging portion of the dialog box and you'll see a dialog box similar to the one shown in Figure 14.18 (the actual name will vary according to the profile you choose).

The four fields in this dialog box give you complete control over the log. Here's a description of each field.

Name Contains the name and location of the file you use for logging. It's possible to create a different log for each profile so that you can track entries by profile.

Size limit (KB) Contains the maximum log file size so that it doesn't end up eating your entire hard drive. The default size of 4MB (4,096KB) is more than sufficient for most needs.

FIGURE 14.17
Modify the overall Windows Firewall settings for a particular profile.

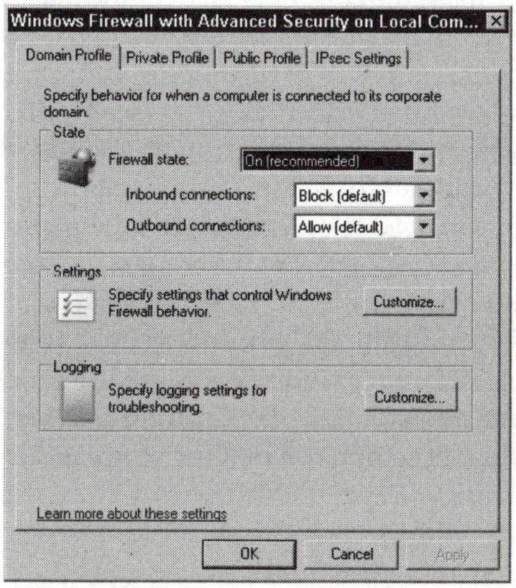

FIGURE 14.18
Set the logging options for a particular profile.

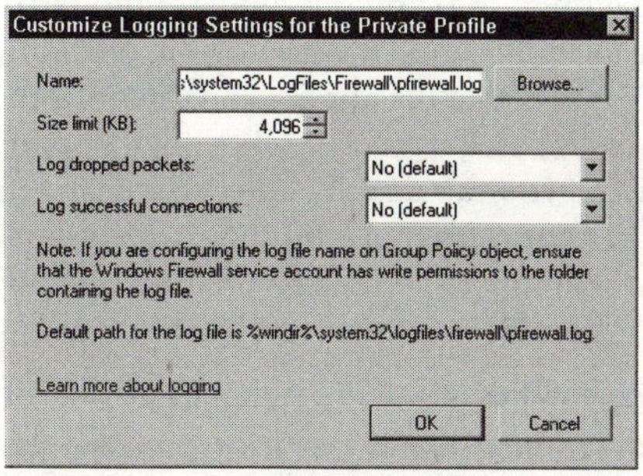

Log dropped packets Tells Windows Firewall to log any failed attempts when set to yes. These entries tell you about people who are probing your defenses, but haven't made it past them yet (at least, not completely).

Log successful connections Tells Windows Firewall to log successful connections to your system. You should only see the applications that you have specifically allowed when you choose this setting. In addition, the entries shouldn't show the application connecting to odd websites. If the connection is unexpected or does unexpected things, then it's suspect and you should investigate further.

Modifying ICMP Settings

ICMP is actually a complex topic for such a seemingly simple protocol and I won't be covering it in detail in this book. The short version is that it provides a means of controlling how the gateways on the Internet route messages. For example, if a message can't get to its destination, then a gateway will send an ICMP message saying that it doesn't know what to do with the message. You can read the specification for ICMP at `http://www.ietf.org/rfc/rfc792.txt`. The Microsoft-specific view of ICMP for Windows Firewall appears at `http://www.microsoft.com/technet/community/columns/cableguy/cg0106.mspx`.

Unfortunately, Microsoft hasn't made life any easier for anyone who needs to work with ICMP in Vista—the settings appear all over the place and you need to know where to find the setting you need, which is the purpose of this section. If you're working with IPSec and want to exempt ICMP from IPSec to improve performance, you can change the setting found in the Windows Firewall with Advanced Security dialog box (see Figure 14.17). The setting appears on the IPSec Settings tab. Right-click the top-level folder in the Windows Firewall with Advanced Security console and choose Properties to access this dialog box.

When you need to control ICMP for a particular rule (inbound or outbound), right-click the rule and choose Properties from the context menu. Select the Protocols and Ports tab. Now, here's the important part. If the Protocol Type field doesn't contain an ICMP entry, you can't change any ICMP values for it. In addition, you need to make sure that you have selected the correct form for ICMP. Windows Firewall provides separate entries for ICMPv4 and ICMPv6 (for newer IP addresses). Click Customize and you'll see the Customize ICMP Settings dialog box shown in Figure 14.19.

The default setting for an ICMP entry is All ICMP Types. However, you can choose the specific ICMP settings shown in the figure by choosing the Specific ICMP Types option. After you change the ICMP settings, click OK twice to make the changes permanent.

Creating Incoming and Outgoing Rules

Incoming (inbound) and outgoing (outbound) rules control how applications communicate outside the local machine. It's essential to create rules that let the application work as it should, yet limit the things that the application can do. The limitation part of the rule might seem superfluous, but it's essential. If a cracker takes over an application by writing a DLL that overwrites an application DLL, you can usually detect the change by observing changes in Internet activity. The limitations in your rules make this happen automatically because Windows Firewall will alert you to the lack of ability to contact an unauthorized website.

The following steps describe how to create a rule using the wizard.

1. Right-click either the `Inbound Rules` or `Outbound Rules` folder and choose New Rule from the context menu. You'll see a wizard similar to the one shown in Figure 14.20. (Inbound and outbound rules use the same wizard, but some prompts and titles differ.)

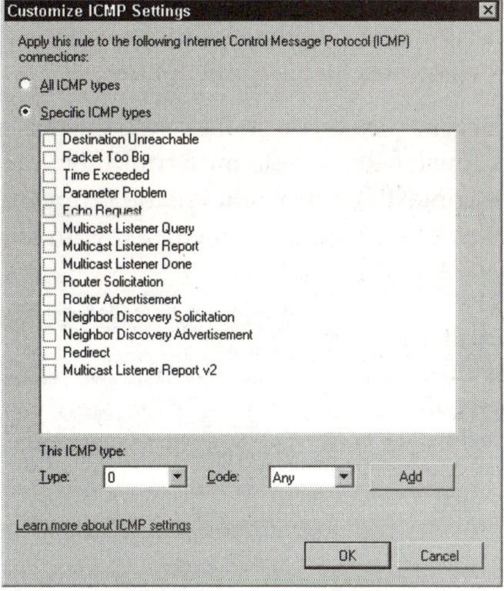

FIGURE 14.19
Define the ICMP settings for an inbound or outbound rule.

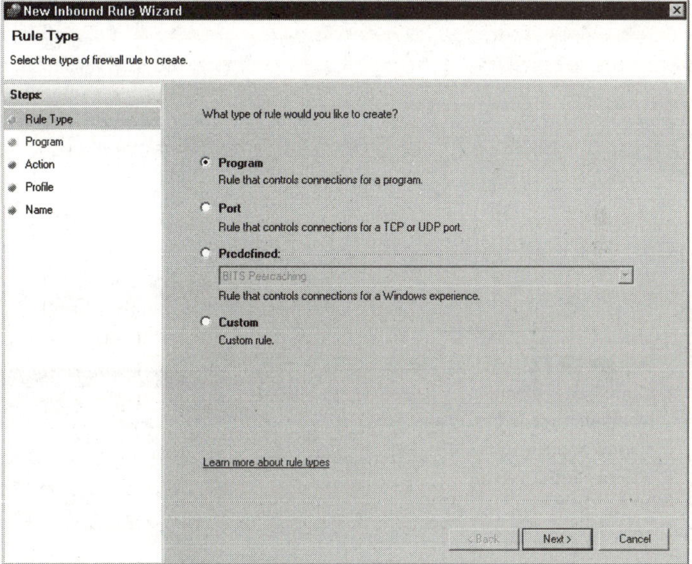

FIGURE 14.20
Create a new rule using the wizard to get you started.

2. Choose the kind of rule you want to create. Notice that the steps that follow change according to the kind of rule you want to create. For example, when you choose Program, the next step is to define the program the rule affects. Likewise, when you choose Port, the next step defines the port you want to use.

3. Follow the steps for the rule you want to create. Eventually, you'll see the list of actions you want the rule to perform as shown in Figure 14.21. This is the essential part of the security setup because it determines the effectiveness of the rule. The second option, Allow Connection If It's Secure, is the focal point of creating a good rule. Select this option and you can determine who can create the connection using the Users and Computers step of the rule.

4. Select an action to perform and click Next. Optionally define which users and computers can use the rule. Continue with the wizard steps until you complete the wizard. Windows Firewall creates the new rule for you.

It would be nice if you could create the perfect rule every time, but that's probably not going to happen. If you need to redefine a rule after you create it, right-click the rule and choose Properties from the context menu. You'll see the Properties dialog box shown in Figure 4.22 where you can change any of the settings you created with the wizard.

FIGURE 14.21
Define security for your rules as often as possible because security reduces system risk.

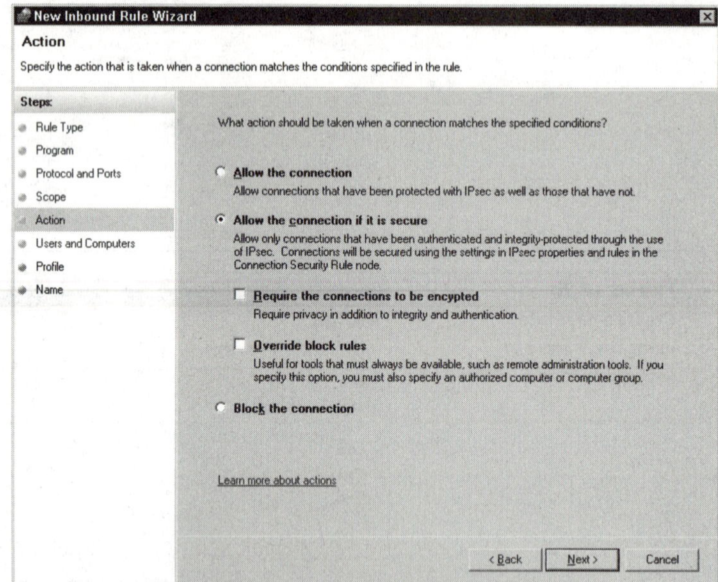

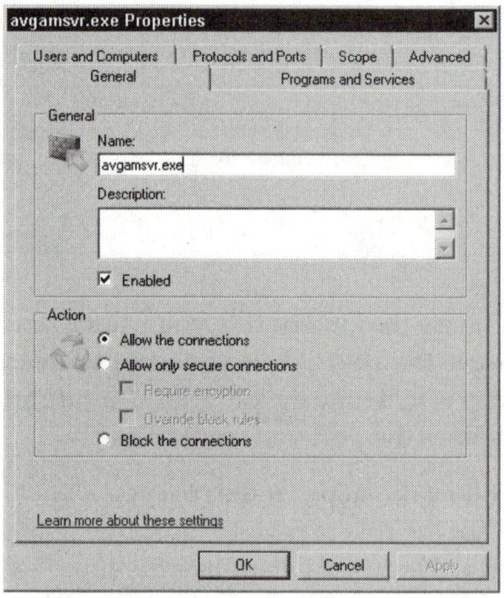

FIGURE 14.22
Change the rules whenever needed to ensure applications work as anticipated.

NOTE Vista makes some settings unavailable for predefined rules. In fact, you'll see a notice about this issue when you open the Properties dialog box (see the General tab). You can still modify some rule properties, but you can't modify them all.

It isn't necessary to delete a rule when you don't need it. If you'll need the rule later, you can right-click it and choose Disable Rule from the context menu. Windows Firewall ignores the rule until you enable it again. To enable a rule, right-click its entry and choose Enable Rule from the context menu.

TIP Make the rules and status information provided by the Windows Firewall with Advanced Security console easier to see by using filtering. All of the entries provide filtering of some type, normally profile and state. If you have defined groups, you can also filter the rules by group.

Creating Connection Security Rules

While the inbound and outbound rules control application communications, the connection security rules control how the machine communicates. For example, you can use a connection security rule to exempt communications from a particular computer from scrutiny or create a communications tunnel between two computers. As with inbound and outgoing communications, you create rules to establish Windows Firewall behavior.

The following steps describe how to create a connection security rule.

1. Right-click the `Connection Security Rules` folder and choose New Rule from the context menu. You'll see the New Connection Security Rule dialog box shown in Figure 14.23.
2. Choose a connection security rule type. Notice that the steps for creating the rule change based on the rule type you choose.

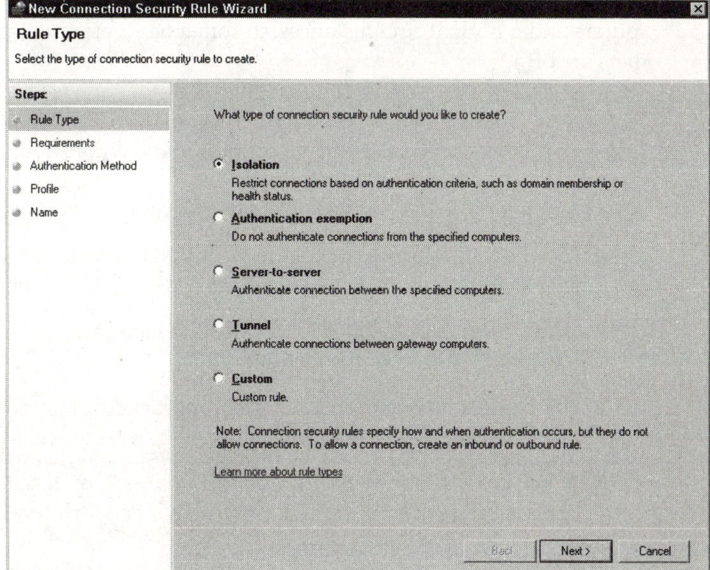

FIGURE 14.23 Determine which connection security rule you want to create.

3. Follow the steps for creating a rule. Make sure you provide complete information at each step. Eventually, you'll reach the Profile step of the wizard.

4. Check the profile options that the rule should affect. This step is especially important for connection rules. While it might be acceptable to create server-to-server connection in the private profile, you may not want to create the connection when using the public profile. Click Next.

5. Type a name and description for the rule. Click Next. Windows Firewall creates the new connection rule for you.

As with inbound and outbound rules, you can reconfigure connection rules after the initial setup by right-clicking the rule and choosing Properties from the context menu. The Properties dialog box you see will vary by connection type, but you can change all of the properties that you configured using the wizard. You can also disable rules by right-clicking the rule and choosing Disable Rule from the context menu. Enable the rule again later by right-clicking the rule and choosing Enable Rule from the context menu.

Using the Network Setup Wizard to Share an Internet Connection

As you may know, Vista lets you share your Internet connection with other computers on your network. Logically enough, the feature that lets you do this is called *Internet Connection Sharing*, which gets abbreviated to ICS.

ICS can be a great way of saving time and money: instead of needing a modem and a phone line (or a DSL or cable modem) for each computer that needs Internet connectivity, you can get by with one modem and one phone line (or the equivalent). ICS is particularly good if you have a fast Internet connection such as a DSL or a cable modem that provides enough bandwidth for several computers under normal circumstances. (If someone's perpetually trying to watch streaming video, all bets are off.)

This is all good—provided your Internet connection is fast enough. It goes without saying that ICS doesn't speed up your existing Internet connection. If your connection is slow with one person using it, it'll be glacial once you've connected the whole household or office through it.

Set Up the Computer That Will Share the Connection

Start with the computer that will share the Internet connection. First set up your Internet connection, and then use the Network Setup Wizard to configure the computer by taking the following steps:

1. Create and test an Internet connection using the information in the "Connecting to the Internet" section of the chapter.

2. Right-click Network and choose Properties from the context menu. You'll see the Network and Sharing Center window.

3. Click the Manage Network Connection link. You'll see the Network Connection window. You must have a minimum of two active network connections to make ICS work. The first

connection is from your computer to the Internet. The second connection is from your computer to the rest of the network.

4. Right-click the connection to the Internet and choose Properties from the context menu. Select the Sharing tab. You'll see sharing options like the ones shown in Figure 14.24.

5. Check the first option to let other people use this connection to access the Internet. If you want to also allow others to manage the connection (a very bad idea from a security perspective), check the second option.

6. Click Settings. You'll see the Advanced Settings dialog box shown in Figure 14.25 where you can control the services that others can use on your system.

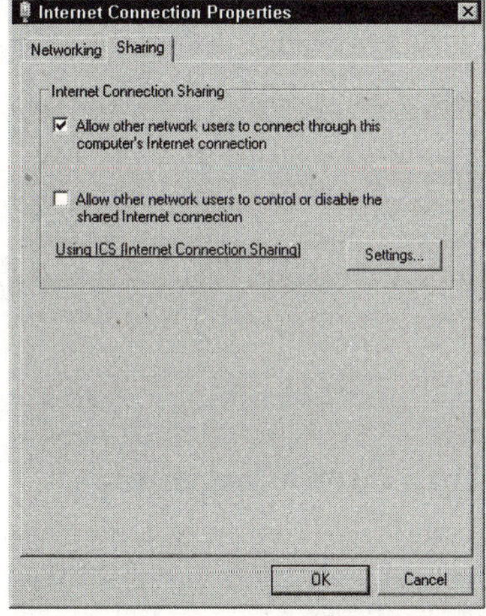

FIGURE 14.24
The Sharing tab has options to share your connection with others on the network.

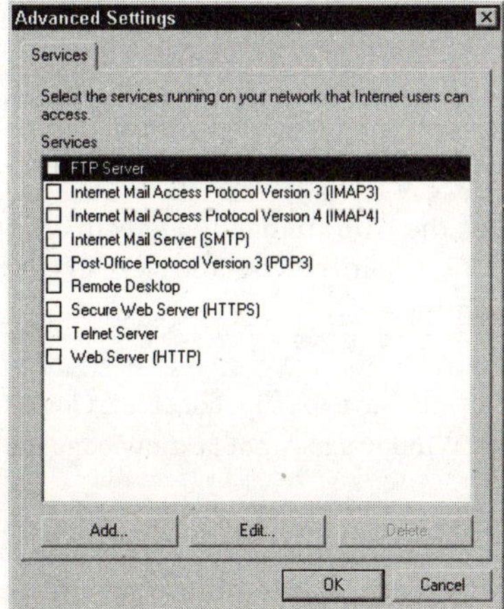

FIGURE 14.25
Choose the services that other people can access from your computer.

7. Check the standard services that you want other people to access.

    1. Click Add to add custom services to the list. You'll see the Service Settings dialog box shown in Figure 14.26. Custom services require that you provide an IP address and port number. You can make your custom service less vulnerable by choosing a different setting for the fourth field, Internal Port number for This Service, to a different value than the external port number.

    2. Click OK to add the custom service. ICS enables the option automatically.

8. Click OK twice to make the ICS connection functional. Vista will ensure that the connection doesn't have any problems such as address conflicts.

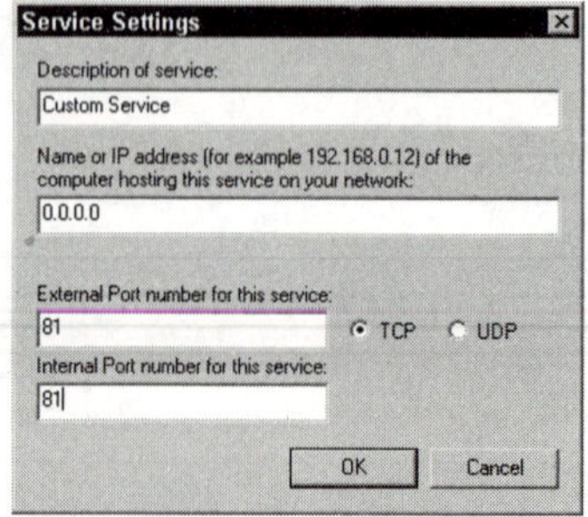

FIGURE 14.26
Create custom services that others can access through your computer.

Setting Up a Client Computer

Next, set up the first of your client computers. Make sure the Internet connection is still open on the computer you set up to share it, and then take the following steps:

1. Open the Internet Options applet in the Control Panel. You'll see the Internet Properties dialog box.
2. Select the Connections tab.
3. Choose the Never Dial a Connection option.
4. Click LAN Settings to display the Local Area Network (LAN) Settings dialog box.
5. Check the Automatically Detect Settings and the Use Automatic Configuration Script options. Clear the Use a Proxy Server for Your LAN option. Click OK twice to change the settings.

NOTE You may have to reboot or at least log out and then back into the system to make the connection work. Windows may not acknowledge the availability of the shared connection otherwise.

What ICS Does

In networking terms, ICS combines several elements: a proxy server, a router, and a Dynamic Host Configuration Protocol (DHCP) server. As such, it's relatively simple—but it comes free with Windows, and it's easy to set up and use.

ICS uses Network Address Translation (NAT), which is also known as *IP masquerading* (particularly in the Linux world). In NAT, the host (in this case, ICS) acts as an intermediary between the client (the PC connected to the network) and the server (the Internet server that is supplying information).

In NAT, the identity of the client submitting a request is hidden: instead, the request appears to come from the host. This can be good and bad. NAT gives you more freedom in the IP addresses you assign within the network. For example, you can use nonroutable internal IP addresses to make sure that incoming packets can reach a computer only through the router. But, if someone on your network takes some illegal or offensive action (for example, posting libelous comments or downloading, uh, *unsuitable* material), the culprit will appear to be the host rather than the individual concerned. (If you had multiple IP addresses, only the specific IP address involved would appear to be guilty.)

NAT Improvements in Vista

The nonroutable IP addresses lead us (indirectly, sure, but that's what happens when you're routing requests) to something that's been more of a problem with NAT in the past: computers not being able to communicate with each other across *two* NAT routers.

That might sound complicated, but it really isn't. You see, what usually happens with NAT is that one of the computers inside the network originates the conversation with a computer on the Internet. For example, consider Figure 14.27. This shows two simple home networks, unimaginatively named West Network and East Network. Each network contains a computer that's connected to the Internet (West 1 and East 1) and running NAT so that it can provide Internet connectivity to the two other computers in its network (West 2, West 3, East 2, and East 3). In the middle of the figure is the Internet, represented by its traditional cloud of uncertainty. And right below the cloud (quite coincidentally) is the Sybex web server, represented by a computer the size of a walk-in freezer.

So far, so good. Now, here's the problem that used to occur with NAT. The computers that connect through the NAT boxes have only internal IP addresses. That means they can originate a conversation with a computer on the Internet, but they can't take part in a conversation originated from beyond their NAT box. For example, West 2 can access the Sybex web server with no problem. It sends its request to the NAT router on West 1, which says the binary equivalent of "ah, an address on the Internet" and shunts the request out through its external connection. The Sybex web server responds to the request and sends back a response to West 1. The NAT router intercepts this response, matches it to the outgoing request, says "ah, it's for West 2" (again in binary), and passes the data on to West 2. And so it continues: West 2 (and the other internal computers) can access Internet sites provided that it starts the conversation.

But if West 3 wants to start a conversation with East 2, it can't, because it can't see East 2 through the NAT router on East 1. It can get as far as East 1, because that computer has an external IP address. But the computers beyond the NAT router are hidden from view. So you can't access them for a quick Deathmatch, for videoconferencing, for chat—well, for anything. And with NAT routers becoming widely implemented, thanks to the rapid spread of broadband availability, that inability to start a conversation quickly becomes a problem. At one end of the connection, the activity has to take place on the computer running the NAT router rather than on the "inside" machine you want to use.

The good news is that Vista fixes this problem, letting you communicate across two NAT routers, from one inside machine to another inside machine. This is quite clever, because both the server (the NAT router) and the client (the inside machine) need to understand what's going on and work together. Some of the software has to be reworked in order to make the connection work, but you'll find that many things work.

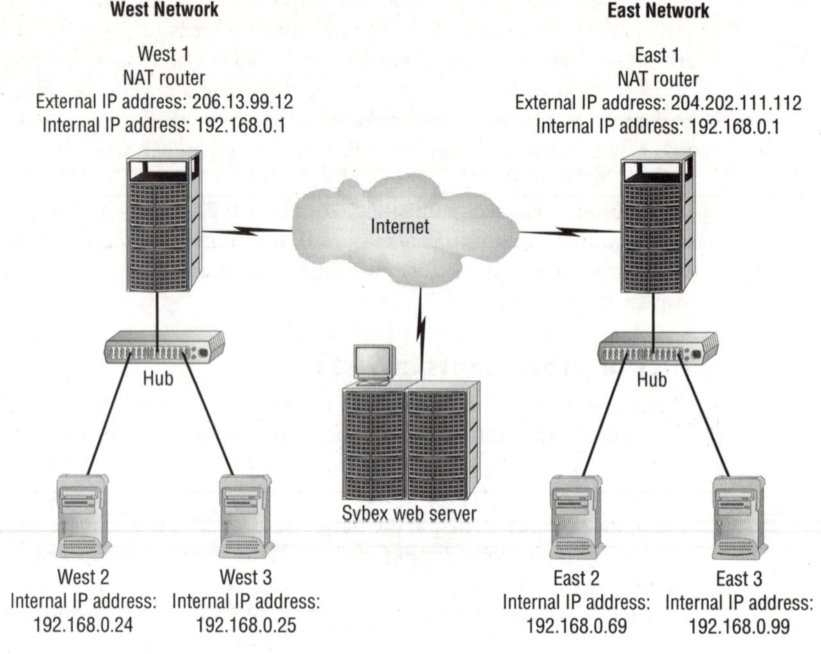

FIGURE 14.27 Two networks using NAT to connect internal computers to the Internet.

ALTERNATIVES TO INTERNET CONNECTION SHARING

The preceding description probably makes ICS sound pretty good. And it is—up to a point. But it has two significant limitations:

- First, you need to keep the ICS computer running all the time so that it can handle the Internet connection and the sharing.
- Second, because of the way ICS is set up, you can share only one Internet connection at the same time on the same network by using ICS. To share two Internet connections, you'll need to set one up manually for sharing via another technology. (Alternatively, you can create two separate networks with an ICS connection in each, but doing so is usually much more work than setting up a second shared connection manually, because those two networks won't be able to talk to each other directly without ICS conflicts.) You can also use unshared Internet connections alongside your shared connections without any problems.

There are better alternatives—*much* better alternatives—to using ICS. Unfortunately, almost all of them want you to pay for them and put some more effort into implementing them than ICS takes. But they're worth a quick mention here in case you're interested.

Depending on your ISP, you may be able to get multiple IP addresses for your broadband connection without paying more for them. Other ISPs consider supplying multiple IP addresses to involve a different category of service than supplying a single IP address and charge accordingly. For example, some ISPs charge around $40 a month for "residential" DSL service (which gives you just one IP address) and $100–$200 for "business" DSL service (which gives you multiple IP addresses—usually between 5 and 20). Apart from the IP addresses and the fistful of dollars, the distinctions between the residential and business services tend to be detectable only under sustained scrutiny through an electron microscope.

If you want the residential service but need to be able to connect multiple computers through your single IP address connection, get a cable router or DSL router designed for this purpose. All these routers have NAT built in, and most can run DHCP as well, which means that you don't need to keep one computer running the whole time to handle DHCP and NAT so that other computers can access the Internet. Some routers have firewalls built in as well, which you can use instead of or in addition to Vista's Internet Connection Firewall (ICF) or Windows Firewall.

Some models are designed to connect to a network switch or hub and have two ports: an internal port for connecting to the switch or hub and an external port for connecting to the cable modem or DSL splitter. Others have hubs or switches built in, so if you haven't yet bought the hub or switch for your network, you can solve all your connectivity needs with a single box.

Setting the IP Addresses of Connected Computers

If your Windows computers are set to get IP addresses via DHCP, they should automatically get IP addresses from ICS within a few minutes after you implement ICS. If you're configuring IP addresses manually, you'll need to set each computer to an IP address in the `192.168.0.2` to `192.168.0.254` range.

Turning Off ICS

To turn off ICS on the host computer, clear the Allow Other Network Users to Connect through This Computer's Internet Connection check box on the Sharing tab of the Properties dialog box for the connection, and then click OK. Windows closes the Properties dialog box and changes your computer's IP address from using `192.168.0.1` to obtaining an IP address automatically.

If you have a DHCP server on your network, Windows grabs an IP address from it on the next go-around of network polling. If Windows doesn't find a DHCP server (which will be the case if ICS was handling DHCP for you before you turned it off), Windows falls back on its alternate TCP/IP configuration, which uses Automatic Private IP Addressing (APIPA) to automatically assign an IP address in the range `169.254.0.1` to `169.254.255.254`.

Using a Shared Internet Connection

Depending on how a shared Internet connection is configured, you can use it in much the same way as you use a regular Internet connection on your computer.

The shared connection appears under the Internet Gateway heading in the Network Connections window with a flashy icon.

If the connection is configured to start automatically on demand, you can start the connection by starting a program that attempts to access the Internet. For example, if you start Internet Explorer or Outlook Express, ICS automatically starts the connection.

If the connection is configured to let you control it, you can start it manually by double-clicking its entry on the Network Connections screen, and you can disconnect the connection by right-clicking its notification-area icon and choosing Disconnect from the shortcut menu.

Troubleshooting Internet Connectivity Problems

The following sections provide some solutions for common problems with connecting to the Internet.

Dial-Up Modem Problems

Here are some issues you might encounter with an analog modem:

No dial tone Make sure the phone line is connected to the Line port on the modem and to the wall outlet. Try plugging a telephone into that jack to confirm that it's working.

Lots of static on the line/slow connection speeds Make sure the phone line is plugged into the Line port on the modem, not the Phone port. It makes a big difference on some modems; on others, none at all. Also make sure you're using a good-quality phone cable, that it isn't overly long (say, over 15 feet), and that it isn't next to any cables or devices emitting electromagnetic interference. Finally, have the phone company run a line quality check on your phone line to make sure there's not undue static interference.

Modem won't dial Check the modem through Phone and Modem Options in Control Panel, as you learned to do in Chapter 10. In the Modems tab, click Properties, and then click the Diagnostics tab; then click Query Modem.

Modem leaves phone off the hook Remove and reinstall the driver for the modem. See Chapter 10.

Frequent disconnects Try a different access number if there is more than one in your area. Also, you might contact your ISP to see whether there are any special modem settings you need to make in order for the connection to be more reliable. Remember from Chapter 10 that you can add extra initialization AT commands to a modem's Properties.

Cable/DSL Problems

Here are some problems you might face with a cable or DSL connection:

Blinking lights on cable or DSL box If there are no always-on lights on the box but just one or two blinking ones, the connection isn't being made from the box to the Internet. Try turning off or unplugging the box, waiting a few seconds, and then turning it on again. Sometimes temporary network outages prevent access and there's nothing you can do about it, so try again in an hour or so. It won't help you after the fact, but if you can catch the cable or DSL box when it's working right, notice which lights are on and which are blinking. Then you'll know what's "normal" for that device.

After reinstalling Windows, no access If the lights on the cable or DSL box indicate it's functioning correctly but you can't get a web page to come up, the problem is between the box and your PC. You probably don't have the right settings in Windows. Check the IP address for TCP/IP to make sure you're using the assigned IP address (if you have one assigned), and check the computer name in the Computer Name tab of the System Properties dialog box. Some cable or DSL connections require you to use a certain computer name.

Satellite Problems

Here are some problems you may encounter with satellite Internet service:

After upgrading or reinstalling Windows, no access You may need to rerun the Setup program. Generally, the satellite vendor's installation directory will have everything you need.

Loss of satellite signal Double-click the satellite vendor's icon in the notification area (when supplied) to open a status box for the connection. (Some vendors provide other means of checking signal strength—see your documentation for details.) If the connection strength is poor (under 50 percent), make sure nobody has bumped your dish out of alignment. Signal strength tends to degrade in rainy or snowy weather. You may need to go out and brush the snow off the dish. (Don't use your hand; use a broom or similar tool.)

Summary

This chapter covered how to install and configure modem and broadband connections to the Internet. You discovered techniques for protecting your computer while on the Internet by using Windows Defender and Windows Firewall. The chapter also gave you step-by-step instructions for implementing Internet Connection Sharing by using the Network Setup Wizard and by setting up this configuration manually.

Vista makes it considerably easier to keep your system protected from prying eyes, but only if you take the time to configure these features. Sure, the default settings do a good job, but they're generic. These settings reflect a best practice of what Microsoft thinks you might need. It's better to configure the software to meet your specific needs, which is what you should do now if you haven't already. Security is your responsibility and Microsoft can't do the whole job for you.

In the next chapter, you'll learn how to configure and use Internet Explorer to surf the Web. Internet Explorer 7 offers a lot of new features, such as a tabbed interface. If you've been wondering what you're missing by not using products such a Firefox, wonder no longer. The next chapter fills you in on all of the details of Internet Explorer 7, which is a big improvement from any previous version of Internet Explorer.

Chapter 15

Web Browsing with Internet Explorer

Obviously, the most important thing about Internet Explorer (IE) isn't the program itself but all the resources you can access using it. And, to be completely honest about it, Internet Explorer is so easy to use that you hardly need a how-to book, a manual, or even this chapter. If you know how to open any Vista program, you know how to open Internet Explorer, and you can start browsing immediately by simply clicking links.

Thus, in this chapter, I'm going to move briskly through the tasks you most commonly perform with Internet Explorer. As I proceed, I'll point out some new features of version 7 and show you how to expand on what comes naturally.

- Starting Internet Explorer
- Touring Internet Explorer
- Moving around the Web
- Finding exactly what you want on the Internet
- Customizing Internet Explorer

Vista: What's New?

There's a lot of new and a lot of old with Internet Explorer 7. Of course, what will strike you first is the new Internet Explorer 7 interface. It looks and feels new. Unfortunately, part of that new look and feel is Microsoft hiding older features you really may want to use. You'll see features that users have been asking for quite some time such as tabs. It's also possible to work with Rich Site Summary (RSS) entries on websites.

The interface uses screen real estate a lot more efficiently. Microsoft has reworked the part of Internet Explorer that people see most often. Of course, this is the default view. Interestingly enough, you can put some of the features from previous editions back into place. I provide a quick discussion of how to do this in the "Recovering Your Toolbars" section of the chapter.

However, some things remain relatively unchanged. For example, you won't notice many changes in the Internet Options dialog box. Yes, it has new entries to support the new Internet Explorer 7 features, but overall it works the same as the previous edition. For example, all of the same tabs are there and you work with older features just as you always have.

All of the old lists are still present. You can still use the History list to review where you have browsed on the Internet. Added to the standard lists is a new Feeds list that you can use to browse the RSS feeds that you have subscribed to on the Internet.

Microsoft has also added a little more security to Internet Explorer 7. Like the rest of Vista, the security is more pessimistic and you'll find that you can perform fewer tasks by default. These new limits are actually good because you'll have to think about whether a particular website really deserves to have increased rights. The new phishing filter also promises to make it significantly harder for websites to fool you into thinking they're something they really aren't (such as a cracker website posing as your bank).

I saved the feature I like best for last. Microsoft has finally made it relatively easy to manage add-ons for Internet Explorer. In addition, you can enable or disable the add-ons as needed. For example, you might only want to enable Macromedia Shockwave on websites you truly trust to avoid some of the well-known exploits crackers use to gain access to your system.

Starting Internet Explorer

When you first start Internet Explorer after installing Vista, you'll see the start page shown in Figure 15.1. (The content of the page changes daily, so yours will look different.)

You can start Internet Explorer by doing any of the following:

- Choose Start ➢ Internet Explorer.
- Choose Start ➢ All Programs ➢ Internet Explorer.
- Click the Internet Explorer icon in the Quick Launch toolbar (if displayed).
- Double-click the icon for a web page from a file management window or from the Desktop.
- Click a hyperlink in an e-mail message, document, or some other data file.

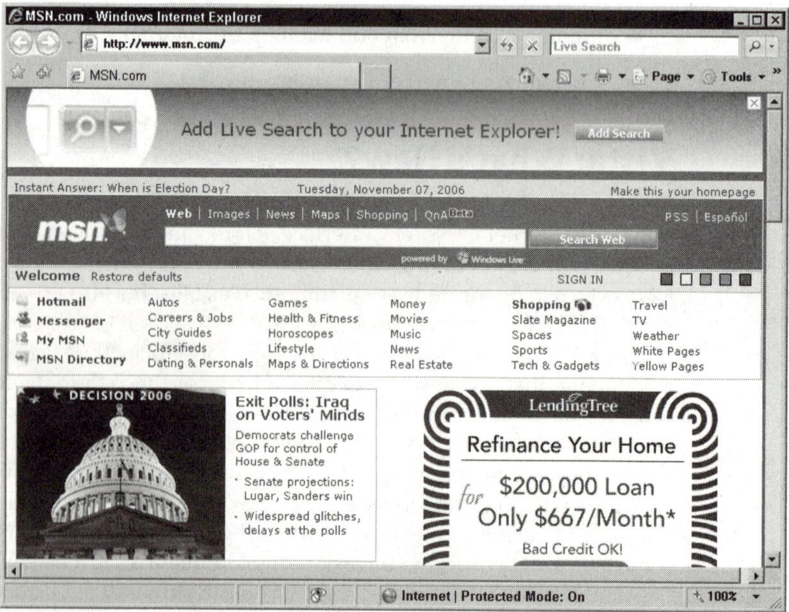

FIGURE 15.1 You can retain the page at `http://www.msn.com` as your start page or select any other page that suits your fancy or interests.

TIP If you use both Internet Explorer and some other browser, such as Firefox, when you start up Internet Explorer, if it's not set as the default browser, you'll see a dialog box offering to "fix" the problem. Clear the Always Perform This Check with Starting Internet Explorer check box to prevent it from doing this in the future. You can also control this preference from the Internet Options dialog box's Programs tab. That'll take care of it from the IE side. Your second browser will also have settings that let you set it as either the primary or the secondary browser. See the help that comes with the browser to determine how to perform this task.

Recovering Your Toolbars

Internet Explorer 7 actually looks more like previous versions of Internet Explorer than you might think. Microsoft has hidden some of the toolbars that you're used to seeing. To display the toolbars you've been missing, right-click the toolbar area and choose Menu bar. Right-click it again and choose Links. Right-click the toolbar again and choose Lock Toolbar. At this point, you can rearrange things to looks surprisingly similar to the old Internet Explorer as shown in Figure 15.2. Of course, you pay a price for having the toolbars back—reduced screen space for website data, which is why Microsoft hid these features from view.

You may have also noticed that some of the buttons are missing from the Command bar. Some of these buttons appear in other places. The Back, Forward, and Search buttons appear at the top of the window now. However, you can add other features in that you might be missing by right-clicking the toolbar and choosing Customize Command Bar ➤ Add or Remove Commands. You'll see the Customize Toolbar dialog box shown in Figure 15.3.

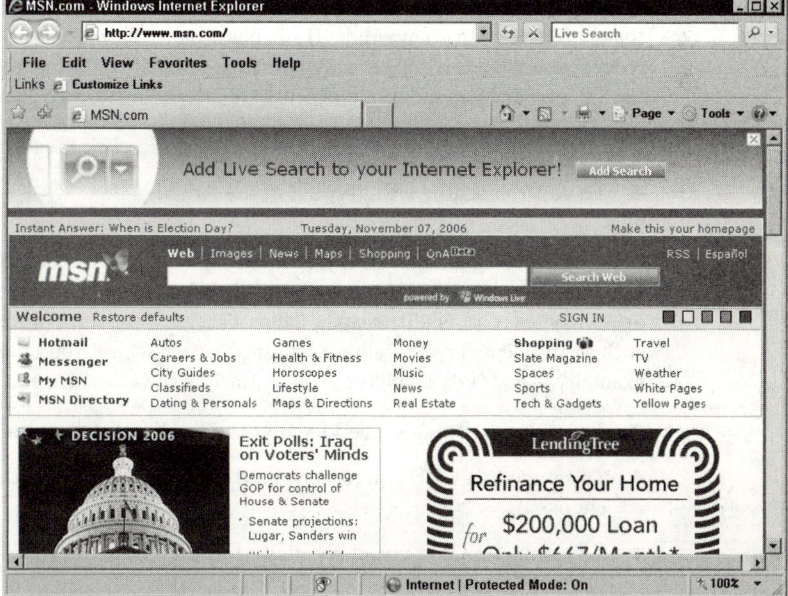

FIGURE 15.2 Microsoft simply hides some of the toolbars you enjoyed using in the past.

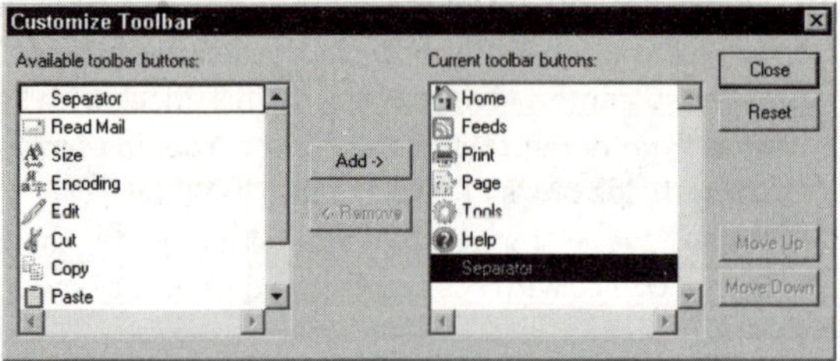

FIGURE 15.3 Add or remove buttons as needed from the Command bar to meet your personal needs.

To add a button, highlight its entry in the Available toolbar buttons list and click Add. Likewise, to remove a button, click its entry in the Current toolbar buttons list and click Remove. You can change the position of a button by selecting its entry in the Current toolbar buttons list and clicking either Move Up or Move Down as needed. Finally, if you find that you want the old setup back, click Reset.

TIP You can temporarily display the Menu bar by pressing Alt. Press the letter of the menu item you want to access, such as F for File. You can then choose a menu item by pressing the underlined letter for it. After you select a menu item, the Menu bar disappears from sight.

Moving around the Web

You probably already use Internet Explorer (or some other web browser) nearly every day, so we won't dwell on the basics of web surfing here, other than to run down this quick list of skills:

NOTE Depending on how you have security set up for your system, Internet Explorer may tell you that it needs to open a new window to display a particular website. This feature is designed to help reduce certain kinds of cracker activity such as cross-site scripting. It's a normal part of using Internet Explorer and you should simply click OK after being warned about the new window.

- To open the page represented by a hyperlink, click the hyperlink.
- To go to a specific URL, type it in the Address box.

NOTE Internet Explorer assumes that when you enter a URL in the Address bar, you want to go to a web page or some other HTML document. Therefore, whether you enter `http://www.sybex.com` or `www.sybex.com`, you'll reach the Sybex website. If you want to access another type of resource, such as an FTP archive, a Telnet host, or a Gopher server, you'll need to enter the full URL, for example, `ftp://ftp.archive.edu` for the FTP site at archive.edu.

- To open a web page saved locally, use the File ➢ Open command.
- To return to a URL you have visited recently, open the Address box's drop-down list and choose it.
- To return to a site you have visited in the last several days, choose Tools ➢ Toolbars ➢ History from the command bar to display the History pane (covered in more detail later in this chapter). You can also press Ctrl+Shift+H to open the History pane.

NOTE The Favorites Center has three tabs, one for each of the Internet Explorer 7 lists: favorites, history, and feeds. When you display the Favorites Center by clicking Favorites Center, the list appears temporarily while you make a selection. You can make the list appear permanently by clicking Pin the Favorites Center (the button in the upper right corner of the Favorites Center).

- To go to a URL you have saved on your Favorites list, open the Favorites pane by clicking the Favorites Center button and selecting it (also covered in more detail later). You can also press Ctrl+Shift+I to open the Favorites pane.
- To see your list of RSS feeds and any new articles they contain, choose Tools ➤ Toolbars ➤ Feeds from the command bar to display the Feeds pane (covered in more detail later in this chapter). You can also press Ctrl+Shift+J to open the Feeds pane.
- To return to the page you last viewed, click Back. To go back multiple steps, open the drop-down list on the Back button and choose the step in which you're interested.
- After having used Back, click Forward to go forward again to the page you started from when you clicked Back. The Forward button has a drop-down list, too, for multiple hops at once.

TIP If you want to edit only part of an address that's already displayed in the Address bar, place the cursor in the Address bar, hold down Ctrl, and press the right or left arrow to jump forward or backward to the next separator character (\\ \ . ? - or +).

A Look behind the Scenes: Viewing HTML Pages

HTML is the abbreviation for Hypertext Markup Language, the language that's used to create web pages. HTML uses tags to tell the browser how to display the page on the screen. Tags are enclosed in angle brackets, and most come in pairs. For example, the <H1> tag defines a first-level heading, like this:

<H1>This is a level 1 heading.</H1>

An HTML file is really just a plain text file that can be created with a text editor such as Notepad or with a program such as Microsoft FrontPage. To view the HTML behind any page you open in Internet Explorer, choose View ➤ Source. You'll see a special warning box that tells you an application is attempting to open web content like this one.

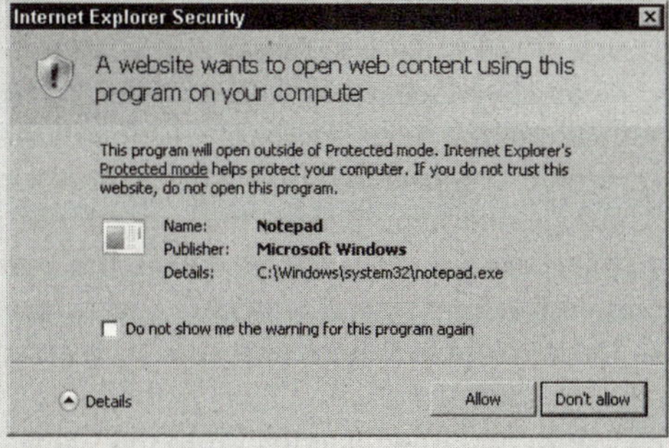

Click the down arrow next to Details so you can see all of the information about the application. If you're sure you want to open the content using the application, click Allow. Since you're simply displaying text using Notepad and there isn't any possibility of executing code, viewing the source code is safe and actually provides one method you can use to check the website for irregularities before you trust it. The file is displayed in Notepad and looks similar to the following:

To return to Internet Explorer and the page displayed in the browser, click the Close button in Notepad.

If you're interested in learning more about HTML and creating web pages, check out the following Sybex titles: *Mastering FrontPage 2002 Premium Edition* and *Mastering HTML and XHTML*.

Working with the Links Bar

One way to keep track of links that you follow and want to revisit is to add them to the Links bar. Unfortunately, you won't even see the Links bar when you first open Internet Explorer. Follow the instructions in the "Recovering Your Toolbars" section of the chapter to display it. In addition, unlike previous editions of Internet Explorer, Microsoft doesn't place any content in the Links bar. Consequently, the only content you'll see is the content you add.

To add a link to the Links bar, simply drag it from the web page to the Links bar. (You can then rename it if the name is too long by right-clicking and choosing Rename.) To remove a link, right-click it and choose Delete from the shortcut menu. To rearrange items on the Links bar, click the item and then drag it to a new location.

You can also add links and folders to the Links bar using Add to Favorites. When you add the link, place it in the Links folder of the Favorites pane. If you want to place the links in a folder, select the Links folder and click New Folder in the Add a Favorite dialog box. See the "Keeping Track of Your Favorite Sites" section of the chapter for more details on this method.

TIP You can put a link to any file on the Links bar, not just a web page. If you maintain a log file where you store interesting information you come across on the Web, for example, you could put a link to that text file there.

Keeping Track of Your Favorite Sites

If you add lots of links to the Links bar, it can get really crowded. You might find that you need a more sophisticated method of keeping track of your favorite sites, and the Favorites list is just the thing. To open it, click the Favorites Center button on the Standard toolbar, or choose Tools ➤ Toolbars ➤ Favorites. Figure 15.4 shows the Favorites pane of the Favorites Center.

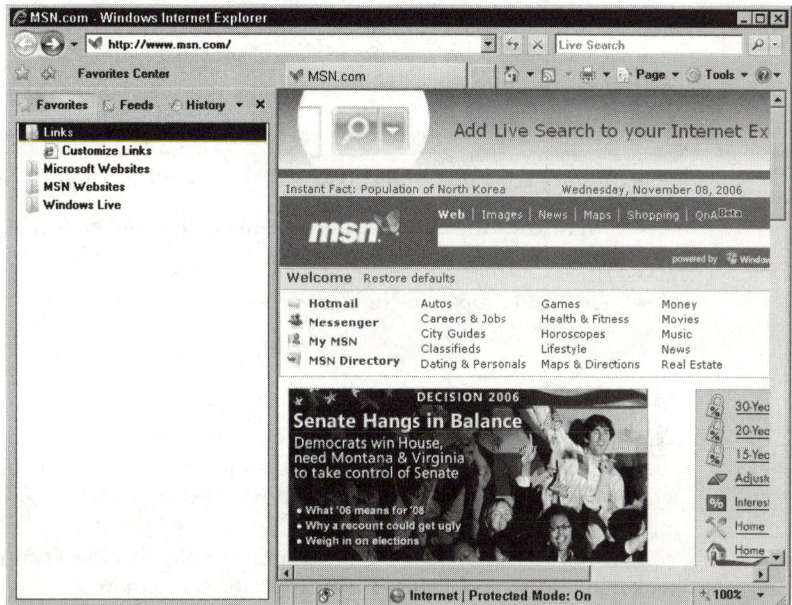

FIGURE 15.4 The Favorites pane contains a list of your favorite websites organized any way you want.

Adding a Site to Your Favorites List

To add a site to your Favorites list, follow these steps:

1. Go to the site you want to add.
2. Click Favorites (the icon that has a golden star with a green plus sign in front of it) ➤ Add to Favorites . . . or press Ctrl+D to open the Add Favorite dialog box shown in Figure 15.5.

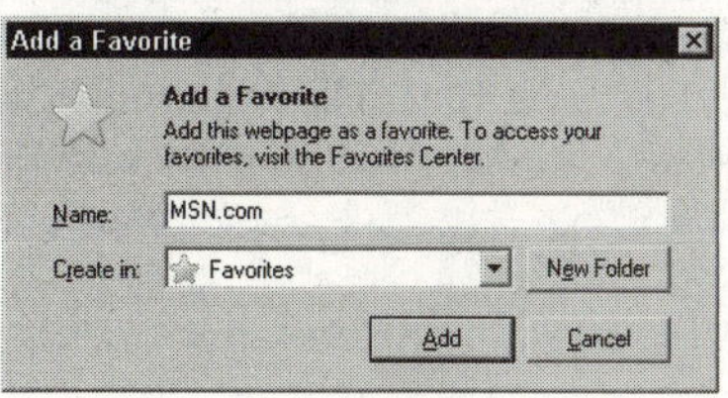

FIGURE 15.5 Adding a new favorite consists of providing a favorite name and a storage folder.

3. In the Add Favorites dialog box, Internet Explorer provides a name for this Favorite site. To give the site another name in your Favorites list, replace the default name with the name you want.

4. If you want to place this page in your top-level Favorites menu, click Add.

   If you want to add the item to an existing Favorites folder, click Create In and select a folder, and then click Add.

   If you want to create a new folder for this item, choose the starting location for the folder in the hierarchy, click New Folder, enter a name for the folder, and click Create. Then click Add to save the link into that new folder.

NOTE On some web pages, you'll see a suggestion that you "bookmark" this page. Netscape and some other web browsers refer to a list of sites that you want to revisit as a *bookmark list* rather than as a Favorites list.

You can also add items to your Favorites list in some other ways:

- Right-click a link, and choose Add to Favorites from the shortcut menu.
- Right-click the current page outside a link, and choose Add to Favorites from the shortcut menu.
- Drag and drop a link on a web page to the Favorites pane of the Favorites Center when displayed.

Maintaining Your Favorites List

You'll find out soon enough that your Favorites list will grow quickly, and before too long, it will become out of date. To keep your list manageable, you need to do some periodic housekeeping, weeding out what you don't want and rearranging or retitling what you do keep so that it's meaningful.

Deleting a site from your Favorites list is simple: open the Favorites bar or Favorites menu, right-click it in the list, and choose Delete from the shortcut menu. You might, however, want to get in the habit of following the link before you right-click—just in case the site is more important than you remembered and you want to keep it in the list.

To move an item to another place in the list or to another folder, simply click and drag it. To rename an item, right-click it and choose Rename from the shortcut menu. Type the new name and press Enter.

You can also do all of this management and more from the Organize Favorites dialog box, shown in Figure 15.6. To access this dialog box, choose Favorites ➢ Organize Favorites. From here, you can rename, delete, move, and so on, plus create new folders.

TIP If your Favorites list gets very long, it may be difficult to wade through. One way to reduce its size is to turn on the Personalized Favorites Menu option. This hides favorites that haven't recently been used, much like the personalized menus feature in Office XP. Choose Tools ➢ Internet Options, click Advanced, and mark the Enable Personalized Favorites Menu check box.

FIGURE 15.6
Organize your list of favorites.

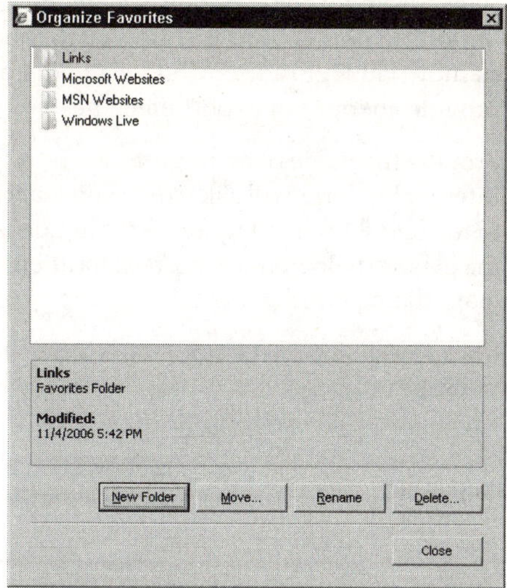

Importing and Exporting Favorites

There are many reasons to import and export favorites. You may want to share favorites with other people or incorporate their favorites into your list. Exporting your favorites and placing them in a safe place on another drive or maintaining them as part of a backup is one way to ensure your favorites won't get lost. Import your favorites after you set up a new system to restore Internet Explorer functionality quickly.

The following steps describe how to import or export favorites:

1. Choose Add to Favorites ➤ Import and Export. You'll see the Import/Export Wizard dialog box.
2. Click Next. You'll see a list of items you can import and export as shown in Figure 15.7.

FIGURE 15.7
Choose the items that you want to import or export from the list.

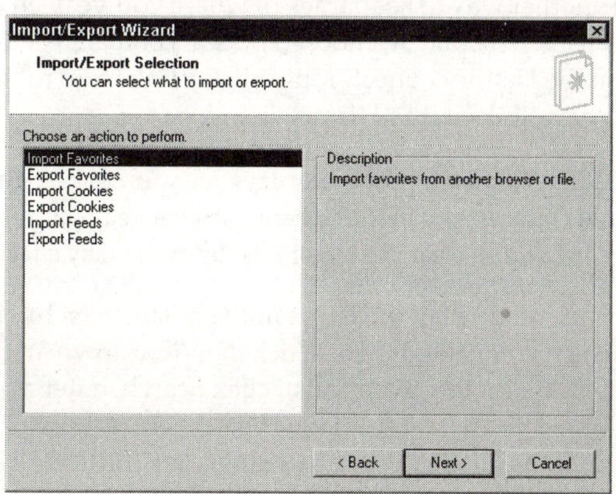

3. Select an import or export task from the list. Click Next. If you're exporting favorites, the Import/Export Wizard will ask you to choose a folder to use as a starting point for exporting as shown in Figure 15.8. Choose a folder and click Next. In all cases, you'll see a request to provide an input or export filename.
4. Provide the name of an import or export folder. Click Next. When working with favorites, Internet Explorer will ask where you want to place the favorites using the dialog box similar to the one shown in Figure 15.8 (the title is different, but the dialog box works the same as the export dialog box). Choose a location for the favorites and click Next. You'll see a summary dialog box.
5. Click Finish. Internet Explorer performs the task that you requested and displays a success message.

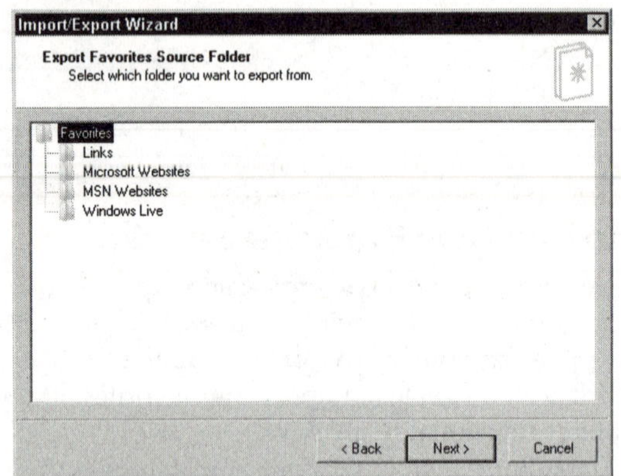

FIGURE 15.8
Select the location for imports or exports in the Favorites folder.

Working with the History List

Yet another way to keep track of where you've been and to quickly revisit sites of interest is the History list. To display it, choose Tools ➤ Toolbars ➤ History (you can also press Ctrl+Shift+H). You'll open the History pane. Simply click a link to go to that page. Click a folder to see pages in that site that have links in the History list.

NOTE To specify how many days you want to keep links in the History list, choose Tools ➤ Internet Options, and in the General tab change the number in the Days to Keep Pages in History box. You can also clear the history list from there by clicking Clear History.

You can display the items in the History list by date, by site, by most visited, and by the order in which you visited them. Click the View down arrow to choose an order. If you want to search for something on the History list, click Search, enter a word or a phrase, and click Search Now.

To delete an item from the History list, right-click it, and choose Delete from the shortcut menu. To clear the History list completely, click the Clear History button in the General tab of the Internet Options dialog box.

NOTE The original version of IE 6 came with a Media bar that you could use to listen to music and play videos from within IE. Lots of people found it annoying, though, especially for video playback because the video would be so tiny. As of Service Pack 2 (SP2), it's no longer a part of IE.

Sending a Link or Page via E-mail

When you find a web page that someone else you know might enjoy, you can e-mail its link to them. To send a link, follow these steps:

1. Open the page.
2. Press Alt if necessary to display the Menu bar. Choose File ➤ Send ➤ Link by E-mail to send just the link or File ➤ Send ➤ Page by E-mail if you want to send the entire page. When you choose the Page by E-mail option, you'll see a content warning dialog box (the same one shown in the "A Look behind the Scenes: Viewing HTML Pages" sidebar). The New Message window opens with the link in the body of the message and the site title in the Subject and Attach lines.
3. Address your message, compose your message, and click Send.

If your recipient is connected to the Internet and has a web browser, they merely need to click the link in the message to open the page when you send a link. Sending the page is convenient when you can't be sure that the recipient will see the message right away and the page has content that changes regularly.

Some e-mail programs block the sending or receipt of e-mail links sent in this manner. If the recipient can't read it, or if you can't send it this way, try sending the page itself. To send the page itself, follow the same steps but choose Send Page (or Send Page by Email). The current page you're viewing will appear in the body of the message.

WARNING Before you willy-nilly include web pages in your e-mail, be sure that your recipient's e-mail program can handle HTML messages. For more information about e-mail and HTML, see Chapter 17.

Saving and Printing Web Pages

If you always want to see the most current version of a web page, you probably want to place a link to it on the Links bar or the Favorites bar. However, in some cases, you'll want to save it to your local hard drive or to a drive on your network. For example, I recently wanted easy access to a rather long U.S. government document. In this case, the document had been written and distributed over the Internet and was not going to change. It was what it was, so I saved it to my local network so that I could get to it quickly without being connected to the Internet. Saving a web page has other practical uses. For example, you can save the web page that contains information about an order that you make online. The saved web page is a good backup in case the website doesn't send you a confirmation email.

Saving the Current Page

To save the current page, follow these steps:

1. Press Alt if necessary to display the Menu bar. Choose File ➤ Save As to open the Save Webpage dialog box shown in Figure 15.9.
2. Click Browse Folders, if necessary, to display a list of locations you can use to save the web page. Select a folder in which to save the page, and in the File Name box enter a name if you want something different from that which Internet Explorer proposes.
3. In the Save As Type drop-down box, select the format in which you want the page saved.
4. Click Save.

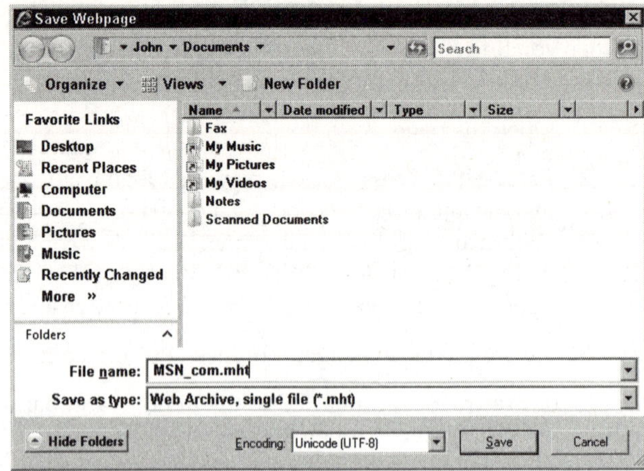

FIGURE 15.9
The Save Webpage dialog box lets you save a local copy of a web page.

You can also save a web page without opening it if its link is displayed. Follow these steps:

1. Right-click the link, and choose Save Target As from the shortcut menu. You'll see a dialog box that shows you that the page is being downloaded.
2. In the Save As dialog box (see Figure 15.9), select a folder, and specify a filename.
3. Click Save.

SAVING PORTIONS OF A PAGE

You can also save only a portion of text from a web page or an image. To save a portion of text to use in another document, select the text, and then press Ctrl+C. Open the other document, place the insertion point where you want the text, and press Ctrl+V.

SAVING AN IMAGE

To save an image, follow these steps:

1. Right-click the image, and choose Save Picture As from the shortcut menu to open the Save Picture dialog box.
2. Select a folder, a filename, and a type, and click Save.

To save an image as wallpaper, right-click the image and choose Set As Background from the shortcut menu. To specify how you want the wallpaper displayed, right-click the image on the Desktop, choose Properties to open the Display Properties dialog box. Click the Desktop tab, and select an option in the Position drop-down box.

PRINTING THE CURRENT PAGE

If you want to quickly print the current page, simply click the Print button on the Standard toolbar. Using Internet Explorer 7, you can also choose Print Preview and Page Setup from the down arrow next to the Print button. If, however, you want more control over what's printed and how, press Alt (if necessary) and then choose File ➢ Print to open the Print dialog box.

For the most part, this is your standard Windows Print dialog box. (For details about printers and printing in Vista, see Chapter 9.) The difference is the Options tab, which you can use to specify how frames and links are printed; it's shown in Figure 15.10.

Here are the specifics:

- Select the As laid out on screen option in the Print Frames section to print the web page exactly as it's displayed on your screen.
- Select the Only the selected frame option to print only a frame you have previously selected. (To select a frame, click inside it in an empty space—in other words, not on a link.) If you're not sure which frame is selected, use File ➤ Print Preview.
- Select the All frames individually option if you want to print each frame on a separate sheet of paper.
- Select the Print all linked documents option if you want to print the pages that are linked to the current page as well. (Be sure you really want to do this; you could need lots of paper.)
- Select the Print table of links option if you want to print a table that lists the links for the page at the end of the document.

When you have all your options selected, click the Print button on any tab to print the document.

To print the target of any link, right-click the link, and choose Print Target from the shortcut menu to open the Print dialog box.

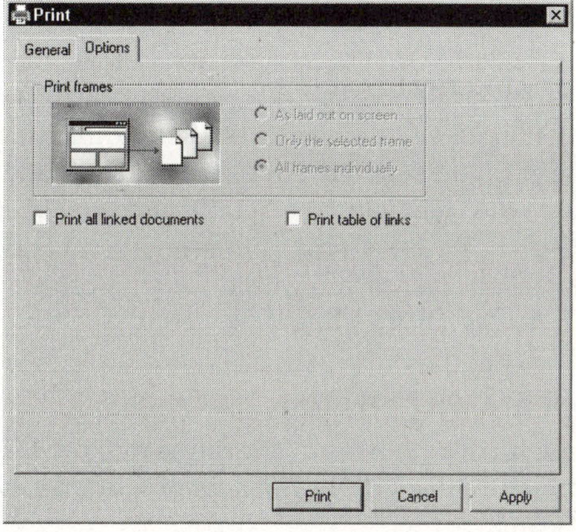

FIGURE 15.10 The Print dialog box, open at the Options tab.

TIP By default, Windows does not print the background colors and background images of web pages. First, the printed output could be illegible, and, second, unless you have a rather powerful printer, spooling and printing could be really slow. If, for whatever reason, you want or need to print the background, choose Tools ➤ Internet Options to open the Internet Options dialog box. Click the Advanced tab, scroll down to the Printing section in the Settings list, check the Print background colors and images check box, and click OK.

Printing Your Favorites List

There's no way to directly print the Favorites list in Internet Explorer, but you can do so indirectly like this:

1. Export it to a file (press Alt, choose File ➤ Import and Export, and use the wizard as described in the "Importing and Exporting Favorites" section of the chapter).
2. Open that file in Internet Explorer (File ➤ Open).
3. Choose File ➤ Print, and in the Options tab, choose Print Table of Links.

Finding Exactly What You Want on the Internet

The serendipitous experience of clicking and following hyperlinks may suffice while you're polishing off your lunch of tuna sandwich and chips or filling the occasional lazy, rainy afternoon, but most of the time when you connect to the Internet, you have something specific in mind that you want to do or find. Regardless of what you're looking for—information about a topic, an e-mail or mailing address, a business, a web page, and so on—the way to find it is to use a search service. *Search service* is a relatively new term for what we referred to in the past as a search engine, a program that can search a file, a database, or the Internet for keywords and retrieve documents in which those keywords are found.

Examples of search services that you may have used include Yahoo!, AltaVista, Google, and HotBot Advanced. To search with one of these services, you go to the site (for example, `www.yahoo.com`); optionally, select a category, enter a keyword or phrase, and click Search (or some similar button). You can also access search services within Internet Explorer. Let's do a simple search to see how this works.

Performing the Search

Internet Explorer 7 is designed to work directly with search engines. It uses whatever search engine you have selected as the default. The name of the default search service appears in the Type to search the web field. The default and only search engine installed with Internet Explorer 7 is Live Search. To use it, type your search term and click Search (the magnifying glass icon). You'll see the results just as you would for any website as shown in Figure 15.11. To access one of the search results, click its link.

Adding Search Providers

You might already have a favorite search provider that you like using. For example, you might be familiar with all of the nuances of working with Google and aren't very interested in using Live Search.

Use the following steps to change a search provider:

1. Choose Find More Providers from the Search Options list (the down arrow next to the Search button). You'll see a list of search providers such as the one shown in Figure 15.12.
2. Click the link for the search engine you want to use. Microsoft provides links for most common search providers such as Google. You'll see an Add Search Provider dialog box that tells you about the search provider. If you don't see the provider you want, proceed to Step 4.
3. Click Add Provider. Internet Explorer adds the new provider to the available list. You're ready to go with your standard search provider.

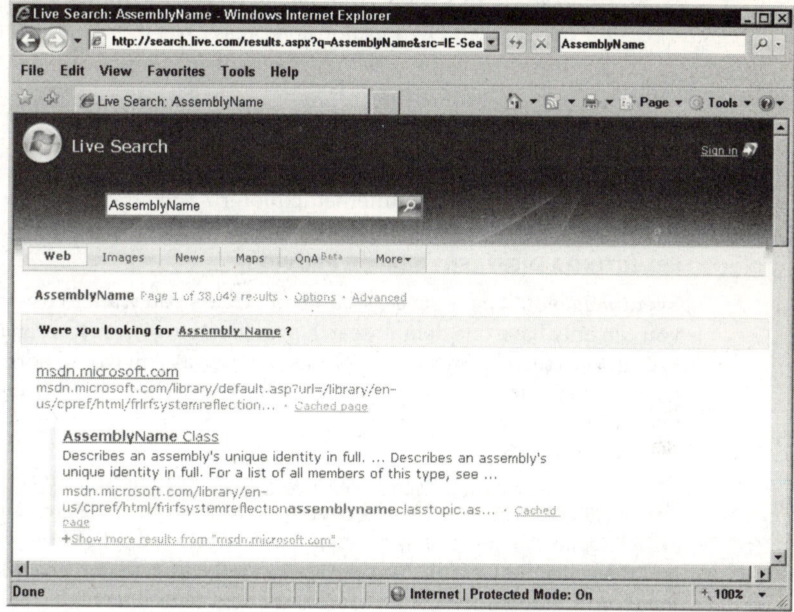

FIGURE 15.11
Searching for and finding specific results is an essential part of the web experience.

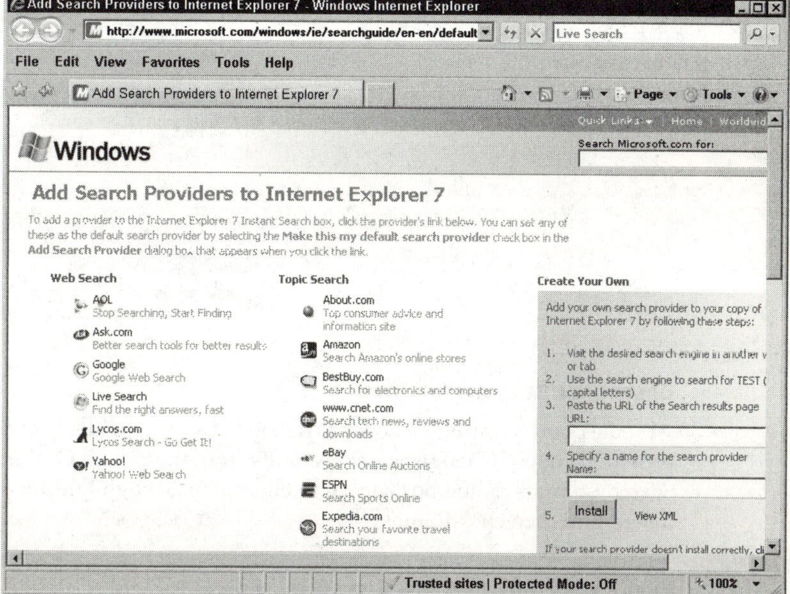

FIGURE 15.12
Microsoft provides a listing of search providers that you can choose or you can create your own.

4. Open the URL for the alternative search provider you want to add in another tab.
5. Perform a search for the word TEST (use all capital letters).
6. Highlight the URL in the Address bar and press Ctrl+C.

7. Select the Add Search Providers to Internet Explorer 7 tab. Select the text box in Step 3 of the Create Your Own section and press Ctrl+V. You see the URL you copied pasted into the text box.
8. Type a name for the alternative search engine in the text box for Step 4.
9. Click Install. You see the Add Search Provider dialog box.
10. Click Add Provider. Internet Explorer 7 adds the new provider for you.

SELECTING A DIFFERENT SEARCH PROVIDER

Eventually, you'll have several search providers you want to use for specific situations. Of course, you can only have one default search provider. However, you can use any search engine you want to perform a search. Simply type the search term as you would normally, and then choose the search engine you want to use from the Search Options list (the down arrow next to the Search button). This feature lets you use a search engine one time and then revert to your normal default search engine for subsequent searches.

If you find that the default search engine isn't to your liking, you can always change it. To change defaults, choose Change Search Defaults from the Search Options list. You'll see the Change Search Defaults dialog box shown in Figure 15.13. Highlight the search provider you want to use, and then click Set Default. You can always tell which search provider is the current default because the word Default appears in parentheses next to its entry.

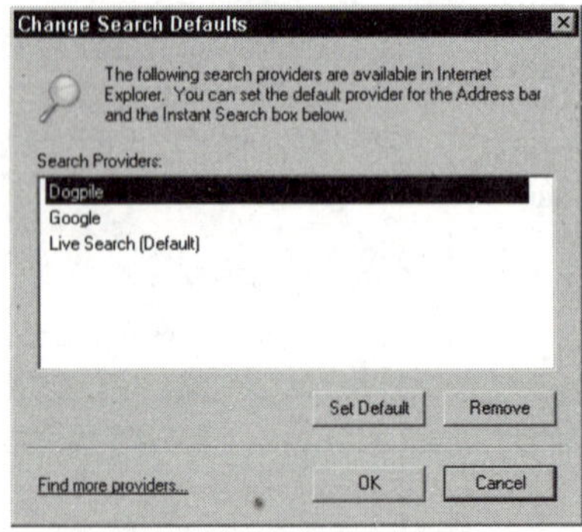

FIGURE 15.13 Change the default search engine for Internet Explorer to match your preferences.

DELETING A SEARCH PROVIDER

At some point, you might choose to delete a search provider you no longer need. To delete a search provider, choose Change Search Defaults from the Search Options list. You'll see the Change Search Defaults dialog box shown in Figure 15.13. Highlight the search provider you want to delete, and then click Remove.

Working with the Feeds List

The abbreviation RSS has at least three definitions and you might see more. Of course, all of these definitions make the term confusing. All that RSS really provides is a means of downloading headers from your favorite website. The headers tell you about the latest news stories. If you decide to read the story, you click a link to go directly to the story on the website. The summary also includes a very short summary and may provide other special features, such as the ability to add the story to other websites such as Digg (`http://digg.com/`).

NOTE Places such as Digg provide yet another alternative for figuring out what to read in our information-overloaded society. As you Digg for stories, they rise to the top of the heap. Theoretically, the main page contains a list of stories that have received the most votes.

Adding Feeds

The following steps tell you how to add a new RSS feed to the list.

1. Click the little orange RSS symbol you see next to a link or as part of the web page. Internet Explorer takes you to a web page that contains additional information about the feed and provides you with some examples of the content.
2. Click the Subscribe to this feed link. You'll see the dialog box shown in Figure 15.14. Adding an RSS feed is very much like adding a favorite.
3. Type a name for the feed in the Name field. Choose a location for the feed or create a new location using the same techniques you use for a favorite.
4. Click Subscribe. Internet Explorer adds the new feed to your list of feeds. Notice that the Subscribe to this feed link changes to a View my feeds link when you don't have the Favorites Center open. You can click this link to open the Feeds tab of the Favorites Center.

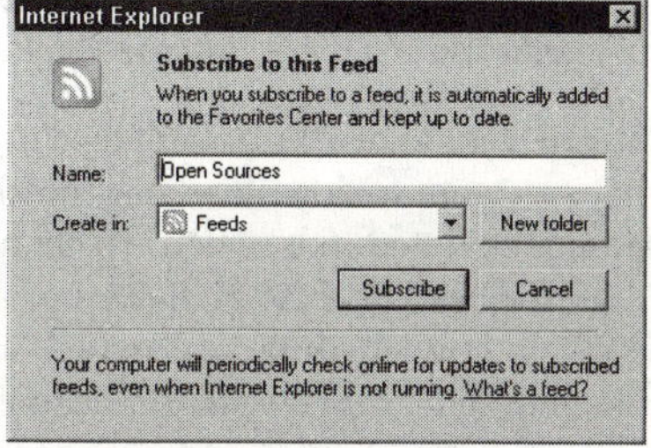

FIGURE 15.14
Provide a feed name and location.

Viewing Feeds

Internet Explorer doesn't automatically tell you when new content is available on your favorite website by default. Instead, you must go down the list of available feeds and view them for new content one at a time. To perform this task, open the Feeds tab of the Favorites Center pane by choosing Tools ➤ Toolbars ➤ Feeds. Click the link for one of the feeds you've added and you'll see a list of headings for it in the window as shown in Figure 15.15.

Notice the Mark feed as read link. The presence of this link tells you that you haven't read the feed yet and it contains new headings. The check mark next to this link lets you determine whether Internet Explorer marks the headings as read when you leave the page. If you click the Mark feed as read link, the check mark disappears and Internet Explorer keeps the current headers marked as unread.

The status panel to the right of the feed listings provides entries you can use to manage the list of headers easier. For example, you can always sort the headings. The sort options depend on the feed, but date and title are always present. You'll normally see author as a sort criterion as well. In addition, many feeds provide the means to filter the articles. For example, you might only have an interest in corporate topics, so you can choose to view only those headers using a filter. Whenever the feed has new articles, you can also click the New link to see the new headers.

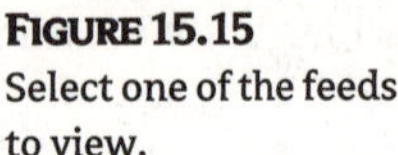

FIGURE 15.15
Select one of the feeds to view.

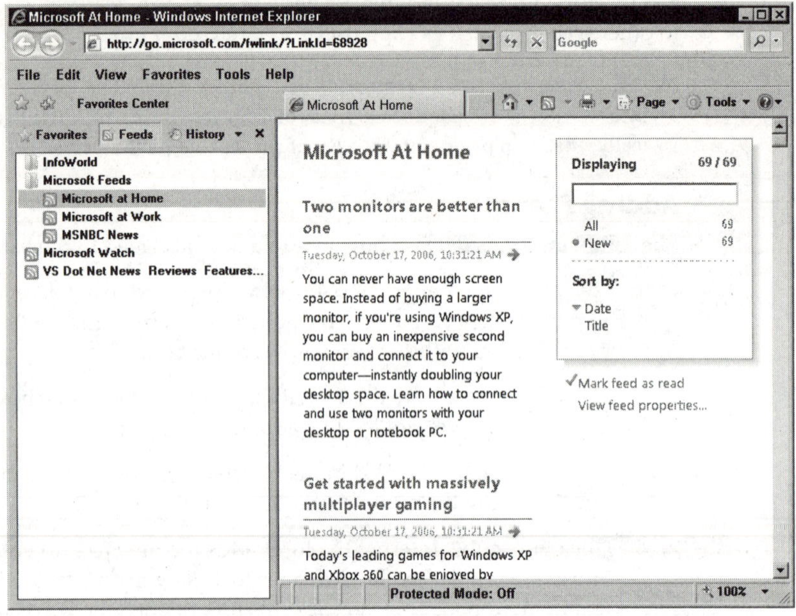

TIP To see the latest headings for a particular feed, right-click any blank area of the page and choose Refresh from the context menu. Internet Explorer will download any new headings for you.

You may not want to use the default feed settings that Microsoft provides. For example, Microsoft assumes that you want to download new headings automatically once a day and you might want to see the headings updated more often. To change the feed properties, click the View feed properties link. You'll see the Feed Properties dialog box shown in Figure 15.16. This dialog box lets you change the feed name, update schedule, and archive schedule. Archiving is important because it keeps your display from getting cluttered with old headings.

It's also possible to ask Internet Explorer to download the content in the Feed Properties dialog box. This convenience feature downloads both the headings and features so that you can read articles while you're away from the Internet. Archiving becomes especially important in this case because the articles can consume a lot of space on your hard drive.

The Feed Properties dialog box does contain a hidden setting that you need to know about. Click Settings and you'll see the Feed Settings dialog box shown in Figure 15.17. The dialog box contains interesting features such as automatically marking a feed as read when you finish with it. However, the last option, Play a sound when a feed is found for a webpage, is perhaps the most important. Just as you hear a sound when mail arrives in your inbox, you can tell Internet Explorer to inform you when there are new headers to read.

Deleting Feeds

You may find that you don't want to subscribe to all of the feeds you've tried. To delete a feed, open the Feeds tab of the Favorites Center pane by choosing Tools ➤ Toolbars ➤ Feeds. Right-click the feed you want to delete in the Feeds tab and choose Delete from the context menu.

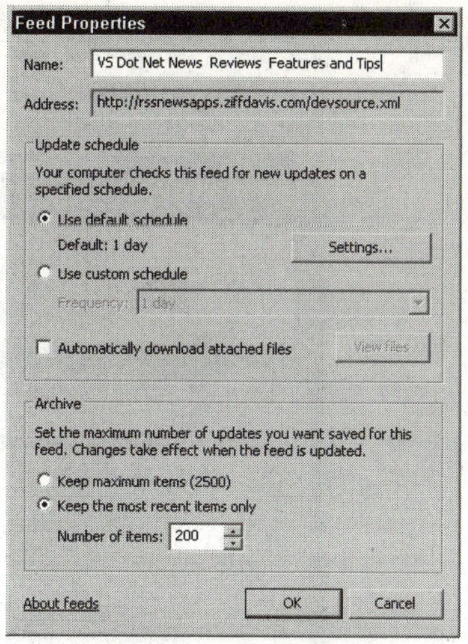

FIGURE 15.16
Change the feed settings as necessary to get the news when you need it.

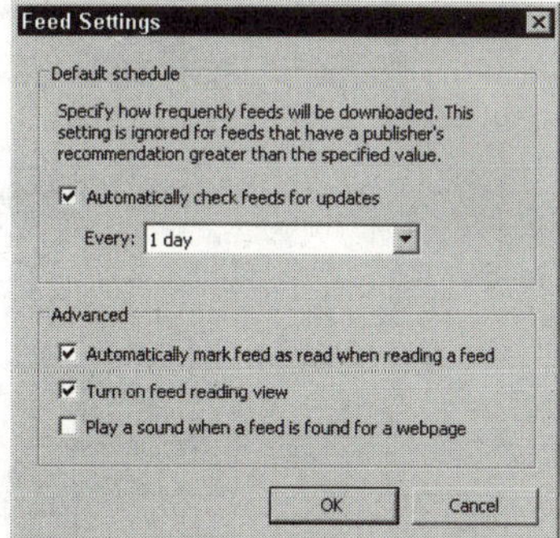

FIGURE 15.17
Add sound to the RSS feed download so you know when new headers arrive.

Downloading Files

Sometimes when you click on a hyperlink, it doesn't take you to another web page; instead, it starts a file download. However, Internet Explorer doesn't let you download files from just anywhere and it might block the download. When this situation occurs, you'll see an Information bar notice first asking whether you noticed that Internet Explorer has displayed it. (Internet Explorer also makes a sound when it displays the Information bar to attract your attention.) Click Close. Click the Information bar and you'll see options for working with the website as shown in Figure 15.18.

Click What's the Risk? to learn more about file downloads from a security perspective. Downloading files from sites you don't trust doesn't make sense. If you decide that the website is trustworthy, click Download File. When you don't click this option, Internet Explorer takes you back to the previous web location and cancels the download. Whether the website is blocked or not, you'll eventually see a download dialog box, as in Figure 15.19.

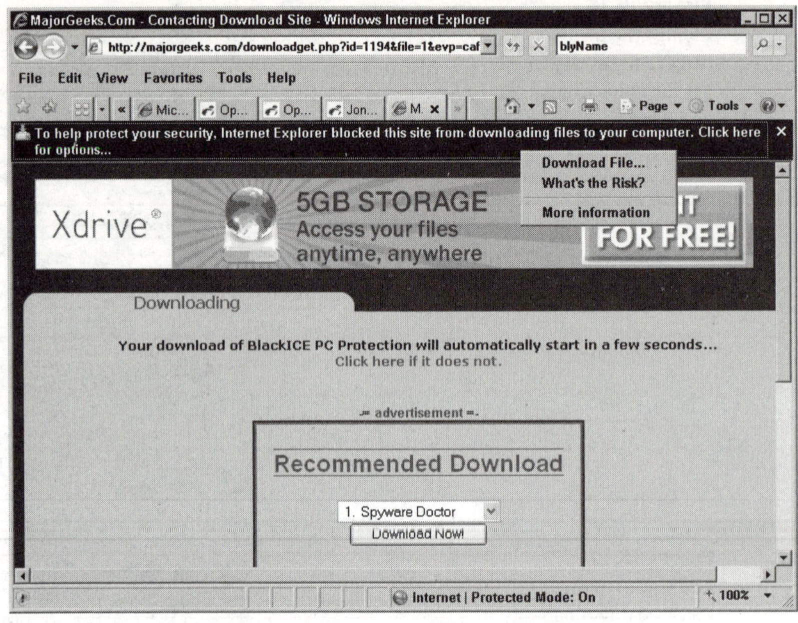

FIGURE 15.18
Internet Explorer may block your attempt to download a file.

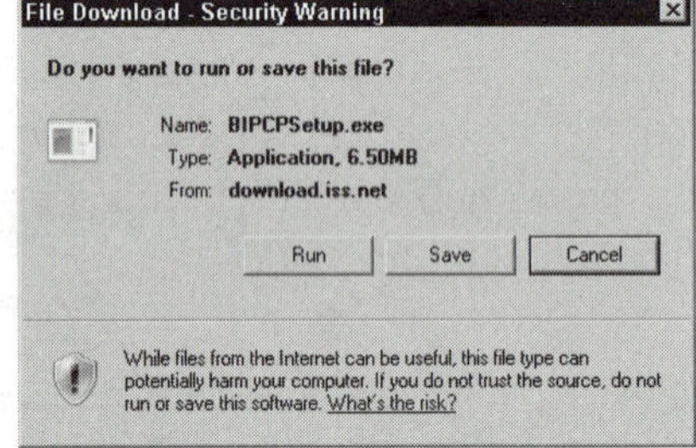

FIGURE 15.19
When a hyperlink points to a downloadable file, this box appears.

If you choose Run (or Open), the file is downloaded to a temporary folder and run from there. This is useful if you're downloading a setup program but you don't need to retain that setup program after you run it.

If you choose Save, it prompts you for a folder in which to save the file, but it does not run it. When the download is finished, you'll see a dialog box where you can choose Run (or Open) to run the program or Open Folder to open the folder into which it was saved.

Customizing Internet Explorer

In Vista, you can view or change the configuration options relating to Internet Explorer in two ways:

- Use Internet Options in Control Panel.
- Choose Tools ➤ Internet Options from within Internet Explorer.

Regardless of which you choose, you open the same dialog box. However, if you open it from Control Panel, it's called Internet Properties, and if you open it from within Internet Explorer, it's called Internet Options. In both cases, the contents of the dialog boxes are identical. In this section, we'll use Internet Explorer. (To open the Internet Properties dialog box, choose Start ➤ Control Panel ➤ Network and Internet Connections ➤ Internet Options.)

The Internet Options dialog box has seven tabs, and in the next few sections, I'll review the most important configuration choices you can make on each of these tabs. I'll start with the General tab.

Configuring the General Tab

The General tab, shown in Figure 15.20, contains these groups of settings:

Home Page Lets you choose which web page opens each time you connect to the Internet. A home page is the first web page you see when you start Internet Explorer. Click Use Current to make the current page your home page (if you're online to the Internet), click Use Default to return to the default setting, and click Use Blank to start each Internet session with a blank screen. To use a different web page as your home page, type the URL in the Address box.

Browsing history Contains a list of the links you have visited so that you can return to them quickly and easily using the History button on the Internet Explorer toolbar. You can specify the number of days you want to keep pages in the History folder; if you're running low on hard disk space, consider reducing this number. To delete all the information currently in the History folder, click the Delete button.

Search Provides access to the Change Search Settings dialog box where you can choose the default search provider. Click Settings to change the search provider defaults.

Tabs Defines how Internet Explorer presents tabs. Clicking Settings displays the Tabbed Browsing Settings dialog box. The options include turning off the tabbed feature if you want to return Internet Explorer to its older configuration. You can also determine how to handle pop-ups and links from other applications.

Colors button Opens the Colors dialog box in which you can choose which colors are used as background, links, and text on those web pages for which the original author did not specify colors. By default, the Use Windows Colors option is selected.

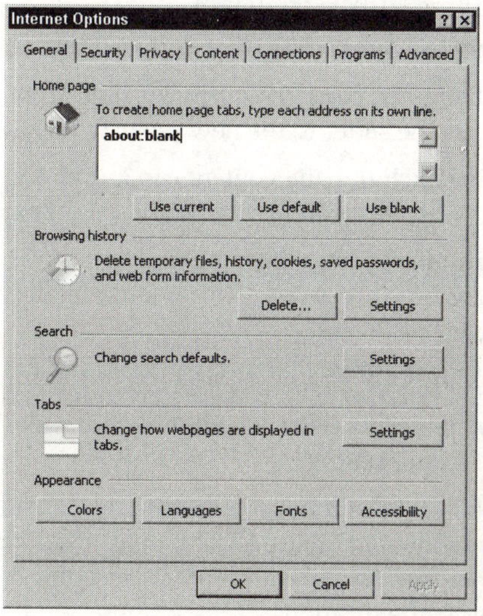

FIGURE 15.20
The General tab in the Internet Options dialog box.

TIP You can always change the Windows colors. In Control Panel, click Display, and then select the Appearance tab.

Fonts button Opens the Fonts dialog box in which you can specify the font style and text size to use on those web pages for which the original author did not make a specification.

Languages button Opens the Language Preference dialog box in which you can choose the character set to use on those web pages that offer content in more than one language. English is rapidly becoming the most common language in use on the Internet, so you may not use this option often.

Accessibility button Opens the Accessibility dialog box in which you can choose how certain information is displayed in Internet Explorer, including font styles, colors, and text size. You can also specify that your own style sheet is used.

Looking at the Security Tab

When you're connected to the Internet, you immediately have a couple of concerns that aren't at issue otherwise: security and privacy. Security concerns involve protecting your computer from unsafe software. Privacy concerns involve protecting your personally identifiable information. To configure the security settings in Internet Explorer, you click the Security tab in the Internet Options dialog box, which we'll look at in this section. To configure privacy settings, you use the Privacy tab, which we'll look at in the next section.

The Security tab, which is shown in Figure 15.21, lets you specify the overall security level for each of four zones. Each zone has its own default security restrictions that tell Internet Explorer how to manage dynamic web page content such as ActiveX controls and Java applets. The zones are as follows:

Internet Sites you visit that aren't in one of the other categories; default security is set to Medium.

Local Intranet Sites you can access on your corporate intranet; default security is set to Medium-Low.

Trusted Sites Websites that you're confident won't send you potentially damaging content; default security is set to Low.

Restricted Sites Sites that you visit but don't trust; default security is set to High.

To change the current security level of a zone, select the zone, click the Default Level button, and then move the slider to the new security level you want to use:

High Excludes any content capable of damaging your system. Cookies are disabled, and so some websites won't work as you might expect. This is the most secure setting.

Medium Opens a warning dialog box in Internet Explorer before running ActiveX or Java applets on your system. This is a moderately secure setting that's good for everyday use and is selected by default.

Medium-Low Same as Medium but without the prompts.

Low Does not issue any warning but runs the ActiveX or Java applet automatically. This is the least secure setting.

Click the Custom Level button to create your own settings in the Security Settings dialog box, which is shown in Figure 15.22. You can individually configure how you want to manage certain categories, such as ActiveX controls and plug-ins, Java applets, scripting, file and font downloads, and user authentication.

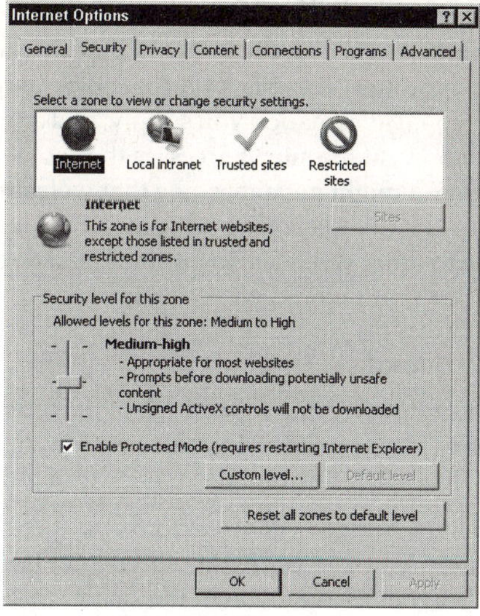

FIGURE 15.21
The Security tab in the Internet Options dialog box.

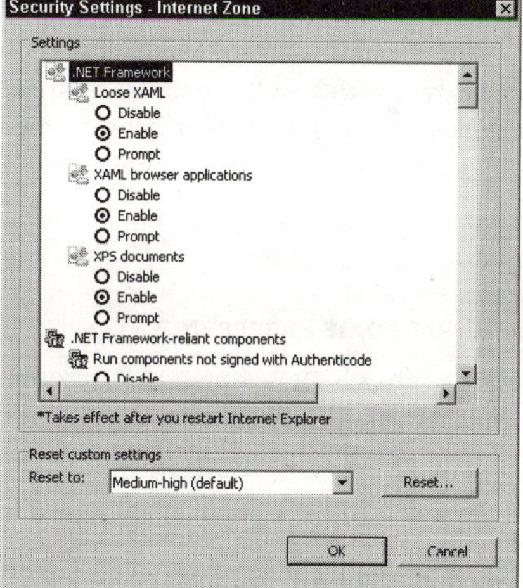

FIGURE 15.22
The Security Settings dialog box.

This dialog box also contains a new security feature for Internet Explorer. The Enable Protected Mode option lets you decide whether Internet Explorer should provide additional protection against websites that try to download files to your system or install executables. It's a good idea to keep this feature enabled because telling Internet Explorer that you really do want to download a file is a single click away. With all of the nefarious websites out there trying to download nasty files to your system, the extra protection is critical.

You'll also see a new Reset all zones to default level button. Clicking this button automatically removes any extra security you've added. If you tend to provide extra heavy security for your system, like I do, then clicking this button will undo every good thing you've every done. This button is only helpful if you've completely messed up the security settings on your system and want to return it to a semi-secure state quickly.

Using the Privacy Tab

When you visit a site on the Internet, that site can store information about you in a file that resides on your computer. This file, called a cookie, might contain your name, your e-mail address, any other personal information you supply, and any preferences you established when visiting the site. When you revisit the site, it accesses the cookie in order to personalize the site for your visit. For example, you might get a message that welcomes you by name.

Once a site saves a cookie on your computer, only that website can access the cookie; it isn't available to other websites. In addition, the website that created the cookie can't access any other information that's stored on your computer.

Types of Cookies

Using the settings on the Privacy tab in the Internet Options dialog box, you can choose to allow all websites to store cookies on your computer, to allow only some sites to do so, or to allow none to do so. Before we look at these settings, though, it's helpful to understand the types of cookies:

Persistent cookies Are stored on your computer and remain there after you close Internet Explorer. You saw earlier in this chapter how to delete cookies using the options in the Temporary Internet Files section in the General tab of the Internet Options dialog box.

Temporary cookies Are stored on your computer only as long as you have Internet Explorer open. When you close Internet Explorer, these cookies are deleted.

First-party cookies Originate on or are sent to the website you're currently visiting.

Third-party cookies Originate on or are sent to a website that you're not currently viewing. For example, a site that's advertising on the site you're currently viewing might create a cookie to track your Internet usage for marketing purposes.

Unsatisfactory cookies Allow access to your personal information that can be used without your knowledge or consent.

Establishing Cookie Preferences

In the Privacy tab, which is shown in Figure 15.23, you use the slider in the Settings section to specify how you'll deal with cookies in the Internet zone. You have the following choices:

- Block All Cookies does exactly that. No website is allowed to store a cookie on your computer, and any existing cookies that are stored won't be able to be read by the sites that created them.
- High blocks all cookies from websites that don't have a compact privacy policy and blocks cookies that collect personal information without your knowledge or consent.

NOTE A *compact privacy policy* is a statement in condensed computer-readable form about how a site handles personal information.

- Medium High blocks the following:
  - Third-party cookies from sites that don't have a compact privacy policy
  - Third-party cookies from sites that use personal information without your knowledge or consent
  - First-party cookies from sites that use personal information without your knowledge or consent

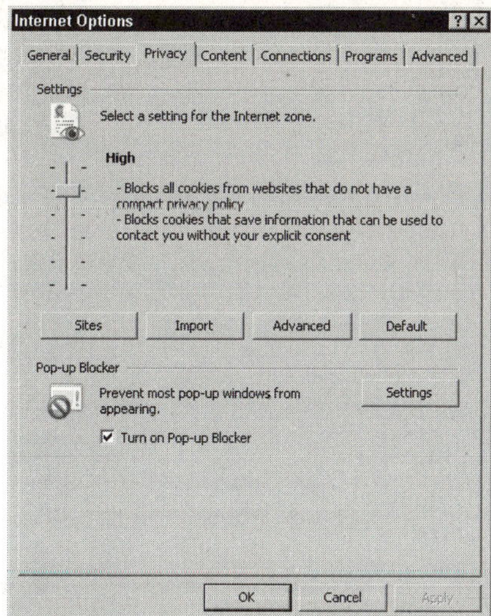

FIGURE 15.23
The Privacy tab in the Internet Options dialog box.

- Medium, the default setting, blocks third-party cookies from sites that don't have a compact privacy policy and from sites that use personal information without your knowledge or consent. This setting restricts first-party cookies that use personal information without your knowledge or consent.
- Low restricts third-party cookies from sites that don't have a compact privacy policy and from sites that use personal information without your knowledge or consent.
- Accept All Cookies does exactly that. All cookies from all sites are accepted and stored on your computer, and any cookies that are already on your computer can be accessed by the websites that created them.

When you use the slider bar to set your preferences, you establish a sort of one-size-fits-all rule that applies to all websites that you visit. You can use the other options in the Privacy tab to take a more granular approach and override the settings established using the slider bar.

To apply custom settings that you have stored in a file on your computer, click the Import button to open the Privacy Import dialog box, which is simply an Open dialog box in disguise and works the same as an Open dialog box.

To choose to Accept, Block, or Prompt for first-party and third-party cookies, click the Advanced button to open the Advanced Privacy Settings dialog box shown in Figure 15.24.

Click the Override automatic cookie-handling check box, and then select the options that you want. If you want to allow session cookies, click that check box, and then click OK.

To establish privacy settings for individual websites, click the Sites button in the Web Sites section to open the Per Site Privacy Actions dialog box shown in Figure 15.25. This is actually a preferable technique to trying the one-size-fits-all approach to cookies. If you set Internet Explorer to disallow all cookies and then allow sites you trust to use cookies, you gain added security without any cost to your browsing.

In the Address of Web Site box, type the complete URL for the site you want to allow or block, and then click Block or Allow. The site's domain name and your chosen setting will appear in the Managed Web Sites list. Use the Remove or Remove All button to delete a site from the list.

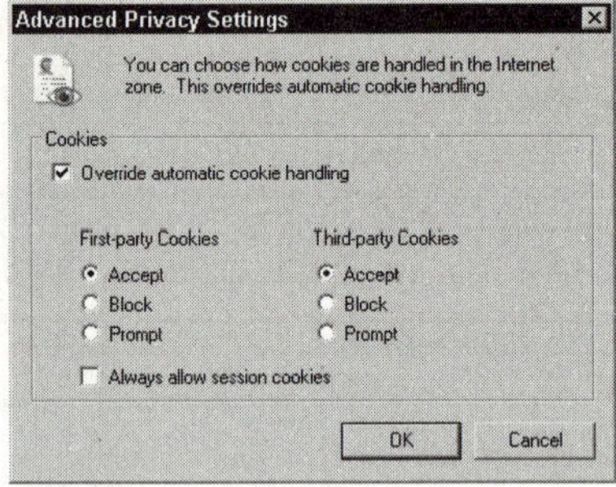

FIGURE 15.24
Use the advanced privacy features to provide specialized cookie handling.

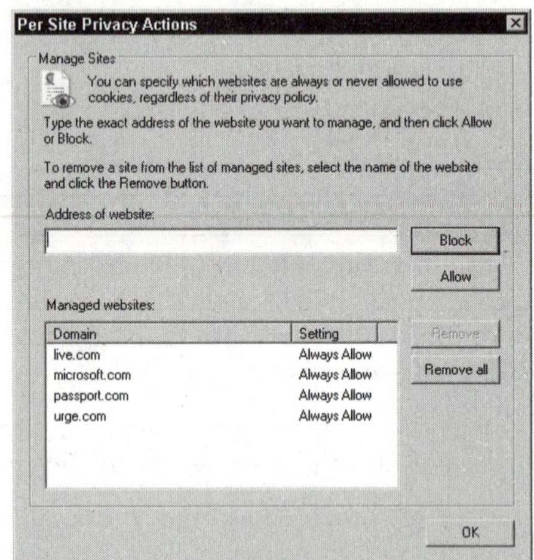

FIGURE 15.25
Per site handling of cookies lets you grant cookie privileges to sites you trust and block everything else.

TIP To back up your cookies, use the Import/Export Wizard (File ➤ Import and Export.)

CONFIGURING THE POP-UP BLOCKER

One of the benefits of Internet Explorer 7 is the built-in pop-up blocker. You can configure it on the Privacy tab by clicking the Settings button at the bottom of the dialog box (Figure 15.26). From the Pop-Up Blocker Settings dialog box, you can enter specific sites that shouldn't be blocked, set other options, and set whether a sound should be played when a pop-up is blocked.

You can also control pop-up blocking on a case-by-case basis as you're surfing the Web. When a pop-up is blocked, a bar appears across the top of the window letting you know. You can click that bar to open a menu containing your choices for that site. If you choose Always Allow Pop-Ups from This Site, the site will be added to the list of allowed sites.

Using the Content Tab

The Content tab, shown in Figure 15.27, contains settings you can use to restrict access to sites and specify how you want to manage digital certificates:

Parental Controls Displays a window where you choose an account to control with parental controls. You can define web filters, time limits, game access, and application access. The setup also provides a reporting feature that lets you know how children are using the system.

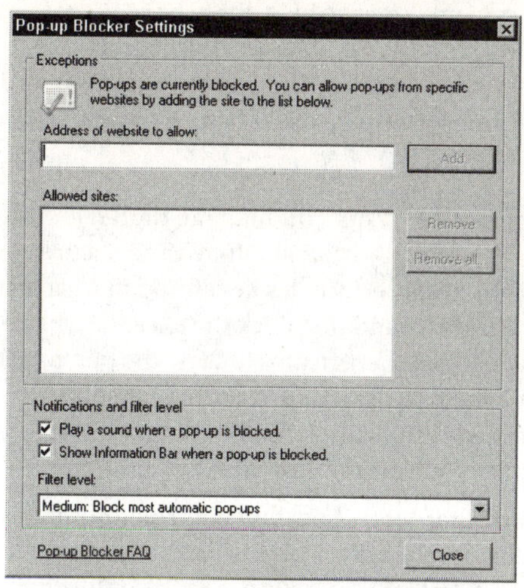

FIGURE 15.26
Use the pop-up blocking features of Internet Explorer to keep extra windows at bay.

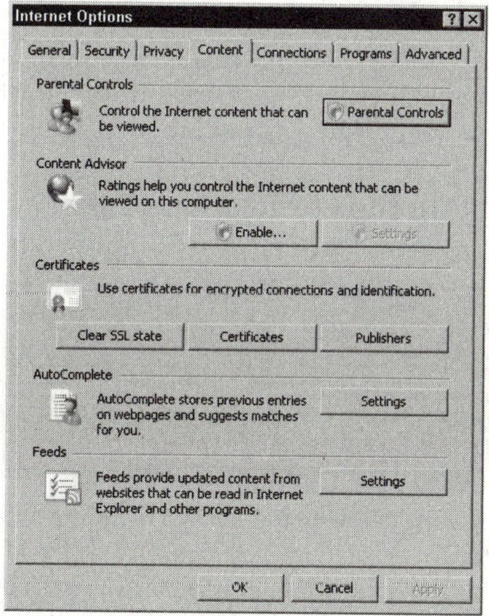

FIGURE 15.27
The Content tab in the Internet Options dialog box

Content Advisor Lets you control access to certain sites on the Internet and is particularly useful if children have access to the computer. Click Enable to open the Content Advisor dialog box. Use the tabs in this dialog box to establish the level of content you'll allow users to view:

Ratings Lets you use a set of ratings developed by the Recreational Software Advisory Council (RSAC) for language, nudity, sex, and violence. Select one of these categories, and then adjust the slider to specify the level of content you'll allow.

Approved Sites Lets you create lists of sites that are always viewable or always restricted regardless of how they're rated.

General Specifies whether people using this computer can view material that hasn't been rated; users may see some objectionable material if the website hasn't used the RSAC rating system. You can also opt to have the Supervisor enter a password so that users can view web pages that may contain objectionable material. You can click the Create Password button to create or change the Supervisor password; remember that you have to know the current Supervisor password before you can change it.

Advanced Lets you look at or modify the list of organizations providing ratings services.

Certificates Lets you manage digital certificates used with certain client authentication servers. When you visit a site that has a secure connection, you can choose to verify that site's certificate. Such certificates are stored in a cache until you reboot your computer. To remove these certificates manually, click the Clear SSL State button. (SSL is an abbreviation for Secure Sockets Layer.) Click Certificates to view the personal digital certificates installed on this system, or click Publishers to designate a particular software publisher as a trustworthy publisher. This means that Vista applications can download, install, and use software from these agencies without asking for your permission first.

AutoComplete Lets you control automatic completion of forms online. Click AutoComplete to change the way that this feature works within Vista, or click My Profile to create an Address Book entry for yourself that represents your profile or to select an existing Address Book entry to represent your profile. You can then send this information to any websites that request information about you when you visit their site.

Feeds Lets you control how Internet Explorer works with RSS feeds. You control update schedule, automatic marking of feeds as read, the feed reading view, and whether Internet Explorer plays a sound when it detects new headers.

Setting Up the Connections Tab

The Connections tab allows you to specify how your system connects to the Internet. Click the Setup button to run the New Connection Wizard and set up a connection to an Internet Service Provider. (See Chapter 14 for complete details on this.) If you use a modem, click the Settings button to open the My ISP Settings dialog box, where you can specify all aspects of the phone connection to your ISP.

Looking at the Programs Tab

The Programs tab, which is shown in Figure 15.28, lets you specify whether Internet Explorer is the default browser, manage add-ons, choose the HTML editor, and set your default program choices. Click Make Default when you want to make Internet Explorer the default browser. You can also choose to let Internet Explore tell you when it isn't the default browser. The "Working with Add-ons" section of the chapter tells you how to work with add-on programs. The HTML editor drop-down list contains the options that Internet Explorer recognizes for editing files. Finally, Internet Explorer 7 changes the method of working with Internet programs completely. Click Set programs and you'll see the Default Programs applet. You can learn more about this applet in the "Setting Program Access and Defaults" section of Chapter 6.

Configuring the Advanced Tab

The Advanced tab, which is shown in Figure 15.29, lets you look at or change a number of settings that control much of Internet Explorer's behavior, including accessibility, browsing, multimedia, security, printing, and searching, and how HTTP 1.1 settings are interpreted. Click a check box to turn an option on; clear the check box to turn the option off.

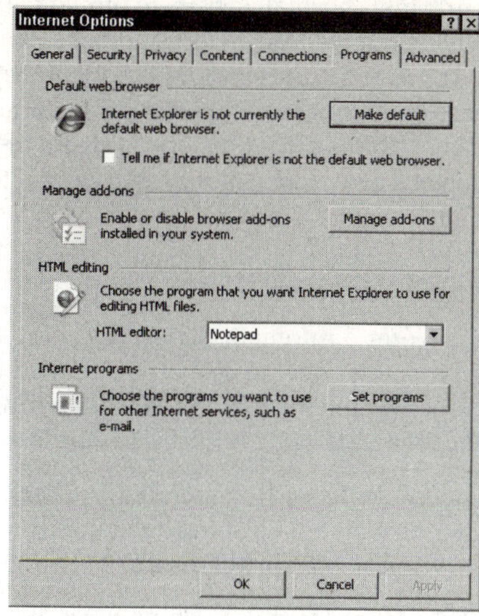

FIGURE 15.28 The Programs tab in the Internet Options dialog box.

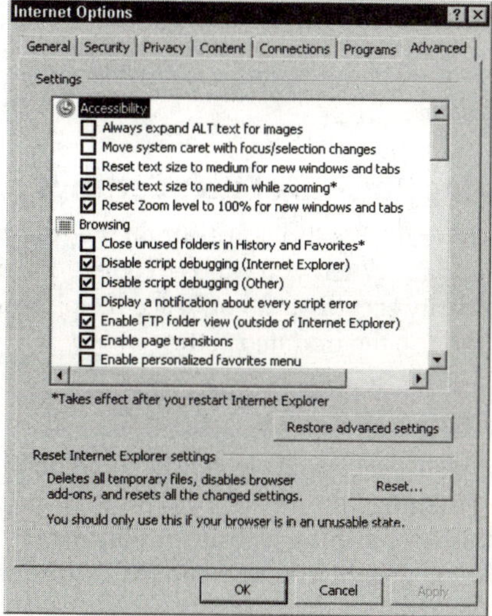

FIGURE 15.29 The Advanced tab in the Internet Options dialog box.

Changes you make here stay in effect until you change them again, until you download an automatic configuration file, or until you click the Restore Defaults button, which returns the settings in the Advanced tab to their original values.

Using the Phishing Filter

Phishing is a serious problem on the Internet today. You receive a notice from your bank that they need to verify your account, so you click a link. The link looks legitimate and the website also looks like your bank's website. With a few small tricks, crackers can easily make it appear that you're using your bank's normal website to put you at ease. Without thinking twice, you'll enter your social security number, birth date, mother's maiden name, and other information to verify your account. At this point, the cracker takes all of the information you've provided and uses it to obtain credit cards in your name. Soon, you're swimming in debt and bad credit. No one ever lends you money again. This is what phishing is all about—it's a kind of identification theft where you participate in your own destruction. A phishing filter helps prevent this form of attack by letting you know when someone is trying to pull the wool over your eyes.

Checking a Website

Internet Explorer 7 automatically checks every website you visit for possible phishing problems. However, it doesn't hurt to be a little paranoid when you visit your bank's website or any other location where you have to provide sensitive information such as a credit card.

Use the following steps to check a website manually.

1. Choose Tools ➢ Phishing Filter ➢ Check This Website. The first time you use the phishing filter, you'll see a Phishing Filter dialog box warning you that using the phishing filter sends the website URL to Microsoft.
2. Click OK to clear the Phishing Filter dialog box. Internet Explorer begins checking the website. At some point, you'll see another dialog box telling you whether this is a phishing site.
3. Click OK to clear the dialog box.
4. Go anywhere else if this is phishing website or proceed with your transactions if the website is safe.

Managing Phishing Filter Settings

The phishing filter settings appear on the Advanced tab of the Internet Options dialog box shown in Figure 15.29. When you choose Tools ➢ Phishing Filter ➢ Phishing Filter Settings, scroll down to the Security section and you'll see the phishing filter settings. You may have to restart Internet Explorer to use the updated settings.

Reporting a Website

When you suspect that a website is going on phishing expeditions, you need to report it. Choose Tools ➢ Phishing Filter ➢ Report This Website to display the Report a Website Wizard. Check the I think this is a phishing website option and click Submit. Microsoft will work with the authorities to determine whether the website really is going on phishing expeditions.

Working with Add-ons

There's a strong third-party market for Internet Explorer add-ons. You use add-ons to add functionality that you feel Internet Explorer is missing. Using add-ons lets you create an Internet Explorer that better meets your needs. The only problem is that you had to look pretty hard to find them in the past. It's not that Microsoft was hiding them, Internet Explorer simply made the task of working with add-ons harder than it should have been. Internet Explorer 7 makes add-ons incredibly easy to add, use, control, and delete when you no longer need them. The following sections describe the add-on features.

Enabling, Disabling, or Deleting Add-ons

Internet Explorer ships with a few add-ons, but you won't want to do anything with them most of the time. Even so, you'll want to know what Internet Explorer is doing in the background, so it's helpful to look at the add-ons even if you aren't adding anything new. Choose Tools ➤ Manage Add-ons ➤ Enable or Disable Add-ons to display the Manage Add-ons dialog box shown in Figure 15.30.

Add-ons are always enabled by default when you install them. Consequently, if you have just installed an add-on, you normally won't need to enable it. However, if the add-on isn't working the way you think it should, then it's a good idea to check its status. The Settings area contains two radio buttons, enabled and disabled. When you highlight an add-on these options show its status. To change the status of an add-on, simply choose the other option. When you click OK, the add-on is either enabled or disabled based on the setting you choose.

You can delete some add-ons when you no longer need them (others are permanently part of Internet Explorer and the best you can do is disable them). To delete an add-on, highlight its entry. If the Delete button is enabled, you can click it to delete the add-on.

Internet Explorer doesn't show all of the add-ons at one time. The Show drop-down list box contains a number of add-on categories. For example, one category shows you which add-ons are currently loaded, while another tells you about add-ons that run without asking your permission. If you don't see the add-on you expect in one view, choose another category from the Show drop-down list box.

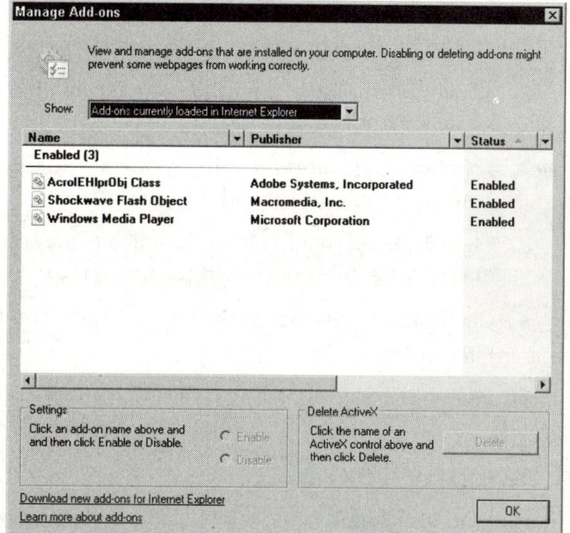

FIGURE 15.30
Enable, disable, or delete add-ons as needed on your system.

Adding New Add-ons

As previously mentioned, you can find many add-ons for Internet Explorer. Of course, you need to know that an add-on is available, so sometimes it pays to search for an add-on when you notice something missing in Internet Explorer. To locate a new add-on, choose Tools ➤ Manage Add-ons ➤ Find More Add-ons. You'll see a website similar to the one shown in Figure 15.31 where you can search for new add-ons.

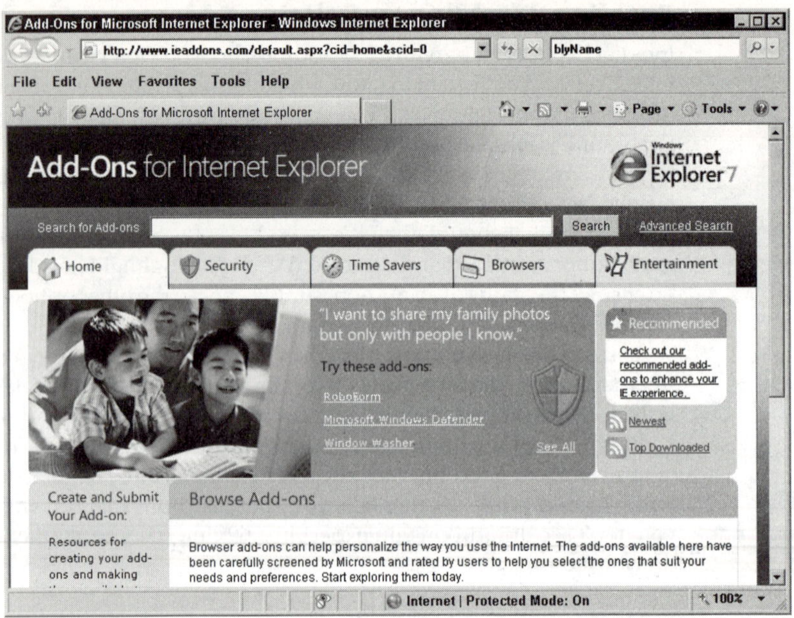

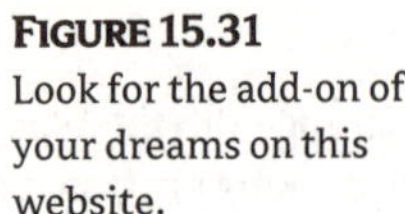
FIGURE 15.31
Look for the add-on of your dreams on this website.

The following steps describe how to install a new add-on.

1. Search for an add-on using standard search techniques or click one of the category tabs to locate a particular add-on type.
2. Locate the software you want to download. Click the Download link for that software. You'll see a File Download dialog box.
3. Click Run. Internet Explorer downloads the software. You may see an Internet Explorer dialog box at this point telling you that it can't determine the application's publisher.
4. Click Run. Vista installs the new add-on. You'll see the software start at some point in most cases.
5. Follow any instructions that the software provides for finalizing installation.

Changing Text Size

In addition to the many customizations you have already learned about, you can control how a web page appears by using commands on the View menu (press Alt to see the View menu if necessary).

One of the handiest ones for people with limited vision is the ability to change the font size for web page content. To do so, choose View ➤ Text Size and then choose Larger or Largest. This works with all web pages that have been formatted with standard HTML tags and aren't encoded to use a particular font size.

If you have a mouse with a wheel on it, you can use the wheel to change the text size too. Hold down the Ctrl key as you roll the wheel. Rolling forward decreases the text size; rolling backward increases it.

Using Built-In Internet Utilities

Vista includes several standard Internet utilities. These programs are, in most cases, functionally identical to the same programs or commands found on pretty much every flavor of UNIX. Although most people aren't going to use these nearly as often as they will their web browsers, I describe each in the following sections so that you at least know what they are. It's useful to acquaint yourself, for example, with FTP—if you're ever on a Vista system that for some reason does not have a web browser, knowing how to use FTP to transfer files enables you to connect to Spry, Netscape, or Microsoft and download a browser.

Following this brief rundown of each of the tools, we'll look at other Internet applications you can download via the Internet. Note that with each of the following programs, you can get help by typing the program name at the command prompt followed by `-?` (hyphen, question mark).

To open any of the following utilities, you type a command at a command prompt. To open a command prompt window, choose Start ➢ All Programs ➢ Accessories. Right-click the Command Prompt entry and choose Run as Administrator from the context menu. You'll see a command prompt open that has a title of Administrator: Command Prompt.

NOTE Vista includes very robust command line protection. You must run the command line in administrator mode or many of these utilities won't work.

Address Resolution Display and Control

The Address Resolution Protocol (ARP) program is used to display or modify entries in the Internet-to-Ethernet (or Token Ring) address translation tables that are used by the Address Resolution Protocol. Various command-line switches are documented in the -? option. To use ARP, type **arp** at the command prompt.

File Transfer Protocol (FTP)

FTP is the standard TCP/IP file transfer protocol used for moving text and binary files between computers on the Internet. If you have an account on a distant computer on the Internet, you can use FTP to download files from the other computer to your PC and to upload files from your PC to the host. In addition, there are tens of thousands of *anonymous* FTP archives all over the Internet that accept logins from anybody who wants copies of their files.

TIP You can do FTP from Internet Explorer; you don't necessarily have to use the command prompt for it. Just type the FTP address in the Address bar, as in `ftp.mysite.com`. However, the FTP capabilities in IE are rather limited. If you do a lot of FTP transferring, consider a stand-alone FTP application.

The Vista FTP program (and the others mentioned here) can be found in the `Winnt\System32` folder, which is included in your search path. Therefore, you don't have to specify the path when you enter an FTP command. To connect to an FTP server, follow these steps:

1. At a command prompt, type the following, and then press Enter:

   ```
   FTP <host name>
   ```

2. Vista displays the `ftp>` prompt shown in Figure 15.32. This figure also shows an attempted login (failed on purpose) and the help menu you access by typing Help and pressing Enter.

FIGURE 15.32
The ftp> prompt provides access to files.

```
Administrator: Command Prompt - ftp ftp.sybex.com

C:\>ftp ftp.sybex.com
Connected to ftp.sybex.com.
220 Microsoft FTP Service
User (ftp.sybex.com:(none)):
501 'USER ': Invalid number of parameters
Login failed.
ftp> help
Commands may be abbreviated.  Commands are:

!               delete          literal         prompt          send
?               debug           ls              put             status
append          dir             mdelete         pwd             trace
ascii           disconnect      mdir            quit            type
bell            get             mget            quote           user
binary          glob            mkdir           recv            verbose
bye             hash            mls             remotehelp
cd              help            mput            rename
close           lcd             open            rmdir
ftp> _
```

3. After FTP connects to the server, the server asks for your username and password. If you're connecting to an anonymous FTP server, type **anonymous** as your username, and type your e-mail address as your password or leave the password field blank and press Enter. For your password, use the standard *name@address.domain* format.

Most FTP servers use the same system of directories and subdirectories that you may be familiar with from DOS and Windows. To see the contents of the current directory, type **dir** or **ls** at the ftp> prompt.

If the FTP server is in UNIX mode, a *d* as the first letter in a listing indicates that the item in that line is a directory. If a dash is the first character, the item is a file. The name of the file or directory is at the extreme right. See Chapter 24 for more info regarding UNIX mode.

Use the command **cd *name*** (typing the name of the subdirectory in place of *name*) to move to a subdirectory.

Use the command **cd ..** to move to the next higher level. (Press the spacebar after you enter the *d* and before you type the first period.)

When you download a file from an FTP server, you must specify that it's either an ASCII text file or a binary file. As a general rule, binary files that you can read on a PC have a DOS file extension (rather than TXT for a text file or PS for a Postscript print file), but you really can't be certain. ASCII text files may or may not have a file extension.

When you initially connect to an FTP server, you're in ASCII mode. Before you try to transfer a binary file, you have to change modes. To switch to binary mode, use the command **binary**. To switch back to ASCII mode, use the command **ascii**. The host acknowledges your mode-change command.

To download a file from the server, use the command **get *filename*** (typing the name of the file in place of *filename*). If you want to store the file on your PC with a different name, use the command **get *filename newname*** (typing the file you want to get in place of *filename* and the name you want to store the file under in place of *newname*). When the file transfer is complete, the host sends you another message.

When you're finished with your FTP session, type **disconnect** to break the connection to the server. You can connect to another host by typing the new server's address.

To close the FTP utility, type the command **quit**.

TIP One handy use for the command-line FTP client is automating file transfers. Because FTP accepts scripts (via the `-s:filename` switch), you can easily create a script (which is just a text file of FTP commands) to log on to an FTP server, switch to a particular directory, transfer a long listing of files in one or both directions, and then log off. You can even set this to occur at a given time of day by using the Vista `at` command. (For details on using the `at` command, type **`help at`** from any command prompt.)

Finger

The finger program can be used to retrieve user-supplied information about a user (or host computer). Unfortunately, many users don't have a finger file for others to retrieve and view (or even know about creating one), and some host computers don't provide finger services, so your mileage will vary. On the other hand, some universities and institutions do use finger services, and on these you can find some useful (or at least interesting) information. To use finger, type **`finger`** ***`auser@someplace.com`***. Enter a valid username or, at least, a hostname, press Enter, and you may get a listing of information.

Ping

Ping is a useful diagnostic utility that tests your ability to connect your computer to another device through the Internet by sending an echo request and displaying the number of milliseconds required to receive a reply. Whenever you need to diagnose your Internet connection problems, pinging a known host computer is a good first test.

To set up a Ping test, follow these steps:

1. At a command prompt, type **`ping`** ***`destination`***. Use the domain name or the IP address of the host you want to test in place of *`destination`*. If you don't get a response when using the domain name of the destination, try the IP address of the destination instead.
2. Ping sends four sets of Internet Control Message Protocol (ICMP) echo packets to the host you specify and displays the amount of time it took to receive each reply, as shown in Figure 15.33.

FIGURE 15.33
Use Ping to locate and test connections to other machines.

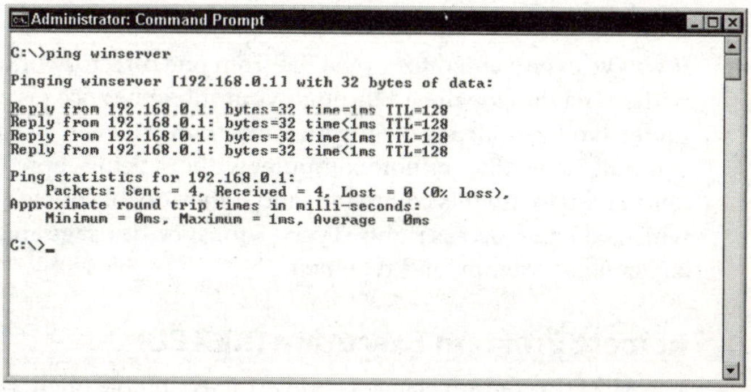

```
Administrator: Command Prompt
C:\>ping winserver

Pinging winserver [192.168.0.1] with 32 bytes of data:

Reply from 192.168.0.1: bytes=32 time=1ms TTL=128
Reply from 192.168.0.1: bytes=32 time<1ms TTL=128
Reply from 192.168.0.1: bytes=32 time<1ms TTL=128
Reply from 192.168.0.1: bytes=32 time<1ms TTL=128

Ping statistics for 192.168.0.1:
    Packets: Sent = 4, Received = 4, Lost = 0 (0% loss),
Approximate round trip times in milli-seconds:
    Minimum = 0ms, Maximum = 1ms, Average = 0ms

C:\>_
```

The important part of the Ping display is the `time</>`*nnnms* section of the Reply lines. Ping's capability to connect to the distant host tells you that your connection to the Internet is working properly; the number of milliseconds can tell you if you have an efficient connection to this particular host (anything less than about 500ms is usually acceptable).

Protocol Statistics (*netstat*)

Use the `netstat` command to display a list of currently active Internet connections. At the command prompt, type **`netstat`**. A list of connections similar to the ones in Figure 15.34 appears.

A `netstat` report includes the following information:

Proto Shows the networking protocol in use for each active connection. For PPP or SLIP connections to the Internet, the Proto column always reads TCP, which specifies a TCP/IP connection.

Local Address Indicates the identity of your PC on the network.

Foreign Address Shows the address of each distant computer to which a connection is currently active.

State Shows the condition of each connection.

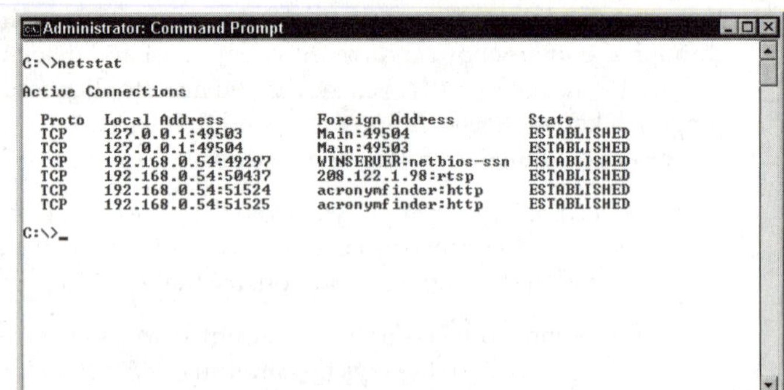

FIGURE 15.34 Netstat tells you about the machines on your network.

Remote File Copy (RCP)

If you've ever wanted to copy a file from one directory or drive to another on a remote computer without having the file go through your modem twice (as a normal copy or xcopy would), you understand the purpose of the RCP program. You can also use RCP to copy files from one remote computer to another remote computer without being copied to your computer first. Not all systems permit you to use this command, and if they do, of course you're limited to the directory areas for which you have access rights. Type **`-?`** for specific usage and option information. To use RCP, open a command prompt, and type **`rcp`**.

Remote Program Execution (REXEC)

The REXEC program is just as powerful as Remote Shell/Script (RSH; discussed in the next section), if not more so, and likewise, it's quite restricted by most system administrators. It functions just like RSH, except that it starts binary programs rather than scripts on the remote host. Vista stations *do* permit remote execution of programs, provided the system administrator has enabled this and has given you the necessary access rights. To run REXEC, type **`rexec`** at a command prompt.

Remote Shell/Script (RSH)

Another potentially powerful utility, RSH is used to start a script program on a remote host. Again, some host computers don't support this, and of those that do, your access rights may preclude or severely limit what you can do. To use RSH, type **`rsh`** at a command prompt.

Remote Terminal (Telnet)

Telnet is one of the utilities you're somewhat more likely to use, particularly in university settings or when data you need to access without using HTML is stored on a remote host (a less and less common scenario, thankfully). When you connect through a Telnet connection, your PC becomes a terminal on the distant system. In most cases, a Telnet login requires an account on the host (remote) machine, but many systems accept logins from anybody who wants to connect. Among the most common public Telnet sites are online library catalogs. Other public Telnet sites let you use certain character-based Internet services that may not be available on your computer.

NOTE Vista doesn't have Telnet installed by default. In fact, if you want full Telnet support, you have to install the Telnet client and server. These two options are separate. Microsoft doesn't install Telnet because crackers have used it in the past to gain unlawful entry to systems. If you don't need Telnet, don't install it.

To set up a Telnet connection, type **`Telnet`** ***`hostname`*** at a command prompt (using the domain name or IP address of the computer to which you want to connect in place of *`hostname`*). Telnet connects your computer to the host whose name you supplied and displays messages from that host in the Telnet window.

Most Telnet hosts display a series of login prompts as soon as you connect. If you're connecting to a public Telnet host, it will probably tell you how to log in.

NOTE Telnet is also used to configure some routers, although many are configured through a web (http) interface.

The *route* Command

You can use `route` to view, add to, or modify a routing table on a Vista computer with more than one network interface. If you have a *multihomed* computer (one with multiple network cards) and have enabled IP forwarding in the TCP/IP Properties dialog box, you can use the `route` command to view and modify the table of information that tells Vista where to direct TCP/IP data from one interface to another. Using this command on a computer with one network interface will also display basic routing information. To use `route`, type **`route`** at a command prompt.

Trace Route (*tracert*)

In most cases, when you set up a connection to a distant computer through the Internet, your signal path passes through several routers along the way. Because this is all happening in a fraction of a second, these intermediate routers are usually invisible. But when you're having trouble making a connection, the trace route command (`tracert`) can help isolate the source of the problem.

To run a trace route test, type **`tracert`** ***`target`*** at a command prompt. In place of *`target`*, type the address of the distant system. A trace route report appears in the prompt window.

In many cases, your connection will pass through one or more backbone networks between your connection to the Internet and your ultimate destination.

`tracert` steps through the connection route, one step at a time. For each step, it shows the amount of time needed to reach that router, in milliseconds. If an intermediate router or a connection between two intermediate routers fails, `tracert` won't display any steps beyond that point in the route. If that happens, you can assume that the failed site is the reason that you're unable to connect to your intended destination.

Summary

Within the space of a very few years, many of us have come to consider access to the Internet an essential component of daily life. It's now the first place I turn when I want information about almost anything, and it's rare that I don't find what I'm looking for. This chapter has demonstrated the many new features of Internet Explorer 7 and has also shown that many old features are still present. Don't let the pretty new face fool you—the old Internet Explorer is lurking just below the surface.

A lot of people don't take their browser very seriously. Yet, considering the importance of this tool to modern computing, it's important to work with the browser to make it the best it can be. Consequently, one of your first tasks after reading this chapter is to configure Internet Explorer so it meets your needs. As you find deficiencies, consider downloading an add-on or two. You'll be surprised at how much better Internet Explorer works with proper care.

Internet Explorer is far from the only tool available for communicating on the Internet. In the next chapter, you'll learn about Remote Desktop Connection; then in Chapter 17, you'll learn about e-mail with Outlook Express.

Chapter 16

Using the Communications Programs

You may never have an occasion to use the programs I'm going to discuss in this chapter, but I'm including information about them so that you'll know they exist, what each is best suited for, and how to access them when the need arises. They're alternatives to the ubiquitous web browser interface for working with data between PCs on a network or the Internet.

- Where are the older applications?
- Using Remote Desktop Connection

Vista: What's New?

Remote Desktop works almost the same as it always has, but like many areas of Vista, you'll see some security enhancements. The security enhancements, in this case, are very much warranted when you need to connect between systems across the Internet or a wide area network (WAN). The systems might be overkill when you're connecting to another machine on your network. Fortunately, Vista lets you choose the level of security to employ with Remote Desktop.

Microsoft has made some good changes to Remote Desktop, even though most people will look at them as unnecessary. For example, you must enter your credentials every time you start a Remote Desktop session. It's too easy for someone to access your machine, create a Remote Desktop session, and perform terrifying deeds in your name otherwise. Consequently, even though you must now take a few seconds to type your name and password, you'll very likely find that the enhanced security isn't much of a problem.

You'll find that Remote Desktop doesn't expose your system to as many potential problems. For example, you must now specifically configure Remote Desktop to work with local disk drives. In addition, you don't have to choose all of your disk drives or anything, as you did in previous versions of Windows. Vista lets you choose specific local drives or even decide that you want to specify which drives to use later as Remote Desktop requires the resource.

Where Are the Older Applications?

You may have noticed that Vista is missing a few of the older applications that you may have used in the past. Gone is HyperTerminal, for example, which was a standby for anyone who wanted to check their modem. A lot of people used HyperTerminal for communication with other systems. Microsoft recommends that you use Telnet (a text-based command line utility) for communication with other systems. If you want to test your modem, they recommend using the testing features provided as part of the device Properties dialog box. The "Configuring a Modem" section of Chapter 10 describes these testing features.

The main reason for not including HyperTerminal is that it's an older utility with several security holes. Microsoft has patched at least some of these holes and you can read about one of them at `http://www.microsoft.com/technet/security/Bulletin/MS00-079.mspx`. Just in case you're not familiar with HyperTerminal, you can read about it at `http://www.microsoft.com/technet/prodtechnol/windowsserver2003/technologies/security/ws03mngd/11_s3hyp.mspx`. You can still download HyperTerminal from the Hilgraeve website at `http://www.hilgraeve.com/htpe/index.html`.

Another application that's missing in action is Windows Messenger. You'll notice that Vista provides a Windows Live Messenger Download link. However, any resemblance between the old Windows Messenger and Windows Live Messenger is purely coincidental. The online program works and acts completely different from the previous program. Unfortunately, the product is still in beta as I write this and not as usable as it could be, so you won't see a complete description of Windows Live Messenger in the chapter.

Using Remote Desktop Connection

Remote Desktop Connection lets you connect via a dial-up connection, a local area network (LAN) connection, or across the Internet and take control of somebody's computer (or your own).

Remote Desktop Connection is designed to let you access and control one computer (say, your work computer) from another computer (say, your home computer or your laptop). It's great for catching up with the office when you're at home, or for grabbing the files that you forgot to load on your laptop before you dived into the taxi for the airport.

TIP Make sure you have the latest version of the Remote Desktop software to ensure you get full connectivity with Windows 95, Windows 98 and 98 Second Edition, Windows Me, Windows NT 4.0, and Windows 2000. You can get the latest update at `http://www.microsoft.com/downloads/details.aspx?FamilyID=80111F21-D48D-426E-96C2-08AA2BD23A49`. Just in case you own a Macintosh and want to use Remote Desktop, you can download the required software at `http://www.microsoft.com/mac/otherproducts/otherproducts.aspx?pid=remotedesktopclient`. Finally, if you want to support a Remote Desktop web connection, check out the software at `http://www.microsoft.com/downloads/details.aspx?FamilyID=E2FF8FB5-97FF-47BC-BACC-92283B52B310`. Since Microsoft frequently updates its software, you'll always want to check the Microsoft Download Center for the latest updates at `http://www.microsoft.com/downloads/`.

Remote Desktop Connection Terminology and Basics

Remote Desktop Connection terminology is a little confusing. Here are the terms:

- The *home computer* is the computer on which you're working. The home computer needs to have Remote Desktop Connection installed. Remote Desktop Connection is installed by default in Vista.
- The *remote computer* is the computer that you're accessing from the home computer. The remote computer needs to have Remote Desktop installed. Remote Desktop is separate from Remote Desktop Connection and is included in Vista, Windows XP Professional, and Windows 2003 Server. Remote Desktop is not included in Windows XP Home.

NOTE You can access more than one remote computer at a time from the same home computer. However, unless you have impressive bandwidth, this results in slow sessions.

In order for you to connect to another computer via Remote Desktop Connection, any active session (whether local or connected via Remote Desktop Connection) on that computer needs to be disconnected. You get a warning about this, but the other user doesn't. If you choose to proceed, the remote computer displays the Welcome screen while your Remote Desktop Connection session is going on. There's no easy way for anyone looking at that computer to tell that you're remotely connected to it.

If a user comes back and starts using the remote computer while your Remote Desktop Connection session is going on, your session will be terminated—with a warning on their side, this time, but not on yours. Frankly, this could be more elegant.

In lay terms, Remote Desktop Connection works as follows:

- Keystrokes and mouse clicks are transmitted from the home computer to the remote computer via the display protocol. The remote computer registers these keystrokes and clicks as if they came from the keyboard attached to it.
- Programs run on the remote computer as usual. (Programs aren't run across the wire—that would be desperately slow.)
- Screen display information is passed to the home computer, again via the display protocol. This information appears on the display as if it came from the video adapter (only rather more slowly, and usually in a window).

Sound can be passed to the home computer as well, so that you can hear what's happening at the remote computer. Transferring sound like this enhances the impression of controlling the remote computer, but sound takes so much bandwidth that transferring it isn't a good idea on slow connections. The default Remote Desktop Connection setting is to transfer sound, but you may well want to switch it off.

Setting the Remote Computer to Accept Incoming Connections

The first step in getting Remote Desktop Connection to work is setting the remote computer to accept incoming connections. Remember that this is the computer that's remote from you and that's running Vista (or .NET Server).

To set your computer to accept incoming connections, follow these steps:

1. Click the Start button, right-click My Computer, and choose Properties from the shortcut menu to open the System window. Click the Advanced system settings link to display the System Properties dialog box.
2. Click the Remote tab, which is shown in Figure 16.1. Notice that Vista provides three options for remote connections.
    - Don't allow connections to this computer
    - Allow connections from computers running any version of Remote Desktop (less secure)
    - Allow connections only from computers running Remote Desktop with Network Level Authentication (more secure)

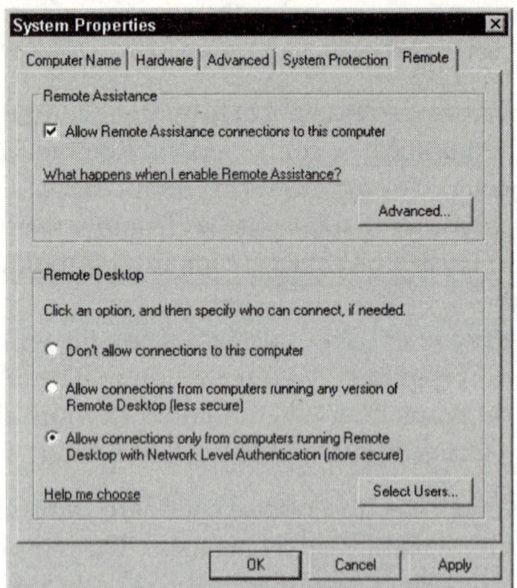

FIGURE 16.1
The Remote tab of the System Properties dialog box.

3. To allow users to connect to your computer, choose the Allow Connections from Computers Running Any Version of Remote Desktop (less secure) or Allow Connections Only from Computers Running Remote Desktop with Network Level Authentication (more secure) option. The option you choose depends on your setup and security requirements. The first option lets you connect to any version of Windows that has Remote Desktop installed. It's also relatively fast, but susceptible to certain kinds of attacks. The second option only works with Vista systems today and you incur a performance penalty to get the extra security that this option provides.
4. To specify which users can connect via Remote Desktop Connection, click the Select Users button to open the Remote Desktop Users dialog box (shown in Figure 16.2). The list box shows any users currently allowed to connect to the computer. Below the list box is a note indicating that you (identified by your username) already have access—as you should have.
5. To add users, click the Add button. Windows displays the Select Users dialog box.
6. Select a user or group, and then click the OK button. Windows adds them to the list in the Remote Desktop Users dialog box.
7. Add further users or groups as necessary.

FIGURE 16.2
The Remote Desktop Users dialog box.

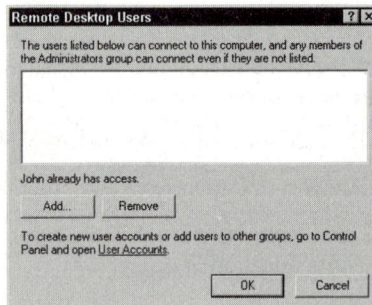

8. To remove a user or a group, select them in the list box and click the Remove button.
9. Click the OK button to close the Remote Desktop Users dialog box.
10. Click the OK button in the System Properties dialog box. Windows closes the dialog box and applies your changes.

That's the remote computer all set. Leave it up and running and return to the home computer.

Choosing Settings for Remote Desktop Connection

Next, choose settings for Remote Desktop Connection on the home computer. Remote Desktop Connection has a modestly large number of settings, but many of them are set-and-forget. Even better, you can save sets of settings so that you can quickly apply them for accessing different remote computers (or the same remote computer under different circumstances, such as when the cable modem is working and when it's flaked out on you).

To choose settings for Remote Desktop Connection, follow these steps:

1. Choose Start ➤ All Programs ➤ Accessories ➤ Remote Desktop Connection. Windows starts Remote Desktop Connection and displays the Remote Desktop Connection window in its reduced state (shown in Figure 16.3).
2. Click the Options button. Windows displays the rest of the Remote Desktop Connection window.
3. The General tab of the Remote Desktop Connection window (shown in Figure 16.4) offers these options:

   Computer drop-down list Enter the name or the IP address of the computer to which you want to connect; or select it from the drop-down list; or click the Browse for More item from the drop-down list to display the Browse for Computers dialog box, and then select the computer in that. Unlike previous versions of Windows, you can't save a username and password. Notice that the dialog box says that the remote system will prompt you for the required credentials.

   Connection Settings section Once you've chosen settings for a connection, you can save the connection information by clicking the Save As button and specifying a name for the connection in the Save As dialog box that Windows displays. You can also save the settings as the default by clicking Save. Remote Desktop Connection connections are saved as files of the file type Remote Desktop File, which by default is linked to the RDP extension, in the `My Documents\Remote Desktops` folder. You can open saved connections by clicking the Open button and using the resulting Open dialog box.

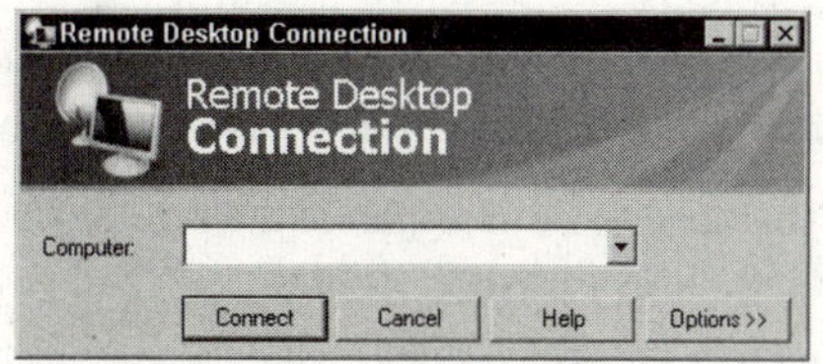

FIGURE 16.3
The Remote Desktop Connection window appears first in its reduced state.

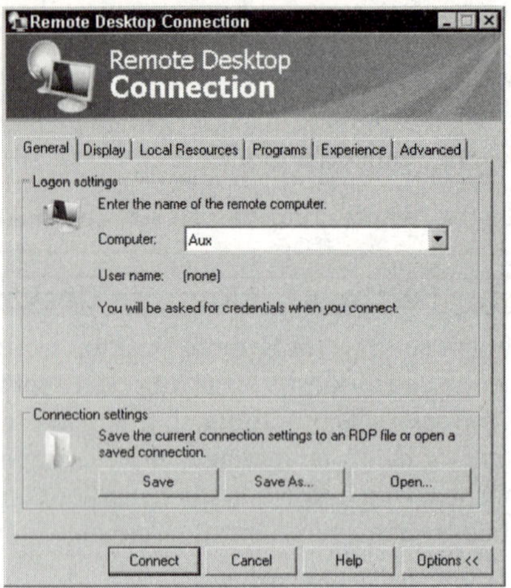

FIGURE 16.4
The General tab of the expanded Remote Desktop Connection window.

NOTE You'll see a file named `DEFAULT.RDP` in the `My Documents\Remote Desktops` folder. Windows automatically saves your latest Remote Desktop Connection configuration under this name when you click the Connect or Save buttons. But, by explicitly saving your settings under a name of your choice, you can easily maintain different configurations for different Remote Desktop Connection settings.

4. The Display tab of the Remote Desktop Connection window (shown in Figure 16.5) offers three display options:

   Remote Desktop Size section Drag the slider to specify the screen size you want to use for the remote Desktop. The default setting is Full Screen, but you may want to use a smaller size so that you can more easily access your Desktop on the home computer. When you display the remote Desktop full screen, it takes over the whole of the local Desktop so that you can't see your local Desktop. (To get to your local Desktop, you use the connection bar, discussed in a moment or two.)

   Colors section In the drop-down list, select the color depth to use for the connection. Choose a low color depth (for example, 256 colors) if you're connecting over a low-speed connection. This choice will be overridden by the display setting on the remote computer if you ask for more colors than the remote computer is using.

   Display the Connection Bar When in Full Screen Mode check box Leave this check box selected (as it is by default) if you want Windows to display the connection bar when the remote Desktop is displayed full screen. The connection bar provides Minimize, Restore/Maximize, and Close buttons for the remote Desktop. (When the remote Desktop is displayed in a window, that window has the control buttons, so the connection bar isn't necessary.)

5. The Local Resources tab of the Remote Desktop Connection window (shown in Figure 16.6) offers the following options:

   Remote Computer Sound section In the drop-down list, specify what you want Windows to do with sounds that would normally be generated at the remote Desktop. The default setting is Bring to This Computer, which transfers the sounds to the home computer and plays them there. This setting helps sustain the illusion that you're working directly on the remote Desktop, but it's heavy on bandwidth, so don't use it over low-speed connections. Instead, choose the Do Not Play setting or the Leave at Remote Computer setting. The Leave at Remote Computer setting plays the sounds at the remote computer and is best reserved for occasions when you need to frighten somebody remotely or pretend to be in your office.

Keyboard section In the drop-down list, specify how you want Windows to handle Windows key combinations that you press (for example, Alt+Tab or Ctrl+Alt+Delete). Select the On the Local Computer item, the On the Remote Computer item, or the In Full Screen Mode Only item (the default) as suits your needs.

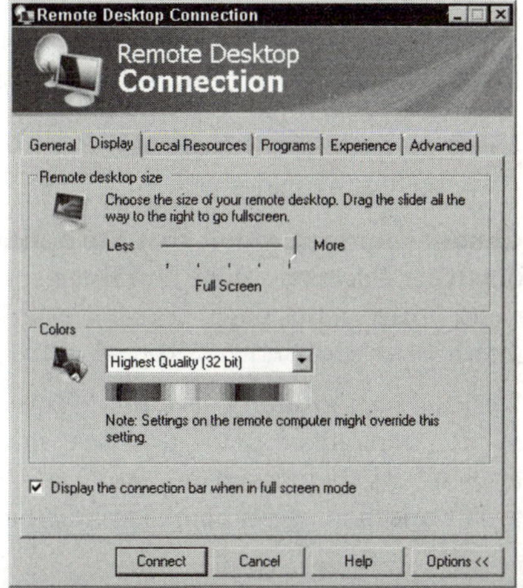

FIGURE 16.5
Choose display settings in the Display tab of the Remote Desktop Connection window.

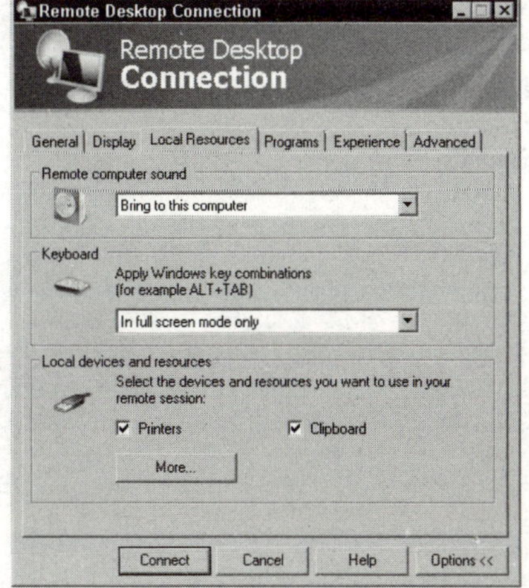

FIGURE 16.6
In the Local Resources tab of the Remote Desktop Connection window, specify how Windows should handle sound, keyboard shortcuts, and devices on the home computer.

Local Devices section Leave the Printers and Clipboard check boxes selected (as they are by default) if you want these devices on your home computer to be available from the remote computer. Click More and you'll see entries for Smart cards, Serial ports, Drives, and Supported Plug and Play devices. None of these options are checked by default, but you may want to choose at least some of the drive selections. Adding a drive and serial port selection means that you can save documents from the remote computer to local drives, print them on your local printer, or transfer them via devices attached to serial ports (for example, a PDA). Local disk drives appear in the Other category in Explorer windows, named *Driveletter on COMPUTERNAME*. Local printers appear with *from COMPUTERNAME* in parentheses after them.

6. The Programs tab of the Remote Desktop Connection window (shown in Figure 16.7) lets you specify that Windows run a designated program when you connect via Remote Desktop Connection. Select the Start the Following Program on Connection check box, then enter the program path and name in the Program Path and File Name text box. If you need to specify the folder in which the program should start, enter that in the Start in the Following Folder text box.

7. The Experience tab of the Remote Desktop Connection window (shown in Figure 16.8) contains the following options:

   Choose your connection speed to optimize performance drop-down list In this drop-down list, select one of the four listed speeds to apply a preselected set of settings to the five check boxes on this page. The choices in the drop-down list are Modem (28.8Kbps), Modem (56Kbps), Broadband (128Kbps–1.5Mbps), LAN (10Mbps or Higher), and Custom.

   Desktop background check box This check box controls whether Remote Desktop Connection transmits the Desktop background. Because Desktop backgrounds are graphical, transmitting them is sensible only at LAN speeds. (If you clear this check box, Remote Desktop Connection uses a blank Desktop background.)

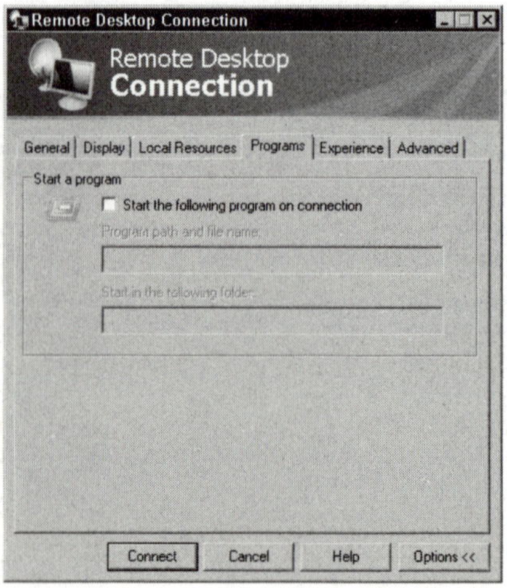

FIGURE 16.7
If you need to have a program run on the remote Desktop when you connect, specify it in the Programs tab of the Remote Desktop Connection window.

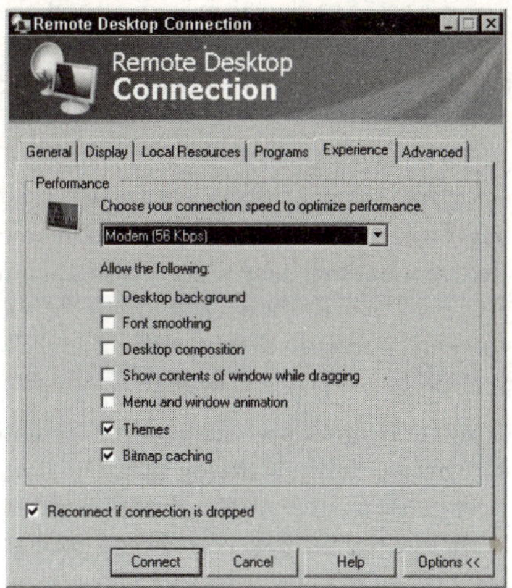

FIGURE 16.8
In the Experience tab of the Remote Desktop Connection window, you can customize which graphical information Remote Desktop Connection transmits in order to balance performance against looks.

Font smoothing check box This check box lets you determine whether the screens you see rely on font smoothing. Remember that font smoothing tends to enhance the display on LCD screens, but doesn't help with CRT screens.

Desktop composition check box This check box determines whether the screens use Aero Glass. Unless you have an extremely high-speed connection (we're talking a 100Mbps or higher LAN connection), don't check this option. You'll see your system crawl to a stop almost immediately otherwise.

Show contents of window while dragging check box This check box controls whether Remote Desktop Connection transmits the contents of a window while you're dragging it or only the window frame. Don't use this option over a modem connection, because the performance penalty outweighs any benefit you may derive from it.

Menu and window animation check box This check box controls whether Remote Desktop Connection transmits menu and window animations (for example, zooming a window you're maximizing or minimizing). Don't use this option over a modem connection—it's a waste of bandwidth.

Themes check box This check box controls whether Remote Desktop Connection transmits theme information or uses "classic" Windows-style windows and controls. Transmitting theme information takes a little bandwidth, so you can improve performance over a very slow connection by clearing the Themes check box. But bear in mind that Windows will look different enough to unsettle some inexperienced users.

Bitmap caching check box This check box controls whether Remote Desktop Connection uses bitmap caching to improve performance by reducing the amount of data that needs to be sent across the network in order to display the screen remotely. Caching could prove a security threat, so you *might* want to turn it off for security reasons. But, in most cases, you're better off using it.

Reconnect if connection is dropped check box This check box tells Vista to reconnect your system automatically when the remote connection is dropped. This feature comes in handy when you have a less than perfect connection to the remote machine.

8. The Advanced tab of the Remote Desktop Connection window (shown in Figure 16.9) contains the following options:

   Server authentication section This section contains a drop-down list box that lets you choose what happens when authentication fails. The default setting, Warn me if authentication fails, tells Remote Desktop to display a dialog box whenever the authentication fails so you can choose an action at that time. The other two selections won't connect when authentication fails or connects even when authentication fails.

   Connect from anywhere section This section contains a pushbutton that displays the Gateway Server Settings dialog box. The default setting automatically detects the Terminal Services gateway and creates the appropriate connection for you. Unless you have a good reason to change the setting, you should probably use this option. As an alternative, you can manually configure the Terminal Server gateway (helpful when you must use a specific server and your LAN has multiple servers available) or not use the Terminal Server gateway at all.

9. If you want to save the settings you've chosen under a particular name so that you can reload them at will, click the Save or Save As button in the General tab of the Remote Desktop Connection window.

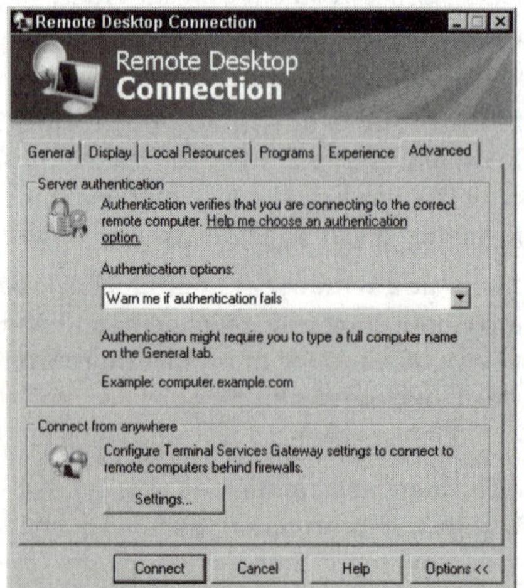

FIGURE 16.9
In the Advanced tab of the Remote Desktop Connection window, you can customize authentication and Terminal Services options.

Connecting via Remote Desktop Connection

Once you've chosen settings as outlined in the previous section, you're ready to connect. If you're connecting via the Internet (rather than a local network) and you have a dial-up connection, make sure it's up and running.

Click the Connect button in the General tab of the Remote Desktop Connection window. Windows attempts to establish a connection to the computer you specified.

If Windows is able to connect to the computer, it displays the Log On to Windows dialog box. Enter your username, password, and optionally domain (when necessary) and click the OK button to log in. Windows then displays the remote Desktop.

If you left a user session active on the computer, Remote Desktop Connection drops you straight into it—likewise if you left a user session disconnected and no other user session is active. But if another user *is* active on the remote computer when you submit a successful logon and password, Windows displays the Logon Message dialog box to warn you that logging on will disconnect the user's session. Click the Yes button if you want to proceed. Click the No button to withdraw stealthily.

If you click the Yes button, the active user gets a Request for Connection dialog box. This tells them that you (it specifies your name) are trying to connect to the computer, warns them that they'll be disconnected if you do connect, and asks if they want to allow the connection.

The active user then gets to click the Yes button or the No button as appropriate to their needs and inclinations. If Windows doesn't get an answer within 30 seconds or so, it figures they're not there, disconnects their session, and lets you in.

If the active user clicks the Yes button in the Request for Connection dialog box, Windows logs them off immediately and logs you on. But if the active user clicks the No button, you get a Logon Message dialog box, telling you that they didn't allow you to connect. Windows displays this Logon Message dialog box for a few seconds, and then closes it automatically, returning you to the Remote Desktop Connection window.

If Windows is unable to establish the connection with the remote computer, it displays one of its Remote Desktop Disconnected dialog boxes to make you aware of the problem. The dialog box you see depends on the problem that Vista encountered. In all cases, the dialog boxes are self-explanatory. For example, you might see a message saying that Vista couldn't find the remote computer or that the remote computer doesn't accept Remote Desktop connections.

Working via Remote Desktop Connection

Once you've reached the remote Desktop, you can work more or less as if you were sitting at the computer. The few differences worth mentioning are discussed briefly in this section.

Using Cut, Copy, and Paste between the Local and Remote Computers

You can use Cut, Copy, and Paste commands to transfer information between the local computer and the remote computer. For example, you could copy some text from a program on the local computer and paste it into a program on the remote computer.

Copying from Remote Drives to Local Drives

You can copy from remote drives to local drives by working in Explorer. The drives on your local computer appear in Explorer windows on the remote computer marked as *Driveletter on COMPUTERNAME*. The drives on the remote computer appear as regular drives. You can copy and move files from one drive to another as you would with local drives.

Printing to a Local Printer

You can print to a local printer from the remote Desktop by selecting the local printer in the Print dialog box just as you would any other printer.

Printer settings are communicated to the remote Desktop when you access it. If you add a local printer during the remote session, the remote Desktop won't be able to see it. To make the printer show up on the remote Desktop, log off the remote session and log back on.

USING DRAG AND DROP

A new feature for Vista is the ability to use drag and drop to move objects between the local and remote computer. My personal experience has been that the feature appears to work better when you connect two Vista systems. However, I'm still working with a release candidate at this point and Microsoft may make additional tweaks that let you use this feature with any two systems.

Returning to Your Local Desktop

If you chose to display the connection bar, it hovers briefly at the top of the screen and then slides upward to vanish like a docked toolbar with its Auto-Hide property enabled. To pin the connection bar in position, click the pin icon at its left end. (To unpin it, click the pin icon again.) To display the connection bar when it's hidden itself, move the mouse pointer to the top edge of the screen, just as you'd do to display a docked toolbar hidden there.

The connection bar provides a Minimize button, a Restore/Maximize button, and a Close button. Use the Minimize button and the Restore button to reduce the remote Desktop from full screen to an icon or a partial screen so that you can access your local Desktop. Maximize the remote Desktop window to return to full screen mode when you want to work with it again. Use the Close button as discussed in the next section to disconnect your remote session.

Disconnecting the Remote Session

You can disconnect the remote session in either of the two following ways:

- On the remote Desktop, choose Start ➢ Disconnect. Windows displays the Disconnect Windows dialog box. Click the Disconnect button.
- Click the Close button on the connection bar (if the remote Desktop is displayed full screen) or on the Remote Desktop window (if the remote Desktop is not displayed full screen). Windows displays the Disconnect Windows Session dialog box. Click the OK button.

Windows disconnects the remote session but leaves the programs running for the time being. You can then log on again and pick up where you left off.

Logging Off the Remote Session

To log off and end your user session, click the Start button on the remote Desktop and choose Log Off from the Start menu. Windows displays the Log Off Windows dialog box. Click the Log Off button.

When someone else bumps you off the remote Desktop (by logging on locally or remotely), Windows displays the Remote Desktop Disconnected dialog box, telling you that the remote session "was ended by means of an administration tool."

If the network connection between the home computer and the remote computer is broken, the home computer displays a Remote Desktop Disconnected dialog box.

Summary

Vista doesn't include some of the old favorites that you found in older versions of Windows such as HyperTerminal and Windows Messenger. Fortunately, you can find alternatives to these older applications. The one application that Microsoft did keep, Remote Desktop, is significantly improved from previous versions. You'll find that the sessions are more secure, which means you have to worry less about someone eavesdropping on your session.

One of the things you should try, at least once, is creating a Remote Desktop connection. This tool can come in handy for a variety of purposes. For example, you can use Remote Desktop to help a user at another location accomplish specific tasks or perform administrative chores. Obviously, you can use it to access a remote computer to perform useful work too.

Now let's turn our attention to something you'll probably use every day—Windows Mail. Everyone needs an e-mail program. Rather than buy a potentially expensive alternative, try the e-mail program that comes with Vista.

Chapter 17

Using Windows Mail for E-mail and News

Of all the features of the Internet, intranets, and local area networks (LANs), e-mail is, without question, the most used. Instead of playing phone tag with colleagues at work, you send them e-mail. Millions of extended families stay in touch via e-mail, and an e-mail address has become an expected component of a business card.

Windows Mail is an Internet standards e-mail reader you can use to access one or more Internet e-mail accounts. An Internet e-mail account isn't the same thing as an account with an online information service. The difference is that an Internet account provides services such as Point-to-Point Protocol (PPP) Internet access and e-mail but doesn't include services such as chat rooms, access to databases, conferences, and so on. Consequently, you can't use Windows Mail to access an e-mail account with Hotmail, MS Mail, cc:Mail, CompuServe, America Online, or versions of Microsoft Exchange Server prior to version 5.

In addition to being an e-mail reader, Windows Mail is also a newsreader. In the first part of this chapter, I'll explain its e-mail features, and in the second part, I'll show you how to access newsgroups and post to them.

- Starting Windows Mail
- Touring Windows Mail
- Using Windows Mail to read, compose, and send e-mail
- Using Windows Mail to read news and post to newsgroups
- Customizing Windows Mail
- Using Windows Calendar

Vista: What's New?

Don't let the new name fool you, Windows Mail is Outlook Express in disguise. Yes, Windows Mail does have a few additional features and improvements of existing features, but if you already know how to use Outlook Express, you also know how to use Windows Mail. The most noticeable change in Windows Mail is that it does provide significant protection from junk e-mail. This change is in line with the rest of Vista in that it provides additional security.

You'll also notice that Windows Mail doesn't have a Contacts area. That's because it uses the new Windows Contacts feature to store e-mail and other information. Microsoft has centralized contact storage in Vista so that you can use it with a number of applications. For example, you'll use

Windows Contacts when you collaborate with other people. However, except for using a separate window now to view contact information, you won't really notice a big change.

The big news for this chapter is Windows Calendar. Users have seen this feature provided in Outlook for years. Now, you get essentially the same feature as part of Vista. I say *essentially* because Windows Calendar definitely doesn't provide all of the bells and whistles that Outlook does. For example, anyone who needs to work in a group setting will probably want to continue using Outlook rather than rely on the free alternative. Even so, Windows Calendar is a welcome addition for home users or anyone who really doesn't need to collaborate with others on schedule.

Using Windows Mail as Your Mail Reader

To start Windows Mail, choose Start ➢ Windows Mail. In addition, if Windows Mail is set as the default e-mail application, you can select it directly from the Quick Launch toolbar.

If Windows Mail doesn't appear there but you would like it to, right-click the Taskbar and choose Properties, and then click the Start Menu tab and click Customize. In the Customize Start Menu dialog box that appears, choose Windows Mail from the E-mail link drop-down list, as shown in Figure 17.1.

FIGURE 17.1
Change the Start menu settings to use Windows Mail as your e-mail program.

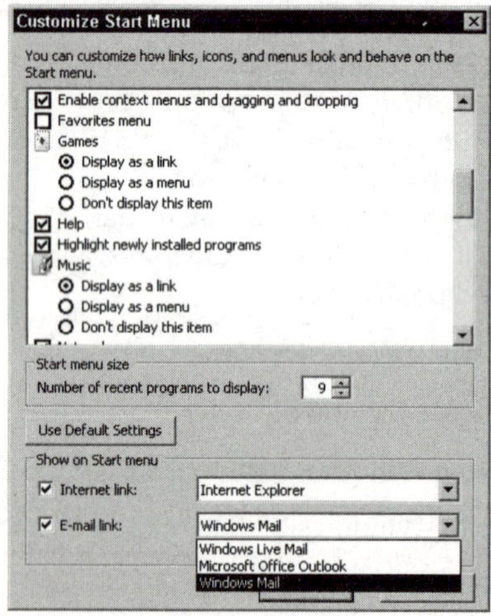

NOTE Before you can open and use Windows Mail to send and receive e-mail, you need to configure your Internet connection. You'll find information on how to do this in Chapter 14.

A Quick Tour

When you first open Windows Mail, you'll see a screen similar to that shown in Figure 17.2.

To read your mail click Inbox in the Folders list. Initially the Preview pane is split horizontally; header information is displayed in the upper pane, and the message is displayed in the lower pane.

TIP To change the arrangement of the Preview pane, choose View ➢ Layout to open the Window Layout Properties dialog box, and select options to show or hide certain parts.

FIGURE 17.2
The opening screen in Windows Mail.

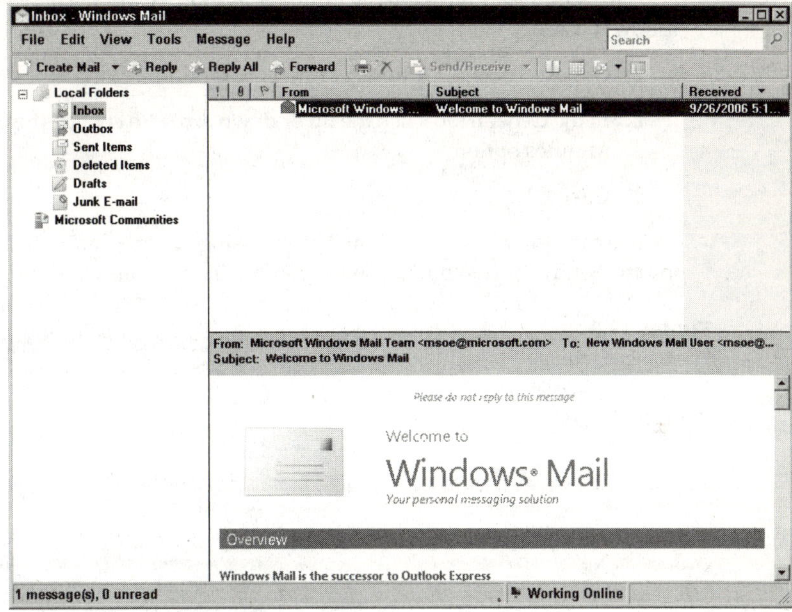

LOCAL FOLDERS

The Local Folders list is a tool for organizing messages. Initially, it contains the following folders, although you can create additional folders, as you'll see shortly:

Inbox Contains newly received messages and messages that you haven't yet disposed of in some way.

Outbox Contains messages that are ready to be sent.

Sent Items Contains copies of messages that you've sent (a handy device if you send lots of e-mail).

Deleted Items Contains copies of messages that you've deleted.

Drafts Contains messages that you're working on but which aren't yet ready to be sent.

Junk E-mail Contains the messages that Windows Mail identifies as junk e-mail.

MICROSOFT COMMUNITIES

The Microsoft Communities folder is your connection to newsgroups. To use this feature, you must download and select newsgroups that you want to view. The newsgroups appear as subfolders, just as e-mail entries appear as folders beneath Local Folders. You can learn more about newsgroups in the "Using Windows Mail as Your Newsreader" section of the chapter.

Retrieving Your Mail

If you're connected to your Internet account, Windows Mail will automatically check the server for new messages and download them when you open Windows Mail. By default, Windows Mail will also check for new mail every 30 minutes, as long as you're connected. To adjust this time interval, follow these steps:

1. Choose Tools ➤ Options to open the Options dialog box shown in Figure 17.3.
2. In the General tab, click the up or down arrow to change the Check for New Messages Every *x* Minutes option.
3. Click OK.

You can also check for new mail by choosing Tools ➤ Send and Receive ➤ Receive All or by clicking the Send/Receive button on the toolbar in the main window.

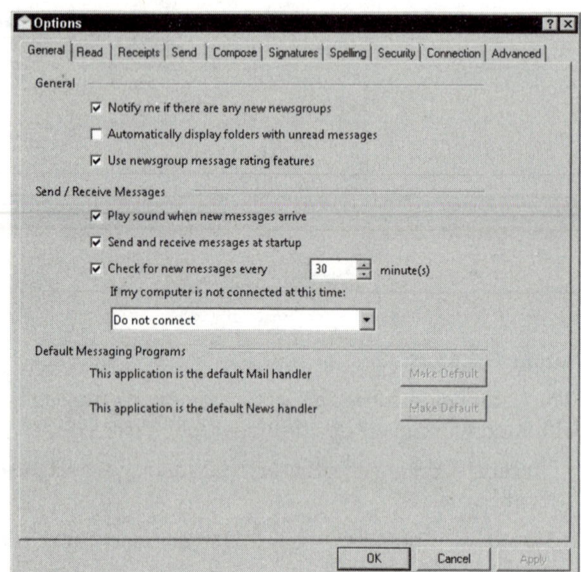

FIGURE 17.3
The General tab contains options for the basic operation of Windows Mail.

Reading and Processing Messages

If you're working in the split Preview pane view, simply click a message header to display the message in a separate window. Otherwise, simply double-click a header to view the message.

PRINTING MESSAGES

For various reasons, it's often handy to have a paper copy of e-mail messages. You can print in a couple of ways:

- To print a message after opening it in the Preview pane, select its header and click the Print icon on the toolbar in the main window. You can also right-click its header and choose Print from the context menu.
- To print an open message, click the Print icon on the toolbar in the message window.

Marking Messages

If you're like me, you don't always handle each message as you receive it or immediately after you read it, and it's easy to forget that you need to take some action or follow up on a message unless it stands out from the others in the header list. One trick that I use is to mark a message as unread even though I've read it (select the header and choose Edit ➤ Mark as Unread or right-click the header and choose Mark as Unread from the context menu). You can also select the header and choose Message ➤ Flag Message to display a red flag to the left of the message header. To remove the flag, choose Message ➤ Flag Message again.

In addition, you can mark a message as read, and you can mark all messages as read.

Moving Messages

You can easily move a message from one folder to another by dragging and dropping it. For example, if you receive a message that you want to modify and send to someone else, select the message header and then drag it to the Drafts folder. Open it, revise it, and then send it on its way.

Saving Messages

You can save messages in folders you created in Windows Explorer, and you can save messages in Windows Mail folders. You can also save attachments as files.

Saving Messages in Windows Explorer Folders

To save messages in a folder in Windows Explorer, follow these steps:

1. Open the message or select its header.
2. Choose File ➤ Save As to open the Save Message As dialog box shown in Figure 17.4.
3. Select a folder in which to save the message. Windows Mail places the subject line in the File Name box. You can use this name or type another name.
4. Select a file type in which to save the message, and then click Save.

FIGURE 17.4
Save messages to your hard drive to later review or archive.

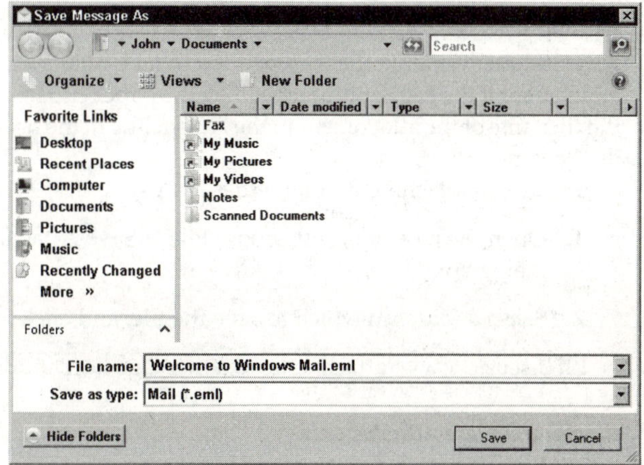

Saving Messages in Windows Mail Folders

As I've mentioned, you can create your own Windows Mail folders. For example, you might want to create folders for people with whom you regularly correspond, or you might want to create folders for current projects. To create a new folder, follow these steps:

1. In the main Windows Mail window, choose File ➤ New ➤ Folder to open the Create Folder dialog box shown in Figure 17.5.
2. In the Folder Name box, type a name for your folder.
3. Select a folder in which to place the new folder, and click OK.

You now have a new folder in your folders list, and you can drag any message to it. You have, however, an even easier and more efficient way to save messages in Windows Mail folders, and I'll look at that in the "Applying Message Rules" section, later in this chapter.

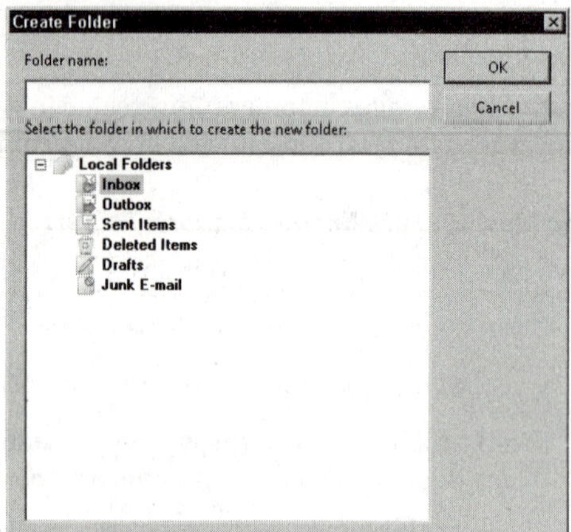

FIGURE 17.5
Specify the location of the new folder you want to create.

Saving Attachments

An attachment is a file that's appended to an e-mail message. You'll know that a message has an attachment if the header is preceded by the paper clip icon. When you open the message, you'll see the filename of the attachment in the Attach line in the header. To open an attachment, double-click its filename.

To save an attachment, follow these steps:

1. Open the message, and choose File ➤ Save Attachments to open the Save Attachments dialog box.
2. Select a folder in which to save the file, and click Save.

I'll discuss how to attach a file to a message later in this chapter.

Blocking Unsafe Attachments

Windows Mail has the ability to block unsafe attachments—that is, attachments that could potentially carry viruses. This includes executable files and scripts. Most of the time, this is a good thing, especially for newbie users who are prone to blindly taking every attachment at face value.

However, advanced users might find that it blocks file attachments that they genuinely need to receive. You can get around this in a couple of ways. One is to ask the sender to zip the file before sending it. Another is to turn off the blocking option in Windows Mail, either temporarily or permanently.

To change the blocking setting:

1. Choose Tools ➤ Options.
2. Click the Security Tab. You'll see a list of security options, as shown in Figure 17.6.
3. Mark or clear the Do not allow attachments to be saved or opened that could potentially be a virus check box.
4. Click OK.

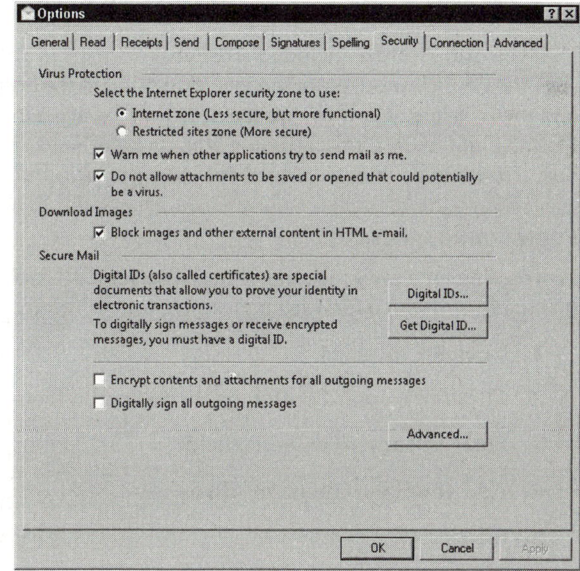

FIGURE 17.6
Specify the security settings you want to use when working with Windows Mail.

REPLYING TO A MESSAGE

To reply to a message, click the Reply button on the toolbar in the message window. If the message is addressed to multiple recipients and you want to reply to all of them, click the Reply All button.

TIP This is a quick and easy way to note the person's e-mail address. By default, Windows Mail automatically places the names of the people you reply to in your Address Book.

By default, Windows Mail includes the text of the original message in your reply. According to Internet tradition, this squanders bandwidth, and it's better not to include the original message unless it's really necessary. When is it necessary?

- When you want to be sure that the recipient understands the nature of your reply and the topic to which it's related.
- When your message is part of a series of messages that involve some sort of question-and-answer sequence.
- When it's important to keep track of who said what when.

An alternative is to include only the relevant portions of the original message in your reply. Many people call this technique quoting and depending on how you edit the content, it can lead to cries of foul by the other person. An essential part of quoting is to ensure you don't quote material out of context and that you always include enough of the original text to make its meaning clear. To use quoting, follow these steps:

1. Open the message and click the Reply button.
2. The message is now addressed to the original sender, and the original subject line is preceded by Re:.
3. In the body of the message, edit the contents so that the portions you want are retained, and then enter your response.
4. Click the Send button.

If you don't want to include the original message in your reply, you can simply open the message, click the Reply button, place the insertion point in the body of the message, choose Edit ➤ Select All, and press Delete. If you're sure that you don't want to include the original message, choose Tools ➤ Options, and in the Options dialog box, click the Send tab. Clear the Include message in reply check box. If, once in a while, you need the message included, simply recheck the option.

Forwarding a Message

Forwarding an e-mail message is much easier than forwarding a letter through the U.S. mail, and it actually works. To forward a message, follow these steps:

1. Open the message.
2. Click the Forward button on the toolbar in the message window.
3. Enter an address in the To field.
4. Add your own comments if you want.
5. Click Send.

Deleting Messages

To delete a message, you can select its header and click Delete, or you can open it and then click Delete. The message isn't yet really deleted, however; Windows Mail has placed it in the Deleted Items folder. And that's where the message stays until you empty the Deleted Items folder or tell Windows Mail to empty it when you close Windows Mail.

If you want to delete items from the Deleted Items folder yourself, follow these steps:

1. Select the Deleted Items folder.
2. Choose Edit ➤ Empty "Deleted Items" Folder.
3. When Windows Mail asks if you're sure you want to delete these items, click Yes.

To set up automatic deletion of the items in the Deleted Items folder, follow these steps:

1. Choose Tools ➤ Options to open the Options dialog box.
2. Click the Advanced tab.

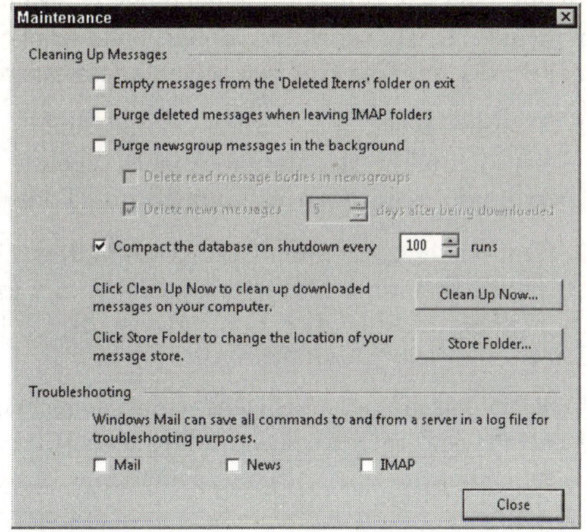

FIGURE 17.7
Define the level of automation you want to use to maintain Windows Mail.

3. Click Maintenance. You'll see the Maintenance dialog box shown in Figure 17.7.
4. In the Cleaning Up Messages section, click the Empty messages from the "Deleted Items" folder on exit check box, and then click OK.

Creating and Sending Messages

In this section, I'll walk you through the steps to create a simple message and send it. You can also create messages in HTML (Hypertext Markup Language) and include hyperlinks, pictures, colorful formatting, sounds, and so on. We'll look at that in the next section.

To begin a new message, you can click the Create Mail button in the main window to open the New Message window, as shown in Figure 17.8. Or, if the intended recipient is in your Address Book, you can double-click that person's name in the Contacts window to open the New Message window; the To line will display the recipient's name.

FIGURE 17.8
You create a new message in the New Message window.

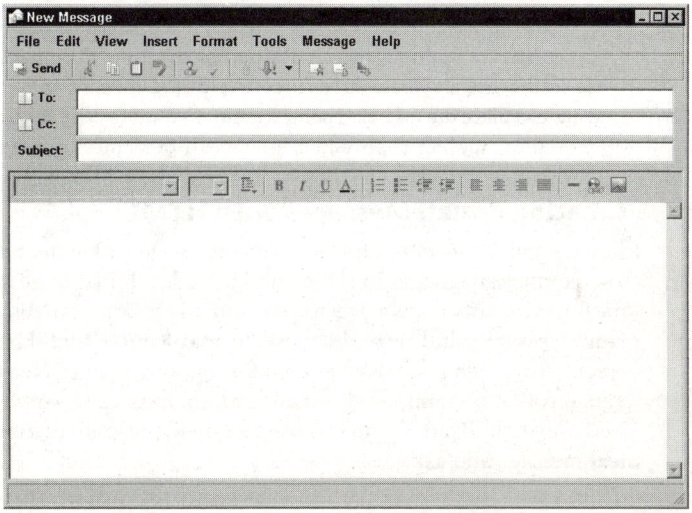

If your New Message window includes a Formatting toolbar, the message you compose will be formatted as HTML. For my purposes here, I want only plain text. If this is what you want, as well, choose Format ➤ Plain Text before you begin composing your message. Now, follow these steps:

1. If necessary, enter the address of the primary recipient in the To field. If you're sending a message to multiple primary recipients, separate their addresses with semicolons. If you choose multiple recipients from your Address Book, they're automatically separated by semicolons.
2. Optionally, enter e-mail addresses in the Cc (carbon copy) and Bcc (blind carbon copy) fields. To enter a Bcc recipient, click the Cc icon, enter the name in the Select Recipients dialog box, and click Bcc. You can also display the Bcc field by choosing View ➤ All Headers.

TIP Recipients in the Bcc field don't appear as recipients to other viewers. Use the Bcc field when you don't want others to know who is receiving the message. In fact, I often use the Bcc field alone when sending informational messages to a mailing list.

3. Enter a subject line for your message.

NOTE If you don't enter a subject line, Windows Mail will ask if you're sure you don't want a subject line. Unless you have a good reason not to do so, enter some text in the subject line. Your recipient will see this text in the header information for the message and will then have a clue as to the nature of your message.

4. Enter the text of your message.
5. If appropriate, establish a priority for your message. Choose Message ➤ Set Priority, and then choose High, Normal, or Low. The default is Normal.
6. Click Send to start your message on its way.

You can send your message immediately by clicking the Send button, or you can save it in your Outbox to send later by choosing File ➤ Send Later. The message will be sent when you choose Send and Receive All or when you choose Send All.

TIP You can use Copy and Paste in Windows Mail just as you use those commands in other Windows programs. For example, to include a portion of a Word document in a message, open the document, select the text, and press Ctrl+C to copy it to the Clipboard. In Windows Mail, open the New Message window, place the insertion point where you want to copy the text, and press Ctrl+V. Use this same process to copy portions of e-mail messages to other messages or to documents in other applications.

Creating E-mail Messages with HTML

In the previous section, I told you how to create a plain text message, but as I mentioned, you can also compose messages in HTML and include all sorts of neat effects. Before you send a formatted message, be sure that your recipient's e-mail program can display it effectively. When you open the New Message window and choose Format ➤ Rich Text (HTML), the message you compose is essentially a web page. Newer e-mail programs such as Netscape Messenger and the commercial version of Eudora, Eudora Pro, can read, compose, and send HTML messages, but others can't. An easy way to find out if your recipient's e-mail program can handle HTML is to send a simple plain text message and ask.

That said, let's look at some bells and whistles you can include in Windows Mail e-mail messages. Click the Create Mail icon to open the New Message window, and be sure that the Rich Text (HTML) option is selected. You'll see the screen shown in Figure 17.8. Notice the Formatting toolbar, which contains many of the same tools you see and use in your Windows word processor. You'll also see the Font and Font Size drop-down list boxes that are present in your word processor.

As you create your message, just pretend that you're using a word processor, and use the Formatting tools to apply emphasis to your message. All the usual design rules apply, including the following:

- Don't use a lot of different fonts.
- Remember, typing in all capital letters in e-mail is tantamount to shouting.
- Don't place a lot of text in italics. It's hard to read on the screen.
- Save boldface for what's really important.

To insert a horizontal line that spans the message window, click the Insert Horizontal Line button on the Formatting toolbar.

To apply HTML styles such as Definition Term or Definition, click the Paragraph Style button on the Formatting toolbar.

Using Stationery

In addition to formatting, you can add some class or some comedy to your e-mail messages in another way: stationery. In the New Message window, choose Message ➤ New Using, and then choose a predesigned format from the list in the submenu, or click Select Stationery to open the Select Stationery dialog box and select from a larger list. Here's one example of what you'll find:

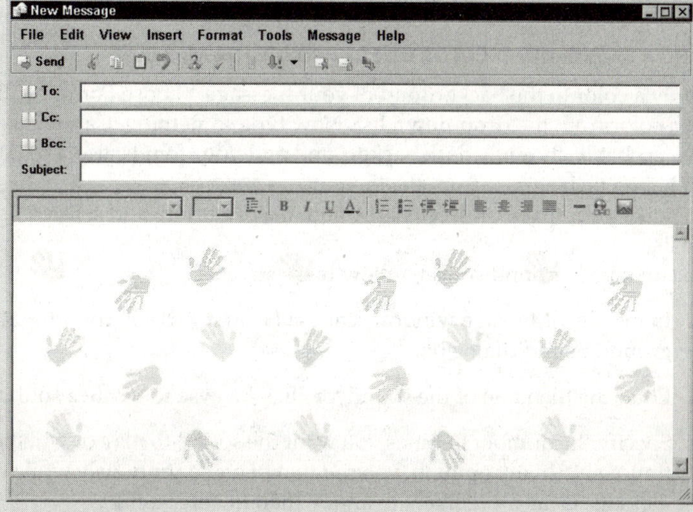

To customize stationery, click Create New in the Select Stationery dialog box to start the Stationery Setup Wizard. Follow the on-screen instructions.

ADDING A PICTURE TO YOUR MESSAGES

You can insert a picture in a message in two ways:

- As a piece of art
- As a background over which you can type text

To insert a picture as a piece of art that you can size and move, follow these steps:

1. In the New Message window, click the Insert Picture button on the Formatting toolbar to open the Picture dialog box.
2. Enter the filename of the picture in the Picture Source text box, or click the Browse button to locate it.
3. Click Open. Windows Mail inserts the new picture into the message for you.
4. Optionally right-click the new picture and choose Properties from the context menu to display the Picture dialog box. In the Alternate Text box, enter some text that will display if the recipient's e-mail program can't display the picture, and specify layout and spacing options if you want. (You can also size and move the picture with the mouse once you place it in the message.) Click OK.

To insert a picture as background, follow these steps:

1. In the New Message window, choose Format ➤ Background ➤ Picture to open the Background Picture dialog box.
2. Enter the filename of the picture, or click Browse to select a predesigned stationery background or locate another file.
3. Click Open, and then click OK to insert the background.

ADDING A BACKGROUND COLOR OR SOUND TO YOUR MESSAGE

To apply a color to the background of your message, choose Format ➤ Background ➤ Color and select a color from the drop-down list. Now type something. Can you see it on the screen? If not, you've probably chosen a dark background and your font is also a dark color—most likely black if you haven't changed it from the default.

To make your text visible, click the Font Color button, and select a lighter color from the drop-down list.

To add a background sound, follow these steps:

1. In the New Message window, choose Format ➤ Background ➤ Sound to open the Background Sound dialog box.
2. Enter the filename of the sound, or click Browse to locate a sound file.
3. Specify the number of times you want the sound to play or whether you want it to play continuously. (In my opinion, a sound that plays continuously while the recipient is reading the message is far more likely to annoy than to entertain.)
4. Click OK.

Including Hyperlinks in Your Message

When you insert a hyperlink in a message, the recipient can go directly to the resource simply by clicking the hyperlink. You can insert a hyperlink in three ways:

- Simply type it in the message body. Be sure to include the entire URL.
- In the New Message window, choose Insert ➤ Hyperlink to open the Hyperlink dialog box, and then enter the URL in the text box.
- In Internet Explorer, press Alt, choose File ➤ Send ➤ Link by E-mail to open the New Message window. The URL of the current page is automatically inserted in the message body.

Adding a Signature to Your Messages

I know people who never sign their e-mail messages. After all, their name is in the From line in the message header. I also know people who append elaborate signatures, touting their accomplishments or advertising their businesses. I usually just sign my first name at the bottom of messages, but what you do depends on your personal style or whether you're sending business or personal correspondence.

To create a signature that's automatically added to all your outgoing messages, follow these steps:

1. Choose Tools ➤ Options to open the Options dialog box.
2. Click the Signatures tab.
3. Click New. Windows Mail will add a new signature, as shown in Figure 17.9.
4. To create a text signature, in the Edit Signature section, enter the content in the box next to the Text option button.

Figure 17.9
Create a signature to add to the bottom of each e-mail message.

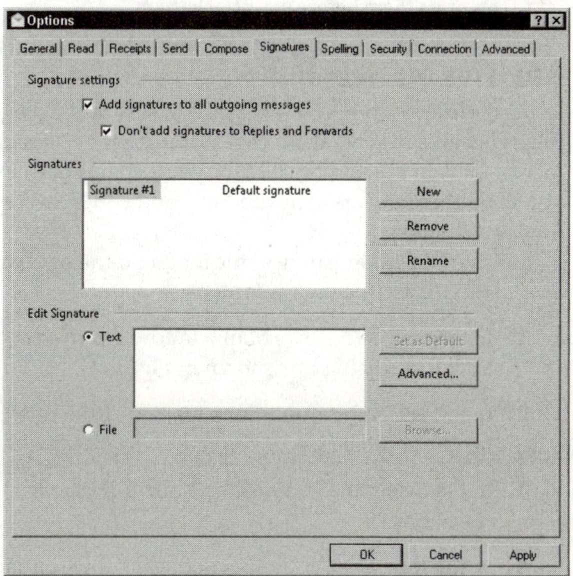

5. If you want to use a file you've already created as your signature, click the File option button and enter the filename, or click Browse to locate it.
6. If you have multiple e-mail accounts, click the Advanced button to open the Advanced Signature Settings dialog box, and specify which accounts should use this signature.
7. Click the Add Signatures to All Outgoing Messages check box, and click OK.

If you don't want the signature automatically appended to all outgoing messages, leave the Add Signatures to All Outgoing Messages check box unselected. Then, to add this signature to a message, choose Insert ➤ Signature in the New Message window.

Attaching Files to Your Messages

In Windows Mail, sending a file or multiple files along with your message is painless and simple. Follow these steps:

1. In the New Message window, choose Insert ➤ File Attachment to open the Open dialog box.
2. Select a file and click Open.

Your message now contains the name of the file in the Attach line.

If the file is large or if you know that the recipient has a slow connection, you'll want to compress it. To do so, in the Insert Attachment dialog box, right-click the file, click Send To on the shortcut menu, and then click Compressed Folder. You'll now see a compressed folder for the file in the current folder (the folder displays a zipper). Vista uses the WinZip program to compress files and folders, and WinZip is compatible with any compression utility your recipient may have. All the recipient needs to do to uncompress the file or folder is double-click it.

TIP Digital picture files can be quite large, so if your recipient has a compression utility, be sure to compress them before you attach them.

Applying Message Rules

Using the Rules Editor, you can specify where messages go after they're downloaded, block unwanted messages, and, in general, manage incoming messages more efficiently—especially if you deal with a lot of e-mail. In this section, I'll give you a couple of examples that illustrate the possibilities, but, as you'll see, there are lots of possibilities, and you'll need to apply the options that make the most sense for your situation.

Let's start by establishing a rule that sends all mail from a particular person to that person's Windows Mail folder. Follow these steps:

1. In the main Windows Mail window, choose Tools ➤ Message Rules ➤ Mail to open the New Mail Rule dialog box shown in Figure 17.10.
2. In the Select the Conditions for Your Rule section, click the Where the From line contains people check box.
3. In the Select the Actions for Your Rule section, click the Move it to the specified folder check box.
4. In the Rule Description section, click the Contains People link to open the Select People dialog box shown in Figure 17.11.

FIGURE 17.10
Define rules for your e-mail messages to automate message-handling tasks.

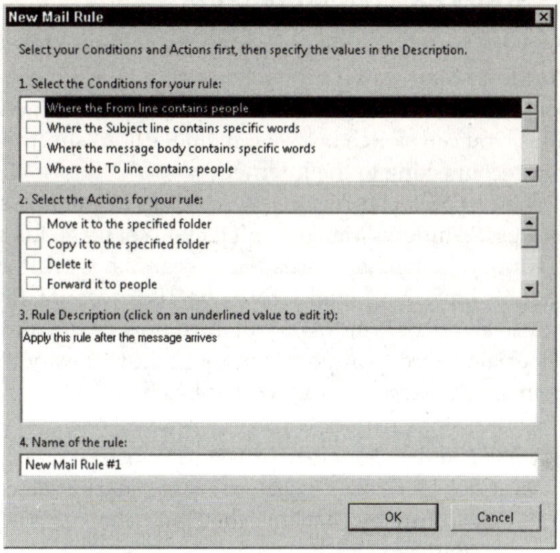

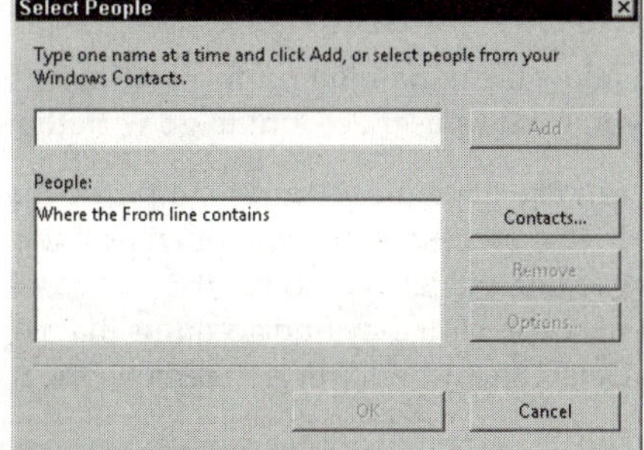

FIGURE 17.11
Choose one or more persons that the rule affects.

5. Enter a name and click Add or select a name from your Contacts, and click OK.
6. Click Specified to open the Move dialog box.
7. Select the folder where you want this person's messages to go, and click OK. If you need to create a folder, click New Folder.
8. Accept the name of the rule that Windows Mail proposes, or type a new name.
9. Click OK.

Now, when messages arrive from that person, you'll find them in their folder rather than in your Inbox. You use this same technique to block messages. For example, if you don't want to see messages from a particular person, you can move the messages to the Deleted Items folder.

TIP To delete a rule, select it and click Remove in the Message Rules dialog box. To modify a rule, select it and click Modify.

Adding and Managing Identities

If several people use the same computer either at home, at the office, or elsewhere, and thus also use Windows Mail, you'll probably want to take advantage of the Identities feature, which lets each person view their own mail and have individualized settings and contacts. Once you set up Identities, you can switch between them without shutting down the computer or disconnecting from and reconnecting to the Internet.

When you install Vista, you're set up in Windows Mail as the Main Identity. Unlike Outlook Express, Windows Mail doesn't let you set up an identity without having a corresponding account to support it. In other words, each account has a different e-mail account associated with it, but you can only have one e-mail account per user account. If you have multiple e-mail accounts from a previous version of Windows, you must now create multiple user accounts to support them. You use a special wizard to import identities that you want to use with Windows Mail. To add an identity from another account, follow these steps.

1. Choose File ➤ Identities. You'll see the Identity Import Wizard.
2. Click Next, if necessary, to get past the initial screen. You can avoid seeing this initial screen in the future by checking the Don't show this again option. You'll see the dialog box shown in Figure 17.12.
3. Choose Import Identities and click Next. If there aren't any other identities on your system, you'll see a message box stating that there aren't any identities to import from this account.
4. Follow the remaining prompts to import the identity you want to use. The wizard will help you create a user account to go with the e-mail account that you're importing.

You can use the same wizard to import e-mail accounts from other user accounts. The only difference in this process is that you must provide credentials to access the other user account before Windows Mail will let you access it.

In some cases, you may find accounts that you really don't need any longer. In this case, you can choose Delete Identities option to remove the unneeded accounts.

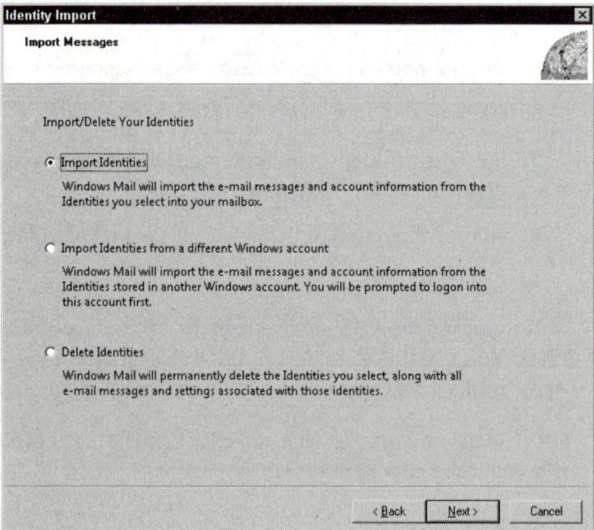

FIGURE 17.12
Choose the action you want to perform.

Using Windows Mail as Your Newsreader

A newsgroup is a collection of articles about a particular subject. A newsgroup is similar to e-mail in that you can reply to what someone else has written (the newsgroup term for this is *posting*), and you can send a question or a response either to the whole group or to individuals.

The primary (but not sole) source of newsgroups is Usenet, which is a worldwide distributed discussion system consisting of newsgroups with names that are classified hierarchically by subject. For example, `rec.crafts.metalworking` is a recreational group devoted to the craft of metalworking. The leftmost portion represents the largest hierarchical category, and the name gets more specific from left to right. Table 17.1 lists the major top-level newsgroup categories and explains what topics each discusses. Currently, there are thousands and thousands of newsgroups on every conceivable topic. For an extensive listing of them, go to `http://www.ibiblio.org/usenet-i/hier-s/master.html`.

You access newsgroups by accessing the server on which they're stored. Not all servers store the same newsgroups. The network administrator or the owner of the site determines what to store, but if you request a particular newsgroup from your ISP, the ISP can forward that request to another server that does provide the newsgroup. Almost all news servers "expire" articles after a few days or, at most, a few weeks because of the tremendous volume. Although they might be archived at the site, these articles are no longer available to be viewed by users.

NOTE Newsgroups are uncensored. You can find just about anything at any time anywhere. Nobody has authority over newsgroups as a whole. If you find certain groups, certain articles, or certain people offensive, don't go there, or use the Rules Editor that I talked about earlier to prevent certain articles from even being displayed. But remember, anarchy reigns in newsgroups, and you never know what you might stumble upon in the least likely places.

TABLE 17.1: The Major Newsgroups

NEWSGROUP	WHAT IT DISCUSSES
alt	Newsgroups outside the main structure outlined in this table
biz	Business products, services, reviews, and so on
comp	Computer science and related topics, including operating systems, hardware, artificial intelligence, and graphics
humanities	Fine art, literature, philosophy, and the like
misc	Anything that doesn't fit into one of the other categories
news	Information on Usenet and newsgroups
rec	Recreational activities such as hobbies, the arts, movies, and books
sci	Scientific topics such as math, physics, and biology
soc	Social issues and cultures
talk	Controversial subjects such as gun control, abortion, religion, and politics

Windows Mail has the Microsoft Communities news server as the default server, so you no longer need to set up a newsgroup account. This news server only provides access to the Microsoft newsgroups, so you can use it to find information on Windows and other Microsoft products. However, you can add more news servers as necessary. Simply follow the instructions in the "Setting Up a Newsgroup Account" section of the chapter.

Setting Up a Newsgroup Account

Before you can read newsgroups, you must set up a newsgroups account. Before you start, get the name of your news server from your ISP, and then follow these steps:

1. Choose Tools ➤ Accounts. You'll see the Internet Accounts dialog box shown in Figure 17.13.
2. Click Add. You'll see a Select Account Type dialog box.
3. Choose Newsgroup Account and click Next. You'll see a Your Name dialog box. The dialog boxes that follow ask you to supply specifics about your account.
4. Type your display name—the name that you want others to use when addressing you. Click Next.
5. Type your e-mail address. Click Next.
6. Type your news server address. Click Next. Windows Mail will check the server connection. When the connection is successful, you'll see a success message.
7. Click Finish. Windows Mail adds the new account to its list of news servers.
8. Optionally, click Set as Default to set this new account as the default news server.

You'll now see a folder in the Folders list for your news server.

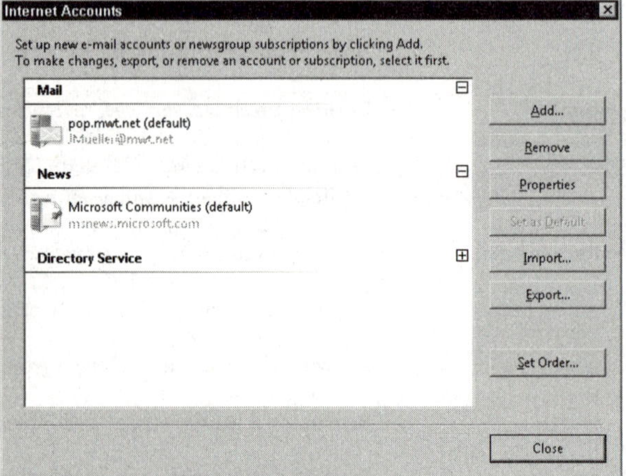

FIGURE 17.13
Create additional mail and news accounts as needed.

Connecting to Newsgroups

The next task is to download the list of newsgroups from your server. When Windows Mail asks if you want to do this, click Yes. This may take a while if you have a slow connection, but notice the incrementing number of newsgroups in the Downloading Newsgroups dialog box. The number available depends on what the server has subscribed to (well over 100,000 for the server I use).

TIP Only the names of the newsgroups are downloaded to your computer; their contents remain on the news server. Periodically, you can update this list by clicking Reset List.

When the list has finished downloading, you'll see the Newsgroup Subscriptions dialog box, as shown in Figure 17.14.

FIGURE 17.14
Use this dialog box to search for and subscribe to newsgroups.

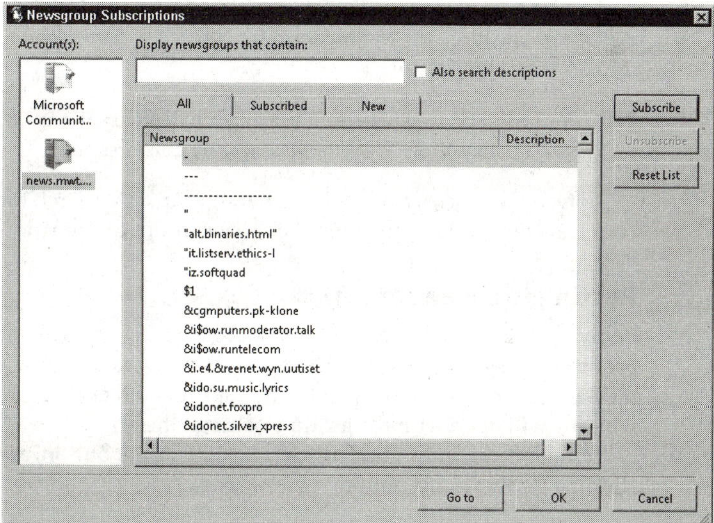

Finding a Newsgroup of Interest

You can select a newsgroup to read in two ways:

- You can scroll through the list (this will take a lot of time).
- You can search on a term.

Just for the sake of doing it, scroll down the list a bit. As you can see, it's in alphabetic order by hierarchical categories. If you don't see anything right away that strikes your fancy, you can perform a search. Enter a term in the Display Newsgroups Which Contain text box, and then don't do anything! In a second, you'll see a list of newsgroups that contain articles about your topic.

Subscribing to a Newsgroup

Subscribing to a newsgroup doesn't involve a fee or any other transaction. Subscribing simply means creating a subfolder for a particular newsgroup in your news folder. Then, instead of selecting it from the Newsgroup Subscriptions dialog box, you can simply click the newsgroup's folder to see the list of articles in it.

Once you've located a newsgroup you want to read, you can select it, click Subscribe, and then click Go To to open it, or you can simply click Go To. To unsubscribe to a newsgroup, right-click its folder, and choose Unsubscribe.

Reading a Newsgroup

To read an article, simply click its header to display the message in the lower pane.

Windows Mail is a threaded newsreader in that it groups messages that respond to a subject line. If you see a plus sign (+) to the left of a newsgroup header, you can click it to display a list of related messages. The more up-to-date term for threads is *conversation.* Newsgroup articles are grouped by conversations by default.

TIP You can also organize mail messages by conversations. With your Inbox selected, choose View ➤ Current View ➤ Group Messages by Conversation.

To read the articles from another newsgroup or to search for another newsgroup, double-click your main news folder, and then click Newsgroups to open the Newsgroup Subscriptions dialog box.

Posting to a Newsgroup

Replying to a newsgroup article or sending a message to a newsgroup is known as posting. You post to a newsgroup in much the same way that you compose and send e-mail. To send an original message to a newsgroup, open the newsgroup and click the New Post button. The New Message window will open with the group's name in the To line.

To reply to an individual article, click the Reply button, and to reply to the entire newsgroup, click the Reply Group button.

TIP You can also access newsgroups on the Internet at `http://groups.google.com/`, and doing so is much easier than using Windows Mail.

Customizing Windows Mail

Throughout this chapter, I've mentioned from time to time ways that you can specify how Windows Mail handles certain features, such as signatures. In most cases, you do this through the Options dialog box, which you open by choosing Tools ➤ Options. Here's a quick rundown of what to use each tab for in the Options dialog box:

General Use this tab to specify settings for how Windows Mail starts and for sending and receiving messages.

Read Use this tab to set options for reading news and mail. For example, you can specify a maximum number of news article headers to download at one time.

Receipts Use this tab if you want to verify that your message has been read by the recipient.

Send Use this tab to set, among other things, the format (HTML or Plain Text) in which you'll send all messages and the format you'll use to reply to messages. You can also specify whether copies of sent messages will be stored and whether you want Windows Mail to put the names and addresses of people you reply to in your Address Book.

Compose Use this tab to specify the font and font size for mail messages and news articles that you create and to select stationery fonts for HTML messages.

Signatures Use to create a signature, as discussed earlier in this chapter.

Security Use this tab to specify your desired Internet Security zone and to get a digital ID.

Connection Use this tab to specify how Windows Mail handles your dial-up connection.

Advanced Use this tab to specify what Windows Mail does with deleted items and to clean up downloaded messages, as well as to specify that all server commands are stored for troubleshooting purposes.

NOTE If you've installed any of the Microsoft Office applications that include a spell checker, you'll also see a Spelling tab in the Options dialog box.

Using Windows Calendar

Windows Calendar is a new Vista application that replicates some, but not all, of the functionality provided by other Microsoft products such as Outlook. You can use it to track both appointments and tasks. Theoretically, you can use Windows Calendar in a group situation by publishing your calendar and subscribing to the calendars offered by other users. In practice, you'll find that this feature isn't as easy to use as the group features found in other products. Yes, you can use Windows Calendar successfully in a small workgroup, but avoid using it for larger group coordination.

To start Windows Calendar, choose Start ➤ Windows Calendar. You'll see the window shown in Figure 17.15 where you can work with appointments and tasks. The following sections tell you more about Windows Calendar.

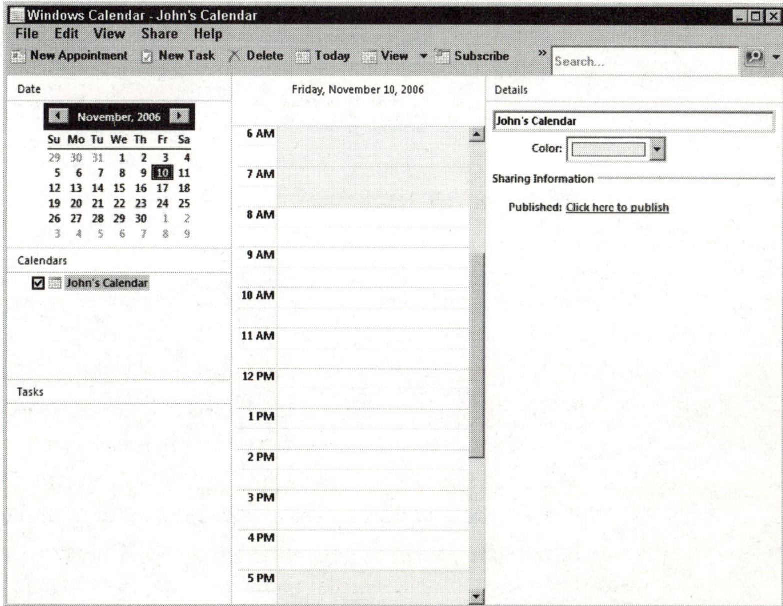

FIGURE 17.15 Windows Calendar helps you manage appointments and tasks.

Adding Appointments

An appointment is a task you must perform at a specific time. For example, a meeting falls into the appointment category. To create a new appointment, highlight the calendar you want to use, select a starting date and time, and click New Appointment. You'll see a new appointment added to the calendar. The Details pane is where you enter specifics about the appointment. Figure 17.16 shows the wealth of information you can add to the Details pane.

You can set the date and time using the fields in the Appointment Information section, or you can resize the appointment in the center pane. If you want Vista to remind you about the appointment, choose a value in the Reminder field. It's also possible to create recurring appointments (such as a monthly meeting) using the Recurrence field. Windows Calendar automatically schedules recurring appointments for you.

TIP **Windows Calendar adds special symbols to the calendar entries so that you know what kind of an appointment you're working with. Appointments with a reminder time have the alarm clock icon attached. When you add attendees to an appointment, you'll see the group icon (which looks like three people). Finally, recurring appointments have a double arrow arranged as a circle.**

Most appointments are with other people, so it's important to invite them. Click Attendees to see a list of people from Windows Contacts. To add a person to the list, highlight their name and click To. Click Cancel and you'll see the names appear in the Participants list. To make the invitations, click Invite. Windows Calendar opens an e-mail with all of the participant names already in place, a topic that corresponds to your meeting title, and a copy of the meeting details from the appointment (not the whole calendar). Type any required message in the e-mail and click Send. All of the invitations are made.

FIGURE 17.16
Enter the information about the new appointment in the Details pane.

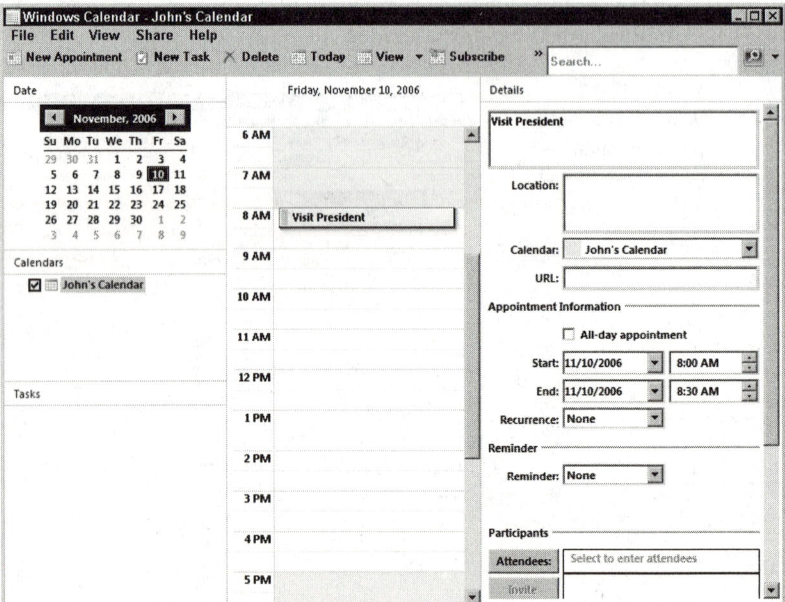

Adding Tasks

Tasks are responsibilities that you don't have to accomplish at a specific time, such as writing a proposal for a business venture. Even though the meeting for presenting the proposal is at a specific time, you can accomplish the task anytime before the meeting. You create a new task by clicking New Task. You'll see the task listed in the Tasks list and see the details for it in the Details pane. Type a name for the task and then fill in the details.

As with appointments, tasks have basic information such as start and end dates. You can assign a priority to the task to make it easier to know which tasks to accomplish first. A task can also include a reminder. However, unlike appointments, you don't invite others to work on the task with you, so the Details pane contains considerably less information than when you work with an appointment.

Viewing Calendar Entries

The center pane shown in Figure 17.15 is the only permanent part of the view. If you don't want to move directly from entry to entry, you can turn off the Navigation (right) pane by choosing View ➤ Navigation Pane. You can view the Navigation pane again by choosing View ➤ Navigation Pane a second time. Likewise, the Details pane is a toggle that you change using the View ➤ Details Pane command.

The default Windows Calendar view is a single day. However, you can also view your workweek or an entire month. Figure 17.17 shows the month view with the Navigation and Details panes closed. You select these alternative views using the View ➤ Workweek, View ➤ Week, and View ➤ Month commands. When you hover the mouse over an appointment, you see some, but not all, of the details. These alternative views don't show you any pending tasks.

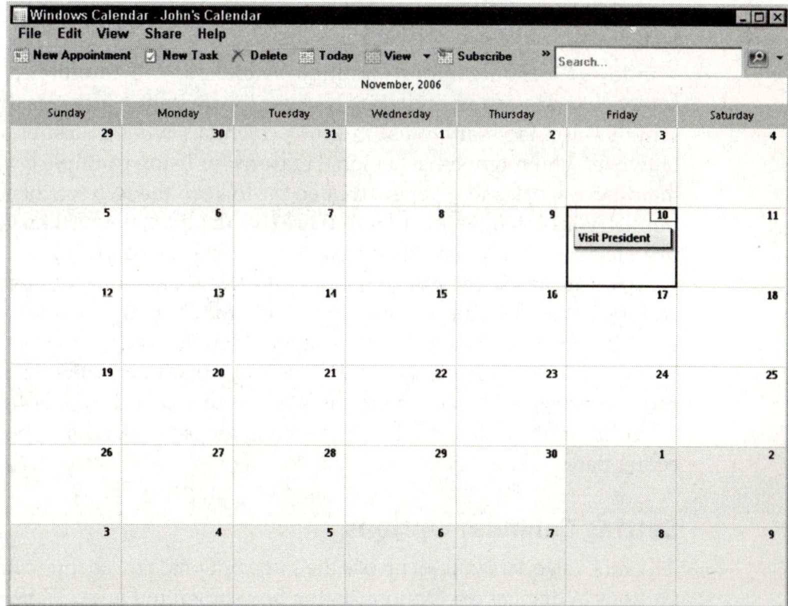

FIGURE 17.17 Use the calendar view that best meets your scheduling requirements at a particular time.

Printing Your Calendar

Printing a calendar is slightly different from printing a Word document. When working with documents, there are natural starting and stopping points. In fact, you often print the entire document since printing only part of it doesn't give the whole picture. When working with a calendar, you're always working with a date and time range. Consequently, the print dialog box for Windows Calendar contains some customized entries. To print a calendar, choose File ➤ Print. You'll see the dialog box shown in Figure 17.18. As you can see, you can print the current day, workweek, week, or month. You can also print a range of dates.

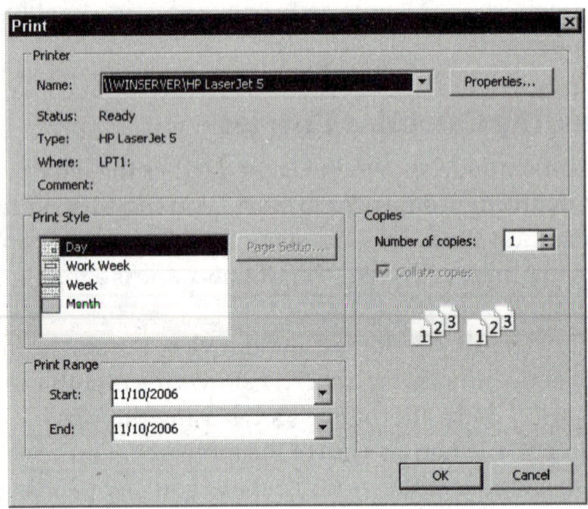

FIGURE 17.18
Choose the date range you need to print.

Creating New Calendars

Windows Calendar supports multiple calendars. You automatically use other calendars when someone sends you an invitation because the invitation includes the calendar that the other person sent. It's also necessary to use multiple calendars when you subscribe to someone else's calendar. However, you might have personal reasons for using multiple calendars. For example, you might maintain a work and a personal calendar to keep the two sets of activities separate. If you plan to publish your calendar, in order to share it with other people, then you should also create public and private calendars so that other people don't know everything that you're doing.

To create a new calendar, choose File ➤ New Calendar. Windows Calendar will add a new calendar entry to the Calendars list. Type a name for your calendar and press Enter. Every calendar has a different color. You can choose the calendar color in the Details pane.

The default settings show every calendar. However, viewing all of your calendars at once can prove confusing. If you want to display just one calendar, clear the check marks next to the other calendars in the Calendars list. The entries for each calendar appear in that calendar's color in the center pane.

Setting Calendar Options

All of the calendars you set up use the same options. You change calendar options by choosing File ➤ Options to display the Options dialog box shown in Figure 17.19.

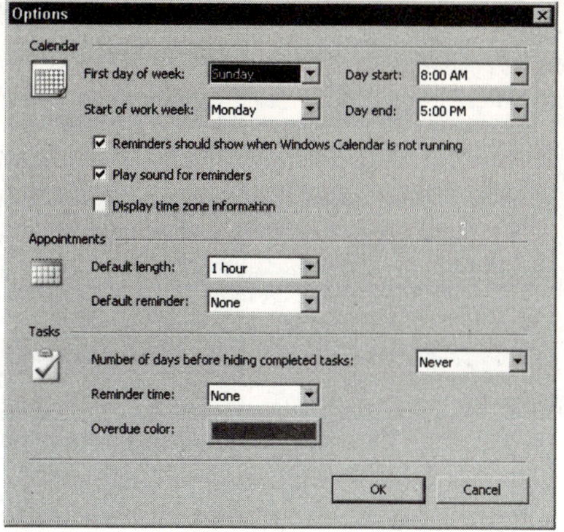

FIGURE 17.19 Define the default settings you want to use when working with calendars.

The options in the Calendar section affect both tasks and appointments. The Day Start and Day End fields contain the time you start and stop work each day. If your workweek starts on Sunday, then you should set the Start of work week field to Sunday. Unfortunately, Microsoft seems to assume that everyone works a five-day workweek because that's what the workweek views always display.

The Appointments section lets you choose the default appointment length and the reminder time. This feature is helpful when you have appointments of a set length and don't want to hand edit every appointment you make.

The Tasks section helps you define the task reminder time and provides the overdue task color. Notice also that this section lets you define the interval from the time a task is completed and Windows Calendar hides it from view.

Publishing Your Calendar

Windows Calendar provides a number of methods for sharing your calendar. One of them is to send an invitation to other people as described in the "Adding Appointments" section. Another method is to send the entire calendar to a third party by choosing Share ➤ Send via E-mail. However, both of these methods are static. Anyone who obtains such a calendar will find that the information is quickly outdated. A dynamic method for sharing calendars is publishing. When you publish a calendar, people can subscribe to it. Any changes you make to your calendar also appear in their calendar.

Use the following steps to publish a calendar.

1. Click Click here to publish in the Details pane when you highlight the calendar or choose Share ➤ Publish. In both cases, you'll see the Publish Calendar dialog box shown in Figure 17.20.

2. Type a name for the calendar when necessary. The Calendar name field always contains the name of the calendar as it appears in Windows Calendar. Although you can change this name, it's usually better to retain the default name to avoid confusion.

3. Provide a location for the calendar in the Location to publish calendar field. The example shows a website, but you can easily use a network drive or other convenient location.

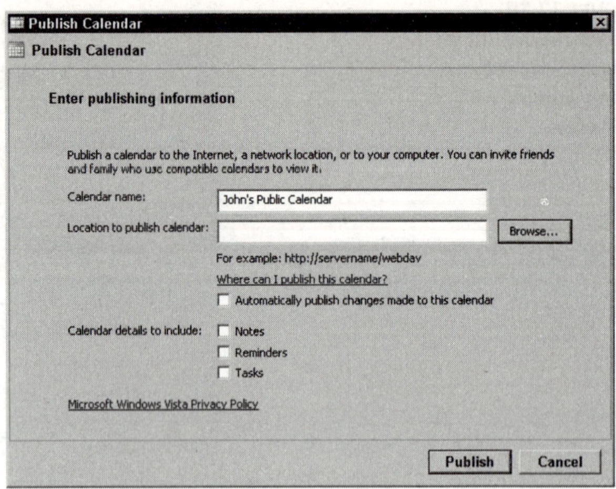

FIGURE 17.20
Publish your calendar to keep others posted on your activities.

4. Check the Automatically publish changes made to this calendar option. If you don't check this option, you might as well choose one of the static sharing options.
5. Choose the details you want to include with the calendar.
6. Click Publish and you'll see a success message.
7. Click Announce. You'll see an e-mail message with the subscription information for your calendar already included. (If you decide to perform this task later, you can choose Share ➤ Send Publish E-mail to display the same e-mail.)
8. Fill out the e-mail details and click Send.
9. Click Finish to close the Publish Calendar dialog box.

If you ever decide to stop publishing the calendar, highlight its entry in the Calendars list. Choose Share ➤ Stop Publishing. Windows Calendar will display a warning message asking if you're sure that you want to stop publishing the calendar. Click Unpublish to complete the action.

Subscribing to Other Calendars

You might need information about the activities of other people in your organization to avoid overlaps in your own schedule. If these other people publish their calendars, you can subscribe to them and keep track of their activities. The other person's calendar appears in the Calendars list and you can see how their activities coincide with your own. If you don't want to see their activities, simply remove the check mark next to their calendar entry.

The following steps describe how to subscribe to a calendar.

1. Choose Share ➤ Subscribe. You'll see a Subscribe to Calendar dialog box with a single entry for the location of the calendar.
2. Type the location of the calendar that you to which you want to subscribe. Click Next. You'll see a Calendar subscription settings dialog box like the one shown in Figure 17.21.

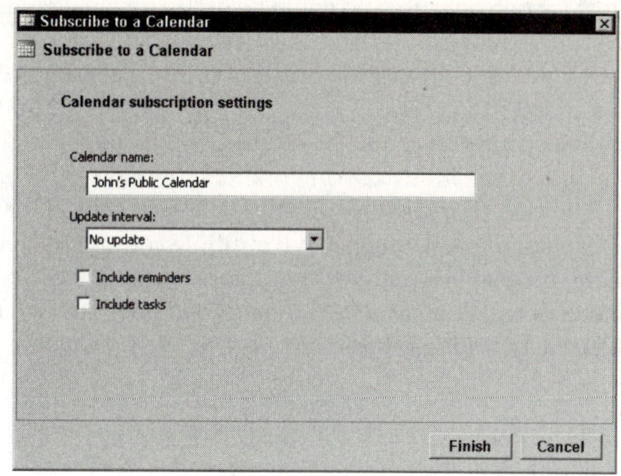

FIGURE 17.21
Determine how you want to subscribe to someone else's calendar.

3. Type a name for the calendar when it conflicts with one of your calendars. Normally, it's a good idea to retain the default name to avoid confusion.
4. Choose an update interval. The interval you choose should match your use of your calendar. If you have to check it every 15 minutes, then make sure the external calendar is updated, too.
5. Choose the optional information you want to see from the external calendar. Click Finish. Windows Calendar adds the new calendar to the Calendars list and assigns it a unique color.

If you ever decide to stop subscribing to a calendar, highlight its entry in the Calendars list and press Delete. Windows Calendar will ask you for confirmation. Click Yes and Windows Calendar will remove the entry.

Importing and Exporting Your Settings and Data

Windows Calendar provides the File ➤ Import command to import data from other calendars and the File ➤ Export command to export data to a file. In both cases, you see a dialog box where you choose a location for either the import or export file, which always has an ICS extension. The calendar file holds all of the information for the calendar, so exporting the calendar also saves the calendar settings. When you import the calendar, Windows Calendar restores the settings.

The import feature also lets you choose how to import the file. You can import the entries to an existing calendar or create a new calendar. Unless you really want those settings to become part of your calendar, it's a good idea to create a new calendar.

Summary

An e-mail program is arguably the most-used program in most businesses today. Though Windows Mail lacks the major features of its more robust sibling, Outlook, it contains everything you need to communicate over the Internet. And, as you've seen in this chapter, it's extremely easy to use. Vista adds an important new capability in the form of Windows Calendar. This application is great for personal use and could be useful for smaller groups as well. The point is that Vista includes the rudimentary features needed to track both appointments and tasks.

If you don't already have an e-mail and calendar program, you'll want to use the information in this chapter to get started now. At least try setting up Windows Mail and Windows Calendar to address your e-mail and scheduling needs. Both programs are surprisingly flexible and you may just find that a little experimentation now saves you considerable money.

The next chapter starts looking at a new subject, networking. Very few computers today are stand-alone. Even homes have multiple computers, making some form of networking necessary. Many people view networks as a terrifying mystery best left to the professionals. Vista actually makes networking nearly automatic and you'll find that this next chapter takes a lot of the mystery out of networking for you.

Part V

Home Networking

In this section, you'll learn how to

- **Understand Different Options for Networks**
- **Configure a Small Network**
- **Set up a Wireless Network**
- **Use Vista Security to Your Advantage**

Chapter 18

Vista Networking and Network Design Primer

You're at home, wondering if you should go through the trouble of connecting your computer with those of your spouse and children. Or maybe at work, your frugal boss says, "Hey, you seem to know a lot about computers. How about you take care of our network along with your other job." (Does that come with a pay raise too?) Before embarking on your journey, whether it's at home or for work, you need to understand the basics of networking.

This chapter is designed to give you the background you need to understand what happens on a network. Networks can do a lot of really cool things, such as allow multiple people to share one printer (so you don't need to spend the money on one for everyone) and exchange files quickly. If you're into computer gaming, then you definitely need to understand the inner workings of networking, just in case something goes wrong when your friends are over and you're racing or blowing each other up.

If you've set up networks in the past, this chapter might just be review to you. But if you've never set one up, the information in this chapter will (hopefully) demystify some of the jargon of computer networking. This chapter covers the following topics:

- Overview of networking
- Networking vocabulary
- Theoretical networking concepts
- Types of networks
- Basic network connectivity
- Building your own network
- Using Network Map to view the network

Vista: What's New?

Each update to Windows has made working with networks a bit easier. Vista continues the trend by simplifying networks even more. In many cases, especially with simple networks, Vista does everything needed to create the network connectivity you need automatically once it detects the network. Given the proper setup, Vista normally detects the network during the initial installation. Consequently, you might complete the Vista setup to find that the network setup is complete as well. Of course, things don't always go perfectly, so an understanding of networks is important.

Vista also makes it easier to see the layout of your network. Network mapping helps you understand how Vista sees your network connections. By understanding the Vista view of things, you can make corrections faster and easier. Network Map also makes it considerably easier to locate devices on your network and even determine when the network (or a part of it) has become unavailable. In short, Vista doesn't keep you in the dark as much as previous versions of Windows did (even though there's always room for improvement).

Perhaps the biggest gain for network users is the support that Vista provides for wireless devices. Not only is Vista considerably more secure because it adheres to the latest networking standards, it also provides the means for overcoming many wireless networking problems. For example, you can now configure a wireless device using a USB flash drive, rather than making direct contact with it. In addition, you have manual configuration options when your wireless device is especially difficult to work with.

One of the less subtle additions to Vista is the concept of network type. When Vista asks you about your network type, it gives you three choices: work, home, and public. The work and home options are both examples of private networks—networks that only trusted people can access. Public networks could possibly be in a Starbucks or a library. These seemingly simple selections change how Vista works. For example, you can't easily shape Windows Media Player files on a public network, but it's quite simple on a private network.

Defining a Network

Simply enough, a network is just two or more computers that communicate with each other. Many businesses commonly connect their networks together in a process known as *internetworking*. The largest internetwork is the Internet.

In most cases, when you connect your computer to the Internet, your computer joins a network that's set up by your Internet Service Provider (ISP). Your ISP is then connected to the Internet. In Chapter 14, you learned about some of the settings you need to connect to the Internet. In this chapter, you'll see what you need to set up a local area network (LAN).

Early Networking: Sneakernet

The oldest form of the computer network is commonly referred to as the *sneakernet*, an official-sounding name for a very unofficial way of sharing information. In this popular networking arrangement, a user copied information to a floppy disk, put on a good pair of sneakers, and carried the file over to another computer or user. Not a very efficient method of networking by today's standards, but it got the job done. For some purposes, it may still be the best way to get information from one place to another.

Health benefits from additional walking aside, sneakernet poses a few serious disadvantages. Losing data is a big risk with this system because if you misplace or accidentally reformat the data disk, you'll lose the information. In an office environment, making sure that everyone who's working on a document or worksheet has the same information is also cumbersome:

- What happens if you have a copy of the original disk and someone makes changes to the original without telling you?
- What happens if more than one person is working on a document and you need to incorporate everyone's changes into one copy?
- How do you keep people from leaving the building with disks full of sensitive information?

Obviously, if you want data integrity, security, and the best use of the creativity of all the people working on a document (and who doesn't?), sneakernet isn't the way to go. What you need instead is some way of tying your network together other than having to rely on people's goodwill and comfortable shoes. What you need is a LAN.

NOTE The last few years have seen a bit of a resurgence of sneakernet. Instead of using floppy disks, which don't hold much information, people will burn CD-ROMs or DVDs and walk them over to their coworkers. In some cases, people also rely on USB flash drives today because you can reuse them in the same way you reused floppy disks in the past. A USB flash drive can also contain a considerable amount of data—2 GB to 4 GB is typical today, but look for the storage space to increase considerably.

LAN: The Better Way

LANs vary greatly in size—you can make a LAN out of two computers sitting across from each other in the same room or out of several thousand computers in the same building. The key parts to the definition of a LAN are that all the computers on the network are *grouped together in some fashion and are connected.*

NOTE A network that extends over a larger area, such as a city block or a country, is known as a *wide area network (WAN).* These networks generally consist of two or more internetworked LANs. A network that's larger than a LAN, but smaller than a WAN, is the metropolitan area network (MAN). A MAN is a special kind of network that extends throughout a town or city. It also connects multiple LANs, but doesn't extend beyond the metropolitan area. The free wireless service offered by some cities today is an example of a MAN.

On most LANs, cables connect the LAN by linking the network cards that reside within each computer or printer on the network. Situations in which cable is *not* the means of connection will be touched on later in this chapter, as well as in Chapter 20.

The preceding definition is the strict, textbook definition. However, in the real world, LANs are generally defined less by their physical characteristics and more by their function. In this sense, a LAN is a system in which linked computers and peripheral devices can share common information, software applications, printers, scanners, and fax services. LANs also enable the use of groupware for scheduling, shared databases, and e-mail. The quick electronic dispersal of computer-generated information to people striving toward a common goal and existing in a single-user-per-computer environment truly defines a local area network.

Most of the functions of a LAN are based on using one or two computers as servers. With a LAN, you can do all the following:

- Share files through a file server
- Share applications from an application server
- Share printers through a print server
- Share schedules, transmit e-mail, and hold electronic meetings through a Groupware server such as Microsoft Exchange or IBM's Lotus Notes
- Share Internet connections
- Utilize a common security platform

Other things that you can do on a LAN include sharing backup media such as tape drives and recordable CD and DVDs, playing multiuser games, and video conferencing with multiple users in a process known as *multicasting*.

File Sharing

One of the primary purposes of a LAN is to provide a common storage area so that several people can access the same files. File sharing can help ensure that anyone who uses that file is always working with the most recent version. Alternatively, if you don't want to share a file with the network but you need someone else to do some work on it, you can transfer the file to someone else—just move it from your folder to theirs or send it as an attachment to an e-mail message.

Note that the act of sharing a file with the network does *not* automatically give everyone on the network access to it. In many network operating systems, you can attach a password to your files so that only people who have the password can access them.

Alternatively, you can grant different levels of access to specific users or a specific group of users. Access can be at levels such as read-only, read and change, and full control. This capability can prevent unauthorized users from seeing your work or making changes to your work. More information on this process is available in Chapter 21.

Sharing, transferring, and securing information between computers on a network is generally known as *file management*. You can share entire drives and folders. If you use an NTFS-formatted drive, you can also share individual files.

NOTE As with individual files, you can restrict access to your shared resources (printers, CD-ROMs, scanners, tape drives, and so on) with passwords. Chapter 21 describes how you can restrict access to specific users.

Concurrent Use of Applications

Many, but not all, software packages will work fine if you install them onto an *application server* and let other users access them from their computers. Here are a few of the advantages to locating software centrally (that is, on an application server):

- It frees disk space on individual computers. The bulk of the application is stored on one or two servers and not at each user's computer.
- Multiple users can use an application simultaneously (almost a necessity in many database applications).
- Upgrading software is easier because the application that needs to be updated is the copy of the software that's installed on the server.

NOTE When upgrading, some Windows applications have a certain number of files that need to be updated at each user's computer even though the major part of Windows is located on the application server. These files usually include configuration information that's specific to each computer system in your office.

WARNING If you store applications on an application server and let users access them from their individual workstations, *you're still required to buy more than one license.* You should have proper software licensing for every user, even if you load only one copy of the software onto the server. Otherwise, you're committing software piracy—stealing from the developers of that software. Software piracy is a federal crime. One exception is software that uses one of the free licenses such as the Free Software Foundation's General Public License (`http://www.fsf.org`).

LAN-dependent applications, such as e-mail, are usually licensed for a specific number of users. When you access the program from the server, a full-blown copy of the program is transported from the hard drive of the server to the memory of your computer. As you interact with the program, you're interacting with the copy that's stored in the memory of your computer. If you activate another program, such as a spell-check feature taken from a word processing program, that feature is transported from the hard drive of the file server to the memory of your computer. You need a license for every program and every computer that will store part of each program in its memory.

NOTE Application servers are also often inaccurately referred to as file servers. Since applications require CPU power, application servers require the fastest possible CPUs. On the other hand, file servers work best with extra RAM. When a shared file is already available in RAM, file access speed is increased.

Print Sharing

Printers are just one of a host of peripherals that you can share. A lot of people get confused about the nature of peripherals these days, but basically a peripheral device is anything that's external to the CPU and memory.

NOTE The words *peripheral device* and *peripheral* are just tech-speak for "a device that attaches to your computer system." Printers, scanners, sound cards, DVD players, PDA cradles, and keyboards are all peripheral devices.

A LAN enables its users to share high-cost peripheral devices such as printers, and manage them so that multiple users do not attempt to use the devices simultaneously.

Print sharing saves you both time and money. Of course, even without a network, you don't have to buy printers for every computer you own. One device will work just fine—if you don't mind standing in line to use it. However, if you must wait for a device to be free, you're spending the money you saved (by not buying the extra printer) on wasted time.

NOTE You don't even need an extra computer to share a printer. Network print servers that are about the size of my hand are available. They have two connections: one to the network, the other to the printer. Once configured, a print server looks just like any other computer to a network.

As with file management, a network administrator can restrict access to the peripheral devices on a network so that only those people authorized to use them can access them. For example, you may not want people to print out rough drafts of your kid's homework or family pictures on the $8,000 color printer you bought for your home business. To set up Vista as a print server, see Chapter 9.

Groupware

Groupware is a type of application that supports group scheduling, e-mail, and possibly other functions such as database management and file sharing. In office environments, this could be one of your office manager's favorite network features. Organizing departmental meetings can be an administrator's nightmare, as they try to sort through everyone's schedules to find a time when everyone can meet. Groupware can make this nightmarish task much more manageable.

Groupware keeps track of all users' schedules, either separately or together as one large calendar. Each person on the network keeps track of their own appointments in the virtual day planner. This information is automatically stored in a central database.

Now, let's say that you want to call a meeting of all the marketing people in your company. All you have to do is list the names of the people who should attend this meeting and then choose a date. The computer can tell you of any scheduling conflicts and let you modify the meeting time accordingly. Some scheduling software packages let you tell the computer to choose the first time that everyone is available, to save you the trouble of having to guess. After you've settled on a time, you can use the scheduling program to send "invitations" and ask people to confirm their attendance.

Groupware also supports input from multiple users to other applications, such as databases. For example, sales input from different stores can be merged on a database using the right kind of groupware. Some groupware packages such as Microsoft Exchange also include e-mail servers.

Internet Connections

Another good reason to set up a network is to share Internet connections. We first looked at Internet Connection Sharing (ICS) in Chapter 14, in which one system acts as a "gateway" for all of the other computers, and only one computer from your network is seen on the Internet.

Alternatively, you can use a hardware firewall router to protect your network as well as connect you to the Internet. As discussed later in this chapter, specialized routers can share one Internet connection and act as a firewall. With the right commands, the router can even block the communication ports used for specialty programs such as instant messaging and networked games. The router becomes the "computer" at risk; since there's no data on the hardware router, your risks are small.

These types of configurations work well in a home network, and not enough people take advantage of them. You have to pay for only one connection, and all computers can access the Internet! Of course, at most businesses, people share Internet connections all the time.

Security Considerations

The Internet can be a dangerous place for a computer. Every computer that connects to the Internet needs some form of security to protect it from attack. This means purchasing filters and virus scanners for every computer and a firewall or proxy server for the whole network. Maintaining these systems can be a difficult and expensive enterprise. With the Windows Firewall, as described in Chapter 14, the computer running ICS is the only one at risk from Internet attacks.

Unfortunately, this does not protect you from risks inside your network. Malicious or poorly trained users can still download e-mail viruses or sabotage your data.

By using a network, you can tightly control security through one common platform as opposed to trying to configure security on each individual system. You'll have fewer concerns about who's logging in and what they can access if and when they do get in.

Networking Vocabulary

Like most other specialized fields, networking has its own jargon. This list is far from exhaustive—in the following chapters, more terms will be introduced—but it gives you a good starting place. Remember these definitions:

Client Any computer with independent processing power (CPU and RAM) that can provide *input* to the network is a client. This definition includes personal computers, handheld scanners, PDAs, and so on.

Server A server is a computer that processes common requests from the network. For example, a print server queues and processes print jobs for a group of computers. The most common server is a file server. A file server is a computer that holds, manages, and secures access to files and data. It provides centralized control for and to your data and acts as a common location for your files for the purpose of centralized backup.

Workstation Any computer physically operated by a user is a workstation. Most workstations are clients. Some workstations, especially in peer-to-peer networks, may also be configured as servers.

Terminal A terminal is a computer-like device from which you can provide input to the network. While a terminal may include graphical processors, it may or may not have a processor or hard drive. Terminals are also known as slave computers.

Node Each client, workstation, terminal, and server has a unique IP address on a TCP/IP network. Specialized hardware items such as routers and print servers also have their own unique IP address on a network. Each of these items is a *node*. Each node associates its IP address with the network interface card.

Packet A packet is the smallest unit of information that can be sent across a network. A packet contains the sending node's address, the receiving node's address, and the data being sent between the two nodes.

Ethernet The trade name for the most common form of networking in use today, Ethernet is more formally known as IEEE standards 802.2 and 802.3. While several other types of networks are available, current network equipment in most computer stores is based on some form of Ethernet. The basic Ethernet standards are listed in Table 18.1. Devices supporting each of these standards are commonly available in major computer stores, with 10-Gb Ethernet being the hardest to find.

TABLE 18.1: Ethernet Standards

COMMON NAME	STANDARD	SPEED
Ethernet	IEEE 802.3	10Mbps
Wireless ("Wi-Fi")	IEEE 802.11a	54Mbps
Wireless ("Wi-Fi")	IEEE 802.11b	11Mbps
Wireless ("Wi-Fi")	IEEE 802.11g	54Mbps
Wireless ("Wi-Fi")	IEEE 802.11n	100Mbps
Fast Ethernet	IEEE 802.3u	100Mbps

TABLE 18.1: Ethernet Standards *(CONTINUED)*

COMMON NAME	STANDARD	SPEED
Gigabit Ethernet	IEEE 802.3z	10,00Mbps
10-Gb Ethernet	IEEE 802.3ae	10,000Mbps

Hub A hub is a box that connects that the computers on a LAN. On an Ethernet network, messages are broadcast to all computers that are connected to that hub. This device can increase traffic on a LAN as a device (or node) broadcasts packets to all devices connected to the hub.

NOTE You'll occasionally hear people refer to networking cable (usually twisted pair, such as Cat 5) as *Ethernet*. This is wrong. Ethernet is a set of rules for network communication and isn't dependent on one specific type of cable (or lack thereof for wireless).

Switch A switch is a box that connects some or all of the computers on a LAN. A switch can determine the destination node for a packet and can send the message directly to the node. Since other computers aren't bothered with that packet, a switch can reduce traffic on a LAN. In addition, a switch often provides significantly better performance than a hub does.

Router A router connects a LAN to other networks such as another LAN or the Internet. If your router has enough connections, it can also connect all of the computers in your LAN. What routers do is called *routing*, which is the transmission of data between networks. Some routers offer special features, such as Dynamic Host Configuration Protocol (DHCP) support.

A Little Theory

In order to understand networks, you need to understand some theory. We'll start with some basics about the OSI model, which can help you understand the functionality of different types of network hardware and software.

The OSI model provides the basis for organizing and classifying network protocols into protocol stacks. Two major protocol stacks are commonly used by Vista for networking: IPX/SPX and TCP/IP. You might also see a third protocol stack, NETBIOS Extended User Interface (NetBEUI), if you work with older Windows-based networks.

OSI Model

The Open Systems Interconnect (OSI) model of networking provides the theoretical basis for all network hardware and software. It provides all of the functionality needed to translate the Word file that you're accessing from the server to the 1s and 0s that are transmitted over computer cables. The seven layers, from top to bottom, are as follows:

- Application (7)
- Presentation (6)
- Session (5)

- Transport (4)
- Network (3)
- Data Link (2)
- Physical (1)

NOTE Some network designers refer to the numeric name for a layer; for example, the application layer is also known as layer 7.

The following sections describe each of these layers in some detail. Perhaps the most important of these protocols form the basis for IP addressing, which is covered in some detail later in this chapter.

NOTE One alternative to the seven-layer OSI model is the five-layer TCP/IP model of networking. The top three layers of the OSI model (5, 6, 7) approximately correspond to the top layer in the TCP/IP model. The bottom four layers in both models are, for our purposes, the same thing. While purists may object, OSI layers are often used to describe the functionality of specific TCP/IP protocols without reference to the TCP/IP model.

APPLICATION (7)

The OSI application layer includes the services and commands that users call to connect to a network. Common application layer protocols that you've seen earlier in this book include HTTP, FTP, and Telnet. One other important application layer protocol is the Domain Name System (DNS), which contains a database of domain names such as `www.mommabears.com` and corresponding IP addresses such as 10.12.213.54.

OSI application layer protocols are different from regular applications. In fact, they translate the programs that you use, such as Microsoft Word, to a format usable by the OSI presentation layer.

One example of application layer hardware is a computer that has direct connections to more than one kind of network. For example, a computer that's connected to a TCP/IP network on one end and an IPX/SPX network on the other end is a true application layer gateway. A more common example of a gateway is a computer configured for ICS/Windows Firewall, as discussed in Chapter 14.

PRESENTATION (6)

The OSI presentation layer is a translator. It formats and encrypts data. For example, some presentation layer protocols can translate the words you type into computer codes such as ASCII.

SESSION (5)

The OSI session layer manages your time and connections on a network. Computers exchange messages at the session layer to keep a connection open. If a user isn't active, session layer messages may stop after a designated timeout period.

TRANSPORT (4)

The OSI transport layer drives the effort used by the network to ensure that your message gets to the destination. Some transport layer protocols keep trying until the receiving computer confirms delivery. Others just use a *best effort*, which means the sending computer spits out the message and hopes that the receiving computer gets it.

Network (3)

The OSI network layer includes the protocols that actually move data, in packets, from computer to computer and from network to network. The most important network layer protocol is IP, which handles computer addressing.

Hardware routers work at the network layer. A router is installed as the interface between two or more networks. There are some hardware routers that are known as *router/gateways*, because they function at both layers 3 and 7.

Data Link (2)

The OSI data link layer translates packets to bits (1s and 0s). The data link layer includes two sublayers:

Logical Link Control (LLC) Supports synchronization and error checking.

Media Access Control (MAC) Allows computers to access a network. MAC addresses are the hardware addresses associated with a network interface card.

Hardware components known as switches work at the data link layer. Normally, a switch divides a LAN into segments. One or more computers are located on each segment. A switch can regulate traffic in a LAN; messages within a segment aren't sent to other segments, thereby reducing traffic on other parts of the LAN.

NOTE Another name for a switch is a bridge. While *switch* is in more common use today, *switch* and *bridge* can be used interchangeably.

NOTE There are a number of hybrid switches on the market. For example, network salespeople may refer to a *Layer 4 switch* or a *Layer 7 switch*. These hybrids have some functionality at multiple layers. Since there's no standard for hybrid equipment, there's no true standard for what they do on a network.

What Do I Really Need to Know about OSI?

The descriptions provided of the OSI layers might appear to be watered down, since they certainly don't outline each layer's complete functionality, but I've done that for a reason. It's handy stuff to know if you're shopping for a device for your home network, and the salesperson tries to display brilliance by referring to some little black box as a "Layer 3 device" or the like. You can also try starting conversations at cocktail parties with this knowledge, but you're on your own there.

While setting up your own network, it's pretty unlikely that OSI knowledge will help you out a great deal, unless you're reading your router's manual. In fact, those of us who troubleshoot networks for a living don't often rely on OSI knowledge either. Problems usually boil down to something like, "The network cable is unplugged," or "The router is dead." Sure, those problems correspond to layers 1 and 3, respectively, but the bottom line is, fix it!

If at some point in your life you want to get a Cisco or Microsoft networking certification, then you'll need to know these layers inside and out. But for now, use them as a reference to understand how the networking puzzle fits together. Pretty much everything relating to network communications revolves around these seven layers.

PHYSICAL (1)

The OSI physical layer defines how messages are to be sent through cables, radio waves, light pulses, and so on, in the 1s and 0s of computer communication. Think of it as the workhorse that does the actual job of getting data from point A to point B.

Protocol Stacks

With seven layers in the OSI model, you can imagine that there are a substantial number of protocols. In fact, there are literally dozens of major groupings of protocols, organized in their own protocol stacks. These two stacks are pretty common and are supported in the Microsoft world:

IPX/SPX Novell developed the Internetwork Packet Exchange/Sequenced Packet Exchange (IPX/SPX) protocol stack for use with the Novell network operating system (NOS). IPX and SPX are just two of the available protocols in this stack. Novell NOSs are still commonly used in larger corporations; however, IPX/SPX use is less common since Novell included TCP/IP as the preferred option in NetWare 5.0, released several years ago. Some network administrators set up IPX/SPX on a LAN for security. Because IPX/SPX is essentially a different language from TCP/IP, it's considerably more difficult for someone using the Internet to break into this type of network.

TCP/IP The language of the Internet is named for two of its component protocols, Transaction Control Protocol (TCP) and Internet Protocol (IP). TCP/IP is routable and scales to any sized network. Most modern networks use TCP/IP exclusively. Since TCP/IP was developed concurrently with Unix, TCP/IP is native to any related operating system (Linux, BSD, Solaris). Specific TCP/IP protocols will be addressed in the next section.

NOTE There's another protocol that you might run across if you're networking with older Microsoft operating systems, such as Windows 98, called NetBEUI. It's relatively fast but not scalable for large networks. Because of its limitations, Vista doesn't support it natively. If you need NetBEUI, the files needed to install it are available on the Vista CD-ROM. For more information, see the Microsoft Knowledge Base article 306059.

TIP Microsoft Knowledge Base articles are readily available online. Navigate to `http://support.Microsoft.com`, and enter keywords or the article number as a search term. Alternatively, if you enter the article number in a comprehensive search engine such as Google (`http://www.google.com`), you'll probably find a direct link to the article.

The TCP/IP Protocol Suite

As inferred in the previous section, TCP/IP and other protocol suites are a collection of interdependent protocols working together to allow computers to communicate with each other. While there are several dozen protocols in the suite, only a handful of TCP/IP protocols are commonly used. Some of the common ones are covered here and are related to what you see in this book. They're listed with their associated OSI layer number.

Hypertext Transfer Protocol (HTTP) (7) Supports transmission of web pages over the Internet. You can see how to set up an HTTP server in Chapter 34.

File Transfer Protocol (FTP) (7) Provides for streamlined uploading and downloading of files. You can learn how to set up an FTP server in Chapter 34.

Simple Mail Transfer Protocol (SMTP) (7) Allows users to send e-mail messages. You can see how to set up an SMTP server in Chapter 34.

Post Office Protocol (POP) (7) Lets users receive e-mail messages. The most common POP in use today is known as POP3.

Transaction Control Protocol (TCP) (4) Sets up a connection between two different computers, with guaranteed data delivery.

User Datagram Protocol (UDP) (4) Sets up a connection between two different computers, with best effort (no guarantee) data delivery. Alternative to, and faster than, its cousin TCP—but less reliable.

Internet Protocol (IP) (3) Allows for unique numeric addresses on a network. Discussed in more detail in the next section.

Internet Protocol Secure (IPsec) (3) Allows for encrypted IP messages. Requires an encryption key. Supports virtual private networking (VPN), which is discussed in more detail in Chapter 31.

Dynamic Host Configuration Protocol (DHCP) (3) Provides automatic allocation of IP addresses and network configuration information to client computers. After a certain period of inactivity, the IP address can be reassigned to a different computer.

Point-to-Point Protocol (PPP) (2) Supports a connection to other networks such as the Internet. Most commonly used for dial-up connections through a telephone modem.

Point-to-Point Protocol over Ethernet (PPPoE) (2) Lets you use broadband connections such as DSL and cable modems to connect your LAN to the Internet.

Point-to-Point Tunneling Protocol (PPTP) (2) Supports virtual private networking (VPN). An option to IPsec.

IP Addressing

In order to communicate on a TCP/IP network, each node needs its own unique IP address. When working with the currently common IP version 4 (IPv4), an IP address consists of four numbers (called octets) between 0 and 255, such as 125.23.252.2. IP addresses can be divided into two portions: a network address and a host address. The network address is shared by all of the nodes on that network. The host address is unique to that node.

There are 32 bits in every IP address. This corresponds to a total of 2^{32} = 4,294,967,296 possible addresses. You might think that four billion IP addresses would be enough for a world of just over six billion people, but that's not the case. Although not all IP addresses are engaged at once, all available IP addresses are taken. See the "IP Version 6" sidebar for some details on the next generation of IP addressing.

There are five different categories of IP addresses available, as described in Table 18.2.

TABLE 18.2: IP Address Classes

CLASS	DESCRIPTION
A	IP addresses between 1.0.0.0 and 126.255.255.255. Suitable for networks with millions of nodes.
B	IP addresses between 128.0.0.0 and 191.255.255.255. Suitable for networks with thousands of nodes.

TABLE 18.2: IP Address Classes *(CONTINUED)*

CLASS	DESCRIPTION
C	IP addresses between 192.0.0.0 and 223.255.255.255. Suitable for networks of up to 254 computers.
D	IP addresses between 224.0.0.0 and 239.255.255.255 are reserved for multicast applications.
E	IP addresses between 240.0.0.0 and 255.255.255.254 are reserved for experimental use.

IP VERSION 6

This chapter focuses on IPv4 because that's the most common addressing scheme in use today on the Internet. Because of inefficiencies in the way IPv4 was designed, and consequently how network addresses are assigned, all available IPv4 network addresses are taken. Many are taken by ISPs that can assign you one of these addresses when you connect to the Internet.

There's another type of IP addressing, known as IP Version 6 (IPv6). Unlike previous versions of Windows, where IPv6 was optional, Vista uses both IPv4 and IPv6 addresses, by default, in preparation for the move to IPv6 on the Internet. Instead of the 32 bits in an IPv4 address, an IPv6 address includes 128 bits. This corresponds to over 3.4×10^{38} addresses, or about 54,000,000,000,000,000,000,000,000,000 addresses for every human on earth. That should last for a few years!

You can view the IPv4 and IPv6 address assigned to your computer using the Local Area Connection Status dialog box. To access this dialog box, right-click Network and choose Properties from the context menu to open the Network and Sharing Center window. You can also open this window by accessing the applet directly in the Control Panel. Click the View status link and you'll see the Connection Status dialog box. Click Details and you'll see both an IPv4 and IPv6 address for your network, as shown here:

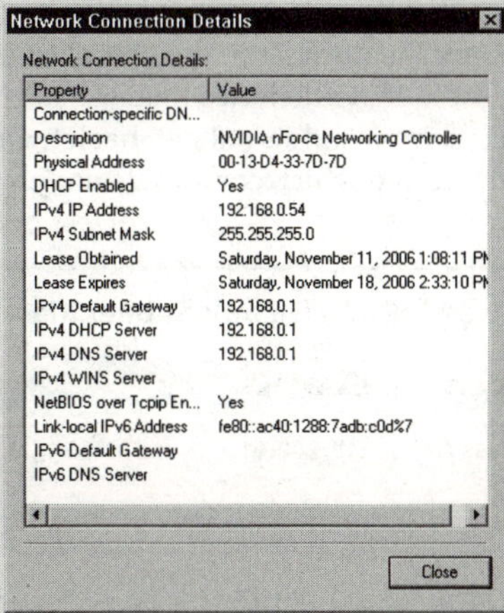

While IPv6 is already in use in some countries, it's taking a long time to take hold, so you must still configure your computer with IPv4 addresses. Every IPv4 address is automatically translated to a unique IPv6 address for these more advanced networks.

Defining a Subnet

A *subnet* is a group of computers whose IP addresses define them as being on the same network. This is determined by your computer's IP address and a parameter called the *subnet mask*. When you set up TCP/IP on any computer, an IP address and a subnet mask are required.

Whether or not a destination computer is on the same subnet as the sending computer is a critical distinction for TCP/IP networking. If they're on the same network, then the message is sent directly to the recipient. If not, then the message is sent to the default gateway, which then has the responsibility of forwarding the message appropriately.

For example, if you're trying to connect to `http://www.sybex.com`, you're actually looking for the web server that contains the files for the Sybex website. This is a specific computer. But your Vista computer doesn't know where the Sybex website is located. It needs an IP address. Chances are that it gets the IP address from your ISP's DNS server.

Once the address is located, the next step is for your computer to determine if the IP address for the Sybex website is on your subnet. If it is, then the message can be sent and communication established. Odds are, though, that you're on a different network than the Sybex website.

All IP addresses that aren't on the subnet are routed to outside networks. If your subnet is properly defined, a request for the Sybex website will be routed outside your LAN (unless you work for Sybex, of course).

IP Addresses and Subnetting

IP addresses have two parts: the network address, which is the same for all computers on your subnet, and the host address, which must be unique. The entire IP address must be unique for each computer on a network. Unfortunately, you can't just look at an IP address and determine which portion is the network and which portion is the host.

For example, take a look at 155.102.16.47. The network portion could be 155.102, or maybe 155.102.16, but you can't tell by looking at it. (If the network address is 155.102, the host address would be 16.47, and if the network address is 155.102.16, the host address would be 47.) The length of the network address is determined by the subnet mask.

There are three classes of IP addresses available to be assigned to hosts on the network, and the classes are determined by the number in the first octet of the IP address. Each class has its own default subnet mask. Table 18.3 illustrates this.

By looking at an IP address and its subnet mask together, you can discern what the network address is and then determine which computers are on the same network.

Table 18.3: IP Addressing and Default Subnet Masks

First Octet	Class	Example	Default Mask	Network Address
1–126	Class A	118.202.61.147	255.0.0.0	118.0.0.0
128–191	Class B	155.188.166.199	255.255.0.0	155.188.0.0
192–223	Class C	201.106.87.1	255.255.255.0	201.106.87.0

Using the IP Address and Subnet Mask

Here's a quick and dirty way to determine the network address. Look at the IP address and look at the subnet mask. For each octet in the subnet mask that has a 255 in it, the corresponding octet in the IP address is the network. If there's a 0 in the subnet mask, the corresponding octet in the IP address is part of the host address.

While this will work in a lot of instances, it's not always that easy. In fact, subnet masks can have other values besides 0 and 255, such as 224 or 240. That makes things a bit more complex. Also notice that in the last section, I said that there's a *default* subnet mask for each class of addresses. Do you have to use the default? Of course not.

NOTE Understand that all of the configurations available with subnet masks can be pretty complex. In this book, I want you to understand it well enough so that you can set up your own network and not have problems.

Let's look at an example. In Table 18.3, we used the address of 118.202.61.147. If you use it with a mask of 255.255.0.0, the network address portion becomes 118.202. If you were to use a mask of 255.255.255.0, then the network address would be 118.202.61. You don't need to use the default, but each computer on a subnet needs to have the same subnet mask.

Okay, so let's cut to the chase. Why should you care? Because if you're setting up a network and the computers won't talk to each other, frustration can set in quickly. And improper configuration is the most common cause of problems.

Here's a list of tips to keep in mind when dealing with IP addressing:

- Each host (computer, printer, router, etc.) needs to have its own unique IP address.
- All hosts on a subnet need to have the same network address, unless you're setting up a more complex, routed network.
- Each host needs to have a subnet mask. The subnet mask determines the network address. Each host on a subnet should have the same subnet mask, or you'll likely have communications problems.

Keeping these tips in mind will help reduce network communications problems. If you set up a network and the computers won't talk, check your connections and check your configurations!

Configuring the Subnet

Now that you know some IP addressing rules, you can define the IP addresses that you can use on a network. For example, take the first example from Table 16.3. That network address is 118.0.0.0. At first glance, you might think that you could assign all addresses between 118.0.0.0 and 118.255.255.255. But there are two more rules governing IP addresses:

- The first address in the subnet is the network address and can't be assigned to any specific computer.
- The last address in the subnet is the broadcast address for that network and also can't be assigned to any specific computer.

In other words, the assignable addresses on the 118.0.0.0 network start at 118.0.0.1, and end at 118.255.255.254. Some other examples are shown in Table 18.4.

TABLE 18.4: Assignable IP Addresses

NETWORK ADDRESS	SUBNET MASK	ASSIGNABLE IP ADDRESSES
12.0.0.0	255.0.0.0	12.0.0.1–12.255.255.254
135.52.0.0	255.255.0.0	135.52.0.1–135.52.255.254
206.35.153.0	255.255.255.0	206.35.153.1–206.35.153.254

Although you can assign any address within the range, it's good practice to start with 1 and work your way up. For example, the first computer could be 12.0.0.1, the second 12.0.0.2, and so forth. This makes it cleaner and easier to remember the numbers you used!

SPECIAL IP ADDRESSES

You might have noticed that I left out a whole range of IP addresses. Some are reserved for special purposes; others are reserved for private IP networks. These addresses include:

0.0.0.0 Used by any computer on a TCP/IP network to refer to the local network.

127.0.0.0 Reserved for loopback purposes. Includes all addresses on this network, from 127.0.0.0 through 127.255.255.255. The loopback address, 127.0.0.1, is used for troubleshooting. We use it in Chapter 19.

224.0.0.0–239.255.255.255 Addresses in this range are Class D and are used for multicasting (sending messages to groups of computers). Some programs use these to communicate, and these addresses aren't available for host use.

240.0.0.0 and up Addresses in this range are Class E and are reserved for future use.

255.255.255.255 Used as a broadcast address to all computers on the local network.

PRIVATE IP ADDRESS RANGES

If you never connect your network to the Internet, you now have all the information that you need to assign an IP address to a specific computer. However, most people with networks do want to connect to the Internet. For your Internet connection, you need a unique IP address. But you don't need an Internet-unique IP address for every computer on your network. For the computers wholly inside your LAN, there are private IP addresses.

For example, when you set up ICS/Windows Firewall in Chapter 14, you assigned a unique public IP address to the NIC or telephone modem connection to the Internet. Now you can assign a private IP address on that computer's connection to your LAN.

A series of private IP addresses are available for this purpose. These four blocks of private IP addresses can't be used "live" on the Internet, because they're officially reserved for private networks.

NOTE I say they can't be used "live" on the Internet, but computers with these addresses often access the Internet. How? These addresses work only on a private network, and in order to get on the Internet, computers with one of these addresses must go through a translator, such as a system running ICS or a router. The ICS system or router will actually make the connection to the Internet-based computer and return the requested information to the client. This process is sometimes called Network Address Translation (NAT).

The official private IP address ranges are shown in Table 18.5.

The 169.254.0.0 network address was originally assigned to Microsoft and has recently been adapted by the Internet Assigned Numbers Authority (IANA) as a private network address. If you have a network of computers where Windows 98 and later operating systems are installed, the Microsoft *Automatic Private IP Addressing* (APIPA) system automatically assigns an IP address from this range to the NIC.

TABLE 18.5: Private IP Address Ranges

CLASS	PRIVATE NETWORK ADDRESS	ADDRESS RANGE
A	10.0.0.0	10.0.0.1–10.255.255.254
B	169.254.0.0	169.254.0.1–169.254.255.254
B	172.16.0.0	172.16.0.1–172.31.255.254
C	192.168.0.0–192.168.255.0	192.168.x.1–192.168.x.254

There are 254 available Class C private network addresses (1–254 in the third octet). With the default Class C subnet mask of 255.255.255.0, you have to pick one of these network addresses. To get the corresponding address range, substitute the number you choose for x.

SETTING UP A PRIVATE NETWORK

When you want to set up a LAN that's connected to the Internet, pick a private network address. Select from the list in Table 18.5. There are three basic ways to assign an IP address to different computers:

Static IP Addressing Allows you to select an IP address and assign it directly to your NIC. For a NIC connected to your internal network, select an IP address from the range on your chosen private IP network. You can often get a static IP address from your ISP for your Internet connection, but you may have to pay more. Static IP addresses are convenient for anyone who wants to connect to your computer from a remote location on the Internet, but they can also be an open invitation to hackers.

DHCP Addressing Lets a DHCP server assign the address. Hardware routers that connect a network to the Internet often include DHCP servers. You can often set up a hardware router with a range of IP addresses from your selected subnet. You can then set up each computer on your LAN to take an IP address from that router.

Automatic Private IP Addressing (APIPA) Assigns an IP address when no DHCP server is available. This is a Microsoft protocol, which uses the 169.254.0.0 network address.

To set up one of these addressing schemes for your NIC, go into its properties. Click Start ➤ Control Panel. In Control Panel, click the Network and Sharing Center applet. Click the Manage network connections link. You should see the Network Connections window with a list of your NICs, similar to what's shown in Figure 18.1.

To see the specifics for a particular network interface card (NIC), also known as a network adapter, right-click the device and choose Status from the context menu. Click Details and you'll see specifics about the connection (see the sidebar entitled "IP Version 6" for details). If you want to make a change, right-click the NIC. In the context menu that appears, click Properties to get the properties window for that NIC, similar to Figure 18.2.

Notice that you can choose to enable or disable any of the protocols in the list. For example, if you really don't want to enable IPv6 in Vista, you can disable it by clearing the associated check box. Some people have reported network problems with IPv6 because other machines on the network aren't prepared for it, so you may have to disable this feature (try to keep it enabled since IPv6 will eventually become standard).

To communicate on the Internet today, you must have IPv4 enabled. Even if you decide to use IPv6 internally within your organization, IPv4 support will be essential for quite some time. The properties window for the NIC should include "Internet Protocol Version 4 (TCP/IPv4)." Highlight it and click Properties to get the Internet Protocol Version 4 (TCP/IPv4) Properties window shown in Figure 18.3.

In this figure, the Obtain an IP Address Automatically option is selected. If you have a DHCP server on your network, this NIC gets its IP address from that server. Otherwise, the NIC gets its IP address through APIPA.

If you want to assign a static IP address, click Use the Following IP Address. Enter the IP address and subnet mask that you selected. For the Default gateway, enter the IP address of the router on your network (if you have one).

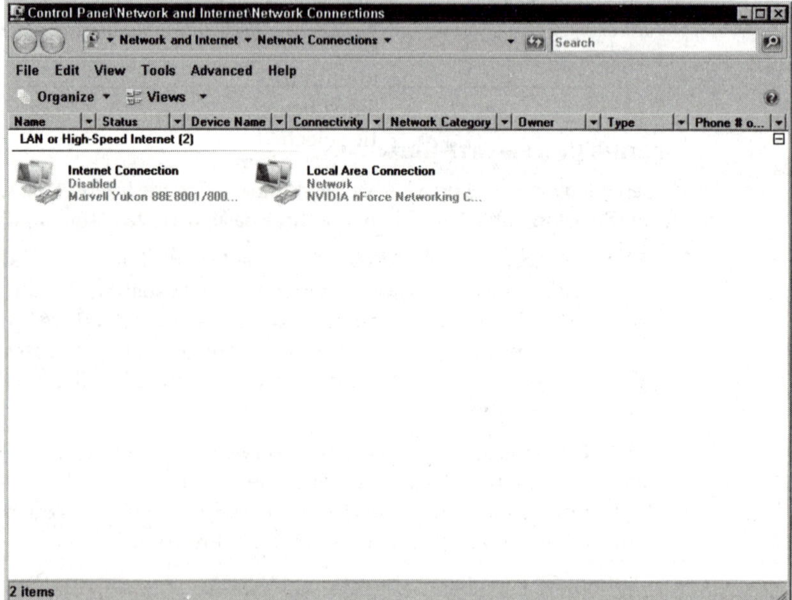

FIGURE 18.1
Vista Network Connections.

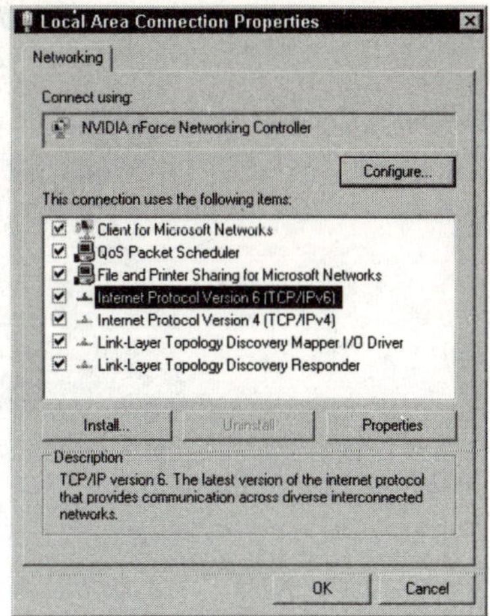

FIGURE 18.2
Properties for a network connection.

Having an assigned static IP address often means that you also have to set the DNS server address. DNS servers translate names like `http://www.sybex.com` to their corresponding IP address such as 63.99.198.12. Internet DNS servers have unique IP addresses, which should be available from your ISP.

NOTE If you have a NIC that supports Universal Plug and Play (UPnP), you may not have to bother with any of this. The UPnP standard supports automatic configuration of the NIC, including IP addressing, on the attached LAN.

Just in case you do need to work with IPv6, you'll find that the dialog box for configuring it works very much the same as IPv4. Select the Internet Protocol Version 6 (TCP/IPv6) entry and click Properties just as you did with the IPv4 entry. You'll see a dialog box like the one shown in Figure 18.4. Notice that this dialog box looks very much the same as the IPv4 dialog box. This dialog box also uses the automatic selections.

FIGURE 18.3
TCP/IP Properties for a network connection.

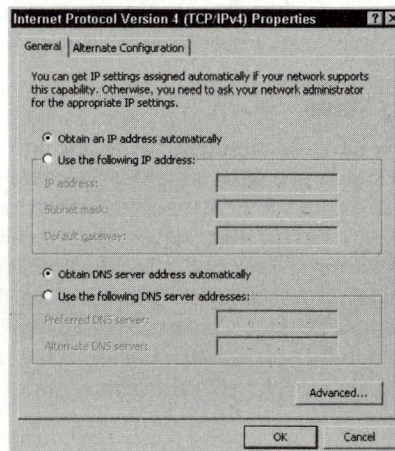

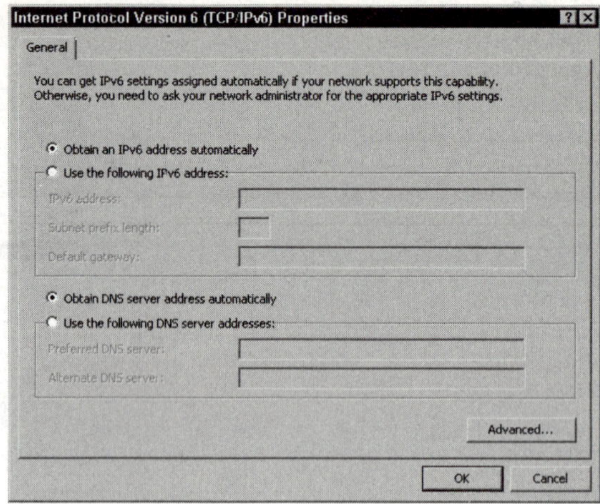

FIGURE 18.4
Working with an IPv6 address is similar to working with an IPv4 address.

You configure a static address using the same technique that you would when working with an IPv4 address. However, instead of a subnet mask, you enter a number that defines the amount of the IP address that defines the subnet prefix. The goal is the same—to define a unique network number. However, this approach is considerably more flexible than the IPv4 approach.

Network Relationships

Now that you know a bit about network addressing, it's time to start thinking about your computers and their relationships to each other. There are three basic ways to set up relationships between computers on a LAN:

- Master/slave
- Client-server
- Peer-to-peer

Most networks depend on servers in some capacity, but not all networks require a server. In fact, in a truly pure sense, a peer-to-peer network has no servers at all.

Master/Slave

In the early days of computing, processing power and memory were relatively expensive. Many users had to share the same computer. The computers were the servers or the masters of the network. Users were stuck with the slaves, also known as terminals. Servers were configured with separate storage areas for every user. In those days, terminals rarely had their own processor or memory.

Today, we may be coming full circle. With the development of the *network computer*, also known as the diskless workstation, it's possible to use Vista on a terminal in a master/slave network.

The Remote Desktop Connection discussed in Chapter 16 is one implementation of this kind of network. In that case, the *home computer* acts as a terminal, and the *remote computer* acts as the master. All signals, including keystrokes and mouse clicks, are transmitted from the slave to the master computer.

Even though this type of configuration is plausible, it's unlikely you'll see many networks like this. Most of the time, you'll see client-server networks in businesses and peer-to-peer networks in home environments.

Client-Server

Client-server networks are similar in some ways to master/slave networks. In each, a central computer is in charge of the network and handles all requests. The main difference is that the client computers are able to compute on their own (assuming that they're PCs), unlike regular terminals. These networks are most commonly used in larger companies.

However, client-server networks are like their peer-to-peer (which is covered next) counterparts in a number of ways. Most important, each client can operate independently as a separate computer and can, by itself, function when the network stops.

Client-server networks are most commonly organized into logical structures called domains, which use centralized databases to store information about users and profiles, as well as security settings (rights and permissions) to specific files and folders.

NOTE Chapter 22 covers the details of connecting Vista through a network to a domain.

Peer-to-Peer

Peer-to-peer networks represent an entirely different concept in networking. Rather than allocating every user on the network a central storage ground, peer-to-peer networking connects a group of totally independent computers. Each computer generally keeps its applications on its own hard disk so that if something happens to the network, the network simply breaks down into a group of individual yet functional computers. If one workstation goes down, life can go on for the rest of the network if all users keep their needed files at their own workstation. In other words, a peer-to-peer network enables every workstation to lead a double life: to be a client *and* a server.

NOTE Chapter 19 goes into the details of using Vista to connect a peer-to-peer network.

Peer-to-peer networks give their users many of the same capabilities that client-server networks do. Each user decides which files, applications, and peripheral devices they'll share with the rest of the network and then shares them. You can attach passwords to your resources so that unauthorized people can't access them. Alternatively, you can share things selectively, saying, perhaps, "Accounting gets to use the C drive, and Personnel gets to use the printer." In that case, Accounting and Personnel would need their own accounts on your Vista computer.

On the subject of sharing resources, remember that because important information on a peer-to-peer LAN is distributed throughout the network, you'll have to leave networked computers on and connected to the network as long as anyone is working who needs the information on those computers.

How does a peer-to-peer network work? On a stand-alone computer, when you ask your operating system to access the drive, it can do so directly. The application talks directly to the operating system, which sends the information to the computer's disk. The operating system needs no go-between to help it access information and peripherals on its own computer.

If you're working on a network, however, the situation is a little different. The operating system needs help accessing information on other computers on the network. Its helper is called the *redirector* (or the *shell*, if you're a Novell user).

Servers

The keys to most large networks are servers. You might even want to set up a server at home, depending on your needs. Servers can be dedicated to certain purposes such as file storage and sharing in a client-server network. And workstations can be set up as nondedicated servers in a peer-to-peer network.

What truly defines a server is the role it plays on a network. Most often, servers have their own specific operating system. For example, Windows Server 2003 and Novell NetWare are operating systems specifically designed to be servers. Most Unix-based operating systems can function equally well as a client or a server. Vista is generally regarded as a client-side operating system, but that's not to say it can't function as a server on a network. It's just not as good at being a server when compared to NetWare or Windows Server 2003.

Generally speaking, servers also have higher hardware requirements in some areas than client computers. For example, a server generally requires a faster processor or even multiple processors, extra memory, and a large hard drive (or multiple smaller drives in a Redundant Array of Inexpensive Disks, RAID, configuration). This makes sense, because servers are used by almost everyone on the network, while clients are typically used by one person at a time. However, servers don't require a fancy display adapter or a sound card because someone who needs such functionality doesn't use them.

A *dedicated server* is a separate computer whose only goal in life is to be a file or application server. By dedicating a computer as a server, you can configure its memory more efficiently. A *nondedicated server*, on the other hand, is a workstation that moonlights as a server—its memory is divided between its role as a workstation and as a server.

NOTE **You won't find some types of servers discussed in this chapter. For example, a database server holds the data for an organization using a product such as SQL Server. A communication server provides access to communication devices such as a fax. Most large organizations have a number of specialty servers that perform specific tasks. This chapter also doesn't explore advanced server topics such as server farms, which appear as a single machine to the user, but actually comprise a number of machines.**

Why would you want a dedicated server? A dedicated server is faster, safer, and more efficient than one also being used as a workstation.

- It's faster because all of the server's memory and processing power are used to serve clients.
- It's safer because no one's using the computer as a workstation and possibly crashing it (everyone crashes *sometimes*). It's also safer because you can control security from one centralized location.
- It's more efficient because it does not have to divide its time between being a server (processing remote requests) and being a workstation (processing local requests).

In short, dedicating a computer as a server can greatly improve your network's performance. Of course, the downside is cost, because you must buy a computer just to hold and maintain the integrity and security of your information. Because your server will have a lot of demands on it, you're going to want something fast with as much RAM as possible and a big hard disk, and that type of computer isn't cheap.

The expense of a dedicated server gives nondedicated servers their place in life. A lower price tag is just about the only advantage you get from using your workstation as a server. Nondedicated servers tend to be slower because any time the server/workstation is in use, the other workstations have to wait to access the server. This wait time can slow down your entire network. If you have only a few computers on your network, though, this is definitely the way to go. You won't notice any major performance degradation unless you approach double-digit clients.

Also, nondedicated servers are much more likely to crash, increasing the risk of data loss all over your network. If you *must* use a server as a workstation, it's best to limit it to a less-risky capacity such as a print or fax server. If one of those servers crashes, it's a pain in the neck but probably won't stop other people from accessing Microsoft Word or getting to their e-mail.

What Type of Network Is Best?

There's no "best" type of network. What's best for you depends on your needs and resources. If you're creating a network from scratch, some of the factors you should consider include:

Number of computers If you have more than one computer, you don't want to have to purchase expensive peripherals for each system. All three types of networks permit you to connect a printer, for example, to one computer and share it on the network. Peer-to-peer networks of more than 10 or 15 computers are difficult to manage.

Number of users If you have more than one user, you may have more than one person making changes to the files on your network. If you can afford it, a dedicated file server can ease the effort in maintaining a single copy of a file. Users who need access to client computers in different locations require a centralized database of users and passwords. Neither a dedicated file server nor a central database of users is possible in a peer-to-peer network.

Shared applications If you have a substantial number of computers on your network, it can make sense to set up a dedicated application server. This isn't an option in a standard peer-to-peer network.

Independent needs If your users need the ability to work independently, even when the network is down, each user needs a separate computer. This isn't possible in a master/slave network.

Centralized control Domains in a client-server network provide a level of centralized control almost equal to that available with a master/slave network.

Cost Dedicated file and application servers can be expensive, especially when applied to small numbers of users. An independent computer for every user creates a different kind of expense.

For home networks, the best choice is usually peer-to-peer. In businesses, client-server is generally the network of choice. However, the facts associated with your particular network may lead you to a different conclusion.

The Look and Feel of a Network

The most common way to set up a LAN is with computers connected to a hub. The predominant choice for network technology is Ethernet. The nodes in most Ethernets are connected with twisted-pair cables. This type of cable contains eight wires and connects as easily as a telephone. This chapter covers the details later. Figure 18.5 gives you a feel for how a network is set up.

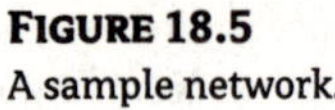

FIGURE 18.5
A sample network.

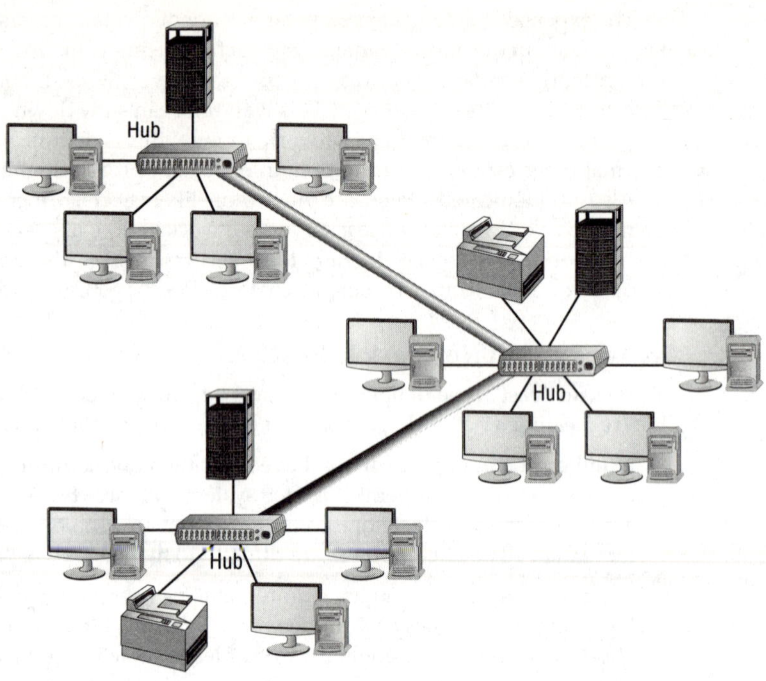

This is one LAN, organized into three different sets of computers. It could represent the setup of a LAN in a three-floor office. Assume that you install a hub in a wiring closet on each floor. You could then install cables between the hub and the computers on that floor. The cables between the hubs would run between floors.

NOTE Of course, if you're setting up a home network, your diagram will look much simpler than this. You'll probably have just one hub, with all devices and your Internet connection attached to it.

The cable that's used to connect one hub to another hub (or a switch or a router) is generally referred to as a backbone. You always want to make sure that the cable that you use for the backbone is rated for speeds that meet or exceed the speed of the cable that you're using throughout the network (from the hub to the nodes).

Building Your Own Network

Now that you've selected the software configuration for a network and have a general idea of the physical layout, you're ready for the hardware. To build a network, you need a network interface card (NIC) for each computer. In most cases, you'll also need cables to connect to each NIC, and hardware such as hubs (or switches) and routers to connect the NICs together.

All of the previously discussed network relationships—master/slave, client-server, peer-to-peer—work well with the various types of Ethernet networks. But before you can select a NIC, a cable, a hub, or a router, you need to know what type of Ethernet network you're going to build.

TIP Always plan out your network before purchasing anything!

Selecting Ethernet Hardware

Several types of Ethernet network equipment are available at most larger computer stores. Before you go out and purchase equipment, you have to make some choices. At minimum, you need to select the speed of your network. If you want a wireless Ethernet, you need to accept the associated higher costs and limited speeds. Whatever choice you make, you can then make sure that your components are consistent with that type (e.g., speed, wired, or wireless) of network.

Ethernet networks can be built to capacities of 10Mbps, 100Mbps, or 1,000Mbps. As illustrated in Table 18.1, these standards are sometimes known as regular Ethernet, Fast Ethernet, and Gigabit Ethernet. Full-duplex versions of each of these standards are available, with twice the speed. Wireless Ethernet offers speeds of 11Mbps and 54Mbps.

The hardware that you select in the following sections—NICs, cables, hubs, switches, routers, and so on—all need to support the characteristics that you select.

Network Cards

The NIC, or the adapter card, is a card that you use to connect your computer to servers or other computers. The NIC you select should be consistent with the rest of your network. NICs are available that vary in the following characteristics:

Installation: Internal or External or PC Card

Internal NIC: PCI or ISA

External NIC: USB or IEEE 1394

Speed: 10Mbps, 100Mbps, 1,000Mbps, 10,000Mbps wired, and 11Mbps or 54Mbps wireless

Duplex: Full-duplex or half-duplex

Connection: Cabled or wireless

NOTE Many better-quality motherboards include one or two NICs as part of the package today. Make sure you check the motherboard statistics before you buy a NIC. In many cases, you can save yourself a little money and time by checking for the NIC in advance. These motherboard NICs won't require any installation on your part, generally work well with Vista, and won't take up a precious slot inside the computer.

SPEED

Transmission speed is measured in millions of bits per second, or Mbps. A bit is short for a binary digit, the 1s and 0s associated with computers. NICs transmit bits of data through a network as a negative or positive electrical pulse.

NIC Installation Options

A NIC can be internal or external to your computer. Internal NICs can fit into PCI or ISA expansion slots. Before you buy an internal NIC, make sure you have the right kind of slot free inside your computer. Some instructions for installing an internal NIC are available in Chapter 19.

Many internal NICs are older *legacy* components. For various reasons, legacy NICs don't always work with Windows Plug and Play. In those cases, you should note the I/O address, DMA channel, and IRQ ports used by your NIC. Some techniques for handling legacy NICs are available in Chapter 10.

NICs today are fairly inexpensive, unless you're setting up a Gigabit network (and it's unlikely that you *really* need that kind of speed at home, even if you're a gamer). If you have a NIC that can't be configured through the Vista Plug and Play system, it's often more cost effective to purchase a Plug and Play NIC. If you have a lot of peripherals, you may not be able to use the techniques described in Chapter 10 to find a free IRQ and would otherwise have to uninstall a different component.

Vista may not recognize all Plug and Play NICs. Other techniques to address this problem are described in Chapter 19.

WARNING When installing any hardware inside your computer, be careful. Computers are sensitive to static electricity. Before touching any electronic components, touch a larger piece of metal, such as a computer case. While firm pressure can be required to install or remove a hardware card such as a NIC, never force a card into a slot. If it's the wrong slot, the crossed wires will likely destroy many of the circuits in your computer.

External NICs may connect to USB or IEEE 1394–enabled ports. Make sure your computer has the port that works with the network card you want. Be especially careful if you want to get a USB NIC. There are two standards: USB 1.0 and USB 2.0. Be sure to match the NIC to the USB standard port available on your computer.

NOTE If you see a FireWire or iLink NIC in your computer store, you should be able to use either of them with an IEEE 1394 connection on your computer. FireWire and iLink are trade names for components that meet IEEE 1394 standards.

Credit card–sized NICs are also available, primarily for laptop computers, which conform to the PC Card standards discussed in Chapter 7. They often come with separate adapters to connect to a cable or exchange signals with a wireless network.

NIC Speed

Ethernet, Fast Ethernet, and Gigabit Ethernet NICs are readily available. Many NICs work at both Ethernet and Fast Ethernet speeds, which allows you to upgrade your network without changing your NIC. Some NICs are full-duplex, which essentially doubles the maximum data transfer speed. If you get a full-duplex NIC, make sure all of the other equipment that you get is also built for full-duplex data transmission.

NIC Connections

NICs are available for regular twisted-pair connections that look like oversized telephone cables. With the latest advances in wiring, even Gigabit NICs can use the same cables. Wireless NICs are also available. Whatever your choice, make sure that your cables and other hardware are compatible.

NOTE The terms *NIC*, *network card*, and *network adapter* all refer to the same thing—the network interface card.

Cables

Cables are the backbone of most computer networks, even though wireless networks have made huge inroads in recent years. All information runs through the cables, either in the form of electrical or light pulses through twisted-pair cable or fiber-optic cable. For your network to work well, information must pass through the cabling (or air) without electromagnetic or other interference. Interference generally won't corrupt the data, but it can slow down the network considerably. When you purchase a cable, you need to consider the following:

- Length
- Distance limits
- Interference
- Cable standards
- Connectors

CABLE LENGTHS

When you calculate the distance between your computer and a hub, remember that you want to keep your cables out of the way. That probably means you'll be routing cables to walls, along baseboards, above ceilings, and more. For example, I use a 100-foot, Category 5 cable to connect two computers in adjacent rooms. This extra length allows me to route the cable along the far ends of walls and avoid doorways.

DISTANCE LIMITS

The rated speed on an Ethernet cable is limited to 100 meters, which corresponds to about 328 feet. If the distance between a computer and a hub is greater than 100 meters, don't use a longer cable. You may not like the result. Instead, get a repeater to maintain the strength of the signal over the extra distance.

INTERFERENCE

To avoid interference, keep your network cables away from anything that may create an electromagnetic field, including fluorescent lights, motors, and other cables or power lines.

Two alternate ways to avoid interference are by shielding your cable, such as with a metal conduit, or by running network cables at right angles to other cables or power lines. Another option is a fiber-optic based network, because light pulses are essentially impervious to electromagnetic interference.

Some judgment is required. For example, if you're using today's standard Ethernet cable for a 10Mbps Ethernet network, a little interference doesn't matter. The Category 5e (the *e* is for enhanced) and Category 6 cables available in most computer stores can handle Gigabit data transfer speeds. However, as your network speed requirements increase, you need to pay more attention to cabling and potential sources of interference.

STANDARDS

The standard for wiring regular Ethernet is known as Cat 6 UTP. This is short for Category 6 standard unshielded twisted-pair cable, a standard of the Electronic Industries Association. While there are shielded cables, and lesser quality cables that support slower speeds, it's difficult to find these in most consumer computer stores today.

Cat 6 supports speeds up to Gigabit Ethernet levels without a problem and is backward compatible with older versions such as Cat 3, Cat 5, and Cat 5e. Cat 5e and Cat 6 cables should be readily available in any self-respecting computer store.

NOTE There are regulations on the network cable that you can use in the workplace. If you install network cables in areas susceptible to fire such as ceilings, many governments require the use of *plenum* cables. These cables include special coatings that do not emit toxic fumes in a fire. Whatever you might think of government regulations, plenum cables are generally a good idea in any network installation.

TIP Most networks can get by with Cat 5 cable, which supports transfer speeds of up to 100Mbps. Sometimes you'll be able to find Cat 5 a lot cheaper than 5e or 6. Whatever you do, though, don't buy anything older than Cat 5!

CONNECTORS

Most Category 6 UTP cable terminates using connectors that look like chunkier versions of the connectors used to plug your telephone into the wall, as shown in Figure 18.6. These are called RJ-45, whereas your telephone uses RJ-11 connectors. One end plugs into your computer's NIC, and the other plugs into a hub. Category 7 cables use different types of connectors than the older categories, but they plug into hubs and NICs in the same way.

Many cables are sold with the connectors already attached. For larger networks, it may make more sense to purchase long lengths of cable, cut the cables to fit the physical layout of your office, and then attach a connector. Crimping tools are available for this purpose.

FIGURE 18.6
RJ-45 connector.

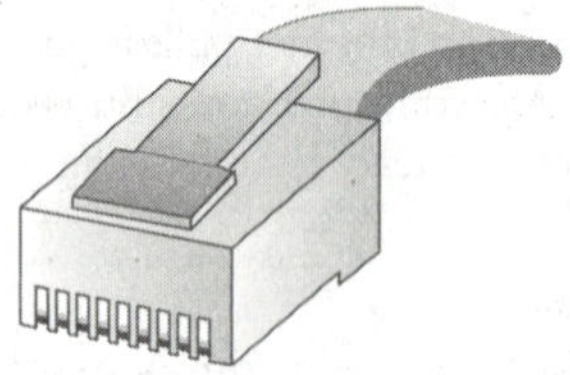

Wireless Considerations

If you're going to create a wireless network, you don't need many cables. Wireless networks work through the air with radio signals, infrared, or even microwaves.

The most common wireless networks are based on the IEEE 802.11b and 802.11g standards, colloquially known as *Wi-Fi*. The 802.11b standard provides for an Ethernet-style network at up to 11Mbps, while 802.11g operates at up to 54Mbps. A number of other wireless networks are available, but most of them don't have the speed or the cost-effectiveness of a Wi-Fi network.

If you set up a wireless network, you need a wireless hub, switch, or router to send and receive the signals. These are radio-style signals. In the frequencies used by IEEE 802.11b/g, (2.4GHz), you may get interference from microwave ovens, wireless phones, and other wireless devices such as PDAs and BlackBerry handhelds. A wireless network on a different subnet can also cause interference. If you're operating a wireless network, keep these sources away from the *wireless access points*, where wireless devices send and receive signals. We will spend more time discussing wireless networks in Chapter 20.

Buying Network Equipment

Purchasing the equipment for your first network does not need to be confusing or difficult. In fact, your choices for Ethernet networks are simple. They're based on speed and cabling, as required. The details are covered in previous sections. Here's a summary of your options:

Speed: 10Mbps, 100Mbps, 1,000Mbps, 10,000Mbps.

Duplex: Full-duplex.

Cabling: Cat 5 UTP can handle speeds up to 100Mbps. Cat 5e and Cat 6 UTP can handle 1,000Mbps networks. If you're going to create custom lengths of cable, you also need a crimping tool to attach the RJ-45–style connectors. If you're using a wireless network, you don't need a cable.

Wireless Standard: Wi-Fi (IEEE 802.11a/b/g/n) or some other standard.

NIC: Internal, External, or PC Card.

Internal NIC: PCI or ISA

External NIC: USB 1.0, USB 2.0, or IEEE 1394 (iLink/FireWire)

Hub: Requires enough ports for each node on your LAN, an uplink port, and any additional computers that you may add in the future.

Switch: Can substitute for a hub. If you have a lot of traffic between several computers on your network, a switch can reduce traffic.

Router: Substitutes for a computer with a NIC on your LAN and a NIC or telephone modem that connects to another network such as the Internet.

Hubs/Switches

Computers on a standard LAN connect to a hub. A hub includes multiple ports to which you can connect RJ-45 or other types of cables. If you have more than two computers on your network, you need a hub. Different hubs are available for different speeds. As described earlier, smart hubs may also include diagnostic functionality. When you purchase a hub, check for the following:

Ports: You need a port for each computer that you want to connect. If your network might grow in the future, you may want additional ports. If you're using a wireless hub, each antenna serves as a port.

Uplink: If you want to connect your network to any other network such as the Internet, you should get a hub with an uplink port. Some hubs use a toggle to change a regular port to an uplink port. You can connect two hubs together by connecting the uplink port on one hub to the regular port on the second hub using a regular patch cable. Alternatively, you can connect two hubs together via regular ports using a crossover cable. A crossover cable is wired slightly differently than a regular Ethernet cable and is used to connect some types of network devices in a daisy-chain fashion.

Speed: Ethernet hubs are available at all currently available speeds. But you need to make sure that the speed rating of your hub and NIC match. Some hubs can *autosense*, or automatically detect, the speed capabilities of a NIC, within limits.

Power: Remember, hubs are external and normally require a separate power supply.

NOTE If you have a network of two computers, you can connect them with a crossover cable, which is a standard UTP cable with the send and receive wires flipped on one end. This simulates what happens to a signal when going through the hub and saves you the additional cost of purchasing a hub.

Switches are basically intelligent hubs. They work like hubs in that they connect multiple devices. However, switches are better at managing traffic and handling heavy data loads.

Routers

Routers can serve the same function as a hub. With the right uplink port, a router can also serve as a junction between networks, such as a small business network and the Internet. In fact, specialized routers are available. Some have embedded telephone modems. Others connect to external ISDN, DSL, satellite, or cable modems.

NOTE The only real "modem" is a telephone modem, because it can translate the 1s and 0s of computer talk to the sound waves transmitted through telephone wires. Broadband modems such as DSL, satellite, and cable modems are more closely related to Ethernet adapters. In fact, you can connect a NIC or the uplink port of a hub or router directly to most broadband modems. Consult your broadband modem manufacturer or ISP for more information.

The ICS/Windows Firewall setup discussed in Chapter 14 assumes that you have a computer that's connected to your LAN and to the Internet. This requires two separate NICs, or a NIC and a telephone modem. Each connection requires its own IP address. Since this computer has a direct connection to the Internet, the Windows Firewall may not always protect it from intruders. You can install a router in place of this computer. Since you don't store any data on the router (other than what's required to configure that router), this configuration is safer.

TIP The IP address on an ICS/Windows Firewall computer that's directly connected to the LAN is important. To other computers on the LAN, that's the default gateway address.

Installation

If you use a cabled network, the biggest cost may be installation. Because bundles of network cables on the floor are often unsafe and unattractive, many people want the cables run through the walls, just like telephone wire. You can see why wireless has taken off!

If you're in the process of building, you may be able to set up the installation of network cables in the same conduits used for your telephone cables. You can then set up your network (RJ-45) and telephone (RJ-11) adapters in the same wall for every room that needs connections.

However, if you already have an existing structure, the time and expense associated with paying a contractor to set up your network can be daunting.

Speed becomes a major consideration now and in the future. If your old cable can't keep up with the transfer rate of your new network, you'll need to replace it when you upgrade parts of the network, and that upgrade could be expensive. Clearly, the need for upgrades is yet another reason to plan your network ahead of time.

Working with Network Map

Network Map is a new feature in Vista that provides you with a picture of what your network looks like to Vista. The Vista picture may not represent the physical setup of your network very well, but it does show you how Vista sees the network, which is quite important when you want to perform troubleshooting. When the Vista view of your network doesn't match the physical reality, consider the following causes:

- The device is malfunctioning.
- A conflict exists between the device's configuration and the Vista configuration.
- The use of IPv6 on Vista is causing a problem.
- The firewall settings on Vista won't let it see the device.
- Your network is configured as public, rather than private.
- The Computer Browser service isn't running.
- The Network Location Awareness service isn't running.
- One or more of the peer network services aren't running.
- The SSDP Discovery service isn't running (SSDP stands for the Simple Service Discover Protocol).
- The NIC isn't running the Link Layer Topology Discovery Protocol (LLDP).
- A device is so old that it doesn't support the required protocols.

The map that Vista provides is relatively straightforward. It shows connections from point A to point B. To display the map, open the Network and Sharing Center applet in the Control Panel and click the View full map link. You'll see a network map that's specific to your network. Figure 18.7 shows a typical example for a simple network.

FIGURE 18.7
Vista provides a map of the network as it sees the network, not as you expect to see it.

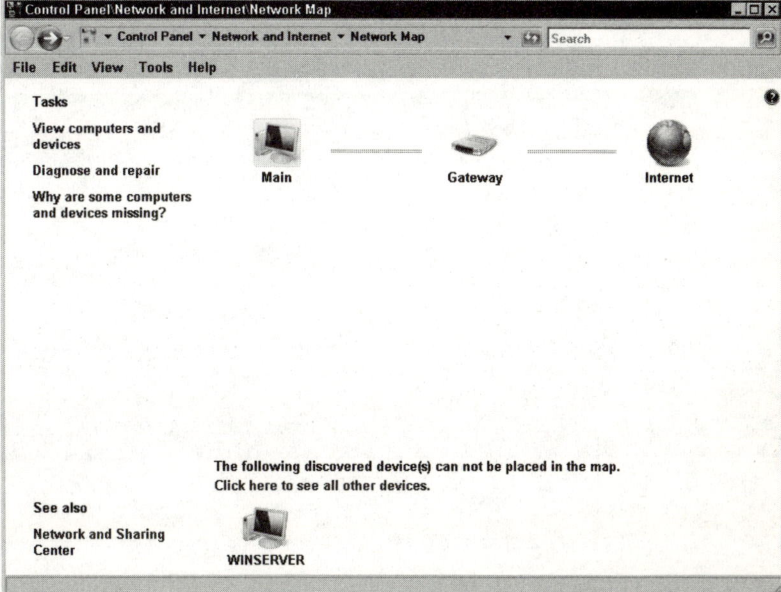

Summary

In this chapter, we looked at the basics of networking. LANs help users share files, applications, and more. We then covered some of the vocabulary and theory behind a network and discussed various network relationships: master/slave, client-server, and peer-to-peer. Finally, we walked through the network components that you might get at your local computer store. After you connect everything, you'll want to get the Vista view of your network using Network Map. This simple tool provides useful troubleshooting information you can use to correct network problems. For example, you can discover whether Vista sees a device and simply isn't connecting to it, rather than not seeing the device at all.

It's important to plan a network. Consider your computing needs before you do anything. For example, you need to know whether you'll run a database and then buy a machine that can handle the database load. If you go out and buy hardware without really thinking about how you want to perform the setup, you'll make mistakes. For example, you need to discover whether the machines you're buying have a built-in NIC, or whether you need to buy them separately. It's also important to consider standards, especially when it comes to wireless devices. Finally, you'll need to consider how everything will fit together to meet specific computing needs.

With all of this information behind you, it's time to start setting up your own network in the next chapter! This next chapter considers the small network. A small network scenario doesn't just apply to your home or a small business. Workgroups within a larger organization can use small networks as well for localized needs and connect to the larger network only when needed to communicate outside the workgroup.

Chapter 19

Setting Up and Configuring Your Own Small Network

One of the most powerful features of Vista is its capability to attach to and become part of a networking environment. In this chapter, we'll look at many of the decisions you'll need to make in order to get the networking features to run reliably in that environment. You'll learn how to set up a simple Ethernet network, including what to do if Vista doesn't detect your network interface card, how to configure your Vista machine using the Connect to a network wizard, and how to manually configure your own IP addresses. You'll also learn how to allow users to share documents and printers and how to create profiles for users and hardware. Finally, the chapter wraps up with a section on troubleshooting your network.

In this chapter:

- Setting up your network
- Physically connecting your network
- Configuring Vista for a network
- Sharing resources
- Connecting to shared resources on the network
- Understanding and using profiles
- Troubleshooting

Vista: What's New?

Vista may do a lot of things wrong (UAC is both a feature and an annoyance) and it may require too much hardware for too much eye candy, but it does do one thing very well. I've never had networks go together as easily as I have with Vista. The detection is automatic, in most cases, and the tweaks, when required, are few. So the big news for this chapter is that you really may not need any of the information you find here except for planning your network. Vista really does an amazing job of making things work as you connect them.

Another new Vista feature is Link Layer Topology Discovery (LLTD). Vista installs this feature by default, so you don't have to do anything special to get it. LLTD builds on the base provided by Universal Plug and Play (UPnP) and Windows Connect Now (WCN), along with a new technology called Windows Rally, to simplify the setup and maintenance of a home network. This technology's responsible for making Vista's network setup nearly automatic. By automatically discovering the hardware on your system with a greater degree of accuracy, Vista reduces the problems of setting a network up in most cases to minor tweaks.

Planning a Network

The whole idea of a network is to share things: space on a large disk drive, a particular file on that disk drive, a printer, and so on. Networks provide two major benefits. One, they can increase user productivity and collaboration. Two, they can save you money on hardware and software. Imagine the cost difference of buying one color laser printer for every person in your family as opposed to buying one for everyone to share. As an example, let's consider a family that needs to do some sharing.

In our happy family, Jennifer has more storage capacity on her machine than Joe does on his, but the laser printer that he convinced her he needed it attached to his (Joe's) PC. Jennifer and Joe work on stuff like their finances and writing letters to family members together, so they need to share some files—or they'll have to pass floppies (or a newer USB flash drive) back and forth via sneakernet. Because Jennifer has more disk space, they store the files on her machine. So, the network problems that we need to solve are as follows:

- Sharing Joe's printer with Jennifer
- Sharing Jennifer's disk with Joe

Let's solve their problem with a basic peer-to-peer network. Microsoft generally refers to peer-to-peer configurations as *workgroups* (as opposed to *domains*). With this type of network, Jennifer makes her hard disk available on the network, and Joe makes his printer available on the network. Assuming that both computers are running Vista, here's how to get Joe onto Jennifer's disk and Jennifer onto Joe's printer:

1. Jennifer tells the Vista networking software, "Offer the Files subfolder on my C drive to anyone who wants it. Call it JenFiles." In Microsoft enterprise networking terminology, JenFiles becomes the *share name* of that folder on Jennifer's machine (GTW09), and it's the name that others will use to access the resource over the network. In a few pages, I'll show you exactly how to share such a resource on the network so others can access it, but for now, remember this: a machine (named GTW09) is sharing a resource called JenFiles with anyone on that network who's able to use it. In this case, it's only Joe.

NOTE Here's an important concept in Microsoft networking: You must name each machine in the network, whether it's a server or a workstation. You'll often hear this name referred to as a NetBIOS name. You also must name each user (in our example, Joe and Jennifer). Because the PCs need names, we may as well name the PCs with their inventory numbers, which in this example are DELL05 and GTW09. Another common naming scheme, used within many companies, is to name the computer based on the physical location within the company. A computer in the east wing, row L, station 6 could be called EL06.

WARNING Naming machines after their users is generally a bad idea, even in a home network, because PCs may be reassigned to other users or given to other family members.

2. Joe then tells the networking software on his PC, "Attach me to the JenFiles resource on Jennifer's machine."

3. Joe, meanwhile, tells his computer to share the printer on his LPT1 port, giving it a name—again, a share name—of JOLASER. Joe's machine is called DELL05, so the Universal Naming Convention (UNC) name of that printer will be `\\DELL05\JOLASER`.

NOTE UNC stands for Universal Naming Convention. In the printer's UNC name, `\\DELL05` is the machine name and `\JOLASER` is the share name. UNCs are used all the time in networking and always follow a `\\computername\sharename` format. Of course, on a hard drive where the share has subdirectories, you can drill down through the subdirectories using `\\computername\sharename\subdirectory`.

4. Jennifer then tells her networking software to make a network connection to JOLASER on Joe's machine and to create it on her LPT1 port.

From now on, whenever Jennifer tells an application program to print to a laser printer on LPT1, the network software will intercept the printed output and will direct it over the network to Joe's machine. The networking software on Joe's machine will then print the information on Joe's printer.

I've left out some of the "how do we do this?" information; it's coming right up.

Ways to Connect a Peer-to-Peer Network

In the next section of this chapter, I'll show you how to connect a network that uses an Ethernet hub, which I discussed in the previous chapter. You can, however, connect a peer-to-peer network in a couple of other ways:

- By using a special network cable called a crossover cable, which allows you to connect two machines' NICs directly to each other and bypassing a hub. This saves you the cost of buying a hub, but they're cheap nowadays anyway. The downside of this type of configuration is that you don't have easy expandability.
- By using a wireless connection, which we'll talk about extensively in Chapter 20.

For some detailed information about these types of connections, from the Start menu open Help and Support Center, click the Table of Contents link, click the Networking – connecting computers and devices link, and then click the Setting up a network link.

Vista is designed to work in a variety of networking situations. Vista makes the perfect network client for both home and office users. It doesn't matter if your entire network consists of Vista computers or if you have servers running NetWare, UNIX, or some other platform; Vista will play nicely with a variety of network operating systems. Vista can also act as a server in a pinch—although you're better off going with a true server product for a long-term solution.

The real key to good networking is good planning. Always draw a basic diagram of what your network will look like, such as where the computers will be, where the hub or router will be, and where the cables will run. In addition, don't forget to put down logical (as opposed to physical) information such as IP addresses, which computer will be the print server, and which files are stored where.

Even Joe and Jennifer mentioned in the earlier example should draw things out. A drawing can eliminate problems before they begin. Let's say that neither Joe nor Jennifer knows a lot about networking, but they make a diagram and take it to a friend who knows computers well. That friend (or a trusted salesperson) might be able to tell them if their plan will work, before they purchase potentially expensive hardware. If Joe and Jennifer want to expand their network at a later time, they have a diagram ready and can see what their possibilities are.

For large and complex networks, planning is even more critical. Still, plan ahead before installing even the smallest network; it will save you troubleshooting headaches in the future.

Connecting Your Ethernet Network

In this section, I'm going to show you how to set up a simple peer-to-peer Ethernet network that solves the problems of Joe and Jennifer that I just described. Using the information in the previous chapter, you first need to design your network, and then you probably need to go shopping—either on the Internet or at one of many computer centers that are springing up all over the place.

You need a network interface card (NIC) for each computer on the network, a hub (cost effective), switch (better performance), or router, and some cables. Many computers that you buy these days come with NICs already installed (depending on your motherboard, you might actually have two NICs installed). If you have an older computer, though, you'll probably need to purchase a NIC. You can even buy a starter kit that contains everything you need—NICs, cables, and a hub—probably for less than $50. With that and a couple of screwdrivers, you're ready to get started. Follow these steps:

NOTE Many people assume that they have a spot in their computer for a NIC and that the NIC will simply fit within whatever slot is available. Both assumptions are recipes for disappointment. Open your computer before you go to the store and determine whether you have a slot available. In addition, make sure you know what kind of slot you have available. The book that comes with your machine (you did save it, didn't you?) usually tells you about the slots. If you can't determine this information, you need to have someone else look at the system and make the determination for you.

1. Turn off and unplug each computer that will be part of your network.
2. At each computer, open the case, ground yourself by touching the power supply case (static electricity will cause damage to your system), and insert a NIC in an empty slot, screwing the card in securely so it won't come loose.
3. Replace the case.
4. Insert one end of the cable into the RJ-45 socket on the card and insert the other end of the cable into the hub. The hub number isn't important as long as you don't plug it into a port labeled "Uplink" or "Crossover"—avoid those.

NOTE One way to avoid using a hub altogether is to buy a *crossover* cable. Plug one end of the crossover into one machine and the other end into your second machine. The major drawback with this is that you can have only two computers on your network. While hubs are pretty inexpensive, this is an alternative if money is really an issue.

5. Plug the hub or switch into the power supply.
6. Turn on the hub and all connected computers. You'll see some lights start blinking on the hub. Most hubs will have a light for each port indicating whether it detects a connection, along with a power light and traffic indicators.

TIP Here's a quick troubleshooting tip. When you have everything plugged in and turned on, look for connection lights on the connecting device. If a computer is plugged into port 2, then there should be a light indicating a connection for port 2. If it's not on, double-check your cables to make sure they're plugged in right. No light generally means no connection, which means no networking.

Because Vista is Plug and Play, when you restart your computer after inserting the NICs, the system automatically loads the device drivers you need for the NICs. For the most part, Vista is very good about automatically detecting network cards after installing them and rebooting. In this respect, Vista is very user-friendly.

TIP Always check to make sure that the hardware you're purchasing is in the Windows Catalog (also known as the hardware compatibility list [HCL] for older operating systems). You can find it at `http://www.microsoft.com/whdc/hcl/default.mspx`.

Configuring Your Network

After successfully installing your network adapters, you need to take some common steps to get the network running properly. Among those steps are to name your computer and workgroup, add protocols necessary for communication (TCP/IP is installed by default; you generally don't need to add more), and configure protocol parameters, such as IP addresses. Using the Network Setup Wizard can help you simplify these configuration processes.

WARNING If you use Internet Connection Sharing (ICS), don't change the IP addresses. The machine that provides the shared Internet connection automatically assigns these addresses for you. Changing the IP addresses could cause your network to stop working.

Understanding LLTD

The new LLTD technology provided with Vista builds on a number of existing technologies and adds a few others to discover your network setup. The technology works with both wired and wireless connections. Generally, Vista will discover any connections and automatically set them up for you. That's why you can perform a setup and find that all of your network connections are already working.

An optional Quality of Service (QoS) extension (installed by default) performs diagnostics for your network. For example, this extension tells you that your network cable is unplugged, rather than simply letting you find the problem cable yourself. In addition, the QoS extension discovers problems such as signal strength, especially in a wireless network. It even discovered a crimped cable I keep around for testing purposes (previous versions of Windows merrily used the cable and significantly hindered network speed).

Although LLTD can do a lot for you right out of the package (hey, I'm impressed so far), you really do require hardware that supports LLTD to get the maximum potential from it. In many cases, this won't mean going out and buying something new. All you need is a firmware update from your hardware vendor. After Vista is released for a while, check out the vendor site, download the firmware upgrade, and follow the vendor instructions to install it. If you can't find the firmware update, you might want to ask the vendor about it.

Eventually, Microsoft plans to provide LLTD for Windows 2003 and Windows XP as a minimum. You'll see the update as either a standard patch or as part of a service pack. By adding LLTD support to these older products, you can get end-to-end diagnostics, something that isn't available now unless you have specialized equipment, such as a Time-Domain Reflectometer (TDR)—a special device for checking cabling problems.

NOTE Microsoft is making LLTD a public specification. If you want to know how LLTD works at a low level, check out the specification at `http://www.microsoft.com/whdc/Rally/LLTD-spec.mspx`.

Using the Connect to a Network Dialog Box

Setting up a peer-to-peer network has never been easier than it is with Vista. In most cases, Vista is going to detect your network, install the required software, and connect to it before Setup is even finished. Even if you create the connection later, Vista will automatically detect it for you before you can create the connection. This feature works great with any version of Windows, UNIX, and NetWare. It will probably work fine with Macintosh and Linux machines as well. In fact, you shouldn't have to do much more than make minor tweaks to any local connection. To check your network connection, open the Network and Sharing Center applet in the Control Panel and click the Connect to a network link. You'll see a Connect to a network dialog box similar to the one shown in Figure 19.1.

In most cases, the dialog box will show that you've connected to any available networks. If there are any other networks that you can connect to, they'll appear in the list in the center of the dialog box. Highlight the connection you want to use and click Connect. That's all there is to creating a new connection.

If you don't see a network connection that you think should appear in the list, click the Diagnose why Windows can't find any additional networks link. You'll see a Windows Network Diagnostics dialog box that contains possible connectivity issues. Click the issue that matches your network and you'll see some troubleshooting steps for it. After you correct the problem, the network connection will appear in the list in Figure 19.1 (if Vista doesn't connect automatically) and you'll be able to make your connection.

Vista doesn't recognize remote connections automatically. If you need to make a remote connection, click the Set up a connection or network link. You'll see four connection options as shown in Figure 19.2. Chapter 14 describes how to work with the Connect to the Internet and Set up a dial-up connection options. Chapter 20 describes how to work with the Set up a wireless router or access point option. Chapter 31 discusses the final option, Connect to a workplace.

Configuring Older Windows Client Machines

When being used on a Vista-based network, Windows 95 and Windows NT Workstation computers need to be configured manually. Windows 98/Me/2000 computers can also be configured manually in nearly the same fashion. To manually configure a down-level network client, follow these steps:

1. Right-click Network and choose Properties from the context menu to open the Network dialog box.

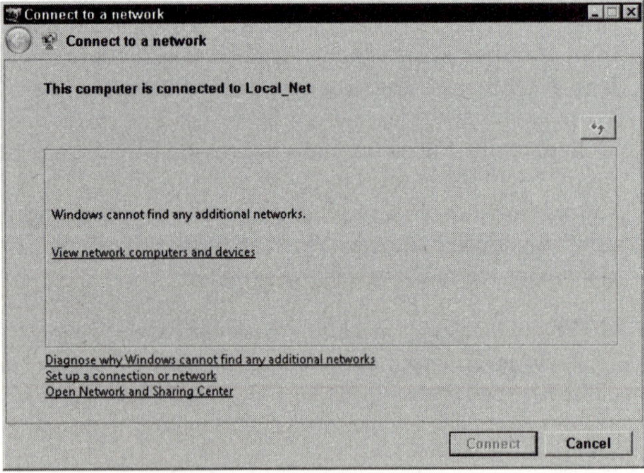

FIGURE 19.1
Verify that your system has connected to any recognizable networks automatically.

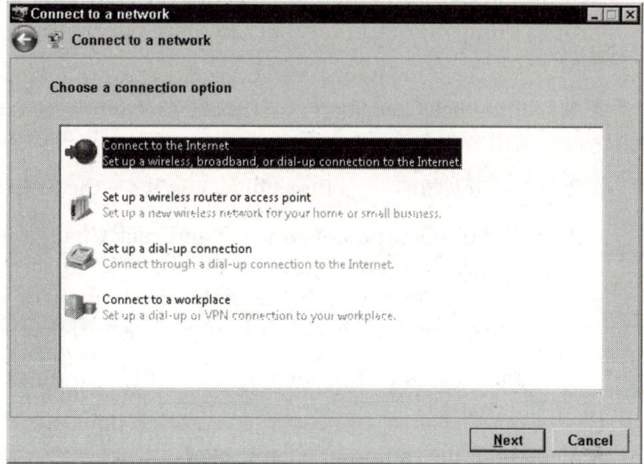

FIGURE 19.2
Vista provides four remote connectivity options that it doesn't automatically detect for you.

2. In The Following Network Components Are Installed list in the Configuration tab, you need to see at least the following (you may see more, and that's okay):
   - TCP/IP
   - Identification
   - File and Printer Sharing for Microsoft Networks

NOTE For the remainder of this discussion, we are going to assume that this is a new installation and none of the required protocols are installed. We will begin by adding TCP/IP.

3. Click Add to open the Select Network Component Type dialog box. Select Protocol and click Add again. Under Manufacturers, select Microsoft. In the right pane, scroll down and click TCP/IP. Click OK twice.
4. Insert the CD-ROM disk for your appropriate operating system. Click OK. At this point, you may have to provide the path to the operating system files. For Windows 95 it should be `x:\Win95`; for Windows 98, `x:\Win98`; for Windows 98 Second Edition, `x:\Win98_SE`; and for Windows NT/2000, `x:\i386`. Replace x: with your CD-ROM drive letter; for example, if your CD-ROM drive is D, replace x: with **d:**.
5. Right-click Network and choose Properties from the context menu to open the Network dialog box.

   In The Following Network Components Are Installed list in the Configuration tab, select TCP/IP *Your network adapter*. Click Properties.

   You will see two choices: Obtain an IP Address Automatically or Specify an IP Address. Select one, depending on the criteria in the "Configuring IP Addresses on a Network" sidebar.

Identification

If you're going to connect your computers to share information, you must configure the Network (or Network Neighborhood or Network, depending on your OS) properties' Identification tab. This tab sets the computer name for the computer and configures your computer in a workgroup (a group of computers that can share information). Follow these steps when working with Vista:

1. Right-click Computer and choose Properties from the context menu. You'll see the System window.
2. Click the Change settings link. You'll see the System Properties dialog box.
3. Select the Computer Name tab and click Change. You'll see the Computer Name/Domain Changes dialog box shown in Figure 19.3. Notice that you can use this dialog box to change the computer name, choose between a domain or workgroup connection, and provide the name of the domain or workgroup to which you want to connect.
4. Type the name of your computer in the Computer name field. Click OK twice to complete the change.
5. Reboot the computer if prompted.

You'll need to follow other steps when working with other versions of Windows. The following steps help you work with Windows XP and other older versions of Windows.

1. Right-click Computer and choose Properties from the context menu. Select the Identification (or Network Identification) tab. Click Properties to display a dialog box similar to the one shown in Figure 19.3.
2. In the Computer Name text box, enter a name. This name can be up to 15 characters long and must be unique within your network.
3. In the Workgroup text box, enter a workgroup name. This name *must be the same* for each computer in the network. If you're at a loss for a name, use WORKGROUP or MSHOME.

NOTE Capitalization of the workgroup name doesn't matter; *computers* is identical to *Computers*, which is identical to COMPUTERS. Also, don't give a machine the same name as any other machine in your environment. This can cause communication problems.

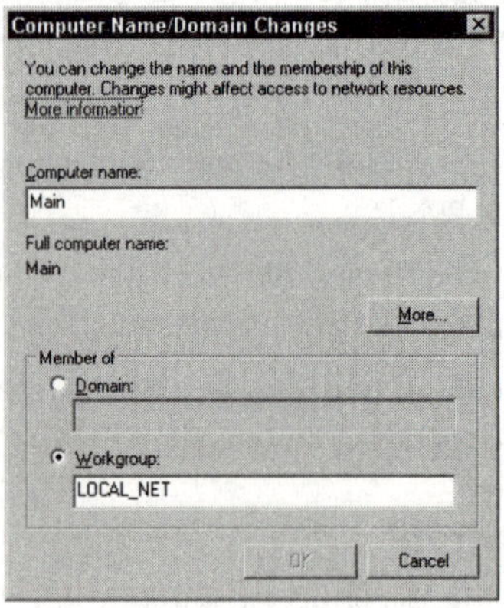

FIGURE 19.3
Type a name for your computer, choose domain or workgroup, and type the domain or workgroup name.

TIP Don't just accept the defaults. The default workgroup name for Vista, MSHOME, differs from the default workgroup name for other Microsoft operating systems, WORKGROUP.

4. Click OK.
5. Reboot the computer if prompted.

Configuring IP Addresses on a Network

There are two basic ways to set up IP addresses for your peer-to-peer network. You can automate the process through DHCP or APIPA, or you can select and assign the IP addresses yourself. These techniques apply equally well to all older Windows operating systems (Windows 98 and above); you don't need the Network Setup Wizard.

Obtain an IP Address Automatically

Use this setting if you have a Dynamic Host Configuration Protocol (DHCP) server (a server that automatically assigns IP addresses to client machines) or if this machine is connected to an Internet Connection Sharing host.

Specify an IP Address

Enter your IP address and subnet mask. If you're designing a network that isn't connected to the Internet, you can choose any IP address you want. For example,

```
IP Address:      131.107.0.102
Subnet Mask:     255.255.0.0
```

The numbers above the 255s in the subnet mask determine the network number. In this example, 131.107 is the network number. The network number *must* be the same for all the computers in the network. The number above the zero in the subnet mask is the host number, which must be *different* on each computer in the network.

On the other hand, if your network will be connected to the Internet, use one of the private network addresses described in Chapter 18. For example:

```
IP Address:   10.X.Y.Z
Subnet Mask: 255.0.0.0
```

or

```
IP Address:  172.16.Y.Z
Subnet Mask: 255.255.0.0
```

or

```
IP Address:  192.168.56.Z
Subnet Mask: 255.255.255.0
```

Of course, X, Y, and Z aren't numbers. Substitute any number between 1 and 254 for X, Y, and Z, as long as each computer gets a unique number. Duplicate addresses on a network can cause a variety of communication problems. After you've made your selection and specified an IP address and subnet mask, click OK.

File and Printer Sharing for Microsoft Networks

File and Printer Sharing for Microsoft Networks doesn't need to be installed on Windows 95/98/Me machines for them to participate on a network. Without it, Windows 95/98/Me machines can still be clients on a network; that is, they can retrieve files from and use printers on remote machines. However, they won't be able to host their own resources.

Windows NT machines also have the ability to share resources. However, Windows NT calls its server service "Server" and its client service "Workstation." These services are installed and configured by default on Windows NT machines.

Both Windows XP and Vista machines have the ability to share resources by default and don't require additional configuration of File and Printer Sharing for Microsoft Networks.

Configuring Vista Manually

Generally, you won't need to configure Vista manually. It does a very good job of performing the required configuration for you in most cases. However, you may encounter a situation where you want to configure Vista manually. You may simply want better control over how Vista interacts with other computers or have a specific problem to solve, such as the need to give each computer a specific address to allow for proper application configuration.

To configure Vista manually, you need to display the Properties dialog box for the affected connection. Right-click Network and choose Properties. Click the Manage network connections link to display the Network Connections window. Right-click a connection and choose Properties from the context menu. The connection's Properties dialog box contains a list of the protocols that you can configure. Figure 19.4 shows a typical example, but your connection will probably vary from the one shown.

The following sections provide some guidelines on common configuration changes. For example, one common change is to modify the Internet Protocol Version 4 (TCP/IPv4) settings. In some cases, you'll need to refer to vendor documentation to discover all of the changes you can make to a particular protocol, especially when working with custom protocols.

FIGURE 19.4
Choose a protocol to configure from the supplied list.

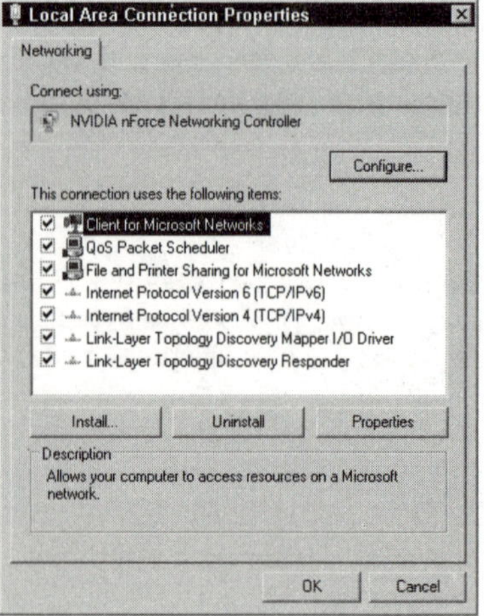

IPv4 Configuration

Vista also has two options for configuring IP addresses, much like previous versions of Windows operating systems. The first option is to obtain an IP address automatically (through a DHCP server or APIPA), and the second option is to configure addresses manually. If you want to configure addresses manually, then the sidebar on IP addressing in the "Configuring Older Windows Client Machines" section in this chapter will help you in Vista.

Automatically obtaining an IP address can happen in one of two ways. First, if your network has a DHCP server, you'll obtain an address from it. Many people don't realize it, but Internet Connection Sharing (ICS) and other Internet sharing software provides a DHCP server, so you may not need to perform any configuration. However, if you have just a small office in your home that lacks an Internet connection, you probably don't have a DHCP server. That's okay. Let's say that you set your Vista machine to obtain an IP address automatically, but Vista can't locate a DHCP server (which makes sense, because you don't have one). Vista will automatically assign an IP address and subnet mask to your machine. The address will be in the 169.254.X.X range, with a subnet mask of 255.255.0.0. This feature is called Automatic Private IP Addressing (APIPA).

NOTE Windows 98, 2000, Me, XP, 2003, and Vista support APIPA.

You should be careful of one thing when using APIPA, though. Let's say that you've manually configured one computer with an address of 131.107.2.102 and a mask of 255.255.255.0. Another computer on the same network gets an APIPA-assigned address of 169.254.225.128, along with a mask of 255.255.0.0. Those two computers won't be able to talk to each other using TCP/IP. The reason for this is they have different network addresses, so they each think the other is physically somewhere else, when they're really on the same physical network. The computers will be confused and won't talk. Manual configuration is normally an all or nothing proposition—you must manually configure all of the computers on your network or none of them.

To manually configure IPv4 addresses on your Vista computer, right-click Local Area Connection, and click Properties again. Highlight Internet Protocol version 4 (TCP/IPv4), and choose Properties. Select the Use the Following IP Address radio button, and enter your IP address, subnet mask, and default gateway (if necessary). You can specify an address for a DNS server as well or obtain that server's address automatically as shown in Figure 19.5.

TIP If you're configuring your network for an Internet connection and assigning IP addresses yourself, ask your ISP for their DNS server addresses. Enter these numbers in each of the computers on your network.

TIP Administrators who want to automate manual IP address configuration can use the NetSH utility at the command line. To use this approach, type `NetSH Interface IPv4 Add Address <AddressName> <AddressValue>` or `NetSH Interface IPv6 Add Address <AddressName> <AddressValue>` and press Enter. The AddressName must already appear in the list of addresses. The AddressValue has to reflect a valid address. You can discover the list of current addresses by typing `NetSH Interface IPv4 Show Addresses` or `NetSH Interface IPv6 Show Addresses` and pressing Enter. Consequently, if you want to provide a custom loopback address for IPv4, you could type `NetSH Interface IPv4 Add Address "Loopback Pseudo-Interface 1" 127.0.0.2` and press Enter. Likewise, if you want to later remove the address, you'd type `NetSH Interface IPv4 Delete Address "Loopback Pseudo-Interface 1" 127.0.0.2` and press Enter.

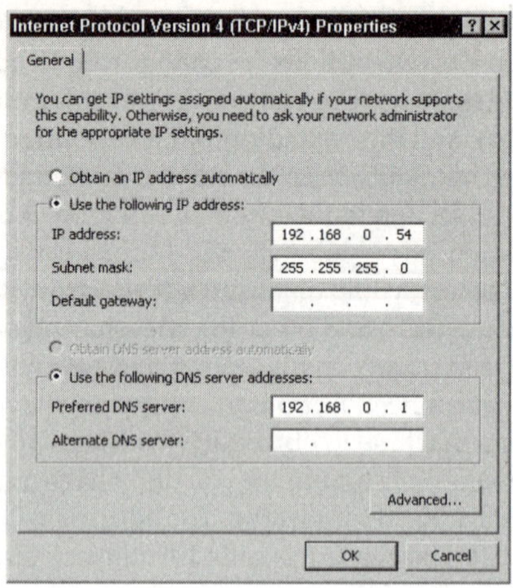

FIGURE 19.5
Manually select an address for your computer.

IPv6 Configuration

In general, IPv6 configuration is the same as IPv4 configuration from a procedure perspective. However, when working with IPv6 addresses, you provide the address and then a length value that shows how long the network address portion of the address is. However, creating the actual address isn't simply a matter of deciding on a network address and a host address. The process of creating an IPv6 can become quite complex and you'll probably want to let Vista create the value for you automatically whenever possible. You can learn more about IPv6 construction at `http://technet2.microsoft.com/WindowsServer/en/library/af7d4a80-cfe8-4d7d-a830-8eb6e6ebd6b71033.mspx?mfr=true`.

Network Bridging

If you have multiple NICs, you could set up a separate IP address for each NIC. Vista looks at an IEEE 1394 adapter as a NIC. If you work with any virtual machine technology such as VMWare, that software also installs separate "virtual" NICs on your computer. Without Microsoft Vista Network Bridging technology, I'd have to maintain four different NICs on just one computer. And managing a network can be difficult enough. With a network bridge, I can easily manage different NICs on the same computer, as shown in Figure 19.6.

To create a bridge, open the Network Connections window shown in Figure 19.6, Ctrl+Click on every connection that you want to include in the bridge, and choose Advanced ➤ Bridge Connections. You'll see the usual UAC message. Click Continue and Vista will create the bridge for you.

Without the network bridge, I'd need two different IP addresses. I'd have to configure two sets of DNS addresses, reconfigure WINS as required, and so on. In addition, since the NICs could be connected to different networks, the computer could become a router, and if I wanted to do that, I would then have to configure IP forwarding to get the NICs to talk to each other. Traffic from any one of these NICs could cause a traffic jam on the network.

With the network bridge, I need only one IP address. All of the NICs plug into Computer in the same way as they plug into a hub. But as a bridge (which is another name for a switch), it regulates traffic on the network. In other words, if I'm downloading a digital video through my IEEE 1394 port, that doesn't stop traffic that goes through Computer to a virtual machine or a USB device.

Sometimes you need separate IP addresses. For example, if you want two separate networks connected to your computer, it's easy to detach one of your NICs from the bridge. From the example shown in Figure 19.6, right-click the Network Bridge icon, and then click Properties in the pop-up menu. In the Network Bridge properties window shown in Figure 19.7, the Adapters area includes the connections that are connected to the bridge. Deselect the connection of your choice and click OK.

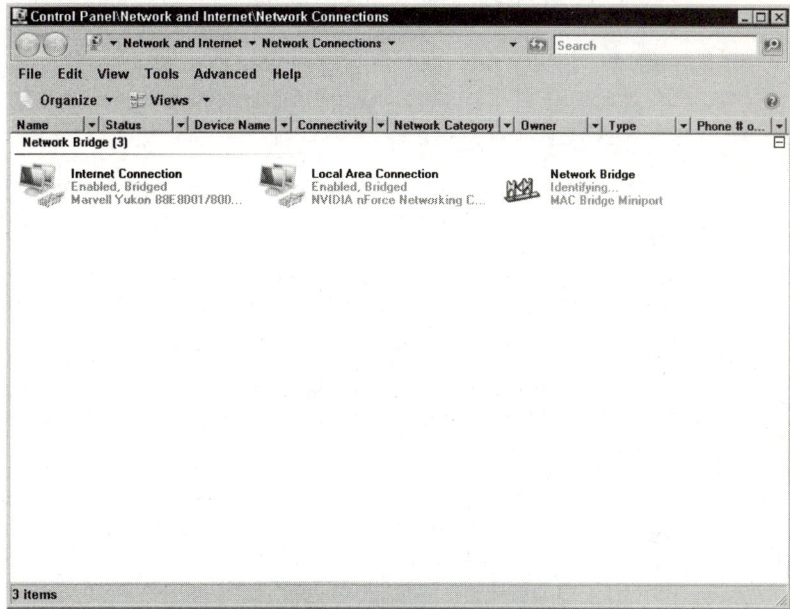

FIGURE 19.6
You can manage multiple NICs with one Network Bridge.

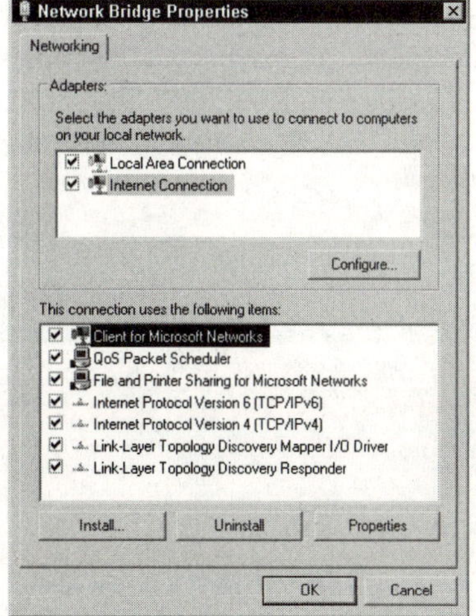

FIGURE 19.7
Just deselect any connection that you want to detach from the properties of the Network Bridge.

Now the Network Connections window is split between regular LAN connections and connections that are part of the Network Bridge. You can now configure the properties of the connections that you just decoupled from the bridge.

Eventually, you might decide you don't want the bridge in place. To remove a bridge from your system, right-click the Network Bridge icon and choose Properties from the context menu. In the Network Bridge properties window, clear all of the adapter check boxes to disconnect all of the adapters from the network bridge. Click OK. The Network Bridge icon will now say that it's disconnected. Right-click the Network Bridge icon and choose Delete from the context menu. Vista will ask if you're sure that you want to delete the bridge. Click Yes and, after the usual UAC message, Vista will delete the bridge from your system.

Creating Shares

Before users on your network can get to resources on your computer you must share those resources. To do this, you must be logged on as an administrator or have a user account with local administrator privileges. In addition, you must have the Server service started (it's set to start automatically by default, but some people stop this service to enhance system security). You can create shares using Windows Explorer or the Computer Management console found in the Administrative Tools folder of the Control Panel. Using Windows Explorer is simple and direct, so in this section, that's what I'll use.

NOTE To open Computer Management, in Control Panel click Administrative Tools and then click Computer Management. Alternatively, click Start ➤ All Programs ➤ Administrative Tools ➤ Computer Management.

A share can be a folder or a drive—any resource on your computer that you want other people to be able to use over the network. Microsoft provides two techniques for creating a share. The first technique uses the File Sharing Wizard, while the second technique is a manual approach. Here are the steps for creating a share with the File Sharing Wizard.

1. Right-click the folder or drive that you want to share and choose Share from the context menu. You'll see File Sharing dialog box like the one shown in Figure 19.8. Notice that the dialog box contains the name of the owner as a minimum. You may also see other names of other people or groups that have access to the folder.

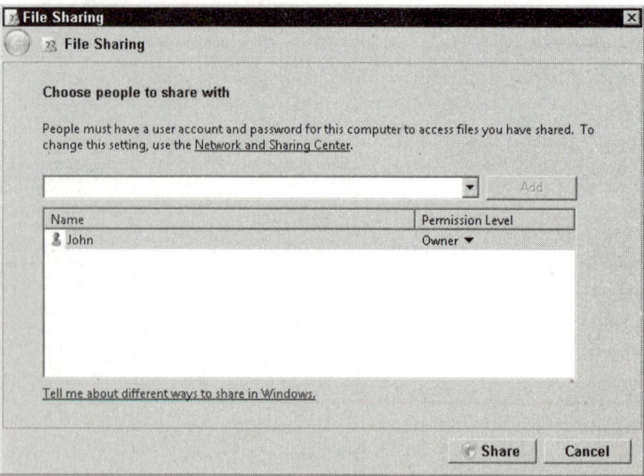

FIGURE 19.8 The File Sharing Wizard makes it relatively easy to share resources.

NOTE If the folder is already shared, you'll see a File is already shared dialog box. Click Stop sharing when you want to remove the existing shares from the folder or drive. Click Change sharing permissions when you simply need to update the sharing information. When you click this second option, you'll see the dialog box shown in Figure 19.8 and the remaining sharing steps work as normal.

2. Choose a name or group from the drop-down list box and then click Add. You'll see the name or group added to the list.
3. Choose a permission level for the entry from the drop-down list in the Permission Level column. Vista provides three permission levels. A Reader can read the files, but not change them. A Contributor can read and write the files. Finally, a Co-owner can read, write, delete, and otherwise manage the files.
4. Click Share. After the usual UAC warning, Vista will share the folder. You'll see a success dialog box like the one shown in Figure 19.9.
5. Optionally, click the e-mail link and Vista displays an e-mail message with the To, Subject, and content already filled out for you. Add any additional recipients and content, and then click Send to let everyone know about the new share.
6. Optionally, click Copy. Vista copies the new share information to the clipboard. You can paste the share information anywhere you like.
7. Click Done. You'll see a group icon next to the folder or drive to show that it's shared.

The File Sharing Wizard is fast and simple, but it doesn't provide you with very good control over the shared features of your folder or drive. To enable manual sharing, choose Tools ➤ Folder Options to display the Folder Options dialog box, select the View tab, clear the check mark next to the Use Sharing Wizard (Recommended) option, and then click OK. Here are the steps for creating a share of any type using the manual method:

1. In Windows Explorer, right-click the folder or drive that you want to share, and choose Share from the context menu to open the Properties dialog box for that folder or drive at the Sharing tab shown in Figure 19.10.

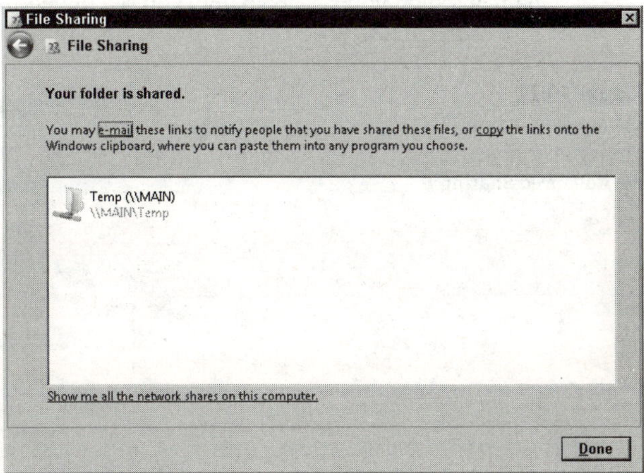

FIGURE 19.9
The success dialog box tells you what you've shared with others.

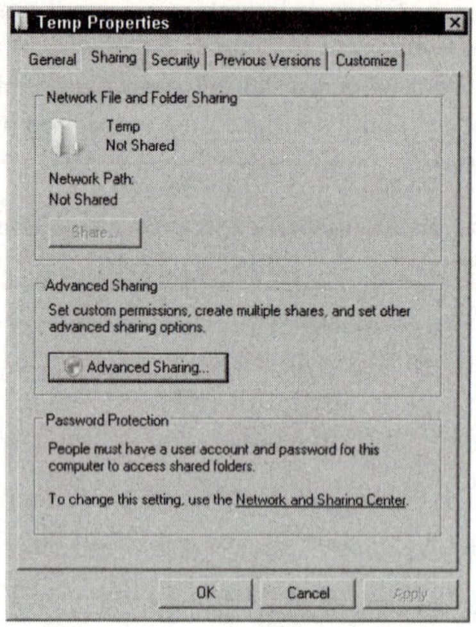

FIGURE 19.10
The Sharing tab lets you share folders with other people.

NOTE Microsoft doesn't recommend sharing drives because they believe it allows too broad of access and a possible security hole. In reality, it's done all the time (especially for sharing CD/DVD drives). If someone else needs to access several folders on your computer, it's more efficient to put all the needed folders on one drive and share the drive. You can then set security at the drive level as opposed to the folder level, and it's easier to manage.

2. Click Advanced Sharing and check the Share this folder option. You'll see an Advanced Sharing dialog box like the one shown in Figure 19.11.
3. Type a name for the share in the Share name field.
4. Type a description of the share in the Comments field.
5. Click Permissions. You'll see a Permissions dialog box like the one shown in Figure 19.12. The Permissions dialog box contains a list of users and groups that have access to the share or that you specifically deny access to the share. The Group or user names list contains the names. When you select a name, you see the permissions in the Permissions list at the bottom of the dialog box.

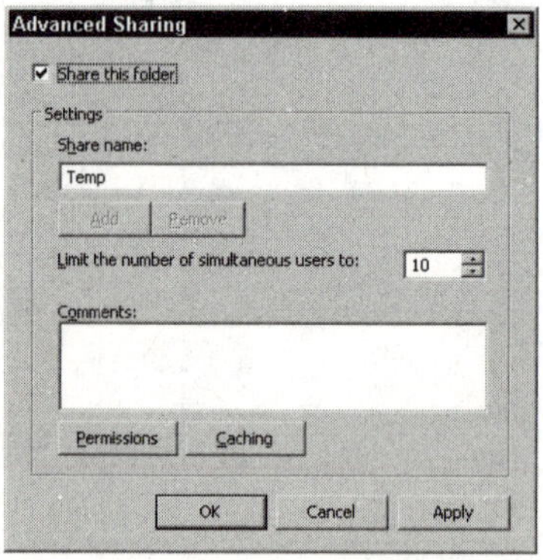

FIGURE 19.11
Choose detailed sharing options using the Advanced Sharing dialog box.

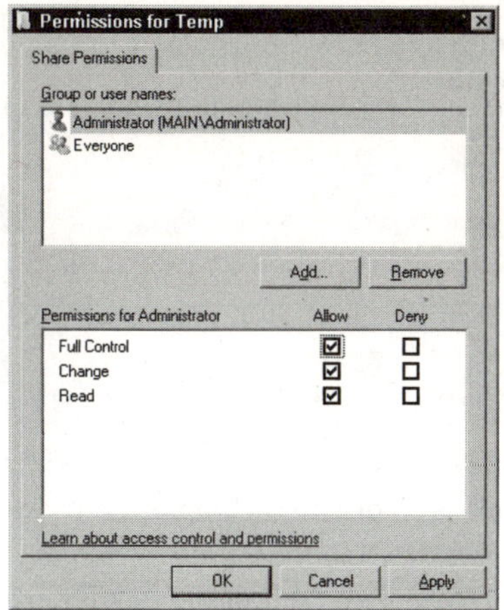

FIGURE 19.12
Select the people and groups that can use the share and define how they can use it.

NOTE To remove share permission for a user or group, highlight the user or group name and click Remove. Vista will remove the name from the list.

6. Click Add to add a new user or group. You'll see a Select Users or Groups dialog box like the one shown in Figure 19.13.
7. Type the names of one or more users or groups in the list. Separate multiple names using a semicolon (;). Click Advanced if you want Vista to help you search for a user or group name.
8. Click OK. You'll see the names and groups you selected added to the list in the Permissions dialog box.
9. Highlight each user or group entry and choose rights for the user or group. If you check an option in the Allow column, the user or group is allowed to perform that action. When you check an option in the Deny column, Vista disallows that user or group from performing the action, even if they'd normally inherit the right to perform that action from a higher object in the hierarchy.
10. Click OK to return to the Advanced Sharing dialog box.
11. Click Caching. You'll see the Offline Settings dialog box shown in Figure 19.14 where you can determine how others can cache content from the share. The first option is the default and lets the user make the decision. The second option forces the user to allow offline caching. The third option doesn't allow any offline caching—a good precaution for sensitive material.

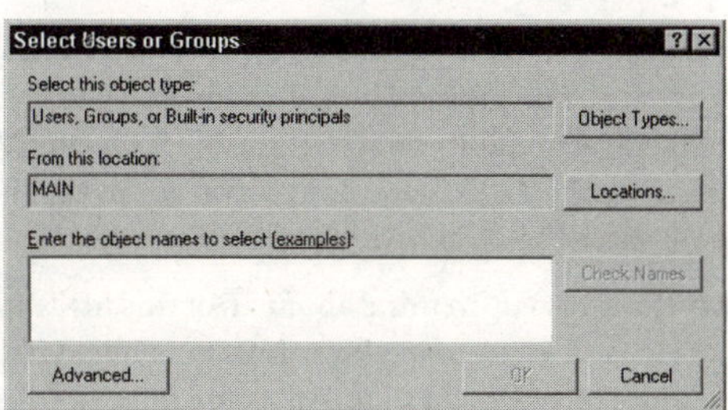

FIGURE 19.13
Add a user or group name to the list.

FIGURE 19.14
Select offline caching options for the share.

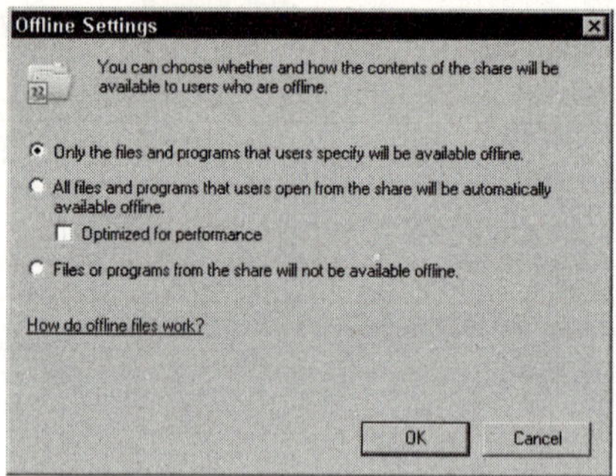

12. Choose an offline caching option and then click OK to return to the Advanced Sharing dialog box.

13. Click OK twice. You'll see a group icon next to the folder or drive to show that it's shared.

You need to know one additional fact about shares. Windows provides a number of administrative shares. These shares let you perform administrative tasks such as backing up the drive or accessing drive data as an administrator, even when the user doesn't share any resources on the system at all. The administrative shares always have a dollar sign ($) attached to them. For example, you can access the C drive of a system using the C$ administrative share as long as you have the proper privileges. Consequently, if the only reason for creating a share is to perform administrative tasks, you don't need it—the share already exists.

To see the administrative shares on a drive, open the Computer Management console and select the `System Tools\Shared Folders\Shares` folder as shown in Figure 19.15. This figure shows all of the default administrative shares for my system. Some of the entries are easy to figure out, such as the drive and printer shares, as well as ADMIN$, which provides access to the Windows folder.

FILE SYSTEMS AND NETWORK SHARING

A common question that I often hear is, "Can my Windows 98 computer access files on my Vista computer using NTFS?" To be sure, Windows 98 doesn't support NTFS, meaning that it has no way of being able to read NTFS volumes. Over a network, this isn't a problem. Your Windows 98 computer can get files off your XP-mounted NTFS hard drive just fine.

Here's why: When you make a request to retrieve a file, Windows (regardless of version) first checks to determine where that file is located. If it's on the local hard disk, the request gets passed to a file system driver, which knows how to read a specific file system (FAT or NTFS). The file system driver gets the file and returns it to Windows. Windows 98 doesn't have an NTFS file system driver.

When the requested file is somewhere else on a network, the request is passed to the network *redirector*, which, if networking is installed, Windows 98 has. (Nice name, huh? It redirects network requests.) The network redirector figures out that the file is on your Vista computer and asks that computer for the file. It's then up to the Vista file system driver to get the file and return it to the network redirector for a safe journey back to the Windows 98 computer.

Another thing to keep in mind about all of this file transferring: when data is being transmitted on a network, NTFS and FAT are irrelevant. Data is just data: 1s and 0s. NTFS and FAT are merely methods of storing those 1s and 0s on a hard disk and have nothing to do with data on the network.

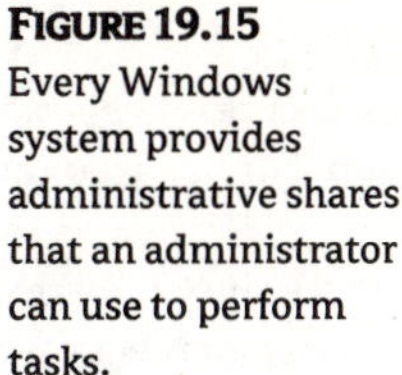

FIGURE 19.15
Every Windows system provides administrative shares that an administrator can use to perform tasks.

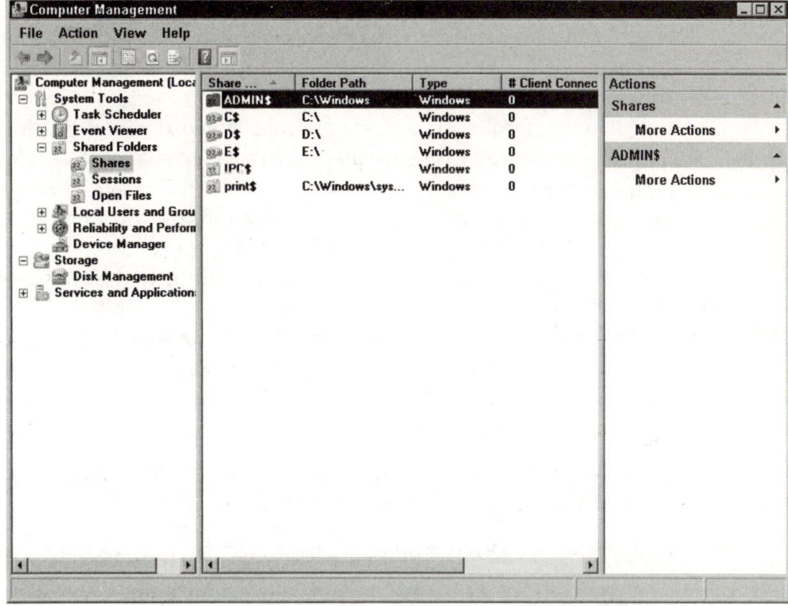

The Inter-Process Communication (IPC) share, IPC$, is a little harder to explain because it involves complex programming issues to explain it fully. The short version is that the administrator needs this share to communicate with processes on the target machine. For example, the administrator may have to kill a task on the system. To perform this task from a remote machine, the administrator requires the IPC share. Unfortunately, any advantage the administrator gains can also provide an advantage to crackers. For example, you can read an article on how to exploit the IPC$ share at `http://www.governmentsecurity.org/articles/HackingaWindows2000systemthroughIPC.php`. By the way, this particular security hole is closed, but it does provide a nice illustration. The security problems of these administrative shares are the reason that many people turn the Server service off unless they really do need to share something.

Attaching to Network Resources

After your network is configured for sharing, one of the easiest ways to test your network connections is to attach to network resources. You can do so in the following ways:

- By browsing Network
- By mapping a network drive
- By using UNCs to connect directly

Browsing Network

To access Network, double-click its entry on the Desktop. You can also choose Start ➤ Network. Then, double-click a computer to view and connect to its shared resources. The Network window only shows shared resources, so you might have to ask the computer's user to share a resource if you don't see it.

Mapping a Network Drive

Mapping a network drive involves assigning a drive letter to a network location. For example, if you frequently connect to someone else's shared folder, you might assign it an unused drive letter on your computer.

When you frequently access particular network resources, mapping a drive to the network share is a great way to ensure that they're easily available. When you map a drive, you're telling your computer, "make the `docs` shared folder on `computer1` my drive letter L." Drive L then appears in Computer under Network Location, and all you need to do to access it is to double-click it. Remember that the information is still physically stored on the other machine. All you've done is make a logical pointer on your machine pointing to the physical resource. It's purely for the sake of convenience.

One of the benefits to networking is being able to back up your files and folders on another computer. You'll find that some applications won't recognize other network drives unless they're mapped—so that's another reason you need to know how to map network drives.

To map a drive, follow these steps:

1. Right-click Network and choose Map Network Drive to open the Map Network Drive dialog box shown in Figure 19.16.
2. From the Drive drop-down list, select an unused drive letter.
3. From the Folder drop-down list, select the folder you want to map to, or click Browse to find the folder on your network.
4. If you want to use this mapping every time you log on, leave the Reconnect at logon check box selected.

NOTE Clicking the Connect using a different username link opens the Connect As dialog box. I'll discuss that option later in this chapter.

5. Click Finish. The drive now appears in Computer under Network Drives along with your local drives.

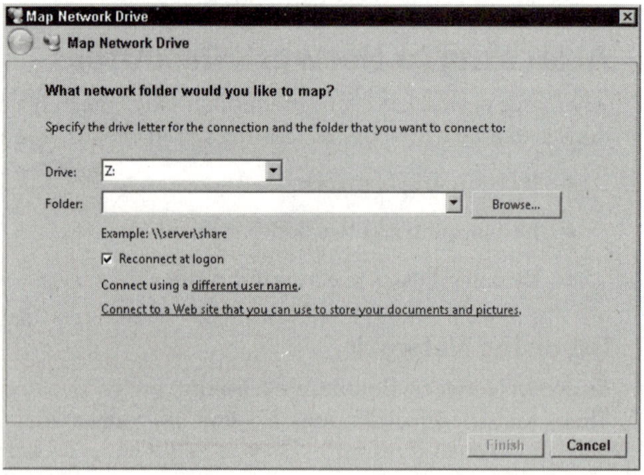

FIGURE 19.16
Create a logical pointer from a local drive to a network resource.

To disconnect a mapped drive, follow these steps:

1. In Computer, choose Tools ➤ Disconnect Network Drive to open the Disconnect Network Drive dialog box.
2. Select the network drive you want to disconnect, and click OK.

TIP If this process isn't working for some reason, the next section provides an alternative method for mapping network drives that's more reliable.

WARNING Here's a situation to avoid: don't disconnect a mapped drive and then map another drive using the same drive letter, telling it to automatically reconnect at login. If the original drive you disconnected is set to reconnect automatically as well, it can cause your system to become confused when remapping the drives.

Making a Direct Connection via a UNC

At the beginning of this chapter, I mentioned UNC names. Using UNC names is yet another way to attach to network resources. You do this in one of two ways. One way is to click the Start menu and choose Run. The other way is by executing `net use` statements at the command prompt. But before you can attach to resources on the network, you need to know which resources are available.

If you're using the `Run` command from the Start menu, type **`\\`*`computername`*** and it will show you the resources available on that machine. For example, if I knew that Joe had shared his printer but I couldn't remember its name, I could type in **`\\DELL05`** and press Enter, and I'd see what he's shared. To attach to a network resource using the `Run` command, use the full UNC name, like **`\\GTW09\Shared`**.

We already looked at how to use Network and the `Run` command to locate network resources, but you can also do so at the command prompt using the `net view` command.

NOTE So far in this chapter, I've been talking primarily about how to set up and configure a Vista peer-to-peer network, although some of the information, such as mapping network drives, applies equally to a client-server network and domains. This section, however, contains information that sometimes applies to workgroups and sometimes applies to domains. You know which kind of network you have, so you'll know which instructions apply to your situation.

NOTE In environments with lots of shared resources, complex group and permission issues can arise. For information on groups and permissions, see Chapter 21.

Here's how to use the `net view` command:

- To display a list of the machines on your network, type **`net view`** at the command prompt.
- To display a list of the resources on a particular machine, append the name of the machine. For example, if the machine name was spiritwolf, you'd enter **`net view \\spiritwolf`**.
- To view the resources of a machine in another domain, for example, the server spiritwolf in the domain hq, you'd enter the following: **`net view \\spiritwolf /domain:hq`**
- To display a list of all the domains on the network, simply enter **`net view /domain`**.

Using Net Use: Connecting to Other Drives and Printers

After you've browsed the network with the `net view` command, you can connect to all the available goodies (or disconnect from those you don't want) with the `net use` command. Use this command to connect to network resources as drives D through Z and printer ports LPT1 through LPT9.

WARNING Drive letters can be used only once. So if your CD-ROM is drive D, you'll have only drive letters E through Z available.

To display information about the workstation's current connections, type **`net use`** without options. You'll see a list of the drives or folders that you've connected to on other machines. However, you won't see the printers listed. This utility only lists printers that you connect to using the `net use` command.

Using Long Filenames in UNCs

If you wanted to connect to a folder called `Wpfiles` on the spiritwolf server and make that your E drive, your command would be **`net use E: \\spiritwolf\wpfiles`**. You get to specify the port name or drive letter that you want to connect a resource to, but again, you're restricted to drive letters D through Z and ports LPT1 through LPT9. To connect to a printer instead of a folder, you'd use a port—such as **`lpt1:`**—instead of a drive letter and the printer name instead of the folder name. Your command may read **`net use lpt1: \\spiritwolf\printer1`**.

If the computer you're getting the resource from has a blank character in its name (that is, the computer name has two words in it), you must put the name in quotation marks, like this:

```
"\\eisa server"
```

If a password (let's say it's "artuser") is attached to the resource that you're trying to connect to, you need to include that in your connection command, like this:

```
net use lpt1: \\ted\hp4m artuser
```

Or, if you want the computer to prompt you for the password so that it isn't displayed on the screen, append an asterisk:

```
net use lpt1: \\ted\hp4m *
```

Using Other Switches

No matter what kind of connection you make, you can make it persistent (that is, have it reconnect automatically every time you reboot your machine) by adding the switch `/persistent:yes` to the end of the command. If you don't want it to be persistent, use `/persistent:no` instead.

If you don't specify one or the other, the default is whatever you chose last. If you want to make all future connections persistent, type the following (or type **`:no`** if you want all future connections to be temporary):

```
net use /persistent:yes
```

Typing `/persistent` by itself at the end of the line won't do anything.

To disconnect from a resource, type the following:

```
net use devicename /delete
```

where *devicename* is the connection (such as D or LPT1). You don't have to provide a password or say anything about persistency to disconnect from a resource.

Using Profiles

In Vista, a user profile is a collection of environment settings that customize a user's interface. It can include display settings, network settings, printer settings, and so on. User profiles are of three types:

- Local
- Roaming
- Mandatory

User profiles are particularly useful when you have multiple people using the same computer. As examples, you and your significant other might share a computer, and some companies don't have assigned desk locations for their employees. If you and I use the same machine (you work days and I work the swing shift), you want to be able to have your settings (wallpaper, icons, printer, and network connections) every time you log in. So do I. User profiles is the answer.

The first time you log on to a computer, whether it's yours or that of someone else on your network, Vista creates a *local user profile* for you that's specific to that machine. Since this is the first time you're logging on to this machine, Vista gives you what's called the *default user profile*. When you log off, any changes you've made to the environment during the sessions are saved in your local user profile. Local user profiles apply only to a local machine, hence their name.

NOTE The *roaming user profile* and *mandatory user profile* configurations require a domain and will be covered in Chapter 22.

To customize the default user profile so that each new user of the machine gets the same settings, follow these steps:

1. Log on to the computer as a new user.
2. Establish the desired settings, such as Start menu options, network connections, and so on, and then log off the computer.
3. Log back on to the computer as Administrator.
4. Right-click Computer, choose Properties from the context menu to open the System Properties dialog box, and click the Advanced system settings link to display the System Properties dialog box.
5. Click the Advanced tab, and then click Settings in the User Profiles section to open the User Profiles dialog box shown in Figure 19.17.
6. Highlight the profile that you want each new user to use, and then click Copy To to open the Copy To dialog box shown in Figure 19.18.

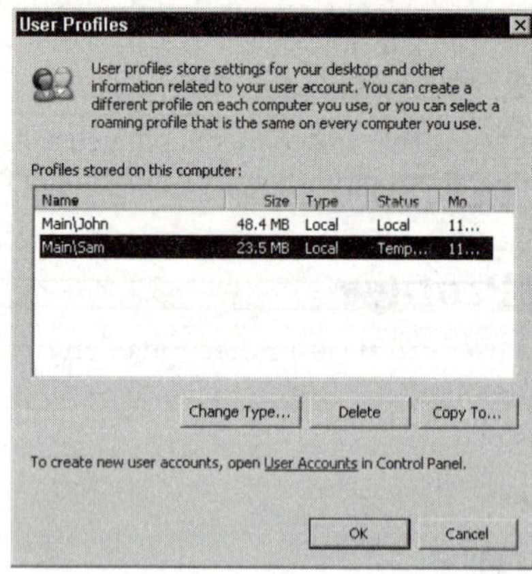

FIGURE 19.17
Display a list of existing user profiles for the current system.

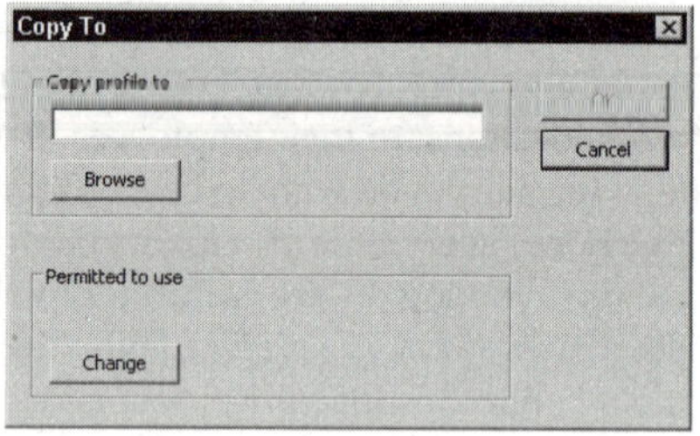

FIGURE 19.18
Copy the profile you want to use for the default user to the default user's account.

7. In the Copy Profile To field, enter the following path:

```
%SYSTEMROOT%\Users\Default
```

8. Click OK, and then click OK again.

If you should happen to delete a profile folder in the Documents and Settings folder, Vista will react as if the user has never logged on to the system before. When the user logs on again, Windows will create a new profile folder for the user. This feature can be useful if the user has placed icons and information all over the Desktop and is now complaining that it keeps coming up as a mess. You can simply delete the profile folder, and a new one will be created the next time that user logs on. It will be the default environment as created in the Default User folder.

Troubleshooting Vista Networking

Because Vista is a network operating system, it makes sense that you'll probably encounter issues with your network from time to time. In most documentation you find today, the troubleshooting text tells you to perform "standard network troubleshooting" without ever telling you what that is. This section lets you in on that secret. Troubleshooting networking is one area in particular where my basic methodology will help you.

First, you start with any error message that Vista gives you. This is always the first step in troubleshooting Vista: Use whatever information it provides. Write the error message exactly as it appears because you can later use that to query the Knowledge Base in Help and Support

Center. Next, you want to see what the Event Viewer can tell you. Event Viewer is probably the best friend you have in troubleshooting Vista. It's not always clear and concise, but it will often tell you exactly what the problem is. It's always worth checking.

TIP The exact error message is important for other reasons too. You can often plug the exact message into a search engine such as Google and find a considerable number of hits, even if the Microsoft Knowledge Base doesn't tell you anything. When working with exact messages, make sure you perform an advanced search, such as the Google Advanced Search at `http://www.google.com/advanced_search`. In this case, you'd type the error message, precisely as Vista presents it, in the with the exact phrase field.

These things are true for any type of troubleshooting in Vista. But basic network troubleshooting goes beyond Vista systems to encompass any network operating system. That's what we need to focus on in this section.

Is It Plugged In?

What do you need in order to have a conversation? You must have some kind of medium to carry the information from one person to another. You must also have some rules to determine how that conversation will take place. Imagine what happens when you meet someone on the street and strike up a conversation. You probably start by making eye contact, then smiling and speaking. If you both happen to speak at least one language in common, you can communicate easily. There may be a few failed attempts before you both find a language you can use, but eventually you'll succeed.

A network is just like that. In its simplest form, a network can be two computers connected by a wire. When one wants to talk to the other, the first computer needs some kind of attention signal; then they both need to negotiate a common language and follow the rules of that language to communicate.

Networks can be simple systems or they can be complex. But however complicated they get, they all have certain things in common. They all have something connecting the nodes, and they all have at least one language. On most networks, the nodes are individual computers as well as intermediary systems such as routers, bridges, switches, and gateways. The language of a network is the protocol.

When troubleshooting any network system, keep these fundamental concepts in mind. Start with the communications medium. Is a proper cable plugged into the computer? Is the other end of the cable plugged into a hub or wall drop? If you're using coax cable, do you have a T-connector and possibly a terminator? Are the drivers for the network card installed and working? Do you have at least one protocol in common with the other computer?

TIP If a network cable is unplugged, or becomes unplugged when it's generally connected, Vista will generally notify you. Look in your system tray for an icon that looks like two small computer monitors. If there's a red X on the icon, that connection has a problem.

These sound like simple questions, and they are, really. You might be surprised how often these simple questions will resolve your networking issues.

WARNING Don't always assume that a physical connection means that the electrical connection is also taking place. Connectors wear out. Sometimes you can plug something in and the physical connection works fine, but the electrical connection is missing completely. Fortunately, Vista displays an unplugged error message when you look at the connection in the Network Connections window.

Configuration Testing

You will want to test your configuration if you can't connect to machines you think you should be able to connect to. Keep the following principles in mind when troubleshooting networks:

- Isolate the problem before fixing it.
- Be familiar with the tools you have available.
- Always check the obvious things (i.e., connections) first, no matter how silly it may seem.

When the system starts, you'll know if Vista can see the network during the logon procedure. You may see error messages, for example, if your TCP/IP address went awry or if the domain controller refuses to validate you into the domain. Even if no errors are immediately apparent, take a look in Event Viewer for potential conflicts. Event Viewer is a great tool for helping track down problems. To open Event Viewer, follow these steps:

1. Click Start ➤ All Programs ➤ Administrative Tools ➤ Computer Management to open the Computer Management window.
2. In the Computer Management pane, expand System Tools, and then expand Event Viewer.
3. Open the Windows Logs folder. Click System to display events in the pane on the right.
4. Look for red stop signs or yellow exclamation points. If you see one of these symbols, double-click it to open the Event Properties dialog box for that event, which will look similar to the one shown in Figure 19.19.
5. If the information in the Event Properties dialog box isn't sufficient to solve the problem, check the configuration of the component. In some cases, you may need to remove and reinstall it.
6. Click the Close button to close the Computer Management window.

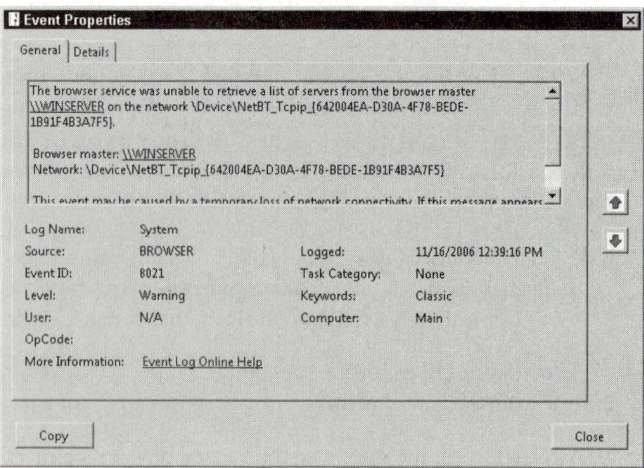

FIGURE 19.19
Warnings and errors tell you about unwelcome system events.

TIP When using Event Viewer to troubleshoot network problems, start at the top of the list and work down until you find event ID number 6005 with a source of eventlog. This represents the last time you booted the computer. The most likely source of your problems will be the event immediately above or immediately below the 6005 event. You should focus most of your efforts on resolving these events before moving on to the others.

Is Anybody Out There?

Most of the troubleshooting I've talked about so far has dealt with working on one computer at a time. Network troubleshooting often involves the connecting systems between the computers as much or more than the computers themselves. I've shown you many ways to work with problems on computers, but how do you see what's wrong with a whole network? That's what this section is about. Here, I introduce you to some of the tools included in Vista to troubleshoot the network.

The ultimate test of your configuration is being able to attach to all the resources you need. In Windows Explorer, look in Network. The icons you see there can give you insight into which parts of the network you can and can't communicate with.

Vista and NetWare's IPX

Many people are wondering where the Internetwork Packet Exchange (IPX)/Sequenced Packet Exchange (SPX) support is in Vista. The bad news is that you won't find it at all if you're using a 64-bit version of Vista. However, even if you have a version of NetWare as old as NetWare 5, you can install standard IP support as a protocol. Sure, you won't get the benefits of using IPX, but you can still connect to your NetWare server. This problem could change if Novell decides to provide a NetWare client update for Vista, but there isn't one as of this writing. You can locate NetWare downloads on the Novell site at `http://download.novell.com/index.jsp`. Read more about this issue on the Microsoft TechNet site at `http://www.microsoft.com/technet/windowsvista/library/plan/26e41adf-f1b6-4ca9-b5d7-adf162300bc3.mspx?mfr=true`.

The 32-bit version of Vista does come with an updated NWLink and Client Service for NetWare that works just like the same feature in older versions of Windows. If Vista detects NetWare or you upgrade from a copy of Windows XP that has the appropriate NetWare support installed, Vista seamlessly installs the required software for you. Read more about this update at `http://www.microsoft.com/technet/windowsvista/library/plan/62ee8100-16b7-429f-a58c-71724339a36e.mspx?mfr=true`. You can't manually install IPX because Microsoft doesn't want you to use this protocol to connect Windows machines. The bottom line is that even though Vista does provide IPX support in the 32-bit version of Vista, it would be a good idea to think about updating your NetWare server to use IP.

Troubleshooting TCP/IP

The single most common network protocol today is TCP/IP. Its popularity is most likely due to the Internet, but it's also because TCP/IP is an industry standard suite of protocols. It isn't just one protocol but rather a group of them designed to perform specific tasks. The part that most people like is the industry standard part. That means that if you have Macs and NetWare and UNIX computers on your network, your Vista computer can communicate with all of them using TCP/IP. TCP/IP is also popular with support people because it has so many troubleshooting tools built into it.

Ping

The packet Internet groper (ping) is the most basic test of network communication over TCP/IP. What ping does for you is bounce a series of packets off a remote host. You're essentially just saying "Hello?" over and over and (you hope) getting a response each time. The basic syntax is `ping www.host.com` or `ping 10.1.0.44`.

So what does this tell you? Getting a response when pinging by IP address means that your network card is installed correctly, the driver is working, the TCP/IP protocol is working, Windows Sockets is working, the other computer is working, and everything in between is working. That's quite a lot of information for just one small command! When you ping by hostname, you get all the previous information, plus you know that your hostname resolution is working.

You can also ping the address 127.0.0.1. This address is reserved for the local host (the local computer) and is a loopback diagnostic test of your installed TCP/IP software. Successfully pinging the local host verifies that TCP/IP is successfully installed on the local computer.

With this in mind, follow this procedure to test your IP configuration and network connection:

NOTE Some of these tests assume that your LAN is connected to the Internet.

1. Test that you've installed the IP software by pinging the built-in IP loopback address. Type **`ping 127.0.0.1`**. If that fails, you know that you've done something wrong in the initial installation, so check that the software is installed on your system. This test doesn't put any messages out on the network; it just checks that the software is installed. By the way, the same thing happens if you ping your IP address, except that pinging your address also tests the network card.

   If that fails, your TCP/IP stack probably isn't installed correctly, or perhaps you mistyped the IP number (if it failed on your specific IP address but not on the loopback), or perhaps you gave the *same* IP number to another workstation.

2. Ping your default gateway to see that you can get to it, because it should be on your local subnet. For example, if your gateway were at 199.34.57.2, you'd type **`ping 199.34.57.2`**, and you should get a response.

3. If you can't get to the gateway, check that the gateway is up and that your network connection is all right. Nothing is more embarrassing than calling in outside help, only to find that your LAN cable fell out of the back of your computer.

4. Ping something on the other side of your gateway, such as an external DNS server. (Ping me, Mark Minasi, if you like: 70.168.214.165. I ought to be up just about all the time.) If you can't get there, it's likely that your gateway isn't working properly.

5. Next, test the name resolution on your system. Ping yourself *by name*. Instead of typing something such as **`ping 199.34.57.35`**, you'd type **`ping test`** (the machine you're on at the moment). That tests your DNS server, or your HOSTS file if you're using one instead of DNS.

6. Then, ping someone else on your subnet. Again, try using a fully qualified domain name on your local network, such as `mizar.Ursamajor.Edu`, rather than an IP address. If that doesn't work, use the IP address. If the IP address works but the hostname doesn't, you've got a problem with the Hosts file or DNS.

7. Finally, ping someone outside your domain, such as `house.gov` (the U.S. House of Representatives), `www.yahoo.com`, or `orion01.Mmco.Com`. If that doesn't work but all the pings inside your network work, you've probably got a problem with your Internet provider.

WARNING While pinging websites can help test connectivity, some websites don't allow pings in to their network. They block pings off as a security measure. So, the site may be up, but you won't get a response from a ping. `Microsoft.com` is a good example of this.

If you're successful on all these tests, your TCP/IP connection should be set up properly.

Hostname

The hostname utility returns the hostname of the local computer. This can be helpful when you aren't exactly sure what it is.

IPConfig

IPConfig is right up there with ping when it comes to valuable TCP/IP utilities. This tool enables you to view some or all of your TCP/IP configuration (as the name might imply). To use it, type **`ipconfig`** at the command prompt to receive your IP address, subnet mask, and default gateway. If you type **`ipconfig /all`**, you'll see a list of every TCP/IP configuration for every interface on your computer. To give you some idea of the scope of information, Figure 19.20 shows the output of the `ipconfig /all` command.

If IPConfig reports an address that's unfamiliar to you, or reports no information at all, then you may have found your problem. IPConfig can also be used to release and renew IP addresses acquired through DHCP. The process for this is `ipconfig /release` and then `ipconfig /renew`.

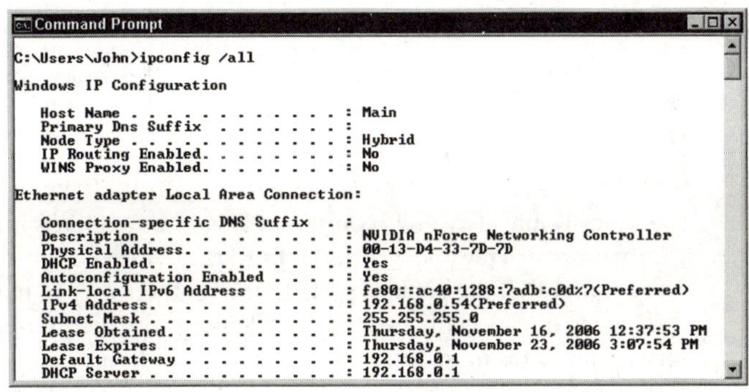

Command Prompt
C:\Users\John>ipconfig /all
Windows IP Configuration
Host Name . . . . : Main
Primary Dns Suffix . . . . :
Node Type . . . . : Hybrid
IP Routing Enabled. . . . . : No
WINS Proxy Enabled. . . . . : No
Ethernet adapter Local Area Connection:
Connection-specific DNS Suffix . :
Description . . . . : NVIDIA nForce Networking Controller
Physical Address. . . . . : 00-13-D4-33-7D-7D
DHCP Enabled. . . . . : Yes
Autoconfiguration Enabled . . . . : Yes
Link-local IPv6 Address . . . . . : fe80::ac40:1288:7adb:c0d%7(Preferred)
IPv4 Address. . . . . : 192.168.0.54(Preferred)
Subnet Mask . . . . : 255.255.255.0
Lease Obtained. . . . . : Thursday, November 16, 2006 12:37:53 PM
Lease Expires . . . . : Thursday, November 23, 2006 3:07:54 PM
Default Gateway . . . . : 192.168.0.1
DHCP Server . . . . : 192.168.0.1

FIGURE 19.20 Use the IPConfig utility to discover the configuration of your network.

ARP

The ARP command views and modifies the Address Resolution Protocol (ARP) cache. ARP is used by TCP/IP to resolve an IP address such as 10.1.0.1 to a unique hardware address or MAC address.

The process that TCP/IP uses to communicate between two computers that are on the same subnet as the host server is shown in Figure 19.21. At the application layer, the user types in a Uniform Resource Locator (URL) to browse a favorite website. The user's computer is configured to use a certain Domain Name System (DNS) server that's responsible for resolving the name in the URL to an IP address. Then TCP/IP uses ARP to resolve that IP address to a unique physical address. Every network card has a unique hexadecimal number assigned to it when it's manufactured. That's the physical address, or MAC address, of the card.

When ARP resolves an IP address to a unique hardware address, it stores the resolution in its cache. One thing you can do to improve the connection speed to a server that you use frequently is to make a static entry in the ARP cache. The command string below will add a static entry for a computer:

```
ARP -s 10.1.0.1 00-40-05-16-DA-8A
```

The -s switch tells the ARP command to make the entry permanent. You should be aware that *permanent* in this case means only until the computer is rebooted. If you want this entry to really be permanent, you must use the ARP command in a logon script or batch file in your Startup group.

FIGURE 19.21
Resolving a hostname to a MAC address in TCP/IP networking.

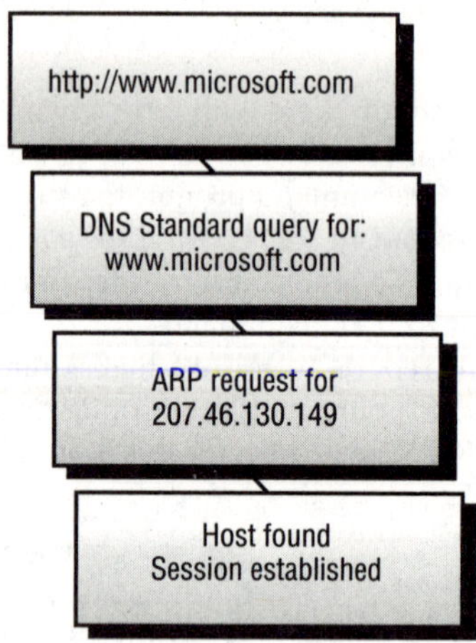

TraceRT

The Trace Route (TraceRT) command is very much like ping in that it bounces several packets of information off a remote computer. But TraceRT does more than that. It also shows a response from every router that the packets go through on their way to the remote computer.

This can be especially useful when dealing with communications issues with a remote host that's very far away (as in many routers away). TCP/IP uses a mechanism called a time to live (TTL) to determine how long a packet of data should be allowed on the network. If it didn't drop packets after a set period of time, packets would still be roaming the Internet from 20 years ago or more. The TTL is decremented automatically by at least one at each and every router it passes through (also called a *hop*). If a packet is forced to wait in a router because of network congestion, its TTL may be decremented by more than one.

TraceRT can reveal when the default TTL isn't high enough to allow for network congestion on the way to the remote host. The TTL setting can be adjusted in Vista through the Registry at this location:

```
HKEY_LOCAL_MACHINE\System\CurrentControlSet\Services
\Tcpip\Parameters

Value name: DefaultTTL
```

The maximum setting for this value is 255.

The following troubleshooting scenario is a common support call in most networks. This time, imagine that you're the support person for a group of users on your company network and are attempting to correct a problem with network connectivity.

NOTE There are some very cool graphical route tracing programs available commercially. One such program is NeoTrace, available at `http://www.neotrace.com`.

Scenario: Unable to "See" My Server

You have just received a call from a coworker, Mary, who's having trouble retrieving e-mail from her server. (She knows you know a lot about computers, and the help desk never seems to answer their phone.) When you talk with her at her office, you learn that she's unable to open her e-mail application without receiving an error that the server couldn't be found. She's using TCP/IP as the only network protocol.

Has it ever worked before? Mary tells you that she was able to get e-mail until yesterday when someone installed the latest version of the e-mail client. Ever since then, no luck.

Track possible approaches. The problem could be the e-mail client but is more likely a simple configuration problem. You decide to do the following:

1. Verify the IP address and configuration.
2. Test communication with the server.
3. Test communication with another computer other than the server.

The first thing to do is run `ipconfig /all` to verify the computer's current settings. You do this and find that the computer's IP address, subnet mask, and default gateway are all correct.

Next, you try pinging the server and get no response. You now try using ping in a methodical process to determine where the failure is. You try pinging the default gateway (router) and you do receive a response. You don't know if there's another router between your default gateway and the e-mail server, but you can find out by using TraceRT. TraceRT returns success messages from three routers but fails to find the e-mail server.

You now know that the local computer's configuration is fine and that the default gateway is up and running. You know that at least three routers between the local computer and the e-mail server are functional. What you need to know is whether the last router is passing the information directly to the e-mail server and the e-mail server is down, or whether there's another router beyond the third router that may be down.

When you pinged the e-mail server earlier, you did it by IP address. Now you try pinging by hostname. The attempt fails, but it does resolve the name to an IP address, so you can tell that name resolution is happening correctly. Looking at the address of the e-mail server, you try another address that should be another server on that same section of the network. The ping attempt to that address does respond.

NOTE Many network designers assign IP addresses in a set, predictable pattern. One common pattern is to assign all routers to the first 5 addresses on a subnet and servers to the last 20 addresses.

What you know now is that the network is working correctly all the way to the remote subnet where the server is located, but the server itself is still not responding. This would be a great time to call the administrator of that server to see if the server is running. Another possible solution is that the server may have an incorrect TCP/IP configuration. If the server *is* running, you should verify the configuration on the server to see if it can communicate with any other computer.

Troubleshooting IPX/SPX

IPX/SPX used to be the protocol of choice on Novell networks, and it still is in many. It's a fine, routable protocol, relatively fast and easy to configure. So why is it being mentioned in a troubleshooting section? Because there are settings that are frequently misconfigured. The problems with the IPX/SPX protocol stem from those options for configuration that must be set correctly for two computers to hold a conversation. Most notable is the setting for frame type.

Frame type refers to the manner in which data is packaged when placed on the physical wire. It describes the header and addressing fields, the error correction, and the overall size of the data that can be sent at one time. IPX/SPX supports five frame types: 802.2, 802.3, Ethernet II, Ethernet SNAP, and Token Ring. The most common are 802.2 and 802.3. Vista (like most operating systems) uses only one frame type at a time. Frame types are important because you must have the same frame type as the computer you're trying to communicate with. Mismatched frame types are probably the most common reason for failed communication over IPX/SPX.

In Microsoft networking, NWLink is called the IPX/SPX-compatible protocol even though it's fully compliant with all IPX/SPX standards. It's different only in that it provides a NetBIOS layer to facilitate name services on Microsoft network operating systems. For troubleshooting, that may or may not be important to know. What is important to know is that it's fully compliant with everyone else's IPX/SPX protocol.

Unlike TCP/IP in Vista, NWLink doesn't ship with a bunch of troubleshooting utilities. That's usually not a problem because most issues will be resolved in the configuration. The primary tool for checking your NWLink configuration will be either the Network Connections applet in Control Panel or `ipxroute.exe`. Using `ipxroute.exe` enables you to view the current configuration of NWLink for each network adapter in the computer and to modify the IPX/SPX routing table if the computer has more than one network interface. Entering the command **`ipxroute config`** at the command prompt will display the current configuration of NWLink.

The properties dialog box for NWLink on Vista covers the essentials—the adapter, the frame type, and the network number. The default setting for the frame type is Auto Detect. Microsoft tells us that this setting enables Vista to scan the frame types being transmitted across the wire and then pick the most prevalent type. In fact, what appears to happen is that Vista uses the very first frame type it comes across. Usually this will be correct. But on a network that utilizes multiple frame types, your Vista computer may choose the wrong frame type when it starts up, causing you to be cut off from the servers you need.

The other important setting on this page is the network number. IPX/SPX handles routing of information by using these network numbers to identify each unique section of a network. Every segment (the section of network between two routers) must be assigned a unique network number. The default setting in Vista takes care of that for you. When you're using Auto Detect for the frame type, it will also detect the local network number. If you change from Auto Detect to a specific frame type, you'll need to enter a valid network number. Contact your network administrator if necessary.

How Do You Troubleshoot Vista Network Architecture?

Although it's true that a good troubleshooting method can work you through almost any problem, at times you need to know more. In fact, I believe that the more you know about how something's put together, the easier it is to find what's wrong. That's certainly true of a complex system such as Vista.

Troubleshooting is the process of going from a big-picture view of things to a small-detail view. Asking questions is the primary tool for accomplishing this, but knowledge is also a valuable tool. Figure 19.22 shows the overall network architecture of Vista.

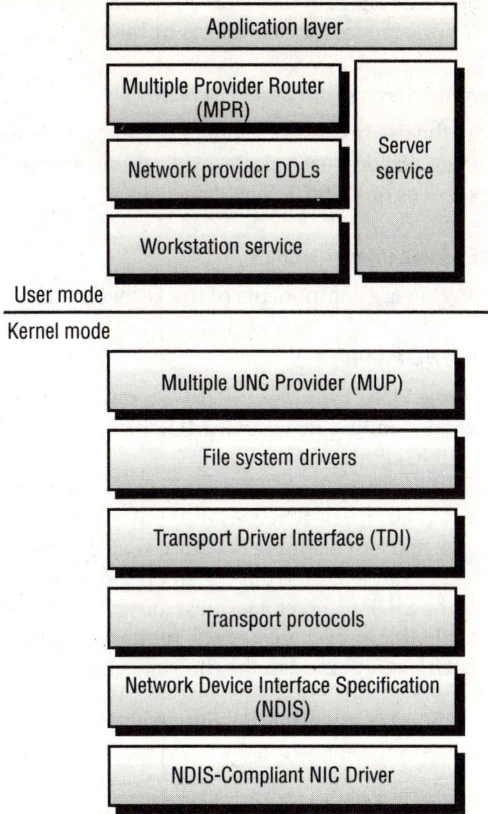

FIGURE 19.22
The network architecture of Vista.

USER MODE COMPONENTS

The following are components of the user mode.

Application Layer

The Application layer is where your program is accepting your network requests. For example, when you type in the URL of your favorite website, you're interacting with the Application layer.

NOTE This application layer is completely different from the OSI or TCP/IP application layer.

Multiple Provider Router

The Multiple Provider Router (MPR) is kind of like a traffic cop in that its job is to direct the flow of communication. Vista uses the MPR only when you're mapping a network drive. Its task is to decide which of the installed network clients will do the best job in making the drive mapping.

The MPR is contained in the file `mpr.dll`.

Network Provider DLL

A DLL is a dynamic link library, which is basically a file that contains support functions for a program. In this case, the library of functions is part of a network client that's installed in Vista.

There will be one provider DLL for each installed network client. The file for the native Vista client, LanmanWorkstation, for example, is `ntlanman.dll`.

Workstation Service and Server Service

These are the user mode components of the Workstation and Server services. Essentially, these are "stubs" that provide user mode applications with access to the kernel mode Workstation and Server services of Vista.

KERNEL MODE COMPONENTS

The following are components of the kernel mode.

Multiple UNC Provider

The Multiple UNC Provider (MUP) is a traffic cop like the MPR, except that instead of directing traffic when mapping drives, the MUP directs traffic when you're using a Universal Naming Convention (UNC) path.

You will be using the MUP's services whenever you click Start ➤ Run and type a path such as `\\Server5\Public`, or when your application connects to a server resource without mapping a drive letter first. An example is your e-mail program, which is configured to talk with one particular server to retrieve mail but doesn't require that you first map a drive to the share on the server.

When the MUP receives a request for service, its job is to decide which file system driver (which network client) can best answer the request and then send the request to that driver.

The MUP is contained in the file `mup.sys`.

NOTE The `.sys` extension files normally appear in `system32` folder subdirectories. In this case, the `mup.sys` file appears in the `\system32\drivers` folder.

File System Drivers

File system drivers are the network redirectors and servers. When you install network support in Vista, you always get two of these drivers by default. The first is the kernel mode component of the Workstation service, your native Vista client. The second is the kernel mode portion of the Server service.

Other file system drivers may be installed for other network clients. One common example is the driver for the Client Services for NetWare in Vista.

Transport Driver Interface

Transport Driver Interface (TDI) doesn't actually exist as a file. It is what its name implies, an interface between the file system drivers and the transport protocols. The TDI is *exposed* by the two layers—that is to say that any file system driver for Vista networking must support the functions used by TDI, and the same for the transport protocols.

This layered approach allows for portability and extensibility. Because of the TDI boundary layer, you can (in theory) install as many network clients and servers or as many protocols as you want on Vista.

Transport Protocols

These are the protocols used to communicate on your network. The files for each should be easy to identify because they're usually just the name of the protocol with a `.sys` extension.

In theory, you can install an unlimited number of protocols in Vista so long as they conform to the two boundaries in the network stack. Transport protocols must expose the TDI boundary on top and the NDIS layer on the bottom.

Network Device Interface Specification

Network Device Interface Specification (NDIS) is a boundary layer between the protocols and the adapter driver. But it has a more important job than that.

Years ago, when you wanted to develop a new driver for a network adapter card, you needed to think about details and settings such as the media access scheme, error detection and correction, frame types, and so on before you ever got to the part of the driver that just ran the card. NDIS was an effort by Microsoft, Intel, 3Com, and other companies to solve this problem. By conforming to a known standard, they could remove the common functions from the driver and load them into a library of functions that every network needs. Essentially, they wanted to stop reinventing the wheel every time they brought out another card.

NDIS, as it's implemented in Vista, is an interesting component. It's both a file and a boundary layer. As a file, `ndis.sys` is a driver file that acts like a DLL in that it loads into memory and anybody who knows how to talk to it can ask NDIS for support. As a boundary, it defines a standard form of communication between the transport protocols and the network adapter card.

NDIS-Compliant Network Adapter Driver

At the bottom of the stack but certainly very important, the network interface card (NIC) driver is responsible for error-free transmission and reception of data on the physical network medium.

Using the NDIS standard enables you to install as many NICs as you want in a computer (of course, you have only so many slots in your computer). As long as the drivers comply with the NDIS standard, you can bind multiple cards to one protocol or multiple protocols to one NIC.

The file containing the driver is named according to the naming convention of the manufacturer, but they all end with a `.sys` extension.

Quick Advice

As with many skills, troubleshooting is best learned by doing. There really is no good substitute for experience. To make things easier, though, keep in mind these quick tips when troubleshooting a network:

- Always check your connections. Try another network cable if possible.
- Check and double-check your IP configuration, including IP address, subnet mask, default gateway, and DNS server addresses.
- Run `ipconfig` and `ping`. Make sure you're set up properly, and see what, if anything, you *can* connect to.
- Look in Event Viewer for any errors.
- Use your help and online resources.
- Delete and reinstall the network adapter if necessary.

Also, the Windows Help and Support center has a lot of good information, including wizards, to assist in your troubleshooting. Take one step at a time, and if you make configuration changes, change one thing, test, and then change another if necessary. Don't change a bunch of stuff all at once, because you'll never know which change was the right one. One last thing—if you see someone troubleshooting a problem, and they say something like, "Huh, that's not supposed to happen," or "That's weird . . .," think about how silly a statement that *really* is. (I catch myself saying it, too!) If everything is working as advertised, then why are they troubleshooting in the first place?

Summary

In this chapter, we've looked at how to set up and configure a network, create shares, attach to network resources, use user profiles and hardware profiles, and troubleshoot your network when things go awry. The best fact you can learn from this chapter is that you need to work through network design, setup, configuration, and troubleshooting methodically. Take one step at a time.

A number of things make life easier when it comes to networks. I maintain a troubleshooting diary and refer to it when I need to troubleshoot a problem. You wouldn't believe the number of times that I see the same failure. Make sure you obtain the tools you need to work with your machines and keep them in one place. Spend some time documenting your network once you get it set up, because you won't have time to figure out the configuration when the system is down.

In the next chapter, we'll dive into a very popular topic these days—wireless networking. A wireless network provides all kinds of convenience, but it can also lay traps for you. One of the biggest issues with wireless is security problems due to incorrect configuration. The next chapter will help you get a good configuration; one that will work well and provide a measure of security for your data.

Chapter 20

Wireless Networking

Let's face it, cables are so yesterday. We live in a society that demands instant communication gratification. If you doubt that, look around at the number of cell phones and PDAs out there. Ten years ago if you had access to the Internet, you were cutting edge. Now, if you don't have your cell phone browser going during your taxi trip to the airport, you feel as though you're somewhat technically inadequate.

There's a lot of fuss about wireless everything these days. Is it all hype? Not really. Cables are bulky and ugly (even if you bought cool neon colors) and a pain to string. And if you ever decide to move your office from one room to another, guess what? Yep, time to rerun the cable.

In the last five years or so, wireless networking has gone from a luxury that only a few could afford (mostly businesses and then only for special needs) to a mainstream form of communication for both home and business. Wireless networking is what this chapter's all about. Here are the specifics:

- Current wireless standards
- Required hardware
- Additional security considerations
- Setting up Vista on a wireless network
- Using Windows Collaboration

Vista: What's New?

One of the biggest problems with wireless connections is that you're sending data using radio waves to anyone who cares to listen. The very feature that makes wireless connectivity so enticing is the same thing that makes it dangerous. Windows has always provided some level of security for wireless connections, but it was often difficult to use and not as complete as it should be. Vista overcomes some of these issues by making wireless connectivity easier to secure and far more automatic.

Vista supports a new technology for making wireless connections nearly automatic. Read about the new Link Layer Topology Discovery (LLTD) in the "Understanding LLTD" section of Chapter 19. In addition to LLTD, wireless users will enjoy the Windows Connect Now (WCN) technology. This new feature is the Microsoft implementation of the Wi-Fi Alliance standard currently named Simple Config.

Microsoft also provides more collaboration tools with Vista. These collaboration tools make it easier for people to know who's present on the network and invite them to work on projects using applications such as Windows Meeting Space. This chapter shows how to make your presence known and how to work with Windows Meeting Space, an application that has special significance in an environment where the connections are always changing.

Wireless Standards and Hardware

If you're unfamiliar with wireless networking, the idea of setting up this type of network might seem a bit daunting. You probably have a lot of questions. Are there extra security concerns? Yes. Do I need different hardware than for my old wired network? Yes. Is it as fast as my old wired network? No, but that probably won't matter much. Will the signals bother my goldfish? Not likely, unless their laptop doesn't have the right NIC.

Although desktop computers can, and often do, participate in wireless networks, this chapter will focus mainly on laptops. That is, after all, where the benefits of wireless networking truly shine. Before you dive into wireless, though, make sure you know what you're getting into by understanding the current standards and the hardware you'll need.

Wireless Standards

In your quest to set up a wireless network, you will undoubtedly come across the term *Wi-Fi* very quickly. It's short for *wireless fidelity*, pronounced "why-fy" (think "why fry," and get rid of the *r*), and it's the most common wireless standard you'll see today. More specifically, Wi-Fi refers to the collection of IEEE 802.11*x* standards; the name has been perpetuated by the Wi-Fi Alliance, a group of over 200 wireless hardware manufacturers and software providers established in 1999. Their goal was to ensure interoperability between wireless devices. They figured (correctly) that by getting together and branding the name Wi-Fi, they could have greater control over the development of the wireless networking business segment, as well as the associated profits.

All of this collaboration has been good for standardization within the wireless industry. Past computer history has shown us that superior technologies can easily lose out to inferior ones if the acceptance isn't there. Today, if a hardware or software product is "Wi-Fi Certified," you're assured that it will work with your existing Wi-Fi setup.

IEEE 802.11*x*

The Institute of Electrical and Electronics Engineers has been around since 1963, setting standards for the computer and electronics industries. The original 802.11 specification was approved in 1997. There are four common 802.11 standards floating around today:

- 802.11a
- 802.11b
- 802.11g
- 802.11n

The most common one you will see is 802.11b. This standard transmits at a frequency of 2.4GHz and provides data speeds of 11Mbps. The 802.11g standard is a newer version of 11b; it uses the same frequency but can provide data speeds of up to 54Mbps (although roughly 20Mbps is more common).

The "oddball" standard is 802.11a. It transmits at 5GHz and allows data speeds of 54Mbps. There's one key thing to note, and it's that 11a uses a different frequency than either 11b or 11g, meaning that it's not interoperable with the other two.

Just in case I didn't hammer that last point home well enough, let me say it again: 802.11a is *not* compatible with either 802.11b or 802.11g. However, because they run on the same frequency and use similar transmission methods, 11b and 11g will work together. This means that if you have a

NIC that supports only 11b but have a router that supports 11g, you won't have any problems. Of course, the NIC running 11b will still be slower than an 11g NIC, but it will still work.

The latest standard to appear is 802.11n. This new standard isn't even approved yet, but it's close and might be available by the time you read this. The 802.11n standard can use either 2.4GHz or 5GHz transmission. It boasts a maximum data rate of 540Mbps; although 200Mbps is typical. The best news is that this standard lets you transmit up to 250 meters—100 meters was the maximum in previous standards.

Bluetooth

The most popular competing standard to Wi-Fi is Bluetooth. Like Wi-Fi, Bluetooth also has a supporting group, called the Bluetooth Special Interest Group. This group includes Microsoft, Intel, IBM, Apple, and Toshiba, as well as cell phone powers Ericsson, Nokia, and Motorola. Although most commonly referred to by the catchy Bluetooth name, it's also occasionally referred to as IEEE 802.15.1.

So far, Bluetooth hasn't achieved quite as much widespread popularity in networking as Wi-Fi. However, Bluetooth technology is not to be discounted. It's being used with a lot of laptops, peripheral devices (keyboards, mice, printers), PDAs, and cell phones, as well as with wireless automobile communications packages. Toyota and BMW are among the auto manufacturers that offer Bluetooth-enabled hands-free phone options.

Bluetooth operates in the 2.4GHz frequency, but because of differing transmission standards, it isn't interoperable with Wi-Fi. In fact, if you have Bluetooth devices and Wi-Fi devices operating in the same space, it's possible you'll experience some communication problems from time to time. It used to be worse, but in recent times, makers of both types of devices have worked on ways to eliminate interference.

Wi-Fi or Bluetooth: Which One Should You Choose?

The makers of Bluetooth devices will tell you that their standard isn't in direct competition with Wi-Fi, and it's for good reason. Although they transmit at the same frequency, Bluetooth's speed (about 700Kbps) is considerably slower than Wi-Fi's. That might make you wonder why anyone would use Bluetooth.

The two technologies really are best used in different applications. Wi-Fi is intended to be used as a wireless local area network (WLAN) technology, whereas Bluetooth is better suited for a wireless personal area network (WPAN). What's the difference? Distance, power, and devices. Wi-Fi signals are pretty reliable for a couple of hundred feet, but Bluetooth signals typically have a strength of about 30 feet. Since Bluetooth isn't designed to transmit as far, Bluetooth devices use significantly less power than Wi-Fi devices. This, in turn, makes them cheaper as well.

Here's the bottom line: for a network, go with Wi-Fi, unless you have found a compelling reason not to. Bluetooth will serve you better with devices such as cell phones, PDAs, and wireless peripherals such as keyboards, mice, and printers.

Hardware

After reading Chapter 18 and Chapter 19, you should be pretty familiar with the types of devices needed for networking. With wireless networking, only a few things change. One, no more talk of Cat 6. Two, the devices have to be wireless enabled, which means they'll be slightly more expensive than their wired counterparts.

Network Adapters

The key to selecting a NIC for your wireless network is to make sure it supports the right standard. For example, if your network is going to run 802.11g, be sure you don't buy an 11a card. It won't work. However, keep in mind that 11b and 11g are compatible, so you won't have problems with those two standards. In fact, a lot of cards are marked 11b/g, just as years ago wired NICs were labeled 10/100.

If you're setting up a desktop computer for a wireless network, make sure you have a free PCI slot available for your wireless NIC. Don't worry if your computer is under a desk; neither Wi-Fi nor Bluetooth requires a line of sight to communicate. That being said, thick obstructions such as steel or concrete walls can hinder wireless signals.

For laptops, you have a lot more wireless NIC options. Many computer manufacturers give you the option to have a wireless NIC built into your case. If you can get it, do it. In these situations, the antenna for the NIC is generally built into the case as well, so you usually get good reception. At the same time, this option frees up your PCMCIA slots and USB ports for other peripherals.

If you don't want to or can't go with a built-in NIC, then your choices are PCMCIA and USB. Both work equally well, so the most important consideration when buying a PCMCIA or a USB wireless NIC is convenience. Most laptops' USB ports are on the side of the computer, but the location of USB ports vary. For example, one of my laptops has only one USB port, and it's located on the back of the system. It's not very convenient to get to, and if I had to push my system up against the back wall of a desk, that would cause problems. Figure 20.1 shows you a USB NIC.

USB NICs are smaller and fit easily into your pocket when you're on the move, but it's not like PCMCIA NICs are huge and bulky either. In the end, your purchase decision will probably boil down to brand and price.

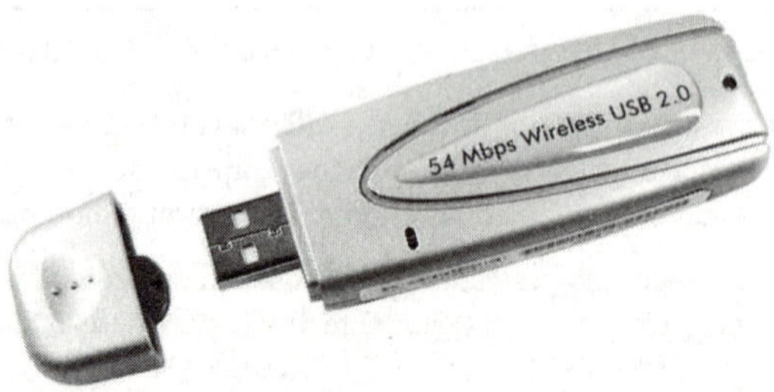

Figure 20.1
USB wireless NIC

WARNING Not all PCMCIA cards are created equal. You may find that your new laptop won't accept older PCMCIA cards. In fact, most newer laptop computers accept only USB or newer PCMCIA Type 2 cards.

Centrino

In the last section, I mentioned that many laptops come with built-in wireless NICs. If your laptop has the Intel Centrino chipset in it, then you are included in this group.

Centrino is Intel's product name for its Pentium M processor, packaged with an Intel 855 chipset for memory management and an Intel PRO/Wireless network card. As of this writing, there are three Intel PRO/Wireless options, summarized in Table 18.1.

TABLE 20.1: Intel PRO/Wireless Network Adapters

VERSION	SUPPORTED STANDARDS
PRO/Wireless 2100	802.11b
PRO/Wireless 2100A	802.11a and 802.11b
PRO/Wireless 2100BG	802.11b and 802.11g

Each of these adapters has Intel's Wireless Coexistence System built in to help reduce interference between itself and Bluetooth devices. In addition, because they're packaged with the power-saving Pentium M, these adapters take less power than a PCMCIA NIC, saving precious battery life.

CONNECTIVITY DEVICES

Once again, wireless networks parallel their wired counterparts. Just as with a wired network, you will need a device to connect the computers together. For wired networks, that choice is usually a hub or a switch, and if you have a larger network (or need segmentation), you connect the hubs and switches to a router. Wireless terminology is pretty similar, but you have slightly different options.

When you go to the computer store, you'll be stunned by the number of devices you can choose from. And for the most part, they each look the same. Which one do you choose?

The two main types of devices you will see are wireless access points (WAPs) and wireless routers. A WAP is basically a wireless hub. Wireless routers do the same thing that wired routers do. On wireless networks, though, instead of "plugging" all of your computers into a WAP and then connecting the WAP to a router, all you need is a router, and the computers can communicate directly with it. Price points for WAPs and wireless routers are usually similar, so the deciding factor will be functionality. If you're setting up a home network and have a few computers that need Internet access through your cable modem or DSL, then the router is the way to go. If you don't want anything to do with the Internet, or if your Internet access is already managed by another router, then a WAP will be just fine.

NOTE The majority of wireless routers have a few wired ports on them as well. This allows you to plug in computers that don't have a wireless card. In addition, there will usually be a wired port for your cable modem or DSL connection.

The prices of wireless routers have come down considerably in recent years, which has probably helped their popularity. If you shop the big electronics retailers, you can find 802.11b devices for around $40–$50, whereas the 11g ones will cost closer to $80–$100. Of course, if you want to, you can probably spend a lot more than that. If you don't have a NIC, and you need that as well as the router, you can find wireless kits for around $30 more than just the router.

Faster Technologies

It seems that we're constantly striving for faster speeds, more storage space, and the like when it comes to computers. Once the latest and greatest fastest technology comes out, it's no longer fast enough. We want more.

To that end, wireless router manufacturers have released products designed to go above and beyond 802.11g speeds. These new technologies promise data transfer speeds of up to108Mbps while maintaining compatibility with 11Mbps 11b and 54Mbps 11g. The caveat is that you have to purchase a more expensive router (of course), along with their special, more expensive NIC that supports those speeds (of course).

There's no official name for this technology yet. D-Link calls theirs "Xtreme G," and Netgear refers to theirs as "Super G." Once again, it just goes to prove that if you want to spend the money, someone is sure to have a product to fit your needs.

Security Concerns

Security on a wireless network is a much, much bigger issue than it is on a wired network. That's not to say that wired security isn't important, either. But when you look at how signals are transmitted—through the air—you really have to stop and think about how much easier it is to intercept those signals as opposed to the ones transmitted over a cable.

When you get your wireless router home and plug it in, one of the first things you will need to do is configure it. The outside port of your router (the one that gets the IP address from your ISP) will have a public IP address, and the inside ports should all have private IP addresses. This is the first step to securing your network, because private IP addresses are not "available" to computers on the Internet. The other thing that you need to take care of immediately is to change the defaults on the domain name used by the router and the password required to gain access to that router. Generally, there are two separate passwords. The first is required to gain administrative access to the router. Obviously, this is a good one to change. The second is the one needed to use the wireless signal. Change that as well. Your router's documentation should have step-by-step instructions on how to do this.

It might not sound like a big deal, but it really is. At the very least, someone sitting in their car on the street outside your house (or in your apartment building) could browse the Internet on your dime. More important, that same person is *on* your network, meaning that with just a little handiwork, they could be accessing files on your system (bank account information, anyone?), reading your e-mail, sending e-mail for you, and performing a variety of other nefarious activities.

Recently, one of my local TV station's news teams went on a security-themed scavenger hunt. They found a local security consultant and, armed with a Wi-Fi–enabled PDA, traipsed through several neighborhoods. The consultant found plenty of signals. That was no surprise. What was surprising was that over half of the networks he located did *not* have the default domain name or password changed. The owner had basically just plugged the router in and let it go. Now, if you're a hacker, this will make you salivate uncontrollably. If you're not, please, please remember that if you're setting up a wireless network, take every security precaution you can lest you get burned.

Any self-respecting wireless router will have a firewall option. Enable it. (Of course, enabling it and leaving the default password settings is still pointless. You might as well leave your front door open, put a sign in your front yard saying, "Take whatever you want from inside!" and go on vacation for two weeks.) Also, don't forget about enabling Windows Firewall, which we covered in Chapter 14.

Wireless Vista

Vista supports wireless networking just as well as it supports wired networking. In this section, we will look at some of the specific Vista features related to wireless networking, as well as how to configure Vista to work on a wireless network.

Vista Wireless Support

The big thing to remember about wireless in Vista is that it's easier. The use of LLTD means that you don't have to fight with Vista to locate and use your wireless device as long as Vista can discover the device at all. Even if your device has low signal strength or other problems, Vista is likely to discover it and even help you correct the problem.

The new WCN technology also means that you don't spend as much time trying to configure your wireless device. You can attach an wireless router to a network with Vista and Vista will use the wired Ethernet connection to discover and configure the device. All you need to do is provide a four-or eight-digit Personal Identification Number (PIN) to verify that you have permission to configure the device. As with LLTD, WCN works best when your hardware has the required firmware installed. Look for vendors to provide updates to their products to support WCN. In fact, Buffalo Technology and D-Link Systems are just two of many vendors working on WCN updates. You can see the detailed WCN specification at `http://www.microsoft.com/whdc/Rally/WCN-UFD_XPspec.mspx`.

NOTE WCN isn't just for Vista users. You can read about the Windows XP WCN update at `http://www.microsoft.com/windowsxp/using/networking/learnmore/bowman_05june13.mspx`.

Of course, wireless doesn't just mean hardware and firmware support, you must also have operating system support. One of the key wireless features Vista provides is its WLAN AutoConfig (Wireless Local Area Network Automatic Configuration) service. This service is designed to help detect wireless networks visible to your network card as well as automatically configure your computer to participate on that network. Vista supports both Wi-Fi and Bluetooth networking.

TO B OR NOT TO G? THAT IS THE QUESTION.

You're at the store. The salesperson is smiling at you. There are literally dozens of different models of wireless routers sitting in front of you. For some reason, the salesperson is recommending one of the more expensive models. What do you do?

Buying computer hardware is always a tradeoff of wants versus needs. Sure, you want the quad flat-screen setup with a separate CD/DVD tower, but do you really need it? Probably not.

In wireless networking, your primary choices are 802.11b and 802.11g, with 11g being up to five times faster than 11b. One of the common reasons I hear for going with 11g is, "Well, I want to speed up my Internet." That's not a good reason. In fact, it's a bit silly. Even if you have great high-speed access, such as a cable modem or DSL, you will be lucky to get 1Mbps. Ever. Even if you run 11b, you will have 11Mbps internally. Boosting that to 54Mbps or even 108Mbps doesn't do anything to make your DSL line transmit or receive data to and from the phone company any faster.

On the other hand, if you do have a lot of internal networking going on, then the upgrade to 11g might well justify the costs. For example, if you transfer a lot of large graphics files internally, or if you are really into multiplayer action games, then 11g makes a lot of sense. Just make sure you get NICs that support 11g as well.

If cost isn't an issue, then there's absolutely no harm in going with 11g, even if you don't need it. Just don't get upset if you aren't able to download music files (legally, of course) any faster.

When 802.11n comes along, you'll have another choice to make. Given Vista's incredible graphics requirements, you might find that 802.11n is a good choice for collaboration or Remote Desktop use. The point is that you shouldn't get more speed than you need to get the job done when cost is an issue.

While Vista is generally very good about detecting available wireless signals, there might be an occasion where you want to look for one manually. Perhaps you're near an Internet cafe and want to look for a signal, or you're in a restaurant that has a hotspot. (Even McDonalds is granting wireless access in selected restaurants as part of its "I'm Lovin' It" program.) To look for a signal, right-click on Network and select Properties, click the Manage network connections link, right-click your wireless connection, and choose View Available Wireless Networks. Vista will look for wireless connections and display a dialog box that contains a list of them. Highlight the connection you want to use and click Connect.

Security should also be on your mind. Vista supports the Wi-Fi Protected Access (WPA) standard, as well as Wired Equivalent Privacy (WEP) encryption. If you use WPA, WEP is optional. WPA has two alternatives for encryption: Temporal Key Integrity Protocol (TKIP) and the Advanced Encryption Standard (AES). They're both newer and more secure than WEP. The wireless access point you connect to will likely support either WEP or WPA, and some will support both as more and more clients transition to WPA. This isn't something you'll probably be actively thinking about when trying to get on a network, but you never know what problems will pop up.

Creating a USB Key Configuration

Even with LLTD and WCN, you might run into a situation where Vista can't detect your wireless network. In this case, you have another alternative as long as your device supports USB. You can copy the required information to a USB key (flash drive or thumb drive) and then place the USB key in the device to configure it.

Use the following steps to create the key.

1. Right-click Network and choose Properties from the context menu to display the Network and Sharing Center.
2. Click the Set up a connection or network link to display the Set up a connection or network dialog box.
3. Click Set up a wireless router or access point. Vista displays an informational dialog box.
4. Click Next. Vista tries to detect the wireless network and fails. Be patient, this step typically requires up to a minute to complete.
5. Click Create wireless network settings and save to USB flash drive.
6. Type a Service Set Identifier (SSID) in the Network name field. Click Next.
7. Type a passphrase in the Passphrase field or use the default that Microsoft provides for you. Clear the Display characters option if you want to maximize security (this option lets you see the characters as you type them, which means you're less likely to make a mistake). Click Next. Click Continue to get past the usual UAC warning.
8. Choose the file and printer settings you want to use with the wireless device. You have the following options:

   Do not allow file and printer sharing Selecting this option means that you won't be able to share files or a printer with the wireless devices. This option works fine with some devices, but not with others. For example, you need to allow file sharing at least when working with a camera. However, setting up a wireless network with a laptop could work fine without file or printer sharing support.

Allow sharing with anyone with a user account and password for this computer Selecting this option means that someone who would normally have access to your computer can share the files and printers. This is a safe option in most cases because the person requesting access would have the required security anyway. However, if the person isn't careful with their username and password, a cracker could still gain access to their machine by stealing the other person's credentials. In short, you must be aware of security problems from both the technical and human standpoint when making this selection.

Allow sharing with anyone on the same network as this computer Selecting this option means that you're opening file and printer access to everyone on your network. Don't choose this option if you disallow access using a wired connection. This is the least secure method of sharing access.

Keep the custom settings I currently have Selecting this option means that the wireless connection will observe all of the security policies you currently have set for your system. This is the most consistent method of sharing the wireless connection. It means that no one will unexpectedly find they can't access your system using a wireless device.

9. Click Next. Vista copies the settings to the USB device.
10. Insert the USB device and follow the device vendor's instructions for modifying the settings.

Connecting Vista to a Wireless Network

The first thing you need to do is to install your wireless network adapter. If you have a desktop computer, follow these steps:

1. Turn off and unplug each computer that will be part of your network.
2. At each computer, open the case and insert a NIC in an empty slot, screwing the card in securely so it won't come loose.
3. Replace the case.
4. Make sure the wireless router (or access point) is turned on and configured (see the "Creating a USB Key Configuration" section of the chapter if Vista doesn't configure the router or access point automatically), and then turn on all connected computers.

Vista supports Plug and Play, so the network card driver should be installed automatically. In addition, the card will normally detect the network signal. If not, you'll want to scan for networks, as mentioned in the "Vista Wireless Support" section.

For laptop computers, the process is even easier:

1. Insert your network card into the appropriate (USB or PCMCIA) slot.

That's it. Plug and Play will detect the card and begin the installation process for you. You'll see a pop-up notification in the notification area (next to the clock), and the drivers will be installed. When the Found New Hardware Wizard is finished, you'll see a successful installation message.

You might need to reboot your computer after installing the card. Subsequently, when you plug in the network card, it will be automatically detected, and you won't need to reboot to use it.

Troubleshooting Wireless Connections

The first thing you should check when troubleshooting an issue that relates to hardware is whether or not your device is listed in the Windows Catalog (known as the Hardware Compatibility List for older Windows versions). It can be accessed at `http://www.microsoft.com/windows/catalog`. If it's not listed, then get a new NIC.

Provided that your NIC is compatible with Vista, check the drivers. It's always important to make sure these are installed properly. Find your NIC in Device Manager.

If there's a red X or an exclamation mark in a yellow circle over the icon for the adapter, there's a problem. Also, a NIC showing up under a category called Other Devices usually indicates a driver problem as well. Right-clicking the NIC and selecting Properties should tell you that the device is functioning properly.

If it's not installed properly, right-click the card, select Properties, and go to the Driver tab. There, click the Update Driver button, and follow the instructions.

Finally, always be mindful of signal strength. By checking your connection's properties, you should be able to see it. Climate conditions, obstacles, and the mood of your network card can all affect signal strength. Poor signals (zero to two bars) can cause severe communications problems.

Other than the suggestions listed here, troubleshooting wireless networks is just like troubleshooting their wired cousins. For more network troubleshooting information, consult the "Troubleshooting Vista Networking" section in Chapter 19.

Using Windows Collaboration

Vista provides a number of collaboration features that makes it easy to create an ad hoc work group. Your friends and you can get together, create a wireless setup, and get to work together almost immediately. Of course, these features also work with desktop computers using a wired connection.

Configuring People Near Me

The People Near Me applet of the Control Panel lets you configure and sign into the People Near Me service. After you sign into the service, other people can find you and send you invitations to join meetings or engage in other activities. The idea is that you sign into People Near Me when you start Vista and sign out when you shut down. Using this approach, people will know when you're available to work with them on a project.

You'll begin by configuring People Near Me. Open the People Near Me applet of the Control Panel and you'll see the Settings tab shown in Figure 20.2. Set your name and picture as desired (the applet defaults to whatever picture you have set for the system or no picture at all). Make sure you select an Allow invitations from option. Unless you're overly friendly, you'll probably want to avoid the Anyone setting. A better setting is Trusted contacts (which means people you have added to your Windows Contacts list) or No one (which means people can still find you, they just can't send you invitations). If you plan to use People Near Me every day, make sure you check the Sign me in automatically when Windows starts option.

Configuring People Near Me won't log you on the first time (or subsequent times if you don't choose the Sign me in automatically when Windows starts option). Select the Sign in tab and you'll see sign in and sign out option. To sign in, choose the Sign in to People Near Me and click OK. If this is your first log in, People Near Me will display a summary dialog box where you can change the default options. Make any required changes and click OK. Likewise, to sign out, choose Sign out of People Near Me and click OK.

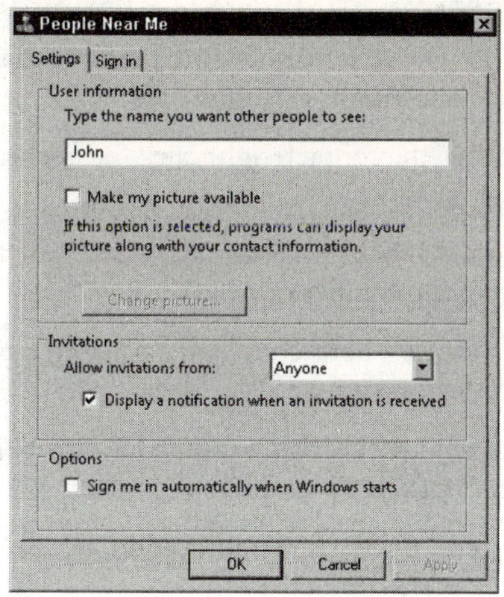

FIGURE 20.2
Configure People Near Me to reflect the invitations you want to accept.

Using Windows Contacts

Windows Contacts is the Vista replacement for Windows Address Book. It offers more functionality and you'll find that many Vista applications rely on Windows Contacts. For example, you'll use it with both Windows Mail and Windows Meeting Space. The actual contact files appear in your Contacts folder with a contact extension. Internally, the files are XML, so you can use any XML technology you wish to view them.

Windows Contacts begins with all of the users on the local machine as contacts. To open Windows Contacts, choose Start ➤ All Programs ➤ Windows Contacts. You'll see a list of contacts in a standard folder as shown in Figure 20.3.

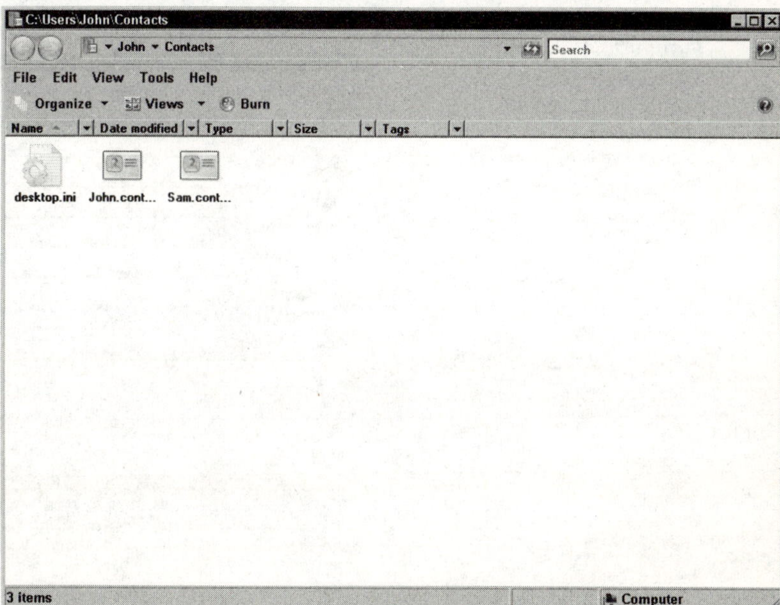

FIGURE 20.3
Add, delete, and use contacts.

USING CONTACTS

You can use Windows Contacts to perform some tasks without opening any other application. The following list contains common uses.

- To call the contact, right-click the contact entry and choose Action ➤ Call This Contact from the context menu.
- To send the contact e-mail, right-click the contact entry and chose Action ➤ Send E-mail from the context menu.
- To create a hard copy of the contact, right-click the contact entry and choose Print from the context menu.
- To send the contact to someone else, right-click the contact entry and choose Send Contact from the context menu.
- To edit the contact information, double-click the contact entry.

ADDING CONTACTS

You'll probably want to contact more than just the people on the local machine, so at some point, you'll need to add contacts. Vista provides a number of options for performing this task. For example, you can add contacts using Windows Mail. Simply right-click the mail entry and choose Add Sender to Contacts. You'll still need to open Windows Contacts and edit the entry afterward, but the new entry will include a name and e-mail address based on the mail message.

A more direct method of entering new contacts is to open Windows Contacts, right-click in any blank area, and choose New ➤ Contact from the context menu. You'll see a Properties dialog box like the one shown in Figure 20.4. As you can see, there are tabs to define the contact's identification, home information (address and telephone number), work information, personal information, notes you need when talking with the person, and even a digital ID so you know that you can trust contact with the person. When you finish filling out the details, click OK.

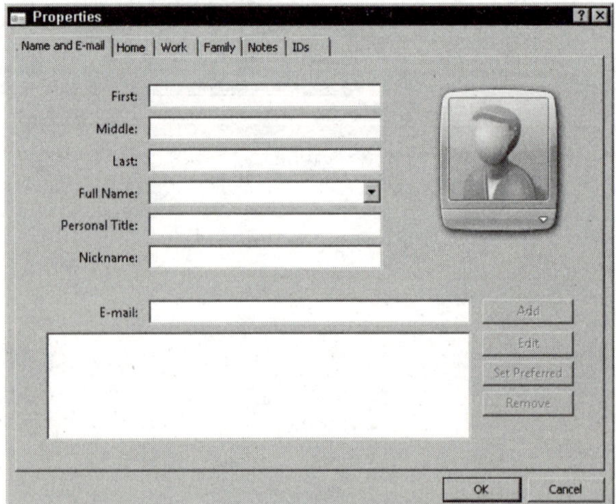

FIGURE 20.4
Vista lets you add a lot of information about new contacts.

Deleting Contacts

Nothing is worse than having a lot of old contacts that you never see anymore. Removing a contact is easy. Right-click the contact entry and choose Delete from the context menu. Windows Contacts will ask if you're sure you want to delete the entry. Click Yes and Windows Contacts will place the entry in your Recycle Bin (where you can recover it if you change your mind).

Summary

Wireless networking is the wave of the present and the future. Wireless installations are growing exponentially, and it's only a matter of time before there are more networks using wireless (at least partially) than completely wired networks. This chapter examined the current wireless networking standards, as well as the hardware required to install a wireless network. Also covered were wireless considerations, such as extra security, and how to make your Vista computer work on a wireless network.

If you haven't tried a wireless setup with Vista yet, now is the time to try. Unlike previous versions of Windows, you'll find that setting up your own wireless network is a pleasure, rather than a pain. Make sure you take time to plan the network out and get the right equipment to match your needs. Consider getting 802.11n if you don't already have an investment in wireless technology, since this updated standard will likely provide good throughput for Vista's graphics-heavy displays.

I've mentioned security several times in this chapter and how security becomes more important on wireless networks. The next chapter will cover many more aspects of Vista security to help you ensure that your files and programs are as safe as they can be.

Chapter 21

Vista Security

In Chapter 19, I walked you through the steps for creating and configuring a network, but one big piece of the networking pie is still missing: securing the resources on your network. From its inception, the NT family of operating systems was designed with security as a primary feature, and, of course, this architectural element is omnipresent in Vista. In fact, with Vista, Microsoft sacrificed backward compatibility and even some applications for the sake of security. Vista is so secure that some people feel Microsoft has gone too far. The sad thing is that even Microsoft can't protect users from themselves—more about this issue as the chapter progresses.

One of the first things you'll notice about Vista security is that Vista requires you to create a user account for yourself right on your PC before you can do anything on that PC. Yes, the idea that you must create your own user account on your own PC before you can do anything with the PC is unusual; most other Windows-based operating systems don't have this requirement (with the exception of Windows XP). If you're accustomed to working in a networked environment, you're probably used to needing individual domain-based user accounts, but not particular accounts on a workstation. But—as your father might say when you complain that something you don't like isn't fair—get used to it!

The user account is an integral part of Vista and has some great benefits. For example, suppose you and Sue share a computer. You can set up the computer so that you own a folder on the hard disk and Sue owns another folder on the hard disk, and *it is completely impossible for Sue to access your data* (and vice versa) unless you give her permission.

In addition, you can restrict access to files and folders by setting permissions. As you may recall, in Vista you can use the FAT, FAT32, or NTFS file system. If you use either FAT system, you can exercise only a limited amount of control over file and folder access, but if you use the NTFS system, you can exercise a great deal of control—whether the files are on your local computer or on your network.

In this chapter, we'll first look at how to set up user accounts, and then we'll look in detail at establishing permissions for shares, files, and folders. Finally, we'll examine Security Center. You'll learn about the following topics:

- Understanding and creating accounts in Vista
- Understanding the New Account Settings
- Setting permissions
- Understanding ownership
- Using Security Center
- Working with BitLocker
- Working with CardSpace

NOTE A single chapter can't possibly provide complete coverage of the huge topic of Vista security. What this chapter provides are the essentials. If you want to see the bigger picture and obtain the full security details, check out *Administering Windows Vista Security: The Big Surprises* by Mark Minasi and Byron Hynes (Sybex, 2007).

Vista: What's New?

The difficult part of Vista security is figuring out where to begin. Microsoft made radical changes to Windows security in Vista, so you'll need to get used to a different way of working. The biggest change to affect the network administrator is that no one has an actual administrator account. Every user has standard user rights. The standard user is a blanket level of security, not an actual group. To perform administrator tasks, the administrator must now request an elevation of rights from standard user to administrator. Windows will ask whether you want this elevation every time you need additional rights to perform a task, or you can tell the system to perform a certain task as an administrator. The result is that any task that might compromise the system requires your permission.

WARNING Every time Microsoft does more of the security thinking for you, it's tempting to think that this security is somehow foolproof. Microsoft can secure the system, secure the user, and even make it difficult to perform certain tasks. However, in the end, Microsoft can't protect a user from bad decisions. A user will always find ways to overcome the security features, view them as unnecessary, and generally disdain any help Microsoft might try to provide. The only way to overcome such thinking is through training, written policies and procedures that you strictly enforce, and, in some cases, coercion. If there aren't any negative effects from disregarding prudent computing, the user has little or no reason to change bad computing habits that result in data loss and other unfortunate problems.

Vista takes a pessimistic view of security. Many of the chapters in this book have discussed these new security procedures. For example, you can't create a file in the root directory of a drive. You must instead create a folder, give yourself permission to access it, and then create files in that folder. Microsoft would actually prefer that you do everything in your own user folder (a kind of sandbox) and not access the rest of the drive at all. In fact, the way Vista is designed, you have to go out of your way to get to other areas of the hard drive.

The Vista pessimistic security view goes even further than local resources. It treats all external drives, even those on the LAN, as Internet zone resources. This means you can't execute an application on a remote drive unless you give yourself permission to do so. In short, even if someone else gets a virus, it's less likely to travel to your machine.

Besides all of the user constraints in Vista, you'll also find new features for protecting your data. One of the most interesting features is BitLocker—an encryption technology that protects an entire disk. This technology makes it incredibly hard (nothing is ever impossible in security) to read your drive, even if the person trying to read it should take the drive out and move it to another system. In order to unlock the drive, you must provide the proper credentials. This feature is a boon for businesses because stolen or lost laptops are no longer the liability they once were. Sure, you still lose the device and any work you had on it, but you don't have to worry about someone compromising your data (and opening you to liability) as well.

Another feature is CardSpace. This tool lets you create a relationship with websites and online services that you trust. Using CardSpace provides a consistent way for websites and online services to request data from you and for you to examine their identification. The first question many people ask is how CardSpace differs from any other identity security mechanism. Crackers have easily overcome past efforts and placed their information as a trusted location within the application. CardSpace uses the secure desktop to perform all tasks. The secure desktop is inaccessible from the outside world and is even secure against local applications. You'll notice when you use CardSpace that you can't access any other application. The isolation of CardSpace means that only you can provide input to it and, therefore, the identities are indeed trustworthy.

Understanding User Accounts in Vista

As you've just read, you must create separate user accounts on a Vista machine before any user can log on to the workstation—and, unlike Windows 9*x*, Vista won't let you get anywhere until you log on. However, even after you log on, your rights are severely limited, which means you can't accidentally cause security problems—at least, not nearly as easily as before. See the "Understanding the New Account Settings" section of the chapter for additional details on these new restrictions and what they mean to you.

If your computer is part of a Vista client-server network, two types of user accounts are available: domain accounts and local accounts. A domain account gives you access to the network and to the network resources for which you have permission. The level of access depends on the zone that you set for that drive, with the Trusted Site zone providing the most access. The manager of the server normally sets up domain accounts, which are stored in a directory on the server. The directory can be either Active Directory or a Windows NT domain directory.

A local user account is valid only on your local computer; local user accounts sit in a database called the *Security Accounts Manager*, or SAM. You create user accounts with the Users and Passwords applet, which you'll meet later in this chapter.

In this chapter, I'm going to talk about local user accounts only. If you happen to be working in a domain on a network and you need help creating domain user accounts, take a look at *Mastering Windows 2000 Server*, Fourth Edition (Sybex, 2002), or *Mastering Windows Server 2003* (Sybex, 2003), depending on the type of domain you have. I also talk about joining domains in Chapter 22.

Before I get into how you change or create an account, we need to look at the types of accounts in Vista. The two broad categories are users and groups. A user account identifies a user on the basis of their username and password. A group account contains other accounts, and these accounts share common privileges. All users run as standard users and elevate their privileges as needed to perform specific tasks. This security feature is a major change from previous versions of Windows. Consequently, even administrators run as standard users, although they're part of the Administrators group. However, an administrator has the option of elevating privileges to perform tasks, such as adding a new user.

User accounts are of three types:

Computer Administrator This account has full and complete rights to the computer and can do just about anything to the computer. However, any advanced task will require that you give yourself permission through the User Access Control (UAC) dialog box. The Computer Administrator account was created during installation and setup of Vista. You'll need to log on as Computer Administrator when you want to create new accounts, take ownership of files or other objects, install software that will be available to all users, and so on.

NOTE Vista also provides an actual Administrator account. This account is disabled and inaccessible by default. It doesn't have the same limits as a user account that is part of the Administrators group—you don't have to give yourself permission to perform any advanced task. However, after months of working with Vista I found no reason at all to activate the Administrator account and feel it might be dangerous to do so giving the current computing environment. If you insist on using the actual Administrator account, however, you can activate it by opening a command prompt with elevated privileges (right-click the Command Prompt entry and choose Run as Administrator from the context menu), typing **`net user administrator P@s$word /active:yes`** (where P@s$word is the password you want to use), and pressing Enter. The reason that the actual Administrator account is so dangerous is that it allows anyone who accesses your machine to perform any task in your name without raising errors.

Limited This account is intended for use by regular users, those who shouldn't be allowed to install software or hardware or change their username. Someone with a Limited account can change their password and logon picture.

Guest This built-in account allows a user to log on to the computer even though the user does not have an account. No password is associated with the Guest account. It's disabled by default, and you should leave it that way. If you want to give a visitor or an occasional user access to the system, create an account for that person, and then delete the account when it's no longer needed.

As I said earlier, a group is an account that contains other accounts, and a group is defined by function. People who want to log in to the computer will never log in as a group; everyone logs in as a user. However, when a user logs in, they receive the permissions and rights associated with any and all groups they belong to. Using groups allows the system administrator to easily create collections of users who all have identical privileges. By default, every Vista system contains the following built-in groups:

Administrators Can do just about anything to the computer. The things that they can do that no other type of user can do include loading and unloading device drivers, managing security audit functions, and taking ownership of files and other objects. All administrators run as standard users until they tell Vista to elevate their privileges to perform specific tasks.

Backup Operators Can log on to the computer and run backups or perform restores. You might put someone in this group if you want them to be able to get on your system and run backups but not to have complete administrative control. Backup operators can also shut down the system but can't change security settings.

Cryptographic Operators Can perform cryptographic tasks, such as encrypting files. The reason for this new group is that some crackers have employed a new scheme to get money out of less technical users. They encrypt all of the data files on a system and hold the data ransom until the user pays the cracker a fee. If a user doesn't belong to the Cryptographic Operators group, crackers will find it impossible to employ this particular scheme.

Distributed COM Users Can access components using DCOM. The Component Object Model (COM) is a technology for using code outside of an application. By letting everyone use a piece of common code, such as the code required to display a dialog box, Windows can conserve resources and work faster. Microsoft calls this external piece of code a *component*. Distributed COM (DCOM) is the same idea. However, instead of accessing the component on a local machine, you access the component on another machine. For example, you might choose to access a common component on a server. The advantages of this approach are many, but for the purposes of this chapter, the biggest advantages are that using a single component makes it easier for a developer to make updates to the code and everyone gets the change at the same time. However, as you might imagine, accessing code on another machine is a security risk. Consequently, Microsoft has added to Vista a new group that has the right to access components on another machine. Since using DCOM is a common practice for business applications, you might find that users who don't belong to this group have a very tough time getting an application that uses DCOM to work, even if they do remember to change settings such as configuring the server as part of the user's Trusted zone. (See the "Understanding Network Access Restrictions" section of the chapter for details on zone requirements.)

Event Log Readers Can read the Event Log. The Vista Event Log is a significant change from previous versions of Windows. You really won't recognize it (see the "Using Event Viewer" section of Chapter 25 for details). Because the new Event Log provides so much information, giving everyone access to it might pose security problems. Consequently, in order to view the Event Log now, you must be part of the Event Log Readers group. Given that most users really don't have a reason to review the Event Log, this restriction isn't going to cause problems.

Guests Have minimal access to network resources. As I mentioned earlier, creating user accounts for occasional users is a much safer bet than using Guest accounts.

IIS_IUSRS Can access the machine anonymously using a web connection. Windows has always provided a special group for anonymous web access to a system. If you install Internet Information Server (IIS), you'll see the IIS_IUSRS group in Vista. This group provides a special level of access for anonymous web users. Generally, you'll restrict access to ensure that no one accessing the system over the Internet can cause havoc on your network. When someone accesses the system anonymously, they receive whatever rights you define for this group. Personally, I recommend against anonymous access. You should require everyone to log in with a fully qualified username and password. Even with full authentication, you'll probably want to restrict the user's rights to maintain a safety factor for the network.

Network Configuration Operators Can manage network configuration with administrative-type access. Although they don't have administrative access to your system, these users can modify network and dial-up connections.

Performance Log Users Can schedule logging of performance counters, enable trace providers, and collect event traces both locally and via remote access to this computer. Performance logs help you perform long-term monitoring of events that occur sporadically or change dramatically over time.

Performance Monitor Users Can access performance counter data locally and remotely. Performance counters are small pieces of application code that monitor an event. For example, a performance counter may track how many times applications request data from the hard drive in a second. Besides monitoring the operating system, you can also use performance counters to monitor applications when the application vendor provides them, such as SQL Server.

Power Users Can create new printer and file shares, change the system time, force the system to shut down from another system, and change priorities of processes in the system. They can't run backups, load or unload device drivers, or take ownership.

Remote Desktop Users Have the right to log on remotely.

Replicator Enables your computer to receive replicated files from a server machine.

Users Can run programs and access data on a computer, shut it down, and access data on the computer from over the network. Users can't share folders or create local printers.

Understanding User Rights

But what's this about shutting down the machine or loading and unloading drivers? Well, actually, the notion of a *user right* is an integral part of how Vista security works. Basically, the difference between regular users and administrators lies in the kinds of actions that they can perform; for example, administrators can create new user accounts but regular users can't. In Vista terminology, the ability to perform a particular function is a user right. To take a look at the user rights in Vista and the types of users to whom they're assigned, follow these steps:

1. In Control Panel, click System and Maintenance, click Administrative Tools, and then click Local Security Policy to open the Local Security Policy console shown in Figure 21.1.
2. In the Security Settings pane, expand Local Policies, and then click User Rights Assignment to display a list of user rights in the pane on the right:

Most user rights are self-explanatory, but a few can use some clarification. Here's a list some of the rights and, where necessary, what they mean and what they're good for:

Back up files and directories Run backup utilities.

Change the system time Because the system time is important to the functioning of a network, not just anybody can change the system clock; it's a right. (Of course, you could always reboot the computer in DOS or go straight to the setup program in CMOS to reset the time, so it's not an airtight security feature.)

Force shutdown from a remote system Some utilities let you select a Vista machine and force it to shut down, even though you're not logged on to that machine. (One such utility comes with the Resource Kit.) Because you wouldn't want just anybody doing a forced shutdown, Microsoft made this a right.

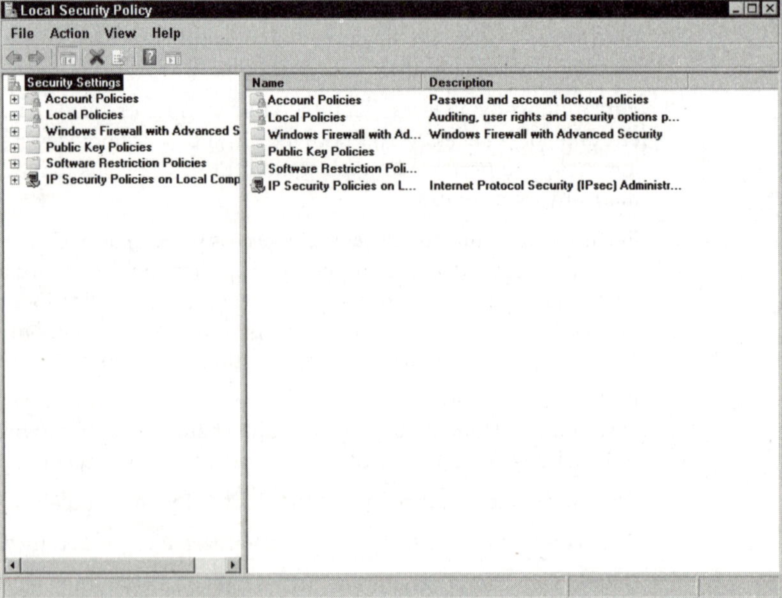

FIGURE 21.1
The Local Security Policy console helps you manage security policies for the local system.

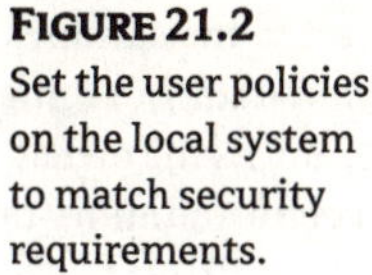

FIGURE 21.2
Set the user policies on the local system to match security requirements.

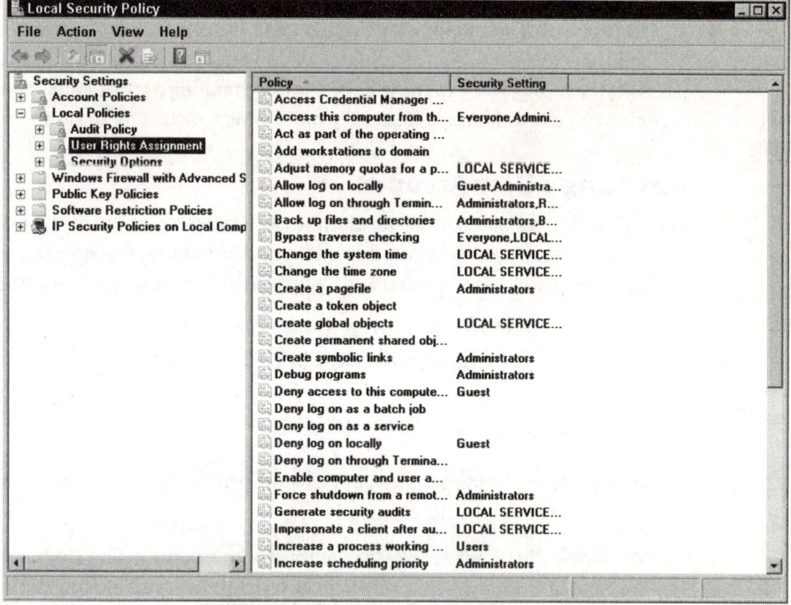

Load and unload device drivers A device driver isn't just a video driver or SCSI driver; a device driver may be part of a software application or operating system subsystem. Without this right, you'll often be unable to install new software, and you'll usually be unable to change drivers or add and remove parts of the operating system.

NOTE Microsoft has removed some older settings that really didn't make sense in the first place, such as Log on locally (after all, why have an account at all if you can't log on), and added new settings that are in line with their new security policies. For example, you'll find separate entries now for Change the system time and Change the time zone since Microsoft now considers the two rights separate. Cracker activity created a need for this separation. Some crackers changed the system time to obtain undesirable system access.

Manage auditing and security log You can optionally turn on a Vista Security Log, which will report every single action that woke up any part of the security subsystems in Vista. In general, I don't recommend using the Security Log because the output is quite cryptic and can be *huge*; logging all security events can fill up your hard disk quickly, and the CPU overhead of keeping track of the log will slow down your computer. You can't enable any security logging unless you have this right.

Restore files and directories As the name states.

Take ownership of files or other objects If you have this right, you can seize control of any file, folder, or other object even if you're not *supposed* to have access to it. This right is obviously quite powerful, which is why only administrators have it.

NOTE The user right to Take Ownership of Files or Other Objects is the secret to the administrator's power. You can do whatever you like to keep an administrator out of your data, but remember that the Computer Administrator can always take ownership of the file, and as the owner, do whatever they want to the file, including changing permissions. You can't keep an administrator out; you can only make it slightly more time consuming to get in.

Creating a User Account

Okay, now that you understand about the types of accounts and the concept of rights, let's create a new user account. You can do so in a couple of ways: using the Users and Passwords applet and using Computer Management. I'll start with the steps for creating a new user account with the Users Accounts applet:

1. Log on using an Administrator's group account.
2. Choose Start ➤ Control Panel to open Control Panel, and then click User Accounts to open User Accounts.
3. Click the Manage another account link. After seeing the usual UAC warning, you'll see the Manage Accounts window.
4. Click the Create a new account link to open the Create New Account window shown in Figure 21.3. Notice that this window contains entries that define the username and the account type. Even though there's an Administrator option, remember that all users run as standard users until the account receives an elevation of privileges.
5. Enter a username for the person, choose an account type, and then click Create Account. Vista creates the new account for you and returns you to the Manage Accounts window.

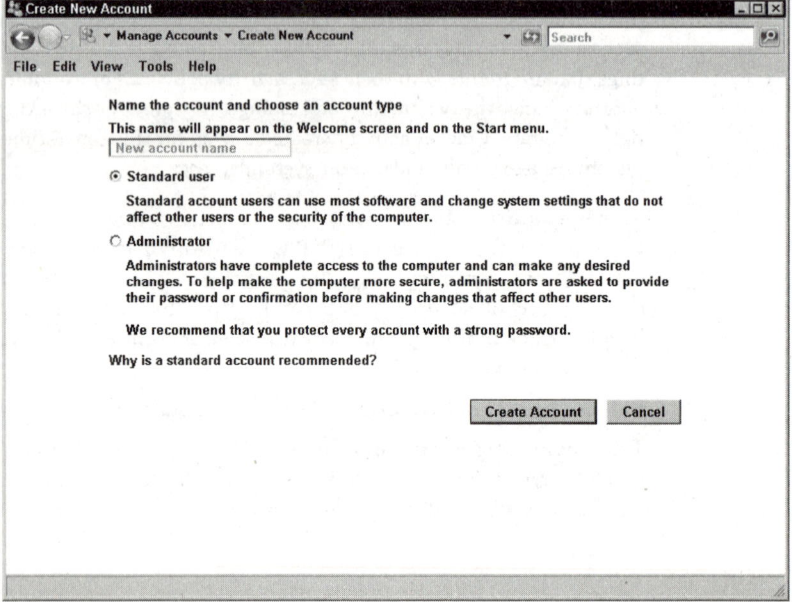
Create New Account
Manage Accounts ▾ Create New Account
Search
File Edit View Tools Help
Name the account and choose an account type
This name will appear on the Welcome screen and on the Start menu.
New account name
Standard user
Standard account users can use most software and change system settings that do not affect other users or the security of the computer.
Administrator
Administrators have complete access to the computer and can make any desired changes. To help make the computer more secure, administrators are asked to provide their password or confirmation before making changes that affect other users.
We recommend that you protect every account with a strong password.
Why is a standard account recommended?
Create Account
Cancel

FIGURE 21.3 Create a new user for the system by providing a name and account type.

NOTE In Vista, a username can be a maximum of 20 characters and isn't case-sensitive.

At this point, you have a new account on the system, but the account isn't configured. It doesn't even include a password, which is a very dangerous situation. The following steps help you configure the account.

1. Click the new user's account entry and you'll see the Change an Account window shown in Figure 21.4, where you can modify every aspect of the account.
2. Click Create a password to open the screen on which you can create a password for the account.

NOTE In Vista, a password can be a maximum of 127 characters if you're in a pure Vista environment. If you have Windows 9*x* machines on your network, keep the password to a maximum of 14 characters. Passwords *are* case-sensitive.

3. Type a password in the New password field, and then enter it again in the Confirm new password field. If you want, you can then type a hint (which can be seen by anyone using this computer) to trigger your remembrance of the password if you forget it.
4. Click Create password to establish the password for the new user account.

To gain more control over the process of managing user accounts on Vista, you'll need to use the Local User Manager. In Control Panel, click System and Maintenance, click Administrative Tools, and then click Computer Management to open the Computer Management console. In the Computer Management (Local) pane, expand System Tools, expand Local Users and Groups, and then select Users to display a list of users in the right pane. Choose Action ➢ New User to open the New User dialog box, as shown in Figure 21.5.

FIGURE 21.4
Define the characteristics of the new user's account before you consider the account finished.

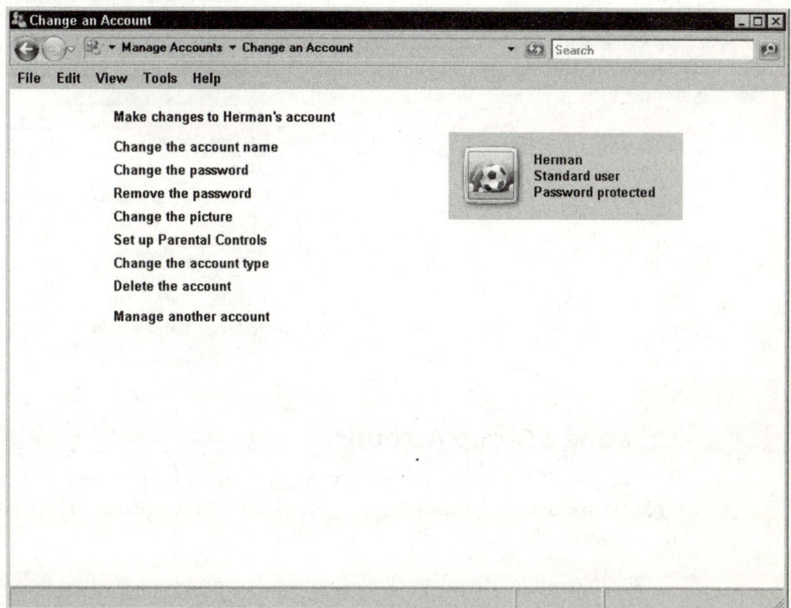

Now follow these steps:

1. Enter a username for this new account.
2. Enter the person's full name.
3. Enter a description.
4. Enter and confirm a password.
5. Set the password options. The default option is User Must Change Password at Next Logon. This option means that only that user will know the password, which means better security. If you uncheck this option, the other two options become available. Select User Cannot Change Password if this account will be used for a service or for someone whom you don't want to give the ability to change their own password. Select Password Never Expires if this password should be considered "permanent" and not have an automatic expiration.
6. The final option is to specify whether the account should be disabled. This is often a good idea if you want to change other properties of the account before it can be used, such as setting permissions on files and folders that this user will use. If this is the case, check the Account Is Disabled box.
7. When all options are selected, click Create to complete the process of making the new user account.

NOTE To enable a disabled account, in the Local Users and Groups window, right-click the account, and choose Properties from the context menu to open the Properties dialog box for that account. Clear the Account is disabled check box.

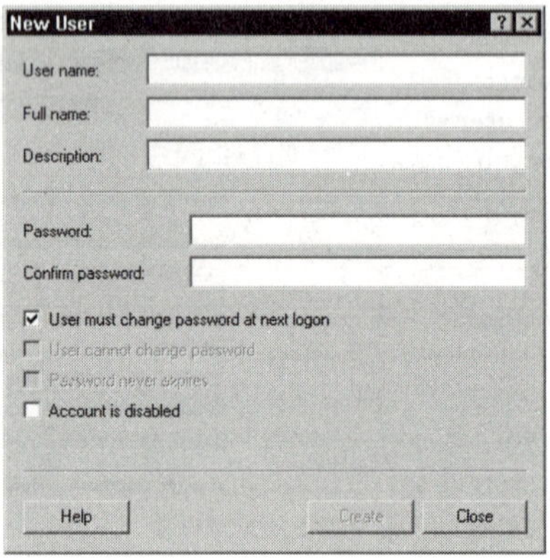

FIGURE 21.5
Use the New User dialog box to add a new user to your system.

Creating a Group Account

The process of creating a new group account is similar to creating a new user account. Local groups are useful for assigning permissions to resources. To create a new group account, follow these steps:

1. In Control Panel, click System and Maintenance, click Administrative Tools, and then click Computer Management to open the Computer Management console.

2. Expand System Tools, expand Local Users and Groups, right-click Groups, and choose New Group from the context menu to open the New Group dialog box shown in Figure 21.6.
3. Type a name for the group in the space provided. The name can contain any numbers or letters and can be a maximum of 256 characters. The name must be unique in the local database.
4. Enter some text in the Description field that will describe the membership and purpose of this group.
5. Click the Add button to open the Select Users dialog box:
6. In the Enter the Object Name to Select box, enter the name of the user that you want to add to the group, and then click OK. Repeat step 5 and this step to add more users to the group.
7. Back in the New Group dialog box, click Close, and then close Computer Management.

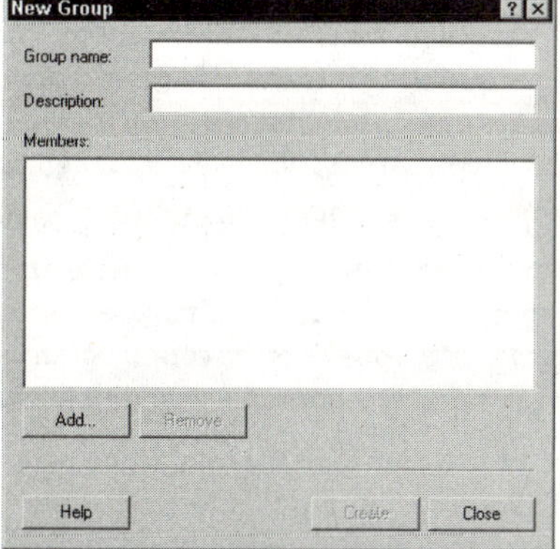

FIGURE 21.6
Use the New Group dialog box to add a new group to your system.

Understanding the New Account Settings

User account settings don't go quite as far in Vista as they did in previous versions of Windows. Microsoft has provided a number of other hurdles for both users and crackers. The problems for users are minimal once you get used to providing the new permission. Hopefully, crackers won't find a way around the new protections immediately (I have no doubt that crackers will eventually find ways around these protections). The following sections describe some new account issues that you must consider as part of the user setup in Vista.

Giving Yourself Permission

You may think that as a member of the Administrators group that you have full access to the system. That fact might be true for Windows XP, but it isn't true for Vista. Even as an administrator, you don't have access to many folders in Windows. For example, you have the same access to the root directory as any other user. To obtain increased access, you must become the owner of the root directory in most cases. However, even owning the root directory doesn't provide increased access to the Windows folder. You must set that permission separately. In short, Microsoft has made it very difficult for even members of the Administrators group to modify system elements accidentally. This feature is actually beneficial and you should leave it in place to help keep crackers at bay.

The problem comes in when you don't have access to a data folder. For example, you might create a shared data folder for your Word projects. This shared directory is outside of the standard shared directory. Perhaps you have an entire hard drive devoted to Word and want to place the files there. In order to access that directory, you must give yourself permission. If you're working with a group, create a group for the Word document folder and assign that group permission. (See the "Creating a Group Account" section of the chapter for details on creating a new group.) After you create the group and give it permission, assign all of the members of your group to the group by clicking Add in the New Group dialog box shown in Figure 21.6. Everyone that you add to the group will have permission to access the Word document folder and make the changes you define to its contents.

UNDERSTANDING CODE-BASED SECURITY

Vista makes significantly more use of the .NET Framework than previous versions of Windows for applications. Vista doesn't use the .NET Framework as much as it could for operating system features, but look for the move to the .NET Framework to continue. One of the features of the .NET Framework is code-based security. This feature places restrictions on code as well as the user. Even if a user has the right to change data in a folder, the code the user is interacting with might not have that right. Consequently, the modification will fail even though the user should be able to make the change.

The purpose of code-based security is to ensure that code can't make changes to the system unless you want it to do so. For example, it may be perfectly fine for the code to make a change to the system when used locally, but not acceptable when used through an Internet connection. An application that uses code-based security considers the context of the application so that no one can use the code externally to perform acts that you normally wouldn't allow.

It's important to understand the interaction between user security and code-based security because settings in Vista will commonly require both. This chapter focuses on the user, so you won't see much about code-based security here. However, you'll find a complete description of the code-based security requirements in the "Configuring the .NET Framework" section of Chapter 33. If the actions you perform for the user don't clear up security problems, consider reviewing the code-based security requirements as well.

Understanding Network Access Restrictions

Vista restricts your access to network drives. When you first set up Vista, every network drive has the same rights as the Internet, which is essentially none at all. You can't even execute a remote application or open a data file without problems. Because many viruses pass through network connections, setting restrictions on network drives you don't access is a good idea. However, it's a problem when you really need to change that shared data file on the file server.

This is one time when having the status bar showing in Windows Explorer is a very good idea. To display the status bar, choose View ➢ Status Bar. The status bar appears on the bottom of any Windows Explorer window. On the right side of this window is an area that shows the current zone for the network drive that you're accessing. These zones are precisely the same as the Internet Explorer zones described in the "Looking at the Security Tab" section of Chapter 15 and you have precisely the same rights. When you need to access a network drive, double-click the zone entry and you'll see the Security tab of the Internet Security Properties dialog box. Choose the zone that best matches your access needs for the network drive and click OK.

Setting Permissions

The capability to restrict access to data is a really great feature of Vista and previous versions of Windows based on the Windows NT operating system core. Prior to Windows NT, my experience with operating systems of all kinds was that if you could gain physical access to a computer, you could get to its data; before NT, the only way to secure data with any confidence was to put the data on a server and put the server behind a locked door.

But network security is only as good as you make it. If a person can gain physical access to your machine, they can remove your hard disk and have all your data in many cases. When working with Vista, BitLocker makes even hard disk removal a less predictable method of gaining access to the system. Even with these improvements though, data security includes educating users to protect passwords and to apply permissions responsibly.

In this section, I'm going to show you how to set permissions at the share level and at the file and folder level. Remember, however, that you can establish file and folder security only if you're using the NTFS file system.

NOTE To set permissions on a shared resource, you need to disable simple file sharing, which is enabled by default. In an Explorer window, choose Tools ➤ Folder Options to open the Folder Options dialog box. Click the View tab, and then in the Advanced Settings list, clear the Use Sharing Wizard (Recommended) check box.

Setting Share-Level Permissions

In Chapter 19, I showed you how to share resources on your computer with others on your network. Now we need to look at what kind of access you want to give those who use your shared resources. To do this, you set the permissions.

To set share permissions, follow these steps:

NOTE This particular sequence of steps works only if you're part of a domain or have turned off the Use Simple File Sharing option. Following this list of steps, I'll show you how to set share permissions using simple file sharing, which is the default if you're part of a workgroup.

1. In Explorer, right-click the shared resource, and choose Share from the context menu to open the Properties dialog box for the share at the Sharing tab.
2. Click Advanced Sharing to display the Advanced Sharing dialog box.
3. Click the Permissions button to open the Permissions dialog box shown in Figure 21.7.
4. Click Add to open the Select Users or Groups dialog box, in which you can select which groups will have access to a shared file or folder as shown in Figure 21.8.
5. In the Enter the Object Names to Select box, enter the name of the user or group to whom you're granting permission, and click OK.
6. Back in the Permissions dialog box, you'll see that the user or group has been added to the Group or User Names list. In the Permissions section, click Allow or Deny to specify the type of permission that you want to grant this user or group. Table 21.1 explains the choices.
7. When you've granted the permissions, click OK.

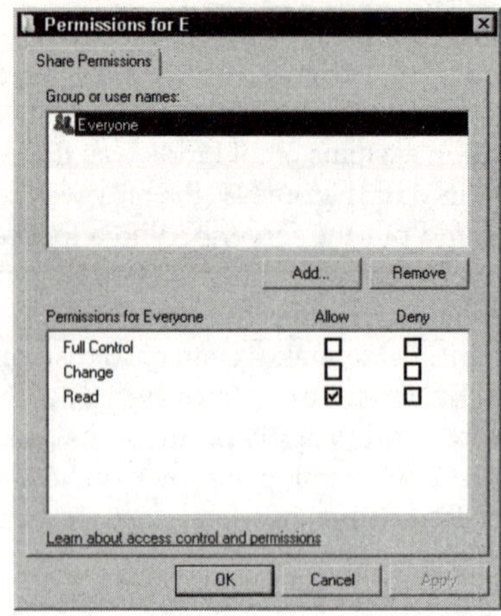

FIGURE 21.7
The Permissions dialog box lets you set permissions for a shared resource.

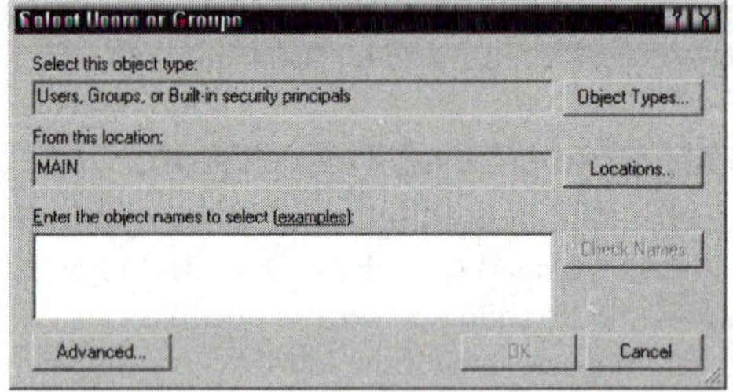

FIGURE 21.8
Choose the users and groups that have access to the shared resource.

TABLE 21.1: File Permissions

PERMISSION	DESCRIPTION
Full Control	The assigned group can perform any and all functions on all files and folders through the share.
Change	The assigned group can read and execute, as well as change and delete, files and folders through the share.
Read	The assigned group can read and execute files and folders but can't modify or delete anything through the share.

As I mentioned in the first note in this section, the steps I gave you to set share permissions are available only if you're part of a domain or have turned off the Use Simple File Sharing option. The "Creating Shares" section of Chapter 19 shows an example of creating a share using the Simple File Sharing Wizard. When using simple file sharing, you set security at the Reader, Contributor, and Co-owner levels, which equates to the three levels described in this section. However, you don't have quite as much flexibility. Chapter 19 provides a full comparison of the two techniques for you.

Types of File and Folder Permissions

Share-level permissions determine who can access resources across the network and the type of access that they'll have. However, you can still assign more detailed permissions to the folders and files that can be accessed through the share. In addition, by using file- and folder-level permissions, you can restrict access to resources even if someone logs on to the system and accesses those resources locally.

You've already seen that network shares have three types of permission levels: Read, Change, and Full Control. The permission types for files and folders are much more extensive, and each primary type includes still other types. Here are the primary types:

Read Allows you to view the contents, permissions, and attributes associated with a resource. If the resource is a file, you can view the file. If the resource is a folder, you can view the contents of the folder. You can't modify anything or execute anything.

Write Allows you to create a new file or subfolder within a folder if the resource is a folder. To change a file, you must also have Read permission, although you can append data to a file without opening the file if you have only Write permission.

List folder contents Allows you to obtain a listing of the files and folders in the target folder. Without this right, you can still read or write files, but you must know the name in advance. Removing this right is helpful when you don't want to user to know what information the folder contains. For example, you could tell the reader to open a specific file in the folder without letting them know about other files. An application could write to a data file without telling the user the name of the file or even them telling where the file appears on the hard drive. Part of security is often keeping information secret and the listing of files in a folder can be a helpful tool to crackers.

Read & execute Allows you the permissions associated with Read and with Write and also allows you to traverse a folder, which means you can pass through a folder for which you have no access to get to a file or folder for which you do have access. In addition, you can execute applications.

Modify Allows you the permissions associated with Read & Execute and with Write and also gives you Delete permission.

Full Control Allows you the permissions associated with all the other permissions that I've listed so far and lets you change permissions and take ownership of resources. In addition, you can delete subfolders and files even if you don't specifically have permission to do so.

Multiple Groups Accumulate Permissions

Imagine running a small network for an auditing firm. You might have one group in your network called Accountants and another called Managers, and they might have different permission levels—for example, the Accountants might be able to only read the files, and the Managers might have Change access, which in NT was called Read and Write access. What about the manager of the Accounting department, who belongs to both the Managers and the Accountants groups—does he have Read access or does he have Change access?

In general, your permissions to a network resource *add up*—so if you have Read access from one group and Change from another group, you end up with Read *and* Change access. However, because Change access *includes* all the things that you can do with Read access, there's no practical difference between having Read and Change and having only Change access.

If these levels of access are a bit coarse for your needs, you can fine-tune someone's access with what Microsoft calls *special access*. To modify the special access permissions for a file or folder, follow these steps:

1. In Explorer, right-click the resource whose permissions you want to modify, and choose Properties from the context menu to open the Properties dialog box for that resource.
2. Click the Security tab, and then click Advanced to open the Advanced Security Settings dialog box. The initial dialog box simply shows the settings. Click Edit to show a second, editable, copy of the Advanced Security Settings dialog box shown in Figure 21.9.

NOTE If you don't see the Security tab in the Advanced Security Settings dialog box, in the Explorer view of My Computer, choose Tools ➤ Folder Options to open the Folder Options dialog box. Click the View tab, and in the Advanced Settings list, clear the Use Simple File Sharing (Recommended) check box, and click OK.

3. Highlight the entry you want to modify, and then click Edit to open the Permission Entry dialog box shown in Figure 21.10.

Here's a description of each of these permissions:

Full Control As its name indicates and as discussed earlier in this chapter.

Traverse folder/execute file Changes folders through this folder, and you can run this file.

List folder/read data Displays the contents of a folder and reads the contents of a file.

Read attributes Displays the current attributes of a file or folder.

Read extended attributes Displays the extended attributes of a file or folder, if there are any.

Create files/write data Writes data to a new file. When applied to a folder, this permission means you can write files into the folder, but you can't view what's already in the folder.

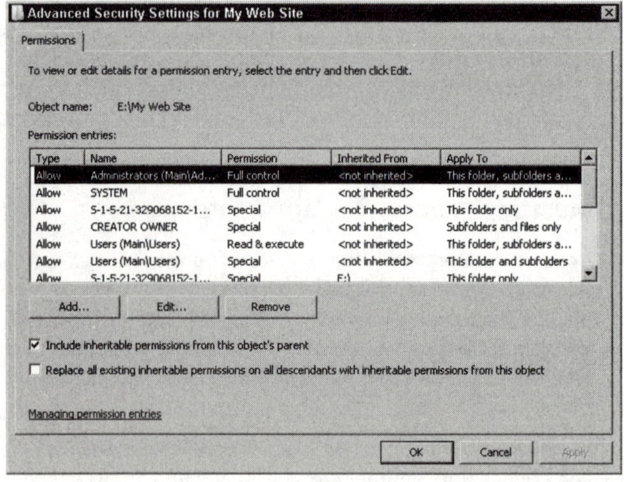

FIGURE 21.9
It's possible to provide very fine security settings to define precisely what the user can do.

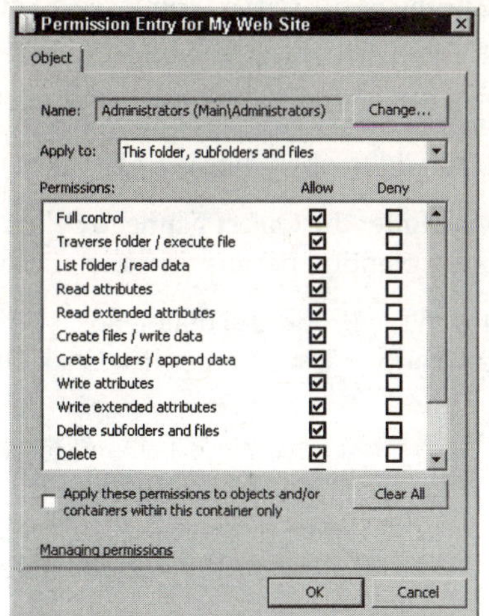

FIGURE 21.10
Select from the list of specific user activities to determine how the system interacts with the user.

Create folders/append data Creates new folders in this location, and you can append data to existing files.

Write attributes Modifies the attributes of a file or folder.

Write extended attributes Creates extended attributes for a file or folder.

Delete subfolders and files Removes folders contained within the folder you're working in, and you can remove the files contained in them.

Delete Deletes files.

Read permissions Displays the current permissions list for the file or folder.

Change permissions Modifies the permissions for the file or folder. This permission is normally included only in Full Control.

Take ownership Claims ownership of a file or folder.

These levels of granularity make security considerations more difficult to grasp initially, but they give a skilled administrator much finer control over how files and folders can be accessed.

To prevent someone from accessing a file or folder, you have two choices. The first, and usually the best, is to simply not grant the person access to the file or folder. That means don't add their account to the list of permissions. The second method is to add the person's account to the permissions list, but check Deny for each permission. This creates an explicit No Access–type permission.

NOTE The special access items are all check boxes, not radio buttons, so you can mix and match them as you like.

Assigning File and Folder Permissions

Now that you know something about the types of permissions that you can place on files and folders, let's walk though the steps to assign them:

1. In Explorer, right-click the file or folder for which you want to establish permissions, and choose Properties from the context menu to open the Properties dialog box for that file or folder.

2. Click the Security tab. You'll see a listing of users/groups and their rights as shown in Figure 21.11.
3. Click Edit to display the Permissions dialog box.
4. Click Add to open the Select Users or Groups dialog box.
5. In the Enter the Object Name to Select box, enter the name of the user or group to whom you're granting permission, and click OK.
6. Back in the Properties dialog box, you'll see that those groups or users have been added to the Group or User Names list. Click OK.

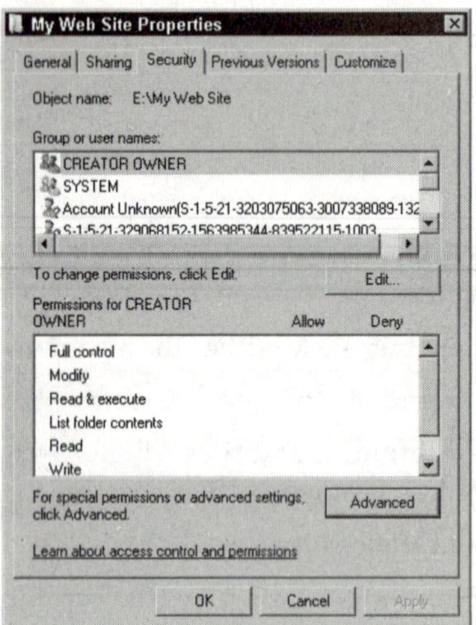

FIGURE 21.11
A list of individual resource users and their rights.

Auditing Files and Folders

In addition to assigning file and folder permissions, Vista lets you keep track of who accessed a file and when. You can audit everyone or only specific users or groups. Follow these steps to add auditing to a resource.

1. In Explorer, right-click the resource you want to audit, and choose Properties from the context menu to open the Properties dialog box for that resource.
2. Click the Security tab, and then click Advanced to open the Advanced Security Settings dialog box.
3. Select the Auditing tab. You'll see a message telling you that you need administrator privileges to add auditing to the system.
4. Click Continue. You'll see an Advanced Security Settings dialog box that looks very much like the one shown in Figure 21.9, except that this one has an Auditing tab, rather than a Permissions tab.

5. Click Add. You'll see a Select User or Group dialog box.
6. Type the name of the user or group that you want to audit and click OK. You'll see an Auditing Entry dialog box that looks very much like the Permissions Entry dialog box shown in Figure 21.10. In fact, all of the check boxes are the same. The difference is that you'll monitor the success or failure of an activity, rather than give permission to do it.
7. Check the entries that correspond to the activities you want to audit, and then click OK.
8. Click OK three times to make the change permanent.

To take a look at the events that you've selected to audit, follow these steps:

1. In Control Panel, click System and Maintenance, click Administrative Tools, and then click Event Viewer to open the Event Viewer console.
2. In the pane on the left, select Windows Logs\Security to display a list of audited events in the right pane.

Understanding Ownership

Ownership—what a confusing concept. *Ownership* is a process by which you can take exclusive control over a file or a folder; and you can do all of this with a click of a button. But before you get power drunk with the possibilities, let's take a closer look at what being the owner of a file really means.

Defining Ownership

Now, having worked with NT since its inception, I don't mind telling you that the whole idea of a folder or file's "owner" seemed a bit confusing until I finally figured out the definition. Here's a definition—and from this point on, let me shorten the term *file or folder* to *object*:

Minasi's Definition of an Owner An object's owner is a user who can *always* modify that object's permissions.

Ordinarily, only an administrator can control settings such as an object's permissions. But users need to be able to control objects in their own area, their own home folder, without having to involve an administrator at every turn. For example, suppose you want to give another user access to a folder in your home folder. Rather than having to seek out an administrator and ask the administrator to extend access permissions to another user, you as the owner can change the permissions directly. Ownership lets users become mini-administrators, rulers of their small fiefdoms.

To find out who owns an object, follow these steps:

1. In Explorer, right-click an object, and choose Properties from the context menu to open the Properties dialog box for that object.
2. Select the Security tab, and then click Advanced to open the Advanced Security Settings dialog box.
3. Select the Owner tab. You'll see the current owner information as shown in Figure 21.12.

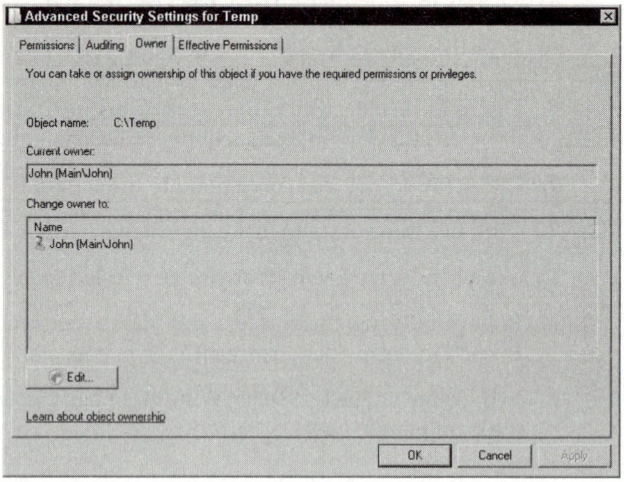

FIGURE 21.12
The object owner can perform any task with the target object.

Taking Ownership

Users can't force themselves onto the permissions list for an object, but if they have the Take Ownership permission, they *can* become the owner, and once they're the owner, *then* they can add themselves to the permissions list. In previous versions of Windows, the question of ownership was problematic because it was quite easy to get the required leverage to circumvent administrator-applied ownership rules.

However, in Vista, only an administrator can change ownership, even if the user is currently the owner of an option. When you click Edit in the Advanced Security Settings dialog box shown in Figure 21.12, you see a UAC dialog box asking for an elevation in privileges. At this point, you'll see a second Advanced Security Settings dialog box where you can change the ownership. If you highlight your name in the Change owner to list and click OK, you can become the owner of the object.

To summarize permissions and ownership:

- By default, new files and new subfolders inherit permissions from the folder in which they're created. However, special Vista folders, such as the Windows folder, don't follow this rule.
- A user who creates a file or a folder is the owner of that file or folder, and the owner can always control access to the file or folder by changing the permissions on it. However, in Vista, only someone from the Administrators group can assign ownership.
- When you change the permissions on an existing folder, you can choose whether those changes will apply to all files and subfolders within the folder.
- Users and groups can be denied access to a file or a folder simply by not granting the users or groups any permissions for it.

WARNING It's possible to lock out everyone, including the operating system itself, if you don't apply permissions correctly. However, given the way Vista locks even administrators out of critical areas, it's quite unlikely that this problem will occur.

As an alternative to using the GUI to take ownership, Vista provides the takeown utility. Using this utility is simple. To take ownership of a particular file or folder, you type **takeown /F <Directory or Filename>** and press Enter at the command line. You can use the /A command line argument to give ownership to the administrator instead of the current user. For example, if you want to give ownership to the C:\Temp folder to the Administrators group, you'd type **takeown /F C:\Temp /A** at the command prompt and press Enter. Use the /R command line argument when you want to apply the new ownership to subdirectories as well as the current directory. This command also works remotely. Simply provide the system, username, and password using the /S <System>, /U [Domain\]Username, and /P <Password> command line arguments.

Security Center

By now, you understand how important security is. Security management can take a lot of time, even if you just have two computers at home. Managing security on hundreds or thousands of computers is often a full-time job. To make it easier to manage security, Vista provides the Security Center applet in Control Panel. It's shown in Figure 21.13.

While this applet doesn't allow you to specifically control user accounts or share, file, and folder permissions, it does give you an interface in which you can help manage overall system security. First, you can manage Windows Firewall, which is critical in the protection against hackers and viruses. Second, you can enable automatic updates. This ensures that you always have the latest software patches from Microsoft, just in case there might be a security hole. Third, Windows checks whether you have an antivirus program and if it's up-to-date. If not, Windows will warn you. Vista can work with and help manage most antivirus applications. Clicking on any of the three sections will give you more details on how to manage your security. Happy securing!

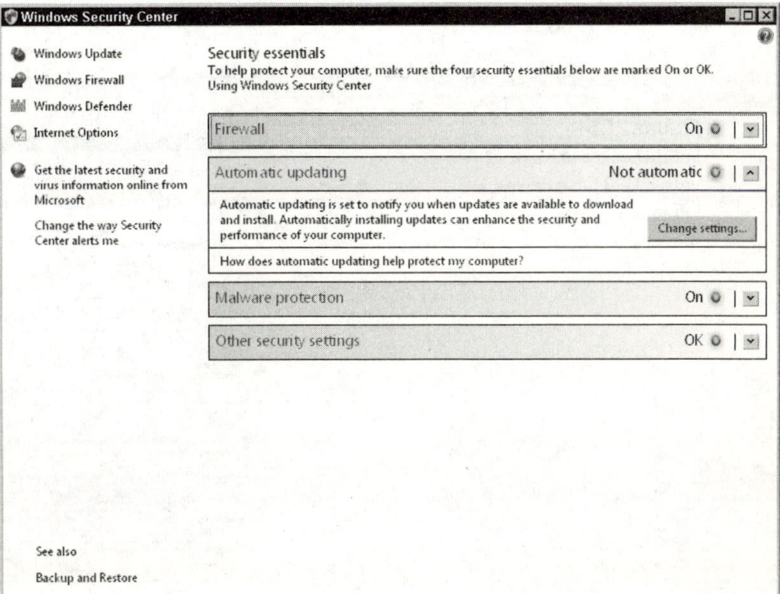

FIGURE 21.13
Use the Security Center to manage the security features that Vista provides.

Working with BitLocker

BitLocker is full drive encryption. The encryption is so secure that even if someone takes the hard drive out of your system, they can't do anything with it. The drive is encrypted in such a way that you have to unlock it as part of the boot process. Consequently, BitLocker is the perfect solution for laptops. Even when the laptop gets lost, you don't have to worry about someone walking away with the data.

Before you begin thinking that BitLocker is the answer to all of your security nightmares, you need to know that the default BitLocker setup for Vista requires that you have a Trusted Platform Module (TPM) chip. The system activates this chip before it begins looking for an operating system to boot. The TPM chip can provide the resources to encrypt and decrypt files on your system at the hardware level. If you're really interested in the inner workings of TPM, you can discover more about it at `https://www.trustedcomputinggroup.org/groups/tpm/`.

Unfortunately, TPM chips are rare in computers today. However, Vista provides an alternative that you can use. It's not quite as secure because the support isn't built into your computer and you must have a USB flash drive that Vista supports to implement it. The USB flash drive (or thumb drive) is the weak link because theoretically, you could move it to another machine. To set up your machine to use the USB alternative, use the following steps:

1. Choose Start ➤ Run, type **`gpedit.msc`** in the Open field, and click OK.
2. Select the `Local Computer Policy\Computer Configuration\Administrative Templates\Windows Components\BitLocker Drive Encryption` folder.
3. Double-click the Control Panel Setup: Enable advanced startup options policy and you'll see the dialog box shown in Figure 21.14.
4. Select the Enabled option, and then check the Allow BitLocker without a compatible TPM option.
5. Click OK, log off your system and then back on to ensure the policy takes effect.

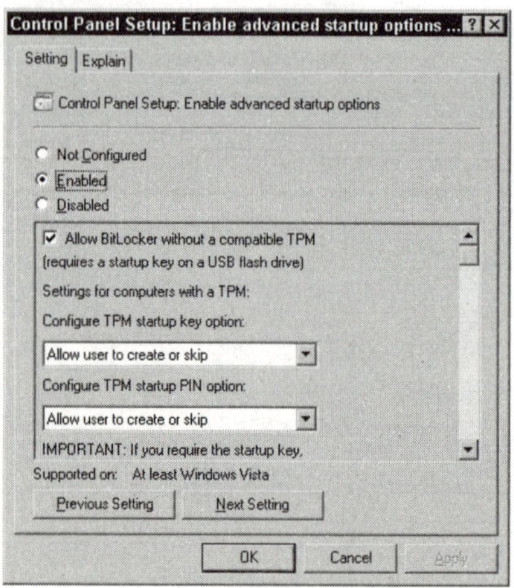

FIGURE 21.14 Set BitLocker to work with a USB flash drive when necessary.

Whichever method you choose, TPM or USB flash drive, you'll need to open the BitLocker Drive Encryption applet of the Control Panel. The BitLocker Drive Encryption window tells you the status of BitLocker on the boot drive. BitLocker only affects the boot drive—not other drives on your machine. If you want to encrypt the other drives, you must perform this task separately. However, since the boot drive is inoperable without the required credentials, anyone obtaining your drive still has a hunk of useless metal and plastic.

To turn on BitLocker, click the Turn On BitLocker link. You'll see the Setup BitLocker startup preferences dialog box shown in Figure 21.15. If you're using a TPM, you can choose from any of the three startup options; USB flash drive users can only choose the third option. Select one of the startup options and then follow the instructions to encrypt your boot drive. After your drive is encrypted, Vista will ask for validation of your identity every time you start the system. The method of validation depends on the startup option you choose in Figure 21.15.

FIGURE 21.15
Choose one of the BitLocker startup preferences to determine how you'll validate your identity.

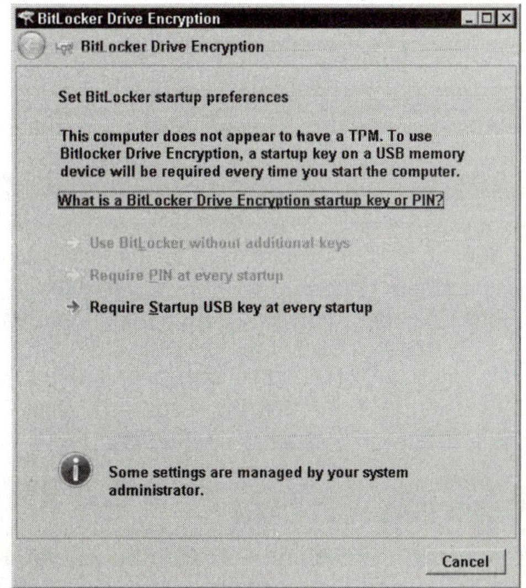

Working with Windows CardSpace

Windows CardSpace is a special applet in the Control Panel that lets you send information to a website without having to supply the information each time. You can also maintain cards from websites so that you can verify the website owner every time you visit. All of this support is performed from the secure desktop, which means that Windows CardSpace is completely inaccessible to third parties. Only you can add, maintain, and remove cards.

To open Windows CardSpace, open the Windows CardSpace applet in the Control Panel. You'll see the normal UAC dialog box. Click Continue and you'll see the Windows CardSpace window shown in Figure 21.16. Notice that everything else becomes inaccessible. The only application you can access is Windows CardSpace.

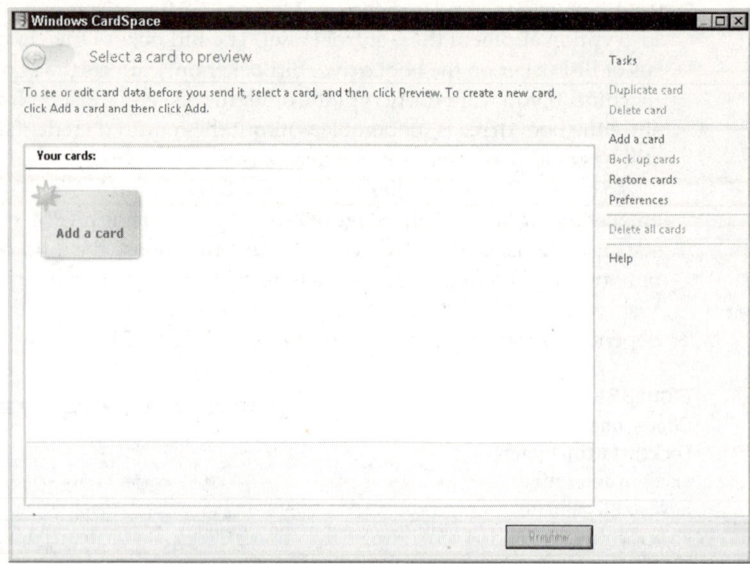

FIGURE 21.16 Windows CardSpace provides safe storage for sensitive information you want to provide to websites.

TIP You can use the Clipboard to transfer text to and from Windows CardSpace. Simply highlight the text to select it, press Ctrl+C to copy it to the Clipboard, select an insertion point for the text, and then click Ctrl+V to copy it from the Clipboard.

Since you have total control over the cards in Windows CardSpace, you can trust the information they provide. The following sections describe how to perform Windows CardSpace tasks. I'm assuming that you've already opened Windows CardSpace.

Adding a Personal Card

Before you can do anything with CardSpace, you must add a card. Your personal card contains your information. On the other hand, a managed card comes from a business. You import it into Windows CardSpace so you know something about the business. The "Adding a Managed Card" section of the chapter describes this second kind of card. The following steps describe how to perform this task.

1. Click the Add a card link. Windows CardSpace will ask you to choose a card type.
2. Choose the Create a Personal card option. You'll see the Edit a new card window shown in Figure 21.17.
3. Fill out the information you feel comfortable sending to a particular website. Don't create a generic card unless you really do want to send the same information to every website. You can't add any additional information to a personal card, so you must manually supply additional information that Windows CardSpace doesn't support.
4. Click Save. The new card appears in the Windows CardSpace window shown in Figure 21.16.

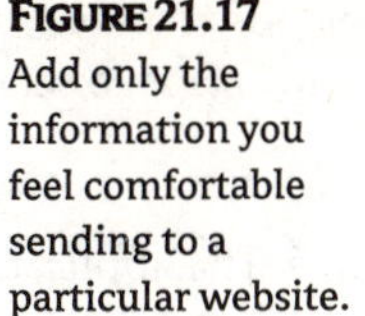

FIGURE 21.17
Add only the information you feel comfortable sending to a particular website.

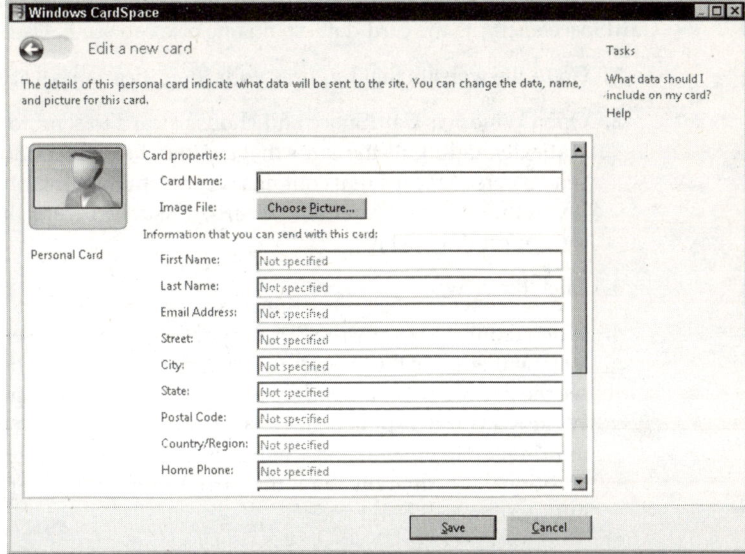

Adding a Managed Card

Managed cards identify businesses and help you ensure that the person you think you're talking to really isn't someone on a phishing trip. Never accept a card from someone you don't trust. The following steps tell how to import a managed card into Windows CardSpace.

1. Obtain the managed card file from the third party that you trust before you open Windows CardSpace.
2. Click the Add a card link. Windows CardSpace will ask you to choose a card type.
3. Choose the Install a Managed card option. You'll see a Choose a file to import window where you can choose a managed card. If you don't see the file you want, click Browse. You'll see an Open Information Card File dialog box where you can choose the file you want to import. Choose a file and click Open.
4. Highlight the file you want to install and click Continue. Windows CardSpace displays the vendor information.
5. Review the vendor information to ensure it comes from a trusted source.
6. Click Install. The new card appears in the Windows CardSpace window shown in Figure 21.16.

Sending a Card

After you create the cards needed for various websites, you can begin using them. You send the card to the website after reviewing the website's identity. The system requires that you review the website's identity the first time. After the first time, you'll only need to review the website's identity when the website's privacy statement changes or any of the website information changes. Windows CardSpace encrypts the card data, so no one else can see it. Use the following steps to send a card.

1. Go to the website that requires your identification.
2. Open Windows CardSpace and choose a card to send to the website. The application automatically highlights the cards that contain the correct information for you. Generally, you'll send a personal card that contains the information that the website requires to identify you. If you find that you can't send a card, it usually means that you've chosen a card that lacks the appropriate details.
3. Click Preview.
4. When required, supply the PIN for your card. You can secure cards after you create them by locking them. See the "Securing CardSpace Entries" section of the chapter for details. You'll see the data that you're sending to the website as shown in Figure 21.18. At the bottom of this Window, you'll also find the card's history—a listing of websites that have received the information in the past and when they've received it. After the card history, you'll find some additional information about the card. Windows CardSpace doesn't send this additional information to the website.
5. When Required, click Edit to modify the card data using the same technique described in the "Adding a Personal Card" section of the chapter. After you save the updated card, click Send. Windows CardSpace sends the card to the website.

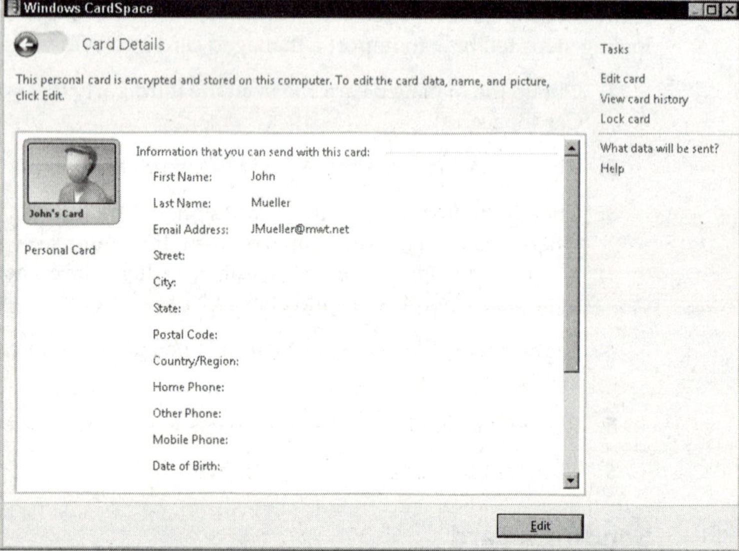

FIGURE 21.18 Review the card information and history before you send it to anyone.

Deleting a Card

Since Windows CardSpace cards contain your personal information and you want to manage that information in a way that reduces risk, it's important to delete cards that you no longer need. The following steps tell how to delete a card.

1. Highlight the card you want to delete and click the Delete card link. You'll see a Delete a card dialog box that contains the card's history.
2. Examine the card's history and click Delete if you want to delete it or Cancel if you want to save it. Windows CardSpace removes the card and its history. You see the Windows CardSpace window shown in Figure 21.16.

You might decide at some point to delete all of your cards. To perform this task, click the Delete all cards link. You'll see a warning dialog box. Check Yes, I want to delete all my cards and card history and click Delete All. Windows CardSpace removes all of your cards from the system.

WARNING All forms of card deletion are permanent. Once you delete a card, the information is gone unless you create a backup of the card information first. See the "Backing Up the CardSpace Entries" section of the chapter for details on creating a backup.

Duplicating a Card

You never want to send a website more information than it requires to identify you. The less information the website has, the lower your risk. Consequently, you might end up with a number of cards that have almost, but not quite all, of the same information. To reduce typing time, you can use card duplication. Create a simple card and add the information you need to it. The following steps describe how to duplicate a card.

1. Highlight the card you want to duplicate and click the Duplicate card link. You'll see the Duplicate card window. This window contains the same information as the original card.
2. Make any changes required for the new card. It's essential to give the card a new name that reflects its purpose.
3. Click Save. The new card appears in the Windows CardSpace window shown in Figure 21.16.

Securing CardSpace Entries

Windows CardSpace can provide additional protection for your card in the form of a PIN. You don't have to assign a PIN to every card, but you can add a PIN to cards that contain sensitive information to add more protection. The following steps tell you how to lock a card by adding a PIN to it.

1. Highlight the card you want to see and click Preview. When required, supply the PIN for your card. You'll see the Card Details window shown in Figure 21.18.
2. Click the Lock card link. You'll see the Lock the card window shown in Figure 21.19.
3. Type the same PIN into the New PIN and Confirm new PIN fields. Click Lock. Windows CardSpace returns you to the Card Details window.

At some point, you might decide to unlock a card or change the PIN. You open the Card Details window as usual to perform this task. However, in this case, the window will look like the one in Figure 21.20. Click the Change PIN link to change the PIN or the Remove lock link to remove the lock from the card. In both cases, you must supply the existing PIN before you can make any changes.

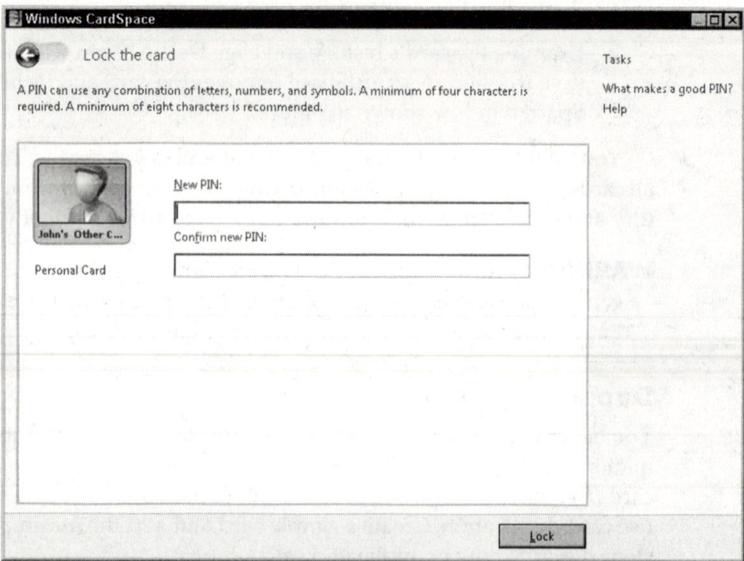

FIGURE 21.19 Provide a PIN to secure the card.

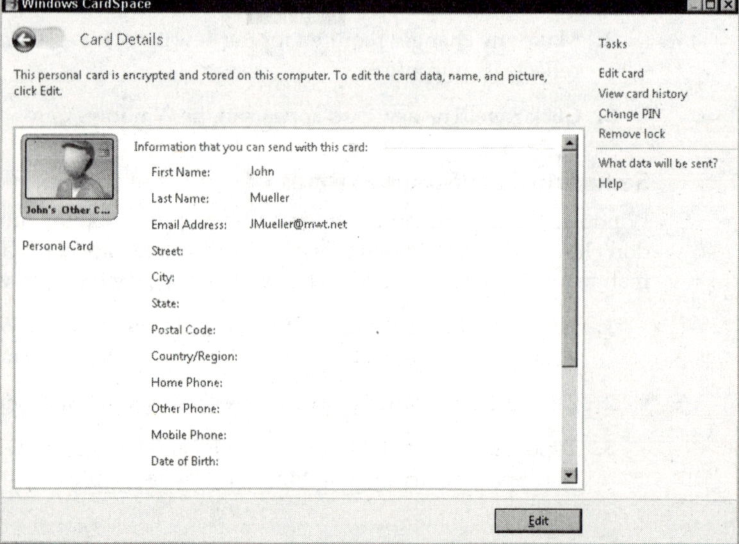

FIGURE 21.20 The links in the Card Details window change to show the card's locked status.

Backing Up the CardSpace Entries

Eventually you'll end up with a number of cards that make it very easy to provide identification to websites and verify that you're working with the party that you think you're working with. Although you could probably duplicate your personal cards without too much effort, you can't duplicate the managed cards with any ease. Consequently, you'll want to create a backup of the cards you create. The following steps describe the backup process.

1. Click the Back up cards link (see Figure 21.16). You'll see the Back up cards window shown in Figure 21.21.
2. Check the cards you want to back up. If you want to back up all of the cards, click Check All.
3. Click Continue. You'll see a Name the backup file window.
4. Click Browse. Type a name for the backup file and choose a location to store it (the default location is with your personal data). Click Save. The filename appears in the Name the backup file window.
5. Click Continue. You'll see a Type a password window.
6. Type the same password in the Type password and Retype password fields.
7. Click Back Up. Windows CardSpace creates the backup for you.

NOTE This process creates a file on your hard drive with your cards. It doesn't back up the file to alternative storage such as another hard drive, CD, DVD, or tape. Consequently, even though you now have two copies of the cards on the same hard drive, you probably don't have a copy of the cards in an alternative location and they aren't truly safe from catastrophic failures such as a hard drive crash.

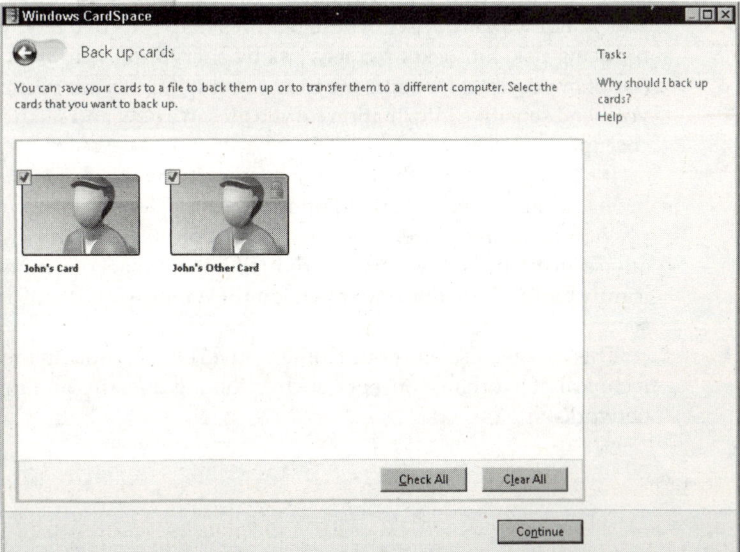

FIGURE 21.21 Choose the cards that you want to back up.

Restoring the CardSpace Entries

If you have a backup, you can always restore your cards when you lose them due to a catastrophic failure or simply because you moved to a new machine. The backup always appears as a file with a `.crds` extension. This file is actually in XML format, but if you open it all you'll see is a seemingly random bunch of letters and numbers. The XML file is encrypted, which means you have to have the password to make any sense of it. Use the following steps to restore a CardSpace backup.

1. Click Restore Cards. You'll see a Restore cards window.
2. Click Browse. Highlight the backup file you want to restore. Click Open. The filename appears in the Restore cards window.
3. Click Continue. You'll see a Type the password window.
4. Type the password in the Type password field. Click Continue. You'll see a list of the cards that Windows CardSpace will restore. The application doesn't let you choose the particular cards. The restore feature automatically overwrites older cards with the new information in the backup file, but leaves files with the same date/time or newer alone.
5. Click Restore. Windows CardSpace performs the restore for you and returns you to the Windows CardSpace window shown in Figure 21.16.

Summary

In this chapter, we looked at creating user and group accounts and at the rights that the various kinds of users and groups can have. We also walked through the steps involved in setting permissions for shares, files, and folders. We also looked at a helpful management feature, Security Center. Understanding and following these procedures is essential if you want the information on your Vista system to be secure. And presumably, that's one of the main reasons you're working with Vista anyway, right? Finally, the chapter discusses two new features of Vista: BitLocker and Windows CardSpace. These features help improve the overall security of your system by reducing risk. BitLocker reduces risk by encrypting your boot drive and making it very difficult (if not impossible) for someone to access it without your permission. Windows CardSpace helps you send sensitive information to websites in a new and secure way that third parties can't easily corrupt.

It's time to explore the many new security features of Vista. You'll very likely find that you have fewer rights than you did under older versions of Windows and that some applications simply don't run any longer. The suggestions provided in this chapter should help you overcome any security difficulties without reducing the impact of the new security features. Vista is significantly more secure than older versions of Windows, but only if you do your part to maintain that security edge.

This chapter also ends our Home Networking section. In the next chapter, we'll dive into more technical networking concepts, such as joining domains and interoperating with non-Microsoft networks.

Part VI

Advanced Networking

In this section, you'll learn how to:

- **Connect to Windows-Based Domains**
- **Work with Windows Server 2003**
- **Interoperate with Non-Microsoft Network Servers**

Chapter 22

Connecting to Domains

Although peer-to-peer workgroups have beauty in their simplicity, there are some limitations. As an example, did you know that with Vista, Microsoft has limited workgroups to 10 computers? For larger networks, you'll need to create a domain.

A Microsoft Windows domain is a network with a single database of usernames, passwords, profiles, and more. Once you get an account on a domain, you can log on through any computer on the network and have access to your files and preferences. You can even log on to the domain remotely from halfway around the world. Except for the limits you might encounter in network speed, everything else would be the same.

In Chapters 18 and 19, you learned to configure and install networks in a peer-to-peer relationship. Chapter 18 also described the client-server relationships that are associated with larger computer networks. The lessons of these chapters apply equally well here. For smaller networks, the required network hardware isn't significantly different between a peer-to-peer and a client-server domain-based network.

Vista is an excellent client on a network domain. In this chapter, we'll look at many of the decisions you'll need to make in order to get the networking features to run reliably in that environment. You'll also learn how to connect documents and printers shared in the domain. To enable the consistent look and feel, you'll also create roving profiles for users and hardware. Finally, the chapter wraps up with a section on troubleshooting your domain.

In this chapter:

- Setting up a domain
- Requirements on the domain server
- Attaching to network resources
- Using profiles
- Troubleshooting

Vista: What's New?

The new domain network features in Vista are essentially the same as the peer-to-peer network features. You'll find that Vista provides improved security for domain networks, just as it does for peer-to-peer networks.

Setting Up a Domain

The basic reasons for having a network are the same for peer-to-peer and client-server networks. A network allows you to share files, printers, applications, and more. However, a domain can let you do even more. With its centralized database of usernames, you can use the same username and password on any computer on the domain.

As with peer-to-peer networks, domains increase user productivity. With their dedicated servers, domains are better at supporting collaboration. The following is an example of how this can work.

In our offices, Leslie is one of several engineers. The engineering office is 50 miles away from the manufacturing plant, but the engineers often need to travel to the plant to check on the product. Sydney is the manufacturing supervisor, who's in constant need of engineering help. So, the network problems that we need to solve are as follows:

- Setting up workstations at the engineering and manufacturing facilities for all users
- Creating a common database for the engineers, accessible by manufacturing

Let's solve their problem with a client-server network on a Microsoft domain. With this type of network, Leslie can easily access her drawings from either facility, and Sydney can review the designs as they're developed. Assuming that both computers are running Vista, here's how to get both users access to Leslie's files from any facility:

1. Using the user account, the computer account, and any folders that are set up for her on the domain controller, Leslie connects her Vista workstation to the domain. She starts saving her engineering drawings on the domain server.
2. The network administrator sets up a roving profile on the server. Whenever Leslie logs on to the domain, she gets the same roving profile. It doesn't matter what workstation she uses.
3. The network administrator gives Sydney a different account on the domain controller. Sydney's username is included in a group with permissions to access Leslie's folder.

Now Leslie can access her drawings and files from either facility. Sydney can view Leslie's engineering drawings as required, so she can plan future manufacturing activity.

MICROSOFT DOMAINS AND INTERNET DOMAINS

Microsoft domains and Internet domains are related but not identical concepts. A Microsoft domain includes a group of computers with a common database of users, groups, files, and so on. The Internet concept of a domain is based on a hierarchical organization of computers in a network, without any requirement for a common database of any sort. However, you can organize a Microsoft domain in the Internet hierarchical style.

For example, if you wanted to organize the Microsoft computers that belong to the `mommabears.com` network, you could give them the following names:

```
w95a.ms.mommabears.com
w98b.ms.mommabears.com
w2000c.ms.mommabears.com
wxpprod.ms.mommabears.com
wxpserver.ms.mommabears.com
```

All five computers (`w95a`, `w98b`, `w2000c`, `wxpprod`, `wxpserver`) would belong to the `ms` subdomain in the `mommabears.com` Internet domain. However, in a Microsoft domain, you don't have to follow Internet domain naming rules. Alternatively, you can follow the rules you used when you installed Vista in Chapter 2, where the name of a computer is limited to 15 characters. This is also known as a NetBIOS name.

These actions apply on a server used as a domain controller. Domain controllers are by definition computers with one of the Windows Server operating systems that participate in managing domain security. (Servers can also be part of a domain but can't control domain security. These are typically file, application, and print servers.) Therefore, many of these steps are for the administrator responsible for the domain and are beyond the scope of this book.

Vista is designed to work in a variety of networking situations. Vista makes the perfect network client for both home and office users. It doesn't matter if your network servers are running NetWare, UNIX, or some other platform; Vista will play nice with a variety of network operating systems. Vista can also act as a server in a pinch—although you're better off going with a true server product for a long-term solution.

Requirements on the Domain Server

As a Vista power user, you'll sometimes need to know the basics of what an administrator does on a domain server. The details of this process are beyond the scope of this book. You wouldn't want to see detailed information about configuring Windows NT Server, Windows 2000 Server, or Windows Server 2003 in a book on Vista, anyway.

A domain controller includes the information that you need to connect to that domain from a workstation. There are four basic steps that an administrator has to take on a properly configured domain controller:

- Create a user account.
- Create a computer account.
- Set up appropriate profiles.
- Identify the new computer.

For more information on configuring domain controllers, refer to *Mastering Windows 2000 Server*, Fourth Edition (Sybex 2002), or *Mastering Windows Server 2003* (Sybex, 2003) and *Mastering Windows Server 2003: Upgrade Edition for SP1 and R2* (Sybex 2007).

User Accounts

You need a user account on a domain controller in order to connect to a domain. By default, that account has a standard set of rights and privileges to certain folders on the server, including a data folder for your everyday work files. In addition, the user account of anyone who needs access to your work should be made a member of a group with appropriate rights to your data folder.

User accounts on a domain controller are different from user accounts in Vista. They're kept on separate databases. Once your computer is configured for a domain, you can log in to either system through your Vista computer. Fortunately, as with peer-to-peer networking, Microsoft has made the task of logging into a domain significantly easier (automatic in most cases) when working with Vista. Generally, Vista will detect the domain and automatically make any settings changes for you. All you provide is your name and password for the domain as you would when logging into a peer-to-peer network.

Of course, all of the same tasks occur in the background as they did before. The system still provides the server with the username, password, and domain when logging into the server. The difference is that you normally don't have to worry about these complexities—they're invisible to the end user. Don't look for the old Windows NT login dialog box for domains in Vista. You won't find it because it no longer exists. The connection you see in the Network and Sharing Center is the connection that your system will use. The "Working with Network Map" section of Chapter 18 tells you how you can use the Network Map feature to understand your network configuration better. See the "Understanding LLTD" section of Chapter 19 to understand how the connection magic takes place. To create other connections, you must change the settings in Network and Sharing Center as described in the "Attaching to Network Resources" section of Chapter 19.

Computer Accounts

If you want your Vista computer to participate in a Microsoft domain, your computer needs a computer account on the domain controller. Once your network administrator creates the account, you'll need to provide the computer account name and password to connect your Vista computer to that domain. You need to do this only once, and then you're part of the domain. (It's very likely that you'll find that you're already part of the domain after you set up Vista because the underlying software detects domains automatically.) Keep in mind that computer accounts are very different from user accounts. You'll always log on as a user; the only time you'll need your computer account name is when joining a domain.

Alternatively, your administrator might give you temporary access to an administrative username on the domain, which you could use to create a computer account when you connect your Vista computer. This doesn't happen very often, though. Administrators shouldn't give out administrative access to non-administrators, even on a temporary basis. It's just too much of a security risk.

Profiles

In Chapter 19, I described the basics of user profiles on a Vista computer in a peer-to-peer network. Two other profiles are available: roaming and mandatory. Both require a domain and are discussed later in the chapter. However, to support access to your files and settings from any workstation on the domain, the domain administrator should set up a roaming or mandatory profile when creating your user account on the domain.

Name of Domain

The final item you need to connect to a domain is the name. It could look like an Internet domain name such as `mommabears.com`, or it could be a NetBIOS-style name such as DOMAIN-COMPANY. You can see the names of your peer-to-peer and domain connections in the Network Map (see the "Working with Network Map" section of Chapter 18 for details on this feature).

NOTE Ever since the introduction of Windows 2000, Microsoft has strongly encouraged administrators to name their domains in an Internet-style scheme. While this is good practice, you don't necessarily need to use an Internet-standard top-level domain name such as `.com`, `.net`, or `.org`. For example, you can call your domain `froggy.pond`, and it will work just fine (although others might find you strange).

Connecting to a Domain

Vista makes it significantly easier than past versions of Windows to connect to a domain. In most cases, all you need is your username and password. Vista automatically detects the domain and connects to it for you. You can access any available resource on the domain just as you would in a peer-to-peer network. However, even though Vista does so much for you, you'll still want to know the following information about your domain before logging in so that you can verify your connection:

- Your domain username
- Your domain password
- The name of the domain that you'll join
- Your computer name (you may have to provide the computer name to the administrator, especially if you configured it in a workgroup)
- IP configuration details for the domain

NOTE With the information shown above, you can set up your computer to join the domain during the Vista installation process.

Configuring Vista for a Domain

In most cases, Vista automatically detects your network configuration and sets up your system appropriately during setup. However, at times you may not be able to just connect. You really only need this section of the chapter in those few situations where Vista isn't able to detect your configuration. First, you need to check to see if your IP configuration parameters are compatible.

When you get the configuration parameters you need from the domain administrator, remember that the domain probably includes a substantial number of computers. There may even be multiple LANs on the same domain. This means you'll probably have a Domain Name Server (DNS), Dynamic Host Configuration Protocol (DHCP), and possibly a Windows Internet Naming Service (WINS) server on the domain. If you don't, or if you recognize a DNS server from an outside network, be skeptical.

IP Configuration

It's easier to configure your computer on a peer-to-peer network. As you read in Chapter 19, it's just a matter of selecting a group of IP addresses for your LAN and typing them in with associated subnet masks, gateway addresses, and possibly the DNS addresses from your ISP.

TIP Most domains include a DHCP server. If this applies to you, consult your network administrator. Depending on your domain's DHCP configuration, you may be able to skip some of the following steps.

There's more to configure when you're getting Vista ready to connect to a domain. To see what I mean, open up the properties for your network adapter. Open the Network and Sharing Center applet in the Control Panel, and then click the Manage Network Connections link to see the Network Connections window. Right-click the connection that you're using and then click Properties in the context menu. For example, Figure 22.1 shows the properties for Computer's Local Area Connection.

Now highlight Internet Protocol Version 4 (TCP/IPv4), and then click Properties. You'll see where you may already have configured your IP and DNS addresses. Figure 22.2 illustrates this window with static IP addresses and DNS server IP addresses. Alternatively, you can select Obtain an IP Address Automatically. Your computer would first look to the DHCP server for an IP address assignment. If none were available, it would use the Automatic Private IP Addressing (APIPA) system. These systems are described in more detail in Chapter 19.

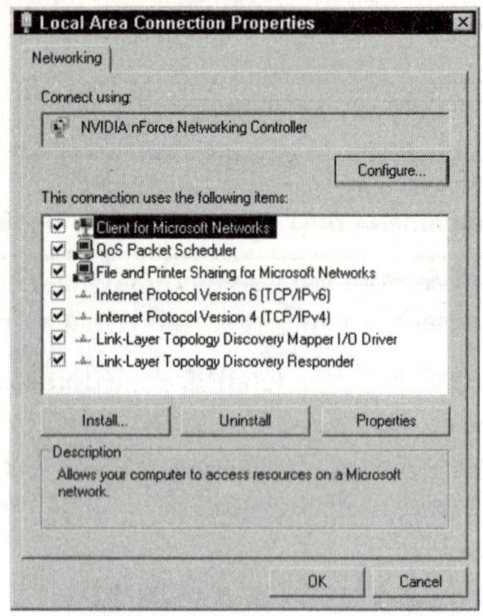

FIGURE 22.1
Local Area Connection properties.

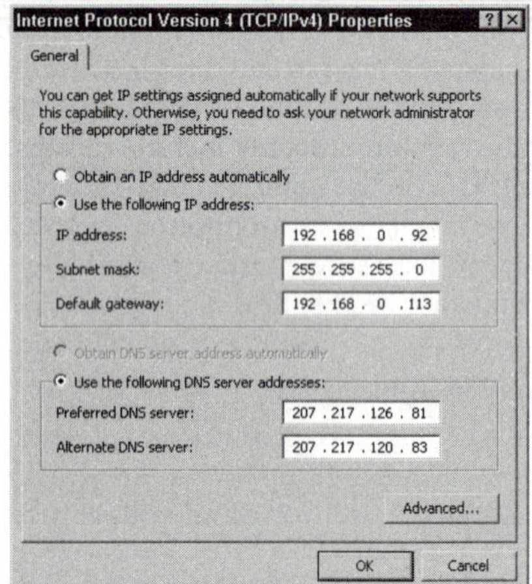

FIGURE 22.2
IP address properties.

Additional IP and Gateway Addresses

Click Advanced to open the Advanced TCP/IP Settings window. It includes three tabs. You should see the IP Settings tab by default, as shown in Figure 22.3. You can assign additional IP addresses to your NIC. If there's more than one way for messages to leave your network, you can also assign additional Default Gateways. Just click the appropriate Add button. Finally, the Automatic Metric setting is checked by default. It's designed to optimize network traffic through your gateways.

NOTE Multiple default gateways are more common in domains than in workgroups. While additional gateways can add to your security challenges, they also provide a backup if you need to ensure reliable connections to other networks or the Internet.

FIGURE 22.3
You can add more IP addresses and gateways.

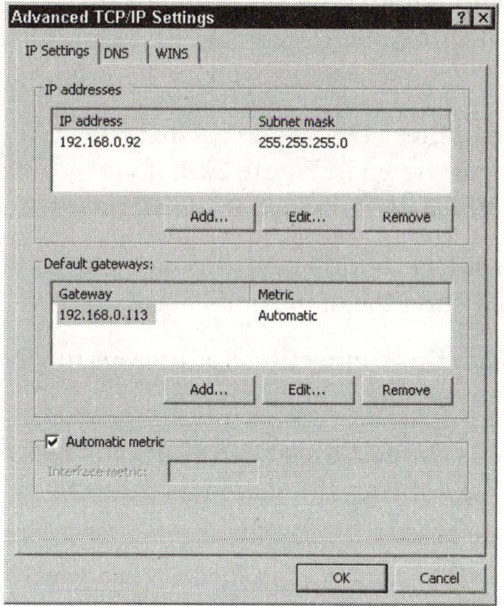

WHAT HAPPENED TO THE OPTIONS TAB?

Earlier versions of Windows provided an Options tab that is completely missing in Vista. The essential purpose of the Options tab in previous versions of Windows was IP filtering, which allows you to block some of the ports and protocols used in TCP/IP communication. The Windows Firewall (described in the "Protecting Your System with a Firewall" section of Chapter 14) performs this task in Vista, so you don't need the Options tab.

It's important to consider Windows Firewall in light of the domain. Over 65,000 TCP/IP ports are available. The first 1,024 ports are reserved for basic communication. For example, port 80 is reserved for HTTP, port 21 for FTP, and port 25 for sending mail (SMTP). It's common for a hacker to use one of these ports to get into a computer. The current list of TCP/IP port numbers is maintained by the Internet Assigned Numbers Authority at `http://www.iana.org/assignments/port-numbers`. Make sure you limit the ports your computer uses based on your company's best practices. Most companies are now severely limiting port access to reduce virus infection and virus transmission among machines on the network.

Additional DNS Information

In a domain, your computers need a DNS server as an address book to figure out how to find other computers. Corporate domains include more than one DNS server. If one goes down or needs maintenance, backups keep a network going. If the domain is large, additional DNS servers help keep any one server from becoming overloaded.

Click the DNS tab. As you can see in Figure 22.4, you can add as many DNS addresses as you might need. The other options in this tab are as follows:

Append primary and connection specific DNS suffixes: Adds the name of your domain to the end of any specified computer name. For example, if you have a computer on the `xp.mommabears.com` network and searched for the laptop2 computer, this option assumes that you're really looking for the computer at `laptop2.xp.mommabears.com`.

Append parent suffixes of the primary DNS suffix: Uses parent suffixes. For example, the parent suffix of `xp.mommabears.com` is `mommabears.com`. Thus, if your computer can't find a `laptop2.xp.mommabears.com` computer, it would then look for `laptop2.mommabears.com`.

Append these DNS suffixes (in order): Adds the suffixes in the text box shown below. For the example shown in Figure 22.4, if you searched for a computer named bigshot, it would automatically look for `bigshot.mommabears.com` and `bigshot.xp.mommabears.com`, in that order.

DNS suffix for this connection: Includes this suffix if all other options fail. Normally, you should enter the name of the local domain.

Register this connection's addresses in DNS: Requests that your DNS server include the name of your computer in its records.

Use this connection's DNS suffix in DNS registration: Requests that your DNS server include the name of your domain in its database.

WARNING If you've specified DNS servers on the Internet, don't select either of the last two options under the DNS tab. At best, your ISP might get annoyed. It also provides an easy way for hackers to bypass your firewall. The exception is if you're using Vista as a server, with a "real" (not private) IP address on the Internet. But most ISPs charge more before they'll allow you to set up a server on their network.

WINS

An alternative to DNS on Microsoft Windows networks is the Windows Internet Naming Service (WINS). Like DNS, WINS provides a database of computer names and IP addresses. The advantage is that WINS servers are automatically updated. However, Microsoft's relatively new Dynamic DNS service also provides for automatic updates. Therefore, you're more likely to use WINS on domains governed by older Microsoft servers such as NT 4.0. Click the WINS tab to review the information shown in Figure 22.5.

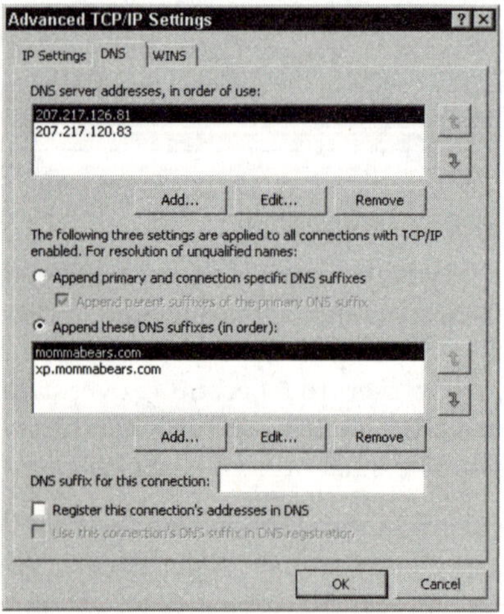

FIGURE 22.4 You can set up DNS resolution in a number of ways.

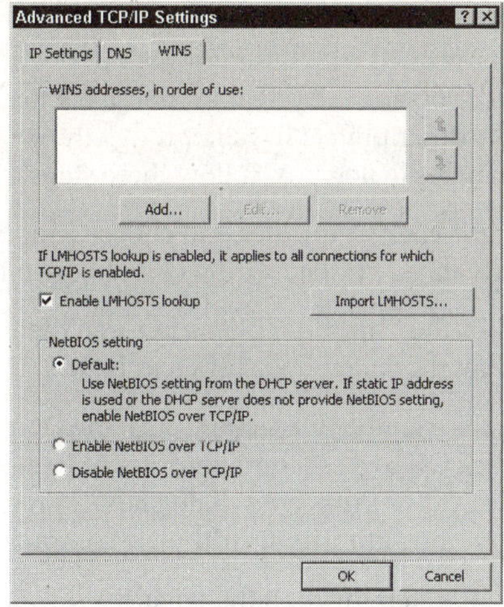

FIGURE 22.5
You can also set up WINS to help find computer names.

Because WINS will eventually become obsolete, I cover it in less detail. Under the WINS tab, you can include the IP addresses of WINS servers. Alternatively, LMHOSTS is a text file that you can substitute for a WINS server.

Generally on a Microsoft network, you want to enable NetBIOS over TCP/IP. However, this may already be set through your DHCP server. In any case, follow the instructions from your network administrator.

IDENTIFICATION

Now you're ready to change the identification of your computer from a workgroup to a domain. The computer name is associated with the properties for Computer. To access these properties, right-click Computer and choose Properties to display the System window. Click the Advanced system settings link to display the System Properties dialog box and then choose the Computer Name tab. As shown in Figure 22.6, you'll see your computer name, as well as the workgroup or domain name. You can also change that information here.

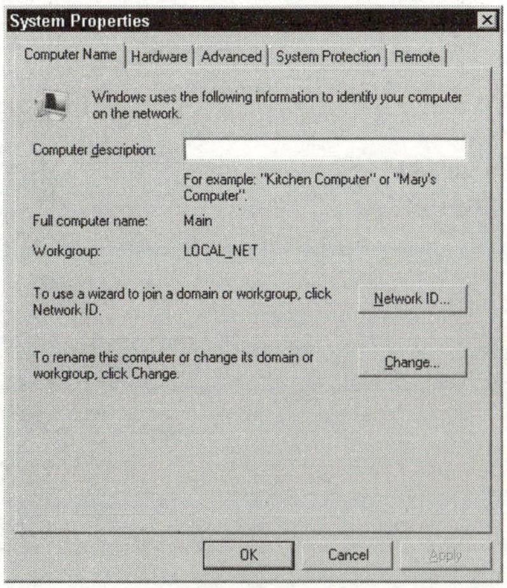

FIGURE 22.6
The Computer Name tab shows whether your computer is part of a workgroup or a domain.

Making the Connection

Once you're armed with this information, you can join a domain using the Computer Name/Domain Changes dialog box in System Properties or the Network Identification Wizard. Since using the wizard is more descriptive, I'll walk through the process of using it next. If you want to use the Computer Name Changes dialog box, follow these steps to open it:

1. Right-click Computer and choose Properties to display the System window. Click the Advanced system settings link to open the System Properties dialog box.
2. Click the Computer Name tab, and then click Change to open the Computer Name/Domain Changes dialog box shown in Figure 22.7.
3. In the Member Of section, click the Domain option, and then enter the name of the domain. Click OK to close the Computer Name Changes dialog box, and then click OK again to close the System Properties dialog box. If prompted, enter a username and password *on the domain* with the authority to add your computer.

Now, let's step through the wizard:

1. Right-click Computer and choose Properties to display the System window. Click the Advanced system settings link to open the System Properties dialog box.
2. Click the Computer Name tab, and then click Network ID to start the Network Identification Wizard shown in Figure 22.8.
3. Click the option that tells Vista that this computer is part of a business network, and then click Next. Vista automatically detects the domain and tells you to reboot your computer.

NOTE Don't try to install management tools from previous versions of Windows on Vista. You might not get a usable installation. See the Knowledge Base article at `http://support.microsoft.com/default.aspx/kb/930056` for details.

After the computer reboots, supply your username and password. Vista will log you into the domain. If you find that you're logged into the wrong domain or the wrong server, you'll need to manually supply the name of the domain using the Computer Name/Domain Changes dialog box shown in Figure 22.7.

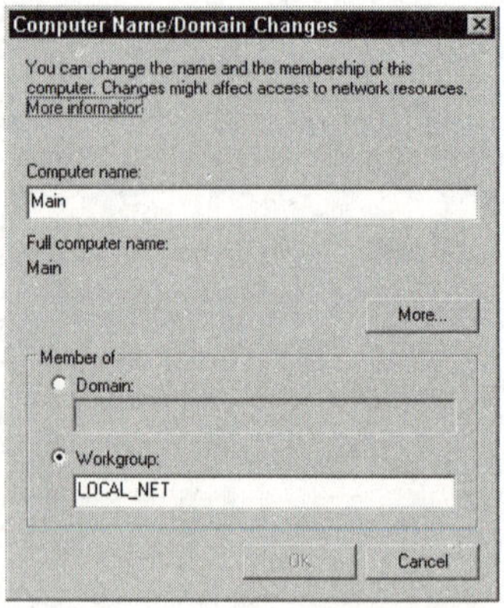

FIGURE 22.7 Switch between a domain or workgroup association using this dialog box.

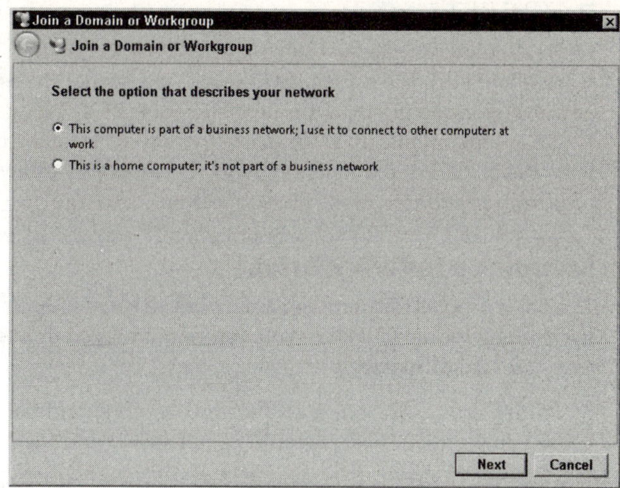

FIGURE 22.8
Join a workgroup or domain using the Network Identification Wizard.

One thing to keep in mind is that these steps work only if the computer and user accounts already exist on the domain. In addition, only domain administrators are authorized to add your computer to the domain. It's not as though they want to give out the domain administrator password to everyone. If your user account doesn't have the necessary rights to join your computer to the domain, you may need some assistance from your network administrator.

REJOINING A WORKGROUP

It's easier to reconfigure your computer from a domain to a workgroup. First, make sure your IP address settings are consistent with other computers on your workgroup. For more information, see Chapter 19. Then return to the Computer Name tab shown in Figure 22.6. Click Change. Select the Workgroup option and then enter the name of your workgroup.

When you click OK, you'll be prompted for your username and password on the workgroup (not on the domain). Once this information is entered, Vista joins the workgroup of your choice.

Attaching to Network Resources

After your network is configured for sharing, one of the easiest ways to test your network connections is to attach to network resources. The process is nearly identical to that for a peer-to-peer network. In fact, if you've read Chapter 19, a lot of the following sections will seem familiar; they're just repackaged for domains. You can test your connections in the following ways:

- By browsing Network
- By mapping a network drive
- By using UNCs to connect directly

Browsing Network

Open Windows Explorer. Click Network to open a window that displays the options on your network. Double-click a computer to view, and connect to its shared resources. You can also double-click Network on the Desktop to open a view of the network.

On a domain, this may not work if you didn't use the domain username and password. However, the other two methods can work, because they allow you to enter the domain username and password in order to make the connection.

Mapping a Network Drive

The basic process for mapping a network drive is essentially identical to that described for a peer-to-peer network in Chapter 19. If you're not logged in with a domain username and password, there are two differences:

Folder: Specify the name of the domain server and the associated share name in the Folder text box. In Figure 22.9, that would be net-server and inetpub.

Username: Select different username. In the Connect As window that appears, type in a domain username and password. An example is shown in Figure 22.10.

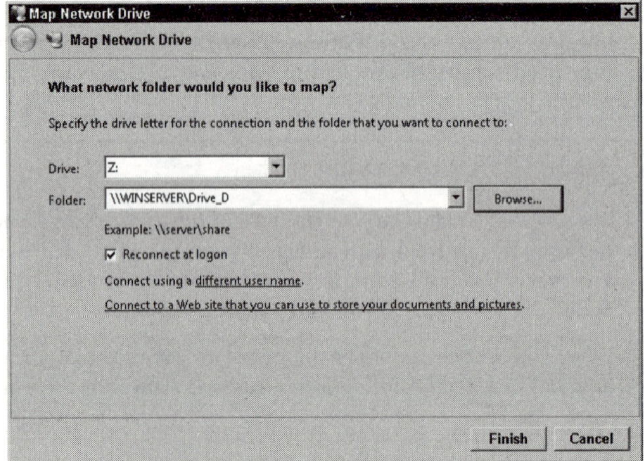

FIGURE 22.9
Just specify the name of the domain server and shared directory.

FIGURE 22.10
If you're an authorized user on a domain, just specify your domain username and password.

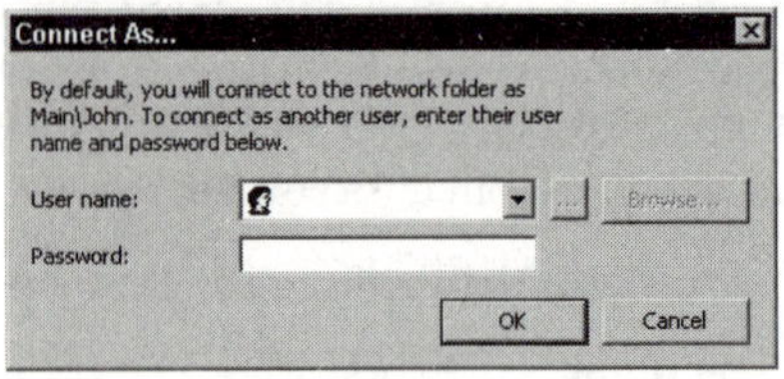

Making a Direct Connection via a UNC

Alternatively, you can use various forms of the `net` command at the command-line interface.

Here's how to use the `net view` command:

1. To display a list of the computers on your network, type **`net view`** at the command prompt.
2. To display a list of the resources on a particular server, append the name of the machine. For example, if the server name is spiritwolf, you'd enter **`net view \\spiritwolf`**. This works even if spiritwolf is the server for your domain.
3. To view the resources of a machine in another domain, for example, the server spiritwolf in the domain hq, you'd enter the following:

   ```
   net view \\spiritwolf /domain:hq
   ```

4. To display a list of all the domains on the network, simply enter **`net view /domain`**.

ALTERNATE DOMAIN ACCOUNTS

But what if you're attaching to another server and you don't have an account on that server? This happens a lot to administrators.

If you have an administrator called Sheila Sanders, Sheila will have an account on her primary server that she logs on to. In addition, Sheila may need to attach to other servers that have resources she wants to use, even though she doesn't have an account on those servers. Another classic example would be that Sheila logs on to a Windows server as Sheila but has an account named SSanders on a NetWare server.

To resolve this issue, Sheila could log on to the Windows server as Sheila, but when she maps a drive to a Novell server, she could use the Connect As dialog box to connect to the NetWare server as SSanders. If Sheila's passwords on the Windows server and the SSanders account on NetWare are the same, Sheila gets direct access to the NetWare directory. If the passwords are different, Sheila will be prompted to enter a password for the NetWare server when she clicks OK to map the network drive.

USING *NET USE*: CONNECTING TO OTHER DRIVES AND PRINTERS

After you've browsed the network with the `net view` command, you can connect to all the available goodies (or disconnect from those you don't want) with the `net use` command. Use this command to connect to network resources as drives D through Z and printer ports LPT1 through LPT9.

WARNING Drive letters can be used only once. So if your DVD player is drive D and your CD burner is drive E, you'll have only drive letters F through Z available.

To display information about the workstation's current connections, type **`net use`** without options, and you'll see something like the output shown in Figure 22.11.

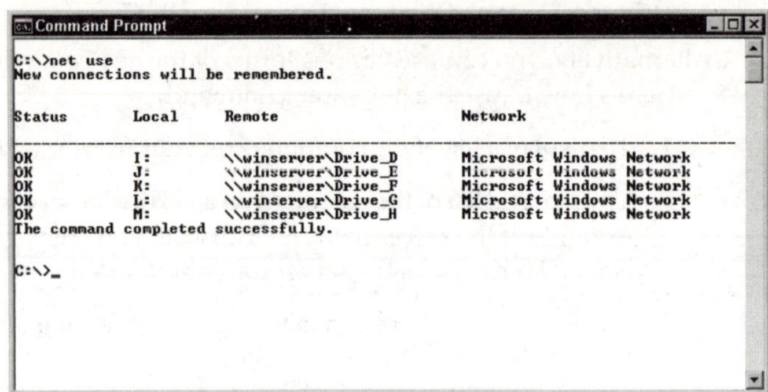
Command Prompt
C:\>net use
New connections will be remembered.
Status Local Remote Network
OK I: \\winserver\Drive_D Microsoft Windows Network
OK J: \\winserver\Drive_E Microsoft Windows Network
OK K: \\winserver\Drive_F Microsoft Windows Network
OK L: \\winserver\Drive_G Microsoft Windows Network
OK M: \\winserver\Drive_H Microsoft Windows Network
The command completed successfully.
C:\>_

FIGURE 22.11
The net use command displays a list of your current connections.

CONNECTING TO A RESOURCE IN THE LOCAL DOMAIN

To connect to a shared resource, such as a printer shared as lexmarko on server spiritwolf, type **`net use lpt1: \\spiritwolf\lexmarko`**. If you want to specify domain username jdoe and password, type **`net use lpt1: \\spiritwolf\lexmarko * /USER:jdoe`**, and then you'll be prompted for a password.

USING LONG FILENAMES IN UNCS

If you wanted to connect to a folder called `Wpfiles` on the spiritwolf server and make that your E drive, you'd substitute **`E:`** for **`lpt1:`** and **`Wpfiles`** for **`lexmarko`** in the preceding example. Your command would be **`net use E: \\spiritwolf\wpfiles`**. You get to specify the port name or drive letter that you want to connect a resource to, but again, you're restricted to drive letters D through Z and ports LPT1 through LPT9.

If the computer you're getting the resource from has a blank character in its name (that is, the computer name has two words in it), you must put the name in quotation marks, like this:

```
"\\eisa server"
```

If a different username and password are attached to the resource that you're trying to connect to, such as on a domain server, you need to include that in your connection command, like this:

```
net use lpt1: \\ted\hp4m * USER:mjang
```

The asterisk tells the `net` command to prompt you for the password.

TIP When you use the `net` command to connect to a share, don't use more than one domain username.

CREATING A DRIVE MAPPING FOR YOUR HOME FOLDER

To connect to your home folder (the folder on the server that has been assigned to you, assuming there is one), type the following:

```
net use /home
```

with the (optional) password and username on the end as just explained.

If you want to make the connection for another user, rather than for yourself, add the user's name (Frank) to the end of the line, like this:

```
net use lpt1: \\ted\hp4m * user:frank
```

The asterisk tells `net` to prompt you for a password. If the user for whom you're making the connection is in another domain, the user part of the statement looks like this:

```
user:domainname/frank
```

where *domainname* is the name of that user's home domain.

Connecting to a Resource in Another Domain

If you want to connect to a resource in a domain that's not your usual one, you must first log on to that domain. One way to do this is to have a user account for yourself in the second domain. Managing multiple accounts for one person can get extremely cumbersome, so it's not the best setup. When a password expires in one domain, and you have to change it, the password doesn't necessarily expire in the other domain. This can cause confusion, and profiles don't span domains either. Another way is to have a trust relationship between your domains. Trust relationships allow users in one domain the potential to access resources in the other domain. I say *potential* because we still have to deal with permissions.

Think of trust relationships in human terms. If I trust you, I may let you drive my car (my resource). However, you still can't drive my car until I give you the keys (permissions). But if I don't trust you, there's no way I'm handing you my keys! After you've logged on to the proper domain, the process of connecting to resources is the same as described previously.

NOTE Trust relationships are set up between domains, not specific computers. Generally, the setting of trust relationships is a domain administrator's responsibility and not something you'll do from Vista; however, it's important to talk about, since you may be part of a domain and need to access resources in another domain.

Using User Profiles

In Vista, a user profile is a collection of environment settings that customize a user's interface. It can include display settings, network settings, printer settings, and so on. User profiles are of three types:

- Local
- Roaming
- Mandatory

Local user profiles apply only to a local machine, hence their name. Since local user profiles apply to the local computer, they're covered in more detail in Chapter 19.

A *roaming user profile* can be created by only your system administrator and is stored on the server. A roaming user profile contains settings that are specific to you and is loaded whenever you log on to any computer on the network. Local user profiles and roaming user profiles contain the same types of information. The only differences are that the main copy of a roaming profile is stored on a server (as opposed to the local machine). Roaming profiles follow you no matter where you log in. (Parts of the roaming profile appear on your local machine for performance reasons, but this copy is only temporary and Vista copies any changes to the server.) You must have a domain to use roaming user profiles.

TIP If your network uses roaming user profiles, don't store large files on your desktop, which is part of your profile. Every time you log on, the profile needs to be copied from the server it's stored on to the local machine. If there are large files as part of that profile, logging on to the network could take an excruciatingly long time.

A *mandatory user profile* specifies settings for an individual or a group of users and can be created or modified only by your system administrator. There's a major philosophical difference between mandatory user profiles and the other two we have discussed. With local and roaming profiles, users are allowed to customize their settings any way they choose. While this allows for freedom and personalization, people are known to abuse these types of privileges. With a mandatory user profile, the user gets a specified environment every time they log on. They're allowed to make changes, but every time they log off and back on, their settings go back to the defaults. Most of the time, when users realize that their changes aren't being kept, they'll simply stop making changes at all.

NOTE Mandatory user profiles will work only if you're implementing them across a network. They won't work locally.

Please note that mandatory profiles do *not* keep users from making changes to their desktop settings. Mandatory profiles just don't save those changes that the user does make. If you want to keep people from changing desktop settings at all, you need to use either Local Security Policy (which affects only your computer) or Group Policies (which can affect an entire network).

Attaching to Network Resources Using Login Scripts

A very common way in which you'll attach to network resources is through network drive mappings that the network administrator created in a login script. Often drive letters such as H and M point to files on a file server on the network. The good news is that login scripts run automatically every time you log in (hence their name); therefore, they require no thinking on the part of the user.

You'll be able to distinguish between network drives and local hard drives by the icon associated with the drive. Network drives have the little T-connector and cable beneath the icon. From time to time, you may see a drive with a red X across it. This symbol indicates that you formerly had a drive mapped to this drive letter, but the system can't find the network location at this time. This situation happens most frequently if you're accessing the network remotely via a modem, but it could also be a sign of connectivity problems.

Troubleshooting Domains

Entire books have been written on the topic of troubleshooting networks. It's such a voluminous topic that it requires a lot of attention. To that end, there's no way this chapter can teach you everything you need to know to troubleshoot network problems. The best training for troubleshooting is simply hands-on experience. That said, this section will give you some pointers to get you started.

Receiving the Error Message "No Domain Server Was Available"

When logging on to the server, you may get an error message stating that no domain server was available to authorize you to log on to a domain. Often this error message will prevent you from seeing some resources in Network and prevent you from accessing the network entirely.

NOTE The title of this section is a good example of a specific error message. Whenever you receive specific error messages, write them down. They're invaluable to have when searching your resources for a solution. You're never going to know how to fix everything right away, but if you know where to look for help, you'll be a lot further ahead in the game.

TIP A good place to get started is Microsoft's Knowledge Base. It has a lot of articles about known error messages and may be able to help you. Go either to Microsoft's web page (`http://www.microsoft.com`) and click the Support link or to `http://support.microsoft.com`. You'll be able to type in your error message and search through all of Microsoft's products or choose the specific product you're interested in. The support page also provides a download area for patches, and newsgroups for you to post questions.

This message appears when the system is unable to contact a domain controller for the domain that you're logging on to. The obvious problem could be that the server is down. Another common cause of this error is that a switch, router, or gateway is malfunctioning in your environment, so check the hub and the bridges to make sure they're operating normally.

Easily the most common occurrence of this problem is when TCP/IP is the primary transport protocol in your environment. If the workstation is on one physical segment of the network and the domain controller is on another segment of the network, often the client machine is unable to see the server via NetBIOS. To test this situation, see if you can ping the server's address. If you can ping the server by using its IP address but are unable to contact the server for domain logon authentication, you have determined the cause of your dilemma.

If your network has a DNS server (which it must if you're running a Windows 2000 or newer domain), configure your clients to use the DNS server. This should already be the case, and if the clients can find the DNS server, and the DNS server has the records it's supposed to have, you won't encounter this error message.

TIP If your client computers are getting their IP configuration information from a DHCP server, the addresses of WINS and DNS servers can be supplied along with the IP address, subnet mask, and other parameters.

Identification

In a network with sufficient extra capacity, no extra work by the domain administrator should be required. However, if you have a problem connecting, have your administrator check the domain controller for the following issues:

Services: If the services related to networking such as DNS aren't running, they can't help your computer connect to the domain.

DNS pointers: If the DNS server on your domain doesn't know about your computer, it can't find you when you try to log on. This includes reverse lookup zones.

DHCP scope: If your domain uses DHCP to lease IP addresses, make sure you have enough available for the computers that are connected to your network.

Subnet: If you've manually assigned IP addresses, make sure each computer on the network belongs to the proper subnet. For examples of the range of IP addresses available on a subnet, see Chapter 19.

Summary

In this chapter, we've looked at how to set up and configure a Vista connection to a domain, attach to network resources, understand roaming and mandatory user profiles, and troubleshoot your network when things go awry.

Although Vista will perform most of the work for you, it's usually a good idea to have a look around. Becoming familiar with your network configuration makes it significantly easier to troubleshoot problems later. For example, you'll want to know how IP is configured on your system. With this goal in mind, check the various settings for your system and consider recording them in a log for future use.

In the next chapter, we'll stick with the domains topic but focus our efforts on understanding Windows Server 2003. Generally, you'll find that Windows Server 2003 hasn't changed, but Vista's ability to work with Windows Server 2003 is an improvement over previous versions of Windows.

Chapter 23

Working with Windows Server 2003

Any discussion of connecting to domains is incomplete without talking about Microsoft's most current offering in the server space, Windows Server 2003. As pointed out in Chapter 22, the true power of networking comes with being able to control resources and security from a centralized location. Windows 2000 introduced Active Directory, which allowed you centralized control while granting flexibility in your management structure as well as providing convenient management tools.

Windows Server 2003 still uses the basic core of Active Directory. But of course, because it's a newer product, there are updated features that didn't come with Windows 2000. Because the structure of Active Directory hasn't changed a great deal, this chapter won't focus on stuffing those types of details into your head. Rather, this chapter discusses new features of Windows Server 2003 and how they'll impact your network.

Here are the topics included in this chapter:

- The Windows Server 2003 family tree
- Integration with Vista
- Two key server additions
- Networking improvements
- Active Directory improvements
- Security enhancements
- Other improvements
- Connecting Vista to Windows Server 2003 domains

Vista: What's New?

The big news with Vista is that Microsoft seems to have worked out most of the kinks of accessing the server from Vista. While writing this book, I tried both Windows 2000 Server and Windows Server 2003 access from the various tools in the Administrative Tools folder of the Control Panel. Amazingly, they all worked flawlessly, which is something that never happened in Windows XP. Just this change alone should make at least some administrators very happy about Vista.

Of course, Vista also continues a trend that Microsoft started with Windows Server 2003. Unlike previous versions of Windows where you started with everything unlocked, Vista assumes that you want every locked for the default configuration. After all, you can unlock items as you need them. This trend continues the start of the locking trend for Windows Server 2003.

The Five Flavors of Server 2003

Microsoft isn't quite Baskin-Robbins yet, but to some administrators, it seems like it's getting that way. In the good old days of Windows NT 3.5, there was only one version. Windows NT 4 also had an Enterprise Edition, which used an enhanced memory model and offered clustering. Because it was more expensive and didn't provide a lot of added value, few people used it.

Enter Windows Server 2003: Now there are five. Well, okay, if you include the 64-bit versions, the embedded versions, and so on, there are actually a lot more. But the main product grouping includes these five flavors:

- Windows Server 2003 Standard Edition
- Windows Server 2003 Enterprise Edition (32-bit and 64-bit)
- Windows Server 2003 Datacenter Edition (32-bit and 64-bit)
- Windows Server 2003 Web Edition
- Windows Small Business Server 2003

Which one is right for you? I'm glad you asked. Let's browse some of the features of each, and that might help you make up your mind.

No More "Plain Old Server"

For the first time since 1983, the basic variety of server has a name; it's now Windows Server 2003 Standard Edition. In general, it has just about all of the features that it did back when it didn't have a name; it just takes twice as long to say.

Standard Edition comes with a bunch of new features that are new to all of 2003's editions, as you'd expect, but it also comes with a bit of quite welcome news: Standard Edition includes Network Load Balancing (NLB) (if you want clustering, you'll still have to pony up for either Enterprise or Datacenter). NLB's not new, since it was included in Windows 2000 Advanced Server, the more expensive version of Windows 2000 Server. But where Microsoft once required you to buy the pricier version of 2000 Server to get this very useful feature, it's now included in all editions of Windows Server 2003. But that's not all that's new in Standard Edition—for instance, how does "You finally get a complete e-mail server free in the box" sound? Like sweet music in a field of daisies.

Just for Web Servers

Windows Server 2003 Web Edition is the first Microsoft server offering specifically for web servers. The idea is that Microsoft really wants their web server, IIS, to completely crush, overtake, and overwhelm the competition: Apache and Sun web servers. So they ripped a bunch of things out of Server and offered it to hardware vendors as an OEM-only copy of Server 2003. It can address only 2GB of RAM (NT has always been able to access 4 or more GB) and supports only 2-way SMP, not 4-way.

- Be a domain controller, although it can join a domain
- Support Macintosh clients, save as a web server
- Be accessed remotely via Terminal Services, although it has Remote Desktop, like XP
- Provide Internet Connection Sharing or Net Bridging
- Be a DHCP or fax server

So it's unlikely that you'll actually see a copy of Web Edition, but if you do, then don't imagine that you'll be able to build a whole network around it. As its name suggests, it's pretty much intended as a platform for cheap web servers.

Enterprise and Datacenter Features

Back in the NT 4 days, Microsoft introduced a more expensive version of Server called NT 4 Server, Enterprise Edition. It supported clusters and a larger memory model. When Windows 2000 Server came around, Microsoft renamed it Windows 2000 Advanced Server. With Server 2003, Microsoft still offers this higher-end version of Server but with yet another name change. Now it's called Windows Server 2003 Enterprise Edition. Yes, you read that right: once it was Enterprise Edition, then it became Advanced Server, and now it's back to Enterprise Edition. Remember, people get paid big money to make naming decisions like these.

Enterprise Edition still does clusters—four-PC clusters now. It also lets you boot a server from a storage area network (SAN), hot-install memory like Datacenter can, and run with four processors (eight if you have Enterprise). As of the writing of this book, only 32-bit versions of Server 2003 support these features (not the 64-bit versions). And, of course, your hardware might limit you on some cool features, such as hot-installing memory.

With Server 2003, Microsoft has finally made me covetous of Datacenter. It has this incredibly cool tool called Windows System Resource Manager (also available in Enterprise) that basically lets you do the kind of system management that you could do on the mainframe years and years ago. How'd you like to say to your system, "Don't let SQL Server ever use more than 50 percent of the CPU power or 70 percent of the RAM?" WRM lets you do that, and it ships only with Datacenter. Datacenter also now supports eight-PC clusters as well as hot-installing RAM—yup, that's right, you just open the top of the server *while it's running* and insert a new memory module, wait a second or two, and the system now recognizes the new RAM, no reboot required. How cool is *that*?

Small Business Server 2003

Based on the title alone, I can hear you thinking, "Gee, I bet this is for people who run small businesses." How absolutely correct you are. Microsoft's rationale behind offering a small business product is pretty simple. Small businesses, by nature, are strapped for resources. Instead of needing to hire an IT professional or worry about domain management issues that they don't have the time or expertise to deal with, why not make it easy? Make Server easy to install, manage, and use: that's the goal of Windows Small Business Server 2003.

Small Business Server 2003 comes in two varieties (see, I told you there were a ton): Standard Edition and Premium Edition. Premium Edition has three primary add-ons: ISA Server (Internet firewall), SQL Server (database), and FrontPage 2003 (design websites). All in all, Small Business Server 2003 has most of the same features as Windows Server 2003 Standard Edition (minus a few), but it's not nearly as stripped down as Web Edition.

Perhaps the biggest advantage to small businesses is that Small Business Server 2003 is cheaper than Standard Edition. Depending on where you buy it, you can generally find it for about 40 percent less than Standard Edition.

Free E-mail Server and SQL Server "Lite"

Thank you, Microsoft.

Not too many people remember this, but back when Server first came out, it wasn't all that impressive in terms of performance. But over time, it took market share away from network OSes that were, in many ways, faster, more flexible, or more reliable. How'd they do it? Many ways, but I've always thought that there were two biggies. First, NT used the Windows interface, which meant that once you'd mastered Solitaire you were well on the way to administering an NT Server.

The second reason was that NT came with a lot of stuff free in the box. From the very beginning, NT contained software that most vendors charged for. At one time, most server OS vendors charged for the TCP/IP protocol, but NT always had it. Ditto remote access tools, or Macintosh support, or a web server, or FTP, or a dozen other things. In terms of features, Microsoft made NT an attractive proposition.

So I could never understand why they didn't include an e-mail server. Well, okay, I understood it—they wanted to sell you MS Mail (you in the back there, stop laughing) or Exchange and didn't want to offer a free alternative. But I've never understood that. Exchange is a mail server that, while powerful, is complex, difficult to set up, and expensive. Why not offer an e-mail server that's nothing more than an SMTP and POP3–based system? It would serve that five-person office well, and they're probably not about to buy Exchange. Nor would it keep the 100-person (or 100,000-person) enterprise from buying Exchange, because they're probably large enough that they want support for shared calendars, IMAP, mailbox forwarding, antivirus add-ons, and so on, and a super-basic POP3 service wouldn't do it.

I got my wish. All versions of Windows Server 2003 include a POP3 service. The other part, SMTP, has always existed, so between the two of them, you've got a complete low-end mail server. Again, there are no hooks for antivirus software, no way to set a mailbox to automatically forward to somewhere else, and no way to create an autoresponse message for a mailbox a la "Jack doesn't work here anymore; please don't send any more mail here to his address," but it may still do the job for you.

The next goodie wasn't on my wish list, but I'll bet it was on a lot of other people's: a free database engine. Even better, it's a free database engine that's a copy of SQL Server 2000, although with a "governor" and no administrative tools.

For years, Microsoft has offered a thing called Microsoft Database Engine, or MSDE. It was never generally available to NT users, but it was available to various groups of developers. The idea with MSDE was that Microsoft took SQL Server 2000—a fairly expensive piece of software—and crippled it in three ways:

- First, they limited the database size to 2GB. That may not sound like a big deal, but a "real" application of any size could grow beyond that very quickly. But it's a great size for testing and developing database-driven apps or for managing a database that will never get very big.
- Second, they put a "throttle" (Microsoft's word) on it so that if more than five people access it, it slows down. Again, it's a barrier to using this for member registration on a thousand-member website, but it's fine for testing and small networks.
- Finally, they don't ship any administrative tools for MSDE. If you want to do something as simple as changing the password on the default "sa" account, you'll have to do some scripting.

None of that's intended to sound negative, even though it's true the MSDE is a severely cut-down version of SQL Server 2000. The price is right and once you get past the basic lack of an admin interface—the hard part—then you'll find that it's a pretty nice add-on.

SQL SERVER 2005 EXPRESS EDITION, BETTER THAN MSDE

You may find that MSDE is nice, but perhaps not as nice as you'd like. It lacks functionality or performance you need to complete simple tasks. Fortunately, you now have another alternative to consider. Microsoft provides SQL Server 2005 Express Edition as a free download. It doesn't provide all of the functionality of SQL Server 2005, but it does provide considerably more functionality that MSDE and there's a good upgrade path should you decide to move to the full version of SQL Server 2005 later. You can download this free product at `http://msdn.microsoft.com/vstudio/express/sql/download/`.

The download for this product is on the hefty side. You'll need to obtain the .NET Framework 2.0 and SQL Server Express Edition as a minimum. (Make sure you obtain any required service packs as well—Service Pack 1 is available as I write this.) If you have a copy of SQL Server 2005 installed somewhere, you can use the same management tools with SQL Server 2005 Express that you use with SQL Server 2005. On the other hand, if you don't have such an installation handy, you can download the optional SQL Server Management Studio Express separately. No longer do you need to write odd-looking macros to accomplish everything as you did with MSDE. In fact, the SQL Server Management Studio Express interface is quite nice and relatively easy to learn. Any time you invest in the express version reduces your time in learning the full version because they're essentially the same.

Make sure you consider the differences between the standard version of SQL Server 2005 Express and SQL Server 2005 Express with Advanced Services. This second product is a huge download, but it also provides considerably more functionality. You really could build a reasonably complex (albeit with limited connectivity) solution with this product. The advanced services are really provided to get you to buy the full version of SQL Server, but don't be fooled, this really is a significant improvement over MSDE and well worth the download time if MSDE isn't serving your needs.

Networking Enhancements

What good is a new server product if it doesn't include networking improvements? When Windows XP came out, it included some networking features that Windows 2000 Server didn't have. That made for an interesting paradox that the client system had more advanced networking features (in some cases) than the server. No longer is this the case, because Windows Server 2003 includes XP's networking functionality. You'll find that Vista offers more security than any previous operating system, but it also works fine with both Windows 2000 Server and Windows 2003 Server. From a low-level networking perspective, Vista is a half step up with terrific IPv6 support and great security as the emphasis. When compared with Windows 2000 Server, Windows Server 2003 networking features include

- NAT traversal (discussed in Chapter 14)
- IPSec NAT traversal (like NAT traversal, but secure)
- Routing and Remote Access Service (RRAS) NBT Proxy
- DNS conditional forwarding supporting multidomain AD-integrated networks

There are others, as well, but these are some of the most useful upgrades.

Active Directory Improvements

For a first try, Windows 2000's Active Directory (AD) was pretty good, not bad for a 1.0, Microsoft. (Of course, they *did* have Banyan and Novell's directory services to learn from, but let's ignore that for this discussion.) In Server 2003, Microsoft dishes up a 1.1 version of AD that solves several irritating problems, makes running branch offices easier, and expands AD's flexibility.

While I don't want this to sound negative, it's a fact that Active Directory still suffers most from its inflexibility—there's no simple way to rearrange the structure of an existing forest, to merge forests into one forest, or to break off a piece of a forest and make it a forest of its own. Don't think that those scenarios are marginal or unusual ones—they're not. The reorganizations that most organizations undergo every year or so often require rearranging a forest. Two firms merging need to be able to merge their forests as well. And a firm divesting itself of a subsidiary would want to be able to detach one or more domains or trees from a forest. But perhaps that will appear in a future version of Server; let's hope so.

Meanwhile, the 2003 edition of AD has, again, some very good news. Here's a look at its high points.

Forest-to-Forest Trusts

Combining a bunch of AD domains into a forest offers two main benefits: first, those domains all automatically trust each other, and, second, the domains share a set of "super" domain controllers called global catalog (GC) servers, which are domain controllers that contain a subset of information not just about their own domains but about every single domain in the forest. Doing away with the unreliability of NT 4 trusts for the convenience and dependability of AD's automatic trusts is a big win for AD users.

But, as I suggested a few paragraphs back, AD forests were and are still pretty inflexible. So suppose you're an organization that finds itself with more than one forest, and you need to get those forests to share things? Well, there's always been the hard way—get a migration tool and copy all of the user accounts, machine accounts, and other objects from Forest 1 to Forest 2 and then just plain delete Forest 1. The problem with that solution is that while migration tools are pretty nice, they don't do the whole job and they're a lot of work to get working.

With a Server 2003–based forest, however, you have a new answer: forest root trusts. With these, you just build one new trust relationship between Forest 1 and Forest 2, and instantly every domain in Forest 1 trusts every domain in Forest 2 and vice versa. Cool; thank you, Redmond.

But I said that forests had two main features—complete trust and a centralized database of forest information called the global catalog. A forest-to-forest trust gives us back the first benefit of a single forest; what about the second? Unfortunately, two forests that trust each other don't share a global catalog. That means that forest trusts won't let applications that are GC-dependent see the trusting forests as one single overall directory. What apps are GC-dependent? Well, the most prominent one is Exchange 2000: it really wants to see your organization as one big forest. Forest trusts don't solve that problem.

I was surprised to learn of another limitation to forest trusts: they're not transitive. Interestingly enough, if Forest 1 trusts Forest 2 and Forest 2 trusts Forest 3, then Forest 1 doesn't trust Forest 3. Bummer. And *none* of this forest trust stuff works at all until you've upgraded every single DC in every single domain of both forests to Server 2003. So, overall the forest trusts are a good step forward but not the whole story.

Group Replication Problem Solved

It's always been ironic that while Active Directory can support a far larger user list than could NT 4 domains, AD couldn't support *groups* as large as NT 4 could. You can create literally millions of users in an AD, but because of a quirk in AD's method of keeping domain controllers' information consistent (AD replication) in combination with the way that group membership is stored in AD, you can't put more than about 5,000 users into a group.

In 2003's AD, Microsoft restructured the way they store group membership, and now the sky's the limit. It also solves another problem wherein it's possible in 2000's AD that you and I work in the same worldwide company and you change a group's membership while sitting in the Edenton office while I change that same group's membership while sitting in the Port Angeles office, and one of our changes overwrites the other person's changes. With 2003, that's fixed.

To get this benefit, you must upgrade all of the DCs in all of the domains in your forest to 2003.

Domains Can Be Renamed

One of 2000's most annoying AD limitations was that it prevented you from renaming a domain; if Bell Atlantic had had an AD forest when it merged with GTE and was renamed Verizon, there would have been no way to rename an AD domain named `bellatlantic.com` to `verizon.com`. Now you can rename a domain, but it's not a simple matter, even now.

First, every DC in the domain to be renamed (not all DCs in the forest, just the ones in the domain) must be running Server 2003. And second, there are, well, I was going to write "a few steps to perform in order to complete the domain renaming," but the truth is that Microsoft has a white paper online explaining how to do it.

The paper is *60 pages long*. So it's *possible*, just not easy, at least not yet.

AD Can Selectively Replicate

Active Directory is a database, and domain controllers are database servers, just like systems running Access, Oracle, MySQL, or SQL Server and holding some other kind of database. (Well, not *just* like DCs don't respond to SQL queries. Instead, their query language is LDAP.) While the AD database was originally designed for storing user accounts, machine accounts, and the like, there's no reason application designers can't take advantage of AD's built-in database engine to store other information.

Microsoft's own programmers did just that when designing 2000's DNS server. As you may know, 2000 introduced you to the option to create a DNS zone that was an Active Directory–integrated zone. A zone of that type stores the DNS info for your systems in the AD itself and replicates it along with the normal domain information from DC to DC. But *only* DCs get copies of the database, so if you choose AD-integrated DNS, all of your DNS servers must be DCs.

But now consider: what if you had a lot of DCs, but only a few of them were DNS servers? Wouldn't that be a bit wasteful? You'd use precious bandwidth to replicate DNS info to every DC, whether it used it or not. Server 2003 solves that problem with the notion of an *application directory partition*. Partitions are subsets of the AD that replicate only to a subset of DCs. Microsoft then applied that notion to their DNS servers, so in a network using AD-integrated zones only the DCs running DNS will get the DNS info. This feature doesn't require any preparation; you get its benefit on any DC running Server 2003.

Better Security

Sometime in late 2001, two things occurred to Bill Gates: first, network security is important and, second, Microsoft software is buggy as heck when it comes to security (among other things), so a lot of Microsoft security is lacking a bit. So he derailed virtually all of Microsoft's coding efforts for two months as Microsoft trained nearly everyone about security.

In the end, this was a good thing. NT has always had a reputation of being an insecure operating system (the joke was that NT was a perfectly secure operating system until you installed the NIC), but it's an inaccurate reputation. NT (3.1–4, and Windows 2000) is an extremely secure OS in that it provides the option to lock many things; a properly tweaked NT server is a secure server indeed. NT's reputation comes, however, from the fact that a default installation leaves the vast majority of those locks unlocked. For Server 2003, that changes. (In Vista, Microsoft continues the trend toward default locking and you'll find that you must unlock at least a few items to get some things to run at all—lock by default has become the default mode for Microsoft.)

For example, NT 4 and Windows 2000 installed an unsecured web server by default on every server you ever installed. Not a good idea, as we learned in June 2001 when a worm called Code Red infected millions of servers—*through the web server*. With Server 2003, in contrast, you don't get IIS unless you ask for it. And even then, it's a pretty locked-down version of IIS.

To see another example, look at the NTFS permissions on the C drive of any Server 2003 computer. Where the default permission for every previous version of NT was Everyone/Full Control—"C'mon in, y'all, we're all friends here!"—Server 2003 gives Everyone only Read and Execute permission on the root of C. The Users group has more power because it can read files and create folders on C, but it can't create new files on the root of C. You can change all of this, of course, but by default Server 2003 is a bit tighter security-wise than its predecessors.

That's a good thing. But it won't be an unmixed blessing. I'm sure that at least once in your life you'll be sitting at the server trying to get something done but getting nowhere. You've got Help open, or a book at your side—this one, I hope!—clicking where the book says to click and dragging where the book says to drag, but it's not working. In that case, you may be doing the right thing but lack the permissions to do it. So Server 2003 offers us one more impediment to getting our jobs done: we'll have to wend a maze of security to do some things.

But don't take that as a negative comment. It's simply a fact of life in the twenty-first century that there are tons of dirt bags out there and the Internet has now given them the chance to come knock at our doors, so we have no choice but to install locks on our doors. Yes, it was nice back in the days when we didn't have to lock our doors or carry keys, but those days are gone forever. Operating systems are just changing with the times.

In addition, other security enhancements dive deeper than the generalities I mentioned already.

Profiles and Policies

When they first arrived, roaming profiles seemed like a great idea but then we tried them. Slow, prone to breaking, auugh! But Windows 2000 made them more palatable, and so has Server 2003.

First of all, there's a new Group Policy that you can apply to a machine (or machines) that says, "ignore all roaming profiles." This is terrific—now I can ensure that just my laptop and desktop get my roaming profile, by setting up all of the public access/shared systems and the servers to "ignore roamers."

Another Group Policy makes roaming profiles better for laptop users. Sometimes I'll check into a hotel and find that it offers Ethernet connections to the Internet (yippee! I'll sleep on a *stone floor* if it means I get high-speed Internet access), so I plug my laptop into the Ethernet and boot it up, only to realize that my stupid laptop is trying to suck my roaming profile over the Internet. A half hour later, it gives up.

Or at least that's what *used* to happen. Now I just set the Group Policy on my laptop that stops and asks, "Do you want to download your roaming profile?" I say no and log on in seconds. (Of course, the laptop must be running Windows XP or higher.)

Those are just two examples of the new things you can do to control profiles; there are many more.

Software Restriction Group Policies

Every help and support desk person has a little list of things they'd like to see. One is almost always "I'd really like to keep users from running particular programs on the system." (If you're having trouble thinking of examples, then see if the names Morpheus and Kazaa ring any bells.) With Windows XP and above desktops, you can do that. In fact, the features in Vista work with the group policies to provide additional levels of restriction.

Windows XP and above, along with Server 2003, include a whole new set of Group Policies called software restriction policies. With them, you can tell a desktop, "Nothing runs except Word, Internet Explorer, Outlook, and the Palm Desktop." It's pretty neat and pretty powerful.

The Group Policy Management Console (GPMC)

After reading the last section, you may be shaking your head saying, "Yeah, that's nice and all, but you're talking about Group Policies? Those guys are a nightmare." Yes, they can be, particularly when a Group Policy refuses to run—"Let's see, I just created this policy that keeps Access from running on Ronnie's desktop and he can *still* run Access!" Several things might keep your new policy from running—Ronnie's desktop might not have refreshed policies, or it might have refreshed policies but your policy might have been overridden by another policy. You look and see that there are only 24 other policies that apply to Ronnie and his desktop, so it's time to start sifting through policies or not.

Microsoft has been working on a really terrific Group Policy troubleshooting tool called Group Policy Management Console. It *didn't* ship with Server 2003 originally, but it's available (for Windows XP and Server 2003) and free at `http://www.microsoft.com/downloads`. Just search for Group Policy Management Console. Vista provides this tool as part of the package, so you don't need to download it for your Vista installations.

Other Improvements

I could literally write an entire book talking about Windows Server 2003 features—wait, I *did*!—but that's obviously for a different book. By now, I hope your curiosity is piqued. Just in case it's not, I'll leave you with three more enhancements that you might find useful: remote administration, reliability, and storage improvements.

Remote Administration Upgrades

For years, remote administration and control of Microsoft operating systems drove me nuts. It seemed only Microsoft OSes required you to be physically sitting down at a computer in order to control the software running on it. Sure, there were third-party alternative tools such as PCAnywhere or VNC, but remote control/admin always seemed like something that really needed to be "in the box," integrated into the OS.

Windows 2000, then, was a great advance, incorporating remote Telnet sessions and a remote control tool called Terminal Services that was a cut-down version of a program from a company named Citrix. Terminal Services ran only on Server, though, so remote control of 2000 Pro boxes was dicey.

Windows XP Professional, Windows Server 2003, and Vista include Microsoft's adaptation of Citrix's remote control product. It and the server version of Terminal Services are built around a tool called the Remote Desktop Protocol (RDP). Microsoft has improved RDP to make it run on slower connections, and I'm not exaggerating when I say that remote control over a 40-kilobit dial-up connection works very well, almost as well as sitting at the computer.

RDP also matures in that it automatically gives your remote control session access to your local printers and drives, something that Terminal Services for Windows 2000 couldn't do. It supports colors beyond the simple 8-bit, 256 color of Windows 2000's RDP, and it transports sound as well.

Perhaps even better, Windows XP Professional, Windows Server 2003, and Vista repackage RDP in two forms: *remote desktop support* and *remote assistance*. These are ways to provide remote control or offer remote assistance, but they're nothing more than new user interfaces placed atop Terminal Services. If you've not used them yet for Vista, try them; they're great! If you want more information, look in Chapter 3 for Remote Assistance and Chapter 16 for Remote Desktop.

Finally, Server 2003 offers a completely new set of remote control tools in the form of web pages. You can install a bunch of modules on your server that will let someone do approximately 80 percent of the administrative functions you'll ever need, all through a secure web connection. The bottom line is that we don't have to put up with those UNIX guys kicking sand in our faces telling us that their OS is more manageable!

Better Reliability

Windows 2000's System File Protection and Driver Verifier made great strides in making Windows 2000 far sturdier than its NT 4 predecessor; XP took that further with System Restore, Application Verifier, and Driver Rollback. As with some other Server 2003 features, they're not exactly new, since they first appeared in XP, but they're new to Server.

Driver Verifier was—and is—a useful tool for checking up on new device drivers and other system-level programs. It was a great addition to 2000 and still is, with Server 2003; smoking out problems with kernel-mode programs is far easier with its help. Vista places additional emphasis on solid drivers by requiring signed drivers for the x64 (64-bit) version and encouraging signed driver use in the x86 version. Driver verification is covered in Chapter 29.

Application Verifier performs a similar service but for user-mode programs. Have a program that ran fine under NT 4 or Windows 9*x* but won't run under Server 2003? Then run it under Application Verifier. When it fails, Application Verifier will tell you what caused it to fail and, even better, it can add information to the application that lets it run under Windows Server 2003.

Another source of operating system instability can be new drivers. You've got the system running fine, but the vendor of one of your pieces of hardware comes out with a new driver. Since it looks like you're running smoothly, you're leery about chancing it with a new driver. There must be some subtle bug that someone found that this updated driver fixes, but this new driver could make your system unstable. What to do? Well, Driver Verifier is a great way to check out a new driver, as it was in Windows 2000. But now it's got a simple partner in Driver Rollback. You load a driver and decide that it's no good now, where did you put the old driver? Just go to Device Manager, find the device with the new driver, right-click it, and choose Properties. You'll see a new button, Rollback Driver. Like XP, Server 2003 and Vista keep the previous version of all drivers.

Improved Storage

Windows XP Professional and Server 2003 brought some much-needed fixes to NTFS and one great new feature: volume shadowing. You'll also find this feature in Vista.

In brief, volume shadowing lets you take snapshots of a file share. At predetermined times of the day, Server 2003 records the status of whatever it's shadowing and lets you roll back to that quickly and easily. For example, suppose you keep your important documents in `share \\serv01\documents`. You could tell 2003 Server to take snapshots—*shadow copies* is the Microsoft term—of the files in that share at 7 AM, 10:30 AM, noon, and 6 PM.

A few days later, at 10:15 AM, you realize that you've accidentally deleted an important document. But all is not lost; just fire up the shadow copy client software (included with Server 2003) and restore the 7 AM version of the document. A few hours' work lost, but that's all. And no need to go find the tape librarian and beg to get a tape with last night's backup mounted. The Previous Versions tab of the Properties dialog box for all files makes choosing a previous version of a file even easier in Vista. You've seen the Previous Versions tab mentioned several times in the book—most notably in Chapter 8 and in the "Fixing Pictures" section of Chapter 12.

Volume shadowing lets you create a kind of imaginary copy of a file, with the state of that file frozen in time. That means that you can take shadow copies of open files and then back up the shadow copy! For example, suppose you have a SQL database that you need to back up every day, but there's never a good time to stop the database server. No problem: take a shadow copy at 3 AM. That copy doesn't change on a second-by-second basis, unlike your real SQL database file, so you can back it up at your leisure.

I told you that NTFS got some other improvements; they include the following:

- NTFS clusters can be any size, unlike Windows 2000, where their cluster size couldn't exceed 4KB or the volume couldn't be defragmented.
- A server can now host as many Dfs (Distributed File System) roots as you like; Windows 2000 allowed each server to host just one root.
- Offline files can now cache encrypted files.
- You can set up encrypted files so that more than one person can view an encrypted file.
- You can now both compress and encrypt a file.
- EIDE drives can now run independently, meaning that you can run a small database server with two EIDE drives rather than SCSI drives—one drive for the database, the other for the transaction log. This was always possible in NT but never made sense, because EIDE drives were limited to run only one at a time—if your SQL software said to the hardware, "Save these bytes to the database file and those bytes to the transaction log," then in actuality the OS would make the EIDE drives take turns. It might first write the bytes to the drive holding the database file while the drive holding the transaction log cooled its heels, and then write to the transaction log while keeping the database idle. The techie term for this would be that EIDE drives are now *asynchronous*, at least when they're on different channels—for example, this works if one hard disk is on the primary EIDE channel and the other is on the secondary EIDE channel.

None of those are truly earthshaking, but they're all quite welcome improvements.

Connecting to a Windows Server 2003 Domain

Vista is the ideal client for Windows Server 2003. The client and server operating system and user interface are the same, and Vista supports all of the great Server 2003 features, including remote administration, remote installation services, and Group Policies. Universal Plug and Play makes installation of your supported network card driver virtually automatic. If your network card is present and detected when the OS is being installed, Vista automatically loads the driver. If you accept the typical network settings during the installation of Vista, setup will go ahead and install TCP/IP Protocol and the Client for Microsoft Networks. If you install the NIC later, Vista automatically detects the new hardware and loads a driver or prompts the user for the location of the correct driver. Either way, once the driver for the NIC is loaded, you're home free. If you need only the TCP/IP protocol and the Client for Microsoft Networks, there's not much for the admin to do except join a domain or specify a workgroup.

Verifying Your Network Configuration

First, log on to the system as a user with administrative rights. Before trying to join the domain, you should at least take a look at the Network Connections window to ensure that the network card was detected and the appropriate software has been loaded. To open this window, right-click Network and choose Properties. Click the Manage network connections link in the Network and Sharing Center window to display the Network Connections window. As shown in Figure 23.1, if the network software has loaded properly, you'll see an icon named Local Area Connection (if you have more than one NIC installed, you'll see more than one Local Area Connection icon).

You should see that the connection is enabled. To verify the connection status, right-click the connection and choose Status from the context menu to display the Local Area Connection Status dialog box. Click Details to display the Network Connection Details dialog box shown in Figure 23.2 and you should also see the IP address that was assigned by DHCP. If you don't see a Local Area Connection icon, your NIC may not have been properly detected. Use Device Manager to isolate the problem, or try to add the network adapter manually using the Add New Hardware Wizard in Control Panel and your OEM-provided disk or CD-ROM.

If everything looks correct, right-click the Local Area Connection icon and choose Properties to view your network configuration information. The Properties page, shown in Figure 23.3, lists installed components: network card type, protocol, and the client software. Both TCP/IPv4 and TCP/IPv6 are automatically configured to use DHCP; to statically assign IP information, select Internet Protocol Version 4 (TCP/IPv4) and choose Properties. Figure 23.4 shows the Internet Protocol Version 4 (TCP/IPv4) Properties page.

NOTE To be absolutely certain that your network card and TCP/IP are working properly, open a command prompt, use ipconfig to verify your DHCP addressing, and then use ping to test network connectivity. Ping your IP address, the IP of the router, and the IP of the server or another node on your network. While you are at it, ping a couple of systems by name to test your DNS resolution. See Chapter 19 for more information on troubleshooting network problems with TCP/IP.

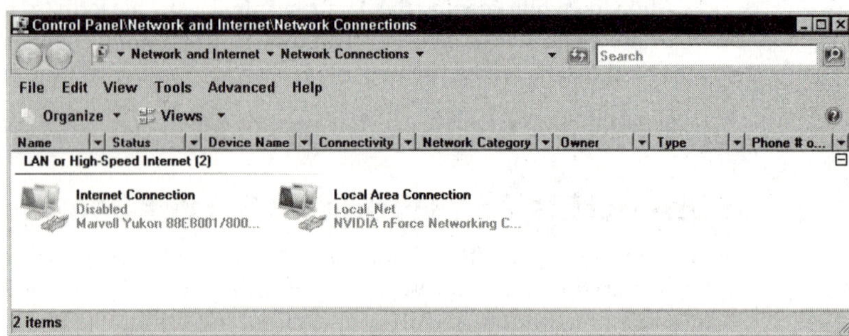

FIGURE 23.1
The Local Area Connection icon in Network Connections.

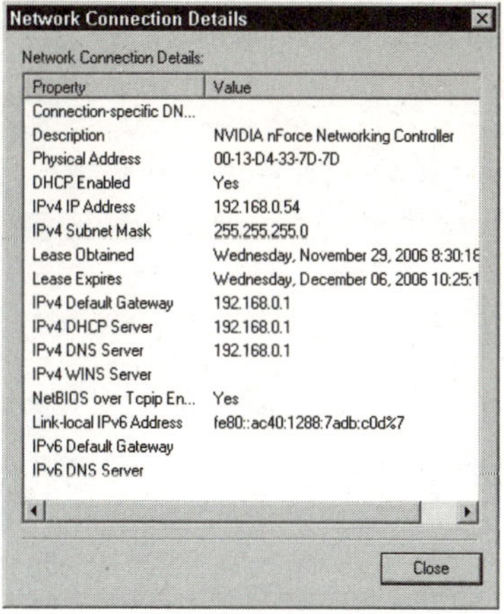

FIGURE 23.2
The Local Area Connection details.

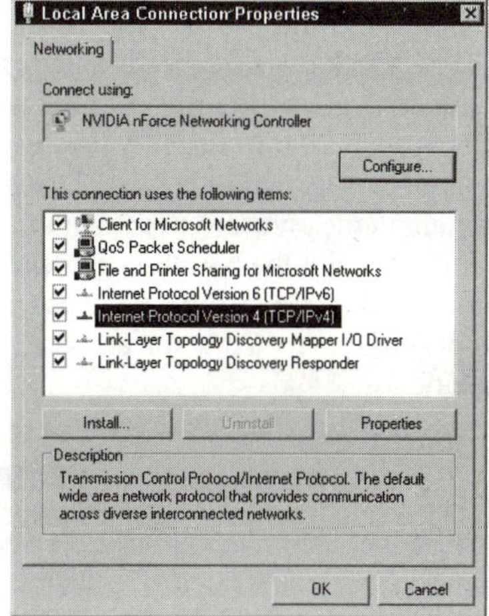

FIGURE 23.3
Local Area Connection Properties page.

Joining a Domain

Now that you know your network card is working properly and you've successfully obtained configuration information from DHCP, it's time to join the domain. If your Vista client will exist in an Active Directory environment, you need to create a machine account for it in the target domain. Members of the Administrators and Account Operators group on the domain can use the Active Directory Users and Computers tool to do this beforehand, and that's the recommended course of action. However, you can also create a machine account from the workstation during the network part of the setup program, or you can use the System Control Panel, if you know the username and password of an account with the ability to create machine accounts in the domain. I'll give you the steps to create the machine account from the workstation as you join the machine to the domain.

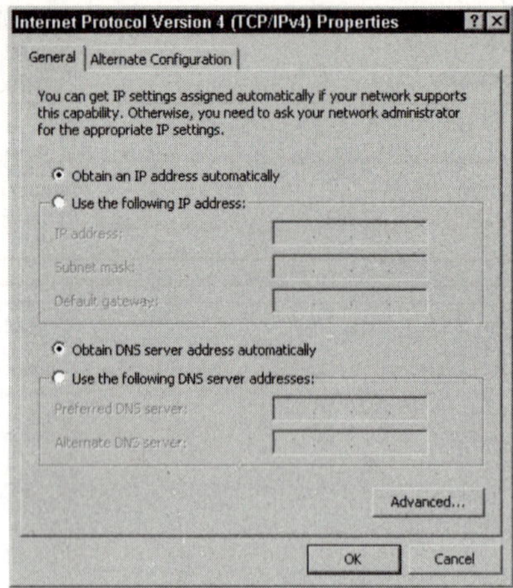

FIGURE 23.4
Internet Protocol Properties page.

To join a domain, open the System applet. The System applet is in Control Panel, or you can right-click Computer and choose Properties. I prefer this to wrangling with the XP Control Panel's Category View. Click the Advanced system settings link to display the System Properties dialog box. Navigate to the Computer Name tab (see Figure 23.5).

The Vista System, Main, currently belongs to a workgroup named LOCAL_NET. Click Change to join a domain. As shown in Figure 23.6, change the radio button selection to Domain and type in your domain name, **`mydomain.com`** in this case. Notice that you use the full Active Directory domain name here, not the NetBIOS name MYDOMAIN. Click OK. If an account for the system doesn't already exist on the domain, Vista prompts you to supply a domain username and password with permission to create the account. If all goes well, you'll see a message welcoming you to the domain.

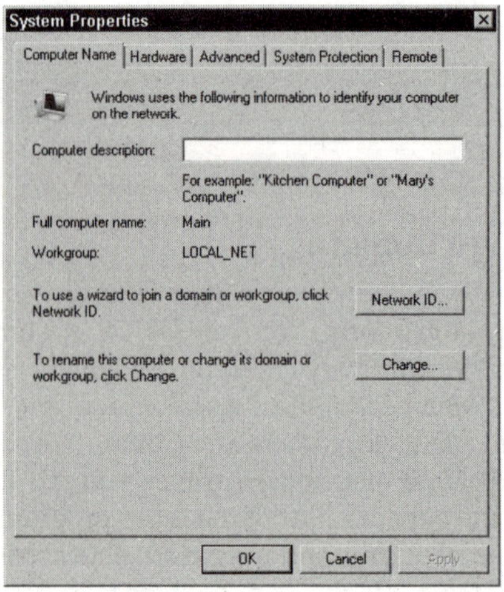

FIGURE 23.5
Computer Name tab in System Properties.

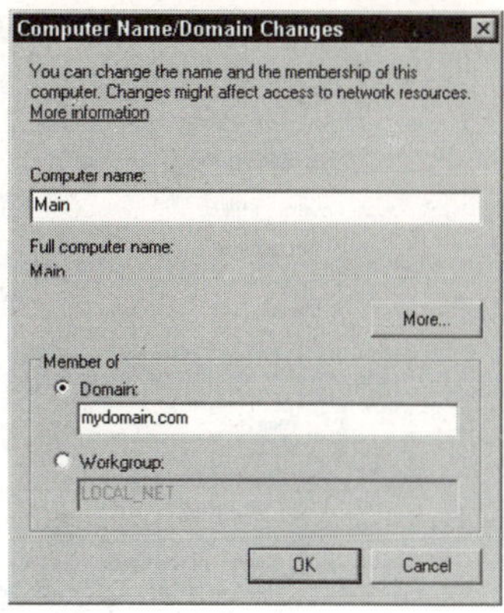

FIGURE 23.6
The Computer Name/Domain Changes dialog box.

Restart the system for the changes to take effect. When the system restarts, Vista will automatically create a connection for you to the domain. All you need to do is provide your username and password. When Vista is finished logging you on and loading your personal settings, it's time to connect to network resources.

NOTE How is it possible to join the workstation to the domain and then log on using a domain account? How does the workstation identify you and assign you rights and permissions? Actually, when the workstation joins the domain, the domain's Domain Users group is added to the workstation's local Users group membership. In addition, the Domain Admins group is added to the Administrators group on the local workstation. By default, then, if a domain controller authenticates you as a member of the Domain Users group, the workstation will accept you as a local user. And if the domain controller recognizes you as a Domain Admin, the workstation will grant you local admin rights as well. This is the default behavior for all NT-based client operating systems: Windows Server 2003, Windows .NET, Vista, Windows 2000, and Windows NT.

Connecting to Network Resources

The easiest way to connect to network resources is to use the Network icon on your Desktop. You can also get to it through Computer, by opening Computer from the Start menu or Desktop and choosing Network from the Navigation pane (see Figure 23.7).

Network, shown in Figure 23.8, offers several different options for finding and connecting to network resources. Here are two of the most common methods:

- Type the location you want to find in the Search field using a UNC name (***SERVER******SHARE***).
- Browse the network by double-clicking entries in the main pane or by opening the hierarchy in the Navigation pane.

Remember, of course, that to connect to a resource, you must have the proper permissions to access that resource.

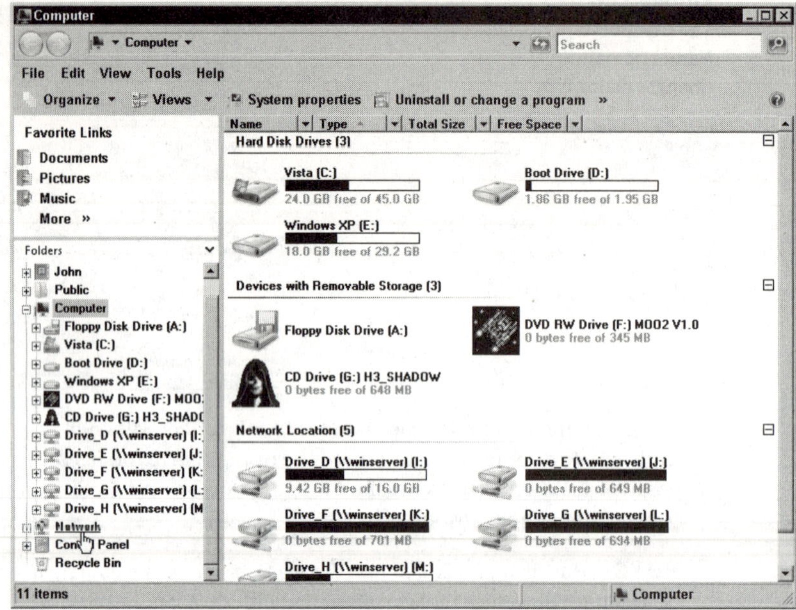

FIGURE 23.7
Open Network from Computer.

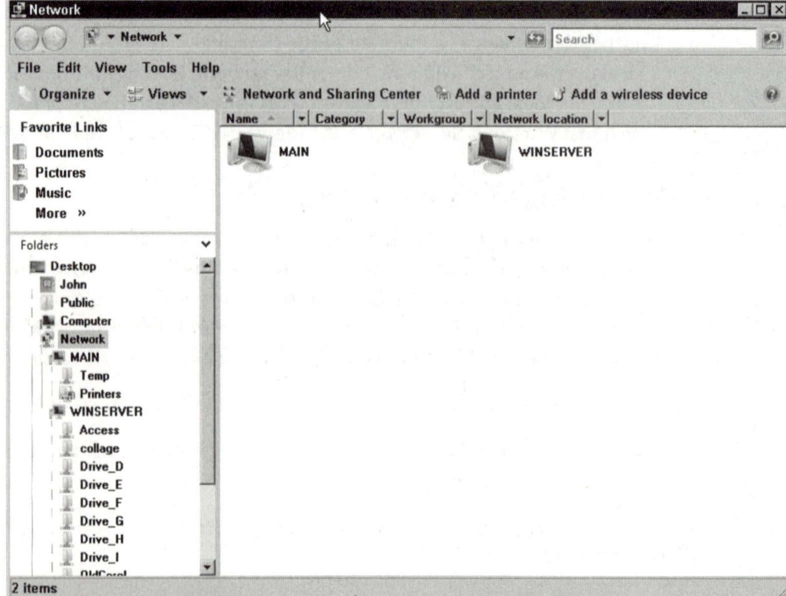

FIGURE 23.8
Finding resources from Network.

Changing Domain Passwords

It's good security practice for users to change their password the first time they log on to the network. It's also a default parameter set when the admin first creates a new user account. So if a user is logging on to the network for the first time, they'll see a message informing them that they must change their password. The Change Password dialog box then opens and the user types the old password and the new one (twice for confirmation). If the old password is correct and the new password meets the password criteria and both new entries match each other, the user sees a confirmation of the password change and the logon process continues.

After the initial logon and password change, administrators can use Active Directory Users and Computers (from Windows Server 2003) to reset a user's password or to expire a password so that the user must change it the next time they log on. Users can change their own domain passwords after logging on by using Ctrl+Alt+Del and the Change a Password link. The Ctrl+Alt+Del sequence is the same one used to lock the computer or shut it down, so it's important that everyone knows about it.

Summary

This chapter covered some basics of Windows 2003, to help you understand how the operating system works, as well as how to join your Vista computer to a Windows Server 2003 domain.

First, we discussed the different varieties of Server 2003. Then, we moved into some of the more notable features of Server 2003, including better e-mail server and database server functionality, networking improvements, Active Directory enhancements, and a few other nifty additions. Finally, this chapter ended with a discussion of how to join a Vista computer to a Windows 2003 domain.

Of course, this book focuses on Vista and doesn't provide a complete discussion of Windows Server 2003. For that, you'll want to get *Mastering Windows Server 2003*.

Now that we've talked a lot about Microsoft-based networks, it's time to turn our attention to the competitors. Not that everyone doesn't love Microsoft, but there are other server products out there, and you need to be able to make your Vista computer communicate with those products as well. The next chapter puts you on the path of cross-platform cooperation.

Chapter 24

Connecting to Non-Microsoft Networks

Thinking that Microsoft-based operating systems are the only ones in existence on networks is shortsighted. Although it's an oversight that Microsoft would surely allow you to maintain, now is a good time to discuss connecting to non-Microsoft operating systems and networks. This section specifically looks at connecting to Novell NetWare, Unix, and Macintosh networks.

Novell's NetWare retains its popularity mainly because of its Novell Directory Services (NDS). NDS is a redundant, scalable, mature distributed directory service that eases administrative tasks and provides unified authentication. Unfortunately, Microsoft's Client Service for NetWare (CSNW) applet is missing in action in Vista, so you'll find that NetWare support is a little lacking when it comes to management unless you use Novell-specific utilities. You can still connect to NetWare using IPX/SPX, use resources on the server, and even manage the server using both command-line and graphical utilities, but the CSNW applet used to control features such as banner printing is gone. Fortunately, you can manage features such as printer banners using the same techniques that you use when working with Windows servers, so what Microsoft has actually done is given you one way to perform a task regardless of server type, which makes Vista actually easier to use, even though it'll be a strange upgrade for users who are used to using the CSNW applet.

Unix has been around practically since the dawn of time. Well, the dawn of computer time, anyway. Although it's a gross generalization to treat all Unix-based operating systems the same, it's the appropriate thing to do in this book. Microsoft provides a client service to attach to Unix-based servers, and we'll look at that.

Finally, contrary to popular belief, Macintosh networks do exist. We'll look at how to make your Vista computer play nice with Macs on a network as well.

TIP When working with multiple platforms, try to keep uniform usernames for all of your users. In other words, Sheila Sanders may have an easier time accessing resources if her account name is SSanders on all platforms, instead of Sheila on one and SSanders on another.

This chapter specifically covers:

- Using Novell administration utilities
- Printing to Novell printers
- Enabling long filename support on the Novell server
- Choosing a Novell client solution
- Understanding interoperation with Unix-based computers
- Working with Macintosh computers on your network

CSNW Features

Even though you might not see the CSNW applet in the Control Panel, the underlying software still exists in Vista. The software sends Network Core Protocol (NCP) packets to NetWare so that Vista and NetWare can communicate. CSNW provides the following features:

Novell script processing CSNW processes the system and individual login scripts created by the network administrator of the Novell network.

Seamless File and Print Services Drive letters can be mapped to NetWare volumes either through login scripts or by using any of the mapping utilities in Vista. These volumes appear just like a local drive, and you can continue using long filenames on NetWare mapped drives since NetWare supports long filenames. You can print to NetWare print queues using conventional UNC naming, or you can capture a queue to an LPT port using standard Vista tools. NetWare servers are *browsable* via the Network Explorer views, which makes it even easier to find NetWare resources, map network drives, or use printer resources.

NDS authentication Versions of NetWare prior to 4.*x* used a server-centric database, called the *bindery*, for authentication. Vista doesn't appear to provide support for the bindery. NetWare versions 4.*x* and later still provide bindery emulation; however, the preferred method is to authenticate with NDS, which is the only method that Vista does appear to support. CSNW can use either of these methods to connect to a NetWare file server, but without access to the CSNW applet, you can't modify the system to use the bindery.

WARNING As mentioned earlier, CSNW is a very basic client for connections to NetWare servers. Microsoft hasn't made a strong effort to update CSNW since it was first released for Windows NT 4. A major drawback of CSNW is its lack of IP support. NetWare administrators will be forced to load the IPX protocol on servers that contain replicas or partitions of the NDS database and any other server providing services to a Vista using CSNW. In addition, Vista for 64-bit processors won't support the Client Service for NetWare because of its dependency on the IPX protocol. If you must use IP as the protocol or if you need a feature-rich client to connect to NetWare, Novell will provide a 32/64-bit client. As of this writing, Novell doesn't provide a Vista-specific client, but expect this situation to change. You can check for a Vista client at `http://download.novell.com`.

Using Novell Administration Utilities

NetWare 3.*x* used various DOS-based utilities for administration. The primary utilities are called SYSCON and Pconsole. SYSCON, short for system configuration utility, is a DOS-based menu-driven program for creating users, groups, and login scripts and for managing accounting, setting directory permissions, and setting user restrictions. Pconsole, short for printer console, is also a DOS-based menu-driven program that allows you to create print queues and printers. You can also use a handful of other administrative utilities and many powerful command-line tools instead of these menu-driven applications. The following list shows them in simple alphabetical order:

Chkvol	Help	rconsole	settts
Colorpal	listdir	remove	slist
Dspace	Map	revoke	SYSCON
Fconsole	Ncopy	rights	tlist

Filer	Ndir	security	userlist
Flag	Pconsole	send	volinfo
Flagdir	Psc	session	whoami
Grant	Pstat	setpass	

You must map a drive to the NetWare volume where these utilities are located in order to run them. Vista won't run them correctly from a UNC path.

Most administrative tasks in NDS require just one tool, the NetWare Administrator (NWADMIN). NWADMIN is a graphical view of NDS that allows you to create organizational units; create users, printers, and groups; modify login scripts; and more. NWADMIN is similar to Vista's Microsoft Management Console (MMC) in that you can extend the capabilities of NWADMIN by "snapping-in" new administration tools. For example, you can snap-in Symantec's Norton AntiVirus (NAV) to administrate NAV on all your NetWare servers. You can launch NWADMIN only from a workstation (running Windows 9*x*, Windows NT, Windows 2000 Professional, Windows XP Professional, or Vista) attached to a NetWare server. However, Novell has released a new administration utility called ConsoleOne (see Figure 24.1) that has many of the same features of NWADMIN and more.

ConsoleOne is a graphical tool for administering network resources, including NDS objects, schema, partitions, replicas, and NetWare servers. The real beauty of ConsoleOne is that it can be launched on the console of a NetWare 5.*x* server or from a workstation. In the past, NetWare servers always required a workstation to begin administrative tasks. Now, you can walk right up to a server and begin adding users and setting permissions. This is particularly helpful in first-time installations and smaller networks.

Another cool feature of ConsoleOne is its web portal to NetWare servers that allows you to use some utilities and view the status of your NetWare file server, as shown in Figure 24.2. ConsoleOne isn't fully baked, especially when running from a NetWare server. This means that not all of the utilities have been blended into ConsoleOne and you must use legacy tools, but it's Novell's intent that ConsoleOne be the complete tool for all administrative tasks, and it does show a lot of promise.

FIGURE 24.1
ConsoleOne will be the one-stop administration tool for NetWare 5 servers and beyond.

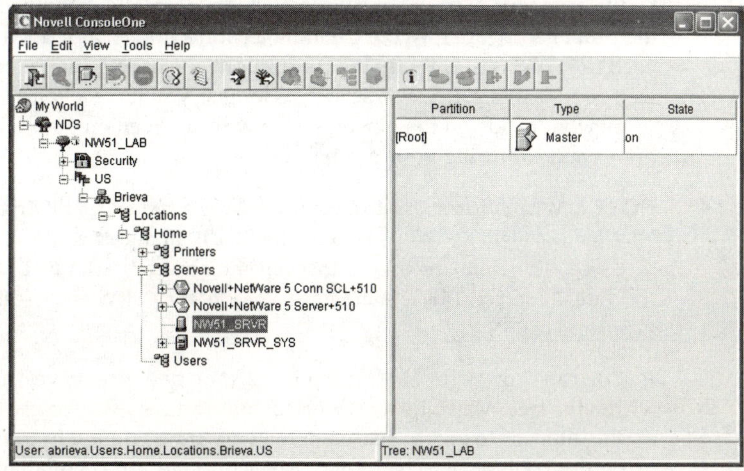

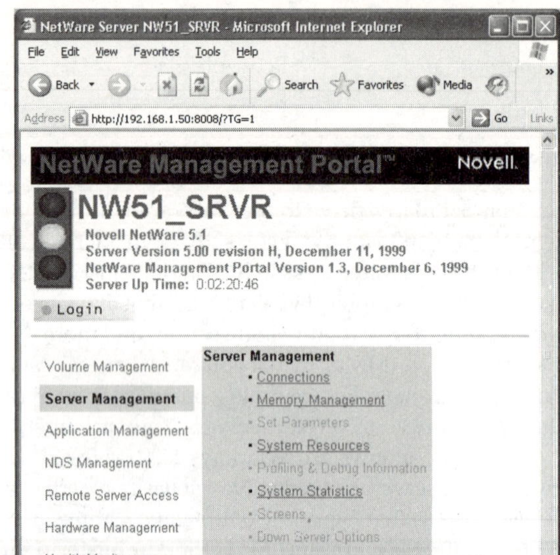

FIGURE 24.2
The NetWare Management Portal accessible through ConsoleOne.

The bad news for people who want to use Vista to manage their NetWare 5 network is that NWADMIN and ConsoleOne won't work with CSNW. NWADMIN and ConsoleOne require several Novell dynamic link libraries (DLLs) that are installed only when using Novell's client software. If you're serious about managing your NetWare environment from within Vista, you should strongly consider downloading Novell's Client for Vista (the Novell client for other versions of Windows are unlikely to run properly). Unfortunately, since this client is unavailable at the time of this writing, I can't tell you much about it.

Accessing a NetWare Server

Unlike previous versions of Windows, Vista normally recognizes the NetWare server and installs the proper software for you. Creating a connection as described in Chapters 19 and 22 is all you need do. After Vista creates the connection, you can access the resources of a NetWare 3 server as well as a NetWare 4, 5, or 6 server, as long as you have a valid login ID and password. The login scripts that reside on the Novell server will run even on your Vista workstation, mapping your drives and capturing your printer ports.

NOTE When Vista starts up and the CSNW is installed, you'll first be prompted for the standard Windows login ID and password. The user ID and password you enter are passed along to the CSNW. Therefore, the user ID that you enter must match the ID that's been created on the NetWare file server. This is another weakness of the CSNW and a reason for using the Novell client instead of CSNW.

You can browse for NetWare servers, map network drives, and browse for network resources within the tree. Mapping a network drive is an easy way to use the same drive letter for common applications or to access shared data every time you log in to the network. You can map drives using the Tools ➤ Map Network Drive command that's available in every Explorer window, or you can browse through the list of server volumes on any given server. To map a network drive, follow these steps:

1. Choose Start ➤ Network or click Network on the Desktop to open the Network window.
2. Choose Tools ➤ Map Network Drive to open the Map Network Drive dialog box shown in Figure 24.3.
3. Click Browse to open the Browse For Folder dialog box and view a list of network resources. Unlike previous versions of Windows, you don't have to scan separate areas for NetWare and Microsoft networks. Any server with a resource to offer will appear at the top of the hierarchy.
4. Double-click a server to which you want to map a network drive.
5. Highlight the resource you want to map. You can map a drive directly to a volume or you can expand a volume to map directly to a folder on the server. Click OK.
6. To make this a permanent mapped drive, click the Reconnect at Logon check box, and then click Finish.

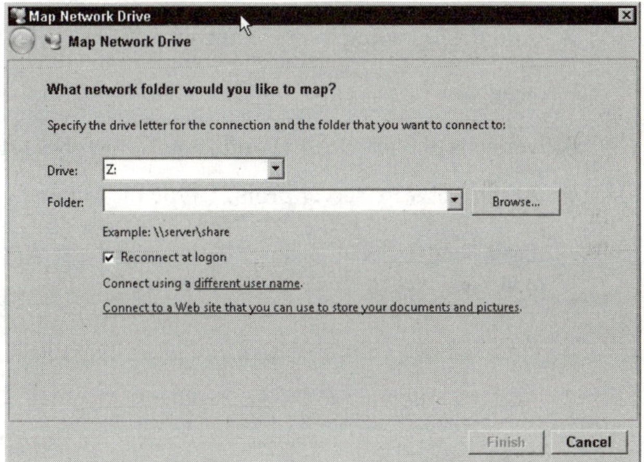

FIGURE 24.3
Create a link between your NetWare drive and a local drive as you would for any sever.

Printing to Novell Printers

Microsoft has made printing considerably easier in Vista. You use a NetWare printer precisely as you would a printer attached to a Windows system. Chapter 9 provides all of the details about working with printers. The short version is that you locate the printer you want to use in Network, right-click it, and choose Connect from the context menu. Vista creates the required connection for you. When working with a NetWare server, you'll likely have to have your printer driver software available because the NetWare server won't be able to download it to your machine.

The only other difference when working with a NetWare printer is that Microsoft doesn't support it through the Print Management Console (described in the "Using the Print Management Console" section of Chapter 9). You use the same utilities that you always have to manage printers on the NetWare server. Consequently, even though having Print Management Console support would be nice, you won't notice any difference if you've worked with NetWare before with other versions of Windows.

Enabling Long Filename Support on the Novell Server

NetWare requires you to enable long filename support on the NetWare servers prior to revision 5. NetWare 5 and 6 file servers have long filename support enabled by default. Different revisions of NetWare require slightly different commands. It isn't necessary to restart the server after entering these commands; however, this process will slow your NetWare server down dramatically. Make sure you perform these tasks after hours.

For versions of NetWare earlier than 4.10, follow these steps:

1. At the NetWare server prompt, type the following:

   ```
   Load os2
   add name space os2 to volume sys
   ```

   (and to every volume where you want long filename support)

2. Add the following to the `startup.ncf` file:

   ```
   load os2
   ```

For versions of NetWare 4.11 and later, follow these steps:

1. At the NetWare server prompt, type the following:

   ```
   Load long
   add name space long to volume sys
   ```

   (and to every volume where you want long filename support)

2. Add the following to the `startup.ncf` file:

   ```
   load long
   ```

Choosing a Novell Client Solution

I've already mentioned that the Novell 32-bit client solution has more features than CSNW and that it will resolve problems with TCP/IP connectivity and using NDS administration tools. Novell's client is a true 32-bit client, and eventually we may see a 64-bit version of the client.

Novell has a package of network tools called Zero Effort Networking, or *ZENworks*. ZENworks gives you complete control over desktop and user management from the NetWare 4 and newer environments. It's actually similar in many ways to Microsoft's Zero Administration Windows (ZAW) initiative in that it uses policies and login scripts to manage users and computers. But in the case of ZENworks, the policies are being applied based on NDS objects across all client platforms, not just one version of Windows.

The full version of ZENworks provides several useful help desk functions as well, including a ticketing system for reporting problems and remote control ability. The version that's supplied with NetWare 5 and newer is the "light" version, which includes everything except the help desk tools and is supported by all the current Novell client platforms.

Entering the Dark World of Unix

Right now, you may be thinking, "But I don't know much about Unix, much less how it networks!" That's okay. By now, you have some knowledge of general networking principles, and the principles don't change from platform to platform. You still need to find a way to make the machines talk, and you still need to make resources available across the network.

NOTE Many people are reporting problems getting Vista to work with Linux using Samba. For the most part, the problems stem from Vista's security setup. The article at `http://www.builderau.com.au/blogs/codemonkeybusiness/viewblogpost.htm?p=339270746` describes a technique you can use to fix the Samba problems with Vista.

Probably the biggest difference if you're using a Unix-based machine is the interface. Although there are some graphical interfaces for Unix (such as KDE and GNOME), most of the time Unix is run from a command prompt. Don't be scared of the dark place; just be able to type and you'll make it through. The good news is that accessing Unix-based resources from a Microsoft Vista machine is incredibly similar to accessing Windows-based resources.

Microsoft offers two Unix interoperability products: Services for Unix 2.0 and Interix 2.2. The one you'll be dealing with most is Services for Unix, which allows you to integrate your Vista machine into a Unix environment. If you want to run Unix-based applications or logon scripts on your Vista machine, you'll need Interix.

NOTE For purposes of this discussion, Unix, Solaris, and Linux support require the same configurations.

The first thing you need to look at when trying to connect to a Unix-based machine is the network protocol. Unix uses TCP/IP by default, and so does Vista. First problem solved. Just make sure the machines are configured properly.

NOTE One of the great things about the TCP/IP protocol is that it's universal. Whether you're using Windows, Unix, or any other operating system, the rules for configuring addresses don't change. Therefore, if you're trying to communicate with a Unix machine, just make sure that all computers have the same network address but a unique host address. If you've forgotten how this works, take a look at the "Configuring IP Addresses on a Network" sidebar in Chapter 19.

The next thing to look at is how the computers make requests. Vista uses a protocol called Common Internet File System (CIFS) to make requests of the server. Unix uses the Network File System (NFS) protocol. Since the two are incompatible, we need to figure out a way to make the two platforms talk. Enter Services for Unix.

NOTE Services for Unix is an umbrella term for four separate products: File Services for Unix, Client for NFS, Server for NFS, and Print Services for Unix. Only Print Services for Unix is automatically included with Vista.

Services for Unix contains many components—more than are necessary to cover here. Probably the most important ones are Client for NFS and Server for NFS. When you install Services for Unix on your Vista machine, these services allow you to not only request stuff from an NFS server but to host resources for NFS clients as well. Specifically, Services for Unix allows you to access files and printers on a Unix server, as well as have Unix machines access your files and printers. Services for Unix is a separate product that can be installed from its CD-ROM.

NOTE Services for Unix is an optional add-on product that must be purchased from Microsoft.

TIP If you're planning to install Services for Unix 2.0, be aware of the telnet vulnerability described in Microsoft Knowledge Base article 286043.

Printing in Unix is also slightly different from Microsoft printing. Installing Services for Unix installs two critical printing components: Line Printer (lpr) and Line Printer Daemon (lpd).

You can install Print Services for Unix using the following steps:

1. Open the Programs and Features applet in the Control Panel. You'll see the Programs and Features window.
2. Click the Turn Windows features on or off link. You'll see Windows Features dialog box shown in Figure 24.4.
3. Expand the Print Services entry as shown in Figure 24.4. Check the LPD Print Service entry if you want to support Unix printing on your machine. This is a server, so it opens your machine to incoming requests. Check LPR Port Monitor if you want to send print jobs to a Unix server. Since this is a client, it doesn't open your machine to outside influences.
4. Click OK. Vista installs the required software for you.

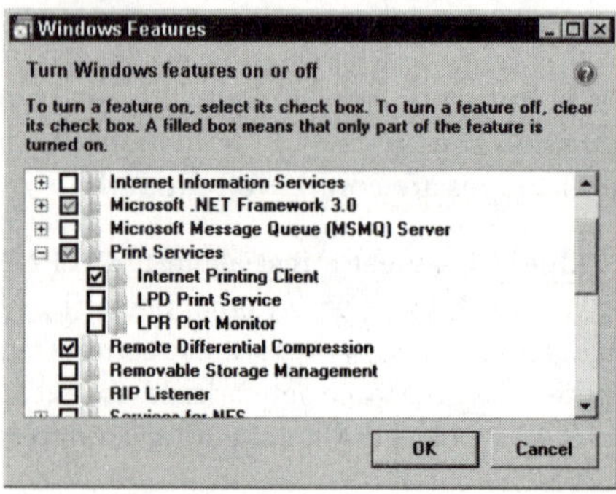

FIGURE 24.4
Locate the special Unix print features that Vista supports.

The lpr utility is used to send print jobs to the print service, which is lpd. Daemon, in Unix terms, simply refers to a service. If you wanted to, you could use lpr from a command prompt to send print jobs through lpd. It's easier to map to the printer, though. Here's how to add an LPT port:

1. Click Start, and choose Printers.
2. Double-click Add Printer, which opens the Add Printer Wizard.
3. Click Add a local printer.

UNDERSTANDING SUBSYSTEM FOR UNIX-BASED APPLICATIONS (SUA)

If you're using Vista Enterprise or Vista Ultimate, you'll find a special feature called SUA that lets you run Vista applications on your system unchanged. In the past, administrators had to run Windows applications on one system and Unix applications on another. With SUA you can run the applications on a single machine. You can learn more about SUA at `http://technet2.microsoft.com/WindowsServer/en/library/695ac415-d314-45df-b464-4c80ddc2b3bc1033.mspx?mfr=true`.

Vista makes it very easy to install SUA support. The following steps describe the process.

1. Open the Programs and Features applet in the Control Panel. You'll see the Programs and Features window.
2. Click the Turn Windows features on or off link. You'll see Windows Features dialog box shown in Figure 24.4.
3. Check the Subsystem for Unix-based Applications entry.
4. Click OK. Vista installs the required software for you.

4. Click Create a New Port, and for the Type of port, choose LPR Port, as shown in Figure 24.5. Click Next. You'll see an Add LPR Compatible Printer dialog box.
5. In the Name or address of server providing lpd field shown in Figure 24.6, enter the DNS name or IP address of the host providing the lpd service (the Unix printer). You'll also need to provide the name of the printer or print queue. Click Next.
6. The wizard will finish the installation for you.

TIP Services for Unix isn't required for Unix and Windows to communicate. Samba is the Unix implementation of the Server Message Block format, which is the foundation of the NetBIOS protocol. If you install Samba on Unix (or Linux or Solaris), you don't need to make any changes to Vista. With Samba, shared Unix directories and printers work in a standard Microsoft Network Neighborhood or domain.

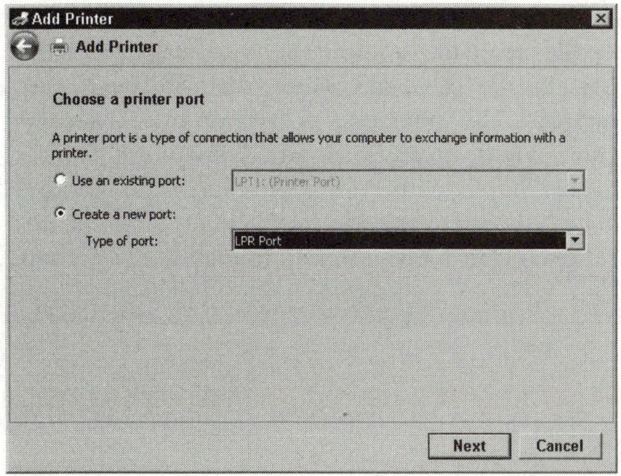

FIGURE 24.5
Create a local printer based on an LPR port when working with Unix.

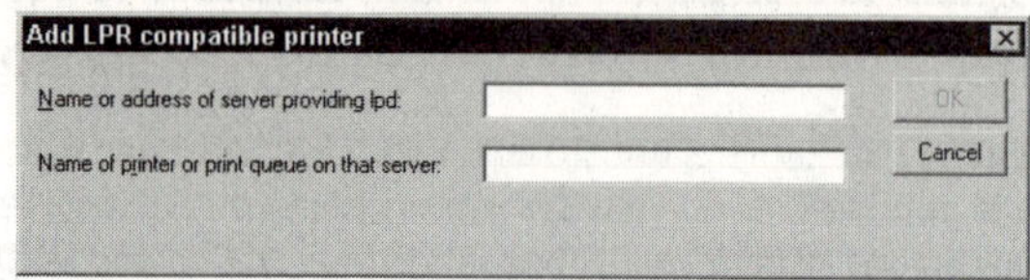

FIGURE 24.6 Provide connection information for the printer.

Macintosh Networks

Networking professionals will tell you that the words *Macintosh* and *network* should never be used in the same sentence. Native Macintosh networking is horribly slow by today's standards, and creating Macintosh-accessible volumes on NT servers could cause crashes and headaches. Because of these issues, Macs don't have a good name in the PC-networking arena.

But for all the flak Macs get regarding networking, they make excellent graphics and design machines. Besides, most of the Macintosh networking components, including the NIC, are built in.

Macintosh computers use the AppleTalk networking protocol by default. Fortunately, however, Macs also support TCP/IP. It's recommended that if you want to network with Macs, you should use the TCP/IP protocol. Vista doesn't support the AppleTalk protocol.

Vista doesn't come with any products or services to support Macs on a network. Windows 2000 Server comes with Services for Macintosh, which allows Mac users to save files on Windows 2000 servers. If you absolutely must get Vista and Macs talking to each other, you'll need a third-party solution. One such solution is PC MACLAN, by Miramar Systems.

NOTE For more information about PC MACLAN, visit `http://www.ca.miramar.com/`.

Summary

Many networks run pure Microsoft operating systems. That's fine, but you need to be aware of other possibilities that exist, in case you must network with other vendors' products. In this chapter, we took a long look at connecting to an existing NetWare network with Vista, including how to connect to a NetWare printer and how to log on to a NetWare system. We also discussed Unix and Macintosh networking.

Nothing works well without planning, especially multiplatform networks. Although this chapter provides you with many of the nuts and bolts of creating a multiplatform network, you still need to create the required plans, infrastructure, and best practices for your network. Before you string the first cable and before you install even one piece of software, plan your multiplatform network carefully. Whenever possible, reduce the number of platforms to reduce the amount of work required to setup and maintain the network.

This chapter ends Part 6, "Advanced Networking." In the next chapter, we begin a new section dedicated to network administration topics. The next chapter begins by looking at administrative and diagnostic tools you need to maintain your network.

Part VII

Network Administration

In this section, you'll learn how to

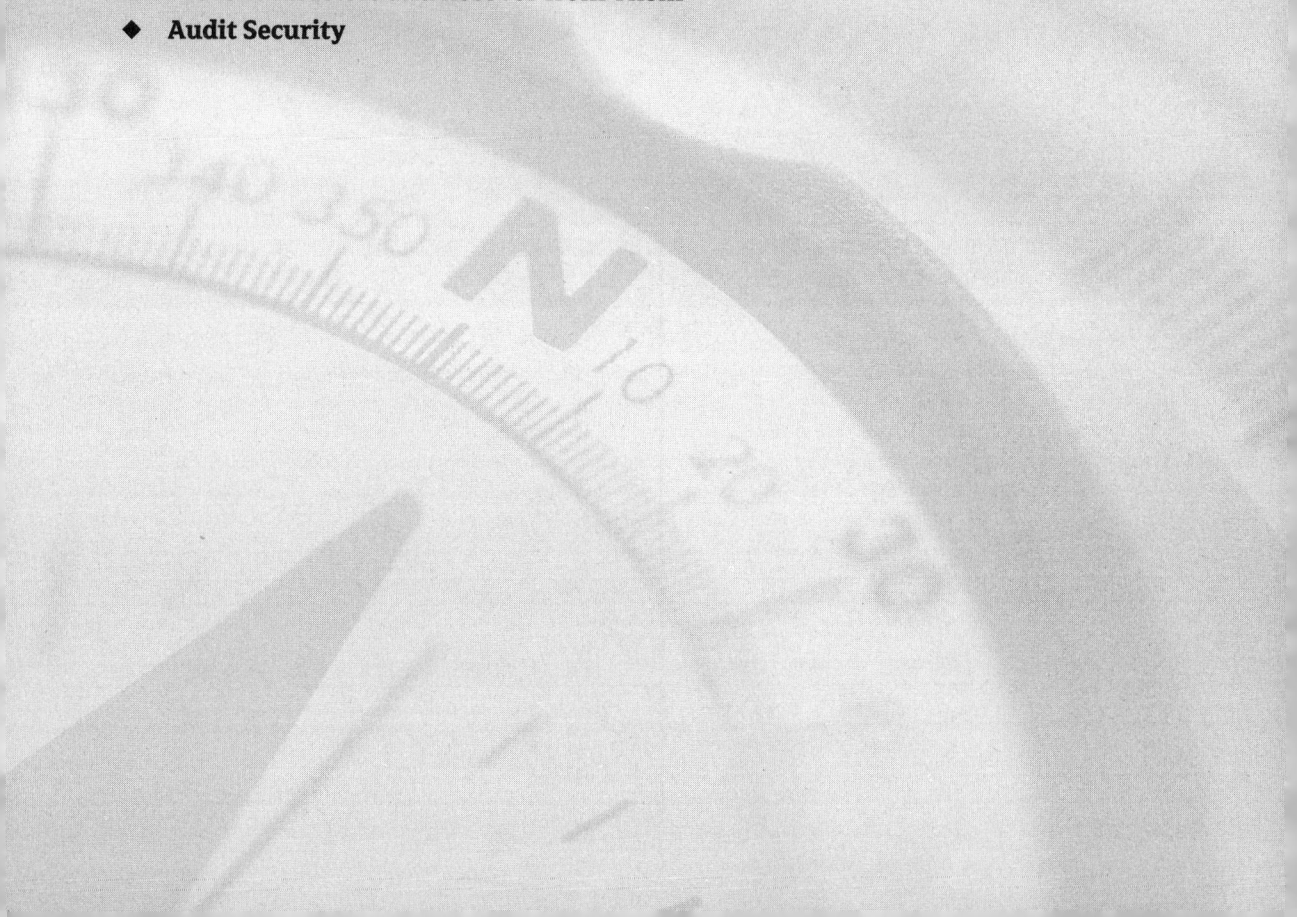

- Manage Administrative and Diagnostic Tools
- Manage Active Directory
- Understand and Use the Registry
- Use Scripts to Automate Tasks
- Prevent Disasters and Recover from Them
- Audit Security

Chapter 25

Administrative and Diagnostic Tools

Vista comes with administrative tools for you to use when you add new disk volumes and check on existing ones, track system events, watch system performance, and run general diagnostics. Let's take a look at these tools and how they can help you keep your system running smoothly.

- Managing hard disks through Disk Management
- Tracking down problems using Event Viewer
- Using Problem Reports and Solutions to track Vista issues
- Automating repetitive tasks using Task Scheduler
- Monitoring system performance
- Managing resources and applications with Task Manager
- Using BCDEdit

Vista: What's New?

Vista changes a lot of features that you used to manage previous versions of Windows. In most cases, you'll find that the change is for the better. For example, the new Problem Reports and Solutions applet helps you track failure events that occur on your system automatically. No longer will you have to guess about some of the failure event information and then record it in your own system. This new applet doesn't quite record everything you should know about your system, but it's a significant step in the right direction.

Anyone who has used Task Scheduler in the past to schedule jobs knows that it does work and it actually works well, but it has limitations. For example, jobs could run forever if you let them. Vista provides a new Task Scheduler that provides an interesting array of new features for working with jobs. You can specify when a job should end now and even tell Vista to kill the job should the time elapse. Unfortunately, this new functionality comes at a price. Vista tasks are invisible to previous version of Windows by default. If you choose not to use the new features, you can still create jobs that other versions of Windows can see. Administrators who are used to creating jobs at the command line using the SchTasks utility will find that the utility has kept pace with Vista, so you'll also see some new features added to it through command-line arguments.

Vista provides about the same level of performance monitoring that Windows XP provided. Microsoft tweaked the interface a little bit, but generally, you'll find that you can perform the same kinds of monitoring as before. What has changed is that Microsoft has also provided a simplified view of performance through the Performance Information and Tools applet in the Control Panel. This new view of performance makes a simple statement of what you can expect of the system.

You may be familiar with the old way of managing the boot arguments for your system using the BootCfg utility. Because of the way that Vista works and new features such as BitLocker, you'll need to use a new utility to manage boot arguments, Boot Configure Data Store Editor (BCDEdit). This new tool lets you do a lot more than the BootCfg utility, but it's also quite complex, so be prepared for a somewhat steep learning curve. The information in this chapter will help you overcome many of the BCDEdit complexities.

Using Disk Management

In Vista, Disk Management is part of the Computer Management console in Administrative Tools. To open Disk Management, follow these steps:

1. Choose Start ➤ Control Panel to open Control Panel.
2. Click the System Maintenance link, and then click Administrative Tools to open the Administrative Tools folder.
3. Click Computer Management to open the Computer Management window.
4. In the Computer Management pane, expand Storage, and then click Disk Management. You'll see something similar to the window shown in Figure 25.1.

FIGURE 25.1
You can change log settings in the log's Properties dialog box.

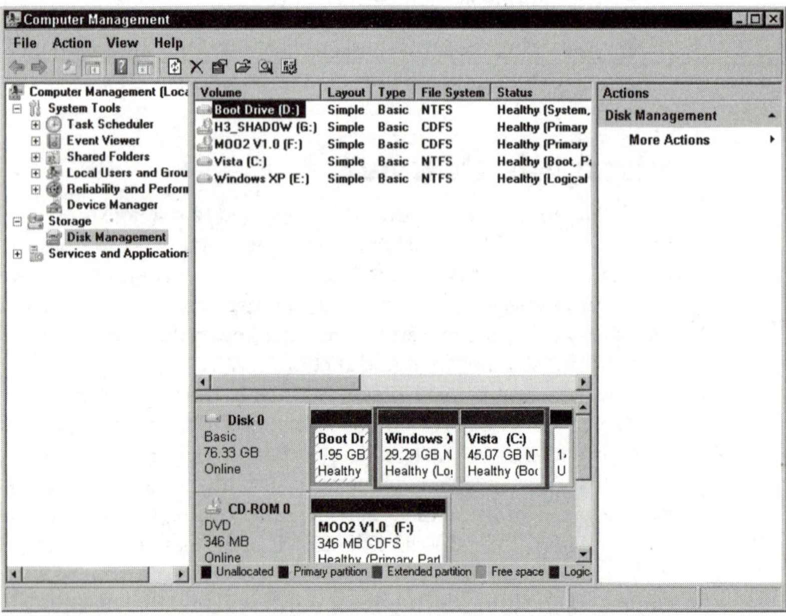

The Disk Management tool, which is displayed in the upper right pane of the Computer Management window, gives you a graphical representation of the hard disks and CD-ROM devices in your computer. You can, however, customize the way information is presented in a variety of ways.

The Disk Management window is in four parts. On the left is the Computer Management pane of the Computer Management console. The lower pane contains the information for all the physical disks installed in the computer, excluding floppy drives. The upper pane contains descriptions of those disks, including data on the amount of space used and free, the type of file system, and the health of that system. The right pane contains a list of actions you can perform. The list changes based on the object you select.

To use Disk Management to create or delete partitions, format drives, and create striped or volume sets, simply click the disk that you want to modify, and select the change that you want to make from the Action menu or Actions pane. Or you can right-click the drive that you want to modify, and then select the appropriate action from the context menu.

Deciding Which File System Is Best

Vista can use the File Allocation Table (FAT) file system supported by DOS and all versions of Windows, the File Allocation Table 32 (FAT32) file system supported by Windows 9*x* and Windows 2000, and the New Technology File System (NTFS) supported by Windows NT/2000/XP/2003 and Vista. Each file system has its respective upsides and downsides. Here's a quick rundown.

FAT's main advantage is its backward compatibility with DOS and with Windows 9*x* systems using FAT. FAT's main disadvantage is that it's a 16-bit file system with a minimum cluster size of 32KB. The result is that FAT can address partitions only up to 2GB. If your drive is larger than this, you'll have to create two or more partitions to use FAT. (And how many hard drives these days are this small?) Also, FAT has no security features, which is a huge problem. As a positive note, under Windows NT/2000/XP/2003, the FAT file system has a maximum file and partition size of 4GB. Still, it's not a good file system to use anymore.

The FAT32 file system evolved from the traditional FAT file system used by DOS and Windows. Vista can format FAT32 partitions up to 32GB and can access FAT32 partitions up to the maximum size (although this isn't recommended for partitions larger than 32GB). One downside to FAT32 is that, like FAT, it doesn't provide any local security.

In contrast, NTFS is a robust, 32-bit file system with many security features, including password protection for specific files, the capability to limit access to specific files, file compression, file recovery, and the capability to address very large partitions. Although a system using NTFS in some cases runs a bit slower than one using FAT, NTFS is your best bet if you want the additional features of Vista. The speed issue isn't usually significant enough for you to even notice.

To add another twist, Vista provides support for usage quotas on NTFS partitions.

NOTE Remember, Windows 98 can still access files on an NTFS volume across a network, but it can't read an NTFS volume locally.

USING COMPRESSION IN NTFS

In Chapter 8, we looked at how to compress files and folders, but Vista can also compress entire volumes. The compression ratio usually winds up being about 1.5:1, or 33 percent.

To compress an NTFS hard-disk volume, follow these steps:

1. Click Start, and then click Computer.
2. Right-click the volume you want to compress, and choose Properties from the context menu to open the Properties dialog box for that drive as shown in Figure 25.2.
3. On the General tab, click the Compress this drive to save disk space check box, and then click OK.

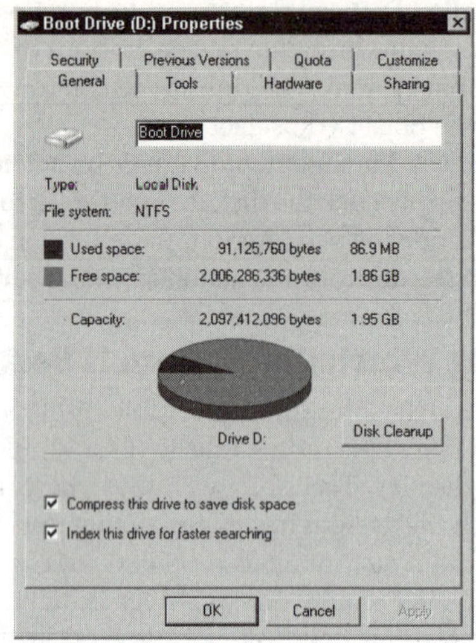

FIGURE 25.2
Compress an NTFS volume to help it use disk space more efficiently.

DUAL-BOOTING CONSIDERATIONS

Let's say you want to run Vista and Windows 98 on the same computer. Why you would want to do this is beyond me, but let's just say that you do. Which do you install first, and what file systems can you use?

Install Windows 98 first and then Vista. When you install Vista, it will create a boot menu so you can choose the operating system you want when you boot up. If you install 98 second, it won't do this for you. Also, it's best to install them onto separate partitions. For this example, Windows 98 will be installed on the C drive (it has to be), and Vista will be on D.

More important, which file systems do you use? For Windows 98, you'll have to use FAT32. So, C will be FAT32. The D drive can be FAT32 or NTFS. For security reasons, it's better to go with NTFS.

Now, when you boot into Windows 98, it will *not* be able to see the D drive, because Windows 98 *cannot* read NTFS. Vista will be able to see both C and D without any problems. If you made D FAT32 as well, then 98 would be able to read it just fine.

USING NTFS FILE SECURITY FEATURES

NTFS file security lets you change settings for disk drives, folders, and even files. These features can be useful if your machine stores many files that you share with other users on your network, as well as your private files.

For information on how to set permissions for NTFS drives, folders, and files, see Chapter 21.

Setting Up a New Disk Drive in Vista

If you've added a new disk drive to your system, Disk Management will be able to see it, but you'll need to create a partition and a volume on it before Vista can use it. The process for setting up a new hard drive in Vista relies on more automation than previous versions of Windows, so you'll find that Vista prompts you to perform certain tasks.

NOTE After you create a partition on a new disk and format it, you can use it in Vista without rebooting. You can even change the size of a partition or extend it across several hard drives without rebooting.

Let's step through adding a new partition and creating a volume on a new disk:

1. Open the Computer Management console in the Administrative Tools folder of the Control Panel. Select the Disk Management folder. Vista automatically scans the disks on the system and opens the Initialize Disk dialog box, shown in Figure 25.3, when it detects a new hard drive. Notice that Vista provides two methods of initializing your hard drive. If you use a dual-boot system, you want to use the Master Boot Record (MBR) option. The MBR option is also good for smaller hard drives (less than 1TB) on Vista-only systems. If you have a large hard drive (1TB or larger) and your system is only used for Vista, the Globally Unique Identifier (GUID) Partition Table (GPT) option is the best idea.
2. Choose a partitioning option. Click OK to initialize the disk. When the initialization is complete, you'll see the Disk Management window again.
3. In the Disk Management window, select the new disk, and choose Action ➤ All Tasks ➤ New Simple Volume to start the New Simple Volume Wizard.
4. Click Next to open the Specify Volume Size dialog box shown in Figure 25.4.

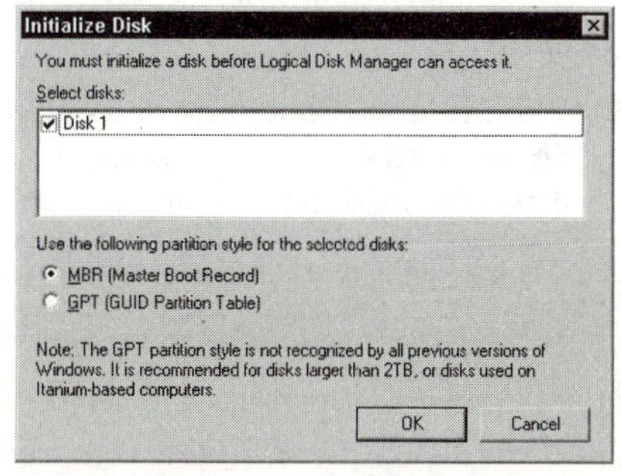

FIGURE 25.3
Vista automatically detects your new hard drive and prompts you to initialize it.

FIGURE 25.4
Determine how large to make the partition on the new drive.

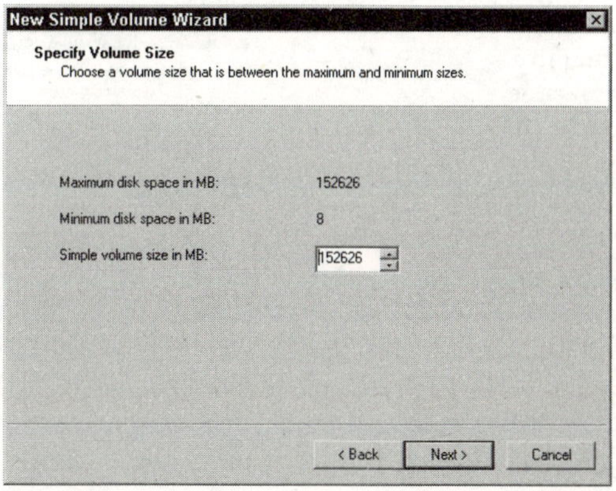

5. Define the size of the volume and click Next. You'll see the Assign Drive Letter or Path dialog box shown in Figure 25.5. Notice the new Mount in the following empty NTFS folder option. Select this option if you want to add this drive to an existing drive. As far as the user is concerned, the existing drive has simply grown larger. You access the drive through the specified empty folder. You can also choose not to assign the drive a letter or mount it as an NTFS folder. In this case, the partition exists, but is essentially inaccessible. You can use this feature for data storage that you want to use for maintenance purposes and don't want the user to see.

6. Choose a drive letter or mounting option and click Next. You'll see the Format Partition dialog box shown in Figure 25.6. Formatting makes the drive usable by your applications. Consequently, if you choose the Do not format this drive option, the drive isn't accessible to your applications. The Format this drive with the following settings option lets you choose how to format the drive. Here are the characteristics you must consider.

   - **File system**: Determines the file system used to format the drive. You can choose FAT (for small drives), FAT32, and NTFS. The safest solution is to choose NTFS so that you gain the security and performance features that NTFS provides.
   - **Allocation unit size**: Sometimes you can make your drive more efficient by choosing a smaller or larger allocation size. For example, if the hard drive will store database records, you can often use a larger allocation size to reduce the number of searches the system has to perform to locate a particular part of the file. On the other hand, you can use a smaller allocation size when working with small files to use hard drive space more efficiently.
   - **Volume label**: Choosing a descriptive volume label makes it easier to work with multiple drives. A label such as Drive 4 doesn't tell you anything about the drive content and could make it more difficult to find the data you need.

7. Choose the file system and allocation unit size. Type a volume label.

8. Check the Perform a quick format option if you've used this drive before and don't need to perform a comprehensive check of the drive surface.

9. Check the Enable file and folder compression option if you want Vista to save space by automatically compressing files and folders for you.

FIGURE 25.5
Define the drive specifics such as drive letter.

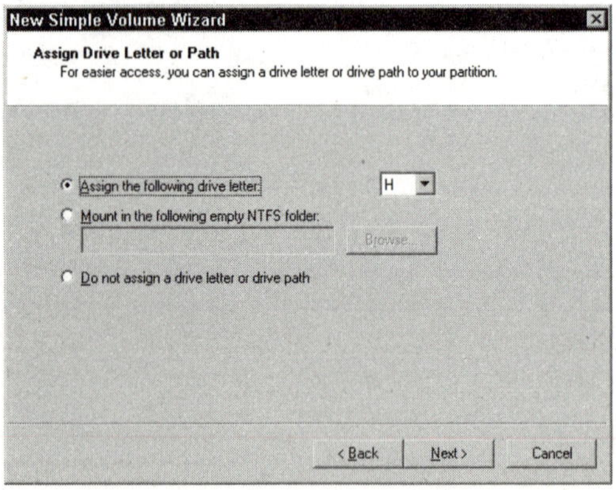

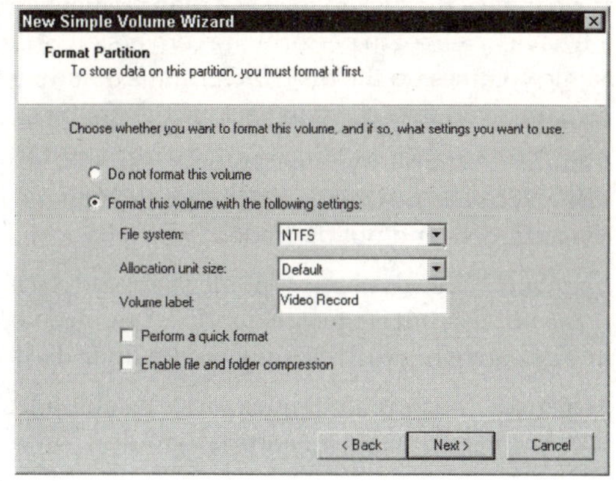

FIGURE 25.6
Format the drive so that it becomes accessible to your applications.

NOTE Don't enable file and folder compression if you want to use the drive for a complete PC backup. Vista will only allow you to use uncompressed drives for backup purposes. See the "Performing a Complete PC Backup" section of Chapter 29 for details on creating a complete PC backup. You need a complete PC backup for certain system restore tasks. If your system is damaged beyond the point where a restore point can fix the problem or your hard drive fails, you need to perform a complete PC restore. See the "Performing a Complete PC Restore" section of Chapter 29 for details on performing this task.

10. Click Next. The New Simple Volume Wizard will display a summary of the options you selected.
11. Check the options you selected for accuracy. If you see an error, you can click Back to fix it. When the summary reflects the choices you want to make, click Finish. Vista partitions and formats the drive for you. When the partitioning and formatting process is finished, you see the new drive appear in the Disk Management display. Vista also opens a new copy of Windows Explorer so that you can access the drive immediately.

ADDING VOLUMES

You might not want to create just one volume on a drive. In this case, you can create a smaller volume in step 5 of the procedure described in the "Setting Up a New Disk Drive in Vista" section of the chapter for new drives. When you finish creating the initial volume, you can right-click an empty area of the hard drive, and choose New Simple Volume from the context menu. The process for adding a new volume is the same one that you follow starting with step 4 in the "Setting Up a New Disk Drive in Vista" section of the chapter.

USING DYNAMIC VOLUMES

Traditional partition types stored their information in a *partition table* that was located in the first physical sector of the hard disk. It was this location and its limited storage space for partition information that limited us to four partitions per physical disk. The partition table stores information for the size and location of each partition and is used to find the bootable partition during the startup procedure.

Dynamic volumes store their partition information in the data portion of the drive, and thus they aren't limited in the amount of information they can store. To convert a basic disk to a dynamic disk, right-click the disk in the Disk Management tool, and select Dynamic from the context menu. You'll have to reboot to perform the conversion. After the restart, you'll be able to create or modify dynamic volumes on the disk, including expanding the volume across multiple disks.

Dynamic volumes come in various flavors:

Simple A simple dynamic volume is similar to a traditional partition in that it exists on a single drive. It can be resized by extending the volume if it's on a dynamic disk that was created as a dynamic disk and not upgraded from a basic disk.

Spanned This dynamic volume spans two or more disks to create one logical volume, as its name implies, but it can be extended. Spanned volumes are the same as volume sets in NT 4, but in Vista, they're available only on dynamic disks.

Mirrored Mirrored volumes provide fault tolerance by keeping an exact mirror image of all data in the volume on a separate hard disk. If you lose one disk, you still have an exact copy of all the data.

Striped Striped volumes are the fastest type of dynamic volume and yield great benefits in performance. They aren't fault tolerant, however. If you lose one disk, you lose all the data in the volume. In that sense, they're actually *less* fault tolerant than a single volume. They're the same as the traditional striped sets available in NT, but striped volumes are available in Vista only on dynamic disks.

RAID 5 RAID 5 is also known as striping with parity. RAID 5 allows the volume to lose one hard disk without failing. It does this by combining the remaining data with the parity information to recreate the data on the fly.

NOTE Dynamic volumes aren't supported on portable computers, removable disks, detachable disks using Universal Serial Bus (USB) or IEEE 1394 (also called FireWire) interfaces, or on disks connected to shared SCSI buses.

Resizing Volumes

Vista makes it possible to resize a volume. You might have space that you set aside for future use on a drive and now need for additional data. In some cases, you might use this option to consolidate volumes or create new volumes to manage your data better. The resizing process takes two forms. The first is extending the volume to add more space and the second is shrinking the volume to make it smaller. Here are the steps for extending a volume.

1. Right-click the volume you want to change and choose Extend Volume from the context menu. You'll see the Extend Volume Wizard.
2. Click Next. You'll see the Select Disks dialog box shown in Figure 25.7.
3. Choose a disk to use for the extension (if necessary, Vista normally chooses the correct disk for you).
4. Type the new size of the volume in the Select the amount of space in MB field. Click Next. Vista summarizes the size change.
5. Click Finish. Vista resizes the volume for you.

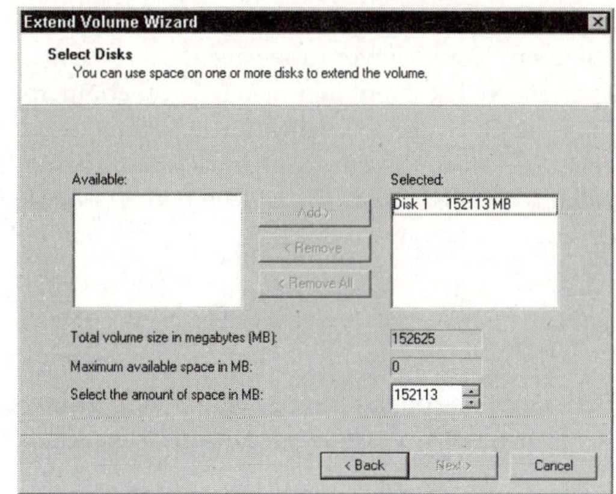

FIGURE 25.7
Choose the disk you want to use for extension purposes and define the new size of the volume.

Here are the steps for shrinking a volume.

1. Right-click the volume you want to change and choose Shrink Volume from the context menu. You'll see the Shrink dialog box shown in Figure 25.8.
2. Define the amount you want to shrink the volume in the Enter the amount to shrink in MB field. This field tells Vista how much smaller to make the volume, not the resulting size of the volume. If you have a 10,240MB hard drive and want to make the new size 8,240MB, then you must shrink the drive by 2,000MB.
3. Click Shrink. Vista reduces the size of the hard drive.

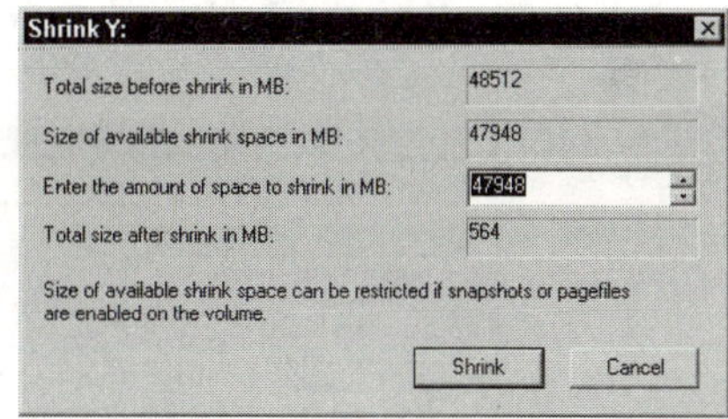

FIGURE 25.8
Define a smaller size for a volume when you want to use the space for other purposes.

Using Event Viewer

One of Vista's more handy tools is the Event Viewer, which can be helpful for troubleshooting a misbehaving PC or for getting a better handle on what Vista is doing behind the scenes. Vista makes significant changes to the Event Viewer. You'll now find that the Event Viewer displays more information in a smaller space. In addition, while you'll still find the common logs from the past, Vista provides a wealth of new logs for applications and services. What used to be called a custom log now outnumbers the standard logs from the past.

Viewing Events

You'll open Event Viewer to see events. An event can tell you about the system and the problems it experiences. The event logs also tell you about application successes, so you know what is working as well. Overall, the Event Viewer is the best place to learn more about what's happening on your machine through the event entries that it provides. To open Event Viewer to the standard logs, follow these steps:

1. Choose Start ➤ Control Panel to open Control Panel.
2. Click System and Maintenance, and then click View event logs in the Administrative Tools section.
3. In the pane on the left, open the Windows Logs folder, and then select Application, Security, or System. If you select System, you'll see something similar to the window shown in Figure 25.9.

System events are logged by Vista's system components, including hardware drivers. For example, if a driver fails to load, it will write a system event to the System log. Or if a Vista service fails to initialize, the service reports its failure in the System log. There are three types of System log events:

Information Logged when a driver or service starts successfully and indicated by the blue letter *i*. For example, each time you boot up Vista, a system event is logged, indicating that the event log service was started.

Warning Logged when a condition occurs that could mean future trouble, for example, a nearly full hard drive. Indicated by an exclamation point in a yellow triangle.

Error Logged when a service or a driver fails to start or load and indicated by an *X* in a red circle. For example, if your network card driver fails, that error is logged, as is an error indicating that any network protocols communicating with that network card have failed.

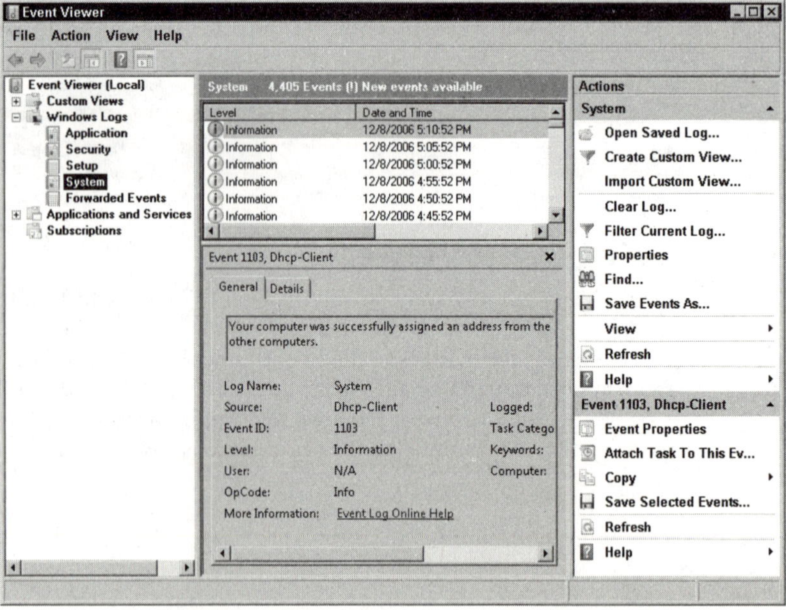

FIGURE 25.9 The new Event Viewer provides more to look at, but similar functionality to the old version.

Security events occur if you've enabled auditing on a shared disk, subfolder, or file. Audited events are written to the Security log when someone accesses your shared area and logs in. An administrator can specify which events are logged into the Security log. There are two types of Security log events:

Success Logged when a user successfully logs on to one of your shared areas: a disk, a subfolder, or a file.

Failure Logged when a user fails to log on to one of your shared areas.

Vista applications write status and error messages in the Application log. If an application is crashing or behaving oddly, it's usually a good idea to check the Application log for error messages. The Application log uses the same three event types as the System log: Information, Warning, and Error. Application developers specify which events to log.

One of the changes that Microsoft has made to Event Viewer is the ability to see both a listing of events and details about a specific event without having to open up anything. The upper pane in Figure 25.9 contains the list of events for the event log that you choose in the left pane. The bottom pane contains details about the event you highlight. If you want to see the details in a separate dialog box so that you can compare two events, double-click the even entry.

With Event Viewer, you can look at only one event log at a time. To change views, select the log you want to see.

TIP **When opening old log files, be careful not to confuse them with your system's actual logs. The system log files live in the `Winnt\System32\Config` subfolder. If you open a log other than one of your system's three primary logs, its name will be displayed in the title bar of the Event Viewer window. Each time you open Event Viewer, it loads all three primary logs, along with the standard application and service logs.**

The Event Viewer doesn't provide all of the available data in the event listing. You can add or remove columns from the listing by choosing View ➤ Add/Remove Columns from the Action pane. The Add/Remove columns dialog box contains a list of all of the unused columns in the Available columns list and all of the columns currently displayed in the Displayed columns list. To change the display, simply select an item in the list and click Add or Remove as necessary. You can also change the display order by clicking an entry in the Displayed columns list and clicking Move Up or Move Down.

You also don't have to stick with the view shown in Figure 25.9, which is the default view for Vista. Click View ➤ Customize to display the Customize View dialog box. Check or clear the items you want to see and click OK. The Event Log view changes to contain any elements that you want.

Arranging and Filtering the Logs

The Event Log provides a wealth of convenient methods of arranging and filtering the event log entries. Arranging the entries means that you still see all of the entries, but they appear in a certain order or within groups. Filtering the event entries means removing entries that don't meet certain criteria from view. The entries still exist, you just can't see them.

The command for arranging the logs appears in View menu of the Actions pane on the right side of the display. Choosing an option from the Sort submenu changes the order of the entries. Choosing an option from the Group submenu places like items together under a heading. You have the following options when you sort or group entries.

- Level
- Date and Time

- Source
- Event ID
- Task Category

To create a filter for an event log, click Filter Current Log in the Actions pane. You'll see the Filter Current Log dialog box shown in Figure 25.10.

The Filter Current Log dialog box contains a wealth of options for limiting what you can see. Choose an entry in the Logged field when you want to limit the time interval you see. You may only want to see the log entries for the last hour, rather than the month of log entries that the event log currently contains. The Event Level lets you filter out less important events or see just the informational events. You can also filter by the event log or source, the event ID, task category, keyword, user, and computer. When you finish selecting filter criteria, click OK and you'll see just the event log entries you selected.

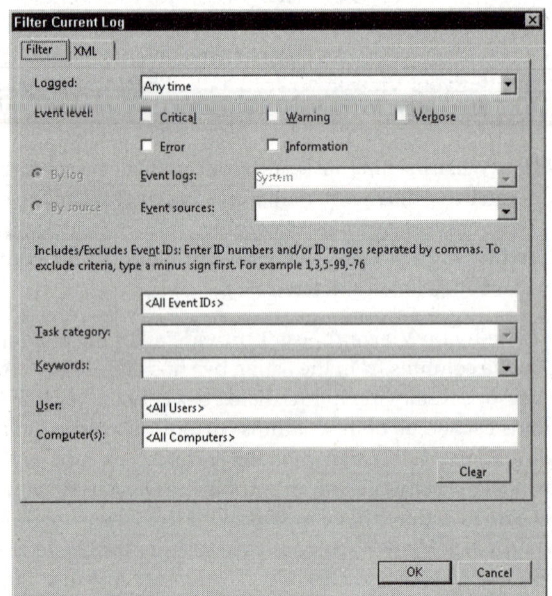

FIGURE 25.10
Filtering helps you to see just the events that you need to work with.

Diagnosing Problems with the Event Log

If a hardware device isn't loading or is behaving oddly, one of the first places to look for the cause is the Event Viewer because a misbehaving device will likely document its problems in the System log. (If you don't see the expected entry, make sure you check the application and service logs as well.) And even though Warning and Error events are sometimes short on specifics, they can often be good indicators of where to begin looking. Here's what a troubleshooting session might look like.

On startup, the driver for a Sound Blaster card fails to initialize; the result is a lack of wave audio in Vista. The first indicator you get is a message informing you that at least one Vista service failed to start.

On opening Event Viewer, you'd see an Error event in the System log reported by Vista's Service Control Manager. After clicking it, you'd see the message "The following boot-start or system-start driver(s) failed to load: sndblst." Although this somewhat terse message doesn't provide any specifics from Event Viewer, you could then check your Sound Blaster driver's status by following these steps:

1. Click Start, right-click Computer, and choose Properties from the context menu to open the System Properties window.
2. Click the Advanced system settings link to open the System Properties dialog box.
3. Click the Hardware tab, and then click the Device Manager button to open Device Manager.
4. Expand Sound, video, and game controllers, right-click Sound Blaster, choose Properties from the context menu to open the Properties dialog box, and check the settings.

Managing Event Logs

Event Viewer has a few other handy features to check out. From the Actions pane, you can clear all events from a selected log. Be careful here, however. Although Vista will issue a warning, there's no Undo for clearing the logs. If you think you might want to access event information contained in the logs, save them as backups in a different subfolder so that you can access them later if need be.

To change the size of a log or overwrite its settings, right-click the log, and choose Properties from the context menu to open the log's Properties dialog box. Figure 25.11 shows the General tab for the System log's Properties dialog box.

Log size can be anywhere from 64KB on up (the default is 20MB or 20,480KB). Vista defaults to overwriting events as needed to keep the log the specified size. It's important to perform backups often enough to maintain a complete catalog of system events.

FIGURE 25.11
You can change log settings in the log's Properties dialog box.

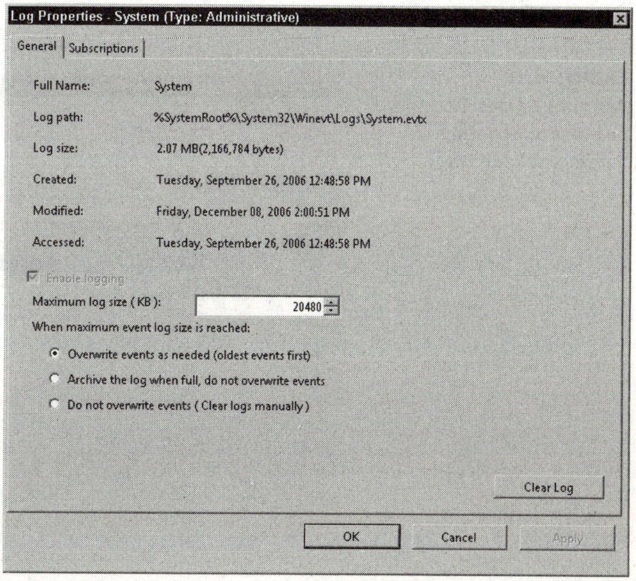

NOTE If you've set Do not overwrite events (Clear logs manually), the Vista System log can fill up and can no longer be updated until you make more room in the log. If your system is having problems and can't update the System log, diagnosing a problem may be more difficult. If your log file has filled, you can't reenable event logging by increasing the logs' file sizes. You'll have to back up your logs, clear all events from them, and then increase the files' sizes.

WARNING Be careful to watch the size of logs as they grow. If you've set the logs to never overwrite and they fill up, Vista may hang. If you're auditing for security events, the recommended setting is to never overwrite because security events should be documented over long periods of time. Clearing and archiving the log should be a part of routine maintenance.

Creating Event Log Tasks

Sometimes you might want to do more than simply view an event. The event might be something special that requires additional work on your part. The Vista event logs let you attach tasks to events. For example, you might want the system to send you an e-mail every time an application indicates a file directory problem, so that you can clear additional space. You could also run an application to perform the clearing automatically. The idea is that you're interacting with the event log in a new way. The following steps tell you how to create an event log task using the Event Viewer.

1. Right-click the event that you want to monitor and choose Attach Task to This Event from the context menu. You'll see the Create Basic Task Wizard dialog box shown in Figure 25.12.
2. Type a name and description for the task. Make sure you provide enough information to know what the task does later. Click Next. You'll see the When a Specific Event Is Logged dialog box. Depending on how you enter the wizard, you may not be able to change the information. The dialog box contains a description of the event—the log used to store the event entry, name of the application or service that generates the entry, and the event ID for the event.

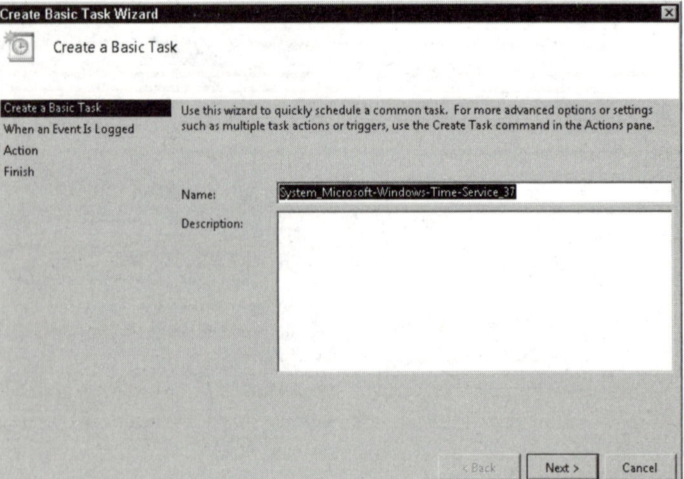

FIGURE 25.12
Associate a task with an event to perform automated handling.

3. Provide the event information, when necessary, and click Next. You'll see the Action dialog box. This dialog box provides three options:
   - **Start a program:** Starts an application of any type (could be a script or batch file) in a certain location using the command-line arguments that you provide.
   - **Send an e-mail:** Sends an e-mail to any number of people. You supply the From, To, Subject, text, attachments, and Simple Mail Transfer Protocol (SMTP) information needed to route the e-mail and describe the problem. This feature doesn't provide carbon copy (CC) or blind carbon copy (BCC) fields.
   - **Display a message:** Displays a message box on the local machine. This option only provides you with a notification—it doesn't solve any problems for you.
4. Choose an action and click Next. Depending on the action you selected, you'll see one of three dialog boxes where you provide the action details. For example, when displaying a message, you must provide a message title and content.
5. Provide the required action information and click Next. You'll see a summary of the task associated with the event.
6. Verify the task information and click Finish. Vista creates the task for you.

Creating Event Log Subscriptions

Event log subscriptions let you track events on other computers. The remote computer publishes an event and you subscribe to it. To use subscriptions, you must start and configure the Windows Event Collector Service. When you try to create your first subscription, Event Log automatically displays a message box telling you about the configuration requirement, and gives you an option to start the service and configure it. Simply click Yes when asked to perform the configuration.

After you perform the required Windows Event Collector Service configuration, you can create a subscription. The following steps tell how to perform this task.

1. Select the Subscriptions folder. You'll see a list of current subscriptions.
2. Click Create Subscription in the Actions pane. You'll see a Subscription Properties dialog box like the one shown in Figure 25.13.
3. Type and name and description for the subscription.
4. Optionally, choose a log for the subscription. Vista defaults to using the System log.
5. Click Add. You'll see a Select Computer dialog box.
6. Choose a computer to use for the subscription. Click OK. Vista adds the computer to the Source Computers list. You can't access computers that don't support Windows Remote Management (WinRM) with this approach. For example, you can't add a Windows 2000 server to the list without a special configuration. The article at `http://msdn2.microsoft.com/en-us/library/aa389290.aspx` describes how to connect to Windows Management Instrumentation (WMI) using WinRM.

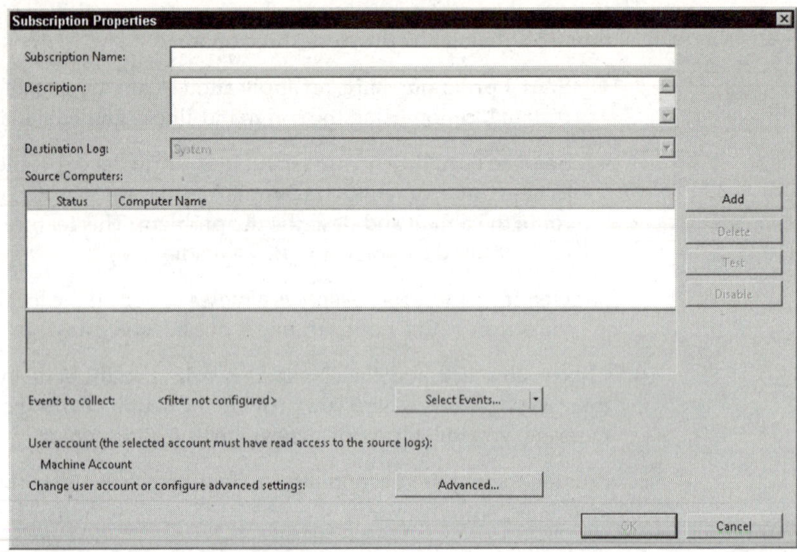

FIGURE 25.13 Create subscriptions to event logs on other machines so you can monitor them remotely.

7. Highlight the new computer entry and click Test. Follow any recommendations for fixing the connection when the connection fails.

NOTE In many cases, the problem is going to be one of not having access to the remote system. Use the WinRM utility at the command prompt to make the connection. The system you want to monitor must appear as part of the TrustedHosts property. For example, if you want to add a server name WinServer to the list, type `winrm set winrm/config/client @{TrustedHosts="WinServer"}` at the command prompt and press Enter. You can learn more about WinRM installation and configuration at `http://msdn2.microsoft.com/en-us/library/aa384372.aspx`.

8. Click Select Events. You'll see a Query Filter dialog box similar to the one shown in Figure 25.14. In this case, the filter will retrieve all critical and warning events in the security and system logs.
9. Select the filtering criteria for the incoming events and click OK.
10. Click OK to create the subscription. You'll see the subscription added to the Subscriptions folder of the Event Viewer.

After you create an event, you can use entries in the Actions pane to manage it. You can delete the subscription when you no longer need it. However, if you only want to suspend the subscription for a short time (such as when you go on vacation), you can click Disable in the Actions pane to disable it instead. When you return from vacation, you can highlight the entry and click Enable to start receiving events again. If a subscription fails to start, you can check for errors in starting it, highlight the entry, and click Retry to try starting it again.

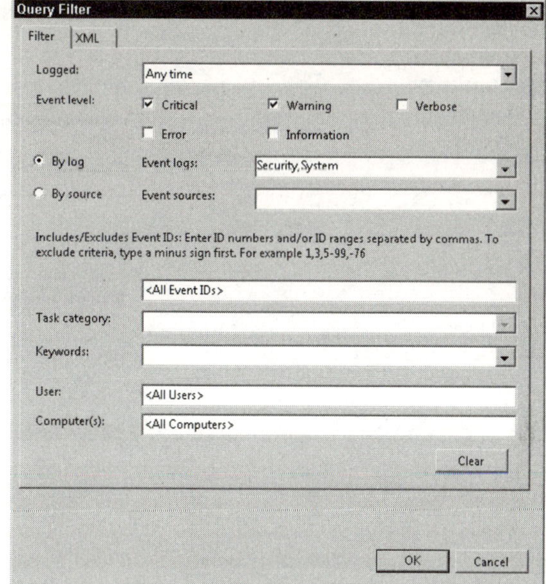

FIGURE 25.14
Choose the information you want to receive from the remote system.

Using Problem Reports and Solutions to Track Vista Issues

One of the problems with reporting errors to Microsoft in the past was the perception that the reports went into a vortex, never to see the light of day again. In some respects, that perception was true. Do you know of anyone who ever received any kind of response from Microsoft regarding a problem report? I certainly don't. However, things have changed in Vista. The new Problem Reports and Solutions applet in the Control Panel helps you track errors and even obtain solutions for them. Figure 25.15 shows a typical display.

Any problems you report automatically appear in a problems list. You see two such entries in Figure 25.15. The application in question failed and the suggested fix was to obtain a new version of the product. Unfortunately, I can't implement the fix today because the new version isn't available. Clicking on the problem link shows the detailed problem analysis and upcoming solution shown in Figure 25.16. At least I know that someone is working on the problem and that I'll eventually see a solution to it. This, in a nutshell, is what this new applet is designed to do. It's there to provide information so that you at least have some idea that someone out there knows you have a problem and is working on a solution.

You can obtain a detailed view of every problem your system has experienced by clicking the See problems to check link. What you'll see is a detailed list of the problems your system has experienced. Click on the View Details link for the problem to see additional information. The amount of information varies by problem, but the additional information often provides clues you can use for self-help. For example, when a driver doesn't install, you can discover what device is failing and why.

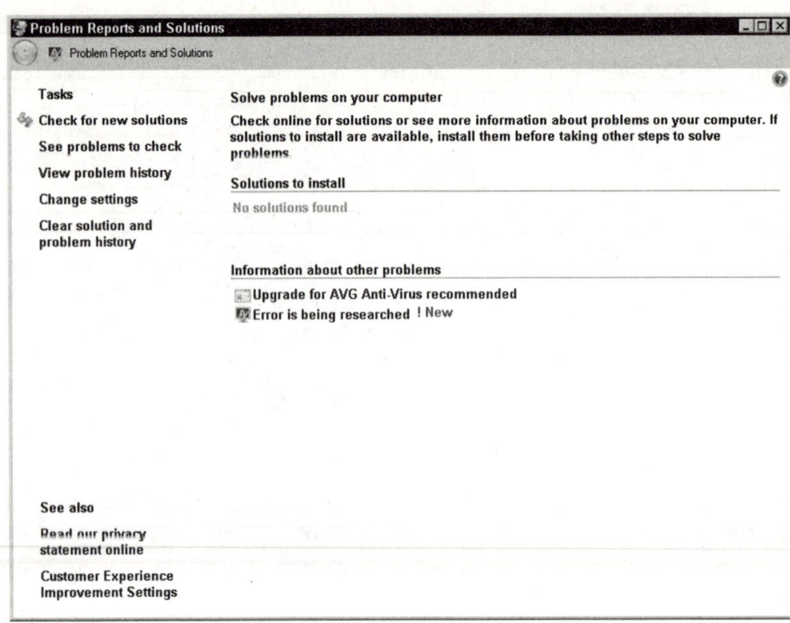

FIGURE 25.15
The Problem Reports and Solutions applet helps you track problems and solutions for your system.

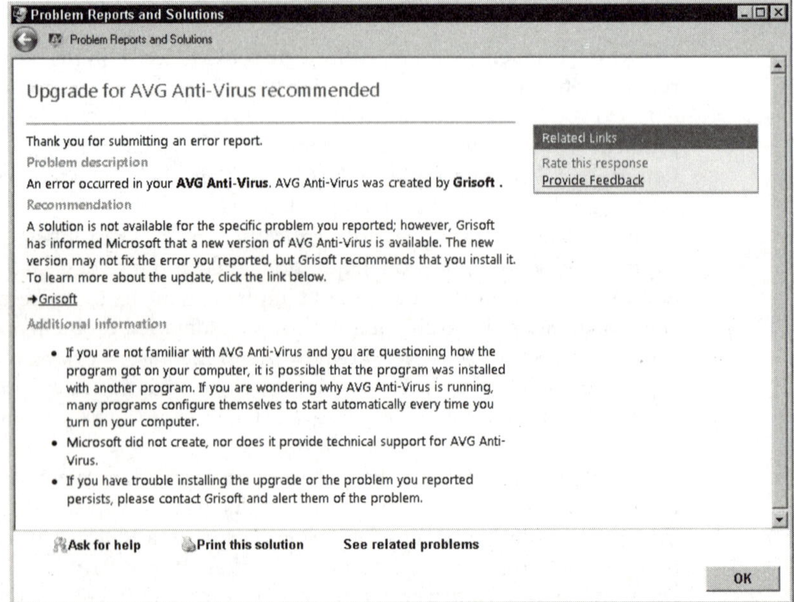

FIGURE 25.16
The information might appear canned (and it is), but at least you know someone is aware of the problem.

As your list of unsolved problems gets longer, you might wonder what the vendor is doing or whether someone has already provided the required fix. To check for problem solutions, click the Check for new solutions link. You'll see a Problem Reports and Solutions dialog box while the Vista checks for solutions. Eventually, the dialog will go away and you'll hopefully see some new solutions. Simply click the link associated with the solution to install it on your system.

In some cases, you'll see a dialog box like the one shown in Figure 25.17 that tells you Microsoft needs more information (at least it tells you that someone is reviewing the problem). Click View problem details to get the specifics on the problems that Microsoft is researching. If you decide to send the additional information, click Send information.

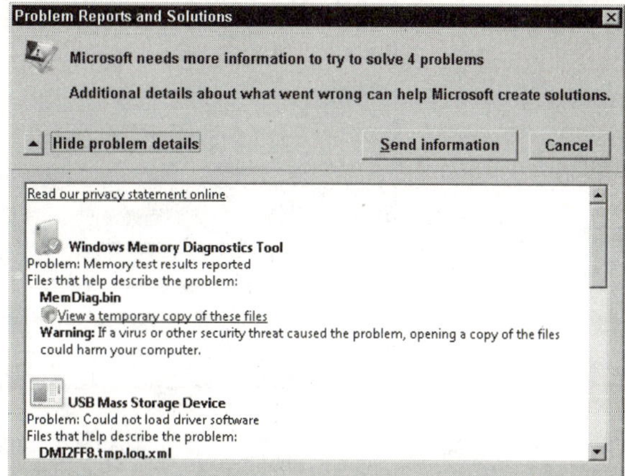

FIGURE 25.17
Microsoft may need additional information to solve the problem on your system.

Automating Repetitive Tasks Using Task Scheduler

The Task Scheduler is an important tool for automating tasks on your system. A big problem for many people is that they don't remember to perform some tasks, even when they know that the task is important. For example, many people never make a backup of their system or fail to defragment the hard drive. Of course, you shouldn't limit yourself to management tasks. Any task that you need to perform routinely and consistently is a candidate for Task Scheduler. In fact, you'll find that many applications on your system use Task Scheduler automatically or as a result of actions on your part.

To start the Task Scheduler, choose Start ➤ All Programs ➤ Accessories ➤ System Tools ➤ Task Scheduler. You'll see a window similar to the one shown in Figure 25.18. If you've used Task Scheduler in previous versions of Windows, you'll notice that the Vista version contains considerably more information. Don't worry about it though, creating and managing tasks hasn't changed in Vista—only the presentation has changed.

In this case, you're seeing tasks for the Certificate Services Client. The hierarchy of task-related folders appears in the left pane. The list of tasks associated with the CertificateServicesClient entry appears in the upper pane. The lower pane contains details for the selected task. The right pane contains a list of actions you can perform on the selected entry. You can change this display by choosing View ➤ Customize. The Customize View dialog box contains a list of application features you can use for viewing purposes. Check or clear any of the options, and then click OK, to change the display. You can also modify the presentation of the upper pane by choosing View ➤ Add/Remove Columns. The Add/Remove Columns dialog box contains a list of columns you can add or remove from the upper pane.

Task Scheduler actually supports two kinds of tasks. A basic task only works with Vista—it's invisible to previous versions of Windows because it relies on XML to describe the task. A standard task can use either XML (making it invisible to previous versions of Windows) or the older task format (which means other versions of Windows can see it). In addition, you gain some flexibility (with associated complexity) when creating a standard task. The following sections describe how to create basic and standard tasks.

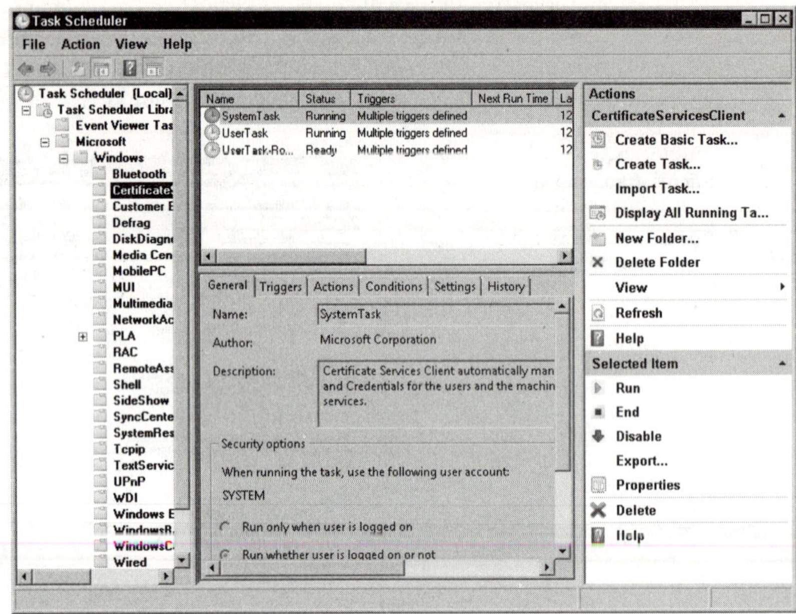

FIGURE 25.18 Task Scheduler might have a new interface for Vista, but the usage details are about the same.

Creating a Basic Task

A basic task only works with Vista. You can create one quite quickly using the wizard that Task Scheduler provides. The following steps describe how to perform this task.

1. Select the folder you want to use to hold the task. You can create a new folder by selecting a parent folder and clicking New Folder in the Actions pane.
2. Click Create Basic Task. You'll see the Create Basic Task Wizard. The Create a Basic Task dialog box asks you to identify the task.
3. Type a name and description for the task. More information is better because a good description helps you remember why you created the task later. Click Next. You'll see the Task Trigger dialog box shown in Figure 25.19.
4. Select an interval (such as monthly) or event (such as logging in) to trigger the task. Click Next. You'll see a dialog box that tells you to define the precise triggering in detail. For example, if you choose monthly, you'll need to define precisely when during the month you want the task to run. For example, you could choose the first Monday of the month as the task time or a specific day, such as the first of each month.
5. Define the interval or event details and click Next. You'll see the Action dialog box where you choose an action to perform as follows:
   - **Start a program:** Starts an application of any type (could be a script or batch file) in a certain location using the command-line arguments that you provide.

- **Send an e-mail:** Sends an e-mail to any number of people. You supply the From, To, Subject, text, attachments, and Simple Mail Transfer Protocol (SMTP) information needed to route the e-mail and describe the problem. This feature doesn't provide carbon copy (CC) or blind carbon copy (BCC) fields.
- **Display a message:** Displays a message box on the local machine. This option only provides you with a notification—it doesn't solve any problems for you.

6. Choose an action to perform and click Next. Task Scheduler will ask you to provide details about the action, such as the location of the application or the content of the message.
7. Provide the required action details and click Next. You'll see a Summary dialog box.
8. Review the task details and click Finish. Task Scheduler adds the task to the list.

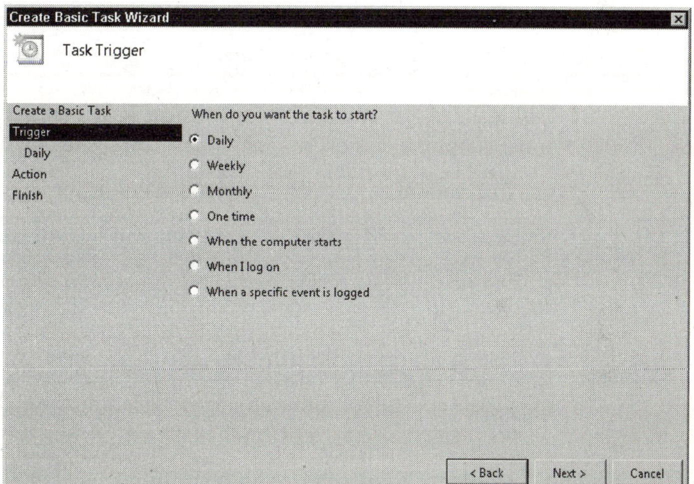

FIGURE 25.19 Choose an interval or event to trigger the task.

Creating a Standard Task

A standard task accomplishes essentially the same thing as a basic task—it schedules some action in response to a trigger you define. However, the standard task lets you define whether the task is visible from other versions of Windows. In addition, you gain a little flexibility in defining the task parameters. The following steps describe how to create a standard task.

1. Select the folder you want to use to hold the task. You can create a new folder by selecting a parent folder and clicking New Folder in the Actions pane.
2. Click Create Task. You'll see the Create Task dialog box shown in Figure 25.20. Notice the Configure for field lets you choose the operating system for the task. If you choose Windows Vista, the task only works on Vista because it relies on an XML data file.

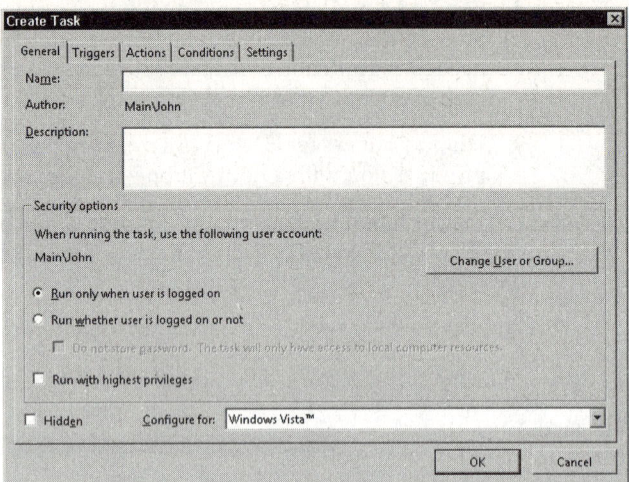

FIGURE 25.20 Creating a standard task provides additional flexibility, but at the cost of more complexity.

3. Define the task particulars using the process described in the "Creating a Basic Task" section of the chapter as a starting point. Here are some flexibility points to consider:
   - You can define user and group credentials on the General tab.
   - Select Hidden on the General tab if you want the task to run in the background.
   - Define multiple triggers on the Triggers tab to perform the task under more that one condition.
   - Define multiple actions on the Actions tab to perform more than one task for a given trigger.
   - Create special conditions for accomplishing the task on the Conditions tab. For example, you can choose to perform the task only when the computer is idle.
   - Modify the task settings on the Settings tab. For example, you can clear the Allow task to be run on demand check box if you only want to run this task at the scheduled interval or in response to a particular event.
4. Click OK. Task Scheduler adds the new task to the list.

NOTE The History tab tells you about the history of the task. You can determine when the task has run and whether it completed successfully. In many cases, you can also learn why a task failed when it doesn't complete successfully.

Monitoring Performance

Vista is designed to "self-tune" for optimal performance but also provides several tools for detecting possible performance bottlenecks. You can use the Vista Reliability and Performance Monitor console to monitor and log the performance of hundreds of variables, including some very esoteric ones intended to be used by developers and network administrators when tracking application and system behavior. In addition to tracking performance on your system, you can track performance counters on other Vista machines on your network. We'll take a look at the

Reliability and Performance Monitor console and some of its components. Rather than cover every variable counter you can assign in Reliability and Performance Monitor, we'll look at about a dozen or so key counters that deliver the most relevant system information.

NOTE If you want only a quick read on Vista "vitals," right-click the Taskbar and select Task Manager from the context menu. Task Manager has a Performance tab that reports CPU usage and memory statistics. Task Manager also lists applications you have open, as well as processes and services that are running (those created by programs and Vista services). Task Manager is discussed in detail at the end of this chapter.

To open the Reliability and Performance Monitor console, in Control Panel click the System and Maintenance link, click Administrative Tools, and then click Reliability and Performance Monitor. Figure 25.21 shows the Reliability and Performance Monitor console.

Performance provides three views of real-time data in System Monitor. To access one of these views, click the down arrow next to the Change the graph type button and choose one of the options. (To display a button's label, simply place the cursor over it.) The three views are simply different displays of the data that Performance can report. Here's a quick rundown:

Line Displays counters graphically. This is the view shown in Figure 25.21. You can add as many counters as you like, although more than about a half-dozen makes for a rather cluttered graph.

Histogram bar Displays bar graphs that dynamically update as the data changes.

Report Displays counters in real time (as Chart view does). Selected counters are listed and their values are updated at a specified rate.

Before getting into detail about each of these views, let's look at some counters you're most likely to monitor.

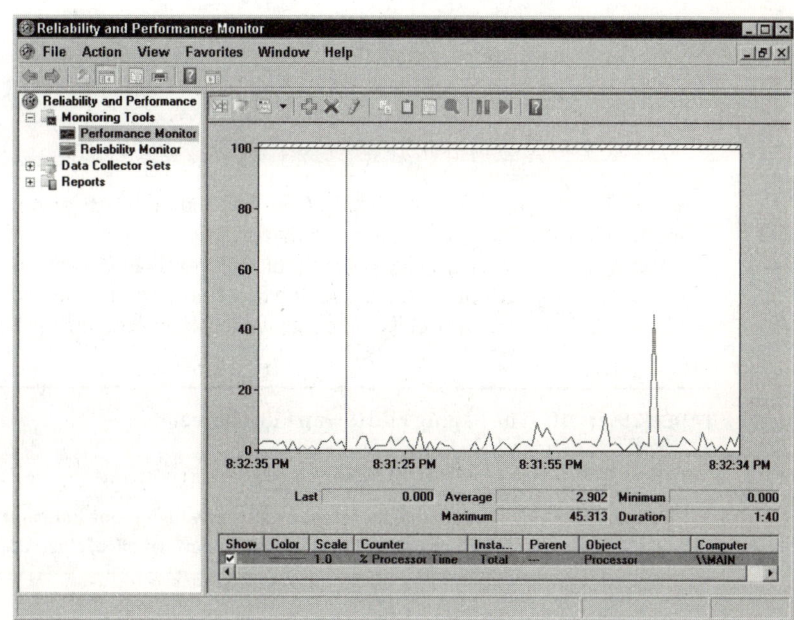

FIGURE 25.21 The System Monitor in the Reliability and Performance Monitor console delivers constantly updated information about the performance of subsystems, and it can update its display dozens of times a second.

Vista classifies its subsystem components into objects, and each object has anywhere from two to more than a dozen counters that you can monitor. In addition, certain objects—such as processors, physical disks, and logical disks—also have instances because your Vista system may have more than one of these types of hardware.

To display an explanation of what any counter monitors, follow these steps:

1. Click the Add button on the toolbar (it has a plus sign) to open the Add Counters dialog box shown in Figure 25.22.
2. Click the plus sign (+) next to an object from the performance object list (the Processor entry in Figure 25.22).
3. Select a counter from the performance object list (the % User Time entry in Figure 25.22).
4. Click the Show description check box.

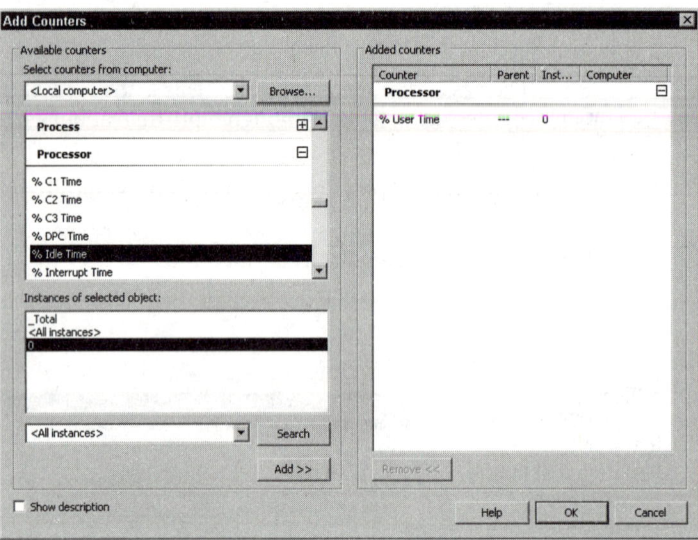

FIGURE 25.22
Add one or more counters to the display to track performance.

Obviously, you also use the Add Counters dialog box to specify which counters you want to monitor, and we'll look at how to do that shortly.

So without further ado, let's take a look at several objects and some of their counters. Tables 25.1 through 25.4 show you the counters, the functions, and the importance of four objects: the Paging File object, the Processor object, the PhysicalDisk object, and the Server object.

TABLE 25.1: The Paging File (Swap File) Object

COUNTER	IMPORTANCE
% Usage	A value that stays persistently high is one indicator that additional RAM would noticeably improve system performance, given the type of work you're doing.

TABLE 25.2: The Processor Object

COUNTER	IMPORTANCE
% Processor Time	May indicate that an application or a service is using the CPU excessively, cutting into overall system performance.
% Interrupt Time	Interrupts execute in Vista's kernel mode; applications execute in user mode. Excessive hardware interrupts can hamper overall system performance.
% Privileged Time	Similar to % Interrupt Time; if your system is spending excessive amounts of time in privileged mode, applications, which all run in user mode, have to wait for the CPU to return to user mode to access the CPU.
% User Time	An indicator of how much CPU time applications have available to them.

TABLE 25.3: The PhysicalDisk Object

COUNTER	IMPORTANCE
Disk Read Bytes/sec	Gives a general indication of a disk's read performance.
Disk Write Bytes/sec	Gives a general indication of a disk's write performance.

TABLE 25.4: The Server Object

COUNTER	IMPORTANCE
Bytes Total/sec	Excessive network access of your system by other users can drag down your overall performance.
Errors Logon	Repeated failed logon attempts may mean a password-guessing program is trying to crack into your system.
Sessions Timed Out	Useful for setting idle time-out values. Each active peer connection to your system slightly diminishes overall system performance.

Adding a Counter in Graph View

Performance defaults to Graph view, which graphically displays any selected counters. Let's go through the steps to add the Processor object and % Processor Time counter and the Paging File object and % Usage counter:

1. In the Reliability and Performance Monitor console, select Performance Monitor, and click the Add button to open the Add Counters dialog box.

2. Click the plus sign (+) next to Processor in the performance object list. You'll see a list of processor-related counters appear below the Processor entry.
3. Select %Processor Time.
4. Highlight the _Total instance in the Instances of selected object list, and then click Add. You'll see the counter added to the Added Counters list on the right side of the display.

NOTE Notice that the Instances of selected object list changes as you choose different objects and counters. An instance is a particular use of an object. In the case of processors, you'll see an instance for each processor in your system numbered 0 through one less than the number of processors in your machine. If you only have one processor, you'll only see the number 0. The _Total instance is an accumulation of the data from each of the individual instances. You can also choose the <All instances> entry to add all of the instances at once.

5. Click the plus sign (+) next to Paging File in the performance object list. You'll see a list of paging file–related counters appear below the Paging File entry.
6. Select %Usage.
7. Highlight the page file instance for your hard drive, and then click Add. The page file instance appears as `\??\c:\Pagefile.sys` in the list, where `c:\pagefile.sys` is the location of the page file on your system. If you have multiple page files, then you'll see multiple `pagefile.sys` entries—one for each page file. You'll see the counter added to the Added Counters list on the right side of the display.
8. Click Close.

Back in the Reliability and Performance Monitor console, you'll see something similar to the display in Figure 25.23. The counters you selected are added to any counters already in place. Eventually, you'll end up with a large number of counters in the display. To remove counters you no longer want, highlight the counter in the list at the bottom of the display and click Delete (the red *X*).

To save this view at any point in time, right-click the chart, choose Save As from the context menu to open the Save As dialog box, give the file a name, and click Save. You can save the view as a web page or as a report.

TIP To highlight a counter, select it at the bottom of the window and press Ctrl+H.

To customize the chart's colors, fonts, and other graphical elements, follow these steps:

1. Right-click the chart, and choose Properties from the context menu to open the System Monitor Properties dialog box shown in Figure 25.24.
2. Click one of the five tabs, and then specify your options.
3. When you've finished, click OK.

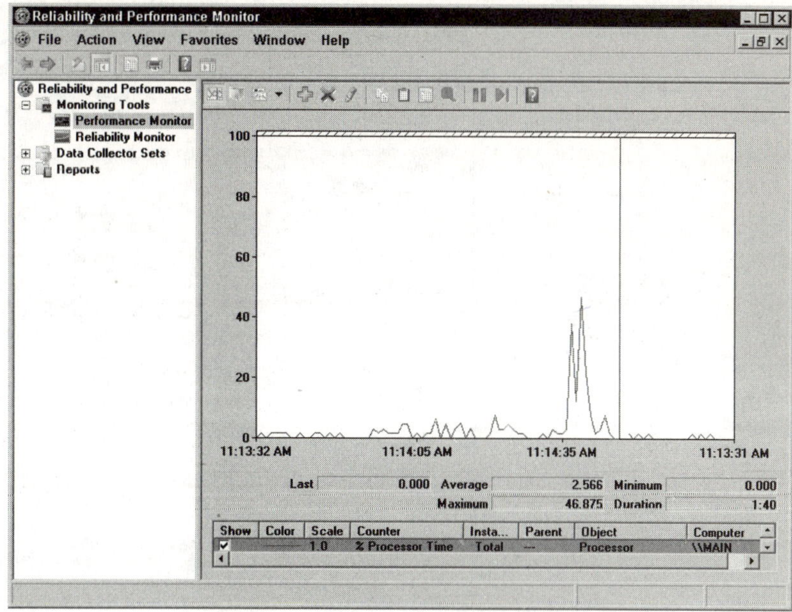

FIGURE 25.23 The graph reflects the counters and instances you've chosen.

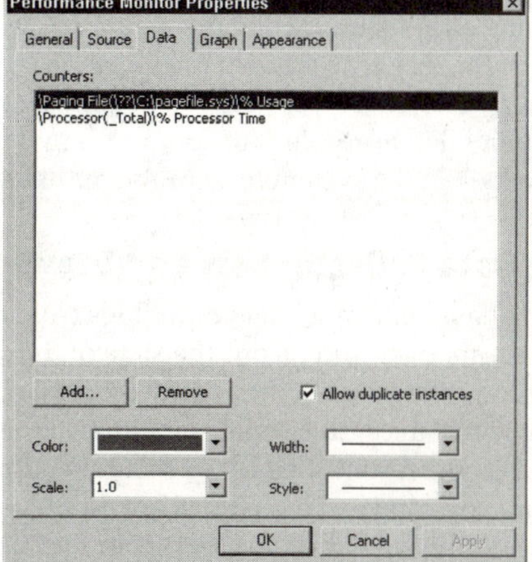

FIGURE 25.24 You can customize the appearance and presentation of data in the chart.

Using the Reliability Monitor

The Reliability Monitor is a new feature of Vista. It monitors the system for problems and tells you about them using the graphic interface shown in Figure 25.25. You don't have to do anything special to use this feature. Vista collects the data automatically and presents you with a reliability index based on the information it obtains.

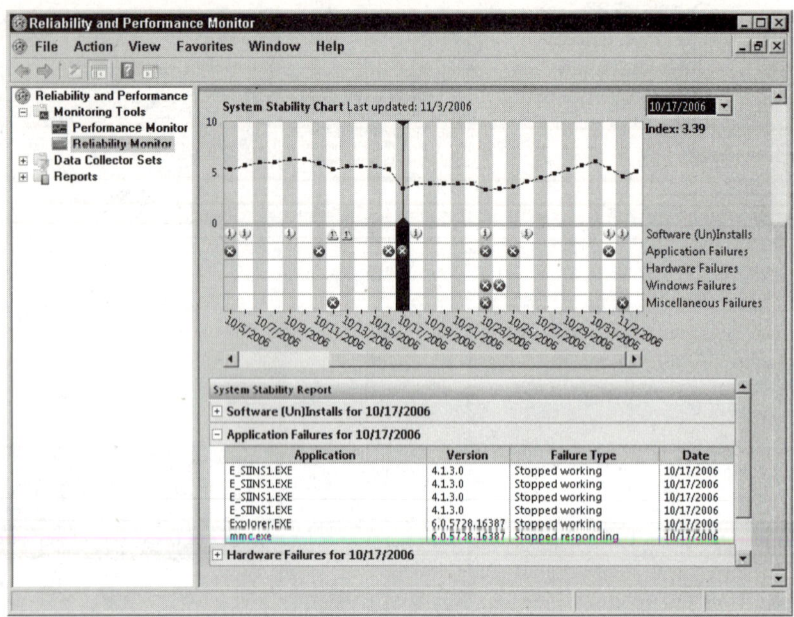

Application	Version	Failure Type	Date
E_SIINS1.EXE	4.1.3.0	Stopped working	10/17/2006
E_SIINS1.EXE	4.1.3.0	Stopped working	10/17/2006
E_SIINS1.EXE	4.1.3.0	Stopped working	10/17/2006
E_SIINS1.EXE	4.1.3.0	Stopped working	10/17/2006
Explorer.EXE	6.0.5728.16387	Stopped working	10/17/2006
mmc.exe	6.0.5728.16387	Stopped responding	10/17/2006

FIGURE 25.25 The Reliability Monitor provides you with an overview of the system state.

Notice the little icons displayed on the screen. They look very much like the icons used for errors, warnings, and information in the Event Viewer. The icons serve the same purpose in this situation. By clicking one of the bars that has an icon, you can see detailed information about that event at the bottom of the display as shown in Figure 25.25.

By observing reliability patterns in your system, you can often detect the cause obscure reliability problems. For example, if the pattern shows that a failure occurs every Friday, you at least know when to look at the system for a problem that might not occur at any other time.

Using Data Collector Sets and Viewing Reports

You may have remembered counter logs from previous versions of Windows. A counter log is a special file that lets you record the state of the system over time in a permanent form. Although counter logs were useful, they really didn't lend themselves to flexible reporting. All you got was a static view of the system from sometime in the past. Data Collector Sets are a new feature of Vista that adds some flexibility into the picture and provide a means of creating useful reports.

Before you can view a report of any kind, you must create the required data. Vista comes with a number of useful data collector sets in the `Data Collector Sets\System` folder. Here are the data collectors you can use immediately:

LAN Diagnostics Collects data about the LAN. All of the LAN events, including standard informational, warning, and error messages, appear in the log. The log differentiates between wired and wireless LANs to make it easier to detect wireless problems with your network.

System Diagnostics Collects data about localized system events. This includes both hardware and software events. You'll see startup events, kernel events, performance counters, and a wealth of other information about the system.

System Performance Tracks all of the standard system performance counters and the NT Kernel counters. This is the closest Data Collector Set to the old counter logs.

Wireless Diagnostics Collects data about all wireless activities for the current system. The device need not be part of the LAN. For example, this diagnostic will collect information about your wireless devices such as a mouse or keyboard.

You can see the information that a Data Collection Set contains by clicking on its entry in the list. Figure 25.26 shows the LAN Diagnostics Data Collection Set content.

To save data from a particular Data Collection Set, highlight its entry and click Start on the toolbar (the green right-pointing arrow). When you finish collecting data, click Stop on the toolbar (the black square). Although you can try to create a report at any time, it's best to wait until after you finish collecting the data. Otherwise, the report screen says that it's collecting data, but never shows the report. To see a report, click View latest report on the toolbar (the green book icon). Figure 26.27 shows a LAN Diagnostics report.

The top-level headings describe data areas, such as the Wired Networking Troubleshooting Information heading, which contains all of the data that the system collected during diagnostics. Drill down into a heading and you'll find test headings, such as Software Configuration (shown in Figure 25.27). Within each of these test headings, are individual tests (or informational entries), such as Wired Networking System Files Versions. Drill down further and you'll find the individual data point, such as `CIM_Datafile.Name`, which tells you the names of the individual files. Finally, you get to the specifics of the file. In this case, you see the full path to the `onex.dll` file and its version number.

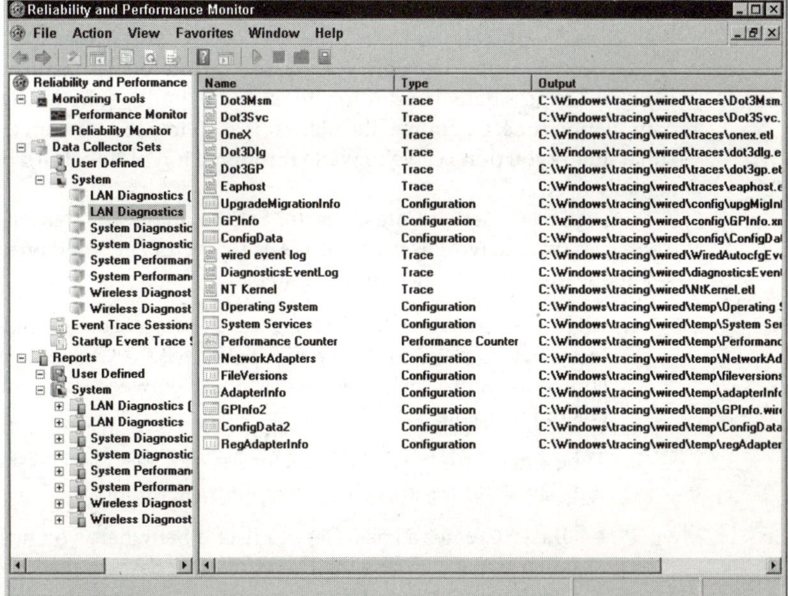

FIGURE 25.26
Data Collection Sets help you obtain and store data about the system in a permanent form.

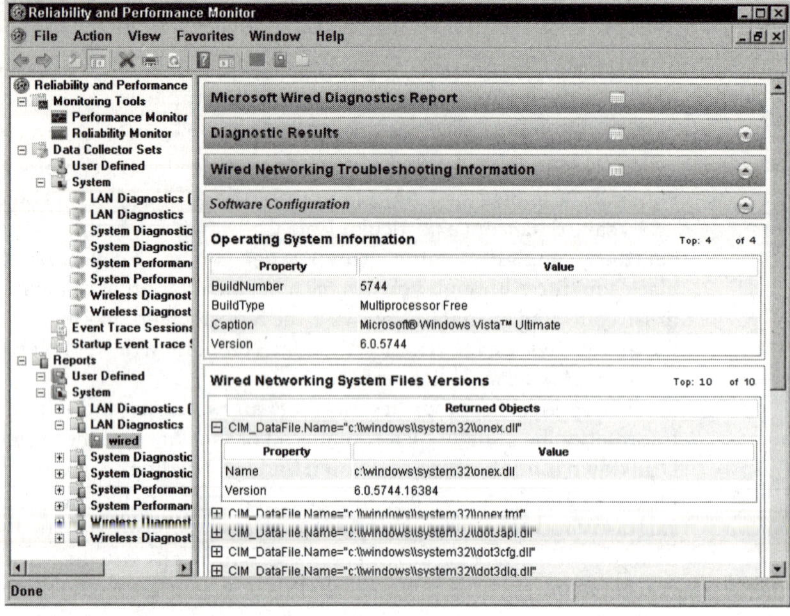

FIGURE 25.27
Reports provide an overview of the data that you can drill down into to locate specifics.

Creating Custom Data Collector Sets

As nice as the predefined Data Collector Sets are, you'll very likely want to create custom sets at some point. By using a custom set, you can create reports faster, since the Data Collector Set will likely collect less data. In addition, the data file will require less hard drive space and less report compilation time. Of course, the biggest reason to use a custom Data Collector Set is to save personal time—you don't have to wade through a ton of unhelpful data to find the one nugget you actually need.

You can base custom Data Collector Sets on an existing template or create your own template. The easiest way to work is to create a Data Collector Set based on an existing template, so that's the technique described in the following steps.

1. Right-click the `Data Collector Sets\User Defined` folder and choose New ➤ Data Collector Set from the context menu. You'll see the Create new Data Collector Set dialog box shown in Figure 25.28 where you choose between using an existing template or creating a custom template.

2. Type a name for the Data Collector Set and click Next. Vista will ask you which template to use. The default setup offers the following options:

   - **Basic**: Creates a basic Data Collector Set where you need to define most of the content such as the counters the Data Collector Set will use. Use this option when you really don't want to spend time removing all of the counters and other features the other templates provide.

   - **System Diagnostics**: Creates a Data Collector Set that matches the System Diagnostics Data Collector Set. You modify the preexisting features to meet your specific needs. This

Data Collector Set focuses on diagnostic and configuration issues with an emphasis on the system hardware.

- **System Performance**: Creates a Data Collector Set that matches the System Performance Data Collector Set. You modify the preexisting features to meet your specific needs. This Data Collector Set focuses on system response times and performance with an emphasis on the system software.

3. Choose one of the templates and click Next. Vista will ask where you want to store the data. Normally you'll want to accept the default location.
4. Optionally type a new location for the data and click Next. Vista will ask whether you're ready to create the new Data Collector Set as shown in Figure 25.29.
5. Click Change if you want to change the account used to run the Data Collector Set. The default setting normally uses the System account, which works fine in most cases. The only time you need to change this setting is if you want to access network resources (in which case, you'll need to Network Service account) or you want to limit the accessibility of the Data Collector Set for security reasons.

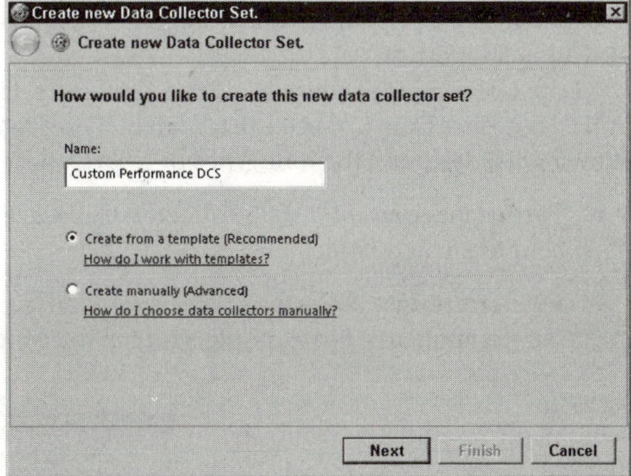

FIGURE 25.28
Create Data Collector Sets based on an existing template whenever possible.

FIGURE 25.29
It's time to create the new Data Collector Set.

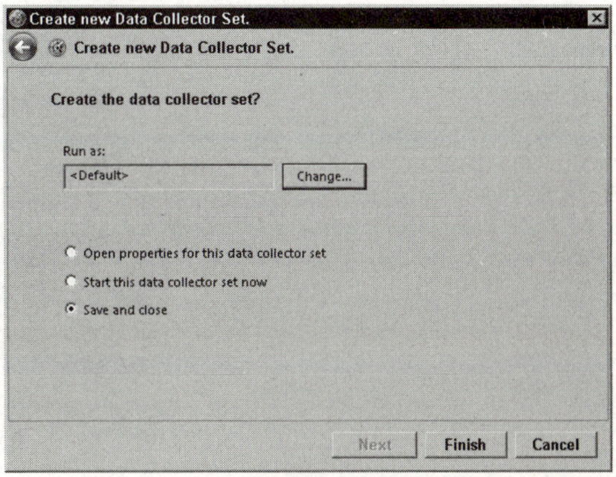

6. Choose one of the postcreation options. You have the following choices:
   - **Open properties for this data collector set**: Opens the Properties dialog box for the Data Collector Set so that you can make modifications to it.
   - **Start this data collector set now**: Immediately starts the Data Collector Set. Because the Data Collector Set mimics an existing Data Collector Set in most cases, the only thing this option accomplishes is creating a second Data Collector Set that collects the same data as one of the existing Data Collector Sets. You could possibly use this option for testing purposes, but that's about it.
   - **Save and close**: Saves the Data Collector Set, but doesn't start it. You'll need to change the Data Collector Set properties later to create your unique configuration.
7. Click Finish. Vista creates the new Data Collector Set and performs the postcreation task you specified (if any).

At this point, you have a new, unconfigured, Data Collector Set. When you open the Properties dialog box for a Data Collector Set, you see the set of tabs shown in figure 25.30. You use these tabs to define the general characteristics of the Data Collector Set, such as which account it uses to run, when it runs, and stop conditions. For example, you can assign a specific runtime to the Data Collector Set. It's also possible to tell Vista to perform a task when the Data Collector Set stops, such as creating a report.

A Data Collection Set consists of Data Collectors. Figure 25.26 shows the Data Collectors for the LAN Diagnostics Data Collector Set. Each of these Data Collectors can perform different tasks. The following list describes the four types of Data Collectors:

- **Performance counter data collector**: Collects information based on the performance counters you define.
- **Event trace data collector**: Collects information based on events that occur with specific system components. For example, you can trace the activity of the audio portion of your system.

FIGURE 25.30
Modify the Data Collector Set properties to match specific data collection requirements.

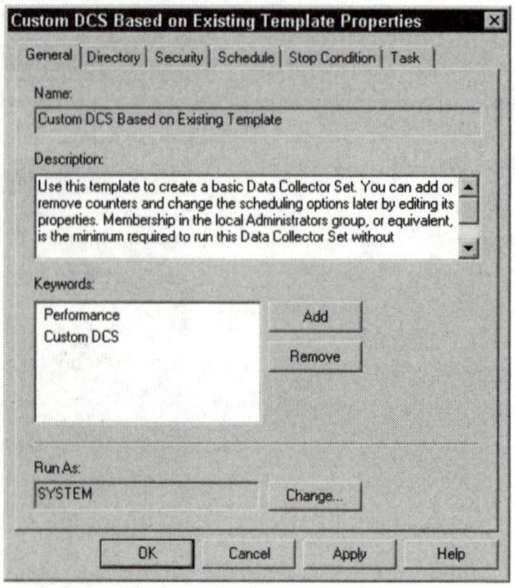

- **Configuration data collector**: Logs any configuration event for the specified system component. For example, you could track application installation or updates.
- **Performance counter alert**: Tracks the specified performance counters and performs an action when the performance counter value matches or exceeds a specific level. For example, you might create an alert when the hard drive's available space falls below a certain level.

NOTE You might remember alerts from previous versions of Windows. The performance counter alert fulfills that purpose in Vista. Because you can combine them with other collectors, the new setup is considerably more powerful than functionality that previous versions of Windows offered. Unlike previous versions of Windows, you can tell a performance counter alert to initiate additional system monitoring through a Data Collector Set.

Now that you have a better idea of how a Data Collectors work with a Data Collector Set, it's time to look at modifying them so you can customize the Data Collector Set you just created. The following sections describe how to modify, add, and delete Data Collectors in your Data Collection Set.

Modifying Data Collectors

When you create a new Data Collector Set, it normally contains one or more Data Collectors. However, these Data Collectors have default settings that probably don't match the data collection goals you have in mind. Consequently, you'll want to modify the existing data collectors to configure them to meet your needs. To modify any existing Data Collector, right-click the Data Collector entry and choose Properties from the context menu. Figure 25.31 shows the Properties dialog boxes for the four Data Collector types.

The figure shows the dialogs you'll use to configure each Data Collector type. When working with a Performance Counter Data Collector, you choose a list of performance counters that you want to modify. The asterisk (*) in the definition tells Vista that you want to monitor everything. The pattern used in this case doesn't follow the order you might think. The object appears first (Processor in this case), followed by the instance in parentheses, followed by the counter for that instance. For example, if you wanted to monitor the print queue jobs for the fax, it would appear as `\Print Queue(Fax)\Jobs`.

In some cases, you need special knowledge to configure a Data Collector. When working with a Configuration Data Collector, you must know the Registry keys you want to monitor. When working with a management path, you must know the WMI object you want to monitor. The Properties dialog box won't help you fill in these entries—you must find the data elsewhere.

Adding and Deleting Data Collectors

At some point, you'll want to add more Data Collectors to your Data Collector Set. Using multiple Data Collectors lets you customize the activities of each one to meet the data collection requirements. For example, when working with a performance counter alert, you might want to react one way when the hard disk space reaches a certain point and in another way when processor performance reaches a peak. You would need two Data Collectors to handle this situation. The following steps describe how to create a new Data Collector.

1. Select the Data Collector Set you want to update. You'll see a list of Data Collectors in the right pane.

FIGURE 25.31
Each Data Collector in a set should accomplish a specific purpose.

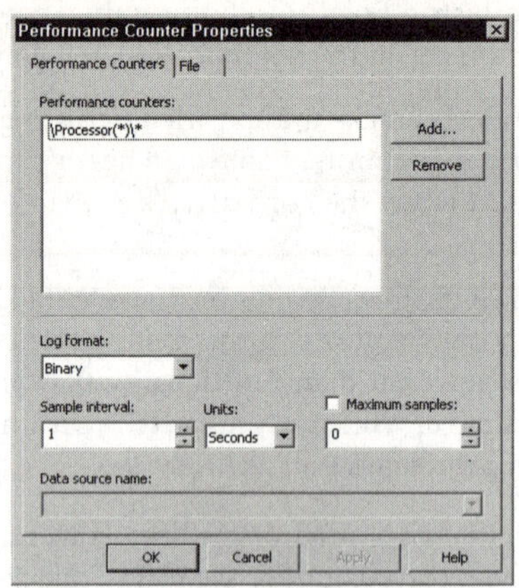

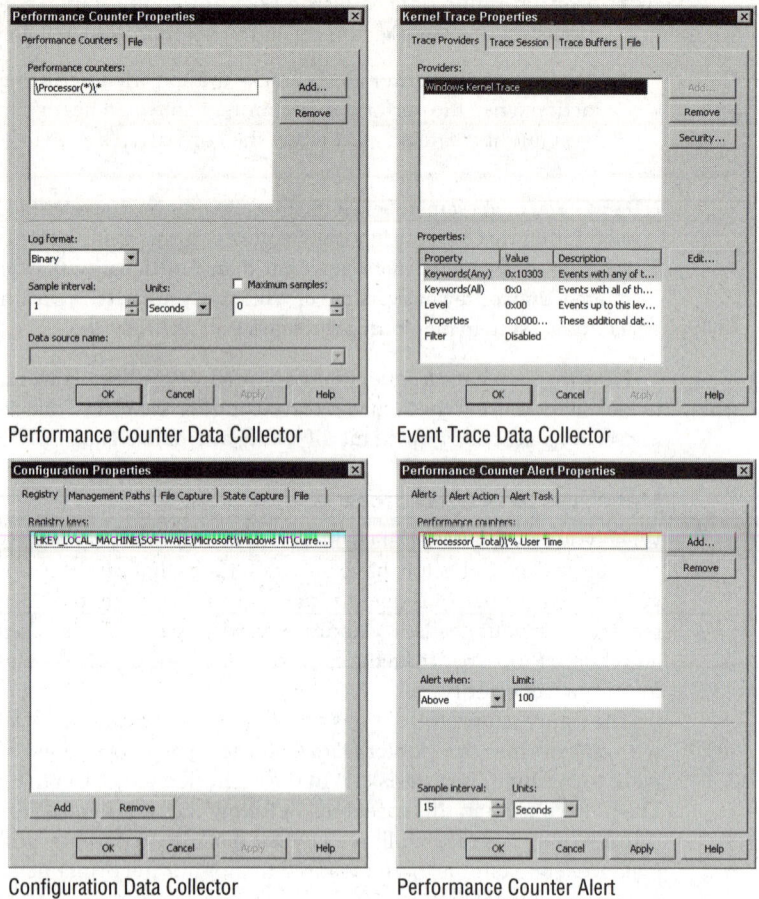

Performance Counter Data Collector

Kernel Trace Properties

Event Trace Data Collector

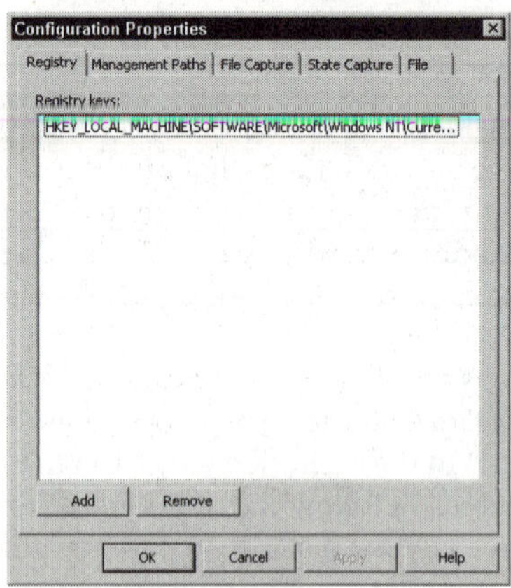

Configuration Data Collector

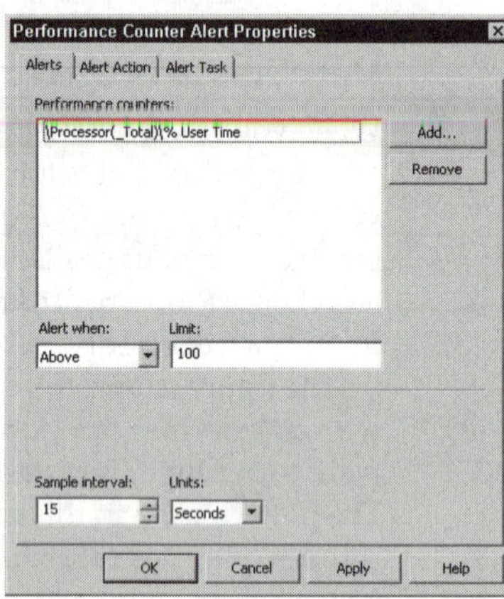

Performance Counter Alert

2. Right-click in any clear area of the right pane and choose New ➤ Data Collector from the context menu. You'll see a list of Data Collector type choices as shown in Figure 25.32.
3. Type a descriptive name for the Data Collector. Select a Data Collector type. Click Next. You'll see a configuration screen for that Data Collector type.
4. Fill out the information required for that Data Collector type. Click Next. Vista asks whether you want to create the Data Collector.
5. Optionally check the Open properties for this data collector option. Click Finish. Vista creates the new Data Collector and optionally opens its Properties dialog box.

Removing a Data Collector you no longer need is easy. Simply select the Data Collector and click Delete on the toolbar (the red *X*).

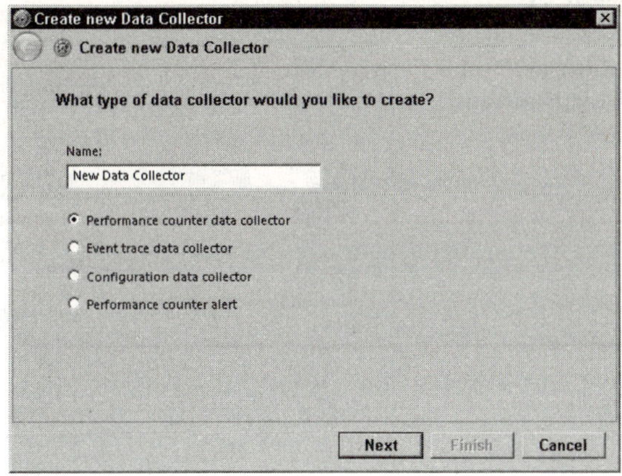

FIGURE 25.32
Select the type of Data Collector you want to create from the list.

Running System Information

When everything on your system works, new devices install painlessly, and services work right the first time, life is good. If only it were always so. Alas, the general headaches of new hardware installation follow—cracking the box open, finding an available I/O slot, dealing with the mysterious force that makes your system's box much easier to rip open than it is to put back together. Then, after you restart the system, there may be I/O resource conflicts or services may fail for whatever reason. The fun never ends.

Fortunately, Vista provides some tools to ease system troubleshooting. Chief among them is System Information, which you can use to display system information ranging from detailed display driver data to the services that are installed and the other services or devices on which they depend. To open System Information, click Start ➢ All Programs ➢ Accessories ➢ System Tools ➢ System Information.

The pane on the right displays the version and build of Vista you're running, your CPU type, a serial number, and registration information, as well as information ranging from the manufacturer on your system and its model number to the amount of memory free or the amount of paging file in use. Figure 25.33 shows information about my system.

To view information on the hardware installed in your computer, expand Hardware Resources. For information about display hardware and drivers, expand Components, and then select Display. You'll see something similar to Figure 25.34.

For information about the drives on your system, expand Storage under Components, and then select Drives. The Drives screen gives detailed information about local floppy, hard, and CD-ROM drives. Although there isn't really any diagnostic information available here per se, the Drives screen can indicate trouble with a drive simply by showing you that Vista can't see the drive. For example, say you have a second hard drive that is *not* displayed on this list. The drive's absence may indicate either a faulty data or power cable connection to the unit. If the drive is a SCSI device, the SCSI chain may be incorrectly terminated. If it's a second EIDE hard drive, there may be an incorrect master-slave configuration on the second drive. Before looking at more complicated problems, always check your physical connections. Often, the solution is simpler than you think.

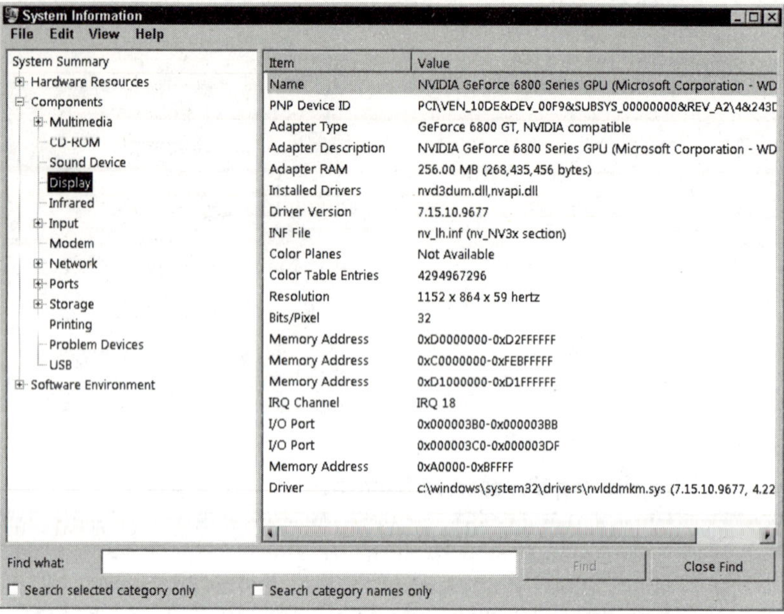

FIGURE 25.33 The System Summary screen displays local configuration details.

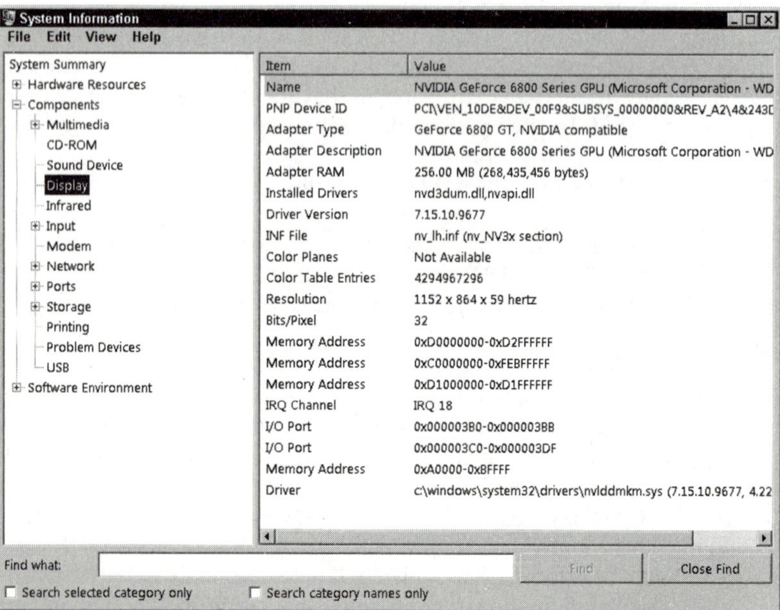

FIGURE 25.34 Obtain information about the display and other system elements in the Components folder.

TIP You can't get information about floppy, removable disk, or CD-ROM drives unless a disk is in the drive. With a disk present, you'll get information about that specific disk.

For information about services, expand Software Environment, and click Services. The information looks very similar to the output of the Services console in the Administrative Tools folder. The difference is that you can't modify the state of any of the entries. Consequently, this makes System Information the perfect tool for working with users. You can ask them questions about the system without any fear that they'll accidentally modify the state of any of the services.

For information about system resources, expand Hardware Resources and select one of the subfolders. Figure 25.35 shows the IRQs in use on my system, which I displayed by selecting the IRQs folder.

NOTE Vista supports interrupt sharing by hardware devices to try to alleviate IRQ conflict problems. But older hardware devices that aren't aware of this feature frequently expect to be the sole possessors of a given IRQ and won't do very well sharing it with another device. The best plan of action is for each hardware device to have its own dedicated IRQs.

Since Vista is a Plug and Play operating system, the values contained in the System Information screen should be correct. But sometimes, a device won't be displayed here because its resources are in conflict with another device. In this case, the two devices in question should be displayed when you click Conflicts/Sharing. It's a good idea to check here before you install a new device so that you can figure out which resources are allocated and which are available. Be sure to check all three resource types: IRQs, DMA, and I/O.

FIGURE 25.35
The IRQs in use on my system.

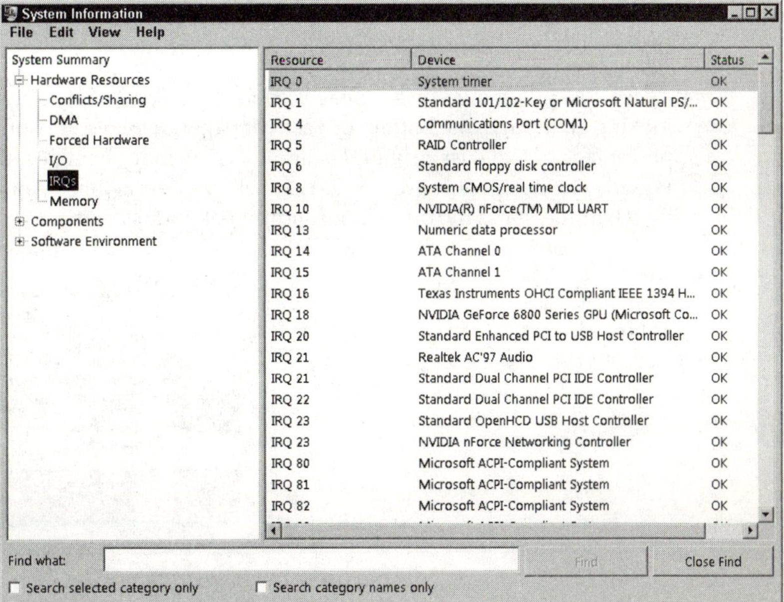

For system environment information, expand Software Environment, and click Environment Variables. The Environment Variables folder is another view-only portion of the System Information screen; it displays system information about CPUs and system paths. You can't edit this information, but it may be valuable to a technical support engineer trying to troubleshoot your system. Windows applications, in addition to using the system's paging file, will often write temporary files for storing less frequently used data rather than using system memory. It's a method of "cheating" on the amount of memory the application allocates or using allocated memory for more immediate or more frequently used tasks.

To create and print a report from any of the System Information screen items, select the item and choose File ➤ Print. Because so much information is generated, you might want to save the information in a file rather than printing it. To save the file, choose File ➤ Save to open the Save As dialog box.

Using Task Manager

Task Manager (see Figure 25.36) is a tool that lets you quickly monitor and troubleshoot Vista, particularly in terms of the programs you're running.

NOTE If multiple users are logged on to your computer, you'll also see a Users tab in Task Manager.

To run Task Manager, do one of the following:

- Right-click your Taskbar, and choose Task Manager from the context menu.
- Choose Start ➤ Run, type **`taskmgr`** in the Open box, and click OK.

TIP If your system is causing some difficulty that makes the above methods unavailable, press Ctrl+Alt+Del to open Task Manager. Go ahead—try it.

Figure 25.36 shows Task Manager open at the Performance tab. Regardless of which tab you're looking at, though, the bottom of Task Manager displays the number of processes being run, the percentage of CPU usage, and the amount of memory being used, including any virtual memory you may be using. This quick reference tells you everything you need to know in order to immediately understand the operating condition of your system.

FIGURE 25.36
Use Task Manager to easily monitor programs you're running.

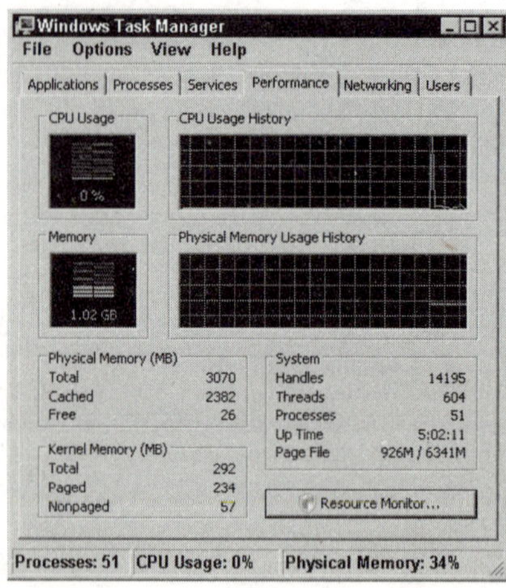

Task Manager Applications

Task Manager's Applications tab lists all running applications and their current status (see Figure 25.37). An application's status will be either Running, if the program is behaving properly, or Not Responding, if the program is having problems.

To close a running application, select it, and click End Task. To switch to a running application, select it, and click Switch To. To start a new application, follow these steps:

1. Click the New Task button to open the Create New Task dialog box.
2. Type the name of the application in the Open box, and click OK.

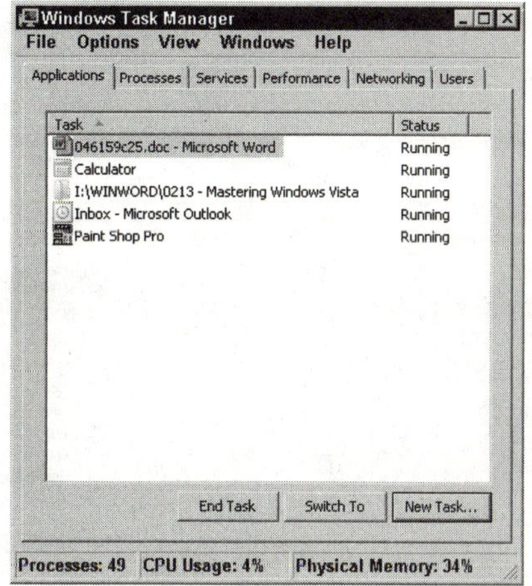

FIGURE 25.37 The Applications tab of Task Manager.

Task Manager Processes

You can use the list on the Processes tab (see Figure 25.38) to monitor and halt any processes that are running on your computer. Processes are measured in all the separate executables that Vista runs concurrently. This includes any applications you're running and all the background executables that Vista runs automatically, including services. To terminate a running process, select it, and click the End Process button.

WARNING Don't end a process unless it's marked as being errant. Ending a process that is running may crash other programs that are running correctly if they depend on that process.

Task Manager Services

In previous versions of Windows, there wasn't any way to monitor the services running on your system for the most part. Services run under a special application called `svchost.exe` in most cases. Consequently, you'd see multiple copies of `svchost.exe` running on your system, but you wouldn't actually know what the service host application was hosting unless you used a command-line utility such as TaskList. Vista fixes this problem by including the new Services tab shown in Figure 25.39.

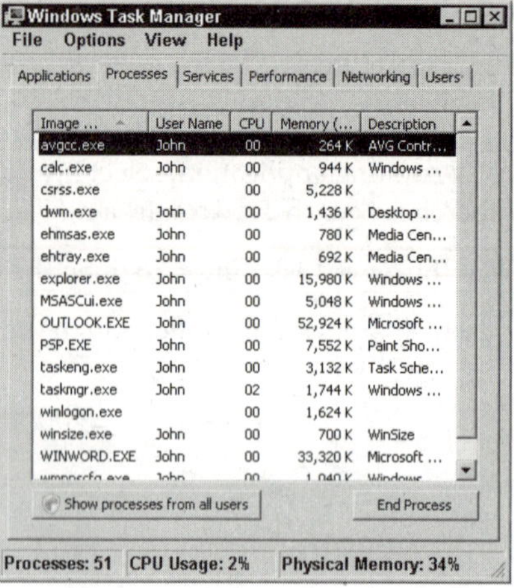

FIGURE 25.38
Task Manager lets you monitor running processes.

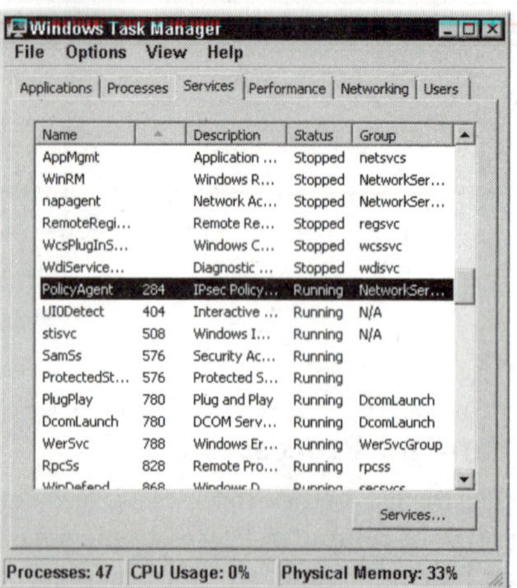

FIGURE 25.39
See which services are running on your system using the new Services tab.

You can't stop the services using this display. To stop a service, you still need to use the Services console found in the Administrative Tools folder of the Control Panel. However, you can see which services are related by clicking the PID (Process Identifier) column. The `svchost.exe` application that is hosting the service will have the same PID, so you can tell how all of these entries are related now.

Task Manager Performance

You use the Performance tab to monitor your computer's usage of memory, processor time, and other resources. The two central graphs on the page measure the amount of memory used and the amount of processor time used. For multiple processors, you can choose to show one graph for each CPU or one graph for combined CPUs. The Performance tab also contains information on how much physical memory is being used and how much memory the Vista kernel is using.

TIP When you run Task Manager, a small green square appears on your Taskbar next to your clock. This is a CPU usage meter. Point to the usage meter to display the percentage of CPU usage at the current moment.

Task Manager Networking

You use the Networking tab (shown in Figure 25.40) to monitor Internet and local area network usage. At the bottom of this tab is information about the link speed and the number of bytes transferred for each adapter.

TIP By default, Task Manager is always on top when you have multiple windows open on the Desktop. If you don't prefer this arrangement, choose Options ➤ Always on Top to clear the check mark. You can also use Task Manager to put your computer in hibernation, turn it off, restart it, log off, or switch users. Choose the appropriate item from the Shut Down menu.

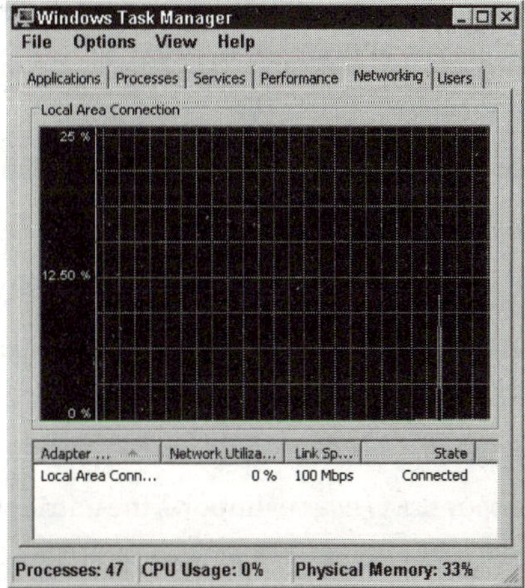

FIGURE 25.40
The Networking tab in Task Manager.

Using BCDEdit

You won't need to do it very often, but you'll eventually need to modify the boot configuration of your system. The boot configuration is the screen that shows up when you boot your computer. When you press F8 and see the diagnostics that Vista provides, you're looking at part of the boot screen. Previous versions of Windows used the BootCfg utility to change the boot configuration. However, Vista needs something a bit more robust because it does significantly more than earlier versions of Windows at boot time. Consequently, to manage the Vista boot configuration, you use the Boot Configuration Data Store Editor (BCDEdit) utility.

The BCDEdit utility isn't for the faint of heart. You can actually cause Vista to stop booting if you make the wrong changes. Consequently, you'll want to spend some time displaying information with BCDEdit before you make any system changes using it. Understanding how BCDEdit works with data is essential to using it properly. To display data using BCDEdit, type **`BCDEdit /enum`** at the command prompt and press Enter. If you want to display information about a specific entry, such as the boot manager, type the name of that entry after the command-line switch. For example, type **`BCDEdit /enum BootMgr`** and press Enter. You'll see a display similar to the one shown in Figure 25.41.

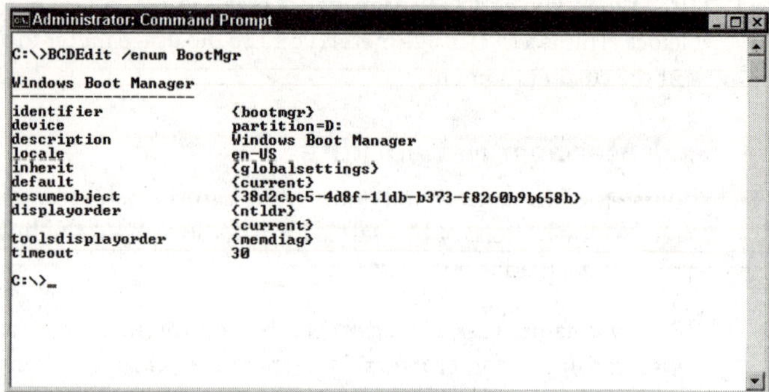
Administrator: Command Prompt
C:\>BCDEdit /enum BootMgr
Windows Boot Manager
identifier {bootmgr}
device partition=D:
description Windows Boot Manager
locale en-US
inherit {globalsettings}
default {current}
resumeobject {38d2cbc5-4d8f-11db-b373-f8260b9b658b}
displayorder {ntldr}
{current}
toolsdisplayorder {memdiag}
timeout 30
C:\>_

FIGURE 25.41
Display specific boot entries for your system by adding the element name to the /enum switch.

Many of the BCDEdit command-line switches that you'll use most often have nothing to do with changing the boot order of your system. You'll use command-line switches to turn on debugging or perform other tasks. With that in mind, here are some common diagnostic BCDEdit command-line switches you should know about.

- `/bootdebug [ID] {On | Off}`: Turns boot debugging on or off.
- `/bootems [ID] {On | Off}`: Turns Emergency Management Services (EMS) on or off.
- `/debug [ID] {On | Off}`: Turns kernel mode debugging on or off.
- `/default` *`ID`*: Specifies the entry to use as the default boot manager.
- `/ems [ID] {On | Off}`: Turns Emergency Management Services (EMS) for the specified boot entry on or off.
- `/export` *`Filename`*: Exports the system's data store to an external file.
- `/import` *`Filename`*: Imports the entries found in an external file into the system data store.
- `/timeout` *`Timeout`*: Changes the time that the boot manager waits for the user to make a selection before booting the default entry.

These are the most interesting command-line switches for common use. To see a complete list of command-line switches, type **`BCDEdit /?`** and press Enter at the command line. You can also find a complete listing of BCDEdit command-line switches at `http://msdn2.microsoft.com/en-gb/library/aa468636.aspx`.

Summary

Vista's suite of administrative tools covers the gamut of system functions, ranging from providing networking settings to detailed information about the operating system's main "plumbing."

Most of the tools are intended to help troubleshoot system problems; using them in concert, you can gather sufficient information to remedy most system hiccups and even avert larger ones by catching them early. Although no set of tools is a panacea for all problems, those in Vista will do a good job of helping you keep your system up and running.

In the next chapter, we'll cover a topic that, although relatively new in Microsoft networking terms (it's been around only since 2000), is critical to understanding the Microsoft domain structure: Active Directory.

Chapter 26

Active Directory Essentials

If you're using Vista in a corporate environment, chances are good that your Vista box is networked and that the network is based on servers running either Windows NT 4, Windows 2000 Server, Windows .NET Server, or Windows Server 2003. Even if you have a home network, you might want to install a server for security purposes or to manage your home business files (tax write-offs are a beautiful thing).

If that's true and if you're networked with Windows NT 4, you have what is (not surprisingly) called an "NT 4 domain." (For details about an NT 4 domain, see my book *Mastering NT Server 4*, Seventh Edition, published by Sybex.) But if your networks are based on Windows 2000 Server or newer, you probably have what is called an "Active Directory" domain. Although I can't make you an Active Directory (AD) expert in one day, I'll introduce you to the basics of AD here.

Not that long ago, networks were small (remember when the only "networks" you cared about were CBS, NBC, and ABC?), and so were their problems. But nowadays it's not unusual to see worldwide networks connecting hundreds of thousands of PCs and users. Managing that kind of complexity brings up big problems—oops, we're supposed to call them challenges; I always forget. One of the answers to the obvious question "Why bother with Windows 2000 Server, .NET Server, or Server 2003, anyway?" is that they were designed with some of those challenges in mind. That's important because NT 4 *didn't* address many of those problems.

You'll notice that, for most of this chapter, I'll be talking about Windows 2000 Server. And, yes, I realize that this book is about Vista and that there are newer Windows Server products out there. I'll stick with Windows 2000 simply because it was the first Microsoft operating system to use Active Directory. Although some new features have been added over the years, the basic concepts remain the same.

If you're using Vista on a stand-alone computer or a small peer-to-peer network that connects Vista, Windows 2000, NT, and Windows 9*x* machines, you don't need to know anything about Active Directory. But if you're part of a large client-server network, and your Vista workstation is connected to a server version that incorporates Active Directory, you do need to understand Active Directory, and the information in this chapter is important to you. After I explain what the hoopla is all about, I'll give you step-by-step instructions for connecting to an AD domain.

NOTE Throughout this chapter, I will refer to "Windows Server" quite a bit. When I use that designation, I am referring to all Windows-based server products that support AD: Windows 2000 Server, Windows .NET Server, and Windows Server 2003.

- Keeping track of who can use the network
- Finding stuff on the network
- Creating new types of subadministrators

- Subdividing control over a domain
- Dealing with connectivity and replication issues
- Building big networks

Security: Keeping Track of Who's Allowed to Use the Network and Who Isn't

A network's first job is

- To provide central places to store simple things such as files or more complex things such as databases, shared printing, or fax services
- To make it possible for people to communicate by means of e-mail, videoconferencing, or whatever technology comes up in the future
- More recently, to make it easier for people to buy things

Fast on the heels of that first job, however, is the second job of every network: to provide security. Once, most computer networks were unsecured or lightly secured, but human nature has forced a change, and there's no going back. Just as businesses have locks on their doors, file cabinets, and cash registers to protect their physical assets, so also do most modern firms protect their information assets. And no matter which vendor's network software you're using, computer security typically boils down to two parts: authentication and authorization. To see why, consider the following example.

Acme Industries sells pest control devices. They've got a sales manager named Wilma Wolf; Wilma wants to see how the sales of a new product, Instant Hole, is doing. Acme's got it set up so that Wilma can review sales information through her web browser—she just surfs over to a particular location on one of the company's internal web servers, and the report appears on her screen.

Of course, Acme management wouldn't be happy about just *anybody* getting to these sales report pages, so the pages are secured. Between the time that Wilma asked for the pages and the time that she got them, two things happened:

Authentication The web server containing the sales reports asked her workstation, "Who's asking for this data?" The workstation replied, "Wilma." The server then said, "Prove it." So the workstation popped up a dialog box on Wilma's screen asking for her username and password. She typed in her name and password, and assuming that she typed them in correctly, the server then checked that name and password against a list of known users and passwords and found that she is indeed Wilma.

Authorization The mere fact that she's proven that she's Wilma may not be sufficient reason for the web server to give her access to the sales pages. The web server then looked at another list sometimes known as the access control list, a list of people and access levels—"Joe can look at this page but can't change it," "Sue can look at this page and can change it," "Larry can't look at this page at all." Presuming Wilma was on the "can look" list, the server sent the requested pages to her browser.

Now, the foregoing example may not seem to contain any deep insights—after all, everyone's logged into a system, tried to access something, and either been successful or rejected—but understanding how Windows 2000/.NET/2003 Server and in particular AD work together requires examining these everyday things a bit. Here's a closer look at some of the administrative mechanics of logins.

Maintaining a "Directory" of Users and Other Network Objects

Every secure system has a file or files that make up a database of known user accounts. NT 4 used only a single file named SAM, short for the less-than-illuminating Security Accounts Manager. It contained a user's username (the logon name), the user's full name, password, allowed logon hours, account expiration date, description, primary group name, and profile information. Of course, the file was encrypted; copy a SAM from an existing NT 4 system and pull it up in Notepad, and you'll see only garbage.

Server versions using AD store most of their user information in a file called `ntds.dit` (think of it as standing for NT directory services directory information table), but `ntds.dit` is different from SAM in a couple of ways:

- First, `ntds.dit` is a modified Access database, and Windows 2000 Server, Windows .NET Server, and Windows Server 2003 actually contain a variant of Access's database engine in their machinery. (Microsoft used to call the Access database engine JET, which stood for Joint Engine Technology—no, the meaning isn't obvious to me either, I think they just liked the acronym—but now it's called ESE, pronounced "easy," which stands for the equally useful name Extensible Storage Engine.)
- Second, as you'll see demonstrated over and over again, `ntds.dit` stores a much wider variety of information about users than SAM ever did.

The information in `ntds.dit` and the program that manages `ntds.dit` are together called the *directory service* (DS). (As a matter of fact, most folks will never say "`ntds.dit`"; they'll say "directory service.") Which leads to a question: What exactly is a "directory"?

It would seem (to me, anyway) that what we've got here is a database of users and user information. So why not call it a database? No compelling reasons, mostly convention, but there *is* one interesting insight. According to some, databases of users tend to get *read* far more often than they get *written*. That allows a certain amount of database engine tweaking for higher performance. This subset of the class of databases gets a name—*directories*. I guess it makes sense, since we're used to using lists of people called office directories or phone directories. I just wish the folks in power had come up with some other name; ask most PC users what a directory is, and they start thinking of hard disk structures: `C:\Windows`—isn't that a directory?

Centralizing the Directory and Directories: A "Logon Server"

"Please, can't we set things up so I need to remember only *one* password?"

Consider for a moment when Windows 2000 Server, Windows .NET Server, or Windows Server 2003 will use that user information located in AD. When you try to access a file share or print share, AD will validate you. But there's more at work here. When fully implemented, AD can save you a fair amount of administrative work in other network functions as well.

For example, suppose your network requires SQL database services. You'll then run a database product such as SQL Server or Oracle on the network. But adding another server-based program to your network can introduce more administrative headaches because, like the file and print servers, a database server needs authentication and authorization support. That's because you usually don't want to just plunk some valuable database on the network and then let the world in general at it—you want to control who gets access.

So the database program needs a method for authentication and authorization. And *here's* where it gets ugly: in the past, many database programs required their administrators to keep and maintain a list of users and passwords. The database programs required you to duplicate all that work of typing in names and passwords, to redo the work you'd already done to get your Novell, Banyan, NT, or whatever type LAN up and running. Yuk. But it gets worse. Consider what you'd have to do if you ran both NT as a network operating system *and* Novell NetWare as a network operating system: yup, you're typing in names and passwords yet again. Now add Lotus Notes for your e-mail and groupware stuff, another list of users, and hey, how about a mainframe or an AS/400? More accounts.

Let's see—with a network incorporating NT, Oracle, NetWare, and Notes, you've got each user owning *four* user accounts. Which means each user has *four* passwords to remember. And, every few months, four passwords to remember to change.

This seems dumb; why can't you just type those names and passwords once into your Windows Server and then tell Oracle, NetWare, and Notes to just ask the local Windows Server machine to check that you are indeed who you say you are rather than making Oracle, NetWare, and Notes duplicate all that security stuff? Put another way, you have a centralized computer that acts as a database server, another that acts as a centralized e-mail server, another as a print server—why not have a centralized "logon" server, a centralized "authentication" server? Then your users would have to remember (and change) only one password and account name rather than four.

Centralized logons would be a great benefit, but there's a problem with it: how would Notes actually *ask* the Windows Server to authenticate? What programming commands would an Oracle database server use to ask a Microsoft "logon server" (the actual term is *domain controller*, as you'll learn later) if a particular user should be able to access a particular piece of data?

Well, if that domain controller were running NT 4, the programming interface wouldn't have been a particularly well-documented one. And third parties such as Oracle, Lotus, and Novell would have been reluctant to write programs depending on that barely documented security interface because they'd be justifiably concerned that when the *next* version of NT appeared (Windows 2000 Server, and then Windows .NET Server, followed closely by Windows Server 2003), Microsoft would have changed the programming interface, leaving Lotus, Novell, and Oracle scrambling to learn and implement this new interface. And some of the more cynical among us would even suggest that Lotus and Oracle might fear that Microsoft's Exchange and SQL Server would be able to come out in Windows Server–friendly versions nearly immediately after a new Windows Server's release.

Instead, Microsoft opted to put an industry standard interface on its AD, an interface called the Lightweight Directory Access Protocol (LDAP). Now, LDAP may initially sound like just another geeky acronym, but it's more than that—what Microsoft's done by putting an LDAP interface on Active Directory is to open a doorway for outside developers. And here's how important it is: yes, LDAP will make Oracle's or Lotus's job easier should they decide to integrate their products' security with Windows Server's built-in security. But LDAP also means that it's (theoretically, at least) possible to build tools that create Active Directory structures—domains, trees, forests, organizational units, user accounts, all of the components. It means that if Windows Server gets popular but Microsoft's Active Directory control programs turn out to be hard to work with, some clever third party can just swoop in and offer a complete replacement, built atop LDAP commands.

NOTE If you really want to learn more about LDAP, check out the specification at `http://www.ipa.go.jp/security/rfc/RFC3377EN.html`. An overview of LDAP appears at `http://www.zytrax.com/books/ldap/ch2/`.

Which, after you spend a bit of time with the Microsoft Management Console (MMC), may not seem like a bad idea—but I'll leave you to make your own judgment about that.

Searching: Finding Things on the Network

Thus far, I've been talking about the directory service as if it contains only user accounts. But that's not true—the DS not only includes directory entries for people, it also contains directory entries describing servers and workstations. And that turns out to be essential, for a few reasons.

Finding Servers: "Client-Server Rendezvous"

Client-server computing is how work gets done nowadays. You check your e-mail with Outlook (the client), which gets that mail from the Exchange machine down the hall (the server). You're at your PC (the client) accessing files on a file server (the server). You buy a shirt at L.L. Bean's web server (the server) from your PC using Internet Explorer (the client).

In those three cases, the copy of Outlook on your desktop had to somehow know where to find your local Exchange server; you couldn't get files from your file server until you knew which file server to look in, and you couldn't order that shirt until you'd found the address of the L.L. Bean web server, `www.llbean.com`.

In every case, client-server doesn't work unless you can help the client find the server, hence the phrase "client-server rendezvous." In the Outlook case, your mail client knows where your mail server is probably because someone (perhaps you) in your networking group set it up, feeding the name of the Exchange server into some setup screen in Outlook. You may have found the correct file server for the desired files by poking around in Network Neighborhood in Windows 9*x* or in Network if your workstation is running Vista, or perhaps someone told you where to find the files. You might have guessed L.L. Bean's address, seen it in a magazine ad, or used a search engine such as Yahoo! or Google.

Those are three examples of client-server rendezvous; many more happen in the process of daily network use. When your workstation seeks to log you in, the workstation must find a domain controller, or to put it differently, your "logon client" seeks a "logon server." Want to print something in color and wonder which networked color printers are nearby? More client-server rendezvous.

In every case, AD can simplify the process. Your workstation will be able to ask AD for the names of nearby domain controllers. You can search the AD for keywords relevant to particular file shares and printers.

Name Resolution and DNS

But merely getting the name of a particular mail, web, print, or file server (or domain controller) isn't the whole story. From the network software's point of view, `www.llbean.com` isn't much help. To get you connected to the Bean web server, the network software needs to know the *IP address* of that server, a four-number combination looking something like 208.7.129.82. That's the second part of client-server rendezvous.

In the case of a public website such as Bean's, your computer can look up a web server by querying a huge network of publicly available Internet servers called the Domain Name System, or DNS. The public DNS contains the names of many machines you'll need to access, but chances are good that your company's internal network doesn't advertise many of its machines' names on the Internet; rather, your internal network probably runs a set of private DNS servers.

After its inception in 1984, DNS didn't change much. But RFC 2052 (introduced in October 1996, see RFC 2052 at `http://www.faqs.org/rfcs/rfc2052.html`) and RFC 2136 (introduced in April 1997, see RFC 2136 at `http://www.faqs.org/rfcs/rfc2136.html`) transformed DNS into a naming system that's good not only for the worldwide Internet but also for internal intranets. Many of the pieces of DNS software out in the corporate world don't yet support 2052 and 2136, so it's a great convenience that all Windows Server DNS server versions support those features.

NOTE RFC stands for Request for Comments, which is a document or a set of documents in which proposed Internet standards are described or defined.

Creating New Types of Subadministrators

The next network challenge becomes apparent after a network has grown a bit. When a network is small or new, a small group of people does everything, from running the cables and installing the LAN adapter boards to creating the user accounts and backing up the system. As time goes on and the network gets larger and more important to the organization, two things happen:

- First, the organization hires more people—*has* to hire more people, because there are more servers to tend and user accounts to look after—to handle all the different parts of keeping a network running.
- Second, networks get political: all of a sudden, some of the higher-ups get clued to the fact that *what those network geeks do affects our ability to retain our power in this organization.*

Both of those things mean that your firm will soon start hiring more network helpers. In some organizations, these newly created positions get to do much of the scut work of network administration, stuff that is (a) pretty simple to train people to do and (b) of no interest to the old-timer network types. Examples of the I-don't-want-it-you-can-have-it jobs in a network include

Resetting passwords For security's sake, network administrators usually require users to change their passwords every couple months or so. Administrators also inveigh against the evils of writing those passwords down, so it's common for users to forget what they set their most recent passwords to. Resetting passwords to some innocuous value is something that really needs to be done quickly—the natives get restless when it takes a week to get them back on the network—and it's a relatively simple task, so it's perfect for the newly hired, minimum-wage network assistant.

Tending the backups For tediousness, nothing matches the sheer irritation of backups. Most people who manage large networks are forced to use tape drives for backups, and, well, some days it seems like tape drives were invented by someone who was abused by network administrators as a small child. They're balky and prone to taking vacations at random times, and you never can predict exactly how much data you can get on 'em—eight gigs one day, three the next, and as a result, *someone's* got to be around ready to feed in another blank tape. And somebody's got to label them and keep track of them; ask most network admin types what job they'd most like to give someone else to worry about, and backups are likely to be at the top of their wish list.

Hiring a few low-wage backup watchers and password fixers also gives a firm a sort of a "farm team," a place to try out folks to see if they're capable of learning to eventually become network analysts with more responsibilities (and, they hope, more salary).

But regular users can't do things such as resetting passwords and running backups—you need at least some administrative powers to do those things. Recall that we'd like to hire this "network scut work" person or persons at a pretty low hourly rate, and that's troublesome from a security point of view. If they can leave this job and go off to one with the same pay level whose main challenge is in remembering to say, "Would you like fries with that, sir?" it might not be the brightest idea to give them full administrative control over the network. Is there a way to create a sort of partial administrator?

NT 4 gave us *some* of that, since there was a prebuilt group called Backup Operators, but there wasn't a Reset Password Operators group, and besides, all NT 4 offered was a small set of prebuilt groups of types of administrators—the groups were called Server Operators, Account Operators, and Backup Operators—with different levels. There wasn't a way to create a new type of group with a tailor-made set of powers. Windows 2000 Server, Windows .NET Server, and Windows Server 2003 change that, offering a sometimes bewildering array of security options.

Delegation: Subdividing Control over a Domain

In the last section, I offered two examples of things that might motivate changing how the network works—a growing set of network duties that require some division of labor (which I covered in that section) and growing attention from upper management as it becomes increasingly aware of the importance of the network in the organization. That second force in network evolution is perhaps better known as "politics." Despite the fact that it's something of a bad word, we can't ignore politics—so how does Windows Server address an organization's political needs?

To see how, consider the following scenario. Some fictitious part of the U.S. Navy is spread across naval facilities around the world, but perhaps (to keep the example simple) its biggest offices are in Washington, DC; San Diego, CA; and Norfolk, VA. There are servers in DC, San Diego, and Norfolk, all tended by different groups. For all the usual reasons, the officers in charge of the Norfolk facility don't want administrators from DC or San Diego messing with the Norfolk servers; the DC folks and the San Diego folks have similar feelings, with the result that the Navy technology brass wants to be able to say, "Here's a group of servers we'll call Norfolk and a group of users we'll call Norfolk Admins. We want to be able to say that only the users in Norfolk Admins can control the servers in Norfolk." They want to do similar things for San Diego and DC. How to do this?

Well, under NT 4, they could do it only by creating three separate security entities called *domains*. Creating three different domains would solve the problem because separate domains are like separate *universes*—they're not aware of each other at all. With a DC domain, a Norfolk domain, and a San Diego domain, they could separate their admins into three groups that couldn't meddle with one another. It's a perfectly acceptable answer and indeed many organizations around the world use NT 4 in that manner—but it's a solution with a few problems.

For one thing, enterprises usually want *some* level of communication between domains, and to accomplish that, the enterprises must put in place connections between domains called *trust relationships*. Unfortunately, trust relationships are a quirky and unreliable necessity of any multidomain enterprise using NT 4. With Windows Server, in contrast, the Navy need only create *one* domain and then divide it using a new-to-NT notion called *organizational units*, usually abbreviated *OUs*.

More specifically, the Navy would solve their problem in this way:

- They'd create one domain named (for example) NAVY.
- Inside NAVY, they'd create an organizational unit named Norfolk, another called DC, and a third named San Diego. They would set up their servers and then place each server into the proper OU.
- Also inside NAVY, they'd create a user group named Norfolk Admins and two others named San Diego Admins and DC Admins. They'd create accounts for their users and place any administrators into their proper group, depending on whether they were based in DC, San Diego, or Norfolk.

At this point, understand that the San Diego Admins (kinda sounds like a baseball team, doesn't it?) don't yet have any power: there's no magic in Windows Server that says, "Well, there's an OU named San Diego and a group named San Diego Admins, I guess that must mean I should let these Admin guys have total control over the servers in the San Diego OU." You have to create that link by *delegating control* of the San Diego OU to the user group San Diego Admins. (Windows Server has a wizard that assists in doing this.) OUs are an excellent tool for building large and useful domains.

Satisfying Political Needs

"That's *my* data, so I want it on *my* servers!" As information has become the most important asset of many firms—for example, I once heard someone comment that the majority of Microsoft's assets resided in the crania of their employees—some firms have been reluctant to yield control of that information to a central IT group. Nor is that an irrational perspective: if you were the person in charge of maintaining a five-million-person mailing list, and if that list generated one half of your firm's sales leads, you might well want to see that data housed on a machine or machines run by people who report directly to you.

Of course, on the other side of the story there is the IT director who wants Total Control of all servers in the building, and her reasoning is just as valid. You see, if a badly run server goes down and that failure affects the rest of the network, it's *her* head on the chopping block.

So on the one hand, the department head or VP wants to control the iron and silicon that happen to be where his data lives, and on the other hand, the IT director who's concerned with making sure that all data is safe and that everything on the network plays well with others wants to control said data and network pieces. Who wins? It depends—and that's the "politics" part.

What do Windows Servers do to ameliorate the political problems? Well, not as much as would be nice—there's no "make the vice presidents get along well" wizard—but Windows Server's variety of options for domain design gives the network designers the flexibility to build whatever kind of network structure they want.

Got a relatively small organization that would fit nicely into a single domain but one VP with server ownership lust? No problem, give the VP an OU of their own within the domain. Got a firm with two moderately large offices separated by a few hundred miles? Under NT 4, two domains and a trust relationship would be the answer, and you could choose to do that under Windows Server, but that's not the only answer. Since Windows Server is extremely parsimonious with WAN bandwidth in comparison with NT 4, you might find that a single domain makes sense because it's easier to administer than two domains but not impossible from a network bandwidth point of view. And bandwidth utilization is our next topic.

Connectivity and Replication Issues

More and more companies don't live in only one place. They've purchased another firm across the country, and what once were two separate *local* area networks are now one firm with a wide area network need. If that WAN link is fast, there's no network design headache at all: hook the two offices up with a T1 link, and you can essentially treat them as one office.

That's beneficial because each site will usually contain a domain controller—one of those servers that hosts the AD database and that acts as a machine to accomplish logins. But those domain controllers must communicate whenever something changes, such as when a user's password changes or when an administrator creates a new user account. This is called *AD replication*. The same thing happened with NT 4, because NT 4 also allowed you to put multiple domain controllers in an enterprise.

In NT 4, suppose you've got two offices connected by a slow WAN link. Suppose further that you've got a domain controller in each of these offices. They need to replicate their SAM database between domain controllers (recall that NT 4 used a user database named SAM; the Windows Server database is called AD). NT 4's domain controller updates happened every five minutes. That means that a domain controller might try to replicate changes to another domain controller every five minutes, even if they're connected with only a very slow link. All that chatter could well choke a WAN link and keep other, more important traffic from getting through.

Windows Server improves on that by allowing you to tell domain controllers about how well they're connected. The idea is that you describe your enterprise in terms of *sites*, which are just groups of servers with fast connections—groups of servers living on the same local area network, basically. You can then define how fast (or probably, slow) the connections *between* those sites are, and Windows 2000 Server will then be a bit smarter about using those connections.

In particular, Windows Server AD servers compress data before sending it over slow WAN links. Taking the time to compress data requires a certain amount of CPU power, but it's well worth it, since AD is capable of a 10 percent compression ratio!

Not only do you often face slow links, you often must live with *unreliable* links, ones that are up and down or perhaps up for only a short period of time every day. Windows 2000 Server lets you define not only a WAN link's speed but also the times that it is up.

NT 4's directory replications require a real-time connection called a Remote Procedure Call (RPC). RPCs are like telephone calls—the domain controller programs on each side must be up and running and actively communicating simultaneously. Inasmuch as domain controllers can be more or less busy as the day wears on, requiring this kind of shared concentration in order to get a simple directory replication accomplished is a bit demanding. It might be nicer if replications could work less like a telephone call and more like a mailing—and to a certain extent, Windows 2000 Server allows this, or rather points to a day in the future when it'll be possible.

It's possible for one domain controller to simply *mail* part of its replication data to another domain controller. Then, even if the receiving domain controller is not currently online, the mail message is still waiting for it, ready to be read when the receiving domain controller is again awake.

Site control will make life considerably easier for those managing multilocation networks.

Scalability: Building Big Networks

Large enterprise networks found NT 4 lacking in the number of users that its SAM database could accommodate. Although you could theoretically create millions of user accounts on an NT domain, it's not practical to create more than about 5,000 to perhaps 10,000 user accounts in a domain. (If you took the MCSE exam for NT Server and are looking at that number oddly, it's because they made you memorize 40,000 as the answer to the question "How many user accounts can you put on an NT domain?" In my experience, that's just not realistic, hence my 5,000 to 10,000 number.)

Five thousand user accounts are more than most companies would ever need. But some large firms need to incorporate more user accounts into their enterprise, forcing them to divide their company's network into multiple domains—and multiple domains were to be avoided at all costs under NT 4 because of the extra trouble in maintaining them.

AD can accommodate many more user accounts than NT's SAM. Furthermore, AD allows you to build larger networks by making the process of building and maintaining multidomain networks easier. Whereas once an administrator of a multidomain network had to build and maintain a complex system of interdomain security relationships—the *trust relationships* I've already referred to—now Windows Server will let you build a system of domains called a *forest*. A forest's main strength is that once a group of domains has been built into a forest, the trusts are automatically created and maintained. Smaller multidomain structures, called trees, also feature automatic trusts.

Simplifying Computer Names or Unifying the Namespace

Devices on a network mainly identify themselves by some long and unique number. On an intranet or the Internet, it's a unique 32-bit number called an *IP address*. Networks also commonly exploit a 48-bit address burned into each network interface card called a *MAC* (Media Access Control) *address*. Any Ethernet, Token Ring, ATM (asynchronous transfer mode), or other network interface has one of these addresses, and some conventions that network manufacturers have agreed on have ensured that no matter whom you buy a NIC (network interface card) from, the NIC will have a 48-bit address that no other NIC has. Some parts of NT identify PCs by their IP address (or addresses—a machine with multiple NICs will have an IP address and MAC address for each NIC), others by the PC's MAC address or addresses.

But people don't relate well to long strings of numbers—telling you that you can send me mail at `mark@11001110111101101111110111001000` is technically accurate (presuming that you can find a mail client that will accept network addresses in binary) but not very helpful. It's far more preferable to be able to instead tell your mail program to send mail to `mark@minasi.com`, which you can do. Somehow, however, your mail client must be able to look up `minasi.com` and from there find out where to send mail for `minasi.com`. In the same way, pointing your web browser to `www.microsoft.com` forces the browser to convert `www.microsoft.com` into the particular IP address or addresses that constitute Microsoft's website. This process of converting from human-friendly names such as `minasi.com` to computer-friendly addresses such as 11001110111101101111110111001000 is called *name resolution*. It's something every network must do.

So, why is name resolution a problem with NT? Because most of the networking world uses *one* approach to name resolution, and up through version 4, NT used a different one.

Most every firm is on the Internet and has an internal intranet, or both. Intranets and the Internet use the DNS form of name resolution. DNS names are the familiar Internet names such as `www.microsoft.com`. PCs resolve DNS names by consulting a group of servers around the world called, not surprisingly, DNS servers. Your company or Internet Service Provider operates one or more DNS servers, and your Internet software uses these nearby DNS servers to resolve (for example) `www.minasi.com` to the Internet address 206.246.253.200.

NT-based networks using Internet software don't use DNS for much of their work. Instead, Microsoft invented its own name servers somewhat like DNS but using NetBIOS names; they called these name servers Windows Internet Name Service, or WINS, servers. The NetBIOS naming system is incompatible with DNS; NetBIOS names are simpler—no more than 15 characters, no periods.

That leads to this problem: nearly every firm is on the Internet—*has* to be on the Internet—and so every firm must give DNS names to their computers. But if they're also using NT, they need to give their systems NetBIOS names. That in and of itself is not a great burden; what *is* a burden is that these names are important to the programs that use them, and programs typically can need one of the two names and can't use the other of the two.

Let's take an example. Suppose someone wants to log on to an NT 4 domain at Acme Technologies. To accomplish that, this person's workstation must find a domain controller for that domain. The workstation does that by searching for a machine with a particular NetBIOS name. Let's say that Acme does indeed have a domain controller around named LOGMEIN (its NetBIOS name), which *also* acts as a web server with the DNS name `reptiles.pictures.animalworld.com`, because it hosts pages of pictures of local reptiles. Let's also suppose that for some reason ACME has no WINS servers but has a great network of DNS servers.

DNS names are of no value to the workstation looking for a logon. You could have the finest set of DNS servers in the world, but it would make no difference—without a functioning WINS server, that workstation would probably be unable to locate a domain controller to log you in. On the other hand, if someone sitting at that very same workstation sought to view the reptile pictures on `http://www.livescience.com/reptiles/`, they'd just fire up Internet Explorer and point it at that URL. Internet Explorer is, of course, uninterested in NetBIOS names, relying mainly on DNS names. The workstation would quickly locate the web server and browse its pages, even as that same workstation was unable to detect that the very same server could perform logins.

Windows Server solves this problem by largely doing away with WINS, using DNS for all its name resolution needs. Unfortunately, however, Windows Server uses DNS for all *its* name resolution needs—older Windows 9*x* and Windows NT 4 systems still rely on WINS. So, while WINS' role is diminished, it'll still be around until you've pulled the plug on the last Windows 9*x* and NT machines.

Satisfying the Lust for Power and Control

Well, okay, maybe it's not *lust*, but it's certainly *need*. Put simply, there just plain aren't enough support people around, and there is no shortage of users to support. In 1987, many firms retained one support person for every 100 users; in many companies nowadays, that ratio is more like one support person for every 2,000 users.

Although it was once possible for a support person to physically visit every user's PC to perform support tasks, it's just not reasonable to expect that anymore. Support people need tools that allow them to get their work done from a central location as much as possible. And, although not every user is all that happy about it, one way to simplify a support person's job is to standardize each PC's desktop. In some cases, support staffs need software tools to allow them to *enforce* that standard desktop. (As you can imagine, it's a very political issue for many firms.)

In NT 4, Microsoft started helping support staffs centralize their desktop control with something called *system policies*. But system policies were lacking in a few ways. AD improves upon system policies with a kind of "system policies version 2" called *group policies*.

Better security, more flexible administration options, wiser use of bandwidth, and providing godlike control to administrators: that's basically what AD is trying to accomplish.

Connecting a Vista Machine to an AD Domain

So now that you know all about Active Directory and what it's for, let's take a look at how you can connect your Vista workstation to an Active Directory domain. The steps are actually quite easy, and if you work along with the examples that follow, you should be connected to an Active Directory domain in no time.

Checklist

Before trying to connect to an Active Directory domain. be sure you have the following information available:

- The name of the AD domain you will be joining.
- Your username and password, as they are defined in the AD.
- Whether an account has already been added to the AD for your machine (each machine has an account, as does each user).
- If an account has not been added for your machine, you will need a login name and password in Active Directory with the rights to create an account for your machine.

Connecting to AD

Once you have verified all of the items on the checklist, you've got what it takes to add your machine to an Active Directory domain. The next step is to verify that the correct components are installed on your Vista computer (and to install them if they're not) and then to add your machine to the Active Directory domain.

Verifying Operating System Prerequisites

In order to connect to an Active Directory domain, two networking components must be in place on your system:

- Client for Microsoft Networks
- An appropriate communications protocol (TCP/IP)

NOTE Previous versions of Windows would let you connect to a Windows server using IPX/SPX. Vista only provides support for IPX/SPX when connecting to NetWare—you can't use it to connect to a Windows server. However, Vista does provide strong support for both TCP/IPv4 (the current standard) and TCP/IPv6, so you can use the flavor of TCP/IP that best suits your company's needs.

Both components are necessary for any Microsoft operating systems to talk to each other, so it is important to make sure they are properly installed before trying to join an Active Directory domain.

To verify that both components are installed, follow these steps:

1. Right-click Network and choose Properties to open the Network and Sharing Center. Click the Manage network connection link to open the Network Connections folder.
2. Right-click the icon that represents your network (Local Area Connection), and choose Properties from the shortcut menu to open the Properties dialog box for your network.
3. In the list of configured components you should see the Client for Microsoft Networks and Internet Protocol Version 4 (TCP/IPv4) or Internet Protocol Version 6 (TCP/IPv6). Make sure that Client for Microsoft Networks and one of the TCP/IP entries are enabled (the check box next to the item is selected).

You now have everything you need to connect to a domain. You just need to tell Vista to do it.

Changing Your Computer Name

To tell Vista to join an Active Directory domain, you change the network identification information on your system. However, the configuration for doing so is a bit hidden. Instead of being with the other networking items, the Active Directory domain items are configuration parameters in Computer. To change network identification, follow these steps:

1. Click Start, right-click Computer, and choose Properties from the shortcut menu to open the System Properties window.
2. Click the Advanced system settings link to open the System Properties dialog box.
3. Click the Computer Name tab, and you will see the current identification of your system consisting of a machine name and the current domain or workgroup your system is configured to use as shown in Figure 26.1. On this tab, you have two choices for joining a domain.

By clicking the Network ID button, you begin the Network Identification Wizard. Selecting Change will get the same job done, but manually.

4. To change this configuration, click the Change button to open the Computer Name/Domain Changes dialog box shown in Figure 26.2.

As you can see, the name of my machine is QDOCLAP, and it was originally a member of a workgroup called MSHOME. I've told Vista to join an Active Directory domain called SUSHIYUM by clicking the Domain radio button and entering the name of the domain that my system should join. After you make the necessary changes to your system, click OK. Either one of two things will happen.

First, you might see a dialog box welcoming you to the domain you specified. What that means is that someone—an administrator or someone else—has already set up an account for the name of your computer within Active Directory. If this is the case, all you will need to do is reboot to complete your changes. You can now proceed to the "Logging In to Active Directory" section of this chapter.

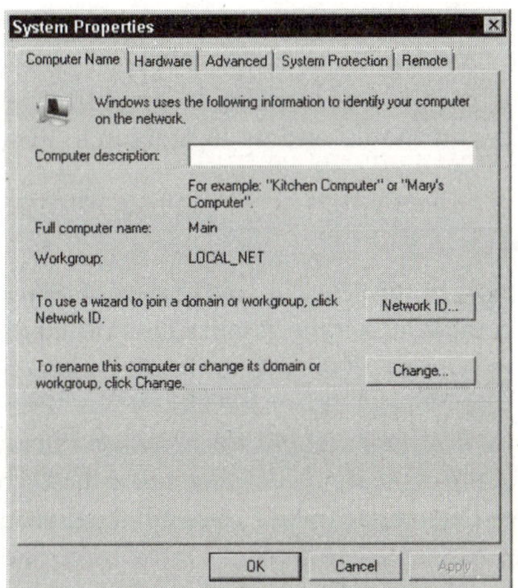

FIGURE 26.1
The Computer Name tab contains the network identification information.

FIGURE 26.2
The Computer Name/Domain Changes dialog box contains the network identification information.

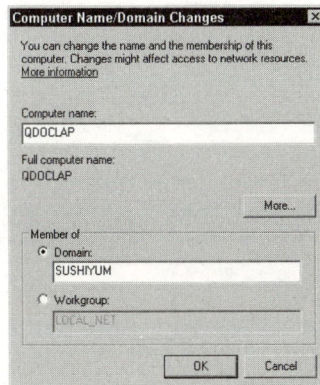

However, more often than not there won't be an account for your computer within Active Directory, so you'll need to add one. You'll know this is the case if you get prompted for a username and password.

Active Directory doesn't let just anyone add machine accounts to its database; you need an Active Directory user account that has the right to do so. The Administrator account will work for these purposes, but depending on your circumstances, you may not have been provided with the administrative password to Active Directory. There are also ways to create special accounts for one purpose—to add machines to domains—but ultimately if you don't know of an account to use at this point, you will need to contact an administrator for Active Directory in order to complete this process (that's why this information was listed in the prerequisites).

Assuming you have the correct username and password to use (or that someone has entered it for you), the next thing you should see is a dialog box welcoming you to the domain you've joined. Your machine will need to be rebooted for the changes to take effect, so go ahead and reboot your system.

Logging In to Active Directory

The next time your computer boots up, it probably won't look much different. You'll be presented with the same login box that you've always seen. Vista automatically logs you into the domain, so you don't have to do anything different from what you did in the past. If everything is configured correctly, you should end up logging in to the Active Directory domain. Congratulations!

Summary

The purpose of this chapter was to introduce you to AD. As you can tell from even these few pages, AD is a complicated topic. If you're interested in learning more, I recommend that you take a look at *Mastering Windows 2000 Server*, Fourth Edition by Mark Minasi et al. (Sybex, 2002), *Mastering Active Directory for Windows Server 2003 R2* by Brad Price, John Price, and Scott Fenstermacher (Sybex, 2006), and *Active Directory Best Practices 24seven: Migrating, Designing, and Troubleshooting* by Brad Price (Sybex, 2004) or *Mastering Windows Server 2003* by Mark Minasi et al. (Sybex, 2003).

Active Directory can be a somewhat nebulous topic; until you get into it, it might not make a lot of sense. The same can be said for the topic of our next chapter: the Registry.

Chapter 27

Understanding and Using the Registry

This chapter covers how to work with one of the most mentioned but least understood components of Windows—the Registry, the giant repository of Windows' knowledge and wisdom about your computer. The chapter starts by discussing what the Registry is, what it does, why you might want to mess with it, and what the dangers are of doing so. It then details the step you *must* take before you make any changes to the Registry: backing up the Registry so that you can restore it if something goes wrong. After that, the chapter shows you how to use the Registry Editor to examine the contents of the Registry, find what you're looking for, and make changes.

In this chapter:

- Understanding the Registry and what it does
- Running Registry Editor
- Backing up your Registry
- Restoring the Registry from backup
- Registry subtrees and data types
- Finding and changing information in the Registry
- Understanding Vista Registry Access Restrictions

Vista: What's New?

The Registry in Vista works just as it has in previous versions of Windows. If you already know how to work with the Registry in Windows XP, you know how to work with it in Vista. However, Registry security has changed. Applications can no longer write just anywhere in the Registry without the proper privilege elevation. Some application vendors used sloppy coding practices in the past. They would write settings at the machine level that only the user cared about. Consequently, you might find that some applications don't work quite the same as they used to unless you run them as an administrator. None of these changes affect the physical configuration of the Registry and you still use tools such as RegEdit to modify the Registry. All you really need to know is that you might need privilege elevation to make certain changes.

What Is the Registry and What Does It Do?

Put simply, the Registry is a hierarchical database of all the settings required by your installation of Windows and the programs you've installed. These settings include information on the hardware installed on your computer and how it's configured; all the programs and their file associations; profiles for each user and group; and property settings for folders and files.

The Registry stores the information needed to keep your computer running. Windows itself stores a huge amount of information in the Registry, and each program you install stores information there too. You can store information in the Registry yourself if you want to, though unless you're creating programs, there's not much reason to do so.

The number of entries in the Registry depends on the number of users of the computer and the software installed, but between 50,000 and 100,000 entries is normal. This multitude of entries makes browsing through the Registry practical only for those with serious amounts of time weighing on their hands. Even searching through the Registry can be a slow process, because many of the entries contain similar information.

The Registry was introduced in Windows 95, and all 32-bit desktop versions of Windows have used it. In Windows 3.*x*, information was stored in initialization files—INI files for short. For example, Windows configuration information was stored in files such as `WIN.INI` and `SYSTEM.INI`. Most programs typically created configuration files of their own.

Centralizing all the information in the Registry has two main advantages. First, all the information is in one location. (Actually, it's in a couple of locations. More on this a little later in the chapter.) And second, you can back up the Registry (though most users forget or fail to do so) and restore it.

Not surprisingly, this centralization has the concomitant disadvantage that damage to the Registry can cripple Windows completely.

Why Work with the Registry?

Paradoxically enough, you *don't* work with the Registry—most of the time. In theory, you should never need to mess with the Registry.

That's why Windows provides no direct way from the user interface to view the Registry and change its contents. If you want to explore and change the Registry, you need to deliberately run the Registry Editor program, which is tucked away in a safe place where no casual user should stumble across it.

Most of the information that's stored in the Registry you'll never need to change. Those relatively few pieces of information that Windows is happy for you to change are accessible through the Windows user interface, which provides you with an easier—if more restrictive—way of changing them than working in the Registry. For example, the settings in Control Panel applets store most of their information in the Registry, so you *could* edit the Registry and change the information there. But for all conventional purposes, you'll do better to work through those Control Panel applets and let them set the values in the Registry for you. Control Panel is designed to be easy to use, while the Registry isn't. Control Panel shows you your options in (mostly) intelligible ways; the information in the Registry is arcane when not incomprehensible. And Control Panel seldom screws up in translating your choices into hex and binary, whereas the Registry will happily accept input that will instruct Windows how to disable itself.

That said, sometimes you may need to access the Registry to change a vital piece of information that you cannot change through the user interface. Sometimes you'll need to access the Registry because something has gone wrong, and you need to change an entry manually. But more often, you'll hear about a cool tweak that you can perform by entering a new value in the Registry or by changing an existing value.

You can also use the Registry to store information of your own that you want to have available to Windows or to the programs you use. You might want to do this if you write your own programs or if you use a macro language to create automated procedures in a program—for example, if you use VBA to automate tasks in Word, Excel, or Outlook. (You *could* also use the Registry to store odd information, such as names and addresses—but there are far better ways of spending your life.)

Preparing to Access the Registry

Before you do anything to the Registry, you need to understand this:

> *If you mess up the Registry, you may disable parts of Windows' functionality. You may even disable Windows itself so that it cannot boot.*

So before you do *anything* to the Registry, back it up by exporting it as discussed later in this chapter. In fact, even if you don't make any changes to the Registry, it's a good idea to keep a backup of your Registry in case a program, Windows itself, or (more likely) a piece of malware makes a change for the worse.

Running Registry Editor

To work with the Registry, you use Registry Editor. Windows provides no Start menu item for Registry Editor, though you can of course create your own Start menu item if you want.

Unless you create a Start menu item or shortcut, the easiest way to run Registry Editor is to choose Start ➢ Run (or press Winkey+R), enter **`regedit`** in the Run dialog box, and click the OK button. Windows starts Registry Editor (shown in Figure 27.1).

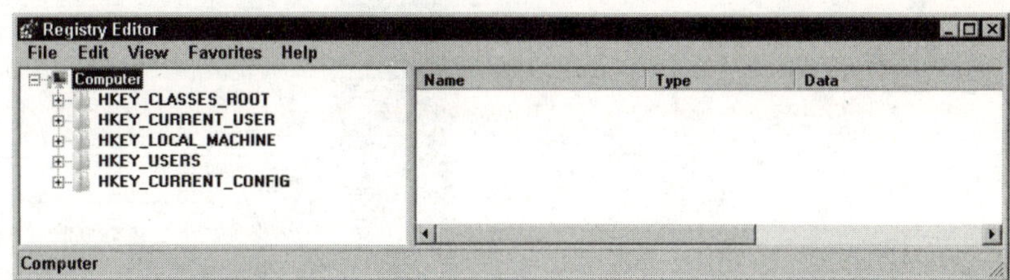

FIGURE 27.1 Launch Registry Editor by choosing Start ➢ Run and entering regedit in the Run dialog box.

NOTE If you've worked with the Registry in Windows 2000 or in Windows NT, you'll recall that those OSes included *two* Registry Editors REGEDIT.EXE and REGEDT32.EXE. Both were functional but offered slightly different features from each other. Vista includes just one Registry Editor (with full functionality), REGEDIT.EXE, but there's a stub for REGEDT32.EXE so you can start the same Registry Editor by using either name.

Backing Up Your Registry

Before you do anything else with Registry Editor—and that includes exploring the subtrees and keys of the Registry, let alone changing any values—back up your Registry.

To back up the Registry, export it by taking the following steps from Registry Editor:

1. Select the Computer item in Registry Editor.

TIP If you want to back up only a subtree of the Registry, select the subtree instead of the Computer item.

2. Choose File ➤ Export. Registry Editor displays the Export Registry File dialog box. As you can see in Figure 27.2, this dialog box is a common Save As dialog box with an extra section tacked on at the bottom to house the Export Range box.
3. In the Export Range section, make sure the All option button is selected. If you chose a subtree in step 1, the Export Registry File dialog box appears with the Selected Branch option button selected and the subtree's name entered in the Selected Branch text box.
4. Specify the filename and location for the file as usual.

TIP Registry files tend to be large—on the order of 20–30MB—so don't try to save yours to a floppy. If you have a CD recorder, save the Registry file to disk, and then burn it to CD.

5. Click the Save button. Windows saves the Registry file.

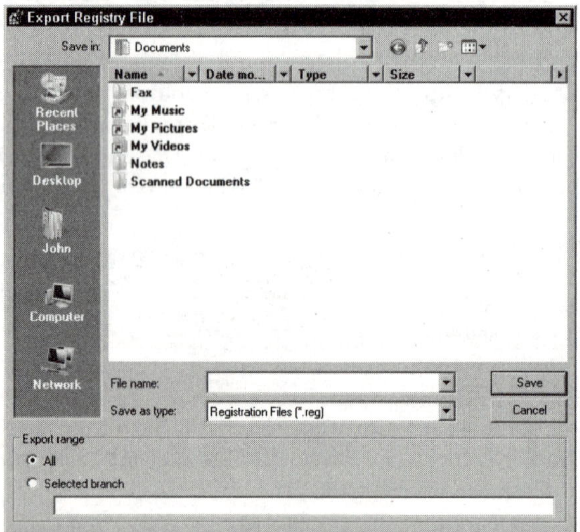

FIGURE 27.2
Export all or part of the Registry to create a backup.

Restoring Your Registry

To restore your Registry (or part of it) from a Registry file you've exported, follow these steps:

1. From Registry Editor, choose File ➤ Import. Windows displays the Import Registry File dialog box, which is a renamed Open dialog box.
2. In the Files of Type drop-down list, select the Registration Files item or the Registry Hive Files item as appropriate.

USING THE REG UTILITY

Most versions of Windows also include the REG utility. This utility lets you work with the Registry from the command line. Normally, you'll want to use RegEdit to make Registry changes because using the command-line utility can increase the probability of errors. However, you might need to use the REG utility in some cases. For example, if Vista won't boot due to a Registry error, you can restore your backup of the Registry using the REG utility. Any task you can perform using RegEdit, you can also perform using the REG utility.

As with all command-line utilities, you use REG by opening a command prompt. However, because you're working with the Registry, you need to open an administrator command prompt by right-clicking the Command Prompt link in Start ➤ Programs ➤ Accessories and choosing Run as Administrator from the context menu.

The REG utility provides several operations that you can perform on the Registry including QUERY, ADD, DELETE, COPY, SAVE, LOAD, UNLOAD, RESTORE, COMPARE, EXPORT, IMPORT, and FLAGS. The operations perform the tasks that you might imagine. For example, if you simply want to obtain information about the Registry, you use the QUERY operation. You can learn more about each operating by typing **REG *<Operation Name>* /?** at the command prompt and pressing Enter.

3. Select the Registry file to import.
4. Click the Open button. Registry Editor imports the Registry file and adds it to the Registry.

Working in the Registry

Now that your Registry is safely backed up, it's time to examine how the Registry works and how you can change it.

As mentioned earlier in this chapter, the Registry is a hierarchical database. It's hierarchical in that its contents are arranged into a hierarchy of folders organized into five main areas called *subtrees* or *root keys*. You'll also sometimes hear them called *predefined keys*, though the term tends to be confusing because the Registry contains thousands of keys that are predefined. As you can see in Figure 27.1, the name of each subtree begins with the letters HKEY.

The Five Subtrees of the Registry

These are the five subtrees and the types of information they contain:

HKEY_CLASSES_ROOT Contains an exhaustive list of the file types that Windows recognizes, the programs associated with them, and more.

HKEY_CURRENT_USER Contains information on the current user and their setup. For example, when you're logged on, all your Desktop preferences are listed in this subtree.

HKEY_LOCAL_MACHINE Contains information on the hardware and software setup of the computer.

HKEY_USERS Contains information on the users who are set up to use the computer, together with a DEFAULT profile that's used when no user is logged on to the computer.

HKEY_CURRENT_CONFIG Contains information on the current configuration of the computer—the hardware with which the computer booted.

Keys, Subkeys, and Value Entries

In Registry Editor, expand the HKEY_CURRENT_USER subtree by clicking the plus sign (+) next to it or by double-clicking its name. Registry Editor displays the items contained within the subtree—an apparently endless list of folder-like objects, many of them containing further objects. Figure 27.3 shows the HKEY_CURRENT_USER subtree and some of its subkeys expanded.

Within each subtree are keys, subkeys, and value entries. A *key* is one of the folders within the subtree. Just as a subfolder is a folder within a folder, a *subkey* is a key within a key. Also as with "folder" and "subfolder," many people say "key" rather than "subkey" except when they need to be specific; this chapter does the same.

Each key or subkey can contain subkeys and value entries. The term *value entry* sounds like a management-consultant way of saying "value," but in fact it's not: a value entry is the current definition of a key and consists of a name, a data type, and the value assigned to the key.

For example, consider the MinAnimate key and value entry that you can see in Figure 27.3 in the HKEY_CURRENT_USER\Control Panel\Desktop\WindowMetrics subkey. As you can see in the Data column, the value of MinAnimate is 1. This value entry controls whether Windows animates windows when you minimize, maximize, or restore them. (The animation zooms the window from its displayed size and position down to its button on the Taskbar, and vice versa, instead of popping it off or back on the screen instantly.) A value of 0 indicates that the animation is off, a value of 1 that the animation is on.

MinAnimate is interesting in that it's an example of a key added to the Registry in Vista in order to implement functionality already in Windows. In earlier versions of Windows, including Windows NT and Windows 2000, this key wasn't included in the Registry, though its functionality was implemented in Windows. These versions of Windows automatically animated windows that you minimized, maximized, or restored.

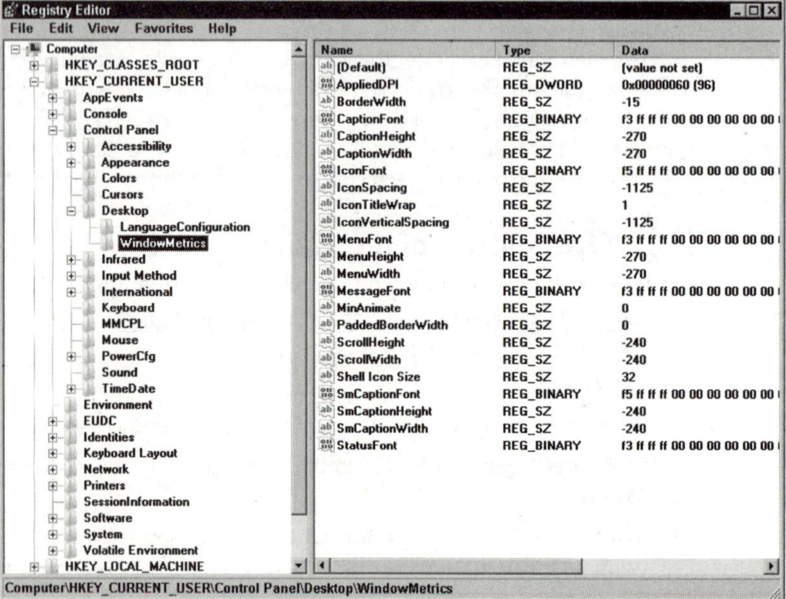

FIGURE 27.3
Each subtree contains keys, subkeys, and value entries.

This animation was (and remains) pure eye candy—and like much eye candy, this animation didn't appeal to everyone. On a slow computer, or one with an underpowered graphics card, it was particularly irritating, because Windows seemed to be running arthritically. To switch off this animation, you needed to create the `MinAnimate` value entry in the Registry, assign it the value 0, and then restart Windows. (You could also implement this change by using a utility such as TweakUI, which created and adjusted the `MinAnimate` value entry transparently for you.)

Vista lets you control this setting via the Animate Windows When Minimizing and Maximizing check box on the Visual Effects tab of the Performance Options dialog box. When this check box is selected, `MinAnimate` has the value 1; when the check box is cleared, `MinAnimate` has the value 0.

Registry Data Types

As you can see in Figure 27.3, the `MinAnimate` value entry is of type `REG_SZ`. `REG` means Registry, as you'd guess; `SZ` means string, indicating that the value entry contains a string of text (text characters, as opposed to, say, binary data). The `WindowMetrics` key also contains value entries of another data type, `REG_BINARY`. You get no prize for guessing that these are binary data.

Strings and binary data are the most widely used of the data types in the Registry. Next comes `REG_DWORD`, a double-word value entry. Figure 27.4 shows the `HKEY_CURRENT_USER\Control Panel\Desktop` key, which contains some double-word value entries as well as string and binary value entries.

The other two most widely used data types are `REG_MULTI_SZ`, multistring entries, and `REG_EXPAND_SZ`, expandable strings. Table 27.1 provides a roundup of the five most widely used data types.

You can create and edit value entries with any of these data types. We'll get to that a bit later in the chapter, after discussing where the Registry is stored and how to find information in it.

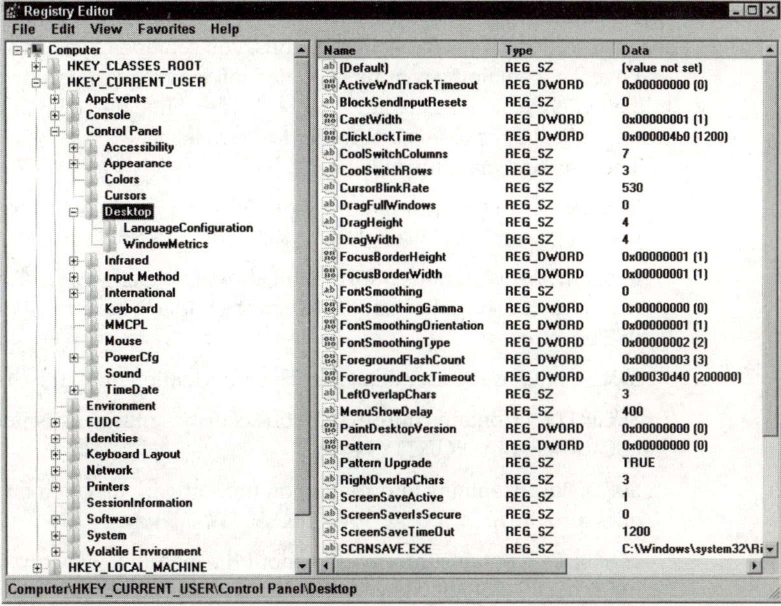

FIGURE 27.4 The HKEY_CURRENT_USER\Control Panel\Desktop key contains a variety of data types.

NOTE Beyond these five widely used data types, the Registry can contain many different data types, such as REG_DWORD_BIG_ENDIAN (a value stored in reverse order of double-word value), REG_DWORD_LITTLE_ENDIAN (another type of double-word value), REG_FULL_RESOURCE_DESCRIPTOR (a hardware-resource list), REG_QWORD (a quadruple-word value), and REG_FILE_NAME (three guesses). You shouldn't need to mess with any of these unless you get into programming Windows—in which case, you'll need a book more specialized than this one.

TABLE 27.1: The Five Most Widely Used Registry Data Types

TYPE	TYPE DISPLAYED	EXPLANATION
String	REG_SZ	Text
Multistring	REG_MULTI_SZ	Text, but with multiple text values
Expandable string	REG_EXPAND_SZ	Text, but expandable
Binary	REG_BINARY	A binary value, displayed as hexadecimal
DWORD	REG_DWORD	Double-word: A 32-bit binary value displayed as an 8-digit hexadecimal value

Where the Registry Is Stored

Most of the Registry is stored in several files on your hard drive. (Part of the Registry is created automatically when Windows boots and discovers which devices are attached to your computer.) These files are called *hives* (think bees, not allergies) or *hive files*. The hives are binary, but (as you'll see in the next section), if you're feeling curious, you can open them in a text editor and peek inside them.

Hive files containing computer-related information are stored in the *Windows*\system32\config folder, where *Windows* is your Windows folder. Hive files containing user-specific information are stored in the Users*Username* folder for each user.

These are the main hive files:

SYSTEM Contains information about the computer's hardware and about Windows. This information goes into the HKEY_LOCAL_MACHINE\SYSTEM key.

NTUSER.DAT Contains information about the user's preferences. Vista keeps an NTUSER.DAT file for each user in the \Users*Username* folder. This information goes into the HKEY_CURRENT_USER subtree.

SAM Contains the user database. This information goes into the HKEY_LOCAL_MACHINE\SAM key.

SECURITY Contains information on security settings. This information goes into the HKEY_LOCALMACHINE\SECURITY key.

SOFTWARE Contains information on the software installed on the computer. This information goes into the HKEY_LOCAL_MACHINE\SOFTWARE key.

DEFAULT Contains information about the default user setup. This information goes into the HKEY_USERS\DEFAULT key.

Each of the hive files has a log file named after it: `DEFAULT.LOG`, `SOFTWARE.LOG`, `NTUSER.DAT.LOG`, and so on. These log files note the changes to the hive files so that, if a change is applied that crashes the system, Windows can read the log, identify the problem change, and undo it.

Having read this, you're probably longing to lift the lid off a hive so you can see what's inside it. Perhaps if you use Notepad or another text editor, you can get a peek inside.

Don't.

Taking a text editor to a hive file would be like taking one of those old-fashioned can openers (you know, the ones that leave those nice jagged edges) to your favorite black box of electronic wizardry: clumsy, messy, and ultimately fruitless. In any case, Windows keeps the hive files open the whole time it's running so that it can write information to them and retrieve information from them whenever it needs, so they're locked. All you'll get for your pains is a message box telling you something like "The process cannot access the file because it is being used by another process." Translation: Windows needs this file. Hands off.

Let's look at what you *can* profitably do with the Registry: find keys and value entries or information in it, change values, and create (and delete) keys and value entries of your own.

Finding Information in the Registry

You can find information in the Registry in two ways: by digging through the Registry looking for it or by using the Find function.

Digging through the Registry takes minimal explanation, because it's very similar to browsing in Explorer in Explore mode. You can expand and collapse keys as you would drives and folders in Explorer, and you can use type-down addressing to reach the next key or entry matching the letters you type. But because of the number of keys and value entries the Registry contains, you'll usually do better by searching through it than browsing.

If you know the name of a key, the name of a value entry, or the data contained in a value entry, you can search for it. For example, if you wanted to find where FTP sites were listed, you might search for FTP Sites. If you wanted to find out what the entry for the AutoCorrect file was called, you might search for .ACL, the extension of the AutoCorrect file. You can restrict the search by selecting only the check boxes for the items you're looking at—Keys, Values, or Data—in the Look At group section of the Find dialog box (shown in Figure 27.5). (Choose Edit ➤ Find to open the Find dialog box.) And you can search for only the entire string by selecting the Match Whole String Only check box. Selecting this check box prevents Find from finding the string you're looking for inside other strings—it makes Find find only whole strings that match the string in the Find What text box.

Because of the volume of information that Windows stores in the Registry, the first match you find may not be the key (or value entry, or value) you need. For example, if you use your company's name as the Find item when looking for the `RegisteredOrganization` key for Windows, you may find another key, such as the registered organization for Internet Explorer. Close examination of the key will usually tell you whether you've found the key you were looking for. If not, press the F3 key or choose Edit ➤ Find Next to find the next instance.

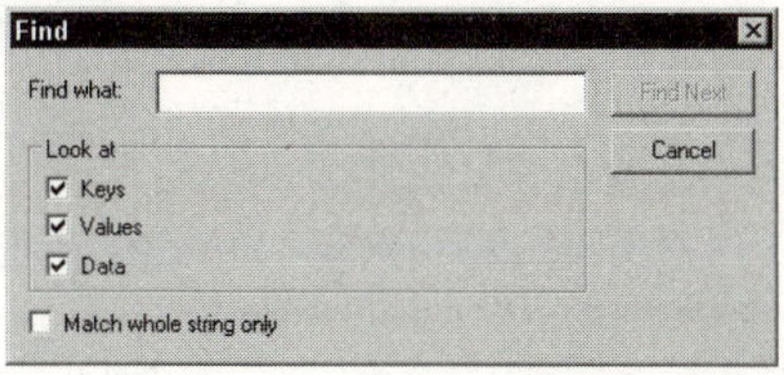

FIGURE 27.5
Use the Find dialog box in Registry Editor to find the keys, values, or data you want to manipulate.

Editing a Value Entry

To edit a value entry in the Registry, navigate to it and double-click it. (Alternatively, select it and choose Edit ➤ Modify.) Windows displays an Edit dialog box appropriate to the type of data the value entry contains.

String values and expandable string values are the easiest values to edit. In the Edit String dialog box (shown in Figure 27.6), enter the text of the string in the Value Data text box, and then click the OK button.

Multistring values are relatively simple to edit. In the Edit Multi-String dialog box (shown in Figure 27.7), enter all the data for the value entry on separate lines, and then click the OK button.

Double-word values are the next-easiest values to edit. In the Edit DWORD Value dialog box (shown in Figure 27.8), enter the data in the Value Data text box, and then choose the Hexadecimal option button or the Decimal option button as appropriate in the Base section. (When you're editing a built-in double-word value, you shouldn't need to change the existing Base setting.) Click the OK button.

Binary values are brutes to change, and you probably won't want to mess with them for fun. In the Edit Binary Value dialog box (shown in Figure 27.9), edit the data in the Value Data text box with great care, and then click the OK button.

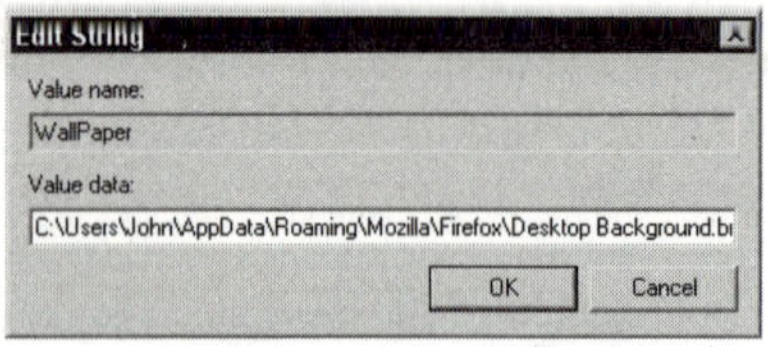

FIGURE 27.6
You can edit both string values and expandable string values in the Edit String dialog box.

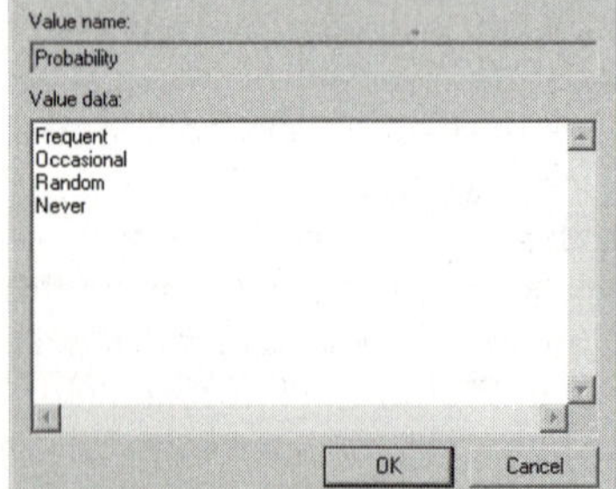

FIGURE 27.7
Editing a multistring value in the Edit Multi-String dialog box.

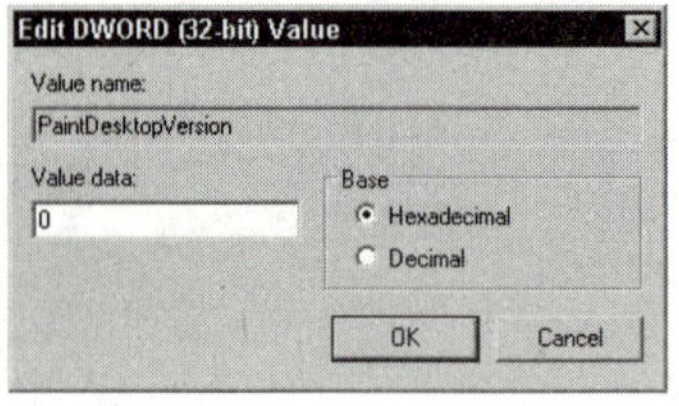

FIGURE 27.8
Editing a double-word value in the Edit DWORD Value dialog box.

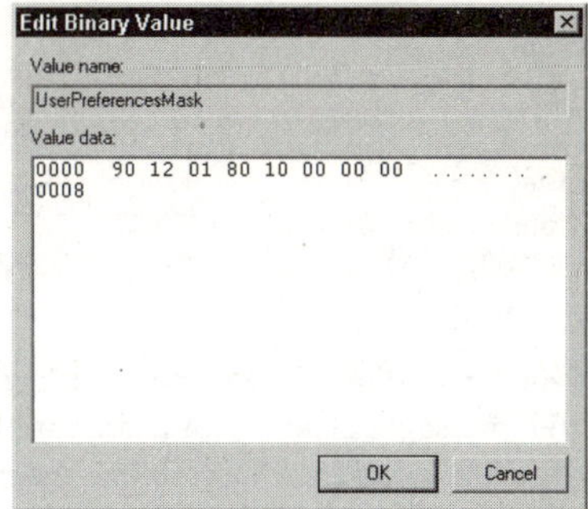

FIGURE 27.9
Editing a binary value in the Edit Binary Value dialog box is hard work.

Adding a Key or a Value Entry

You can add a key or a value entry to the Registry either automatically or manually.

To add a key or value entry to the Registry automatically, double-click a REG file that you've received. For example, some programs sold via download use Registry keys to implement a license: you pay for the program and download it. The company then e-mails you a license and a REG file. To add the registration data to your Registry, double-click the REG file. Windows adds the necessary keys and value entries to the Registry.

To add a key or a value entry to the Registry manually, follow these steps:

1. Right-click the key in which you want to create the new key or value entry, choose New from the shortcut menu, and choose the appropriate item from the submenu: Key, String Value, Binary Value, DWORD Value, Multi-String Value, or Expandable String Value. Registry Editor creates a new key named `New Key #1` or `New Value #1` (or the next available number) and displays an edit box around it.
2. Type the name for the key or value entry.
3. Press the Enter key or click elsewhere in the Registry Editor window. Registry Editor assigns to the key or value entry the name you specified.

If you created a value entry, double-click it. Registry Editor displays the Edit dialog box appropriate to its type. Enter the data for the value entry as described in the previous section.

Deleting a Key or a Value Entry

Just as you can create keys and value entries, you can delete them. Generally speaking, it's a bad idea to delete any keys other than those you've created. Windows itself and Windows programs protect some keys in the Registry, but you'll find a surprising number that aren't deleted and that you can therefore delete freely.

To delete a value entry, right-click it and choose Delete from the shortcut menu. Registry Editor displays the Confirm Value Delete dialog box (shown in Figure 27.10) or the Confirm Key Delete check box. Click the Yes button to confirm the deletion.

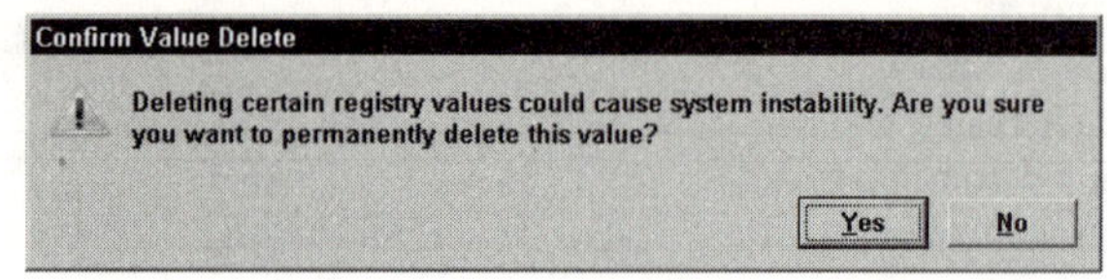

FIGURE 27.10
Confirm a deletion in the Confirm Key Delete dialog box (shown here) or the Confirm Value Delete dialog box.

NOTE If you've used previous versions of Registry Editor, you'll notice that Microsoft has made some of the messages clearer. For example, the Confirm Value Delete dialog box now tells you that deleting the value could destabilize the system.

If the key or value entry is locked against deletion, Registry Editor displays an error message box.

Copying a Key Name

If you're describing to someone how to find particular information in the Registry, you'll need to get the key name right. But you don't need to type it painstakingly—you can copy it instead.

To copy a Registry key name, select it in the left pane in Registry Editor and choose Edit ➤ Copy Key Name. You can then paste it from the Clipboard into a program.

An Example: Changing Your Windows Name and Organization

As mentioned at the beginning of the chapter, Microsoft reckons you should seldom (or preferably never) need to make changes to the Registry directly. But you'll probably run into tips and tweaks, online or in magazines, that promise to improve Windows' performance, compatibility, or behavior with a judicious change or two.

For example, say you misspelled your name or your organization's name during setup. Or perhaps you've bought a computer loaded with Windows from someone else. Either way, when you display the General tab of the System Properties dialog box, there's the misspelling or the wrong name laughing at you.

You'll want to change the name or organization name so that they're correct. There's no way to do so through the Windows user interface, but by navigating to the `HKEY_LOCAL_MACHINE\SOFTWARE\Microsoft\WindowsNT\CurrentVersion` key and changing the `RegisteredOwner` and `RegisteredOrganization` value entries as appropriate, you can fix the problem in a minute or two.

Using Registry Favorites to Quickly Access Keys

If you find yourself using the Registry a lot, there's another feature you should know about: Registry favorites. To access the keys you need to work with frequently, you can create favorites in Registry Editor much as you can in Explorer and Internet Explorer.

To create a favorite, follow these steps:

1. Select the key to which you want the favorite to refer.
2. Choose Favorites ➤ Add to Favorites. Registry Editor displays the Add to Favorites dialog box shown in Figure 27.11.

FIGURE 27.11
Create a list of favorite locations in the Registry to make it easier to find a location when you need to edit it.

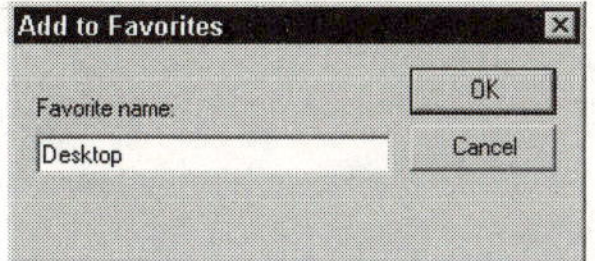

3. In the Favorite Name text box, enter the name for the favorite. (By default, Registry Editor suggests the key name, but you may well want to change this to more descriptive text.)
4. Click the OK button. Registry Editor adds the favorite to your Favorites menu.

To access a favorite, display the Favorites menu and choose the favorite from the list.

To remove a favorite from the Favorites menu, choose Favorites ➢ Remove Favorite. Windows displays the Remove Favorites dialog box. Choose the favorite in the Select Favorite list box and click the OK button.

Understanding Vista Registry Access Restrictions

As previously mentioned, some applications run into problems with Vista because they don't access the Registry correctly. The most common problem comes into play when an application tries to place user data in the HKEY_LOCAL_MACHINE hive. All user changes should appear in HKEY_CURRENT_USER. If your application uses HKEY_CURRENT_USER, you'll never see any messages when working with it. Most changes to HKEY_LOCAL_MACHINE require a privilege elevation, which means you'd have to have an administrator account to use the application.

You may also find restrictions to some keys and values. Unfortunately, Microsoft hasn't documented these restricted areas of the Registry. I've never personally run into any key or value that I actually needed to access that Microsoft restricted in some way. The restricted keys and values usually deal with a sensitive system function and you'll want to steer clear of them anyway. If you run into a problem accessing a key or value, you need to consider when you really want to access it anyway.

Summary

This chapter has discussed what the Registry is, what it does, why you *must* back it up before messing with it, how to mess with it, and why you shouldn't mess with it most of the time.

The next chapter will dive into a concept that can make administration easier if you have a large network: scripting. Scripting allows you to automate common repetitive tasks in order to ease your administrative burden.

Chapter 28

Scripts for Automation

Virtually every administrative task we've performed so far has, in one way or another, involved utilizing Windows' many GUI tools such as the MMC, System Applet, Network Applet, and the like. Microsoft has gone to great pains to ensure that we have a variety of tools at our disposal for performing administrative functions. However, certain tasks—particularly common, repetitive tasks—can become quite tedious when executed one at a time using the GUI tools. It is in these instances that leveraging scripts can be advantageous. Not only does scripting save time, it can also allow you to accomplish certain tasks that are difficult, or even impossible, with the standard GUI tools. This chapter covers the following topics:

- Brief overview of scripting
- Writing shell scripts
- The Windows Scripting Host
- Advanced scripting concepts
- Sample scripts for common tasks

Vista: What's New?

The biggest issue with Vista and scripting is security. Many of the scripts you now have will probably run, but you'll have to open an administrator command prompt to do it. To open an administrator command prompt, right-click Start ➤ All Programs ➤ Accessories ➤ Command Prompt and choose Run as Administrator from the context menu. The resulting command prompt window will say Administrator: Command Prompt and have additional privileges.

Another problem with Vista is that Microsoft changed some of the commands. For example, the `Choice` command works a little differently than it did in the past. Here's an example of the Windows XP and earlier form of the `Choice` command.

```
CHOICE /C:N /N /T:N,15
```

The Vista equivalent of the same command appears here:

```
CHOICE /C N /N /T 15 /D N
```

This second form does precisely the same thing as the Windows XP and earlier form. Just why Microsoft decided to make the change is a mystery. However, you need to be aware of these changes when moving old scripts to Vista because many of them result in unrecoverable errors.

The help associated with each command tells you about changes to that command. To see the new command-line syntax for `Choice`, simply type **`Choice /?`** at the command line.

What Is Scripting?

Quite simply, *scripting* is the process of arranging individual commands such that they follow a logical course and produce a desired result. These commands can be DOS commands (shell scripting) or commands specific to a particular scripting engine (Windows Scripting Host [WSH] scripting). Scripting is a form of computer programming. Notice that I didn't say "simple form" or "small form" of programming. Indeed, while most scripts are comparatively small and designed to perform quite specific, limited tasks, the differences between scripts and fully functioning computer programs have more to do with how they are deployed than what they do. Here's a brief comparison.

Scripts are interpreted. Scripts must be interpreted by a script engine during execution. Computer programs are generally precompiled into the bytecode (also known as machine code) of the target platform.

Scripts provide limited functionality. Most of the available scripting engines are subsets of larger programming languages. VBScript, for example, is based on Microsoft's more powerful Visual Basic language. While it simply can't do some things, there are ways to give your scripts power that rivals "professional" development languages. We'll discuss these techniques in the "Advanced Concepts" section.

Scripts are "cleartext." Once a computer program is compiled to bytecode, it is very difficult (but not impossible) to view the original code. Scripts are stored as ANSI text so the script engine can parse the file and translate each command into the appropriate operation. For security reasons, scripts should be kept in a secure location on an NTFS partition with limited access. The script files themselves can also be encoded to make deciphering contents somewhat more troublesome.

Even with these limitations, scripting can be a powerful weapon in your administrative arsenal. The rest of this chapter will cover some of the basic concepts of scripting and will include sample scripts to help you apply this knowledge.

Shell Scripting with BAT and CMD Files

Many people look at shell scripting as a basic entry point into scripting—something to use to get their feet wet until they graduate to the more advanced scripting available with the Windows Scripting Host. While it's true that the WSH does provide a more powerful scripting environment, I tend to view the differences between the two based on the task I am trying to accomplish at the time. I believe it was Confucius who said, "Don't use a cannon to kill a mosquito." If the task at hand can be completed with a batch script, then there's no reason not to use one.

NOTE It doesn't matter whether you use the extension `.bat` or `.cmd`—there's no difference. I use the `.cmd` extension for the scripts in this section.

A *shell script* (also known as a *batch file*) is essentially a group of shell commands encapsulated into a file and executed in sequence. Shell commands are those commands that are typed directly at the Vista command prompt. These can include standard DOS commands such as `copy`, `dir`, `mkdir`, etc., as well as any executable applications that are capable of receiving command-line arguments, such as `cacls` and `net`.

In addition to OS commands and programs, shell scripts can contain additional code to aid in executing the script, including commands to perform script logic such as comparisons, loops, and so on. Shell scripts have the extension of either `.bat` or `.cmd` and can be executed simply by typing the name of the script (with or without the extension) on the command line.

Tools for Scripting

Before you can begin creating scripts, you'll need an editor to get your code into the computer. The perennial favorite for creating batch scripts (and scripts for the Windows Scripting Host, for that matter) is Notepad. Veteran scripters refer to this simple text editor as "Visual Notepad," as in *Visual* Basic or *Visual* Studio—Microsoft's integrated development environment. While this sarcasm may be justified (Notepad does not perform any syntax checking, error handling, or even simple text formatting), virtually every scripter I've met relies on Notepad almost exclusively.

Many third-party script editors are available, as well. Feel free to experiment with them. Some are shareware and some are "professional" products. Each has its own distinct advantages and disadvantages. I'm sure you'll find one that suits you just fine.

WARNING Notepad always tries to save a new script as a TXT file. You have to remember to Save As ➢ Save As Type ➢ All Files (*.*), and then type the filename along with proper extension.

For creating XML-based WSH scripts, an XML editor comes in handy. I like to use FrontPage, because it came with my Office 2003 software. I don't much fancy buying software when a tool I already have will work just fine. We'll discuss this in further detail in "XML-based Scripts" later in this chapter.

Your First Shell Script

An unwritten law of computer programming states that your first application in any environment must be "Hello World!" Let's write a batch script to print "Hello World!" on the screen. (See Figure 28.1.)

```
rem HelloWorld.cmd
rem Displays "Hello World!" on the command line
echo off
echo Hello World!
```

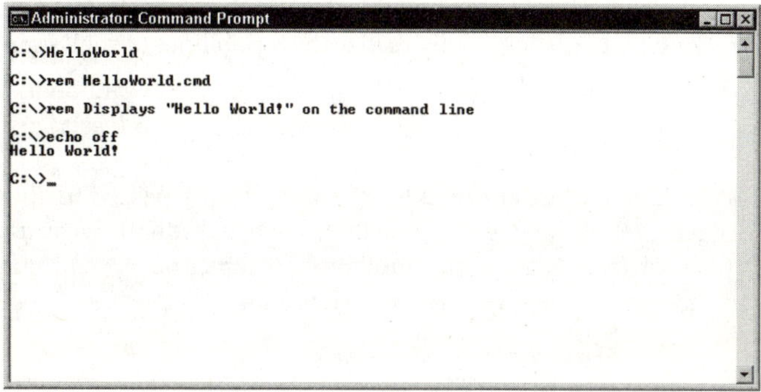

FIGURE 28.1 Output from HelloWorld.cmd.

This simple script shows us some very important features of shell scripting. First, we can include remarks to help us understand what the script does. The rem keyword causes the rest of the line to be ignored, allowing you to comment your code.

Text is displayed using the echo function. Echo is also used to turn automatic echoing on or off. By default, the command interpreter automatically echoes each command to the screen, thus allowing you to follow the execution of the script. Sometimes this is advantageous, but it can quickly get out of hand. Turning this feature off allows you to limit output to only the text that you specify, so that important information doesn't get lost in a sea of echoes.

Adding Logic to Shell Scripts

While printing "Hello World!" on the screen can provide endless hours of entertainment for the whole family, let's see if perhaps we can write a batch script to do something a bit more productive. At the same time, we'll learn some of the advanced logic available to batch scripts.

Since batch scripts can include any shell command, the possibilities are limitless. Don't believe me? Go to a command prompt and, after the C:\, simply type **help**. Quite a list, no? And that's just the tip of the iceberg. At the time of this writing, Microsoft hasn't provided a Resource Kit for Vista (they likely will in the future). However, you can find useful tools in the Vista Software Development Kit (SDK) at http://www.microsoft.com/downloads/details.aspx?familyid=C2B1E300-F358-4523-B479-F53D234CDCCF.

Any and all of these commands can be placed in a batch file to be invoked whenever necessary. That alone is worth the price of admission, in my opinion! May I enthrall you with a personal example? I have a batch file called Connect.cmd that stays on my Desktop. Although small (it contains only two lines), it really comes in handy:

```
nbtstat -R
ping myinternalserver
```

I use this script every time I travel and need to tunnel into my private network over the Internet. The first line purges and reloads my remote cache name table (causing my LMHOSTS file to be parsed, which contains the IP addresses of computers in my internal network). The second line attempts to make a connection based on an internal name (invoking my firewall-security login screen). It sure is a lot easier to simply double-click this file on my Desktop than to open a command-prompt window and type both lines.

The real power of scripting, however, is its ability to perform repetitive operations. In order to do this effectively, you need to be able to pass arguments to the script, store data in variables, perform comparisons and loops on this data, and control the flow of the script. Actually, quite a bit more is involved in order to fully realize the capabilities of shell scripts, but the following list should get you off to a good start.

Arguments

Command-line arguments are automatically passed to your script when you run it. All that is required is that you include the code to capture these arguments. These arguments are stored, in the order entered, in the numbered variables *%1*, *%2*, *%3*, and so on. The arguments on the command line are separated by a space. Here's an example:

```
C:\ShowArgs arg1 arg2 arg3
```

If you need to include more than one word as an argument, enclose the whole thing in quotes (just remember that the quotes themselves become part of the argument). You can strip out the quotes by referring to the variable as `%~x`:

```
C:\ShowArgs2 arg1 arg2 "This is argument 3"
```

Figure 28.2 shows these arguments being displayed in a script, both with and without the quotation marks removed.

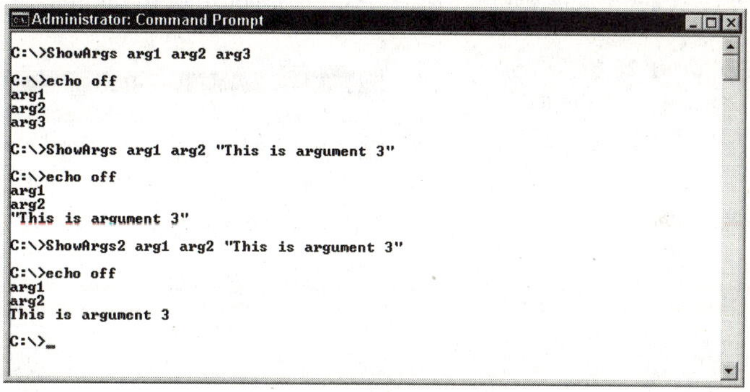

FIGURE 28.2
Passing arguments to batch scripts.

```
Administrator: Command Prompt
C:\>ShowArgs arg1 arg2 arg3

C:\>echo off
arg1
arg2
arg3

C:\>ShowArgs arg1 arg2 "This is argument 3"

C:\>echo off
arg1
arg2
"This is argument 3"

C:\>ShowArgs2 arg1 arg2 "This is argument 3"

C:\>echo off
arg1
arg2
This is argument 3

C:\>_
```

VARIABLES (THE *SET* COMMAND)

Quite often the need arises to create variables to store additional data. This can be accomplished by using the `set` command to create an environment variable. Just remember to reset the variable back to empty before the script terminates.

```
rem The following line creates an environment variable
rem named 'var1' and assigns it the value of 'MyData'
set var1=MyData
rem the following line resets the environment variable to nothing
set var1=
```

The `set` command can also solve numerical expressions and assign the data to a variable. The expression can include both real numbers or other variables. This is accomplished using the /A flag:

```
echo off
rem The following line adds the two command-line
rem arguments together and multiplies them by 10
set /A var1=10*(%1 + %2)
echo %var1%
Set var1=
```

When I run this script as `C:\ShowSet 5 4`, the script echoes 90 to the screen, just as it should. In addition to "standard" math, these numerical expressions can include logical shift; bitwise AND, OR, and XOR; and more.

You can even use the `set` command to take user input from the command line. The `/P` flag allows you to prompt the user for input:

```
echo off
rem The following line prompts the user to enter their name
set /P var1=Enter your first name:
echo %var1%
Set var1=
```

Figure 28.3 shows the output from both of the previous scripts.

FIGURE 28.3
Output from the set command.

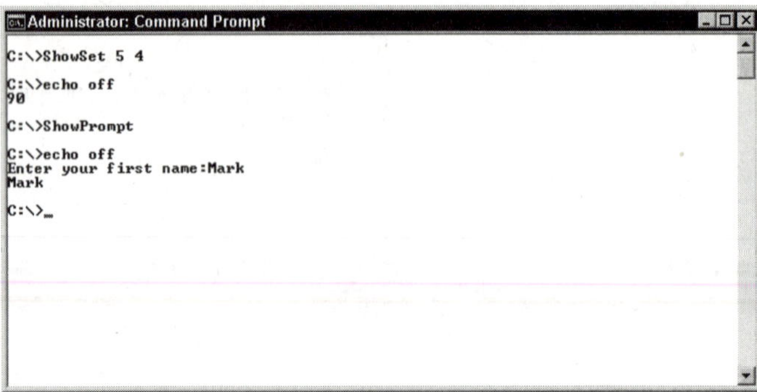

COMPARISONS AND LOOPS (THE *IF* AND *FOR* COMMANDS)

The real "logic" of a script is found in the ability to perform operations selectively. The `if` and `for` commands allow you to perform two very important logical operations:

- Ensure that a particular criterion has been met prior to executing a section of the script (`if`)
- Execute the same operation over and over using different criteria (`for`)

The `if` command allows you to check for the existence of a file, compare the values of two strings or sets of numbers, and more. This is particularly useful when you have several subroutines set up to perform different operations. Depending on the result of the `if` comparison, a particular subroutine can be called. When checking for files, the process is simple:

```
If exist file.tmp del file.tmp
```

Or you can use variables:

```
If exist %1 del %1
```

If necessary, you can specify the path, drive, and so on. The `if` command also evaluates a variable and determines script flow:

```
If %1==delete goto :DeleteFiles
```

The `for` command enables you to perform operations on each file in a set of files:

```
For %%i in (*.txt) do copy /a All.txt+%%i All.txt
```

I said earlier in this chapter that scripts allow you to do some things that are impossible to do using GUI tools; this is one of those times. The above code takes every TXT file in the current directory and copies them all into one big file called `All.txt`. You can't do that in Explorer!

The `/R` option allows you to specify a root directory and perform the specified operation on every file in that directory and all subdirectories.

The `/D` option performs the command specified on all directories (rather than files) in the current directory.

Finally, as with the `set` command, you can strip the quotes out of the variable (*%%~i*), expand it to a path only (*%%~pi*), and expand it to a file extension (*%%~xi*).

Flow Control (the *call* and *goto* Commands)

As your scripts become more complex, you need to maintain control over script execution. Remember, doing the same things over and over are what scripts do best. If you find yourself using the same code again and again, you can use `call` or `goto` to save a *lot* of typing. The `goto` command is pretty straightforward. It simply causes the script to jump to the specified label:

```
rem Just a hop, skip, and a goto
echo Hello There!
goto :goodbye
echo How are you?
:goodbye
echo Goodbye
```

In this script, `Hello There!` and `Goodbye` are the only things echoed to the screen. The `goto` statement caused us to skip over the line to echo `How are you?` When using `goto`, each jump is final. If you want to get back to where you were, you have to use another `goto` (and another label).

The `call` command allows you to either run another script (complete with arguments) or jump to a label in the current script and execute it as if it were a separate script. Once the code has executed to the end of the script (or the command `goto :EOF` has been executed), control is passed back to the line directly following the initial `call` command. Figure 28.4 shows the output from using `call...goto` for flow control.

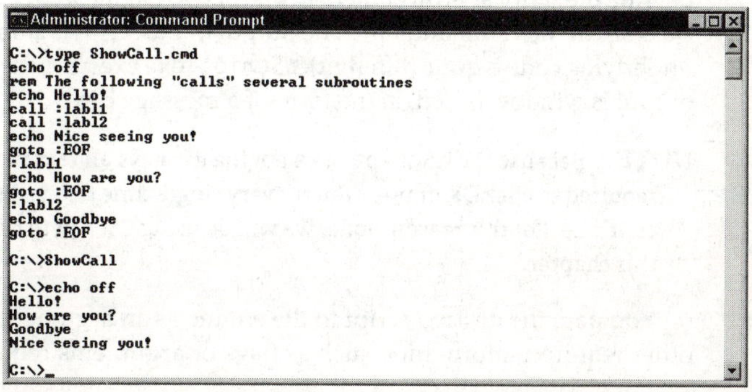

Figure 28.4
Using call...goto for flow control.

```
Administrator: Command Prompt
C:\>type ShowCall.cmd
echo off
rem The following "calls" several subroutines
echo Hello!
call :labl1
call :labl2
echo Nice seeing you!
goto :EOF
:labl1
echo How are you?
goto :EOF
:labl2
echo Goodbye
goto :EOF

C:\>ShowCall

C:\>echo off
Hello!
How are you?
Goodbye
Nice seeing you!

C:\>_
```

NOTE EOF is programming shorthand for End of File. You might also see BOF on occasion. If you guessed that it means Beginning of File, you are correct.

```
echo off
rem The following "calls" several subroutines
echo Hello!
call :labl1
call :labl2
echo Nice seeing you!
goto :EOF
:labl1
echo How are you?
goto :EOF
:labl2
echo Goodbye
goto :EOF
```

Using `call...goto :EOF` in this manner is very similar to using subs and functions in VBScript, which we discuss a bit later. It allows you to create procedures you can call over and over. To ensure proper execution, you merely need to place these subroutines at the end of your script and place a `goto :EOF` on the line just prior to the first routine.

Introduction to the Windows Scripting Host

While batch scripts can be very effective, there's no substitute for the power and flexibility of the Windows Scripting Host (WSH). The WSH is a COM-aware scripting environment (COM is Microsoft's Component Object Model) that not only allows you to create scripts in various languages, such as VBScript or JScript, it also enables you to extend the functionality of your scripts by directly accessing external COM components. (More on this topic in the "Advanced Concepts" section.)

The WScript and CScript Executables

A significant difference between shell scripts and WSH scripts is that the latter must be executed by passing the script as an argument to one of two engines: `CScript.exe` or `WScript.exe`. `CScript.exe` executes at the command line. The output of the script is similar to that of shell scripts (although the underlying code is quite different). `WScript.exe` executes the script within the Vista GUI. As such, all output is window based, in the form of a message box.

NOTE Because the `WScript.exe` engine displays all text in the form of a message box, you are required to click OK or press Enter every single time text is displayed before script execution will continue. For this reason alone, we will be using CScript to run the scripts we write for the rest of this chapter.

You pass the desired script to the engine as an argument on the command line, along with any other required information such as flags or arguments required by your script:

```
cscript helloworld.wsf
```

Scripts can also be started directly, either by typing their names at the command prompt or by double-clicking the script file from Windows Explorer.

WARNING Directly executing scripts causes them to run under `WScript.exe` (i.e., in the GUI). The only way to invoke scripts with CScript is to explicitly specify it when running the script.

Script File Languages

A key advantage to writing scripts for use in the WSH is the choice of scripting languages available. Vista includes scripting engines (not to be confused with the script host engines `WScript.exe` and `CScript.exe`) for the VBScript and JScript languages. Additional ActiveX scripting engines, created by third-party vendors, are available for other languages. For the purpose of consistency, we'll stick to VBScript for the scripts we feature here.

VBScript

As I've mentioned, VBScript is a subset of Visual Basic. While it derives its functionality from a full-featured development language, there are quite a few limitations. Rather than discuss them here, I'll highlight them as they become apparent in our scripts. However, I try to follow these rules religiously when writing scripts in VBScript:

Option Explicit This command should be placed at the beginning of the `<script>` section of every script you write. It forces you to declare variables before you use them. Variables are declared using the `dim` statement. This helps immensely when debugging. You'd be surprised how many times I've spent hours trying to figure out why a script isn't working properly, only to find that I misspelled a variable name at a critical stage.

Hungarian Notation When you declare a variable, it is customary to have the variable name include a prefix that indicates the type of data it will hold. While VBScript does not allow you to specify the data type of variables, using Hungarian Notation will help keep your scripts more readable and less confusing.

`strMyVariable` Indicates that the variable will hold a string of text.

`intMyVariable` or `iMyVariable` Indicates an integer (whole number) value.

`bMyVariable` Indicates a Boolean (True/False or Yes/No) value.

`objMyVariable` Indicates that the variable will contain an object. We discuss objects in the "Advanced Concepts" section.

There are others, but these will pretty much cover the variables we will be using in our scripts.

XML-based Scripts

WSH 2.0 introduced the capability to write scripts in XML format. Prior to this, all scripts were single language, with the script's file extension indicating the language: `.vbs` for VBScript, `.js` for JScript, and so on. By contrast, all WSH 2.0 scripts have the extension `.wsf`; they can contain multiple scripts, with each script having the capability of being in a different language. WSH 2.0 scripts offer some rather unique features not found in their WSH 1.0 counterparts.

Multiple jobs WSH 2.0 scripts can contain several jobs, each identified by a particular job ID. When a job is specified at runtime, only that job executes. If no job is specified, the first job is executed and the script terminates.

Multiple scripts Each job can contain multiple scripts, specified by the `<script>` tag. The language of the script is also determined by this tag, allowing a single script job to utilize scripts in any (or all) of the supported languages.

Objects A significant XML tag is `<object>`. It allows you to specify an object that will be used by the entire job. This allows you (among other things) to persist data between several scripts.

Runtime tags These XML tags allow you to specify the usage requirements of a script. They also allow you to name your command-line arguments, enabling you to enter them in random order when running the script. As your scripts become more complex, the ability to ask the script what it does and what data it is expecting becomes invaluable.

Editing Since the scripts are in XML format, you can use a standard XML editor to create and edit them. Most editors of this type perform basic text formatting and color coding to make the scripts easier to debug. Microsoft's FrontPage has an HTML view that you can use for this purpose.

Your First WSH 2.0 Script

In Listing 28.1, we have modified the `HelloWorld` script for use in the WSH. Figure 28.5 shows the output from this script when each job is executed individually.

LISTING 28.1: *HelloWorld.wsf*

```
<?xml version="1.0" ?>
<package>
  <comment>
  Hello World.wsf
  This script contains two jobs:
  Hello and Goodbye
  </comment>
  <job id="hello">
    <script language="VBScript">
    <![CDATA[
    'This script prints "Hello World!"
    WScript.Echo "Hello World!"
    ]]>
    </script>
  </job>
  <job id="goodbye">
    <script language="VBScript">
    <![CDATA[
    'This script prints "Goodbye World!"
    WScript.Echo "Goodbye World!"
    ]]>
    </script>
  </job>
</package>
```

FIGURE 28.5
Output from HelloWorld.wsf.

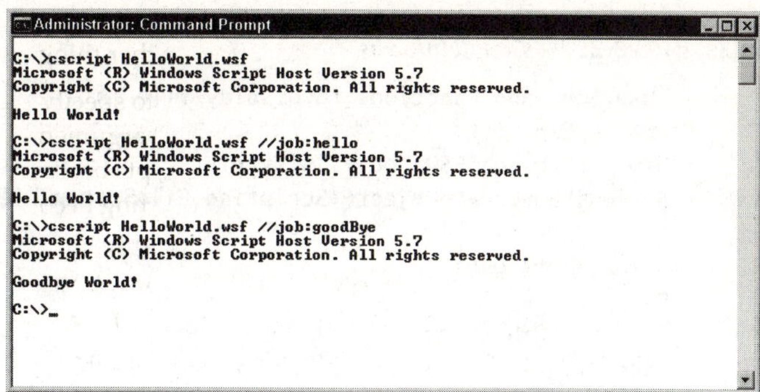

Listing 28.1 shows us quite a bit about XML-based scripts:

XML version The `<?xml?>` tag tells the script parser that this file needs to be strictly parsed (i.e., attribute names are case-sensitive, values are enclosed in quotes, etc.) By contrast, HTML files are loosely parsed. This tag is not required but may be necessary for your scripts to be displayed properly, depending on which XML editor you are using.

Package The `<package>` tag tells WSH that one or more jobs follows. It is optional if your script only has one job.

Comments (XML) The `<comment>` tag allows you to include comments that pertain to the entire script. You can still comment individual lines of code, which we will see next.

Job IDs The `<job id="xxx">` tag specifies the name of each job in the script. The ID is optional if the script contains only one job. Figure 28.5 shows how this job is specified on the command line. If no job is specified, the first job in the script is executed.

CDATA This tag causes the data contained within it to become opaque to the XML parser. It is necessary only when combined with the `<?xml?>` tag. Without this tag, logic from your script might "confuse" the XML parser. It might, for instance, read this script code, `If intA < intB`, and think that the "is less than" comparator is actually the beginning of an XML tag.

Comments (inline) You can add comments inline with your script code, as well. The keyword is the same as for shell scripts: `rem`. However, VBScript provides a shortcut—a single quote mark (').

Adding Logic to Your Scripts

The XML tags I just listed notwithstanding, the real meat of the script is what resides inside the `<script>` tag. This is where you *get stuff done*. One of the best ways to get that stuff done in a structured, logical manner is through the use of procedures: subs and functions. The difference between the two is that a function may return a value, but a sub does not. These are similar to the `call...goto :end` subroutines we used in our batch scripts, except that they are quite a bit more robust. For one thing, they don't execute unless they are called. You can place them anywhere in your script and rest assured they won't get in the way until you need them. Listing 28.2 uses both types of procedures to take a filename from the command line and display that file's properties. I've left out the "standard" XML in the interest of space. To use it in a `.wsf` file, simply place it between the `<script>...</script>` tags. It can also be saved as is to a `.vbs` file and used directly. Figure 28.6 shows the message box output by this script.

LISTING 28.2: *GetFileInfo.vbs*

```
'Use Subs and Functions to display file info
Option Explicit
Dim strArg, objFSO, objFile, strTxt
Set objFSO=CreateObject("Scripting.FileSystemObject")

strArg=GetArgs()
Display
Set objFSO=Nothing
WScript.Quit

Function GetArgs()
  If Wscript.Arguments.Count < 1 Then Wscript.Quit
  GetArgs=objFSO.GetAbsolutePathName (Wscript.Arguments(0))
End Function

Sub Display()
  'Display file information
  Set objFile = objFSO.GetFile(strArg)
  strTxt="Drive:" & objFile.Drive & vbCRLF
  strTxt=strTxt & "File name:" & objFile.Name & vbCRLF
  strTxt=strTxt & "Path:" & objFile.Path & vbCRLF
  strTxt=strTxt & "Size:" & objFile.Size & vbCRLF
  strTxt=strTxt & "Date created:" & objFile.DateCreated & vbCRLF
  strTxt=strTxt & "Date last modified:" & objFile.DateLastModified
  msgbox strTxt
End Sub
```

I threw a curve ball at you, did you notice? I used the FileSystemObject (FSO) to access information about the file specified on the command line. We discuss the FSO in more detail in the "Advanced Concepts" section. I included it in this script to give you a practical demonstration of subs and functions and, at the same time, show you how to perform a very useful task.

TIP **Indenting your code is important. Without it, tracing your logic can be a real pain! The general rule is to indent the code inside procedures, `If...Then` statements, and loops (`For...Next`, `Do...Loop`, etc.).**

I also used another common technique designed to keep my code readable. You'll notice in both the `GetArgs` function and the `Display` sub that I have some long lines of code. When viewed in Notepad (with Word Wrap off, of course), the line can be as long as you want (but it can make it hard to follow the logic.) On a page in a book, there is limited width to work with. In either case, when you want to break a long line of code, simply type a space followed by an underscore (_) and a carriage return. This tells the VBScript parser that the following line of code is a continuation of the previous line. It's also customary to indent the following line so you know it is part of the previous line.

Structuring your code into subs and functions not only keeps things organized, it also aids in debugging your code (something we all have to deal with, no matter how long we've been scripting).

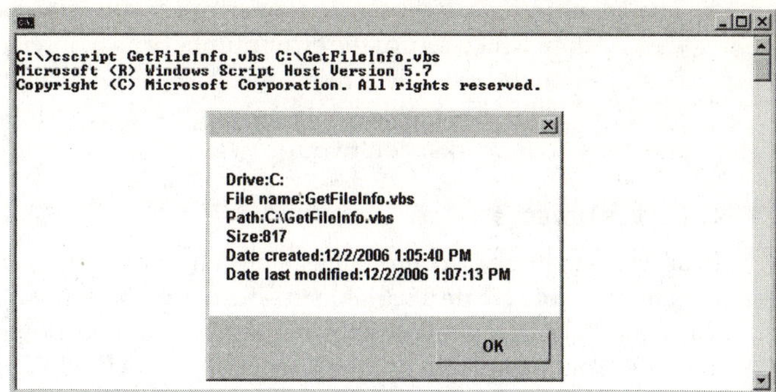
C:\>cscript GetFileInfo.vbs C:\GetFileInfo.vbs
Microsoft (R) Windows Script Host Version 5.7
Copyright (C) Microsoft Corporation. All rights reserved.
Drive:C:
File name:GetFileInfo.vbs
Path:C:\GetFileInfo.vbs
Size:817
Date created:12/2/2006 1:05:40 PM
Date last modified:12/2/2006 1:07:13 PM
OK

FIGURE 28.6 Detailed file information using the FileSystemObject.

Advanced Concepts

As discussed earlier, the WSH is a COM-aware scripting environment; COM provides a mechanism that allows for interoperability. It is the foundation of such things as object linking and embedding (OLE), a magic feature that allows you to drag a spreadsheet from Excel and drop it into a Word document. I could go into a bunch of boring details about the inner workings of COM, but space is limited and I'm sure you'd rather get to the good stuff. Suffice to say, COM allows us to access COM-enabled components (aka, objects) from our scripts. This section also discusses scheduling your scripts to run at a specified time.

Objects

Objects are COM-enabled components that can be accessed from within scripts. Components are a special kind of binary file. They are not executable on their own but can provide their functionality to COM environments via exposed interfaces. Two main interface types pertain to scripting:

Properties Properties hold data. This data can be as simple as a value that determines how the object works. A property may also store (persist) user data when necessary. Let's assume you have a component that allows you to perform symmetrical encryption on a file. This component would require a property, likely named "key," that specifies the key used to encrypt the file.

Methods Methods perform a function. In the encryption example I just used, the component would likely have a method called EncryptFile that, when executed, uses the key specified in the "key" property to encrypt the file. There's an example of both properties and methods in the "Callable Objects" section later in this section.

INTRINSIC OBJECTS

Intrinsic objects are built in to the Windows Scripting Host. Every time you execute a script, these objects are created and sit waiting for you to use them. They can be referenced directly, without ever having to be assigned to variables or created. You will likely use two intrinsic objects quite often:

The WScript object Used to print information on the screen (WScript.Echo) and to access command-line arguments (WScript.Arguments). Other methods include Quit and Sleep. Properties include Name, ScriptName, and Version. This object also contains several child objects that are not intrinsic but can be called to perform other functions such as editing the Registry or mapping network drives.

The Err object Allows you to trap errors in your scripts. Its main properties are Number and Description, which return the error number and a description of the error. It also has two methods: Clear and Raise. Clear resets the Err object. Raise actually allows you to cause an error to occur, which is invaluable when debugging your scripts. You want to make sure your error handling code works, don't you?

CALLABLE OBJECTS

In addition to intrinsic components, you can access external components, as well. To call a component, you simply create a variable to house it and execute the `CreateObject` method. Once this is done, the object is referenced via the assigned variable. Properties and methods are specified using a dot (`.`). For example, to call the `EncryptFile` method of the previously discussed encryption component, I would simply execute the following code:

```
Dim objMyObject
Set objMyObject=CreateObject("MyEncrypt.Encryption")
objMyObject.File="C:\MyConfidentialData.mdb"
objMyObject.Key="secret"
objMyObject.EncryptFile
```

Many callable objects come built in to Vista. One such object that you are likely to use extensively is the FileSystemObject. The FSO actually consists of a parent object and several child objects. Once you have created the "main" component, additional components are called by executing specific methods. This is demonstrated in Listing 28.2. Once I created the FileSystemObject, I simply executed the `GetFile` method `Set objFile=objFSO.GetFile(strArg)` to create an instance of the `File` object (a child object of the FSO).

Another useful built-in object is the Active Directory Services Interface. ADSI enables you to perform a gazillion useful tasks. Listing 28.3 in the next section demonstrates how to perform one very useful task with ADSI.

AUTOMATION

Certain applications can be utilized in the same manner as components. Indeed, the entire Office suite can be automated from within a script. In order to support automation, the application must have an exposed object model. This object model must be represented in a file called a *Type Library*. Type Libraries usually have the file extension of `.tlb` (the Office Type Libraries use `.olb` as their extension).

NOTE Each version of Office has a different set of type libraries. The type library names usually include the version number of Office that they're associated with, so you can easily tell one from another. However, since each version of Office has different type libraries, you'll have to update your scripts to match the version of Office that you use.

Utilizing the Type Library, you can, for example, start Word, create a new document, enter text, and save it. Or you can launch Internet Explorer and load a specified web page! Or you can read information from an Excel spreadsheet and process it with your script! Or well, you get the point.

Scheduling Scripts

A key advantage to using scripts is the ability to schedule them to run at any time. With the Task Scheduler, you can schedule a script to run every night, on a specific day every week, or on the next occurrence of a day and time. Scripts are scheduled using the `AT` command. You must remember to include all of the command-line arguments required by your script when scheduling it.

Scripts for Common Administrative Chores

No discussion of scripting would be complete without including a nice selection of sample scripts for you to use and learn from. The scripts included in this section cover different administrative tasks you are likely to perform quite frequently. Following each script, I've highlighted the salient code sections.

AddUser.wsf

This script (see Listing 28.3) uses the Active Directory Services Interface to automate adding users to your computer. It illustrates how useful ADSI can be even if you aren't part of a domain. You specify the username and password via the command-line arguments.

LISTING 28.3: *AddUser.wsf*

```
<?xml version="1.0" ?>
<package>
<comment>
AddUser.wsf
This script adds a user to the local computer
Using the ADSI interface
</comment>
  <job>
  <runtime>
    <description>
    Add a user to the local computer
    and place it in a group
    </description>

    <example>
    C:\cscript AddUser.wsf /uname:[username] /group:[group]
    </example>

    <named
      name="uname"
      helpstring="The username of the new user"
      type="string"
      required="true"
    />
    <named
      name="group"
      helpstring="The group in which to place the user"
      type="string"
      required="true"
    />
  </runtime>
  <script language="VBScript">
  <![CDATA[
  ' Add a user and place him/her into a group
  dim objADSI, objGroup, objUser, strUser, strGroup
```

```
    strGroup=WScript.Arguments.Named.Item("group")
    strUser=WScript.Arguments.Named.Item("uname")
    Set objADSI=GetObject("WinNT://mycomp,computer")
    Set objUser=objADSI.Create("User",strUser)
    objUser.SetInfo
    Set objGroup=GetObject("WinNT://mycomp/" & strGroup & ",group")
    objGroup.Add(objUser.ADsPath)
    objGroup.SetInfo
    ]]>
    </script>
    </job>
  </package>
```

The only "hard-coded" parameter in this script is `mycomp`, the name of the local computer. The script could be easily expanded to accept this information as an argument as well, making it capable of adding a user to an NT domain. The usage of the `<runtime>` tags is explained following the next script.

You'll notice that once I create the user, I still have to execute the `objUser.SetInfo` method. This finalizes the deal. Once that's done, I can pass that user information to the `objGroup.Add` method to place the user into the group. Lots of possibilities exist using this script as a starting point. You could even use the application automation we discussed earlier to add a list of users from a spreadsheet.

ChangeRole.wsf

This script (see Listing 28.4) uses the `WScript.Shell` object to make a change to the Registry—specifically, the Win32PrioritySeparation value. When you use the System applet to change your computer's performance option to adjust for Programs or Background Services, it utilizes this Registry entry. It's this value that determines the role of your computer: Server or Workstation. No, it can't convert Vista to Windows 2003 Server. What it does is determine how Vista handles background processes in relation to foreground processes. If you're using Vista as, say, an intranet server in your organization, specifying a Server role will increase its performance in this capacity.

LISTING 28.4: *ChangeRole.wsf*

```
<?xml version="1.0" ?>
<package>
<comment>
ChangeRole.wsf
This script updates the Win32PrioritySeparation
key in the registry to change the performance
of applications running in the foreground
</comment>
  <job>
  <runtime>
    <description>
    This script allows you to change the
```

```
    performance role of your computer
    </description>

    <example>
    C:\CScript ChangeFGPerf.wsf /Role:[W/S]
    </example>

    <named
    name="Role"
    helpstring="The role for the computer"
    type="string"
    required="true"
    />
  </runtime>

  <object id="objShell" progid="WScript.Shell"/>

  <script language="VBScript">
  <![CDATA[
  'Change foreground performance
  Option Explicit
  On Error Resume Next

  Dim strRole, strKey, strDataType
  strKey= _

"HKLM\System\CurrentControlSet\Control\PriorityControl\Win32PrioritySeparation"
  strDataType="REG_DWORD"
  strRole=UCase(WScript.Arguments.Named.Item("Role"))

  Select Case strRole
    Case "W"
    objShell.RegWrite strKey, 38, strDataType
    WScript.Echo "Priority Control has been set to optimize foreground
      applications."
    WScript.Quit

    Case "S"
    objShell.RegWrite strKey, 24, strDataType
    WScript.Echo "Priority Control has been set to optimize background services."
    WScript.Quit
  End Select

  WScript.Arguments.ShowUsage()
  WScript.Quit
  ]]>
  </script>
  </job>
</package>
```

This script uses the `<object>` tag to create an instance of the `WScript.Shell` object. The computer's role is specified via a `<named>` argument. It also includes the `<runtime>` tags `<description>` and `<example>`. These tags specify the information that is displayed whenever the script is run using incorrect (or no) arguments or when it's run using the `/?` argument. Figure 28.7 shows this output.

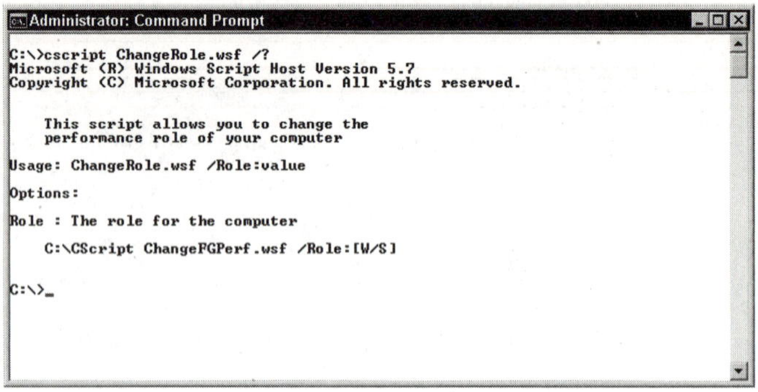

FIGURE 28.7
WSF scripts can display usage information describing how to run the script.

```
Administrator: Command Prompt
C:\>cscript ChangeRole.wsf /?
Microsoft (R) Windows Script Host Version 5.7
Copyright (C) Microsoft Corporation. All rights reserved.

    This script allows you to change the
    performance role of your computer

Usage: ChangeRole.wsf /Role:value

Options:

Role : The role for the computer

    C:\CScript ChangeFGPerf.wsf /Role:[W/S]

C:\>_
```

LogEvent.vbs

This script (see Listing 28.5) allows you to log an event to Vista's Application Event Log. While not terribly useful on its own, it can be invaluable when added to an existing script. As we discussed in the "Advanced Concepts" section, one of the joys of scripting is that you can schedule a script to run whenever you want it to. An event log entry noting whether or not the script completed successfully may be your only indication of potential trouble. Since you'll likely add this code to an existing script, I have put the script in the `.vbs` file format.

LISTING 28.5: *LogEvent.vbs*

```
'Logs an event to the XP application log
Option Explicit
Dim objShell
Set objShell=CreateObject("WScript.Shell")
objShell.LogEvent 0, "Script: " & WScript.ScriptName & " Completed Successfully."
```

We use the WSHShell object to write the log entry. The `LogEvent` method requires two arguments, with a third optional argument:

Event type In this script, we logged an event type of 0, which is a "Success." Other types include `Error`, `Warning`, `Information`, `Audit_Success`, and `Audit_Failure`.

Message This is the text that is entered into the event log. If a script error happened to trigger the LogEvent method, you would want this text to include that error information.

Target (optional) This allows you to log an event to another computer. This is useful for aggregating all of the logged events on every computer in your organization to one central location.

Figure 28.8 shows this event viewed in the application log of the Event Viewer.

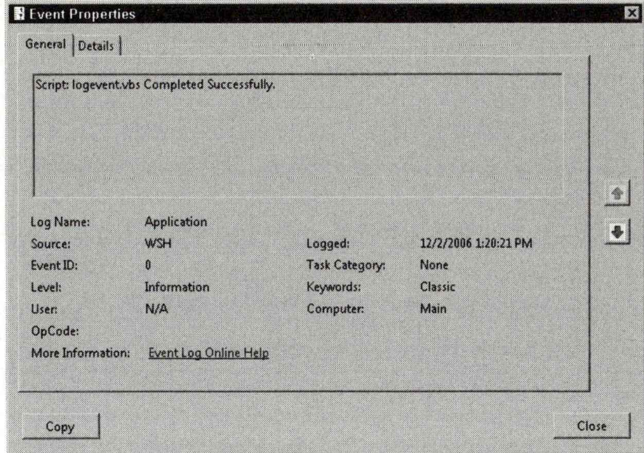

FIGURE 28.8
Log events to the application log.

Summary

We've crammed quite a bit into this chapter. I hope it's given you a good foundation of knowledge to build on, as well as provided some useful code that you can put to work right away.

Shell and WSH scripts allow you to automate some (or all!) of the redundant and not-so-redundant tasks that you face each day. Repetitive tasks can be accomplished much faster than is possible using the GUI tools. Scripts can be scheduled to run during off-hours and, through the use of COM objects, can perform some very powerful operations. For more information about WSH scripting, go to `http://msdn.microsoft.com/scripting`. It is my scripting home-away-from-home. You'll find downloads for the scripting engines, tutorials, a VBScript reference, and much more.

The next chapter will change gears and focus on yet another critical administrative responsibility: disaster prevention and recovery. Make sure to pay close attention, because even the most reliable networks can fail from time to time.

Chapter 29

Disaster Prevention and Recovery

Despite Vista's resilient nature, it still sometimes crashes. Some crashes are caused by random events: it really *is* possible for a cosmic ray to hit a critical part of a chip and freeze up a PC (and, in that case, there's not much to do other than to turn the machine off and then back on). But if you find Vista crashing *regularly*, you have to do something about it, because it's not supposed to. Of course, to do something effective about system crashes, you'll need a method, and that's what this chapter offers.

I'll avoid trotting out all the old an-ounce-of-prevention bromides (though there *is* a lot of truth to those old saws). I start off with a discussion of preventing trouble in the first place and then look at techniques you can use to gather the information needed to ascertain, attack, and fix problems that may sooner or later arise.

- Avoiding Vista crashes
- Defragmenting files, cleaning up disks, and checking disks
- Restoring a configuration
- Using the Recovery Environment
- Using Vista's built-in diagnostics
- Using the Driver Verifier
- Using System File Checker
- Forcing a core dump
- Backing up and restoring

Vista: What's New?

Microsoft has put a lot of work into making Vista more reliable than previous versions of Windows. Some of these changes are quite noticeable to everyone that uses the computer. For example, the Previous Version feature makes it significantly easier to recover from an accidental overwrite of a file. This feature is also incredibly easy to use, which means that you won't spend hours trying to fix a seemingly simple problem.

You'll also find that the Recovery Console has changed. It's now called the Recovery Environment and you can use it to perform memory diagnostics, as well as record complete PC backups and perform other recovery tasks. Vista provides access to this feature in a number of ways. One way to begin a recovery is during startup. However, you can also run the Vista Setup application to gain access to the recovery features. As with previous versions of Windows, you can also gain access to a command prompt from the Recovery Environment, which means you literally have access to all of the command-line utilities you normally use to maintain the system.

The number of built-in diagnostics has also improved considerably. You could always check your hard drive with relative ease. However, you can now perform one of the tasks that used to require a specialized application—a RAM diagnostic. As systems gain increasingly more RAM, the probabilities of a particular piece of RAM breaking also increase. Performing RAM checks can reduce the probability that a RAM error will cause unexpected application behavior. Finally, you can check your network for problems with greater ease.

The one area of disappointment in Vista is system backup. The NT Backup utility provided with previous versions of Windows was fairly complete, but it lacked a few key features, such as the ability to back up to a CD/DVD. The Vista backup, WBAdmin, is significantly less functional. Unlike NT Backup, you can't even choose what to backup on a system when working with the GUI utility. It's as if Microsoft took a step back and tried to figure out the least functional backup they could provide. I'd recommend getting a third-party backup program because you're going to be disappointed by the backup functionality that Vista provides. Yes, the backup now runs automatically and you can backup to a CD/DVD, but the new backup application really doesn't serve the user very well.

If you liked the other tools that Windows provided in the past, such as the Disk Defragmenter, you'll find the Vista alternatives disappointing. In the past, you could select the drive to defragment and monitor its progress. Vista simply provides you with a button for defragmenting and doesn't bother to tell you what is defragmented. You can't monitor the progress. The whole idea seems to make Vista absurdly simple to work with, but at the significant cost of lost flexibility. I see a big opportunity for third-party developers who want to give users back the flexibility they had in the past.

Avoiding Vista Crashes

You can keep Vista trouble at bay in a few basic ways:

- Buy reliable hardware, preferably hardware that is on the Vista Windows Catalog.
- Protect the machine from environmental hazards, most notably substandard electric power.
- Install Vista properly, or, in some cases, *re*install Vista properly.
- Obtain the latest Microsoft-certified drivers for your hardware.
- Always shut down Vista properly.
- Back up your hard disk.
- Be sure you have the proper security level for whatever function you're performing.

Let's look quickly at each of these.

Buy Reliable Hardware

One of the things that cause instability for *any* PC operating system is the hardware that the operating system must sit atop. PCs made by IBM were once the standard and, right or wrong, "PC-compatible" meant that they "did the same thing that the IBM machines did, including the bugs." Nowadays, there *is* no standard, and so no two brands of computers work exactly the same way.

A major point of difference between makes and models of computers is the expansion bus, the slots on a PC motherboard into which you plug expansion cards such as video boards, sound cards, and network boards. Because these slots must accommodate the connectors on the bottom of the expansion cards, the person who designs the motherboard and the person who designs the expansion card must agree on how that interface should work; the interface must be *standard*.

That's where the problem arises. A common PC interface standard is called the Industry Standard Architecture, or ISA, board. The *problem* with the ISA standard is that it's not really a standard; there's no carved-in-stone specification for it, just an informal industry consensus. The result is that if you take a "standard" ISA board and plug it into a "standard" ISA slot, it may not work perfectly 100 percent of the time. It'll probably work most of the time, but some small percentage of the time, data may get lost passing between the expansion card and the motherboard. If that data is crucial, the PC may lock up.

What can Vista do about that? In other words, how can an operating system that wants to be stable work around an inherently unstable hardware platform? To a certain extent, there's nothing that the operating system can do, and some crashes are unavoidable. But some ISA boards are designed better than others, and only experimentation will separate the good from the bad. Further, the operating system can incorporate drivers for the hardware that are a bit more "forgiving." By forgiving, I mean that the driver is built to *anticipate* a certain number of hardware errors and to simply step around them.

"Aha!" you cry. "If they can make drivers 'forgiving,' why don't they *always* do that?" Well, for one thing, it's harder to write such drivers. For another, most driver authors resent writing drivers to support hardware that isn't really standard. Talk to them for a bit, and they start muttering about hitting moving targets and the like. Finally, and most important, adding forgiveness to a driver *slows it down*, and as all PC speed freaks know, slow is bad.

Again, what can you do about it? For one thing, stay as far away from ISA boards as you can. Yes, they're the most common and the cheapest boards, but there's usually a reason why cheap things are cheap.

TIP **Buy systems that have PCI slots (at least three slots), and use only PCI boards Generally speaking, you can find motherboards that still include one or two ISA slots if you look hard, but you'll want to steer clear of them. It's better to replace any ancient piece of ISA hardware than to keep using it in your new system.**

The Peripheral Component Interconnect (PCI), Extended Industry Standard Architecture (EISA), MicroChannel Architecture (MCA), and Accelerated Graphics Port (AGP) buses were all designed by a central authority that published specifications, which, if followed, yield an expansion board that works predictably. That's why I strongly recommend staying with those expansion slot types. In reality, however, you won't find many of today's systems with the MCA bus; it's ancient history. Again, you'll find EISA slots on many multiprocessor systems, but not many EISA expansion boards are on the market. PCI has been the de facto standard for several years. AGP is a very common standard for video adapters, and FireWire (IEEE 1328) and USB are fast and readily available.

Vista users will also probably want to get a system that uses PCI Express for the graphics card. PCI Express provides higher graphics performance, which is a plus for Vista. Some motherboards that support PCI Express also provide support for Scalable Link Interface (SLI), a technology that lets you place to graphics adapters in one system and use them in tandem. An SLI configuration provides the fastest graphics available on a PC today, but the graphics adapters tend to be expensive, and you need a special motherboard and power supply to support SLI. You can learn more about these various bus technologies and their differences in the ARS technical article at `http://arstechnica.com/articles/paedia/hardware/pcie.ars/1`.

Guard against Environmental Hazards

A decent number of PCs die each year because they get bad power. It's not something you can easily detect; it just happens. But you can prevent it.

PC power problems fall into three categories:

- Incorrect voltage—usually too low. Low voltage is called a voltage sag or brownout.
- Loss of power altogether.
- Extremely brief (under one 1/100 of a second) increases in voltage and power, called surges or spikes.

Low voltage causes your PC's power supply to try to compensate by drawing more current, which heats up the PC components and shortens their lives. You change voltage on an electrical circuit with a device called a transformer. A transformer that's smart enough to know whether to move the voltage up or down is called a *voltage regulator*, and for most PC applications, the name of the device that contains a voltage regulator is a *power conditioner*.

Loss of power altogether requires a battery of some kind. The two kinds of battery backup are *standby power supply* (*SPS*) and *uninterruptible power supply* (*UPS*). An SPS has a battery that "wakes up," so to speak, when power to the PC is interrupted. Because an SPS doesn't always wake up fast enough, you need an SPS with a switching time (wake-up time) of 4 milliseconds or less. A UPS, in contrast, is always supplying power from the battery (while refilling it, of course) and so has no switching time. Clever marketers call their SPSs "UPSs." If in doubt, ask about the switching time.

Surges and spikes can be brushed aside by a power conditioner. Do *not* buy a surge protector, a cheap device that does little to protect you from power problems. A surge protector is based on a device called a Metal Oxide Varistor (MOV), which is a "kamikaze" device: After you get a little surge, the MOV stops the surge but dies in the process. The *next* surge goes through without trouble.

NOTE To read more about PC power problems and solutions, pick up the latest edition of my book *The Complete PC Upgrade and Maintenance Guide*, 16th Edition (Sybex, 2005).

Install Vista Properly

A look back at Chapter 2 will remind you that you've got a lot of choices to make when you install Vista. If you end up with a bad installation, reinstall Vista or your Vista applications. If you reinstall a piece of software, however, don't install it on top of an existing installation; that often doesn't wipe the old installation clean. Before reinstalling any software, remove it completely and check the Registry for any leftover pieces.

In Chapter 2, I tell you how to upgrade from an earlier version of Windows or NT, but the truth is, the most stable and reliable installations are built from the ground up. This usually means installing on a freshly formatted hard drive and then installing applications. If you simply must perform an upgrade, be sure to disable all third-party services. Heck, disable all the services you can easily live without for a while. The less that Setup has to worry about, the fewer things that can go wrong.

Obtain Tested, Certified Drivers for Your Hardware

Although Vista was a solidly built system, it does have one fairly large Achilles' heel (or maybe a whole Achilles' foot): drivers. During the development of Vista, Microsoft took a hard line with hardware vendors, insisting that they write "good" drivers that would pass Microsoft certification. In some cases, you may even see a warning message if you attempt to install new hardware or software with drivers that aren't certified. Take this message to heart. A poorly functioning driver can be difficult to track down and can crash your system.

Always Shut Down Vista Properly

Most people seem to know this by now, but it's worth repeating that you should *shut down Vista properly*. Don't just turn off the computer; choose Start and then Turn Off Computer.

If you don't do that, not only do you stand to lose data from your applications, but you may damage the operating system. If you are using only NTFS-formatted disks, the damage will be less than it would be with a FAT disk (NTFS incorporates fault-tolerant features), but you could lose data nevertheless.

Back Up Your Disk Regularly

I shouldn't have to say this, but . . .

The hard disks in most people's PCs aren't backed up. And there are as many excuses for this as there are PCs. But there's no reason for it, at least not anymore. Iomega's Zip drives are a terrific way to quickly and easily save up to 750MB of data onto a thing that *looks* like a floppy but that stores much more data. Tape drives get cheaper all the time. And I just can't say enough about the value of CD-ROM and DVD burners for backups.

Vista even comes with its own backup program that I'll discuss later in this chapter. This very limited program does perform automatic background backups of critical Windows files for you. Unlike the NT Backup program provided in previous versions of Windows, the Vista backup program is extremely limited and inflexible. Even so, there's no excuse *not* to back your stuff up.

Be Sure You're Authorized to Do Something before Doing It

As you've read elsewhere in this book, living with Vista means thinking differently because you're now living in a more secure world. That means that you may run into a kind of trouble fairly new to PC users—the inability to do a particular function on your system.

For example, imagine that when someone logs on to your network, they run a logon batch script that synchronizes their PC's clock with the time on the server; the command is `net time\\`*servername/set/yes*. When you log on to a Vista workstation as a simple domain user, you get an error indicating that you don't have the right to set the PC's clock.

Now, if you're a network techie, you'd likely understand this error message and where it comes from—again, the account you used to log on is too low on the network's totem pole, so to speak. But for a regular, less-technical user, it could be somewhat disconcerting.

In general, remember that a Vista computer runs different kinds of user accounts—administrators, users, power users, and so on. You'll make your life easiest if you remember to log on as an administrator for that particular workstation before trying to change permissions on files or do anything with the Administrative Tools.

An Ounce of Prevention

Before I get into what you can do to fix Vista before it breaks, I want to point you toward some tools you can use from time to time that might well prevent some common, everyday problems: Disk Defragmenter, Disk Cleanup, and Check Disk.

Defragmenting Files

As files on your computer grow, they won't fit back into their original locations on your hard disk, so Vista divides the files into pieces and spreads the files over several different disk locations. This is how Windows is designed to work and how the system juggles constantly changing file sizes. An unfortunate side effect is that as a file is divided into more and more pieces, it takes longer and longer for your system to find and retrieve the whole file when you open it. A disk defragmenter keeps your hard disk performance at its peak by finding fragmented files on your system and rewriting them into contiguous, continuous areas of your hard disk.

Disk Defragmenter works behind the scenes; although the files on your hard disk have actually been moved, you'll still find them in the same folders. To start defragmenting your hard drive, choose Start ➤ All Programs ➤ Accessories ➤ System Tools ➤ Disk Defragmenter. You'll see a Disk Defragmenter display where you can choose between manual and automatic defragmentation. Click Defragment now. Vista will start degragmenting your hard drive. Unlike previous versions of Windows, you only have one option for stopping Disk Defragmenter once you start it—clicking Cancel Defragmentation, which stops the process completely.

TIP You can certainly perform other work on the computer while Disk Defragmenter is running, but the response time will be much slower, and Disk Defragmenter will start over each time you write a file to your hard disk. The best time to run Disk Defragmenter is while you're out for lunch or after you've finished your work for the day.

Vista also makes it possible to defragment your drive automatically at a specific time. To use this feature, open the defragmenter as usual by choosing Start ➤ All Programs ➤ Accessories ➤ System Tools ➤ Disk Defragmenter. Check Run on a schedule (recommended). If you want to change the schedule, click Modify schedule. You'll see a Disk Defragmenter: Modify Schedule dialog box. Choose the defragmentation interval in the How often field (daily, weekly, or monthly). Select a day to perform the defragmentation in the What day field when using weekly or monthly defragmentation. Select a time to perform the defragmentation (when the machine is on, but not in use) in the What time field. Click OK twice to finish configuring the automatic defragmentation.

NOTE You can gain some defragmentation flexibility by using the Defrag utility. The Defrag utility lets you choose the volume to defragment. It's also possible to simply analyze the drive using the `-a` command-line switch or perform a partial (quick) defragmentation using the `-r` command-line switch. To learn more about this utility, open a command prompt with administrator privileges, type **`Defrag /?`**, and press Enter. You'll see a complete list of command-line switches provided by this utility. The Defrag utility in Vista isn't the same as the Defrag utility provided with previous versions of Windows. Make sure you update any batch files you have to reflect the new command-line switches.

Cleaning Up Disks

Have you ever wished there was some way you could just wave a magic wand and get rid of all the unused or temporary files that take up space on your hard disk? Well, there is such a tool, and it's called Disk Cleanup. Choose Start ➤ All Programs ➤ Accessories ➤ System Tools ➤ Disk Cleanup to open the Select Drive dialog box. Select My files only or Files from all users on this computer. Disk Cleanup will perform some background tasks at this point and then display a Disk Cleanup: Drive Selection dialog box. Choose the drive you want to work with, and click OK to open the Disk Cleanup dialog box shown in Figure 29.1.

You'll only see the Disk Cleanup tab when you choose to clean up your own files. The More Options tab appears when you choose the Files from all users on this computer option. The Disk Cleanup dialog box has these tabs:

Disk Cleanup Displays the amount of free space that could be recovered by deleting temporary files in certain categories or by emptying the Recycle Bin on your Desktop. As you check the boxes to delete files, a running counter tells you how much disk space will be recovered.

More Options Lets you remove applications or Windows components that you don't use. In the Windows Components section, click the Clean Up button to start the Windows Components Wizard, which you can use to add or remove components. In the Installed Programs section, click the Clean Up button to open the Add or Remove Programs dialog box and change or remove a program. In the System Restore section, click the Clean Up button to remove all but the most recent restore point. I'll talk about System Restore later in this chapter.

FIGURE 29.1
The Disk Cleanup dialog box.

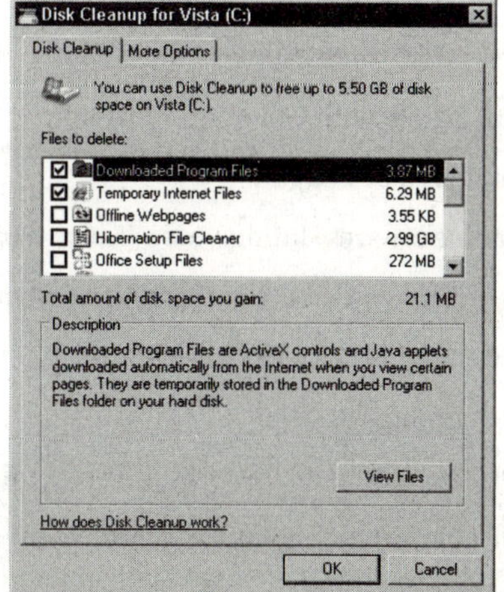

Checking Disks for Errors

Another disk-management task you might have to perform from time to time is to check a hard disk for errors, and Vista includes a tool for checking FAT32 volumes. All NTFS volumes log file transactions and replace bad clusters automatically. To check out a hard disk, open Explorer or My Computer, right-click the disk you want to work with, and then choose Properties from the context menu. In the Tools tab, click the Check Now button to open the Check Disk dialog box, which contains these two options:

- Automatically Fix File System Errors
- Scan For and Attempt Recovery of Bad Sectors

Check the appropriate boxes, and then click Start to begin scanning the disk. A status bar across the bottom of the Check Disk dialog box indicates the progress of the tests, and you'll see a message when the disk check is complete.

Restoring a Configuration

Sometimes, no matter how vigilant you've been, mistakes happen or something just goes wrong, and you need to fix your system. These fixes range from easy to horrific.

One thing that you *could* do is reinstall Vista, a time-consuming process. But not only do you have to do the installation process itself, you have to set up all services and user accounts again, and this gets very boring or frustrating very quickly. Fortunately, there are other ways to fix your setup when something's gone wrong.

Using the Last Known Good Configuration

If you've changed your system so that it can't boot Vista, one of these better solutions can be seen while you're rebooting. If you watch while your machine's booting up, you'll see a message on a black screen that says "For troubleshooting and advanced startup options for Vista, press F8." If you press the F8 key, you'll see a menu with the following choices:

- Safe Mode
- Safe Mode with Networking
- Safe Mode with Command Prompt
- Enable Boot Logging
- Enable low-resolution video (640 × 480)
- Last Known Good Configuration (advanced)
- Directory Services Restore Mode
- Debugging Mode
- Disable automatic restart on system failure
- Disable Driver Signature Enforcement
- Start Windows Normally

These options cover most of the possible troubleshooting scenarios involving the boot process. If your machine won't boot, you probably don't want to use the current configuration; so choose the Last Known Good Configuration. This should make your machine bootable.

NOTE The Directory Services Restore Mode is for domain controllers only. In other words, you won't use this option in Vista. Nothing bad will happen if you accidentally select it, but since Vista isn't a domain controller, you'll find that the Directory Services Restore Mode has nothing special to offer.

When Does (and Doesn't) It Work?

What are the criteria for a configuration being the Last Known Good one? To qualify, a configuration must not have produced any critical errors involving a driver or a system file, and a user must have been able to log on to the system at least once.

The Last Known Good Configuration can't always help you. If any of the following are true, you'll have to use another solution:

- You made a change more than one successful boot ago and want to restore things as they were before the change.
- The information that you want to change isn't related to control-set information—user profiles and file permissions fall into the category of information that can't be changed with the Last Known Good Configuration item.
- The system boots, a user logs on, and then the system hangs.
- You change your video driver to an incompatible driver, restart the system, and then log on with the bad driver (you can still type, even if you can't see).

NOTE The key to getting Last Known Good to work is knowing what constitutes a *successful logon.* A successful logon occurs when you've entered your username and password and *have been authenticated.* Ever seen the message that a domain controller couldn't be found but you've been logged on with cached credentials? Vista considers that a successful logon. If you suspect, even for a moment, that the change you made might not work, don't log on. Let the computer sit at the Ctrl+Alt+Del prompt for a couple of minutes. If you don't receive any messages about failed services, then log on.

Using System Restore

If Vista has been working correctly but you suddenly, inexplicably can't boot into Windows, you can use System Restore. In a nutshell, System Restore creates restore points, such as the following:

- System checkpoints, which are scheduled and created by your computer
- Manual restore points, which you create
- Installation restore points, which are automatically created when you install certain programs

You use these restore points to revert to a system configuration that was working properly. (System Restore doesn't recover changes to personal data files.) You can change some System Restore settings, and we'll look at how to do that next. First, though, let's walk through a typical scenario.

You turn on your computer, Vista starts to boot, but then just sits at the opening screen, doing nothing. You turn off your computer and turn it back on, and the same thing happens again. Turn your computer off again, turn it back on, and this time boot into Safe Mode, as described in the previous section.

After Safe Mode loads, you'll see a help window that displays all kinds of options for correcting problems in Vista. Figure 29.2 shows a typical help window. You can see the largest number of options by clicking the Diagnostic tools to use in safe mode link. To start working with System Restore, click the Click to open System Restore link in the Diagnostic tools to use in safe mode window.

When the System Restore dialog box opens, you'll see two options: Recommended restore and Choose a different restore point. Normally, if you're trying to recover from an error that occurred during the last boot, you'll want to use the Recommended restore option. However, if the problem is minor and you didn't notice it immediately, you'll want to select the Choose a different restore point option instead. When you click Next, you'll see a list of restore points for your system. The restore points will tell you what action occurred to create the restore point, such as installing an application or a system scheduled restore point. Choose the restore point you want to use and click Next.

TIP Sometimes all you need to do to get your system back in shape is to boot into Safe Mode and then restart the system. Safe Mode loads only a minimal number of drivers, thus simplifying the boot process.

If you are ready to restore, click Next. When the restoration is complete, you'll see a message to that effect. Vista will restart, using the settings in the restore point you selected. With a bit of luck, everything will be working properly.

NOTE During the restoration process, don't fiddle with your computer. Let Windows do its thing.

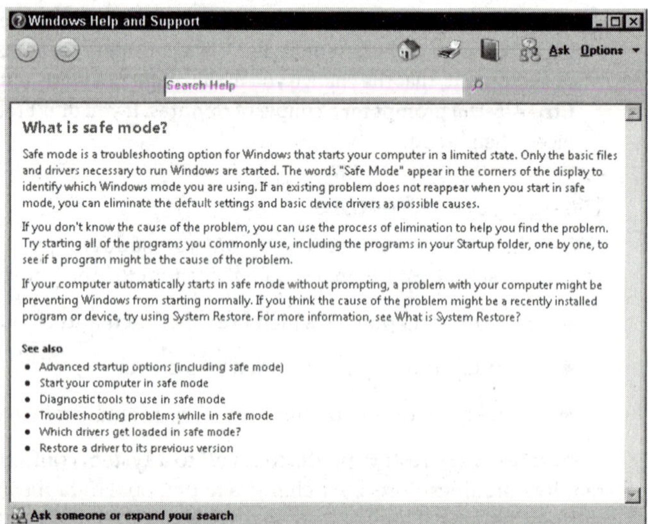

FIGURE 29.2
Vista provides quick access to a number of tools you can use to fix problems.

CREATING YOUR OWN RESTORE POINTS

You can also run System Restore from a working Vista system and use System Restore to create your own restore point. To open System Restore, choose Start ➤ All Programs ➤ Accessories ➤ System Tools ➤ System Restore. At first, it might appear that this dialog box only allows you restore the system. However, when you click the open System Protection link, you'll see the System Protection tab of the System Properties dialog box as shown in Figure 29.3.

Notice that only the Vista boot drive is checked in Figure 29.3. By default, Vista only creates restore points for the boot drive. To disable System Restore, simply remove all of the checks from the hard drives. Protect additional hard drives by checking that drive. When you want to create the restore point, click Create. You'll see a System Protection dialog box where you must type a description of the restore point. Type a description and click Create. It's important that you type a description that you'll recognize later when you need to restore the system. After Vista creates the restore point, you'll see a success dialog box. Click OK to clear the success dialog box.

NOTE Unlike previous versions of Windows, Vista doesn't allow you to control the amount of disk space that System Restore uses. The amount of space required depends on the amount of free disk space on your system. As disk space decreases, so does the number of restore points you can create. System Restore requires a minimum of 300MB for each hard drive you want to protect. This feature won't work on hard drives smaller than 1GB. As the hard drive begins to fill, System Restore removes older restore points automatically. System Restore uses up to 15 percent of your hard drive for restore points.

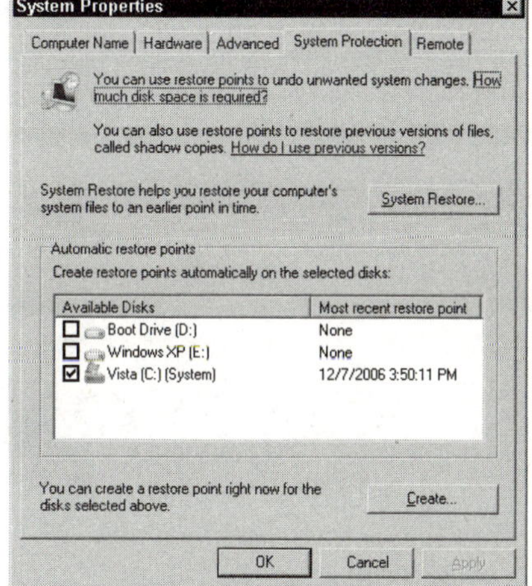

FIGURE 29.3
The System Protection tab determines what Vista protects when you create a restore point.

Restoring a Single File Using a Previous Version

Every time you create a restore point of your hard drive, Vista saves shadow copies of your files. The shadow copies include all of your data files. Consequently, you can protect your data by creating a restore point before you make any changes. You make changes to the file as you normally do, but the shadow copy of the file remains.

If you decide later that you don't want to retain the modified version of your file, you can restore it to the same state it was in when you created the restore point. The file will appear as if nothing had happened. To restore the previous version of the file, follow these steps.

1. Right-click the file and choose Properties. You'll see the file's Properties dialog box.
2. Select the Previous Versions tab and you'll see a list of previous versions similar to the list shown in Figure 29.4.
3. Highlight the previous version you think you want to restore. At this point, you have three options:

   Open Lets you view the contents of the file without actually restoring it. Use this feature when you aren't sure which version to restore.

Copy Lets you create a copy of the file to a different location. The copy reflects the shadow copy's content, not the current file content.

Restore Deletes the current version of the file and copies the shadow copy of the file in its place. This option restores the original version. Any changes you made to the file are lost.

4. Click OK to close the Properties dialog box.

FIGURE 29.4
Restore points save your personal data as well as the system state.

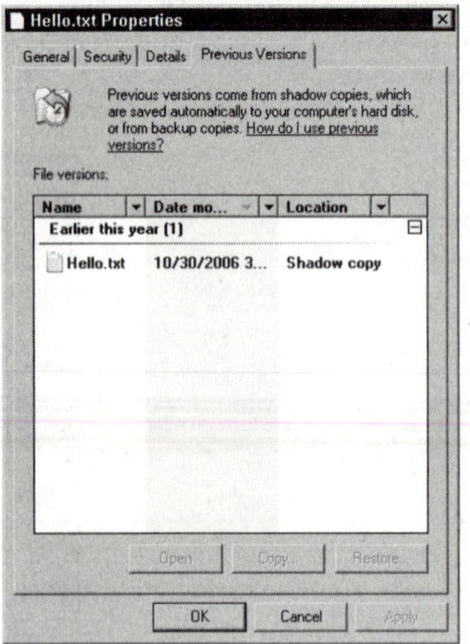

Using the Recovery Environment

Unlike previous versions of Windows, Vista uses a Recovery Environment. The Recovery Console is no longer available as a repair option. This environment is available when you boot from the Vista DVD. Unlike previous versions of Windows, you don't have to install the Recovery Environment or do anything special to use it. The following steps display the recovery environment.

1. Insert the Vista DVD and boot from it. You'll see a loading file screen, and then the installation screen appears.
2. Select your keyboard layout, language, and other particulars. Click Next. You'll see an installation screen.
3. Click the Repair your computer link. You'll see the System Recover Options dialog box. Setup searches for valid installations and displays them in the operating system list.
4. Highlight the installation you want to repair, and then click Next. Setup displays a number of repair options including:

   Startup Repair Fixes problems with the startup sequence for Vista.

   System Restore Repairs any damage to the Vista system files by using a restore point. The restore point works as normal, so you might find changes to your applications and user settings as well.

Windows Complete PC Restore Uses a backup to restore everything on the PC including the Vista system files, your applications, and user settings.

Windows Memory Diagnostic Tool Performs a diagnostic of the system memory to determine whether there are any problems with it.

Command Prompt Displays a command prompt so that you can perform low-level repairs and use administrator tools to perform additional diagnostics.

The Recovery Environment includes a wealth of new tools that make it easier to perform diagnostics on your system, as well as all of the old favorites. The following sections describe the Recovery Environment and tell you how to use it.

Performing a Startup Repair

A startup repair performs checks on the system to ensure it can boot properly. To use this feature, click Startup Repair. Vista performs the diagnostics automatically and tells you the result. You don't have to do anything special to perform the required repairs—everything is automatic. If you want to see what tests Vista ran, click the View diagnostics and repair details link. You'll see the Startup Repair dialog box, which contains a complete listing of the tests and their results.

Performing a System Restore

A system restore repairs damage to the Vista system files by using a restore point to modify the system to a known good state. Obviously, using a restore point can also affect applications and your user settings because the system returns to that previous condition. Consequently, when you use this feature, you might find that applications are missing, don't have the required settings, or simply don't work the same as when you booted Vista last. The following steps help you perform a system restore.

1. Click System Restore. You see the System Restore wizard.
2. Click Next. You'll see the Choose a system restore point dialog box.
3. Highlight the restore point you want to use (newer is usually better, unless the new restore points have problems). Click Next. You'll see a Confirm disks to restore dialog box.
4. Place a check mark next to each of the drives you want to restore. You must restore the system drives—Vista doesn't provide a choice when it comes to the system drive.
5. Click Next. You'll see a Confirm your restore point dialog box.
6. Click Finish. Vista performs the restoration for you.

Performing a Complete PC Restore

A complete PC restore uses a backup to restore the files on your system. You can use this option when the system has suffered major damage. For example, you could use this option to return your hard drive to a previrus state should you get attacked by a virus. Of course, you'll lose any data that you changed since the lack backup, so consistent and frequent backups are a plus when using this feature. This feature will even let you recover from a failed hard drive very quickly. The following steps describe how to perform a complete PC restore.

1. Click Windows Complete Restore. You'll see the Windows Complete PC Restore dialog box. This dialog box contains two options. The first lets you use the most current backup to

restore your hard drive. The second lets you select from any backup that the Windows Recovery Environment can access.

2. Select the recommended backup or choose to restore a specific backup. If you choose to restore a specific backup, you need to follow the additional steps listed here.

   1. Click Next. You'll see the Select the location of the backup dialog box. This dialog box lists all of the locations that the Recovery Environment can find with backups. You'll find that you can't access backup DVDs unless you have two DVD drives on your system and that network drives are likewise inaccessible.

   2. Highlight a location. Click Next. You'll see the Select the backup to restore dialog box.

   3. Highlight the backup you want to restore.

3. Click next. At this point, you'll see a dialog box that contains the selected backup and the two options described here:

   Format and repartition disks This option will repartition the disk and then format it before it begins the restore process. You won't be able to set the partition size or formatting because the Recovery Environment uses the same partitioning and formatting found with the backup. This option is a perfect way to set up your new hard drive after a hard drive failure.

   Only restore system disks The backup may contain data from any number of disks on your system. This option tells the Recovery Environment to restore the system disk only. It ignores any data drives that appear as part of the backup.

4. Click Finish. The Recovery Environment begins the restore process.

Using the Windows Memory Diagnostic Tool

The Windows Memory Diagnostic Tool performs a comprehensive test of your system memory. This test can require a considerable amount of time to complete, so you don't want to run it unless you really have time to wait for it to complete. The actual completion time depends on your system. I have a relatively fast system with 3GB of RAM and the test requires about 20 minutes to complete.

Testing your memory is automatic. All you need to do is click Windows Memory Diagnostic Tool to display the Windows Memory Diagnostic Tool dialog box. The dialog box contains two options: Restart now and check for problems and Check for problems the next time I start my computer. Generally speaking, the only difference between the two options is that the second one doesn't restart your system immediately.

When your system does restart, you'll see a Windows Memory Diagnostics Tool screen. This screen provides status information as the tool examines your machine's memory. The tool performs two complete testing passes. When the test completes, Vista boots as normal. After you log in, you'll see a results dialog box that tells you about any problems that the Windows Memory Diagnostic Tool finds.

Using the Command Prompt

The command prompt you open by clicking Command Prompt in the Recovery Environment looks very much like the command prompt you've used in Vista. However, this command prompt places a few limitations on that tasks you can perform. First, it only supports local commands—this isn't a network tool. To confirm this limitation, open the command prompt, type **`NET CONFIG`**, and press

Enter. The resulting output shows there aren't any network services running, which means that you don't have any access to the network.

Second, those commands are specialized for this interface and perform only a limited set of functions. Unlike the Recovery Console of old, you do have complete access to every resource on the system. Within the ability of the system to execute the command, you can use any command or utility that you would normally use at the command prompt. However, open RegEdit and you'll notice that a considerable number of keys are missing. Anything you'd want to monitor from the Recovery Environment is there, but a number of other keys aren't. That's because you aren't logged into the system, so you don't have access to items such as user keys.

Beyond these minor limitations (they really are minor when you consider the limits the Recovery Console used to place on you), you can perform just about any task you want at the command line. For example, you can use the DiskPart utility to gain low-level access to the partitions on the system, create new partitions with specific features, and even install Vista there. The limits placed on you at the command prompt are reasonable considering the environment in which you're working.

Using Vista's Built-in Diagnostics

You don't necessarily have to use the Recovery Environment discussed in the "Using the Recovery Environment" section of the chapter to perform diagnostics. Vista provides access to a number of these features directly within the GUI. The following sections describe how to access these features.

Performing a RAM Diagnostic

It's possible to perform a RAM diagnostic anytime you want. Not only is this option available when you boot the machine (if you have a multiple boot machine, the option to run a memory diagnostic appears as part of the boot menu), but it's also available within Vista. All you need do is open the Memory Diagnostics Tool entry found in the Administrative Tools folder of the Control Panel. You'll see a dialog box with the same two entries you'll find in the Recovery Environment. See the "Using the Windows Memory Diagnostic Tool" section of the chapter for details.

Checking a Drive

Hard drives experience wear and tear. Checking your hard drive from time to time will provide you with some advance notice of failure or help you recover when minor problems occur. The following steps help you perform a check of your hard drive.

1. Open a copy of Windows Explorer.
2. Right-click the drive you want to check and choose Properties from the context menu. You'll see a drive Properties dialog box.
3. Select the Tools tab. You'll see three diagnostic aids for the hard drive. The buttons on this tab let you check for errors, defragment the drive so it works more efficiently, and back up the drive's data.
4. Click Check Now. You'll see a Check Disk dialog box with two options:

   Automatically fix file system errors This option tells Vista to fix any errors it finds automatically. Otherwise, you must provide input for fixing every error that Vista locates.

Scan for and attempt recovery of bad sectors Whenever Vista sees what it thinks is a bad sector (a bad physical location) on the hard drive, it marks the sector and doesn't use it. Some of those sectors are actually good. Scanning for the bad sectors and testing them can help you recover some space on the hard drive that Vista originally thought was bad, but actually isn't.

5. Choose the error-checking options you want to use and click Start. Vista performs a check of the hard drive and tells you about the drive's status.

6. Click Close to clear the results dialog box. Click OK to clear the drive's Properties dialog box.

The Driver Verifier—a Babysitter for Your Drivers

It goes without saying that reliable hardware is the number one most important consideration when building reliable Vista systems. However, equally as important is making sure that reliable drivers are used.

A hardware device—as far as Vista is concerned—is only as good as its associated driver.

If you've been lucky, all the hardware on your system has well-behaved drivers that don't cause any problems. But what if you wanted to add an old, slightly outdated card to your system? How would that impact your system's stability? Or what if you found a new driver on the Internet for some existing hardware you have? Will the new driver be as stable on your system as your current driver? How can you be sure that updating to a new driver won't compromise your system stability in some way?

The Driver Verifier, first released in Windows 2000 Professional and included with Vista, is the answer to all these questions and more. In reality, what the Driver Verifier does is quite simple. During normal Windows operations, all the drivers on your system reside in the kernel of the Vista operating system and are supposed to play nicely together and with the operating system. Vista doesn't really look at what they are doing. It more or less assumes that the drivers will be on their best behavior as long as they respond appropriately when called on. As an analogy, imagine a bunch of children playing around unsupervised in a backyard. Now, as long as they respond when you call to them, would you assume that they aren't doing anything they shouldn't be doing? I should hope not!

As anyone who has children knows that just because you don't find out that your kids are misbehaving doesn't mean that they're not causing trouble. Kids need supervision. Well, sometimes the drivers in your system need supervision. That's basically what the Driver Verifier does—it acts as a babysitter for your drivers. It puts them under a microscope and scrutinizes every single thing they do. Using our children analogy, imagine taking one of the children, putting them in their own private sandbox, and standing over them watching every single thing they do.

In effect, this is what the Driver Verifier does. By keeping an eye on how the drivers on your system utilize and access memory, your system will display a blue screen if a driver misbehaves. So, what does Vista consider misbehaving? Well, the list is rather long—and *extremely* technical—to the point where addressing those issues would take up far more pages than are allocated to this book. Therefore, let's just take a look at the common circumstances in which you would want to use the Driver Verifier and how to use it.

Running the Driver Verifier

As I mentioned before, you'll probably want to use the Driver Verifier if you want to add a new piece of hardware to your system or if you want to update an existing driver. In any case, if you're concerned about system stability, run the Driver Verifier in order to place the new (or updated) driver in its own private sandbox for the first few weeks.

WARNING During the course of writing this chapter, I placed the driver for my network adapter in the Driver Verifier to make sure it was behaving appropriately. For whatever reason, when I took the driver back out, my system would no longer access the Internet without causing a blue screen. Eventually, I figured out that this was due to a conflict with some personal firewall software that I was using. The personal firewall software worked fine before I started testing the Driver Verifier, but after I took my network adapter in and out of the Driver Verifier, my personal firewall would no longer work consistently. I'm sure that this was an atypical symptom of using the Driver Verifier program—and more likely a problem with my personal firewall software—but it does warrant a bit of caution. Even though this is a great diagnostic utility, unless you have something specific that you want to troubleshoot, it may not be wise to play around with it. And just in case you do want to use it, you might want to back up your system first.

You can start the Driver Verifier in two ways:

- At the command prompt, type **`verifier`**.
- Choose Start ➤ Run to open the Run dialog box, and in the Open box, type **`verifier`**.

In either case, the Driver Verifier Manager opens, as shown in Figure 29.5.

On the first screen of the Driver Verifier Manager, you select the settings you want the program to use, create custom settings, delete existing settings, display existing settings, or display information about verified drivers. Unless you're the developer of a driver, click the Create Standard Settings option if you are ready to place a driver "in its sandbox," and click Next.

You can then select which driver or drivers you want to verify. Select an option to display a description of what that option will do at the bottom of the screen. If you select Automatically Select Unsigned Drivers, the Driver Verifier Manager will immediately search your system for any unsigned drivers and display a list of any it finds. Driver Verifier Manager will do the same if you select the Automatically Select Drivers Built for Older Versions of Windows option.

FIGURE 29.5
The Driver Verifier Manager program.

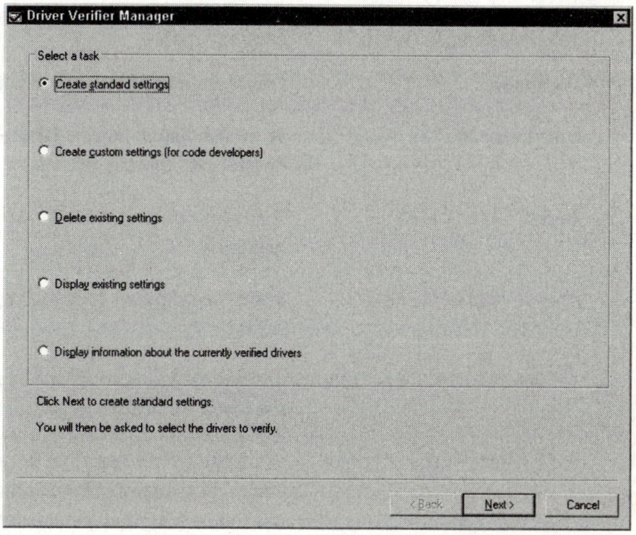

If you want to verify all drivers on your system, click that option, and then click Finish. If you just want to see a list of drivers, click Select Driver Names from a List. When you've made your choice, click Next, and Driver Verifier Manager will take care of the task.

System File Checker

One of the things that Microsoft has learned over the years is that, more often than not, unreliable behavior in Windows can be directly attributed to missing, corrupted, or conflicting versions of critical system components. In an effort to resolve this problem, Microsoft has included a utility in Vista called the System File Checker (SFC).

The System File Checker is a command-line utility that will scan the critical system files on your computer and replace any suspicious files with original copies either from your installation media or a special folder on your system. If you suspect that a Windows file on your system might have been damaged, run the System File Checker to find out for sure.

Running the SFC

The SFC will check approximately 2,700 files on your system—namely most of the SYS, DLL, EXE, TTF, FON, and OCX files that were originally installed. When you run the SFC, you are in effect telling the utility to compare all the files on your system against the original installation media. Therefore, the SFC will need a copy of the original files to work from. Make sure that you have your original Vista CD-ROM handy when you need to run this utility.

The SFC is a command-line utility, so you won't find it on any of the menus in your system. To launch the SFC, type **SFC** at a command prompt. If everything is working correctly, you should see a help screen giving you the available command options. The options are listed in Table 27.1.

TABLE 29.1: SFC Command-Line Options

COMMAND-LINE OPTIONS	DESCRIPTION
`/scannow`	Forces an immediate scan of your system. Repairs any damaged files.
`/verifyonly`	Scans the system for any damaged files. You only see a list of problems—SFC doesn't attempt any repairs.
`/scanfile=<file>`	Scans the referenced file for damage. SFC repairs the damaged file if necessary.
`/verifyfile=<file>`	Scans the referenced file and reports any damage. SFC doesn't attempt a repair.
`/offbootdir=<directory>`	Scans the referenced offline boot directory for damage. This is the option to use if you think an external application is affecting online results.
`/offwindir=<directory>`	Scans the reference offline Windows directory. This is the option to use if you think an external application is affecting online results. You should also use this option when you have trouble scanning files that are in use.

Since you're reading this chapter, you're most likely looking for troubleshooting information, either to repair a system that is currently experiencing problems or for future reference. For most troubleshooting purposes, a simple SFC `/SCANNOW` will suffice. It begins checking each of the critical system files on your computer, comparing them against the original copies, and determining if any of the files have been corrupted.

As the tool is running, a status monitor will keep you informed as to how far the system has proceeded with its checking. If the SFC finds any files that are missing or corrupted (when compared with the Vista source media), it will replace the file with the original version either from its cache on your hard drive or from the original media.

Just for giggles, I tested this capability on my system by overwriting one of the True-Type Font (TTF) files. Sure enough, once I ran the SFC, it saw that one of my files was corrupted and replaced it with an original copy of the file. I can definitely see where the SFC is useful in the case of corrupted files, virus infections, or just plain ol' human error. The SFC is a lifesaver!

The Registry Entry That Lets You Force a Blue Screen (Core Dump)

Okay, so far in this chapter, I've been talking about ways to avoid blue screens or at least to minimize their impact. But what if you actually *want* to cause a blue screen?

Although unusual, on occasion you might want to force your system to crash via a blue screen. For example, you might want to test that Vista will reboot itself properly and that all the necessary services on your system will start again. Or you might want to see how well an application that is running on your system will perform in the event of a critical failure. For whatever the reasons, if you want to force your system to blue screen, you can do it.

All you need is one simple Registry modification. To modify the Registry in Vista, you use RegEdit. As always, before making *any* modifications to your Registry, back it up.

After you back up your Registry, you'll need to navigate to the `HKEY_LOCAL_MACHINE\SYSTEM\CurrentControlSet\Services\i8042prt\Parameters`. In there, you'll create a key called CrashOnCtrlScroll as a DWORD type. Enter a value of 1 for the Registry key, and then reboot your system.

So what does this do? Well, the `i8042prt` service is responsible for handling your keyboard input. So this Registry entry allows you to force the system to crash through the use of a special keystroke. Useful for both diagnostic testing purposes and practical joking! Once you have this Registry key in your system, a simple Ctrl+ScrollLock+ScrollLock will cause your system to immediately blue screen (you must use the Ctrl key on the right side of the keyboard and press the ScrollLock key twice).

Backing Up and Restoring

A lot of what I've talked about in this chapter won't do you any good unless you've backed up your system. As previously mentioned, backups in Vista are all-or-nothing affairs. You don't have any options about the backup type and can't determine what the system backs up. A backup in Vista is simply a means of providing a complete PC repair later (see the "Performing a Complete PC Restore" section of the chapter for details) and you'd be well advised to obtain a third-party backup product. Here are the steps for backing up and for restoring.

Making a Backup

The next thing you can do to make life easier for yourself is to back up important files. Yes, we know you've heard all this before; everybody's heard about making backups, but why should *you* make a backup?

To protect against hard disk failure A hard disk can fail at almost any time, but when it does, it's always at the most inconvenient moment.

To protect against accidental deletion of a file If you work on many projects, your chances of accidentally deleting a file are far higher than if you work on only one at a time.

To create an archive at the end of a project You can make a backup that contains all the files relating to a single project when the work is done; then if you need to refer to the files again, you know where to find them.

These are the main reasons to make a backup, but there are others. You might back up the files of a terminating employee in case the computer is reassigned within your department or is transferred to another department. In either case, the new user will likely clean up the hard disk—in other words, delete all the most important files. In addition, making a backup is one way to transfer a large number of files from one computer system to another. Finally, you should always back up before making a substantial change to your system such as installing new hardware, upgrading the operating system, or making a major configuration change to your application software.

Once you decide to make a backup, you need to plan your backup strategy and, most important, stick to it. With no plan, you'll simply accumulate floppy disks or tapes haphazardly, you'll waste tapes, and you'll waste time looking for a file when you need to restore a file deleted by accident.

So how often should you make a backup? For an answer that fits the way you work, answer these questions:

- How often do your data files change? Every day? Every week? Every month?
- How important to your day-to-day operations are these files? Can you work without them? How long would it take you to recreate them?
- How much will it cost to replace lost files in terms of time spent and business lost?

In our computerized world, it takes hours to create an HTML page with just the right look or a budget spreadsheet that everyone agrees to, but either can be lost or destroyed in milliseconds. A hard-disk failure, a mistaken delete command, overwriting the file with an earlier version with the same name—these can destroy a file just as surely as fire, flood, or earthquake. You just have to lose one important file to become an instant convert for life to a program of regular, planned backups.

Unlike previous versions of Windows, Vista performs backups automatically. The backup is complete—you have no choice about what Vista backs up. The only choice you have is to enable or disable the backup and when the backup occurs. You can also perform a manual backup whenever you want.

To start the Vista backup program, choose Start ➢ All Programs ➢ Accessories ➢ System Tools ➢ Backup Status and Configuration.

Configuring the Automatic Backup

The first time you start Backup Status and Configuration, you must set up the automatic backup. You can change these settings as desired to meet personal needs. The following steps tell you how to perform the automatic backup configuration.

1. Click the Set up automatic file backup link. Vista will ask where you want to store your backup. You can choose a local hard drive, network drive, CD drive, or DVD drive as storage locations. To use the CD drive or DVD drive options, you must have a writeable CD or DVD and a drive capable of performing the writing tasks.
2. Select a backup location. Click Next. Vista asks you which disks you want to back up. The backup process will back up the complete drive by default.
3. Choose the drives you want to back up by placing a check next to the drive. Click Next. Vista asks you which personal files you want to back up. You can choose to back up individual categories of information including pictures, music, videos, e-mail, documents, TV shows, compressed files, and additional files.
4. Select the personal items that you want to appear in the backup. Click Next. Vista will ask how often you want to perform the backup.
5. Choose options in the How often, What day, and What time fields. Click Save settings and start backup. Vista begins creating a backup of your files.

NOTE **After you perform the initial configuration, you can change the backup settings by clicking the Change backup settings link. Start with step 2 of the procedure in this section.**

Performing a Manual Backup

You can perform a manual backup at any time. Open Backup Status and Configuration as normal and then click the Back up now link. Vista will perform a backup using the settings you provided for automatic backups.

Performing a Complete PC Backup

A complete PC backup saves everything on your hard drive. You can use the backup to create a mirror image of your system on another machine and restore your disk after a hard drive crash. This isn't the best option to use when you simply want to back up your data. You should rely on a file backup (described in the "Configuring the Automatic Backup" and "Performing a Manual Backup" sections of the chapter) for this purpose.

To perform a complete PC backup, follow these steps:

1. Click the Complete PC Backup option on the left side of the Backup Status and Configuration dialog box.
2. Click the Create a backup now link. You'll see the Windows Complete PC Backup dialog box where you can choose the destination for a backup. You can choose to backup the system to an uncompressed local hard drive or a DVD or CD drive with writing capabilities.

NOTE If you're planning to use the backup for restoration purposes, choose the backup media with care. You won't normally have access to a network drive when using the Complete PC Restore found in the System Recovery Environment described in the "Performing a Complete PC Restore" section of the chapter. In addition, since the Vista DVD is in your DVD drive, you might not be able to use a DVD backup either. The best solution for situations where you want to be able to access a backup from the System Recovery Environment is to use an uncompressed volume. To reduce the risk of not being able to access the backup due to a hard drive failure, place the backup on a different hard drive than the one you use for your data (a hard drive set aside specifically for the purpose is a good idea).

3. Choose either the On a hard drive or On one or more DVDs option. Select the drive you want to use from the associated drop-down list. Click Next. Vista asks which drives you want to include in the backup.
4. Check each of the drives you want to appear in the backup. Click Next. Vista will ask you to confirm your backup settings.
5. Review the backup settings, and then click Start Backup. Vista will begin the backup process. At some point, Vista displays a successful completion dialog box.
6. Click Close to close the dialog box.

Restoring a Backup

Vista lets you perform a restore of your data using one of two techniques. The first technique is a simple restore of user data. The second technique is an advanced restore where you choose what to restore to the system. The following sections describe both techniques.

Performing a Simple Restore

The following steps describe how to perform a simple restore:

1. Click the Restore Files option on the left side of the Backup Status and Configuration dialog box.
2. Click the Restore files link. You'll see a Restore Files dialog box. This dialog box has two options:

   Files from the latest backup Lets you choose files from the most current backup of your system.

   Files from an older backup Lets you choose from any of the backups on the system. When you choose this option, you must perform an additional step to select the backup that you want to use.
3. Choose one of the restore options and click Next. If you're using an older backup, you'll need to choose the backup you want to use and click Next. You'll see a Restore Files dialog box. This dialog box helps you perform several tasks:

   Add files Lets you add files to the list of items to restore.

   Add folders Lets you add entire folders to the list of items to restore.

Search Helps you locate the file or folder you want to restore.

Remove Removes a single entry from the restore list.

Remove all Removes all of the entries currently in the restore list.

NOTE If you want to restore all of the files in a backup, check the Restore everything in this backup option. Vista will change the Restore Files dialog box so you can't make any file or folder selections.

4. Select the files and folders you want to restore, and then click Next. Vista will ask where you want to restore the files. If you choose the In the original location option, Vista will place the files into the locations that they appeared in during the original backup. However, if you select the In the following location option, you must tell Vista where to place the files. Click Browse to find a location. The Browse for Folder dialog box lets you choose any location you can access, including network drives. Click the Restore files to their original subfolders when you want to create a mirror image of the original setup. If your backup contains multiple drives, you'll also want to check the Create a subfolder for the drive letter option so that each drive has its own folder (to avoid possible conflicts).
5. Click Start restore. Vista restores the files for you. When the restoration is complete, you see a success message.
6. Click Finish to close the Restore Files dialog box.

Performing an Advanced Restore

The following steps describe how to perform an advanced restore:

1. Click the Restore Files option on the left side of the Backup Status and Configuration dialog box.
2. Click the Advanced restore link. You'll see a Restore Files (Advanced) dialog box with three options:

   Files from the latest backup made on this computer Lets you choose files from the most current backup of your system.

   Files from an older backup made on this computer Lets you choose from any of the backups on the system. When you choose this option, you must perform an additional step to select the backup that you want to use.

   Files from a backup made on a different computer Lets you restore a backup found on another computer—effectively duplicating the setup on the remote computer on the local computer if desired. When you choose this option, you must provide the location of the remote machine, click Next, select the backup you want to use, and then click Next again.
3. Choose one of the restore options and click Next. If you're using an older backup, you'll need to choose the backup you want to use and click Next. If you're working with data on another system provide the location of the remote machine, click Next, select the backup you

want to use, and then click Next again. You'll see a Restore Files dialog box. This dialog box helps you perform several tasks.

Add files Lets you add files to the list of items to restore.

Add folders Lets you add entire folders to the list of items to restore.

Search Helps you locate the file or folder you want to restore.

Remove Removes a single entry from the restore list.

Remove all Removes all of the entries currently in the restore list.

4. Follow the procedure in the "Performing a Simple Restore" section, starting with step 4.

Summary

This chapter introduced you to some of the vital skills needed for troubleshooting Vista when things go wrong. I discussed how to avoid Vista crashes, which is the best troubleshooting technique of all, and how to restore a configuration. We then looked at System Restore and Recovery Environment. Following that, we took a look at the Driver Verifier, the System File Checker, and the Registry entry that lets you force a core dump. Fixing Windows is no fun, but at least now you have an idea of how to go about it. You also know why it's important to back up your files, you know how to back up, and you know how to restore.

As with many tool type chapters, this one contains a lot of information that you're going to need in a crisis. Unfortunately, when the crisis arrives, you might not remember to look here and run around not knowing what to do. Exploring these tools before you need them is the key to making Windows at least a little easier to fix. Take time now to explore the functionality of the tools in this chapter. You might be surprised and find a problem with your system that you didn't know about (subtle problems often accumulate until they become quite noticeable, making repair much more difficult).

In the next chapter, I'll show you how to perform a critical administrative task that is often overlooked—auditing security. Auditing security is important because you can't assume the settings you create today are the ones that Vista has tomorrow. Continual monitoring is one of the most important elements of a good security plan.

Chapter 30

Auditing Security

Back in Chapter 21, we took a detailed look at how Vista security works. If securing your computer is a primary concern to you, then the obvious first step is to know how to apply security settings. However, you can't just assume that since you set up security on your machine all is well. There are many things you could have overlooked. Maybe you forgot to set security on a specific folder. Perhaps the security you set isn't as strict as it should be. Things like this happen because, after all, we are human.

This is where auditing comes into play. After you have established security measures, auditing can help you check to make sure that no one is getting access to resources that they shouldn't. Auditing can act as a watchdog, if you will. In this chapter, we'll look at the many benefits of auditing, a few inconveniences of auditing, and how to set up auditing. We'll also look at

- Reasons to use and not to use auditing
- Implementing auditing through policies
- Auditing folders, files, and printers
- Monitoring audited events

Deciding What to Audit

Vista gives you a great deal of flexibility in auditing. You can decide to audit every time any user opens any file on your machine. You can also go to the other extreme and choose no auditing whatsoever. But if you're like most people, you'll choose a position somewhere in the middle.

NOTE Most home networks have no auditing enabled. It's mostly because people aren't worried about their home network. After all, who would want to break into it? Plenty of people would. In the workplace, a company that does not audit security is asking for serious problems. At the very least, unauthorized people could be poking around in sensitive areas. At the worst, there could be legal problems, thanks in part to the Sarbanes-Oxley Act of 2002. Information on Sarbanes-Oxley as it relates to IT can be found in a variety of places. A good one to start with is the Information Systems Audit and Control Association (ISACA) at `http://www.isaca.org`.

Although many factors may play into your decision to enable auditing, the most important consideration is the security of your computer. If you don't care about security and could care less who sees your files or uses your printers, then auditing isn't for you. There's no sense in enabling it. However, if the files on your machine are confidential, then you'll likely want to know if someone is trying to get to them or, worse yet, has gotten to them.

Benefits of Auditing

Auditing provides increased security for your computer. No, auditing won't actually keep someone out of your files. That's what permissions are for. Auditing is there to let you know about potential security breaches. For example, you can audit logon attempts to your computer. If someone has tried to log on to your machine a dozen times, using your username but the wrong password, auditing can track that. By reviewing your security logs, you'll notice attempts to hack your machine. If you didn't have auditing, you might not know until it's too late.

You can use auditing to track almost everything that happens on your computer. You'll know what happened (log on, file access, printer access), when it happened, and who did it. This way, if something bad does happen, you'll have a culprit. In this way, auditing can be thought of as supplemental security. It won't keep a specific event from happening but will leave a detailed electronic paper trail.

A discussion of the benefits of auditing wouldn't be complete unless you knew what types of things were available to audit. After all, how do you know it's good for you if you don't know exactly what it does? Nine different types of events can be audited in Vista. These events are listed in Table 30.1.

TABLE 30.1: Vista Audit Events

EVENT	DESCRIPTION
Account logon events	Audits when a user logs on to or off of another computer from this computer. This typically happens only in domains, so you won't likely use this event in Vista.
Account management	Audits when changes are made to a user or group. These changes can include creating, deleting, renaming, disabling or enabling, and password changes.
Directory service access	Audits whenever a user accesses a directory service object other than a file, folder, or printer. Used only in Windows 2000 and above domains.
Logon events	Audits whenever a user logs on or logs off of this computer. Very helpful.
Object access	Audits a user's access to files, folders, and printers. Very helpful.
Policy change	Audits changes made to user rights policies, audit policies, and trust relationships.
Privilege use	Audits whenever a user executes a user right, other than logon, logoff, system shutdown, or network access events.
Process tracking	Tracks changes made by programs in Vista. Generally not very useful.
System events	Audits system shutdowns and restarts or any attempted changes to the system's Security log. Sometimes useful.

Some of the events may seem redundant and can be confusing as to their purpose. Let's try to clarify them now:

Account logon events vs. logon events Account logon events are useful if someone uses your machine to log on to a Windows 2000, Windows .NET, or Windows Server 2003 domain. If you don't have a domain, you won't need to use these events. Logon events will track who logs on to your individual machine.

Directory service access vs. object access Directory service access tracks whenever someone accesses a specific object in the Windows 2000, Windows .NET, or Windows Server 2003 directory. Object types include, but aren't limited to, shared folder objects, user objects, and group objects. Once again, this is not generally useful for Vista because it implies that a domain is present. Object access tracks access to files, folders, and printer objects specifically. Implementing tracking on these three types objects is a two-step setup process, which we'll cover in the "Setting Up Auditing in Vista" section of this chapter.

The events listed in Table 30.1 can be quite a lot to absorb. The two most commonly used audit events are logon events and object access. Account management, privilege use, and policy change are common in environments where there are multiple users with administrative privileges. Account logon events and directory service access are used only when you have a domain. Process tracking and system events are rarely audited.

The Dark Side of Auditing

When deciding what to audit on your Vista computer, you'll want to be aware of two negative aspects. The first one is performance overhead, and the second one is the volume of audited information.

Auditing adds overhead to your computer. Auditing is a process, much like an application, in that it performs a task based on a specific event happening on your computer. So if you have enabled auditing on every file on your machine, your computer needs to make a note of *who*, *what*, and *when* every time someone opens a file. This extra work slows down the machine. The more you audit, the more overhead you'll have. Overhead becomes a more extensive issue when you are auditing servers, because they generally have more people accessing them than do workstations. Even so, overhead is still something to keep in mind when deciding what to audit on your Vista workstation. Too much auditing can cripple your system's performance.

The sheer volume of audit records that your computer may generate can become overwhelming. Once again, the more you audit, the more you will have to deal with. With so many audit events to sort through, it can be difficult to find the specific piece of information you're looking for. Fortunately, Vista allows you to restrict your display to specific types of events through filtering. We'll look at how to filter events in the "Monitoring Security" section later in this chapter.

All in all, the benefits of auditing far outweigh the drawbacks. As long as you apply your auditing judiciously, you should be able to enjoy the benefits without causing any serious performance problems.

Setting Up Auditing in Vista

Auditing is enabled in Vista through the Local Security Settings console. Local Security Settings is part of Administrative Tools located in Control Panel. Figure 30.1 shows where Audit Policy is located within the security console. You must have administrative privileges to enable auditing.

Notice in Figure 30.1 that we have enabled a few of the more common auditing events. Also, when you enable auditing, you have the choice of auditing successes or failures of each type of event. Auditing logon failures could warn you about a potential hacker, whereas logon successes may just show you that you've indeed logged on every day for the last month. Once again, you have to decide on an appropriate auditing level for your computer. To set up auditing of an event, double-click it in the right pane, and check the Success and/or Failure box. An example is shown in Figure 30.2.

WARNING If you are part of a Windows 2000, Windows .NET, or Windows Server 2003 domain, domain-wide security policies set with Group Policy objects will override your local settings. Check with your domain administrator to see if this is going to be an issue.

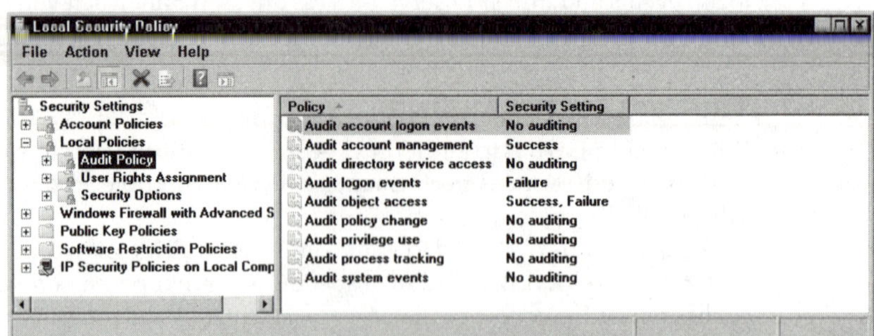

FIGURE 30.1
Local Security Settings.

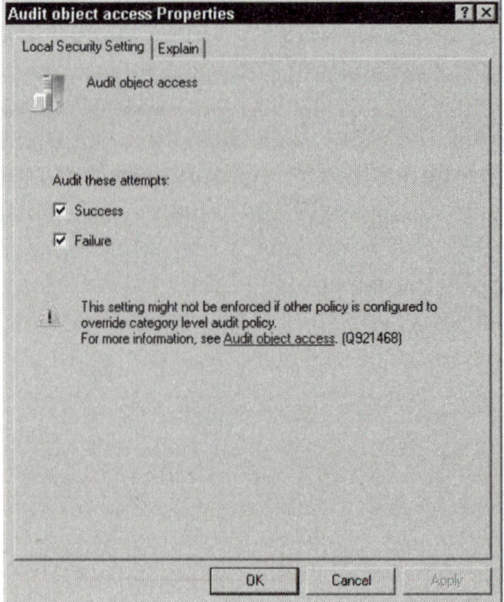

FIGURE 30.2
Auditing object access.

For most audit events, all you need to do is open up Local Security Settings, find the event you want to audit, and select the Success and/or Failure boxes. It's a relatively painless procedure. However, for object access, specifically auditing folders, files, and printers, you will need to perform an additional step.

The first step to auditing objects is just like auditing anything else. Open Local Security Settings and check Success and/or Failure for the Audit object access event. For object access, it's recommended that you always check both the Success and Failure boxes. By performing this first step, you have set up your machine to allow the auditing of folders, files, and printers. Now you have to tell your computer *which* folders, files, and printers you want to monitor.

There is logic in Microsoft making this a two-step process. If all you needed to do were to check the boxes in Local Security Settings, you would automatically enable auditing on *all* folders, files, and printers. In most cases, this is completely unnecessary—definite overkill. This two-step process lets you fine-tune audit control over your machine.

NOTE In order to audit folders and files, the folders and files must be on an NTFS partition. FAT partitions do not support auditing. If you don't have a Security tab on your folder's Properties, check to make sure your partition is NTFS.

For the second step, start by finding the folder, file, or printer you want to audit. Generally, it's best to audit folders rather than specific files, much like Microsoft recommends setting permissions at the folder level rather than the file level. Once you have found the folder that you want to audit, right-click it and choose Properties. In the Security tab, click the Advanced button and then the Auditing tab. Click Continue on the Auditing tab. You will see a screen similar to the one shown in Figure 30.3.

Unless you have set up auditing before, it's likely that your text box will be blank, as opposed to having the Everyone group in it like Figure 30.3 does. To add a group of people to audit, click the Add button. You will get a screen similar to Figure 30.4. Select the group or user you want to watch in the Name box by clicking the Change button, and then check the boxes for which actions you would like to audit. Clicking the Full Control box will enable the whole column. If you want to be safe, choosing Full Control is the best option, but keep in mind that this increases the amount of overhead for the workstation. In order to audit multiple groups, click the Add button in the Auditing tab again, and add the additional group. You can specify separate auditing policies for different groups.

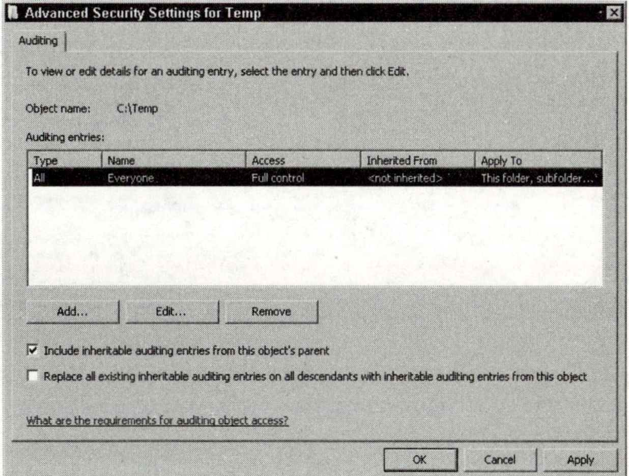

FIGURE 30.3
The Auditing tab for the Temp folder.

You can further customize your auditing preferences with the drop-down menu shown in Figure 30.5.

For the most part, setting up auditing in Vista is pretty simple. It does get more complex when you want to audit folders, but if you remember to complete both steps, your auditing setup will turn out fine.

But now that you've enabled auditing, where do you go to see who has tripped audit events? Setting up auditing isn't enough. You need to periodically monitor your security logs to see if anything has gone awry.

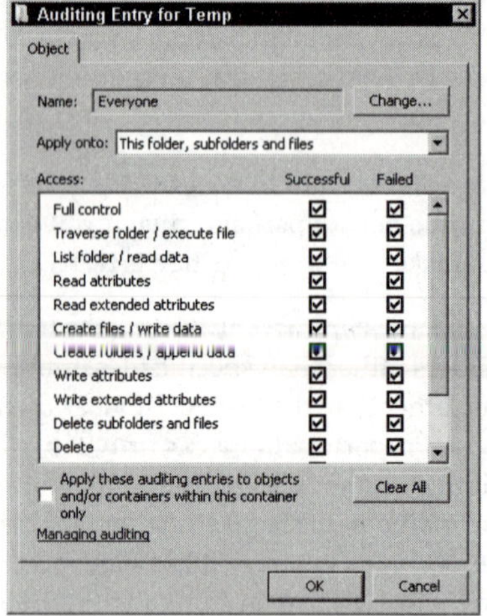

FIGURE 30.4
Enabling audit entries for the Temp folder.

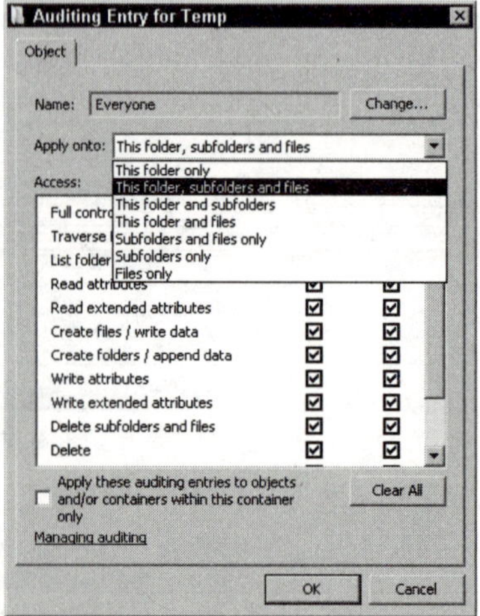

FIGURE 30.5
Fine-tuning audit entries.

Monitoring Security

The Event Viewer utility is used to monitor your security audits. Event Viewer is located in Administrative Tools in Control Panel. To see the security entries, select the `Windows Logs\Security` folder. Event Viewer's Security log is shown in Figure 30.6.

NOTE In order to view the Security log, you must have administrative privileges.

A quick look at the Security log will tell you whether the logged event was a success or failure, the date, time, category, event number, user performing the action, and computer that it was performed on. It's an electronic paper trail of what's happened on your computer—at least what's happened in regard to what you've been auditing. The details about the highlighted event appear at the bottom of the display, so you don't have to do anything special to get all of the information you require.

As I mentioned earlier, your Security log can quickly acquire a large number of events. It can be difficult, if not impossible, to find the specific types of events you want to look at. Fortunately, Vista Event Viewer comes with an ability to filter events based on almost any criteria you choose. As an example, if you wanted to find events that related to the user JSmith only, you could filter for the username JSmith (see the "Arranging and Filtering the Logs" section of Chapter 25 for details on filtering).

Because the Security log can get quite large, Microsoft recommends that you periodically clear out the log. You can choose to delete all old security records or save them for future reference. For details on how to do this, and more Event Viewer management topics, see Chapter 25.

FIGURE 30.6
The Security log in Event Viewer.

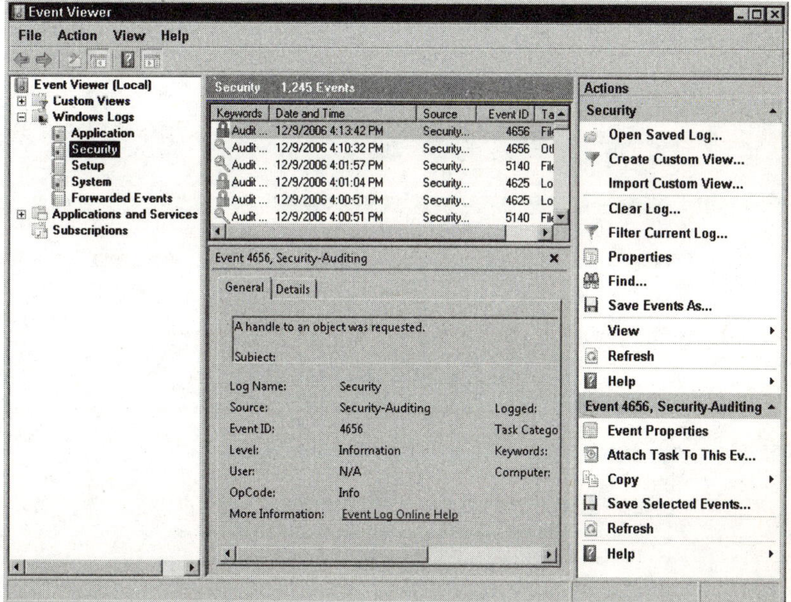

Summary

Auditing allows you to monitor various security-based aspects of your computer. You can see if someone logged on or off, made changes to security settings, created or modified users, or accessed system resources.

Perhaps the biggest benefit of auditing is how it affords you the ability to check for potential system abuses. By enabling auditing of logon and logoff events, you can see if someone has been trying to hack your account. By auditing your folders, you can see who has accessed critical files.

Auditing is enabled through Local Security Settings in Administrative Tools in Control Panel. Once you have enabled auditing, you can check your Security log in Event Viewer to see if any events have happened. Although auditing itself will not keep people out of your resources—that's what permissions are for—auditing can tell you what actions were performed on your machine, allowing you to further control your security.

This chapter ends our section on network administration. Within these pages is a plethora of information that can help you effectively manage small and large networks alike. Keep in mind, though, that the best administrators are the "best" because of their experience. They've been there, done that, and seen it all. Well, maybe not "seen it all," but seen enough to have a good idea where to go when there's a problem. Practice and experience are the keys if you want to be a solid administrator

In the next chapter, we begin a journey into additional advanced topics. These include things that you might or might not use Vista for, such as telecommuting and web services, as well as a few more management tools. We will begin with setting up secure telecommuting.

Part VIII

Advanced Topics

In this section, you'll learn how to:

- **Configure Safe Telecommuting**
- **Use the Microsoft Management Console**
- **Manage Services within Vista**
- **Configure and Host Web and FTP Servers**
- **Troubleshoot Vista**

Chapter 31

Secure Telecommuting

This chapter begins the final part of this book. Each topic in this part is one that you likely won't have to deal with on a daily basis. However, failure to understand how to deal with these issues when you need to can cause serious problems for your Vista computer and your network.

In this chapter, we'll take a look at a common scenario—a corporate user who wants (or needs) to telecommute a portion of the time and needs to do so as securely as possible. We'll look at some of the common threats that a telecommuting user must face, along with what Vista can do to protect against those threats.

- Overview of telecommuting
- Protecting against data interception
- Protecting against user impersonation
- Protecting against data abduction

Vista: What's New?

Vista goes a long way toward securing telecommuting. Past chapters have already discussed a considerable number of these features. All of the new security makes your system more secure as a whole. These security features also make it very difficult for anyone to access your machine or do anything too terrible with it even if they do gain access as long as you maintain the default Vista security settings. Unfortunately, you can override many of the security settings, which means you can become your own worst enemy. Although features such as User Account Control (UAC) seem like a painful way to ensure security, they really do work.

The use of telecommunication features also makes a big dent in the telecommunication threat. For example, because Windows Firewall now provides two-way security, it's a lot more difficult for crackers to make any use of your machine, even if they should gain access to it. Vista starts with the firewall completely locked down, which means that almost no communication occurs. As you begin using more Vista features, you have to open additional ports (points of access) to your system. Every open port is a potential security hole, so like other Vista security features, Windows Firewall only works effectively when you cooperate.

Telecommuting Overview: Risks and Rewards

As telecommuting becomes more commonplace, the risks and rewards associated with it are becoming more apparent. The rewards are obvious: no dealing with traffic jams, being able to work in your bathrobe (if you want to), no office distractions, and so on. The risks, however, are a little less obvious. One of the biggest problems is the risk involved when corporate data is moved outside the corporation's walls.

The risks of telecommuting fall into three distinct areas:

- Interception of corporate data
- Impersonation of an authorized user
- Potential abduction of confidential data

It's interesting to look at the irony of the situation. Corporations are increasing their efforts to secure their data within their walls, but at the same time they're allowing more and more employees to telecommute. I can imagine that people who want to steal corporate data will eventually start to focus their efforts on telecommuting workers instead of the corporation's main systems, because most telecommuters make much easier targets.

The interception of data is an obvious threat: as data passes from your Vista computer into your corporation's main systems, someone eavesdrops on the data transmission and reads the data. If your transmission is crossing the Internet, it will travel through many systems outside your company's control before it reaches its final destination. The same is true with dial-up modems, although the risks are slightly less because your traffic is being carried over the telephone network (a bit more secure). Still, risks do exist, and the main way to deal with the risk of data interception is through data encryption between the source and destination computers. I'll talk about some of the ways you can protect against data interception by encrypting transmissions leaving your Vista computer.

Impersonation of a user is also a threat. If someone obtains your username and password, and if your account has dial-in access, that person can log in to your company's systems under your account, effectively impersonating you. Although the problem of account/password discovery happens within the corporation's walls as well (for example, users writing passwords on yellow sticky notes and attaching them to their monitors), it becomes more of a problem when a user's account is granted dial-in access. The pitfalls of this type of security breach are many—corruption of data, deletion of data, abduction of data, and the introduction of malicious viruses, just to name a few. You can take steps to prevent user impersonation. Some of them are built into Vista, and others are security measures that your corporation must implement. We'll take a look at a number of possible solutions later in this chapter.

Finally, the risk of having data abducted is also a threat. Corporate espionage is a significant problem in many large organizations (although corporations usually keep silent about it since reporting it would have a negative impact on the company's stock price). Again, although corporations are taking significant steps to increase the security of their data within the company's walls, they're allowing users to keep copies of some data on their own home computers or laptops. Instead of targeting a corporate network, it will eventually be easier for someone to target a telecommuting user if they want to obtain a copy of sensitive corporate data. After all, which would be more difficult—breaking into a company and trying to steal a computer, or breaking into someone's home and stealing their computer or laptop? We'll take a look at some of the utilities provided in Vista that will allow you to secure data on your system so that even in the worst-case scenario—your computer is completely stolen—your company's sensitive data won't fall into the wrong hands.

Protecting against the Interception of Data

If you're telecommuting, odds are you're connected to your corporation's network in one of three ways: directly—through some sort of wide area network connection, indirectly—through an analog dial-up networking connection, or through a high-speed digital connection or possibly a virtual private network (VPN). Some companies are also starting to use web services for data communications. Web services require custom applications to access and they can be very secure. Since web services are so specialized, we won't discuss them in the book. No matter how you're connected, you can take steps to secure your communications.

Securing RAS Dial-In Sessions

The dial-in scenario is probably familiar if you've been using computers for any length of time. You install a modem, you define a dial-up networking entry to call into a remote network, and then your computer initiates a connection over your phone line. This is a relatively secure means of communicating with a remote network, but it still could be compromised: someone could tap into your phone line and record the data conversations traveling back and forth between your computer and the remote computer. Therefore, the primary means to protect RAS (remote access server) dial-in sessions is via encryption. Vista makes it easy to implement (and require) encryption on any dial-up networking connection.

NOTE Encryption is the process of encoding information so that it's secure from unauthorized access. Decryption is the reverse of this process.

Assuming you have a working dial-up networking connection, setting up encryption is relatively easy. Follow these steps:

1. Choose Start and right-click Network. Choose Properties from the context menu. Click the Manage network connections link to display the Network Connections window.
2. Right-click the icon for your dial-up connection, and choose Properties from the shortcut menu to open the Properties dialog box for that connection.
3. Click the Security tab. Select the Advanced (custom settings) option, and then click the Settings button to open the Advanced Security Settings dialog box shown in Figure 31.1.

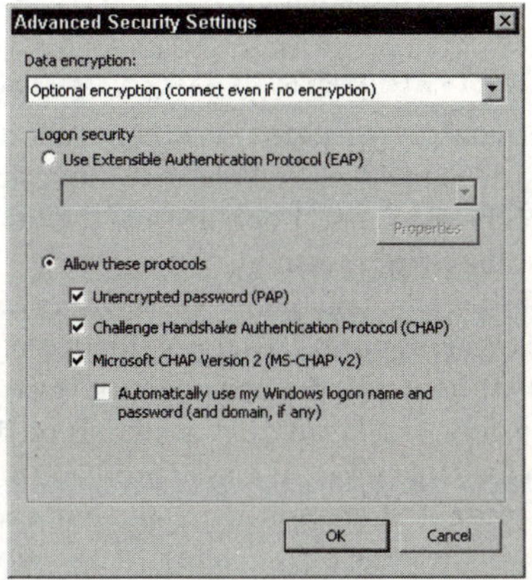

FIGURE 31.1
Modify the advanced connection properties as needed for your network.

NOTE Previous versions of Windows provided additional security options that don't appear in Vista. You can't use the Shiva Password Authentication Protocol (SPAP) at all. In addition, you'll find that Vista doesn't support older versions of the Challenge Handshake Authentication Protocol (CHAP). This limitation means that you'll experience problems establishing a connection to older versions of Windows, such as Windows 95. Microsoft made these changes for security reasons—the old protocols were simply too weak to provide good security. For example, SPAP is susceptible to playback attacks—a scenario in which the cracker records the session and plays the information back later to gain access to the system without really know what information the two systems exchange. Newer versions of CHAP overcome this security problem by using a challenge message that changes every time communication takes place so that a response that worked previously won't work during the next authentication sequence.

You'll notice that the very first item in the Advanced Security Settings dialog box is the Data Encryption drop-down list box. This option has four possible settings:

No Encryption Allowed This setting will attempt to force your computer into a nonencrypted communication session. If the remote system that you're dialing into will allow any type of connection (encrypted or not), you'll be able to connect. However, if the remote system will accept only encrypted connections, you won't be able to connect.

Optional Encryption This setting will defer to whatever is required by the remote system you're calling into. If the remote system doesn't require encryption, this setting will let you connect. If the remote system does require encryption, this setting will also let you connect.

Require Encryption Enabling this setting will implement a 40-bit encryption channel between your Vista computer and the remote system. If the remote system can't support encryption, your session will immediately disconnect, and you'll see a disconnection error message.

Maximum Strength Encryption Enabling this setting will require a strong (128-bit) encryption channel between your Vista computer and the remote system. You'll see this option only if you purchased Vista in the United States. If the remote system can't support strong encryption, your session will immediately disconnect with an error message.

Enabling a data encryption option ensures that all your communications are kept private, even if someone is able to intercept them.

To enable encryption on your dial-up connection, select one of the protocols in the Logon Security section of the Advanced Security Settings dialog box.

Virtual Private Networking Connections

Virtual private networking (VPN) connections are, by definition, meant to be private. VPNs were originally developed as a means to route confidential, private data across untrusted networks. As a result of the reach and popularity of the Internet, VPNs have enjoyed a considerable amount of success in the current market.

One of the better analogies I've found for explaining the concepts of a virtual private network is to refer to them as "pipes." To conceptualize VPNs, think of two pipes, one large and one small. Now, imagine that the small pipe actually runs *inside* the large one. It starts and ends at the same places the large pipe does, and it can carry materials on its own completely independently of whatever is happening in the large pipe. As a matter of fact, the only thing the small pipe is dependent on the large pipe for is the determination of the start and end points. Beyond that, the small pipe can operate independently of the large pipe in terms of direction of travel, materials it carries, and so on.

To add another layer to this analogy, let's assume that the large pipe is made of a transparent material and that the small pipe is made of metal. Anyone taking a look at the pipe-within-a-pipe would easily be able to see whatever is moving through the outer (large) pipe. However, whatever is traveling through the inner pipe would remain a mystery.

Finishing off this analogy, think of the large pipe as representing the unsecured network (that is, the Internet) and the small pipe as representing the virtual private network. VPN is a way of tunneling data packets through a connection that already exists but that can't be used on its own for privacy reasons. Obviously, the Internet is a perfect example of a network that often can't be used on its own for privacy reasons.

To establish a VPN connection to your corporate network, your company must have set up a VPN server capable of receiving those connections. (More information on setting up a virtual private networking server is available in *Mastering Windows 2000 Server*, Fourth Edition, Sybex, 2002, and *Mastering Windows Server 2003*, Sybex, 2003.) If your company has set up a VPN server for you to dial in to, you'll need to know the answers to the following questions:

- Which authentication type does it require?
- Which encryption strength does it require?
- What's the IP address or DNS (domain name service) name to connect to?

Once you know the answer to these questions, you can set up a VPN connection on your Vista computer.

Since a VPN (typically) runs over the Internet, the first thing you must have on your system is a functional Internet connection. Whether your connection is a dial-up modem or a dedicated cable/xDSL connection is mostly irrelevant. Assuming you have an Internet connection in place, you can easily create a VPN connection. Follow these steps:

1. Choose Start and right-click Network. Choose Properties from the context menu. Click the Setup a connection or network link to display the Setup a connection or network wizard.
2. Highlight Connect to a workplace in the Choose a connection option list. Click Next. Vista asks whether you want to use an existing connection for the VPN. If you have an existing connection, choose the Yes, I'll choose an existing connection option, select the connection you want to use, and click Next. Vista will attempt to create the connection using your existing connection. Follow company policies for establishing your connection. You can exit this procedure.
3. Select the No, create a new connection option and click Next. Vista asks you what kind of connection to create as shown in Figure 31.2.

   Use my Internet connection (VPN) This connection uses the public Internet to make the connection to the remote system. This is the connection type described in this section of the chapter.

   Dial directly Uses the telephone line to create the connection. See the "Securing RAS Dial-In Sessions" section of the chapter for details on this technique. When you choose this option, you use the same procedure you would use for creating any other modem connection.
4. Click the Use my Internet connection (VPN) link. Vista asks you about the particulars of the connection as shown in Figure 31.3. You'll need to obtain all of these particulars from your administrator before you can make the connection.

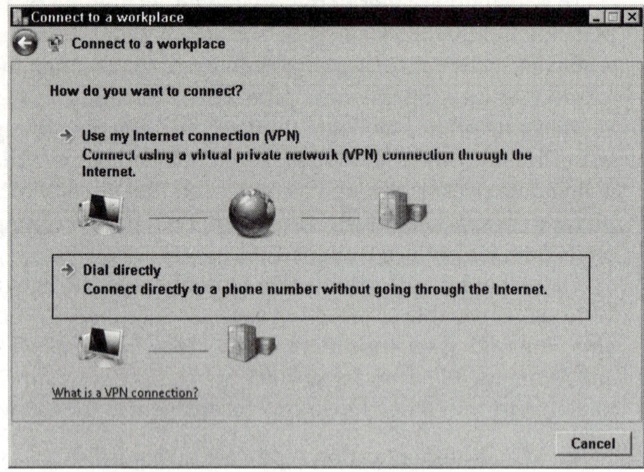

FIGURE 31.2 Choose the kind of connection you want to use to connect with the workplace.

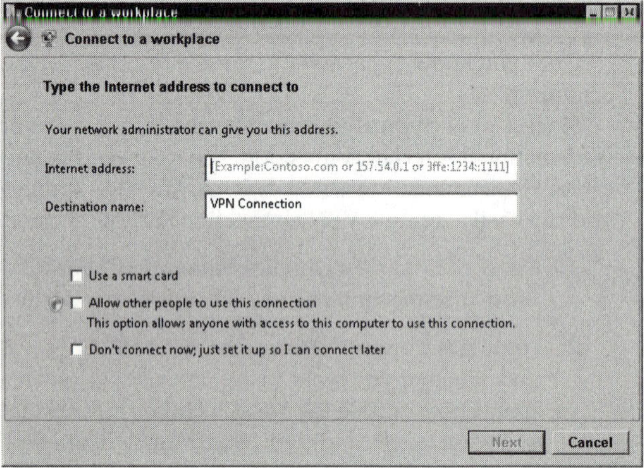

FIGURE 31.3 Provide the particulars of the VPN connection for your company.

5. Type the Internet address. You can use any one of the three following options to provide this information:

   URL Type the URL for the company such as `https://www.mycompany.com`. In some cases, you might need to include a port number as part of the address such as `https://www.mycompany.com:80` for port 80.

   IPv4 address Type the IPv4 address for the server, such as 154.0.54.1.

   IPv6 address Type the IPv6 address for the server, such as 3FFE:1234::1111.

6. Type the connection name. If you use multiple workplace connections, make sure you use a descriptive name that differentiates this connection from other connections on your system.

7. Choose one or more of the following connection options:

   Use a smart card Prompts you for a smart card, instead of a name and password, when creating the VPN connection.

Allow other people to use this connection Allows other people who use your machine to use the connection you created.

Don't connect now; just set it up so I can connect later Use this option when you want to create the connection, but don't want to use it immediately.

8. Click Next. Vista asks you to provide the credentials for connecting to the remote system, which include your name, password, and domain name as shown in Figure 31.4. In addition, you can choose from the following options.

   Show characters Displays the password characters as you type them. Although this option can make it easier to type the password, it's also a security risk because anyone can see what you type.

   Remember this password This option tells Windows to store the password, which means you won't have to enter it the next time you make the connection. Unfortunately, this option is also a huge security risk because anyone with access to your machine can use the connection, perform terrifying acts in your name, and then leave your signature on the actions. In general, you should choose to enter your password every time you make the connection to ensure good security.

9. Type the required credential information, choose the required options, and click Create (or Connect if you plan to connect immediately). Vista creates the required connection and optionally establishes the connection for you.

FIGURE 31.4
Enter the name, password, and domain required to establish the connection.

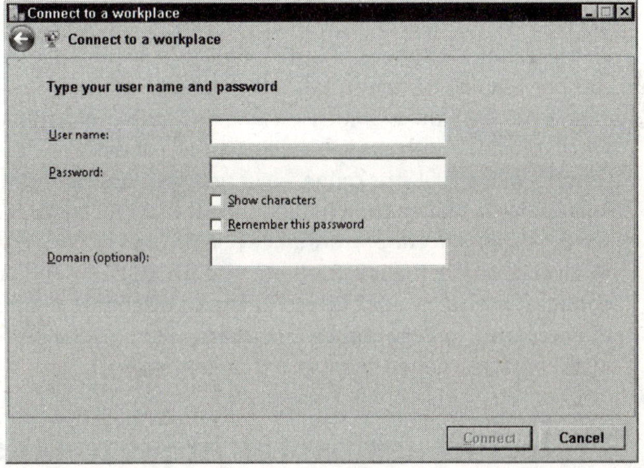

Once you've got everything correctly defined on your system, you should be able to double-click your VPN icon on your Vista system and get connected—securely—to your corporate network. Once you're connected, you should be able to navigate throughout your company's corporate network just as if you were sitting in the office.

VPN Performance Considerations

Our look at virtual private networking wouldn't be complete without taking a bit of time to discuss performance issues. Although virtual private networking is a neat technology, some performance drawbacks are associated with it.

In the right set of circumstances, virtual private networking can provide fast, reliable, and secure connections to your company's network from across the Internet (or another unsecured network). However, in the wrong set of circumstances, virtual private networking can make an already slow dial-up connection seem even slower.

So what are the right circumstances? In my professional opinion, high-speed connectivity on the corporate side of your VPN, and preferably high-speed connectivity on both the corporate side and your personal connection. On occasions when I've been able to implement VPN circuits at locations with a T1 or better available at both the company and client ends, performance has been wonderful and the connections reliable. However, due to the protocol overhead involved with PPTP (Point-to-Point Tunneling Protocol) and L2TP (Layer 2 Tunneling Protocol) and the inherent latency of the Internet, don't have high-performance expectations if you're planning to implement a VPN with a dial-up modem.

If you're using a dial-up modem, nothing will ever be faster than a direct dial-in connection. Period. Dial-in connections are simple. There's no encryption, and there's no VPN protocol overhead involved. Plus, your traffic doesn't have to cross through a countless number of routers before reaching its destination. Simply put, with a direct dial-in connection your packets go out of your computer, across the phone line, and directly into the corporate network.

If you're implementing a VPN connection over a dial-up modem, your packets must first be encrypted. They must then be bundled into a VPN protocol and then bundled again into another TCP/IP packet. After that, they're transmitted across the Internet, where they'll probably pass through anywhere from 4 to 12 routers before reaching the VPN server at your corporation. Once the VPN server receives the packet, it must unpackage the entire payload and then decrypt it. Although computers can do this quickly, it does add overhead to the process.

How much overhead? Well, there are no official numbers to go by, but I'd say you can expect a decrease in your performance ranging anywhere from 10 to 50 percent. Now, without getting into all the technical details, it's worthwhile to note that this isn't entirely Microsoft's fault; after all, they can't be blamed for the fact that the Internet can be inherently slow at times (or can they?). However, even with the worst-case scenario of a 50 percent reduction in performance, if there's 1Mb worth of bandwidth available on each side of the VPN, the effective speeds of the network are still roughly in the 500Kbps range—a very respectable amount. However, if you're using a 56K modem on your Vista workstation (which probably won't connect much faster than 48Kbps), you can easily see how a 50 percent performance penalty can make a connection go from "slow" to "unusable."

Everything in life is a tradeoff, and it will be up to you to decide if this will work adequately enough for your needs. After all, what's adequate to one person might be great to another and unacceptable to yet another. In either case, expect a performance penalty when implementing virtual private networking and plan accordingly.

Protecting against the Impersonation of a User

Compromising a valid user's account name and password is a network administrator's worst nightmare. An unauthorized user—posing as a valid one—can steal, compromise, or sabotage data from the company's network. If that user has remote dial-in access capabilities as well, the problem is even worse because someone can dial in from anywhere in the world and make trouble for the network. Therefore, it's important to prevent your user ID and password from falling into the wrong hands.

Commonsense Guidelines

It still amazes me how many times I run into users who have written their usernames and passwords on a yellow sticky note and then stuck the note to their monitor. Talk about a security nightmare!

Even if people don't stick their passwords on their monitors, users have a tendency to write them down on cards in their wallets or put them into an organizer such as their PDA. The first measure of good security is to never write down your username and password. If, for some reason, you must do so, at least write them on separate sheets of paper and store them in different places. Don't store them with each other.

Another common security problem is users who choose passwords that are easily guessed. For example, it's common for many people to use simple things for passwords, such as the type of car they drive, their favorite sport or a favorite athlete, their mother's maiden name, their middle name, other family names, pet names, and so on. All those types of passwords can be easily guessed if someone is determined enough.

Better types of passwords are complex combinations that have nothing whatsoever to do with you. Even better yet is complete gibberish. You can make your passwords a bit more complex—but still easily remembered—by substituting letters, numbers, or symbols in place of actual words. This is the same type of logic that people use to spell out phrases on custom license plates. For example, you could use the phrase "No soup for you today!" as a password (with all due respect to the *Seinfeld* "Soup Nazi" episode) by using "nosoup4u2day." Such a password is still easy to remember, but is much more difficult to guess. Other suggestions for substitutions are

- Instead of the word "to" or "too," use the number 2.
- Instead of the word "for," use the number 4.
- Instead of the word "at," use the @ symbol.
- Instead of the word "and," use the & symbol.
- Instead of the word "you," use the letter U.
- Instead of the word "are," use the letter R.

I'm sure you get the point. The object is to keep the password something that you can remember while making it difficult to compromise. I've had good success using this formula. At the very least, always use a combination of upper- and lowercase letters, numbers, and symbols if possible.

Encrypted Authentication

If you're dialing into a remote network—either via a direct dial-in line or a VPN connection—Vista must pass your user credentials (your username and password) to the remote system for authentication. The remote system will then check those credentials to determine if your account has been granted dial-in access. But how does Vista send your credentials to the remote computer?

The answer can be found in the Advanced Security Settings dialog box. As you can see in that dialog box, Vista can send your user credentials to the remote system in a number of ways, as long as the remote system is able to understand them. Some of these authentication methods are encrypted, and some aren't.

Extensible Authentication Protocol (EAP) Since security and authentication is a constantly changing field, embedding authentication schemes into an operating system is impractical at times. To solve this problem, Microsoft has included support for Extensible Authentication Protocol, which is simply a means of "plugging in" new authentication schemes as needed. Presumably, any type of extensible authentication would be encrypted, but that could vary from one case to the next.

Unencrypted Password (PAP) Password Authentication Protocol (PAP) is one of the first options and is also one of the least secure. It's no more secure than a simple conversation from your server saying "What's your name and password?" to the client, and the client responding with "My name is Mark and my password is 'let-me-in.'" There's no encryption of authentication credentials whatsoever.

Shiva Password Authentication Protocol (SPAP) SPAP is an encrypted password authentication method used by Shiva LAN Rover clients and servers. Vista doesn't provide support for SPAP because it's a weak protocol that crackers overcome quite easily.

Challenge Handshake Authentication Protocol (CHAP) Defined in RFC (Request for Comments) 1334, and later revised in RFC 1994, CHAP is a means of encrypting authentication sessions between a client and server. Since this protocol is defined by an RFC, it enjoys a broad base of support among many operating systems and other devices.

Microsoft CHAP (v1 and v2) (MS-CHAP) Microsoft's derivative of CHAP, or Challenge Handshake Authentication Protocol, is an encrypted authentication method that also allows you to encrypt an entire dial-up session, not just the original authentication, which is important when it comes to setting up virtual private networking sessions. Vista doesn't provide support for CHAP version 1 because of security problems with it. If your system is old enough that it doesn't provide CHAP version 2 support, you probably shouldn't use it as a means to connect to work.

Caller-ID/Callback Security

Although Caller-ID/callback security isn't an option for Vista, it's worth discussing in terms of security. Simply put, let's assume that you have dial-in access to your corporate network, and the worst-case scenario comes true—someone obtains your user ID and password. Caller-ID and callback security can still provide your corporation with some level of protection. Both features work by verifying that you're actually calling from an authorized phone number—a phone number that has been predefined by the administrators of your corporate network.

Caller-ID security If the dial-in systems on your corporate network can support it, your account can be set up with a Caller-ID–based security option. In this scenario, when the computers on your corporate network receive your incoming call, they take note of the phone number. Once you provide a username and password authentication, your username is checked for an associated Caller-ID number. If the two numbers match, your call is granted. If the two numbers don't match, your call is denied. Therefore, even if someone has your username and password, this type of security can protect your corporation's computers. The drawback is that whenever you want to connect to your company's network, you must be calling in from the approved number.

WARNING Using Caller ID really isn't very secure. Someone can buy a SpoofCard (`http://spoofcard.com/`) and tell your system that you're really talking with someone else. The SpoofCard is easy to use and anyone can employ it. You can learn more about the problems of Caller ID as a security measure at `http://www.eweek.com/article2/0,1895,2004482,00.asp`.

Callback security This functions in a similar manner to Caller-ID security but is a bit more secure. With callback security enabled, your user account is associated with a callback number. When you initiate a dial-in session to your company's network, you'll provide your username and password. The system that verifies your dial-in credentials will see that you have a callback number associated with your account and immediately disconnect you. After it disconnects you, it will then initiate a call to your system and establish the connection. This is a very secure method of verifying a dial-in user; however, it comes at the price of having to always log in from the same phone number.

If you're concerned that your account credentials might fall into the wrong hands, talk to your network administrators to see if either of these options is available for your dial-in system. Windows 2000 Server and Windows Server 2003 support both of them.

Third-Party Products: SecurID, SafeWord

Although this is a book about Vista, I want to mention two products that fall into the "extremely cool" category of security products: SecurID from RSA Security and SafeWord from Secure Computing.

The nature of these two products is similar—they're what's known as a "second factor" authentication method. What that means is that your "first factor" of authentication—your username and password—isn't good enough to obtain access to a resource; you must authenticate yourself in another (second) manner before access is granted. You can think of a second factor authentication as being similar to having two different locks on a door—a regular one and a deadbolt. You won't be granted access until you can provide the correct authentication (a key) for both.

How they work—from a user perspective—is quite simple. When you start a dial-up networking session, you're prompted for your username and password. That's your first authentication. After successfully negotiating a dial-in connection to your corporation's network, you're then prompted for a second authentication—a second "password," if you will. What's unique about this second password is that it's a different password every time.

SecurID works through a small key fob that has a digital readout on it. Every 60 seconds, a new number appears on the readout. The key fob is given to a user and must be used to gain access to the company's network. Let's take a look at a typical example.

Let's assume that a user named Wendy is trying to dial in to her company's network. Now, Wendy has a password for her account—let's assume that it's "arlington." Wendy also has a SecurID key fob that has been assigned to her. At the moment she is trying to sign in, her key fob is displaying the six-digit number 378265. As an added measure, Wendy also has a four-digit "pin" number assigned to her. Let's assume that she used 1234 for her pin number.

When Wendy dials in, she'll type in her username and password (wendy/arlington) just as in a normal dial-up connection. Her Vista system will dial in to the company's network and negotiate a connection. Once the connection is negotiated, Wendy will be prompted for her SecurID passcode. At the moment she is logging in, the correct passcode for her will be "1234378265". Her passcode is validated by a SecurID server within the company's network, and if the passcode is correct, she's granted access to the network. The SafeWord system also functions on a similar, one-time password concept.

As you can see, this is an *extremely* secure means of authenticating a user. If someone manages to obtain Wendy's username and password, they're useless without her SecurID key fob. And even if someone were to obtain the key fob itself, it would still be useless without knowing Wendy's individual pin number.

Protecting against the Abduction of Data

Okay, I'll admit it, the word "abduction" sounds a bit too much like an *X-Files* episode, but the word just fits so well with the concept I'm trying to get across. In any case, the abduction of data is simply someone without authorization copying corporate data off your system. You know, your typical corporate espionage stuff.

As I stated earlier in the chapter, I can imagine that this will become more and more of a problem as companies allow increasing amounts of data outside their corporate walls. After all, who is it more difficult to steal data from—the well-guarded and physically secured corporate network or Joe, the account executive, walking out of the building late at night with his laptop? A quick bop on Joe's head and a grab of the laptop would compromise all the data stored on the laptop.

Or would it? Vista contains encryption technologies that specifically address this type of situation. The encrypting file system (EFS) can ensure that no one other than you'll be able to read your encrypted files if your computer is ever stolen.

The encryption capabilities available in Vista (right out of the box) are very good. And with a few additional precautions, you can make sure that they're absolutely secure—that no one will be able to ever read your encrypted files.

NOTE It goes without saying that if someone gets hold of your username and password, all bets are off. As far as Vista is concerned, if someone logs in with your username and password, it must be you! Vista will gladly decrypt all your files in that scenario. So, it's critical to make sure that your password isn't discovered.

Encrypting Files with EFS

Encrypting data is merely a matter of a few clicks of the mouse, and an entire folder or folder structure can be protected from prying eyes. Having said that, you should try to follow a few "best practices" principles when working with EFS:

Don't encrypt the Vista folders. This would have a significant impact on your system—most likely it wouldn't boot. Fortunately, EFS will always try to prevent you from encrypting system files, but you probably shouldn't even try to in the first place.

Don't encrypt your *My Documents* folder. This runs 100 percent contrary to Microsoft's suggested practices. The reason I recommend that you *don't* encrypt your `My Documents` folder is because there are almost no visual clues in the Windows interface that a file or folder has been encrypted. I've already read a few accounts of users who were "playing around" with EFS and followed Microsoft's suggestions to encrypt the `My Documents` folder, but months later they forgot that they'd done it. Because of some sort of failure (in one instance, a simple HAL [hardware abstraction layer] upgrade), the users reloaded Vista. Guess what? Since they hadn't taken the additional step to back up their recovery keys, all their documents were irrecoverable. Gone. Personally, I like to make a folder called `Encrypted Stuff`, which gives me an obvious visual reminder that anything within that folder is encrypted.

Encrypt your *Temp* folder. Your temporary folder (which can usually be found by typing **SET** at a command prompt and looking for the `TEMP=` and `TMP=` folders) is often a repository for fragments of your data, documents, and so on. Sometimes programs don't properly clean up after themselves, and they leave fragments of your files in this folder. If this folder is encrypted, no leftover fragments can be used by anyone else.

Encrypt entire folders, not just files. As I mentioned earlier, I like to make a special folder on my machine and call it `Encrypted Stuff`—then I just copy everything into it that I want protected.

Encrypting files and folders is really quite simple. Follow these steps:

1. Click Start, right-click Computer, and choose Explore from the shortcut menu to open an Explorer-type window.
2. Right-click the file or folder, and choose Properties from the shortcut menu to open the Properties dialog box for that item.
3. Click the Advanced button to open the Advanced Attributes dialog box as shown in Figure 31.5.

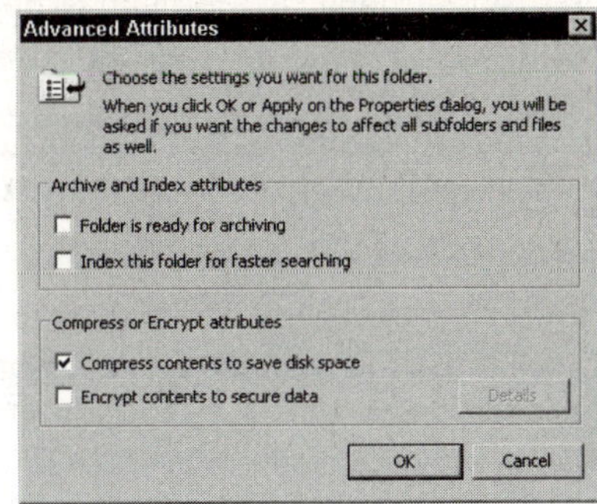

FIGURE 31.5
Encrypt data files to make the data inside them more secure.

Notice the two check boxes at the bottom of this dialog box: Compress contents to save disk space and Encrypt contents to secure data. These two items are mutually exclusive, meaning that if you compress a file you can't encrypt it, and if you encrypt a file, you can't compress it.

4. If necessary, uncompress the file, and check the Encrypt Contents to Secure Data check box.
5. Click OK, and then click OK again to encrypt the file.

It almost seems too easy, doesn't it? Well, don't take my word for it—try logging in as someone else and see if you can read the file. You can't. Even if you have full access to the file under another user account, you won't be able to open the file, copy it, or do anything else with it. Only the user account that encrypted the file can decrypt it, so use encryption carefully.

Summary

In this chapter, we talked about the security of corporate data once it moves outside your corporation's walls. We covered how to encrypt the data as it's transferred to your computer and even how to encrypt the data once it's stored on your computer. We talked about how to protect your account credentials and proposed solutions that you can provide to your corporate network administrators if an additional level of security is necessary.

It's important to know how the various security features in Vista work. Even if you don't have to create a workplace connection today, you should at least become familiar with the options in case you need to make a connection tomorrow. Make sure you understand the security ramifications of connecting to your workplace from a remote connection. In addition, become familiar with any company policies in place for remote connections. You don't want breaking a seemingly minor rule to result in a huge security breach.

The next chapter will cover the Microsoft Management Console (MMC). This single tool is inherently powerful and can be complex. You should make yourself intimately familiar with it if you're managing a number of Vista computers.

Chapter 32

The Microsoft Management Console

This chapter addresses the Microsoft Management Console, the Swiss Army knife of administrative tools for Microsoft Vista.

Starting with Windows 2000, individual administrative tools—such as User Manager, Server Manager, Event Viewer, and even Disk Administrator—were assimilated into the Microsoft Management Console (MMC). This all-in-one administrative tool can be set up to include everything that you need to administer Vista, including Internet Information Server (IIS), which is covered in Chapter 34.

MMC is a framework for management applications, providing a unified interface for Microsoft and third-party management tools. MMC doesn't replace management applications; it integrates them into one single interface. (However, you can still access many tools through their original interfaces.) There are no inherent management functions in MMC at all. It uses component tools called snap-ins, which do all the work. MMC simply provides a user interface; it doesn't change how the snap-ins function.

To become a true power user, you must fully understand the MMC. This chapter covers the following topics:

- MMC structure
- MMC terminology
- Exploring MMC snap-ins
- Using the MMC
- The Computer Management Console

Vista: What's New?

MMC is essentially the same in Vista as it was in previous versions of Windows. The new MMC 3.0 simply makes it easier to perform some tasks. For example, creating a new console is easier than it was before and you'll find that you use fewer clicks to accomplish a given task.

Of course, the most noticeable change in MMC 3.0 is the Action pane. The Action pane makes it easier to access the features of snap-ins. Again, this is a good addition because you use fewer steps to accomplish something and the steps required to perform a task are much more obvious.

The Basic Features of MMC

The following benefits are associated with MMC:

- You have to learn only one interface to drive a whole mess of tools.
- Microsoft is encouraging software vendors to use MMC snap-ins.

- You can build your own consoles, which is practical and fun. Administrators can even create shortcuts on the console to non-MMC tools such as executables, URLs, wizards, and scripts.
- By customizing MMC consoles, an administrator can delegate tasks to underlings without giving them access to all functions and without confusing them with a big, complicated tool.
- Help in MMC is context sensitive; it displays subjects for only the appropriate components. Okay, that's not really new, but it's still cool. Context-sensitive menus are available through the Action and View menus or by right-clicking the snap-in.

WHY ONLY ONE TOOL?

In the first years of Windows NT, administrators had to master multiple administration tools. A whole set of built-in tools, plus independent third-party tools, made administration sort of a mess. Although many administration tools functioned remotely, you had to install some of them separately (unless your desktop happened to include Windows NT Server), and with third-party tools, you often had to jump through hoops to get them to work remotely, if at all. Even worse, with menus, buttons, toolbars, wizards, tabs, HTML, Java (you get the picture), just learning how to navigate new software was a chore. Also, there was no simplified version of the User Manager that could be given to account operators and no way to hide menu items in administrative tools for those without full administrator rights.

So we complained. "As administrators, we need to be able to administer our networks from the comfort and luxury of our cubicles. And we don't want to waste time exploring all the windows, wizards, and tabs in every new tool. And we need more flexible tools," we said. Behold, Microsoft heard our cries, and their response was the MMC. It's even available for Windows NT 4 if you've installed some of the later service packs.

The MMC turned out to be so popular that Microsoft expanded the number of available tools. Third-party vendors also create tools that can be installed in the MMC as snap-ins.

MMC Terms to Know

This section defines important terms you'll need to know when working with MMC.

A *console*, in MMC-speak, is one or more administrative tools in an MMC framework. The prebuilt admin tools, such as Active Directory Users and Computers, are console files. You can also make your own consoles without any programming tools—you needn't be a C++ or Visual Basic programmer, as I'll discuss a bit later. The saved console file is a *Microsoft saved console (MSC)* file and it carries the `.MSC` extension.

NOTE It's important to distinguish between Microsoft Management Console and console tools. MMC provides a framework to create customized console-based tools. `MMC.EXE` is a program that presents administrators (and others creating console tools) with a blank console to work with. It might help to think of a new instance of `MMC.EXE` as providing the raw material for a tool. In that case, Microsoft Management Console provides the rules and guidelines for building the tool, and the new console you create is the finished product.

Snap-ins are the name for administrative tools that are added to the console. (Other companies use a similar process: *plug-ins*. Of course, Microsoft couldn't use that term.) For example, the Disk Management tool is a snap-in. Snap-ins can be made by Microsoft or by other software vendors. (You *do* need programming skills to make these, in other words.) A snap-in can contain components that allow us to manage various facets of our computer, such as hard drives, users, and security. Although you can load multiple snap-ins in a single console, most of the prebuilt administrative tools contain only a single snap-in (except the Computer Management tool).

TIP By default, all MMC consoles, including the ones you create, are accessible through the Start menu. Click Start ➢ All Programs ➢ Administrative Tools and select the console of your choice.

An *extension* is basically a snap-in that can't live by itself on the console but depends on a stand-alone snap-in. It adds some functionality to a snap-in. Some snap-ins work both ways. For example, the Event Viewer is a stand-alone snap-in, but it's also implemented as an extension to the Computer Management snap-in. The key point is that extensions are optional. You can choose not to load them. For example, Local Users and Groups is an extension to the Computer Management snap-in. If you remove the extension from the `COMPMGMT.MSC` file used by your support folk, or simply don't include it in a custom console that uses the snap-in, those who use the tool won't have the option to create or manage users and groups with the tool. They won't even see it. (Please note that this won't prevent them from creating users and groups by other means, if they have the correct administrative privileges.)

Administrators can create new MSC files by customizing an existing MSC file or by creating one from a blank console. `MMC.EXE` plus the defined snap-ins create the tool interface. Also, it's possible to open multiple tools simultaneously, but each console runs one instance of MMC. Open an MSC file and look in Task Manager while it's running—you see only the `MMC.EXE` process running, not the MSC file, just as you'd see `WINWORD.EXE` running in Task Manager but not the Word document's name.

The MMC Console

Microsoft Management Consoles (MMCs) can be configured and run in one of four different modes:

Author mode Allows you to create your own consoles with the snap-ins of your choice.

User mode–full access Allows you almost total control of installed snap-ins, except you can't install or remove a snap-in.

User mode–limited access, multiple window Allows you to use MMC with multiple embedded windows. However, you can't open a new window or close any of the preconfigured windows.

User mode–limited access, single window Allows you to use MMC with a single embedded window.

Author mode is where you create and customize a console. But you shouldn't manage your system from any MMC Author mode. Instead, you can save the console in one of the User modes. Different User modes are suitable for different types of users. The following sections describe the snap-ins and each mode in more detail.

What Are Snap-ins?

Snap-ins include the essence of different Vista administrative utilities. You can add the snap-ins of your choice to the MMC. Some are already included with Vista. More can be added through other applications such as Internet Information Server.

Many of the following snap-ins are the same as those used on Windows 2000. Some of these snap-ins can be used on local or remote computers. Successful remote access depends on configured rights and permissions on that computer. Available snap-ins include the following:

NOTE You might not see all of the snap-ins shown in this list. Some snap-ins require that you have special Windows features installed. For example, you won't see any web administration tools until you install Internet Information Server (IIS).

ActiveX Control Allows control of the list of ActiveX objects that help Vista applications share information and more.

Authorization Manager Lets you set authorization levels for applications that support the Authorization Manager. These applications provide role-based security—a form of protection that relies on a user's role in an organization. For example, an administrator fulfills a different role than a manager or a regular user.

Certificates Permits browsing of your computer's collection of digital signatures associated with applications, drivers, websites, and more.

Component Services Allows configuration of COM components based on Microsoft's Component Object Model and related COM+ applications.

Computer Management Installs the standard Computer Management Console, which is described later in this chapter. It can also be installed as a snap-in in a customized console.

Device Manager Configures the manager of hardware devices as an MMC snap-in. This tool is covered in Chapter 10.

Disk Management Sets up Disk Management, which can help you manage the file systems and partitions on your drives. This tool is discussed in Chapter 25.

Event Viewer Installs the Event Viewer, which is one of the key troubleshooting tools for Vista. This tool is described in Chapter 25.

Folder Installs the Folder snap-in, which can help you organize your other snap-ins into different categories. Once it's installed, you can rename the Folder snap-in. When you add new snap-ins, you can select this folder before adding the new snap-in.

FrontPage Server Extensions Sets up the snap-in that can help you administer FrontPage Server Extensions for web servers.

Group Policy Manager Installs the Group Policy manager, which can help you administer Vista policies for computer and user accounts on local or remote computers.

Group Policy Object Editor Helps you manage group policy objects.

Indexing Service Includes the Microsoft Indexing Service, which collects information from documents on local or remote computers in a separate database for quicker searches.

Internet Information Services (IIS) Adds the management tool for IIS, which is the Microsoft server for web, FTP, and mail services. IIS is addressed in more detail in Chapter 34.

IP Security Monitor Allows you to monitor traffic on local or remote computers based on various IP Security Policies. Associated with the IPSec protocols that require encryption keys and can support virtual private networking (VPN).

IP Security Policy Management Allows you to set up specific policies for monitoring traffic on your network from a local or a remote computer.

Link to Web Address Prompts you to enter a website or web file. This allows you to use MMC as a browser based on the given location. You can also use this as a link to a specific e-mail address. For example, if there's a remote administrator who needs information from your console, you can set up their e-mail address in the following format: `mailto:administrator@abc.cba`.

Local Users and Groups Lets you view and manage the users and groups on a local computer. With the right permissions, you can also set up users and groups on remote computers.

NAP Client Configuration Performs Network Access Protection (NAP) configuration for the specified client machine.

Print Management Helps you configure printers and printer servers on your network.

Reliability and Performance Monitor Allows you to configure counters, traces, and alerts. This snap-in can be used to manage the Performance console discussed in Chapter 25. You also use this snap-in to monitor system reliability, as described in Chapter 25.

Removable Storage Management Allows you to manage the information from removable media such as CDs, tape drives, and more. Can be configured for a local or a remote computer.

Resultant Set of Policy Allows you to check or test the effect of multiple policies on specific users or computers. On a domain, you can use this to check the effect on remote computers.

Security Configuration and Analysis Includes configuration and analysis tools to let you configure and analyze the effect of your security policies. This snap-in is covered in more detail in Chapter 21.

Security Templates Includes the Vista security templates that you can use in your security configuration and analysis. You can also set up the import (and export) of custom templates for your workgroup or domain. This snap-in is covered in more detail in Chapter 21.

Services Permits you to monitor and manage services on local or remote computers. This snap-in is covered in more detail in Chapter 33.

Shared Folders Allows you to monitor and manage shared files and folders on local or remote computers. As an administrator, you can disconnect users who are connecting to a share over a network. For more information on setting up a shared folder, see Chapter 19.

Task Scheduler Creates and schedules tasks that run automatically based on the criteria you provide. This snap-in is covered in more detail in Chapter 25.

TPM Management Helps you manage the Trusted Platform Module (TPM) components on a system.

Windows Firewall with Advanced Security Helps you manage the Windows Firewall, which includes configuring access for applications that require outside access using special ports. This snap-in is covered in more detail in Chapter 14.

WMI Control Installs the control tools for the Windows Management Instrumentation service, which includes VBScript objects that can further help you manage the Vista Environment. For the latest information on WMI objects, use an Internet search engine such as Google and enter the following search phrase: "Managing Windows with WMI."

Working in Author Mode and Adding Snap-Ins

When you open the MMC without snap-ins, Vista takes you to MMC Author mode to allow you to customize the administrative tool that you need. To start MMC, type **MMC.EXE** at a command prompt.

Start configuring your administrative tool. Add some of the available tools by following these steps:

1. Click File ➤ Add/Remove Snap-in to open the Add or Remove Snap-ins dialog box shown in Figure 32.1.
2. Select a snap-in of your choice. Click Add. You may see a configuration dialog box for the snap-in, such as the Device Manager dialog box shown in Figure 32.2. The most common configuration is to choose a local or remote computer. However, when working with the Certificates snap-in, you'll need to choose your account, the service account, or the computer account. The configuration dialog box you see depends on the features of the snap-in you choose.

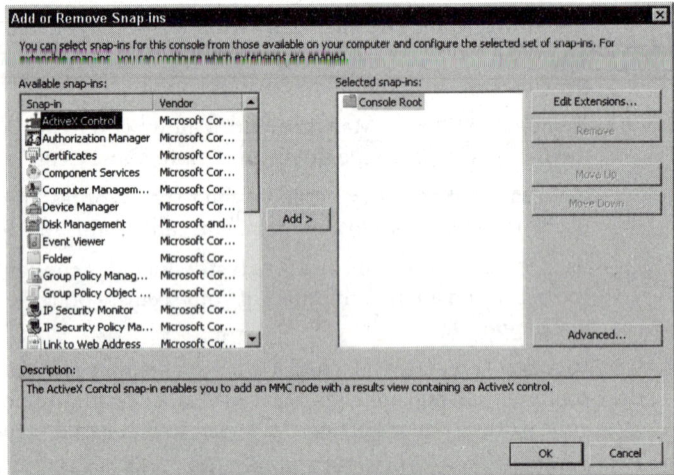

FIGURE 32.1
Use the Add or Remove Snap-ins dialog box to create a custom console.

FIGURE 32.2
Define the configuration options for the stand-alone snap-in you choose.

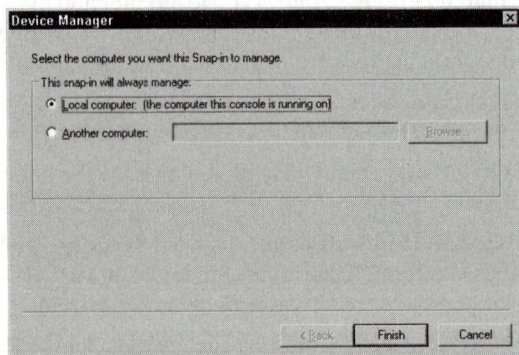

3. Repeat step 2 with as many available snap-ins as desired. The snap-ins that you selected are shown in the Selected snap-ins list on the right side of the Add or Remove Snap-ins dialog box. If you want to delete a snap-in, highlight it and click Remove.

    1. Some snap-ins, such as Shared Folders and Computer Management, include extensions that are usually other snap-ins that are normally grouped together. When a snap-in has extensions, MMC enables the Edit Extensions button. Click Edit Extensions to see the list of extensions for a particular snap-in, such as those shown for Computer Management in Figure 32.3. At this point, you need to decide whether to use all or just some of the extensions.

    2. Choose the Always enable all available extensions option when you want to use all of the extensions available with a stand-alone snap-in. Choose the Enable only selected extensions option when you want just a few of the extensions available to console users. Check any extensions that you want to make available and clear the check from any extensions you want to hide.

4. When you're ready, click OK to add these snap-ins to your console. MMC displays the snap-ins you've selected as shown in Figure 32.4.

5. Save the result under another name. Choose File ➤ Save As. In the Save As window, enter a descriptive name such as **`Cert-Device`**, and click Save. The console is saved with the `.MSC` extension by default.

Note that the title bar now reflects the filename that you used. You can now close this window, because it is also saved in your Start menu. Click Start ➤ All Programs ➤ Administrative Tools ➤ Cert-Device.MSC (or the name that you used to save your console). Vista opens the console that you've set up.

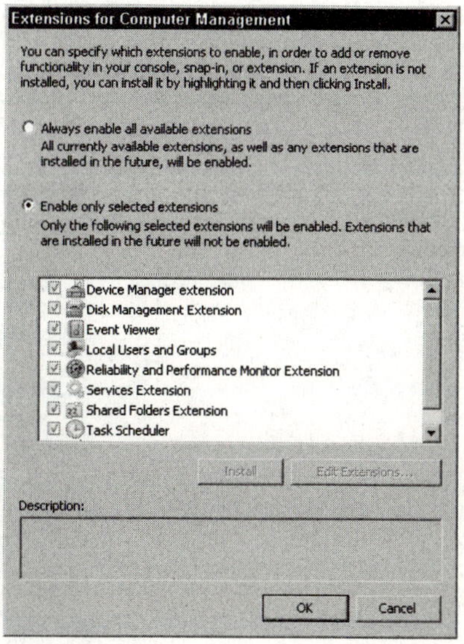

FIGURE 32.3
Snap-in extensions extend the functionality of the stand-alone snap-in you've selected.

Once you're happy with your new administrative tool, you'll want to save it in one of the User modes to prevent further changes. Choose File ➤ Options. The Console tab of the Options page opens, as shown in Figure 32.5.

You can select from the four previously mentioned modes in the Console Mode drop-down box. The different user modes are discussed in following sections. For each mode, you can choose whether to allow the user to customize the tool with the other check boxes in the Options page:

Don't save changes to this console If checked, this option prevents users from making any permanent changes to this console.

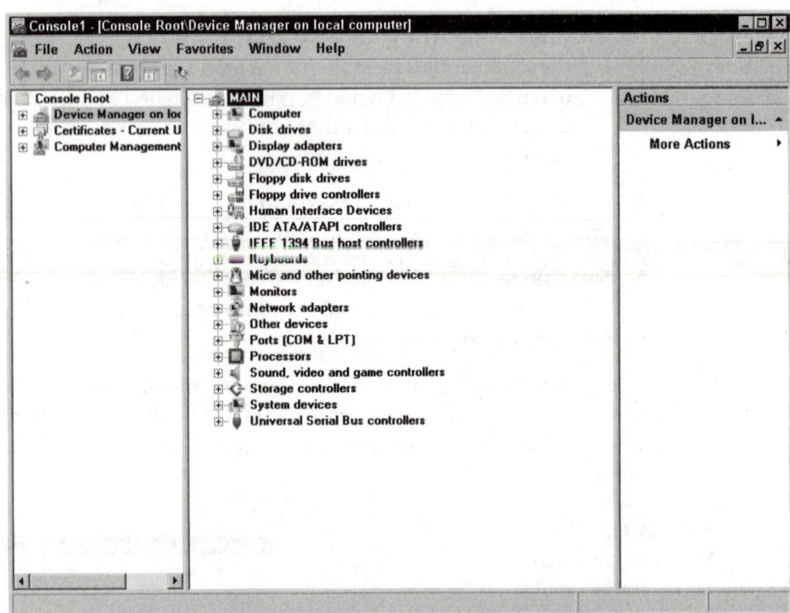

FIGURE 32.4
MMC displays the snap-ins you've selected for the custom console.

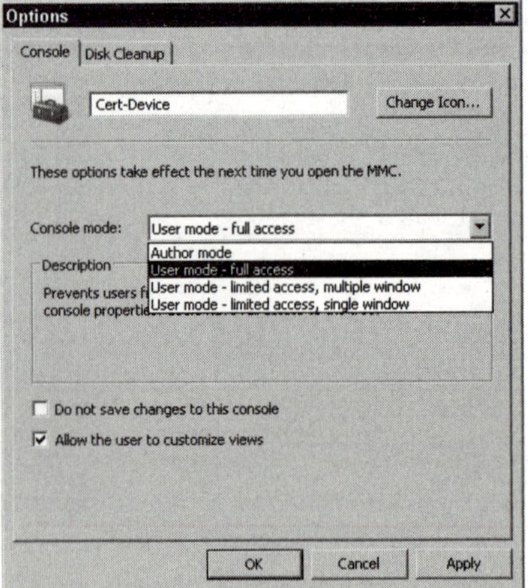

FIGURE 32.5
Consoles can be saved in different modes.

Allow the user to customize views If checked, this option allows users to access the Customize View window.

Once you've created the options of your choice, click OK to exit the Options window. Choose File ➤ Save As and enter the name of your choice.

Customizing MMC Views

If you set up a console that allows users to customize views, they can modify the look and feel of that console. To access the Customize View window shown in Figure 32.6, choose View ➤ Customize. Each of the options is described below:

Console tree Displays a list of snap-ins that are included in the console.

Standard menus Includes the Action and View menus in the console toolbar. The Action menu allows you to see a context-sensitive list of options associated with the highlighted snap-in. Alternatively, you can just right-click the snap-in. The View menu allows you to customize the look and feel of the details associated with each tool.

Standard toolbar Activates typical toolbar icons for navigation, help, and other context-sensitive options.

Status bar Shows a message associated with the highlighted tool at the bottom of the console window.

Description bar Provides information about the selected snap-in option in the details pane of the console.

Taskpad navigation tabs Allows the user to use context-specific commands associated with snap-ins. See the "Taskpad" section for more information.

Action pane Displays the Action pane on the right side of the window. This pane provides quick access to all of the actions that a user can perform with any given object.

Snap-in menus Displays menus associated with a particular snap-in. Some snap-ins don't have individual menus.

Snap-in toolbars Includes toolbars associated with a particular snap-in. Some snap-ins don't have individual toolbars.

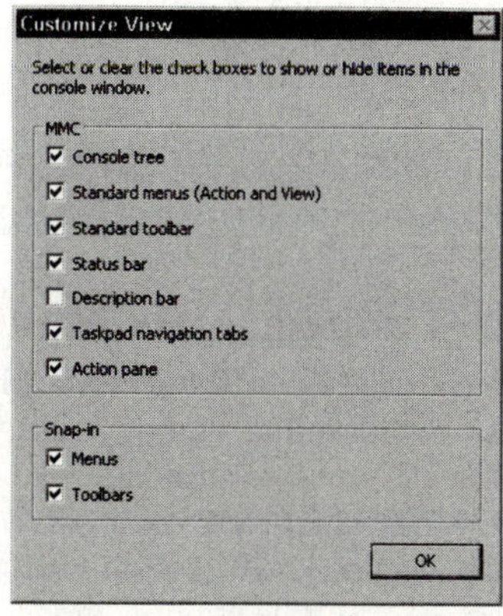

FIGURE 32.6
You can customize the look and feel of an MMC console.

User Mode–Full Access

By default, prebuilt console tools such as Computer Management open in *User mode – full access*. This is the best setup for junior system administrators or power users. Changes can't be made to the console design. They can't add or remove snap-ins, for example. When a user is running a tool and not configuring it, it should be running in one of the User modes. The tool actually looks different in User mode than it does in Author mode.

The most prominent example of a prebuilt console tool is the Computer Management Console. To start it, click Start ➤ All Programs ➤ Administrative Tools ➤ Computer Management. Figure 32.7 shows the Computer Management Console in User mode – full access.

In User mode, File menu options are limited. You can't add or remove snap-ins or change the mode of the console. But full access allows you to add windows or change the format of the console, such as the columns of data associated with a specific snap-in.

If you need to change a User mode tool, open `MMC.EXE` at the command line. Use the File menu to open the tool you want to change in Author mode. Console files are normally stored in either the `\Users\<User Name>\AppData\Roaming\Microsoft\Windows\Start Menu\Programs\Administrative Tools` or the `\Windows\system32\` directory.

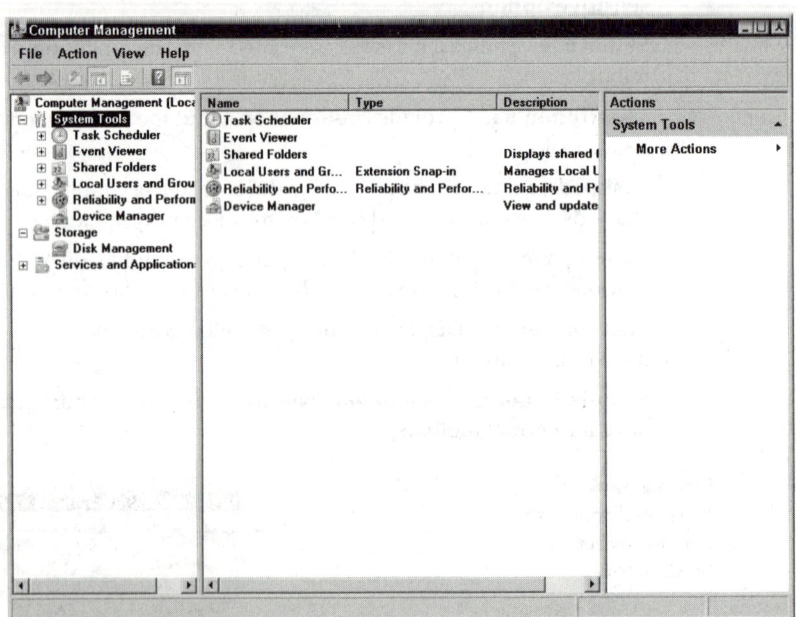

FIGURE 32.7 Computer Management in User mode.

User Mode–Limited Access, Multiple Window

In Author mode, you can restrict access further to different parts of the console. And you can set up limited access with multiple windows by default. This mode is known as *User mode – limited access, multiple window*. As you can see in Figure 32.8, multiple windows are open by default, and the close button (the X in the upper-right corner) in both windows is disabled. However, you can open additional windows. When you exit and return to this console, the changes are automatically saved.

Limited access, multiple window mode is best for users with specific dedicated tasks such as monitoring various print servers.

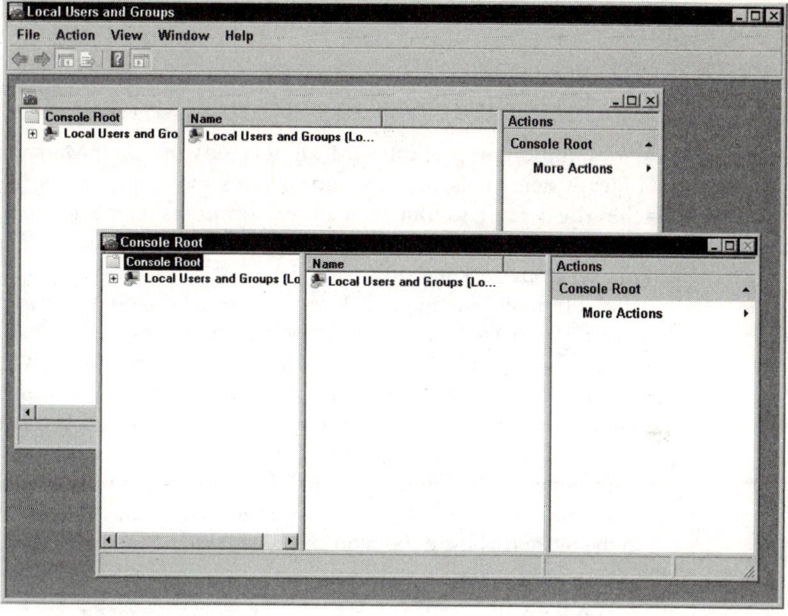

FIGURE 32.8
Sample console in User mode - limited access, multiple window.

User Mode–Limited Access, Single Window

You can restrict console access to a single window. You can't open new windows in this type of console. The controls associated with multiple windows are disabled. Not surprisingly, this mode is known as *User mode – limited access, single window*. An example of this mode is shown in Figure 32.9.

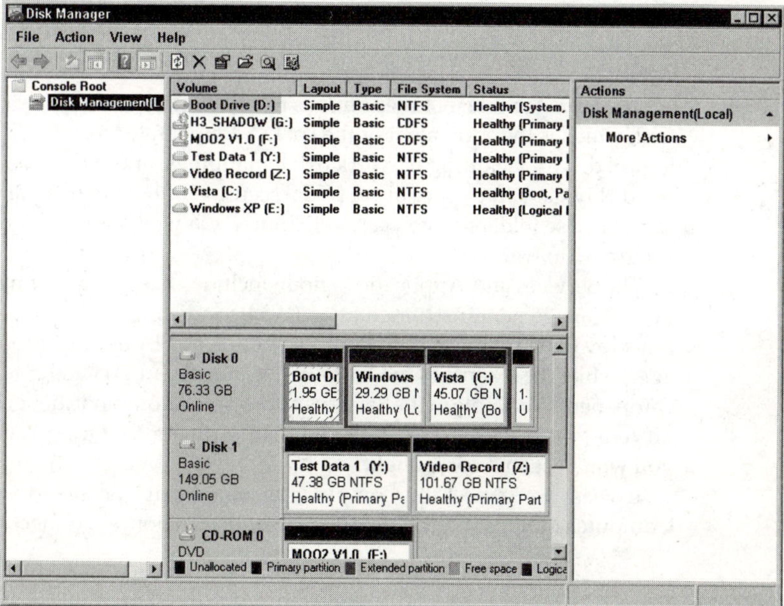

FIGURE 32.9
Sample console in User mode – limited access, single window.

Limited access, single window mode is best for less-experienced users. The limited flexibility associated with this type of console reduces the risk to your system.

The Computer Management Console

The most important prebuilt MMC tool is the Computer Management Console. The console tree includes System Tools, Storage, and Services and Applications. Notice that the focus is on the local machine by default; to connect to other computers on the network, right-click the Computer Management icon at the root of the tree (or click the Action menu) and choose Connect to Another Computer from the shortcut menu.

The Computer Management Console is *the* main tool for administering a single server, local or remote. If you have only one server on your network and you want to use only one admin tool, Computer Management fits the bill. To open the Computer Management Console, click Start ➤ All Programs ➤ Administrative Tools ➤ Computer Management.

Expand the nodes in the Computer Management Console tree to reveal the configuration tools and objects, as shown in Figure 32.7. Most of the core functions are under System Tools. Some functions even work remotely on NT 4 machines (you can view a remote machine's event logs, for example), but new features require the remote machine to be a Vista box.

In the System Tools node, you can complete the following tasks:

- View events and manage the event logs. Basically, the Event Viewer tool is turned into an MMC snap-in.
- Manage shared folders. You can view, create, and manage shares; view sessions and open files; and disconnect sessions.
- Manage devices. Device Manager is a great place to track down information about your hardware, update drivers, and troubleshoot resource conflicts.
- Configure Performance Logs and Alerts. You can create, configure, and monitor various performance settings.
- Create and manage local users and groups.

The Storage node includes options for managing removable storage and the Disk Management tool, which is the equivalent of the Disk Administrator in NT 4. There's also a component to view logical drives, including network drive mappings, and their properties. This is useful if you want to quickly view free space or set NTFS security at the root of a partition, for example. Too bad you can't browse folders as you can in Explorer. Oh well, I guess we don't need *another* desktop shell program, do we?

The Services and Applications node includes telephony settings, services configuration, Windows Management Instrumentation (WMI), indexing, and IIS management stuff, the last of which is also available in the Administrative Tools group by itself (the tool is called Internet Services Manager, while the extension in Computer Management is called Internet Information Services). The components available in the Services and Applications node depend on which services are installed on your system. For instance, if Internet Information Services isn't installed (and it isn't by default), you won't see that component.

It's easy to connect the Computer Management Console to a remote computer. Highlight Computer Management (Local), then choose Action ➤ Connect to Another Computer. In the

Select Computer window, enter the name of the other computer. The format depends on whether you've set up Vista in a workgroup or a domain:

Workgroup Use the name of the workgroup and the computer in the format `workgroupname\computername`.

Domain Use the fully qualified domain name for the computer, such as `\\xpcomp.windows.mommabears.com`.

What you can do on a remote computer depends on the applicable permissions and access rights associated with each tool. These concepts are explained in Chapter 21.

Additional Customization Options

Author mode in MMC is quite flexible. You can even use it to modify prebuilt tools such as the Computer Management Console. To open up this tool in Author mode, start the MMC. Type **`MMC.EXE`** at a command prompt. Choose File ➢ Open and select `compmgmt.msc` from the `\Windows\system32` directory.

Whenever you change a standard tool, it's a good practice to make a backup before you begin. To back up the Computer Management Console, choose File ➢ Save As and save it as another file such as `compmgmt-rev.msc`. Now you can experiment and still have the original Computer Management Console in reserve. The following sections address other available Author mode options, menu by menu from the toolbar. The exceptions are the Window and Help menus, which you already know because they work in the same way as the Window and Help menus in other Microsoft applications.

File

The File menu should look familiar. You've already added snap-ins to other consoles and used the Options window to save customized consoles in one of the four different modes.

In any User mode, most File menu options are disabled. The File ➢ Options command opens the Options window. The Delete Files button in this window deletes the changes that you've made to other User mode consoles. For example, if you've opened new windows, they're normally saved. If you click Delete Files, the original console configuration is restored.

Action

Action menus in MMC are partially context sensitive. For example, in the console tree, navigate to Local Users and Groups ➢ Users and then select the Action menu. As you can see in Figure 32.10, you can set up new users from this menu. The options that you'll see in every Action menu (except a User mode - limited access, single window console) are as follows:

New Window from Here Opens a new window within the available console.

New Taskpad View Starts the New Taskpad View Wizard that helps you create a different view of the snap-in.

Rename Allows you to rename the top-level folder in the console tree.

Export List Creates a text file with a list of plug-ins. You can share this information with other users for more standard consoles.

Help Opens help topics on MMC and any plug-ins that you've installed.

Only context-sensitive options are available in a User mode - limited access, single window console.

FIGURE 32.10
The Computer Management Action window.

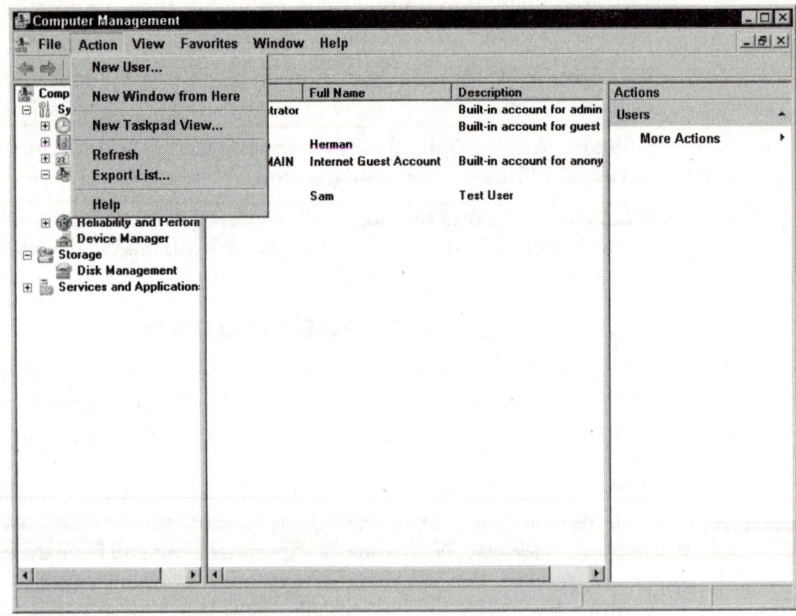

Taskpad

A *taskpad* is a graphical HTML window customized for a specific MMC plug-in. Taskpad options are available only in Author mode. To open a new console in Author mode, type **`MMC.EXE`** at a command prompt. Use the File menu to open the console of your choice. Highlight the desired plug-in and then choose Action ➢ New Taskpad View. This starts the New Taskpad View Wizard. Click Next to start the wizard, and navigate to the Taskpad Display page shown in Figure 32.11.

In the Taskpad Display page, you can set up the way the tasks are shown in the console. The options are divided into three categories:

Style for the Details Pane Organizes the tasks and configured options for this snap-in. If you deselect Hide Standard Tab, you can easily switch from the taskpad display to the standard pane by clicking the appropriate tab near the bottom of the console window.

FIGURE 32.11
The New Taskpad View Wizard.

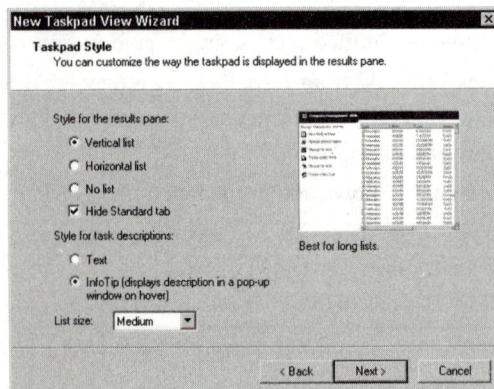

Style for Task Descriptions Determines whether the descriptions are shown on the screen or in a pop-up window.

List Size Sets up the columns associated with each task. The Small, Medium, and Large options are associated with the number of columns shown in the taskpad display.

Make your choices and click Next to continue. In the Taskpad Target page, you can set up whether this will apply to just the selected snap-in. Make your selection and click Next to continue.

In the Name and Description page, enter a name and description for the taskpad, and then click Next to continue. This completes the New Taskpad View Wizard, as shown in Figure 32.12. To continue, select the Start New Task Wizard and then click Finish.

You're taken to the Welcome to the New Task Wizard page. Click Next to continue. As shown in Figure 32.13, three types of commands are available:

Menu Command Allows you to select a task from the Action menu associated with the snap-in.

Shell Command Helps you configure a text command at the command-line interface based on what you might use at the MS-DOS–style prompt. This is appropriate if you've set up a script such as for automated monitoring of disk activity.

Navigation Allows you to select from a list of favorite snap-ins. The associated list of Favorites is different from any that you may have saved in your web browser.

FIGURE 32.12
Transition between wizards.

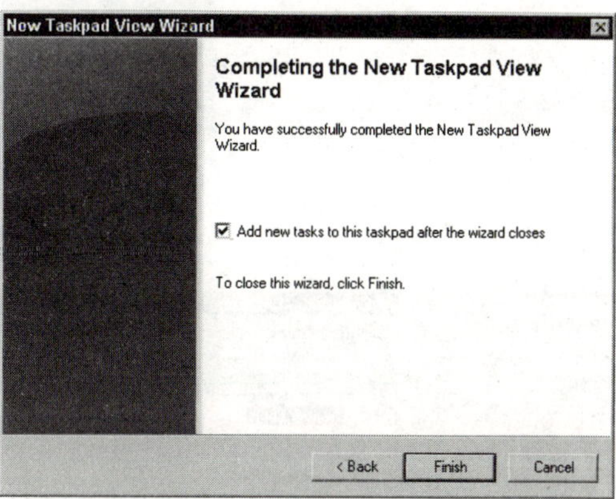

FIGURE 32.13
Select the right command type.

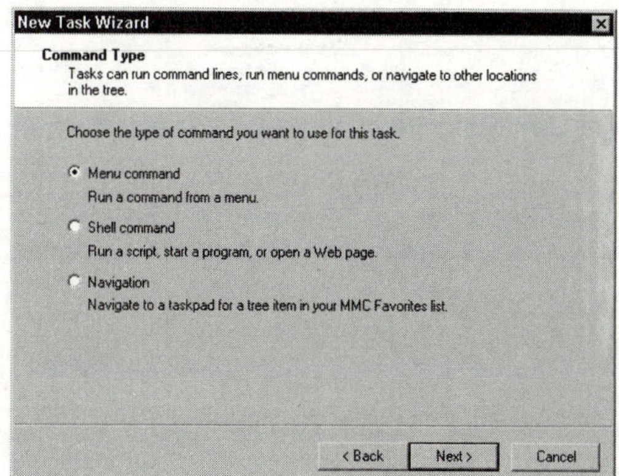

Click Next to continue. Depending on your selection, you'll need to choose a menu command, type in a shell command, or select a favorite.

Click Next to continue. Enter a task name and description. If the tool isn't familiar to your users, the description can be quite important.

Click Next to continue. Select an icon appropriate to your task.

Click Next to continue. You're shown a list of tasks that you've selected. If you need additional tasks, select the Run This Wizard Again check box, as shown in Figure 32.14. Click Finish.

Now the tasks that you've selected are shown in the right pane. As you can see in Figure 32.15, they don't have to be related to the task at hand. Now you can start the selected tasks by clicking them just like any link in a web browser. Alternatively, you can return to the original view by clicking the Standard tab near the bottom of the console.

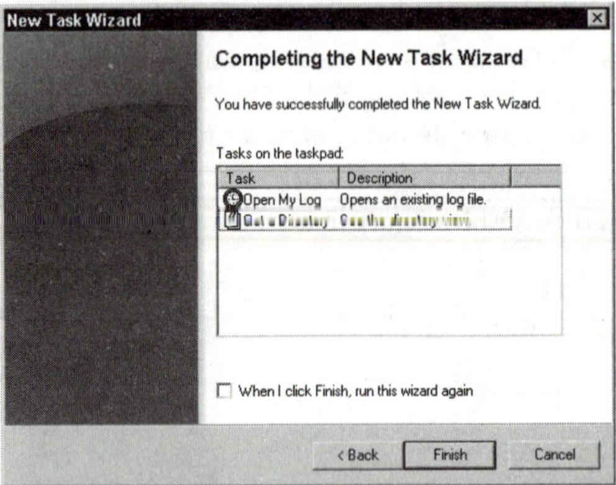

FIGURE 32.14 Selected tasks are shown before you complete the New Task Wizard.

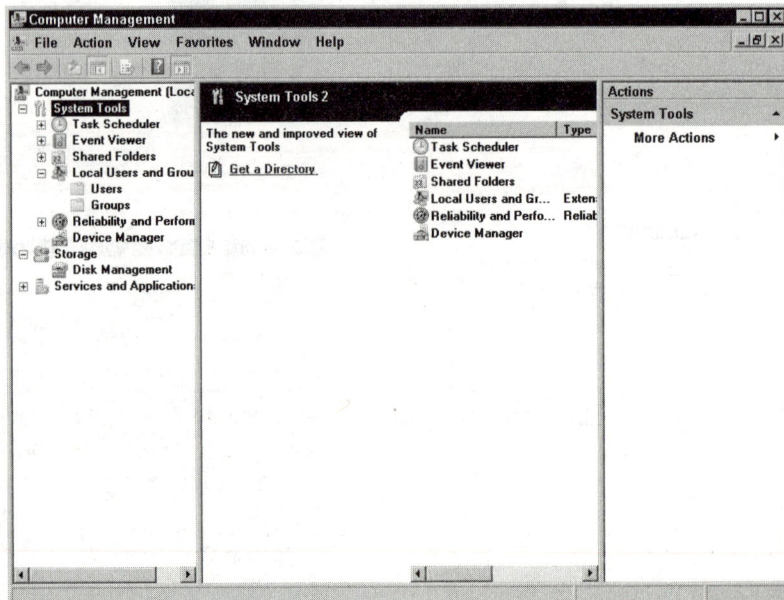

FIGURE 32.15 A console with some tasks.

NOTE If you don't see tabs at the bottom of the console, you selected Hide Standard Tab near the beginning of the New Taskpad Wizard, as shown in Figure 32.11.

If you want to change the taskpad, click the Action menu. You can now select Edit Taskpad View or Delete Taskpad View to edit or delete the task of your choice.

View

The View menu allows you to customize the look and feel of the options associated with each snap-in. The basic options (Large Icons, Small Icons, List, and Detail) work in the same way as from the Windows Explorer View menu. Two other options are unique to MMC:

Add/Remove Columns Allows you to customize the displayed columns for each snap-in.

Customize View See the "Customizing MMC Views" section earlier in this chapter.

In many cases, you can also open a View menu by right-clicking the snap-in of your choice.

Favorites

You can set up Favorite tools in MMC the same way that you set up Favorite websites in Internet Explorer. (They're separate lists.) Select the snap-in of your choice and then choose Favorites ➤ Add to Favorites and follow the prompts in the windows that appear. You can then quickly navigate to Favorite snap-ins or add a Favorite through the taskpad.

Summary

In this chapter, I've given you the basics of the Microsoft Management Console (MMC). It's a complex tool, so it's useful to recount the basic steps associated with creating or modifying a console:

- Open an existing console. Click Start ➤ All Programs ➤ Administrative Tools and select the console of your choice.
- Open a new console in Author mode. Type `MMC.EXE` at a command prompt.
- Add a snap-in in Author mode. Choose File ➤ Add/Remove Snap-in.
- Add Taskpad views with links to other tools. Choose Action ➤ New Taskpad View and follow the prompts.
- Set up a console in one of the four modes. Click File ➤ Options and select a Console mode with the settings of your choice.
- Save the console with the File ➤ Save As command. Saved consoles are accessible through the Start menu.

The next chapter dovetails quite nicely with the material presented here. It covers a lot of Vista services that you need to be familiar with to manage Vista. Most of the time, you won't need to manually tweak services, but there are times when something goes wrong and you have no other choice.

Chapter 33

Managing Vista Services

A service is a program that runs in the background to support basic activities, everything from automated updates through website connectivity. Everything important in Vista depends on one or more services. As with many other critical systems, you can manage your services through the Microsoft Management Console, which was covered in Chapter 32. Properly managed, many services allow Vista to continue operating without reboots. Properly configured, Vista turns on only the services that you need. This chapter covers the following topics:

- Why services exist
- Service management consoles
- Types of services
- Managing and configuring Vista services
- Troubleshooting service issues

Vista: What's New?

Services work essentially the same under Vista as they have for all previous versions of Windows since Windows NT. Yes, each version of Windows seems to add a little something to services, but in general, even the dialog boxes don't change much. Some of the service names have changed in Vista. Whenever possible, I'll let you know about the old name of the service.

Vista does add two features of note to services. First, you'll now find that some services provide a delayed start feature. Using a delayed automatic start means that the service is less likely to fail due to a lack of support from other services. In addition, the service will have more of the operating system features available during startup. This change will help with some types of Windows errors. For example, if you commonly receive the 80246008 error during a Windows Update, you can set the Background Intelligent Transfer Service (BITS) to a delayed start as described at `http://windowshelp.microsoft.com/Windows/en-US/Help/5f3f02f4-69bc-47a5-9e40-8c9b86ffb2fd1033.mspx`. Likewise, a delayed start can help fix the 80070643 error that results from the Office Source Engine (OSE) service during Windows Update as described at `http://windowshelp.microsoft.com/Windows/en-US/Help/e5304fc1-9264-4d97-9c35-3c3ad167e1701033.mspx`.

The second feature is an emphasis on automatic service restarts. Services have always had the ability to restart automatically. However, the default setting of previous versions of Windows was to take no action at all. Vista changes the default to restarting the service automatically. In addition, should you decide to reboot the computer, rather than simply restart the service, you can now send messages to other computers on the network so that others who rely on services your computer provides can act accordingly.

The Purpose of a Service

Services run in the background. Most are started automatically when you start Vista—some start and stop automatically as the result of an application request or environmental need. Among other things, services provide the interfaces that allow you to connect to the Internet, manage interfaces to an uninterruptible power supply (UPS), and more.

Vista services are similar to *daemons* in the world of UNIX and Linux. In either case, these are programs that run in the background and provide the interfaces required to run programs such as Internet connections and print servers.

It's practically unheard of to find a Vista computer that needs to run every service (in reality, you can't actually run every service because some services stop automatically when they don't have work to do). Each service takes up space in RAM and places demands on your CPU. Even if you have the fastest computer and gigabytes of RAM, you generally don't want all services to run simultaneously. Some services have been known to conflict with each other.

In fact, if you have a relatively small amount of RAM (64MB–128MB), you'll want to disable as many services as possible. The following sections highlight several services that you may be able to disable if you're not using the associated applications.

Specialized programs come with their own services that may cause problems. For example, some database programs explicitly state that you should turn off all but a few services on Vista before starting the installation process.

The Service Management Console

Take a look at the installed services in Vista. To open the Service Management Console shown in Figure 33.1, click Start ➢ All Programs ➢ Administrative Tools ➢ Services. By default, it opens this console in User mode - limited access, single window, which means you can use it just for your services. It also opens with a taskpad that can allow you to start, stop, pause, or restart different services with a single click.

Note the two tabs at the bottom of Figure 33.1. The Extended tab is configured with a taskpad to allow you to manage the highlighted service with ease. In contrast, the Standard tab includes no such feature. When working on the Standard tab, you right-click the service and choose the management option from the context menu.

NOTE This chapter assumes that you've read Chapter 32 and are comfortable with the basic operation of the Microsoft Management Console.

TIP The Services snap-in is also available as part of the Computer Management Console. Alternatively, click Start ➢ Run and type `services.msc` to start the Service Management Console.

Click the Extended tab if required, and then click a service. Note the options for what you can do with this service. Repeat this with other services. Figure 33.1 shows the Interactive Services Detection service selected, which helps the user work with interactive services. The links allow you to quickly stop, pause, or restart that service.

WARNING Some services don't provide a Stop or Pause option. After they start, they continue to run while the computer is running. One way to shut down such a service is to disable the service and restart the computer—the service won't start. However, using this technique is counterproductive in most cases. If the service doesn't provide a Stop option, you should normally leave it running.

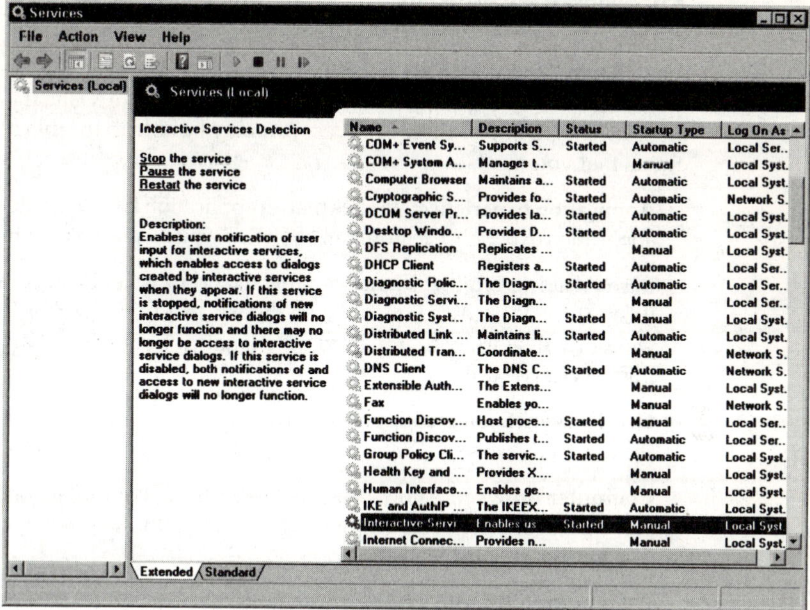

FIGURE 33.1
The Service Management Console.

Vista Services

A large number of services are installed on Vista. The following lists are based on a standard computer with IIS installed. I've divided these services into five categories:

- Services that are started automatically
- Services that are started automatically after a delay
- Services that you start manually
- Services that are disabled
- Services that you can add after installing Vista

Since required services vary with the hardware and software configuration of your computer, this may not be a complete list. Based on previous work on your computer, the service may be in a different category. Other services that you might see, such as VMware Authorization Service, are associated with a particular program, in this case, with VMware. New services are under constant development. If you don't see your service here, consult the developer of the associated application, or check the Microsoft Knowledge Base, available at `http://support.Microsoft.com`.

In the section "Configuring Services," you'll learn how to change the status of a service. Automatic services are started when you boot Vista. Specific programs often start manual services. Disabled services aren't available to support any programs that might need them. And other programs, such as IIS and VMware, add additional services that fall into one of the other three categories.

Automatic Services

The following is a list of services that are started automatically when you boot Vista. The list you see will vary by configuration.

While this is a long list, it can help you learn a lot about Vista. If you're not using the applications associated with one of these services, you may be able to disable it and save resources for the programs that you need.

Application Experience: Verifies that an application is compatible with Vista before running it. The application experience feature can often help you fix possible problems to make the application run.

Base Filtering Engine: Manages firewall and Internet Protocol security (IPsec). If you turn off this feature, Windows Firewall won't work. In addition, other Vista security features might not work or will work with impaired functionality. Some third-party products may eventually use this service as well.

COM+ Event System: Supports the System Event Notification service discussed in the previous section. In this case, COM is the Component Object Model, required for ActiveX programs.

Computer Browser: Allows Vista to keep a list of computers on the LAN. If there are Windows servers on your network, they generally take on this task. A Vista computer can take on a backup role for this service.

Cryptographic Services: Manages the certificates that you need to verify the authenticity of critical files and programs.

DCOM Server Process Launcher: Lets the system launch Distributed Component Object Model (DCOM) processes, which are bits of code that reside on another machine that provide some specific functionality. For example, an application might need to request information from a database on a server using a DCOM component.

Desktop Window Manager Session Manager: Provides the Desktop Window Manager with startup and maintenance services. You must enable this service to obtain most of the new graphics features of Vista.

DHCP Client: Lets your computer get an IP address from a DHCP server. See Chapter 22 for more information on DHCP, which is the Dynamic Host Configuration Protocol. Don't disable this service unless you have a fixed IP address.

Diagnostic Policy Service: Provides diagnostic and troubleshooting services for the system. Every time an application, piece of hardware, or part of the operating system experiences a problem, this service provides support for troubleshooting it.

Distributed Link Tracking Client: Allows your computer to maintain the links between files on your computer or network. One example of a link is an Excel spreadsheet embedded in a Word document. If you don't have an NTFS partition, you can disable this service.

DNS Client: Permits contact between your computer and Domain Name System (DNS) servers. This is usually a requirement for computers on larger networks or with a connection to the Internet. For more information, see Chapter 19.

Function Discovery Resource Publication: Publishes the presence of this computer and the resources it provides across the network. If you don't want the presence of your computer known and have no resources to share with others, you can stop this service.

Group Policy Client: Applies settings defined by administrators using the Group Policy Object Editor console. If you stop this service, Vista won't apply any group polices, which means that you might not have access to system features.

IKE and AuthIP IPsec Keying Modules: Provides security using the Internet Key Exchange (IKE) and Authenticated Internet Protocol (AuthIP) keying modules. Vista uses the keying modules for authentication and key exchange when using IPsec. Stopping this service means that some peer exchange functionality may not work and you won't be able to access resources on remote systems.

IP Helper: This service provides IPv6 connectivity over an IPv4 network. This service doesn't affect native IPv6 connectivity. You don't need to keep this service running if you don't use IPv6 over IPv4.

IPsec Policy Agent: Manages security on TCP/IP networks. It's required to support virtual private networks. Older versions of Windows called this service IPSEC Services.

NOTE Microsoft has eliminated some older services that you found in other versions of Windows. One of the most notorious services was Messenger. This service let administrators send alerts across the network before performing maintenance tasks or shutting down systems. Even though Messenger was a helpful and useful service, the security flaws it included prompted Microsoft to remove the service from Vista.

Multimedia Class Scheduler: Manages multimedia tasks on a system so that each task obtains the required number of resources and processing time. If you stop this service, the applications will still run, but they'll default to their programmed priority levels, which means that multimedia may not play as efficiently as before.

Network List Service: Identifies the networks to which the computer has connected. In addition, this service collects and stores properties for each of these networks and notifies applications when the properties change.

Network Location Awareness: Maintains information on connected logical networks.

Offline Files: Performs maintenance on the offline file cache. This service also reacts to user logon and logoff events to make offline files available for use. Finally, this service sends out messages to applications whenever the status of the offline file cache changes.

Plug and Play: Supports most modern hardware on a Plug and Play operating system such as Vista.

Portable Device Enumerator Service: Enforces group policy for removable devices. Retrieves the serial number of portable music players that are connected to your computer. If you're not using a portable digital music device such as a Rio player and don't use removable media in a group setting, deactivate this service. This is an extension of the Portable Media Serial Number service found in previous versions of Windows.

Print Spooler: Loads files that are translated to your printer in memory. If you print, you need this service.

Program Compatibility Assistant: Provides support for the Program Compatibility Assistant feature of Vista.

ReadyBoost: Enhances system performance using the ReadyBoost feature of Vista. You can read about this feature in Chapter 1 and the "Get Plenty of RAM" sidebar in Chapter 2.

Remote Procedure Call (RPC): Supports communication between applications on a client-server network. Many other services depend on RPC. If you plan to be on a network, you should always enable this service.

Secondary Logon: Allows users to log on more than once to the same system. This important security feature is described in more detail in Chapter 22.

Security Accounts Manager: Stores security information for local accounts. See Chapter 21 for more information.

Server: Permits access to the local computer as a server, typically for sharing files and printers.

Shell Hardware Detection: Allows the AutoPlay feature to automatically run a CD that you've just inserted into a drive. AutoPlay is described in Chapter 1.

Software Licensing: Enables you to download licensed content from the Internet. This service downloads the required license, installs it on your machine, and enforces the terms of the license.

SuperFetch: Helps improve system performance over time by monitoring system activities and optimizing resource usage. You can learn more about SuperFetch in Chapter 1.

System Event Notification: Supports connectivity for mobile devices. For example, this service allows you to enter e-mail on a laptop computer. Your mail is sent when you connect to a network.

Tablet PC Input Service: Provides support for the Tablet PC pen and ink features included with Vista. You can learn more about these features in the "Working with Tablet PCs" section of Chapter 7. Stop this service if you don't intend to use any of the Tablet PC functionality.

Task Scheduler: Permits you to schedule a task to run automatically on a specific time and date.

TCP/IP NetBIOS Helper: Allows Windows computers to communicate on a TCP/IP network. For more information on NetBIOS and TCP/IP, see Chapter 19.

Terminal Services: Enables the use of Terminal Services Advanced Clients (TSAC) such as the Remote Desktop Connection discussed in Chapter 16.

Themes: Supports the basic themes and desktop backgrounds shown in Vista.

UPnP Device Host: Supports many home and small business network devices. Depends on the SSDP Discovery Service. This service isn't related to Plug and Play. Older versions of Windows call this the Universal Plug and Play Device Host service.

User Profile Service: Loads and unloads user profiles. Stopping this service prevents users from logging into or out of a network, and means applications may not function properly and the user might not be able to access important data.

WebClient: Lets you create, access, and modify files on the Internet.

Windows Audio: Supports sound. If you want sound, you need this service.

Windows Audio Endpoint Builder: Manages audio devices for the Windows Audio service. If you disable this service, the audio devices on your system may not function properly.

Windows Defender: Scans your system for unwanted software, schedules software scans, and downloads the latest software definitions. Essentially, this is a very basic spyware and virus protection. You can learn more about this Vista feature in Chapter 14.

Windows Driver Foundation - User-mode Driver Framework: Manages the user-mode device driver features. This is the part of the device driver software that you would use to configure a device.

Windows Error Reporting Service: Allows error logs from nonstandard applications. This service may not be necessary unless you need logs to help troubleshoot a specific application. This service was called Error Reporting Service in previous versions of Windows.

Windows Event Log: Sends notification of major events and errors to the Event Viewer. This is a critical troubleshooting tool discussed in Chapter 32. It's also required to support IIS, which is covered in Chapter 34. This service was called Event Log in previous versions of Windows.

Windows Firewall: Provides both incoming and outgoing filtering of Internet messages to protect your system. This feature used to be part of the Windows Firewall (WF)/Internet Connection Sharing (ICS) service.

Windows Image Acquisition (WIA): Enables communication with some image devices such as scanners and digital cameras. Associated with the Scanners and Cameras Wizard in Control Panel.

Windows Management Instrumentation: Sets up a common model for administering local and remote systems.

Windows Search: Allows the organization of the contents of local and remote files into a database. Supports the organization of data in web searches. Required for the Fast Find feature associated with Microsoft Office. Since this service uses a substantial amount of resources, don't use this feature unless your users need this level of access to data on your system. Older versions of Windows call this the Indexing Service.

Windows Time: Synchronizes the time between computers.

Workstation: Manages network connections from a client computer on a network.

Automatic (Delayed Start) Services

Automatic (Delayed Start) services work essentially the same as Automatic services. The only difference is that they start a few seconds after all of the Automatic services start. In general, the delayed start reduces problems with services starting correctly. The following list of services is usually set up for an automatic, delayed start, startup.

Background Intelligent Transfer Service: Manages network file transfers through unused bandwidth; allows for interrupted file transfers.

KtmRm for Distributed Transaction Coordinator: Coordinates communication between the Microsoft Distributed Transaction Coordinator (MSDTC) and the Kernel Transaction Manager (KTM). Essentially, transactions ensure that data gets from one location to another. When the data fails to arrive, the system rolls back the tasks used to create it. Using this technique helps ensure the system remains in a known good state.

Security Center: Monitors the system security settings and configurations. You can learn more about Security Center in Chapter 21.

Windows Event Collector: Manages the subscriptions to events from remote sources. This is part of the Data Collector Sets described in the "Monitoring Performance" section of Chapter 25.

Windows Media Center Service Launcher: Starts the Windows Media Center Scheduler and the Windows Media Center Receiver when you enable the TV feature of Windows Media Center. You can disable this service if you don't use Windows Media Center.

Windows Update: Permits automatic Vista updates. You can safely disable this service and still run Windows Update manually. Keep it if you're configuring Vista for users who wouldn't run Windows Update on their own. This service used to appear as Automatic Updates.

Manual Services

Manual services normally aren't activated when you boot Vista. However, associated programs and utilities can usually start these services on an "as needed" basis. The following list of services is usually set up for manual startup:

Application Information: Helps you run applications that require administrator privileges. Although this service is set to run manually, it always runs for an administrator account. If you stop this service, Vista won't provide the prompts to elevate your privileges, which makes using some applications impossible.

Application Layer Gateway Service: Allows you to use the Internet Connection Sharing (ICS) features on the local computer. Don't let the Service console's reference to third-party plug-ins confuse you; this is required for ICS. For more information on ICS, see Chapter 14.

Application Management: Allows for the installation and updating of certain types of applications.

Block-Level Backup Engine Service: Used by the backup applications your system to perform backup and recovery of data.

Certificate Propagation: Used with smart cards to spread certificates as needed within the system.

CNG Key Isolation: Provides Cryptographic Next Generation (CNG) key support for data storage and applications. CNG is the eventual replacement for the CryptoAPI and provides significantly better security. You can learn more about this low-level security feature at `http://msdn2.microsoft.com/en-gb/library/aa375276.aspx`.

COM+ System Application: Manages the configuration and tracking of COM+-based components. Closely related to the COM+ Event System service.

DFS Replication: Performs Distributed File System (DFS) tasks, such as keeping files on various machines synchronized.

Diagnostics Service Host: Provides detection, troubleshooting, and resolution for service-related errors.

Distributed Transaction Coordinator: Allows resource communication between programs that manage databases, even on non-Windows operating systems.

Extensible Authentication Protocol: Provides Extensible Authentication Protocol (EAP) authentication for wired, wireless, virtual private network (VPN), and Network Access Protection (NAP) connections. This service normally starts when the system needs to perform authentication and stops immediately afterward, so there isn't any reason to change its settings.

Fax: Allows you to send and receive faxes. If you have trouble sending a fax, this service might be disabled and need restarting.

Function Discovery Provider Host: This service supports the Function Discovery feature of Vista. This feature helps applications enumerate system resources. In most cases, you won't want to change this service's settings. You can read more about this feature at `http://msdn2.microsoft.com/en-us/library/aa814070.aspx`.

Health Key and Certificate Management: Provides X.509 key and certificate management functionality for the Network Access Protection Agent (NAPAgent).

Human Interface Device Access: Associated with hot buttons on input devices such as keyboards and mice.

Interactive Services Detection: Provides the user with notification of interactive services. The interactive services normally interact with the user through special dialog boxes. Normally, this service starts itself when specific system events occur and you won't need to worry about it.

Internet Connection Sharing (ICS): Supports the sharing of an Internet connection. For more information see Chapter 14. This feature used to be part of the Windows Firewall (WF)/Internet Connection Sharing (ICS) service.

Link-Layer Topology Discovery Mapper: Provides automatic networking services by using various new technologies in Vista. This is the piece of magic that makes networking connectivity so automatic in Vista. You'll find discussions of this technology throughout Parts 5 and 6 in the book.

Microsoft .NET Framework NGEN v2.0.50727_X86: Provides support for the Native Image Generator (NGen) tool provided with the .NET Framework. This tools changes a .NET application from a series of tokens into an actual executable for your system. The version number part of the service name will vary by platform and version of the .NET Framework you have installed. You can read more about the NGen tool at `http://msdn.microsoft.com/msdnmag/issues/05/04/NGen/`.

Microsoft iSCSI Initiator Service: Provides support for the Internet Small Computer Systems Interface (iSCSI) functionality found in Vista. You can learn more about this feature in the "Working with iSCSI Devices" section of Chapter 10.

MS Software Shadow Copy Provider: Manages a special type of dynamic backup known as a shadow copy. Closely related to the Volume Shadow Copy service.

Net.Tcp Port Sharing Service: Provides the ability to share TCP ports using the Net.Tcp protocol. Generally, the software that uses this service is a custom application that relies on the Windows Communication Foundation (WCF) portion of.NET Framework 3.0. You can learn more about Net.Tcp at `http://msdn2.microsoft.com/en-us/library/ms734772.aspx`.

Netlogon: Supports sending usernames and passwords to a domain controller on a network. If you're not on a domain as described in Chapter 22, you can disable this service. Previous versions of Windows called this service Net Logon.

Network Access Protection Agent (NAPAgent): Enables Network Access Protection (NAP) support on the client computer.

Network Connections: Supports network connectivity. Don't disable, unless your computer never connects to another network. Even Internet connections require this service.

Office Source Engine: Saves the Office installation files and uses them for updates and repairs. You must also have this service enabled to download Setup application updates and Watson error reports.

Parental Controls: Provides Parental Control support under Vista.

Peer Name Resolution Protocol: Lets you use Peer Name Resolution Protocol (PNRP) over the Internet without an intervening server. This server supports such Vista features as Windows Meeting.

Peer Networking Grouping: Provides peer networking grouping services.

Peer Networking Identity Manager: Provides peer networking identity services.

Performance Logs and Alerts: Allows collection of performance data. If preconfigured benchmarks are met, this service triggers an alarm. If you're troubleshooting through the Performance console, enable this service.

PnP-X IP Bus Enumerator: Provides Plug and Play (PnP) X bus enumeration services. The service uses the Simple Service Discovery Protocol (SSDP) and WS-Discovery protocol to perform the required enumeration. If you disable this service, the system will stop recognizing any Network Computing Devices (NCDs). You can read more about this feature at `http://msdn2.microsoft.com/en-us/library/aa814083.aspx`.

PNRP Machine Name Publication Service: Publishes the system's name using PNRP.

Problem Reports and Solutions Control Panel Support: Provides support for sending, viewing, and deleting system-level reports using the Problem Reports and Solutions applet in the Control Panel. You can read more about this feature in the "Using Problem Reports and Solutions to Track Vista Issues" section of Chapter 25.

Protected Storage: Allows password protection for the files you specify.

Quality Windows Audio Video Experience: Creates a more pleasing audio and video experience in Vista. This service also provides streaming support for IP home network.

Remote Access Auto Connection Manager: Supports network connections that require a search through a database of computer names based on a DNS server or NetBIOS names.

Remote Access Connection Manager: Supports Internet connections. Required for ICS.

Remote Procedure Call (RPC) Locator: Supports remote administration from the local computer.

Remote Registry: Allows users with appropriate rights to modify the local Registry from a remote computer. Disable this service unless you absolutely need to manage the Registry from a remote computer.

NOTE Microsoft changed the automatic startup status of some services in Vista. The Remote Registry service used to start automatically. However, allowing access to your system from a remote machine, especially access to the Registry, isn't a very good idea. Consequently, Microsoft has made the Remote Registry service a manual startup in Vista for security reasons.

Routing and Remote Access: Enables configuration of the local computer as a router, which acts as the interface between your network and another network such as the Internet. If you're using ICS/ICF, you don't need this service.

SL UI Notification Service: Provides a user interface (UI) for software licensing (SL) activation and notification.

Smart Card: Enables the use of smart card readers, which may become the standard for remote identification.

Smart Card Removal Policy: Allows you to configure the system to lock the desktop automatically when the user removes a smart card.

SNMP Trap Service: Allows the receipt of messages through SNMP traps such as those associated with the Performance console.

SSDP Discovery Service: Allows the use of Universal Plug and Play (UPnP) devices such as those related to small business or home networks. As strange as it sounds, UPnP isn't related to Plug and Play.

TCP/IP Print Server: Enables clients with Line Print Daemon (LPD) software to print to the local computer. LPD is common in UNIX/Linux systems as well as Windows NT computers that are connected through TCP/IP.

Telephony: Supports the Telephony Application Programming Interface (TAPI), which is required for communications programs such as Microsoft Fax. For more information on these programs, see Chapter 16.

Telnet: Allows remote access through Telnet clients on a TCP/IP network. For a description of the Remote Terminal (Telnet) service, see Chapter 15.

Terminal Services Configuration: Performs Terminal Services (TS) and Remote Desktop related configuration and session maintenance activities that require the SYSTEM account. The features include session temporary folders, TS themes, and TS certificates.

Terminal Services UserMode Port Redirector: Performs redirection of ports, printers, and disks when using the Remote Desktop Protocol (RDP).

Thread Ordering Server: Performs ordered execution of threads at the same priority and created during the same time frame. Orderly execution ensures that each thread can perform a given amount of its task during each processing session.

TPM Base Services: Manages access to the Trusted Platform Module (TPM) chip used for Vista features such as BitLocker. You can learn more about BitLocker in the "Working with BitLocker" section of Chapter 21.

Uninterruptible Power Supply (UPS): Supports the management of a UPS that's connected to and controlled by your computer. For more information, see Chapter 10.

Virtual Disk: Configures disks. Manages the status of disk drives automatically. Allows Vista to see removable drives when they're installed. Permits different applications to share access to removable storage devices such as tape drives. This service is a superset of the Logical Disk Manager, Removable Storage, and Logical Disk Manager Administrative Service services found on older versions of Windows.

Volume Shadow Copy: Supports the dynamic backups associated with the Microsoft Backup utility. Closely related to the MS Software Shadow Copy Provider. For more information on backups, see Chapter 29.

Windows Backup: Provides backup and restore functionality. For more information on backups, see Chapter 29.

Windows CardSpace: Provides digital identity management. You can learn more about this feature in the "Working with CardSpace" section of Chapter 21.

Windows Color System: Provides a means of extending the native color system in Windows to perform additional color matching tasks. The specifics of the additional color rendering functionality depend on the third-party product. See the vendor documentation for additional details.

Windows Connect Now - Config Registrar: Issues a network credential to the person or object requesting access.

Windows Installer: Supports the installation and maintenance of any application that uses instructions configured in MSI files such as Microsoft Office.

Windows Media Center Extender Service: Provides the means for Media Center Extender devices to locate and connect to the computer.

Windows Media Center Receiver Service: Lets your computer receive TV and FM broadcast transmissions.

Windows Media Center Scheduler Service: Starts and stops recording of TV shows within Windows Media Center.

Windows Media Player Network Sharing Service: Lets you share the media on your system with other people. This service relies on UPnP to provide connectivity and discoverability.

Windows Modules Installer: Lets you add and remove Windows components. In most cases, the component software is still in place; Vista simply makes the software inaccessible, so you really aren't adding or removing software as you would have in previous versions of Windows.

Windows Presentation Foundation Font Cache 3.0.0.0: Optimizes the performance of the fancy graphics that Vista provides, such as the Aero Graphics. Microsoft calls this feature the Windows Presentation Foundation (WPF). It's one of the additions provided by.NET Framework 3.0. The version number of the service will vary as Microsoft provides updates to the original .NET Framework 3.0.

Windows Remote Management (WS-Management): Provides the services required to perform maintenance on a system through an Internet connection using a web services interface. WS-Management is a multi-vendor specification hosted by the Distributed Management Task Force, Inc. You can find the specification for WS-Management at `http://www.dmtf.org/standards/wsman`. The Windows view of WS-Management appears at `http://www.microsoft.com/whdc/system/pnppwr/wsm/default.mspx`. You can learn about the enabling technology in Vista, Windows Remote Management (WinRM), at `http://msdn2.microsoft.com/en-us/library/aa384291.aspx`.

WinHTTP Web Proxy Auto-Discovery Service: Implements the HTTP functionality you need to make requests and receive responses using the Internet. This feature includes support for using remote software, such as the COM Automation components used by some Microsoft websites, such as Windows Update. Finally, this service provides support for the Web Proxy Auto-Discovery (WPAD) protocol. You can learn more about WPAD at `http://wpad.org/draft-ietf-wrec-wpad-01.txt`. The most visual effect of WPAD is the Local Area Network Settings dialog box (open the Internet Options applet of the control panel, select the Connections tab, and click LAN Settings). When you check the Automatically detect settings option, Internet Explorer relies on WPAD to locate a proxy server automatically.

Wired AutoConfig: Configures compatible wired network adapters automatically. It automatically authenticates connections using Institute of Electrical & Electronics Engineers (IEEE) 802.1X authentication.

WLAN AutoConfig: Configures compatible wireless network adapters automatically. Older versions of Windows call this the Wireless Zero Configuration service.

WMI Performance Adapter: Enables the high-performance (HiPerf) class of data associated with the Performance Monitor discussed in Chapter 25.

Disabled Services

Disabled services aren't activated when you boot Vista. Unless you activate them in the Services console, associated programs and utilities can't start these services. Unlike previous versions of Windows, Vista doesn't disable any services by default. In some cases, you'll actually need to disable a service to stop it from running when you don't want the service it provides. You may also see disabled services when you install other software when the functionality that the service provides isn't needed immediately or is used intermittently.

Additional Services

Additional services are added to the Services console when you install the associated application. They can fall into any of the above categories (Automatic, Manual, Disabled). In preparation for Chapter 34, the services described here are associated with Internet Information Server (IIS):

FTP Publishing: Supports the configuration of an FTP site for sharing files with others. Information on accessing FTP sites is available in Chapter 15.

IIS Admin: Enables administration of IIS through the Microsoft Management Console.

Simple Mail Transfer Protocol: Allows the setup of a mail server through IIS. Don't confuse this with SNMP.

SNMP Service: The Simple Network Management Protocol (SNMP) allows you to use services such as the Performance console discussed in Chapter 25 to monitor network activity. It also supports network monitoring from other computers, even through other operating systems such as Linux.

World Wide Web Publishing: Permits the setup of local website files, accessible through the network with IIS.

Configuring Services

You can modify how a service works on Vista. The properties for each service include General, Log On, and Recovery properties. The dependencies of each service are listed on the Dependencies tab of the service's Properties dialog box. Finally, you can stop or start a service through the console or at the command line.

These are all tabs in the Properties window associated with each service. A few services such as SNMP include other tabs that support the special configuration requirements of that service.

General

In the Services console, highlight the service of your choice. Choose Action ➤ Properties to open a Properties window named for your service. (You can also right-click the service entry and choose Properties from the context menu.) The properties for the Background Intelligent Transfer Service are shown in Figure 33.2. The basic information is consistent for all services.

As you can see in Figure 33.2, this window opens to the General tab by default. It lists the basic parameters of the service: the name, description, and the location of the associated executable file.

NOTE Note the actual file associated with the service. It will come in handy later in the "Service Commands" section.

The Startup Type can be set to Automatic, Manual, or Disabled. As described earlier in this chapter, Automatic startup means this service starts when you boot Vista. Manual startup leaves the service available for other programs or applications to start on an as-needed basis. Disabled startup means that service is unavailable for such programs.

As shown in the Service Status section, you can Start, Stop, Pause, and Resume each service. When a service is stopped, you can specify Start parameters as you would at the command-line interface.

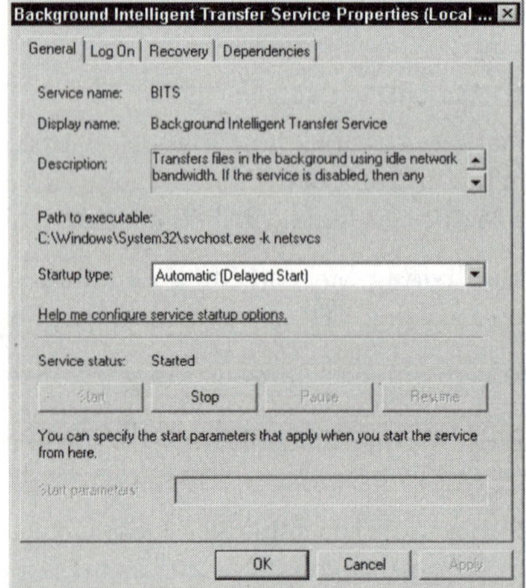

FIGURE 33.2
Service properties.

Log On

Every running service needs to log on before it starts. In the Properties window for your service, click the Log On tab, which is shown in Figure 33.3. Most services have their own generic account, known as the Local System account. The options are listed here:

Local System Account: Allows most services to be set to log on to their own account, known generically as the Local System account. You won't find this account in the User Management list.

Allow Service to Interact with Desktop: Supports special configuration for services such as the Print Spooler service. Alternatively, may allow some services to send messages to your desktop.

This Account: Many services can be configured to use a different local or remote account. Some need special accounts, especially if network access to other computers is required. Two exceptions are the DNS and DHCP services.

Hardware Profile: Configured services can vary by the hardware profiles.

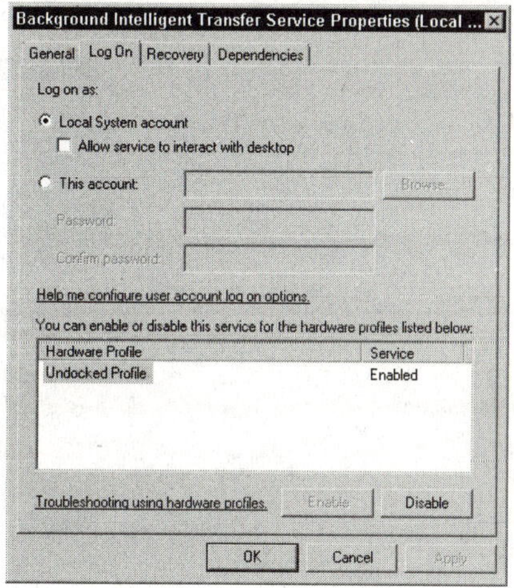

FIGURE 33.3
Log On properties.

Recovery

If you install just a few applications, you may have over 100 configured services on your computer. Many services fail for "ordinary" reasons, such as a broken network connection or a modified configuration file. You don't want to have to restart the computer every time a service fails. Under previous versions of Windows, the default action was to take no action at all, which means that if the service didn't start, you wouldn't know about it until such time as you actually needed to use it. The default action in Vista is to restart the service. This action is a better default because it makes the service available even if a minor glitch occurs during startup.

Click the Recovery tab on the Properties window for a service. As you can see in Figure 33.4, you can set different actions for the first, second, and subsequent failures. You can set each service to take one of the following four actions in any of these cases:

Take No Action: Allows a noncritical service to fail. Unless you use this option, some services such as IIS will automatically restart after a failure. If you're having a problem with IIS, you may want it to stop to give you a chance to maintain the associated web or FTP server.

Restart the Service: Allows a service to be restarted, which is appropriate if the problem is temporary. For example, some network services fail if there's a temporary problem with the connections. Many of these services will work again if restarted. This is the default setting for Vista.

Run a Program: Permits you to run the program of your choice, as shown in the Run program box. For example, you can automate a logging program to document the problem or send a message to your users stating that a service is down. Use a batch or a script file as the program when you want to perform multiple actions.

Restart the Computer: Lets the failure of a service restart your computer. If you set this option, the configured service failure automatically restarts the computer based on the Restart Service After text box. Click the Restart Computer Options button. As you can see in Figure 33.5, the Restart Computer Options window allows you to send a message to computers on the network. The message shown in the figure appears when you select the Before Restart, Send This Message to Computers on the Network check box. You can rewrite the message as desired.

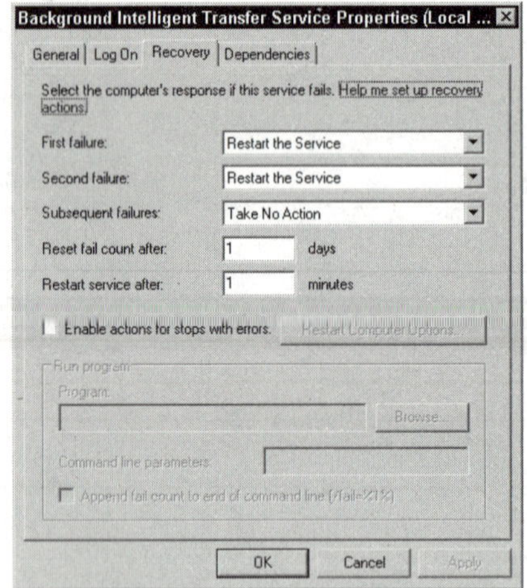

FIGURE 33.4
Recovery properties.

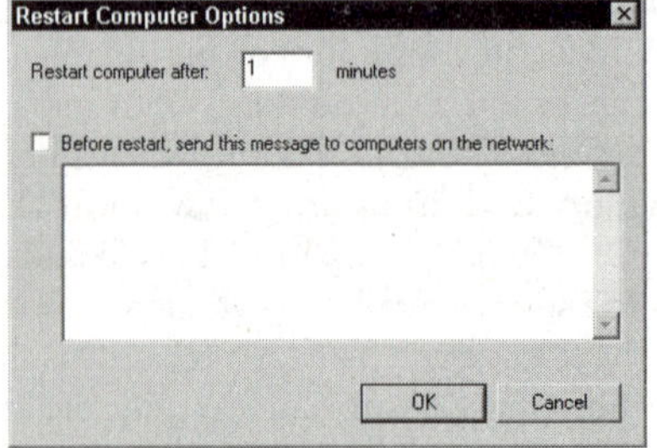

FIGURE 33.5
You can warn remote users that you're about to restart your computer.

Dependencies

Many services depend on others. For example, you can't run a DNS Client service without TCP/IP. Click the Dependencies tab in the Properties window for your service. The Dependencies tab of the COM+ Event System service is shown in Figure 33.6. The two text lists under this tab are described here:

This service depends on the following system components: Lists the services required by the current service. You'll see in Figure 33.6 that the COM+ Event System service depends on the Remote Procedure Call (RPC) service. Notice that there's a plus sign (+) next to this service entry when you first open the tab. Click the plus sign and you'll see that the Remote Procedure Call (RPC) service relies on the DCOM Server Process launcher service. So, if the DCOM Server Process launcher service fails, not only will the Remote Procedure Call (RPC) service but this service will fail too. It's important to review the entire hierarchy of services when troubleshooting a problem.

The following system components depend on this service: Lists the services supported by the current service. You'll see in Figure 33.6 that the following services, Background Intelligent Transfer Service, COM+ System Application, DFS Replication, SL UI Notification Service, and System Event Notification Service, won't run without the COM+ Event System service.

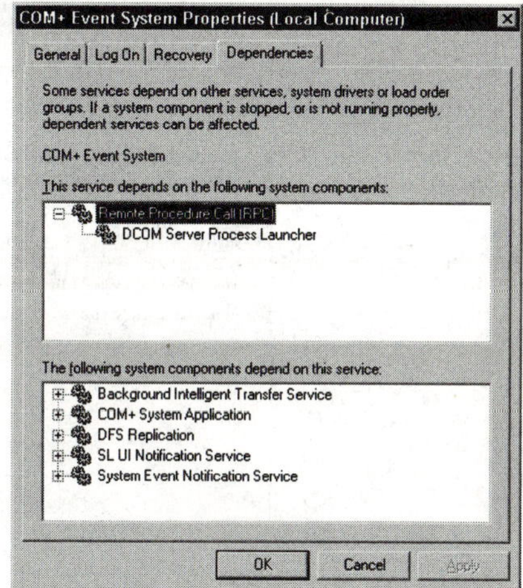

FIGURE 33.6
Dependencies of a service.

Service Commands

You don't need the Services console to manage your services. In fact, you can use the `net` command at the command line to manage just about any Vista service. The basic commands are fairly straightforward: `net start` *`service`* starts a service; other commands include `net stop` *`service`*, `net pause` *`service`*, and `net continue` *`service`*. The only twist is the `net start` command by itself, which lists currently running services.

Now try some of the `net` commands. If you want to see a list of open services, try `net start | more`. A partial list of open services is shown in the screen, similar to what you see in Figure 33.7. Press the spacebar to scroll through additional open services.

You can start, stop, pause, or resume any installed service. For example, if you wanted to stop the IIS Admin service, type **`net stop "COM+ Event System"`**. The quotes apply if the name of the service is more than one word. As you can see in Figure 33.8, Vista warns you about any dependent services that must also be stopped and gives you a chance to cancel the operation. If you continue, Vista will stop the dependent services as well. Generally, you'll want to say **`n`** (for no) as shown in the figure.

TIP When maintaining a service, you can use the service name or the display name. For example, since the service name for the World Wide Web Publishing service is W3SVC, the `net start w3svc` command has the same effect as `net start "world wide web publishing"`.

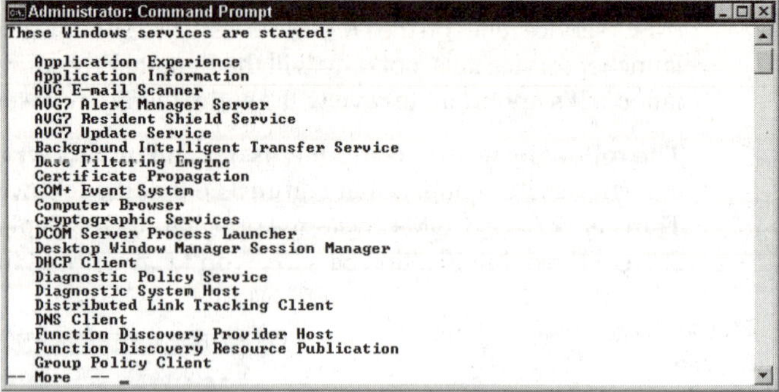

FIGURE 33.7
A Telnet view of open services.

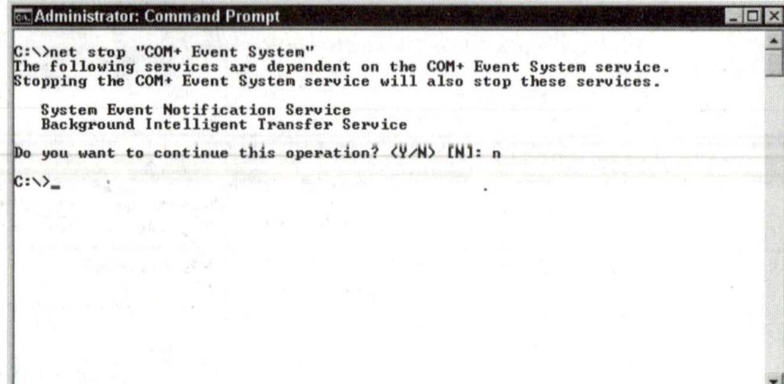

FIGURE 33.8
Remotely stopping a service through the command line.

Troubleshooting Service Issues

Managing services is like maintaining a network. If you have a problem with a service, you troubleshoot it. Based on the troubleshooting methodologies discussed in Chapter 35, it's best to check the simplest things first. On a network, you'd check the connections between computers and power to the hubs, switches, and routers. Sometimes rebooting a computer or resetting a hub, switch, or router will address a problem on a network.

But if others are connected to your computer, they're depending on the connection. If your computer goes down, they can lose data. Therefore, you don't want to have to reboot it unless absolutely necessary.

This system applies equally well to services. For example, if you have a problem accessing web pages on your Intranet, you may not have to reboot. First, you'll want to make sure your IIS Admin and World Wide Web Publishing services are actually active. Then you might try resetting these services by setting them to stop and then start again. The next step would be to check your connections and network as discussed in Chapter 18. You should also check other network-related services. For example, if the computers on your network rely on DNS to find each other, you need to make sure that the DNS service is active.

Other applications may have the same solution. If you're having problems printing, you can try stopping and restarting the Print Spooler service. If you're having problems printing from a Linux computer to a printer that's connected to a Vista computer, try stopping and restarting the TCP/IP Print Server service.

Summary

The basic low-level programs that form the backbone of Vista are also known as services. There are many different kinds of services that help you manage the basic functions of the operating system, as well as the way it interacts with a network. Some are started automatically when you start Vista. Others can be manually started by specific applications. Unlike previous versions of Windows, Vista doesn't disable and services by default, but you can disable them if you don't need them. You can manage Vista services through the preconfigured MMC Service console. Alternatively, services can be managed at a command-line interface, even from a remote computer.

One of the first steps in troubleshooting many problems is to check the associated service. Sometimes you just need to turn it on. Sometimes resetting the service by turning it off and back on is sufficient.

Now it's time for you to spend time with services. The lists in this book tell you about services that you'll commonly see installed in Vista. Do you see any other services in the lists? If so, you should find out more about them and document them in some way so that you know where to look when you have a system problem. Begin looking at dependencies as well. Often, it appears that one service is having a problem when it's really a dependent service that's the cause of all of the problems.

In the next chapter, I'll describe two specific services that are implemented all over the Internet: web (HTTP) and FTP. Microsoft doesn't install HTTP and FTP services by default in Vista because doing so could open your system to outside attack. In fact, you only need to review the next chapter if you actually need HTTP and FTP services on your machine. One common situation that requires installation of HTTP and FTP services is application development. You don't want to install the HTTP and FTP services if your only need is to display some pictures of the family—it's better to use the hosted service for that need.

Chapter 34

Hosting Web/FTP Servers

Internet Information Server (IIS) has seen a significant change in Vista. The old IIS 6.0 provided a friendly interface that made it relatively easy for anyone to host and configure a website. IIS 7.0 is definitely all business and you need quite a bit of knowledge to configure it completely. Microsoft has changed IIS to serve the needs of developers first, administrators second, and doesn't really consider the small user at all. Theoretically, you can host a small website on your Vista computer with Internet Information Services (IIS), but it's better to use a website hosted by your ISP for those family pictures or small business needs. While the number of connections is limited, IIS is easy to install. You can also use IIS to host a File Transfer Protocol (FTP) site for sharing files.

Both services are highly configurable, but the emphasis in IIS 7.0 is on working with the .NET Framework. If terms such as role-based security and Code Access Security (CAS) are unfamiliar, you probably won't get much use out of IIS 7.0. You can use the IIS console to manage these services locally or remotely, but the interface couldn't be more different from IIS 6.0 (in other words, anything you know today is useless).

A full description of everything that IIS 7.0 can do is outside the scope of this book. You need good application development skills to use IIS 7.0 at any level of detail. The purpose of this chapter is to show how to perform some basic tasks with IIS and create some simple content for a local website. I won't be showing you how to write ASP.NET applications (or CGI or ASP applications for that matter). This chapter addresses the following topics:

- Installing Internet Information Services
- Vista limits on IIS
- Working with websites
- Configuring the FTP server

Vista: What's New?

Vista comes with IIS version 7.0, which is a significant change from previous versions of IIS. Gone are the easy configuration features and the Properties dialog boxes that provided a straightforward method of configuring a monolithic web server. Missing in IIS 7.0 are some older favorites. For example, you won't find Network News Transport Protocol (NNTP) support in IIS 7.0—at least not the version that installs with Vista. SMTP support now relies on ASP.NET, which means that you require a good working knowledge of ASP.NET to use it. Look in the ASP.NET section of the server and you'll find an icon for SMTP. Since this book isn't for developers, you won't find a discussion of SMTP in this chapter.

Microsoft has deprecated (ended support for) the Internet Server Application Programming Interface (ISAPI) extensions and filters. ISAPI has been around for quite a few years and many web applications use them. You can still install ISAPI support today, but it's no longer mandatory. If you don't have any ISAPI applications to support, you don't need to install ISAPI support as part of IIS. If you suddenly find that a beloved IIS application stops working, it's a good idea to check into its need for ISAPI support.

IIS 7.0 replaces ISAPI with modules created using the .NET Framework. Administrators will find that ASP.NET has more focus in IIS 7.0, so you won't run into as many problems where IIS 7.0 forgets to support ASP.NET applications. I remember having to reinstall ASP.NET support more than once in older versions of IIS because they would simply stop working for apparently no reason.

Negative issues aside, IIS does come with a significant number of features that make it a delight for developers and administrators who have worked with the .NET Framework (everyone else is going to have a significant and frustrating learning curve before they can appreciate even a modicum of what IIS 7.0 offers). One of the features that administrators will like most is that IIS 7.0 uses a simplified XML configuration file that provides site-wide functionality. If you already know how to work with the CONFIG files for ASP.NET applications, then you have a good handle on the files that IIS 7.0 uses. Each application can also have a configuration file that overrides the side-wide configuration. In short, you can create general rules and then override them as needed in IIS 7.0—all without the complexity of the configuration files used in previous versions of the product.

IIS 7.0 is also significantly more modular than previous versions of IIS. Figure 34.1 shows the relatively long list of IIS features you can install. Notice that even the security features are individual entries. If you don't use the Common Gateway Interface (CGI), then you don't need to install it. Unlike previous versions of IIS, IIS 7.0 doesn't load unused features. The increased modularity and the new loading functionality means that IIS is less susceptible to global errors that hackers can employ to attack anyone, even if they aren't using that feature. Of course, the best news about the improved modularity is that the memory footprint of IIS is significantly smaller and it uses fewer other resources as well.

It's important to realize that previous versions of IIS focused on the administrator and provided a monolithic server environment. IIS 7.0 is very modular (meaning that it uses completely independent pieces of code for each feature) and it's designed to make life easier for both the administrator and the developer. The setup is designed to help the administrator and developer work together productively. For example, those configuration files I mentioned earlier in this section actually come from the developer as part of the application programming process for the most part. The administrator need only tweak the files to meet specific requirements or adjust system performance. Here's a list of the new module categories in IIS 7.0.

- HTTP Modules
- Security Modules
- Content Modules
- Compression Modules
- Caching Modules
- Logging and Diagnostics Modules

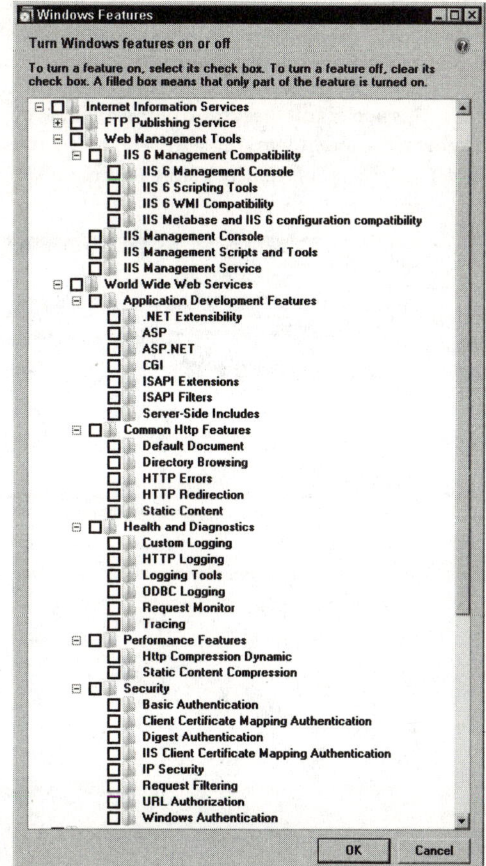

FIGURE 34.1
IIS 7.0 sports considerable modularity, which means you only load what you need.

I won't get into the specifics of each module type and you don't really need to worry about them much since each IIS handles the modules for you automatically. However, you'll notice that IIS now loads fewer DLLs than it did in the past. A typical load in the past could include up to 75 DLLs—an IIS 7.0 load might include as few as 25 DLLs.

If you found that the old IIS management utilities were cumbersome, you'll probably like the new interface that IIS 7.0 provides as shown in Figure 34.2. Microsoft has completely rewritten the management tools to work better with the Microsoft Management Console (MMC)—at least for web services (FTP sites still use the old MMC interface). Along with a better management interface, IIS 7.0 provides significantly improved diagnostics. No longer do you need to look from screen to screen to locate the one configuration item you forgot, but IIS won't tell you about. In general, you'll find that IIS 7.0 consumes far less time in troubleshooting and diagnostics.

As you can see from Figure 34.2, IIS 7.0 lets you control ASP.NET application functionality such as how the Common Language Runtime (CLR) compiles the application. You can add users using standard .NET techniques and assign them to roles that your .NET application will understand. When using these new features, you'll need to have a copy of SQL Server or SQL Server Express for

IIS to use (IIS stores user and role information in SQL Server). This chapter doesn't discuss the nuances of .NET configuration, so you won't need to install SQL Server or SQL Server Express to use this chapter, but you also need to be aware of this requirement should you decide to go further.

NOTE This book can't discuss all of the nuances of writing an ASP.NET application. If you want to know more about working with ASP.NET 2.0, check out *ASP.NET 2.0 Website Programming: Problem - Design - Solution* by Marco Bellinaso (Wrox, 2006).

FIGURE 34.2
The new IIS 7.0 interface uses icons that let you perform the required configuration of .NET features.

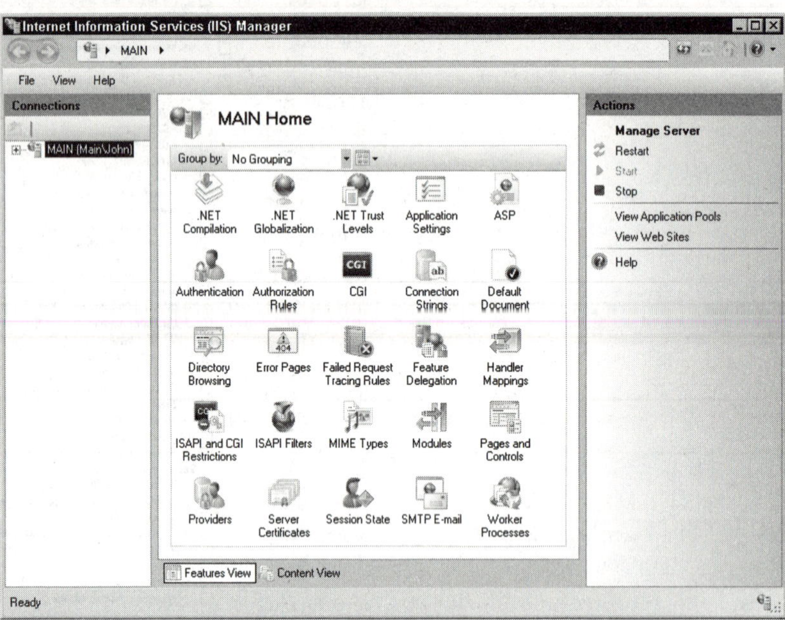

Installing Internet Information Services

IIS is not installed by default. Unless you've upgraded from a Windows operating system with IIS or Personal Web Server, you need to install IIS to set up a web, FTP, or SMTP site on your computer. This is a fairly easy process. Just use the Windows Components Wizard described in Chapter 6. Have your Vista CD available and then follow these steps to install IIS:

1. Click Start ➢ Control Panel to open Control Panel.
2. Click the Programs link and then the Turn Windows features on or off link. You'll see the Windows Features dialog box shown in Figure 34.1.
3. Click the plus sign (+) next to Internet Information Services. As discussed in Chapter 6, you need to select the desired components. See the "IIS Components—to Install or Not to Install" sidebar for more information on the available choices.
4. Click OK to continue. The Windows Components Wizard proceeds to install IIS on your computer. Be patient, the installation process can require a few minutes to complete.

IIS Components—to Install or Not to Install?

You don't have to install all of the features associated with IIS. In fact, you should install just what you need. The more services you install, the more doors you open for hackers to get into your computer. For example, if you install the FTP service, some hackers may be able to get into your computer through the associated TCP/IP port. If you install FTP and don't use it, you may not even be paying attention when a hacker uses your computer for malicious purposes. With that in mind, the IIS components shown in Figure 34.1 have the following purposes:

FTP Publishing Service Lets people upload and download files from your system using the File Transfer Protocol (FTP). Normally, you won't need to use this feature if you only want to let people download files since you can create a link on your website for the file and the browser will download it automatically. IIS provides separate entries for both the FTP Server and the FTP Management Console. You'll need to install both features if this is your only FTP server.

Web Management Tools Provides the tools needed to set up, configure, and maintain websites. The following list describes the web management components.

IIS 6 Management Compatibility Lets you manage systems that have IIS 6.0 installed on them. You only need to install these tools when you plan to manage older remote machines.

IIS Management Console Helps you manage both local and remote IIS 7.0 servers.

IIS Management Scripts and Tools Provides the tools required to manage a local IIS user using scripts.

IIS Management Service Provides support for managing this server from a remote location.

World Wide Web Services Includes all of the modules required to support a website. You could install just this part of IIS and have enough software to run a web service. Of course, you'd still need management tools on one of the machines on your network.

Application Development Features Provides support for web applications. IIS provides support for Active Server Pages (ASP), ASP.NET, CGI, and ISAPI applications, as well as server-side includes. Don't confuse ASP and ASP.NET. Despite the similarity in names, the first is a scripting environment and the second is a complex managed environment based on the .NET Framework. Server-side includes are common across most products (including Apache) and you can learn about them at `http://www.microsoft.com/WINDOWS2000/en/server/iis/htm/core/iisiabt.htm`.

Common HTTP Features Supports common features found on most HTTP servers including a default web page, common error support, directory browsing (akin to using an FTP site), redirection, and static content (normally pages with an HTM or HTML extension).

Health and Diagnostics Provides all of the tools you need to maintain the health of your web server. Most of these options either log requests/responses or trace the events that occur on the web server. The Request Monitor used to be a command-line tool in older versions of IIS—you can read about it here: `http://technet2.microsoft.com/WindowsServer/en/library/c94f11d8-b054-430e-913f-6ca151d1e6ad1033.mspx`. Vista has simply made it possible to add or remove the tool as needed.

Performance Features Makes your older applications run faster, but doesn't do anything for newer applications based on the .NET Framework. The HTTP Compression Dynamic feature compresses older ASP applications so that they consume fewer resources and transfer their data to clients faster. The Static Content Compression feature compresses your web page data so that it gets to the client faster, which reduces the load on network bandwidth.

Security As with most areas of Vista, IIS includes additional security features. All of the old favorites are still there. For example, you can still perform basic authentication. However, now you can perform client certificate monitoring with greater ease and you also have access to new features such as URL authorization, which gives the client access to the specific URLs that comprise a web application.

If you want to remove one or more of these services, repeat the basic steps you used to install IIS. Just deselect the components you no longer need during the process.

Assuming that you've installed the World Wide Web service, IIS should now be installed and active on your computer. It's easy to verify a successful installation. Open up Internet Explorer and enter `localhost` in the Address text box. Assuming you don't already have a web page, you'll see the default shown in Figure 34.3. Notice that the default display shows an Information Bar dialog box. Vista doesn't even trust the website on your local machine. You'll need to add this website to the list of trusted sites using the procedures discussed in Chapter 15. When you click the big blue square in the center of the display (the one with all those words of welcome), you go to a website that contains information on how to configure your new IIS setup.

FIGURE 34.3
The IIS default web page is visible only on the local computer.

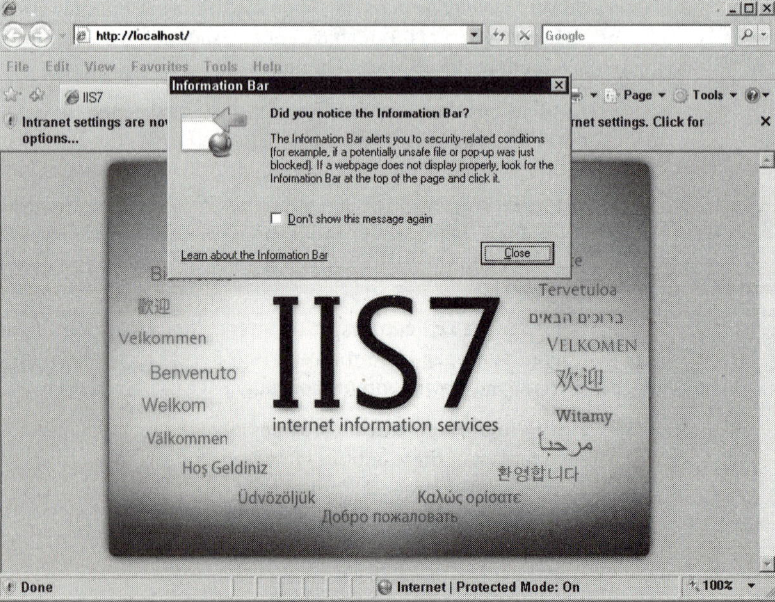

Vista Limits on IIS

The IIS that you just installed on Vista is essentially the same software that you can install on Windows Server products, with one major exception: Vista limits access to 10 simultaneous TCP connections. That includes all connections made to your web, FTP, and SMTP servers. Very few Internet web or FTP sites would be practical with this limit. Obviously, Vista wasn't designed to be a full-fledged web server. It does fine for small sites (such as your family home page), however.

NOTE In fact, some connections to a website open multiple pages that require more than one TCP connection. In other words, access to your website on a Vista computer may be limited to fewer than 10 users.

However, Vista with IIS is still useful in the following ways:

As a test bed You can load a website on Vista and test its look and feel over your LAN. However, you won't be able to test the response of your website to any serious traffic. For that purpose, you need to test your website on an operating system such as Microsoft's .NET Web Server.

With an intranet IIS on Vista can be great if you're communicating with a small number of users, especially within a LAN or a domain.

For a small group IIS on Vista can be used to share information with a small group, such as for a project.

These are common uses on an intranet. You can also connect IIS on Vista to the Internet. Before you do this, talk to your ISP. Many ISPs, especially those that provide broadband service, may not even allow you to set up an Internet web server on your home computer.

However, many ISPs do provide space for a small website with a limited amount of traffic with your ISP membership. If desired, you can pay your ISP (or another company) for more space and larger amounts of traffic.

Working with Websites

After you install IIS, you can access your personal web server using a browser as you would with any other website. Simply open a browser and type **`localhost`** as the address. Figure 34.3 shows the results. Of course, seeing a display that takes you to a help page isn't that useful. What you really want to see is the content you want to provide for the website. When working with IIS 6.0, you could perform a significant amount of tasks using the Internet Information Services (IIS) Manager; however, that has changed with IIS 7.0. To avoid having to overcome the difficulties of configuring your site with the Internet Information Services (IIS) Manager, you can use static, or HTML, pages for your website. A standard HTML page can include all of the features you've come to expect including links, pictures, special fonts, graphics, sounds, and so on. In fact, a standard HTML page can include ActiveX controls, so you can even add special features such as a Macromedia Shockwave Player.

So, why don't the big guys use static HTML pages? It's important to understand that static pages retain the content you provide until you manually change them. Although it's very easy to change the 40 or 50 pages on a personal website, trying to change several thousand pages on a commercial website is a nightmare. In addition, it's very difficult if not impossible to create a shopping cart and other complex applications using static HTML pages. Consequently, the technology of choice for creating a complex websites requires programming talent that you don't need to create a personal website.

The IIS web page content appears on your hard drive in the `\inetpub\wwwroot` folder. If you want a particular web page to appear as the default web page, then you need to name it `default.htm`. Now, when you type **`http://localhost/`**, the browser will show your default web page, rather than the help page shown in Figure 34.3. You don't need anything complicated to create a web page. It's possible to use Notepad to create simple web pages if you like.

In fact, try this out. Right-click any blank area within the `\inetpub\wwwroot` folder and choose New ➤ Text Document. Change the filename to **`default.htm`** and press Enter (make sure you don't keep the old `.txt` extension or the file won't work). Right-click the new web page you just created and choose Edit from the context menu. Notepad will open the file, which is going to be blank. Type the following tags (a special name for the instructions in a static HTML page) into the file and save it.

```
<html>
<head>
   <title>My Test Web Page</title>
</head>
<body>
   <h1>Test Web Site</h1>
   <a href="iisstart.htm">Original Help</a>
</body>
```

Congratulations! You just created your first web page. Wasn't that easy? Figure 34.4 shows what this web page looks like. The tags you types are important. Every HTML page begins with an `<html>` tag. The `<head>` tag contains any header information that doesn't appear as part of the content. The `<body>` tag contains all of the page content. In this case, the `<head>` tag contains an optional `<title>` tag that defines the page's title as shown in the title bar of the browser. The `<h1>` tag contains a level-1 heading for the web page. The `<a>` tag contains a pointer to the original help file for the website, which shows up as a link in the web page.

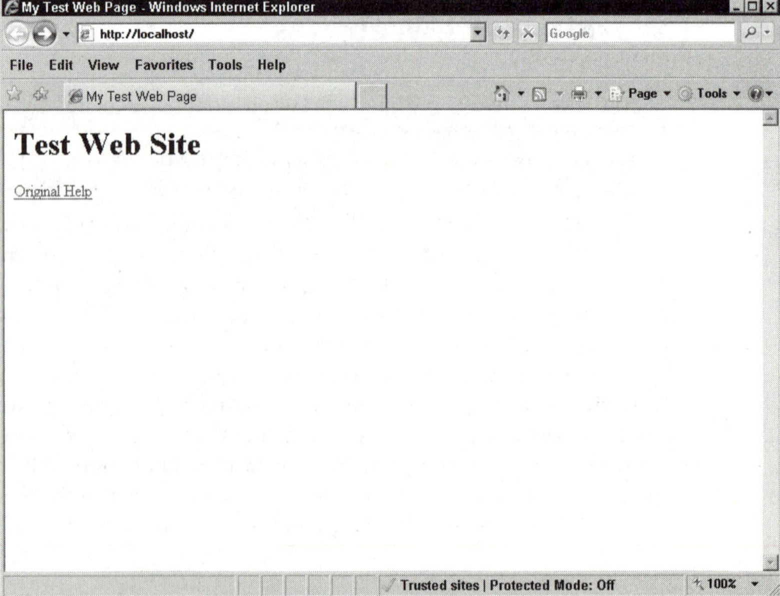

FIGURE 34.4
A few simple tags will get you started with static HTML pages.

Any static HTML page you create will start out the same way. You'll create the required framework and add tags to it. The user will normally start with a default page that contains links to other pages on your website. You can connect everything together and provide features such as site maps to make navigation easy. As with any other documentation task, you can use folders to organize material and provide special locations for pictures. In short, working with web pages is similar to completing any reasonably complex documentation project.

Of course, you'll eventually want to get a special HTML editor and not use Notepad for everything. An HTML editor should provide highlighting to show the tags and it should provide hints on using them. For example, Web-Design-Toy (`http://acme-web-design.info/free-web-design-toy.php`) provides excellent functionality and you can download it at no cost. I can't provide a complete list of HTML editors because you can find hundreds of them quite easily. The list of features they provide varies and you might find that you like a particular editor that would never fulfill someone else's needs (editors are a very personal thing). As another example, you might try the EasyHtml editor at `http://www.javascript-page.com/easyhtml/` as a starting point. It's easy to use, provides reasonable functionality, and, best of all, is free. However, consider this editor a good a starting point—you'll want to experiment with other editors too.

OBTAINING MORE INFORMATION ABOUT STATIC HTML

The Internet includes a wealth of information about HTML. In fact, the accumulation of information is staggering. This chapter provides a quick start on working with IIS 7.0 and static pages, but you'll very likely want more specifics than I can provide in a single chapter. If you're a complete HTML novice, then you'll want to start with the W3School.com tutorial at `http://www.w3schools.com/html/`. This is a step-by-step tutorial that assumes you know absolutely nothing about HTML.

Most web pages today use the HTML 4.01 specification as a standard for working with various tags. The biggest new addition to your web page when you use this standard is the `<!DOCTYPE HTML PUBLIC "-//W3C//DTD HTML 4.0 Transitional//EN">` tag. You can find the HTML 4.01 specification at `http://www.w3.org/TR/REC-html40/`. This document contains complete instructions for using the various tags associated with a web page and provides links to other useful documents.

Eventually, after you experiment with a few web pages, you'll want to add special fonts and formatting. Rather than individually format every web page, you can use a special methodology called Cascading Style Sheets (CSS). A CSS file provides a central location to store style information for your web page. Default styles affect the specified tags, so you don't need to do anything special to use them, other than to tell the browser where to find the CSS file using the `<link rel="stylesheet" type="text/css" ref="http://www.mysite.com/My.css">` tag. Interestingly enough, the W3CSchool also has a CSS tutorial at `http://www.w3schools.com/css/default.asp`.

Working with ActiveX controls isn't hard. However, you're starting to get into an area where some programming is required. You need to provide scripts to interact with the controls you provide on the web page. Microsoft provides a good overview of working with ActiveX controls at `http://msdn.microsoft.com/library/?url=/workshop/author/dhtml/overview/activating_activex.asp`.

Configuring the FTP Server

When the first pre-Internet networks were developed in the 1970s, there was a lot of trust in the computer world. There was little need for computer security; few people made money from computer data. Most of the people working on this network were university researchers; they just wanted to exchange information. Anonymous connections allowed for the quickest possible exchange of data. The File Transfer Protocol (FTP) was developed to help make this possible.

For some odd reason, Microsoft decided not to include the FTP server as part of the IIS 7.0 configuration. Consequently, you don't even use the same MMC console to work with FTP servers, you use the Internet Information Services (IIS) 6.0 Manager in Vista instead. Because the FTP server provides the same basic IIS 6.0 functionality as before, you actually can use it to perform useful work.

It's easy to configure an FTP server. Since multiple FTP sites on a single server are uncommon, you'll be configuring just the default FTP site. Open the Internet Information Services (IIS) 6.0 Manager console and highlight Default FTP Site. Choose Action ➤ Properties. This opens the Default FTP Site Properties window, as shown in Figure 34.5.

As you can see, the five tabs shown in Figure 34.5 address basic configuration (FTP Site), security (Security Accounts), messages to users (Messages), the configuration of the FTP server home directory (Home Directory), and security for the FTP directory (Directory Security). The options on the Directory Security tab are disabled for Vista. When working on a server system, you can use the features on this tab to deny or grant access to specific computers.

FIGURE 34.5
It's easy to set up an FTP site.

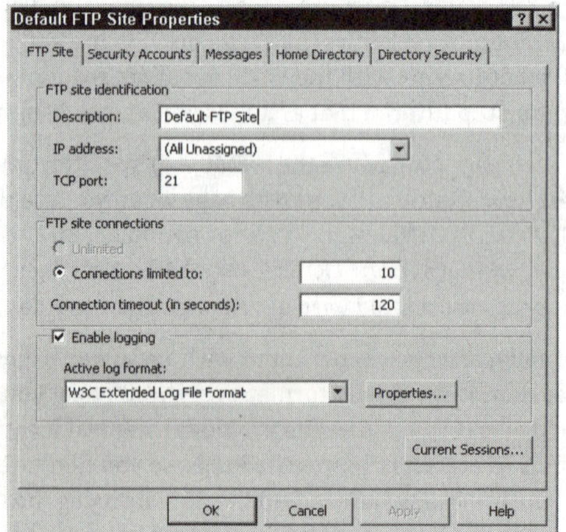

FTP Site

You have already seen the information associated with the FTP Site tab. As shown in Figure 34.5, the information appears quite similar to the Web Site tab that you configured earlier in this chapter for the default website. You can configure four sections:

Identification Describes the name of the FTP site, the IP address used to connect, and the TCP port. (The default TCP port for FTP communication is 21.)

Connection Allows you to regulate the number of connections, as well as the amount of time the connection can be inactive before it's disconnected. Remember, for Vista, the total number of connections is limited to 10. If you've configured a website as well, you may want to reduce this number further so your website is accessible by at least one user.

Enable Logging Permits logging per W3C Extended Log File Format or the Microsoft IIS Log File Format, based on the general criteria described earlier in this chapter. The default directory with the actual FTP log files is slightly different from that for other servers.

Current Sessions Lets you monitor currently connected users. Click this button, and you can disconnect currently logged on users in the FTP User Sessions window that appears.

Security Accounts

Click the Security Accounts tab. You see the options normally associated with FTP security, as shown in Figure 34.6. The default is Allow Anonymous Connections. While people who log on to FTP anonymously get a generic username, passwords aren't even required.

If you deselect Allow Anonymous Connections, only people who have a username and password on your system can log on to your FTP server. Even if they're administrative users, they don't automatically have Write access through your FTP server.

NOTE Older versions of Windows provided an Allow IIS to control password option. Because IIS is so different in Vista, the FTP server doesn't provide this option. Consequently, you must always configure the password when working with FTP in Vista.

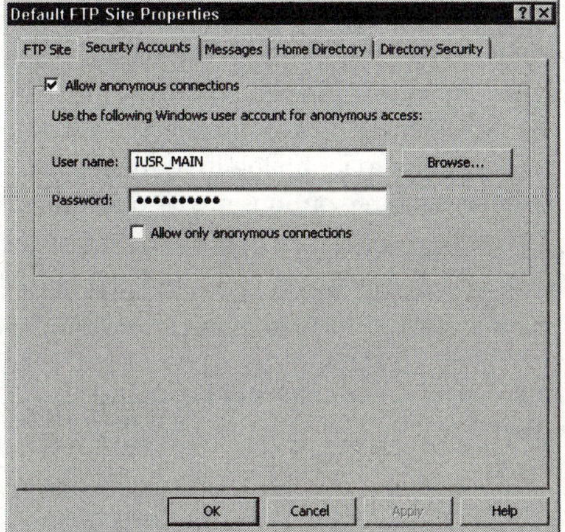

FIGURE 34.6
IIS uses standard FTP security requirements.

Messages

You can set up various messages for your FTP users. Click the Messages tab. The message boxes shown in Figure 34.7 are fairly self-explanatory.

Banner Lists the message you see when you connect to the FTP server, before you log in.

Welcome Sends a message to a user after a successful login.

Exit Sends a message to a user after exiting from the server.

Maximum Connections Sends a message to the user if there are already too many other connections to the server.

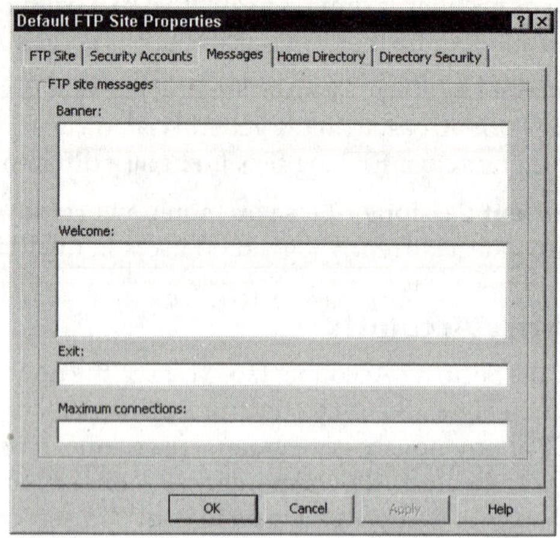

FIGURE 34.7
Creating messages for your FTP users.

Home Directory

A number of options are available for the home directory for your FTP server. Click the Home Directory tab, and you'll see that the options shown in Figure 34.8 are fairly straightforward.

The first option is whether the files on your FTP server should come from the local or a remote computer. If you keep A Directory Located on This Computer selected, the FTP Site Directory section allows you to type a path in the Local Path text box. If you select A Share Located on Another Computer, the Local Path text box turns into a Network Share text box, where you can enter the share in the `\\Servername\sharename` format. In that case, you'll also see a Connect As button, which you can use to let IIS log in to the remote computer.

In either case, three options are associated with configuring a specific FTP site directory:

Read Gives you Read access to the home directory. Allows you to use various directory commands such as `dir` and `ls` to list the files in that directory. Read access is required at least on the home directory; otherwise, your users won't be able to log in to your FTP server.

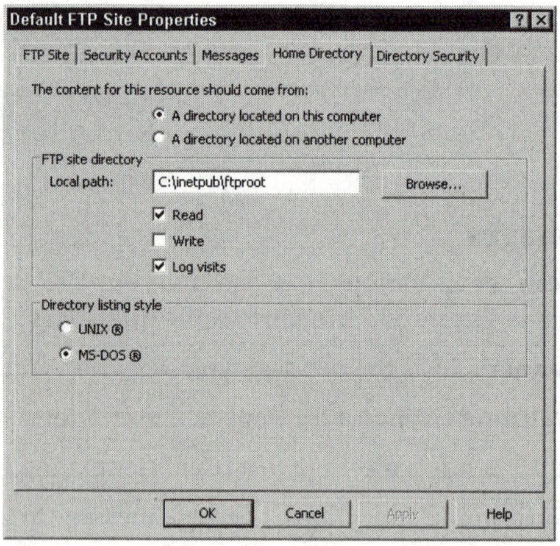

FIGURE 34.8
Setting up the FTP home directory.

Write Permits you to upload files to the FTP server. Since users with Write access can overwrite the files on your FTP server, this would create a security issue.

Log Visits Data from visitors is collected in log files, as described earlier with the FTP Site tab and in related information discussed in configuring a web server.

There are two different Directory Listing Style options, UNIX and MS-DOS. The style you select determines the FTP server response to the `ls` command, which is an FTP command from UNIX used to list the contents of directories. If UNIX style is selected, the `ls` (and `dir`) command gives you a file list with permissions, ownership, file size, file type, and creation date. If your users are more comfortable with a UNIX-type operating system such as Linux, BSD, or Solaris, consider using a UNIX directory listing style. It does not change anything else related to your FTP site. For more information on FTP as a client, see Chapter 15.

Virtual Directories

If you want to share files in a specific directory, you don't have to copy them to the FTP server home directory. You can set it up as a virtual directory. You won't have to move your files. To create a virtual directory in the IIS console, highlight your default FTP site. Choose Action ➤ New ➤ Virtual Directory to start the Virtual Directory Creation Wizard, and then click Next to continue. This takes you to the Virtual Directory Alias page shown in Figure 34.9, where you can enter the virtual directory name of your choice. Just remember the name that you use.

Click Next to continue. Enter the path to the directory containing the files you want to put on the FTP server, and then click Next to continue. This takes you to the Access Permissions page shown in Figure 34.10, where you can set Read and Write permissions on your new virtual directory.

While you need to select Read permissions to let FTP users read the contents of your new virtual directory, remember that Write permissions may be a security risk. Click Next to continue, and then click Finish to complete the Virtual Directory Creation Wizard.

Before you can use your new virtual directory, you need to create a "mirror" as a subdirectory of your FTP home directory. The default FTP home directory as shown in Figure 34.8 is `C:\Inetpub\ftproot`. Navigate to this directory in Explorer and create a new folder with the same name as your virtual directory alias. Don't add any files to this folder. The FTP server automatically mirrors the files through your virtual directory. Now you're ready to use the new virtual directory.

FIGURE 34.9
Setting up a virtual directory alias.

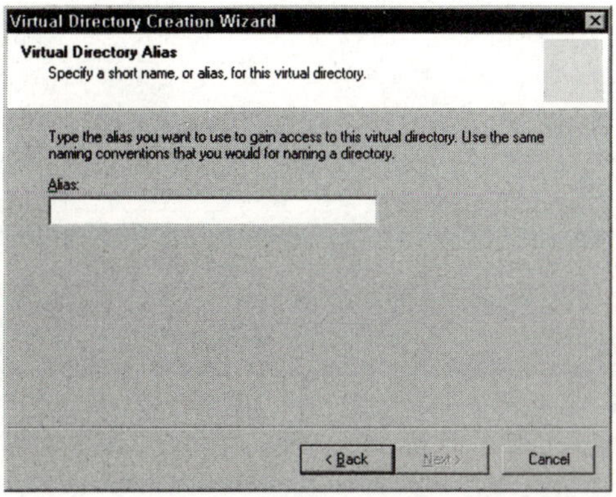

FIGURE 34.10
Setting up permissions on a virtual directory.

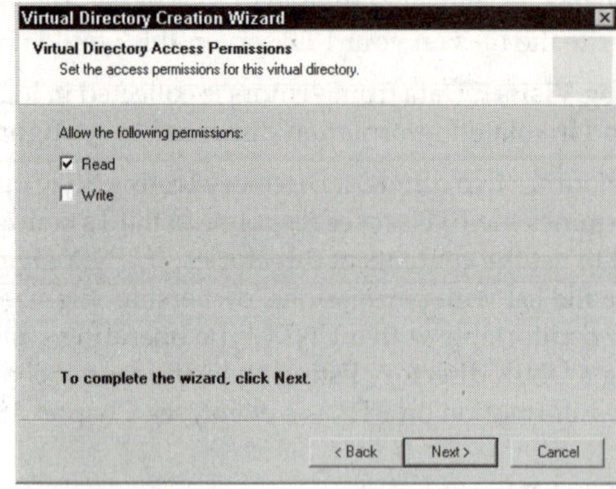

Summary

This chapter addressed the two basic services that you can set up and configure with Internet Information Server (IIS): web service and FTP service. IIS and associated services are easy to install through the Add or Remove Programs link in Control Panel. Vista limits the number of connections to your IIS services to 10, which makes it impractical for a full-scale business websites but perhaps adequate for your own personal sites. However, given the complexity of using IIS 7.0, you're probably better off hosting anything personal on a website established through your ISP. It's important to remember that Microsoft is targeting IIS specifically at developer needs.

FTP site configuration is a bit less complex. Configurable settings include connection control, logging, security, status messages, and directory settings. You can even customize the site for UNIX users.

In the next chapter, we'll wrap things up by hitting the topic everyone loves to hate: troubleshooting. Using these tips will decrease the time you spend looking for a problem. However, it's always important to remember two concepts: patience is a virtue (after all, the computer won't lose its cool) and one step at a time. The next chapter discusses both concepts.

Chapter 35

Advanced Troubleshooting Methodology

Ever have one of those days? A day when nothing seems to go right with your computer? Unfortunately, an operating system such as Vista is extremely complex, and any complex system will inevitably have those days. Just remember this quote from a favorite Scottish engineer: "The more they over-tink the plumbing, the easier it is to stop up the drains." With a system such as Vista, things can go wrong in so many places that it's often difficult to find a place to start.

Troubleshooting always seems to get pushed to the back of every technical book. It's almost as if we authors say, "If they make it this far, *then* we'll finally give them the Holy Grail." Just because troubleshooting seems to be hidden away in the cobwebs of a book, don't assume it lacks importance. In fact, it's just the opposite. Someone with good troubleshooting skills is a valuable person indeed. It's here at the back of the book because so much of troubleshooting depends on understanding what you're dealing with (in our case, Vista). Once you have an understanding of your product, *then* you can dive in and try to fix it.

In this chapter, we take a look at the "how" of troubleshooting Vista. I want to give you a workable method for finding your way through the maze. You'll learn about the following:

- Troubleshooting principles and procedures
- Troubleshooting printing
- Troubleshooting Vista Setup
- Dealing with SCSI problems during setup
- Windows Memory Diagnostics Tool
- Troubleshooting Stop errors

Vista: What's New?

Microsoft has included a number of new diagnostics in Vista, most of which you don't even have to worry about using because they're automatic. Whenever a problem occurs, Vista documents it, sends the error information to Microsoft, and helps you look for a solution. You can even track the error using the Problem Reports and Solutions applet in the Control Panel (see the "Using Problem Reports and Solutions to Track Vista Issues" section of Chapter 25 for details). In addition to automation, Microsoft is fighting problems by supporting signed drivers to a greater degree and additional testing before the software even arrives to you. The bottom line is that you'll theoretically need to use the troubleshooting procedures in this chapter less often with Vista than with any other version of Windows.

Of course, Microsoft recognizes that errors happen and that automation won't fix them all. One part of the solution for this problem in Vista is the Recovery Environment, which is discussed in the "Using the Recovery Environment" section of Chapter 29. One of the key features of the Recovery Environment is the Windows Memory Diagnostic Tool. In fact, you can access this tool from several locations. You'll find it in the Vista GUI and as part of the boot options when you start your machine. That's one of the reasons that this key tool also appears as part of the discussion in this chapter.

The Tao of Troubleshooting

At first, it seems that troubleshooting mostly involves memorizing a lot of details about everything. When working with an experienced troubleshooter, you've probably even found yourself thinking, "How do they know that?" Truth is, most people never do well by simply trying to memorize everything. Human beings succeed best when working from their strengths; we all have problems when working from our weaknesses. To make troubleshooting a strength, you need to find the pattern in the chaos.

NOTE **The process of troubleshooting is the process of moving from the big picture to the small details. Asking questions is the tool for breaking the big picture into small details.**

Consider this scenario: A friend tells you he's having trouble getting a vending machine to accept a dollar bill. If you happen to be a vending machine expert, you might know everything about how the dollar bill is drawn into the machine, every detail of the mechanisms that control the entire process. But you probably aren't a vending machine expert. Instead, being a good troubleshooter, you consider the directions on the machine. Then you start asking questions: "Has it ever worked before?" "Did you put the dollar in facing the right direction?" "Is the dollar bill folded?"

With this last question, your friend admits that the corners of the bill are a bit folded. So you try straightening them out. Then you test your solution by reinserting the bill. It works, and you're a hero. Of course, solving a problem like this has a low glory quotient, but it serves to illustrate the basics.

Define the Problem: "It's Broken."

The first step to successful troubleshooting is to define the problem accurately. Many times people will define a problem in very simple terms and expect you to know what they're talking about. Your job as a troubleshooter is to define the details of the problem: "So, *exactly* what's broken?" This is a good question to start the conversation. (Incidentally, this may be a conversation with yourself if you're trying to solve your own problem.) Start by getting a clear description of what the person who's reporting the problem feels is the issue. It's often a good technique to take the time to write these points out on paper.

Try to get all the details that describe the problem as the user sees it. Ask such questions as "Has it ever worked before?" or "When did you notice that it stopped working?"

Explore the Boundaries

This can be a painful lesson to learn. Often the person you're working with to solve a problem (yes, this can even be yourself) leaves out important details. This is almost never because they want you to fail, but rather because they don't think a particular detail is relevant. This is a painful lesson because you may spend a great deal of time pursuing irrelevant issues when the real problem is very simple. Consider the following illustration.

You're talking with a friend about their computer problem. The issue, as reported, is that their new modem isn't working. So right away you dig into the settings and configuration for the modem. You eventually discover that the friend has disabled the COM port in Device Manager because they didn't think they needed it!

Exploring the boundaries means finding out everything that may be wrong with the system. The extra information you get here *may* be unrelated to the problem, but it may be exactly the piece you need to solve the puzzle.

Brainstorm and Document

Now that you have a clue about where the problem lies, it's time to come up with some ideas to help focus on the real issue. While you're gathering your thoughts, write them down. It's a good idea to have at least three things to try before proceeding.

Writing down your ideas is important. You'll be trying each possible approach, and this may take time. It may be difficult to remember each idea when you're in the heat of battle (figuratively speaking). Don't be afraid to add to this list as you go. Often you'll discover the best approach while trying one of your initial ideas.

DOCUMENT EVERYTHING!

One piece of advice I give to anyone who's new to troubleshooting (or anyone who'll listen, for that matter) is to keep a notebook handy. It can be a simple 3×5 notebook or a full-sized one. That's up to you. But in your notebook, write down any problems, what you did, and what fixed the problem. Later, if you run into a similar problem, you'll have a record of what worked last time. Eventually you might become less and less reliant on the notebook, but it will pay dividends almost immediately if you do a lot of troubleshooting.

Test Your Ideas

This is a critical point: Test each approach—one at a time.

It's impossible to overemphasize this point. Many troubleshooters will try the "shotgun" approach, meaning they test every idea they can muster all at once. Most likely one of the ideas will work, but which one?

During the course of troubleshooting an operating system, you'll frequently be disabling certain functionalities. If you try every idea at the same time, you may fix the problem, but you'll be left with an operating system that's been crippled by your actions. Worse yet, you won't know which areas to reenable and which one to repair. So, test your ideas one at a time, and if the idea doesn't work, change your setting back to the way it was before trying your next fix. You don't want to cause more problems for yourself!

Testing each idea one at a time enables you to discover clearly what's broken and to easily find your way back through the maze of settings that have been changed.

Repair the Problem

This is the easy part—usually. Finding the problem can often be a time-consuming process, but repairing the broken portion of the system can be as simple as replacing a corrupt file. Perhaps the issue arises from bad hardware. This is easy to fix; just replace the hardware. (The hard part, here, is to find the money for the replacement.)

Clean Up after Yourself

Remember how I said earlier to test each possible solution individually? This is the phase where you undo some of the ideas that were unsuccessful, if you haven't already done so. Never leave the system worse than you found it. There are few support issues worse than a customer who's upset that the previous support person made their problems worse or caused new ones.

Again, it's helpful to have documented the approaches you tried—especially if you kept notes about what you did during the troubleshooting phase. If you did, it's simple to backtrack and turn features back on.

Provide Closure

If you're dealing with other people in your troubleshooting process, providing closure means informing them of what the problem was and what you did to resolve it. If you're going through this process to solve your own problem, it means reviewing what you did and understanding how to avoid this problem in the future.

Nearly every person you work with when supporting an operating system will want to know what the problem was and how to fix it. We all like to feel that we've been included in finding a solution, that we're part of a team effort. A word of advice here: If you're supporting people on Vista as part of your job, always try to include the customer in the troubleshooting process. It helps them to feel better about the incident and about your presence. That, in turn, helps them to participate by giving you good information. And that makes everyone's day go better.

Now a moment for the darker side of support. If the problem was caused by the user's ignorance, getting closure is your opportunity to educate. If you do this with some sensitivity, you can turn this into a positive experience. If you give in to the temptation to tell the person that they're an idiot, you'll be burning bridges that will be difficult to rebuild later. Your choice. If *you* are the customer, this is where you can ask advice or discover an opportunity for education.

Document the Situation

The problem's fixed, and the customer's happy. You've explained to them what went wrong, and they promised to never touch that button again. You're finished, right? Not quite.

The last step, and one that most people often forget, is to document the situation. What was the problem? How did you fix it? It may even be helpful to leave brief notes about what you tried that didn't work. The question is, where do you document all of this? It really depends on your work situation. Some companies require server and workstation maintenance logs. Generally, they're stored in an easily accessible area so the network administrators can find them in a hurry.

If you work for a company that has multiple administrators (or network troubleshooters), keeping notes on a fixed problem is critical. If the problem happens again, you don't want to be the person who spends three hours trying stuff that someone else already tried to no avail. Nor do you want to be the person who has to look at your coworker who just spent three hours doing what didn't work for you last time either. Common logs are a great way to keep track of issues and expedite troubleshooting.

If you're the only troubleshooter, or if it's otherwise possible, keep your own logbook of your activities, especially if you're new to troubleshooting. No one can possibly know or remember everything. The book can help your memory. Eventually, you may rely on it less and less, but when you need it, it's an invaluable tool.

No matter what your situation, the documentation rule is simple. Document what you do, and do what you document. It will save everyone time and headaches in the long run.

Troubleshooting Printing

Printing is one of those areas that are most important to users of computer systems. Remember the promise of the "paperless office"? Anyone ever seen one? Printing is one of the highest causes of support calls, and it's one of the hardest areas in which to get good support. This area in particular is one in which you need to think simple. Don't forget to ask yourself the easy questions such as "Is it plugged in?" "Is it turned on?" and "Is the correct driver properly installed?" If they're answered up front, these three questions can save you a lot of time troubleshooting printing issues. Just remember to ask diplomatically when troubleshooting someone else's printing problem. No one likes to feel dumb.

Let's work through a scenario to get a feel for how to apply the methodology to printing issues in Vista. Here's your trouble ticket:

User:	Bob
Telephone:	12345
Problem:	Can't print
Description:	Nothing comes out when I try to print.
Priority:	URGENT!

As you can see, your user Bob is having trouble trying to print a document and feels it's urgent that this be resolved quickly. The first step is to define the problem, so you contact Bob at his cubicle. Bob informs you that the job he's trying to print is a monthly profit-and-loss report for The Boss. Sounds pretty important, so you get right to work on the problem.

Troubleshooting Scenario 1: Printer Is Unplugged

Simple questions first. Has it ever worked? Bob tells you that the printer worked fine the last time he tried to print, which was yesterday. What happened when he tried to print this time? He clicked Print in Word and got a message that the printer was offline or out of paper.

Test the approach. You look at the print device that's on Bob's desk, and you see that the lights are on. This indicates that the printer is plugged in and can access electricity. Next, you try toggling the online/offline switch and find that the print device is online. Still thinking simple, you next check the back of Bob's print device to make sure the parallel cable is firmly attached. It is. Bob's computer is a tower and is located under his desk. You crawl under the desk to check the parallel cable and find that it's fallen off the back of the computer. You reconnect the cable and try to print a test page. It works!

Provide closure. The closure comes with the determination that Bob may have accidentally kicked loose the cable when he stretched his feet out under his desk. One possible solution to avoid this is to be sure that the retaining clips of the parallel cable are correctly fastened on the computer's parallel port. Providing an explanation of the cause along with a solution gives the customer some closure on the issue.

This sounds ridiculously easy, right? You might be surprised to find out that this ticket, or a slight variation thereof, is a very common answer for help desks. Don't forget to document!

Troubleshooting Scenario 2: Nothing in the Print Queue Will Print

Explore the boundaries. When you contact Bob regarding his printing issue, he tells you that he's been trying to print for the last two hours but nothing's coming out of the printer. Bob tells you that there were no messages when he tried to print other than the pop-up message that the job was successfully printed. Vista is accepting the print jobs when he submits them, but nothing's coming out.

Ask the simple questions. You investigate the simple issues first. The print device is connected and plugged in. It does display indicator lights, so you know that it's turned on and getting power. The cables are connected. Bob tells you that it printed fine yesterday, but it hasn't printed at all this morning. He insists that nothing's been changed on his computer, no software added, no hardware changed.

Track the possible approaches. You decide that some of the possibilities are that he might be printing to a different printer and doesn't realize it or that something's wrong with the print queue.

Test the approaches. You check the Printers and Faxes folder on Bob's computer and verify the setting for his locally attached printer. Next, you verify that this printer is set as the default and that he hasn't redirected the output to another network printer. Opening the printer icon, you discover a long list of jobs that Bob submitted earlier today. Every job he's tried to print is listed, and the job on top of the list is a report from Excel.

You try checking to make sure that the printer hasn't been paused. Everything looks fine, but no print jobs will process. You determine that the queue itself has become either corrupted or jammed.

Repair the problem. After closing the Printers and Faxes folder, you open the Administrative Tools folder and double-click the Services icon. You scroll down the list to find the Print Spooler service and highlight it. You stop the service, wait a few seconds, and then start it again.

TIP When the Print Spooler service becomes corrupt, or a job gets jammed in the queue, stopping and restarting the service may be enough to resolve the issue with no further effort.

After restarting the Print Spooler service, you examine the queue and find that the jobs are unchanged. At this point, the most likely cause is a corrupted document stuck at the top of the queue. Make a note as to the document size and timestamp. Stop the Print Spooler again, and then open Explorer.

Using Explorer, open the `WINNT` folder and find the `system32\Spool\Printers` folder. Find the files with the approximate timestamp of the print job that was stuck at the top of the queue. There will be two files, one with the extension `.spl`, the other with the extension `.shd`. If you have trouble deleting the SPL file, you may still be able to fix the problem by renaming the SHD file and restarting the Print Spooler service.

NOTE Vista uses two files for each print job submitted. The first is the actual spool file (`*.spl`), which contains the formatted data to be printed. The second is the shadow file (`*.shd`), which is basically a transaction file for the print job.

After successfully deleting the two files, you restart the Print Spooler and immediately the print jobs begin to print.

Provide closure. Talking with Bob, you describe the issue as a corrupted print job that acted like a cork in a bottle, plugging up the queue. This could have been caused by a problem with the printer settings, the queue itself being corrupt, or, most likely, the document being corrupt. In the last case, Bob could open the document in the original program and select Save As from the File menu to save a new copy of the document without the corruption. Once again, don't forget to document.

Other Print Troubleshooting Steps

There are several standard troubleshooting steps that you can add to your support toolbox. We've already discussed one of the most important—asking simple questions. Believe it or not, verifying that the print device is plugged in and turned on can solve many problems. This is no reflection on either the intelligence of the user or their knowledge of computing. Some *very* experienced people have called support with printing issues that were solved by either plugging in the print device or turning it on. We've all done it at some time.

Assuming that the print device is plugged in and turned on and that you've verified the parallel cable as well, you need to test the print subsystem directly. To do so, follow these steps:

1. Choose Start ➤ Control Panel ➤ Printers to open the `Printers` folder (if you're using the Classic view of Control Panel, and as a system administrator or power user, you surely are).
2. Right-click the icon for your printer, and choose Properties from the context menu to open the Properties dialog box for your printer.
3. In the General tab, click Print Test Page.

If you're troubleshooting a non-PostScript print device that's been redirected to LPT1, you can try the following command at a command prompt:

```
Type dir > lptl:
```

This copies the output of a `dir` command directly to the print device and bypasses the spooling provided by Vista. If this fails or if the output is garbled, the issue may be a bad cable, faulty parallel port, or other hardware problem. If it works, you know the problem exists in Vista or in the program.

NOTE Redirecting the output of a command to the port won't work if you're testing a PostScript device.

If any devices are connected to the computer's parallel port between the computer and the print device, you should remove them and try printing again. Vista is often not very forgiving about sharing ports with multiple devices.

Try a generic driver for the print device. If you're using a PostScript device, try installing the Apple LaserWriter driver. This is a very basic PostScript driver. If it works, you've identified the problem as a bad `*.ppd` driver for the PostScript print device. If it's a non-PostScript device, try the Generic-Text Only driver.

NOTE PostScript printers don't really have a printer driver. Instead they use a PostScript Printer Description file (`*.ppd`), which is essentially a text file that describes how to send print jobs to the print device.

An issue that's often overlooked is the amount of space available for the spool file. Check to make sure that plenty of free space remains on the partition where Vista is installed. If you run out of room for the spool file, one of two things will happen: Either the jobs won't print, giving you an error message about being out of memory; or the jobs will print, but the printing process will be incredibly slow. If you have multiple partitions on your hard drive, or multiple hard drives in your machine, you can move your print spooler to a location with more free space. To do this, open the Printers window, and choose File ➤ Server Properties. In the Advanced tab, you'll see a location for the spool folder. Type in an alternate folder location (on a different drive), and then click OK.

Another thing to try is printing from another operating system on the same computer if there's a dual-boot configuration. Or, you could even try printing from the same application on a different computer.

One last possibility is that there's a problem with your document. It's possible that you'll be able to print a less-complex document from the same application. If this is the case, the problem is probably within the application.

Troubleshooting Vista Setup

Many people encounter problems during the installation of Vista, though most of the problems are minor and can be easily avoided. This section helps with troubleshooting the more difficult Setup issues.

In this section, we talk about troubleshooting Setup on the Intel and compatible platforms. The techniques work well for machines that are on the Hardware Compatibility List (HCL) and also for most machines that aren't on the list. Why would you want to install Vista on a "noncompatible" system? Ever build your own computer? It wouldn't likely be on the HCL unless you want to pay Microsoft to test your computer and certify it for Vista.

I've broken this section into parts that address problems you might encounter when planning for or during the text mode portion of Setup, during the transition to GUI mode, and during the final phase of rebooting.

Planning

If you can restrain yourself from simply tearing the shrink-wrap from the box and whipping the CD-ROM out to start Setup, you should think about some things before you begin. Does your computer meet or exceed all the requirements? You may want to take the time to consult Chapter 2 again for setup guidance and hardware requirements. Assuming that you've done this and your computer meets all the requirements, there are some additional points you'll want to document before starting.

What cards are installed in your computer? Do you have a network card? A sound card? What about a 3D accelerator card? Do you have the settings for all these devices written down? Remember that Vista is a Plug and Play operating system; it can find the settings for most of your hardware on its own, but you should still know what those settings are in case it can't find them. Do you have the latest, certified drivers for Vista? Are the drivers on floppy disk or CD-ROM where you can get to them easily? Or are they on a network share? By the way, it won't do you any good to have your network card drivers out on a network server somewhere if you don't already have a functioning network card. Keep these handy on a USB flash drive, rewriteable CD/DVD, or floppy disk. Use Table 35.1 as a guide for the information you should have on hand prior to running Setup.

TABLE 35.1: Useful Information for Setup

DEVICE	INFORMATION TO GATHER
Video display	Adapter brand and model, chip set
Network adapter	IRQ, I/O address, DMA, transceiver type
SCSI adapter	Manufacturer and model, chip set, IRQ, bus type
Mouse (pointing device)	Manufacturer and model, bus type, port
I/O ports	Serial, parallel, IRQ, I/O addresses
Internal modem	Port, IRQ, I/O address
Sound card	Manufacturer and model (or compatible model), IRQ, I/O address, DMA
Other devices	Hardware resources, device type, drivers

Now let's look at another troubleshooting scenario involving Setup issues. In this situation, imagine you're the person responsible for installing Vista and for providing general technical support to a group of users.

Troubleshooting Scenario 3: Drives Not Found

You're responsible for installing Vista on a computer for one of the users in your department. You insert the installation CD and begin Setup. When Setup reaches the point where it displays your current disk and partition information, Setup displays the following error message:

```
Setup did not find any hard drives on your computer.
```

You know there are two hard disk drives in this computer and you can hear them spinning, so you know that they're receiving power. The first step in your troubleshooting methodology is to explore the boundaries of the problem.

You open the case of the computer to find out exactly what kind of hard disk drives are installed (after turning off the power, of course). You find that the drives are SCSI-2 2.1GB and that they're attached to an Adaptec 2940 controller. No other SCSI devices are installed in this computer. When you investigate, you find that the computer had IDE drives and has recently been updated with a new SCSI controller and SCSI disks.

What you know and don't know at this point:

- The computer has never worked before in this configuration.
- The drives are SCSI, which require electronic termination and unique ID numbers on each bus.
- You don't know the state of the termination.
- You don't know the SCSI ID numbers for each drive.

Based on this information, you should already be suspecting that something's wrong with the hardware configuration. You reach into the case to ensure that the cables are tightly attached and find that they are. On these hard disks drives, the SCSI IDs are set by jumpers on the rear of the drive (you'll probably have to remove the drives to get at them).

Your plan of attack:

1. Verify the SCSI ID numbers of the drives and controller.
2. Verify the termination of the drive chain.
3. Check the BIOS settings of the controller.

Before you go through the work to remove the hard disk drives to check their ID numbers, you boot the computer to run the SCSI BIOS program. This program enables you to view and modify the configuration of the devices, as well as run diagnostics and other utilities. This utility tells you that it sees both hard disk drives, one as SCSI ID #0, the other as SCSI ID #1. This means the ID numbers aren't the issue. SCSI ID #0 and #1 are usually reserved for hard drives.

NOTE SCSI ID numbers are important. Having a conflict between two or more devices on the same SCSI bus can cause Setup to fail to recognize installed hard disk drives. It can also cause the system to fail when booting or to hang after booting.

The BIOS utility on the Adaptec controller also provides the capability to enable or disable termination on the controller card itself. You check and find that it's enabled correctly. Now you've verified the SCSI ID numbers, the controller settings, and half of the termination. The only thing left on your list is termination. To do this on older hardware, you have to pull out the last hard disk drive on the ribbon cable and check its termination. Newer drives are self-terminating, and normally the termination is on the ribbon cables.

Checking the last drive on the chain, you find that its terminator packs (resistors) aren't set. This means that the SCSI bus isn't terminated at one end. This may or may not be the problem, but it certainly needs to be fixed. You correct the termination and are ready to test the setup again. You start Setup, and this time everything runs fine.

Today, many SCSI drives are self-terminating, and you can also terminate on the ribbon cable instead of the drive. Today's SCSI is usually terminated on the SCSI controller and on the ribbon cable if building internal (to the PC) SCSI chains.

When you're troubleshooting problems on a SCSI-based system, always remember to check the termination. With SCSI, both ends of each drive chain must be terminated. Vista is so sensitive about the stability of the hardware components that improper termination can be fatal to Setup. Even if you succeed with Setup, termination issues can result in hanging or even a blue-screen error. Even mismatched termination levels can cause this situation. If your controller has active termination and your hard disk has passive termination, you may have problems. Upgrading your SCSI chain to active termination or even forced-perfect termination at both ends can relieve the problem.

SCSI Troubleshooting

In the previous scenario, we looked at the possible importance of SCSI termination. In my experience, nearly 90 percent of the troubleshooting issues of Vista Setup on SCSI-based computers involve termination problems. But there are other issues to be aware of as well. For instance, is the BIOS of the SCSI controller activated? This is another problem that would cause the preceding scenario.

A low-level format that's incorrect for the current drive geometry could cause file corruption, drives not being recognized by Setup, and system crashes. If you're installing a new SCSI drive or changing to a new make or model of SCSI controller, you should perform a low-level format of the drive to assure that the drive geometry will line up correctly.

In simpler terms, the drive controller performs a format of the disks within the drive so that the operating system will be able to write data to the individual sectors on the drive. In a way, sectors are like tiny boxes that are meant to contain information. Imagine trying to drop golf balls into small boxes. If you're lining them up correctly, it's easy. The balls simply drop right into place every time. But imagine now that you're slightly off your aim. The balls usually go in the boxes, but sometimes they bounce off the edges and roll away. That's what's happening when your drive isn't low-level formatted correctly for the specific controller. Each SCSI controller has its own geometry, its way of laying out those little boxes.

If multiple SCSI controllers are in the computer, does more than one of them have an active BIOS? If so, they may be competing for Int13 calls. This means that the "wrong" controller may be trying to boot the computer and therefore prevents the "right" controller from doing its job.

It's common today for people to try to mix SCSI device types—that is, to add 50-pin SCSI-2 devices to the same chain as SCSI-3 devices with 68 pins. That means that the cable has to change sizes from 68 wires to 50 wires. If you mix these devices, be certain that you buy the proper cable to make the conversion. If you don't, or if you try to convert from 68 to 50 wires and then back to 68, you'll have wires that aren't being terminated correctly. It's better, by far, to have only "wide" devices with 68 pins on one chain and "narrow" devices with 50 pins on a separate chain.

One other major factor with SCSI disks involves the controller. If the SCSI controller to which your drives are attached isn't on the Vista HCL, you could run into major problems during installation. It's difficult, if not impossible, to install any operating system on a drive it refuses to acknowledge. To work around this, Vista will prompt you to provide any required disk drivers early in Setup.

Addressing Initial Boot Issues

During this phase of Setup, Vista installs drivers and configures the system. Problems in this portion of Setup are typically fewer and generally related to configuration rather than failing hardware or drivers. This is also where Vista will try to load the network for the first time in a full configuration.

It's possible to encounter video problems at this phase of Setup. On some computers, the display won't reset correctly during a warm boot under Vista. If this occurs, your display will be black or very distorted. Try turning off the power to the computer (yes, this is one of those rare cases where you power down without shutting down first) and then restarting it. If this resolves the issue, you'll have to power down the computer every time you reboot. This is a hardware issue related to the video and system BIOS and not a Vista problem.

USB Device Errors

As people add more and more devices to their systems through the Universal Serial Bus (USB) connectors on their machine, the potential for potentially crippling problems increases. My system has the potential to support up to 10 USB devices directly. With additional hubs, you could add a considerable number of devices to the system and not all of these devices are Vista friendly.

During the setup process, you'll normally want to remove the USB devices that you don't need. For example, you need a mouse, but you don't need your camera connected to the system. Complete the setup with a minimal number of devices and then add them one at a time to your Vista setup. Let Vista recognize the device and configure it. Test the device to make sure it actually works before you add the next device.

Be especially wary of USB devices that don't appear as part of Microsoft's HCL. For example, I tried plugging one brand of USB flash drive (thumb drive) into Vista and it amazed me to see the almost instantaneous blue screen of death (BSOD) that appeared. The drive was good. It worked fine under Windows XP on the same machine, but the drive simply wasn't Vista compatible. (See the "Troubleshooting Stop Errors" section of the chapter for more information about handling the BSOD.)

Windows Memory Diagnostics Tool

You wouldn't believe how often problems end up being something that you think doesn't go bad, such as memory. One of the reasons that Microsoft included the Windows Memory Diagnostic Tool is that memory does go bad. In fact, given the amount of memory in many machines today, the memory probably goes bad more often than you think. We've already discussed the mechanics of the Windows Memory Diagnostics Tool in the "Using the Windows Memory Diagnostic Tool" section of Chapter 29. This section looks at the Windows Memory Diagnostic Tool as a troubleshooting aid and helps define when you should use it.

How do you determine when to use the Windows Memory Diagnostic Tool? You could simply run the Windows Memory Diagnostic Tool at predefined intervals. If you ran it once a week, you'd probably find most memory problems before they have a chance to destroy your data. However, given the time that it takes to run this tool, many people would start using it with good intentions and then stop at some point, so it's probably better to view this as an "as needed" tool.

Memory is a very hard piece of hardware for many people to grasp because it sits in the background without much of a physical presence at all. When a hard drive fails, you know it's failed because the system won't boot. Likewise, display adapters and monitors are very easy to spot, as are CD and DVD drives. All of these features have a very prominent presence and failure is unmistakable, but not so with memory.

TIP Memory errors commonly occur during startup. The power surge that occurs during the power on sequence can make toast of marginal memory.

Very often, memory problems show up as flaky applications. An application may load properly and run well one day, but not the next. Sometimes an application will load and fail for seemingly no reason at all. You might see unexplainable data corruption one day and it doesn't show up the next. In fact, one of the most prominent features of a memory failure is uncertainty. A key point to remember is that computer programs aren't inconsistent. If you perform the same steps day after day, the program should produce the same results. When you see your system suddenly doing something that seems absurd, unreasonable, inconsistent, or unexplainable, you might want to run the Windows Memory Diagnostic Tool.

The reason that memory errors are so hard to diagnose is that applications load in different places each time you run them. An application could load into a good section of memory one day and a section of memory with errors the next. Sometimes the memory will contain code and others times it contains data, so even the presentation of the error can change. The size of an error could be as small as a single bit, which means that the error might not even show up if the application doesn't use that bit for some reason. In addition, sometimes a memory glitch occurs due to unknown reasons—a voltage spike or even alpha rays (you can read about single event upsets at `http://en.wikipedia.org/wiki/Single_event_upset`). The fact that memory glitches are extremely hard to pin down without a diagnostic aid is well known and that's the reason you need the Windows Memory Diagnostics Tool.

Troubleshooting Stop Errors

As I mentioned earlier, Vista is an incredibly complex operating system. And with anything this complex, problems are bound to occasionally occur. The good news is that Vista is very stable. Problems are generally kept to a minimum, and the operating system itself should rarely crash. The bad news is, because of its stability, when a problem *is* serious enough to make it crash, Vista crashes hard.

Some people call Stop errors the "Blue Screen of Death," or BSOD, although you should be aware that there may be hundreds of possible blue-screen errors in Vista. None of us will likely ever see them all; at least we can hope that we never see them all.

When you first see a Stop error, you may be overwhelmed with the information in front of you. Most of the time, the ominous blue background is a placemat for a horde of binary and hexadecimal information that is indecipherable to mere mortals. This information is provided for developers and debuggers. The first thing you want to look for is near the top of the message: the word STOP followed by a message. Depending on the Stop error, you may also find the name of the offending driver or application on the screen as well.

Stop errors can occur at almost any stage of Vista installation or operation. The errors can be broken into three categories, based on when they occur:

During Vista installation If a Stop error happens here, it may indicate a BIOS incompatibility issue, failing hardware, or a faulty device driver. Make sure that all of your hardware is on the HCL.

During Vista startup If Vista has been installed and working for some time, but an error occurs during startup, it could mean a couple of things. Generally, the culprit is a device driver or system service. If you just installed a new service, application, or driver and you get a BSOD when rebooting, the new software could be your problem. Make sure you also consider the possibility of failed memory.

During Vista operation This is the most ambiguous time an error can happen. The error could be practically anything. A Stop error during operation can be caused by failing hardware (particularly memory and processor), system services, device drivers, and applications. The text of the Stop message will give you valuable information as to the cause of the problem.

Common Stop Errors

The title of this section, "Common Stop Errors," doesn't mean to imply in any way that Stop errors are common. In fact, it's quite the opposite. However, if you're one of the unlucky souls to encounter a Stop error, these are some of the more common ones that appear. They're listed in hexadecimal order for convenience.

```
STOP: 0x0000000A
IRQL_NOT_LESS_OR_EQUAL
```

This Stop message can appear at almost any time. Most of the time, this error points to a problem device driver, service, or application. On the Stop screen, it will usually tell you the name of the offending driver, service, or application. Be sure to write down the name of the offender, because this can be invaluable for troubleshooting.

```
STOP: 0x0000001E
KMODE_EXCEPTION_NOT_HANDLED
```

This Stop message occurs when the processor receives an instruction that it doesn't understand. Many times, this is caused by invalid memory access violations. This Stop error often lists the name of the offending device driver.

```
STOP: 0x00000023
FAT32_FILE_SYSTEM
```

A problem has occurred with the FAT32 file system driver. This could indicate a hard disk connectivity problem or a hard disk failure.

```
STOP: 0x00000024
NTFS_FILE_SYSTEM
```

This is the same as the 0x23 error, except it's for the NTFS file system.

```
STOP: 0x0000002E
DATA_BUS_ERROR
```

This is most often caused by failing physical memory (including video memory) but could also indicate a physical problem with the motherboard.

```
STOP: 0x00000077
KERNEL_STACK_INPAGE_ERROR
```

If Vista tries to read information from the page file and doesn't locate the information it expects, you'll receive this error message. Failing physical memory, failing hard disks, corrupted data, and viruses can cause this error message. A similar error message is the `STOP: 0x7A KERNEL_DATA_INPAGE_ERROR` message.

```
STOP: 0x0000007B
INACCESSIBLE_BOOT_DEVICE
```

This error almost speaks common English. Your computer can't find the boot device. Check your physical connections. This could also indicate a failing hard disk or disk controller.

One of the most interesting causes of the STOP: 0x7B message is adding an IDE drive to a SCSI-based system. IDE controllers are enumerated before the SCSI controllers, meaning that the BIOS of the computer looks for them first. If you add an IDE drive to a computer that is already working fine with SCSI hard disks, you may very well see this blue screen. That situation can be fixed in the computer's BIOS. If your BIOS supports the option, set the boot order to go to the SCSI drives first and then to the IDE.

```
STOP: 0x0000007F
UNEXPECTED_KERNEL_MODE_TRAP
```

Hardware failure generally causes this error message. If you're running an over-clocked processor, you can expect to see this Stop error at some point.

```
STOP: 0x000000D1
DRIVER_IRQL_NOT_LESS_OR_EQUAL
```

This cryptic message is actually one of the more common Stop errors. It happens when a device driver tries to access a memory address that it's not supposed to. Poorly written drivers are generally the culprit, although software applications (particularly antivirus programs or backup programs) can cause this error as well.

```
STOP: 0x000000D8
DRIVER_USED_EXCESSIVE_PTES
```

Once again, this is caused by a faulty driver. We can gather that from the error message, even if we have no idea what a PTE is. PTEs are page table entries, which Vista uses to keep track of memory information. Poorly written or corrupt drivers can cause this error. Another related error is STOP: 0x3F NO_MORE_SYSTEM_PTES.

```
STOP: 0xC000021A
STATUS_SYSTEM_PROCESS_TERMINATED
```

This error message usually indicates that a Vista user-mode subsystem has been compromised in some way. This is a serious problem. You may also see this error message if a backup has been only partially restored or if permissions have been modified so that the System account no longer has access to required system files and folders.

```
STOP 0xC0000221
STATUS_IMAGE_CHECKSUM_MISMATCH
```

This error message usually points to a corrupted file or hard disk. You'll usually see the name of the offending file on this blue screen.

This list is by no means intended to be complete. It's here to give you a general idea of what types of problems may cause your Vista machine to blue screen. As you can see, most Stop errors are caused by failing hardware, device drivers, services, or applications. If you encounter an error message not listed, or just want more information on blue screens, you can go to Microsoft's support site at `http://www.microsoft.com/support` and search for your specific error message.

One more thing to mention about blue screens applies more to upgrading Vista from an earlier version than to a fresh installation. During an upgrade, Setup will notify you with a blue-screen error that you must remove an application before you can continue. As soon as the application is removed, Setup will proceed normally.

Responding to Stop Errors

You can configure Vista to respond in a variety of ways once it encounters a Stop error. To do this, you need to go to System Properties (either open the System icon in Control Panel or right-click the Computer icon in your Start menu and choose Properties, and then click the Advanced system settings link). Then in the Advanced tab, choose Startup and Recovery ➢Settings. You should see a screen similar to Figure 35.1.

In Figure 35.1, take a look at the System Failure section. In the event of a system failure, you can configure Vista to do any of the following tasks:

Write an event to the system log Writing an event to the System log will create an event for you to look at in Event Viewer. While this event may not tell you everything you want to know, it will list the Stop error code so you have a point from which to start troubleshooting.

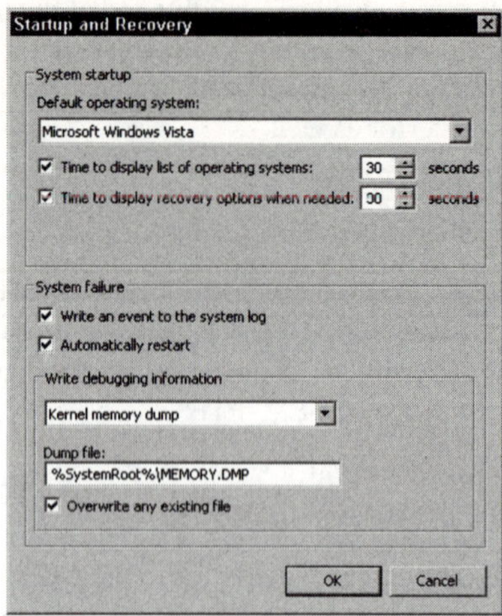

FIGURE 35.1 Customizing Stop error response.

Automatically restart Automatically restarting is self-evident. If you don't choose this option, you'll have to restart your computer manually after a Stop error occurs.

Write debugging information Writing debugging information doesn't really help you much, but it does provide a log of the event that you can send to Microsoft for analysis. The debugging information is basically the contents of physical memory when the system crashed. Although the information may not be incredibly relevant for most of us, it can be useful to programmers or to the technicians at Microsoft's help desk.

TIP If you choose to have your system automatically restart, make sure to have Vista log an event in the System log as well. Otherwise, you may never know what went wrong, other than the fact that your computer just rebooted itself.

Fixing Stop Errors

Fixing a Stop error is no different than troubleshooting any other problem with your computer. First and foremost, don't forget about your list of good troubleshooting procedures: define the problem, explore the boundaries, brainstorm, test your ideas, repair the problem, provide closure, clean up after yourself, and document the situation. Here are some general guidelines for fixing Stop errors:

- After you write down the message, reboot your computer. If the error doesn't come back, it's not a problem. This may sound cynical, but it's true. Sometimes the computer will "hiccup" and produce an error. Things happen. If the error keeps happening, then you have a problem.
- Suspect recent changes. If you just added hardware (including drivers) or software, it could be causing the problem. Try removing the hardware or application or trying an alternate device driver.
- Check your system BIOS. Sometimes incorrect BIOS settings, especially with an ACPI-compliant BIOS, can cause blue screens. If possible, reset the settings to BIOS defaults.
- Search Microsoft's Knowledge Base. This site often has specific fixes for the problem you've just encountered. Remember, good troubleshooters don't necessarily know everything. They just know where to look to find answers.

Most of the time, you can find a fix for your Stop error. The fix may be replacing hardware or installing different drivers or software. In more extreme cases, you may need to restore from a backup. In a worst-case scenario, you can always reinstall the operating system.

Summary

No matter what your interest is in Vista, there will be times when understanding the process of troubleshooting will be helpful to you. Even if troubleshooting is never going to be part of your responsibility, things may go wrong. If you have even a basic understanding of the process, you'll convey much more meaningful information to the person who *is* responsible for the troubleshooting.

Use the methods listed in this chapter when troubleshooting your own computer. Follow the guidelines for documenting the steps taken and the possible approaches to use. Always remember to think simple at first, and then move on to the more exotic as you eliminate basic possibilities.

The next and last part of this book details Microsoft's tools for deployment of Vista in an organization. Chapter 36 is an overview of the tools that Microsoft offers, tools that are organized by and supported by the Business Desktop Deployment solution accelerator. Subsequent chapters take a closer look at the different deployment scenarios, as well as explore in depth the individual tools that you can use for your deployments.

Part IX

Enterprise Installation Setups with Business Desktop Deployment (BDD)

In this section you'll learn:

- **How to Use the Business Desktop Deployment Solution**
- **Set Up and Manage a Large-scale Deployment Using Teams and Projects**
- **Determine and Create a Deployment Scenario with which to Run WAIK**
- **Create, Maintain, and Deploy System Images for a Large Number of Desktops**
- **Perform Network Installations Using Windows Desktop Services**

Chapter 36

An Overview of Business Desktop Deployment (BDD)

When an organization makes the decision to migrate or upgrade a fleet of client computers to a new operating system, it has large economic repercussions. An upgrade can cost companies up to $1,000 per client to implement, which in most cases is more than the cost of the computer and software license itself. When implemented with automated tools such as the ones described in this chapter, it's possible to reduce that cost by a factor of 10. Upgrades save organizations money over time by offering improved operations, but it may take some time to realize those savings. More often than not an upgrade adds new capabilities that provide business opportunities as the primary motivation to perform the upgrade.

Still, the upgrade process carries a certain level of risk (which speaks to the real costs involved); and upgrades for an organization are always complex to manage. A first step may be a cost-justification project that results in estimated return on investment (ROI) or total cost of ownership (TCO) calculation, a statement of the business case for the project, as well as the specification for the overall estimated cost and length of the deployment—all of which management must sign off on.

Many factors influence a large-scale Vista deployment: infrastructure must be evaluated, systems must be inventoried, hardware may need to be upgraded, applications must be tested and validated, and client systems must be standardized, imaged, and rolled out to the correct systems. To work out the details of an enterprise deployment, a test lab or sample subnet is often created to support the initial development efforts. The key to a successful deployment is careful planning, testing, and stepwise implementation.

This chapter describes the Microsoft Solution Accelerator for Business Desktop Deployment solution or BDD, which is available in both a Standard Edition and an Enterprise Edition. The BDD is an application management framework that provides an organizational structure to a large-scale Vista deployment, informational resources for those teams, and some of the utilities that I discuss in this chapter to allow you to perform the deployment itself. Using those tools and the BDD guidance, you can inventory your software and hardware, set up a lab environment for testing, and create and manage system images, as well as check and manage the security settings of your systems and network.

The BDD uses the Microsoft Application Compatibility Toolkit 5.0 to perform software inventories and check for known compatibility issues. The BDD requires access to SQL Server for its services, uses ImageX technologies to create system images, stores and manages images from master computers (model setups) with the System Image Manager, and relies on the Windows Automated Installation Kit to install images to systems that have been booted with the Windows Pre-Installation Environment. This chapter introduces these tools, so that you have the context in which to understand their use when they are discussed in much greater detail in the chapters to come.

Microsoft considers the Office Professional 2007 suite a core application, and that application suite, along with other applications, can be packaged into images as part of a deployment. The BDD offers access to templates and scripts that allow Office to be part of the base desktop computer image.

In this chapter I provide an overview of the BDD, which explains the following:

- Performing large-scale deployments of Vista with the BDD
- Analyzing client hardware and software requirements
- Setting up project teams to execute the deployment
- Creating and managing system images with ImageX and the System Image Manager
- Using WAIK to deploy system images of Vista with and without Office 2007
- Migrating user state data to new Vista installations with the User State Migration Tool (USMT)
- Performing remote installations in the Windows Pre-installation Environment (Windows PE)

Vista: What's New?

Microsoft has changed deployment technology substantially since Windows XP and Windows Server 2003. A new image-based file format called Windows Imaging Format (WIM) and the technology to deliver those images to desktops makes the tools used previously much more powerful and, most importantly, much more flexible. Nearly all of the utilities used in desktop deployments have been refined and upgraded. In this chapter, you'll also see that many new tools have also been introduced to help you deploy large-scale Vista systems.

Understanding the Concepts behind Scaled Desktop Deployment

In Chapter 2 you saw how easy it is to do a clean install of Vista on a single computer when the hardware is "Vista ready." There are a few options to set, such as time zone, but other than being in front of the computer for a short time to set those options, the OS install doesn't take that much time or demand too much from you.

Even in a single system installation, you are still faced with prospect of installing and setting up the applications you need postinstallation. You can migrate your old settings from a previous version of Windows using the Windows Easy Transfer utility and, with luck, most of your work is complete.

When you upgrade Windows XP SP2 to Vista the process is both a little harder and a little easier. You will have to worry about application compatibility, but if those applications are compatible at least you don't have to reinstall them when the upgrade to Vista is complete, nor do you have to migrate files and settings. Your files and settings are (hopefully) still there and successfully applied.

Installing Vista on multiple systems very quickly turns a chore into a vocation. Multiply the time involved by the tasks just mentioned by several systems that need to be upgraded and it's easy to see that the problem becomes exponentially harder. Your interest in standardizing and automating the Vista installation process should also grow exponentially. Common wisdom in the industry suggests that 10 computers are about the upper limit of the number of systems that most people want to install on a one-at-a-time basis. Beyond 10, people stop describing the job as "installation" or an "upgrade" and begin to describe the experience as a "deployment." Without automation, the number of systems that any one administrator can upgrade in a month is rather limited.

If you are familiar with the details of automated deployment technology in Widows XP or 2000, you will be pleasantly surprised by the many improvements in deployment technologies that Microsoft has made for Vista. Other improvements like the Aero Glass interface may get more press, but from the standpoint of businesses, easier deployment may make the difference between Vista's being deployed or not. Microsoft has made a great effort to improve this area and has largely succeeded.

At the heart of scaling your Vista deployment is the notion of standardization. The more uniform the systems you are installing Vista on, the fewer the number of configurations that you have to create. In previous versions of Windows administrators who wanted to perform unattended installs had to grapple with a large set of files such as `Unattend.XML`, `Sysprep.inf`, `Winbom.ini`, and others. These multiple files, along with the way Setup worked on a network share, made large-scale deployment more difficult.

Windows Image Technology

Images are a much easier way to deploy an operating system than a setup program acting on a collection of cabinet files. Symantec's Ghost, Altaris, and many other utilities have used system images with their deployment modules to automate previous Windows installations for a while now. With Vista Microsoft has now adopted this system. Microsoft's system image technology creates a highly compressed container file called a Windows Imaging Format (a WIM file) that is easy to create, can be edited directly with the right tool, and minimizes the hit to a network's bandwidth when it is copied over a network.

NOTE Even compressed Vista images are still larger than Windows XP images were. For XP, system images were between 1GB and 3GB. Visa images tend to start at 2GB and can be as large as 5GB depending on what has been added to the operating system. The uncompressed sizes of images between 2GB and 5GB would be between 6GB and 15GB.

By making the Windows Imaging Format file rather than sector based, it is possible to create a file that uses what is called a Single Instance Storage or SIS technology. (An ISO file is an example of a sector-based image format.) An SIS file stores only one copy of a file within the WIM container and uses references to that file whenever multiple copies were used by the source. As a system is imaged, the elimination of duplicate files along with the compression used compresses the content of an image to around 35 percent of its uncompressed size. When you use a WIM file you do not have to delete the original partition or the original directory before its use. The Business Desktop Deployment system creates and uses WIM files.

By modularizing the files contained within the WIM image it is possible to ship one single image of all versions of Windows Vista, along with all languages. A core component called MinWin contains about 95 percent of the code and is the base Windows Vista OS. To that are added modules that extend MinWin by adding the Home features, or the Pro features, or a particular language. It is this modularization that enables a single master image for all the versions of Vista, including all of the language packs, and more importantly from the standpoint of this discussion enables Microsoft to finally offer imaged-based deployment technology.

To summarize, here are some characteristics of the WIM file that you will want to know:

- WIM images are hardware independent, so you can store different platforms in single file.
- WIM is a container format and can store multiple images in the same file.

- Many versions of the same family of products can be stored under the same file unifying all versions of Vista.
- WIM is highly compressed, about 35 percent.
- WIM is single instancing and stores only one copy of the same file.
- WIM allows for offline editing on a file-by-file basis for files contained inside the WIM file.
- WIM has no size limitations for its creation.
- WIM imposes no size restrictions on the target storage medium beyond its being big enough to fit the uncompressed contents of the WIM file.
- WIM installs without altering the contents of a disk; it does not overwrite existing files.
- WIM is supported by an API called WIMGAPI so that software can support this format.

Image Deployment Tools and Scaling

The whole idea behind successful large-scale deployments is to automate them. The less you have to touch the systems you are upgrading to Vista, the more time an organization saves, the more money they save, and if done correctly the fewer mistakes get made. It's not always true that an organization gets these benefits, but when a deployment is done carefully and tested prior to application, the odds are highly in their favor.

Therefore, the central issue for medium and large-scale deployments is the creation of "master" images from the hardware standards that your organization will support. You create a standard system (called a master) with the hardware, software, and settings you desire; Sysprep the result to remove any unique identification; and then deploy that image. Then, with a tool like ImageX, you create the image and store that image in a network share. The process is one where you have an original system and you are cloning that system to clients.

Since images are a managed collection of files rather than a stored collection of disk sectors, you can mount an image to a folder. ImageX can be run from the command line or from within the Windows Pre-installation Environment (Windows PE).

More importantly, as you collect new device drivers, service packs, and applications that you want to update or install, you can add them directly to your images without having to rebuild your master system and imaging it again. WIM is also Windows operating system independent, so using imaging technology you can also install Windows XP, Windows Server 2003, and future versions to come.

With your images prepared from your master computers, you can use tools like the Windows Automated Installation Kit (WAIK, or Windows AIK) to install Vista. WAIK is a package of components containing the Windows System Image Manager, Windows PE, and related help files. As described later in this chapter, WAIK is distributed with the Business Desktop Deployment solution. For a small number of computers that's as easy as preparing a disk or flash media with Window PE, the WIM file, WAIK, and ImageX. When you boot system from this media, Windows PE loads into memory and opens a command prompt that lets you run the ImageX command to apply the image.

To automate the process, you can script the installation, mount the images on a distribution share, and run the installer. You'll also need to create an `Unattend.xml` answer file using the Windows System Image Manager or WSIM and place that file onto your master computer prior to making that system's image. When a system runs the Pre-boot eXecution Environment (PXE) it obtains a network address through DHCP Discover, finds the distribution share, and applies the image. For small to medium deployments of less than 100 computers, you can use your images to perform an unattended setup as described in this paragraph. However for larger deployments, a more automated system is required.

In order to scale your Vista deployment, you need a tool that allows you to automate the migration of files and settings from previous systems to your new freshly installed ones. Remember, for upgrades your settings and files are already there. Windows Easy Transfer, which is the preferred method to use when you can manually install systems, isn't convenient for scaled deployments. Large-scale deployments use the User State Migration Tool 3.0 (USMT), which allows you to migrate many systems from a single interface.

For installation of Vista on hundreds or thousands of systems, you will also need a server-based approach to manage the operation. The Windows Deployment Services (WDS) is now used in Vista as the deployment engine, and this application replaces the Remote Installation Service (RIS) used with previous Windows deployments.

Tools of the Trade

Vista introduces a number of new tools to help you create images, modify images, deploy images, migrate user state information, set up security, and in doing so obsoletes tools you might be familiar with. Just to keep track of what's being used now, below is a summary listing of the tools that are used in Vista deployments.

Tools in current use include:

ACT The Application Compatibility Toolkit 5.0 was revamped for Vista. This tool not only determines what is compatible, but also can serve to monitor your systems and push out applicable updates.

BCDEdit Use Boot Configuration Data Store Editor to modify the Vista boot configuration.

BDD Workbench This management tool is part of the BDD framework solution for managing images used in a deployment.

BitLocker BitLocker provides volume drive encryption and is included in Vista Enterprise and Vista Ultimate editions.

ImageX ImageX is the command-line utility that creates WIM system images, usually applied in the Windows PE environment.

OCSETUP OCSETUP installs Windows components and replaces SYSOCMGR used in its online mode. OCSETUP is a command line tool that lets you install or remove system MSIs or pacakages.

PEIMG PEIMG is used to modify Windows PE images.

PKMGR This tool is used to modify the operating system. It replaces SYSOCMGR in its offline mode.

PNPUTIL The PNPUTIL is used to manage the driver store, allowing you to add or subtract drivers as required.

SETUP This is the installation tool for Vista and replaces the previous installers WINNT and WINNT32.

SYSPREP The System Preparation Tool, or SYSPREP, has been updated for Vista. This tool removes system identification prior to cloning.

USMT 3.0 The User State Migration Tool 3.0 captures and restores user state data including files, profiles, settings, and other information. This version migrates from Windows 2000, and XP to Windows XP or Vista.

Windows Deployment Services Windows DS replaces RIS and is use to deploy Vista, XP, and PE boot images.

Windows SIM The Windows System Image Manager or is used to create and modify the `Unattend.xml` files that are used to control image installations. This system replaces the use of the Setup Manager and a text editor as the editor for answer files.

Although this chapter and the chapters that follow document Microsoft's deployment technologies, undoubtedly third-party vendors will begin to offer their own deployment tools over time. The above list includes Microsoft utilities only.

Application Compatibility

Vista was designed to be as compatible as possible with the largest number of Windows applications. However, changes in the operating system often break important applications that organizations rely on for system and network configuration, security, and peripherals. In the upgrade from Windows 2000 Professional to Windows XP Professional it was estimated that perhaps 15 percent of all applications tested were incompatible and needed to be replaced. So something similar might reasonably be expected to be the case for a Vista deployment or migration.

As a general rule the lower the level that the application hooks into the operating system, the more likely it is that you may encounter problems with Vista. You might reasonably expect problems if you don't update or replace your antivirus or antispyware applications. Those applications often must check for viruses, worms, spyware, and other forms of malware at all levels of the operating system. However, you can also expect to find issues with scripts, macros, and other forms of automation; problems when applications that request services that have changed; and a certain percentage of device drivers. Testing your Vista system build for application compatibility is a very important part of planning for a Vista deployment.

What to Test

To create your base Vista images—the ones that you will deploy in your enterprise, you want to test any application that is added to Vista. That includes the following:

Productivity applications Microsoft considers Office to be a core application and offers guidance as part of the BDD Workbench solution.

Line-of-business (LOB) applications This includes all client software for enterprise applications, for example, databases, messaging, CRM, ERP, and so forth.

Utilities As a group it is de rigueur to upgrade and replace your antivirus, backup, compression, and remote communications tools.

Automation Carefully check logon and startup scripts, macros, and other forms of automation.

NOTE Microsoft notes that you shouldn't assume that applications that run on 32-bit Vista will run correctly on 64-bit Vista. This is particularly true for older applications as 64-bit operating systems do not support 16-bit applications. You can add an x86 emulator such as WOW64 (Windows 32-bit On Windows 64-bit) to get these applications to run, but you definitely need to check out this issue if you are running 64-bit Vista.

BDD considers application compatibility testing to be one of the central tasks in an operating system deployment. The BDD solution recommends that an Application Compatibility Feature Team be created, and provides a guide for their use. The findings of this team are communicated formally to the Project Management Team, which is considered to be the lead team in a Vista deployment. However, as is the case with all deployment teams, it is expected that the Application Compatibility Feature Team will communicate their results with all the other teams.

The BDD recommends a four-phase approach to application compatibility testing:

Planning phase During the planning phase an application inventory is taken, and any agents of framework applications (such as SMS, LANDesk, Altaris, ZENworks, and others) required to create this inventory is deployed. The team then determines which applications they intend to support on each of the supported system images.

Developing phase This phase tests the migration or deployment of Vista images to systems in a test lab. This testing should lead to any necessary changes required to make these applications work (mitigation), as well as creating the necessary packages that will be part of the Vista image (WIM file).

Stabilizing phase In this phase of the solution, the application's compatibility to user state data is tested and improved. All the methods needed to make applications work correctly once the image is deployed are communicated and documented. A database should be established to collect incident reports from testers that help correct application incompatibilities.

Deployment phase In this phase the Application Compatibility Feature Team hands off their work to the Deployment Feature Team, and all of the mitigation packages are deployed to their target systems.

APPLICATION INVENTORIES

To begin to test your application portfolio for compatibility with Vista, you should run the Application Compatibility Toolkit 5.0 (ACT) on current working versions of your systems. This utility runs whenever an application is launched or installed by matching that application to a set of database files stored at `\systemroot\AppPatch`. Those files list applications with known issues as well as potential solutions for those problems. The current version of ACT supports not only Vista, but Windows XP and Windows Server 2003.

NOTE For a more complete and operational discussion of ACT, see the "Testing Applications with Microsoft Application Compatibility Toolkit 5.0" section of Chapter 39.

One of ACT's functions is to perform a software inventory using its Inventory Collector. You may choose to use your enterprise framework to create an inventory, but it may still be useful to run the Inventory Collector to cross-check your results. ACT also contains several other inventory tools, including: Internet Explorer Compatibility Evaluation (IECE), which can uncover compatibility and security issues for intranet and Internet sites; Update Impact Analyzer (UIA), which will test for any compatibilities with Microsoft's Windows Update site; and User Account Control Evaluator (UACCE), where problems relating to user rights and access permissions are tested.

The SMS Software Inventory will also collect application data, but SMS stores that data in its own database. ACT's inventory data is separate from SMS, which for SMS is a SQL Server database file, or in the case of ACT either a SQL Server database file or a SQL Server Desktop Engine (MSDE) database file. SMS Software Inventory must run on existing systems and is usually performed when a large sample or complete inventory is desired. Since SMS doesn't specifically offer application compatibility information for Vista, ACT doesn't really overlap with SMS in this regard.

ACT is updated from the Internet so that it is always current. You can use SMS to deploy the ACT Inventory agents.

If you are performing an inventory using a lot sample in which you select representative systems, then make sure you select ones that differ in the following ways:

- System hardware by model and type
- Version of the operating system, including any service packs
- Applications installed, and the specific version that are in use
- Department or LOB division
- Geographical location
- User role on that system

A lot sample is a collection of systems that provide either an exact set of systems that will be supported, or enough systems to create a representative matrix from which all parameters may be determined. For example, if all client systems at a location are identical, than one of those systems will be representative. If the client configurations deployed are the same for each user type, than selecting one system for each user type supplies the necessary components of a lot sample even if those systems are found in different geographical locations.

Application Remediation

The net result of your application inventory and the analysis of compatibility is a document or database that is called the *application portfolio*. Each application's incompatibility should be listed, as well as prioritized so that itspossible to generate an ordered To Do list for remediation of all critical or serious issues. In order to mitigate applications to make them compatible, either:

- Update the application, modify the application's configuration, or upgrade the application to one that is compatible.
- Modify the application; change the program code. This change is particularly applicable when the organization is running a custom software package or solution, such as a database application.
- Alter security settings to make the application compatible. This change requires that the Application Compatibility Feature Team work with the Security Team to vet the changes.
- When necessary, substitute another application that is compatible with Vista in place of the one that is currently installed and problematic.

The application portfolio, which is the key deliverable for application compatibility testing should also present a prioritized list for the order in which applications should be deployed in the organization.

NOTE Migration and deployment projects are an excellent time to standardize specific application and specific versions of those applications. If your desktops are running a collection of Office versions such as Office 2003, Office XP, and Office 2000, then standardizing based on Office 2007 (for example) and eliminating older versions will lower administrative costs and may pay for the upfront cost of the upgrades. A total cost of ownership (TCO) analysis will quantify the costs and benefits of this approach.

The application portfolio should also list not just those applications that are found by the inventory but those applications that couldn't be inventoried and are missing. Missing applications include those found on mobile systems or on secured systems. Those missing applications should come up in a review of the application portfolio, which should be considered to be a "live" document until the deployment is completed and past its final review. Once the application portfolio is past its final review, it should be signed off by the appropriate parties.

Application compatibility testing is best done in a limited environment, a test lab, or with a small subset of the systems that will be converted to Vista. Since most organizations both upgrade systems from previous versions of Windows as well as do fresh installs or deploy brand new equipment your application compatibility testing in a test lab may need to examine all of the different deployment scenarios.

Test Beds

Microsoft Framework solutions, which are described in greater detail and of which the BDD Workbench is an example, stress a few fundamental principles. Functions are organized into teams that have specified deliverables One essential part of the project begins with the Application Compatibility Feature Team, which covers testing. Testing is an essential factor in the overall chances of success in many deployment projects.

The general rule is to test from most significant application to least significant application. Don't forget that you want to be forward looking as well. If applications aren't currently installed on your systems that you know will be at some point in the future, make sure to test those applications as well—even if you have to install a timed out version or demo of the future application. The compatibility testing phase is a much cheaper and more efficient place to make changes.

The guidance that the BDD Workbench solution gives you stresses the need to set up a testing facility, which is sometimes called a test bed, and is really a pilot project. Your test facility could be in a separate room, or it could be a collection of systems on its own subnet, but it must be a representative sample of systems.

As a simple example of a test bed, consider Figure 36.1, which shows the basic lab setup for image-based deployment under the Windows Automation Installation Kit (WAIK). There are four separate components:

Technician computer The technician computer contains the tools needed to create images. With ImageX you create images from your system builds. With Windows SIM you can collect, edit, and manage your system images.

Master computer The master computer or reference computer is a fully configured system with Vista and any other components desired already installed that is imaged. It's a "master" in the sense that it is the original copy of the configuration that is rolled out

Network share The network share is a repository for saved system images.

New Vista systems The destination or target computers are the cloned copies of the master computer.

To summarize the testing process, it consists of the following steps:

1. Create a test bed consisting of the components described above.
2. Use Windows System Image Manager (SIM) to create `Unattend.XML`, the new imaged-based version of the answer file.
3. Build your master computer from the Vista installation disks and the `Unattend.XML` file.

FIGURE 36.1
A setup for a test bed or lab environment for image based deployment of Vista.

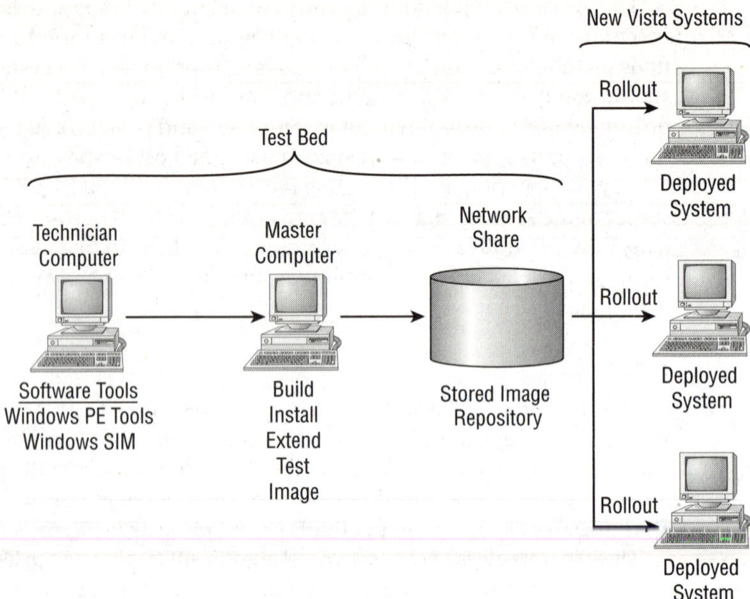

4. Boot the master computer from Windows Preinstallation Environment and use WAIK to create an image of that system that is stored on a distribution or network share.
5. Deploy new Vista systems by copying the image to the destination computer using Windows PE and ImageX.

You can use the test environment to continue to make changes to your deployment setup. As you discover bugs, need to change settings, and add or remove software on the master computer, you can reimage the system. You can also edit the WIM file directly. In the sections and chapters to come, you'll get a much closer look at these technologies, with hands-on procedures.

COMPATIBILITY CHECKLIST

The first place to test is the compatibility of your hardware with Vista itself. With your hardware inventory and compatibility tests in hand, it is a good idea to install Vista alone onto systems and determine whether the systems operate correctly. It is recommended that you test your systems for both a clean install and as an upgrade from Windows XP SP2.

A *clean install* is when you format the system's hard drive and install Vista. Testing an application against a cleanly installed Vista system allows you to test the application's installation routine, as well as its operational condition after installation without interference from another previously installed program or from a modified system setting.

It's important to test the application installation because installations can fail if they don't have the necessary permissions and, because even if the installation fails, it may be possible to run the installer inside a compatibility box within Vista.

There are three possible outcomes to your testing an application's installation on a clean install of Vista:

1. A normal install proceeds without issue once you give the install permission to continue.
2. The application installer fails, but you can perform an elevated install without any further issues. To perform an elevated install, right-click the installer executable file and then use the Run this program as command to set your rights to an administrator.

NOTE To learn more about elevated rights read "Understanding and Configuring User Account Control in Windows Vista" found at: `http://www.microsoft.com/technet/windowsvista/library/00d04415-2b2f-422c-b70e-b18ff918c281.mspx`. A resource page on application compatibility may be found at `http://www.microsoft.com/technet/windowsvista/appcompat/default.mspx`.

3. Your installation fails, but you can run the installer correctly within a compatibility layer. To run a compatibility layer install, right-click the installer executable file, select Properties, click the Compatibility tab, and select Windows XP as the layer to run in.

If none of these three outcomes occurs you'll need to check with your software vendor to see whether there is a new version of the program that will work with Vista. Even if the application's installation succeeds, it's worthwhile to check for new version of any mission critical application under the assumption that a newer version should be more compatible with Vista and less prone to difficulty. That's not always the case, but is in the greater majority of cases.

When you upgrade systems from Windows XP SP2 to Vista the installation of the application isn't the main issue. What you need to check is whether any of the new features in Vista has broken your application. Microsoft recommends, rather than test a Windows XP SP2 system loaded with multiple applications, that the following procedure be done:

1. Create a fresh install of Windows XP SP2 with all of the updates applied.
2. Install the application of interest onto that system.
3. Perform the Vista upgrade, applying all updates to that as well.
4. Then perform functional testing just as you would on a system that didn't have XP previously installed on it.

In either case, a fresh install or upgrade of Vista, the functional testing of your applications should reveal whether or not it runs correctly. Pay extra attention to the following areas, as these are the areas in which Vista differs from Windows XP significantly:

- Security, and in particular User Account Control (UAC) issues. Since Vista limits users, even those with administrator privileges are asked for permission before allowing a number of operations, you may find that your application breaks.

  Security is a particular problem when programs do updates, access online or network resources, or perform other tasks where process rights elevation is required. The recommendation is that applications be configured to run without requiring elevation—although this isn't always possible. For a discussion of UAC compatibility issues see: `http://www.microsoft.com/technet/windowsvista/library/00d04415-2b2f-422c-b70e-b18ff918c281.mspx`.

- Windows resource protection (WRC). This feature locks down the kernel, critical system files, and protected Registry keys. The most common incompatibilities due to WRC are found with installers and updaters, but any program that tries to access protected Registry keys can be denied access.

  Up until RC2 only trusted installers such as Windows Servicing got to modify protected resources. Under pressure from the European Union, Microsoft made some concessions to security vendors to open up WRC somewhat.

- x64 modifications. The x64 Vista requires the WOW64 emulator to run 32-bit applications and will not run 16-bit applications. This version also requires that any driver installed be signed as compatible with Vista. The inability to get suitable drivers is probably the greatest obstacle to using this version. If an application requires that it find its files at a particular location, the application may fail because x64 Vista will install a 32-bit program in a different Program Files folder than the 64-bit version of the same program.

- Obsolete functions. Vista makes a number of important changes to the API that impact applications. In Windows XP you could load some device drivers into the kernel mode, in particular printer and display drivers. Vista printer drivers must use the User-Mode Driver Framework (UDMF) to operate correctly, and display drivers use the new Windows Vista Display Driver Model (WVDDM). Of the two types of drivers, the issue with printer drivers is the more serious of the two.

  The XP and Server 2003 Help and Support Center (and .CHM files), Network Dynamic Data Exchange (NetDDE), Direct3D (D3DRM), FrontPage extensions, and Services for Macintosh will fail during exception handling due to a change in the calls to the Safe Exception Handling (SEH) API. Applications must also now be able to handle multisessions and terminal server in order to support Fast User Switching (FUS), since that is now turned on in Vista.

User State Migration

One of the least pleasant aspects of moving to a new version of Windows is the task of capturing all of the user files and settings from the old system and successfully copying and applying them to the new computer. When users show up at their new Vista systems, they want to see that their files are on the system in the same folders, their personal user settings have been applied, their application and application settings are still there, and other that their other personalizations have been applied. From the standpoint of a user doing a migration themselves, their approach to migration is to transfer everything over using the Migration Assistant.

One of the keys to a successful large deployment is the implementation of a standard operating environment (SOE). In an SOE, hardware, drivers, operating system settings, and applications are standardized. Even though standardization may not be popular with workers, from the standpoint of IT, a small set of SOEs can dramatically lower the complexity of a deployment, improve the stability of new systems, and lower overall costs. It doesn't make sense to migrate settings for applications or obsolete user profiles.

USMT supports three different migration scenarios :

Upgrade or in-place installation User data is already on the system and data does not need to be migrated, but the data must be captured and stored as a backup. In an upgrade, Vista makes appropriate changes to user settings; if a problem's identified prior to the first logon, Vista will roll back the installation.

It is rare for large deployments to perform system upgrades because the end result tends to be systems that aren't as stable as those where Vista has been installed without legacy data and settings.

Side-by-side computer replacement In this scenario, a new Vista system is prepared and user data is migrated from their old system to their new system.

Side-by-side migration is the most common migration scenario since it allows an organization to migrate a user from their old computer to a new computer of their choosing.

Clean or wipe-and-load installation In situations where the computer the user has already can support Vista and a decision is made to deploy Vista on that computer, the wipe-and-load scenario allows user data to be migrated off the system and then back onto the system once the Vista installation has been completed.

The advantage of a wipe-and-clean installation is that you get to use the same computer (as you would with an upgrade), and you still get a fresh system without legacy settings that might make that system unstable as the result.

An Overview of BDD Editions

In order to create a working environment in which deployments can be organized, created, and executed, Microsoft has created the Microsoft Solution Accelerator for Business Desktop Deployment. The BDD installs a GUI called the Workbench that organizes a large deployment into a number of steps. It recommends the formation of teams focused on accomplishing milestones, and provides resources in the form of suggested procedures and guidance, white papers, and access to the deployment tools that the teams need to accomplish the job. Figure 36.2 shows the BDD Workbench.

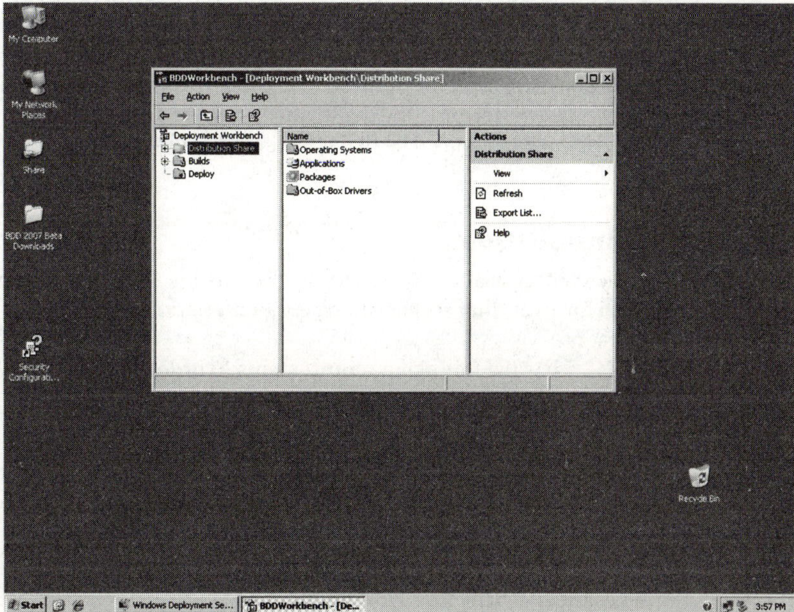

FIGURE 36.2
The BDD Workbench lets you manage your images and set up the Unattend.xml file.

The Microsoft Solution Accelerator for Business Desktop Deployment version 1.0 was a framework that supported the deployment of Windows XP (desktop and tablet versions) and Office 2003. BDD is a collection of best practice guidance (basically recommendations and procedures), templates, and scripts, with a UI that provides access to installation utilities.

Version 2.0 of BDD appeared prior to the release of Vista in two editions: Standard and Enterprise. Both versions share the same basic features in that they allow administrators to plan, build, test, and deploy system images and both rely on the same sets of tools, such as the Microsoft Application Compatibility Toolkit, Microsoft User State Migration Toolkit, Windows PE, and the Windows Enterprise Learning Framework. With the introduction of Vista, BDD 2.5 became the current version. Version 2.5 of the BDD supports the deployment of Vista, Office 2003, Windows XP Professional, and Office 2003.

The differences between the Standard Edition and the Enterprise Edition versions of BDD are:

- The Standard Edition enables the automated deployment method called Lite Touch desktop deployment method. Lite Touch deployment delivers system images over a network from one or more servers. All of the images and support files are stored on a network share that is a distribution point for the installation.

  While it isn't formally required of the deployment, the use of Active Directory and Windows Deployment Services is recommended. Prior versions of BDD used either PowerQuest DeployCenter or Symantec Ghost along with Windows PE.

- The Enterprise Edition is used for large-scale deployments, and requires the use of Active Directory, Windows Deployment Services, SQL Server, along with Microsoft System Management Server to create what is called a Zero Touch desktop deployment.

  For deployments using provisioning, BDD Enterprise Edition will also use Microsoft Operations Manager (MOM), Exchange Server, and even BizTalk Server.

BDD Standard Edition is meant for medium-sized companies, usually between 100 and 500 clients. BDD Enterprise Edition is meant for large companies, typically over 1,000 desktops and with enough IT staff to support the additional server products required for that product. For organizations between 500 and 2,000 desktops, the decision to use BDD Standard or BDD Enterprise is largely a matter of the costs involved performing the deployment, current IT staffing capabilities, and the server products that the organization has. The BDD framework will scale up to deployments of many thousands of workstations.

BDD Installation

The Microsoft Solution Accelerator for BDD is installed on a computer that is referred to as the server. However, that server can be either a Windows 2003 Server or Windows XP Professional workstation.

BDD 2.5 has the following requirements in order to run properly on the server:

- Microsoft Core Extensible Markup Language (MSXML) version 6.0.
- Microsoft .NET Framework 2.0.
- Microsoft Management Console (MMC) 3.0.
- Microsoft Windows Installer 3.1.
- Windows Scripting Host (WSH) 5.6.

For a Lite Touch Installation (LTI), which the Standard Edition supports, a set of deployment scripts must run on the client system. Client systems eligible for in-place upgrades to Vista are limited to Windows XP SP2 or later, with the further restriction that you can't upgrade Windows XP x64 to Windows Vista x64. Although BDD only supports in-place upgrades from Windows XP SP2, it is possible using Windows Easy Transfer and the User State Migration Tool you can migrate to Vista from Windows 2000 SP4 as well as Windows XP SP2.

The software requirements for the client are:

- Microsoft Internet Explorer 5.0 or later
- WSH 5.6
- MSXML 3.0

All of the packages mentioned above may be downloaded from the Microsoft Download Center at `http://www.microsoft.com/download`, with the exception of Internet Explorer.

NOTE **Since BDD will not work properly unless these components are in place, make sure that you have them all properly installed before proceeding to install the BDD framework software.**

To install BDD:

1. Obtain the current copy of the BDD software from Microsoft, which is currently `BDD2007.msi` (either the 32-bit or 64-bit version).
2. Double-click the `.MSI` file to launch the installer or right-click on the file and select Install.
3. On the Custom Setup page, select all features desired and install the features on your local hard drive. Features include Documents, Tools and templates, and the Distribution share.
4. To complete the installation, click Install, and then Finish.
5. Install the Windows AIK by double-clicking on the `WAIK.MSI` file.

Unless you change the default locations for the program or distribution share in the Custom Setup dialog box, you'll find these features installed to `C:\Program Files\BDD 2007` and to `D:\Distribution`, respectively. The Distribution share located at `D:\Distribution`, which will not necessarily be your D drive, but is the drive with the largest amount of free space available for use.

The program folder contains the following subfolders: the Bin folder, in which the BDD Workbench MMC and related files are found; the Documentation, Scripts, and Templates folders, which contain the documentation, scripts, and templates for BDD Workbench; USMT, for the User State Migration Tool program files; and WAIK, in which the Windows Automated Installation Kit is contained. The distribution share contains the following subfolders: OEM, where files copied to the new computer are stored; Applications, for application binary files; Captures, where images are drawn from; Control, which contains system configuration data where each build is a nested (subsubfolder) folder; Operating Systems, where the operating system source files are stored; Out-of-Box Drivers, for additional or updated device drivers; Packages, where installable packages are stored; Scripts, for deployment scripts; and finally Tools, where tools like the BDD Task Sequencer are found.

Standard Edition

The Standard Edition of the BDD solution is meant for small- to medium-sized organizations that do not have or will not install SMS server to help them manage their network. Organizations from

50 to 500 desktops would be included in this range. In practice, however, many organizations from 500 to 2,000 desktops use the BDD Standard Edition since all of the deployment tools other than the SMS management are included. In the sections that follow some of the components of BDD are introduced.

BDD Explorer

When you install the Business Desktop Deployment solution on a server or workstation, the BDD Documentation Explorer is the central application of that solution. The BDD Explorer is an interface for launching the deployment utilities that are part of the BDD Microsoft Solution Framework. The BDD Explorer also provides you with access to resources such as white papers, techniques, tips, FAQs, and other information that is offered in the form of guidance to help each of the project groups perform their tasks and reach their milestone most efficiently.

To open the BDD Explorer, click Start ➤ All Programs ➤ BDD 2007, and select BDD Explorer from the menu. Figure 36.3 shows the user interface of the BDD Explorer for the Standard Edition.

The BDD Explorer is used by each of the teams that is executing aspects of the deployment for individual guidance.

Figure 36.3
Each icon in the BDD Explorer represents a process, and when clicked will display process overviews, process guidance, and a variety of assistance in the left pane.

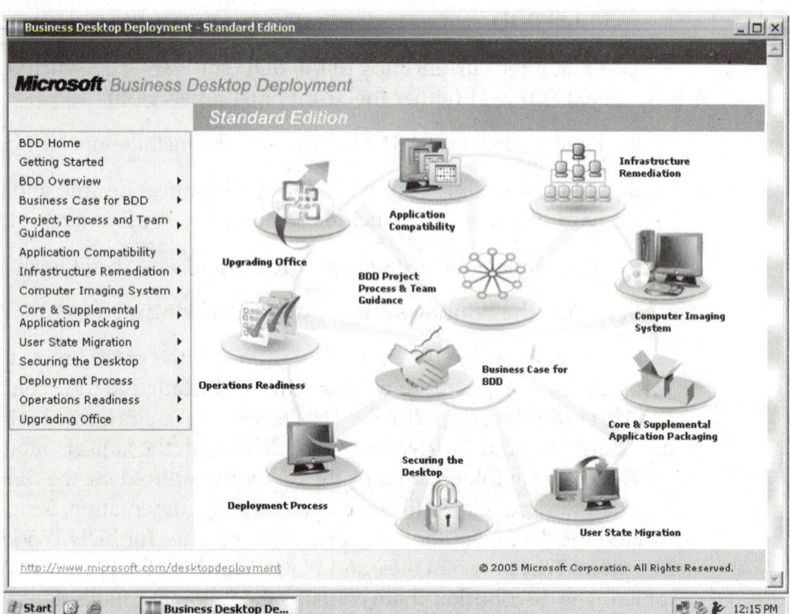

Microsoft Application Compatibility Toolkit 5.0

The Application Compatibility Toolkit included with BDD Workbench allows you to inventory your company's assets and analyze that inventory to determine the effect that deploying Vista will have on them. Applications, websites, and computers are discovered by a set of agents and potential issues are collected and compared to the ACT application database to be analyzed. I described ACT in some detail early in the chapter from an operational standpoint.

When you run ACT, the resulting comparison produces a report and an action plan for remediation of these issues. The report includes ratings of suggested actions by Microsoft and third-party vendors, as well as a community of IT users and providers. Community ratings, called the Microsoft Compatibility Exchange, is similar to feedback that you get on websites and helps calibrate the information supplied, a feature that is new to version 5.0.

The third function of ACT is to provide solution packages that will mitigate and fix the issues identified in the inventory and analysis, and to push those packages out to client systems to get them deployed.

ACT also wants to play as an operating system life cycle tool. With this system in place, the organization can be managed to respond to new versions of operating system, installing service packs, updates, and security patches as they become available. The service can also evaluate the impact that these changes can have on your existing application portfolio.

Microsoft User State Migration Tool 3.0

The need for careful selective migrations makes the Migration Assistant inappropriate for large-scale deployments and problematic even for multiuser systems. To automate remote migrations, the BDD Workbench organizes a technical User State Migration Feature Team and guides them in the use of the Microsoft User State Migration Tool 3.0 (USMT). What USMT provides is a command-line interface that can be scripted and has many more capabilities than the Migration Assistant.

USMT 3.0 supports not only Vista as the data source but Windows XP and Windows 2000 systems as well. Target systems can be either Vista or XP. To get some sense of what is migrated and isn't migrated, consider the lists below.

USMT migrates:

- Accessibility options
- Classic desktop
- Command prompt settings
- Desktop
- Dial-up connections
- Favorites
- Folder options
- Fonts
- Microsoft Internet Explorer settings
- Microsoft Outlook Express store
- Mouse and keyboard settings
- My Documents folder
- My Music folder
- My Pictures folder
- My Received files
- My Videos folder
- Phone and modem options

- Quick Launch settings
- Regional options
- Screen saver selection
- Sounds settings
- Taskbar settings

USMT doesn't migrate:

- Applications
- DLL files
- Device drivers
- Encrypting File System (EFS)
- Certificates (for Windows XP and 2000 as the target)
- Executable files
- Hardware settings
- Passwords
- Synchronization files

Since Windows XP and Vista store user data in different folders, and indeed it is possible for users to have additional data in XP that is stored in folders outside of their profile in the Documents and Settings folder, USMT 3.0 lets you customize the XML files that it uses as its inputs to the migration process to let you customize the process.

For side-by-side migrations use the following steps:

1. USMT uses the ScanState command to collect user state data from the source computer.
2. The user data is compressed and then copied to an intermediate data store (network share) on another system.
3. Vista is installed on the target system. Although it isn't required, most organizations load the applications to be used prior to migrating user data as it seems to give more compatible systems.
4. USMT uses the LoadState command to restore the user state on the target computer from the data on the intermediate data store.

For wipe-and-load migrations use the following steps:

1. USMT uses the ScanState command to collect user state data from the computer.
2. The user data is compressed and then copied to an intermediate data store (network share) on another system.
3. The hard drive is reformatted and the Vista SOE image is installed on the same system the data was collected from.
4. USMT uses the LoadState command to restore the user state on the system from the data on the intermediate data store.

Whereas the Migration Assistant could be used to perform a side-by-side migration, and the two interactive command (ScanState) in the wipe-and-load migration above, USMT lets you script the process and batch process it for any number of PCs.

NOTE For more information on the User State Migration Tool 3.0, refer to the article of the same name on the Technet site at `http://www.microsoft.com/technet/WindowsVista/library/usmt/91f62fc4-621f-4537-b311-1307df010561.mspx?mfr=true`.

In order for USMT to work best, an inventory of the application on a system and the applications that are in current use needs to be done prior to running this utility. The unwanted applications and their data should be removed prior to migration. That will ensure that obsolete data is not transferred, and it will make the resulting system leaner and more stable. Once all of this work is completed, it is possible to write a script to perform these actions.

USMT also uses a set of component manifests to migrate operating system settings. Component manifests are a set of statements in an XML file that lists the desired settings for a particular operating system set of functions. System states that are captured by USMT are compared to the settings in a component manifest and only those settings that can be migrated successfully will be. There are several manifest files for the different operating system components, and they are documented in the BDD Explorer. Essentially the supporting XML files are recipes for USMT to step through to determine what to migrate and what setting to apply.

Microsoft Windows Enterprise Learning Framework User Kit

When administrators have a Vista deployment go live on a network, they still have the problem of educating the users so that they are familiar enough with Vista to do their work. Without some kind of training, the release of Vista into the enterprise can lead to a lot of time spent answering questions that a little training would answer. Microsoft's answer to this problem was to create a learning tool that could be rolled out just prior to the completion of deployment and that would give different types of users information that would help them successfully make the transition by themselves.

The Enterprise Learning Framework (ELF) lets a team create a training and communication plan to train users to adapt to newly deployed Vista and Office 2007 systems. The framework matches topics in the Windows Online Help and Office Online and to the different types of users in your organization.

IT departments can use ELF to identify the topics that they can then pass on to their user community. Topics are prepared as a set of links to the appropriate help system pages, categorized as to importance, and then sent to users in the form of an email. You can stage the information that is sent out based on the deployment date.

Although there are different levels of users (information workers, influential information workers, etc.) who are matched to appropriate information, ELF is not a tool meant to educate the technical staff of an organization. However, one option does allow IT staff to monitor the information that was sent to each user and see the topics that were provided to them.

Windows Preinstallation Environment

Windows PE is a Vista-specific feature, meant to support Vista systems. You get Windows PE 2.0 in Vista installation disks, in the BDD Workbench installation, and, if you have an appropriate service agreement with Microsoft, from Microsoft directly as a separate download. Windows PE 2.0 is not a product you can purchase, so these are the only ways to get this lightweight environment. Figure 36.4 shows the difference between Windows XP and Server 2003's basic architecture, and what's contained in Windows PE 2.0.

FIGURE 36.4
Windows PE 2.0 is a lightweight version of the Vista operating system. Shown here are its major architectural components as compared to Windows XP and Windows Server 2003.

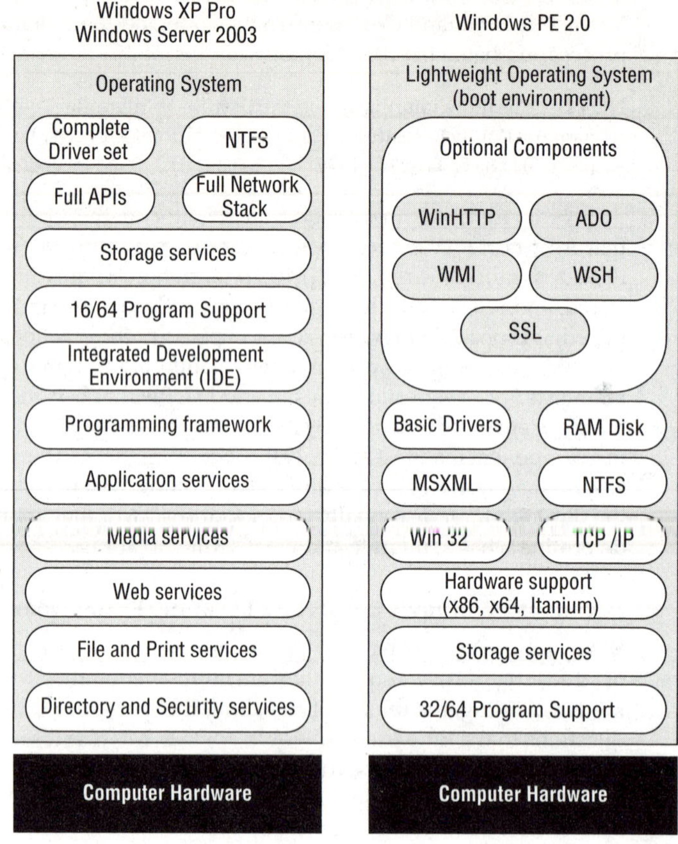

Just like you can install Vista directly from an image because that image has the requisite Vista system files in it, you can create images containing Windows PE within the WIM file.

NOTE A more complete description of the Windows Preinstallation Environment is contained in Chapter 40, in the "Windows PE 2.0" section.

Windows PE's role in automated (Zero Touch) deployments works as follows:

1. A target system boots up and launches the Pre-boot eXecution Environment (PXE) client, which then finds the Windows Deployment Service (WDS, or Windows DS) server and downloads Windows PE 2.0 into RAM.

NOTE In order to run the PXE, your motherboard must support that feature, and you must have it turned on in the system's BIOS.

2. The configuration script runs, does a hardware compatibility check, and then checks the status of the data on the hard drive.
3. If this is a fresh install, Windows PE runs Diskpart, which is Vista's disk partition and format utility.

4. Or, if this is an upgrade, the script can run a backup of the hard drive's contents to a specified share on another system. You customize the way PE starts up by making changes in the `Unattend.xml` file.

5. This script continues identifying the Windows Vista Setup files, which for BDD Workshop are found in the various Distribution folders.

6. Setup continues to complete the unattended installation.

Although this chapter focuses on deployment, Windows PE has important uses in troubleshooting and repairing Vista I want to mention. You can use PE to replace corrupted system files from your installation disk or media, gain access to your system so that you can back up a drive, and run diagnostic and configuration tools. Although PE will back up both FAT and NTFS partitions, keep in mind that backed up data using the Encrypting File System cannot be backed up for easy access. Among the utilities that come with PE are Diskpart, Drvload, Net, and Netcfg, all of which have been covered in more detail in Chapter 40.

TEAMS AND GUIDES

The Microsoft Solution Accelerator for BDD breaks down major tasks into milestones that are assigned to a group of individuals. BDD calls these groups feature teams and provides access to resources to them.

The overview section of the BDD Documentation Explorer that you saw in Figure 36.2 offers an overall guide called the Getting Started Guide, which should be consulted when you begin a project and need to organize your teams. Managers, team leaders, and indeed all team members should also consult the Plan, Build, and Deploy Guide during the early planning phase to match these teams to the skills and milestones required. The Plan, Build, and Deploy Guide is a general guide that describes the project flow.

Each team has a guide that contains the sections: planning, developing, stabilizing, and deploying. Planning describes the resources that the team will have. Developing offers guidance or advice on how to get their task done. Stabilizing is a testing and verification procedure. Deploying is the role that this milestone plays in the overall scheme. In addition to their own particular guide, additional guides are offered as noted below.

The following feature teams are contained in the BDD solution for the Standard Edition:

Application Compatibility Feature Team Inventories applications and tests their compatibility.

Application Management Feature Team Plans and executes the migration of applications to Vista.

Computer Imaging System Feature Team Responsible for creating, modifying, and managing images.

Deployment Feature Team Executes the deployment, and is perhaps the central team in the process. There are more guides for this team than any other. Their additional guides include the Deployment Configuration Guide, Deployment Configuration Samples Guide, Lite Touch Installation Guide, Zero Touch Installation Guide, and Zero Touch Installation Management Pack.

Desired Configuration Monitoring Feature Team Monitors the computer settings in deployed systems to see whether they are in line with specifications.

Infrastructure Remediation Feature Team Upgrades systems, networks, and any other hardware that impacts the deployment. The Volume Activation Guide is offered to this group.

Operations Readiness Feature Team Manages the network during the deployment and are part of the handoff to IT of the solution.

Security Feature Team Defines the security settings that will protect the organization once Vista during and after the deployment.

Test Feature Team Sets up the test bed environment or lab and performs the tests required to support the deployment.

User State Migration Feature Team Moves all appropriate user customizations and state information from a user's old system to their Vista system.

In addition to guides, the BDD solution provides templates that are sometimes document files (DOC), but are more often spreadsheet files (XLS). The document files can be checklists, sign-offs, or documentation structures. Templates in the form of spreadsheets are often counting tools, such as inventory collection.

BDD Deployment Wizard

The BDD Deployment Wizard is a feature in BDD Workbench that allows an IT staff member, a user with administrative rights, or a user who has been granted temporary administrative rights to run a deployment from a GUI in a step by step fashion. Since a number of steps involve some technical knowledge, usually an IT staff member performs the task. In the BDD Standard Edition, the wizard walks you through a Lite Touch deployment, where you can select either an upgrade or in-place OS replacement, a refresh or a wipe-and-load, or a replace which creates a new computer.

Using the BDD Deployment Wizard is very straightforward. Here are the basic steps involved:

1. Right-click on the Deploy folder in the left pane and click New. The BDD Deployment Wizard appears, as shown in Figure 36.5.
2. Select the deployment point, and then click Next.
3. On the Specify a descriptive name screen, enter the name desired; then click Next.
4. In the Allow Application Settings during Upgrade, keep the default choice, which allows users to select application during installation; then click Next.
5. Select the image to be captured, and click next.
6. On Specify the location of the network share screen check that the correct server that has the Solution Accelerator for BDD is specified and that that is the server you want.

   You can specify another server that has the BDD solution on it, although the one you are currently on is usually the correct selection. Once a selection is made, BDD Workbench will share the deploy point using the default name of Distribution and the default share name of Distribution$.
7. Enter the deployment parameters into the Specify user data defaults screen; then click Finish. You can change different aspects of the deployment you just created in the wizard by going to the Properties page of the deployment point.

Table 36.1 lists the information that you'll need to supply the wizard in order to initiate the deployment. Use of the wizard is straightforward, so most of your work goes into specifying the parameters of the deployment.

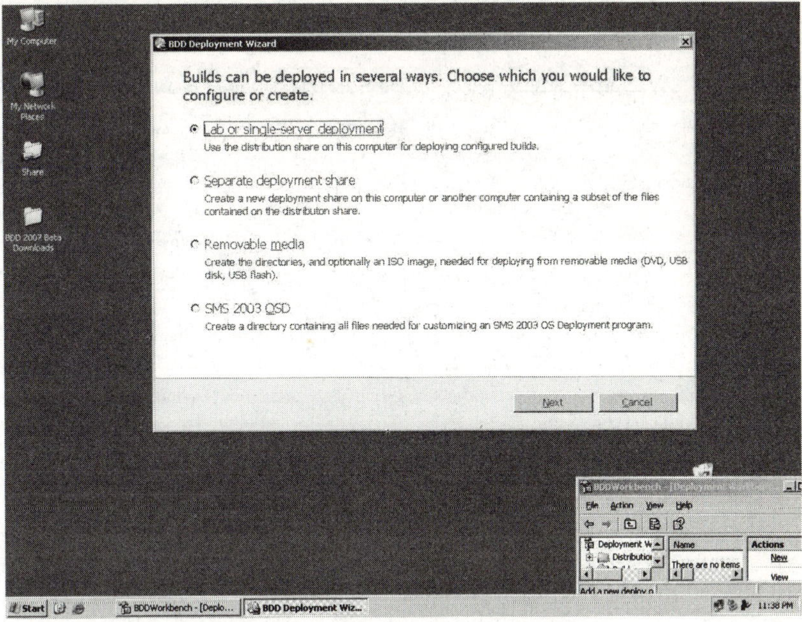

FIGURE 36.5
The first screen of the BDD Deployment Wizard in a Lite Touch deployment.

TABLE 36.1: Table 36.1. BDD Deployment Wizard Options

WIZARD SCREEN	OPTION	PURPOSE	SETTING LOCATION
Credentials for network connection (in bare metal, this is the first screen)	Username	User ID of an account that can connect to the required network shares.	`CustomSettings.ini`
	Domain	Domain name for the account.	`CustomSettings.ini`
	Password	Password for the account.	`CustomSettings.ini`
Computer name and domain or workgroup	Computer name	Computer name the new image should be given. This is a required field.	`Unattend.xml`
	Join a domain	Radio button supporting a domain join for the workstation.	
	Domain	Domain name for the new image.	`Unattend.xml`

TABLE 36.1: Table 36.1. BDD Deployment Wizard Options *(CONTINUED)*

WIZARD SCREEN	OPTION	PURPOSE	SETTING LOCATION
	User Name	Username of an account that can join the new image to the domain.	`CustomSettings.ini`
	Domain	Domain name for the account.	`CustomSettings.ini`
	Password	Password for the domain join account.	`CustomSettings.ini`
	Join a workgroup	Radio button supporting a workgroup join for the workstation.	
	Workgroup	Workgroup name for the new image.	`Unattend.xml`
Data and Settings	Do not restore user data and settings	This is not a replacement computer.	`CustomSettings.ini`
	Specify a location	Type in the location to store the data in UNC format, or click the Browse button to select it.	`CustomSettings.ini`
Operating System Image	Image name	Radio button listing available images.	`CustomSettings.ini`
Packages	Language packs	Radio button listing available languages.	`CustomSettings.ini`
Locale Selection	Locale	Select the locale from the list.	`CustomSettings.ini`
	Keyboard	Select the keyboard from the list.	`CustomSettings.ini`
Applications	Application names	Select the applications to install.	`CustomSettings.ini`
Capture Image	Capture image	Capture an image of this reference computer.	`CustomSettings.ini`
	Location	Type in the location to store the image in UNC format, or click the Browse button to select it.	`CustomSettings.ini`

TABLE 36.1: Table 36.1. BDD Deployment Wizard Options *(CONTINUED)*

WIZARD SCREEN	OPTION	PURPOSE	SETTING LOCATION
	File name	Type in the file name of the new image to capture.	`CustomSettings.ini`
	Do not capture image	Perform a normal system deployment.	`CustomSettings.ini`
Summary	Ready to begin	Lists a summary of the decisions made using the wizard.	

Source: "Lite Touch Installation Guide," `http://www.microsoft.com/technet/desktopdeployment/bdd/2007/LTDFTGuide_5.mspx`

Enterprise Edition

The Enterprise Edition of BDD differs from the Standard Edition through the addition of SMS as the execution engine of the deployment. With SMS as part of the deployment structure, you can leverage the services of this management application to inventory the hardware and software, package the images, and add applications as needed. Organizations of 2,000 or more typically use BDD Enterprise. However, in some instances organizations with as few as 500 users may choose to avail themselves of this architecture.

ZERO TOUCH INSTALLATION

The Zero Touch Installation is perhaps the primary difference between deployments done with the BDD Standard Edition versus the BDD Enterprise Edition. The concept and implementation of provisioning is another feature offered through this technology. Zero Touch Installation (ZTI) is a process by which large numbers of Vista desktops are rolled out to systems using a completely automated process. It's called Zero Touch because no user intervention is required to have the process start and run.

The Enterprise Edition of BDD Workbench supports Zero Touch Installation, but the Standard Edition does not. That is one of the fundamental differences between the two editions of BDD. ZTI makes use of SMS, which isn't assumed to be available to BDD Standard Edition.

Here's a high-level overview of the steps in a ZTI installation:

1. Inventory your systems with SMS to determine what needs to be done to set up target systems for deployment.
2. Create the ZTI processing rules that will match desktops to images and create appropriate custom settings.
3. Setup and run the Windows Deployment Service (Windows DS) server. This server is used to start the Widows PE environment on target systems. (This function used to be done by the Windows Remote Installation Service or RIS.)
4. Install BDD. BDD specifically supports ZTI and contains ZTI scripts, ZTI configuration files, and a set of wizards that manages the ZTI process. When you install BDD, you also get the Windows User State Migration Tool 3.0, which requires an additional installation step.

NOTE BDD comes with a number of scripts to run ZTI. These are provided to users with their source code so that they may be modified and used in custom installations.

5. Prepare the accounts needed to support ZTI deployment. You'll need to add those accounts and their correct permissions as Microsoft Systems Management Server 2003 clients in SMS and have the SMS Operating System Deployment (OSD) Feature Pack in place and other required resources prior to imaging the new Vista system.

6. OSD creates and deploys system images under ZTI. Configure ZTI to run the appropriate phases of an OSD installation: Validation, State Capture, Preinstall, Postinstall, and State Restore phases.

7. Initiate the deployment, and use Microsoft Operations Manager (MOM) 2005 to monitor the operation.

From here the procedure varies a little depending on what type of deployment you are doing. ZTI supports three different types of deployments:

Refresh The computer is taken from Windows 2000 or Windows XP to Vista and the user state data and profile is preserved. This is called an upgrade or in-place installation scenario by USMT as we saw earlier.

New computer Vista is installed on a freshly formatted system with no user state data retained or migrated to it. USMT is not used in this deployment.

Replace A new computer is prepared with Vista on it and the user state data and profile is migrated to that computer. Replace corresponds to the side-by-side computer replacement scenario that we saw previously with USMT.

NOTE A fourth deployment commonly referred to as a bare metal installation is where you run the installation without any regard to the previous data it contains, and the installer validates that the system is capable of having Vista installed before it proceeds.

From an operational standpoint, here's how an example of how ZTI processes a refresh computer deployment:

1. As part of the Validation phase, the client gets and responds to an invitation to initiate Vista deployment from SMS and OSD; the correct image is identified and USMT is set up to run.

2. The State Capture phase runs and the captured user state is copied to the data store by USMT.

3. The client is then booted into the Windows PE environment.

4. The correct WIM is copied to the client and installed.

5. In the Post Install phase, a script executes that runs Sysprep, MiniSetup, and then reboots the client.

6. A State Restore phase runs where SMS installs the appropriate applications and adds custom settings for Vista.

7. As a second step in the State Restore USMT runs and restores user state data to the client or target system.

8. SMS then sends the successful refresh event to a MOM Server 2005 where it is logged in.

NOTE A deployment wizard exists in the Enterprise Edition of the BDD, but it's run from the SMS Administrator console. You'll find that wizard in the OSDImage section, where OSD is the particular SMS OSD Feature Pack OS image that you are going to deploy. Once launched, you'll need to supply the distribution point, the application used to advertise availability to the client, and the place where user state data is stored. Check SMS documentation for further details.

A Lite Touch deployment differs from Zero Touch in that it requires that a user initiate and monitor the deployment. However, Lite Touch doesn't use SMS or any other special infrastructure to run, and it depends on a deployment wizard to enter any settings that haven't already been set in BDD Workbench or in the `CustomSettings.ini` file. In terms of the overall number and kinds of steps involved, Lite Touch deployment is rather similar in operation to the steps shown just above, only without SMS. Lite Touch was completely rewritten for Vista, and the details are documented in BDD Standard Edition.

Zero Touch Provisioning

Zero Touch Provisioning is another feature of BDD Enterprise that is part of some major deployments. In large organizations that want to roll out a deployment so that administrators and managers can review and approve who can upgrade to Vista or who gets what application, they need a system where the application is available to the user once the user indicates that they want it deployed (and it was approved). Provisioning is the term used to define a system where administrative tasks are pushed out to users and they are given the right to initiate the installations

Zero Touch Provisioning is enabled by a service called ZTP services where the rights to administrative tasks are delegated to users. With ZTP services, organizations can also let a manager or user decide if they want to upgrade the OS or add an application. ZTP then proceeds, and when the installation is done it will log the event and accrue charges for the changes.

The following services can be provisioned by ZTP:

- Operating system upgrade
- Installing/uninstalling an application
- Adding/removing users from groups
- Resetting a user's password
- Adding/removing a user from an email distribution list

To perform the tasks mentioned above, an approved user needs to connect to the User Self-service Provisioning (USSP) web portal as follows:

1. Launch Internet Explorer and enter **`http://provisioningserver/sites/ztp`** as the address. The ***`provisioningserver`*** is the server where Zero Touch Provisioning was installed.
2. Request the service desired.
3. Or, if you are the manager and need to approve a change, go to the ZTP Navigation Web Part, and under Zero Touch Services, Service Catalog click the type of action pending and approve the action. Managers will be asked to confirm the change.
4. Users and manager can, if desired, review the status of the request by going to the web page at `http://provisioningserver/sites/ztp/info/status/aspx`.

Solution Accelerators

The Microsoft Solution Accelerators have a number of implementation frameworks that help organization implement complex solutions. The Business Desktop Deployment is but one of a family of solutions.

Other Microsoft Solutions include the following:

- Microsoft Solution Accelerator for Intranets
- Microsoft Solution Accelerator for Server Consolidation
- Microsoft Solution for Exchange Consolidation and Migration
- Microsoft SQL Server Accelerator for Business Intelligence (BI)
- Microsoft Office Solution for Sarbanes-Oxley Workspace
- Microsoft Office Solution Accelerator for Recruiting
- Microsoft Office Solution Accelerator for SMS 2003
- Patch Management Using SMS Accelerator 3.0
- Notification Workflow Solution Accelerator for MOM 2005
- Microsoft Solution for Proposals
- Microsoft BizTalk Accelerator for Suppliers
- Microsoft Office Solution Accelerator for Six Sigma
- Microsoft Office Solution for XBLR (Extensible Business Reporting Language)
- Microsoft Identity Management Solution Accelerator
- Microsoft Solution Accelerator for Consolidation and Migration of Line of Business (LOB) Applications.

As you can see, some solution accelerators involve general Microsoft technologies, such as desktop deployment, server consolidation, intranets, and so forth. Other solutions offer more specific guidance in general areas, and those would include an accelerator for recruiting, proposals, and suppliers. The last area of solution accelerators that are available are those meant for specific Microsoft partner solutions, and some examples of that class of solutions would include the accelerator for Six Sigma. Microsoft has been releasing solution accelerators since 2003 for server technologies and for Microsoft Office.

Why Use BDD?

The Microsoft Solution Accelerator for BDD is a framework that allows an organization to plan and execute a complex and expensive deployment project. It's also a resource center that offers information and practical advice to help guide each aspect of the project on a milestone-by-milestone basis. With BDD you also get several tools that you need to perform a deployment, including BDD Workbench, WAIK, USMT, and the others that were mentioned earlier.

One reason to use BDD is that it is proven technology that Microsoft has used to create large-scale deployments with success. However, that may not be the most important reason. Over time other third-party vendors will introduce deployment tools that will compete with BDD and will present you with options and choices.

What makes BDD a good choice is that it's not only a method for deploying Vista but it's also philosophy on how to go about a deployment. BDD organizes a deployment in a way that separates different milestones, organizes teamswith the skill sets to accomplish those milestones, and provides a methodology to execute the steps required to achieve the result. However, the solution doesn't insist on the exact procedure that a team uses—that is left up to them. In the sections that follow, some of the unique features of BDD are discussed.

Packaged Best Practices

Microsoft's BDD system is what is often referred to as an automated standard operating environment, or SOE process. An SOE system is an automation tool for enforcing a set of policies and procedures that represent the current best practices for software distribution. In that sense, SOE goes beyond the capabilities of the enterprise framework products such as ZENworks, LANDesk, Altaris, Tivoli, and TNG Unicenter—all of which support Windows operating system deployments—to codify a set of principles. Conchango (`http://www.conchango.com`) is better example of an SOE system that competes directly with the BDD Enterprise Edition.

You've already seen the set of best practices that BDD implements, but let's summarize them briefly here as well as put them into a logical order of execution. The best practice methodology in BDD (as far as Vista is concerned) includes the following:

1. Create an inventory of hardware and software.
2. Run an application compatibility database, and test applications to determine their compatibility with Vista. Reconfigure, upgrade, or replace any applications that are required.

NOTE Vista retains the compatibility box that will run applications as if they were running in a previous version of the Windows operating system: Windows 2000, Windows ME and 98, and so forth. To that list Vista adds Windows XP. So you may find that you can run older applications by adjusting the Vista run state alone.

3. Analyze your infrastructure and remediate any deficiencies that would affect your Vista deployment.
4. Create a test or laboratory environment that contains your imaging and deployment systems.
5. Build a master installation that includes the Vista operating system and any software applications that you want to be part of a core package.

   You'll need to have installations for each of the hardware platforms and software collections that you want to deploy, so for any organization with a large number of images to create you'll need to automate the image making and collection process.
6. Image your master installations and collect those images on your deployment servers.
7. Study your desktop and network security policies to determine any policies you wish to implement in order to harden your deployed desktops.
8. Perform the deployment for a small group of desktops, and then roll out the deployment to additional groups of workstations. In this step you'll want to make sure that you locate your deployment servers appropriately and so that you don't saturate your network's bandwidth at inappropriate times.

There are two additional steps that aren't incorporated in the BDD that you may wish to consider after completing any large deployment.

1. Since it is common in large organizations for the staff that manages the network to be different from the staff that deploys the new operating system, there needs to be a documentation and handoff process.

   The need for a documentation and handoff process will certainly be obvious if you use outside consultants to help you with your deployment. However, even when in-house staff is used it is best to incorporate this practice as there is no guarantee that the staff you used will be around at some point in the future should questions arise.

2. Last, since your investment in deployment technology is large and this probably won't be the last time you use it (can you say XP SP3, Vista SP1, Vista SP2, etc.) it's a good idea to create a formal review process to determine what practices need to be refined and how well the project met its timeline and budget.

Out-of-the-Box Imaging Technologies

Disk image technologies have been around for a very long time and are used as an archival backup format, to access virtual disks, for disk cloning, and for many other purposes. The WIM file format is then seen to be the latest in a long line of formats that have appeared over the years. An image is a file containing the whole contents of a disk or device. An image can be held in memory and doesn't need to be stored to disk to be considered an image.

As I noted earlier, most image technologies are sector based and store files on the basis of their physical location. Sector-based images store information about the sectors as their primary data identifier; file-based images store only file information. WIM is file based. CD-ROM images in the form of ISO files are sector based and are defined under the ISO 9660 file system for single track data. Other disk image file formats include BIN/CUE, CCD, PoweISO's DAA, DMG, IMG, NGR, MDF/MDS, and MagicISO's UIF.

Some images are bootable and some are mountable just as if they were physical disks. The ISO format is one of the most widely used formats for images, and ISO files are bootable. Linux images are mostly distributed as ISO files. A mountable image provides the opportunity to use them as a "virtual disk." With virtual disk technology it is possible to create a clone of a game disk and play that game just as if you had the physical disk in your computer.

Many programs create and work with disk images. Nero and Roxio are examples of disk-burning and copying software. The best-selling image software for deployment is Norton Ghost, which is now owned by Symantec (now at version 10.0). Another commonly used program is Acronis True Image 10.0. I am particularly fond of Drive Snapshot, which is lean, spare, and a fast performer.

Image Engineering

Microsoft ships two tools that allow you to create and manage WIM files. The first is the command-line utility ImageX, which is the primary tool used to create images for Vista. Use ImageX to image a system that has been booted in the Windows PE environment.

The second image application for Vista is the Windows System Image Manager that lets you collect, edit, and manage your WIM files; you also create answer files within the Windows SIM application. Both of these utilities are covered in detail in Chapter 40.

Large organizations find themselves supporting many different types of desktops. It's possible with Vista's new imaging technology, a little discipline in choosing which hardware to support, and careful scripting to reduce the number of system images that have to be created from hundreds down to a handful. While the ideal goal of reducing all images down to a single master image is probably impractical for very large global enterprises, it should be possible to get to a number below five images.

The more images you have to support, the more you have to spend on development, test, storage, and network costs. There's more time spent creating the images, more equipment and staff time to test them, the proliferation of large images and deployment to distribution points can consume a lot of disk space, and you'll need to have a thick enough network pipe to transport the images without negatively impacting operations. OS image-based installations is relatively new technology for Microsoft, and some of the features you might want to see, such as multicasting, aren't yet available.

Microsoft differentiates images into three types:

Thick image A thick image contains not only the operating system, but all core applications, and any other additional files that the Computer Imaging System Feature Team wants to install. Most teams opt for this kind of image at the moment because thick images are easy to build and don't require much scripting to deploy. However, thick images are not only costly in terms of their size, but any time any application changes, the entire image must be tested and revalidated. Thick images present network bandwidth challenges, storage challenges, and additional staff development challenges post–image creation.

Thin images If the Imaging Team wants to narrow the number of images it supports, they may opt for what is called a thin image. Thin images minimize the number of core applications that they contain. Once the image is deployed, applications are installed at a later date. Using thin images has the tendency to make the deployment take longer, but lowers the amount of network bandwidth needed at any one time. Methods to manage long network transfers such as the Background Intelligent Transfer Service (BITS) can be employed.

Thin images require some thought and planning to build. Once built, they tend to be stable longer and require less testing over time. Files are smaller, a savings to the organization. However, there are additional costs and complexities to installing the applications post-imaging a system, and security may be compromised if they are not installed correctly. Either the Imaging Team must script the application installations, or the organization must have an infrastructure that will push these applications down to the appropriate desktops. Many companies have deployment systems in their enterprise framework applications (SMS, LANDesk, etc.) and will want to consider this approach of using thin images.

Hybrid images You can mix both thin and thick images together by creating a hybrid image. This approach places the necessary files to start an application installation within the system image, but uses the files the application installer needs to run in a network share. So it appears that the image contained the application, when an additional installation runs at the time the system is image. Hybrid images are relatively easy to create and, provided that a software distribution mechanism exists within the organization, they can leverage that mechanism. The additional installation will, however, make system preparation time longer.

NOTE If the Computer Imaging System Feature Team adopts a hybrid image approach, the organization must deploy applications around the network and other teams must install those applications. This significantly changes the group's milestone and alters the approach taken by BDD to have a milestone completed by the team that is specifically tasked and skilled to complete the task. This is one factor to consider when selecting an image type during image engineering.

Another way to approach a hybrid image is to create a thin image and then create versions of the thin image with additional applications. Since the thick image changes infrequently, it doesn't need to be tested. This approach only works well when the applications added are image friendly.

New *Unattend.XML* Format

With the image-based Vista deployment technology, the text-based answer file used in Windows XP installations has been replaced by a new `Unattend.XML` file. `Unattend.XML` replaces not only the answer file but `Sysprep.INF`, `Wimbom.INI`, and `Cmd.TXT` used in previous installations.

The XML file is a tagged set of definitions and values that Windows Setup uses during an installation to specify various setup settings. Among the settings in `Unattend.XML` are:

- The partition information
- Where to find the image stored in the distribution network share
- The product key
- User account information
- Display settings
- Internet Explorer home page and favorites

Anything that you enter into a manual installation can be entered into the `Unattend.XML` file as an XML tag. The following code shows the beginning and end a sample `Unattend.XML` file. The code shown here is truncated in the middle, as a fully configured `Unattend.XML` file generates code five pages long. This code is taken from an example given in Microsoft's TechNet Magazine in October 2006.

```
  <?xml version="1.0" encoding="utf-8" ?>
- <unattend xmlns="urn:schemas-microsoft-com:unattend">
- <settings pass="windowsPE">
- <component name="Microsoft-Windows-Setup" processorArchitecture="x86"
publicKeyToken="31bf3856ad364e35" language="neutral"
 versionScope="nonSxS" xmlns:wcm="http://schemas.microsoft.com/WMIConfig/2002/
State">
- <ImageInstall>
- <OSImage>
  <WillShowUI>OnError</WillShowUI>
- <InstallTo>
  <DiskID>0</DiskID>
  <PartitionID>1</PartitionID>
  </InstallTo>
- <InstallFrom>
  <Path>.\Operating Systems\Windows Vista 5536\Sources\install.wim</Path>
- <MetaData>
  <Key>/image/index</Key>
  <Value>4</Value>
  </MetaData>
  </InstallFrom>
  </OSImage>
  </ImageInstall>
```

```
- <UpgradeData>
  <Upgrade>false</Upgrade>
  </UpgradeData>
- <Display>
  <ColorDepth>16</ColorDepth>
  <HorizontalResolution>1024</HorizontalResolution>
  <RefreshRate>60</RefreshRate>
  <VerticalResolution>768</VerticalResolution>
  </Display>
- <ComplianceCheck>
  <DisplayReport>OnError</DisplayReport>
  </ComplianceCheck>
- <UserData>
  <AcceptEula>true</AcceptEula>
- <ProductKey>
  <Key>XXXXX-XXXXX-XYXXX-XXXXX-XXXXX</Key>
  </ProductKey>

**************** Code continues … **********************

- <component name="Microsoft-Windows-Shell-Setup" processorArchitecture="x86"
 publicKeyToken="31bf3856ad364e35" language="neutral" versionScope="nonSxS"
xmlns:wcm="
http://schemas.microsoft.com/WMIConfig/2002/State" xmlns:xsi="http://www.w3.org/
2001/XMLSchema-instance">
  <DoNotCleanTaskBar>true</DoNotCleanTaskBar>
  </component>
  </settings>
  <cpi:offlineImage cpi:source="catalog://mniehaus-m400/distribution$/operating
systems/windows vista
5536/sources/install_windows vista ultimate.clg" xmlns:cpi="urn:schemas-
microsoft-com:cpi" />
  </unattend>
```

Each `Unattend.XML` file is usually associated with a single installation or IMG file, but any `Unattend.XML` file can be used with any IMG file. However, if setup doesn't find a component with a setting specified in the `Unattend.XML` file, that setting is ignored and the installation continues without failing at that point.

An `Unattend.XML` file contains two sections, one for components and another for packages. Components are the settings that are entered or selected in the Vista installation. Vista installations use seven different configuration passes that the setup routine makes during which settings are applied.

In the order that they are execute those passes are called:

1. *WindowsPE*. Data entry is performed for setup selections, Disk Prep runs, the image is applied, and boot data is prepared.
2. *OfflineServicing*. Packages are added, security is applied, and drivers are configured.
3. *Generalize* (On-Line Configuration). Components are configured allowing the system to boot to the basic OS. The license files are added.

4. *Specialize* (On-Line Configuration). `Unattend.XML` runs, setting up both common and optional components.

5. *AuditSystem* (FirstBoot). At the start of First Boot the actions done here make the device unique.

6. *AuditUser* (FirstBoot). Sysprep specialization runs and specialization is added.

7. *OobeSystem*. The EULA is accepted, Registration, Machine Name, Users, Connectivity, and Regional settings are applied. (OOBE means out-of-box experience.)

Packages are container files in which service packs, updates, and language packs are distributed. Packages are applied in the offlineServicing configuration pass.

An MSI file is one example of a package. When the `Unattend.XML` file specifies that a package is used in the package section, it means that software is added to the installation along with any settings specified. If a package isn't specified, it is ignored. One package central to Vista is the Windows Foundation Package, which contains Media Player, Windows Backup, games, and other key Windows features. You can choose to disable the Foundation Package, and if you do, Windows Media Player won't be available. The package is retained in your Windows image, but it isn't applied during the installation.

XML-Based Migration

One of the important features of Vista's new deployment tools is that you can modify the way images are deployed through scripting and by changing the XML files that control the deployment. Without this capability it wouldn't be possible to be flexible enough to support large deployments.

The User State Migration Tool (USMT) is the main application used to move user data from one system to the other. It addresses several XML files to obtain the needed settings and configuration information necessary to execute its ScanState and LoadState commands. Modifying those text-based files is the first place to start when you want to customize a particular deployment.

Below is a list of the XML migration files that can be modified to change the way migrations are performed:

`Config.xml` This file is created by the ScanSate `/genconfig` command to generate a custom configuration file. Create this file when all of the applications that are part of your master system are already installed. The command embeds the operating system identification, applications, and a list of the users that are migrated. `Config.xml` is used to migrate either to or from Vista.

`MfgApp.xml` In this file that is used for migration to or from Vista or XP, and contains the application settings. You can edit this file to change which applications get installed or ignored.

`MfgUser.xml` Inside this file are a list of the user folder, desktop settings, and files and file types to migrate to or from Vista or XP. Its name is a little misleading, as it doesn't control which users are involved.

`MfgSys.xml` This file is mostly used to target XP systems and contains the operating system and browser settings. When a migration to Vista is performed, the information on these required settings is drawn from the Windows XP/2000 repositories. If the target is Windows XP, the `MfgSys.xml` file must be included.

To create a custom script for migration, you first create and then edit the `Config.xml` file. The format is easy for work with, as each setting in the file has a conditional statement that contains a "migrate = yes (or no)" statement. To include a component "yes" should be in that statement, and to exclude it a "no."

Understanding the Microsoft Solutions Framework (MSF) Connection

The Microsoft Solutions Framework (MSF) is a collection of deliverable business solutions that have been created by Microsoft through their consulting group, client work, and more lately with in-house testing. Microsoft collects the results of this work as a set of best practices, and then provides an organizational framework of principles, models, concepts, guidelines, organizational design, and best practices that can be rolled out to customers and consulting groups. The BDD solution is but one example of a solution from this Microsoft program; the Visual Studio 2005 Team System is another one. Solution frameworks exist for Exchange rollouts, mobile deployments, web and e-commerce system rollouts, web services, ERP, n-tier transaction systems, operations management system deployments, and even mainframe projects.

NOTE To learn more about MSF, visit their home page on Microsoft TechNet at `http://www.microsoft.com/technet/itsolutions/msf/default.mspx`. On that site you will find a number of white papers, access to MFS newsgroups, sample templates, and small collection of MSF case studies. Microsoft also offers a three-day course called MSF Essentials (MS 1846A) that trains people in organizing, managing, and participating in solution delivery.

MSF owes its creation to the realization that a significant percentage of large IT projects fail completely to be deployed or have such large cost and timeline overruns that the deployment is thoroughly impaired. During the run up to the Y2K boundary (December 31, 1999) when a large number of timed IT systems were being implemented, some studies estimated that as many as 50 percent of large enterprise deployments were abandoned. In 1994, Microsoft's consulting group (Microsoft Services) began to collect their best practices in order to provide solutions, and the first MSFs were offered. Since that time, MSFs have been applied to Microsoft's internal Operations and Technology Group (OTG), and a number of large in-house projects.

There have been several versions of the Microsoft Solutions Framework. The current version, MSF 3.0, added several new features, most notably a significant update to the Team and Process models, better integration with the Microsoft Operations Framework (MOF), support for various industry management standards, and a new support program for project managers trained in this methodology. The Project Management, Risk Management, and Readiness Management disciplines were all added in this latest version of the MSF, as described in the section below.

Regardless of the current versions of these two frameworks, the concept of a framework requires that the guidance that they offer be the current state of a "work in progress." As new best practices are identified, the solutions that these frameworks support are modified to include the new information. So it is always best practice to make sure that you have the latest version of your solution to work with before, during, and even after a project has been delivered.

Framework Organizations

Philosophically, MSF is described as a framework rather than a methodology because no specific set of instructions (recipes) are delivered to the solution teams. Rather, the software organizes large software deployments into functional teams and describes the reduction of best practices as they relate to different organizational requirements; the process is referred to as "guidance." So MSF's guidance is meant to apply to a broad range of circumstances, with the discretion for implementing specific practices left up to the individual project teams within the context of what needs to be accomplished in their particular deployment.

FUNDAMENTAL PRINCIPLES

What is at the heart of an MSF solution such as BDD is a set of core or foundational principles that each framework is based on. Each proven practice is meant to expose a key concept that results in a set of recommendations (guidance). Underlying the MSF are the following foundational principles:

Share the vision. Work for a shared vision in each team and for the project as a whole. It may be worthwhile to have each team craft a vision statement for their particular project.

Keep communication open. Information should flow freely to all deployment staff. Strong open communication is essential to the successful operation of each team and is equally important between different project teams.

Clearly assign accountability and responsibility. There should be a clear understanding who is responsible for each deliverable, and responsibility for each deliverable should be shared among the team.

Empower team members. The ultimate responsibility for any single project rests with those team members.

Deliver business value. Successful projects match a business need with a set of delivered capabilities. The MSF Team Model establishes roles for Product Management and User Experience roles that take the viewpoint of the client or customer and advocate for the user's viewpoint to the various teams.

Invest in quality. Quality is something that can be measured. For the Vista development team, quality was measured by the number of overall bugs that remained at the shipment date. (Reputedly that number was 500 bugs with the elimination of all the critical bugs.) Quality in a Vista deployment scenario would include making sure that the right hardware is in place

Manage risk. There should be continuous risk assessment, and a Risk Management discipline exercised by all team members that continually monitor risks. It is important to have agreed on remediation available should a problem arise.

Learn from experience. Each team project that is completed under the Team Model should be subjected to a post-project review.

Stay agile. Organizations need to be agile and open to change based on their actual experiences.

MODELS AND DISCIPLINES

For BDD the foundational principles (described above) result in segmenting the solution of any framework into project teams. You saw that in earlier sections where we detailed the project teams that the BDD uses for a Vista deployment. MSF describes this segmentation as a concept that it calls a "model." The best way to think of a model of as map to the organizational structure imposed on a solution that creates teams and processes.

MSF describes two different types of models: the Team Model and the Process Model. Each model defines elements of a framework solution. Each area in a framework requires a specific set of methods, a common vocabulary, and an agreed on approach based on proven practices—this organization of a framework is referred to as an MSF discipline. Figure 36.6 describes the organization of the MSF Team Model into functional groups.

A large deployment project is best staged in logical steps using a defined process. The progression of processes is the product life cycle. A well-developed process can greatly improve an enterprise deployments chances for success, which is why the MSF has a highly defined and fully developed Process Model. The MSF Process Model, shown in Figure 36.7 for an enterprise deployment using the BDD takes its inspiration from earlier process models that used a waterfall or a spiral-type topology.

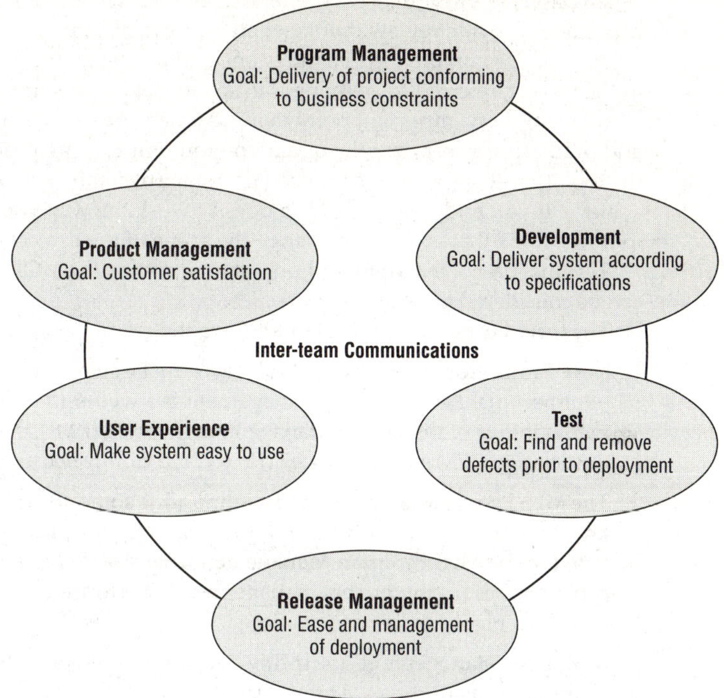

FIGURE 36.6
The MSF Team Model breaks down a complex IT project into a number of functional teams, each of which has measurable deliverable with key quality goals.

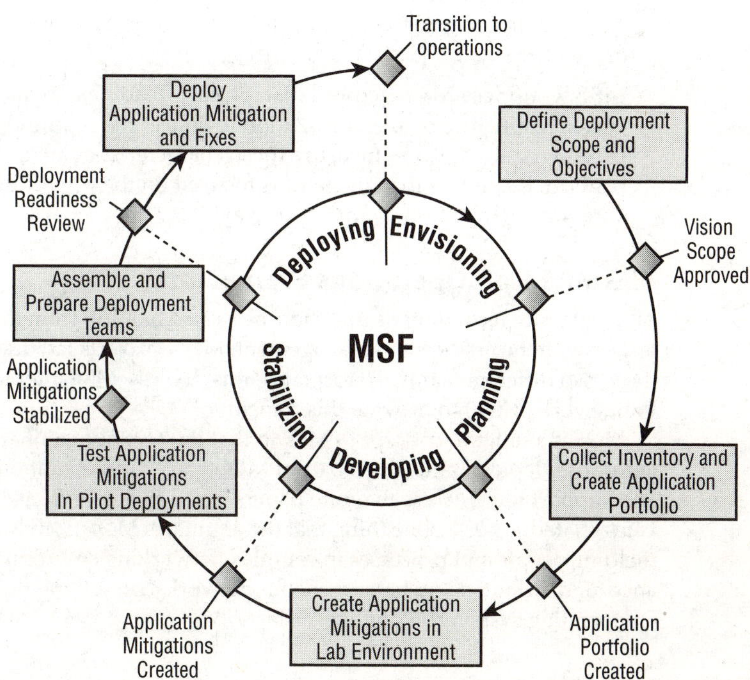

FIGURE 36.7
The MSF Process Model uses phases and milestones to deliver a project in progressively refined iterations.

A phase in the MSF Process Model is a set of activities relating to one of five stages in the project. Milestones provide review points where success or failure as well as risk going forward can be measured. The completion of a milestone and its review provide an opportunity to make changes in the project, referred to as changes in scope that are meant to keep a project on the right track.

Keep this very important point in mind when you do a deployment. Your ability to lower costs and dramatically improve the quality of your effort is greatest at the beginning of the project. In the too-often-than-not-underutilized first stage of creating the project vision, changes are easier to achieve. If you find that something doesn't work the way you want, later in the project it costs a lot more to fix that issue or to change the scope of the project the further as you proceed.

The final part of the MSF solution—shared also by the MOF—is the MSF disciplines. Disciplines can be considered to be areas of practice.

The three current disciplines in MSF are the

MSF Project Management discipline Any large project needs a project manager, or a team of project managers. Project management is a well-established discipline and MFS follows the methodology of the Project Management Institute (PMI), the International Project Management Association (IPMA) and Prince2 (Projects In Controlled Environments).

The MFS Project Management discipline adds some additional features to what is essentially a knowledge area, and not a role or title. Although the role of "project manager" may be designated in the MFS Program Management role cluster (an assignment hierarchy), in MFS as a project scales up the project management is performed at several levels by a team with an emphasis placed on consensus decision making.

MSF Risk Management discipline Risk management attempts to balance projected gains against a measured risk. At the start of a project the team makes a list of the things that can become a problem, and then assigns a relative cost and probability to that issue in the form of a set of risk statements that are collected into a risk knowledge database. Strategies are then put into place to mitigate the risks. As the entire project proceeds, the risks are tracked and changes are made to the project plans accordingly.

MSF Readiness Management discipline Readiness management is the measurement of the current capability of an organization to collect the required knowledge, skills, and abilities (KSAs) required. KSAs measure these characteristics against project milestones and system handoff. Readiness management is focused on the project itself and does not attempt to measure the organization in any other way.

The Microsoft Operations Framework

MSF guidance recommends that there be a clean handoff from the deployment teams to the people tasked with the new system management. Many projects fail due to poor communication between these two different teams. To formalize this process, MSF interacts with the Microsoft Operations Framework (MOF) to provide this transition.

MOF is similar in concept to MSF in that it offers operational guidelines for different types of enterprise deployments. So as part of MOF you'll find operational guides, templates, assessment and support tools, access to white papers, courseware, and case studies. Microsoft also offers services related to MOF. One thing that differentiates MOF from MFS is that more emphasis given to melding people and processes in complex networking environments. Thus, you'll find MOF guidance for distributed and heterogeneous networks, something that isn't really the case for BDD and an operating system roll out like Vista.

NOTE To learn more about the Microsoft Operations Framework, go to `http://www.microsoft.com/mof`.

MFS is a solution delivery framework, while MOF is really a service management framework. So you'll find that whereas the BDD is functionally organized around groups executing projects with known ends and deliverables, an MOF for Vista management would be open-ended and process oriented. Microsoft's slogan for the two: MSF = "Build IT Right" and MOF = Run IT Right."

Systems that fall under MOF purview are those that require high reliability and availability, central management, and support. MOF is a standards-oriented effort, drawing on the work of a set of best practices called the IT Infrastructure Library (ITIL), which was developed in the United Kingdom by the Office of Government Commerce (OGC). Microsoft describes MOF as a superset of the ITIL.

Summary

I gave you a general overview of large-scale Vista deployments in this chapter. With a new image-based installation technology and new and refreshed set of tools, it is possible to support many different types of Vista systems with a limited number of images and by using a set of automated tools: WIM file format, the Windows PE environment, and different installation and migration schemes and scenarios.

The chapter focused on the Microsoft Solution Accelerator for Business Desktop Deployments. This solution creates a framework in which an organization can successfully deploy Vista. The chapter described the different teams, the resources that this solution gives them, and the tools that are part of the overall solution.

Now that you understand the basic technology, the next chapter takes a closer look at the BDD, performs some of the operations, and discusses various templates and tools.

Chapter 37

Getting Started with BDD

In the previous chapter, you were introduced the components that are part of Microsoft's BDD solution. Future chapters go into finer detail on the operational aspects of the different tools. In this chapter, the focus is on the process involved, specifically, getting started:

- BBD organization, tools, and process
- Skills, selection, and management of team members
- Sample deployments
- Deploying Microsoft Office alongside Vista

Vista: What's New?

In the previous chapter you were introduced to the Microsoft Solution Accelerator for Business Desktop Deployment 2007 or BDD. This downloadable collection of tools installs informational and organizational tools, as well as a set of utilities for deploying Vista and Microsoft Office 2007. Some of the tools include BDD Explorer, which is a team-based information and guidance framework; BDD Workbench, where images, distribution shares and deployments are managed; the Windows Automated Installation Kit, which contains the Windows PE 2.0 environment, the User State Migration Tool, and the Windows System Image Manager tools; and the Microsoft Application Compatibility Toolkit 5.0, which has a collection of tools for analyzing existing applications. Some of these tools are new to Vista, and all of the preexisting tools have been significantly reworked and upgraded.

Considerations for BDD

Taken together, the tools of the BDD represent Microsoft's complete solution to deploying Vista in medium to large enterprises. From the standpoint of someone considering a Vista deployment, the BDD becomes valuable in situations where there are too many systems for the installer to individually touch each system. While the minimum number of systems managed before BDD is useful may vary, as a floor most people would find value in some of the tools of the BDD for a deployment with as few as 20 to 50 systems. For people managing less than 50 systems, typically a single administrator, I recommend reading the information in the BDD Document Explorer in order to set up and create images; capture, store, and install user states; and perform a manual or Lite Touch Installation.

If the organization involved is larger, the need for more of the tools in the BDD is greater. The next step up in size would be a medium-sized deployment. Microsoft considers a medium-sized organization to be one that has outgrown a platform such as the Small Business Server, which has as a floor around the 100-client level where SBS must be upgraded to the Windows server architecture, but one that does not have a management framework application such as Microsoft Systems Management Server (SMS) installed. The installation of SMS (or a similar application) depends in part on the nature of the business and the sophistication of the IT staff, but as a general rule medium organizations are considered to top out at between 500 and 1,000 clients. In an organization of this size, typically several IT staff are involved in a deploymentbut generally not enough to form large teams.

In a medium-sized organization Vista deployments are required to support a wider range of hardware platforms and applications. The tools for determining compatibility become significantly more important and the number of images being managed rises. Medium-sized organizations employ manual and Lite Touch deployments, but lack the network services required for fully automated deployments.

The ability of the BDD to scale is evidenced by the successful use of this tool to deploy Vista in large organizations. Large organizations are ones that have between 1,000 and 2,000 desktops, organized deployment teams with specialized skills for each of the different aspects of deployment, and the necessary network services required to run fully automated deployments. For large organizations, the full range of deployment types are available, including manual, automated, Lite Touch, and Zero Touch.

The BDD Process

The BDD provides a structured process for deploying Vista based on functional teams. You'll find the latest version of the BDD along with the current Microsoft recommendations and deployment tools at `http://www.microsoft.com/desktopdeployment`. Since the BDD is always a work in progress and, you'll find incremental changes to the package over time, the best place to start a BDD project is the Getting Started Guide. This guide is available from a link at the bottom of the Business Desktop Deployment: Overview page of the BDD Documentation Explorer.

All of the guides and templates associated with the BDD are in Microsoft DOC format, and they open correctly with recent versions of Microsoft Office, as well as with Wordpad. When you click the link for a document you'll be given the choice of opening the document or saving the document to a convenient location, which may be a network share or a location on your technician system. If you wish to examine the contents of the BDD's documentation en masse or copy them to another location, they are installed by default at: C:\PROGRAM FILES\BDD 2007\DOCUMENTATION.

You may also want to read the release notes of the BDD for late information that couldn't be included in the formal documentation. You can access `Release Notes.DOC` from a menu selection off of the BDD Overview menu in the left menu pane of the BDD Explorer. The release notes document known issues covering the BDD, the Deployment Workbench, Lite Touch Installation and Zero Touch Installation Procedures, and any issues relating to the current versions of the Feature Team guides.

Any BDD process begins with the organization of the Core Team, whose goal it is to specify the deployment project, and to create and organize the remaining teams. The Core Team also works to establish the business case for Vista deployment, which ideally results in a pre-project brief that assesses the following factors:

- Business case based on Vista features
- Quantitative costs of the project

- Projected Vista system life cycles
- Appropriate Vista deployment timing options

Details for developing a business case for BDD Vista deployments can be found on the Business Case for BDD page of the Documentation Explorer. From this initial assessment the decision to deploy Vista using BDD can be made.

The Core Team is meant to be consultative and doesn't direct other teams. Rather, after the teams are organized, all teams are expected to contribute to developing the project plan and providing input as the project is refined and the timeline and resource budgets are assigned. The teams are organized into what could best be described as a "representative democracy." All team members are part of the defining and execution process for that feature team's goals, but one team member has the overall responsibility to make the final team decisions and to consult with team leaders of the other feature teams.

Table 37.1 details the contents of the BDD documentation for each of the feature teams. You'll notice that there are a collection of guides for each group. The other aids include templates, plans, vision scopes, knowledge sheets, inventory lists (of various kinds), build requirement lists (for images), and other tools that are either Microsoft Word files, Excel files, Adobe Acrobat files, and even a PowerPoint file detailing the case study that comes with the version of BDD that you're using.

NOTE If you're using a server that doesn't have Microsoft Office installed on it and you wish to view those files on that system, you can download Microsoft Office Viewers in place of those applications. A jump page to the viewers may be found at `http://www.microsoft.com/office/000/viewers.asp`. Adobe Acrobat may be downloaded from `http://www.acrobat.com`. As an alternative to Acrobat, Foxit Software's Foxit Reader 2.0 will read PDF files and has a much smaller footprint. If you need to open a PPT file from within Outlook Express, check `http://www.soniacoleman.com/FAQs/FAQ00198.htm` for a solution.

TABLE 37.1: BDD Feature Team Resources

TEAM	GUIDANCE	TEMPLATES
Core	Plan, Build, and Deploy Guide	Inventory Template
	Enterprise Learning Framework User Guide	Communications Plan
	Woodgrove Enterprise IT Archetype	Functional Specification
		Migration Plan
		Risk Template Tool
		Training Plan
		Vision Scope
		Site Deployment Project Plan
Application Compatibility	Application Compatibility Feature Team Guide	

TABLE 37.1: BDD Feature Team Resources *(CONTINUED)*

TEAM	GUIDANCE	TEMPLATES
Application Management	Application Management Feature Team Guide Office Deployment Guide	Application Knowledge Sheet Office Assessment Template Office Budget Plan Office Communications Plan Office Configuration Plan Office Current State Assessment Template Office Distribution Plan Office File Migration Plan Office Functional Specification Office Hardware Upgrades List Office Inventory Template Office Management Plan Office Pilot Plan Office Project Plan Office Risk Template Tool Office Test Plan Office Training Plan Office Vision Scope
Computer Imaging System	Computer Imaging System Feature Team Guide	Client Build Requirements
Deployment	Deployment Feature Team Guide Lite Touch Installation Guide Zero Touch Installation Guide Deployment Configuration Guide Deployment Configuration Samples Guide Zero Touch Installation Management Pack	Pilot Plan
Desired Configuration Monitoring	Desired Configuration Monitoring Feature Team Guide	Sample Manifests
Infrastructure Remediation	Infrastructure Remediation Feature Team Guide Volume Activation Guide	Assessment Template Current State Assessment Template Network and Workstation Hardware Upgrades

TABLE 37.1: BDD Feature Team Resources *(CONTINUED)*

TEAM	GUIDANCE	TEMPLATES
Operations Readiness	Operations Readiness Feature Team Guide	
Security	Security Feature Team Guide	
Test	Test Feature Team Guide	Test Cases Workbook Test Plan Test Specification
User State Migration	User State Migration Feature Team Guide	

Source: Microsoft BDD Getting Ready Guide.

Of the guides and plans listed above, I recommend that deployment staff read the Plan, Build, and Deploy Guide found on the BDD Project Process & Team Guidance: Overview page. That guide offers important guidance on organizing the deployment process, selecting teams and team members, and coordinating the project.

The home page of the BDD Documentation Explorer shows a schematic of the deployment cycle, illustrating how the different feature groups relate to one another. That page was shown as Figure 36.3. Figure 36.7 showed the Microsoft Solution Foundation project flowchart for the BDD. You may want to take a look back at those two figures before reading further about the organization of a BDD deployment project.

The BDD 2007 allows a team to deploy Windows Vista (Ultimate and Professional), and Microsoft Office (2007 and 2003), and Windows XP Professional and Tablet). To deploy Vista successfully, the BDD follow these steps:

1. Create a project plan and manage it throughout the deployment.
2. Inventory hardware and software assets.
3. Create a test bed or laboratory with supported system configurations, referred to as reference or master systems.
4. Test for application compatibility and determine the steps needed to remove any incompatibilities.
5. Install the operating system and desired application packages on the reference systems.
6. Harden the desktops to make them more secure.
7. Create a technician computer that has the tools of the BDD installed.
8. Build a Windows PE boot image for the systems you will support.
9. Image the master systems and store those images for deployment.
10. Capture user states so that they may be migrated to newly imaged systems (upgraded systems already have user state data on them).

11. Plan the actual deployment with an eye to the available network resources.
12. Image the target systems and apply the appropriate user state data.
13. Hand off the deployed system to the operations support team.
14. Do a post mortem analysis of the deployment project.

The key to a successful deployment is in planning your deployment and standardizing conditions as much as possible. Thus, the goal of the BDD is to supply the automation tools needed to provide these conditions.

Performing the Hardware Inventory

System inventory is a central module in many network framework products. As an alternative to using ACT you could inventory your systems using SMS or some other third-party tool. The goal of a system inventory is to provide information about the systems that are available for upgrade or need to be replaced. The BDD relies on the Application Compatibility Toolkit 5.0 (ACT) to inventory your current systems and collect that information into an SQL database. You can use either SQL Server or the SQL Server Desktop Edition (MSDE) for the repository, and once the database is populated you can analyze the data it contains in a set of reports.

ACT installs an agent, or what the BDD refers to as a "small collector program," on your network clients. To have the agent report information back to ACT, you need to have the program run on the target system, which you can do by either placing a run command in that system's logon script, or the program can be called from either a web page or a file share and applied to the target computer over the network.

When the program runs, it creates an inventory cabinet file and that file is communicated to the database where it is added to the data from all other systems that have previously reported in. ACT provides information about the systems' hardware configuration, specifically the amount of memory, processor type, and available hard drive space. From this information, you can derive the necessary information that helps you plan which systems to upgrade and which systems to replace.

Considering Application Compatibility

The second part of the inventory operation is that it provides a listing of your installed applications. That application database can be compared with an online Microsoft database that contains the known compatibility status for particular applications using ACT.

After examining your application inventory, you can decide which applications need to be replaced or upgraded. This new version of ACT has a vendor and user forum that can be particularly useful in a deployment, as it contains the most up-to-date information, as well as a window on other people's experience.

You can access the information on application compatibility from the Application Compatibility page of the BDD Document Explorer, which is shown in Figure 37.1. The main information document is the Application Compatibility Feature Team Guide. You should note that the ACT is required for this part of the BDD. You can get information about the latest version of ACT from `http://technet.microsoft.com/en-us/windowsvista/aa905072.aspx`, as well as general application compatibility information from the Vista TechCenter at `http://technet.microsoft.com/en-us/windowsvista/aa905066.aspx`.

The Application Compatibility Toolkit 5.0 is covered in detail in Chapter 39.

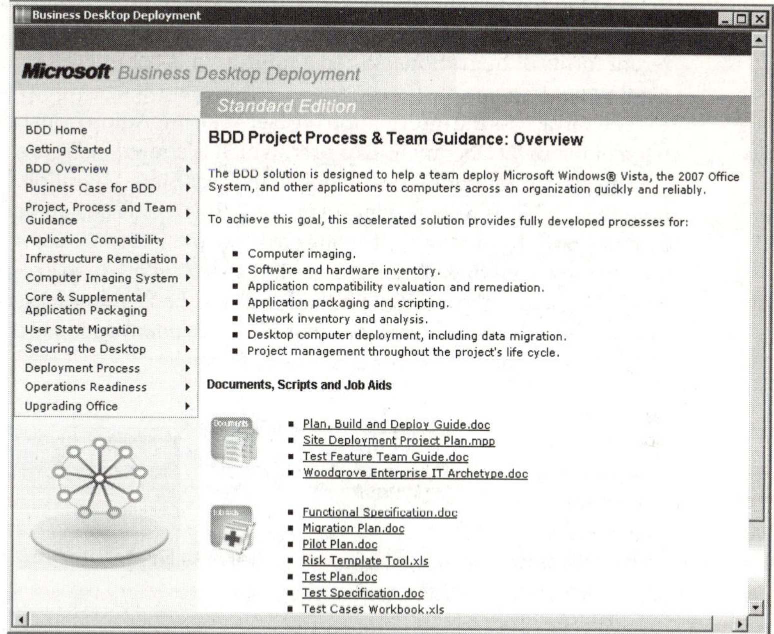

FIGURE 37.1
The Application Compatibility Remediation: Overview page of the BDD Document Explorer offers an overview of the application compatibility testing features, and worksheets to record your testing results.

Performing User State Migration

Migrating user state data, the bulk of which is normally part of a user's profile, is one of the most important tasks in any operating system deployment. However, it is also one of the most critical steps in terms of preserving the work done by users in customizing their environment. One of the critical factors in how clients judge your deployment is whether their data has been migrated successfully. Migration is one of the more difficult and tedious tasks in the Vista deployment scenario.

The User State Migration Team is tasked with the goal of moving user state data from old systems to new Vista systems. In order to successfully perform this task, the information gleaned from the application inventory needs to be examined in order that the required data is transferred correctly.

Migrating state data is tricky because you're often dealing with the data for multiple users stored in multiple profiles on the same system. Some of those profiles may be obsolete; others may require pruning. While you want to migrate some system settings such as favorites, cookies, desktop settings, folder options, and all of the different required data folders, you do not want to migrate many other settings such as hardware-related settings, drivers, applications, old DLLs, and passwords.

The tool used by the BDD to migrate user settings is the Windows User State Migration Tool 3.0 (UMST). UMST is covered in detail "Saving Settings with the User Setting Migration Toolkit (USMT)" section in Chapter 39, The USMT command line ScanState and LoadState tools provide the automation necessary to capture and restore these desired user settings and data while ignoring the kinds of data that you don't want to migrate. Data is captured to an intermediate data store, and when the Vista system is created, user state and data are transferred to the new system.

USMT 3.0 uses a set of migration rule XML files to control the migration process. Part of the lab work that the User State Migration Team must do is to work with these XML files (`MigApp.XML`, `MigUser.XML`, and `MigSys.XML`) to determine whether the default settings apply or whether they need to modify the control files for different behavior. These files actually control the logic and rules used for automated migration, so customizing them allows the team to adapt USMT for different forms of migrations. When a migration is complete, the BDD hands off execution to the Deployment Team.

You can access the information on user state migration from the User State Migration: Overview page of the BDD Document Explorer, which is shown in Figure 37.2.

The main information document is the User State Migration Feature Team Guide. You should note that USMT is required for this part of the BDD. You can get information about the latest version of USMT from `http://technet.microsoft.com/en-us/windowsvista/aa905115.aspx`, as well as view a getting started guide at `http://technet.microsoft.com/en-us/windowsvista/aa905114.aspx`. The latest download page for the Windows User State Migration Tool (USMT) 3.0 may be found at `http://www.microsoft.com/downloads/details.aspx?FamilyID=799ab28c-691b-4b36-b7ad-6c604be4c595&displaylang=en`.

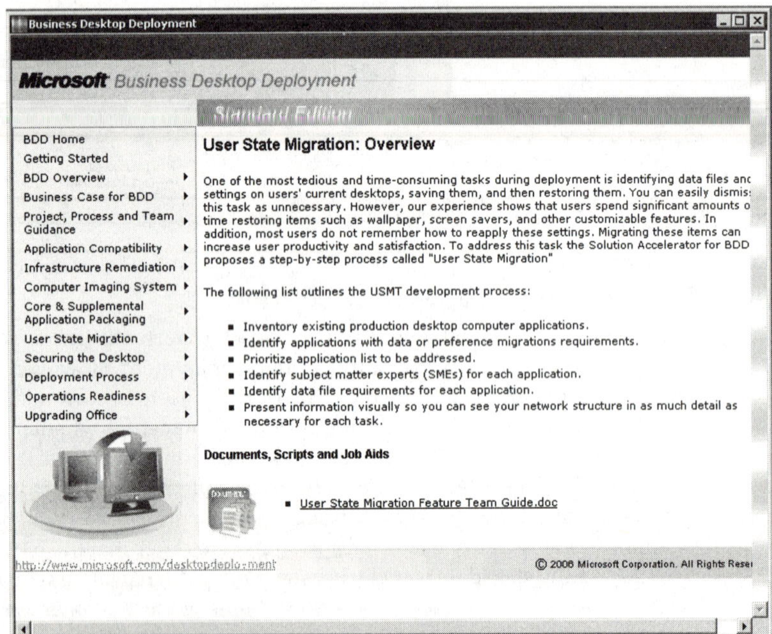

FIGURE 37.2
The User State Migration: Overview page of the BDD Document Explorer offers an overview of the application compatibility testing features and worksheets to record your testing results.

Setting Up a Computer Imaging System

In order to capture system images that can be applied during a deployment, the BDD recommends that a test lab or test bed be created. The laboratory contains at least two systems. One is the technician system on which the BDD and its tools are installed. The second system is the reference or master computer system that contains all of the hardware and software that the organization will replicate and support. In the laboratory, issues such as application compatibility, driver support, and other critical issues are addressed.

In reality most organizations choose to support multiple systems, each of which requires a separate image. It's rare to be able to simply freeze an image, so multiple images may have to be stored for each of these multiple systems. Sometimes images simply need to be updated; other times images may simply be replaced. Since each system image is at least a couple of gigabytes in size to tens of gigabytes, often a large amount of disk storage is required to support the library of images. Deployments rarely are a one shot deal. System rollout is often:

- Done in stages
- Done over time at user request
- Done as new systems become available through purchase
- Done when systems are freed up from prior use
- Done at some other time that makes organizational sense

Vista images are also an important component in backup and disaster recovery scenarios. Therefore, many images may be stored and saved over time.

With the ImageX technology and the new Windows Image Format or WIM file and its single instancing feature, many fewer images need to be stored, but a large amount of storage may still be required. That image store can be on the same technical system as BDD is installed on another server or a network attached storage device usually in the form of a network share. It is the responsibility of the Computer Imaging System Feature Team to create and manage the image store.

The tools used to image Vista systems are part of the Windows Automated Installation Kit (WAIK). WAIK is installed as part of the BDD, but it is also possible to install the WAIK on a different system. To be precise, the system that contains ImageX is referred to as the "build server." WAIK comes with Windows PE and Sysprep as well. It is also the responsibility of the Computer Imaging System Feature Team to create the Windows PE 2.0 boot images, which are deployed either on media inserted into the target Vista system or in the form of a PXE request from the client, which sends the boot images over the network to the client when the client boots up.

You can access the information on system imaging from the Computer Imaging System: Overview page of the BDD Document Explorer, which is shown in Figure 37.3. The main information document is the Computer Imaging System Feature Team Guide. You should note that the WAIK is required for this part of the BDD and is installed with the BDD. If you need to download a copy of WAIK, you can get the latest version of WAIK from `http://www.microsoft.com/downloads/details.aspx?FamilyID=993c567d-f12c-4676-917f-05d9de73ada4&displaylang=en`.

The topics of WAIK and imaging is covered in detail in Chapter 39. The imaging plan describes the methods used to roll out Vista images and is created in concert with other feature team groups.

Securing the Desktop

Vista was designed from the start to be much more secure than previous versions of Windows. For example, the TCP/IP stack was completely rewritten to make it perform better, improve support for IPv6, and most importantly make Vista more secure. However, Vista installs without modification making the default user an administrator, nor does it automatically simply fit into the security schemes that your organization has implemented.

The Security Feature Team is tasked with performing a risk analysis in order to identify system vulnerabilities and deploy desktop security settings. Security settings must be restrictive enough to limit system vulnerability while not being so restrictive that desired system functionality is impaired. The more secure client systems are the less likely client applications are to run without modification, the more testing the Security feature team may have to do, and the more problems your users may have.

FIGURE 37.3
The Computer Imaging System: Overview page of the BDD Document Explorer offers information about imaging and access to the BDD Workbench tool that manages images.

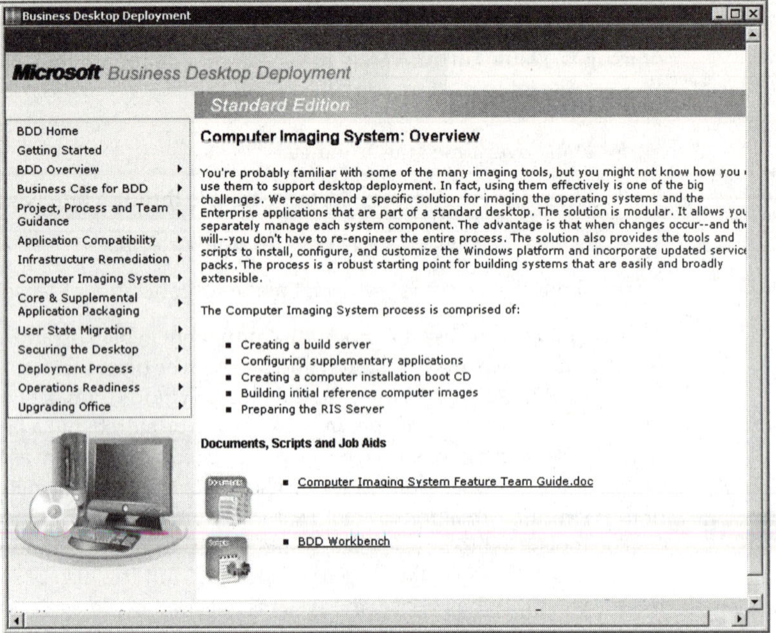

Broadly speaking, the desktop is secured by setting appropriate system policy settings. Account policy should include:

- Strong password settings
- Setting users and groups privileges
- Application access and settings
- File access
- Network access policies (which includes firewall settings)

Since these settings will impact operations, it is important that the Security Feature Team consults with the IT operations staff to gauge the impact of these settings.

Some applications can have their settings migrated, such as Windows Internet Explorer, but many third-party applications require study and testing. New and improved features also need to be considered for their impact on the organization. Those features include:

- BitLocker
- Drive Encryption
- EFS
- Digital Rights Management
- Windows Defender

Just as with Windows XP and Windows Server 2003, you can harden Vista desktops by turning off or limiting running system services, something that is referred to as "Windows service hardening."

You can access the information on security from the Securing the Desktop: Overview page of the BDD Document Explorer, which is shown in Figure 37.4. The main information document is the Security Feature Team Guide.

If you want to read more about the security risk analysis process that Microsoft recommends, you may want to read the Security Risk Management Guide, which you can find at `http://www.microsoft.com/technet/security/topics/policiesandprocedures/secrisk`. A general introduction to Windows security features can be had on TechNet's Security Guidance page at `http://www.microsoft.com/technet/security/guidance/default.mspx`. TechNet's Vista-specific security information may be found at `http://technet.microsoft.com/en-us/windowsvista/aa905062.aspx`.

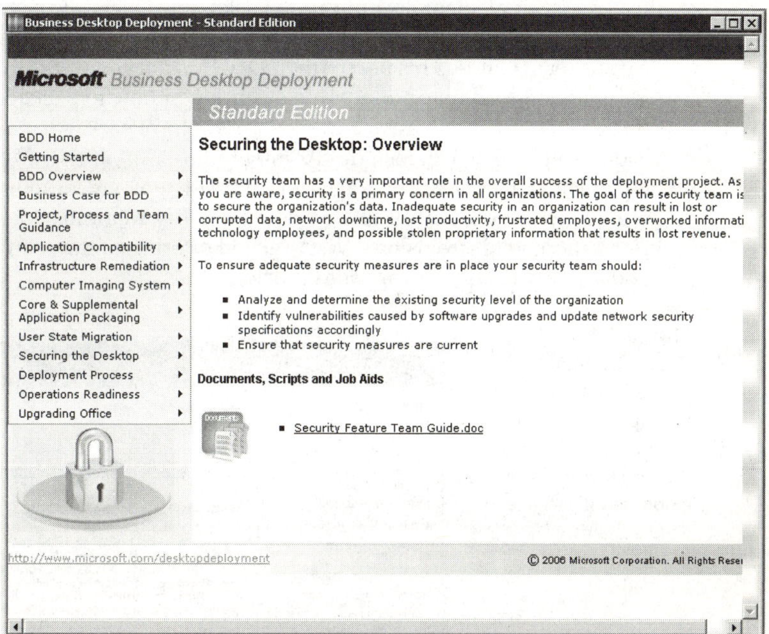

FIGURE 37.4
The Securing the Desktop: Overview page of the BDD Document Explorer offers guidance on how to configure and test Windows Vista's security features.

Packaging the Applications

The BDD recommends that a test lab be set up to create reference or master systems that will have the exact hardware and software configurations that will be created during deployment. The Application Management Feature Team is responsible for determining which applications are to be installed on the reference systems and to work with the User State Migration Team to ensure that all required settings and data for those applications can be migrated successfully. Either concurrently with this effort, or more often after the reference systems are successfully tested and their feature sets frozen (all packages, packages, and upgrades applied), the Application Management Feature Team will then hand off their work to the System Imaging Feature Team.

The BDD separates application installation and testing into two project goals: application compatibility testing and application packaging. Compatibility testing helps decide which applications will be installed; the goal of application packaging is to install the application as a "core" package or as an additional supplemental packages.

Core packages are those that are installed as part of the reference system and imaged as part of its base WIM file. The most widely deployed core application is probably the Windows Office suite. It is possible, of course, to treat Office installation as a separate installation, but most organizations usually choose to eliminate the extra steps and complexity.

A supplemental application is one that is packaged separately from the core Vista image, for example, an MSI file. Deployment is good time to prune the application portfolio. When packaged, applications can still be installed without user intervention, provided the deployment staff supplies the necessary setting such as file locations and application settings. It is also possible to provide the package for on-demand installation by the user, as an executable file. The BDD supports both of these approaches.

Guidance on application packaging for the Application Management Feature Team is found on the Core & Supplemental Application Packaging: Overview page of the BDD Document Explorer, which is shown in Figure 37.5. The main information document is the Application Management Feature Team Guide. This part of the BDD does not come with any tools, but does come with a set of guides and road maps to provide examples of how to package and repackage applications.

The BDD also promotes Macrovision's portfolio of package creation and management tools. Macrovision's software, which includes AdminStudio, AMS, and their Patch Impact Manager, is used to help organizations create packages for different deployment solutions. Macrovision advertises compatibility with SMS, Novell ZENworks, LANDesk, Marimba, ManageSoft, and Tivoli software. For information on Macrovision's Vista-related offerings, refer to `http://www.macrovision.com/products/windows_vista/index.shtml`.

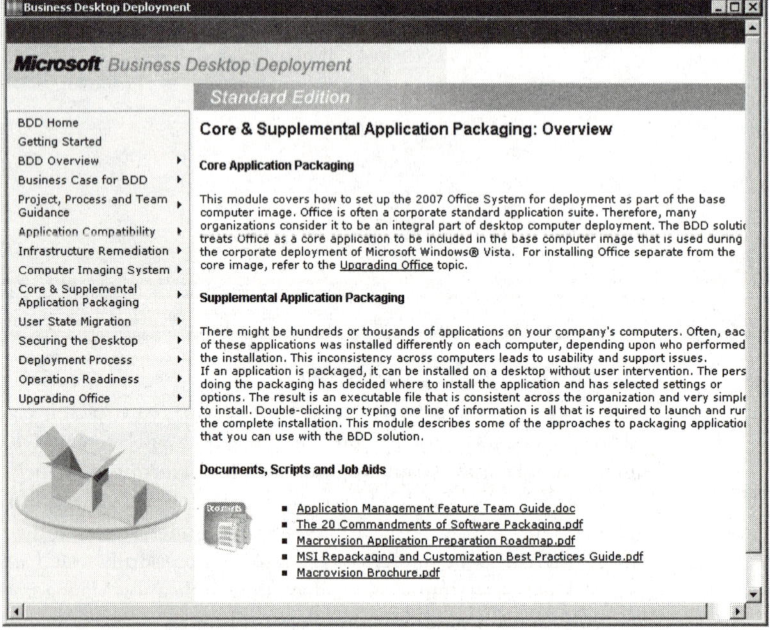

FIGURE 37.5
The Core & Supplemental Application Packaging: Overview page of the BDD Document Explorer offers guidance on package development.

Deployment

Deployment in BDD is performed by the Deployment Feature Team. Deployment is the next to the last step in the framework's guidance for an organization. As Vista systems are deployed, the support of those systems is handed over to the IT operations staff. For this reason, many organizations choose to have an operations staff member be part of the Deployment Feature Team. (Feature teams are meant to be cross-functional.)

The Deployment Feature Team performs one of the most critical aspects of the BDD process. They create the deployment servers, use the infrastructure remediation work to determine how to use the available servers and network capacity to support Vista deployment, set up the deployment tools, and then manage the deployment.

The purpose of the BDD is to provide an automated method for Vista deployment, and so although it is possible to set up deployment to be a manual affair, most small or medium deployments use the Lite Touch Installation method, and most large deployments use a network framework management tool to support the deployment. The Zero Touch Installation relies on Windows System Management Server to automate the installation of Vista.

It's possible to combine automation and manual features by setting up a deployment scheme so that users must initiate a deployment by calling in the request to a help desk. The IT staff will then initiate a remote installation. The BDD supports the old Remote Installation Service, as well as the newer Windows Deployment Service. Both services provide a way to support PXE boot requests for Vista deployment. Chapter 39 describes the Lite Touch Installation and the Zero Touch Installation, LTI and ZTI, respectively. Chapter 41 discusses remote installations and describes both WDS and RIS and how they are used to set up both automatic and manual installations. WDS has a number of interesting and new options that can tailor the deployment process.

Guidance on deployment for the Deployment Feature Team is found on the Deployment Process: Overview page of the BDD Document Explorer, which is shown in Figure 37.6. The main information document is the Deployment Feature Team Guide.

Since installation of any form of Windows requires conforming to licensing requirements and those requirements have changed substantially with Vista, the Deployment Team must provide the necessary information for Vista to conform. Vista licensing can be provided within 30 days of installation, but nearly all organizations perform this task prior to handing over a system to their users. The key document for guidance in activation is the Volume Activation Guide, where volume activations using Multiple Activation Keys (MAK) or the Key Management Service (KMS) are described. That document also describes how OEMs should approach activation.

Vista uses the Software Protection Platform (SPP) for support of large-scale deployments. SPP is a combination of an activation service, client services, and an API that is in Vista and will be in Longhorn Server. It also supports a new digital license activation system called Volume Activation 2.0 that is used by:

- Vista Enterprise
- Vista Enterprise K
- Vista Business

FIGURE 37.6 The Deployment Process: Overview page of the BDD Document Explorer offers guidance on deployment configuration as well as licensing and activation information.

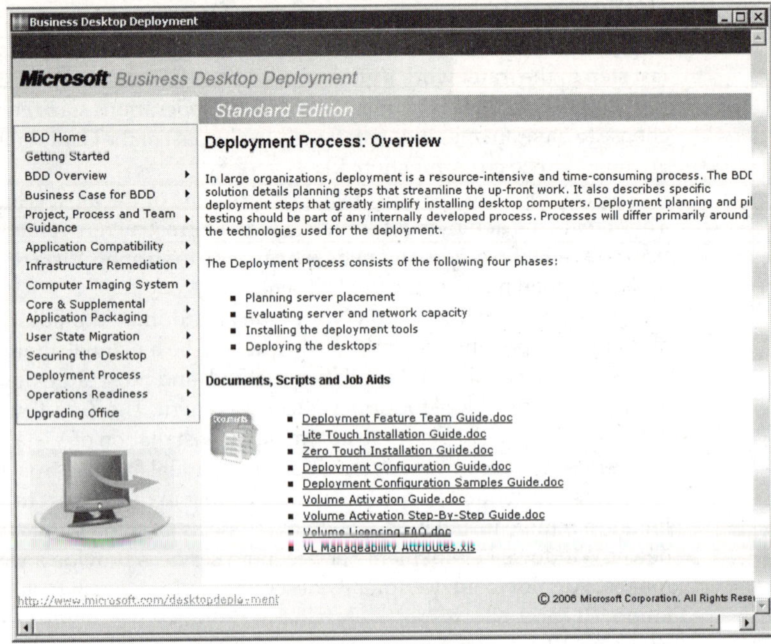

- Vista Business N
- Vista Business K
- Vista Business KN
- Longhorn Server Itanium Edition
- Longhorn Server Web
- Longhorn Server Computer Cluster
- MMS Standard (MAK only)
- MMS Premium (MAK only)
- Longhorn Server Standard/Standard Core
- Longhorn Server Enterprise/Enterprise Core
- Longhorn Server Datacenter/Datacenter Core

The N designation above refers to the European Union version that has multimedia features removed. The K designation above refers to the Korean version which has the same functionality as Windows Business except that it contains links to the Media Player Center Web site and the Messenger Center Web site. These sites have links to 3rd party sites where other media players and messaging software may be downloaded or purchased. The KN version has both sets of features.

You can't deploy Windows Vista Home Basic, Home Premium, or Ultimate as part of Volume Licensing.

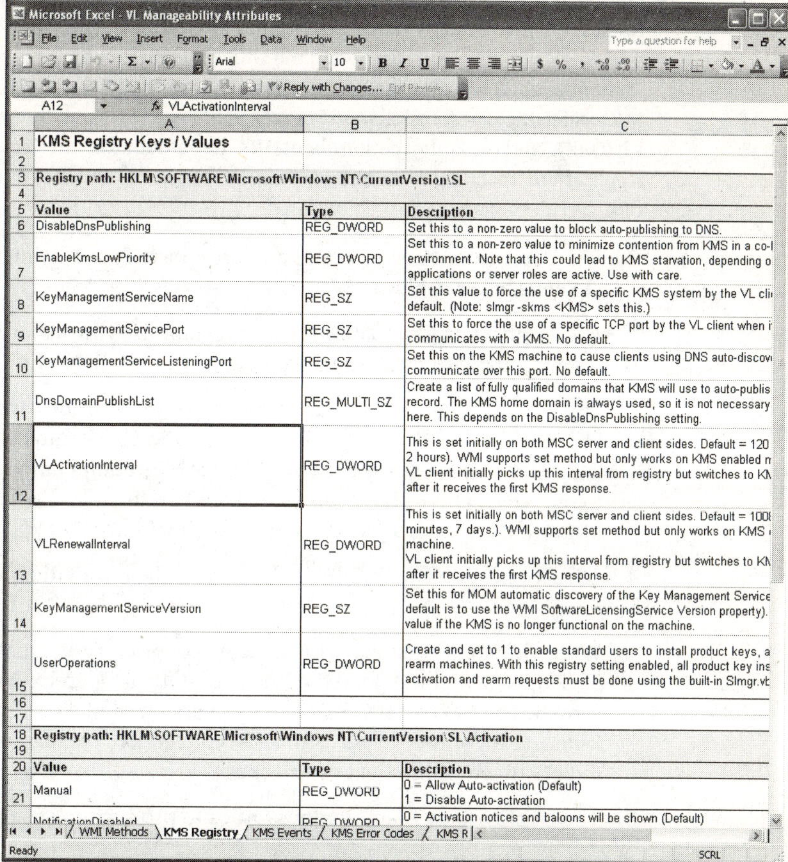

Value	Type	Description
DisableDnsPublishing	REG_DWORD	Set this to a non-zero value to block auto-publishing to DNS.
EnableKmsLowPriority	REG_DWORD	Set this to a non-zero value to minimize contention from KMS in a co-l environment. Note that this could lead to KMS starvation, depending o applications or server roles are active. Use with care.
KeyManagementServiceName	REG_SZ	Set this value to force the use of a specific KMS system by the VL cli default. (Note: slmgr -skms <KMS> sets this.)
KeyManagementServicePort	REG_SZ	Set this to force the use of a specific TCP port by the VL client when i communicates with a KMS. No default.
KeyManagementServiceListeningPort	REG_SZ	Set this on the KMS machine to cause clients using DNS auto-discov communicate over this port. No default.
DnsDomainPublishList	REG_MULTI_SZ	Create a list of fully qualified domains that KMS will use to auto-publis record. The KMS home domain is always used, so it is not necessary here. This depends on the DisableDnsPublishing setting.
VLActivationInterval	REG_DWORD	This is set initially on both MSC server and client sides. Default = 120 2 hours). WMI supports set method but only works on KMS enabled n VL client initially picks up this interval from registry but switches to KN after it receives the first KMS response.
VLRenewalInterval	REG_DWORD	This is set initially on both MSC server and client sides. Default = 100 minutes, 7 days.). WMI supports set method but only works on KMS machine. VL client initially picks up this interval from registry but switches to KN after it receives the first KMS response.
KeyManagementServiceVersion	REG_SZ	Set this for MOM automatic discovery of the Key Management Service default is to use the WMI SoftwareLicensingService Version property). value if the KMS is no longer functional on the machine.
UserOperations	REG_DWORD	Create and set to 1 to enable standard users to install product keys, a rearm machines. With this registry setting enabled, all product key ins activation and rearm requests must be done using the built-in Slmgr.vb

Value	Type	Description
Manual	REG_DWORD	0 = Allow Auto-activation (Default) 1 = Disable Auto-activation
NotificationDisabled	REG_DWORD	0 = Activation notices and baloons will be shown (Default)

FIGURE 37.7
The VL Manageability Attributes worksheet is a reference for issues with volume licensing and activation services.

The Deployment section comes with an XLS file (Excel worksheet) called the VL Manageability Attributes that provides reference data on WMI Properties and Methods, KMS Registry Entries, KMS Events and Error Codes, and KMS RPC Messages. Figure 37.7 shows a sample page of this worksheet. If you're involved in volume activations, you'll want to consult this document as you go forward.

Office Upgrades

The BDD considers Microsoft Office to be a core application and recommends that it is installed as part of a master system's image. However, many organizations upgrade their systems to Vista before deploying the Office 2007 system. So you'll find that the Upgrading Office page of the BDD offers guidance for both approaches.

The BDD recommends the following steps in an Office 2007 upgrade:

1. The Office Deployment team creates the project plan based on test lab results.

   The testing should result in selecting an Office package, establishing required settings, and identifying any required Office tools that are needed. Different versions of Office that could be considered are Microsoft Office Professional 2007, Microsoft Office Professional Plus 2007 (which adds InfoPath 2007), or Microsoft Office Groove 2007.

NOTE To review the current versions of Office available for deployment, take a look at the Microsoft Office System Packaging web page found at: `http://www.microsoft.com/office/preview/suites.mspx`. To obtain the Office installation tools mentioned in this section (Office Customization Tool, Microsoft Office Setup Controller, Microsoft Office File Conversion Tool, and Microsoft Office Local Installation Source), you'll need to install the Microsoft Office 2007 Resource Kit (ORK). The latest information about ORK may be found on the TechNet Microsoft Office Desktop Applications TechCenter at: `http://www.microsoft.com/technet/prodtechnol/office/ork/default.mspx`.

2. The Deployment Team creates an Office Installation Point, usually a network share such as `\\`*`Servername`*`\Office 12`.
3. The Application Compatibility Team customizes the installation routine and propagates the changes made to the installation point.

   This phase of the upgrade identifies any upgrade issues, works with staff to determine how Office will be used, and feeds this information back into the Office deployment project plan (step 1). You can use the Microsoft Office Migration Planning Manager to scan your systems to see which clients have Office installed on them and what Office system files exist. The Migration Planning Manager creates an inventory that you can use as part of your planning.
4. The Application Compatibility Team tests the installation to check its compatibility on master systems.

   While previous versions of Office used proprietary Microsoft document file formats, Office 2007 moves documents to the Microsoft Office Open Extensible Markup Language (XML) format. The Microsoft Office File Conversion can take the output of the Office Planning Manager inventory to perform a file conversion, creating new XML files while leaving the old document files intact as a backup.
5. The Deployment Team deploys Office to production systems.
6. Support for Office is handed off to the IT operations staff.

The Office deployment plan needs to address the type of Office system settings the deployment supports. Some organizations enforce a single Office configuration throughout the deployment, while other organizations customize Office for each group of users. Settings are distributed as part of a patch file (MSP) or in an Office XML configuration file. For instances where the organization allows users to create their own Office settings, you can create a Vista policy that enables users to do so.

When the Office installer runs in quiet mode, it automatically removes previous versions of Office that it finds. It is possible to change the installer to leave earlier versions of Office.

Unlike Vista, deployments of Office 2007 can be staged so that applications from within the Office suite are installed at different times. The Office Customization Tool (OCT) lets you control which programs get installed. With the Office Setup Controller, you can also add programs to an installation. Think of OCT as a tool for stepping through and modifying the Office Setup program.

The Office Customization Tool for the Office 2007 system is described in detail at `http://technet2.microsoft.com/Office/en-us/library/8faae8a0-a12c-4f7b-839c-24a66a531bb51033.mspx?mfr=true`. OCT is a command-line tool that runs as a switch for Office `Setup.EXE`. The four parts of OCT are modifications to:

Setup Modifications can be made to installation location, organization name, network sources, licenses, the user interface, removing previous Office versions, and any additional programs to be installed, as well as programs to run, the Office security settings, and changes that can be made to the Setup program properties.

Features Feature changes are limited to changing user settings and to the set feature installation states.

Additional Content OCT can install and remove files, alter and remove registry entries, and create and configure shortcuts.

Outlook Among the modifications possible are altering the Outlook profile, which Exchange settings enforce; create or remove accounts; export Outlook settings; and specify send receive groups.

The prime example where OCT is valuable is when an organization wants to delay the installation of the new version of Microsoft Outlook until an organization's new mail server is installed. The release of Microsoft Exchange Server 2007 was meant to be coincidental with the release of Vista and Office 2007.

The Microsoft Office Setup Controller program can be used to modify the installation routine. This program checks that the installation source exists, that a client is ready to have Office deployed, and that the correct settings are made in the Registry and file system. With the Microsoft Office Local Installation Source (Office LIS), a compressed copy of all of Office's distribution is created and then sent to the target computer for later use. While LIS was introduced by Microsoft as part of Office 2003, it is now required for an Office 2007 installation.

Guidance is given on office upgrades from the Upgrading Office: Overview page of the BDD Document Explorer, which is shown in Figure 37.8. The main information document is the Office Deployment Guide. Deploying Office is one of the more challenging aspects of a Vista deployment, so this part of the BDD offers numerous templates and aids that the feature teams can use to either plan or document their work. Table 37.1 lists the different documents, templates, and job aids that ship with the BDD to support this aspect of the deployment work.

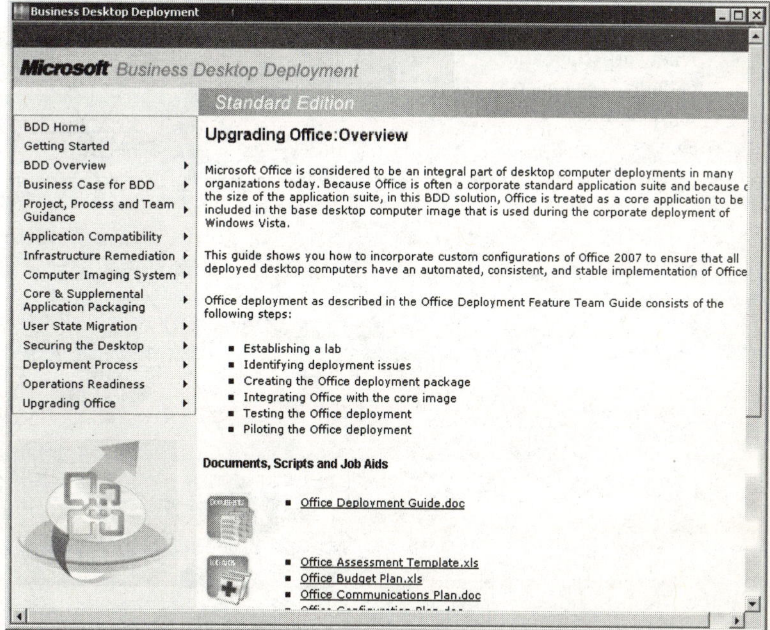

FIGURE 37.8
The Upgrading Office: Overview page of the BDD Document Explorer helps plan an Office deployment and configure Office on clients. Some of the important tools required in this work are part of the Office Resource Kit 2007.

Deployment Samples

As much as possible, the Business Deployment Desktop framework tries to create actual tools that you can use in your own deployment efforts. Tools include planning documents, inventory spreadsheets, and so on. However, the BDD goes further in providing a complete deployment sample, based on a hypothetical company, of the process that a deployment team would go through in order to deploy Vista in that type of company. Previous versions of the BDD created a company called Trey Engineering, which is hypothetical company comprised of 50 clients.

In the more recent version of the BDD the example given is the Woodgrove Bank. The deployment sample that ships with the BDD is documented on the BDD Project Process & Team Guidance: Overview page as one of the aids offered for overall project planning. The Plan, Build, and Deploy Guide; Site Deployment Project Plan; and Test Feature Team Guide are all general documents that aren't tied to either of the sample projects mentioned in the sections below. They are valuable for the Core Feature Team and their project planning.

Trey Engineering Sample Project

Trey Engineering is a hypothetical department of the Trey Company that has three 50-client subnets connected to the company's network. Figure 37.9 shows a schematic of the Trey engineering department that was developed using Visio's network discovery tool, where only one of the three subnets are shown. In the diagram only 15 of the 50 clients on the subnet are drawn. The Cisco Catalyst 8500 connects the subnet to the two other engineering subnets as well as to other parts of the company's network.

The deployment server is shown at the top left side of the diagram inside a circle. The project specification allows for a 12-hour window during which the subnet can be down for the deployment. After inventorying the subnet and creating the diagram, the deployment teams performs a risk analysis where any factors that could jeopardize the deployment's critical deployment window are examined.

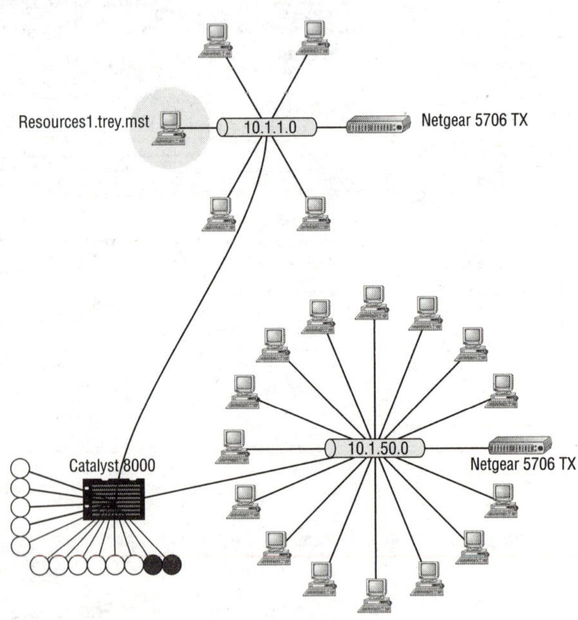

FIGURE 37.9
A network schematic of the Trey engineering department.

The planning process recommends the appointment of an individual to create an action plan that remediates risks prior to the deployment effort. Risks include network bandwidth issues, server capacity, problems accessing needed resources, and so forth. The action plan identifies that moving the deployment server inside the subnet will improve the deployment server's throughput as a key change. Alternatives such as adding more deployment servers, getting a longer downtime window, and creating a phased deployment are also considered. With this planning in hand, the development plan is fashioned.

The Trey Engineering project offers deployment staff the following tools that they can adapt to use in their own deployment:

- Trey Site Deployment Project Plan
- Test Feature Team Guide
- Trey Upper MORG IT Archetype
- Trey Functional Specification
- Trey Migration Plan
- Trey Pilot Plan
- Trey Risk Template Tool
- Trey Test Plan
- Trey Test Specification
- Test Cases Workbook
- Trey Training Plan
- Trey Vision Scope
- Trey Business Case Document
- Trey Business Case Presentation
- Trey Client Build Requirements
- Application Knowledge Sheet
- Trey Communications Plan
- Trey Network and Workstation Hardware Upgrades List
- Inventory Template
- Assessment Template
- Current State Assessment Template

The Trey plan relies on Microsoft SMS to roll out the deployment and is an example of an XP deployment. Therefore, part of the example discusses how the SMS distribution server is placed and configured.

With the introduction of Vista and the new version of the BDD, the sample deployment has been modified to highlight some of the new Vista deployment features. This version is described in the section that follows.

Woodgrove Bank Sample Project

The Woodgrove Bank sample project begins with the IT Archetype described in the next section. The Woodgrove Bank project highlights the deployment of Vista and the Office 2000 system in a large corporate environment. This hypothetical business is a subsidiary of a holding company called WG Holding in London. WG owns five companies, each with over 5,000 employees. One of the five companies is Woodgrove Bank, which has 15,000 employees in 60 worldwide offices. Their headquarters are in New York, with divisional headquarters located in London and Tokyo. The company maintains 57 worldwide offices with 13 of them large enough to be regional hubs.

The Woodgrove Enterprise IT Archetype

The goal of the Enterprise IT Archetype document is to define the nature of the company's organization. The main features are that it documents system inventory, staff inventory, IT budget, IT staff and its organization, and network architecture. Using the information provided in the case study should enable you to project the information to your project needs in order to support the project plan.

Woodgrove's IT infrastructure includes a corporate WAN on leased T3 lines over which an intranet is deployed. Geographic localities within Woodgrove each have their own LAN. Figure 37.10 shows the graphic of Woodgrove's network topology from the Microsoft case study.

Woodgrove's line-of-business or LOB applications are deployed on a combination of Unix and Windows servers. Enterprise applications use either Oracle or SQL Server and a browser-based client. The directory services applications include the PeopleSoft ERP application, iPlanet directory service, and the Microsoft Identity Integration Server. LOB and ERP applications use a Windows client application, or one that can be opened in a console session. The profile specifies that Woodgrove is a very heavy enterprise email user and uses Microsoft Exchange Server as their messaging platform.

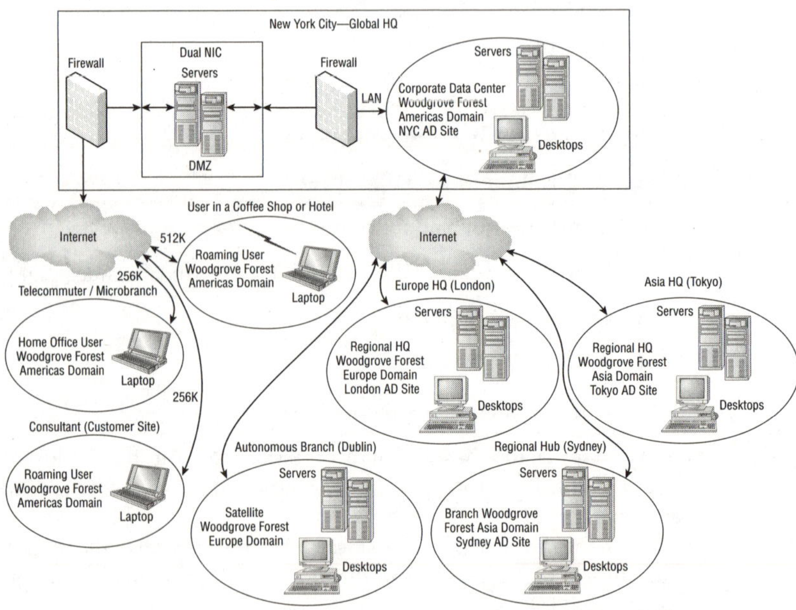

FIGURE 37.10
Woodgrove Bank's network topology.
Source: Woodgrove Enterprise Archetype document (Microsoft Corp.)

The following applications are considered to be mission critical:

- A proprietary trading system, which is an Oracle application on Unix with web client
- An online banking system, which is also based on an Oracle application on Unix with web client
- The Microsoft Exchange Server messaging system
- Business process management through the PeopleSoft application
- Electronic data interchange (EDI)
- Specialized LOB applications that the company has developed

An inventory of Woodgrove Bank shows there to be 1,712 servers, and the project generates a table showing the server applications broken down by the network operating system type. An inventory of personal computers shows that nearly each employee of Woodgrove has at least one computer, with a total of 17,000 systems. Of that 85 percent are desktops and 15 percent are laptops. The great bulk of clients are Windows systems, with a handful of Macintosh and Unix clients also installed. The inventory also specifies the location of the 1,712 servers in the different worldwide offices. Tables of servers by usage type (applications and infrastructure) and servers by location are shown in the case study. The percentages aren't random, although the company is fictional. Microsoft bases these percentages on a collection of its largest clients as a representative example.

Keep in mind that the entire corporate infrastructure is reported because the BDD is meant to support not only Vista, but Windows Longhorn Server. Therefore, information that you might not need for Vista deployment is fully developed. From the standpoint of Vista deployment, the inventory of number and distribution of client operating systems was similarly fully developed and the information of server support for deployment, Microsoft MOM servers, the IT groups exemplified by the "IT Personas" toward the end of the document are particularly valuable.

Functional Specification

The Woodgrove Functional Specification is a developed template that contains documents that specify the solution deliverables for the Woodgrove project. The functional specification represents the promised deliverables that the deployment organization gives its customer. Many consulting groups that do projects for clients staple the functional specification to the back of their contract so that the goals, milestones, and payments are tied to the information that the specification contains.

Depending on the complexity and scope of a deployment, the functional specification is a single document with eight sections or a set of eight separate documents. For Woodgrove Bank, the size of the organization requires fully developed individual reports. The documents are:

- Usage Scenarios
- User Requirements
- Business Requirements
- Operations Requirements
- System Requirements
- Conceptual Design
- Logical Design
- Physical Design

Each section in the functional specification document has a description of the purpose of the section, as well as a short or very short summary of what might be put into Woodgrove's deployment. Use this document in your own project by replacing the green Woodgrove text with your own project's specifications, and by removing the blue description information. You may find it valuable to rephrase the description section so that it summarizes the purpose of the section for your client.

Migration, Pilot, Test, and Training Plans

The plan documents are templates that describe how a part of the deployment process is accomplished and managed. The template uses the Woodgrove Bank project to provide brief samples that you can replace for your own project. The plans include:

Migration Plans Migrations include infrastructure deployment, application development and support, and data that need to be moved onto newly deployed systems.

Pilot Plan A pilot plan creates a test bed or laboratory to test the deployment on a small scale and to establish feasibility for the larger deployment. For very large deployments it is advisable for the deploying group to define a pilot plan as a first separate project before attempting a full-scale deployment.

Test Plan A test plan is described the technique use to test the features of the deployment. Bug fixing, application compatibility, user state migration validation, and other factors that impact the quality of the deployment that can be tested are part of this plan. It should identify the resources required, tools, methodology, responsibility, and expected results of a Test Feature Team.

The test plan will lead to the Test Specification and Test Cases document. This document is similar in purpose to the functional specification, but here it details the testing process as it was developed through the test plan. In essence it is a recipe for enforcing quality control as the deployment moves forward.

Training Plan The training plan document details who will be trained and who will do the training for the subjects that the Program Management staff decide need to be supported.

The different plans should be summarized in the functional specification, as well as supported by the Vision Scope document, which describes what the organization hopes to achieve and why the organization exists. Plans are templates that describe:

- Justification for the task, migration in this instance
- Team roles and responsibilities
- Executive summary
- Objectives and goals
- Strategies, including tools and impacts
- Migration environmental impact, which describes changes in hardware, software, or user interactions
- Guidelines
- Migration process: test environment, deployment, decommissioning, and rollback plan (if needed)

This general scheme is repeated in all of the plans. You can summarize the description in your version of these plans (the blue text), and replace the Woodgrove Bank specific plan text, which is in green in the document.

Vision Scope Document

Although listed last, the Vision Scope template might be one of those tasks that is done at the beginning of a deployment project. The Vision Scope details four different concepts:

- Business opportunity
- Solutions concept
- Project scope
- Solution design strategies

The Vision Scope statement might be part of the organization's attempt to justify a Vista deployment to management and may therefore be required prior to the deployment proceeding. Usually the Project Management Team provides the strategic justification and seeks input on the technical specification from other teams.

Summary

In this chapter the overall parts of the Business Desktop Deployment Document Explorer framework tool was described. This tool offers each of the teams in a Vista deployment information in the form of guidance to help them organize for their task. Most of the topics—Application Compatibility, Computer Imaging System, Core & Supplemental Application Packaging, User State Migration, and others—offer templates that you can use to collect and organize the information that that team develops as part of their work. The chapter also described overall process guidance, which takes the form of sample solutions. For Vista, that sample is a large multinational, multilevel banking company called Woodgrove Bank.

In the next chapter, "Defining Deployment Scenarios," you will see the three different deployment scenarios: upgrade, bare metal, and side-by-side deployments explained. The chapter further examines the tools used in the pre-image stage of a deployment, including the Windows Automated Installation Kit and the Windows System Image Manager.

Chapter 38

Defining Deployment Scenarios

Windows Vista image-based deployments allow for rapid system creation. However, to accomplish this task there needs to be appropriate planning and testing of systems, appropriate imaging of reference systems, and creation of the automation tools needed to perform a system installation automatically. In addition, three different deployment scenarios need to be considered. Deciding which scenario to use depends on whether you are trying to create entirely fresh installations, preserve as much existing user environments as possible, or allow for a stepwise migration.

In this chapter you'll find an overview of the pre-image stages of Windows Vista deployment. The emphasis here is on the overall process and not on the details of using any one of these tools. The topics covered in this chapter include:

- Performing the WAIK setup
- Performing the Windows System Image Manager setup
- Determining your deployment scenario

Vista: What's New?

Vista's deployment tools are upgraded versions of tools that were previously deployed in first Windows 2000 and then Windows XP. If you've deployed Windows XP using Windows PE, you'll find that the newest version incorporates Vista technology and enhances PE's capabilities. Similarly, the command-line tool ImageX and the Windows System Image Manager tool are both new in Windows Vista, as is the XML answer file. All of these new tools mean that the Windows AIK emerges as a new technology for image-based deployment.

The Windows Automated Installation Kit, which contains Windows PE, ImageX, and Windows SIM, has been integrated into the Business Desktop Deployment framework; although it is available on its own. The Deployment Workbench is also new for Windows Vista deployment, and this tool leverages the Windows AIK to intelligently build images for rapid Vista system deployment.

This chapter looks at these new tools and the role they play in various Windows deployment scenarios.

Performing the WAIK Setup

The Windows Automation Installation Kit, Windows AIK, or WAIK is a central tool in Microsoft's image deployment technologies. When you install the Windows AIK onto a technician system, you also install its components:

Windows PE Tools Allows you to build bootable Windows PE environments.

ImageX Lets you create system images from master or reference computers

Windows SIM Enables you to manage a collection of images; and more importantly build an answer file (`Unattend.XML`) for each image. The answer file is the key to automating system deployment.

Windows PE, ImageX, and Windows SIM are covered in detail in later chapters, but in this chapter let's consider an overview of the deployment process so that you can put the material of the next few chapters in context as you read along.

The Windows AIK is downloadable from Microsoft website (`http://www.microsoft.com/downloads/details.aspx?FamilyID=993c567d-f12c-4676-917f-05d9de73ada4&displaylang=en`) as a stand-alone package from the Microsoft Connect site. It is also part of the BDD package and is part of distributions sent to OEMs and enterprise customers as part of their service packages.

Windows AIK is installed by the Microsoft Installer 3.1 program and as such does not differ in detail from other Windows component installations that you are familiar with. After the installation, you will find the Windows AIK program group on the Start menu, as shown in Figure 38.1. From there you can access the Windows PE command prompt, the Windows SIM tool, documentation, and a set of white papers.

Since the Windows AIK is a central part of the Business Desktop Deployment tool, you will find that WAIK is used by:

- Computer Imaging System
- Core & Supplemental Application Packaging
- Deployment Process modules of the BDD

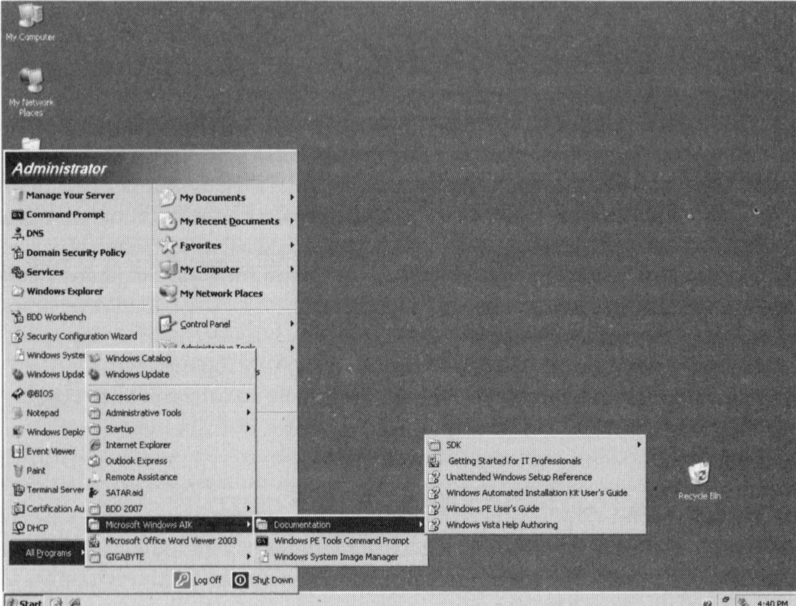

FIGURE 38.1
The Windows AIK program group provides access to the Windows PE command prompt, Windows SIM, and the documentation set.

That means that of the eight modules of the BDD, nearly half of them, and the teams that implement those features, rely on the Windows AIK.

As you learned in the previous chapter, the Windows AIK is valuable for any organization that is rolling out Vista to a large number of desktops. It is even more valuable when that organization is supporting multiple reference system configurations. Recall that in a staged deployment, it is recommended that the organization build a test or lab environment, create appropriate master or reference systems, and test against those systems prior to imaging them. The Windows AIK plays a central role in all steps up to the actual rollout, where the tools that the Windows AIK created take over.

If you follow along with the recommended BDD process, a deployment starts out with the following fundamental steps:

1. Create a lab environment with technician systems and master or reference systems. The technician system contains the BDD, imaging, and deployment tools, while the master systems are systems with Vista and all supported applications, utilities, and settings installed on it.

2. Install the BDD and the Windows AIK on the technician systems, which can be Windows XP Pro, Windows Server 2003, or Windows Vista systems.

3. Create the master or reference systems in each of the configurations that your organization intends to support; then image those systems.

   Large organizations may be able to simply install Vista on individual systems already deployed and test Vista live in their organizations. As a minimum, a single system can be built, configured, imaged, and then rebuilt with the next configuration and imaged. For systems that don't share the same basic components, such as motherboards, individual system types will have to be used.

4. Master systems that have been tested and validated and Sysprepped are imaged with ImageX, and the images are stored typically to a network share.

5. The "A" in Windows AIK stands for "Automated," and the way you automate a deployment is to create the answer files that let Vista installations proceed unattended. To build the answer files you would open the image inside Windows SIM and set the configuration required.

   Windows SIM makes building the `Unattend.XML` file easy by capturing settings in a template and provides a place where scripts and other automation tools can be integrated into the deployment process.

6. Once images and `Unattend.XML` files are created, deployment of the images from the network share or image store uses the Windows PE and ImageX technologies that are part of the Windows AIK, but coordination moves to the Windows Desktop Services application, Windows SMS OS Deployment Feature Pack, or some other third-party enterprise framework application that supports Windows Vista deployment.

Figure 38.2 illustrates the process described above.

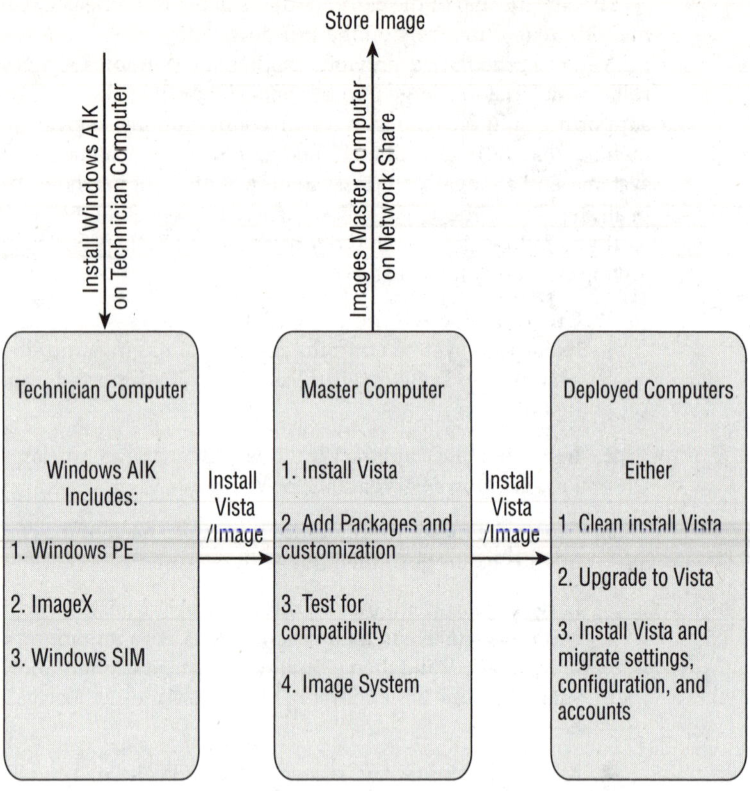

FIGURE 38.2
The Windows AIK programs create the necessary components for performing Windows Vista deployments and are managed by deployment tools during the rollout phase.

Performing the Windows System Image Manager Setup

The Windows SIM utility is Microsoft's tool for creating answer files. An answer file is a text file that contains the settings and configurations that Windows Vista Setup requires to complete itself. The answer file replaces the interaction of the operator sitting in front of a computer monitor (or terminal session) while the installation runs. With an image-based installation not only is Windows Vista installed but any supported applications or utilities are installed as well. That means that the answer file may have to supply the settings for applications such as Microsoft Office, and any other components that you choose to add to any reference system.

The basic steps involved in creating an answer file are:

1. Open Windows SIM and locate the Windows installation image on the Vista distribution media. The image that you use to begin with is the image you would use to create the initial Vista installation and not the custom image that you create with ImageX once your master system is built.

2. Create a new answer file in Windows SIM.

3. Add any additional installation packages or components that you wish to install as part of a Vista installation. Components include special packages such as drivers that are specific to your hardware configuration, such as the critical driver that might be required to access a RAID set or a specialized mass storage device.

4. Add the appropriate values of each configuration setting in the answer file.

5. Use Windows SIM to validate the answer file, `Unattend.XML`.

6. Save the answer file to the media that you will use in your build.

The Answer File Build Process

With the answer file in hand, you can take your Windows Vista distribution as well as any of the other required media and build a reference or master system that you will image. Chapter 40 contains a detailed description of how to create an answer file in Windows SIM once you have the master system image or WIM file. Windows SIM opens an `Install.WIM` file and from the WIM file it can create the required catalog file (CLG) that is an inventory of all of the packages and components that are part of your image installation. Only when you have both the WIM file and its catalog is it possible to create the answer file.

Each Windows Vista installation therefore must have the following three components:

1. The image or WIM file you create with ImageX

2. The catalog or CLG file you create with Windows SIM

3. The answer file or `Unattend.XML` file you can create once you have both an image and the related CLG file using Windows SIM. Sometimes the answer file is given the name `Autoattend.XML` for certain automated Vista installations.

Keep in mind that an image of WIM file is a container, and each WIM file can contain any number of installations. Since WIM files are single instance file databases, there's little penalty in having as many installations contained inside the WIM file as you might need. With Windows SIM you can look inside the WIM file to create the catalog file appropriate to the installation you need, and the corresponding answer file as well.

As you will learn in the "Windows System Image Manager," section of Chapter 40, a Windows Vista Setup installation runs through a set of seven configuration passes. Each configuration pass accomplishes a different part of the installation, and some phases reboot your system. Some settings are mandatory, such as the ones in the Windows PE phase (phase 1) that setup the disk configuration, partitions, and so forth. Some settings are optional, such as the ones that modify the shell for an OEM that is part of phase 4. Refer to Chapter 40 and to the documentation that comes with Windows SIM for further information.

The final step prior to saving the `Unattend.XML` or `Autounattend.XML` file is to validate the file. The Validate Answer file that is found on the Tools menu of Windows SIM then checks the settings that you have specified in order to determine that the settings exist and can be specified. When the validation is completed Windows SIM posts a success notice.

NOTE **Just because a setting exists and is valid doesn't mean that it can be successfully employed during an installation. The classic example is when you specify a partition size that is greater than the available space on the hard drive. So it is important to stay alert to issues such as these until you have fully implemented enough master systems to have confidence in your answer file.**

The Image Build Process

With an answer file in hand, you are now ready to begin installing Vista on the master or reference computer. You run the Windows product DVD against the answer file to create the master installation.

Here are the basic steps used to create the master image:

1. Build, buy, or assemble your reference or master computer hardware.
2. Start up from the Windows Vista distribution media and the answer file.
3. Check that the installation proceeds correctly and that it adds the appropriate OS customizations.
4. Complete the installation, reboot, and open a command prompt.
5. Prepare the system for a new user by running the Sysprep command, as follows:

   ```
   C:\WINDOWS\SYSTEM32\SYSPREP\SYSPREP.EXE /OOBE /GENERALIZE /SHUTDOWN
   ```

   This command generalizes or reseals the computer removing specific system identification.
6. Reboot the system into Windows PE.
7. Use ImageX to save an image of the master system to a network share or to the media of your choice.

The exact commands are described in full in Chapter 40.

With your reference system image now built, you are ready to decide how to deploy the image in a manner that is appropriate for your organization The next section describes some of the basic scenarios for system image deployment.

Determining Your Deployment Scenario

There's no getting away from it: any deployment carries with it potential benefits, which are supposed, and risks, which are unknown. You are replacing something that "isn't broken" with something that supposedly fixes it. No wonder that enterprises are so reluctant to begin new deployments of operating systems.

With Windows Vista, Microsoft has radically changed the way deployments are done. They've given administrators new tools and technologies to aid their deployments and hopefully made the process easier, less error prone, and less painful. What Microsoft hasn't done though is to remove the important element of planning. Since Vista can be brought to clients a number of different ways, and each method has both benefits and drawbacks, it is important to take some time to consider which type of deployment might work best for any particular situation.

Deployments are not the same thing as installations. An installation for the purposes of this discussion is when a person must initiate the installation and maintain control of that installation in order to get the desired result. At worst the person is answering configuration questions as they come up; and at best the installation has an answer file that allows the process to proceed to its conclusion without user intervention.

So a deployment is different from an installation in the following critical aspects:

- Deployments are planned and based on standard recipes for supported system types.

- Deployments are server based and have the ability to scale in the way installations do not.
- Although deployments may still require an operator to initiate a single or group of installations, the process is highly automated.

With those characteristics in mind, let's further consider the types of deployments that are available for Vista, what we are calling "deployment scenarios." For server-based deployments of Vista, three basic types of deployment scenarios are available:

Bare metal, fresh, or new system deployment Most often a bare metal deployment has Vista installed onto a newly formatted boot partition. No previous data is retained.

System upgrades In a system upgrade Vista is installed *over* a system with an older operating system so that as much as possible the applications still operate, and files, the file system, and system settings are retained.

Side-by-side deployments A side-by-side deployment is a migration of applications and data from the older system to a system that has had Vista newly installed.

Figure 38.3 shows an overview of the three separate types of server-based deployments.

It's likely that for large deployments no one type of deployment will suffice. So it makes sense to test these system configuration definitions against your deployment servers in a lab environment prior to rolling them out.

FIGURE 38.3
There are three main server based deployment types for Windows Vista.

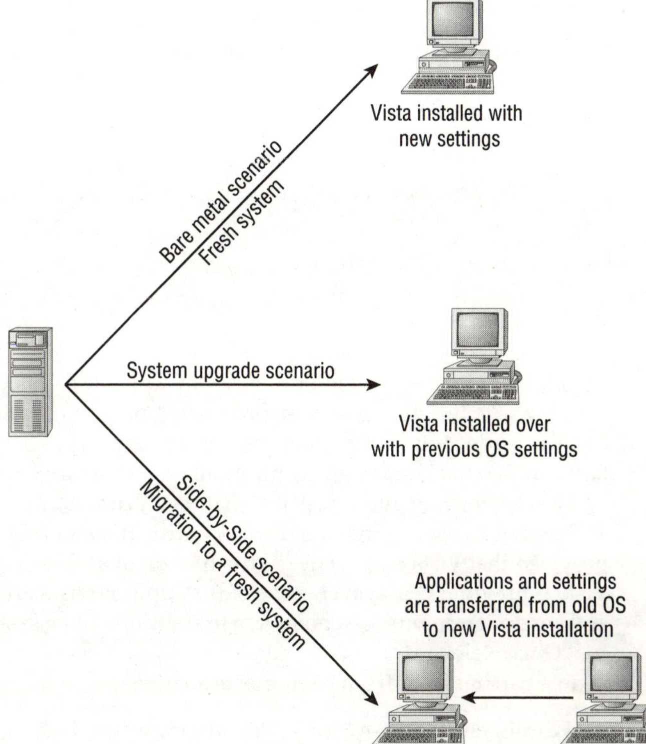

Bare Metal Scenario

In a bare metal or fresh computer scenario, the Vista installation completely overwrites all data on the system and creates a new configuration. A bare metal installation installs a Vista image onto a freshly partitioned and formatted hard drive. Everything that the user finds on their system after a bare metal installation is from the Vista installation, along with any additional settings or applications that were part of the installed image. This type of deployment is often referred to as a *wipe-and-load deployment*.

In a wipe-and-load deployment, you'll need to migrate user state data from their current system to the newly created Vista system, using the User State Migration Tool that you saw in the two previous chapters. When you wipe the system, that data is gone. One way to migrate user data is to capture the user data first and then save that data onto an intermediate data store. Once the new Vista system has been created, you would then restore the user state data. Figure 38.4 shows the steps involved in a wipe-and-load user state migration.

FIGURE 38.4
To migrate user state data in a wipe-and-load Vista deployment, you need to capture that data and store it on an intermediate system.

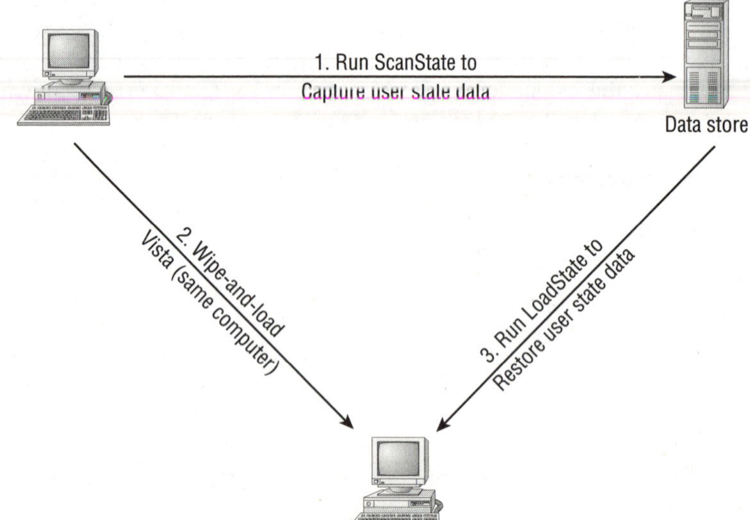

A bare metal scenario isn't the only way to create a system with Vista-only system settings. You can choose to install Vista over a preexisting operating system, but as a fresh installation and not as an upgrade. A new system or fresh system deployment therefore is similar to a bare metal installation in that the Vista image controls all system settings.

The user logging into a fresh installation will find that their old file system is intact, that they can find and navigate through the directory structure and find all of the files that were there before—provided that Vista doesn't overwrite files because they have the same name and location as files Vista is providing. However, none of the applications work, none of the old system settings exist, and an configuration file or pointer in the new operating system is derived from the newly installed Vista image alone.

In a bare metal or fresh computer scenario:

1. All system files are Vista files, all settings and configurations are Vista's alone.
2. The file system may or may not be new.

3. All installed and operating applications are ones that are part of the deployed Vista image. Any application files that are part of a retained file system are data files and no more. If an application file is an executable file (.EXE) file and is retained on disk, that file may still launch and operate provided it doesn't require any Registry data to run correctly. The application won't appear on any system menus, or be part of any Vista interface elements.
4. The Vista Registry is newly created and contains no entries derived from anywhere else.

System Upgrade Scenario

In a system upgrade scenario all user data, applications, and configuration settings are migrated from the old system to the new system. This type of deployment is equivalent to installing Vista *over* the previous operating system. In that sense, a system upgrade is a merging of Vista with all of the components of the old operating system that can be merged.

When an upgrade is completed what a user will find is that:

- Previous data files are still intact.
- Many, if not most of their previous applications will launch with a varying degree of compatibility. You can minimize the number of applications that are incompatible with Windows Vista by running the Application Compatibility Test utility (ACT) first, as you learned about in Chapter 3. For deployments, the ACT should be run on test systems in your laboratory or testing environment prior to roll out.
- Many, if not most, of their previous system settings will be retained in Vista.
- That an Upgrade to a system can take several times longer than a fresh install to complete. (For a fresh install on a system of 30 minutes, a system with a large number of applications on it may take as much as two hours to complete.)

The system upgrade scenario is the most widely used deployment scenario, and the reasons for this are not hard to discern. With current technologies computer hardware tends to have a longer duty cycle than software. During the lifetime of any deployed computer, chances are that the organization will replace the operating system on the computer at least once with a completely new version of the operating system, and perhaps even a couple of major service packs. Major application software often revises every 18–36 months, and therefore those packages will also often get replaced at least once in their lifetime.

NOTE It is highly recommended that systems should be backed up completely prior to a Vista upgrade. With all of the files backed up to other media, the chances of significant data loss are dramatically reduced.

Given all of these factors, there's one more consideration that makes a system upgrade preferable for operating system deployments over other deployment scenarios. That factor is one of timing. If the release of a new major version of Windows such as Vista doesn't coincide with the release of other major software packages, then chances are that the organization may not choose to start a deployment with a fresh system.

The advantages of the system upgrade scenario are obvious. A successful upgrade retains valuable system functionality and preserves large investments in infrastructure and intellectual capital that the organization has made. This is as true of the cost in software and hardware as it is with the investment made in staff training. With an upgrade scenario, you can continue to upgrade clients as you go along, as more compatible applications and device drivers get released. An upgrade scenario has the potential to disrupt an organization's operations less than the other types of Vista deployments will, but requires more care after the deployment to eliminate bugs and incompatibilities that remain from previous drivers and applications.

The disadvantage of the system upgrade is that it creates the largest number of issues that need to be resolved. System upgrades tend to be the most complex of the deployment scenarios. When you migrate applications and settings to a new Vista system (as described in the next section), you have the opportunity to migrate things a little at a time or to control what gets migrated. However, when you upgrade a system, all of the applications and settings that the upgrade allows are part of the new system and can interact in complex manners that can lead to hard-to-diagnose problems.

Side-by-Side Scenario

The side-by-side scenario is a combination of a new system installation followed by a managed migration from the older system. The new system is created on separate hardware, which allows the newly installed Vista installation to exist at the same time that the original system is being used. From a deployment viewpoint, this is a good scenario when you are testing new systems, or when a new upgrade isn't possible because the original system doesn't have the required compatibility.

A side-by-side migration is a little more complicated initially than installing Vista over a preexisting operating system because it forces the operator to perform an additional step or set of steps. However, since the administrator can control what gets migrated and when there are many advantages to the side-by-side scenario. As you may recall you can use the Windows Easy Transfer utility to migrate users' settings for a single computer or for a small number of computers. For a larger number of computers, you can migrate user data using the Windows User State Migration Tool (USMT) 3.0, which can be automated. USMT will migrate user accounts, desktop contents, application settings, favorites, cookies, user files, and other profile information. USMT is used both for side-by-side and for wipe-and-load scenarios.

In a side-by-side migration, the administrator has the task of migrating user state data from the old system to the newly deployed Vista system. The scenario is similar to the one you saw a couple of sections ago for user state migration in a wipe-and-load scenario. However, since there are two individual systems involved here—the old system with the previous version of the operating system and Vista installed on a new system, there is more flexibility involved in performing a user state migration. What this scenario offers is the ability to decouple the task of user state collection from Vista's installation. You collect user state data either before Vista is installed or at a later time of your own choosing prior to handing the new systems off to users. Consider the state transfer shown in Figure 38.5.

In Figure 38.5 you collect data from each of the old systems using ScanState and store that data in an intermediate data store. By storing state data in a single location, you can automate the restoration of state data at a later point. Once Vista, Office, and any other applications comprising the organization's standard environment are loaded onto new systems, the LoadState command migrates the user state data to their new systems. The old systems can then be turned into Vista systems using a wipe-and-load deployment.

Side-by-side migrations don't necessarily require two separate sets of systems. If users share a single system, as might be the case for a Windows Terminal Server or with a Citrix server, then the user state data for multiple users is stored on that server. In that instance, the ScanState process would collect the user state data as part of a batch process, and after the Vista systems are created use the LoadState command to put those users' state data on their new Vista systems. To use ScanState and LoadState for this type of migration, you could use Microsoft Management Server (SMS), a third-party deployment tool, a batch file, or a logon script.

FIGURE 38.5
To migrate user state data in a side-by-side Vista deployment, you can capture user data on an intermediate system at any time prior to handing the Vista systems off to users.

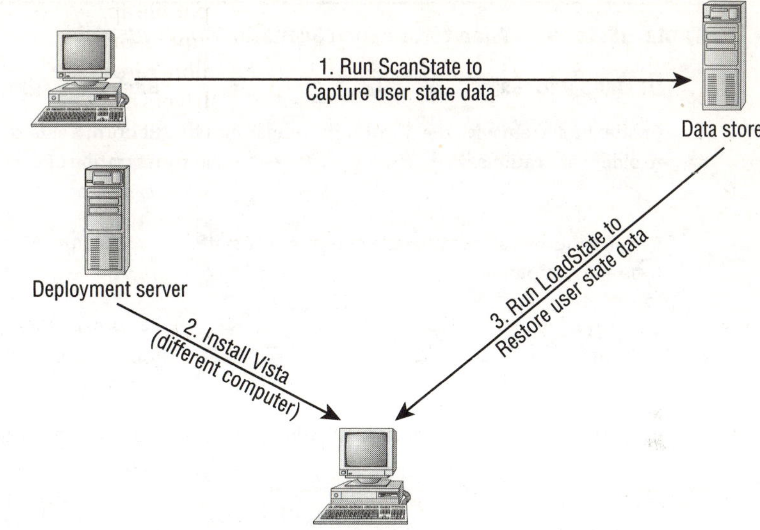

The advantage of a migration is that (depending on the quality of the migration software) it offers the possibility of selectively migrating the applications that are known to work with Vista, and that it allows the operator to preserve applications and data from a broader range of older Windows operating systems.

When to Use Each Scenario

Having considered the three different scenarios, let's briefly consider which ones are best to use in which circumstances. In large organizations, the IT staff doing the deployment is likely to find that they need to support all three types of deployments.

Table 38.1 summarizes the advantages of the different deployment scenarios.

TABLE 38.1: When to Use Each Scenario

DESIRED PROPERTY	BEST SCENARIO
Prepare new computer systems for use by a user	Bare metal or wipe-and-load scenario followed by user account migration.
Preserve user's environment with the least amount of work	System upgrade scenario.
Preserve user's environment to create the most stable Vista system	Side-by-side scenario followed by individual installation of certified applications and drivers.
Create the most stable Vista system	Bare metal scenario followed by individual installation of certified applications and drivers.
Recycle old systems while migrating to new systems	Use the side-by-side scenario; perform a migration of user accounts, applications, and settings. Then reformat old system and install an OS.

TABLE 38.1: When to Use Each Scenario *(CONTINUED)*

DESIRED PROPERTY	BEST SCENARIO
Create the system with the maximum compatibility to older applications.	Perform a side-by-side scenario followed by careful migration of compatible applications, settings, and user account.
Perform the lowest cost upgrade in terms of IT staff time and equipment.	Use the upgrade scenario.
Perform a deployment that allows you to migrate users from older legacy Windows OS (pre-Windows XP, etc.).	Perform a side-by-side scenario followed by careful migration of compatible applications, settings, and user account.
Create the best user experience for Windows Vista.	Start with new hardware and perform a fresh system or bare metal installation.
Extend the useful duty cycle of the organization's current set of computers.	Perform a side-by-side scenario followed by careful migration of compatible applications, settings, and user account.

Summary

In this chapter you saw an overview of the preinstallation phase of a Vista deployment. Microsoft makes available to system builders, OEMs, and enterprises, tools that help build the required system images that can be applied to the various systems onto which Vista will be deployed. The Windows Automated Installation Kit or Windows AIK is a set of tools that let you create a Windows PE build environment, image systems, and the answer files necessary to automate Windows deployments. Windows AIK is an integral part of the BDD solution, and contains Windows PE, ImageX, and Windows SIM. You can use three basic deployment scenarios: wipe-and-load, system upgrade, and side-by-side deployments.

Chapter 39 focuses on more pre-imaging tasks. You'll see how to create an imaging plan, two of the more commonly used deployment technologies: Lite Touch and Zero Touch deployments. Windows Vista also supports 64-bit installations, which offers some interesting advantages. In the next chapter you'll see how to address the concerns for creating stable and useful Vista 64-bit installations.

Chapter 39

Performing Pre-imaging Tasks

A successful Vista deployment hinges on careful planning and setup. In this chapter you will learn about some of the primary tools for validating images and for creating stable reference systems. Then, two of the methods for automated deployment, Lite Touch and Zero Touch installations, are introduced. Of the two the Lite Touch Installation is more flexible but requires more hands-on guidance during the installation process. Zero Touch Installations offer more automation, less administrative oversight once they are set up, and scale more easily. ZTI also involves the use of SMS and the Operating System Deployment Feature Pack.

In this chapter you'll learn about:

- Testing applications
- Saving settings with the User Setting Migration Tool (USMT)
- Working with Windows Automated Installation Kit User's Guide
- Using the guides to create an imaging plan
- Working with solution accelerators, Lite Touch Installation (LTI) and Zero Touch Installation (ZTI)
- Addressing 64-bit installation concerns

Vista: What's New?

The Business Desktop Deployment 2007 is a new version of Microsoft's solution framework. It includes several new tools, as well as updates of all of the previous versions of the tools that came with previous editions. Among the tools described here that have been significantly updated are ACT that comes with a new set of evaluators (agents) and enhanced capabilities, and improved user settings migration with USMT. Both the Lite Touch Installation (LTI) and the Zero Touch Installation (ZTI) once set up through the preinstallation part are now initiated by a wizard that will guide you through the setup process.

Testing Applications

Application compatibility testing is an essential part of any well-planned deployment. You can choose to test your company's applications beforehand in the lab; or you can accept that your clients will be testing deployed applications many times over. When clients test their applications for errors, the process is haphazard and very time consuming for all involved. It's guaranteed that the latter case will cost your organization many times the former case.

As you briefly saw in Chapter 36, the Business Desktop Deployment tool recommends that an Application Compatibility Feature Team be organized and that the team be tasked with the following four goals:

1. Create a database of applications that require testing.
2. Test each application for its compatibility, and if possible debug the application.
3. Resolve incompatibilities by identifying new versions, modifying source and recompiling the application if necessary.
4. Add compatible applications as part of your reference or master system build.
5. Collect the required installation packages and add them to the standard images so that they can be deployed by applications such as SMS Operating System Feature Pack.

The primary tool used by the Application Compatibility Feature Team is Microsoft's Application Compatibility Toolkit (ACT), which is described in the next section.

Microsoft Application Compatibility Toolkit 5.0

ACT 5.0 is the Vista-compatible version of this test application for Enterprise customers. (Version 4.1 was released to support Windows XP.) What ACT does:

1. *Collects information* from systems using automatic diagnostic agents on the client environment.
2. *Inventories the applications* on the tested computers and creates an ACT Application Database.
3. *Analyzes the information* to determine which applications or sets of applications may be a problem. The Application Compatibility Manager is the tool in ACT that is used to analyze the information that is captured in the database.
4. *Prioritizes your application portfolio* in each client environment. You can determine which applications will have the greatest impact on your clients when you roll out Vista (or another new operating system).
5. *Reports issues* in an Application Compatibility Report, which contains the recommendations of Microsoft, vendors, and the user community as part of the online Application Compatibility Exchange.
6. *Mitigates problems* by rolling out solutions packages during or after your migration. The Compatibility Administration tool lets you modify an application's installation routine in order to make that application more compatible with Vista.

Notice that although ACT will help you locate, prioritize, and identify compatibility issues that are known to exist, it does not do the actual testing nor will it find any new issues specific to your client environments. To do actual compatibility testing, you must set up and run the applications on your test systems. What ACT really does is to help you determine what issues to test for.

Although many people first learn about ACT during an OS deployment, the utility of this free solution framework means that it has great value as an operating system life cycle management tool. Indeed, Microsoft intends to make ACT their primary tool for compatibility assessment in the enterprise. The extensible architecture of ACT means that third-party vendors can supply their own agents to operate inside ACT in order to avoid future deployment problems related to their applications.

The applications that you deploy—be it a new version of Microsoft Office, an Oracle database, or Lotus Notes messaging and collaboration servers—don't go away once your deployment is completed. You will need to manage these applications in order to assess how they are impacted by future changes in your reference or master systems' client environment over time. You can and should therefore use ACT in any large organization going forward to analyze the impact of hot fixes, services packs, and other updates to your reference or master client environment prior to those incremental employments for all the same reasons that you test for application compatibility before deploying a brand-new operating system.

NOTE The home page for the Microsoft Application Compatibility Toolkit is found at `http://www.microsoft.com/technet/prodtechnol/windows/appcompatibility/default.mspx`. The ACT requires that you install a SQL Server database (either the full product or Microsoft SQL Server Express) as well as the current version of the .NET Framework. You can download these additional resources from this same URL.

ACT Architecture

ACT 5.0 is a very extensive application testing system that greatly automates the testing process well beyond what would be possible for any stand-alone tool. ACT is server-based, three-tiered framework application that installs a set of agents on master systems that are being tested. Agents are meant to be lightweight and nonintrusive, and the agent framework is extensible. With an agent technology, it is possible to modify the agent's actions (they are small programs themselves) and select when and against what criteria the agents run. Therefore, you might have an agent that runs only on a certain department's system, in a certain domain, and so forth.

Agents can be distributed using self-installed EXE files, through Microsoft SMS, or using Tivoli, Alteris, LANWorks, and other third-party tools. You can also use Group Policy for members of an Active Directory and logon scripts when a user logs onto a domain to install an agent. Microsoft SMS can also perform application inventories and can be used to deploy agents to clients, provided that the client is inventoried in SMS.

NOTE If you want to review the group policy method for installation software deployment, review the article, "Best Practices for Group Policy Software Installation" at `http://technet2.microsoft.com/WindowsServer/en/library/5f065962-a6e3-422a-8db7-20a57f40f9f51033.mspx?mfr=true`. For more information about deploying inventory agents using a logon script, refer to the articles "Logon Scripts How To. . ." at `http://www.microsoft.com/technet/prodtechnol/windowsserver2003/library/ServerHelp/84b5457b-1641-4707-a1f4-887b5f9471dd.mspx` and "How to Automate Logon Processes Using Scripts" at `http://www.microsoft.com/technet/archive/ittasks/tasks/logscrpt.mspx`.

Multiple client systems can be tested at the same time, and the information that ACT collects using its Log Processing Service running on your technician system from the deployed agents on client environments is entered into an enterprise database where it can be analyzed further.

ACT saves its data to a SQL Server database, or if SQL Server isn't available, you may want to use Microsoft SQL Server Express (see `http://www.microsoft.com/sql/editions/express/default.mspx`). SQL Server Express and its management console are distributed freely by Microsoft. The other requirement for ACT 5.0 is that Microsoft .NET version 1.1 or later be installed on the server that is running the software.

In the version 5.0 release of ACT the development team has attempted to address the key problems with application compatibility testing environments in the past. Microsoft's goal is to release upgrades more regularly, integrate testing across multiple product lines, and provide for a positive feedback loop that incorporates the experience of a larger number of current users of any particular application. Application Compatibility Manager (ACM) can synchronize to the web service to get up-to-date information about the applications in your environment.

The use of an enterprise SQL Server database means that the log size can be as large as you need it to be and that you can monitor large numbers of systems even after deployment is completed. Log sizes vary depending on applications. For example, an inventory log file typically runs about 400KB (compressed) to monitor around 100 applications.

With data stored in the SQL Server database, information can be retrieved by the Application Compatibility Manager. ACM is a distributed client/server application that displays a console for managing ACT. Users can log into the application, request reports, and generate their own process or workflows. You can use ACM to have the Log Processing Service run separately against different groups or locations in the organization, as well as perform many other setup tasks.

With ACM you compare data in the database with the Compatibility Exchange on a Microsoft web server. (The Compatibility Exchange is the successor to the Microsoft Application Information Exchange Web Service that was used in ACT 4.1.) The matching system uses a DLL to compares a list of application known problems with a set of instructions to remedy the problem when the user either tries to install or run an application. The matching mechanism is part of not only Vista, but Windows Server 2003 and Windows XP as well.

This system maintains database files stored in the \%SYSTEMROOT%\APPPATCH directory; where you will find:

Migration databases During an OS system upgrade Microsoft writes migration databases to the system.

Prepackaged databases When you install an application, it can install a database of known issues and suggested solutions. Among the solutions are an application compatibility fix where a code segment can replace code in the running application. A second solution runs the application in a compatibility box. Finally, if neither approach works, the database might display an application help message to identify the problem when the user tries to run the application.

Custom databases Administrators can create custom databases, which are similar to prepackaged databases. Usually custom databases are created for applications that didn't include a prepackaged database and, although they should be stored in the AppPatch directory, they can be stored anywhere.

NOTE Both prepackaged and custom databases have an SBD file extension. Migration databases have an INF file extension.

Figure 39.1 shows the topology of ACT 5.0. ACM queries the Microsoft Compatibility Exchange database to pull down the latest information, user questions and answers, FAQs, and other resources for the particular applications of interest. The Compatibility Exchange works just like the feedback mechanism on eBay. People can enter their experiences with applications into the database, issues and solutions, as well as their general acceptance of the technology.

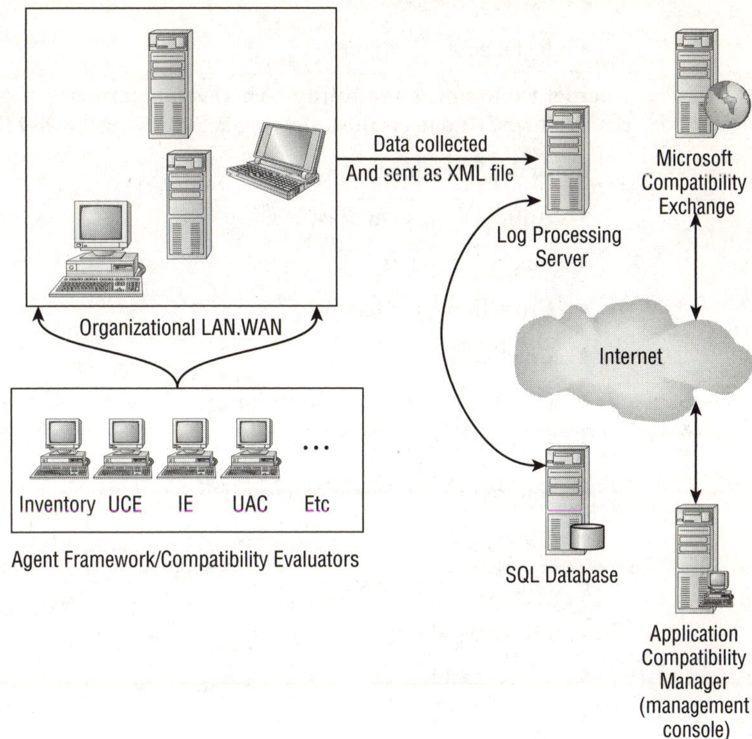

FIGURE 39.1
ACT 5.0 is a three-tiered application compatibility testing framework.

COMPATIBILITY EVALUATORS OR AGENTS

At the time Vista was released to enterprise clients in December 2006 four agent technologies were part of the initial release of ACT:

Inventory Collector This agent runs on Windows Vista, XP, and 2000 and looks at applications it finds in the Program Files folder, ones listed in the Add/Remove Programs control panel, the MSI database, referenced shortcuts in the Start Menu, the App Path environmental variable, and references to registrations in the file extension handlers database (the application used to open a specific file type). From these sources, the Inventory Collector creates a listing for the computer tested.

Among the important inventory items that the Inventory Collector collects are:

- OS version, including the service pack level
- System model and type
- Domain and organizational unit

- Geographic location
- Installed applications

Internet Explorer Compatibility This evaluator runs on XP SP2 as well as Vista running Internet Explorer 7. It detects the following activities for IE6 and IE7:

- ActiveX blocking
- Antiphishing activities
- Binary behaviors
- Cross-frame navigation
- CSS fixes
- CURL (Centralized URL Parsing)
- Download blocking
- International Domain Names (IDN) support
- LMZL
- Managing add-ons
- MIME handling
- Object caching
- Popup blocking
- SSL
- Windows restrictions
- XDOM barrier (XDOM is an open source XML parser)
- Zone elevation

And for Internet Explorer 7 only it detects the list above plus attempts at protected-mode access and UIPI activities. The log created by the IECE is based on the websites you visit and the activities you perform while you are on those websites.

User Account Control Compatibility This evaluator runs on Windows XP (all versions). It monitors which applications work under standard user run levels and which applications need to be elevated to admin mode. It determines which applications are trying to modify files and Registry settings that are in protected locations. In Vista, the operating system will automatically redirect the application if a higher security level (run level) is required to request it from the user, such as admin mode.

The Update Compatibility (Security) This agent captures all application activities relating to files and the Registry that are affected by the Windows Update service. Since there can be quite a few calls to these APIs, the Update evaluator can create very large log files. The settings in the Update agent lets you control when or if an update is installed.

The ACM matches the Update Manifest against the Update (file/Registry) data files to determine what application *could be* affected by a Windows update modification. ACM then creates a report that administrators can then use to test the application prior to deploying the Windows update.

Microsoft emphasizes the words *could be* in the sense that you will only know for sure if you test the application yourself. The Update Manifest contains situations that Microsoft knows about through its own testing and the input of users. However, your client environment might be considerably different and the fact that the ACM flags an application doesn't always mean that a problem exists for you.

The net result of running these agents is that you have collected data that can be organized by client system, business unit, software version, or nearly any form that you can query by SQL. What ACT 5.0 adds is a much more graphical reporting agent that is both easier and more powerful than previous versions.

Common Deployment Compatibility Problems

Administrators should check the Hardware Capability List (HCL) for Vista prior to creating a reference or master system onto which Vista is deployed. You'll find the Vista HCL at `http://technet2.microsoft.com/WindowsVista/en/library/ed1e3b7d-5ea7-4ad3-be3f-af29f7b48dde1033.mspx?mfr=true`.

The Vista HCL (like all of Microsoft's HCL) is somewhat deceptive. It lists hardware and associated drivers that have been submitted to Microsoft for the certification. So you should assume that any item on the list is more likely to be compatible than not. However, many items you can purchase are equally good and often better than items on the HCL but whose vendors didn't pursue the listing due to cost or time constraints. Also, not every compatibility issue can be tested.

Additional subtleties crop up with the selection of one type of component over another. For example, you'll often find unbuffered DDR memory on list of compatible memory. While unbuffered memory will work well, ECC or error-checking memory often works better—at a nominally higher cost. Therefore, you should take a very conservative approach to testing Vista on reference hardware and make sure that you are entirely satisfied with Vista's installation before testing for additional application compatibility issues.

Applications written for previous versions of the Windows operating system fail in a deployment of Vista for many reasons. Some of the more commonly encountered reasons are:

- Issues with Setup and Installation such as inappropriate access or settings. An application that is installed under a user account can write to the Registry subkey HKEY_CURRENT_USER, except \Software\Policies and \Software\Microsoft\Windows\CurrentVersion\Policies, to the current user profile directory, the Shared Documents folder, or any new directory (folder) at the top-level or root of the system hard drive. When an application tries to write elsewhere during an installation on Vista, it can fail.
- New operating system features and API changes. One Vista change is that the Windows Messaging System (WMS) has been removed. Any application that relied on that service will fail.

  Another change is to the Microsoft Component Object Model (COM) or its distributed network version DCOM. Vista modifies COM and DCOM to allow an administrator to override weak security settings by setting a general authorization policy that requires that an application get authorized for any launch, activation, or any particular type of call. That authorization can interfere with an application's automation behavior, and prevent the application from operating correctly.
- New security features

- Windows resource protection of Vista, including system files and protected Registry locations. An example of this type of protection is what is called in Vista Windows Resource Protection, and was called in Windows XP Windows File Protection. This system routine protects shared system files from being replaced by applications. When WRP detects that a protected system file like a DLL has been altered, it restores the approved version of that file essentially overwriting the changes.
- Code fails to return the correct operating system type
- User account control limits user permissions
- Restricted Internet Explorer rights. Windows Vista comes with Internet Explorer 7 (which can be installed on Windows XP), and that version tightens up many security settings.

  In the Internet zone when IE 7 is connected to a website online, Vista runs in protected mode at a level now referred to as "Medium-high." That is, applications won't have access to administrator settings. When connect to a Trusted Site zone such as an intranet, the level is Medium by default. However, another change in IE 7 limits access to a system on home networks by other peers on that network.

  ActiveX controls are also more limited; through a feature called ActiveX Opt-in requires that the user approve ActiveX controls before they run.

  Firewall and antivirus software reliance on kernel access and new APIs. Kernel mode drivers are a particular problem for applications migrating to Windows Vista. Applications that sit been the Windows kernel and file I/O are called file filters. Examples of file filters are firewalls and antivirus programs. At least through Vista Service Pack 1 Microsoft's decision to lock down the kernel will substantially limit older programs access and functionality. Any application that relies on redirection should be carefully tested.

  You may wish to refer to The Cable Guy's January 2006 article describing firewall changes for Vista and Longhorn found at: `http://www.microsoft.com/technet/community/columns/cableguy/cg0106.mspx`.
- Certified 64-bit Windows Vista driver requirement. Only certified drivers will work with the 64-bit OS, so device compatibility and any application that relies on a device may be limited or not functional.

Saving Settings with the User Setting Migration Tool (USMT)

When you deploy Vista, you need to retain user state settings in order to preserve the many hours of work that users spent customizing their system. Unhappy clients equal unsuccessful deployments, particularly when some of those users write the checks that makes the deployment possible. If you do a clean install (or wipe-and-load) or a side-by-side deployment, then you will need to capture user settings and move those settings over to the new system. For an in-place upgrade where Vista installs over a previous version of the operating system, the user settings are retained and migrated for you.

The primary tool used to migrate user settings in the Business Desktop Deployment framework is the Windows User Settings Migration Tool (USMT). Version 3.0 has been released to support migrations onto Vista. USMT is a command-line tool that is scriptable, can run in batch mode, and offers a number of useful options for deployment. For example, USMT can migrate all or some of the profiles it finds on a system. If the option is set to ignore profiles that have not been logged onto recently, then any profile that doesn't meet that requirement is ignored.

NOTE For user-based settings, migration of individual systems (not a deployment) users can use the PC Migration Assistant, which provides a GUI to aid in the migration process. The PC Migration Assistant allows a user to migrate their own user profile and cannot be automated. A system with multiple profiles would require multiple runs of this assistant. The Migration Assistant can map the profiles to new user accounts in a domain.

USMT 3.0 has added a number of new features that are meant to support Vista, as well as improve an administrator's control over migrated settings. Among the more prominent changes are the use of XML format scripts that can run ScanState and LoadState, the ability to migrate EFS encrypted files (in some instances), a number of new command options, and the migration of operating system settings. USMT 3.0 analyzes the Vista component manifest files on the target system to determine which settings captured by ScanState will actually get migrated—the remainder are ignored. To learn more about the new features that were included with USMT 3.0, take a look at `http://technet2.microsoft.com/WindowsVista/en/library/91f62fc4-621f-4537-b311-1307df0105611033.mspx?mfr=true`.

When migrating to Vista, you can control USMT using XML files, each of which has a different purpose:

`MigApp.XML` Specifies which applications are migrated, and therefore which settings should be migrated.

`MigUser.XML` Determines which directories, files, file types, and desktop settings get migrated and, not as you might think, which user is migrated. The user is specified as part of the ScanState command and not its XML file.

`Config.XML` Created by ScanState `/genconfig`, it creates a custom configuration file that you can create from a reference or master system to control which application settings are migrated. If ScanState doesn't find this XML file when it starts processing, it will migrate all of the default components that are part of Vista.

The `Config.XML` file is the easiest way to create a custom migration. If you open this file in a text editor (e.g., Notepad), what you see is that each component is listed in a section and has a very simple tag for determining migration actions, that is, MIGRATE = YES or NO. If you examine that file, you can quickly tell whether the migration is performing the actions you expect.

A special XML file `MigSys.XML` is created when you want to migrate user settings to Widows XP.

What Gets Migrated

In addition to migrating all appropriate user profiles, you'll need to migrate the All Users profile, as it contains a set of universal settings. The Windows profiles in Windows XP and Windows 2000 are stored as a folder in the Documents and Settings folder, as shown in Figure 39.2.

USMT and the PC Migration Assistant will only migrate settings from source systems running Vista, Windows XP (both versions), and Windows 2000. USMT 3.0 can migrate the settings to target systems running Vista and Windows XP. The PC Migration Assistant can only migrate settings to a target Vista system.

In theory any modern application will store its settings into the profile folder, but in practice you'll find a few that don't. Most of the applications that bypass the profile folders are typically older legacy applications that have been upgraded partially, but enough to run under these later versions of Windows. A migration is a good time to prune away older applications that might be problematic, remove profiles that are no longer needed or are duplicated, and reduce the amount of settings and data that aren't needed.

Active Directory can store roaming profiles, and you can use those profiles as your source of user settings provided that both the source and target of the user profiles are Vista systems. You might also consider that you could use a Group Policy to provide folder redirection of a profile to a network share and use that redirected data as the source of a migration to Vista, but that method will not include items such as Favorites or Templates and will be incomplete. That's why it's important to use a tool like USMT. By default USMT 3.0 will migrate:

- Personal data files and directories:

  My Documents folder

  My Music folder

  My Pictures folder

  My Received files

  My Videos folder

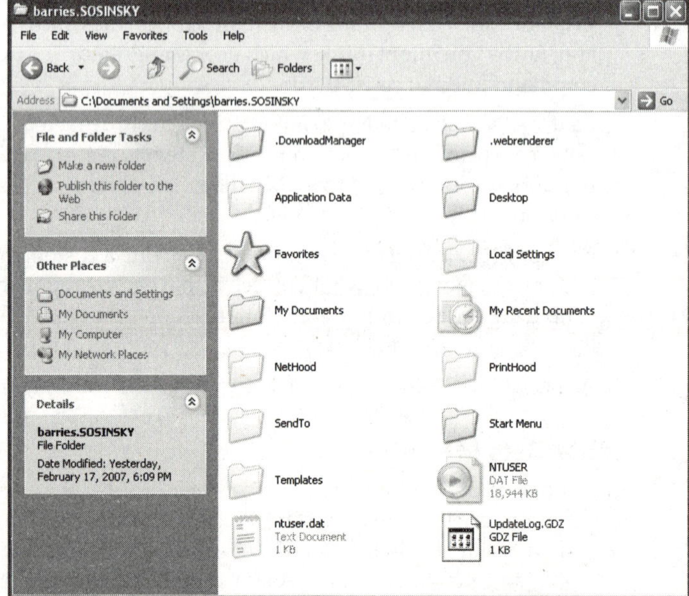

FIGURE 39.2
A typical user profile from Windows XP.

- Personal user settings such as:

  Accessibility options

  Dial-up connections

  Desktop settings, and classic Desktop settings

  Folder options

  Fonts

  Mouse and keyboard settings

  Phone and modem options

  Quick Launch settings

  Regional options

  Sound settings

  Taskbar settings

- Applications and application settings:

  Command prompt settings

  MSIE settings, cookies, favorites, home page, and more

  MS Outlook store

What USMT doesn't migrate includes:

- Applications
- DLL or EXE files
- Encrypting File System (EFS) certificates (in some cases)
- Drivers
- Hardware settings
- Synchronization files

Although this is the default list, USMT takes as its input an XML file that specifies what gets migrated, and therefore it is possible to customize USMT to account for different scenarios.

You'll find that profiles for mobile users are typically larger than desktop users. The size of a profile is often dictated by the way large data stores are handled. In particular if your organization stores email not only in a server store but on client systems as well, then a user's profile can be quite large. It's a good idea to test for the average size of the profile that will be migrated. You can do this by using the USMT ScanState `/p` option, which creates a space estimate file (`USMTSIZE.TXT`).

The USMT ScanState command is used to collect user state data and store it in the location of your choice. Usually the intermediate data store is a network share that will be available to deployment staff. When the target Vista system has been prepared and all applications and packages are installed, then user state data is restored to the target system using the USMT LoadState command. The previous chapter went into some detail on deployment scenarios and illustrated the different types.

You might be surprised to note that USMT doesn't attempt to migrate applications, because some third-party migration tools do perform application migrations. They attempt to match applications that are allowed to be migrated against a database that the vendor maintains. However, Microsoft doesn't support migration of its Office suite and recommends that you do a fresh installation of applications on new systems. There is a strong argument to be made for this point of view, but it isn't the only approach.

Therefore, when using USMT, it is best to install all applications on the target system prior to migrating user settings. Many applications will not function correctly if they haven't been installed first, and then have the migrated settings applied to them later.

The Migration Process

A new operating system deployment is a good time to get rid of old applications and data that serve no purpose on your systems going forward. While you certainly can migrate all settings, if the settings no longer apply because the applications aren't installed on the target, it's best to delete them. Doing so makes the target system faster and leaner. Eliminating user profiles entirely can save gigabytes of storage space.

Since each working desktop is usually backed up in multiple locations, then each gigabyte saved actually eliminates many more gigabytes and improves backup windows, network performance, and many other factors.

In a careful migration of user settings, you'll want to work with the actual users of the systems to determine their needs. The inventory agent in ACT collected a list of systems and applications, and that inventory is a good place to start the process.

The migration process includes the following steps:

1. Use application inventory to migrate, eliminate, or upgrade applications during your deployment.

   Verify which applications are required, which applications need to be updated, and which applications are no longer needed. Applications that are required are migrated; applications that must be updated are tested in the lab as to their suitability and the affect that user setting migration has on them; and finally applications that are no longer needed should not be installed on the target Vista systems and their settings, data files, and folders deleted.

   Be careful when deleting data files for an out-of-date application as users may need the data from that application and may use a new application to work with them. Always check with the system owner and with subject matter experts to validate your decision to migrate, eliminate, or upgrade.

2. Create a transfer script.
3. Use USMT ScanState to capture user settings and store them to a data store. ScanState copies data to the interim store in a compressed format. It does so to lower both the size of the data stored as well as the network bandwidth required. Although ScanState has a switch that will copy data in an uncompressed form, there's little reason to do so.

4. Install the application onto the target Vista system. The application can be installed on Vista as part of a system image, or installed separately after the Vista image has been deployed.
5. Run USMT LoadState to restore the user settings to your target Vista system.
6. Test the data restore to see if the application works correctly and the process can be validated. A thorough test of an application's migration requires the analysis of a subject matter expert to run the application under a variety of scenarios to see that all of its important functions operate correctly.
7. Once tested, the User Settings Migration for this application can be included in the deployment process.

The Windows Automated Installation Kit User's Guide

The Windows Automated Installation Kit is the primary tool that the BDD framework uses. Therefore, one of the primary sources of guidance for Vista deployment is the Windows Automated Installation Kit User's Guide. When you install the WAIK, the User's Guide is installed as a Windows Help file in the Documentation folder, as shown in Figure 39.3. What makes the User's Guide so useful is that it contains set of recipes for the steps described in the BDD's white papers.

The guide is meant to provide the methodology needed to create a consistent deployment that is scalable, fully functional on completion, customizable by OEMs for branding, and conforms to Microsoft's licensing requirements. As such, the guide is organized into sections that start with general planning and move logically through the five phases of deployment.

The five phases covered by the User's Guide are:

1. Preinstallation Planning
2. Preinstallation Preparation
3. Preinstallation Customization
4. Image Deployment
5. Image Maintenance

Additionally, there is a reference section that describes the tools included in the Windows AIK, specifically ImageX, Sysprep, Windows SIM the Windows PE, and others. Figure 39.4 shows the table of contents of the Windows AIK User's Guide expanded to show some of the important sections.

It's highly recommended that anyone doing a large deployment of Vista read the Windows AIK User's Guide prior to performing the deployment. It's particularly valuable in the planning process, as described in the next section, but in addition to theory and overviews, you will find a number of walkthroughs that provide a step-by-step procedure of the tasks described elsewhere.

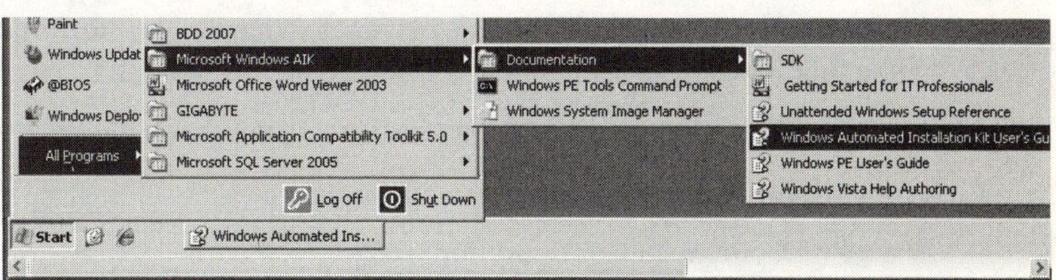

FIGURE 39.3
The Windows AIK User's Guide is installed as a Windows Help file documentation set.

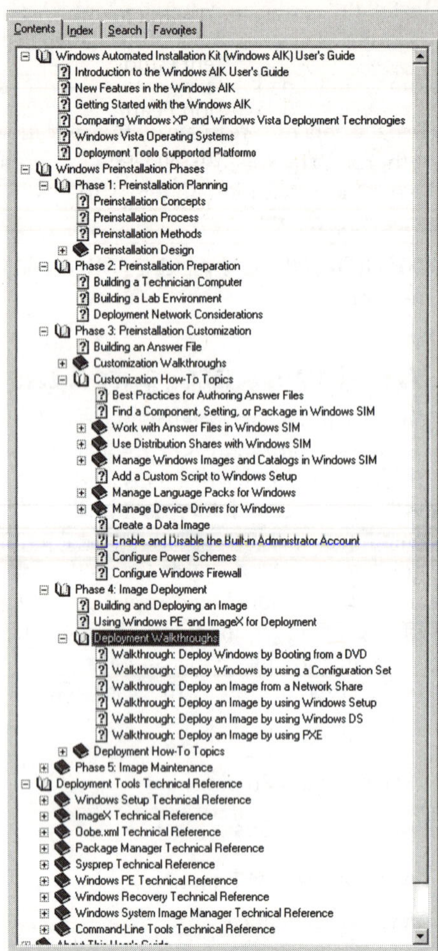

FIGURE 39.4
The Table of Contents of the Windows AIK.

Using the Guides to Create an Imaging Plan

The BDD 2007 comes with a set of guides for several of the key teams, as well as a set of solution guides. These guides contain information that will help you formulate an imaging plan, which should be based on the resources you have available as well as the number of systems you want to deploy. Other factor in the imaging plan is the number of images that you have to manage as part of the deployment.

The current set of guides you will want to consult while formulating an imaging plan in BDD are the following:

- Computer Imaging System Feature Team Guide
- Configuration Reference
- Deployment Configuration Guide
- Deployment Configuration Samples Guide

- Deployment Feature Team Guide
- Lite Touch Deployment Guide
- User Settings Migration Feature Team Guide
- Windows Deployment Services Update, Step-by-Step Guide
- Zero Touch Deployment Guide

Working with Solution Accelerators

BBD 2007 is a framework of best practices, providing of tools and guidance for using those tools. As part of the BDD, Microsoft includes a set of what they call "solution accelerators." A solution accelerator contains the instructions necessary to use some of the tools to structure different types of deployments. The two most important solutions accelerators are the Lite Touch Installation (LTI) deployment, and the Zero Touch Installation (ZTI) deployment solution accelerators, which are described in the next two sections.

A solution accelerator includes the following components:

- Instructions on how to create a specific type of deployment
- The software necessary to implement the plan
- The requirements of a testing facility and the methodology to test applications to certify them as compatible for that solution
- How to customize applications and package them as part of a deployable image
- The means to use to harden deployed desktops so that they are secure
- Applying the software and hardware inventory to a deployment plan based on the solution accelerator
- Managing the deployment according to the solution accelerator that you chose

Previous versions of the BDD (2.0 and 2.5) came in Standard and Enterprise editions. The Standard Edition focused on Lite Touch deployments and was meant to operate in situations where the impact of deployment on your network and management infrastructure must be minimized. The Enterprise Edition of BDD explained how to do Zero Touch deployments and included instructions on working with SMS 2003 and the Operating System Deployment Feature Pack (an add-on to SMS).

BDD 2007, which is the version that supports Vista deployments, only comes as a single edition in which you will find both sets of solution frameworks. In BDD 2007, the tools for both deployment types have been merged and it is now up to you to decide which of these two methodologies (LTI or ZTI) is best for your organization. LTI and ZTI now share a common set of scripts in BDD 2007.

Lite Touch Installation (LTI)

A Lite Touch Installation is so-called because deployment of Vista is set up so that administrators must initiate the installation and specify which systems will have Vista on them. It is different from a Zero Touch Installation in that ZTI creates a system where Vista is installed automatically by policy. The administrator controls an LTI and therefore can determine when and where installation occurs. For ZTI, a person logs onto their system and is informed that their system can be upgraded and asked if they want to do so now.

NOTE To learn more about LTI, see the Lite Touch Installation Guide that is distributed with the Business Desktop Deployment solution.

The preinstallation steps of a Lite Touch Installation is performed as follows:

1. The infrastructure required for LTI is put in place.
   - Install the BDD solution accelerator.
   - Deploy the Windows DS in a Windows domain, and configure it to allow Windows PE to boot by PXE over the network. You'll need to have a functioning DNS, DHCP, WINS, and remote access services available.
   - Verify that a network share exists with the required available space. Microsoft recommends that you allow from 500MB to 4GB for each unique image that you create when you allow for required disk storage. You may also wish to run USMT's ScanState `/p` command to determine average profile sizes as part of your disk space calculation. You also need to accommodate the deployment logs in your space calculations; those logs should be located on a network server that is connected to the target computer over fast network connection.
   - Verify that you have the appropriate privileges to access the appropriate resources and services.
2. Create the required images.
   - Inventory the systems and hardware to be migrated using ACT's Inventory evaluation, SMS, or some other third-party application. One purpose of the inventory is to determine that you have the required Vista hardware. Check that the software in the inventory is appropriate to installing Vista.
   - Use USMT 3.0 to store user profiles to a network share. For a Refresh computer scenario, store the profile on the local system to greatly reduce your network requirements and speed up the deployment.
3. Create master systems with required applications (such as Office 2003 or 2007) installed and tested for compatibility using BDD Workbench, BDD scripts and so on. You may wish to use a management application such as Microsoft Operations Monitor (MOM) 2005 and the Solution Accelerator for BDD Management Pack to track the deployment.
4. Add any additional packages such as drivers that are required to your master systems.
5. Run Sysprep to prepare systems for deployment.
6. Use Windows PE to image your reference or master systems,
7. Store the images to a deployment point (network share) or on media such as DVDs or USB flash cards. Keep in mind that if your BDD operations traverse a firewall that you'll need to make sure that the appropriate ports are open. See the article "Ports that Systems Management Server 2003 uses to communicate through a firewall or through a proxy server" at `http://support.microsoft.com/default.aspx?scid=kb%3Ben-us%3B826852`.

8. Set up Windows DS to boot systems from your Windows PE environment making sure that there is a fast network connection from the deployment point to target computers. Alternatively, prepare a Windows PE CD to boot the installation environment on the target system should Windows DS not be available.

Windows DS must operate in either the mixed or native mode, and will not work correctly for an LTI in legacy mode. Windows DS supports all three typical Vista deployments: New or Fresh Computer (and Wipe-and-Load), Upgrade Computer, and Replace Computer (Side-by-Side). Windows DS can have install (WIM, RIPREP, or RISETUP), boot (Setup and Capture), and Discover images installed on it. For LTI, you'll want a WIM image installed.

The BDD scripts that run the installation of Vista require that you have correctly verified the hardware and software configuration of the target system. For example, you want to make sure that you are installing a 32-bit Vista image on a 32-bit system and a 64-bit Vista image on a 64-bit image. Since a deployment may perform a format and partition, you'll need to make sure that the required disk space exists or deployment may fail.

With the initial setup steps for LTI completed, the Deployment Team then may prestage target computers in the Active Directory by creating the computer accounts for them. It isn't absolutely necessary to prestage target systems, Windows DS can deploy "unknown computers," but a prestaged deployment is easier. At this point in LTI, the Windows DS Windows Deployment Wizard is run to specify the type of deployment scenario desired: New or Fresh Computer, Upgrade Computer, or Replace Computer; and that the folders used by the Windows Deployment Wizard aren't populated with a previous deployment.

To setup a Lite Touch Installation using the LTI Wizard, follow the steps below:

1. Start the LTI Wizard by either running the CSCRIPT LITETOUCH.VBS script in Windows DS; or by navigating to the deployment point (\\servername\Distribution$\Scripts) and running the same script from within a command prompt.

2. Supply the username, domain, and password for the user of the target computer.

3. Specify the deployment point to be used by LTI.

4. Specify the migration type in the LTI Wizard.

   Refresh saves user state data, does the deployment, and then restores the user state data all on the same computer.

   Upgrade leaves user state data intact.

   Replace saves the user state data from that user's current system, stores it, deploys Vista on the new computer, and then restores the user state data to the new computer.

5. The wizard then asks you to name the computer, and specify a domain, where to store user state data, whether or not to restore user state data, and whether and where to back up the system prior to deployment.

6. On the Select an operating system to install page, you will need to specify which image and then enter the product key. If you use the Key Management Service, you can assign multiple keys, or if you have a Multiple Activation Key, you can enter MAK into the key.

7. Specify a language pack (if needed), the locale, and any applications to install based on the packages that are in the image you indicated previously.
8. Supply the Administrators password, and then indicate whether LTI must capture an image from a reference computer (in which case LTI runs Sysprep and then stores the location).
9. Enter your credentials in the Specify credentials for connecting to network shares page (username, domain, and password).
10. After reviewing the information that has been previously entered on the Ready page click the Begin button the LTI deployment starts and runs to completion.

Zero Touch Installation (ZTI)

Many of the steps performed in an LTI above are repeated when setting up a ZTI deployment although the details can be quite different. ZTI automates a deployment by creating the infrastructure necessary to perform unattended installations using a set of processing rules. Although both LTI and ZTI both use the Windows DS to start Windows PE and initiate deployments, ZTI runs a set of scripts that are coupled to a set of ZTI configuration files. SMS OSD Feature Pack is part of a ZTI. What SMS does is to manage the process of creation and delivery of Vista images for the multiple computers that are specified.

NOTE To learn more about LTI, see the Zero Touch Installation Guide that is distributed with the BDD solution.

A Zero Touch Installation has the following preinstallation requirements:

1. The required infrastructure for ZTI (Windows DS, Active Directory, and SMS) exists.
2. Set up a configuration settings database for use with SMS and create the ZTI processing rules. The processing rules match the images to be deployed with the configuration settings to be used, just as you would an `Unattend.XML` answer file. The net result of the configuration work is to create a `Customsetting.ini` file.
3. Install BDD and the Windows DS server. Ensure that ZTI can access network shares and other resources using the administrator accounts you supply. Use the BDD Deployment Point Wizard if needed to create the needed deployment points. BDD creates a default distribution point (the Distribution$ share) that will be used as a deployment point if you don't specify otherwise.
4. SMS OSD Feature Pack is configured so that it performs validation, state capture, pre- and postinstallation, and state restore phases of deployment. ZTI provides the means to configure each of these part of the SMS deployment.
5. Create a ZTI OS image and burn it to an image CD.
6. Create the required Windows PE disks, and the images required for deployment by Windows DS.

   Windows DS must run in the legacy or mixed modes in a ZTI deployment. (In LTI you can run Windows DS in mixed or native modes.) During a ZTI deployment, you need to disable the creation of computer accounts in the Active Directory by Windows PE, as well as PE logging.

When you run a ZTI, you can use the Windows DS to automate the process for a single image deployment by using the Windows DS Client Installation Wizard. The Choice Options dialog box in the Tools menu of the Client Installation Wizard allows you to modify the `Tools.osc`, the `Login.osc`, `Welcome.osc`, `Install.osc`, and the `Oschoices.osc` files to enable this automation. Refer to the ZTI User's Guide for specific details on how to modify these files.

During a ZTI deployment, the SMS client must access network shares, and so the SMS advanced client network access account must be configured in the SMS Administrator Console to present the correct access credentials (username and password) to allow this to happen. ZTI scripts also need access to the SMS 2003 Advanced Client Network Access Account, and may need to connect to database servers such as SQL Server, SQL Server Express, or even a database maintained by Exchange Server 2003 using a Connect to UNC authentication.

With all the settings specified, a ZTI deployment is initiated using the Windows Deployment Wizard that you can find in the SMS Administrator Console in the OSD Feature Pack.

An outline of the ZTI deployment follows:

1. Determine that the folders `boot:\MININT` and `boot:\_SMSTaskSequence` don't exist as they store the information from a previous deployment. If these folders are detected by the Windows Deployment Wizard, the deployment will fail when it tries to write them.
2. Open the SMS Administrative Console.
3. Select the Vista image to deploy, the distribution points, the applications to list, and the target systems to deploy.
4. Initiate the ZTI deployment.

Just to bring the discussion of LTI and ZTI to completion, Table 39.1 summarizes the differences between LTI and ZTI at a glance.

TABLE 39.1: LTI vs. ZTI Deployments

CHARACTERISTIC	LTI	ZTI
Best Used By	Small deployments of 25 clients or more and with low network bandwidth available.	Deployments where SMS 2003 is used
Deployment Method	New computer, Upgrade computer, Refresh computer, and Replace computer scenarios with network deployment. Or a stand-alone installation installed using a DVD driver or USB flash media-based image installation.	New Computer, Refresh Computer, and Replace Computer scenarios implemented within Microsoft SMS 2003
Server Requirements	Windows 2003 Server in a domain with Active Directory, network share, and network.	SMS 2003, Windows Server 2003, domain and Active Directory, and Windows Deployment Services (Windows DS installed)
Microsoft Tools Required	Microsoft .NET Framework 2.0	Microsoft .NET Framework 2.0

TABLE 39.1: LTI vs. ZTI Deployments *(CONTINUED)*

CHARACTERISTIC	LTI	ZTI
	Microsoft Application Compatibility Toolkit 5.0 (part of BDD)	Microsoft Application Compatibility Toolkit 5.0 (part of BDD)
	Microsoft Core XML Services (MSXML) 6.0	Microsoft Core XML Services (MSXML) 6.0
	Microsoft Management Console 3.0	Microsoft Management Console 3.0
	User Settings Migration Toolkit 3.0	SMS 2003 SP 2
	Windows Automated Installation Kit	SMS 2003 Operating System Deployment Feature Pack
		User Settings Migration Toolkit 3.0
		Windows Automated Installation Kit

Addressing 64-bit Installation Concerns

From an operational standpoint, installing the 64-bit version of Vista isn't any different than installing the 32-bit version. To get the 64-bit version of Vista installed properly, you need to make sure that the processor is 64-bit capable, which means that it's either in the Intel EM64T or AMD64 family of processors, and that you have access to the appropriate 64-bit drivers and applications. BDD 2007 does not currently support the installation of Vista on either the Intel Itanium or ia64 platforms.

It's recommended that you run the BDD script `ZTIPrereq.VBS` on any 64-bit target system to check whether it meets the requirements of the Vista deployment scripts. In order to for `ZTIPrereq.VBS` to run correctly, you need to have the following services installed and running on the target system:

Windows Scripting Host 5.6 (WSH) Should you need to you can download this software from `http://www.microsoft.com/downloads/details.aspx?FamilyId=C717D943-7E4B-4622-86EB-95A22B832CAA&displaylang=en`.

Microsoft Core Extensible Markup Language (MSXML) Service version 3.0 Currently MSXML 4.0 and 6.0 will not work with BDD scripts. MSXML 3.0 SP 5 is downloadable at `http://www.microsoft.com/downloads/details.aspx?familyid=4A3AD088-A893-4F0B-A932-5E024E74519F&displaylang=en`, but any service pack level of version 3.0 will work with BDD scripts.

Microsoft Data Access Components version 2.0 (MDAC) or later MDAC is distributed in many products, but if you want to download the latest version, which in early 2007 was MDAC 2.8 SP1, then go to `http://www.microsoft.com/downloads/details.aspx?familyid=78CAC895-EFC2-4F8E-A9E0-3A1AFBD5922E&displaylang=en`.

Windows operating system versions Windows XP SP2, Windows 2000 Pro SP4, or later.

If `ZTIPrereq` finds that the target system can have Vista deployed on it, a subsequent script of BDD called `ZTIValidate.WSF` can determine whether the target system meets the resource requirements for a 64-bit Vista installation. Those requirements are that the system must have a 64-bit capable processor that runs faster than 990 MHz (1.0 GHz), 64 MB VRAM with enough disk space for the image, and that the target computer isn't running a Windows server operating system. The actual minimum amount of RAM required is 448MB of system RAM and 64MB VRAM. Also, for a Refresh Computer scenario (Side-by-Side), the target system must run the operating system on C drive and that must be the first partition on the first disk of at least enough size to hold both the Windows PE log files, Windows PE, and the 64-bit image of Vista, which is 150MB, 150MB, and from 500MB to 4GB, respectively.

When installing onto a 64-bit platform you need to create the 64-bit version of Windows PE. The 32-bit version of PE won't successfully install 64-bit Vista on supported processors. Keep in mind that although 64-bit Windows Vista can run 32-bit programs, 64-bit Windows PE 2.0 can't. With Vista you can install both the 32-bit and the 64-bit versions of an application, and when you do so you'll find that the 32-bit programs are installed into the `C:\Program Files (x86)` folder. Additionally, not only do you need to have 64-bit drivers for 64-bit Vista but those drivers must be signed and certified as being compatible with Vista. Vista will not run unsigned drivers.

There is one peculiarity of the current version of Windows DS that you should know about when it comes to 64-bit Windows Vista. There are instances where Windows DS will not recognize a 64-bit processor. In a situation where you know that the target system is a supported system for 64-bit Vista, you can force Windows DS to deploy 64-bit Vista images by entering the following command:

```
WDSUTIL /SET-SERVER /ARCHITECTUREDISCOVERY:YES
```

The WDSUTIL is covered in more detail in Chapter 40.

Summary

This chapter covered many of the preinstallation steps you need to take to create stable images. With ACT you have a powerful tool to inventory your hardware and software, test applications, and provide updates and remedies for programs that will cause compatibility issues. Two types of automated deployments LTI and ZTI were overviewed in this chapter.

In the next chapter you will learn about image engineering in more detail, including the tools necessary to create, modify, and manage system images.

Chapter 40

Using Image Engineering

Vista deployments make good use of system imaging technology to automate installation and make the process more efficient. A range of tools are available to you to create images, including the Windows PE 2.0 boot and build environment, Windows DS, and the WDD Workbench. In this chapter, we explore how to use these Microsoft tools to achieve a single local system deployment, a small set of the same system deployment and a large number of systems deployed from multiple system images.

In this chapter, the overview of the image engineering covers the following topics:

- Understanding the Windows PE 2.0 technologies
- Using Windows PE to boot systems, install the OS, and capture images
- Working with ImageX and PEIMG to manage and modify WIM files
- Creating different deployment scenarios
- Using the Windows DS service to perform PXE boot installations of Vista
- Managing a range of deployments using the BDD Deployment Workbench

Vista: What's New?

With Vista, system image technology has become central to the OS deployment, not only for large organizations with lots of systems to deploy but to individual systems as well. Windows PE, Windows DS, and BDD Workbench have all been works in progress. The new versions of these tools that leverage the Vista and Longhorn kernels add powerful new capabilities that streamline installations. There is now only a single distribution of Windows for Vista, with the capability of selecting just the files needed for your particular version and system.

Understanding the Technologies

In this chapter, we'll start out looking at the individual tools such as Windows PE, ImageX, PEIMG, and WIM files that are at the heart of image engineering. With the use of images, there is additional flexibility for quickly creating new and modified system types. The tools that follow add automation features such as scripting, automated unattended installation technologies, image validation, and staging and deployment controls. Windows DS and BDD Workbench build on these simpler tools, allowing you to apply what you learn at the beginning of the chapter to larger and more complex scenarios.

Windows PE 2.0

Microsoft Windows Preinstallation Environment (Windows PE) is a lightweight version of the Windows operating system. Windows PE has many uses, but its central uses are as a boot disk for operating system installations and for system recovery and troubleshooting. PE isn't a product. Microsoft distributes PE on a bootable CD to organizations with an enterprise license; the tool is also contained in the Windows Automated Installation Kit (WAIK). Most administrators who need to support specific system-type deployments will want to take the opportunity to learn how to modify Windows PE, adding and removing components such as drivers as required.

Characteristics of Windows PE

Central to the role that Windows PE must play as a boot disk is the fact that PE has been built to be hardware independent. You can put Windows PE on a system that contains an Intel 32-bit or 64-bit processor, or even on a 64-bit Itanium system, and the system will be recognized and boot into the preinstallation environment.

Windows PE is also small. That means that not only will PE fit on a CD-ROM, but given the recent advances in flash memory, you can also load PE on a USB key or memory card or stick. So PE is very portable, and when you store Windows PE on a network share that small size is also an advantage in terms of minimizing the network bandwidth required for remote installations.

You can boot a system with Windows PE stored on a:

- Magneto-optical drive (CD-ROM or DVD drive)
- Flash memory
- USB keys
- A network share

The size of PE on disk varies depending on the version you use, but the 32-bit version of PE 2.0 based on the Vista kernel requires less than around 140MB of storage on disk. The 64-bit version of PE is somewhat larger than the 32-bit version, and the size grows when you add language packs and other customizations to PE. You can even make Windows PE smaller. To reduce the size somewhat, you can compress PE, even within a WIM file, and it will still run correctly.

Since PE is loaded into RAM, the more important fact is that only 40MB to 60MB in RAM gets loaded. That light footprint means that the remainder of your RAM can be used as a virtual disk, and PE automatically creates a RAM drive labeled drive X that is 32MB in size and for compressed NTFS can address up to 60MB of RAM.

You can remove the Windows PE disk once the program is loaded into RAM and put in another disk, such as the one containing your installation WIM file or additional software. Since you don't need to write PE to disk, you can work in the environment even if a drive fails.

There is an IP network stack (IPv4 and IPv6) built into PE that lets you access other systems on a network or connect to the Internet. That stack relies on network services such as DHCP and DNS to find distribution shares, but using the network utilities that come with PE you can modify a system's address.

Many applications that run under Vista will run under Windows PE 2.0, and PE can find and support most of the common hardware installed on recent systems. Most of the drivers in Vista are found in PE, and if the driver you need isn't one of them you can add drivers either by customizing PE beforehand or by using the `DRVLOAD` command to add the driver once in the PE environment.

Unlike Vista itself, when Windows PE 2.0 is the operating system contained inside a WIM file, a system can boot from that file without Windows PE having to copy itself to disk. However, a system that is running PE can't be accessed from another system on a network, and doesn't support key features like 16-bit applications, .NET, or DFS access beyond a DFS root.

NOTE Just to make sure that you don't try and use Windows PE as a viable operating system, a system running Windows PE 2.0 will shut down automatically 72 hours after it starts up. Prior versions of Windows PE were programmed to shut down after just 24 hours, making it harder to resolve installation problems with tech support.

If you look at the PE specification, you'll also find that it's missing many I/O disk and networking W32 APIs. The missing features disable or won't support:

- Access control
- NetShow Theater Administration
- OpenGL graphics rendering
- Power settings modification
- Print services
- Still image
- Tape backup services
- Terminal services and sessions
- User profile modification
- Windows station and desktop services
- Multimedia services
- Windows shell

However, none of these matter when it comes to installation, troubleshooting, or recovery.

Figure 40.1 shows a system schematic of Windows PE.

What Windows PE does come with is a set of utilities for disk management, driver loading, and image creation. The most important of these built-in tools are the following nine tools:

Boot Configuration Data (BCD) Provides the instructions and settings for boot applications and replaces the `BOOT.INI` file used in Windows versions prior to Vista. BCD is new to Windows PE version 2.0.

BCDEdit is a command-line tool that can access and modify the BCD data store. With BCDEdit there are more options than with `BOOTCFG.EXE`, which BCDEdit replaces, and BCDEdit is more easily scripted. You'll find BCDEdit in the Vista `%WINDIR%\SYSTEM32` directory.

BOOTSECT Modifies the boot sector of a hard drive allowing the use of BOOTMGR or NTLDR. It's the replacement tool for FixFAT and FixNTFS.

DISKPART Creates and modifies disk partitions and volumes. Since it's a command-line tool, you can work with it directly or script actions that run the command automatically.

DRVLOAD Loads additional device drivers.

ImageX Captures and can modify system images as WIM files that are to be deployed. Images that you create can be deployed using Setup for Vista, Windows Deployment Services (Windows DS), or as part of the SMS Operating System Feature Deployment Pack.

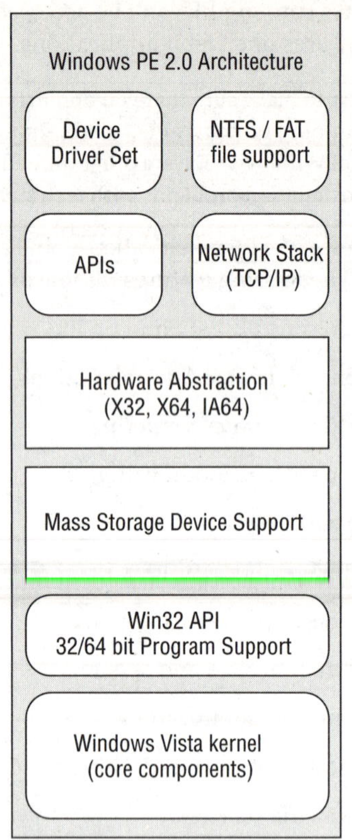

FIGURE 40.1
Windows PE 2.0 is a mini-version of Vista specifically designed for system installs and recovery operations.

OSCDIMG.EXE Creates an image or ISO file of Windows PE.

PEIMG.EXE Modifies a Windows PE image.

WINPESHL.INI(Windows PE Shell) Contains the loading instructions for the PE command prompt. In the new [LaunchApps] section you can specify which command-line options are enabled at boot time.

WPEINIT.EXE Initializes Windows PE when it boots. In previous versions of Windows PE this function was performed by the FACTORY.EXE `-WINPE` command.

ImageX is a central tool that will be described in more detail later in the chapter. Together with the Windows Image File System Filter (WIM FS Filter) driver, ImageX allows PE 2.0 to boot from either:

- Windows OPK CD
- ImageX `/BOOT` command
- Windows AIK CD

These boot options are also a new feature in Windows PE 2.0.

THE BUILD ENVIRONMENT

The goal of image engineering is to create images for the specific systems you wish to deploy. This is a four-step process:

1. Create a PE Build Environment on your technician computer.
2. Image the system.
3. Burn that image onto removable media.
4. Customize the base image.

To start off, you'll need to obtain the Windows PE source files and create the build environment. Keep in mind that you'll need to repeat the procedure below for each processor architecture that you want to deploy.

There are three places where you can get Windows PE:

- Windows OPK
- Windows AIK
- Windows PE distribution disk from Microsoft.

Each of those packages contains the files you need to create a PE build environment on a Windows Server 2003, Vista, or XP system for each of the three different processor architectures that Windows PE supports: X86, AMD64, or Itanium 64.

To create a Windows PE build environment on the technician computer, do the following:

1. Click Start ➤ Run, enter **CMD** followed by the Enter key to open a command prompt.
2. Enter **CD `C:\Program Files\`*`<version>`*`\Tools\PETools`** to move to the directory containing the custom build script, `COPYPE.CMD`. The variable *`<version>`* is either Windows PE kit, Windows AIK, or Windows OPK, depending on which version of PE you have.
3. Enter the command **`COPYPE.CMD`** ***`<architecture>`*** ***`<destination>`***, then press the Enter key.

Figure 40.2 shows the `COPYPE.CMD` script running in the command prompt window for the x86 environment on a Windows Server 2003 system.

The *`<architecture>`* variable is either: X86, amd64, or ia64, and refers to the directories that contain the ImageX source files for each of these different processor types. The *`destination`* variable is any valid directory into which you create the Windows PE build environment, usually on your local drive. The source files for Windows PE 2.0 are installed into the `C:\Program Files\`*`<version>`*`\Tools\` directory, which contains the following subdirectories: `\x86`, `\amd64`, `\ia64`, `\PETools`, and `\Servicing`.

When the `COPYPE.CMD` script runs it uses the Windows PE source files to create the following directory structure:

`<destination>``\winpe_`*`<arch>`*

`<destination>``\winpe_`*`<arch>`*`\ISO`

`<destination>``\winpe_`*`<arch>`*`\mount`

FIGURE 40.2
COPYPE.CMD is the script that creates a Windows PE build environment in which you can create a PXE boot system.

Where the ISO subdirectory contains the files that OSCDIMG uses to create ISO files. ImageX uses the files in the `\mount` subdirectory to mount Windows PE images. At the top of the new directory is the `WINPE.WIM` file, which is the based WinPE image file that you customize for a specific installation. Then, applying ImageX again, you create an ISO directory with the files necessary to create the WinPE ISO image, as well as the BIN file that makes the ISO image bootable.

WINDOWS PE IMAGES

Once you've created the Windows PE build environment, you'll need to create a custom Windows PE image that contains the tools and driver files your installations need. This is done by first extracting the base Windows PE image from the `WinPE.WIM` file with the command-line tools ImageX. The Windows PE image is customized by `Peimg.exe`, and once the customized image is prepared, you again use ImageX to capture the customized Windows PE image into a `BOOT.WIM` file that you can use with your deployment. At that point you prepare your custom boot image for the particular method that you'll use to deploy Vista. Those methods include a bootable CD or DVD disk, an image on a hard drive, or an image on a network share that is used by the Windows Deployment Services (Windows DS) server. Figure 40.3 illustrates the key steps in the customization process.

To create a custom Windows PE boot image, do the following:

1. At the command prompt, change directories to the one containing the base `WinPE.WIM` file. Or click Start ➤ All Programs ➤ *`<version>`* ➤ Windows PE Tools Command Prompt.
2. Enter the command **`IMAGEX /APPLY WINPE.WIM 1 C:\`*`PE_BUILD`***, where *`PE_Build`* is the name of your PE build environment directory.

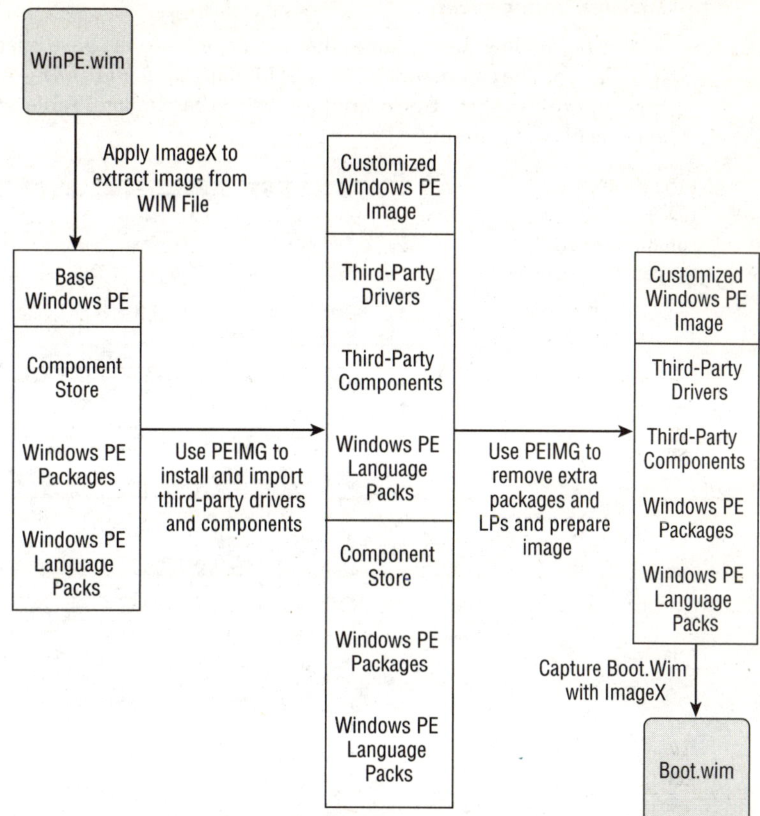

FIGURE 40.3
To create a Boot.wim file you customize the base WinPE.wim file from the Windows PE build environment.

ImageX extracts the WIM file to create the base Windows PE Image and displays its progress in percentages. When the image has been extracted from the WIM file, you'll see the message "Successfully applied image" displayed, and your build environment will have the structure shown in Figure 40.4.

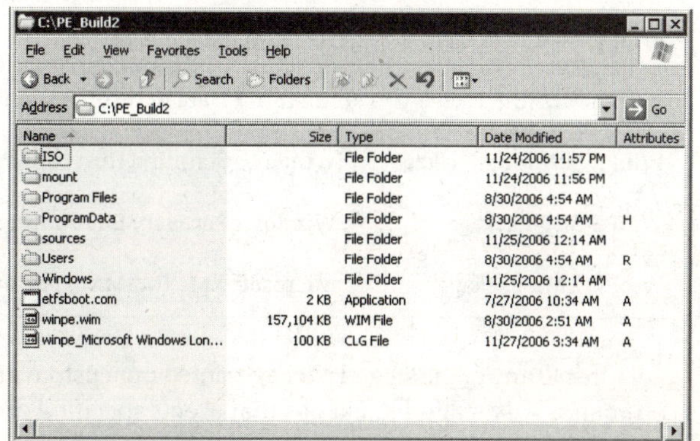

FIGURE 40.4
The build environment containing the base Windows PE Image. Note the appearance of the Program Files, ProgramData, Users, and Windows folders associated with the image.

Package Management

At this point view the packages that are staged into the base image and that could be part of your installation. The command PEIMG /LIST *<BUILD_DIRECTORY_PATH\WINDOWS>* performs this function. Figure 40.5 shows the output for the x86 base image. Table 40.1 shows what the different packages displayed contain.

FIGURE 40.5
Use the PEIMG /LIST command to display the packages installed in an image.

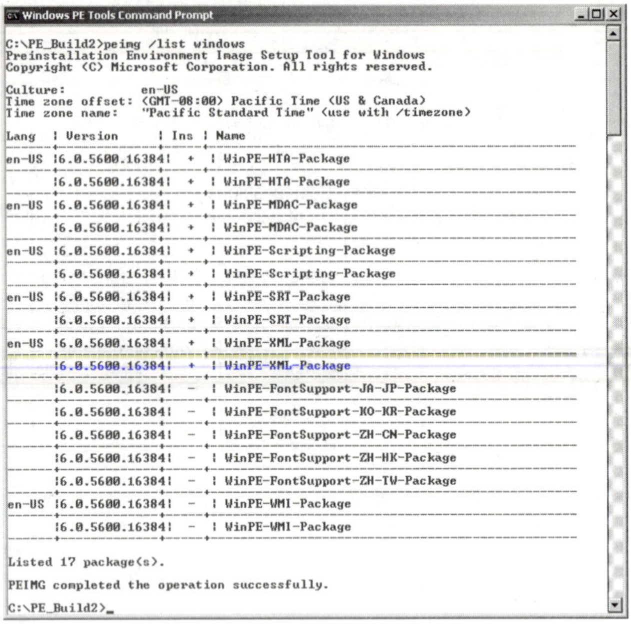

```
Windows PE Tools Command Prompt

C:\PE_Build2>peimg /list windows
Preinstallation Environment Image Setup Tool for Windows
Copyright (C) Microsoft Corporation. All rights reserved.

Culture:          en-US
Time zone offset: (GMT-08:00) Pacific Time (US & Canada)
Time zone name:   "Pacific Standard Time" (use with /timezone)

Lang  | Version          | Ins | Name
en-US |6.0.5600.16384|  +  | WinPE-HTA-Package
      |6.0.5600.16384|  +  | WinPE-HTA-Package
en-US |6.0.5600.16384|  +  | WinPE-MDAC-Package
      |6.0.5600.16384|  +  | WinPE-MDAC-Package
en-US |6.0.5600.16384|  +  | WinPE-Scripting-Package
      |6.0.5600.16384|  +  | WinPE-Scripting-Package
en-US |6.0.5600.16384|  +  | WinPE-SRT-Package
      |6.0.5600.16384|  +  | WinPE-SRT-Package
en-US |6.0.5600.16384|  +  | WinPE-XML-Package
      |6.0.5600.16384|  +  | WinPE-XML-Package
      |6.0.5600.16384|  -  | WinPE-FontSupport-JA-JP-Package
      |6.0.5600.16384|  -  | WinPE-FontSupport-KO-KR-Package
      |6.0.5600.16384|  -  | WinPE-FontSupport-ZH-CN-Package
      |6.0.5600.16384|  -  | WinPE-FontSupport-ZH-HK-Package
      |6.0.5600.16384|  -  | WinPE-FontSupport-ZH-TW-Package
en-US |6.0.5600.16384|  -  | WinPE-WMI-Package
      |6.0.5600.16384|  -  | WinPE-WMI-Package

Listed 17 package(s).

PEIMG completed the operation successfully.

C:\PE_Build2>_
```

TABLE 40.1: Windows PE Base Staged Packages

PACKAGE NAME	DESCRIPTION
WinPE-FontSupport	Installed fonts; optional packages for Japanese, Korean, Chinese, and so forth.
WinPE-HTA-Package	HTML application support
WinPE-MDAC-Package	Microsoft Data Access Component packages
WinPE-Scripting-Package	Windows Scripting Host support
WinPE-SRT-Package	Windows Recovery Environment packages
WinPE-XML-Package	Microsoft XML (MSMXL) parser packages

To install any of the staged packages into your custom image, you'll need to use the PEIMG /INSTALL command. Any staged packages that aren't specified are not included in your final custom Windows PE image.

```
PEIMG /INSTALL=<packagename> <build_directory_path>
```

Or, for example:

```
PEIMG /INSTALL=WinPE_Scripting-Package C:\PE_Build.
```

You can use the PEIMG /INSTALL command to install additional packages, language packs, and drivers. Additionally, you can add files and applications using the command below:

```
C:\<BUILD_DIRECTORY_PATH>\PROGRAM FILE\<APPLICATION_DIRECTORY>\<APPLICATION.EXE>
```

Image Device Drivers

Device drivers can be added to a Windows PE Image during the image building process, or slipstreamed later inside a running Windows PE environment. Microsoft refers to the former as an offline addition and the latter as an online one.

To add a device driver to a Windows PE image offline:

1. Extract the PE image as you have seen previously:

   ```
   IMAGEX /APPLY WINPE.WIM 1 C:\<BUILD_DIRECTORY>\MOUNT\
   ```

   or use,

   ```
   IMAGEX /MOUNTRW WINPE.WIM 1 C:\<BUILD_DIRECTORY>\MOUNT\
   ```

2. Specify each driver using the PEIMG /INF command below, which copies the driver to the PE Windows folder:

   ```
   PEIMG /INF=<INF_FILE_PATH> C:\<BUILD_DIRECTORY>\MOUNT\WINDOWS\
   ```

   or use,

   ```
   DRVLOAD.EXE /OFFLINE <INF_FILE_PATH1, INF_FILE_PATH2, … >
   ```

You'll need to perform the procedure above for each device driver you want to add, and certainly prior to the PEIMG /PREP step, as shown in Figure 40.6. After preparation, you'll no longer be able to add a device driver offline. The one driver you definitely want to include in any PE image is any mass storage device driver. If your build includes a RAID setup, your installation won't proceed without supplying that driver to Setup. Although you can add it after the fact as an online installation, it's much more convenient to add it once in an offline installation.

However, you can always add a device driver online within Windows PE using the DRVLOAD command. The basic command for online device driver injection is:

```
DRVLOAD.EXE <INF_FILE_PATH1, INF_FILE_PATH2, … >
```

Adding Language Packs

Language packs are normally applied offline to an extracted PE image file prior to preparing the image. What a language pack does is to change the language used in the Windows GUI so that it supports the other language. For example, you might add the Spanish or Chinese language to your WinPE image to install those languages during deployment.

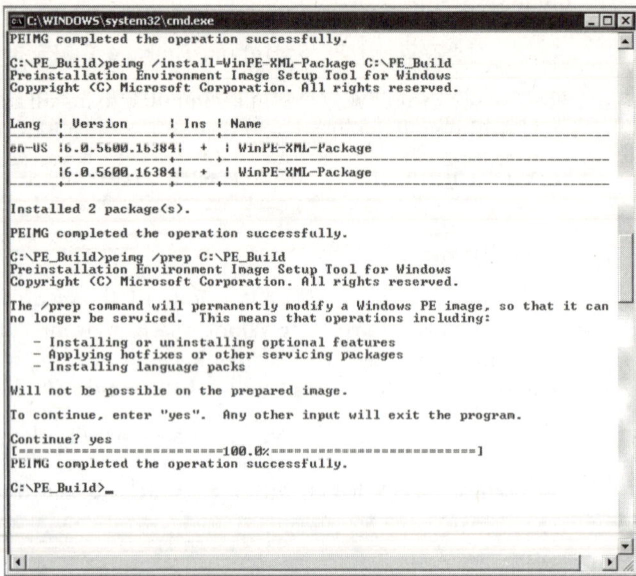

FIGURE 40.6
Use the PEIMG /INSTALL command to add packages to an image, and the PEIMG /PREP command to finalize the image.

Now that Vista ships as a single WIM file, language packs are contained in each install disk. You saw several language packs listed earlier when PEIMG /LIST was used to display the language packs contained in the \WINDOWS directory.

To add a language pack to your image:

1. Extract or mount the image using the ImageX /APPLY or ImageX /MOUNT command, as shown in the previous section.

2. At the command prompt move to the build directory, then import the language pack into your build, as below:

```
CD <BUILD_DIRECTORY_PATH>\WINDOWS>
PEIMG /INSTALL=<PACKAGE_NAME> C:\<BUILD_DIRECTORY>\MOUNT\WINDOWS
```

If you want to install a language pack from a location other than the build directory, you should specify the PATH*PACKAGE_NAME* in the line above in place of just the *PACKAGE_NAME*.

With the desired language pack installed, you can specify that Vista Setup uses a particular language by using the PEIMG /LANG command, as follows:

```
PEIMG /LANG=<culture> <BUILD_DIRECTORY_PATH>
```

Once you prepare the image (PEIMG /PREP) and create your boot media Windows PE will boot using the language that was assigned by the /LANG switch.

Once you have added all of the components that will make up your custom Windows PE 2.0 image, you'll need to prepare the final image, and then capture it as a bootable image using ImageX. You'll probably want to add some of the optional components described in the next section to your PE boot image, so before committing to the preparation step below take a look at the next section.

If you want to add an application to a customized Windows PE image, you can create an application directory such as \\<APPLICATION_NAME>, \TOOLS, or \UTILITY and copy the application to that folder prior to the PREP command. You can also copy the application to the \WINDOWS\SYSTEM32 directory. To have the application start up during a Windows PE session, embed a startup script into the WINPESHL.INI file.

The two final steps in the boot image build process are:

```
PEIMG /PREP C:\<BUILD_DIRECTORY_PATH>\MOUNT\WINDOWS
```

In the step above the image is prepared and packages that haven't been specified are removed. PREP cannot be undone, so be sure that the image is in the form you want it to be in prior to running the command above.

Once prepared, the next step is to commit the modifications that were made back to the original WINPE.WIM image file, as shown below.

```
IMAGEX /UNMOUNT C:\ <BUILD_DIRECTORY_PATH>\MOUNT /COMMIT
```

Microsoft recommends that you use ImageX to capture your custom base image prior to running the PEIMG /PREP command. That allows you not only to save your modified based image but also to check the image size prior to use. Save that copy; then proceed to run the command below to create your bootable image.

```
IMAGEX /BOOT /COMPRESS MAX /CAPTURE C:\ <BUILD_DIRECTORY_PATH>
➥C:\BOOT.WIM "Custom WinPE Image"
```

The COMPRESS MAX switch is optional, but recommended. Once you prepare the image you won't be able to add packages or modify the image, so PEIMG will post a warning requiring that you acknowledge this fact, as shown in Figure 40.06. (You can add language packs and drivers to a built boot image at a later time.) During the build you'll see a message that ImageX excludes the following folders:

```
\WINDOWS\CSC
\RECYCLER
\System Volume Information
\PAGEFILE.SYS
\HIBERFIL.SYS
\$NTFS.LOG
```

These system folders contain temporary information that isn't needed, and these folders are recreated on the fly by Windows. With no language packs installed and the Microsoft Data Access Component packages omitted, ImageX creates a BOOT.WIM file that is 262MB in size.

PE Boot Scenarios

One of the common scenarios for installing Vista proceeds by booting a system from Windows PE from a CD-ROM. When Windows PE boots, it loads a portion of the operating system into RAM, creates a RAM disk that is assigned the drive letter X, and installs Vista from a WIM file. As noted earlier in the chapter, there are several different means for using a Windows PE image to boot a fresh system: CD-ROM, UFD, a hard drive, or on a network share. To prepare Windows PE on a CD-ROM, a UFD, or hard drive so that the image loads into RAM, an ISO file needs to be created and that file is burned to the CD-ROM.

The tool used to create an ISO file from your WIM image file on the technician computer is the OSCDIMG command-line utility. The following command creates the appropriate ISO file for an x86 system:

```
OSCDIMG -N -B C:<BUILD_DIRECTORY>\ETFSBOOT.COM
➥C:\<BUILD_DIRECTORY>\ISO C:\<BUILD_DIRECTORY>\WINPE_X86.ISO
```

The command switch `-B` specifies the location of the boot file and `-N` enables long filenames. OSCDIMG has many options. When using an Itanium ia64 boot disk you need to substitute the `ETFSBOOT.COM` with the `ETFSBOOT.BIN` file.

You'll then need to burn the ISO file to disk. In order to do so, you need to have a CD or DVD burning program such as Nero InCD or Roxio Drag-to-Disk installed, as Windows doesn't offer this utility out of the box. You can also find disk-burning software on the Windows 2003 Resource Kit, which contains the CDBURN and DVDBURN utilities.

If instead of using a CD-ROM or DVD disk you want to put your Windows PE image onto flash media (a UFD device), you'll need to use Vista's disk-partitioning utility DISKPART to format the UFD drive as a FAT32 volume since UFD doesn't support NTFS. From either Vista or Windows PE, insert the UFD device and then at the command prompt perform the following operation:

```
DISKPART
SELECT DISK #
CLEAN
CREATE PARTITION PRIMARY SIZE=<device_size>
SELECT PARTITION 1
ACTIVE
FORMAT FS=FAT32
ASSIGN
EXIT
```

The Disk # is the number of the UFD device. Finish the installation by moving the entire ISO directory structure over to the UFD device; or if you prefer you can use the XCOPY command below:

```
XCOPY C:\<BUILD_DIRECTORY>ISO\*.* /S /E /F F:
```

The C drive is on the technician computer, and the F drive is the UFD drive.

The procedure for creating a bootable Windows PE RAM disk on a hard drive doesn't use the ISO file, runs DISKPART to create an NTFS disk, and lets you set the partition size at any size greater than the image itself. The command prompt session looks like the following:

```
DISKPART
SELECT DISK #
CLEAN
CREATE PARTITION PRIMARY SIZE=<partition_size_in_GB>
SELECT PARTITION 1
ACTIVE
FORMAT
EXIT
```

You'll need to copy both the \BOOT and the \SOURCES directories to the hard drive, either graphically through the Windows GUI, or at a command prompt with the following XCOPY command:

```
XCOPY D:\*.* /s /e /f C:\
```

Here the D: drive is the CD-ROM disk containing Windows PE, or a UFD media with the same, and C: is the hard drive that you are loading the Windows PE image on.

All three of the above solutions described so far in this section load Windows PE into RAM and boot a system from the RAM disk. However, it's also possible to put Windows PE on a freshly formatted hard drive and boot Windows PE from the hard drive itself. Doing so allows you to have more flexibility during deployments and recovery operations in that you can modify the contents of the hard drive on the fly and add additional utilities as you need to.

To boot Window PE from a hard drive:

1. Set the BIOS of the system to boot from either the DVD drive or a USB drive first.
2. Load Windows PE and at the command prompt enter the following commands to format the hard drive:

   ```
   DISKPART
   SELECT DISK 0
   CLEAN
   CREATE PARTITION PRIMARY SIZE=<#_of_GB>
   SELECT PARTITION 1
   ACTIVE
   FORMAT FS=NTFS
   EXIT
   ```

   The partition size must be larger than the size of the Windows PE image.
3. Extract the Windows PE WIM file to the hard drive using `ImageX /apply` as follows:

   ```
   D:\IMAGEX /APPLY D:\SOURCES\BOOT.WIM 1 C:\
   ```

   where D: is the DVD drive and C: is the hard drive.
4. Then copy BOOTMGR to the root C:\ directory:

   ```
   COPY D:\BOOTMGR C:\.
   ```

5. Enter **XCOPY D:\BOOT*.* /E /F C:\BOOT** to copy the BOOT directory to the hard drive.

When you copy the BOOT directory, you also copy the boot configuration data information in the BCD file that is specific to your CD-ROM, DVD, or UFD media. BCD is Vista's replacement for the `BOOT.INI` file. In order to have Windows PE successfully boot from the hard drive, you'll need to rewrite the BCD file using the BCDEdit, which is located in the BOOT folder you just copied over to the hard drive.

To rewrite the BCD file, do the following:

1. Move to the BOOT folder: `CD D:\BOOT`.

2. Enter the following BCDEdit commands:

```
BCDEDIT -CREATESTORE C:\TEMP\BCD
BCDEDIT -STORE C:\TEMP\BCD -CREATE {BOOTMGR} /D "BOOT MANAGER"
BCDEDIT -STORE C:\TEMP\BCD -SET {BOOTMGR} DEVICE BOOT
BCDEDIT -STORE C:\TEMP\BCD -CREATE  /D "WINPE" -APPLICATION OSLOADER
BCDEDIT -IMPORT C:\TEMP\BCD
```

BCDEdit displays a GUID that needs to be used by the various devices in order for the partition, Windows loader, and WinPE to correctly recognize each other at boot. The code needed to set this system identification uses a set of `BCDEdit -store` commands, as follows:

```
BCDEDIT -STORE C:\BOOT\BCD -SET GUID DEVICE PARTITION=C:
BCDEDIT -STORE C:\BOOT\BCD -SET GUID OSDEVICE PARTITION=C:
BCDEDIT -STORE C:\BOOT\BCD -SET GUID PATH \WINDOWS\SYSTEM32\WINLOAD.EXE
BCDEDIT -STORE C:\BOOT\BCD -SET GUID SYSTEMROOT \WINDOWS
BCDEDIT -STORE C:\BOOT\BCD -SET GUID WINPE YES
BCDEDIT -STORE C:\BOOT\BCD -SET GUID DETECTHAL YES
BCDEDIT -STORE C:\BOOT\BCD -DISPLAYORDER GUID -ADDLAST
```

Once the GUID has been replaced, restart the system and set the BIOS to boot from the hard drive first. Windows PE then loads correctly from the hard drive as soon as you reboot.

Just to summarize, the basic steps that you must take to create a custom Windows PE image is shown below in Table 40.2.

TABLE 40.2: Steps to Build a Custom Windows PE Image

STEP	TASK	NOTES
1	Create a Windows PE build environment	From the Windows AIK or OPK open a command prompt and use the `COPYPE.CMD` command.
2	Mount the Windows PE base image	Run `ImageX /MOUNTRW` to make the base image editable
3	Add packages	Run `PEIMG /INSTALL` to add staged packages to your custom image.
4	Add additional utilities (ImageX, Package Manager, etc.)	These additions are covered in the section "ImageX and Custom PE Images" in a following section.
5	Prepare the image	Use `PEIMG /PREP` to finalize the custom image (similar to running Sysprep).
6	Unmount and commit the image	Use `ImageX /UNMONUNT` <*BUILD_ENVIRONMENT PATH*>`\MOUNT /COMMIT`
7	Overwrite the BOOT.WIM file	Replace the `BOOT.WIM` file in the `SOURCES\ISO` directory of your build environment with your custom `WINPE.WIM`

TABLE 40.2: Steps to Build a Custom Windows PE Image *(CONTINUED)*

STEP	TASK	NOTES
8	Create a bootable CD-ROM	Use the OSCDIMG -N -BC command to create an ISO file.
9	Burn the ISO file to your disk	
Or		
8	Create a bootable UFD drive	Format using DISKPART into FAT32 partition.
9	Copy the ISO directory	Use xCopy to copy the \ISO directory to the UFD drive.

Modifying PE Boot Behavior

You can alter the manner in which Windows PE starts up by adding or altering three important startup files with embedded scripts and by modifying their settings. The three files of note are:

- STARTNET.CMD, which alters Windows PE's network behavior
- WINPESHL.INI, which can launch a shell application that allows administrators to use PE tools and services, as well as any additional applications that you added
- UNATTEND.XML, which is the Vista answer file for unattended installations that replaces WINBOM.INI and WINPEOEM.SIF

The STARTNET.CMD script found in %SYSTEMROOT%\SYSTEM32 (usually \WINDOWS\SYSTEM32) of all Windows PE images is used in its default configuration to start up WPEINIT.EXE. WPEINIT.EXE performs the following functions: it detects PnP devices, installs the correct device drivers, reads the UNATTEND.XML file, acts on the settings it finds there, and loads and configures the network stack.

To modify STARTNET.CMD, open the file with Notepad and add your own commands and scripts. However, do not remove the line WPEINIT.EXE, or the device and networking functions won't operate correctly. One modification to STARTNET.CMD is important for Zero Touch Installations in BDD Enterprise where WINS is not used. To correctly access network services in that type of installation, Windows PE uses DNS for its IP address resolution, DHCP for addressing, configures the LMHOSTS file, and adds Active Directory schema extensions so that SMS works correctly with BDD. The following code is added to both the technician system and the deployed systems' START.CMD file:

```
regsvr32 /s netcfgx.dll
factory -minint
netcfg -v -winpe
net start dhcp
net start nla
net start lmhosts
```

The last line is used to use the LMHOSTS file in place of WINS name resolution. For more information on Zero Touch without WINS, see: http://www.microsoft.com/technet/desktopdeployment/bdd/enterprise/ZTIDFTGuide_23.mspx.

The STARTNET.CMD file can also be set to load Windows components that aren't part of the default Windows PE environment, such as WMI. In versions of Windows PE prior to Vista, WSH and ADO were packages that you could add to your customized version and they could be enabled through commands in STARTNET.CMD (see http://www.windowsitpro.com/Article/ArticleID/45736/45736.html).

The second configuration file is the WINPESHL.INI file that controls the WINPESHL.EXE shell program that launches during Windows PE's boot. That is, WINPESHL.EXE is the command prompt that you would normally see if you don't further customize Windows PE. By default, there is no WINPESHL.INI file in Windows PE; you have to add one if you want to alter WINPESHL.EXE's behavior. You create this file in Notepad and save it to the %SYSTEMROOT%\SYSTEM32 directory. Since a shell can hand off execution to another shell, you can call the shell of your choice from WINPESHL.INI.

One place where WINPSEHL.INI is used is in the SMS Operating System Deployment (OSD) Feature Pack. When the Image Capture Wizard finishes running Sysprep and reboots, the system is ready to be captured, the Windows PE Image Capture CD loads, and the WINPESHL.INI on the CD is read. That INI file contains the following two sections:

```
[LAUNCHAPP]
APPPATH=%SYSTEMROOT%\SYSTEM32\OSDSHELL.EXE
....
[SHELL]
RUN=OSDICWP.EXE
```

The first section launches the OSDSHELL, which provides a runtime command environment for OSD, particularly for Image Capture and Image Installation. OSDSHELL also sets environmental variables for OSDICWP.EXE which is OSD's Windows PE Image Capture Wizard, and which becomes the shell application with access to the WIM DLLs necessary to save the image to a location on the network that is specified.

UNATTEND.XML, the answer file that is used to make setting selections during installation, is another method for modifying Windows PE's startup behavior. This file is located in the root directory of the boot device. You can control which UNATTEND.XML runs by adding a command in the STARTNET.CMD and modifying WPEINIT.EXE's behavior.

ImageX

ImageX is Microsoft's primary tool for creating, modifying, and applying system images based on the Windows Image file format. ImageX comes into play whenever Vista is installed on a single system using Windows Setup, in concert with Windows Deployment Services over a network, or with large-scale deployments using SMS OSD, the Operating System Feature Deployment Pack.

You've seen how ImageX extracts a WIM file using the /APPLY switch, and how the /BOOT switch created the boot image. ImageX is the key command-line utility for creating and modifying images, and the /CAPTURE switch is the method used to create the master images you need.

NOTE ImageX consists of the ImageX.exe file, the WIM System Filter (WIMFLTR.SYS and WIMFLTR.INF), and the WIM API (WIMGAPI) all of which support the WIM file format. Since the WIM API is published, you can expect to see third-party applications appear that leverage this technology in the future.

ImageX is a file-oriented file manager, in the same way that Windows Explorer is file-oriented manager. Provided that the Windows Image Filter Service is running, you can open images and view the contents of an image. ImageX allows you to control what's in an image at a granular level and deploy images selectively. That is, ImageX doesn't force you to overwrite an entire image to get the contents you desire. Also, since ImageX knows about files, it supports single instancing, storing just one copy of a file no matter how many times the file would appear in the deployed image contents.

ImageX frees Windows deployment from a number of issues that have plagued deployment systems in the past. Image preparation on the technician computer can provide images for destination systems that have different processor architectures. Sector-based deployment requires that an entire partition be recreated, which limits how the deployment can be staged and modified. ImageX is most often used to capture and apply an image from a network share, once a system has booted into Windows PE, or to modify WIM files.

Although this chapter is concerned with Vista deployment, ImageX can:

- Mount an image from Vista, Windows XP SP2, and Windows Server 2003 SP1 and later
- Capture an image from any version of Vista, Windows XP, and Windows Server 2003
- Capture an installation image created by the Windows System Image Manger (Windows SIM); described later in this chapter
- Take an image that's had its identification data removed ("prepared") by Sysprep and create an installation image from it

When ImageX captures a system image, it captures the entire operating system and all installed applications. ImageX won't capture part of the system's deployment, nor can it be used to install an upgrade to a deployed system. You can use ImageX to upgrade Windows PE from an upgrade package, although it's probably wiser to obtain the most up-to-date version of PE rather than upgrade it as you would a deployed system.

ImageX Options

ImageX is a rich command-line tool with 11 major options, each of which have some additional features. The command syntax is as follows:

```
IMAGEX [FLAGS] {/APPEND | /APPLY | /CAPTURE | /DELETE | /DIR |
➥/EXPORT | /INFO | /SPLIT | /MOUNT | /MOUNTRW | /UNMOUNT} [PARAMETERS]
```

Each command option must be specified individually. That is, you can combine more than one switch into a command. Briefly, the ImageX options provide the following utility:

APPEND Appends a volume image to a WIM file, maintaining single instancing.

APPLY Applies a volume image to a device, usually a hard drive.

CAPTURE Capture reduces a system volume image to a WIM file. All extended attributes are lost. Two compressions are possible with the /COMPRESS switch: MAXIMUM and FAST. Only one can be used at a time, or NONE can be specified.

DELETE Deletes a volume image from a WIM file containing two or more images. Delete only operates on the pointers to the data and not on the file data contained in the WIM file.

DIR Displays the files and directory structure of a volume image in a WIM file.

EXPORT Exports a copy of one WIM file into another WIM file. Requires Windows PE.

INFO Displays XML data of a WIM file, including file sizes, image numbers, directory and file counts, and descriptions.

MOUNT Mounts a WIM file so that it may be read (viewed—provided that WIM FS is running), but a mounted WIM file cannot be written to (modified).

MOUNTRW Mounts a WIM file with both read and write permissions.

SPLIT Allows ImageX to run from within Windows PE and can split a WIM file into separate parts (given a .SWM extension).

UNMOUNT Unmounts a mounted image from the mount directory.

There are many flags (switches) associated with these options. To get a more complete description, enter IMAGEX /<*OPTION_NAME*> /?, and complete help for each of the options is displayed.

You can create a configuration file that modifies the behavior of ImageX, by determining:

- An exclusion list of files and directories that are ignored during a CAPTURE
- The files, file types, and directories that are ignored by COMPRESS
- A WIM file aligns on a 64K or 32K boundary (the default)

The /CONFIG flag or switch tells ImageX to read the CONFIGURATION_LIST.INI text file, which should be placed into the ImageX working directory. This INI file has the following sections:

```
[ExclusionList]
[ExclusionException]
[CompressionExclusionList]
[AlignmentList]
```

Without the /CONFIG flag the CONFIGURATION_LIST.INI is not read and the settings described in it are ignored. If you want to have a configuration automatically run every time you use the /CAPTURE option, then create a WIMSCRIPT.INI file in the ImageX directory, as described more fully in the section below.

ImageX and Custom PE Images

The reason for creating a custom Windows PE boot disk on the technician computer is to capture an image for the master Vista systems that you are going to deploy en masse. Therefore, it's quite helpful to have both ImageX and the Package Manager available on your custom Windows PE boot disk. These two programs are not included in base PE image and need to be added manually prior to PEIMG /PREP command.

When you add ImageX, you're copying the executable file to the ISO folder of your build environment, as follows:

```
COPY C:\PROGRAM FILES\<VERSION>\TOOLS\X86\IMAGEX.EXE C:\<BUILD_DIRECTORY_
➥PATH>\ISO
```

Remember, the version refers to the version of the package that you use to obtain Windows PE: the Windows AIK, the Windows OPK, or the Windows PE Kit.

When you run ImageX to create the custom Windows PE boot image (as was done in the previous section), the program knows to omit the temporary folders listed in that section. When you run ImageX against a master Vista system, it comes to an excluded folder and cannot process it. Thus, ImageX's capture operation fails and an error message is returned. To avoid this problem you have to configure ImageX beforehand.

The method used to exclude folders as well as exclude previously compressed files that can't be compressed further by the COMPRESS switch is to create a `WIMSCRIPT.INI` text file. That file gets read automatically before ImageX operates if it's found in the ISO directory.

To create the `WIMSCRIPT.INI` file, you open a text editor such as Notepad and enter the following code:

```
[ExclusionList]
hiberfil.sys
ntfs.log
pagefile.sys
"System Volume Information"
RECYCLER
Windows\CSC

[ExclusionException]
```

List any of the files in the section above that you want to process, thus overriding the default exclusion list used by the `CAPTURE` switch.

```
 [CompressionExclusionList]
*.cab
*.mp3
*.zip
\WINDOWS\inf\*.pnf

[AlignmentList]
```

This section specifies whether the WIM file that is created has files that align to the 64K boundary or the default 32K boundary.

Save the `WIMSCRIPT.INI` file as a text file into the `<`*`build_directory_path`*`>\ISO` directory. Now when ImageX runs with the `CAPTURE` switch, these settings will automatically apply. If you need to create a custom configuration file and access it at another location outside of the ImageX directory, you'll need to specify that file as part of the ImageX command when you run it. For example, you can use the following command to point to a custom file:

```
ImageX /CONFIG C:\<Image_directory>\CONFIGURATION.INI /CAPTURE D:
➥D:\<Image_directory>\DATA.WIM "Drive D"
```

The command above also works with the `IMAGEX /APPEND` switch. The alternative to using a configuration file is to specify the `IMAGEX /CONFIG` switch and then enumerate the options in the INI file above, which is a very clumsy procedure indeed.

In order to copy over the Package Manager tool, you not only have to copy the executable file `PKGMGR.EXE` but you must copy over the entire Servicing directory as well. That means that you have to use the `XCOPY` command in place of the `COPY` command, as shown below:

```
XCOPY C:\PROGRAM FILES\<VERSION>\TOOLS\SERVICING
➥C:\<BUILD_DIRECTORY_PATH>\ISO\SERVICING /S
```

The final `/S` switch specifies that `XCOPY` not only copy the entire contents of the Servicing directory, but the contents of all nested subdirectories as well. *`VERSION`* refers to the source of the program, which is either the Windows AIK or Windows OPK.

When Windows PE boots and loads into RAM neither ImageX nor the Package Manager will load into memory unless you alter your Windows PE configuration files to launch them. Alternatively, you can have these tools load into RAM automatically when Windows PE boots if you copy the `ImageX.exe` file and the Servicing directory into the mounted Windows directory of your custom Windows PE image.

So far you've seen the tools used for Vista deployment that are appropriate for an attended deployment. You create a custom Windows PE image, boot a fresh system from that image, and run your installation from that image. Alternatively, you boot a system into Windows PE and specify that the installation use an image found in another location such as a network distribution share. In the sections that follow you'll see how this technology can be extended to accommodate and manage multiple system images, set up remote installations, and automate the procedure to enable unattended deployment of large numbers of systems.

Network Installations

Let's put what you've learned so far together to consider how a network installation of Vista is structured when it isn't highly automated. You've already created a custom Windows PE Image that you'll use to boot a fresh system into a state where Vista can be installed. In the lab or through your trials you've also created a master installation of Vista running on hardware that your organization supports. To perform a network installation the remaining steps are:

1. Capture an image of the master systems.
2. Store that image on your network share.
3. Boot a fresh system into Windows PE.
4. Apply the image from your network share.

Two methods are used to create a master system: booting from a Vista installation disk (DVD) or through the use of a Configuration Set within the Windows SIM tool described below. After the master system is fully validated and in the condition in which you wish to deploy it, you should turn off the computer and proceed to capture an image of the system.

To capture an image of a master system:

1. Turn on the master system, and insert your custom Windows PE CD-ROM or flash disk.
2. At the Windows PE command prompt, use ImageX to capture the image with the following command:

    ```
    IMAGEX /COMPRESS FAST /CHECK /SCROLL /CAPTURE C: C:\SYSIMAGES.WIM
    ```

3. Copy the image to the network share, as follows:

    ```
    NET USE Y: \\NETWORK_SHARE\
    COPY C:\IMAGE1.WIM Y:\NETWORK_SHARE\IMAGES\
    ```

To deploy the image over the network:

1. Turn on the fresh computer, and insert your custom Windows PE CD-ROM or flash disk.
2. At the Windows PE command prompt enter the `DISKPART` command and format the hard drive.

3. At the Windows PE command prompt, map the network share, as follows:

```
NET USE Y: \\NETWORK_SHARE\IMAGES
```

4. Use ImageX to apply the image:

```
IMAGEX /APPLY Y:\\NETWORK_SHARE\IMAGES\SYSIMAGES.WIM 1 C:
```

ImageX extracts the imaged files contained in the WIM file and copies them over to the C: drive of the fresh system. The number 1 in the command above indicates that this is the first image in the WIM file, and is necessary if more than one image is contained in the WIM file. Larger-scale deployments automate the various parts of the process above.

Windows System Image Manager

The Windows System Image Manager (Windows SIM) is the primary tool used to create the new Windows Setup XML answer files. An answer file contains the necessary configuration settings to allow Setup to create the correct partitions and install the right device drivers and language packs, updates, third-party applications, and more.

An answer file draws its settings from a Windows Image or WIM file and a catalog (CLG) file, and if it can't find a catalog file associated with the WIM file it will create one for you. A catalog file is a small binary file that stores the settings and the condition of included packages. When you modify a Windows image it's a good idea to update the catalog file. A Vista retail distribution's catalog files may be found in the Sources directory, one catalog for each image contained in the WIM file.

An answer file is in essence a "script" for the answers that you would provide to the dialog boxes that Windows Setup would post if you were monitoring the setup manually.

Windows SIM doesn't change a Windows image—its only use is to modify Windows Setup when it's running. In addition to creating an answer file, Windows SIM offers the following capabilities with regards to Windows images:

- It can display the configurable component settings contained within a WIM file.
- It can validate an answer file against the contents of a WIM file.
- It can be used to create a configuration set that allows Setup to run unattended across a network.

A configuration set is the files that are referenced in the answer file and that need to be found in the distribution share for a single installation. That's a smaller subset of the total installation files in a more portable form than the complete set of files that are in the Windows Image File format. To build a configuration set, you create a distribution share, add drivers and applications to that share, create an answer file (see below), add any required device drivers (out-of-box) and third-party applications to the answer file, and validate the answer file. Once all those steps have been taken, you can create the configuration set specifying both the location of the configuration set and the OEM folder that contains the files it references.

Windows SIM uses the Component Platform Interface or CPI to mount a WIM file, create a Vista Catalog file of the components and packages that are installed, and from these two sets of data create either the answer file (`Unattend.XML`) or the configuration set. Windows SIM can also be used to create a distribution share that stores the files used to customize Windows installations.

Windows SIM is distributed in the Windows AIK and can be launched from that kit's program menu. Figure 40.7 shows the Windows SIM interface with a Windows PE WIM file displayed in the

Windows Image pane. The key to building the answer file is found in the Answer pane in the center of the window where Windows Setup configuration passes are displayed.

As you build or modify an answer file, each setting of a package or component is displayed and can be edited in the Properties pane at the right side of the dialog box. Since WIM files can contain more than one Windows system image and because images can change over time, having the ability to edit an answer file rather than having to build each one from scratch every time is very valuable.

The distribution share that contains a set of subdirectories with files needed to customize a Vista installation is an optional feature. You can create a distribution share from within Windows SIM, and the path to the share is part of the settings stored in an answer file. When Windows SIM creates the distribution share, it creates three subdirectories, as follows:

OEM This directory contains files referenced by the answer file that Setup uses to customize an installation when an installation proceeds using a configuration set. Contained in this directory are items like logos and third-party applications. Vista doesn't support many subdirectories that were part of previous versions of the OEM directory .

Out-of-Box Drivers Any drivers added to an installation through the use of `.INF` files are placed into this folder. They are differentiated from "in-box" drivers that are installed from `.MSI` files, and therefore leverage Windows Installer technology. Boot-critical drivers such as SATA or RAID drivers are added as part of the Windows PE configuration pass.

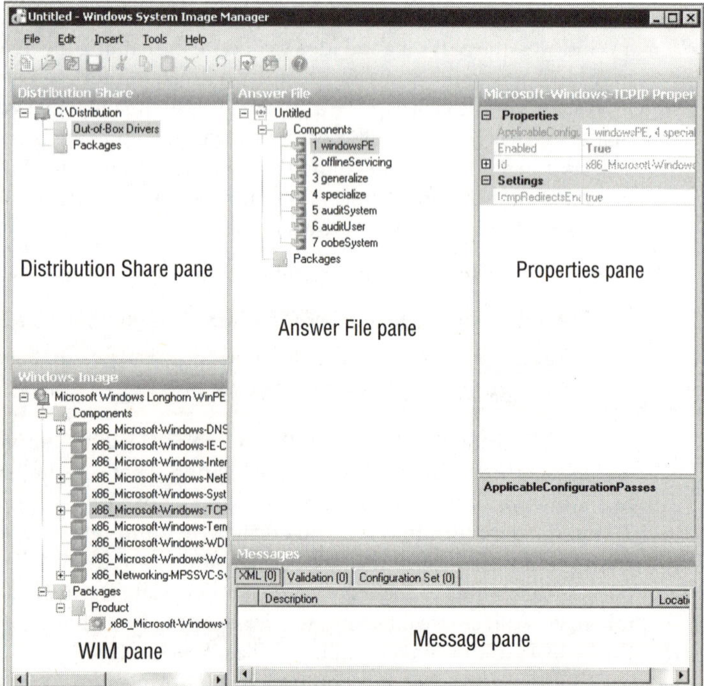

FIGURE 40.7
The Windows SIM user interface.

Packages Windows software updates, features, service packs, security updates, language packs, and other Microsoft updates are imported by Windows SIM into the Packages directory, and can be made available for inclusion in the answer file. An examples of a packages would be the Windows Foundation Package, which contains Windows Media Player, games, and the Windows Backup utility.

If you examine a sample answer file for a Windows image, you'll notice that not only does it store settings in two sections, components and packages, but that components are installed in a set of configuration passes. Each pass is a different stage of any Windows Setup installation. The different configuration passes occur in the following order:

1. WindowsPE
2. Offlineservicing
3. Generalize
4. Specialize
5. AuditSystem
6. AuditUser
7. OobeSystem

Some settings can be applied in more than one configuration pass, in which case you can use the answer file to determine in which pass that setting can be installed.

The basic steps in creating an answer file are the following:

1. On the technician computer insert the Vista DVD.
2. Click Start ➤ Programs ➤Microsoft Windows OPK (or Windows AIK) to open Windows SIM.
3. Click File, select Windows Image, and open the WIM file desired. You may be asked to create a catalog file (`.CLG`) if one does not exist.
4. Create the Windows Image catalog file, or update the catalog if you have modified the image.
5. Add all required source files, packages, drivers, and applications to the distribution share. As a minimum check that the following are included:
   - `Microsoft-Windows-Setup\DiskConfiguration\Disk\CreatePartitions\CreatePartition` (pass 1, windowsPE)
   - `Microsoft-Windows-Setup\DiskConfiguration\Disk\ModifyPartitions\ModifyPartition` (pass 1, windowsPE)
   - `Microsoft-Windows-Setup\ImageInstall\OSImage\InstallTo` (pass 1, windowsPE)
   - `Microsoft-Windows-Setup\UserData` (pass 1, windowsPE)
   - `Microsoft-Windows-International-Core-WinPE` (pass 1, windowsPE)
   - `Microsoft-Windows-Shell-Setup\OEMInformation` (pass 4, specialize)
   - `Microsoft-Windows-Shell-Setup\OOBE` (pass 7, oobeSystem)

6. Add the settings required in the answer file shown in Table 40.3 as they are apply to your Vista installation.
7. Click Tools ➤ Validate Answer File to see if the answer file is valid. Errors are listed in the Messages pane at the bottom of the Windows SIM windows. Fix any errors that are listed.
8. Click File ➤ Save Answer File, and save the file as `Autounattend.XML` into the root directory of a floppy disk or flash drive (UFD). With an Autounattend file stored on removable media, Windows Setup will search for it on start up and run the setup automatically from a DVD without requiring operator intervention.

TABLE 40.3: Unattend.XML Settings

COMPONENT OR PACKAGE	SETTINGS
Microsoft-Windows-International-Core-WinPE	InputLocale = <Input Locale>; SystemLocale = <System Locale>; UILanguage = <UI Language>; and UserLocale = <User Locale>.
Microsoft-Windows-International-Core-WinPE\SetupUILanguage	UILanguage = <UI Language>
Microsoft-Windows-Setup\DiskConfiguration	WillShowUI = OnError
Microsoft-Windows-Setup\DiskConfiguration\Disk	DiskID = 0; WillWipeDisk = true
Microsoft-Windows-Setup\DiskConfiguration\Disk\CreatePartitions\CreatePartition	Extend = false; Order = 1; Size = 15000; (You can adjust size accordingly. This example uses 15 GB.); Type = Primary
Microsoft-Windows-Setup\DiskConfiguration\Disk\ModifyPartitions\ModifyPartition	Active = true; Extend = false; Format = NTFS; Label = OS_Install; Letter = C; Order = 1; [PartitionID = 1
Microsoft-Windows-Setup\ImageInstall\OSImage\	WillShowUI = OnError
Microsoft-Windows-Setup\ImageInstall\OSImage\InstallTo	DiskID = 0; PartitionID = 1
Microsoft-Windows-Setup\UserData	AcceptEula = true
Microsoft-Windows-Setup\UserData\ProductKey	Key = <product key>; WillShowUI = OnError
Microsoft-Windows-Shell-Setup\OEMInformation	Manufacturer = <company name>; HelpCustomized = false; SupportPhone = <support number>; SupportURL = <support URL>; SupportHours = <support hours>
Microsoft-Windows-Shell-Setup\OOBE	HideEULAPage = true; ProtectYourPC = 3; SkipMachineOOBE = true; SkipUserOOBE = true

Source: Windows Automated Installation Kit (Windows AIK) User's Guide (Microsoft Corp.).

Keep in mind that Table 40.3 is a minimal set of packages. When this installation runs, Windows final restart won't show Windows Welcome (OOBE) and the system will require additional steps to prepare it for either becoming a master system or for use by users. Specifically Sysprep must be run to have Windows Welcome appear when the system next starts.

Windows Deployment Services

The Windows Deployment Services (Windows DS) is a component of the Windows AIK or Windows OPK that is a Windows Server 2003 service and deploys Vista to bare metal computers. It's possible to use Windows DS to install both Windows XP and Vista from Microsoft Windows Server 2003 and from the upcoming Windows Longhorn Server; however, the setup is somewhat different depending on which configuration you intend to support.

Three Windows DS functionality modes are supported:

- Legacy RIS
- Windows DS Mixed mode
- Windows DS Native mode

The characteristics of each are shown in Table 40.4.

Windows DS replaces Windows Remote Installation Services (RIS) by installing over RIS and updating it. RIS needs to be installed, but does not need to be running or configured in order to install the Windows DS update.

Windows DS has three separate components:

- A server service that includes a Pre-Boot Execution Environment (PXE) and Trivial File Transfer Protocol (TFTP) service
- A GUI that runs on top of Windows PE at the client
- A set of tools that you can use to change server settings, use system images (Vista particularly), and work with computer accounts

The Windows Deployment Services Update Step-by-Step Guide may be found at `http://www.microsoft.com/technet/WindowsVista/library/9e197135-6711-4c20-bfad-fc80fc215130.mspx`. To install Windows DS find the `WINDOWS_DEPLOYMENT_SERVICES_UPDATE.EXE` file in Windows AIK or Windows OPK and run that executable file. If Windows Server 2003 Service Pack 2 detects that RIS is installed, it will automatically install Windows DS.

TABLE 40.4: Windows DS Server Modes

MODE	BOOT ENVIRONMENT	IMAGE TYPES	ADMINISTRATION TOOL
Legacy RIS	OSChooser	RISETUP and RIPREP	RIS toolset
Mixed	OSChooser and Windows PE	WIM, RISETUP, and RIPREP	RIS toolset and WDS MGMT
Native	Windows PE	Windows PE	WDS MGMT

Windows DS and PXE

Windows DS is used to boot a destination system into Windows PE using that system's Pre-Execution Environment (PXE). Therefore, it requires that Active Directory, DHCP, and DNS all be available to the Windows DS, and a distribution share on an NTFS volume be available to store the required images. Not all systems BIOS support PXE (most modern motherboards do) and systems may need to have the option enabled. However, when a client system starts up with PXE, it searches for a DHCP server for an address and then downloads the files necessary to configure the client. One of the configuration tasks is to set up the answer settings of the PXE Listener service so that it can service client PXE boot requests.

There are two methods for configuring Windows DS: the WDSUTIL command from the command prompt and the Windows DS Setup Wizard.

To access the Windows DS Setup Wizard and configure the service:

1. Click Start ➤ Administrative Tools ➤ and WdsMgmt.
2. Then right-click the Servers node in the MMC, select Add Server from the context menu, select the DS server system, and click OK.
3. In the Add Server Warning dialog box, click Yes.
4. Right-click on the server in the Servers section of the MMC and select Configure Server. The Windows DS Configuration Wizard appears.
5. Click Next on the Welcome page; and Next again on the Remote Installation Folder Location. The Windows DS files are copied to the `C:\RemoteInstall` directory, which is the default location.
6. When the Windows DS service and the DHCP service is on the same server, the DHCP option 60 should be set to PXEClient (port) and Windows DS should be set to Do not listen on Port 67.
7. Move to the PXE Server Initial Settings page, click on Respond to all client computers, then select Advanced, and in the Advanced Settings dialog box click on Auto-add the client computer and mark it as known. Click the OK button to close the dialog box.
8. Click the Finish button to complete your settings.
9. Click and clear the Add Images to Windows Deployment Services now, then click the Finish button to complete the Setup wizard.

Figure 40.8 shows the console for the Windows DS server.

WdsMgmt and System Images

The boot image you'll use for PXE installation must be added to the WdsMgmt MMC. You can add this image by right-clicking on the DS server in the MMC and selecting Add Boot Image from the Boot Image node of that server. The boot image should be one of the boot environments above, but for Vista you want to use the Windows PE custom environment that you've created to support your installations. If you specify multiple boot images (for different Vista architectures, for example), they show up in a BCD boot menu when the PXE client boots (see below).

FIGURE 40.8
The Windows DS console lets you create and manage system image deployment to PXE clients.

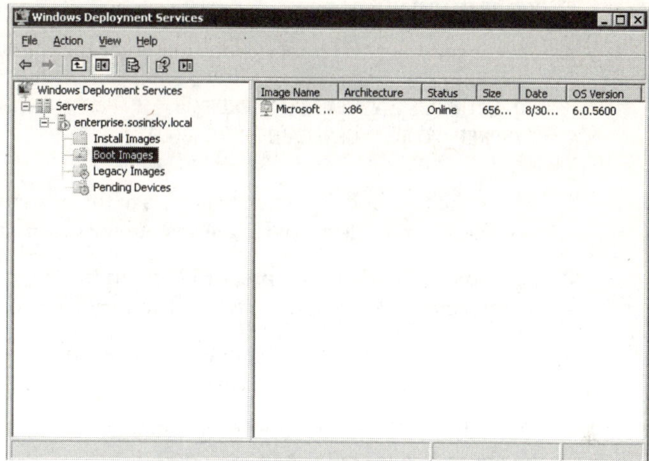

You'll also need to specify the install image in the MdsMgmt MMC. An install image is one that is captured from a master system (or reference installation) and then prepared with `Sysprep.exe`.

Alternatively, you can use WDSUTIL to configure the Windows DS at a command prompt using the following steps:

1. Create the shared folder:

```
WDSUTIL /INITIALIZE-SERVER /REMINST: <SHARED_FOLDER_PATH>
```

2. Set the answer policy to all clients:

```
WDSUTIL /SET-SERVER /ANSWERCLIENTS:AL
```

3. Specify the boot image:

```
WDSUTIL /ADD-IMAGE /IMAGEFILE:\\SERVER\SHARE\SOURCES\BOOT.WIM /IMAGETYPE:BOOT
```

4. Specify the install image:

```
WDSUTIL /ADD-IMAGE
➥/IMAGEFILE:\\SERVER\SHARE\SOURCES\INSTALL.WIM /IMAGE TYPE:INSTALL
```

You can quickly see the advantage of WDSUTIL is that it's easily scriptable. There are many more options to WDSUTIL than can be described here. Use the `WDSUTIL /?` command to see a complete listing of available options.

You can create an install image from within the WdsMgmt console, as well as with the WDSUTIL command. Similarly you can also create a boot image with the same two tools. You create a boot image by opening the Boot Image folder, selecting the image you desire, right-clicking that image and selecting the Create Capture Boot Image command. You'll need to use Add Boot Image to make that image available. The install image has just a few more steps to it.

To create an install image:

1. On the master or reference computer enter the following at the command prompt:

   ```
   CD \WINDOWS\SYSTEM32\SYSPREP
   SYSPREP /OOBE /GENERALIZE /REBOOT
   ```

   where the first line changes directories to the one with `Systemprep.exe` and `Setupcl.exe`, and the second line prepares the system for imaging.

2. After the system reboots, press F12 and in the Windows Boot Manager select the captured image, and click Next in the Image Capture Wizard.

3. Enter the location where the image will be stored in the Image Capture Destination page; then click Save and Upload image to WDS server.

4. Enter the WDS server name, click connect, and select the Image Group that will store the image and choose Finish.

At this point you have installed and configured Windows DS. To complete the automated installation, you need to configure the client system's BIOS so that it enters the PXE boot state, and set the boot order so that the Boot from network option is first in the boot order. Follow the steps below to complete the remote installation.

1. Restart the client system.
2. After PXE launches and requests it, press F12 to start the PXE boot process.
3. Select the Windows PE boot image on the menu. The Windows Setup Wizard Welcome appears.
4. Click Next, enter the username and password of someone who can access the Windows DS menu.
5. Select the operating system to be installed, then Next.
6. Enter a product ID, then Next and proceed to partition the disk as you would in Windows Setup. Don't forget to press F6 if you need to specify a special driver for RAID or SATA or another mass storage device.

At this point the image is copied over, Windows reboots for the next configuration pass, and Windows Setup carries on. The client computer has been configured.

UNATTENDED WINDOWS DS INSTALLATIONS

Windows DS is a two part system: operations run on the server and a different set of operations run on the client. You shouldn't be surprised, therefore, to discover that in order to run unattended installations you'll need two different unattend files. The server-side file is stored at in the `\WDSClientUnattend` directory and answers the first part of an installation. The second unattend file for Widows Setup is stored in either `$OEM$structure` or `\Unattend` for each image; that file stores the answers needed to run Setup through passes 2 through 7.

As before, you can use Windows SIM to create the two answer files. The contents of the unattend file will depend on the type—whether it supports a Windows DS client, the Windows Setup routine, or is a legacy setup. Each unattend file is also architecture and image specific.

To create the Windows DS server unattend file, you need to associate that file with the specific WDS client in the WdsMgmt console. Do the following:

1. Create a `\RemoteInstall\WDSClientUnattend` directory for a specific image.
2. Create the `Unattend.XML` file (with settings for pass one of Setup), rename that file `WDSClientUnattend.XML`, and copy that file to the directory in step 1.
3. In WdsMgmt, expand Servers, right-click on the DS server, and select Properties.
4. Click the Windows DS Client tab, then the Enable Unattend Mode check box, and then Browse to specify the `WDSClientUnattend.XML` you just created.
5. Close the MMC to apply your settings.

The same action above can be accomplished using WDSUTIL.

Having associated a WDS client unattend file to an image and architecture, you now need to create and configure the client-side part of an automated installation that controls the actions of passes 2 through 7 of Setup.

To configure the client-side unattend file, do the following:

1. In the WdsMgmt MMC, right-click on the image to be installed, then click Properties.
2. Click the Allow image to install in unattend mode.
3. Click Select File, then navigate to and select the unattend file associated with passes 2 through 7 of Setup on the client side.
4. Click OK twice to close the Image Properties dialog box.

NOTE You'll also need to associate `Sysprep.inf` with a legacy image installation to have an unattended installation run successfully. Since we are concerned with Vista installations, this isn't of particular interest here. However, you can find information on this topic either in the Windows AIK User's Guide, or at `http://go.microsoft.com/fwlink/?LinkId=66136`.

Windows DS and Non-PXE Clients

Windows DS can also be used with client systems that don't have the ability to boot into PXE. Windows DS supports a feature called "discover image." You can specify an image to be a discover image in the boot image folder of the MMC, or through WDSUTIL. From the Windows PE build environment you can open the Windows PE command prompt.

For non-PXE clients you can also create a CD or DVD that is a bootable discover disk by copying the `WinPE\Boot` and `WinPE\Sources` directories to that disk using `XCOPY`. Then to create an ISO file and burn that image to disk, use:

```
OSCDIMG -N -BC:\WINPE\BOOT\ETFSBOOT.COM C:\WINPE C:\WINPE.ISO
```

Using BDD Workbench

The BDD Workbench Computer Imaging System provides a framework for network-based Vista deployment using the tools that have already been described in this chapter. The main task of the Imaging Team is to setup and operate a distribution share that contains a complete set of unattended Vista installations. By "complete" I mean that the build server has all of the Vista versions, required device drivers, applications that are part of an installation, and the necessary automation or scripts necessary to support the different reference systems that an organization is willing to support. Computers then would boot to Windows PE and then need only connect to the build server to copy the appropriate Vista system image over.

The BDD Computer Imaging System Feature Team is a standard component of the Microsoft Solutions Framework (MSF) model. We've described this model in some detail in Chapter 36, so let's just take a quick look at the imaging portion of the BDD project. Figure 40.9 shows how system imaging relates to the overall project goals and timelines. Image development, testing, and validation can be seen to be one of the most important steps in any large-scale Vista deployment, and must conform to the functional specification that was created by the Product Management and Program Management teams for deployment, scope, and objectives.

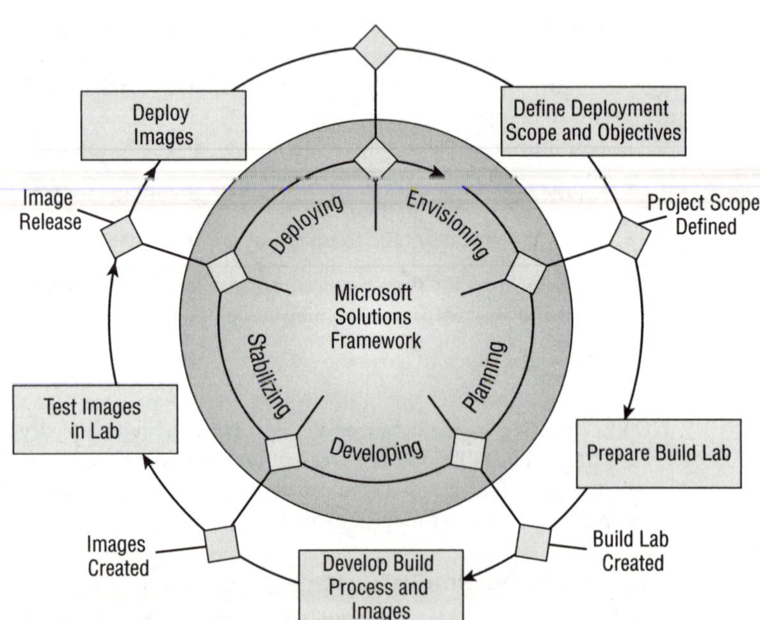

FIGURE 40.9
The BDD framework organizes a team to image and deploy Microsoft Vista over a network. Source: *Computer Imaging System Feature Team Guide* (Microsoft Corp.).

Using the BDD Workbench Interface

The BDD Workbench 2007 provides a means to access the tools needed to create distribution shares and system images. The Workbench is installed on the build server, which is a computer that houses the source files, as noted in the section above. Although BDD refers to this system as a "server," it doesn't need to be a server system running Windows Server 2003 or Longhorn. You could use a desktop PC or laptop running Windows XP or Vista as your build server. Furthermore, there are no restrictions on the type of network computer system that can be a build server. If it's a server, it can be a stand-alone server, a domain member, or even a domain controller. However, the current version of the BDD Workbench cannot run on a 64-bit version of Windows.

Figure 40.10 shows the Overview page for the BDD Imaging System module. Many of the steps should be familiar to you already from what you have read previously.

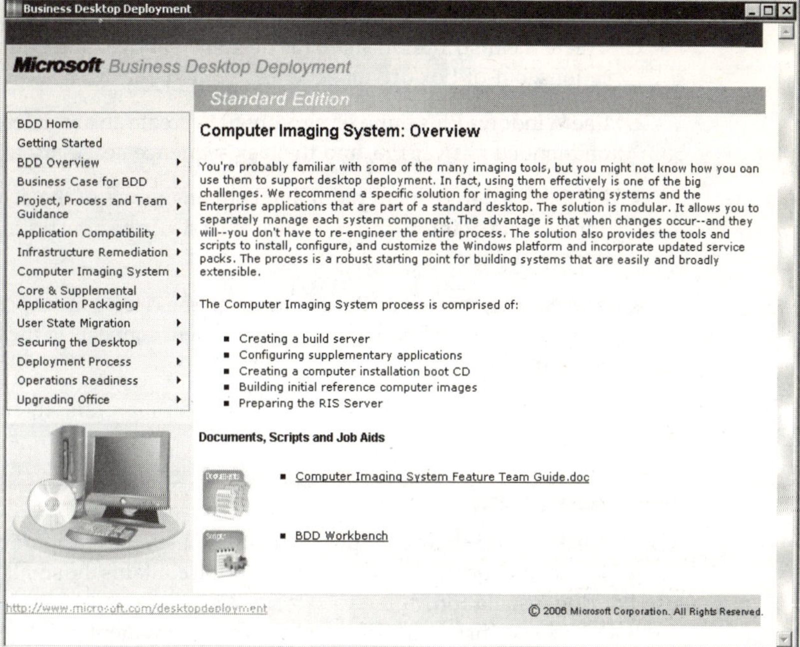

FIGURE 40.10
The Imaging process overview in a Microsoft Solutions Framework deployment of Vista.

DISTRIBUTION SHARE

When you install BDD 2007, it creates the necessary directories and distribution shares that it needs as part of the installation. Previous versions of BDD required the Imaging Team to create the shares manually, so this is a welcome change.

Since a Vista disk contains all versions of the OS in the `INSTALL.WIM` file, the Imaging Team adds the Vista media to the distribution share. You can also add custom Vista images created in Windows DS into the distribution share. When an image is added from Windows DS, the image catalog must be current and referenced properly. BDD 2007 also requires that `Wdsclientapi.dll`, `Wdscsi.dll`, and `Wdsimage.dll` be copied to the `C:\Program Files\BDD 2007\bin` directory from the `\Sources` directory found on the Vista media.

From within the Deployment Workbench you can manage the contents of the distribution share. You can add, remove, and modify operating systems, applications, packages (updates and language packs), and out-of-box drivers. It's recommended that the distribution share be located on a drive that's not a system's boot drive, and particularly a volume with sufficient available disk space. The files in the distribution share are used in builds.

If you want to check the inventory of the distribution share, open the following files in that share's Control directory: `Application.xml`, `Drivers.xml`, `OperatingSystem.xml`, and `Packages.xml`. All metadata on the objects in the share are stored in those files.

BUILDS

The purpose of the build process is to create reference images that can be used by BDD to deploy to support client systems. Builds combine OS files, a configuration of those files or a custom image, the answer file necessary to install and configure the OS on the destination computer, and, in the BDD imaging solution, the task sequence that automates the deployment.

The steps listed below are required to stock the distribution share with the needs system images:

1. Create the distribution share (as described above) and add all supported OS media, applications, out-of-box drivers, and any related packages.
2. Use Windows PE's build environment to create an architecture-specific build, an associated unattended answer file, and the task sequence necessary to stage the deployment.
3. Establish a deployment point that contains copies of the distribution share files, along with appropriate pointers and references that describe how the automation will access files in the deployment point.
4. As required, use the updated images in the deployment points to build Windows PE boot images, which on booting on a client system connects to the deployment point to initiate the client installation.
5. Install a build attained from the distribution share, and then use ImageX to capture the build to a custom install image.

Deployment Points

While a distribution share contains all the files needed to support builds on all types of computers and processor architectures, a deployment point contains the smaller subset of files that are actually used during installation.

BDD 2007 specifies four different types of deployment points:

1. Single system deployment points, also called a lab type. Here the deployment point must contain pointers to all the content contained in the distribution share.
2. Replicated network deployment points. A subset of the distribution share is created, and that subset is then rolled out to multiple servers using a replication scheme.

   A replicated deployment share is often used and necessary because image files are large and deployment can swamp network resources, particularly across WAN links. OS deployments can often swamp even high-speed LANs, causing some teams to create temporary subnets meant to isolate deployment traffic.
3. Distribution on portable and distributable media such as DVDs, flash drives, USB keys, and other devices. This type of deployment point is particularly useful for stand-alone network disconnected deployments.
4. SMS Operating System Deployment (OSD). The OSD Feature Pack is used to perform a Zero Touch Installation (ZTI) deployment where rollout is fully automated. Therefore, OSD require a copy of all the files, tools and scripts that OSD needs to configure the systems it's deploying to. OSD must maintain images, third-party applications, and any out-of-box drivers as part of the replica.

With each type of deployment point, there can be an associated WIM file from which ISO images may be created from Windows PE image files. Those ISO files can be used to be the source of system installations.

Performing BDD Workbench Tasks

All BDD Workbench tasks are done through the graphical user interface of that console. To launch the BDD Deployment Workbench, do the following:

1. Click Start ➢ All Programs ➢ BDD 2007 ➢ Deployment Workbench.
2. To add builds, right-click on Builds and select New. Use the wizard. To examine a build's details, click on Properties.
3. To add deployment points, right-click on Deploy and select New. Use the wizard. To examine a deployment points' details, click on Properties.

BUILDING AND MANAGING MULTIPLE OS CONFIGURATIONS

Figure 40.11 shows the New OS Wizard, which is accessed by right-clicking the Operating Systems collection in the Distribution Share and selecting the New command. Each collection: Operating System, Applications, Packages, and Out-of-Box Drivers all have wizards of this sort associated with them.

The New OS Wizard lets you add one or more operating systems' source files to the distribution share from a variety of sources. You can choose to:

- Copy over all OS files.
- Move files from a location.
- Reference the files in a location you specify.

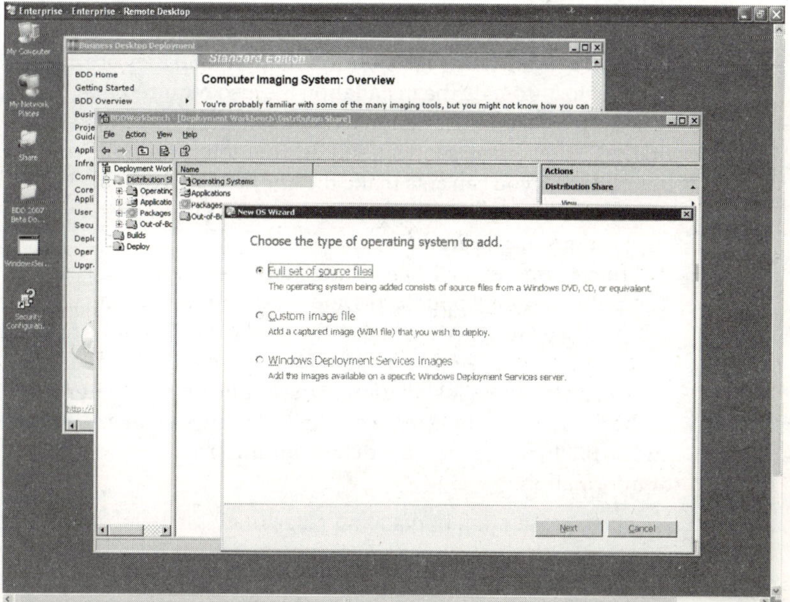

FIGURE 40.11
The New OS Wizard lets you add source files to the BDD's Distribution Share.

Each operating system added to the distribution share appears in an Operating Systems subfolder or subdirectory. From within the Deployment Workbench console tree, you can click on the Operating Systems directory and examine all of the operating systems it contains.

If you want to delete an operating system, right-click on that OS and select the Delete command. Keep in mind that when you delete an OS from the BDD Workbench, you are also deleting the operating system from the server's file system.

If you want to alter the properties of the operating system as it appears in the console, right-click on the OS and select the Properties command. You can use the Properties dialog box to rename the OS, for example.

You can also use the images you create with Windows DS and add them to the Workbench's distribution share, as follows:

1. Add the complete set of Vista source files to the distribution share, as described just above.
2. Copy `Wdsclientapi.dll`, `Wdscsi.dll`, and `Wdsimage.dll` from the Vista `\Sources` directory to the `C:\Program Files\BDD 2007\BIN` directory.
3. Right-click on Operating Systems in the console; then select New to view the New OS Wizard shown above in Figure 40.11.
4. Select Windows Deployment Server Services images on the Choose the type of Operating system to add page, then click Next.
5. On the Select the Windows Deployment Services server page indicate which Windows DS server and image you want to add then click Next to complete the addition.

APPLICATIONS

If you want to add applications as part of a BDD image deployment, the application's source files should be added to the distribution share so that they are available for installation during builds. In order to automate the installation it's also required that the installation commands and all necessary options to those commands be known so that they can be added to the task sequencer. BDD executes a task sequence on destination system. When you add an application to the distribution share, you can also make the application available within the Windows Deployment Wizard, where the installer is offered a set of applications that can be installed and can choose which applications are desired.

From an operational standpoint, adding applications is similar to adding an operating system. You right-click on Applications and select the New command to initiate the New Application Wizard. You need to specify whether the application's source files are copied to the distribution share or references to those files in another location are stored instead.

In order to aid in installation of the application at a later time, it's important to provide details of the application since there can be different versions, different languages, different platforms, and so on. In the Specify the details for this application page have available the following pieces of information:

- Version down to the point level
- Language support
- Supported platforms

Once you've supplied this information above you'll need to specify the directory (folder) that contains the application. When the application's source files are on the same system as the distribution share that contains the staged OS, the option to move the files instead of simply copying them is available.

As a final step, create the folder that will contain either the source files or the metadata pointing to the installation path. Enter the command needed to install the program on the Specify installation details page. Keep in mind that it's important that you not only offer the command with the correct syntax but that you have that command pointed correctly to the Working directory, which is entered into the Working directory text box.

At that point the application will appear in the `Application` subfolder under the name of the directory that you just created. Once an application is listed, you can work in the console to:

- Edit the application's information.
- Change its dependencies on the Dependency tab of the Properties dialog box.
- Enable or disable the installation of the application.
- Remove the application entirely.

Packages and Drivers

Adding packages, language packs, and updates to the distribution share in the Deployment Workbench is very similar to the procedure that you just saw for adding applications. When you right-click on Packages and then click on the New command, the New Package Wizard launches and prompts you for the required information. Specify the location of the package, general information about the package, and create a subfolder for the package. Be prepared to supply the following pieces of information:

- Package name
- Type
- Processor architecture
- Language
- Public key token
- Version
- Product name
- Product version
- Package path

Once you've added the package you'll be able to edit the information you just supplied, enable or disable a package's use, or remove the package entirely from within the Workbench console tree.

Out-of-box drivers are often a critical item to include in a distribution share. As noted earlier, without the drivers that let you access mass storage, devices an installation can fail. Adding drivers follows the same pattern as applications and packages. When you right-click on the Out-of-Box Drivers folder and click the New command, the New Driver Wizard launches. You'll be prompted to supply the location of the driver files, and when you do so, the Deployment Workbench will add all of the drivers found in that folder and any nested subfolder to the distribution share. You should be prepared to supply the following driver information:

- Driver name
- Manufacturer
- Version
- Driver type (class)
- INF path
- Platforms
- Supported OS versions
- Supported PnP IDs

The correct identification of versioning information for drivers is particularly critical and needs to be entered with care. Critical out-of-box drivers can impact the stability of your operating system. Indeed, 64-bit Windows now requires that drivers be signed for compatibility, with the promise that someday this protection will extend to the other more popular versions of Windows.

Once you've added the driver you'll be able to edit the information you just supplied, enable or disable a driver's use, or remove the driver entirely from within the Workbench console tree.

BUILDS

Builds are added to the Deployment Workbench in the same manner that OS, applications, packages and drivers added. The New Build Wizard that appears is different from what you've seen before, in that you not only have to supply build information but you have to create your builds from within the BDD Workbench. So let's take a closer look at this particular operation.

To create a new build:

1. In the Workbench, right-click on Builds, and select the New command to open the New Build Wizard.
2. Provide the information required on the Specify general information about this build page: Build ID, Build name, and Build comments. The Build ID must be unique and can't be altered once you create it.
3. On the Select an operating system image to use with this build, make your choice and click Next.
4. In the Specify the product key for this operating system, either enter your product key or leave it blank.

   Vista lets users add the product key at a later time. Microsoft recommends that volume users with more than 25 Vista systems to deploy should select Do not use a product key when installing. For Windows XP or Vista Multiple Activation Keys (MAKs) the recommendation is to select Use the specified product key and then enter your Product Key in the text box.

5. On the Specify settings about this build page, supply the name of the Organization, the owner of the build's Full Name, and the Internet Explorer Home Page URL.

6. In the final step, specify the local Administrator password for the build. You can either enter the password required or leave it blank if the local Administer password is added when Vista is deployed.

The build you just created appears as a subfolder in the Builds folder labeled with the build ID you supplied, as well as appearing in the `Control\<build_ID_subfolder>`. As before, builds can be edited (but not the Build ID), enabled or disabled, or deleted.

Builds have two other important options that you haven't seen before:

1. The ability to edit the answer file.

2. The ability to edit the task sequence associated with that build.

To change the answer file for unattended setup that is associated with that particular build, go to a build's Properties dialog box and click Edit `Unattend.xml`. The Windows SIM opens and allows you to change the settings of that builds answer file.

A task sequence is the listed order of steps that are taken during the image preparation, installation of the image on the destination computer, and the configuration of the build on a reference computer. To alter the task sequence, you click on the Task Sequence tab in the build Properties dialog box and perform your edits there. You have the following options in the Task Sequence:

- Add, edit, remove, or reorder an application.
- Add, edit, remove, or reorder a group.
- Add, edit, remove, or reorder a reboot.
- Add, edit, remove, or reorder a task.

IMAGES

BDD 2007 installs Windows AIK with Windows PE 2.0. No customizations or modifications of AIK and Windows PE are required to create Windows PE images and from them ISO files.

Several different Windows PE image and ISO types are possible within BDD. The four most commonly used are:

1. A Lite Touch Installation or LTI flat bootable ISO image

2. An LTI ISO image on a bootable RAM disk

3. A generic flat bootable ISO image

4. A generic bootable RAM disk ISO image

The Deployment Workbench recognizes when a deployment point is updated and then uses Windows PE to create new WIM files to be used by the deployment point as well as the optional ISO images. By default these images appear in the Boot directory of the distribution share. The new WIM files can be added to Windows DS or burned to DVDs.

Part of BDD's function is to automatically add network interface device drivers to the distribution share, so it isn't necessary to add those files to your Windows PE image. However, BDD doesn't add video drivers and other system device drivers to the distribution share, so you'll need to add them to your Windows PE image to support the specific hardware you have.

To capture an image of a reference or master system within the BDD Workbench, you would start up that system using a Windows PE boot image that was created by the deployment point. The image can be either on a DVD, or placed in the `\Boot` directory of the distribution share. If you choose the latter method, then you need to use a Windows DS server and add the LiteTouchPE WIM files (32-bit or 64 bit) to the Boot Images node of that server so that during PXE the boot environment can be created.

With the PE environment running on the master system, you are prompted to enter your user credentials and, when validated the Windows Deployment, Wizard will appear. To complete an image capture, you are going to need to be able to enter the following pieces of information:

- Computer name
- Domain or workgroup
- Whether to restore user data
- Operating system image desired
- Product key, or for Vista no product key
- Desired packages
- Locale
- Applications to install
- Image capture name and stored location (UNC path)

When you complete the wizard, the Task Sequencer starts, partitions and formats the hard drive, installs the build, applies Sysprep, and then restarts the system into Windows PE. Once Windows PE is running, an ImageX command captures the image and stores it into the distribution share's Captures folder.

The point of capturing a system image is to be able to "publish" it to other systems. Therefore you'll want to add that image to the Deployment Workbench as an operating system choice. When you start the New OS Wizard you can add your newly captured system state by selecting Custom Image file on the first Choose the type of operating system to add page and then completing the image.

Using BDD Deployment Wizard

All four types of deployment points, a lab deployment point of a single standalone server, a replicated set of network deployment points, creation of deployment media, and an SMS 2003 OSD deployment point, are all created using the Windows Deployment Wizard.

When you right-click on Deploy in the BDD Workbench and select the New command, the BDD Deployment Wizard's first step, shown in Figure 40.12, lets you choose among the four choices. The choices that the wizard displays next depend on the type of deployment point you selected.

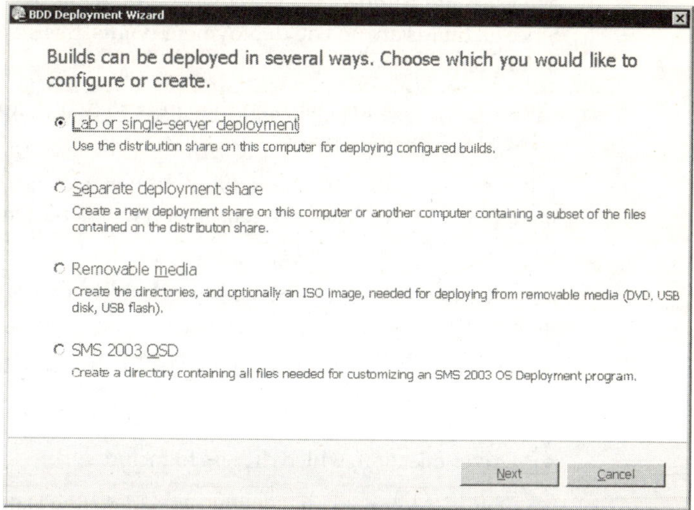

FIGURE 40.12
The BDD Deployment Wizard lets you create one of four different types of deployment points.

After selecting a deployment type, you'll be asked to provide the following information and make the following selections:

1. Name of the deployment point
2. Whether to allow application selection during upgrade
3. Specify whether to prompt for image capture
4. Allow user to set Administrator password
5. Allow user to specify a product key
6. Specify the location of the network share to hold the files and folders necessary for this deployment type
7. Specify user data defaults

The choices shown in each step are somewhat different for each of the deployment points, but the overall number steps and the type of steps doesn't change. Once you've specified the type of deployment point and created it, the deployment point appears in the Deploy section of the BDD. Deployment continues with your configuring the deployment point.

To configure a deployment point:

1. In the Deploy folder, right-click on the deployment point and click the Properties command.
2. Click on the General tab and, if desired, edit the Deployment point name, the Network Path (UNC), Local path, and Platforms supported.
3. Click on the Rules tab to edit the settings found in the `CustomSettings.ini` file. The Configuration Reference contains information about the different rules and their actions.
4. Click the Builds tab, and then select the builds that should be included in the selected deployment point.

When a build is added, the Workbench copies the OS for that build to the deployment point. Since all builds are on Lab deployment points, this step isn't offered for that kind of deployment point.

5. Click the Applications tab, and then indicate which applications should be included in the selected deployment point.

   When an application is added, the Workbench copies that application's file to the deployment point. Since all applications are on Lab deployment points, this step isn't offered for that kind of deployment point.

6. Click the Drivers tab, and select the out-of-box device driver that are to be copied to the deployment points.

   Again, this selection is not available for a Lab deployment point.

7. Click on the Windows PE tab to edit the following settings:

   - Driver injection, which drivers to include.
   - Optional components, whether to add Active Data Objects (ADO) or the Windows Recovery Environment.
   - The type of images to generate Lite Touch bootable ISOs, bootable RAM disk ISOs, or generic versions.
   - Customizations, such as a background image or custom folder.

Changes you make should be propagated to the deployment points by selecting the Update command from the deployment point's context menu in the Deploy details pane of the Deployment workbench. The Update process does the following things:

- For a lab deployment point, the distribution share is duplicated and Windows PE boot images are created.
- For a network deployment point, the folder that was described is created, but only the necessary files are copied over to the deployment point based on the configuration.
- For media deployment points, the folder is created on that media and a bootable ISO image with the necessary set of files are copied to that media.
- For an SMS OSD deployment point, the folder is created and the files required by the OSD Feature Pack are copied to it.

Summary

In this chapter you learned about the many different methods that you can use to automate a Vista installation. With Microsoft's new image-based installation technologies you have a variety of new tools that you can use to rapidly and remotely deploy the installation of Vista. Central to the successful deployment of Vista is the Widows PE 2.0 environment. In this chapter you learned about the characteristics of Windows PE, the tools that come with PE, and how to create and manage images.

There are several different methods you can use to perform network installations. In this chapter you learned how to setup and manage network and remote installations. With the Windows System Image Manager you can create and manage automated unattended installation files. Answer files automate Setup by providing the necessary selections and customizations that would normally be provided by a user.

For larger deployments two tools have been described. The first is Windows Deployment Services, which is an extension of the Windows Remote Installation Services. Windows DS allows clients to boot into the PXE boot environment, and have the server service deliver the necessary image to the client. The BDD Deployment Workbench provides an MMC framework that collects the various tools described into a coherent collection. For large-scale deployments of Vista the Deployment Workbench is a valuable tool.

In the last chapter of this book we examine the final part of an enterprise Vista deployment, which is the ability to remotely deploy Vista. Any medium or large organization soon outgrows the ability of the staff to do hands on installations at each client. With Windows Deployment Service you can perform remote installations that let you leverage your Active Directory, use tools for inventorying and management such as SMS, as well as setup and manage unattended installations. The chapter presents two types of remote installations: Light Touch Installation and Zero Touch Installation.

Chapter 41

Performing Remote Setups

In this final chapter we examine how to use Windows Deployment Service and SMS to remotely deploy Vista. There are many settings that let you control the remote deployment process. Deployments can be automatic, unattended, validated against a system's identity, and even performed manually as a response to a call to a help desk. With all of these options, you can control how and when your clients get Vista, rolling out your deployment in a manner that makes the most sense to your organization.

This chapter explores the steps necessary to create a remote deployment of Vista using automated server-based deployment technologies. You'll learn the following:

- Installing Windows Deployment Service
- Determining what program or image is booted, unattend file is used, and image is used for the deployment
- Use image groups to set security settings for a particular installation
- Using Active Directory to support remote deployments
- Using SMS to support remote deployments in the Zero Touch Installation

Vista: What's New?

Vista's release coincides with the release of a new tool for automated server-based remote deployment, the Windows Deployment Service. Windows DS replaces Windows Remote Installation Service and Windows Automated Deployment Service for imaged-based installations. The good news about Windows DS is that you can transition to it. If you have many RIS images you can continue to use them, using RIS. You can do this from within Windows DS in legacy mode, or support both RIS and WDS installations in mixed mode.

There are so many advantages to using Windows Deployment Service that you'll most likely want to make the transition from any older deployment services to Windows DS as soon as it is practical for your organization to do so. For the largest deployments where additional services and control over the participation of Active Directory is required, System Management Server is the Microsoft deployment method of choice.

Using Remote Installation and Deployment Services

Previous editions of Microsoft Windows clients relied on a server-based solution for remote deployment called Remote Installation Services or RIS. With the introduction of Vista and Windows Longhorn Server the Windows Deployment Service or Windows DS replaces RIS and should be used in its place. You were introduced to Windows DS earlier in Chapters 36 and 40.

Windows RIS was the original bundled solution of client OS deployment. In Windows Server 2003 you can install Windows RIS as you would any system service by going into the Add or Remove Programs control panel and selecting that service from the Add/Remove Windows components. Windows RIS is covered in the detailed Step-by-Step Guide to Remote OS Installation found on the Microsoft TechNet website at: `http://www.microsoft.com/technet/prodtechnol/windows2000serv/howto/remoteos.mspx`.

Windows RIS has the following issues:

- It does not support the deployment of Vista, and changes in the OS loader or the many of the updated components that are part of Vista.
- The management capabilities of Windows RIS are rudimentary and needed improvement.
- There is little OS localization or accessibility support. OS Chooser is not localizable.
- There are a number of PXE boot strategies that Windows DS unifies.

If you intend to do remote deployments of Vista clients, you'll need to use Windows DS. Windows DS provides not only a remote boot capability but is extensible with a plug-in model for PXE Server extension with a client/server communication protocol. With DS you'll also use an enhanced MMC to deploy WIM images.

Microsoft developed Windows DS to consolidate three different deployment solutions that had different infrastructures and addressed different deployment methodologies. Those technologies were:

- SMS 2003
- ADS 1.0 (Automated Deployment Services)
- Windows Server 2003's RIS

In 2004, SMS 2003 OSD FP (Operating System Deployment Feature Pack) and VSMT (Virtual Server Migration Tool) was added to ADS. ADS was updated to version 1.1 in 2005. The intent with Longhorn was to take ADS 1.1 and transfer some of its technologies to Windows DS and the rest to SMS 4.0.

If you are transitioning from RIS Server, you can run Windows DS in three different modes:

Legacy mode The PXE component is replaced by Windows DS, with all components operating as it did in Windows RIS Server. All RIS functionality is retained

NOTE If you want to continue to use RIS images for Vista with your RIS server, you will need to create those images with the new version of RIS Prepare that Microsoft released when it released Vista.

Mixed mode A boot menu appears that lets you go to your old RIS images, or list the new images on the Windows DS server.

Native mode In Longhorn this is the only mode that is supported; only Windows WIM files are supported.

Getting Windows DS

WDS is then meant to be used by IT staff in medium or large organizations and for OEMs in computer system manufacturing scenarios. SMS is the advanced deployment solution for medium and large organizations where Active Directory is used as part of the deployment scenario.

These are the ways that you can get Windows DS installed:

- A downloadable hot fix to install it on Windows Server 2003 SP1
- As an in-the-box part of Windows Server 2003 SP2
- As an in-the-box part of Windows Server Longhorn (Longhorn offers a role migration tool which makes it easy to install Windows DS)
- As part of Vista

In the first two cases, you get both the WDS Server and the WDS Management Console as part of the installation. Vista ships with the WDS Client. Finally, Windows Server Longhorn has all three components: the server, the console, and the client. The Windows DS client is actually a special version of Windows Setup, with extra flags turned on. The new client application replaces the older OSChooser.

With Windows DS you can use bare metal or machine reprovisioning deployment of

- Vista
- Windows Server Longhorn
- Windows XP
- Windows 2003
- Windows 2000

Thus, you can use WDS to capture an XP sysprepped images in the WIM format in place of using RIS Setup or RIS Prep.

Remote Deployment Setup

Windows DS supports both PXE boot and non-PXE boot options. For a client that isn't PXE capable, you can use a CD to boot up the WDS client to access the WDS server and initiate the installation. One option lets you use a boot file to do fully automated installs from the moment the client system powers on using a PXE boot file that skips the F12 required at system startup.

Windows DS has integrated support for booting with Windows PE. Windows PE 2.0 doesn't require Active Directory to boot (but does require pressing F12 during boot). The Windows DS client on the other hand does require Active Directory to run correctly.

The steps involved in setting up and running a remote deployment using Windows DS are the following:

1. Install the Windows DS Server. The installation copies over the server executable and DLLs and creates the services.

2. Configure the Windows DS Server. During installation the REMINST share (Remote Installation Share) and folder structure is created. A TFTP root is established and the services are turned on. Unlike Windows RIS, Windows DS does not require that the server be authorized in DHCP. Authorization in DHCP is optional for Windows DS.

3. Add your images in any of the following four forms in the Windows DS capture GUI:

   - Supported image types are boot images, Windows PE 2.0 in WIM, the WDS client (setup files) and the PXE boot binaries. Boot images appear in the Windows DS boot menu.
   - Install image (the Sysprep OS image in WIM)
   - Image contained on a distribution DVD
   - Custom specified WIM file

   Of the four types of images, the boot image is the one used to boot the client in PXE booting, and the install image or custom WIM files are the images copied over to the client and extracted.

After you install Windows Deployment Service, you can open that service by clicking Start ➤ All Programs ➤ Administrative Services. The Windows Deployment Services and the Windows Deployment Services MMC console opens as shown in Figure 41.1. WDS is, after all, a service in the sense that it's always turned on at the server to service PXE requests when they become available. You can configure the service in Windows Server 2003 or Windows XP by opening the Services Control Panel and setting the options for the service there.

Notice the menu choice called Windows Deployment Services Legacy. That version of the Windows DS service only runs on a server that is running in mixed or legacy modes (which can work with RIS files or the RIS service), or a server that hasn't been configured for Windows DS yet.

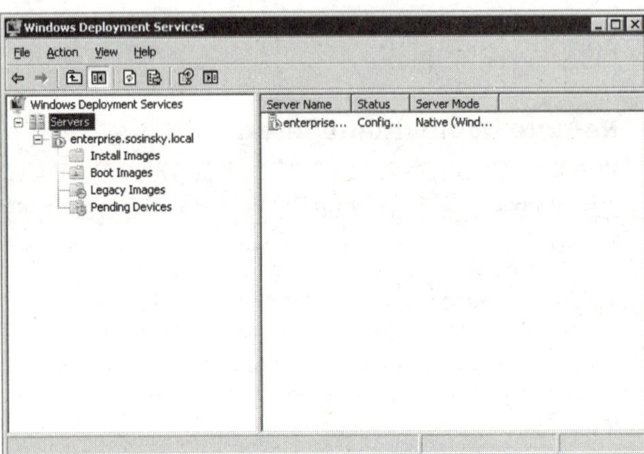

FIGURE 41.1 Windows Deployment Services runs as a Windows service and opens inside an MMC for further configuration.

PXE Boot Deployment

For a remote deployment, boot the WDS clients into PXE. The image deployment runs through the WDS client installation, completes the initial boot sequences, and then runs the OOBE phase. Settings are installed using the `Unattend.XML` answer file, which is created with Windows SIM. The place where you create the kind of automated deployment sequence is in the Server Properties dialog box. A PXE install request that Windows DS can be set to three distinct responses, and are found in the Deployment Service dialog box's PXE Response Settings (see Figure 41.2):

- No response
- Respond only to known client computers
- Respond to all (known or unknown) client computers.

A further setting forces a client to notify the administrator in order to obtain approval. These three settings give you very fine control over how a deployment proceeds. These are the critical settings that determine whether a deployment runs unattended, or must be manually run.

In the first case, the deployment runs at a time of your own choosing, the client is not involved. The second case limits Vista deployment to already established systems (as in an upgrade in place), while the third case essentially makes Windows DS an automatic option for any computer that can access the WDS server. However, the last setting returns Vista deployment to an interesting and interactive manual mode.

If you chose the PXE option that requires a manual remote deployment, then a deployment begins with a call to the help desk by the client's operator. Once the user's installation ticket is validated at the help desk, an IT staff member can initiate the deployment from the WDS management console where that system is added to the Pending devices node of the management console.

The prior notification type of deployment allows for a phased rollout of Vista in an orderly manner if and when the users are ready to accept the upgrade. So in terms of when the users work is interrupted, this is the least disruptive method.

The details of the PXE boot process are:

1. The client boots into PXE and the network boot client `PXEBoot.com` is copied over the network to the client. When the client is PXE enabled (in the BIOS), press the F12 key to go into PXE. If you copy over a PXE boot file, the process can proceed unattended, that is, pressing the F12 key is no longer required.

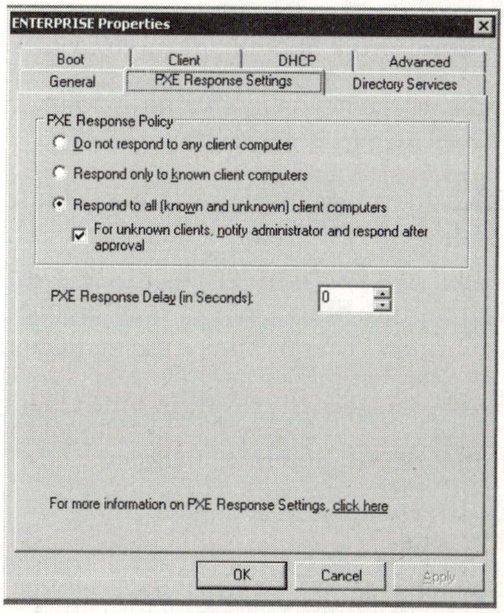

FIGURE 41.2
The PXE Response Settings tab of the Windows DS Properties dialog box allows you to control the type of automated deployment that occurs.

2. `PXEBoot.com` then directs that the new Windows boot loader `Bootmgr.exe` and the BCD file (Boot Configuration Data, which replaced `Boot.ini`), which tells the client how to RAM disk boot Windows PE (the Windows DS client).

3. Then it copies the WIM file over the network to the client and decompresses files sequentially using the WIM mini–file filter.

For a totally unattended Windows DS install, you actually need two unattend files, the client `Unattend.XML` and the image `Unattend.XML`. The client unattend file contains the first two stages of setup and can be associated with a device. The image unattend file contains all of the other stages of setup and can be associated with a WIM file. Together they allow you to customize and completely run an unattended setup.

WDS Management Console

In the original implementation of Windows RIS, the only thing you could do from a management standpoint was to add images. A little extra functionality was added in later versions of RIS, but not much. With Windows DS it is another story entirely.

In Windows DS, the management console is much more fully developed with many more functions. One feature of the WDS console is that it can be remotely accessed. The console contains about 85 percent of the functionality that can be accessed from the command-line interface (CLI) WDSUTIL.

Prior to PXE deployment, you will need to indicate a number of settings in the WDS console. The console allows you to:

- Add a deployment server, as long as that server is registered in the Active Directory.
- Set policies on the Server Properties dialog box such as the PXE response setting (how to handle a PXE request from a client) that you saved in the previous section.
- Set the port settings for PXE communications. WDS and DHCP both listen on port 67 for a DHCP discover signal at the client unless you alter it. If WDS and DHCP are on the same system, then WDS should be blocked on port 67, and DHCP Option Tag 60 should be set to the PXE client can come back with a response on port 4011.
- Determine the boot image (architecture) that gets sent to the client on the boot tab.
- Indicate the new client naming policy that is used in the Pending Devices policy and the Directory join functionality.
- Select the image to deploy. Usually the image is one from an image group as described below. Adding a WIM file to an image group can be as simple as taking the WIM file from the distribution media and copying it into the WDS server. In most cases, WIM files will be the ones you capture from a master or reference system that you build using BDD in your laboratory environment. You can use the management console to capture the image.
- Set the client unattend file on the Client tab.
- Initiate the deployment process.

WDS Settings

The setting tabs for a Windows DS server are critical to controlling most of the different aspects of your remote deployment. To open the WDS server settings dialog box, simply right-click on the server in the left panel of the WDS Management Console and select Properties.

The settings on the following tabs are critical:

General tab The General tab has no settings, but tells you the location of the server, the mode WDS is being used in, and the location of the remote installation files.

PXE Response tab Shown previously in Figure 41.2, the importance of this tab is described above.

Boot tab Shown in Figure 41.3, you enter the different boot programs for different system architectures, which are either COM or EFI files. Standard BIOS use COM files, while systems (such as ia64 and future versions of x86 and x64) require EFI support. If you are booting a system from a system image, then you can use the default boot image section to specify which images to use. Typically these images are WIM files that you developed using your reference or master systems, imaged with ImageX and stored on a network share.

Client tab This essential tab (shown in Figure 41.4), is where you enable an unattended installation. An unattended installation requires that you specify the two answer files that are required by Windows DS to run an installation. The first file runs the first phase of setup, and the second file runs the remaining phases 2 through 7. Typically the first unattend file is found in the `\WDSClientUnattend` folder on the server. The second file is stored either in the OEM structure or `\Unattend` directory for each image.

Directory Services tab. On this tab, shown in Figure 41.5, you can create a naming policy for new systems, as well as determine where the computer account is created. You can use system variables to create a naming convention that is consistent with your organization's need.

For example, use `%Username` to have the computer name be the same as their username; `%MAC` to have the computer take for its name the network interface card's (NIC) MAC address; or `%[0][n]#` to have the computer name become an incremented number in n digits, padded by the number of zeros required to pad the number (e.g., `%03#` results in 001 through 999).

Accounts can be created in the user's domain, the domain of the Windows DS server, in the users OU (organizational unit), or some other location you specify. The advantages of creating a new domain is that you can cleanly move newly deployed systems into it.

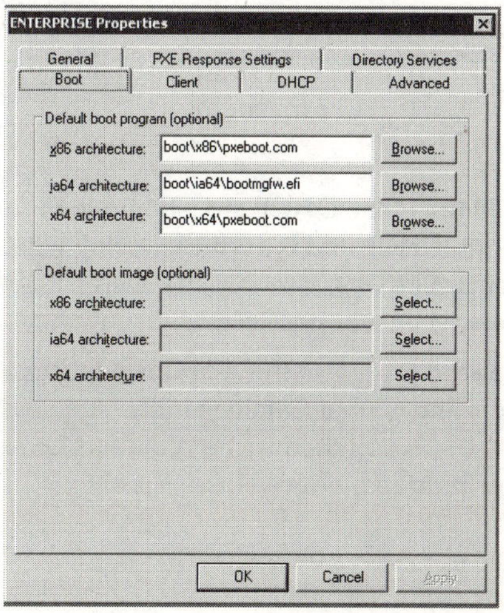

FIGURE 41.3
The Boot tab of the Windows DS Properties dialog box allows you to specify which program or boot file to use to boot a system in a PXE installation.

FIGURE 41.4
The Client tab sets the unattend file used in an unattended installation, as well as enables the process.

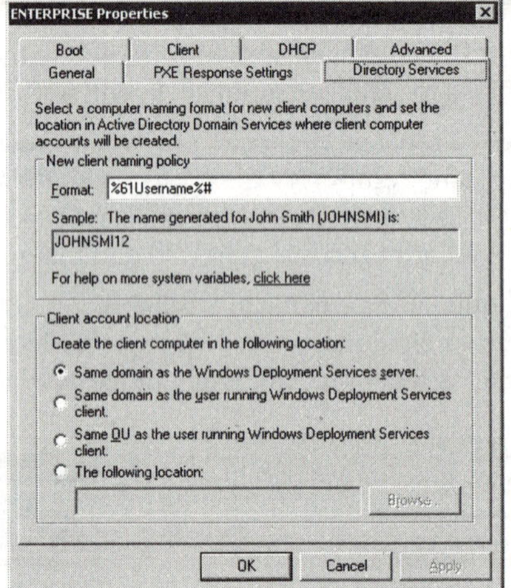

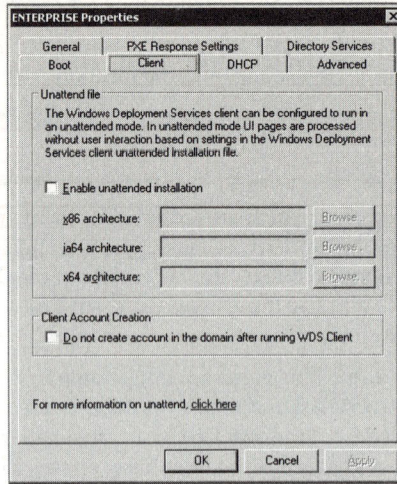

FIGURE 41.5
The Directory Services tab provides the new client naming mechanism, as well as the machine account location.

DHCP tab The DHCP tab (shown in Figure 41.6), allows you to alter the listening ports for PXE and DHCP and is a critical setting whenever the Windows DS server is located on the same system as the DHCP server. In general, it is recommended that these two services be on separate servers whenever possible.

Advanced tab Use the Advanced tab, as shown in Figure 41.7, to determine which domain servers and Global Catalogs in the Active Directory are used by the Windows DS server. You can also specify whether the Windows DS server is authorized in DHCP, something which is no longer required, but can be desirable.

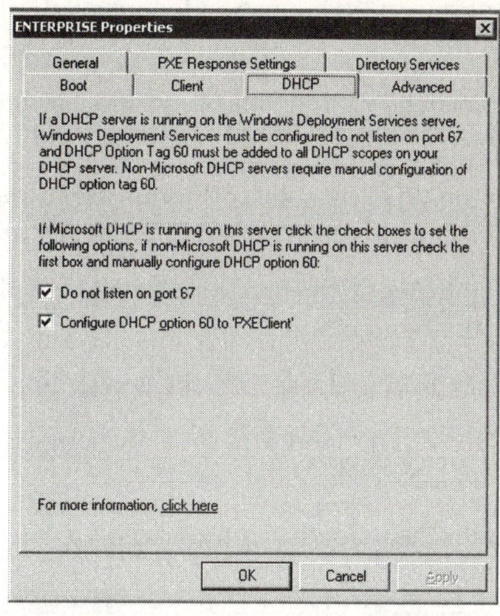

FIGURE 41.6
The DHCP tab allows you to alter port listening settings so that Windows DS and DHCP don't interfere with one another when those two services are located on the same server.

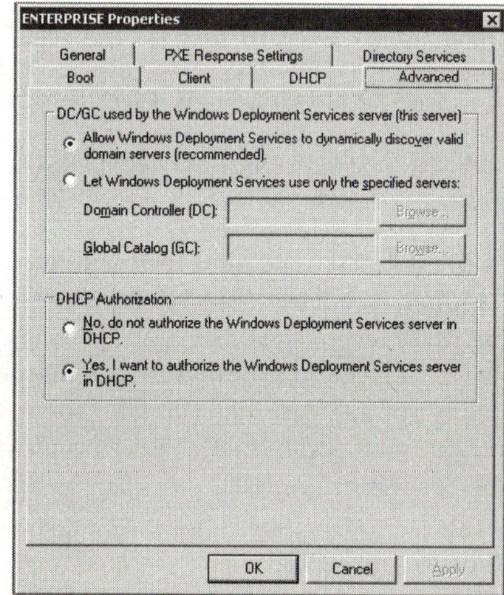

FIGURE 41.7
Use the Advanced tab to specify the domain controller or global catalog in AD that is used by the Windows DS server, as well as DHCP authorization behavior.

WDS and Unattended Installations

You have seen the important settings required by Windows DS for an unattended installation in the previous section. Provided you set up Windows DS correctly, the hard part of the deployment is accomplished. You'll need to make sure that all of the correct files are in place to support an unattended installation, that you've configured Windows Setup unattend, and that a `Sysprep.INF` file is specified. Although you've already seen those steps individually in previous chapters, let's review and overview those steps in full here.

To configure a WDS unattended installation:

1. Create an `Unattend.XML` file for the WDS client for each of the supported architectures, name it `WDSClientUnattend.XML`, and place a copy in `RemoteInstall\WDSClientUnattend`.
2. In the WDS console, specify unattend mode in the Client tab and specify the architecture. You can also use WDSUTIL to specify an unattended installation and configure its settings.
3. Right-click on the image you want to deploy, click Properties, and then Allow image to install in unattend mode.
4. Click Select File, specify the image file, and then click OK
5. Open a command prompt and change directories to the one that contains the image group with a down level image.
6. Enter the following commands:

```
MD C:\REMOTEINSTALL\IMAGES\IMAGEGROUP\IMAGE
MC C:\REMOTEINSTALL\IMAGES\ IMAGEGROUP\ IMAGE \$OEM
```

   which creates the directory for the WIM file and the OEM directory tree, respectively.

7. Then copy `Sysprep.INF` as follows:

```
COPY C:\SYSPREP.INF C:\REMOTEINSTALL\IMAGES\ IMAGEGROUP \
➥IMAGE \$OEM$
```

At this point you should alter the contents of the OEM directory as required, and when the image is applied it will be copied to this new folder.

With all these settings in place, your Windows DS server advertises its PXE service to any client that boots into a PXE environment. What happens next depends on how you set up your servers PXE Boot Environment on the Boot tab shown in Figure 41.03; either the client boots using the image you specified and with the unattend files indicated in this section, or it is checked first for its identity before it is upgraded.

Image Groups and ACLs

The concept of image groups for WIM files is important to understand from the standpoint of correct image assignment. The exact image you chose from an image group is the recipe file for constructing the image into the file stream that gets sent down to the client out of the single sourced RWM resource file that is contained in the WIM file. Consider an OS image that runs about 2GB in size and has perhaps 10 WIM files that reference it. The resource WIM RWM file might be 3GB in size, and each WIM install files might be 2MB in size. A WIM file is like a directory file for the resource file that is the actual file store.

The real utility of an image group is that you can set security ACLs for each specific WIM so that the installation of a WIM can be filtered by users and groups. Therefore, Windows DS can validate that a user is an administrator and uses client X, and then send the WIM file for administrators down to that client during the deployment. A database administrator, clerical worker, communications specialist, doctor, lawyer, and Indian chief can all get their appropriate WIM files as well.

To set the security ACLs of a WIM file:

1. Open the image group.
2. Right-click on the WIM file of interest and select Properties.
3. Click on the Security tab.
4. Set the users and groups desired for that WIM.

When a client PXE boots and the deployment is set to show a menu of possible images that can be installed, only the images that match the user's credentials will be displayed to them for their selection. The dialog box a client sees is similar to the selection box you see in the Vista installation from the distribution media (e.g., Vista Basic, Vista Premium, Vista Ultimate, and so on), except here the choices are the different builds that are available with different language packs, options, and whatever customizations you created.

Understanding Active Directory Requirements

In the previous sections you saw how Active Directory plays in Windows RIS and Windows DS automated deployments. Let's just summarize the information that these deployment services require in order to successfully automate Vista deployment.

Among the AD resources Vista requires are:

- Windows DS and Windows RIS servers need to be registered in the Active Directory.
- Computer accounts either exist in AD or must be created and stored.
- User accounts must exist in AD and their security settings must be stored.
- Group accounts must exist in AD and their security settings must be stored. As you have seen, users and groups are checked prior to displaying a list of available images in the PXE client boot menu during a deployment.
- The Windows domain structure must exist and be specified so that Vista systems can be joined to the domain.
- Administrators must be capable of being validated in AD so that they can access network resources, such as share point or remote access to the WDS management console.
- Any group policies that are pushed out to Vista clients must be correctly supported in the Active Directory.
- Migration of Windows RIS roles to Windows DS roles must be stored in AD.

In order to support these functions Windows DHCP and Windows DNS, servers must be properly configured under the Active Directory.

Using Systems Management Server (SMS)

At the time of Vista's release, SMS was undergoing a transition from SMS 2003 to SMS 4.0. With the addition of the Operating System Deployment Feature Pack (OSD FP) to SMS 2003, SMS is able to patch the PXE boot process and perform large-scale Vista deployments in concert with Active Directory Server (ADS 1.1). SMS 4.0 incorporates the OS deployment functions found in Windows

DS to allow for automated deployments of Vista without needing the OSD FP or any other additional functionality. As a general rule, when you want fine control over a large-scale deployment of Vista, then SMS is the solution to use.

Keep in mind that SMS is Microsoft's technology, and that you should expect to find alternative good (perhaps better) solutions for Vista deployments appearing from various third-party network framework vendors. Deployment modules are a core upgrade from most, if not all, of the successful network frameworks such as LANDesk, Alteris, ZENworks, Unicenter TNG, IBM Tivoli, HP OpenView. You may want to check with your vendor of choice regarding availability.

Much of the functionality you've already seen is integrated into SMS OSD. The main features are:

- Image capture management in the WIM format
- OS package management for the settings of a deployment including administrator notification, network, and distribution settings
- USMT to migrate user state settings to a newly deployed OS

To the features above, SMS adds theses specific functions:

- An enhanced system hardware/software inventory system beyond what is offered in the Windows AIK. The features for inventory include the Inventory Tool for Custom Updates, Custom Updates Publishing Tool, and the Scan Tool for Vulnerability Assessment that were part of the SMS 2003 R2 release.
- Customizable user/group task based Vista image deployment based on your preexisting SMS 2003 infrastructure
- Reporting on deployment status and condition

As you saw in the previous chapter, SMS is the central tool in the Zero Touch Installations (ZTI) that you perform from within the Business Desktop Deployment 2007 framework.

Summary

This section concludes the last part of this book in which you learned about how to use Windows Deployment Services and Windows System Management Server to perform remote deployments of Microsoft Vista. Remote deployments can be unattended or manually initiated. With these tools you can determine which images get deployed and how deployment proceeds. Through the use of these tools, you can save countless hours installing Vista on many systems without having to spend much time on any one system. Without these tools the enterprise deployment of Vista wouldn't be practical.

Index

Note to the reader: Throughout this index **boldfaced** page numbers indicate primary discussions of a topic. *Italicized* page numbers indicate illustrations.

Symbols and Numbers

A

B

E

F

G

H

I

J

K

L

N

O

Q

R

S

T

U

V

W

X

Z